Handbook of
Organization
Development

Handbook of
Organization
Development

Thomas G. Cummings, Editor
University of Southern California

SAGE Publications
Los Angeles • London • New Delhi • Singapore

For information:

Sage Publications, Inc.
2455 Teller Road
Thousand Oaks, California 91320
E-mail: order@sagepub.com

Sage Publications India Pvt. Ltd.
B 1/I 1 Mohan Cooperative Industrial Area
Mathura Road, New Delhi 110 044
India

Sage Publications Ltd.
1 Oliver's Yard
55 City Road
London EC1Y 1SP
United Kingdom

Sage Publications Asia-Pacific Pte. Ltd.
33 Pekin Street #02–01
Far East Square
Singapore 048763

Printed in the United States of America

Library of Congress Cataloging-in-Publication Data

Handbook of organization development/editor, Thomas G. Cummings.
    p. cm.
Includes bibliographical references and index.
ISBN 978-0-7619-2812-6 (cloth)
   1. Organizational change. 2. Organization. 3. Industrial organization. 4. Organizational effectiveness. I. Cummings, Thomas G.

HD58.8.H3613 2008
658.4′06—dc22   2007021508

This book is printed on acid-free paper.

07   08   09   10   11   10   9   8   7   6   5   4   3   2   1

Acquisitions Editor:	Al Bruckner
Editorial Assistant:	MaryAnn Vail
Production Editor:	Diane S. Foster
Copy Editor:	Carol Anne Peschke
Typesetter:	C&M Digitals (P) Ltd.
Proofreader:	Penelope Sippel
Indexer:	Kathy Paparchontis
Cover Designer:	Candice Harman

Contents

1

Introduction

THOMAS G. CUMMINGS

Organization development (OD) has grown enormously since its inception more than 50 years ago. Driven by organizations' increasing needs to adapt to rapidly changing environments and to manage change almost continuously, OD has spawned diverse approaches and methods. From its origins in helping organizations cope with internal social problems, OD has expanded to address more strategic issues of how firms structure and manage themselves for competitive advantage in a rapidly changing global environment. OD applications have moved beyond interpersonal relations and group dynamics to such varied perspectives as sociotechnical systems, global management, organization design, human resource management, corporate strategy, and knowledge management. Similarly, OD's humanistic values have been augmented with economic interests and societal concerns about environmental sustainability, employee welfare, and corporate governance.

Although this extraordinary growth attests to OD's robustness and practical success, the field is far more diffuse and complex today than it was just a few decades ago. Many of the new methods and perspectives have emerged from disciplines far removed from the psychological origins of OD, including anthropology, business administration, economics, engineering, industrial relations, international relations, and sociology. This diversity makes it hard to define the boundaries of the field and to keep abreast of significant developments. Moreover, many of these newer approaches have evolved independently of each other, with little attention to how they fit with existing methods or relate to one other. This makes it difficult to accumulate wisdom in the field and to develop a coherent knowledge base to guide practice and research.

This handbook maps the broad terrain of OD from multiple viewpoints. It seeks to explain what is currently known, what new

1

developments are occurring, and how different methods and approaches are related. The contributors were chosen to represent the key perspectives in OD. They include prominent scholars and practitioners who have unique insights about the field and understand its evolution and challenges. The chapters are not exhaustive summaries of all the relevant literature and research but emphasize basic knowledge and how it applies to the problems facing contemporary organizations and to how OD is conceptualized and practiced.

The handbook is organized into four parts that flow from an overview of the field, to the process through which OD is applied in organizations, to specific interventions and change approaches, and finally to special applications of OD. These parts are meant to broadly organize the contributions, and there is some overlap and interaction across them.

Part I presents an overview of OD. It addresses the nature of the field and provides contemporary and historical perspectives. In Chapter 2, W. Warner Burke provides a comprehensive review of the OD field. He takes stock of where the field stands today while reviewing its definitions, its content, and the education of practitioners. Burke contrasts OD to other forms of planned change and identifies its unique features. He describes OD's success to date yet raises a troubling paradox for its future: Given the growing need for organizations to manage change, why is OD less prolific and important than it should be? This question is a recurrent theme in this volume, and contributors offer a range of answers and promising solutions.

In Chapter 3, Edgar H. Schein reflects on the concepts and research findings that have shaped his thinking and practice of OD, from the 1940s to today. Schein provides a fascinating picture of OD's progress by recounting his own development as a scholar and practitioner. He describes how his intellectual curiosity, personal experiences, and research all contributed to OD concepts and approaches that he helped introduce to the field: "organizational psychology," "coercive persuasion,"

"career anchors," "process consultation," and "organization culture."

Chris Argyris explains his learning approach to OD in Chapter 4, a perspective that underlies much current thinking about the field. He proposes that learning—the correction and detection of error—is fundamental for successful OD and change. Learning is effective when organization members engage in productive reasoning that promotes free and informed choice, learning as a key objective, and acknowledgment of personal causal responsibility. Unfortunately, as Argyris so vividly describes, learning usually is ineffective in organizations, especially when members deal with problems that are difficult, embarrassing, or threatening. In these situations, members revert to defensive reasoning, resulting in counterproductive behaviors that resist the transparency and open inquiry needed for effective learning. Argyris argues that OD practitioners may inadvertently reinforce such defensive behaviors, and he presents specific steps to reduce this problem and facilitate learning.

In Chapter 5, Robert E. Quinn and Scott Sonenshein examine traditional strategies for changing people and organizations and present a new approach based on self-transcendence of the change agent. They show that existing strategies for change—empirical–rational, power–coercive, and normative–reeducative—all have potential limitations that can thwart meaningful change, particularly when people are deeply committed to the status quo. Quinn and Sonenshein propose a new yet more demanding approach in which change agents study their own integrity gaps and commit to a higher purpose. This helps them transcend their self-interests and become more purpose centered and other focused. Quinn and Sonenshein argue that this transforming change strategy can be directed outward to the whole organization. It can help change agents engage members in analyzing the organization, clarifying a common vision, and committing to move in that direction. It can produce a more productive organization that is more closely tied to external reality and the needs and aspirations of members.

Manfred Kets de Vries and Katharina Balazs provide a clinical orientation to OD in Chapter 6. It is based on concepts from psychoanalytical theory, development psychology, neurology, family system theory, and cognition. They describe the irrational or latent processes underlying organization dynamics and show how they can be surfaced, understood, and addressed. This perspective adds depth to the traditional approaches to OD, which mainly focus on observable behaviors and processes. It can help organizations deal with the deeply entrenched causes of their problems.

Part II addresses the OD process. It includes perspectives on how OD is carried out in organizations, from diagnosis to implementation to assessment. In Chapter 7, David W. Jamieson and Christopher G. Worley present an overview of how OD is practiced. They review current debates that affect choices about practice, including definitions and conceptualizations of OD, credentialing and education of practitioners, and OD effectiveness. Based on these discussions, Jamieson and Worley provide an integrative theory that views OD practice as a process involving both science and art. They explain how the OD process is designed and managed; how it involves learning cycles that are punctuated by varying forms of support, inertia, and resistance; and how learning can produce change that both develops people and improves organization performance.

Kate Louise McArdle and Peter Reason discuss the key role that action research plays in developing people and organizations in Chapter 8. Action research has long been a cornerstone of OD practice. It is a highly participative and collaborative process that enables participants to gain practical knowledge to improve their organization by trying to change it and assessing the results. Reason and McArdle argue persuasively that this cyclical process of action and critical reflection can be both developmental and liberating. It encourages continual inquiry and improvement while

enabling members to create their own knowledge of how things work and can be changed. Reason and McArdle describe different variants of action research and show how this form of inquiry can be applied at multiple levels, including the individual, group, organization, and society.

In Chapter 9, Craig C. Lundberg describes diagnosis as an essential step in the OD process. It involves collecting and analyzing information about the organization to understand how it is functioning or to identify and clarify problems. Because diagnosis is intended to inform the creation of appropriate interventions to improve the organization, it must provide an accurate and useful picture of the situation. Lundberg shows that how diagnosis is conceived and practiced in OD is highly variable, with questionable results. He argues that diagnosis is essentially a "sense-making" process guided by preexisting frames or mindsets that determine what and how information is collected and from whom. Lundberg questions whether the frames that have traditionally guided diagnosis can accurately capture how organizations function in today's rapidly changing and complex environments. He describes several challenges that future OD diagnosis must overcome if it is to keep pace with the realities it is trying to assess.

In Chapter 10, Jean M. Bartunek, John R. Austin, and Myeong-Gu Seo discuss the intervention phase in the OD process, which typically follows and is based on diagnosis. It involves the design and implementation of particular change programs aimed at solving problems and improving the organization. The authors first differentiate between the process of intervening and the content of particular interventions. They then provide conceptual clarity to the myriad interventions used in OD by explaining them in terms of the "motors of change" or mechanisms through which they produce results. Bartunek, Austin, and Seo describe three overlapping generations of OD interventions and show how the application, meaning, and combination of their motors of change have evolved over time. They show that interventions that appear different often share underlying change mechanisms. Such understanding is essential in combining interventions correctly to fit their implementation contexts.

J. Richard Hackman and Amy C. Edmondson explain in Chapter 11 how groups can serve as powerful agents of change in organizations. They show how groups can be used as both diagnostic and intervention tools in OD. Hackman and Edmondson describe different types of diagnostic teams and tasks. They discuss how groups can intervene to change individuals, to improve work and organization processes, and to lead organization change efforts. Based on extensive research, Hackman and Edmondson identify what it takes to use groups as agents of change in OD.

Richard W. Woodman, John B. Bingham, and Feirong Yuan address the final stage of the OD process in Chapter 12, the often difficult and complex process of evaluating OD interventions. They show how evaluation can play a valuable role in implementing interventions and assessing their overall effectiveness. Woodman, Bingham, and Yuan identify technical and sociopolitical impediments to effective evaluation. They describe major types of OD evaluation and their respective settings and methods. Exemplar studies are presented to show how the different approaches are applied. Woodman, Bingham, and Yuan conclude with valuable suggestions for how OD evaluation can be improved to contribute better to development of intervention theory and the application of actionable knowledge.

Part III presents major OD interventions used in organizations today. In many ways, these change programs are the core of OD. They help to define the field by providing concrete descriptions of OD in action. OD interventions focus on the issues organizations need to address to be effective; they are the key targets that OD seeks to change to improve the organization. The contributions in this part are organized broadly around four major change targets: human process interventions, technostructural interventions, human resource management interventions, and strategic interventions.

Human process interventions involve social processes occurring among organization members. They address issues related to communication, decision making, interpersonal relations, and group dynamics. These change programs are the oldest and most enduring in the field and represent to many of us the heart of OD. In Chapter 13, Peter B. Vaill explains the fundamental role of social process in OD and change. He traces its history in the social sciences and provides a working definition of what social process is all about. Vaill makes a strong case that understanding and working with social process, what he calls "process wisdom," is the principal skill of OD practitioners and the field's major contribution to organization change. He outlines numerous benefits that derive from process wisdom and identifies barriers or threats to applying it in organizations. Vaill speculates how OD's understanding and application of social process can be enhanced.

In Chapter 14, R. Wayne Boss and Mark L. McConkie discuss team building, probably the most popular human process intervention in organizations today. They describe the roots of team building and identify its different approaches and methods. Boss and McConkie review the research about team building and its effectiveness. They present guidelines for making team building work better and provide remedies for the common problem of regression, by which teams gradually revert to old habits and poor performance after participating in this change program. Boss and McConkie discuss the special team-building needs of virtual teams, whose members do not work together face to face. They go on to distinguish team building from other team interventions and to identify problems that continue to plague team building.

In Chapter 15, Ronald E. Purser and Thomas J. Griffin describe large group interventions (LGIs), a new and rapidly growing form of human process intervention. LGIs typically bring together for short time periods large numbers of organization members to engage in real-time problem solving, visioning, and planning for large-scale change. Purser and Griffin review the theory and assumptions underlying LGIs, a combination of group dynamics, systems thinking, participative management, and social construction. They identify variants of this approach to change, focusing on the search conference and the appreciative inquiry summit. Purser and Griffin suggest new directions for LGIs and propose that they should help organizations treat the future as a unique temporal dynamic, not simply a projection from current visions.

Technostructural interventions involve organizations' task methods and work designs and the structures that place them into departments and coordinate them to achieve overall performance. These change programs have helped to transform how work is designed in modern organizations and how firms structure themselves to compete in a rapidly changing environment. It has led to self-managed work systems and to structures that are lean and flexible and empower the workforce. In Chapter 16, Frans M. van Eijnatten, A. B. (Rami) Shani, and Myleen M. Leary discuss sociotechnical system (STS) design, an intervention that designs work so it jointly satisfies human needs and technical demands. Starting more than 50 years ago in Great Britain, STS design has spread globally as the main alternative to traditional forms of work that are narrowly defined and highly routine. It has led to widespread application of highly flexible, empowered work teams and, in a broader context, to participatory democracy in the workplace. Eijnatten, Shani, and Leary review STS theory, design, and change processes; they identify variants of this intervention in Australia, the Netherlands, North America, and Scandinavia. The authors offer a reflective critique of STS knowledge and suggest key areas that need further understanding. Based on current changes in society, technology, and commerce, they suggest emerging areas where STS can further develop to remain relevant to the times.

In Chapter 17, Gretchen M. Spreitzer and David Doneson focus on empowerment, a change program aimed at moving decision making and control downward in organizations, closer to where the work is done. Empowerment has been a mainstay in OD that helps organizations enhance employee motivation, response to problems, and commitment to change. Spreitzer and Doneson review and synthesize the extensive literature on empowerment from three perspectives: social–structural, psychological, and critical. They explain how empowerment can be a powerful incentive for personal and organizational change and lay out new directions for its development and application.

In Chapter 18, Jay R. Galbraith discusses organization design, a large-scale intervention aimed at designing the firm's structure, people, rewards, and processes so they align with its strategy and with each other. He reviews the practice and research origins of organization design and shows why new organization forms are proliferating at a rapid rate. Galbraith makes a strong case for the role that OD can play in providing the social skills and change management needed for organic, flexible designs with lateral coordination mechanisms that are so prevalent in organizations today. He explains how organization designs can vary on multiple dimensions having to do with products, geography, and customers. Galbraith describes designs that combine multiple dimensions in novel ways to account for firm growth and environmental change. He speculates about the next generation of designs, which may split organizations into cost-centric, product-centric, and customer-centric parts.

Human resource management (HRM) interventions focus on the personnel side of organizations, including selecting employees, training and developing them, assessing and rewarding their performance, and helping them plan and manage their careers. These interventions typically are associated with the personnel function in organizations and are carried out by specialists with expertise in that area. There is much interplay between HRM and OD, however. For example, many technostructural interventions strongly affect how employees are selected, trained, and rewarded. Similarly, HRM programs increasingly rely on change management for successful implementation.

In Chapter 19, Edward E. Lawler III makes a strong case for greater integration between OD and HRM. He shows how rapid changes in information technology and the amount of knowledge work in organizations place a premium on human capital. This requires HRM to be far more involved in strategic planning, organization design, and change management. Lawler outlines the major functions of HRM and shows how they are evolving from mainly administrative tasks to working closely with line managers to support their operations to partnering with top executives to develop corporate strategy. He argues that these value-adding functions are new to HRM and require a system-wide focus, a good understanding of business issues, and knowledge about the effectiveness of different HRM approaches and the feasibility of various strategic paths. Lawler describes how HRM can be organized to perform these roles and identifies specific steps for linking HRM more closely to the strategy process.

In Chapter 20, Ayse Karaevli and Douglas T. Hall discuss career development, an intervention aimed at helping employees plan their careers and organizations manage the career paths of their members. Career development is increasingly tied to corporate strategy to ensure that sufficient talent is developed to enact it. Karaevli and Hall provide an integrated model of career development that includes career planning at the individual level and career management at the organization level. They review methods for both career planning and career management and show how the success of career development contributes to organization effectiveness.

Karaevli and Hall make a compelling argument that organizations with diverse talent pools and varied career experiences will be highly adaptive to environmental shifts while maintaining a strong identity. This requires career development programs that emphasize people's potential for future roles and performance, individual needs and personal development, and lateral promotion policies.

Strategic interventions are among the most recent and publicized change programs in OD. They involve large-scale change that is organization-wide and often radical. They are applied to organizations that need to change strategic direction or transform themselves to keep pace with a complex and rapidly changing environment. In Chapter 21, Larry Greiner explains how OD can be integrated with strategic planning, a process in which senior executives determine how the organization will gain competitive advantage. He shows why OD has traditionally ignored or been excluded from strategic decision making and reviews recent attempts to remedy this problem. Greiner explains that these efforts deal mainly with the process or social side of strategic planning and tend to ignore the content or business side. He argues that if OD is to contribute fully to strategic planning it must address both sides. Greiner presents an OD approach to strategic planning that integrates process and content and results in strategic plans that are realistic, flexible, and likely to be implemented. He proposes future directions that OD will need to take to become a full partner in strategic planning.

In Chapter 22, Michael Beer shows that in today's rapidly changing environments organizations need to be adaptable and capable of transforming themselves into high-performance and high-commitment systems. He presents two opposing approaches to organization transformation: "Theory E," which focuses on economic and financial goals and changes in strategy, structure, and systems, and "Theory O," which emphasizes organization effectiveness and changes in organizations' culture and people. Beer argues strongly that successful corporate transformation must embrace the paradox represented by these two theories of change. Yet executives tend to lock into one approach without considering what can also be gained from the other. To overcome this myopia, Beer proposes a disciplined strategic change process led by an effective top team with diverse perspectives. It includes open dialogue across organization levels so top management can test its approach to transformation and revise it to incorporate elements of both Theory E and Theory O. Beer provides a set of principles to guide this change process and presents evidence about their efficacy in helping organizations embrace the paradox of the two theories.

In Chapter 23, Kim Cameron describes OD interventions for changing organization culture, the taken-for-granted values, norms, and beliefs that are shared by members and affect how they think, feel, and behave at work. A strong culture provides organizations with a unique identity, and when it effectively guides behaviors in the right strategic direction, it helps firms sustain success. Cameron conceptually defines organization culture and shows how it can be measured using a competing values framework. It assesses culture on two dimensions—flexibility versus stability and internal versus external orientation—which can be combined to identify four types of culture: clan, adhocracy, market, and hierarchy. Cameron describes how organizations can profile their existing and preferred culture and, when a gap is discovered, how they can go about changing it.

In Chapter 24, David A. Nadler explains how OD is applied at the top of the organization to help senior executives transform the entire firm, a process called enterprise change. He identifies the elements of such large-scale change and explains the key role of top leaders. Nadler proposes that OD practitioners must be both change architects and trusted advisors when working with CEOs and their executive teams on enterprise change. He describes the kinds of change issues that CEOs

and their teams are likely to face and explains how these OD activities can help resolve them. Nadler devotes special attention to boards of directors and describes their unique and changing role in corporate governance and the problems they tend to face. He identifies an emerging role for OD in helping boards become more effective.

George Roth describes OD interventions aimed at helping organizations learn in Chapter 25. Application of these change programs has grown rapidly in OD because in today's environments, the capacity to learn faster and more effectively than competitors can provide organizations a sustainable competitive advantage. Roth reviews the major perspectives in organization learning, presenting their core concepts, pathways and barriers to learning, and relevance to OD. He pays particular attention to applied work on the learning organization, where much OD intervention has taken place. Roth identifies the principles or disciplines that enable organizations to learn and shows how OD can facilitate their application. He speculates on future directions in organization learning and how OD can evolve along this path.

In Chapter 26, A. B. (Rami) Shani and Peter Docherty address how learning mechanisms can be embedded in OD interventions. They argue that many OD programs fail to sustain change and improved outcomes because learning methods are not designed into the change process itself. Shani and Docherty define learning mechanisms, identify their key features, and describe three broad types: cognitive, structural, and procedural. To illustrate this material, they present case studies of specific OD interventions from each of the four broad categories used in this handbook and show how learning mechanisms were explicitly designed into them. Shani and Docherty discuss the inherent connection between OD, learning mechanisms, and collaborative research. They suggest how organizations can enhance their learning capabilities by building on existing learning methods or developing entirely new ones.

Susan Albers Mohrman describes how organizations can be designed for knowledge management in Chapter 27. She shows how knowledge management adds value to the firm when it is a core competence embedded in the organization's routines and design features, not simply an add-on program or set of techniques. Mohrman presents a strong case that knowledge is practice based and is created by employees as they interact in the workplace. She explains how the various features of an organization can be designed to promote knowledge construction and sharing. This includes building knowledge capabilities into the organization's strategy, work processes, structure, management processes, rewards, and people. Mohrman concludes that knowledge-based views of the organization must be included explicitly in OD diagnosis and intervention and that practitioners need to be constantly alert for opportunities to design knowledge capability into the firm.

Part IV extends OD to issues and settings that differ from those related to large business corporations, where so much of OD has been applied. These special OD applications address such topics as ecological sustainability, community development, and social change in developing nations. They take place in the public sector, in family-owned firms, in nongovernment organizations, and in networks of organizations. In many ways, these special OD applications are not simple extensions of current OD theory and practice but require entirely new concepts, methods, and skills.

In Chapter 28, Robert T. Golembiewski and Gene A. Brewer review how OD is applied in the public sector. They examine several intellectual traditions that guide thinking and administration in government. Although these different perspectives identify particular needs for change in public organizations, they offer only limited encouragement that OD can work successfully there. Golembiewski and Brewer contrast this bleak conceptual picture of OD in the public sector with the positive results of a large panel of OD interventions in

government agencies and business firms in 61 countries. The success rate of public change programs was substantial and on par with those in the business sector. Golembiewski and Brewer speculate on why OD was so successful in these public organizations and challenge the common assumption that OD does not work well in the public sector.

In Chapter 29, Ernesto J. Poza discusses OD's role in firms that are owned or controlled by families, a significant part of the economies of many nations. He describes the unique features of these organizations and the special challenges they pose for OD. Poza presents systems and resource-based frameworks for diagnosing family businesses to assess how they are functioning. Based on diagnosis, he reviews four OD applications that are particularly appropriate to family firms and shows how they work in these settings: change management, leadership succession, strategic planning, and governance. Poza pays particular attention to the skills and knowledge that OD practitioners need to engage successfully with family businesses.

In Chapter 30, Dexter Dunphy describes how OD can contribute to sustainable organizations capable of developing human resources and operating in a way that does not damage the natural environment. He reviews how OD has evolved to keep pace with the key issues facing organizations and makes a compelling argument that the challenge to organizations and OD in the current century will be sustainability on both human and ecological dimensions. Dunphy explains how human and ecological sustainability contribute to organization effectiveness and shows the phases for accomplishing it. He describes what sustainability means for how organizations are designed and managed and for how OD is conceived and practiced. Dunphy clarifies the key role that OD can play in helping organizations achieve sustainability.

In Chapter 31, L. David Brown, Mark Leach, and Jane G. Covey explain how OD can be used in the service of social change, which generally involves large-scale problem solving and transformation aimed at improving the lives and prospects of impoverished and marginalized groups in society. Drawing on their extensive national and transnational work in this area, the authors conceptually define social change and identify four leverage points where OD can help: improving the functioning of social change organizations, scaling up their impacts, creating new systems for social change that transcend existing organizational and institutional arrangements, and influencing the contexts, and thereby the activities, of agencies that are critical to social changes. Brown, Leach, and Covey describe the unique challenges in applying OD to social change. They draw emerging lessons for OD interventions and practitioner skills in this area and suggest implications for making the OD field more relevant to social change.

Rajesh Tandon shows in Chapter 32 how OD applies to nonprofit, nongovernment organizations (NGOs) that in many nations have taken on developmental activities typically carried out by government agencies. He identifies the many variants of NGOs in the world today and explains their growing importance in addressing societal problems. Tandon makes a strong case that OD can help NGOs deal with a number of external and internal pressures for change. He outlines the steps in applying OD to NGOs and identifies several prerequisites for success. Because application of OD to NGOs is new yet growing rapidly, Tandon clarifies issues that OD practitioners and NGO leaders need to address to move the field forward in this area.

In Chapter 33, Rupert F. Chisholm applies OD to interorganizational networks, which are composed of multiple organizations that have joined together to perform tasks and solve problems that single organizations cannot do acting alone. He describes the features of interorganizational systems and provides examples of networks engaged in regional development and social problem solving. Chisholm explains the growing importance of interorganizational networks in the context of societal conditions giving rise to complex, messy problems that single organizations cannot resolve. He identifies the unique developmental problems facing networks and describes the steps for applying OD to help resolve them. Chisholm shows the key role that action research plays in network development and argues strongly for more OD knowledge and practice related to this complex form of problem solving.

In Chapter 34, David M. Boje and Mark E. Hillon describe transorganizational development (TD), a form of planned change applied to multiorganization networks. They review the history of TD and propose a storytelling approach to its practice. Boje and Hillon argue that storytelling binds network members together and facilitates their collective memory. They identify two models of storytelling and explain what they mean for TD theory and practice: One focuses on knowledge management and learning in networks and the other on dialogue and multivoiced participation in networks. Boje and Hillon review storytelling approaches to TD practice and propose a new method that can help in analyzing and developing multiorganization networks.

In Chapter 35, Thomas G. Cummings presents an interview with Warren Bennis, one of the founding fathers and leading scholars of OD. Conducted especially for this handbook, the interview asks Warren a series of questions in which he reflects on how the field has evolved and speculates on where it is heading.

PART I

The Nature of Organization Development

2

A Contemporary View of Organization Development

W. WARNER BURKE

Organization development (OD) originated in about 1958. Many of the first-generation of OD academics and practitioners—the pioneers of the field—are now gone: Richard Beckhard, Robert Blake and Jane Mouton, Sheldon Davis, Douglas McGregor, Herb Shepard, and Bob Tannenbaum, to list some of the more recognizable names. With the gradual passing of this first generation of OD pioneers it is clear that the field of OD is now in the hands of second-, third-, and fourth-generation practitioners and academics. Much has changed since 1958, yet many of the original roots of OD remain: promoting humanistic values, developing leaders, and attempting to deal in a systemic way with an organization as a whole, a total entity.

In addition, OD remains a field, not a profession. OD is a domain of study and practice. Even though attempts have been made to relate the practice of OD to statements if not standards of values and ethics (Gellerman, Frankel, & Ladenson, 1990), there is nevertheless no adopted code of ethics, which helps to define a profession. Moreover, there are no entry requirements or licenses. Anyone can choose to call herself (there are currently as many if not slightly more female practitioners in the field) an OD consultant (or OD professional). Thus, the competence level in the field is wide ranging. Of course, charlatans and incompetents do not last very long. The market for OD work is quite demanding. Fools are suffered for perhaps an hour or two, hardly longer. Yet when fools can enter without credentials or sufficient and relevant experience, the field can have a tainted reputation.

And after all these years we still have a problem of simply defining what OD is. Definitions abound, to be sure, but few are the same.

Yet the field is alive and active. The OD Network has a membership of 4,000, the OD

Institute has 300, and the International OD Association has 300. Even the New Jersey OD Network, essentially a virtual organization, has 1,200 members. The American Society for Training and Development has an OD Division, as does the Academy of Management, and both of them have hundreds of members. There is overlap between all these memberships, and there are undoubtedly some competent OD practitioners who belong to none of these networks and divisions. In any case, the number of people who call themselves OD people today is at least 6,000 and may be much more.

OD is taught in many universities, with a number of schools offering advanced degrees in the field. Books and articles on OD continue to be published, and although many organizations do not have formal OD positions, quite a large number do, including the U.S. Postal Service, and whether it is called OD or not, practice that relies on OD knowledge and techniques is widespread (see Tichy & DeRose, 2003).

Thus, OD emerged in the late 1950s, grew rapidly, particularly in the 1960s and 1970s, and to some extent has become established with a body of literature, university and professional programs, and acceptance in many organizations in the United States (Wirtenburg, Abrams, & Ott, 2004) and a number of other countries (Fagenson-Eland, Ensher, & Burke, 2004). At present, however, OD is somewhat stagnant, with growth leveled and new technology sparse (Bradford & Burke, 2005). With such promise from the 1960s and 1970s and with the need for competence in the world of organization change greater than ever before, it is somewhat puzzling and paradoxical that OD is not more prolific and influential than it is.

The purpose of this chapter, then, is to take stock: to consider OD definitions, OD content, and OD education and professional development, to summarize the strengths and limitations of the field, to compare OD with other forms of organization change, to take a close look at the internal practitioner (where does OD reside in the organization?), and, finally, to consider in more depth the apparent paradox of the field today, with such promise and need, yet limited impact.

DEFINING OD

As noted earlier, definitions of OD are known more for their variety, especially with respect to what they emphasize, than for consensus. Different definitions stress the importance of such things as management from the top (Beckhard, 1969); long-range improvement, particularly regarding the ability to change with the help of consultants (French, 1969); a plethora of system-wide processes (Beer, 1980; his exuberant definition consists of 59 words); planned change with emphasis on the organization's culture (Burke, 1982); and the transfer of behavioral science knowledge to planned development for greater organization effectiveness (Cummings & Worley, 2005).

Among these and other definitions of OD there are nevertheless some commonalities. Most definitions include one or more of these terms: *planned, applied behavioral science, system-wide,* and *improving an organization's capacity for change and development*. And although not always specifically mentioned, implicit in many definitions are these three notions: *change, values* (humanistic, participative, collaborative), and *time* (e.g., long-range process).

Most practitioners in the field therefore probably would incorporate into their definitions the ideas that OD is planned, a long-term process, based on commonly held values, and essentially about change and development through application of the behavioral sciences.

The Content of OD

The content and substance of OD that are found in textbooks, articles, and book chapters and in the curriculum of university courses and programs can be considered in three categories: *theory, conceptual frameworks,* and *practice.*

Theory. There is no singular, all-encompassing theory of OD, or organization change in general, for that matter. Open system theory comes the closest. Most experienced OD practitioners, whether explicitly or implicitly, subscribe to the idea that an organization is metaphorically an organism, with the four identifying features being *input* from the organism's external environment, *throughput* (the organism's use of the input), *output* (the results of the use the organism made of the input), and a *feedback* loop that links the output back with the input (Burke, 1982; Cummings & Worley, 2005). This means that astute OD practitioners realize that for survival an organization depends on its external environment, and they conduct their consulting efforts accordingly. Open system theory comes from cell biology (vonBertalanffy, 1956), and comparisons between a living cell and a large, complex organization can be beneficial in terms of key concepts (equilibrium, chaos, self-organizing, and unforeseen consequences) to bear in mind when working with executives of organizations, particularly regarding change (Burke, 2002; Capra, 1996; Pascale, Millemann, & Gioja, 2000).

A number of mini-theories also underlie OD thinking and practice. *Mini* in this case means that the theory touches on aspects of OD (e.g., structure and interfaces) but does not address all facets or how these aspects interact. Examples of mini-theories that help to provide a foundation for OD practice include the *individual* perspective, including motivation based on need theory (Herzberg, 1966; Herzberg, Mausner, & Snyderman, 1959; Maslow, 1954), expectancy theory of motivation (Lawler, 1973; Vroom, 1964), job satisfaction (Hackman & Oldham, 1980; Herzberg, 1966), and positive reinforcement (Skinner, 1953, 1971); the *group* perspective, including group norms and values (Lewin, 1948, 1951), interpersonal competence, changing values, and organizational learning

(Argyris, 1962, 1971; Argyris & Schön, 1978), and the group unconscious (Bion, 1961; Rioch, 1970); and the *total system* perspective, including participative and consensus management (Likert, 1967), contingency theory regarding structure and the importance of interfaces (organization with external environment, strategy with structure, interunit relations, and the employee–organization implicit or psychological contract Lawrence & Lorsch, 1967, 1969), and the organization as a family (Levinson, 1972a, 1972b). For more on these mini-theories see Burke (2002) and Plovnick, Fry, and Burke (1982), and for a self-assessment instrument based on these theories see Plovnick et al. (1982).

Conceptual Frameworks. Perhaps *the* framework for OD practice is action research, meaning that OD work is databased, with a bias toward action that is derived from the data. As Brown (1972) notes, the words *action research* are actually reversed. Research is conducted (data are collected), and then action is taken as a direct result of what the data are interpreted to mean. Lewin's (1946) bias serves as a guide for OD practice: "No action without research and no research without action." The classic study by Coch and French (1948) serves as a model for what action research is and how to conduct it. The accepted framework for action research applied to OD has been provided by French (1969).

Conceptual frameworks also come in the form of organization models (i.e., representations that are usually metaphorical) and organization change (i.e., how change occurs). OD practitioners love models, and practically everyone in the field at only a moment's notice can explain his or her framework for understanding an organization. After all, models help us to categorize myriad bits of information, understand the organization we are trying to help, interpret data about the organization, provide common shorthand language (e.g., the term *culture* covers a lot of ground), and guide action for change. And most OD practitioners conform to some mode of open system thinking. Short of using one's homegrown version, OD practitioners rely on four organization models: Weisbord's (1976) six-box model, probably the most popular one for OD practitioners; Nadler and Tushman's (1977) congruence model; Tichy's (1983) technical, political, and cultural model; and the Burke–Litwin (1992) model of organization performance and change. All four of these models are grounded in open system theory and are both descriptive and prescriptive: Weisbord argues that everything should be coordinated by the leadership box; for Nadler and Tushman, congruence between their categories (boxes) is critical; Tichy's boxes are viewed as levers for change; and Burke and Litwin argue that performance and change must be seen as either transformational or transactional in order for the appropriate action to be taken.

There are also conceptual frameworks for thinking about how organization change occurs or should occur. Kotter (1996) has an eight-stage process: establishing a sense of urgency, creating the guiding coalition, developing a vision and strategy, communicating the change vision, empowering broad-based action, generating short-term wins, consolidating gains and producing change, and anchoring new approaches in the culture. This framework is based on Kotter's observations and experience, which makes sense, but is essentially atheoretical. A more sophisticated model is one by Porras and Silvers (1991), which posits that interventions into the organization (some change initiative) must affect vision, purpose, mission, and work settings (e.g., organization structure), which in turn affect organization members' thinking (cognitive change), which then leads to behavior change and ultimately to improved organization performance and enhanced individual development. Burke (2002) challenges this thinking and argued that behavior change should *precede*

cognitive change (i.e., that the latter occurs as a consequence of behavioral action, as the earlier James–Lange theory suggests). Moreover, Burke (2002) argues that organization change, though typically planned in a linear fashion, actually occurs nonlinearly.

Practice. The practice of OD may be considered in terms of the steps or phases of planned change, a consulting sequence on the part of the OD practitioner, and interventions that OD practitioners use.

Most OD practitioners think in Lewinian (Lewin, 1947) terms. Organization change follows a three-step (*three-phase* probably is the more accurate and accepted term today) sequence: *unfreezing* (creating motivation and readiness to change), *changing* (behavioral movement toward the change goal), and *refreezing* (integrating the change into daily operations and management of the organization). Lippitt, Watson, and Westley (1958) expand the three steps to five, and Schein (1987) elaborates on how Lewin's original three can be understood and implemented. Other phased models have been developed also. The two most prominent are the transition model by Beckhard and Harris (1987), that is, defining the *present state* of an organization, moving toward a change goal (the *transition state*), and defining the *future state,* (the change goal); and another transition model developed by Bridges (1980), defined in terms of *endings,* proceeding through a *neutral zone,* and then embracing *new beginnings.*

A number of slightly different sequences of the consultant's process have been delineated. Most follow a sequence of *entry* (establishing contact and initial rapport with the client), *contracting* (agreeing on what the consultant will do, what the client will do, and what the outcomes are expected to be [Weisbord, 1973]), *data gathering* (collecting information from and about the organization), *diagnosis* (analyzing and interpreting these data), *feedback* (reporting back to the client the data, organized and analyzed), *intervention* (taking action on the diagnosis), *evaluation* (determining whether the intervention had the intended outcome), and *separation* (ending the consultation in a satisfactory manner for both the consultant and the client). This sequence is useful to follow but in reality can only serve as a guide. When a consultant enters a client system and begins to collect data, an intervention is already under way. Moreover, with today's emphasis on speed, the luxury of conducting a comprehensive and thorough diagnosis is rare (Burke, Javitch, Waclawski, & Church, 1997). Again, Lewin's (1947) remark that the best way to understand an organization is to try to change it still applies today. In other words, the nature of resistances to the change and behavioral forces that attempt to return the organization from disequilibrium to equilibrium are very diagnostic.

With respect to OD interventions one might argue that whatever initiative and technique that will move the organization toward the change goal is an OD intervention. Many OD practitioners may endorse this argument. But then we are back to definition, criteria, and boundaries about just what OD is. For example, Argyris (1970) specifies that an *effective* OD intervention must meet three important criteria:

• The intervention must provide valid and useful information; that is, the data collected and reported back to the client should accurately reflect what organization members perceive and feel, what they consider to be their primary concerns, what they experience as complexities and perhaps accompanying frustrations of living within and being a part of the client system, and what they would like to see changed. With respect to this first criterion, Argyris emphasizes that if several independent diagnoses lead to the same intervention, the data collected by the OD practitioner are valid.

• The intervention must be one of free choice; that is, the client makes the decision regarding action to be taken. The OD practitioner's responsibility is to provide alternatives for action. No particular action is automatic, preordained, or imposed. Argyris (1970) put it this way:

> A choice is free to the extent the members can make their selection for a course of action with minimal internal defensiveness, can define the path (or paths) by which the intended consequence is to be achieved; can relate the choice to their central needs; and can build into their choices a realistic and challenging level of aspiration. Free choice therefore implies that the members are able to explore as many alternatives as they consider significant and select those that are central to their needs. (p. 19)

• The intervention must lead to internal commitment; that is, the client owns the choice made and feels responsible for implementing it. One may think of this third criterion as a distinction between compliance and commitment. With the former the organizational member "salutes" but may or may not have any motivation to follow through with action that will ensure the successful implementation of change. With the latter organization members act on their choice because it responds to needs, both individual and on behalf of the organization.

One way to distinguish an OD intervention for change from other interventions is via the three criteria that Argyris provides. Another way is to consider usage: What are the interventions that most OD practitioners use most of the time? Two sources help to answer this question, one from a prominent textbook and the other from research. The textbook source is French and Bell (1995). They created a typology of OD interventions based on target groups. Table 2.1 is a sample of their typology.

Table 2.1

Target Group	Type of Intervention
Individual	• Coaching • Work redesign • Training and development
Dyads and triads	• Process consultation • Role negotiation • Gestalt organization design
Teams or groups	• Team building • Appreciative inquiry • Responsibility charting
Intergroup relations	• Intergroup conflict resolution • Organizational mirroring • Cross-functional task forces
Total organization	• Large group interventions • Survey feedback • Strategic planning and implementation

For a more complete picture of their typology, see page 165 in their text (French & Bell, 1995).

The research by Fagenson and her colleagues provides another source for understanding the kinds of interventions associated with OD practice (Fagenson & Burke, 1990a, 1990b; Fagenson-Eland et al., 2004). These studies were based on practitioners' responses to surveys asking them to indicate which interventions they used the most. A factor analysis of these practitioners' responses showed that a rough comparison could be made with the typology of French and Bell (1995); that is, many of the specific interventions were similar, but the overall categories were not the same (they did not load together according to the target group). The factors accounting for most of the variance included human resource planning and development (e.g., management development, succession planning, and designing and redesigning reward systems), management-style development (e.g., developing a style that enhances productivity, transforming technical experts into managers), vision facilitation (e.g., conducting visioning or futuring activities, process consultation), job and structural design (e.g., job redesign, providing structural change in the organization), high-technology integration (e.g., integration of technology into the workplace, integration of automatic data processing into the organization), managing diversity (e.g., managing cultural differences, integrating women and minorities into the organization), and planning and forecasting (e.g., strategic planning, long-range forecasting).

At the risk of being overly interpretative, one could conclude that the Fagenson-Eland et al. data, though similar in some respects to French and Bell's typology, are more closely associated with the business of the organization and less related to traditional OD interventions such as team building, conflict resolution, and action research. The most recent Fagenson research (Fagenson-Eland et al., 2004) was a cross-cultural study and showed that many typical OD interventions travel to other nations, but, as might be expected, there are differences. For example, multirater feedback is not exactly welcomed in Asian countries, and even though collectivist cultures embrace team building, it is done more according to the group as a whole and less interpersonally; boss–subordinate relationships usually are avoided.

In terms of intervention type and usage, it may be that OD is moving gradually away from its roots. If true, this may not be bad for the field because OD practice could be related more to the business at hand and to the so-called bottom line. Yet the further it moves from its roots, the more difficult it will be to define OD, and because one of its roots has been the tie to academia and scholarship, this loosening may not bode well for future innovation in the field.

So where do aspiring OD practitioners learn about the field, and where do experienced consultants go for renewal and additional learning?

OD Education and Professional Development

Education. There may be the odd undergraduate course in OD at a college or university, but this would be rare. OD is taught predominantly at the graduate level. There are basically three options. First, a person may simply take a course in OD, usually as an elective, in an MBA, MPA, or other master's-level program. Doctoral students could take the class as well, but it is usually an elective in a master's program. Second, one can be enrolled in a master's or doctoral program in organizational psychology, organizational behavior, or industrial–organizational psychology and opt for a concentration in organization change and development, taking such courses as organization change and development, group dynamics, conflict management and resolution, coaching and counseling, and organization dynamics and theory. Programs at universities such as Case Western Reserve, the Columbia University Teachers College, and the University of Southern California provide such options. Third, some universities offer a full degree program, master's or doctorate, in OD. Universities such as American University/NTL, Benedictine, Bowling Green, Fielding Institute, George Washington, Johns Hopkins, and Pepperdine are good examples of this

third option. Some of these programs are cohort (American University/NTL, Benedictine, George Washington, and Pepperdine), but most are residential, yet the curriculum is very similar. And so are the textbooks: Block (1999), Burke (1994), Cummings and Worley (2005), and French and Bell (1995). However, it would be a safe bet to declare that the actual practice of OD is more varied than a given curriculum or textbook would indicate.

Professional Development. Programs for personal and professional development may be classified as either basic or advanced. Although the staff of the basic program offered by Columbia University Teachers College, "Principles and Practices in Organization Development," prefer that an applicant has had group experience (e.g., T-group, a group dynamics course, or a human relations conference), it is not required. Other programs, such as those offered by the NTL Institute, also prefer a background in group dynamics but usually do not require it. Advanced programs such as the "Advanced Program in Organization Development and Human Resource Management," sponsored by Columbia University Teachers College and the University of Michigan Graduate School of Business Administration do presume group experience and typically want participants with at least 5 years of experience. The Gestalt Institute of Cleveland also provides an advanced offering, "The Organization & Systems Development Program."

If one does not have the time, money, or inclination to attend one of these programs, there are other, less intense options such as participating in workshops, often preceding larger conferences, or attending conferences such as the OD Network, the Organization Development Institute, and the Annual Summit on OD sponsored by Linkage, Inc. Related professional organizations such as the Academy of Management, the American Society for Training and Development, and the Society for Industrial and Organizational Psychology also sponsor preconference and postconference workshops that are often germane to OD.

Because OD is a field of study and practice rather than a profession, choices for education and professional development are not clear-cut. One must seek advice from more experienced and trusted practitioners. Also, sticking one's toe in the water by attending a workshop sponsored by a reputable professional or academic society often is a good way to see whether OD is a path worth pursuing.

Let us now consider the content of OD in more depth by examining the field's strengths and limitations. This consideration will take the form of what we know (strengths) and what we need to know (limitations).

More specifically, the purpose of these next two sections is to provide a current statement of what we know about the practice of OD (i.e., what the OD practitioner can rely on) and what we need to know for the future (i.e., what new knowledge and skills are lacking yet are likely to be required).

OD: WHAT WE KNOW

Although this is not an exhaustive list, the following seven areas—OD process and content, change leadership, organization structure, reward systems, training and development, teams and teamwork, and organization performance—constitute a large proportion of the field of OD and represent primary categories of practice.

The Process and Content of OD

As noted earlier, the practice of OD begins with Lewin's three steps: unfreeze, change, and refreeze. These steps have been expanded and elaborated on. We know the importance of determining the organization's readiness for change and what it will take to make the organization malleable for initial movement toward a change goal. *Malleability* means at the outset some form of education, that is, communicating a need for change based on

changes that are occurring in the organization's external environment (the open system concept). This unfreezing stage therefore means making the case for change and helping organization members to see and feel the need for change.

The second step in Lewin's framework, change or movement toward the goal, typically involves an emphasis on behavior, that is, getting organization members to conduct their work differently, to manage and reward people in new ways, and to be guided by a new vision, and perhaps mission, that will lead to a revised culture and to greater organization, work unit, and individual effectiveness.

Refreezing means finding ways of rewarding and sustaining the new desired behaviors that will ensure ultimate realization of the organization change goal and the purpose: the desired future state.

Also as noted earlier, another aspect of process is the consulting sequence followed by the OD practitioner (e.g., entry, contracting, data gathering). OD practitioners have followed these processes for decades. We understand them and trust them (e.g., the importance of good contracting with a client). By trusting our processes, we are likely to succeed as consultants.

OD content may be considered in two ways: organizational and interventional. *Organizational content* refers to the domains of the organization that OD practitioners focus on for purposes of data gathering and diagnosis: organization mission, strategy, culture, morale, motivation, and performance, to name some of the primary ones. OD practitioners are expected to know, and highly experienced and competent ones do know, what strategy means, the difference between leadership and management, the nature of organization culture, how systems (e.g., rewards, information technology) affect behavior and vice versa, and what are the primary antecedents of performance (e.g., motivation, abilities, and context).

Interventional content refers to initiatives and activities that provide leverage for change. This form of OD content means know-how (e.g., how to collect valid information for a proper diagnosis, how to conduct team-building activities, how to conduct a survey and provide feedback that is useful for action, how to select potential leaders and develop them, how to translate concepts such as values, cultural norms, mission, and vision statements into behavioral language, how to conduct executive coaching, and how to relate any of these interventions to business objectives and performance).

For experienced and competent OD practitioners, these two categories of OD, content and process, are familiar territories.

Change Leadership

It is difficult to comprehend organization change, at least change that actually works, without effective leadership. In organization change efforts OD practitioners work with leaders, some of whom are truly leaders and some of whom try hard but are not especially successful. This latter group consists occasionally of people who have succeeded as managers but have trouble when thrust into a significant leadership role. Leadership is more about personal influence and persuasive abilities, whereas management is more about role and task accomplishment. Astute OD practitioners know about these distinctions and how to work differently with each. Organization change, especially at the outset, requires leadership. As the changes gets under way, management becomes more important.

As we know, the change leader needs to have a vision of the future that can be translated into clear directions and goals, must be articulate and persuasive about the need for change, and embodies the change with her or his story (linking the leader's journey with that of the organization) and with consistency between words and actions. We also know the importance of self-awareness for effective leadership (see Church, 1997).

And, finally, we know that it is easier to be directional, even unilateral, regarding the establishment of change goals in the first place than it is to be unilateral about how to reach the goals. After all, for every goal there are numerous paths to get there. In other words, the probability of disagreement is much higher for determining a path, that is, implementation. OD practitioners know how important it is to coach a change leader to be participative and involved in implementation.

Organization Structure

By *structure* we mean the organization chart, the design of the accountability and decision-making processes, the span of control, and how steep or flat the hierarchy is. We know that there is no one best way to organize, so contingency theory is *the* theory for organization design. Structure depends on strategy, the nature of the business and the overall industry, and the current business model.

We are familiar with the three fundamental organization designs—functional; product, business unit, regional, or by market; and matrix—and understand that most structures, particularly for large, complex organizations, follow a mixed design. Often the mix is one of functional at the top (e.g., executive vice presidents of finance, administration including human resources and legal operations, information technology, public relations) and product or business unit in the middle (e.g., product or business unit heads reporting to the executive vice president of operations). We also know that a pure matrix design is rare. Solid-line and dotted-line accountabilities—direct accountability (dotted line) to a functional head—are more common and not a pure matrix (individuals having two bosses with comparable authority). Being steeped with contingencies, we are therefore well aware that there is no perfect design; there are advantages and disadvantages for each.

We also know that whether to centralize or decentralize is no longer the right question; the right question to ask is which organization functions should be centralized and which decentralized.

Finally, it has been said that the only aspect of all organizations that is common throughout history, and remaining today irrespective of culture or society, is hierarchy. Although recent trends have leaned more toward flatter hierarchies and larger spans of control, hierarchy itself is not likely to fade away.

OD practitioners may be normative regarding certain values, such as the belief that every organization member has a right to learn, grow, and be treated fairly, but experienced practitioners know that when it comes to organization structure they cannot advocate a normative view; OD practitioners are all contingency theorists in this regard.

Reward Systems

People do at any given moment what they have been rewarded for doing before that moment. We know this. But we also know that in the workplace what organization members do and what they are rewarded for doing are not always the same (see Kerr's [1975] classic article, "On the Folly of Rewarding A, While Hoping for B"). Astute OD practitioners, particularly those internal to the organization, therefore are diligent about discerning which kinds of behavior are rewarded, whether intended or not. Corrective action is then taken to link rewards with desired behavior, especially behavior that is performance related.

These statements may sound simple, but incentive systems in particular are fraught with complexity. Do they work? Sometimes they work only too well, that is, they can motivate organization members to focus almost entirely on doing what they need to do to get the rewards, even in lieu of other activities that might contribute to organization performance. Although pay-for-performance schemes (and there are many: profit sharing,

cash bonus, gain sharing, and skill-based pay, to name a few) are problematic, many executives continue to subscribe to one form or the other. There are many barriers to any effective pay-for-performance system, including those associated with linking performance to effort and linking pay to performance. Consider the following:

> Potential barriers to linking performance to effort include difficulties in measuring performance; factors outside the control of individual and groups being paid for that performance; and that managers and peers are uncomfortable with rating employees differently. Potential barriers to linking pay to performance include the following: employees can come to rely on the additional compensation; employees are biased toward over estimating their own contribution; corporate budget for bonuses often limit payout; and managers can lose commitment to the pay system if it pays out more than anticipated due to problems in payout standards and if there are changes in performance standards due to changes in technology and organizational arrangements and unanticipated learning curves. It is changing circumstances that make it difficult for managers to sustain links between pay and performance in a way that will avoid perceptions of unfairness and inequity. Such perceptions can undermine the perceived link between pay and performance so important to sustain its motivational power. (Beer & Cannon, 2004, pp. 4–5)

This quote is from a special issue of the journal *Human Resource Management* leading with the article by Beer and Cannon and followed by seven individual commentaries. Forty-five journal pages were devoted to the exploration of "Promise and Peril in Implementing Pay-for-Performance," resulting in two major conclusions: Managers tend to believe that the costs of pay-for-performance programs outweigh the benefits, and better investments are likely to include developing effective leadership programs, establishing clear objectives, coaching, and training. These are managers' beliefs and opinions, which are not surprising, but we remain short of facts regarding the cost–benefit ratio of pay-for-performance programs.

Much more could be stated about reward systems. The two areas addressed here—linking pay to behavior and pay-for-performance schemes—represent some of the most problematic ones. We know about these problems, but much more remains to be known, as addressed in a subsequent section of this chapter.

Training and Development

Much of OD evolved from training and development, particularly experiential learning methods. Though a clear strength of the formative years of the field, they have also been a problem. Many of the activities included under the rubric of OD are really "ID": individual development. In more recent years, old hands at OD have raised the question of where the *O* is in *OD*.

In any case, we know that our training and development roots grew from both sides of the Atlantic Ocean: the T group or sensitivity training in the United States and the group relations conference from the Tavistock Institute in London. Combining feedback with experiential learning methods, these initiatives evolved from interpersonal relations and group dynamics to team building and from face-to-face feedback to more structured and somewhat distant forms (e.g., multirater feedback programs). We know how important feedback is to learning, and the more current and structured versions are still attempts to help individuals learn and develop. And when applied properly, activities such as multirater feedback processes can be used as leverage for organization change— more toward the *O* in *OD*. But all is not well regarding multirater systems, as we will see later in this chapter.

In general, then, we know a lot today about how adults learn, including the importance of involvement in the learning process and choice of methods. OD practitioners who on occasion double as trainers usually are well equipped. Important as it is to ensure that the *O* is central to OD, we also know that in the end, individual behavior change is key and the end result of organization change. Thus, individual development cannot be separated from OD, but to be OD, individual development must be in the service of or leverage for system-wide change, an integral aspect of OD's definition.

Teams and Teamwork

Among the many roots of OD, the main root is group dynamics. It is therefore not surprising that early OD emphasized group learning activities, which gradually emerged into the form of team building. The dominant intervention of OD in the 1960s was team building, that is, OD practitioners working with a work unit to improve boss–subordinate relationships, goal and role clarity, decision-making and conflict resolution procedures, and interpersonal relations in general (Beckhard, 1972). It is probably not an exaggeration to declare that most OD practitioners enter the field via their use of group facilitation skills. The cornerstone of OD was team building and may remain so today.

Organization Performance

Ultimately OD is about organization change and improving organization performance. We know that the latter usually takes the form of financial outcomes, balancing the budget in a nonprofit organization and having a robust return on investment and net profit in a profit-making, commercial enterprise. We also understand the importance of considering performance across different levels of the organization: individual, work unit, and total system. We are also aware of the measurement problem: What are the true indices of effective performance? Who are the measures for: owners, employees, boards of directors, the Securities and Exchange Commission and other regulatory agencies? How do we measure? Is it just the difference between sales and the cost of goods and services sold before taxes? Or is it multiple (e.g., return on investment, return on assets, and earnings per share)? Answering these questions and making choices between them for a corporation are somewhat contingent on the nature of the business model: How do we make money in this kind of industry and how do we differ—or want to differ—from our competitors? And how can we ensure that our business model incorporates methods of superior customer service?

With regard to rewards, experienced OD practitioners will concentrate on systematic issues in attempting to wrestle with pay-for-performance programs. Clear ideas about what counts in organization performance must be incorporated into any incentive system.

These last two statements illustrate that these seven areas of OD knowledge are not discrete. After all, we are dealing with a system, an open and ever-changing one, whether we dictate the change or not. In concluding this section, it should be repeated that although these seven are highly important to our understanding of OD, other important areas could have been included, such as strategic planning and implementation, information technology, culture change, and communication processes. Thus, these seven areas are somewhat arbitrary but represent mainstream OD. As we proceed to what we need to know, some of the omitted areas will be addressed to some extent.

OD: WHAT WE NEED TO KNOW

What follows is a fairly lengthy list of organization change areas that OD practitioners need to know more about. This list of 14 areas touches on the previous, more comprehensive 7 areas regarding what we know but is more specific and covers new ground. Though lengthy, this list is certainly not exhaustive.

The list is more directly related to recognizable areas of OD practice rather than, say, coverage of business domains such as strategy, information technology, or budget processes, all of which OD practitioners need to know more about.

Planned Change and Unplanned Consequences

An interesting paradox about organization change and development is that we plan the process in a linear fashion following perhaps an expanded version of Lewin's three steps—unfreeze, change, and refreeze—yet the implementation of the plans is anything but linear. The actual change process is rather chaotic and messy. Murphy's Law reigns: If anything can go wrong, it will. Many reactions to the launch of a change effort are unanticipated (e.g., some of the organizational members that we thought would be supportive are resistant, and some we expected to resist actually embrace the changes). Much of implementing change is, or should be, spent on fixing unanticipated problems, backing up to correct consequences of the change that were unexpected. But as long as the change goals and vision remain clear and in place, positive movement can be expected if unanticipated consequences to the change are confronted immediately and action taken to get the effort back on track. This process could be called change management, that is, dealing with reactions to and consequences of change initiatives. So OD practitioners need to know conceptually that change implementation is nonlinear, even though the planning may be linear, and need to learn more about how to help change leaders react to and deal with seemingly chaotic conditions, to persevere, and to be patient during messy, trying times to allow creativity to emerge—leading on "the edge of chaos," as Pascale and his colleagues (2000) call it. For more on the nonlinear aspects of organization change, see Burke (2002).

Momentum

After describing and explaining the significant changes of British Airways (BA) in the 1980s, Goodstein and Burke (1991) conclude their article with the following:

> It may be that BA's biggest problem now is not so much to manage further change as it is to manage the change that has already occurred. In other words, the people of BA have achieved significant change and success; now they must maintain what has been achieved while concentrating on continuing to be adaptable to changes in their external environment—the further deregulation of Europe, for example. Managing momentum may be more difficult than managing change. (p. 16)

We know that after a long and arduous journey down a change path, organization members can experience "change fatigue" and ask, "When will it be over?" Of course, today organization change is never really over. Change has been added to the list of death and taxes. But once a major change effort has been launched and is well under way, say, for a year or two, sustaining the process becomes difficult and sometimes tedious. We need to know more about how to sustain change to manage momentum. This entails, for example, holding celebratory events to recognize milestones reached and the individuals and teams who made it happen. It also entails finding new ways to reward the behaviors that support the change and to plan and implement new initiatives that will move the change effort to yet another level of accomplishment, such as conducting a training program to provide new skills and techniques for organization members. Managing momentum therefore is about continuous innovation and initiating activities that will energize people to battle "change fatigue."

Communication

In a survey that Blake and Mouton (1968) conducted to establish a basis for their approach to OD, they asked managers from 198 companies (66 each in the United States, the United Kingdom, and Japan) representing a wide variety of businesses to state what they thought were the foremost barriers to corporate excellence. At the top of the list of barriers was communication. Other barriers included planning (the lack of), morale, and coordination. Blake and Mouton contend that when you dig deeper for understanding, the managers' statements about communication problems were really not about communication. The statements were symptoms of far deeper and more significant causal factors. Blake and Mouton's main conclusion was that the deeper issue concerned managerial approaches and styles.

No doubt Blake and Mouton's conclusion had merit. Even to this day people in organizations blame a lot on communication when at a deeper level they are likely to be concerned with bad boss behaviors and issues of trust, fairness, and stupid bureaucracy. But to dismiss communication issues as mere symptoms is to overlook some actual problems that need to be addressed directly.

In times of organization change there are always issues of what to communicate, how much to communicate, and when to communicate. Moreover, in the midst of change things happen rapidly, rumors spread like a fast-moving virus, and ambiguity trumps clarity. People want to know what's going on and who's calling the shots. If the change leader communicates too much, expectations on the part of organization members become unrealistic ("Now we're going to get a big raise in pay!"). If the change leader communicates too little, paranoia sets in, and the leader is accused of conducting "secret deals." If the change leader communicates too much too soon in the process, misunderstandings are likely to occur. If the change leader communicates too little too late, organization members are likely to have concluded that the change effort was not working and the whole thing should be abandoned. So what is a change leader to do? Communicate in an open and honest manner, but do so in a careful, balanced fashion. The OD practitioner's job is to help the change leader with these decisions and with the process. There are no clear-cut rules. Much more learning is needed about what, how much, and when to communicate about the organization change process.

Leader Personality and the Organization's "Personality"

Over a long lunch, a friend who has been in the executive search business for more than two decades revealed that even though his business had been highly successful with placements, he felt nevertheless a sense of failure. What he meant was that most of the placements lasted no more than 2 or 3 years. Continuing to place executives, some he had placed before, was obviously good for the business, but it left him with a feeling of unease. He attributed the turnover to a lack of adequate fit between the executive's personality and the new (for the executive) organization's culture. In other words, decisions were made on the strength of the executive's technical abilities, experience, and initial impressions of interpersonal competence. Yet over time in most cases, the strength of the organization's culture and the strength of the executive's personality began to clash, and the executive eventually moved on. Although this clash is one of an individual with the larger organization, it is not unlike the clash of cultures when two organizations attempt a merger. There is much to learn about these culture and personality clashes. This should be ripe territory for OD practitioners.

Power and Politics

Although Greiner and Schein (1988) addressed some time ago the dynamics and importance of power and politics for successful OD, many practitioners remain reluctant to get involved in these kinds of issues, or they are rarely in a position to do so. There are two issues here. One concerns values and perhaps discomfort, and the other is structural. With respect to the former, many OD practitioners subscribe to humanistic values, including openness, honesty, and equality. There is also a positivistic bias incorporated into these values. Power and politics often are associated with the darker side of humanness and therefore not to be emphasized. Moreover, it is likely that some OD practitioners avoid such interactions because they simply feel uncomfortable with attempts to confront the misuse of power in particular or simply to be involved in the political process in general.

The structural issues concern where internal OD practitioners are located on the organization chart. Most are buried in the human resource function and rarely have the opportunity to sit at the same table with executives who run the organization and thereby wield power (Burke, 2004).

Yet the reality is that organization development and change do not occur without the use of power, in the form of leaders making decisions. Furthermore, and particularly in times of significant organization change, internal politics become paramount. Connecting with and attempting to influence opinion shapers, people who have informal status, and those who keep their ear to the grapevine are important activities for facilitating organization change. The point is that OD practitioners need to learn more about organization power and politics and be less reluctant to engage in these kinds of dynamics.

Coaching the Change Leader

OD practitioners need to help change leaders to be as effective as they can be. But effective at what? One could probably construct a long list of "whats." Let us consider at least six. These might be called critical requisites for effective change leadership.

• *Above-average self-awareness:* There is evidence that the more self-aware one is, the more likely one is to be a high performer; in other words, there is a positive relationship between self-awareness and managerial performance (Church, 1997). OD practitioners need to know how to help people in positions of leadership to learn more about themselves, particularly in how they affect and are affected by others, what their strengths and limitations are, and what their biases are.

• *Conceptual abilities:* Change leaders must know how to help organization members understand what is happening and will happen to them during the change process, explain in clear terms what the change is all about and why they are taking this course of action, and help organization members see what the future is likely to be. Conceptualizing and making sense of what to expect before and during the change effort is critical to being successful. OD practitioners need to know how to help change leaders to conceptualize, to provide frameworks for understanding.

• *Tolerance for ambiguity:* There are individual differences in how tolerant people are of matters that are not clear and structured. Change leaders need to be more tolerant of such ambiguity than most people. Organization change, by definition, generates circumstances that are not predictable. Dealing effectively with this lack of predictability and orderliness is the mark of a skillful change leader. OD practitioners need to know how to help change leaders deal with ambiguity, to be patient when things go wrong or not as predicted, and to manage unanticipated consequences to change interventions quickly so that movement toward the goals will be sustained rather than derailed.

• *High energy and enthusiasm:* Change leaders who are slow moving and more pessimistic than optimistic are not likely to succeed. OD practitioners need to know how to help change leaders manage their time so that their energy will be deployed well and to give them ideas about how to keep morale high in the face of setbacks.

• *Conflict management:* Organization change tends to breed conflict between individuals and groups. Organization members before the change is launched may disagree about goals, but they will certainly disagree about how to reach the goals. Also, turf protection will emerge, value differences will be debated, and arguments will occur about space, positions, and budgets. OD practitioners must know how to help change leaders deal with these conflicts as effectively as possible, to help them listen, understand different viewpoints and perspectives, and facilitate resolution of differences.

• *Taking the heat:* This final requisite is related to the previous one but is more personal. In times of organization change, especially when things are perceived to be going wrong, the change leader is likely to be criticized if not vilified. OD practitioners need to know how to support the change leader during these times— to help the leader to understand that defensive feelings are normal but that it is not wise to act on them, to listen and ask questions rather than make speeches, and to seek suggestions about how matters could be improved.

These six requisites are by no means the only ones but do represent some of the more necessary ones for successful change leadership.

Self-Directed Groups and Virtual Teams

Richard Hackman (1992, 2002) has contributed more to our understanding of self-directed groups than practically anyone else, but he has only scratched the surface. Much more needs to be known. Therefore, it behooves OD practitioners to learn as much as they can because they are likely to be sought for help in facilitating the work of self-directed groups.

With the business world particularly becoming more global and travel budgets less liberal, many organization teams today interact via teleconferencing and e-mail rather than face to face. Virtual team dynamics are not quite the same as those of teams who meet around a table in the same room. As Bunker, Alban, and Lewicki (2004) underscore, OD practitioners need to learn more about these different dynamics and how to help with virtual team building. For more on this topic, see Gibson and Cohen (2003).

Organization Structure

Three subareas of organization structure have recently emerged that need the attention of OD practitioners. They are boundary spanning, cells and networks, and unit size.

Boundary spanning. We know that as organizations grow, so does differentiation; labor and organization functions keep dividing (Greiner, 1972). The problem then becomes one of integration and coordination. In the latter years of his tenure as CEO of General Electric, Jack Welch argued for the boundaryless organization. Having absolutely no boundaries between functions and work units would lead to chaotic working conditions, with responsibilities, roles, and authority becoming meaningless. Welch may have overreacted in this cry for a boundaryless company, but his motivation came from frustration with structures that looked like silos and smokestacks. Nothing could get resolved across units until it landed on his desk; in other words, there was entirely too much differentiation. OD practitioners usually are good at bringing people together, but they need to know more about integrating and spanning boundaries for purposes of improving the business and overall organizational performance, not just to get people together.

Cells and networks. With everything that is happening in the world today, isn't it obvious

that we need to know more about these seemingly informal ways of organizing and working together? Cell biology has much to teach us about the larger system. Consider the concept of autopoiesis, or self-making, which means that a living system continuously produces itself. The function of each human cell is to participate in the production of other components in the system so that it continually makes itself. Are there parallels to our understanding of organizations? No doubt. For more on these parallels, see Burke (2002) and Capra (1996).

Networks can be considered as an interaction of cells, whether the cell is singular or acts in pairs, trios, or larger groups. Within and across organizations, informal networks emerge, evolve, serve some purpose, and may then be dissolved. But networks can last for years; the OD Network is a case in point. OD practitioners know some things about networks, such as the apparent paradox that the more one attempts to change an informal network (the OD Network is closer to a formal organization such as a professional society), the greater the risk of destroying it. Informal networks appear to be delicate, if not ephemeral. OD practitioners need to know more about these informal systems and how to work with them.

Unit size. When is a work unit within a larger organization—a department, division, factory, or regional unit—the right size? It appears to be no more than 150 people. If you have read Gladwell's (2000) book *The Tipping Point,* then this idea will sound familiar. Gladwell referred to two notions from the behavioral sciences: social channel capacity and transactive memory. The former concerns the maximum number of people with whom we can have a social relationship, that is, to remember who the others in our group are and something about them. The research conducted by Dunbar (1992) showed that the maximum number was 147.8; we would not violate the finding by rounding up to 150. Gore Associates, a high-tech company headquartered in Delaware, never has a manufacturing site that is populated by more that 150 workers.

Transactive memory, explained by psychologist Daniel Wegner (1991), means that as people get to know one another fairly well, they gradually develop a "transactive memory system," that is, knowledge of who knows what and who may be best suited to do a particular kind of task. So this memory is about knowing what others are capable of, their skills, and their degree of reliability. And apparently the limit of our transactive memory is 150 other individuals.

Interestingly, the research and the ideas of Dunbar and Wegner (and made so readable and understandable by Gladwell, 2000) represent the best of applying knowledge from the behavioral sciences to organizations, an integral component of the definition of OD.

Rewards and Motivation

As noted earlier, much has been written and no doubt discussed at the water cooler in most corporations about incentives and pay-for-performance programs. We hang on to pay-for-performance schemes that we know are not really working, yet to scrap them seems sacrilegious. We've done them for many years, and expectations are difficult to change. But we know that, done properly, incentive systems can work. OD practitioners simply need to work harder on what "done properly" means and act accordingly.

With respect to motivation (we may never learn enough about this human quality), there is some evidence that incentive systems that are largely extrinsic, such as monetary bonuses, can have a detrimental effect on intrinsic motivation, which is more powerful for enhancing motivation. Showering organizations with money for their performance may reduce the psychological meaningfulness of their work. OD practitioners need to learn more about these complex dynamics of human motivation in the workplace.

Action Learning and the Integration of Content and Process

As stated before, the distinction between content and process is important "because the former, the *what,* provides the vision and overall direction for the change; and the process, the *how,* concerns implementation and adoption" (Burke, 2002, p. 14). But the distinction is not as pure as it may sound. Consider a simple example: When we are speaking to another person, the topic of discussion is the content and how we speak—forcefully or softly—is the process. How strongly or passionately we feel about the topic and how the person to whom we are speaking reacts will affect both the nature of the content (we may bring in another point we would not have otherwise considered) and how forcefully we continue to speak to the other person. In other words, there is a constant interaction between content and process; each affects the other.

Action learning, a fairly recent entry into the practice of OD, is a blending of content and process. Action learning is essentially what Argyris and Schön (1978) call "double-loop learning," in contrast to single-loop learning. Single-loop learning is fixing a problem, accomplishing a task, whereas double-loop learning is solving a problem and learning more about the problem-solving process itself. OD practitioners can make the mistake of acting on the belief that they really do not need to know the content, the product or service of the organization; whether it is a potato chip or computer chip really doesn't matter. After all, OD is about process. But how organization members talk and interact at work differs depending on whether they are producing potato chips or computer chips, and this difference creates a distinctive process for each work setting. OD practitioners therefore must learn more about this interaction of content and process and intervene accordingly, showing a work team how the nature of the task affects their work processes. For example, if solving a particular task is linear and largely a matter of logic, a consensual process for the work team may not be all that effective. If the task is not a linear one and is anything but obvious, a consensual process is more likely to be facilitative.

Individual Development and Organization Development

In terms of practice, early OD emphasized individual, interpersonal, and small group levels in the organization. An implicit belief early on was that developing individuals and reaching a critical mass of them would eventually affect the organization; see, for example, an early article by Argyris (1964). In addition, the value roots of OD are humanistic (e.g., "Everyone has a right to learn and grow"). Therefore, much of what is labeled as OD is concerned with individual and team development. Or, put another way and staying with our definition that OD is about system-wide change, most OD practitioners use OD techniques and tools but do not do OD. There is nothing wrong here. Using OD technology to help individuals and teams improve is fine. The bias being expressed here is the importance of not being deluded about what doing OD means.

But can individual development be in the service of organization development? Yes, absolutely. It's a matter of leverage. A leadership development program aimed at providing feedback on behaviors that have been designated as key to culture change is an example; see the case of organization change at a bank in Chapter 10 of Burke (2002). The point is that OD practitioners need to know more about how to leverage individual development for organization development and change.

Synergy

We know that synergy is expressed as $2 + 2 = 5$, that a group outcome on a task is more than the simple sum of individual outcomes. But these expressions are about outcomes. What is the process like? Can an OD practitioner actually help a team to achieve synergy? If so, how?

Yes, members need to listen to one another and build on one another's ideas, and using appreciative inquiry techniques may contribute, but what else?

Personal observations of videotapes of seven- or eight-person groups that had achieved synergy on a task that had measurable outcomes based on sound criteria for success yielded surprising evidence. The tapes revealed that there appeared to be little order to the groups' processes. Group members talked over one another, with listening seeming to be incidental. The picture was chaotic as the groups struggled to meet the time deadline and complete their task. Yet in the end their performances, their outcomes, were outstanding. They achieved what we define synergy to be: more than the simple sum of the individual parts. But what is synergy really? What is unique about the process of groups that achieve synergy compared with those who do not? Being more effective as a group consultant in OD practice is, at least in part, a function of learning more about the synergistic process.

Organization Performance

For OD purposes at least, two aspects of organization performance need more attention. First is the "balanced score card." There is much talk about the use of the balanced score card but much less action. Yet from an OD perspective, Kaplan and Norton's (1996) contribution makes sense. In addition to financial factors, as we would expect, there are measures of customer satisfaction, innovation, and internal business practices. Kaplan and Norton stress the importance of balance, giving equal weight to all four measures. People in the field of OD have for many years lamented the definition of organization performance being limited to financial indices only. This is a movement that OD practitioners need to learn more about and support.

Second, there is a need to learn more about how mission, strategy, and especially organization culture influence all levels of performance:

individual, work unit, and total system. Not since the research of Kotter and Heskett (1992), in which they demonstrated a line between culture and performance, have we had systematic work on understanding more about this linkage and influence. Being clearer about the most important antecedents to performance is a highly worthwhile endeavor.

Multirater Feedback and Coaching

Multirater feedback can be a powerful tool for OD practice, but there are problems. It looks as though multirater feedback does not harm individual performance, but there seems to be little or no evidence that it helps. It appears that once managers and executives receive feedback from multiple sources, they either avoid taking any action (perhaps denying or resisting the feedback) or may simply not know what to do. In any case, what seems to make a difference is coaching. Three recent studies report that when multirater feedback is supported by coaching, individual performance is more likely to improve than in a no-coaching condition (Luthans & Peterson, 2003; Seifert, Yukl, & McDonald, 2003; Smither, London, Flautt, Vargas, & Kucine, 2003). OD practitioners, then, need to know more about coaching in the context of multirater feedback.

Final Comments About the Need-to-Know Areas

As stated earlier, the 14 areas about which OD practitioners need to know more are not exhaustive. The list could have been much longer. Whether this is the definitive list or not, the message is this: The notion of self as instrument applies as much to OD practice as to practically any other field one could mention. The field of OD is only as good as what the OD practitioner knows and can apply competently. And the world of organization change keeps changing (Burke, 1993). Therefore, lifelong learning is an absolute necessity if one wants to be as competent in this field as one can be.

ADDITIONAL PERSPECTIVES

We will now consider additional perspectives concerning OD with the intent of understanding in more detail the nature of the field today. These perspectives include a comparative view of OD with change management and other forms of organization change, internal OD practitioners, and the promise of OD, realized and unrealized.

A Comparative View of OD

Change Management

The emergence of what currently is called change management has caused some confusion. Is it the same as OD? After all, OD is about managing and leading organization change. A few observers even think that change management will replace OD (Worren, Ruddle, & Moore, 1999). Although there is much overlap between OD and change management, differences do exist. Marshak (2005) describes and clarifies the differences.

First, it should be noted that most of change management practice comes from large management consulting firms such as Accenture, Bearing Point, Cap Gemini, Ernst & Young, and IBM Business Consulting Services. Second, as Marshak points out, there are value differences. Change management has a strong business and economic emphasis, whereas OD is more humanistic. Other comparisons made by Marshak are that change management emphasizes outcomes, whereas OD emphasizes processes; and change management stresses engineering and directing the change effort, whereas OD stresses facilitation, participation, and coaching. In short, change management is oriented more to the bottom line, and OD is more concerned with the factors or antecedents that affect the bottom line.

Additional Comparisons

First, OD is planned change. Most change in organizations is unplanned, and OD practitioners often are called on to help with change that may be already in progress but is haphazard and not being managed well. But if it's OD, it's a planned process focused on the total system.

Second, OD is one among other forms of organization change. Change management is similar to but not the same as OD. Considering briefly the history of organization change, broadly speaking, helps to provide perspective. We could begin with ancient China or episodes from the Old Testament, but the beginning of modern organization change occurred at the turn of the 20th century with the work of Frederick Taylor and what he called scientific management. The McKinsey consulting firm began with this mode of change work. Subsequently, the Hawthorne studies had a significant influence on how organization change was defined, as did the early work of industrial psychologists, especially during and immediately after World War II. Other forms of change that emerged were sensitivity training, sociotechnical systems, survey feedback, and OD circa 1958. Other forms of organization change fall within methods of coercion and confrontation, such as the work of Saul Alinsky (1946). For more coverage of these methods and other strategies and techniques of organization change, see Hornstein, Bunker, Burke, Gindes, and Lewicki (1971).

OD has incorporated and to some extent modified some of the methods listed earlier, namely, sociotechnical systems, sensitivity training, survey feedback, findings from industrial psychology and the Hawthorne studies, and to some extent Taylor's scientific management, but in the main, OD's distinctiveness rests with a planned, system-wide focus that relies on applying the behavioral sciences and humanistic values.

The Internal OD Practitioner

External–Internal Practitioner Relations

Often internal OD practitioners bring into their organization an outsider, an external consultant to help with special issues and interventions or a large system-wide change effort. This combination can result in some problems, such as the external person not really delivering what the internal person needs or competitive feelings between the two that may reduce the effectiveness of the consulting process, but the potential benefits outweigh problems that may occur. These benefits include the following:

- The external practitioner may bring expertise that the internal practitioner does not have but the organization needs.

- The internal practitioner may have an opportunity to learn from a more experienced external practitioner

- The external practitioner can work with high-level executives, whereas the internal practitioner may not be as acceptable for this higher-level work because the executives might consider the relationship a violation of status and respect, or what the executives want help with may be too confidential for the internal practitioner to know about.

- The change effort may be so large, diverse, and complex that the internal practitioner simply cannot deal with everything that needs attention.

Finally, an effective working relationship between an internal and external practitioner occurs when reciprocal needs are met; for example, the external practitioner must rely on the internal practitioner for the knowledge that the latter has about the system, its culture, where the skeletons are buried, and who has power. The internal practitioner relies on the external practitioner for additional expertise and perhaps broader experience.

Issues of Organization Structure: Where Does the Internal OD Practitioner Belong?

It had been argued that OD practitioners, particularly those who are internal, do not sit at the tables of power in organizations and therefore have little influence on large-scale change efforts (Bradford & Burke, 2005). Assuming that this is at least partially true, why might this be so? One reason is clearly structural, that is, a matter of where the internal OD practitioner is positioned functionally and within the hierarchy of the employing organization. Most internal OD practitioners are buried in the human resource function and have to go through many hierarchical channels to get to the seats of power. This positioning is not true of all internal OD practitioners. There are other arrangements. What follows is a brief description of five such structural arrangements.

- The *traditional* model: This arrangement is labeled traditional because it is the most common and historical one. Here OD is a subfunction of human resources and has accountability within the system accordingly. If there is a group of internal OD practitioners, the head of this group is likely to report to the human resource development subfunction of human resources or to the senior manager in charge of human resources overall.

- The *independent* model: OD here is a freestanding unit and does not report to human resources but rather to some other executive, such as the head of administration or perhaps operations.

- The *decentralized* model: OD practitioners in this arrangement are part of a business or regional unit and report to either the head of human resources for that unit or to the unit head. There are usually a small number of OD practitioners at the head office or headquarters who coordinate OD work, but the authority for that work rests with the decentralized unit.

- The *integrated* model: In this arrangement every human resource person, except for the subfunctions that are outsourced (e.g., payroll, benefits, or even training) is also an OD practitioner and vice versa. In other words, the primary human resource people are all trained in OD skills and competencies. This model is not widespread, but some organizations are moving in this direction.

- The *strategy* model: OD practitioners are an integral part of the strategic planning function of the organization. In essence, OD is concerned with strategy implementation, helping to make these plans work, so the strategy function is a natural home in the organization for OD.

Recall that there is no perfect organization structure. The optimal structure depends on the organization's mission, strategy, and goals. As in any contingency, there are advantages and disadvantages. So it is with these five models. A sample follows:

- *Traditional:* Because human resources is a legitimate function in the organization, OD as a subfunction becomes legitimate, too; however, a number of operations managers and executives do not respect the human resource function, and therefore OD becomes tainted as well.

- *Independent:* A plus here is that specialists of similar values and like mind work and learn together; however, a free-standing unit is vulnerable to scrutiny and political processes.

- *Decentralized:* The OD practitioner has autonomy and significant challenge, both of which contribute to strong motivation to perform well; however, it is difficult for the practitioner to grow and develop as a professional when working alone.

- *Integrated:* Overspecialization is avoided when the practitioner has multiple skills and competencies; however, integrating can dilute the competency base for both human resources and OD.

- *Strategy:* OD is central to the business of the organization and consequently has influence; however, the practitioner must learn and develop new knowledge and skills and perhaps must adopt stronger business values.

There is no easy answer as to what is the best structural arrangement for internal OD practitioners. The strategy model may be the most attractive one because it is aligned well with the definition of OD. Moving toward this model is not easy, however. It requires an acceptance of OD people by strategic planning experts who are steeped in economic and business traditions, for example. And it requires an acceptance of these business types by OD practitioners. There are stereotypes and value conflicts to overcome if such a model is expected to work. For a more comprehensive discussion of these five models and their advantages and disadvantages, see Burke (2004).

The Promise of OD:
Realized and Unrealized

Much of what the field of OD promised in the 1960s has been realized. OD practitioner groups are alive and well (e.g., the OD Network), workshops and conferences are well attended, graduate programs in OD are plentiful, and the literature about the field is prolific. Some of this literature even contains success stories; see Bauman, Jackson, and Lawrence (1997), Burke (2002, 2000), French and Bell (1995), and Goodstein and Burke (1991).

Yet today there is little OD that conforms to Beckhard's (1969) definition, perhaps the most widely accepted one. The main ingredients of this definition are planned, organization-wide, managed from the top, and applying behavioral science knowledge. Many OD practitioners use OD processes, techniques, and tools but in the end do not practice OD according to Beckhard's definition. Moreover, there is the paradox of need versus action and results. Without question there is more need for effective organization change than ever before (Foster & Kaplan, 2001), yet the majority of efforts to change fail. The failure rate for mergers and acquisitions is essentially the same (Burke & Biggart, 1997), that is, a majority. So the promise unrealized is OD work

not matching the need. As mentioned earlier, there is currently an outcry about this paradox (Bradford & Burke, 2005).

What needs to happen for OD to become more involved in and relevant to the great need for organization change and improvement? Greiner and Cummings (2004) cite six red flags for OD, each beginning with the words "neglected involvement in." What needs to happen for OD, in their view, is to be more involved in these six arenas. Their red flags are neglected involvement in

- Top management decision making
- Strategy formulation
- Mergers and acquisitions
- Globalization
- Alliances and virtual organizations
- Corporate governance and personal integrity

Although such involvement is not easy, OD practitioners have much to offer in each of these six arenas. Regardless of the degree of involvement by OD practitioners today, these six are highly appropriate goals to strive for because they capture most of the central issues for businesses at the present. Involvement in these arenas would ensure OD's relevance.

CONCLUSION

Although practically every practitioner has her or his own definition of OD, there is a coherence to the field, this particular if not unique world of study and practice. There is accepted content for OD, including theory (open system), conceptual frameworks (action research), and practice (planned phases of change and consultation and a typology of interventions), and there are programs, both academic and professional, that teach this content. The field has come a long way since 1958. We know some things about organization change and development; seven selected broad areas (e.g., change leadership) were summarized in this chapter. And we recognize that there is still much to learn. Fourteen areas were identified, including the need to know more about sustaining a change effort once the process is under way, power and politics, and synergy, to name just three. Coming full circle, an attempt was made to clarify further what OD is through some comparisons.

OD practitioners work as external consultants, and perhaps most work in organizations as employees. Special attention was given to the latter group regarding where they reside functionally within their organizations. Five different scenarios were considered, with their respective advantages and disadvantages.

Finally, the promise of OD was briefly reviewed. Although much has been learned since the late 1950s, a paradox remains: What OD has to offer does not measure up to what is needed. The six red flags from Greiner and Cummings (2004) help to focus our attention. To be more relevant and influential, OD practitioners must become more involved in executive decision making, strategic planning, mergers and acquisitions, the global movement, alliances and virtual organizations, and issues of governance and personal integrity. These red flags have a corporate language ring to them, yet all seem to apply to nonprofit organizations as well. Perhaps a list of red flags for government organizations might be slightly different, for example, emphasizing the relationship of mission to constituent satisfaction, but most of the red flags would still apply.

The field of OD is not dead, nor is it in decline. Yet OD, at least as defined long ago by Beckhard (1969), is rarely practiced. If OD practitioners focus more diligently on the six red flag domains, OD the Beckhard way is more likely to be realized.

REFERENCES

Alinsky, S. (1946). *Reveille for radicals*. Chicago: University of Chicago Press.

Argyris, C. (1962). *Interpersonal competence and organizational effectiveness*. Homewood, IL: Dorsey.

Argyris, C. (1964). T groups for organizational effectiveness. *Harvard Business Review, 42*(2), 60–74.

Argyris, C. (1970). *Intervention theory and method*. Reading, MA: Addison-Wesley.

Argyris, C. (1971). *Management and organizational development*. New York: McGraw-Hill.

Argyris, C., & Schön, D. (1978). *Organizational learning: A theory of action perspective*. Reading, MA: Addison-Wesley.

Bauman, R. P., Jackson, P., & Lawrence, J. T. (1997). *From promise to performance: A journey of transformation at SmithKline Beecham*. Boston: Harvard Business School Press.

Beckhard, R. (1969). *Organization development: Strategies and models*. Reading, MA: Addison-Wesley.

Beckhard, R. (1972). Optimizing team-building efforts. *Journal of Contemporary Business, 1*(3), 23–32.

Beckhard, R., & Harris, R. T. (1987). *Organizational transitions: Managing complex change* (2nd ed.). Reading, MA: Addison-Wesley.

Beer, M. (1980). *Organization change and development*. Santa Monica, CA: Goodyear.

Beer, M., & Cannon, M. D. (2004). Promise and peril in implementing pay-for-performance. *Human Resource Management, 43*, 3–48.

Bion, W. R. (1961). *Experiences in groups*. New York: Basic Books.

Blake, R. R., & Mouton, J. S. (1968). *Corporate excellence through grid organization development*. Houston: Gulf Publishing.

Block, P. (1999). *Flawless consulting: A guide to getting your expertise used* (2nd ed.). San Francisco: Jossey-Bass/Pfeiffer.

Bradford, D. L., & Burke, W. W. (Eds.). (2005). *Reinventing organization development: New approaches to change in organizations*. San Francisco: Pfeiffer/Wiley.

Bridges, W. (1980). *Transitions: Making sense of life's changes*. Reading, MA: Addison-Wesley.

Brown, L. D. (1972). "Research action": Organizational feedback, understanding, and change. *Journal of Applied Behavioral Science, 8*, 697–711.

Bunker, B. B., Alban, B. T., & Lewicki, R. J. (2004). Ideas in currency and OD practice: Has the well gone dry? *Journal of Applied Behavioral Science, 40*(4), 403–422.

Burke, W. W. (1982). *Organization development: Principles and practices.* Boston: Little, Brown.

Burke, W. W. (1993). The changing world of organization change. *Consulting Psychology Journal: Practice and Research, 45*(1), 9–17.

Burke, W. W. (1994). *Organization development: A process of learning and changing* (2nd ed.). Reading, MA: Addison-Wesley.

Burke, W. W. (2000). SmithKline Beecham. In D. Giber, L. Carter, & M. Goldsmith (Eds.), *Best practices in organization & human resources development handbook* (pp. 103–118). Lexington, MA: Linkage.

Burke, W. W. (2002). *Organization change: Theory and practice.* Thousand Oaks, CA: Sage.

Burke, W. W. (2004). Internal organization development practitioners: Where do they belong? *Journal of Applied Behavioral Science, 40,* 423–431.

Burke, W. W., & Biggart, N. W. (1997). Interorganizational relations. In D. Druckman, J. E. Singer, & H. Van Cott (Eds.), *Enhancing organizational performance* (pp. 120–149). Washington, DC: National Academy Press.

Burke, W. W., Javitch, M., Waclawski, J., & Church, A. H. (1997). The dynamics of midstream consulting. *Consulting Psychology Journal: Practice and Research, 49,* 83–95.

Burke, W. W., & Litwin, G. H. (1992). A causal model of organizational performance and change. *Journal of Management, 18*(3), 532–545.

Capra, F. (1996). *The web of life.* New York: Anchor.

Church, A. H. (1997). Managerial self-awareness in high-performing individuals in organizations. *Journal of Applied Psychology, 82,* 281–292.

Coch, L., & French, J. R. P. (1948). Overcoming resistance to change. *Human Relations, 1,* 512–532.

Cummings, T. G., & Worley, C. G. (2005). *Organization development and change* (8th ed.). Mason, OH: Thomson/South-Western.

Dunbar, R. I. M. (1992). Neocortex size as a constraint on group size in primates. *Journal of Human Evolution, 20,* 469–493.

Fagenson, E. A., & Burke, W. W. (1990a). The activities of organization development practitioners at the turn of the decade of the 1990s. *Group & Organization Studies, 15,* 366–380.

Fagenson, E. A., & Burke, W. W. (1990b). Organization development practitioner's activities and interventions in organizations during the 1980s. *Journal of Applied Behavioral Science, 26,* 285–297.

Fagenson-Eland, E., Ensher, E. A., & Burke, W. W. (2004). Organization development and change interventions: A seven nation comparison. *Journal of Applied Behavioral Science, 40*(4), 432–464.

Foster, R. N., & Kaplan, S. (2001). *Creative destruction: Why companies that are built to last under perform the market—and how to successfully transform them.* New York: Currency Books.

French, W. L. (1969). Organization development: Objectives, assumptions, and strategies. *California Management Review, 12,* 23–34.

French, W. L., & Bell, C. H. Jr. (1995). *Organization development: Behavioral science interventions for organizational improvement* (5th ed.). Englewood Cliffs, NJ: Prentice Hall.

Gellerman, W., Frankel, M. S., & Ladenson, R. F. (1990). *Values and ethics in organization and human systems development.* San Francisco: Jossey-Bass.

Gibson, C. B., & Cohen, S. G. (Eds.). (2003). *Virtual teams that work: Creating conditions for virtual team effectiveness.* San Francisco: Jossey-Bass.

Gladwell, M. (2000). *The tipping point: How little things can make a big difference.* Boston: Little, Brown.

Goodstein, L. D., & Burke, W. W. (1991). Creating successful organizational change. *Organizational Dynamics, 19*(4), 5–17.

Greiner, L. (1972). Evolution and revolution as organizations grow. *Harvard Business Review, 50*(4), 37–46.

Greiner, L. E., & Cummings, T. G. (2004). OD: Wanted more alive than dead. *Journal of Applied Behavioral Science, 40*(4), 374–391.

Greiner, L., & Schein, V. (1988). *Power and organizational development: Mobilizing power to implement change.* Reading, MA: Addison-Wesley.

Hackman, J. R. (1992). The psychology of self-management in organizations. In R. Glasser (Ed.), *Classic readings in self-managing teamwork* (pp. 143–193). King of Prussia, PA: Organization Design and Development.

Hackman, J. R. (2002). *Leading teams: Setting the stage for great performances.* Boston: Harvard Business School Press.

Hackman, J. R., & Oldham, G. R. (1980). *Work redesign.* Reading, MA: Addison-Wesley.

Herzberg, F. (1966). *Work and the nature of man.* Cleveland, OH: World Publishing.

Herzberg, F., Mausner, B., & Snyderman, B. (1959). *The motivation to work.* New York: John Wiley & Sons.

Hornstein, H. A., Bunker, B. B., Burke, W. W., Gindes, M., & Lewicki, R. J. (1971). *Social intervention: A behavioral science approach.* New York: Free Press.

Kaplan, R. S., & Norton, D. P. (1996). *The balanced scorecard: Translating strategy into action.* Boston: Harvard Business School Press.

Kerr, S. (1975). On the folly of rewarding A, while hoping for B. *Academy of Management Journal, 18,* 769–783.

Kotter, J. P. (1996). *Leading change.* Boston: Harvard Business School Press.

Kotter, J. P., & Heskett, J. G. (1992). *Corporate culture and performance.* New York: Free Press.

Lawler, E. E. III. (1973). *Motivation in work organizations.* Monterey, CA: Brooks/Cole.

Lawrence, P., & Lorsch, J. (1967). *Organization and environment.* Boston: Harvard University Business School, Division of Research.

Lawrence, P. R., & Lorsch, J. W. (1969). *Developing organizations: Diagnosis and action.* Reading, MA: Addison-Wesley.

Levinson, H. (1972a). The clinical psychologist as organizational diagnostician. *Professional Psychology, 3,* 34–40.

Levinson, H. (1972b). *Organizational diagnosis.* Cambridge, MA: Harvard University Press.

Lewin, K. (1946). Action research and minority problems. *Journal of Social Issues, 2,* 34–46.

Lewin, K. (1947). Frontiers in group dynamics: Concept, method, and reality in social science; social equilibria and social change. *Human Relations, 1,* 5–41.

Lewin, K. (1948). *Resolving social conflicts.* New York: Harper.

Lewin, K. (1951). *Field theory in social science.* New York: Harper.

Likert, R. (1967). *The human organization.* New York: McGraw-Hill.

Lippitt, R., Watson, J., & Westley, B. (1958). *Dynamics of planned change.* New York: Harcourt, Brace.

Luthans, F., & Peterson, S. J. (2003). 360-degree feedback with systematic coaching: Empirical analysis suggests a winning combination. *Human Resource Management, 42,* 243–256.

Marshak, R. J. (2005). Contemporary challenges to the philosophy and practice of organization development. In D. L. Bradford & W. W. Burke (Eds.), *Reinventing organization development: New approaches to change in organizations* (pp. 19–42). San Francisco: Pfeiffer/Wiley.

Maslow, A. H. (1954). *Motivation and personality.* New York: Harper & Brothers.

Nadler, D. A., & Tushman, M. L. (1977). A diagnostic model for organization behavior. In J. R. Hackman, E. E. Lawler III, & L. W. Porter (Eds.), *Perspectives on behavior in organizations* (pp. 85–100). New York: McGraw-Hill.

Pascale, R. T., Millemann, M., & Gioja, L. (2000). *Surfing the edge of chaos: The laws of nature and the new laws of business.* New York: Crown Business.

Plovnick, M. S., Fry, R. E., & Burke, W. W. (1982). *Organization development: Exercises, cases and readings.* Boston: Little, Brown.

Porras, J. I., & Silvers, R. C. (1991). Organization development and transformation. *Annual Review of Psychology, 42,* 51–78.

Rioch, M. (1970). The work of Wilford Bion on groups. *Psychiatry, 33,* 56–66.

Schein, E. H. (1987). *Process consultation, Vol. 2: Lessons for managers and consultants.* Reading, MA: Addison-Wesley.

Seifert, C. F., Yukl, G., & McDonald, R. A. (2003). Effects of multisource feedback and a feedback facilitator on the influence behavior of managers toward subordinates. *Journal of Applied Psychology, 88,* 561–569.

Skinner, B. F. (1953). *Science and human behavior.* New York: Macmillan.

Skinner, B. F. (1971). *Beyond freedom and dignity.* New York: Alfred A. Knopf.

Smither, J. W., London, M., Flautt, R., Vargas, Y., & Kucine, I. (2003). Can working with an executive coach improve multisource feedback ratings over time? A quasi-experimental field study. *Personnel Psychology, 56,* 23–44.

Tichy, N. M. (1983). *Managing strategic change: Technical, political, and cultural dynamics.* New York: John Wiley & Sons.

Tichy, N. M., & DeRose, C. (2003). The death and rebirth of organizational development. In S. Chowdhury (Ed.), *Organization 21C: Someday all organizations will lead this way* (pp. 155–173). Upper Saddle River, NJ: Financial Times–Prentice Hall.

vonBertalanffy, L. (1956). General system theory. *General Systems, Yearbook of the Society for the Advancement of General System Theory, 1,* 1–10.

Vroom, V. (1964). *Work and motivation.* New York: John Wiley & Sons.

Wegner, D. (1991). Transactive memory in close relationships. *Journal of Personality and Social Psychology, 61,* 923–929.

Weisbord, M. (1973). The organization development contract. *OD Practitioner, 5*(2), 1–4.

Weisbord, M. R. (1976). Organizational diagnosis: Six places to look for trouble with or without a theory. *Group and Organization Studies, 1,* 430–447.

Wirtenburg, J., Abrams, L., & Ott, C. (2004). Assessing the field of organization development. *Journal of Applied Behavioral Science, 40*(4), 465–479.

Worren, N. A. M., Ruddle, K., & Moore, K. (1999). From organization development to change management. *Journal of Applied Behavioral Science, 35,* 273–286.

3

From Brainwashing to Organization Therapy

The Evolution of a Model of Change Dynamics

EDGAR H. SCHEIN

In this chapter I describe and analyze the evolution of concepts of change based on my own experience as a researcher and consultant. I put this into a historical context, drawing on the research findings from social psychology, sociology, and anthropology that influenced my thinking. This is not intended to be a history of the change field but rather an analysis of how my own thinking evolved around the critical research findings I encountered in the late 1940s and early 1950s and my experiences as a consultant from the 1950s to the present.

I have come to realize that concepts have roots, in both our personal and our academic histories. Inasmuch as I have been instrumental in introducing into the organization development (OD) field the concepts of organizational psychology, as differentiated from industrial psychology (Schein, 1965, 1970, 1980), coercive

persuasion (Schein, 1956, 1961a), career anchors (Schein, 1977, 1978, 1985a, 2006), process consultation (Schein, 1969, 1987, 1988, 1999b), and organizational culture (Schein, 1984, 1985b, 1999a, 2004), the questions arise in my own mind of how I came upon these concepts and what common theme runs through my 50 years of thinking about these things.

The common theme, of course, is personal change, especially change induced by others. In thinking about change in various different settings and contexts, some of them in the extreme contexts of prisoner of war (POW) camps or political prisons, I evolved a model of the essential components of change based on Kurt Lewin's seminal model (Lewin, 1947; Schein, 1961a). But I have come to realize through seeing how others interpret my change model that abstractions are easy to misinterpret and that the model has elements that are not yet understood well enough without examining particular change programs in some detail. The context in which this becomes crucial is in our work as OD consultants when we engage in what is essentially organization therapy.

ACADEMIC ROOTS (1948–1952)

My own academic career started with experimental research on social influence and imitation, focusing on the question of whether one of the mechanisms by which people changed their own behavior was to mimic or be influenced by the behavior of another. We take this change mechanism for granted when we advocate role modeling but have not really examined exactly what takes place when one person replaces his or her own response with something that he or she sees another person doing. Psychiatric theory would draw on the defense mechanism of identification for a deeper analysis of this phenomenon, but that implicates another often overlooked element of change: What is actually being changed, and does the change entail replacing an element that is already there? Is it new behavior, new attitudes, new values, new perceptions, or new thought processes that we are analyzing? Can we assume that the change mechanisms are the same for each of these response categories, and if something present needs to be replaced, is the mechanism of unlearning the same for each response category?

My experiments in imitation focused on whether imitation on cognitive judgments would generalize to other kinds of judgments. In pursuing my master's degree in social psychology at Stanford, I had worked with professor Harry Helson on how judgment was ultimately determined by adaptation level, the neutral point in our subjective scales of judgment (Helson, 1948). For example, in working with weights, at what weight would I shift my judgment from "light" to "heavy"? We had

students in groups judge weights and asked one or more to make extreme judgments to see whether the adaptation level of others who heard these judgments could be influenced. They were, confirming what Sherif (1936) had already shown with the research on autokinetic phenomena, that when an ambiguous stimulus is presented to several people, a group norm develops around their joint adaptation level.

In my PhD work I pursued this line of research. I put groups of five people into a situation in which each person was to make perceptual judgments of how many dots appeared briefly on a screen, something that was very ambiguous but for which there was a correct answer. Respondents were to give their responses in order and could hear each other. At the end of each trial I announced the correct answer. I manipulated the situation so that the task was sufficiently ambiguous to allow me to choose as "correct" a preponderance of the answers of the second person in the sequence, to see whether the third, fourth, and fifth person would begin to repeat whatever the second person had said. Over a number of trials there was a clear trend toward imitation. The crucial question was whether such imitation would continue if the task were switched to something different. On a similar cognitive judgment task, imitation continued, but on a dissimilar task involving aesthetic judgments imitation declined sharply (Schein, 1954).

These experiments were done at a time (1940–1952) when social influence was very central in social psychology, based on the classic experiments by Sherif and the subsequent research by Asch that showed that even in the face of clear empirical evidence, many people could be swayed to deny what they saw if others reported something different (Asch, 1952; Sherif, 1936; Sherif & Sherif, 1969). In other words, we are more dependent on the judgments of others than we might at first realize, even in unambiguous situations. Although this clearly established the importance of social influence, there were individual differences in the degree to which people were influenced, which led psychologists to become more preoccupied with determining the individual variables that would account for these differences rather than pursuing the social side of it, which was being explored thoroughly by the Chicago school of sociology under Everett Hughes, Erving Goffman, and many others (Goffman, 1959; Hughes, 1958). The psychologists had discovered how group norms form through mutual influence in reducing uncertainty but did not really consider the subsequent impact of such norms on individual behavior. The sociologists had discovered that once norms exist in a group, they are quite coercive. In the industrial sector the classic Hawthorne studies were showing clearly how powerful group norms can both stimulate and inhibit production levels (Roethlisberger & Dickson, 1939). In summary, group pressure is one of the components of how change occurs.

In the post–World War II effort to understand the nature of Nazism and its ability to get ordinary people to do extraordinarily brutal things, social psychologists also examined the nature of authority and leadership, culminating in the drastic experiments of Philip Zimbardo (Zimbardo & Ebbesen, 1969) and Stanley Milgram (1983). Zimbardo showed how ordinary college students could begin to behave in cruel ways within a matter of days if given the role of prison guard in a simulation of prisons on campus. Milgram showed that students could be made to give what they believed to be severe electric shocks to fellow students who were giving wrong answers in a learning test just by being ordered to do so by the experimenter. In this same era, the early work of Kurt Lewin on different leadership styles was receiving increasing attention because of two major findings (Marrow, Bowers, & Seashore, 1967). Groups that worked under an autocratic leader could be just as productive as groups that worked under a more participative "democratic" leader, but if the leader departed, the participative

groups continued to function well and remain productive, whereas the autocratically managed groups deteriorated and became less productive. If change was to be self-sustaining, participation and democratic leadership appeared to be necessary. When these findings were coupled with the findings of experiments on changing the work habits of production workers, it became clear that behavior change was more likely to occur if the workers were involved in designing the change. In fact, if workers were not involved, they resisted change. Resistance to change became a popular concept as something to be taken for granted, but how to overcome it remained controversial and ambiguous despite the findings that group forces, authority, and participation were clearly proven to be beneficial in inducing change.

These findings were problematic because they did not reveal the relative importance of these different factors. On one hand, there was plenty of evidence that people respond to peer group and authority pressures ("just show them examples, tell them what to do"). On the other hand, there were plenty of findings that argued that people will not change unless they are personally involved in the change process. Clearly, change was a more complex process than what either set of these classic experiments revealed. This complexity was revealed to me in depth through my fortuitous involvement in the study of repatriated prisoners of war and civilians who had been subjected to "brainwashing."

BRAINWASHING OR COERCIVE PERSUASION (1952–1961)

After earning my PhD under the aegis of the Army Clinical Psychology Program, I was fortunate enough to be assigned to the social psychology and psychiatry section of the Walter Reed Army Institute of Research, run by Dr. David Rioch. Rioch was a brilliant psychiatrist who believed in truly interdisciplinary work. At one extreme the lab had endocrinologists, ecologists, statisticians, and behavioral psychologists, and at the other extreme were psychiatrists who had worked at the front lines in World War II, social psychologists, and anthropologists. We were trying to figure out everything from how people got ulcers to how breakdowns occurred in combat stress. Psychologists such as Leon Festinger and sociologists such as Erving Goffman were invited regularly as consultants to help all of us broaden our perspectives.

My own interest at that time was the organizational network research that had been launched by Alex Bavelas at the Massachusetts Institute of Technology (MIT) in the late 1940s and pursued by Harold Leavitt (1951). This research was a departure from the work on imitation and influence in that it focused more on leadership and organization dynamics. At this time we were involved in the Korean conflict and had lost several thousand men to the North Korean and Chinese POW camps. The Chinese communists were in a frenzy to show everyone how valid their version of communism was, so they were bent on indoctrinating as many military and civilian captives as they could. In the exchange of sick and wounded prisoners in 1953 it was revealed that some prisoners had signed false confessions and in other ways collaborated with the enemy. Edward Hunter wrote a book called *Brainwashing in Red China* (Hunter, 1958) and introduced into English a word that has now become common usage. It was based on the Chinese concept of cleansing the mind of middle-class values.

When the armistice was signed and the United States was scheduled to receive more than 3,000 repatriates, the question arose of whether and how these POWs might have been indoctrinated and what help they might need to reintegrate into the U.S. ideology. The three services pulled together all the psychiatrists, psychologists, and social workers in the service, made them into teams, and placed them aboard ships that would carry several hundred repatriates from Inchon, Korea, to San Francisco. The 16-day voyage would provide time to give tests and do what therapy might be appropriate. But no one really knew what we were facing.

It turned out that my ship was delayed, so I found myself in Inchon, Korea, for 3 weeks with nothing to do but wait. Because something had happened in the POW camps that had to do with drastic influence and shocking changes of political or personal values, I set up shop to interview people as they were coming through to find out what had happened since they were captured. The intellectual problem was to find out what would lead a captive to sign a false confession, march in a "peace march" for obvious propaganda reasons, and even make false allegations against a fellow POW. The social psychology of the day (mid-1950s) was preoccupied with models of attitude change based on experiments with changing different appeals. None of this literature could explain the more dramatic behavior changes of POWs and subsequently the even more dramatic changes undergone by civilian captives on the Chinese mainland. Many of them came out of China stating that they had been spies and had been leniently treated considering their crimes in being released after 3 to 5 years. These were students, businessmen, and priests, so we found their admissions incredible and took comfort in the vague explanation of "brainwashing."

What the interviews of repatriates and Chinese civilians revealed is that the Chinese communists were sincere in their beliefs in their own version of reality and that they were willing to manipulate the social and psychological setting of prisoners to get their message across. Manipulating mail, removing leaders from groups, constantly repeating the new message, and other techniques that prisoners were unable to avoid led to what Lewin had earlier called "unfreezing" or destabilizing the quasistationary equilibria that we count on to make sense of our world. This led to an important insight about managed change: the concept of coercive persuasion (Schein, 1961a).

If you can coerce the person to stay in the setting, you can eventually get him or her to open him- or herself to considering alternative points of view toward an issue. In other words, if you can hold a person captive, you can sooner or later motivate him or her to change.

Coercing people into behavioral change such as signing false confessions or marching in peace marches is not a change comparable to civilians coming to believe that they were spies and were leniently treated. In these mainland prisons, if they offered to sign false confessions, the interrogators became furious and argued that they wanted "sincere" understanding and adoption of the communist point of view. Prisoners were told that they were guilty because they had been arrested, and no amount of protesting of innocence would shake the captor's conviction of their guilt. So the paradox of this kind of change is that the prisoner becomes motivated to change through the constant battering but does not really know what the captor expects because of his or her own cognitive structure, which differs from that of the captor.

The Chinese communists understood this dilemma and put captives into group cells in which some cellmates were farther along in their change process and therefore could help the new cellmate to understand what was wanted. This process is best conceptualized as cognitive redefinition and involves changing the semantic meaning of concepts and changing the adaptation level, or standards by which things are judged. The key was for prisoners to come to understand that the Western concept of "crime" as demonstrated harm to some victim and the principle that you are innocent until proven guilty were not shared by the communist ideology. From the Chinese point of view, a crime was any behavior that could be harmful to the state, which involved totally different tacit assumptions about the role of the state as a potential victim. The prisoners learned that sending postcards home describing local wheat fields could under some future war scenario be useful information to an enemy and therefore was "espionage." Jesuit priests who had run missions learned that they had violated their own Christian values and communist egalitarian principles by employing houseboys in inferior servant roles, which was defined as "imperialist exploitation."

On the matter of standards of judgment, prisoners learned that what they might regard as trivial was considered very serious from the point of view of an aspiring political movement that was still very young and very insecure. When prisoners demonstrated some understanding of these different standards of judgment, they received immediate positive reinforcement from cellmates and interrogators. With the appropriate degree of admitting guilt and with active self-criticism, prisoners were treated better. The interrogators became more encouraging that the changes were now sincere, and prisoners were relieved to learn that their 3 to 5 years in prison might be enough of a prison sentence. If they were released despite their serious crimes of espionage and exploitation, they felt they had been treated leniently. So the next big insight about change can be stated as follows:

> Change in beliefs or attitudes involves cognitively redefining certain concepts and changing one's standards of judgment through shifts in the semantics of what things mean and changes in the adaptation level.

Coerced behavioral change alone may or may not lead to such cognitive change, depending on the degree of coercion and the possibilities of getting insight into what is really wanted. Thus, for example, the coerced political behavior in the Soviet Union did not change certain attitudes toward political freedom but did change some attitudes toward the role of the state in providing full employment and other social services. Dissonance theory argues that eventually we adopt concepts and attitudes that justify our behavior, but what the prison experience illustrated is that developing new concepts and changed standards may require help from others. We cannot automatically think up new concepts or standards of judgment, but once we are motivated (unfrozen), we seek justifications and rationalizations for what we are coerced into doing by looking to others and identifying with them. This often gives the indoctrinators the illusion that they are powerful conveyers of the message. The truth may be that the coerced victim is eager to latch onto whatever makes sense of his or her present situation. This analysis leads to a third critical insight:

> People will resist cognitive redefinition and changes in their standards of judgment unless they have been unfrozen or find themselves coerced into remaining in a situation that requires new concepts and standards.

This principle requires us to unpack Lewin's concept of unfreezing. Other than the kind of severe coercion that we saw in the prisoner situation, what would motivate a person to consider learning some new way of looking at things? My formulation is that several things have to occur for such motivation to arise, and two kinds of anxiety have to be managed:

- *Disconfirmation:* Something must be felt to be going wrong that produces survival anxiety, or there must be a feeling of not achieving something that is expected or hoped for, which produces some form of disappointment or guilt.
- *Learning anxiety:* However, the prospect of learning something new produces learning anxiety because the new behavior, attitude, or value may be too hard to learn, may undermine present sense of identity, or may cause one to lose membership in a valued group. Learning anxiety is the basis for resistance to change, usually in the form of denial of the disconfirming data.

- *Psychological safety:* The resistance to change can be overcome only if the change target feels that learning is possible, that the new can be integrated into the current identity, and that group membership will not be lost or will be suitably replaced.

These forces in combination create the motivation to change that then leads the person to seek new sources of information or new role models with which to identify. Cognitive redefinition and adaptation level change then become possible.

In the case of prisoners, the disconfirmation and experienced anxiety were obvious. But the motivation to change did not really arise until the cellmates were provided a more psychologically safe environment that allowed the prisoner to sincerely ask, "What do they want from me? I just don't understand; I am innocent." Only when the prisoner genuinely inquired in this way could he or she learn what the communist concepts of crime and espionage were.

This same multistep process has to be present in *all* cases of change. For example, I am working with a power company that was under criminal indictment for failing to report some environmentally dangerous materials. The court mandated that they would create a program of environmental responsibility and put a monitor into the organization to report quarterly on their progress. This was severe disconfirmation. The inability to manage their own affairs without the interference of the court created great survival anxiety, which motivated a host of programs to change the culture. Management used incentives and harsh discipline to impose new behavioral rules for identifying, reporting, and remediating oil spills and asbestos, polychlorinated biphenyl, and mercury dangers, a learning process that produced a great deal of learning anxiety and resistance to change. Not only did immediate behavior have to change, but the organization knew that the real change had to be defined as getting internalization of these norms to the point that the court would trust them enough to lift the probation (Schein, 1999a).

From my point of view as a consultant, this change required a cognitive shift in the self-image of the employee from someone who kept the power on reliably to someone who took environmental responsibility as well as keeping the power on. For this shift to occur, the employee had to have extensive training in diagnosing environmental hazards and figuring out what to do about them (cognitive redefinition through new semantic meaning of what it meant to be an employee). In addition, the employee had to accept new standards of judgment (i.e., that even a few drops of oil had to be reported and dealt with and that this was as important as keeping the power on). This was not an easy shift. Some employees resisted the change because they felt insecure in dealing with environmental matters. It was the extensive training that created enough psychological safety to get those employees on board. Employees were formed into labor–management groups that were encouraged to invent ways of dealing with environmental spills and other hazards. For them, psychological safety came through participation in fixing the problems. Some employees left rather than accepting this new concept of their work. Some 7 years later, employees accept their new role, believe that environmental responsibility is important, and deal responsibly with environmental hazards. No doubt some of the old timers would regard these employees as having been "brainwashed."

To conclude this section, I am arguing that most organization change involves changes in attitudes and beliefs, although it usually begins with coerced behavior change. If that is a correct view, then the change agent must understand clearly how unfreezing and eventually cognitive redefinition works. Most theories of change talk about the tactics of creating change without any real understanding of unfreezing as a sociopsychological process or cognitive redefinition as the ultimate change goal to be achieved.

LEARNING THE TECHNOLOGY OF CHANGE (1957 TO THE PRESENT)

A decade of work with the National Training Labs (1957–1967) exposed me to a whole other way of looking at change management. Kurt Lewin's legacy gave us useful experimental data and theories, and his point of view spawned some crucial change tools, the most powerful of which was force-field analysis.

Force-Field Analysis to Diagnose the State of Unfreezing. By specifying the direction of desired change and then analyzing what forces are already pushing in that direction and what forces inhibit movement in that direction, the change agent can decide whether the change target is really motivated to change. The adding of driving forces can then be thought of as disconfirmation or increasing survival anxiety, and the removal of inhibiting forces can be thought of as creating psychological safety by reducing learning anxiety. What such analysis typically reveals is that the change target's psychological field usually is quite complex, and there are many forces on both sides, which create the so-called quasistationary equilibrium.

In deciding to do a force-field analysis, the change agent is also encouraged to think very carefully about the level of change desired. Are we trying initially just to produce behavior change, and what forces are operating to inhibit that? Can we coerce the target to remain in the field if the disconfirming forces get to be too uncomfortable? Are we assuming that behavior change will by itself automatically lead to attitude and belief change, or do we need a separate analysis of the present cognitive field and what it would take to get cognitive redefinition? That probably would entail a separate force-field analysis.

Role-Set Analysis and the Power of Reference Groups. The most common inhibitor of change is the target's unwillingness to break the norms of the group that he or she identifies with or uses as a reference group for his or her own behavior (Katz & Kahn, 1966; Sherif & Sherif, 1969). Our core identities are very much a product of past and present group memberships. Our cognitive structures, our beliefs and attitudes are the result of those memberships, and they are maintained by our desire to continue to get confirmation from our present reference groups that we are okay, that we are not violating some norms or standards that the group holds. The civilian prisoners in Chinese communist camps did not change their understanding of crime, espionage, and lenient treatment until they began to identify with their cellmates. The cellmates became the key reference group and the source of cognitive redefinition. When these prisoners were repatriated, most of them underwent a second change back toward U.S. concepts of crime and espionage, except in the case of one couple who maintained their pro-communist views because they reinforced them in each other. Keeping true to each other became more important than fitting in with Western society and concepts.

For this reason, an important diagnostic for change agents is to figure out what the role-set of the change target is. Who are his or her key reference groups and stakeholders? Who would be upset if the change target exhibited new behavior, beliefs, or attitudes? By analyzing the role-set, the change agent locates what may be some of the most important restraining forces. This process enables the change agent to develop a more refined strategy for how to create psychological safety for the target. It also reveals role dynamics that enable the change agent to compensate for what the change target may feel as *role ambiguity* (not really knowing what is expected with regard to some role senders), *role overload* (realizing that the sum total of what is expected of any one person far exceeds what they are able to respond to, allowing the change agent to recognize the need to get the change agenda high in the change target's "inbox"), and *role conflict* (realizing that

the change target may be experiencing that two critical role senders [e.g., management on one hand, peers and subordinates on the other] have conflicting expectations). Probably the most common version of such conflict occurs when the expectations of the role sender are in conflict with the target person's own expectations of himself or herself.

In my own experience, one's own self-concept and sense of ethics—what we want to call integrity—rests heavily on our integration into membership and reference groups. What this means is that the strongest source of resistance to cognitive redefinition will inevitably come from those group affiliations. It is for this reason that one can state the following principle:

> Change in attitudes and beliefs can occur only if the individual is physically and psychologically separated from his or her membership and reference groups or if the change program is targeted at the group itself.

The reason team learning, family group change programs, and total system change programs are so necessary is because in the end these are the only kinds of programs that can overcome valid resistance to change and lead to genuine cognitive redefinition. However, the focus on groups, team building, family group change programs, and total system change programs overlooks the fact that individuals differ in how vulnerable they are to group forces.

CAREER ANCHORS (1961–1973 AND ONTO THE PRESENT)

When my research on coercive persuasion was coming to an end, the question arose as to what this had to do with management and business organizations. As it happened, the late 1950s were filled with books about corporate indoctrination. The G.E. center at Crotonville was called the G.E. Indoctrination Center, and IBM had a management development system that taught the "correct" IBM response to various kinds of business situations. It seemed logical to me to study corporate indoctrination by tracking Sloan School MBA alumni into their careers and track their changes in beliefs and attitudes as they joined organizations. I had previously developed attitude questionnaires that compared faculty, Sloan fellows, senior executives, and incoming students and found that student attitudes overall showed a drift away from faculty attitudes toward business attitudes (Schein, 1967). It seemed logical to study this process more intensely in a panel of alumni to see how it worked in detail.

Three panels of 15 students were interviewed and surveyed in 1961, 1962, and 1963 with the intention of comparing their responses 1 year out with the responses of their supervisors and peer groups in their companies. Unfortunately, no clear patterns emerged in any of the three years, but it became apparent that a great deal of job and company shifting was taking place not only in the first year but thereafter. Another survey 5 years out again showed no consistent patterns, so I abandoned the project until 1973, when I asked all panel members to return to MIT for a debriefing and found career anchors (Schein, 1977, 1978, 1985a, 1990). Almost all alumni, now 10–12 years into their careers, talked about finding what they were really good at, what they valued, and what kind of career motivated them. These elements were forged through successive experiences into a self-image that began to constrain career choices, set career directions, and specify what kind of organization or work setting was preferred. Once such a self-image began to jell, it operated like an anchor, keeping each alumnus in his or her safe harbor.

The reason I had not found patterns of attitude change overall is because the first 10 years of the career involved a lot of searching, which the U.S. open labor market made possible. This search revealed that the group that had originally all said they wanted to be CEOs and "captains of industry" really evolved into eight different patterns or career anchors. One group wanted independence and autonomy, which led them into teaching, consulting, or other freeform occupations; one group wanted security and stability, which led them into large, "safe" organizations with good benefit programs; one group wanted technical or functional competence, which led them to search for jobs where they could grow and develop the particular skills that defined their identity, whether that was sales, engineering, software design, or whatever; one group wanted to climb the corporate ladder and was busy working their way up in various organizations; one group wanted to be entrepreneurs, to found and build enterprises that were entirely their own; one group wanted an occupation in which they felt they were improving something, working out some important personal values by providing a service; one group wanted pure challenge in the sense that the only kind of work that appealed to them was work that solved impossible problems or was intensely competitive; and one group become more concerned about lifestyle, or how to integrate their own career concerns with the needs of a fully career committed spouse and how to find a setting in which family and personal needs could both be met.

Once formed, career anchors remained quite stable and determined most of the career choices that continued to be made. The practical implication of this concept was the importance of knowing one's career anchor so that choices would be made that would not be regretted later. For me the important insight was that in an open society such as the United States there is a perpetual tension between the needs and requirements of the organization and the needs and requirements of the individual. One of the best ways for a person to resist change is to move out of the situation in which change is required. One of the best ways for an organization to force change is to prevent the person from leaving, whether by physical coercion or "golden handcuffs."

PROCESS CONSULTATION AND ORGANIZATION THERAPY (1960S TO THE PRESENT)

From the point of view of the researcher, the work on coercive persuasion was an adequate model to understand how an organization or a captor could design a set of circumstances that would produce behavior and ultimately attitude change. However, this model did not sufficiently explain how a change agent, whether in the role of consultant, teacher, or therapist, can create conditions for change if the power to coerce is not available. My own understanding of the consulting and therapeutic role came primarily from work with the National Training Labs running T (training) groups. The participants who signed up to learn more about leadership, groups, and their own impact on others were partially unfrozen by virtue of their decision to attend the labs. Feedback from others in the form of how their behavior came across had the further potential of disconfirming what a person believed about himself or herself. The staff member (trainer) was responsible for creating a milieu in the group that would make it safe to reveal anxiety- or guilt-producing data and to ensure that such data would lead to learning rather than psychological damage.

The critical insight in becoming an effective trainer was the realization that telling the group members what to do, taking an active trainer role, would not work. Group members would not feel safe enough to reveal what was really bothering them. Therefore, any advice or direction was likely to be off target in terms of what group members needed. Instead the trainer had to help the group create psychological safety for itself by gradually building up enough mutual acquaintance and trust to be able to tolerate what could be quite threatening feedback.

The essence of this process was the management of the two kinds of anxiety previously identified: *survival anxiety* (if I accept these disconfirming data about myself or my situation,

I may lose power, identity, or group membership, so I have to change or learn) and *learning anxiety* (learning something new may not be possible for me, I may not have the skill or motivation, or learning something new may make me lose power, identity, or group membership). As previously noted, it is the learning anxiety that produces resistance to change, most often in the form of denying the data that would produce survival anxiety. We rationalize the disconfirming data away until the learning anxiety is reduced enough to enable us to learn something new. The management of these two kinds of anxieties is the essence of good consultation and therapy, and the operating principle that worked for me can be stated as follows:

> The key to producing change is to reduce the learning anxiety, to create the conditions where the change target can accept the need to learn because he or she can see a safe direction in which to move without feeling a loss of power, identity, or group membership.

As I was learning how to be a trainer, I was also learning how to be a consultant in organization settings, and I discovered in those settings that advice or direction tended to be ignored or subverted even if it was based on my good intentions and my sincere belief that I knew enough about the situation the client was in. The problem was that either my advice did not take into account the culture of the organization and hence was irrelevant or, more often, it was premature in the sense that the client had not yet really revealed what was bothering him or her because I had not built a relationship of trust that enabled the client to feel psychologically safe in being more open. What I learned both in the T groups and in consulting was that I had to manage the initial process of building a relationship and that the best way to do that was to focus on the interpersonal dynamics of communication processes (Schein, 1969, 1987, 1988, 1999b). Making clients aware of these processes then turned out to be productive for building a trusting relationship and for starting the client on an important learning process of his or her own. Whatever organization problems were ultimately worked on, communication and conversation were always at the root of everything, and the sooner clients learned about the subtleties of listening and conversing, the better off they were.

Once a relationship with the client had been built, it was more likely that clients would reveal what was really bothering them, what kind of disconfirmation they were experiencing, so that the consultant and client could then decide together what the next intervention should be. By deciding together they avoided the trap of designing next steps that would be culturally incongruent, or if some aspects of the culture itself were the problem they could design a culture change program. These thoughts can be summarized in the following generalization:

> The primary role of a therapist, consultant, or teacher is to create an environment in which a relationship with the client can be built that will make the client feel safe enough to deal with prior disconfirmations and the further disconfirmations that may occur in the learning situation itself.

Some words have to be said about prior disconfirmations. All of us have had some kind of negative feedback or failure experiences in our lives. These are repressed, suppressed, and denied until we feel psychologically safe enough to admit what happened or what we heard. A parent has told us that we are very selfish, and we have steadfastly denied that to ourselves until a situation in therapy or in a normal life situation or a T group makes us feel safe enough to admit it and begin to work on it. All of us in adulthood have a storehouse full of those kinds of prior disconfirmations ready to enter consciousness and be dealt with once we feel safe enough to deal with them. Therefore, it is no surprise when someone

"suddenly" begins a change process without appearing to have been disconfirmed. In the training groups we found participants regressing and seeming to get psychologically more disturbed because in the security of the T group, they were able to let down their defenses and allow past and present disconfirmations to be experienced. Invariably these participants became "well" again much quicker than if they had had their regression at work or in a real-life situation.

GROUP AND ORGANIZATION FORCES

The next and final step in fully understanding change is to come to terms with what happens when we go beyond the dynamics of an individual client to small group dynamics and ultimately to intergroup and interorganizational dynamics. The main point to be made here is that in OD we have tended to look only at the impact of groups and larger systems on individuals and have failed to note that some of the toughest problems of change derive from intergroup and interorganizational forces. The people who are the targets of change often are locked into positions within their own groups that make it impossible for them to move. They appear to be logical and rational, but in fact they are functioning as representatives protecting their turf and their people. Change dynamics then move into another arena of diplomacy, negotiation, mediation, arbitration, and ultimately resolution by the hierarchy. I saw this dynamic play out especially in my 35-year analysis of the history of Digital Equipment Corporation (Schein, 2003). The ultimate economic demise of that organization could be directly related to irresolvable intergroup competition for resources in combination with neutralizing of the founder and CEO and the board by powerful engineering groups. The irony is that early success breeds growth, and growth breeds subgroups and subcultures that will inevitably compete with each other for resources.

The implication for OD is that interventions have to be geared to the level at which a problem is being experienced, as Coghlan and Rashford (2006) so ably argue. OD practitioners have to be able to make interventions at the individual, interpersonal, group, organizational, and interorganizational level. This is especially true when we have to take culture into account.

ORGANIZATION CULTURE

The final piece of the change puzzle is culture. For reasons that are not entirely clear, most change programs nowadays claim to be culture change, but when one examines what is actually being changed it is revealed that the change agent is not using *culture* in any kind of clear or appropriate manner. Culture is the learned residue of past experiences and manifests itself at the level of behavioral regularities, espoused values that usually reflect aspirations more than realities, and tacit, shared assumptions that drive daily behavior (Schein, 1985b, 1992, 2006). The essence and most stable element of culture is the shared, tacit assumptions.

When change agents announce "culture change" they usually refer to the promulgation of some "new" values such as teamwork, customer focus, or quality. It is not clear whether cultural assumptions will be involved at all, nor is it clear what actual change is being promoted in the sense of new behaviors or new attitudes. To sort this out entails going back to the change model: What is being disconfirmed, what is the new behavior that is required, and how will the present culture promote or hinder this change? If there are cultural elements that will hinder the change, how will they be dealt with? In the Power Company the court mandated environmental responsibility, and the company announced new responsible behavior and then concluded that this required more openness, personal responsibility, and teamwork. Each of these new values then had to be translated into new behavior, which created a need for training, new reward systems, and new disciplinary processes, which in each case were completely consistent with and derived from the present culture. The only culture change required was to forge a new identity for the electrical worker in the field and to abandon a tradition of assigning jobs to "old boys" who often were not competent to deal with the environmental issues. These changes could be achieved only through the paternalistic training-oriented culture that existed. The court eventually took the company off probation, and 7 years into the program there is some evidence that not only has the behavior changed, but employees have internalized the environmental values. As this internalization continues and as the new behavior is reinforced both internally and externally, it will gradually become a shared, tacit assumption that doing electrical work now includes environmental responsibility. Some elements of the culture will have changed. The implication for change management is clear:

> Culture is both a facilitating and a restraining force. In change programs the focus should be on what behavioral practices are being changed, how the culture will aid or hinder the desired change, and how cultural forces can be harnessed to make the necessary behavioral changes.

CONCLUSION

Human change is a complex process, whether we are talking at the level of the individual, the group, the intergroup, the organization, or the interorganizational set. Yet the core process of managing the components of unfreezing—disconfirmation, survival anxiety, learning anxiety, and the creation of psychological safety—will ultimately be the same at whatever level we are analyzing the process. Similarly, attitudinal or value change processes will always involve some cognitive redefinition—semantic changes in concepts, learning new concepts through identification with others or trial-and-error learning, and shifts in the adaptation level that determine how we make our judgments. Change at this level often entails coercing the change target into remaining in the change situation. If exit is possible, career anchor theory argues that some people will leave rather than change. All of these processes are heavily influenced by the dynamics of membership and reference groups, and all of them take place in cultural settings that derive from country and occupation. The successful change agent will be able to design successfully the tactics of a change process only if he or she has a clear understanding of these underlying dynamics.

REFERENCES

Asch, S. (1952). *Social psychology.* Upper Saddle River, NJ: Prentice Hall.

Coghlan, D., & Rashford, N. S. (2006). *Organizational change and strategy.* London: Routledge.

Goffman, E. (1959). *The presentation of self in everyday life.* New York: Doubleday.

Helson, H. (1948). Adaptation-level as a basis for a quantitative theory of frames of reference. *Psychological Review, 55,* 297–313.

Hughes, E. C. (1958). *Men and their work.* Glencoe, IL: Free Press.

Hunter, E. (1958). *Brainwashing in Red China.* New York: Vanguard.

Katz, D., & Kahn, R. L. (1966). *The social psychology of organizations.* New York: John Wiley & Sons.

Leavitt, H. J. (1951). Some effects of certain communication patterns on group performance. *Journal of Abnormal and Social Psychology, 46,* 38–50.

Lewin, K. (1947). Frontiers in group dynamics. *Human Relations, 1,* 5–42.

Marrow, A. J., Bowers, D. G., & Seashore, S. E. (1967). *Management by participation.* New York: Harper & Row.

Milgram, S. (1983). *Obedience to authority.* New York: HarperCollins.

Rashford, N. S., & Coghlan, D. (1994). *The dynamics of organizational levels.* Reading, MA: Addison-Wesley.

Roethlisberger, F. J., & Dickson, W. J. (1939). *Management and the worker.* Cambridge, MA: Harvard University Press.

Schein, E. H. (1954). The effect of reward on adult imitative behavior. *Journal of Abnormal and Social Psychology, 49,* 389–395.

Schein, E. H. (1956). The Chinese indoctrination program for prisoners of war: A study of attempted brainwashing. *Psychiatry, 19,* 149–172.

Schein, E. H., with Schneier, I., & Barker, C. H. (1961a). *Coercive persuasion.* New York: W.W. Norton.

Schein, E. H. (1961b). Management development as a process of influence. *Industrial Management Review, 2,* 59–77.

Schein, E. H. (1965). *Organizational psychology.* Englewood Cliffs, NJ: Prentice Hall.

Schein, E. H. (1967). Attitude change during management education: A study of organizational influences on student attitudes. *Administrative Science Quarterly, 11,* 601–628.

Schein, E. H. (1969). *Process consultation: Its role in organization development.* Reading, MA: Addison-Wesley.

Schein, E. H. (1970). *Organizational psychology* (2nd ed.). Englewood Cliffs, NJ: Prentice Hall.

Schein, E. H. (1977). Career anchors and career paths: A panel study of management school graduates. In J. Van Maanen (Ed.), *Organizational careers: Some new perspectives.* New York: John Wiley & Sons.

Schein, E. H. (1978). *Career dynamics: Matching individual and organizational needs.* Reading, MA: Addison-Wesley.

Schein, E. H. (1980). *Organizational psychology* (3rd ed.). Englewood Cliffs, NJ: Prentice Hall.

Schein, E. H. (1984). Coming to a new awareness of organizational culture. *Sloan Management Review, 25,* 3–16.

Schein, E. H. (1985a). *Career anchors: Discovering your real values.* San Diego, CA: University Associates.

Schein, E. H. (1985b). *Organizational culture and leadership.* San Francisco: Jossey-Bass.

Schein, E. H. (1987). *Process consultation, Vol. 2: Lessons for managers and consultants.* Reading, MA: Addison-Wesley.

Schein, E. H. (1988). *Process consultation, Vol. 1 (Rev. ed.): Its role in organization development.* Reading, MA: Addison-Wesley.

Schein, E. H. (1990). *Career anchors* (Rev. ed.). San Diego, CA: Pfeiffer.

Schein, E. H. (1992). *Organizational culture and leadership* (2nd ed.). San Francisco: Jossey-Bass.

Schein, E. H. (1999a). *The corporate culture survival guide.* San Francisco: Jossey-Bass.

Schein, E. H. (1999b). *Process consultation revisited: Building the helping relationship.* Reading, MA: Addison-Wesley-Longman.

Schein, E. H. (2003). *DEC is dead; long live DEC: The lasting legacy of Digital Equipment Corporation.* San Francisco: Berrett–Koehler.

Schein, E. H. (2004). *Organizational culture and leadership* (3rd ed.). San Francisco: Jossey-Bass.

Schein, E. H. (2006). *Career anchors* (3rd ed.). San Francisco: Pfeiffer/Wiley.

Sherif, M. (1936). *The psychology of social norms.* New York: Harper and Brothers.

Sherif, M., & Sherif, C. (1969). *Social psychology.* New York: Harper & Row.

Zimbardo, P. G., & Ebbesen, E. B. (1969). *Influencing attitudes and changing behavior.* Reading, MA: Addison-Wesley.

4

Learning in Organizations

CHRIS ARGYRIS

This chapter describes a theory of action perspective on organization development (OD) and change. I begin with the premise that learning is key to effective organization change and development. Learning is defined as the detection and correction of error. In order for learning to occur it is necessary to implement four phases: the diagnosis of a problem, invention of a solution, implementation of the solution, and evaluation of the effectiveness of the implementation.

There is one key requirement if effective learning is to occur. The claims made in each phase must be testable for their validity. Briefly, *validity* means that we can present compelling evidence that the claims made are not based on unrecognized or recognized inconsistencies and gaps in the reasoning used and the methods used to produce the claims. Scholars, professionals, and practitioners are responsible for doing their best to ensure that the processes they used to arrive at the conclusions were not flawed. Put simply, *validity* means

that one strives not knowingly or unknowingly to kid oneself or others.

In order to establish validity it is necessary to test all claims as thoroughly as possible. These tests are especially necessary if we are as professionals, leaders, or followers attempting to influence people's thoughts and actions, especially about learning.

The chapter begins with four examples that exemplify four key challenges to producing learning: leader or follower spinning or designed lying, leaders or followers protecting their incompetence by asserting that they are victims of others or of culture, leaders and followers withholding information and denying that they are doing so, and blaming hierarchies and asymmetrical power for ineffective performance.

These examples are not new. They have been documented in the literature by practitioners and scholars who see them as causes for actions that are counterproductive to learning. But why do they persist, and why do those who condemn them also cause their persistence?

CHALLENGE TO PRODUCING LEARNING

Leadership That Espouses Learning yet Acts in Ways That Inhibit Learning

One of the most common problems identified in the literature is leaders espousing learning but acting in ways that inhibit it.

Secretary of State Dean Rusk organized a conference of senior State Department officials in 1966 to explore ways of reducing the dysfunctions described by many as "foggy bottom." In one session an assistant secretary of defense described how Robert McNamara's program on planning and budgeting could help make the State Department more effective. Immediately after his thoughtful presentation, Secretary Rusk asked me to respond. I predicted that the State Department officials would resist. Secretary Rusk said that he found both presentations of value and asked others to give their reviews. Silence. Rusk then asked one of our country's most senior ambassadors to respond, especially about the concerns that I mentioned. The ambassador thought for a moment and then said, in effect, "Mr. Secretary, if you and the president ask us to implement these new programs, we will do so." After the session ended the ambassador came to me and said that he agreed with me and he would say that to the secretary at a meeting later. I asked him why he did not say so during the meeting. He replied that doing so would be counterproductive and inappropriate.

The next day the secretary told me that he was surprised that the ambassador did not speak out during the meeting. After all, he selected him to attend because he (Rusk) thought the ambassador would be candid and honest. I asked the secretary whether he said that to the ambassador. The secretary said it would have been inappropriate.

Both men covered up their feelings and views on very important issues. At that time Secretary Rusk was pleading with the Foreign Service officers to be candid and honest, yet he was not honest with the ambassador whom he had personally selected to attend the meeting because he believed that the ambassador would speak candidly. The ambassador knew that he was flown in to attend the meeting because the secretary counted on him to help lead a lively and candid discussion. Yet he too covered up his view during the meeting. Neither the ambassador nor the secretary was honest with the group.

In order for a cover-up to be effective, it must be covered up by a cover-up. The actor must act as if he is not covering up. Minimally, this is accomplished by spinning or, at worst, by designed lying. Both of these men disliked spinning, and both were against designed lying. They lived with this personal inconsistency by believing their actions were necessary to show concern and caring, to minimize upsetting the other, and to minimize being held responsible for making the other defensive and to set the stage for a successful implementation.

Culture That Rewards Spinning and Cover-Ups

The aforementioned case is more than a problem of leadership. It is a problem of culture.

About the same time that incident occurred, I was working with a dozen of the most senior foreign services officers (assistant secretaries of state and top ambassadors, including several career ministers). I found much evidence that these men believed that a culture existed that required them to be incompetent and to cover up when dealing with issues that could be upsetting and embarrassing to them or to the State Department. The examples are taken from transcripts of our sessions (Argyris, 1968).

Withdrawal From Conflict

A: If I sense that I am not getting through, if the other person has his hearing aid shut off, I find myself feeling irritated. Then, I quickly sober down and begin to calculate how I can get through. I find out his weaknesses by talking with others. I may seek a third party who might be held in higher esteem and who might get my message across to him. I may hold off until I can have a particular meeting held in which he has to listen. . . .

B: Let me cut you off and add when I use that I usually see to it that the right people are invited so that the weight of unanimity of opinion hits him. . . .

C: Yes, but I've been on the receiving end of such meetings and could sense they were loaded so I mistrusted what was going on. I therefore asked for more time to study the issue.

D: Come on, now, do all of you mean to say that you wouldn't confront the man directly?

E: Well, if he is a very close friend, I wouldn't mind. . . .

B: Like hell! Let's admit it: We rarely even confront our very close friends if we think they're turning us off.

Minimal Defenses

A: If I were to be very honest, I think that one reason I have succeeded is that I have learned *not* to be open; *not* to be candid. Do the powers that be realize what you fellows are implying—that we should strive to be more open? That's like asking us to commit organizational suicide.

B: I agree with A. I have experienced situations where I sensed the superior was not leveling. I figured that he was trying to set up either a psychological situation which would predispose me to his point of view, or he was trying to set up a situation where only one conclusion was possible.

C: And what did you say?

B: Not a darn thing—I let him continue.

F: Another problem is that many of us have been taught never to level so that we can negotiate. I frequently feel that the man is not leveling, not because he lacks ideas but because he is negotiating. He is not presenting all the relevant factors because he is intent on achieving certain results.

A: Over the years, I developed a lot of evidence that my superior wasn't really leveling. It got so bad that one day I seriously thought of resigning. But, I didn't have the courage. I didn't ever tell him this.

B: Why not?

A: It would upset him.

Distrust of Aggressive Selling Actions

A: I tend to distrust people who enjoy selling and fighting. I can remember several cases which we lost because they were using these tactics.

B: What did you do?

A: Nothing. What can you say—you resent competing and fighting? You know their answer would be, "Well that's the trouble with you State Department types."

The existence of these features, if they are to work, must be covered up, and the cover-up is covered up. The most powerful cover-ups are making the features undiscussable while they are being produced in actual settings. The undiscussability of the undiscussable must also be covered up.

Under these conditions, much important dialogue goes underground. As a result a powerful circular loop forms, a process within the Foreign Service culture that tends to reinforce minimizing interpersonal threat by minimizing risk taking, being open, and being forthright and minimizing their feelings of responsibility and their willingness to confront conflict openly. This, in turn, tends to reinforce those who have decided to withdraw, play it safe, not make waves, in their behavior and their writing. Under these conditions people soon learn the survival value of "checking with everyone," of developing policies that upset no one, of establishing policies in such a way that the superior takes the responsibility for them. It also coerces "layering" because subordinates prepare for a crisis, more people are needed to make a decision, and protection of one's bureaucratic skin becomes critical for survival.

Hierarchies and Poorly Trained Participants

Another cause often mentioned for spinning and cover-up is unclear goals, poorly trained participants, vertical hierarchy (power), and horizontal hierarchy (task differentiation).

Snook and Connor (2005) report that hesitation to be honest existed in three organizations considered best in their class. They were composed of highly educated and trained participants (medical doctors, elite Army Special Forces troops, and engineers and scientists at the National Aeronautics and Space Administration). In all three cases the people worked in physical closeness with each other, indeed were able to observe the censorship that was going on. In the first case a child died. In the second case elite troops were killed. In the third case the *Columbia* blew up just before landing. In all cases, the goals were clear, and the participants were highly trained, educated, and committed to excellence in their jobs. Yet the tragedies occurred.

Clear Goals, High Self-Confidence, yet Blindness to Skilled Incompetence and Victim Mentality

Thirty-four CEOs (many of whom owned their own companies) were asked during an executive program to help Andy. Andy left his previous organization because he was invited to be CEO of another organization. After several months he was fired by the board. They cited his leadership style, his blindness toward organization realities (read *politics*), and apparent unwillingness to change (Argyris, 2002). Andy was stunned. After several weeks he began to recognize the validity of the negative evaluations. The one that troubled him the most was that he was unaware and blind.

I asked the CEOs to act as consultants to Andy. Andy sought help to overcome his blindness and to begin to learn new leadership behavioral strategies. I told them that I would role play Andy responding to their advice.

An examination of the transcript of the session (Argyris, 2002) showed that the CEOs acted in ways that Andy did not find helpful, Andy pleaded for more help, the CEOs responded by becoming defensive, and the CEOs acted in ways that created, in the classroom, problems similar to those identified by the board. The major difference was that the CEOs exhibited arrogance, blindness, and unwillingness to change. After reflecting on what was going on in class, the CEOs blamed Andy. They claimed they were the victims of his arrogance.

The point of the story is that people create counterproductive consequences that they do not intend under the following conditions:

- The setting was a classroom. The pressure to make decisions about company problems under everyday time and resource constraints was not present.

- The CEOs acted as individual contributors (consultants) and did not have to develop consensus within their group.

- The learning setting did not contain horizontal or vertical hierarchical structures.

- The CEOs faced an Andy who began by recognizing that he had to change his leadership actions.

- Most probably would not see each other again.

- The CEOs began the session by asserting the problem was real, that they thought they could be of help. At the end of the session there was consensus that I role played Andy effectively.

WHY?

Let us review the questions raised by these four cases.

• Why do leaders (Secretary Rusk) who are genuinely committed to developing organizations that are effective at solving problems, especially problems that may be upsetting, embarrassing, or threatening, seek to genuinely delegate power except the power to spin, cover up, and cover up the cover-up? Why do they appear unaware of this while they are doing it?

• Why do senior leaders (State Department) who recognize how their culture inhibits learning and who commit to changing it continue their counterproductive actions? Why do they explain why they act inconsistently by saying that they are victims of the cultures and helpless to make relevant changes? Why do they continue to assure Secretary Rusk that his important vision on change is courageous and promise that they will support it?

• Why did the medical doctors, elite Special Forces troops, and highly educated engineers and scientists, dedicated to the goals of their organization, withhold their views even though they were situated close to each other and could monitor their actions as they were occurring?

Snook and Conner cite a series of studies (Latané, 1981; Latané & Nida, 1981) that suggest that the reason people behave in these ways is that they fear that if they intervene and they fail, they could embarrass or threaten the others. As a result they would also feel embarrassed or threatened.

But how do they develop such fears when they are members of world-class organizations? I am not aware of any organization that formally educates its top people to spin, cover up, hold a victim mentality, and distance themselves from their responsibility to correct what they admit are counterproductive actions.

• Why did CEOs who voluntarily entered a learning situation act in ways that inhibited their own and Andy's learning? Why did this occur when the ideas in good currency about

inhibiting learning (e.g., hierarchies, unilateral power, poorly trained people, unclear goals and tasks) were not operative? Why did this occur when Andy admitted his blindness and pleaded for help?[1]

HOW CAN WE BEGIN TO ANSWER THESE QUESTIONS?

I begin with the following premises. All the factors identified in the exemplar cases are causally relevant to diagnosing and correcting the errors that are relevant to learning. The challenge is to discover the relevance of each factor and the pattern of interdependency between them. At least two types of knowledge are needed to meet this challenge. First is the knowledge in good currency about the factors in whatever managerial decisions are involved (e.g., accounting, finance, strategy). It is beyond the scope of this chapter to specify this knowledge.

What can be specified is the knowledge and the skills needed to diagnose the factors that inhibit learning and how to decrease them. This means that the problem solvers must know how such factors as spinning, cover-ups, undiscussables, victimization, and helplessness arise. They must also have the knowledge and the skills to reduce these factors and to increase a set of factors that facilitates the learning necessary to solve the problems described in the cases. Finally, they need the skills to test the validity of their diagnosis, the solutions, their implementation, and their effectiveness.

Our research suggests that people in organizations do not have the knowledge and skills to produce these consequences, even though they believe that the factors are counterproductive. Our research also illustrates that these gaps exist in most organizations and with most people (Argyris, 1990a, 1990b, 1993, 2000, 2004; Argyris, Putnam, & Smith, 1985; Argyris & Schön, 1996). Finally, our research suggests that whatever skills people have will tend to exacerbate the problems if implemented ineffectively.

For the problems we are addressing, people are skillfully incompetent and skillfully unaware of the counterproductive consequences while they are producing them. Organizations contain behavioral systems that reinforce these consequences. We thus have a self-fueling set of activities that are counterproductive in solving the problems illustrated in the exemplar cases.

How do people become skillful at these counterproductive actions? How are organizations built to support and reinforce them? I suggest two answers. First is the mindset people have when they create and attempt to correct these types of problems. Second is the theory of effective action that people have stored in their heads that informs their action.

Defensive Reasoning Mindset

Defensive reasoning was used in all these cases. Reasoning is defensive when its purpose is to protect actors (groups, organizations) from being embarrassed or threatened. They do not test the validity of their diagnosis and actions in the service of discovering some semblance of truth on which they can base their diagnosis, design corrective actions, and evaluate the effectiveness of their implementation.

Because the primary reason for testing is to protect the actors, self-referential logic is a key reasoning process. The logic used to create the claims is the same as the logic used to test the claims (e.g., "Trust me, I know this person [group or organization]. He will never agree."). Rusk and the ambassador believed that cover-up and undiscussables are necessary to deal with the problems they faced. The dominant reason why they did not say publicly what they believed was true was that it would be inappropriate. When asked how they knew this claim to be true, their answer was, in effect, "Trust me."

Another underlying feature of the defensive reasoning mindset is that most of it is kept private. Transparency is poor, and asking for transparency is dangerous. Self-referential logic combined with a lack of transparency and bolstered with the belief that all is done in the name of concern and caring is a recipe for disaster for the learning needed to correct the problems described in the exemplar cases. Unfortunately, the degree of the disaster is not transparent. If it ever becomes public it usually is because of a disaster that becomes public (e.g., the child dying, the Special Forces personnel killed, the *Columbia* disaster).

Theories of Action

All people hold what might be called microtheories of action that specify what is effective action and how to produce it. The theories of action people espouse vary widely. To our initial surprise, the theory in use does not vary. We have shown that it is the same regardless of gender, race, education, or wealth and in private or public, large or small organizations (Argyris, 1985, 1990a, 1990b, 1993, 2000, 2004; Argyris, Putnam, & Smith, 1985; Argyris & Schön, 1996). The governing values of the theory in use instruct the leader to be in unilateral control, to seek to win and not lose, to suppress negative feelings, and to deny personal responsibility under conditions of embarrassment or threat. The dominant action strategies are to advocate one's position in ways that do not encourage inquiry into them, to deny that this is the case because one's unilateral actions are in the service of effectiveness. The consequences are self-reinforcing error, a self-reinforcing and self-sealing process.

People using this master program create organization defensive routines. They sanction and reward the self-protective actions that participants used in the exemplar cases. Thus they reinforce the unilateral, top-down model people use, and they in turn reinforce the organization defensive routines. These consequences create an underground world that competes with the aboveground world in organizations. Defensive reasoning mindsets and unilateral theories in use make it unlikely that the underground world will be dealt with.

HOW ORGANIZATION CHANGE PROFESSIONALS REINFORCE ANTILEARNING PROCESSES

It is fair to say that the early founders of OD strove to develop theories and practices that were inconsistent with defensive reasoning. Beginning with the personal growth movement, the argument was that the requirements for rigorous testing were too rational and too scientific (Argyris, 1967, 1968, 1972). The underlying reasoning used by these practitioners was that their orientation was humanistic.

Independent Testing

A humanistic orientation did not require independent testing of claims. Indeed, independent testing probably was not possible. The difficulty with this position is that it is not possible to test the claims made or the effectiveness of the actions produced. It is not possible to determine how you know that you are not kidding yourself and others because the logic is self-referential and self-sealing. The theory underlying this position leads to important inner contradictions. For example, contrary to its claim that the humanistic approach encourages learning and competence, it may do neither.

For example, John, an active senior consultant, holds that an approach that emphasizes rigorous testing inhibits the expression and understanding of emotions. We jointly designed an experiment to test his claim. I became the client. I claimed that John's position would inhibit learning. I also acknowledged that I could be wrong and blind that I was wrong. That is why I "hired" him as my consultant. The experiment we designed was for John to help me to see that my approach inhibited learning and emotions. We held our dialogue over the Internet. It lasted about 6 months (Argyris, 2005).

The dialogue began with John's premise that there are two basic mindsets in consulting.

One is scientific and analytical. The other is subjective and humanistic. The former places feelings in the background; the latter gives feelings a foreground position. He characterized my approach as objective and his as subjective.

Each of us held a different position. I was objective and scientific. He was subjective and humanistic. He would then add, "This in no way makes your position wrong."

If my position was not wrong, I asked, how could I learn about my potential blindness? Isn't one of the key purposes of OD consultants to help people see how their position may lead to ineffective actions? How would I, as a consultant, help my clients learn how to test the validity of their claims? Would not the clients understandably expect me to model such an approach? If I accepted his reasoning processes—in effect that each of us is correct—how would I ever learn that I may be kidding myself and others? How would he ever help to generate such learning for me?

Here are some illustrative comments taken from the e-mails.[2]

- It must be obvious by now, if the claims that I [John] am making are correct, your request (of how do I test for the validity of my claim) is impossible to fulfill. There should not be a way to describe objectively a subjective mindset.

- I [John] believe that objectivity is likely to ruin the effect of emotional understanding. Making and sharing analytical observations will interfere with the conditions required to achieve the outcome that the client and the consultant want.

- My [John's] hypothesis is that people would trust you more, like you more, and feel better about their relationship with you when you adapt what I [John] have been describing as an empathetic–subjective mindset as opposed to a distant–objective one.

- I [John] am arguing that we cannot obtain objective answers regarding [emotional experiences] and that I cannot provide objective reasons why these objective answers are impossible.

• Because I [John] experience my own subjective feelings directly, a test [of their validity] is unnecessary.

• My [John's] reasoning is that if you feel something then for you, ipso facto, it is true.

As I read these claims I expressed the following questions about how John could help me discover any blindness that I have. For example,

• I [Chris] agree that there are consultants [illustrated by John] who believe their position is correct. I do not agree when they claim that analysis of emotion necessarily ruins the experiences of these emotions. I could be wrong.

• How can I learn from John about my errors if he tells me that objective understanding of his claims is not possible and that he cannot provide reasons that his "impossibility" claim is valid?

• If I were to accept John's position as correct, would it not require that I accept his reasoning processes that he uses to produce effective action? Would this not lead to my becoming dependent on him?

• If I were to accept John's advice that thinking about my position "too much" is counterproductive, what criteria would I use to judge when I am thinking "too much" or "too little" (if there is such a state as too little)?

This dialogue continued throughout the experiment. I finally concluded that I could not learn about my possible blindness and how to correct it. John responded in a way that surprised me. He said, in effect, that he did not understand that our experiment was to help me to see and correct my blindness. I referred to our early e-mails where I said this was the reason that I "hired" him. He said that there was a misunderstanding.

I do not think there was a misunderstanding. I interpret the claim of "misunderstanding" as a self-protective defense. I expressed feelings to John of betrayal. John responded to those feelings by repeating his claims that he never intended such an agreement with me.

From my perspective, John distanced himself from having any responsibility to deal with my feelings by claiming there was an obvious misunderstanding. The irony is that his defense of "misunderstanding" was based on rational–objective reasoning. As his client, I felt that he reasoned in ways that made it possible for him to be blind to his part in the causal responsibility for the failure in our relationship.[3]

Participation

The second fundamental assumption of the humanistic approach is that genuine participation could lead to effective problem solving. Consultants often tell their clients that they represent hundreds of years of experience that can help them to find new and practical solutions to their problems; consistent with the humanistic approach, the consultants do not test the validity of this claim.

For example, Tom is a senior OD consultant in a very large corporation (Argyris, 2000). He was enthusiastic about a request by senior line management that the OD problems and the business problems be integrated. Tom and some line managers designed such a change program.

The enthusiasm and commitment of the line managers deteriorated. Over time Tom became upset. He felt that the line managers were going back on their commitment. Tom decided to confront the line managers. The line managers agreed that they were no longer enthusiastic because they felt that the integration of the human and business issues was not succeeding. They admitted that they did not know how to accomplish the goal of integration. Moreover, they told him that they concluded that he also did not know how to accomplish the objective.

Tom admitted that this was true. However, he expressed confidence that with genuine participation these problems could be overcome. The line managers disagreed. As one put it, it meant having confidence in participative processes of the blind leading the blind.

The Tom case illustrates two fundamental problems. Tom activated his defensive reasoning mindset when he was having trouble. He acted in ways that, in his leadership skills workshop, he recommended against using.

The second problem was that Tom had no theory of genuine integration. There was little basis for the activation of productive reasoning mindset. Yet the line managers were using productive reasoning in dealing with the business and technical problems.

During the past 5 years I have used the Tom case in workshops that are attended by OD and other human resource (HR) professionals. The attendees are asked to read the Tom case ahead of time. I then ask the attendees to act as consultants to advise Tom how to prevent this problem from recurring. Here are several excerpts from the taped transcriptions of their responses (Argyris, 2000).

- "I think the key [for Tom] is not to respond, but to be responsive."
- "Yes, I agree. Tom should try to develop, in some kind of a conversation, a real sense of what the survival issues are for the client."
- "Yes, and help the client to feel that all is not lost."
- "These are some ways that working to get this can really build some shared view of what it is that might be possible."
- "And try to frame that in terms that are pretty understandable for folks (which it is difficult to do) to connect directly to business performance."

Let us reflect for a moment on their advice.

- The advice is phrased in terms of end results: Be responsive, develop a real sense of the survival issue, encourage the client not to

feel lost, and craft the conversation in understandable language.

- The contributions do not specify what Tom might say to produce these end results. For example, what is the difference between responding versus being responsive? What is the nature of "some kind of conversation" or building "shared views" of what is possible? And what is "understandable language"?

- The causal theory in each bit of advice is not made explicit. This makes it difficult to test the validity of their advice. The speakers appear to believe that their advice is valid. They do not strive to test the validity of their advice. The features are similar to those produced in the previous two cases.

- The HR professionals were unable to produce the very positive consequences they espoused in dealing with Tom. For example, I asked them to produce the conversations that they would use with the "resisting" line managers. The conversations were consistent with an easing-in process. Easing in means asking the line managers questions that, if they answer correctly, would lead them to become aware of the ineffectiveness of their actions.

There were two negative consequences of this easing-in strategy. First, the line managers did not believe their actions were ineffective. They believed that it was Tom who was ineffective, and that is why they refused to attend further sessions with him.

The second consequence was that the HR professionals sought data from the line managers about their pain and disappointments on their job. The line managers responded that their major pain was dealing with Tom. For example:

HR: First, I would start by asking the "resisting line managers" what is really on your mind at the moment. What keeps you awake?

Line
Manager (LM):   I'll tell you. I want to make sure that I get those darn business processes done because that is how I am being evaluated. I am a loyal manager—by that I mean, a manager who produces the numbers, especially those I agree to.

A Different HR: I would not talk that way.

Faculty
Member (FM):   Fine, what would you say?

HR: I would ask what other things are on his mind.

LM: I am bewildered. You asked me what was on my mind. I told you. Did you hear me?

HR: I think that I am trying to understand how come these ideas are on your mind. I want to understand why that thing is on your mind now.

LM: I am doubly bewildered. I thought I made it clear. I am striving to be a productive manager. So, I am going to produce according to the targets that I helped to set.

HR: What kind of targets are we talking about?

LM: You know. Produce X and Y with Z quality and do so persistently.

HR: What I am trying to understand is, given the targets, what is the disappointment at this point?

LM: The idea of disappointment is in your head, not mine. I am quite happy to do what I am doing. I am not feeling disappointed. In fact, if you would let me get on with my work, I would be quite happy.

I halted the role play and asked the group members to reflect. I said, "One of you began the session with the advice, 'be responsive.' How responsive were you when you crafted this advice to Tom?"

HR: Not very.

FM: Would you please illustrate?

HR: Maybe Tom was not totally listening to the line managers. I would be ready to roll up my sleeves and ask, "How can I really help these guys? How can we really enter some meaningful dialogue to address their problems?"

HR: And do so in a way to find out what's wrong. There has to be something wrong, or else there is not much leverage.

HR: I start with a different premise. I do not go to "sell" to anyone. I require that they come to me. It's not manipulative. It's just the way it is.

The discussion here again becomes abstract. What does it mean, concretely, to "roll up one's sleeves" and "enter into meaningful dialogue"? The discussion also illustrates two assumptions often held by professionals: In order to make progress, the client must feel some pain, and HR experts should not "sell" but await initiatives from the line. In both cases, it is fair to ask why. The HR professionals seemed bewildered that I would question their two fundamental assumptions.

As the discussion continued, more of the participants began to make explicit their own sense of limitations:

HR: I am sitting here thinking, "Okay. Let us admit that we do not know. Maybe we should say so and ask them to work with us to figure it out."

HR: Yes, if we can admit that what we are doing isn't working, we would then all be aligned on that. We have no idea what the hell the right "what" is, but let's figure it out together.

When the HR professionals realized that they did not know as much as they should if they were to be helpful, they recommended shared dialogue and participation in order to figure out possible answers. But how can the blind responsibly hope to lead the blind? Imagine if other types of professionals—say, accountants—were to admit that they did not know how to produce a balance sheet and then ask their clients to participate jointly to prepare one.

To summarize, the HR professionals used defensive reasoning to craft their interventions. Their advice was abstract, it lacked explicit specification of how to produce the consequences they advised, therefore it was difficult to produce robust tests of the validity of their claims, and therefore they gave themselves little opportunity to test where they may be causing the very consequence that they advised against (e.g., making others defensive, acting inauthentically, bypassing their own defensive reasoning and actions, and being skillfully unaware that they were producing these consequences while doing so).

Finally, the HR professionals had no theory that was valid and implementable about how to integrate the technical features of organizations with the leadership, learning, change, and commitment that they espoused.

It may be of interest to the reader that socialist planners in the old Soviet Union made similar errors. They used participation by the workers as a key feature of their society. Many workers had doubts that were similar to the blind leading the blind. The socialists insisted that the workers participate and created the Red Guards to monitor their actions (Argyris, 2004).

THE WORLD OF SCHOLARLY RESEARCH

When we examine scholarly research on such issues as openness, trust, honesty, and concern, we find that such research produces generalizations that, if used *correctly,* will necessarily lead to cover-up spinning, denial of the cover-up spinning, undiscussability, and cover-up of the undiscussability.

The causes of these consequences are the rules in good currency about conducting rigorous research and generalizations whose validity is testable (disconfirmable) (Argyris, 1980, 2004). For example,

- Some highly regarded studies on communication and trust (Hovland, Janis, & Kelly, 1953) conclude that if you are communicating to a large audience that you believe is smart, present more that one alternative if you seek to generate trust. If you believe the audience is not so smart, present only one recommendation. Let us assume a practitioner seeks to use these findings. Does he or she tell the "smart" audience that they are getting several alternatives because that is the way to establish trust with them? If a member of the dumb group asked why the other group got several alternatives, would the practitioner tell the truth? I suggest that a politically correct lie is activated in the name of trust (Argyris, 2004).

- Studies of frustration and regression concluded that mild frustration increases creativity. Beyond the threshold of mildness, the frustration leads to regression.

Let us assume that a manager wants to encourage creativity in her group meetings. Would she tell them ahead of time of her intention to frustrate them mildly? How would she measure when the threshold is reached? How would she deal with any feelings on the part of the group members that they were being manipulated? Would they tell her?

In both examples, the scholarly research leads to advice to spin, cover up, cover up the cover-up, and do all this in the name of not upsetting others and increasing the likelihood of defensive reactions.

INTERVENTIONS

It is not possible to present a detailed description of the interventions used in various organizations that are based on the theory of action. Such descriptions are available (Argyris, 1982, 1985, 1990a, 1990b, 1993, 2000, 2004; Argyris,

Putnam, & Smith, 1985; Argyris & Schön, 1996). Here I present an overview of the more fundamental ideas used to design the interventions and implement the designs.

• The major focus is to obtain data from which it is possible to infer the theories in use of each participant and the degree to which they use a defensive reasoning mindset. This means that the data obtained should describe the actions and conversations that the participants use when they are actually dealing with the problems (e.g., tape recordings, actual observations of dialogue). Instruments such as questionnaires are adequate to infer espoused theories of action but not theories in use.

One advantage of generating directly observable data is that such data make it more likely that one can make valid interferences about the reasoning processes used to design actions and to implement the designs. A second advantage is that making the reasoning processes transparent makes it difficult for people to deny their personal causal responsibility in producing their actions. For example, it is difficult for them to claim that they did not interpret the researcher's inquiries differently because the researcher's and the subjects' inferences were generated from the same directly observable data (e.g., conversation).

A third advantage is that the subjects realize that if they attempt to deny their causal responsibility (e.g., blame any misunderstandings on the researcher), the researcher is able to activate an inquiry into the validity of the inference processes the subjects and the researcher use.

• Whatever instruments are used should be able to capture data that they keep private as well as the conversations that they crafted. Any discrepancies between the two become an important basis for examining possible defensive reasoning and organization defensive routines.

For example, subjects are asked to complete a simple case that describes an important issue they are facing. They are asked to recall the conversations between themselves and others and any thoughts and feelings that they had that they did not express. Typically, for the kinds of problems that can be or are embarrassing or threatening, we find significant differences between the private and the public. We also find that the subjects cover up the differences and act as if they are not covering up. For example,

Private	Public
I am going to be attacked straight out of the box.	I'm so happy to meet you and get to know you. I think we will have a great working relationship and can learn a lot from each other.
What a bunch of crap. I don't want to get drawn into this discussion.	I'd like you to know that I believe in open, direct communication.
Did he say *our* plan? He must have meant *his* plan. Doesn't he know I disagree with his decision?	No problem. It seems like we are at a crucial point.
Winning the Nobel Prize will not help the company. Perhaps it is time to expand the development stuff and downsize the research stuff.	I am sure you all realize that we work in a for-profit industry and must be realistically oriented.

Making the spinning and the undiscussables public makes it legitimate to examine the discrepancies. Typically, the subjects react that they have to hide the discrepancies in the name of caring and concern and of not getting mired in organization defensive routines. This, in turn, often activates their stance that they are victims and helpless to change the situation.

As was shown in the cases, there is validity to claim that they are victims of the culture. But in making public their unilateral theories in use and their defensive reasoning mindset, they realize that they have built-in modes of reasoning and designs for action for which they are causally responsible. They would reason and act as they do in other situations such as family, friendship, or learning settings such as the one that CEOs created in trying to help Andy.

Often this surfaces a double bind. If they make their private thoughts and feelings public, they would probably make others defensive. If they maintain their privacy, they create relationships that inhibit learning. This is one reason that we recommend starting at the top of the organization. But Rusk was at the top, and the ambassadors were very close to the top.

It is time that we face up to the ethical and moral issues involved. After all, problems of cover-up and spinning have been found to exist in the Catholic Church with regard to abusive priests. According to Colin Powell, former secretary of state, analysts systematically manipulated the data on Iraq's military capabilities that they sent to him and George Tenet, director of central intelligence. On the organizational side, Enron and Arthur Andersen were given rewards for leadership and ethical courage when dealing with human development even as they violated accounting and securities regulations, manipulated energy markets, and cheated customers and employees.

- Designing for change means that people have to become skillful at a new theory in use (ironically one that many espouse). The governing values of this theory are creating informed choice, enabling learning as a key objective, and acknowledging personal causal responsibility. A productive reasoning mindset is used. The purpose of productive reasoning is to test for validity of any claims made. The test should be as independent as the reasoning used to create the claims. Self-referential logic is not used because of its self-sealing weak tests (Argyris, 2000, 2004). The key to making these requirements part of the theory in use is practice so that the participants develop the requisite skills, both in the seminars and, more importantly, in everyday life.

If Tom were skillful at productive reasoning, he would have recognized what the line managers reported, namely that his theory of effective intervention was the equivalent of the blind leading the blind. If the OD and change professionals had been skillful in productive reasoning they would have recognized that they adhered to a theory of organization change that was ineffective and that when used made them skillfully unaware.

If the *Challenger* Commission had realized the importance of changing theories in use and defensive mindsets, they would also have realized that their recommendations were incomplete. They also could have predicted that the *Columbia* disaster was likely.

- An important advantage of focusing on the theory in use that requires productive reasoning is that this is the direction information science is going. Information technology professionals tell us that truth (even with a small *t*) is a good idea. Garbage in, garbage out. Information technology is also grounded in the idea of rigorous testing of claims.

To summarize, whatever interventions are designed for organizations with the intent of encouraging learning around substantive issues whose diagnosis and correction may be embarrassing or threatening (double-loop learning), they require at least the following properties:

• Collect data from which theory-in-use inferences can be made about the degree of defensive reasoning mindset and the degree of unilateral, win–lose suppression of feelings.

• Make public the degree of nontransparency, especially when issues are crucial yet activate cover-up and cover up of the cover-up.

• Specify the organization defensive routines. Specify the degree to which people enter organizations skilled with defensive reasoning mindset and unilateral, top-down theories of action.

• Realize that ethical choices are needed if people go with the status quo or if they seek changes in organizations that are nontrivial.

• It is also important to realize that double-loop learning in theories in use and defensive mindsets cannot be produced without people becoming skilled at producing these features, especially when the issues are difficult, embarrassing, or threatening.

• Practice is necessary to develop skills. The development of these skills is most likely to be effective when it is connected with actual substantive problems. The good news is that the theories of managerial disciplines are increasingly being informed by the powerful developments of information science. The use of information science generates an ethical and moral flow. When information technology claims truth is a good idea, it means that information technology cannot produce its potentials if people agree that truth is a good idea and then add, "if it is not upsetting, embarrassing, or threatening." Under these conditions, people massage the truth, spin it, cover up these defensive strategies, and deny that is what is being done.

CONCLUSION

The exemplar cases in this chapter illustrate that behavioral systems exist in organizations with a way of reasoning and a theory of action that are counterproductive to the learning needed to deal effectively with problems that are difficult, embarrassing, or threatening. This behavioral system may be characterized as an underground organization. It resists transparency and open inquiry because it violates the theories and practices acceptable to the aboveground organization.

It is likely that aboveground organizations will try to deal with the underground organizations by surfacing features that are counterproductive to learning. Unfortunately, this tends to occur when there is a tragedy such as the *Challenger* explosion, the church sex scandals, the 9/11 dots that were not connected, the schools that encourage students to cheat on performance tests, and the Enron–Arthur Andersen fraudulent actions.

Once the underground features are surfaced, the strategies tend to be to create new controls, to produce new measures, to design new structures that specify responsibility. These strategies are helpful, but as the *Columbia* tragedy illustrates, they are limited. When we try to correct these tragedies, we must include a thorough analysis of the underground organization.

NOTES

1. The Andy case and a new one called Joe and Bill (about sexual harassment) have been used in seminars with more than 1,000 participants in total (female, male, minorities), and so far the results have been the same.

2. John has read all the statements of his position in this chapter and approved them as valid representations of his position.

3. For a recent example of how the expression of emotions is encouraged and the role that they play in developing sound decisions, see Edmonson and Smith (2006).

REFERENCES

Argyris, C. (1967). On the future of laboratory education. *Journal of Applied Behavioral Science, 3*(2), 153–183.

Argyris, C. (1968). Conditions for competence acquisition and therapy. *Journal of Applied Behavioral Science, 4*(2), 147–177.

Argyris, C. (1972). Do personal growth laboratories represent an alternative culture? *Journal of Applied Behavioral Science, 8*(1), 7–28.

Argyris, C. (1980). *Inner contradictions of rigorous research*. San Diego, CA: Academic Press.

Argyris, C. (1982). *Reasoning, learning and action*. San Francisco: Jossey-Bass.

Argyris, C. (1985). *Strategy, change, defensive routines*. New York: Putnam.

Argyris, C. (1990a). *Overcoming organizational defenses*. Needham, MA: Allyn & Bacon.

Argyris, C. (1990b). Inappropriate defenses against the monitoring of organization development practice. *Journal of Applied Behavioral Science, 26*(3), 299–312.

Argyris, C. (1993). *Knowledge for action*. San Francisco: Jossey-Bass.

Argyris, C. (2000). *Flawed advice*. Oxford, UK: Oxford University Press.

Argyris, C. (2002). Double-loop learning, teaching and research. *Academy of Management Learning and Education, 1*(2), 206–219.

Argyris, C. (2004). *Reasons and rationalizations: The limits to organizational knowledge*. Oxford, UK: Oxford University Press.

Argyris, C. (2005). On the demise of organizational development. In D. L. Bradford & W. Burke (Eds.), *Reinventing organizational development* (pp. 113–130). San Francisco: Pfeiffer.

Argyris, C., Putnam, R., & Smith, D. (1985). *Action science*. San Francisco: Jossey-Bass.

Argyris, C., & Schön, D. (1996). *Organizational learning II*. Reading, MA: Addison-Wesley.

Edmonson, A. C., & Smith, D. (2006). *Too hot to handle*. Working paper, Harvard Business School, Cambridge, MA.

Hoveland, C. I., Janis, I. L., & Kelly, H. H. (1953). *Communication and persuasion*. New Haven, CT: Yale University Press.

Latané, B. K. (1981). The psychology of social impact. *American Psychologist, 36,* 343–356.

Latané, B. K., & Nida, S. (1981). Ten years of research on group size and helping. *Psychological Bulletin, 89,* 308–324.

Snook, S. A., & Connor, J. C. (2005). The price of progress: Structurally-induced inaction. In W. H. Starbuck & M. Farjoun (Eds.), *Organization at the limit* (pp. 178–201). Oxford, UK: Blackwell.

5

Four General Strategies for Changing Human Systems

ROBERT E. QUINN

SCOTT SONENSHEIN

I n this chapter we articulate a new general strategy for effecting change in human systems. To do this, we return to the fundamental assumptions of organization development (OD). In examining the early arguments in the field, we identify an essential strategy that has never been made explicit. By developing this strategy, we open avenues for research and provide an action framework that will increase the effectiveness of change agents.

FOUNDATIONS OF OD

We begin with a review of the seminal paper published in 1969 by Chin and Benne, "General Strategies for Effecting Changes in Human Systems." In the paper, Chin and Benne outline three general strategies for changing human systems: empirical–rational, power–coercive, and normative–reeducative.

The empirical–rational strategy considers people to be rationally self-interested. An organization member adopts a proposed change if the following two conditions are met: The proposed change is rationally justified, and the change agent demonstrates the benefits of the change to the change target. In short, the rational–empirical approach emphasizes that if the target has a justifiable reason to change (i.e., if it is in his or her self-interest), change comes from simply telling the target about the change.

Chin and Benne call their second strategy power–coercive. This approach focuses on change efforts in which a more powerful person imposes his or her will on a less powerful person. The change agent ostensibly exercises coercion that ranges from subtle manipulation to the direct use of physical force. The main advantage of this approach is that it delivers effective results rapidly. However, these benefits come at the expense of damaging relationships, destroying trust, and forfeiting voluntary commitment.

The normative–reeducative strategy also views people as rationally self-interested. But unlike the previous two strategies, the normative–reeducative view emphasizes changes in a target's values, skills, and relationships. This is in contrast to transmitting information or exercising force. The normative–reeducative view understands people as inherently social, guided by a normative culture that influences behaviors. For change to occur under this view, the target not only undergoes rational informational processing (as in the empirical–rational view) but also reconsiders habits and values, normative structures, institutionalized roles and relationships, and cognitive and perceptual orientations. In order to guide the change agent through the complex process of normative reassessment, the normative–reeducative method usually relies on trainers, therapists, or other change agents. These experts' success depends in part on how well they learn to work collaboratively with the client. Collaboration is essential because the normative–reeducative approach focuses on experience-based learning, whereby the expert works with the client to help the change targets learn from their own experiences.

Chin and Benne argue that the empirical–rational and power–coercive strategies are well established but that the normative–reeducative strategy had emerged more recently. The normative–reeducative strategy, which stresses participation, trust, emergent processes, and win–win negotiation, serves as a foundation for OD.

THE NORMAL AND THE EXCEPTIONAL

For simplicity, we refer to these three strategies as the telling strategy, the forcing strategy, and the participating strategy. For most people, everyday experiences with change usually involve the telling or forcing strategies. When we

seek to change others, our first tactic involves explaining why the target needs to change (telling; e.g., "Pat, if you do not put your bike away, someone may run over it."). This strategy works when a target has only loose ties to a given behavioral pattern. However, in many cases people hold stronger commitments to their behavioral patterns (Staw & Ross, 1987). Consequently, the telling strategy routinely fails. When the telling strategy fails, frustration increases, and most people's inclination leads them to use their resources, such as power (forcing). Power may range from subtle manipulation to brute force (e.g., "Pat, if you do not put your bike away right now, I am going to lock it up for a month."). This increase in leverage works initially, but it comes at the expense of trust and undermines commitment. When monitoring ends and the change target is beyond the reach of the change agent, the target tends to revert to the original behavior.

The telling and forcing strategies are so frequently used that they make up what we call normal patterns of change. In a social world where we assume self-interest and transactional norms of exchange (i.e., based on self-interest), we expect to see people using these first two strategies. They are quick and easy and focus on solving short-term problems. They become part of normal or natural patterns of action. People use the normal strategies within and outside the corporate world.

The normative–reeducative or participating strategy is less common than the other two strategies. When change agents successfully use the participating strategy, we view the results as extraordinary or even unnatural. Why? The participating strategy is more time-consuming, takes greater skill, and defies our normal assumptions about the need for control. Stephen Covey tells the story of a CEO who told him, "Every time I try win–win, I lose." Covey replied, "Then you did not do win–win" (Covey, 1989, pp. 204–234). It is difficult for even the best educated and most experienced managers to comprehend that surrendering control and pursuing the common good can result in a positive outcome for both parties. In OD interventions, we often hear the phrase "trust the process." To most people, this phrase is incomprehensible.

Given managers' need for control, we often see the participating strategy corrupted and used as a form of manipulation. It is reduced to a forcing strategy. An authority figure presents himself as open and tolerant. But these attributes become contingent on the participants' arriving at the authority figure's predetermined answer. The manager espouses participation only to the extent that the results of the change process cohere with what the manager would have forced the change targets to do in the first place.

As difficult and rare as the third strategy may be, there is an even more difficult fourth strategy, an approach that takes greater effort and commitment but will lead to long-term, sustainable, and deep change. We also consider this strategy to be more basic, essential, and powerful than the other three strategies.

THE FOURTH STRATEGY

In their original paper, Chin and Benne observe that a minority can change a majority. They do this by using a power–coercive or forcing strategy. The minority uses moral power to shame the majority into changing. In illustrating the argument, Chin and Benne cite the examples of Gandhi and Martin Luther King Jr. However, Chin and Benne overlook the most unique aspect of the change strategies used by Gandhi and King. A deeper examination reveals a fourth strategy that cannot be accessed from transactional assumptions. It can be seen and understood only if we leave the normal assumptions of transaction and self-interest and move to the extraordinary assumptions of transformation.

Quinn (2000) reports an analysis of the common change practices of Gandhi, King, and Jesus Christ. He does not focus on their religious orientation but on the change practices they held in common. From this examination, he articulates a body of change principles called advanced change theory (ACT). At the heart of ACT is what we call self-transcendence or the transforming strategy. Here is the fundamental argument.

First, we begin with the assumption that all systems must acquire energy from the external environment. To do this the system must be aligned with the continuously changing external environment. As a system loses such alignment it tends toward entropy, or the loss of productive energy. All individuals, groups, and organizations tend toward entropy or slow death. Individuals and collectives seek to avoid change and preserve equilibrium. As a result, we all move toward entropy or slow death (Quinn, 1996).

Second, we are all hypocrites. We espouse values at one level and exhibit incongruent behaviors at another (Argyris, 1991, 1998). We all have integrity gaps. Hypocrisy is rampant in organizations. We claim to be committed to certain ends, but we are committed only when those ends are consistent with our self-interests. Instead of making self-sacrifice to create extraordinary realignments for the betterment of the system, we collude with others in politically acceptable behavior. Our actual goal is not extraordinary achievement but the preservation of the status quo. We all seek to stay inside our zone of comfort (Quinn, 2000). We live on the path of least resistance (Fritz, 1989). Thus, it is perfectly normal for each of us to live in a transactional, reactive state, in which we are determined by our environment. It's simply easier.

Third, we can all become more effective change agents. We can enter a proactive state in which we begin to co-create our environment and our future. We do this by reducing integrity gaps. We enter what Quinn (2004) calls the fundamental state of leadership. He argues that leadership is not a function of formal position such as CEO or prime minister but a result of our state of being. Anyone can be a leader or change agent, but most of the time none of us are. We lack the necessary moral power. In OD, if we are to be effective change agents, we must enter this state of leadership.

Fourth, we become effective leaders or change agents when we examine our integrity gaps and make a fundamental commitment to pursue a higher purpose. We then transcend the existing self. In entering the state of leadership, we transcend two polarities: We become more internally driven and more externally open. We become more purpose centered and other focused.

Fifth, when we enter the state of leadership, in the existing transactional system, we become a positive deviant. As we act with greater moral power, we distort the existing system, and others must make sense of us. In the process, some of them join us in the co-creation of new relationships and emergent organizing. We launch an emergent social movement that transcends the current system. This nonlinear process begins with increased integrity and personal risk taking.

NORMAL REACTIONS

We are so steeped in the assumptions of self-interest, and defensive of our hypocrisy, that the fourth strategy tends to be met with cynicism, exemplified by such responses as "Such things never happen," "This may occur occasionally, but it is unrealistic and impractical," "It could never be used in my setting," "People who do such things are heroes; normal people cannot engage in such behavior," or "Why would anyone expose himself or herself to such painful demands?"

The fact is that self-transcendence occurs with some frequency. It is not only practical but essential to individual health and collective well-being. Self-transcendence or a transforming strategy can be used in any setting. It can be and is used by the most ordinary people (Quinn & Quinn, 2004). Yet once we use it, we become temporarily extraordinary.

To not embrace the painful demands of self-transcendence is to collude in our own decay or slow death. These are powerful claims but are unlikely to influence the cynic. For this reason we present one of many cases in which normal organization actors report using the fourth strategy. What follows is the case of an internal consultant. Roman J. Wally is an ordinary person who practices self-transcendence and then begins to make surprising changes in a major corporation (Quinn, 2004, pp. 10–11, 190).

CASE: AN INTERNAL CONSULTANT CHOOSES TO LEAD CHANGE

I have always been afraid to make waves. Growing up in a large family with a quick-tempered, domineering father, I chose the peacemaker and jokester roles. I used self-deprecating humor to deflect undue scrutiny, to cover up my fear of inadequacy. Much of that has changed, but the self-deprecating humor remains.

I first read *Deep Change* when I attended a workshop at the University of Michigan. It happened 5 months after my first wife died, and I felt empty inside. The instructor's life story resonated with my own, but the reflection was twisted as though seen through a melted mirror.

His father died when he was an infant. My first wife, Theresa, died of a rare form of breast cancer when my children were small (ages 10 and 3). He lost a sister he never knew. I almost lost my son to meningococcal encephalitis a year earlier. My sister, Meg, whom I loved dearly and whose spirit, humor, faith, and medical knowledge sustained Theresa and me through her long illness, was in the early stages of a mysterious illness that would eventually take her life. I felt like I was moving through life as a spectator, I was watching a play that I didn't like, but I had no power to change the script, or so I thought. I needed meaning, but life seemed to be devoid of it.

It is hard to describe the power and emotional freedom I felt after reading the book and going through the Leading Change seminar. I looked at the script of my life with new eyes. I began to make changes in how I approached my work. I had assumed a new role as an organization effectiveness consultant in Shell and Texaco's new retail marketing business. I began to ask tough questions of myself: Did I care enough about the business to risk my job? What was more important: my self-respect or the respect of others? As I reflected on these questions the answers came back with certainty and unassailable logic. It truly was slow death to be working in an organization where I felt uncomfortable asking questions that should be answered. If my self-respect came first, the respect of others would naturally follow.

I began to ask tough questions of senior and executive-level leaders. There was surprise in their eyes when they were asked these questions or presented with data they weren't comfortable with. They began to look at me in a new light. I was increasingly asked to consult on more complex and strategic issues. It was a case of tough love at work.

Another example of tough love stands out in my mind. I was asked to coach a team that was not meeting its deadlines. After opening a meeting with the team, I asked the members what was holding the project back. The answers came back quickly: Upper management kept changing the target. They weren't empowered to make decisions. They were hamstrung. There was no guidance. There were too many demands on their time. I listened for about 5 minutes and then reflected back what I heard. I told them that I didn't have any answers, but as an outside observer I felt I could provide an accurate reflection of their current reality.

Their language was the language of victims. Did they want to own the problem and the outcome? Or did they want someone else to make the decisions for them? Did they want to be creative and come up with solutions that hadn't been considered before, or did they want to arrive at predictable outcomes? There was an uncomfortable silence in the room, the unspoken question hung in the air: Slow death or deep change? The team was staffed by ambitious and bright managers who worked very hard but who hadn't confronted their collective behavior yet. One by one, they all admitted they hadn't dedicated themselves to the project. A new energy flowed into the room. After a series of meetings the team came to realize its potential. We completed the project on time and received high praise from the executive sponsors.

I am now the training manager of Shell's commercial marketing and distribution business. I achieved this new level of responsibility because of my willingness to ask tough questions, even the ones that I didn't necessarily want to hear the answers to. But the battle to remain true to the concepts of deep change stays with me.

Even now, I am faced with redesigning a new human resource organization that may eliminate my position and roll my responsibilities into another training manager's organization. Our team of four managers has been meeting, trying to decide what our structure should look like. After the first meeting, our initial design still showed four distinct areas of practice, one for each of the managers to head. I have to step back and ask myself, "Is this the right answer or are we all just trying to protect ourselves?" We four, all experienced in "change management," have been resisting change, putting up barriers, and denying our current reality. The irony of the situation is overwhelming if we just let ourselves see it.

Slow death or deep change? The sacrifices that I saw Theresa and Meg make to live their lives to the fullest while they experienced slow death left me with no real choice. They had to face slow death and chose to live life, celebrating its gifts. I should do at least as much, celebrating their gifts to me and celebrating their memories.

The book has had a profound effect on me. I trace much of my professional transition and personal transformation to trying to live the elements that are outlined in the book. I highly recommend it to all who are confronting the moral dilemma of deep change or slow death—in other words, everybody who is open to the quest.

SOURCE: Quinn, R. E. (2004). *Building the bridge as you walk on it: A guide to leading change.* San Francisco: Jossey-Bass.

CASE OBSERVATIONS

Note some unusual things about this case. First, Roman is an ordinary man who is not one to make waves. He experiences a series of powerful trigger events. These cause him to reflect on his most deeply held assumptions, and he comes to admit something that most people are unwilling to admit: His life is devoid of meaning. At that point he begins to make some fundamental decisions and then begins to ask tough questions: "Did I care enough about the business to risk my job?" "What was more important: my self-respect or the respect of others?"

As he reflects, he concludes, "It truly was slow death to be working in an organization where I felt uncomfortable asking questions that should be answered. If my self-respect came first, the respect of others would naturally follow."

He commits himself to the good of the company, becomes more internally directed, and begins to ask tough questions of senior management. Normally we would expect such questions to get a person like Roman fired. Instead Roman reports that authority figures began to define him in a new light, and they began to invite him to consult on more complex and strategic issues. Roman also challenges other people to stop acting like victims. Again, we are surprised to read that he is successful. In the end Roman is able to question whether his own job should be preserved.

When Roman applies the strategy of self-transcendence or the transforming strategy, he reduces hypocrisy, increases integrity, and begins to attract people to the committed state. Committed people forgo transactional patterns in favor of transformational patterns. Roman was an internal consultant, a change agent. Yet until he engaged the strategy of self-transcendence, he was far from extraordinary. Because he reached a committed state, he was empowering and empowering to his community.

A COMPARISON OF THE FOUR STRATEGIES

In order to get a better grasp of the strategy or self-transcendence, or what we call the transforming strategy, consider Table 5.1.

Table 5.1   A Comparison of the Four General Strategies

	Telling	Forcing	Participating	Transforming
Target	Change target	Change target	Relationship	Change agent
Motivation	Self-interest	Self-interest	Common good	Common good
Levers	Facts	Power	Dialogue	Integrity
Time	Short	Short	Long	Long
Impact	First order	First order	Second order	Second order
Perceived control	High	Highest	Low	Lowest
Actual control	Low	Low	High	Highest
Outcomes	Compliance	Compliance	Emergence	Emergence

Target. In the first two strategies the focus is on the change target. Information is used in the telling strategy and coercion is used in the forcing strategy, with the expectation that the target will change. In the participating strategy, the target is not the other person but the relationship between the agent and the target. As people join in a win–win focus and trust the process, a new relationship emerges. In the transforming strategy, the focus is on self-transcendence. The change agent is the person who is expected to change by reducing hypocrisy and moving into the committed state. The change agent is the change target.

Motivation. The telling and forcing strategies are based on the transactional view of exchange and consequently involve rational, self-interested motivations. The participating strategy becomes less transactional and more transformational because of the win–win emphasis. Yet from the perspective of critics, the participating strategy is based on a *modus vivendi*—a strategic compromise between the parties. The strategy works as long as there is a win–win outcome for self-interested parties to pursue. Proponents argue that if participants trust the process, the win–win solution will always emerge. In the transforming strategy, the change agent shifts from self-interest to the collective interest. Because there is a total commitment to creating a given result, the contingency in the participating strategy disappears. Critics argue that the collective interest has simply become the self-interest. Nevertheless, there is a clear shift from simple self-interest in the first two strategies to the collective interests in the latter two strategies.

Levers. In the first two strategies the levers of change wielded by the change agent are facts or information for the telling strategy and leverage or coercion for the forcing strategy. In the participating strategy, the change agent relies on dialogue and the co-creation of a commonly owned future. In the transforming strategy the lever is personal integrity, which gives rise to moral power. By moral power, we are not presenting a single view of the good life. Quite the contrary, each person must find his or her own moral power. This derives from reduced defensiveness, examination of personal hypocrisy, and commitment to a higher purpose such as the good of the relationship or the organization.

Time. The four change strategies require different time investments. The telling and forcing strategies take little time commitment. In the former strategy, the change agent simply transmits more persuasive information to the change target. In the latter strategy, the change agent simply exercises legitimate or illegitimate authority to institute change. The participating strategy takes more time investment. Establishing a win–win, participative dialogue takes much time and effort. The transforming

strategy is also highly time consuming. The change agent has to go through self-reflection and then repeat the process on a regular basis.

Impact. The first two strategies tend to lead to incremental changes, and the second two tend to result in transformational changes. Incremental changes are smaller changes that happen within the underlying paradigm or meaning system. Transformational changes tend to be larger and more dramatic alterations in which the underlying paradigm or meaning system is altered. The modifications in the meaning system lead to new behaviors, and these give rise to new structures and processes. Occasionally one of the first two strategies can lead to transformation, and occasionally the latter two can result in only incremental differences.

Perceived Control. One of the most important dimensions of comparison is the perceived control of the change agent. In the telling and forcing strategies the change agent tends to believe that he or she is in control. This is one reason why these first two strategies receive widespread support. In the telling strategy we control the information we dispense. In the forcing strategy our perceived control seems to reach a peak. The change target must do what we demand. In the participating and transforming strategies, perceived control appears minimal. In the participating strategy, we allow the change targets to influence us, and we trust the dialogue to result in an emergent win–win relationship. In the transforming strategy, we engage in self-change and then allow others complete agency in determining whether they want to respond to the attraction of our increased moral power. We then wait for an emergent process to unfold, recognizing that we have little control over the process at all.

Actual Control. The irony of the telling and forcing strategies is that although these approaches have high perceived control, they result in little actual control. Recipients of the telling strategy rarely change deeply rooted behaviors. In the forcing strategy, where perceived control appears extremely high, we damage the relationship with change targets.

Consequently, as soon as monitoring ceases, compliance disappears. As we become skilled in the participating strategy, we develop an enormous sense of control in that we can turn most situations into win–win outcomes. In the transforming strategy, we have the ability to reach complete control because we are both the change agent and the target. As we reduce our hypocrisy and increase our commitment, others are free to choose their course of action.

Outcomes. The strategies also differ along the dimension of desired outcomes. The first two strategies seek compliance. In the telling strategy, for example, we may provide factual information, such as the scientifically verified relationship between smoking and cancer. We do this hoping that the change targets will comply with our enlightened understanding of healthy living. In the forcing strategy we may seek to pass laws that demand compliance with our understanding of healthy living. In both strategies we have a paradigm of the desired state, and we push change targets to conform with our expectations. In the participating strategy we do not assume that we know the answer or desired outcome. We engage in a process in which the desired future emerges over time. We co-create it. In the transforming strategy we clarify the common good or higher purpose and embrace it. This increase in moral power distorts the existing system and causes others to make sense of us and then make decisions about their own reality. This distortion gives rise to an emergent social system or productive community, one that is more closely tied to external reality and is full of committed people doing what needs to be done when it needs to be done.

IMPLICATIONS FOR TEACHING AND PRACTICE

Courses and workshops in OD provide two main benefits: theoretical background and applied tools and techniques. What makes a traditional OD course unique is that most of the theories, tools, and techniques usually reflect the values of the participating strategy.

Because the values of the transforming strategy are in many ways similar to the values of the participating strategy, we suggest that the fourth strategy should be more readily accepted in OD than in other fields. Given the value congruence between participating and transforming, it is surprising that OD has little focus on self-transcendence. Increasing the emphasis on transforming may lead to increased change effectiveness as change agents harness additional moral power. Consider a common pattern.

It is normal for a change agent or consultant to act out of self-interest. On occasion, powerful figures hire a consultant to help bring about an organization change. As the change process unfolds, it becomes clear that the behavior of the power figure is part of the problem. The behavior of the power figure needs to change. At this point, the power figure sends implicit messages that call for alternative courses of action. The consultant, who seeks to preserve the relationship with the client for financial and professional reasons, then tends to consciously or unconsciously collude with the power figure. In colluding, the two undermine the best interests of the system. When this happens, none of the first three strategies is likely to work. The consultant or change agent lacks the necessary moral power.

The ideas articulated in this chapter can help. In Figure 5.1 we list questions reflecting the self-orientation of the change agent using each of the four strategies. We place particular emphasis on the self-orientation in the transforming strategy. The other strategies often fail. The political perspective, for example, leads to compliance with a set of rules and uses authority to reach goals. But such behaviors are not a long-term strategy that induces commitment to change. The telling strategy also has difficulties. Although using logical arguments is an effective way of persuading, it does not lead to the widespread change often needed. And the interpersonal perspective, though often useful, can be co-opted by the change agent and internal interests to promote

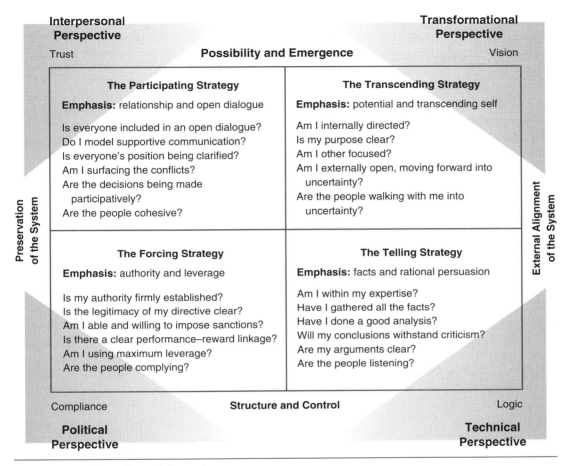

Figure 5.1 Four General Strategies

their own self-interests. On the other hand, the transformational perspective has the capability of leading to the requisite widespread change. Questions such as "Am I internally directed?" and "Is my purpose clear?" are difficult. But these questions lead to the articulation of a vision in which the change agent transcends self-interest. A change agent can use these questions to get into a state of increased moral power and increase the likelihood of organization change (Quinn, 2004).

For the novice, the list of questions is likely to be useful but inadequate. The conceptual jump is large, and people in the normal state of denial have many rationalizations for avoiding the fourth strategy. For this reason Quinn and Quinn (2004) have proposed a process for

helping the novice embrace the fourth strategy. The assumption is that just as it is normal for each of us to live in hypocrisy, it is also normal for each of us to have past experiences in which we have actually experienced self-transcendence. A careful search for and analysis of such moments proves to be a valuable exercise. It gives us vision and courage.

IMPLICATIONS FOR RESEARCH

The fourth general strategy also has implications for research. To date, OD scholars have not carefully considered the assumptions of self-transcendence. Scholars have also not given due attention to the literature on transformational leadership. Most theories do not conceptualize change agents as transformational leaders. We suggest that OD researchers reexamine the literature on transformational leadership and reframe that literature around the assumptions of self-transcendence. Afterwards, researchers can look at the questions and propositions that emerge to raise a set of related questions for OD. Although such research will depart from the norm, we contend that a change in the fundamental assumptions of human behavior toward transformation will provide theoretically rich and meaningful approaches to change, leadership, and OD.

REFERENCES

Argyris, C. (1991, May–June). Teaching smart people how to learn. *Harvard Business Review, 69,* 99–109.

Argyris, C. (1998). Empowerment, the emperor's new clothes. *Harvard Business Review, 76,* 98–105.

Chin, R., & Benne, K. D. (1969). General strategies for effecting changes in human systems. In W. G. Bennis, K. D. Benne, & R. Chin (Eds.), *The planning of change* (pp. 32–59). New York: Holt, Rinehart & Winston.

Covey, S. (1989). *The 7 habits of highly effective people.* New York: Fireside Press.

Fritz, R. (1989). *The path of least resistance: Learning to become the creative force in your own life.* New York: Fawcett.

Quinn, R. E. (1996). *Deep change: Discovering the leader within.* San Francisco: Jossey-Bass.

Quinn, R. E. (2000). *Change the world.* San Francisco: Jossey-Bass.

Quinn, R. E. (2004). *Building the bridge as you walk on it: A guide to leading change.* San Francisco: Jossey-Bass.

Quinn, R. E., & Quinn, S. E. (2004). Becoming a transformational change agent. In L. Greiner & F. Ponfett (Eds.), *Handbook of management consulting: The contemporary consultant— Insights from world experts.* Cincinnati, OH: South Western.

Staw, B. M., & Ross, J. (1987). Behavior in escalation situations: Antecedents, prototypes, and solutions. *Research in Organizational Behavior, 9,* 39–78.

6

Where's the Beef?

A Clinical Perspective on Organization Consultation and Change

MANFRED KETS DE VRIES

KATHARINA BALAZS

Ignorance is the night of the mind, but a night without moon and star.

—Confucius

The greatest obstacle to discovery is not ignorance—it is the illusion of knowledge.

—Daniel Boorstin

Better to keep your mouth shut and appear stupid than to open it and remove all doubt.

—Mark Twain

NEVER SAY NEVER: ORGANIZATION DEVELOPMENT AND BEYOND

Although organization development (OD) has a long and reputable tradition, it finds itself at a crossroads in present-day society. Its original claim to fame had to do with its ability to disentangle knotty group and interpersonal problems, such as employee retention, employee job satisfaction, work–life balance, employee productivity, team performance, conflict management, and organization effectiveness (Burke, 1982; Carter, Giber, & Goldsmith, 2001; Cummings & Worley, 2001; French & Bell, 1999; Worley & Feyerherm, 2003). With a belief in each person's self-actualizing potential and an emphasis on humanistic and ethical concerns such as democracy and social justice, OD became a social movement of optimism and hope. Using its positive *Weltanschauung* as a tool, it aimed to transform the belief systems of individuals and work groups to help organizations adapt to their environment. The ultimate aim was to create better places to work.

In the rough-and-tumble of the global organizational jungle, where the rallying cry of shareholder value is all too often the sole slogan heard, these concepts no longer seem sufficient. Yet the interests of other constituencies must be taken into consideration to make organizations viable. The question becomes how to go beyond simply guarding shareholder value to an outlook that recognizes more effective ways to manage for the long run.

In this era of accelerated change, organizations are not interested in idealistic interventions; rather, they are interested in realistic interventions. Humane concerns are all well and good, but organization leaders want to know what effect any strategy will have on the bottom line. To be able to meet these new challenges, the OD interventionist may be required to go beyond the traditional building blocks of OD, such as humanistic psychology, group dynamics, and traditional management and organization theory. Used in conjunction with traditional OD methods, the tool that offers much promise is the clinical orientation to organization analysis and intervention. This orientation, solidly grounded in concepts of psychoanalytic psychology (specifically, object relations theory), developmental psychology, neurology, family system theory, and cognition, is often glaringly absent in the OD toolbox. Furthermore, when OD practitioners use clinical concepts, these concepts typically are implied rather than explicitly stated. One

reason may be that the humanistic orientation, with its can-do, optimistic attitude, is not always compatible with the more pessimistic *Weltanschauung* of many clinically trained professionals.

Given the intention to foster organizations in which people are at their best, feeling alive and being productive, there is a great need for convergence between the more traditional OD approaches and the insights provided by advocates of the clinical orientation to organization analysis and change. This enhanced need for realism fits with the trend toward greater convergence between the various schools of psychology.

To illustrate the advantages of such convergence in the process of organization intervention and change, we offer a consulting assignment that benefited from a marriage of OD technology and the clinical approach. Although it seemed to be only a limited success by both the consultant's and the organization's standards, it would have been even more difficult with only the traditional OD practitioner's toolbox.

THERE'S MORE TO IT THAN MEETS THE EYE

Most of the partners of one of the local offices of TechDiag, a global consulting firm, had concluded that the partner group was no longer functioning effectively. Partner meetings were poorly attended; the general feeling was that no meaningful decisions were made during these meetings anymore. Many partners had also expressed their concern about a lack of leadership. Although the partner group had a nominal head—the managing partner—nobody seemed to be in charge. To many, it had become evident that the office was no longer functioning at optimal capacity.

And it was not only the partners who were complaining. The malaise of the partner group had spread throughout the office, and the more junior consultants were also commenting about a decline in morale. What once had been an exciting, stimulating place to work had become just another ordinary consulting firm. Some of the consultants feared that this would cause problems in the long run because it would make the search for talent more difficult. There were already signs of trouble in the short term. For example, transfer of knowledge—in the past a major source of competitive advantage in the group—was no longer handled effectively, in large part because backstabbing had become the order of the day. Many of the partners felt like ships passing in the night. They had so little contact that they barely knew each other anymore, and they had lost touch with what the others were doing.

Because of the accelerated growth in opportunities in the geographic region in which the office was located, the number of partners at TechDiag had grown rapidly over the last decade. What had once been a small group of people who understood each other almost intuitively, collaborated intimately, and spent long hours together building up the office into its present form, had changed into a large, loosely connected group. The collegial atmosphere that was TechDiag's hallmark in the early days had all but disappeared. Rather than working to maintain good relationships in the office, the partners now focused almost exclusively on their clients. As a result, claimed some old-timers, the office had become a way-station on the career path. No longer was it a place where people shared common experiences about client successes and defeats; no longer was there a free flow of information for the benefit of clients and partners alike.

The anonymous atmosphere at the office was exacerbated by the fact that some of the partners were not "home grown"; that is, they had not gone through the usual career trajectory of the firm (moving over time, and in many stages, from associate consultant to partner). Instead, they had been hired from the outside at full partner level. These lateral hires had been brought in to help the firm gain a speedier entry into specific market segments.

However, some consultants had observed that the firm had never been very good at integrating lateral hires.

This growing malaise was reflected in the bottom line. The findings of a recent company-wide study had shown that the revenue per partner at this particular office was much lower than at most other offices of TechDiag. This finding was disturbing to many of the partners; in the past they had always been leaders in revenue generation.

There were outside pressures as well: A number of competing companies had entered what had been TechDiag's traditional niche in the consulting market in this office's region, putting great pressure on the partner group to be more effective. After enjoying a period in which they could operate on autopilot regarding marketing and sales, they now had to work hard to bring in new customers.

Senior partners felt that a number of the new partners—insiders and lateral hires alike—were responsible for the present malaise, wondering how much these new partners were really contributing to the bottom line, whereas many of the newer partners felt that some of the senior partners were "fat cats," complacent in their tenured seniority.

At one of the monthly partner meetings the discontent bubbled up into a consensus that the present state of affairs could not continue. The group decided to hire Joni Steiner, a well-known consultant who specialized in human resource management. The assignment given to her was to address the question of how to become more effective as a partner group.

After a series of interviews to get a better understanding of the salient issues, Joni suggested the use of a set of instruments—including 360-degree feedback tools—as the basis for a group discussion during a culminating team-building event. Joni described to the two partners who had given her the original invitation how she had used these instruments effectively in the past to create high-performance teams. The two partners had given her the official go-ahead, expressing their view that the use of such material would be a good idea.

However, during the interviews Joni became aware of an enormous amount of resistance on the part of various partners toward the 360-degree instruments. This puzzled her, given that all the partners, without exception, had strongly stated that something needed to be done to help them work more effectively as a group. She suspected that something was going on beneath the surface. After all, the feedback instruments were intended only as an icebreaker to highlight some of problems in the partner group. Why, when she talked about the use of the survey instruments, did some of the partners get a pained look on their faces and question the use of this kind of material? Personally, they said, they had no problems with the material and would be happy to complete the questionnaires, but they wondered how some of the others would feel using such instruments in a group setting. When pressed about what they saw as the problem, they explained that some of the senior partners had had bad experiences with using personal material before.

TRUTH LIES AT THE BOTTOM OF A WELL

Joni decided to discuss her problem with a colleague who had clinical training. He pointed out to her that she had been looking at the problem at the superficial level, where there was consensus about what needed to be done to have the partner group work more effectively. At what he called the manifest level, all the partners acknowledged that the office had lost its sense of direction (a paradoxical finding for a strategic consulting firm) and that transfer of best consulting practices was taking place clumsily, if at all. At that manifest level, the whole group agreed that some kind of structure had to be introduced to facilitate the decision-making process and the lack of leadership in the company.

Having reviewed with Joni these manifest concerns, Joni's colleague suggested that she dig for latent, significant, but unexpressed problems that would help Joni determine why the partners were so reluctant to take the steps that seemed to be so obvious—steps that, in their own consulting work, the partners would surely recommend to their clients.

Joni's colleague introduced to her the concept of secondary gain, which says that manifest malfunctioning (in this case, the present malaise at the office) can offer psychological advantages. As an example of a secondary gain, he pointed out that the dysfunctional nature of the partner meetings (though painful for all in attendance) guaranteed that some of the firm's most critical issues, such as the declining revenue per partner, would not be addressed.

During Joni's interviews, many people had hinted that not all of the partners were still pulling their weight, that some of the older partners wanted time to smell the roses and were bringing down revenues as a result. This seemed to contradict two primary corporate myths: that TechDiag liked to hire "insecure overachievers," true workaholics, and that the team worked together as a happy community.

Yet Joni had not been able to get anyone to do anything more than hint at this contradiction. To openly state that a problem existed, that some partners were no longer sufficiently contributing to the firm, was apparently perceived by the TechDiag partners as being too anxiety inducing because the discussion that would inevitably result would break the myth of mutuality, the illusion that they were a collaborative and cooperative community. Furthermore, some partners apparently lived under the fear that by entering into such a dialogue, they would be opening a Pandora's box so full of complaints that the office would implode and the most important partners would take their talents elsewhere. At such a price, conflict avoidance was preferable, despite the backstabbing that was its consequence.

Moreover, a number of the partners saw greater accountability as a threat to their present autonomy. In their eyes, although things were bad, the creation of a corporate governance structure that demanded greater clarity about their own contribution, that asked what each person was doing and established controls on activity, would be far worse. Many of the partners liked their freedom; they enjoyed not having to explain how they spent their time, and they liked working at home and putting in odd hours without having to defend these practices.

Joni's colleague said that it looked to him as if the partners were using what he called a social defense: a way of dealing with the anxiety that is part and parcel of life in organizations. Social defenses can be viewed as systems of relationships, reflected in the social structure, that function like individual defenses but are woven into the fabric of an organization. They are ways of dealing with the angst and unpredictability of life in organizations. Their purpose is to transform and neutralize strong tensions and affects such as anxiety, shame, guilt, envy, jealousy, rage, sexual frustration, and low self-esteem. When there is no containment of these feelings—that is, when there are no opportunities to discuss and deal with heartfelt concerns—people in organizations are inclined to engage in defensive routines such as splitting (dividing the world into black-and-white, us-versus-them categories) or projective identification (assigning to other people the negative feelings one has but cannot acknowledge). Although these social defenses can be seen as adaptive at one level—in this case, for example, they helped maintain the illusion of being a happy family and helped avoid potentially disruptive conflict—at another level they contributed to a distortion of inner and outer reality, derailing effective organization functioning. At TechDiag, social defenses allowed the partners to withdraw partially from the responsibility that came with their ownership position.

As suggested earlier, the present impasse had been triggered by diseconomies of size. With the recent growth of the office, the partners were not as close as they had been. Instead of making an effort to combat the situation, the partners chose to pursue more personal agendas, and as a result they forfeited the trust that been built up over the years among personnel. In the absence of trust, a political climate flourished in the office: Subgroups developed, and backstabbing became the communication tool of choice. Constructive conflict resolution went out the window as well because its key ingredient is trust. Thus, whenever the newly politicized TechDiag faced a difficult decision, the partners chose denial over resolution. In abandoning conflict resolution, they gave up commitment and accountability as well, factors essential to a healthy bottom line.

The key to resolution of the present impasse, Joni's colleague told her, lay in openness. TechDiag could reinvigorate itself only if the partners were prepared to deal with their problems head on, to discuss the undiscussables, to stop the infighting, and to air out the increasingly politicized atmosphere at the office. Being willing to deal with the problems that burrowed at a more latent level would also imply that the partners had to bite the bullet and accept a more comprehensive form of corporate governance, even if that intervention meant restriction of the freedom they had enjoyed before. With the growth of the office rendering the old intuitive governance of the partner group ineffective, control systems were needed to enhance the quality of decision-making processes, and a select number of colleagues had to be empowered to make meaningful decisions on behalf of the group.

To overcome the latent problems, the partners also needed to address the level of transparency of accountability acceptable to all, increasing it to ensure fair process. As a group, they needed to spell out the role expectations for each partner, and they needed to discuss frankly whether all partners were pulling equal (or at least adequate) weight. If they concluded that they were no longer an "A" team—that is, if certain partners were found to be pulling down the bottom line—the stronger majority would need to pressure the laggards to shape up or leave the company.

None of these necessary steps could happen, Joni's colleague pointed out to her, until the partners realized that it was their own prevailing social defenses that had prevented such a discussion from taking place. They needed to acknowledge that their defensiveness had impeded the work process. They needed to recognize that, paradoxically, their rational manifest "solutions" to their fears and concerns had contributed to a great deal of irrationality at the latent level. In order to make TechDiag a high-performance organization again—an organization ready and able to take on the future—they would have to address these more subtle latent processes as well.

IT'S NOT OVER 'TIL IT'S OVER

Joni decided to go ahead with her planned team-building session—a 3-day workshop—despite the resistance the partners had shown to her 360-degree feedback instruments. When she called the managing partner to firm up the details, however, he told her that the session would have to be curtailed to just a half day. A number of the senior partners had decided that the days the group would spend together would be more effectively used to discuss the future strategy of the office.

Joni was frustrated by the curtailment of the workshop. It bothered her even more, though, that the human resources partner (a junior partner) wanted to know in advance every detail of the presentation she planned to make. More than once, both he and the managing partner cautioned her not to be too direct in giving certain types of feedback in order not to irritate some of the senior partners. Joni deeply resented being micromanaged by the two of them, but against her better judgment she decided not to object. At the

time, however, she wasn't prepared to analyze her feelings of anger and irritation about being micromanaged.

At the meeting, Joni gave a general presentation about high-performance teams and organizations and then pointed out salient issues she had observed in the office. During the first part of her presentation, the atmosphere was icy; the partners listened to the presentation stone-facedly, without making any comments. During the second part of the presentation, however, matters started to change. After much prompting from Joni, a lively discussion developed, with a number of the partners willing to address the elusive latent issues so that some form of corporate governance could be put into place and they could all work more effectively.

But all too soon, Joni's time was up. Without having had a chance to help the partners arrive at any action recommendations, she was thanked and dismissed; the partners would have to tackle the latent issues themselves and formulate their own recommendations. Leaving the hotel where the meeting had been held, she had a bitter taste in her mouth. She felt as if she had been made the scapegoat. In retrospect, she wondered how she might have dealt with the situation differently.

A number of weeks later, one of the senior partners, in town on business, called Joni and asked whether he could meet with her. Over coffee, he told her that a number of the partners had been disappointed with her intervention. Given her reputation, he said, they had expected more of her. As they talked, though, Joni sensed that the atmosphere at the office had improved. It sounded as if the partners were now more willing to interact with each other. Moreover, the noncharismatic managing partner appeared to have become more assertive. For example, he had created a task force that had already put a governance structure into place. According to the visiting partner, morale at the office was much better than it had been in a long time. He mentioned the existence of a much more collegial atmosphere.

It seemed that the partners no longer used the office as a way-station but were once more exchanging ideas about projects in progress. Maybe, she thought, her efforts had been somewhat effective after all, although taking on the role of scapegoat was not what she had had in mind when she accepted the assignment.

OUT OF SIGHT, OUT OF MIND

As this example illustrates, many people are unaware of irrational processes when dealing with issues of leadership, group processes, and change; in fact, they are typically unaware that such processes even exist, that people engage in activities that have a rationale beyond the obvious. For proof of irrational processes, however, we need look no further than self-destructive behavior. People choose to engage in self-destructive activities that defy logic. People do not generally like to hear about irrationality, despite its ubiquity, and often deny even the clearest evidence of it.

Given the human tendency to view with suspicion and disbelief processes that take place under the surface of consciousness, it comes as no surprise that many scholars of organizations (including many OD practitioners) studiously avoid any immersion in the unconscious and deny its impact on business and political behavior, social dynamics, and outcomes. They like to believe that all organization decisions are based on rational economics. They also—like Joni initially—do not know how to use their own feelings as an additional source of data when such a consultation is going on. They have no idea how to take advantage of the attributions made by their clients during such a management intervention.

Unfortunately, confronting what we see without pursuing where it comes from is dealing with the symptoms, not the causes. By denying the reality of latent processes in organizations, by refusing to make such processes conscious and incorporate them into our conceptual maps, we are institutionalizing the chasm between reality and rhetoric. In a highly

mechanical, two-dimensional, black-box view of humanity, the intrapsychic world of the individual—the richness of a person's inner theater or mental map—is either oversimplified or totally disregarded. Yet that individuality does not disappear: In each black box there is a highly complex person, one whose ways of dealing with processes such as perception, learning, and memory are highly variable. Reducing human beings to simple calculators of pleasures and pain results in an incomplete explanation of human behavior and action.

More and more management scientists and practitioners have come to accept the fact that there are limitations to rational action, that extrarational forces play a major role in work situations. Unconscious intrapersonal, interpersonal, and group-related dynamics account for many decisions and policies in organization life and are a powerful force in explaining human motivation and action. Students of organizations have come to realize that to further organization effectiveness, they have to pay attention to these internal and social dynamics. They start to recognize that there is an intricate playing field on which leaders and followers operate, that there are unconscious and invisible psychodynamic processes and structures that influence the behavior of individuals, dyads, and groups in organizations. People who dismiss the complex clinical dimension in organization analysis cannot hope to move beyond an impoverished understanding of what life in organizations is all about. As a result, they engage in interventions that are less effective than they should be.

DEAD MEN NEVER BITE

Although it has become fashionable to attack Freudian views of the early 20th century, psychoanalytic theory has become increasingly sophisticated, incorporating the findings from domains such as dynamic psychiatry, developmental psychology, ethology, neurophysiology, cognitive theory, family system theory, and individual and group psychotherapy. Although various aspects of Freud's theories are no longer valid in light of new information about the workings of the mind, fundamental components of psychoanalytic theory have been scientifically and empirically tested and verified, specifically as they relate to cognitive and emotional processes (Barron, Eagle, & Wolitzky, 1992; Westen, 1998).

As an archaeologist of the mind, Freud believed that neurotic symptoms could be used to decode why people behave the way they do. As conspicuous signifiers of a person's inner world, they can be seen as the royal road to an understanding of the unconscious, he believed. In an organizational context, an analogy can be made with Freud's observation: Just as every neurotic symptom has a history, so has every organizational act. The repetition of certain phenomena in the workplace suggests the existence of specific motivational configurations. Just as symptoms and dreams can be viewed as signs with meaning, so can specific acts, statements, and decisions in the boardroom. The identification of cognitive and affective distortions in an organization's leaders and followers can help us recognize the extent to which unconscious fantasies and out-of-awareness behavior affect decision making and management practices in that organization. If these factors are not taken into consideration, many management models lose their predictive validity.

Psychoanalysts such as Melanie Klein (1948), Wilfred Bion (1959), and Donald Winnicott (1975) first applied Freud's theories to the workplace. The ideas of these psychoanalysts have been further explored by clinically informed scholars of organizations (Baum, 1987; Czander, 1993; Diamond, 1993; Gabriel, 1999; Hirschhorn, 1990; Jaques, 1951; Kernberg, 1998; Kets de Vries 1984, 1991, 2000, 2004, 2006; Kets de Vries & Balazs, 1999; Kets de Vries & Schein, 2000; Levinson, 1972, 1982; Maccoby, 1976; Obholzer & Roberts, 1994; Schwartz, 1990; Zaleznik, 1966; Zaleznik & Kets de Vries, 1975). The work of these scholars has gone a long way toward creating a deep and rich understanding of life in organizations. Their insights have also opened the way to more effective consultation and intervention in organizations.

FOOTPRINTS ON THE SANDS OF TIME: THE INNER THEATER

In contrast to traditional organization theory, Sigmund Freud focused on the human unconscious—the part of our being that, hidden from rational thought, affects and interprets our conscious reality (Freud, 1900, 1921, 1929, 1933). The impact of unconscious processes is great in the world outside work—in the domains of creativity, love, and friendship, for example—as most people would readily acknowledge, but it also has a great effect on behavior, thought, and outcomes in life in organizations. Each participant has to deal with what can be described as his or her inner theater: the programming that person has incorporated from his or her genetic inheritance and early childhood experience (McDougall, 1985, 1989). Although everyone has a unique script, it is the inner theater of executives that concerns us here. Given the power executives wield, the influence of their inner theater on the rest of the organization is great.

As noted earlier, our inner theater results from a combination of nature and nurture. Although our brains are genetically hardwired with certain instinctual behavior patterns, this wiring is not entirely fixed. Especially over the crucial first months and years of our life (and in later years as well, to a lesser extent), rewiring occurs in response to developmental factors we are exposed to. It is during this developmental period that mental representations of our self, others, and relationships are established, and these representations gradually form the script in our inner theater. We carry this script within us for the rest of our life, guiding our subsequent relationships with others. It helps us make sense of all aspects of reality, serves as the standard by which we judge what we see and decide what we want, and governs our motivations and actions.

How this inner theater evolves depends on a person's responses to his or her motivational need systems in the context of genetic and developmental dispositions (Emde, 1981; Erikson, 1963; Freud, 1933; Lichtenberg & Schonbar, 1992; Sullivan, 1953). Through the nature–nurture interface, these highly complex motivational systems (physiological needs, sensual needs, aggressive needs, attachment needs, and exploratory needs) eventually determine the unique internal theater—the stage on which the major themes that define the person are played out. These motivational systems are the rational forces that lie behind behaviors and actions that are perceived to be irrational. As gasoline fuels an engine, the cognitive and emotional patterns that develop out of these interrelated motivational need systems fuel our behavior. Thus they undergird what can be described as the triangle of mental life: cognition, emotion, and behavior (Kets de Vries, 2002, 2006).

Taking this basic triangle of mental life, with its linking of cognition, emotion, and behavior, as our point of departure, we can see that for any organization change effort to be successful, the key executives in the organization have to be swayed both cognitively and emotionally; in other words, they have to be affected in both the head and the heart if their behavior is to change. Affect and cognition go hand in hand; they are inseparable in all things, including the determination of behavior.

WHAT'S PAST IS PROLOGUE: THE CLINICAL PARADIGM

In our consultations, we attempt to decode the inner theater of individuals to improve organization health and performance. Toward that end, we apply what we call the clinical paradigm, a paradigm grounded in a body of knowledge focused on personality functioning (taking a psychoanalytic perspective in its widest sense) (Kets de Vries, 2000, 2001; Kets

de Vries & Miller, 1984). Using the findings of clinical research on human behavior and on the triangle of mental life as its conceptual base, this paradigm helps us understand all forms of behavior, however irrational they may appear to be. Paradoxically, it could be argued that management scientists who rely on the clinical paradigm, with its emphasis on the nonrational, are the ultimate rationalists, bringing a dose of rationality to irrationality.

This clinical paradigm is based on a number of premises. First, it argues (based on what researchers have learned about motivational need systems) that a rationale can be found behind every human act, even those that are apparently irrational. This somewhat deterministic point of view suggests that all behavior, no matter how strange, has an explanation. Because that explanation often is elusive, one has to be something of a detective to find the rationale behind confusing behavior.

The second premise on which the clinical paradigm rests is that much of mental life—thoughts, feelings, and motives—lies outside conscious awareness. As mentioned before, people often behave in ways that are mysterious even to themselves. The defensive structures they develop over time make them blind not only to their motivation for a certain behavior but also to the behavior itself. Whereas others may notice someone's dysfunctional behavior, that person, because of his or her defense mechanisms, may not see it. And people who fail to see their own dysfunctional behavior certainly will not take responsibility for it.

The third premise underlying the clinical paradigm is that nothing is more central to who a person is than the way he or she expresses and regulates emotions. Along with cognition, emotions determine behavior; and characteristic patterns of emotion, thought, and behavior shape personality. The emotional reactions of infancy are primarily biological, and they are tied to the most basic need systems. From early on, however, socialization occurs through the mediation of the primary caretakers. As socialization progresses, developmental processes enable the person to take on the various emotional roles—sadness, joy, and so on. Although all humans are born with a particular temperament, this constitutional quality gives us only a predisposition to certain emotions. By the time we reach adulthood, affect regulation has become an intricate part of one's personality, and mood state can be used as a barometer of psychological and physical well-being.

The fourth premise underlying the clinical paradigm is that human development is an interpersonal and intrapersonal process. As we have seen, we are all products of our past, influenced (via our motivational need systems) until the day we die by the developmental experiences given by our caretakers (Emde, 1981; Erikson, 1963; Kagan & Moss, 1983). Childhood experiences play an important role in personality development, particularly in the way people relate to others. These experiences contribute to specifically preferred response patterns that in turn result in a tendency to repeat certain behavior patterns.

ALL THE WORLD'S A STAGE: DECODING LIFE IN ORGANIZATIONS

In-depth organization consultation and intervention implies making inferences from the observable to the less observable. Using the clinical paradigm, such consultation can be particularly effective at understanding leadership behavior, interpersonal relations, group behavior, organization culture, strategic decision making, and the dynamics of organization transformation and change. Organization consultants using the clinical approach must pay attention to the following factors.

The Wolf Is at the Door: The Vicissitudes of Leadership

Anyone wanting to create or manage an effective organization needs to understand the dynamics of leadership. Although most of the literature on leadership depicts the leader as a paragon of virtue and speaks in glowing terms of the attributes that constitute leadership, we have learned from experience that there is another side to the coin. We can all name many political leaders tainted by the darker side of leadership; Adolph Hitler, Idi Amin, Joseph Stalin, Pol Pot, Saddam Hussein, and Slobodan Milosevic all come readily to mind. We are far less likely to recognize leadership's shadow when it falls on the workplace, however, even though that shadow can darken the lives of many. But failure to acknowledge and examine the dark side of leadership can distort efforts to learn about the leadership process and may encourage a blind-eye approach to examining the results of influence attempts. The question a consultant always needs to keep in mind is, "What impact will the leadership of an organization, be it functional or dysfunctional, have on corporate culture, organization structure, and patterns of decision making?"

Narcissism. If we hope to understand organizations, we cannot avoid the issue of narcissism, which lies at the heart of leadership (Kernberg, 1975; Kets de Vries, 1989, 2004; Kohut, 1971, 1977). Although leaders need a solid dose of narcissism to be effective, being in a leadership position can drive healthy narcissism over the edge, bringing disaster to the leader and his or her constituency. In other words, disposition in conjunction with position can have a very detrimental effect.

It is helpful to make a distinction between constructive narcissism and reactive narcissism. Leaders characterized by constructive narcissism had an upbringing that helped them develop a solid sense of self-esteem. As adults, they are confident about their abilities and their role in the world; they radiate self-confidence. Reactive narcissists, on the other hand, were not so fortunate in their early years. Many of them had an upbringing that made them into "walking wounded." As adults, they devote much of their energy to overcoming the unresolved frustrations of childhood. Their difficult upbringing deprived them of a solid sense of self-esteem and identity. Because their self-esteem can so easily be shaken, they make a continuous effort to shore up its defenses. Haunted by the ghosts of childhood, they are easy to throw into disequilibrium.

Leaders who are constructive narcissists are driven to create something significant, to leave a legacy that benefits others. But as they pursue greatness in a transformational way, they are prepared to share the stage with others. Their secure sense of self-esteem allows them to see their activities as part of a team effort. Thus, in their role as leaders, they take advice and consult with their followers. Such leaders often are inspiring and seem larger than life, energizing others to be better at what they do and creating life-changing experiences for others.

Although at first glance reactive narcissists often seem to be ideal choices for leadership positions, their narcissistic tendencies may be so reinforced by their position of power that those tendencies become dysfunctional. In many instances, reactive leaders are driven toward achievements and glory not for the good of their followers or the organization but out of a need to get even for perceived slights experienced in childhood. (Again we see the pervasive effects of childhood experiences.) Reactive narcissists often are intolerant of criticism, unwilling to compromise, and vindictive. Having a strong a sense of entitlement, they believe that rules are for others, not for them. They typically lack feelings of empathy and therefore do poorly in relationships, treating their subordinates cruelly and even abusively. Unwilling to tolerate disagreement and criticism, they often surround themselves with sycophants. Reactive narcissistic leaders lack the capacity to deal constructively with failure; if things do not go well, they immediately scapegoat others in the organization to avoid the blame. Although all of these characteristics may be readily apparent to others, reactive narcissists who display them generally cannot see them; they are not aware of the impact of

their actions. They are what we might call psychological illiterates.

Emotional Intelligence. Emotional intelligence is the label we give to an understanding of the motivational forces of self and others. Given the importance of each person's internal theater on cognition, affect, and behavior, emotional intelligence plays a vital role in the leadership equation. People who are emotionally intelligent are more likely to be effective as leaders. Their interpersonal skills make them more successful than others as change agents. Becoming more emotionally intelligent is an experiential process, however. It is not something you can learn by reading a book.

Some leaders—the minority, it must be said—are simply unable to differentiate and verbalize emotion. Suffering from alexithymia (a Greek-based word meaning "no words for emotions") (Kets de Vries, 1999), these emotional illiterates do not respond at all to their own emotions and thus are easy prey for the distortions of others. These extreme emotional illiterates closely resemble the stereotypical bureaucrat. Because they are controlled, structured, and dispassionate, they are viewed in certain organizations as ideal candidates for leadership positions. However, they lack the emotional ability to empathize, energize, foster creativity, and respond appropriately to conflict. They also lack the passion that makes organizations exceptional. The mediocrity they foster drives out any excellence that may be lurking, untapped, in the workforce.

Succession. Some leaders, on reaching retirement age, cannot let go of the reins. They may be so strongly identified, in their own minds, with the organization that they cannot conceive of life on the outside. In addition, they may suffer from the "edifice complex," the fear that their legacy will be destroyed if they leave. They are so addicted to the position and power to which they are accustomed that the thought of living without those perks gives rise to a nightmare of emptiness and futility. Such leaders counter their anxiety the only way they know how: by devoting themselves with intensity, single-mindedness, and persistence to their job.

A Pandora's Box: Collusive Superior–Subordinate Relationships

Many forms of dyadic relationships can be differentiated in organizations. In most work relationships, personal interaction (though occasionally stressful) can contribute to maturation, creativity, peak experiences, transformation, and change. Many work relationships possess the qualities of intimacy and autonomy that set the stage for further personal and professional development. At times, however, superior–subordinate interaction patterns take on a collusive nature and thereby contribute to various forms of dysfunction.

Generational Envy. Generational envy sparks one sort of dysfunctional two-person relationship. The mythological King Cronos is alive and well and living in many organizations. In these organizations, the leader tolerates talented younger subordinates as long as they behave as narcissistic extensions of the CEO. As soon as they want more independence or strive to become people in their own right, the senior executive finds ample excuses to undermine their positions.

Mirroring. One interesting pattern in the leader–follower interface is mirroring: the tendency of leaders to see themselves as they are perceived by their followers and then to feel that they must act to satisfy the projections or fantasies of those followers. A certain amount of mirroring is a normal part of human existence. Indeed, followers always react to leaders at least in part on the basis of their own unconscious scripts. These scripts, as we saw earlier, have their foundation in experiences with childhood authorities, especially parents. Our understanding of the world will always reflect some shared

perceptions of what is real. But in a crisis, even the best of us is likely to engage in distorted mirroring. Lack of reality testing at the top can have disastrous consequences for the organization if leaders choose to use their authority and power to initiate actions that have serious negative consequences for the organization.

Folie à Deux. Occasionally, we discern a phenomenon known as folie à deux, mental contagion or shared madness, in interactions between leaders and followers. Leaders whose capacity for reality testing has become impaired shift their delusions and unusual behavior patterns to a number of associates who are closely associated with them. The truth is sacrificed—for the purpose of minimizing conflict and disagreement—on the altar of a connection with someone who has lost touch with reality (Kets de Vries, 1989). These associates not only take an active part but also often enhance and elaborate on these delusions. The irony is that people willing to share the delusions of their leader prefer the resulting closeness despite the mental acrobatics they need to engage in to stay in the orbit of the delusional leader. As in many forms of collusions, the lack of reality testing by people touched by folie à deux can have serious repercussions.

Nature Abhors a Vacuum: Dysfunctional Group Processes

We turn now from the dyad to the group. The work of Wilfred Bion has been extremely influential in fostering an understanding of the psychodynamics of malfunctioning groups. Bion's insights have proved to be very helpful in structuring psychodynamic interventions in organizations. He lists various shared fantasies that trigger the breakdown of healthy work groups. Such processes impede effective work in organizations. Bion also makes a distinction between three basic "assumption groups" (i.e., categories into which all employees fit, depending on their underlying assumptions about the world): fight–flight, dependency, and pairing (Bion, 1959).

Basic Assumption Groups. People in the fight–flight mode assume that the world is a very dangerous place. Executives who fall into this group use fight-or-flight patterns as defense mechanisms, externalizing internal problems. "Fight" reactions are expressed through aggression against others, taking the form, for example, of fighting for a position in the group, defying authority figures, and scapegoating. Typically, inflexibility and a lack of vision follow from fight-oriented workers' concern with external enemies. In contrast, "flight" reactions often are expressed physiologically, taking the form, for example, of psychosomatic illness or withdrawal at work.

People in the dependency mode (a group that swells in times of crisis) are plagued by feeling of inadequacy. Rather than taking charge, they look for leadership to come from without. Leaders characterized by reactive narcissism are only too glad to cater to followers looking for a hero to lead them. Sometimes, though, even leaders fall into the dependency assumption group: A leader whose childhood dependency needs were not met experienced feelings of frustration and helplessness in the early years, and those feelings continue to guide him or her in the workplace. Such a leader, anxious and insecure, wants to take orders from someone in charge. Failing that, the leader may go overboard with structure, offering rule after rule to provide guidance. Eventually, bureaucratic inertia takes hold.

People in the pairing mode, often found in high-tech companies, tend to elevate grandiosity and innovation over practicality and profitability. In order to cope with anxiety, alienation, and loneliness, individuals or groups often try to pair up with perceived powerful individuals or subgroups. The unconscious need to feel secure and to create something of value results in the unconscious fantasy that creation will take place in pairs.

Big Brother Is Watching You: Neurotic Organizations

The unconscious agendas of executives often are mirrored in the dilemmas of their organizations (Kets de Vries, 1994; Kets de Vries & Miller, 1984, 1988). In our organization consulting work, we have identified recurrent syndromes that seem to be intimately connected to the underlying psychological issues of the power holders in the firm. Different kinds of dysfunction in organizations can be classified, particularly as characterized by individual styles of managers, superior–subordinate relationships, group styles, and overall adaptive character of the organization. These schemas can then be used to design intervention strategies for change.

We have identified five dysfunctional organization types that parallel common neurotic styles: suspicious, compulsive, dramatic–cyclothymic, depressive, and detached. In brief, they can be characterized as follows:

- The suspicious or paranoid organization is pervaded by distrust, with energy focused on external threats. Power is centralized, and the business strategy is conservative and reactive.
- The compulsive organization is marked by a lack of flexibility. Initiative is stifled, and inappropriate and rigid responses become common.
- In the dramatic–cyclothymic organization, boldness, risk taking, and flamboyance mark corporate decision making. The chief executive often is an entrepreneur who follows his or her own intuitions and dreams. Unfortunately, other people in the organization have very little voice, contributing, at times, to a lack of reality testing.
- Inactivity, lack of confidence, extreme conservatism, and insularity are the chief features of the depressive organization. Because of a tendency toward extreme bureaucracy and hierarchy, meaningful change seldom occurs.
- The detached or schizoid organization often has a leadership vacuum that leads to destructive gamesmanship among lower-level executives.

As individual fiefdoms are established, barriers are set up that prevent the free flow of information.

FIRST DO NO HARM: CLINICALLY ORIENTED INTERVENTION

The clinically oriented consultant driving a change effort in an ailing organization faces the same challenges as his or her counterpart in psychoanalysis, but on a bigger scale. As with individuals, psychological awareness in an organization is the first step toward psychological health. It is important, then, that people at all levels of the hierarchy become aware of the unconscious currents underlying observable work behavior. Because unconscious currents are by definition outside ordinary awareness, the task of making them visible falls to the outside consultant. Simply pointing out salient issues and collusive processes is rarely enough. Typically, the consultant has to make such issues more explicit, perhaps through some form of confrontation. The client is presented with specific problem areas. Inconsistencies in activities are highlighted. Conflicts are pointed out. He or she then works through a clarification process, with the help of key members of the organization, analyzing problems more closely and bringing them into sharper focus.

Clinically informed consultants use as one crucial source of data the ways in which members of the organization interact with them, a process to which Joni (in our case example) could have paid more attention. What differentiates them from more traditional consultants is their skill at using transferential and countertransferential manifestations as a basic experiential and diagnostic tool (Etchegoyen, 1991; Greenson, 1967; Malan & Osimo, 1992). The ever-present triangle of relationships—in these situations, the person, the significant past "other," and the consultant—provides a conceptual structure for assessing patterns of response, enabling them to point out the similarity of past relationships to what happens in the present. Anyone hoping to make sense of interpersonal encounters on anything but a superficial level needs to understand these transferential processes that are major part of the consultant's intervention toolbox.

Furthermore, as in any form of organization consultation, multiple resistances are at play. After making a list of the primary symptoms and problems, the consultant needs to move on to what we call resistance interpretation, pointing out the various defense mechanisms (social and individual) used by power holders to prevent unpleasant insights from coming to the fore. The consultant works backward from there, going behind symptoms and defenses to offer conjectures and interpretations about the roots of any dysfunctional processes that have come to light.

BACK TO SQUARE ONE

Organization consultation by a clinically informed consultant usually starts with a contact made by one of the organization's executives, often the CEO, who describes a problem he or she is facing. As any consultant with experience has learned the hard way, the original, stated problem often is not the real problem but only a signifier of other, deeper problems. They know that the presented problem often covers up something far more complex. As the saying goes, "When people complain about the weather, they are often talking about something else." The challenge for the consultant is to integrate the manifest problem with the problems that are concealed by it. Although most organizations exert pressure to come up with instant answers, the consultant must take adequate time to reflect on the problem. That reflection is enhanced if the consultant shares the assignment with a colleague and can discuss observations and analyze transference and countertransference reactions.

After the initial contact, the consultant typically continues discussions about the problem with other key members of the organization to obtain a wide spectrum of perspectives. Complete access to everyone in an organization is essential to the success of such a consultation. Any thwarting of access (whether done subtly or directly) is grist for interpretation. Because in psychoanalytically informed consultation there is little difference between the diagnostic stage and the intervention stage, such interpretation is both diagnostic and therapeutic. The mere fact of data gathering implies that the intervention has begun (Levinson, 2002). The participants' fantasies have been set into motion.

Typically, suggestions for change start at the surface, reaching a deeper level only when a measure of trust has developed between the consultant and the client. A solid working alliance between the various parties is essential if the consultant hopes to clarify issues, confront the principal players effectively about emerging problems, identify resistances, and make interpretations. Thus interventions typically progress from suggestions to key people about structural changes, to observations about various means of communication, to the pros and cons of a particular leadership style.

CONCLUSION

Many business leaders have become more emotionally astute in recent years. Having seen organization fads come and go, they now realize that most problems are deeply ingrained and therefore not susceptible to quick-fix formulas. These experienced leaders have become wary of snake oil salesmen and their simplistic but costly interventions. The "downsizing, rightsizing, capsizing" formulas of many organization consultants have made these leaders aware of the price of faulty intervention. Many of them have paid their dues many times over, in the form of dysfunctional leadership, ineffective culture integration programs, poorly planned leadership development, and inadequate succession planning.

Clinically informed consultation brings a dose of realism to organization intervention, although it should not be seen as a catch-all and certainly does not herald the coming of a new messiah. Still, it makes sense that in-depth approaches to organization consultation have a greater chance than superficial solutions to address the deeply entrenched causes of organization problems. Life in organizations is like a mirror: What we see out there we first have to discover inside.

Clinically trained consultants, unlike many traditional consultants, do not simply make a diagnosis and provide a set of recommendations, leaving it to the client to implement the suggestions. Rather, such consultants help the client make their recommendations a reality. The aim of the psychoanalytically informed consultation is not a temporary high but a lasting change. The consultant wants to move beyond reductionistic formulas to sustainable transformation. Such an orientation often makes for enduring client–consultant relationships. Although the aim of every consultation is greater autonomy for the client (rather than an ongoing situation of dependency), the consultant's services may be asked for repeatedly on an as-needed basis over a period of years. However, the aim of the consultant is to help clients engage in self-analytic activities so that they can learn how to implement interventions on their own.

OD practitioners who have the courage to include the clinical approach in their repertoire, who are willing to tackle the submerged psychological dynamics that characterize any organization (and that threaten, wherever they are found, to derail effectiveness), are in for a pleasant surprise. They come to realize that life in organizations is not to be wept over or laughed at but to be understood and then improved. The deep understanding that the clinical perspective offers lays the building blocks for effective intervention. Unfortunately, although understanding enigmatic riddles is the rallying cry of many consultants, few know, as of yet, the ins and outs of such a deciphering activity.

REFERENCES

Barron, J. W., Eagle, M. N., & Wolitzky, D. L. (Eds.). (1992). *The interface of psychoanalysis and psychology*. Washington, DC: American Psychological Association.

Baum, H. (1987). *The invisible bureaucracy: The unconscious in organizational problem-solving*. New York: Oxford University Press.

Bion, W. R. (1959). *Experiences in groups*. London: Tavistock.

Burke, W. (1982). *Organizational development: Principles and practices*. Boston: Little, Brown.

Carter, L., Giber, D., & Goldsmith, M. (2001). *Best practices in organizational development and change*. San Francisco: Jossey-Bass/Pfeiffer.

Cummings, T., & Worley, C. (2001). *Organizational development and change*. Cincinnati, OH: Southwestern College Publishing.

Czander, W. (1993). *The psychodynamics of work organizations: Theory and applications*. London: Guilford Press.

Diamond, M. (1993). *The unconscious life of organizations: Interpreting organizational identity*. New York: Quorum.

Emde, R. N. (1981). Changing models of infancy and the nature of early development: Remodelling the foundation. *Journal of the American Psychoanalytical Association, 29*, 179–219.

Erikson, E. H. (1963). *Childhood and society*. New York: W.W. Norton.

Etchegoyen, R. H. (1991). *The fundamentals of psychoanalytic technique*. London: Karnac.

French, W., & Bell, C. (1999). *Organizational development*. Upper Saddle River, NJ: Prentice Hall.

Freud, S. (1900). The interpretation of dreams. *The Standard Edition of the Complete Psychoanalytical Works of Sigmund Freud, 5*. London: Hogarth.

Freud, S. (1921). Group psychology and the analysis of the ego. *The Standard Edition of the Complete Psychological Works of Sigmund Freud, 7*. London: Hogarth.

Freud, S. (1929). Civilization and its discontents. *The Standard Edition of the Complete Psychological Works of Sigmund Freud, 21*. London: Hogarth.

Freud, S. (1933). New introductory lectures. *The Standard Edition of the Complete Psychological Works of Sigmund Freud, 22*. London: Hogarth.

Gabriel, Y. (1999). *Organizations in depth*. London: Sage.

Greenson, R. R. (1967). *The technique and practice of psychoanalysis*. New York: International University Press.

Hirschhorn, L. (1990). *The workplace within: Psychodynamics of organizational life*. Cambridge: MIT Press.

Jaques, E. (1951). *The changing culture of a factory*. London: Tavistock.

Kagan, J., & Moss, H. A. (1983). *Birth to maturity: A study in psychological development*. New Haven, CT: Yale University Press.

Kernberg, O. (1975). *Borderline conditions and pathological narcissism*. New York: Aronson Press.

Kernberg, O. (1998). *Ideology, conflict, and leadership on groups and organizations*. New Haven, CT: Yale University Press.

Kets de Vries, M. F. R. (Ed.). (1984). *The irrational executive: Psychoanalytic studies in management*. New York: International Universities Press.

Kets de Vries, M. F. R. (1989). *Prisoners of leadership*. New York: John Wiley & Sons.

Kets de Vries, M. F. R. (Ed.). (1991). *Organizations on the couch*. San Francisco: Jossey-Bass.

Kets de Vries, M. F. R. (1994). The leadership mystique. *Academy of Management Executive, 8*(3), 73–92.

Kets de Vries, M. F. R. (1999). Managing puzzling personalities: Navigating between "live volcanoes" and "dead fish." *European Management Journal, 17*(1), 8–19.

Kets de Vries, M. F. R. (2000, February). The clinical paradigm: Manfred Kets de Vries' reflections on organizational theory—Interview by Erik van de Loo. *Academy of Management Executive & European Management Journal, 18*(1), 2–21.

Kets de Vries, M. F. R. (2001). *Struggling with the demon: Essays in individual and organizational irrationality*. Madison, CT: Psychosocial Press.

Kets de Vries, M. F. R. (2002). *Can CEOs change? Yes but only if they want to*. INSEAD Working Papers Series. Fontainebleau, France: INSEAD.

Kets de Vries, M. F. R. (2004). *Lessons on leadership by terror: Finding Shaka Zulu in the attic*. Cheltenham, UK: Edward Elgar.

Kets de Vries, M. F. R. (2006). *The leader on the couch*. Chichester, UK: John Wiley & Sons.

Kets de Vries, M. F. R., & Balazs, K. (1999). Transforming the mind-set of the organization: A clinical perspective. *Administration & Society, 30*(6), 640–675.

Kets de Vries, M. F. R., & Miller, D. (1984). *The neurotic organization*. San Francisco: Jossey-Bass.

Kets de Vries, M. F. R., & Miller, D. (1988). *Unstable at the top*. New York: New American Library.

Kets de Vries, M. F. R., & Schein, E. (2000). Crosstalk: Transatlantic exchanges. *The Academy of Management Executive, 14*(1), 30–51.

Klein, M. (1948). *Contributions to psychoanalysis, 1921–1945*. London: Hogarth.

Kohut, H. (1971). *The analysis of the self*. New York: International Universities Press.

Kohut, H. (1977). *The restoration of the self*. Madison, CT: International Universities Press.

Levinson, H. (1972). *Organizational diagnosis*. Cambridge, MA: Harvard University Press.

Levinson, H. (1982). *Executive*. Cambridge, MA: Harvard University Press.

Levinson, H. (2002). *Organizational assessment*. Washington, DC: American Psychological Association.

Lichtenberg, J. D., & Schonbar, R. A. (1992). Motivation in psychology and psychoanalysis. In J. W. Barron, M. N. Eagle, & D. L. Wolitzky (Eds.), *Interface of psychoanalysis and psychology* (pp. 11–36). Washington, DC: American Psychological Association.

Maccoby, M. (1976). *The gamesman*. New York: Simon & Schuster.

Malan, D., & Osimo, F. (1992). *Psychodynamics, training, and outcome in brief psychotherapy*. Oxford, UK: Butterworth Heinemann.

McDougall, J. (1985). *Theaters of the mind*. New York: Basic Books.

McDougall, J. (1989). *Theaters of the body*. New York: W.W. Norton.

Obholzer, A., & Roberts, V. Z. (Eds.). (1994). *The unconscious at work: Individual and organizational stress in human services*. London: Routledge.

Schwartz, H. S. (1990). *Narcissistic process and corporate decay: The theory of the organization ideal*. New York: New York University Press.

Sullivan, H. S. (1953). *The interpersonal theory of psychiatry*. New York: Norton.

Westen, D. (1998). The scientific legacy of Sigmund Freud: Toward a psychodynamically informed psychological science. *Psychological Bulletin, 124*(3), 333–371.

Winnicott, D. W. (1975). *Through paediatrics to psycho-analysis*. New York: Basic Books.

Worley, C. G., & Feyerherm, A. E. (2003). Reflections on the future of organizational development. *The Journal of Applied Behavioral Science, 39*(1), 97–115.

Zaleznik, A. (1966). *Human dilemmas of leadership*. New York: HarperCollins.

Zaleznik, A., & Kets de Vries, M. F. R. (1975). *Power and the corporate mind*. Boston: Houghton Mifflin.

PART II

The Organization Development Process

7

The Practice of Organization Development

DAVID W. JAMIESON

CHRISTOPHER G. WORLEY

As a field of applied practice and research focus, organization development (OD) has a mercurial history, marked at times by growth, criticism, acceptance, resistance, and adaptation. Early in its life cycle, individuals and small groups were the targets of change, and it became known for its missionary zeal concerning values derived from humanistic psychology and democratic principles. However, when organization leaders faced significant environmental and performance challenges, they often viewed OD's individual focus as irrelevant. Some OD practitioners adapted their methods to deal with these broader strategic and design issues. Their efforts helped to develop a broader platform for improving organization effectiveness and a new breed of practitioner combining the behavioral sciences with management and organization theory. Others continued to concentrate on work with individuals and groups. Debates over the proper focus for the field ensued. With little agreement and solidarity in the field, anyone and anything could be called OD, adding to a less than stellar reputation in some client systems.

A variety of debates continue unabated. Some of them are the same (e.g., "What is OD?"). Other debates, such as who is an OD practitioner, whether credentialing is important, and whether OD is a profession, have emerged. However, there is general agreement that it is time for the debates to come to a productive end (Bradford & Burke, 2005). Impetus for this view comes from the increase in OD educational options, student applications, and jobs with OD in their descriptions. Many people and organizations still clearly want something from OD.

Therefore, timeliness justifies a chapter on the practice of OD and the development of practitioners. This chapter begins with a discussion of the roots and evolution of OD practice. It then explores the dominant debates in the field and suggests resolutions. In the third section, we present an original theory of OD practice. It overviews what good practice entails and clarifies what makes OD practice different from some other change approaches. The final section provides recommendations for how OD educators can more effectively develop future practitioners.

ROOTS AND EVOLUTION OF OD PRACTICE

The practice of OD is more than 50 years old. Before World War II, organizations typically operated on principles of mechanistic and bureaucratic systems, including authority and obedience, division of labor, hierarchical supervision, formalized procedures and rules, and impersonality (and many still do). After the war, increasing interest in social change, attitudes about democracy, and self-actualization brought distinctly different values that were a counterforce to the extant organizational values in use. OD grew in popularity by offering a more holistic view of people and organizations, with an emphasis on humanistic and democratic values and the belief that this different perspective was better not only for people but also for organization performance. The conclusion of French and Bell's (1999, p. 332) text on OD states, "We believe future OD efforts increasingly will be aimed at *both* high organizational performance and a sense of community. In many ways, the pioneers and major thinkers in the field have been saying this same thing all along."

Behavioral science and management research findings influenced the earliest values, philosophy, and methods of practice. For example, the action research method (as created by Lewin, 1948) tried to solve real-world problems by applying group process knowledge to contemporary issues. Initial OD change methods were clearly connected with

- Early leadership work that brought legitimacy to participative and democratic methods (Follett, 1941; Lewin & Lippitt, 1938; Likert, 1961; Tannenbaum & Schmidt, 1973).
- Early human relations work that highlighted the primacy of social factors, attitudes, and feelings in organization behavior, influencing productivity and morale (Homans, 1950; Mayo, 1945; Roethlisberger & Dickson, 1939)
- Early work on group dynamics and laboratory training bringing attention to group behavior, interpersonal relations, and self-awareness (Bennis & Shepard, 1956; Bradford, Gibb, & Benne, 1964; Cartwright & Zander, 1954; Schein & Bennis, 1965)
- Changing views of the person, motivation, and interpersonal communication (Argyris, 1965; Maslow, 1954; McGregor, 1960; Rogers, 1961)
- Early use of data and diagnosis to guide change, including survey research methods and action research (Bowers & Franklin, 1972; Mann, 1957; Nadler, 1977; Whyte & Hamilton, 1964)
- Early work on environments, structures, systems, and sociotechnical principles helping to bring design and process into the picture (Burns & Stalker, 1961; Katz & Kahn, 1966; Lawrence & Lorsch, 1967; Trist & Bamforth, 1951)

Thus, as a social and organization change practice, OD has always been closely associated with the behavioral sciences, which added greatly to our understanding of organizations, human behavior, and change. Moreover, OD brought to the management of organizations a clearer focus on how values operated in managing, intervening, and changing organizations. The use of data to guide decisions; involvement and participation of people in decisions that affected them; more effective conflict management; use of teams and team building; and the importance of climate and culture increased across organizations in the first 30 years of OD (Kleiner, 1996).

However, OD did not evolve as quickly or in the same direction as many would have hoped. While mainstream management thinking was integrating the influence of complex, faster-changing environments, performance concerns, and economic issues, the "love, trust, and truth" model remained the central strategy for many in OD. These traditionalists continued to focus on individual and group problems as the means to change organization performance.

However, others responded to calls for OD to adapt its methods and tools to organization-level challenges. They argued that for a more comprehensive approach to organization improvement and change to emerge, OD needed to balance the value of an improved human system orientation with the economic, strategic, structural, and power realities. The integration of strategy and organization design with behavioral science has been the most important evolution in the practice of OD and has broadened the playing field and impact (Cummings & Worley, 2005).

Recent trends in the field reflect the continued response to organization conditions, the complexities of change, and the broadening of practice. They include working with larger and larger groups, focusing on strengths and appreciative orientations, using natural sciences to better understand organizations and behavior, integrating principles of organization design with organization change, and deepening human connections and relationships. For example,

- Bunker and Alban (1997, 2005) and Holman and Devane (1999) have chronicled the trend of involving larger and larger numbers of stakeholders in the OD process, including such interventions as future search (Weisbord, 1987) and open space (Owen, 1992).

- Cooperrider and his colleagues (Cooperrider, Sorenson, Yeager, & Whitney, 2001; Cooperrider & Srivastva, 1987; Ludema, Whitney, Mohr, & Griffin, 2003; Magruder-Watkins & Mohr, 2001) have developed methods of practice using appreciative philosophy, which has spawned a further stream of research into positive scholarship (Cameron, Dutton, & Quinn, 2003).

- Wheatley (2001) and Stacey (2001) have begun the important work of translating concepts from the complexity and natural sciences into practical change techniques.

- Mohrman, Galbraith, and their colleagues have been integrating the principles of organization design with organization change (Galbraith, 2001; Lawler & Worley, 2006; Mohrman & Cummings, 1989).

- There has also been a renewed emphasis on deepening relationships and connections by creating real dialogue for understanding and influence and structuring critical conversations as tools for change (Block, 2003; Brown Issacs, and the World Café Community, 2005; Ellinor & Gerard, 1998).

Some of today's trends may pass, as others have. But some will become integrated into our theory, education, and practice and become part of the evolving field of OD.

PERPETUAL DEBATES IN OD PRACTICE

Bradford and Burke (2004, 2005) and Worley and Feyerherm (2003) outline a set of critical debates related to the practice of OD. These debates often splintered the field but also attracted talent and stimulated its development. We may never fully understand which effects are more prominent, but their continuation appears distracting when the field needs centering, relevance, and advocacy. Understanding the debates also helps us understand the evolution of OD practice and some of the choices people make to shape their practice. These debates include

- Definition of OD

- Conceptualizations of OD

- Credentialing of OD practitioners

- Effectiveness of OD practice

Although it may be valuable for the field to always continue some debate in the spirit of continuous improvement, it's important for individual practitioners, those who train them, and the field itself to draw some conclusions and decide where they stand. Growing their practice, mentoring others, and developing the field require clear perspectives on these issues.

Definition of OD

The first and perhaps most interesting debate has been around the definition of OD. In fact, some argue that the term itself is inaccurate.

Asserting that the practice is oriented around the behavioral sciences, Tannenbaum and others have argued that the field should be called human systems development (Tannenbaum, Margulies, Massarik, & Associates, 1985). Our preference is to stick with the current term. We recognize that any organization will involve people interacting across numerous levels of analysis (from individual to interorganizational).

Surprisingly, and despite a number of well-accepted definitions from founders, acknowledged gurus, and academics, there seems to be a never-ending stream of complaints that the field is not defined. Worse yet, there are a wide variety of definitions across firms. Whereas some firms have sophisticated OD capabilities and policies, other firms define OD as "communication." Box 7.1 provides a sample of formal definitions.

BOX 7.1   Definitions of OD

- OD is a planned process of change in an organization's culture through the use of behavioral science technology, research, and theory (Burke, 1982).
- OD is a long-range effort to improve an organization's problem-solving capabilities and its ability to cope with changes in its external environment with the help of external or internal behavioral science consultants, or change agents, as they are sometimes called (French, 1969).
- OD is an effort planned, organization-wide, and managed from the top to increase organization effectiveness and health through planned interventions in the organization's processes, using behavioral science (Beckhard, 1969).
- OD is a system-wide process of data collection, diagnosis, action planning, intervention, and evaluation aimed at increasing congruence between organization structure, process, strategy, people, and culture; developing new and creative solutions; and developing the organization's self-renewing capacity. It occurs through collaboration of organization members working with a change agent using behavioral science theory, research, and technology (Beer, 1980).
- OD is the attempt to influence the members of an organization to increase their candor with each other about their views of the organization and their experience in it and to take greater responsibility for their own actions as organization members. The assumption behind OD is that when people pursue both of these objectives simultaneously, they are likely to discover new ways of working together that they experience as more effective for achieving their own and their shared goals. And that when this does not happen, such activity helps them to understand why and to make meaningful choices about what to do in light of this understanding (Neilsen, 1984).
- OD is a system-wide application and transfer of behavioral science knowledge to the planned development, improvement, and reinforcement of the strategies, structures, and processes that lead to organization effectiveness (Cummings & Worley, 2005).

From a practice perspective, the commonalities between the definitions provide good guidance about OD's essence. For example, most or all of the definitions describe OD as

- A planned process intended to bring about change
- Through the use of various interventions
- Using behavioral science knowledge (theory, research, technology)
- Having an organization or system-wide focus
- Typically involving a third-party change agent

However, the differences in the definitions are important because they can lead to confusion over the purpose of intervening. For example, the definitions vary on the intended outcomes of OD. At the broadest level, they differ on whether interventions increase the organization's capability for change or problem solving or increase the system's effectiveness. There is also little agreement within these broad categories. In the effectiveness category, for example, the outcomes include changes in culture, performance, candor, alignment, and health.

Finally, the breadth of potential change targets may be the most important difference. They can range from a generic label of organization processes to more specific targets such as organization culture or the congruence between structure, strategy, processes, people, and culture. As Greiner and Cummings (2004, p. 384) summarize, OD has evolved by expanding change targets and adapting to new internal and external strategic issues of organizations, and "the enormous growth of new approaches and techniques has blurred the boundaries of the field and made it increasingly difficult to describe."

These definitions also help to distinguish OD "from change management" and to highlight the important issue of values in OD definition and practice. For example, OD and change management both address the effective implementation of planned change. They are concerned with the sequence of activities, processes, and leadership issues that produce organization improvements. Both have developed useful concepts and methods for helping organizations to deal with changing environments, competitor initiatives, technological innovation, globalization, and restructuring.

However, they differ in their underlying value orientations. It is not that OD is unique because it is value driven. All professions and occupations have value bases. What distinguishes OD from change management is its choice of values and the way it enacts those values in practice. Its concern with the transfer of knowledge and skill such that the system is able to manage differently and more able to manage change in the future is part of those values. In addition, OD values the whole person; the well-being of multiple stakeholders; the participation of people in decisions and actions that affect their quality of life; the concepts of free choice and responsibility; the authenticity, openness, integrity, and fairness of interaction; treatment of differences with respect, dignity, and inclusion; and collaboration and community (Jamieson & Gellermann, 2006). These values help to determine the appropriateness of particular planned changes (ends) and methods for getting there (means). Change management, on the other hand, focuses more narrowly on values of cost, quality, and schedule (Davis, 2001; Marshak, 1996; Worren, Ruddle, & Moore, 1999). It is more closely aligned with project management than OD. In short, all OD involves change management, but change management may not involve OD.

Based on these definitions and distinctions and on discussions with OD practitioners, Worley and Feyerherm (2003) suggested that for a set of activities to be called OD, they should meet the following criteria. First, OD involves change. There must be evidence that individuals, groups, or organizations have changed (or are in the process of changing). Unless one is willing to adopt a very constrained view of change, a diagnosis of a system would not constitute an OD process per se. Second, OD involves learning and development. One of the enduring values in the field is that the behavioral sciences can help build the system's capacity to change in the future. In short, the system and the people in it had to learn; they had to develop an increased capability to change. Finally, OD is not about change for change's sake. Its intent has always been to improve the effectiveness of a system. Such a set of criteria provides practical guidance for defining OD.

In consideration of this analysis, we define OD as a process of planned interventions using behavioral science principles to change a system and improve its effectiveness, conducted in accordance with values of choice, participation, human dignity,[1] and learning so that the organization and its members develop.

The definition one uses, especially its breadth, has significant implications for practice. First, it highlights what a practitioner must be able to understand and do. Second, it focuses attention on different targets of change. Third, it provides a basis for determining desired outcomes and measures of effectiveness.

Conceptualizations of OD

Is OD a discipline, field, community, or profession? Practitioners, researchers, professors, and associations use these labels to describe OD. The labels clearly overlap, but each connotes a slightly different way of describing the work and a different way of thinking about the people who affiliate with OD. Each label also suggests different implications for the kind of education and experience that OD practitioners should have and how they should do the work.

Our review recognized a convenient nesting of the terms that might help clear up some of the ambiguity. The root concept is discipline: a field of study or branch of knowledge, instruction, or learning. Disciplines have a body of knowledge and a set of values. Although some argue that there is no agreement on the body of knowledge and values (e.g., Church, 2001) that

make up OD, the definition does not require that. Moreover, there is significantly more overlap than disagreement on textbook content, course syllabi, and other indicators of a body of knowledge (Cummings & Worley, 2005; French & Bell, 1999) and on values (Egan & Gellermann, 2005; Jamieson & Gellermann, 2006; Worley & Feyerherm, 2003).

A field is a "topic, subject, or area of academic interest or specialization; a profession, employment, or business" (dictionary.com, 2006). According to that definition, if OD is a field then it is also a profession. In fact, *field* and *profession* are synonyms. Burke (1982) and Beckhard (1997) support the view of OD as a field of study or a field of practice. Similarly, a community of practice is an informal network with a common sense of purpose, shared values, and a desire to share work-related knowledge and experience. OD has long operated as a tightly knit group of people sharing experiences, knowledge, and language; using common methods; adhering to similar norms and values; and helping the development of others.

There are varying definitions of *profession* that differ on a couple of items, including whether it is a calling or directly influences human well-being. But they agree that it is an occupation or practice and that it involves academic preparation. Certainly, OD has been a calling for many as they have been attracted to the value base, and its concern for human welfare in pursuit of organization performance has long been a distinguishing factor.

A profession involves the application of specialized knowledge gained through education and experience. The importance of the academic preparation before OD practice has been gaining ground, but has never been a requirement or universally accepted. However, thousands of people are hired into jobs in organizations with OD in the position description, and just as many operate as external consultants using the OD label, so it is a recognized occupation for many people.

Cole (2005), Weidner and Kulick (1999), and Church (2001) have all argued that OD should be a profession but generally believe that it is not. They argue that the label *profession* generally connotes images of doctors, teachers, lawyers, and clinical psychologists who complete a lengthy education process, often are required to pass proficiency exams (certification) to practice, and have agreed on quality standards and ethics with effective governing mechanisms. Therefore, many suggest that important characteristics of a profession, not actually found in the definition of the term, are a credentialing mechanism that qualifies one to practice, continuing education requirements, and governance mechanisms that regulate entry, exit, and ethics violations. The OD field today seems far from having the capacity to implement such an infrastructure.

Before we turn to a discussion of the very practical issues associated with credentialing, we close this discussion of conceptualizations of OD by noting that most of these terms have little real effect on the practice of OD. However, certification or regulation would affect practice if professionalization required it. Otherwise, whether OD is a discipline, industry, community of practice, or field has little relevance. Because continuing to use different terms to mean the same thing only contributes to internal and external confusion, we support the adoption and use of the following terms: OD is a field of practice from the perspective of education and a community of practice when describing the practitioners, researchers, and professors who affiliate with OD.

Credentialing of OD Practitioners

The thorniest aspect of OD's conceptualization is whether professionalization necessarily implies regulation and certification. For some, the debate over professionalization focuses on the implications of certification (for proficiency or knowledge), regulation (as in governance and enforcement mechanisms), standards of quality in education and practice (similar to certification discussions), and codes of conduct or ethics (which seems to be one of the enforcement functions of professional governance). The "profession" concept seems to entail setting the standards, certifying that one meets the requirements, enforcing or renewing standards (decertification or periodic recertification), and establishing and enforcing codes of ethics (managing behavior to retain the integrity of the profession). In short, some argue that a profession establishes itself and maintains itself from within.

OD is likely to face continued disagreement over the implications of professionalization. Championed by some OD professional associations and several change management practices at large consulting firms, certification is driven partly in response to a growing number of people marketing themselves as OD practitioners without any formal training or education in the field and a lack of consistency in applying OD's core theories, skills, and interventions. "Bad" OD can be damaging to people, organizations, and OD's reputation. To make matters worse, distinguishing between qualified and unqualified OD practitioners can be difficult for organizations. Professionalization of the field could help remedy those problems and improve quality. By creating a common body of knowledge and defining minimum levels of skills, certification can ensure that OD practitioners have an acceptable level of competence to practice. It has the added benefit of helping the client know that the practitioner is credible. Experience-based professions have developed a variety of methods (e.g., exams and supervised practice) for doing front-end certification. Professionalization and certification would thus create boundaries between who is (and is not) an OD professional and what is (and is not) OD practice.

However, the experience of other professions does not support the quality argument. Despite heavy regulation and certification of engineering, medicine, architecture, teaching, and other fields, there are bad engineers, lousy doctors, inept architects, and ineffective teachers. Moreover, because certification requires a set of consensual ethics, values, and standards, the inability of the field to converge on these issues (despite much overlap in the lists) makes regulation and certification all the more problematic. Finally, without a central, acknowledged professional association, there is no judge or jury. Unless a groundswell of support for a common set of standards emerges, different groups will continue to quarrel over judgments about qualifications. Prior attempts to professionalize the field or to accredit practitioners, including the OD Institute's registration process (Registered OD Practitioner, Registered OD Consultant) and an early attempt by the National Training Laboratory (NTL) and Herb Shepard's certification program (the International Association of Applied Social Scientists), have had limited success. They provide ample evidence of the difficulty of resolving such differences. That may not be so bad, however, because it may allow more innovation and less involvement of government and political bodies.

In essence, professionalization attempts to control the supply side of the OD profession. One alternative we support is to educate the demand side and include education as an informal proxy for certification. First, organizations, managers, and other potential clients should be made fully aware of what OD is, how it works, and what it can contribute to their organization. We think educating clients and potential clients of OD practitioners is a more manageable strategy. It would allow the field to focus on the agreement that exists in a number of areas. Professional association Web sites, advertising, and other marketing efforts could easily spread the word. Why do professional organizations exist if not to provide a mechanism for promoting their membership and the field of practice? Second, agreeing on a set of core issues in OD education would also provide some minimal assurance that an OD practitioner had the requisite knowledge

and skill to conduct an effective OD process. In fact, there is now much similarity in OD textbooks used, curricula, and adoption of basic competencies by OD education programs. Finally, a theory of practice can clarify and differentiate the methods and help to provide stronger criteria to ensure that practitioners are carrying out effective OD processes.

Without credentialing or an acceptable proxy, the field will struggle with the unqualified, mismatched, and fraudulent. High-quality education programs for practitioners and clients, strong professional associations, more visibly shared values and ethics, a better theory of practice, and better evaluation research will all improve practice and help establish greater relevance for OD.

Effectiveness of OD Practice

Yuchtman and Seashore (1967) noted multiple, legitimate definitions of organization effectiveness. The same certainly can be said of the views of OD's effectiveness. At a minimum, one could evaluate whether an OD process produced improved organization performance (using accepted industry metrics), improved individual and organization capability to manage and change in the future, an organization that operated more in line with OD values (a different culture), or acceptable return on investment. Although it is beyond the scope of this chapter to conduct a full review of the debate over OD's effectiveness, we can summarize the critical and supportive views.

Critics of OD's effectiveness point to several important deficiencies in the literature. First, with respect to one of the espoused values and purposes of OD, there are no studies we are aware of monitoring the transfer of OD-related skills and knowledge to a client during an OD process. This statement does not refer to the large body of work evaluating training and leadership development. These educational interventions clearly increase the knowledge and skill of client systems with respect to change competence. In general, however, these interventions are not

OD per se, and there is no evidence that the way they were conducted led to increased change competence in the organization. So does OD actually develop an organization or its members in the developmental sense implied by the term? Although the number of studies demonstrating organization learning is increasing, we still do not know whether an organization actually learns to change better in the future because of an OD process. This is a curious omission.

Second, critics of OD's effectiveness point to the difficulty of associating change with performance improvement, whether performance measures productivity, satisfaction, results, efficiency, or other measures of effectiveness. In particular, a variety of messy research method questions exist (Bullock & Svyantek, 1987; Golembiewski & Munzenrider, 1976; Macy & Mirvis, 1982; Seashore, Lawler, Mirvis, & Cammann, 1983; Terborg, Howard, & Maxwell, 1982; Thompson & Hunt, 1996). Does the research gather longitudinal data (supposedly required for a prima facie evidence of change)? Can the research isolate the impact of the OD process from other influences, such as changes in technology, changes in strategy or structure, or other content-oriented aspects? Most of these issues can be grouped under the dilemmas associated with field research and quasiexperimental methods. In addition, few studies actually assess the return on investment of OD.

On the other hand, there is a strong argument that OD has had a tremendous impact on organization practice. Qualitatively, OD interventions, such as survey feedback, team building, conflict management, sociotechnical system design, culture change, coaching, diversity, large group conferences, employee involvement, self-managed work teams, and open system planning are common, routine, and institutionalized in many organizations. Kleiner's (1996) account of the influence and dissemination of OD practices is a compelling read.

In addition, the number of OD and OD-related jobs is growing both in the United States and internationally. Many organizations recognize OD's value added and often attach these positions structurally to senior line managers. There is also a strong trend in many organizations to incorporate OD qualifications and responsibilities into a wide variety of human resource positions. Worren, Ruddle, and Moore (1999) note how large management consulting firms quickly acquired a variety of small and medium-sized OD practices when clients demanded more change management services from them. Finally, most large organizations remain committed to tuition reimbursement for OD-related educational programs.

Quantitatively, Golembiewski (2002), Porras and Robertson (1992), Anderson (2003), Neilsen (1984), and others have provided substantial evidence (much of which can meet the challenging methodology questions listed earlier) that OD processes have consistently resulted in improvements in organization effectiveness. Golembiewski is perhaps the most outspoken advocate of the research support for OD. He notes that roughly 75% of the cases studied showed attractive success rates across a broad range of interventions, in that all or nearly all pre- and post-measures were in the intended direction. Moreover, nearly two-thirds of the differences achieved statistical significance.

In the end, the qualitative, quantitative, and historical evidence yields decent support for the conclusion that OD has a net positive influence in organizations. However, it is clear that practitioners and researchers need to spend more time and effort on evaluating OD efforts. The field has matured to the point where the rate of new intervention techniques has slowed. It could benefit from more refined assessment processes. We can improve practice substantially by clarifying effectiveness criteria, defining process and outcome variables, gathering more data on processes and outcomes, sharing research results more widely, and connecting theory to practice in our discussions and literature.

Table 7.1 summarizes the implications that result from the OD debates and their resolution.

Table 7.1   OD Debates and Implications for Practice

OD Debates	Implications for Practice
Definitions	Influences the scope, depth, and breadth of practice and the knowledge base and skill requirements.
Conceptualizations	No practical impact on practice.
Credentialing	If credentialing were instituted, it could affect education requirements, accuracy in labeling, ethical behavior, and skill mastery.
Effectiveness	Research results should affect what one does and how. Over time should eliminate less effective methods and increase the best practices.

TOWARD A THEORY OF OD PRACTICE

The purpose of this section is to integrate our own experience as consultants, researchers, and educators into an original theory of OD practice. At this stage of the field's development, there is room for wide variety in the practice of OD. Yet there are also minimum distinguishing characteristics and intended ideals that can define the basis of theory and bring some coherence to this part of the field. Although any theory or model can be only a simplification of reality, it can be highly useful in separating one field from another and one type of practice from another. For example, models of human cognition and culture distinguish psychology from anthropology. An OD practice theory should distinguish it from other applied disciplines, such as engineering, innovation, or operation management. OD has long suffered from the lack of any such theory and consequently has been subject to the definitional and credibility debates outlined earlier. The description and specification of this theory are necessarily tentative but can serve as an important starting point for development of a more codified framework of practice. A theory of OD practice can be helpful in

- Identifying what practitioners need to do well
- Making design, intervention, and behavior choices
- Determining what belongs in OD education
- Distinguishing OD from other types of consultation and especially from other change practices

In proposing this theory, we assume that OD is an imperfect field of practice devoted to combining applied behavioral science and the art of change. It involves both subjectivity and objectivity. Given the values of the field—choice, participation, human dignity, and learning—and its history, we also assume that the practitioner's use of his or her own emotions and cognitions—the use of self as the instrument of change—is essential in executing the art and science. Who you are—your own psychosocial state, character, knowledge, skills, and experiences—is the instrument through which data must pass and many interventions must be executed.

Figure 7.1 organizes the minimum distinguishing characteristics and intended ideals of OD practice. OD practice always involves an OD process in which people participate over time. The design and management of the process and the desired behaviors expected from the client and the practitioner characterize this element of the theory. The result of launching an OD process is a series of individual and organizational action cycles. These cycles include learning, addressing various forms of support, inertia, and resistance, and changing some or all of the features of the organization. During an OD process, these intertwined dynamics begin to create changes first as trial and error and later as adjustments and adaptations. Finally, OD practice always intends to produce two kinds of outcomes: individual development and organization improvement. We describe each of these three characteristics and ideals in more depth in this section.

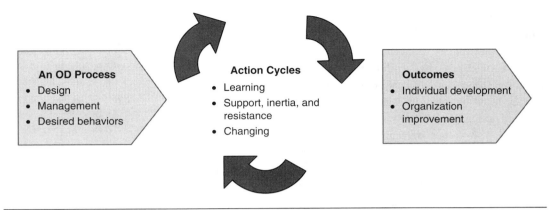

Figure 7.1   A Theory of OD Practice

An OD Process

An OD process involves design, management, and desired behaviors.

Design. As shown in Table 7.2, the design of an OD process always includes five characteristics: a cyclical method, an open system orientation, a specific value base, a set of interventions, and desired roles. First, a cyclical method, such as action research (Reason & Bradbury, 2001) or self-design (Mohrman & Cummings, 1989), requires that a series of data collection, reflection, action, and reflection activities be followed by further data–reflection–action–reflection cycles. OD is a journey, not an event. This orientation recognizes that complex human systems go through state changes with each

intervention and therefore need new data to determine the next appropriate action. This belief in the changing state of human systems is core to OD and will show up in a wide variety of methods with cyclical characteristics.

Second, OD processes also depend on an open system orientation, which starts with an understanding that any system exists as part of a larger system that constitutes its environment. Basic system principles and dynamics (e.g., interacting parts, boundaries, exchanges across system boundaries, transformation processes, inputs and outputs, adaptation, cause and effect) are used in planning the process in terms of whom to include, sequence and simultaneity, and feedback mechanisms (Miller, 1978; von Bertalanffy, 1969). A system orientation also suggests that OD processes adopt a diagnostic

Table 7.2   Characteristics of an OD Process

Design	Cyclical method (e.g., action research, self-design)
	Open system orientation
	Value base (choice, participation, humanism, development)
	Interventions (structure, speed, depth, sequence)
	Roles and relationships
Management	Process path
	Execution
	Intended and unintended effects
	Emergent situations
	Behaviors and relationships
Desired behaviors	Intended consultant behaviors
	Intended client behaviors

and contingent perspective. Context is an important consideration in design (Gladwell, 2001). The client's capacity and readiness for change, the type of change issue addressed, the complexity of the system, and the consultant's competence must be taken into account and derive from this open system orientation.

Third, the values determining the choices made and built into an OD process differentiate it from other change methods. OD practice's core values are choice, participation, human dignity, and learning. In OD, there is a bias that will always show up in what is done and how it is done that will favor people having choice; being able to participate in decisions that affect their lives; promoting norms of authenticity, honesty, openness, respect, and fairness; and providing opportunities to develop their potential.

Fourth, any OD process represents a series of interventions that are defined as purposeful injections of information, activity, or interaction aimed at targets of change. These interventions vary in their sequence, complexity, speed, and psychological depth. Each intervention within a series serves one or more of several purposes, including

- Changing a "what" or a "how"
- Disrupting the status quo (unfreezing)
- Producing valid data, providing free choice, or building client ownership and internal commitment
- Developing individual or organizational capacity and helping the client learn
- Engaging people in developing their desired future
- Identifying, surfacing, or working with support, inertia, or resistance

The process of designing this series of interventions also involves a series of choices usually made jointly by the consultant with the client. A set of specific considerations guide these choices and center around

- The appropriate type of diagnostic and evaluative data that allow for and suggest action options

- The client's capacity to understand and take action on what's happening in the present state
- The client's readiness and motivation to change
- The type, level, and complexity of problems and opportunities, or the breadth and depth of a desired future state or vision
- The system's complexity in terms of number of moving parts, interacting players, or relationships
- The consultant's competence, confidence, and willingness to execute a particular change

Finally, an OD process requires certain roles and relationships. Minimally, there are client and consultant behaviors needed for conducting any OD process. Certain behaviors distinguish these roles in an OD process. The size and scope of the undertaking may require additional roles (Axelrod, 2001; Mohrman, 2002; Old, 1995). These could include project leaders, centers of excellence, program management offices, design teams, change managers, and evaluation specialists. Members of the client system or the consulting team can fill these roles.

OD practitioners design OD processes with the guidelines outlined earlier and operate them with the characteristics discussed. Designs or methods that do not operate on these principles and values probably are not OD. For example, innovation also involves a variety of roles and actors, but the set of values and behaviors during change are not the same.

Management. Managing the OD process is the second major element. A series of interventions defines an intended path of change. However, because the interventions are executed during the cycles of action, an actual path of change emerges that rarely follows the intended path. Thus, an important part of OD work is managing the process by

- Monitoring and managing the actual path, including making midcourse corrections, building in adaptations to unanticipated forces, or changing the path completely, if the change purposes shift significantly
- Ensuring the quality and timing of execution

- Evaluating the intended effects and monitoring unintended consequences
- Incorporating emerging conditions, environmental influences, and erratic client behavior
- Managing client and consultant behaviors and relationships

These management tasks are crucial to success because human systems are continuously changing entities with both predictable and unpredictable actions. Therefore, although design is an important part of the front end of an OD process, the ongoing design and management of the change process in response to new data and changing conditions will make or break an OD practitioner's work.

Desired Behaviors. Certain core behaviors are needed in OD to differentiate it from other forms of consultation. This is true in both the intended role of the consultant and the intended role of the client. The ideal client–consultant relationship does not just happen naturally. It requires continual management, reflection, and intervention. In the ideal relationship, the client and consultant operate in partnership (Block, 1999; Old, 1995). Each one models the importance of human dignity, participation, choice, and learning, and each joins in the design and management of the OD process. However, most clients do not start where they need to end up, and most OD consultants have difficulty with one or more aspects of their role. As a result, the desired behaviors need to be specified, clarified, discussed, and managed along the way.

The OD practitioner brings expertise on the process of design, change strategies and methods, intervention, and facilitation. The core behaviors the consultant needs to master in an OD process include

- Education through modeling and influence
- Collaboration through partnership
- An authentic, open, and trustworthy style
- The display of systemic and strategic thinking
- Suggestions about design and execution processes and interventions

- Inquiry and the ability to diagnose a system
- Facilitation behaviors that structure, frame, question, support, and confront the system

The client brings more expertise in the business of the organization, better understanding of the content of the work, and accountability for the results. Therefore, it is critical that the client engage in, lead, and own the process and outcomes. The core behaviors the client needs in an OD process include

- Leadership and decision making
- Commitment and engagement to actively own the change work
- Openness to learning and feedback
- An authentic, open, and trustworthy style
- Collaboration through partnership
- The display of systemic and strategic thinking

Action Cycles

As shown in Table 7.3, the result of launching any OD process is a cycle of activities that generally involve individual and collective learning; various forms of support, inertia, and resistance; and initial changes in individuals and organizational components. All three are natural and to be expected. They are necessary in any transformation or change of state. The iterative, intertwined processes of learning, working with support, inertia, and resistance, and changing individual perspectives and organizational components ultimately create the desired outcomes of individual development and organization improvement.

Learning can occur on multiple levels (e.g., individual, group, organizational) and in either cognitions or behavior (Tenkasi, Mohrman, & Mohrman, 1998). Learning can be limited to some individuals or more collectively and deeply internalized by the organization in the form of new cultures, systems, processes, and structures. Common types of learning include changed mindsets (perspectives, orientations, or ways of thinking); better understanding of their system's strategies, structures, processes, cause and effect relationships, and real strengths

Table 7.3   Characteristics of Action Cycles

Learning	Individual or collective
	Mindset changes
	System knowledge
	New skills
Support, inertia, and resistance	Individual
	Political
	Cultural
	Systems
Changing	Individual
	Organizational system

and vulnerabilities; and new skills in leading, managing, and changing their organization.

Various forms of support, inertia, and resistance can operate in the different stages of an OD process. In tangible or intangible, conscious or unconscious ways, people can create either positive energy toward or negative energy away from the achievement of the intended outcomes. Support or resistance can originate from an individual's self-interest, political bases of power or entitlement, or cultural forces rooted in operating values or derive from system reactions to the stresses of misalignments during change or the relief of fit when components fall into alignment.

The initial changes can be minor or major; in parts of the organization or organization-wide; and easy or very difficult. Changes need to occur in the people who will work in the changed system, the organization's strategy, structure, culture, and systems, and the alignment between them. Changes first occur as trial and error, adjustments, and adaptations before they become institutionalized or operational

changes. In line with our definition of OD, the organization must make these changes explicit. It is not enough to say that things have changed. Such fuzziness thwarts evaluation of an OD effort.

The actual path of change, with its twists and turns, adaptations, and conscientious management, emerges over time. Learning, encountering inertia, working with support and resistance, responding to environmental shifts and emerging situations, and executing the intended changes create the opportunities for real-time problem solving. As partners, the consultant and client are the architects guiding the organization and its various stakeholders along the path.

Outcomes

As shown in Table 7.4, at least two classes of outcomes, along with any other project-specific outcomes, distinguish an OD effort. Outcomes occur primarily toward the end of the actual change path. The first important

Table 7.4   Outcomes of the OD Process

Individual development	Knowledge
	Skills
	Behaviors
	Attitudes
Organization improvement	Performance
	Capacity
	Culture

class of outcome is individual development. OD processes help individuals grow and increase their potential. Part of the learning that occurs involves improving people's capacity to lead and manage change in the future and their potential to do what they can do best. These outcomes usually show up in knowledge, skills, behavior, and attitudes.

The second important class of outcome is organization improvement. OD efforts specifically target three types of improvement: performance, capacity, and culture.

First, although performance and improvement often are in the eye of the beholder and can be viewed through a wide variety of measures, OD efforts always expect to help the organizations get better at what they exist to do. Performance involves a variety of mission-related results that could include revenues, profit, customer service, production, clients served, environmental or social impact, market share, firm valuation, costs, cycle time, and quality. Often, other internal factors become metrics used as precursors or intermediate indicators of performance and include employee satisfaction, quality of work life, alignment, and various operational measures. The client–consultant contracting process should clarify the specific performance improvement outcomes sought.

Second, OD efforts differ from other forms of consultation and change in that the clients' learning, or the capacity to manage change in the future, is an important part of the work. Increasing an organization's collective capability to lead, design, and manage change has always been central to OD consultation. This outcome differs from the individual development outcome. It focuses on a critical mass of people in the organization knowing how to work together differently in their efforts to manage changes.

Finally, OD operates according to a specific set of values. These values not only guide the design of change processes but also describe intended ways of life in the organization. Therefore, each engagement attempts to create workplaces where choice, participation,

human dignity, and learning are characteristic of the culture. When early pioneers talked about OD as culture change (e.g., Beckhard, 1969; Bennis, 1969), their vision was one in which all organizations would internalize basic OD values into their way of operating. Culture was an appropriate target for OD because it was a reflection of the values operating to guide and shape the behavior of organization members.

CORE OD PRACTICE

Out of years of experience and the evaluation of effectiveness, a core practice has evolved to which most experienced professionals would concur. Most of the schools providing comprehensive OD education teach this core practice. It differs from change management, management consulting, operation research, industrial engineering, and other applied approaches to organization improvement, primarily through (Jamieson, 2006)

- Its value base
- Its integration of behavioral sciences with leadership, strategy, and organization design
- The nature of the consultation role and the use of the client–consultant relationship as part of the change
- Its series of client-centric (capability and readiness) interventions in action cycles
- Its inclusion of individual and organizational learning, development, and capacity building in the desired outcomes

To the extent that this theory of OD practice reflects the appropriate categories and characteristics of knowledge and skill, the question remains, "How do we best develop practitioners of change?" For the past 20 years, the authors have been intimately involved in the development of practitioners through both formal educational programs and internal management and leadership development projects. The final section of this chapter brings our experiences and beliefs to bear on the issue of educating and developing OD practitioners.

EDUCATING FOR OD PRACTICE

Our theory of OD practice suggests that certain areas of knowledge and skill are necessary for good practice. Table 7.5 presents the categories and characteristics of practice and their associated educational needs.

In the context of the practice theory presented here, exactly how does one learn to become an effective OD practitioner? Answering that question requires an understanding of the necessary competencies and a process for acquiring those competencies.

Competencies for OD Practice

Recent research suggests convergence on the competencies necessary for good OD practice

Table 7.5   OD Practice Theory and Educational Needs

	Aspect of Theory of Practice	Educational Need
OD process	Design	Action research, self-design Organization environments, open system theory Assessing client capacity, readiness, emotional intelligence OD value base OD intervention methods to work with individuals, small groups, large groups, and organizations Planning methods (vision, goals, action) Consulting skills
	Management	Leader coaching, facilitation Project management Data collection, research methods Interpersonal relations, group dynamics Presentation and communication skills
	Behaviors	Consultation skills, self as instrument, influence Openness, collaboration, authenticity Designing, inquiry, facilitation Strategic thinking Interpersonal relations, communication, decision making
	Learning	Adult learning Instructional design
Action cycles	Support, inertia, and resistance	Culture Group dynamics Motivation Physics
	Changing	Change theories, system theory Causal analysis Individual psychology Strategy Job and work design, organization design, culture
Outcomes	Individual development	Measurement, assessment
	Organization improvement	Organization effectiveness Organization economics Finance Operation management

(Eisen, Cherbeneau, & Worley, 2005; Worley, Rothwell, & Sullivan, 2005; Worley & Varney, 1998). They include organization behavior, group dynamics, organization theory, and different functional areas and skills in organization design, facilitating change, research methods, personal growth and cross-cultural communication, managing the consulting process, and developing client capability to help systems change over time.

The broad range of skills, knowledge, and competencies envisioned for OD practitioners and the broad overlap between most of them suggest that educational programs should have an easy task of ensuring that their curricula meet some minimal level of coverage and can emphasize certain facets of OD that fit with institutional or school missions and faculty capabilities.

Education Programs to Acquire Competencies

OD education can come from three sources: experience and mentors, workshops and certificate programs, and formal degree programs, especially master's and doctoral education. Experience and mentorship are important sources of OD competencies. As an applied field, OD is a little like playing golf or riding a bike: You cannot just read a book and be able to conduct effective OD processes. Knowing how organizations work, understanding the pressures organization members and managers feel, and navigating the range of technical and ethical choices available is best learned by doing.

Workshop and certificate programs are also very common sources of knowledge about OD. They can range from one-day seminars on specific subjects, such as group facilitation, culture change, training design, or change theory, to multiple-session certificate programs in organization design, OD, or specific interventions. These programs can be aimed at beginners in the field (e.g., OD Network, University Associates, and Linkage conferences) or advanced practitioners (e.g., the University of

Southern California Center for Effective Organizations and Columbia University).

Formal educational programs in OD have existed since the mid-1970s, when the first master's degree programs were created at Pepperdine, Benedictine, and Bowling Green State universities. Since that time, undergraduate curricula in schools of business, education, psychology, sociology, communication, and public policy have expanded to include OD and other organization change-related courses as electives. However, the focus of most OD education has been at the master's and, increasingly, the doctoral levels. The number of master's degree programs grew in the 1980s and has remained stable (Varney & Darrow, 1997, identified more than 22 programs). Most of the master's programs are based in the United States, but a few, including the University of Monterrey (Mexico), are international and have existed for more than 25 years.

Many of the master's and doctoral programs have formally or informally adopted the OD competencies model developed by Varney and his colleagues (e.g., Worley & Varney, 1998), and there is an increasing homogenization of basic curriculums. This is both good and bad for the field. It is good because there is an emerging agreement about the skills and knowledge needed to be a competent practitioner, and the educational system is working to build this foundational level of competence.

It is also a potential problem because too much homogenization could stifle creativity and innovation in both education and practice. The field is broad enough to warrant specializations. Fortunately, and despite some homogenization, program designs are retaining a certain level of uniqueness. Curriculums at different schools are focusing on traditional process skills, international and cross-cultural OD, strategy, positive scholarship, research, and environmental sustainability. For example, Case Western Reserve University has recently redesigned its master's degree program around sustainability and positive scholarship, and Pepperdine University has been implementing a design emphasizing the integration of strategy and OD in an international context. American University/NTL focuses more on group dynamics and small systems interventions, and Eastern Michigan University has developed an extensive program integrating human resources and OD. A similar diversity in thought seems to be pervading the doctoral programs; both alternative and traditional designs offer a variety of academic emphases.

Although the current master's programs seem to be coalescing around the key competencies, their biggest struggle is the focus of this chapter. How exactly is a person interested in OD to get the experience needed to become proficient at the practice of OD? Some schools offer internships or practicum courses that provide opportunities to conduct change projects in real settings. Other schools leverage fieldwork during week-long classes or require full-time employment to allow application of the concepts. This helps in the practical application of interventions but still leaves open opportunity to apply what is arguably one of the more important and central aspects of OD practice: the interpersonal. T groups and other forms of sensitivity training that formed the early base of practice have fallen out of favor. Most master's degree programs (Pepperdine University and American University are the two prominent exceptions) no longer require any form of clinical training. This seems unfortunate given the field's social science traditions and the importance of self-mastery.

Doctoral degree programs have been the fastest-growing segment of OD education. Although OD classes have always existed in traditional doctoral curricula in many business, education, and psychology schools (e.g., Case Western Reserve University), the specialized (or executive) OD doctoral program has become more popular. Degrees at the Fielding Institute, Benedictine University, Pepperdine University, University of St. Thomas, Alliant University, Cranfield University, and others are building strong reputations in developing scholar–practitioners.

The term "scholar–practitioner" has emerged and captures well the intent of most graduate degree programs in OD. That is, there is a balanced focus on developing participants. They should have the competencies to conduct effective OD processes in practical and applied settings. In addition, they should be aware of and capable of contributing to the body of knowledge through various methods of research.

The major differences in education programs and in practice seem to be the emphasis placed on specific methods versus a broad strategy of change technologies, the emphasis on diagnostic depth versus the use of techniques, and the use of self and consultative skill versus programmatic application of semistructured methods.

To be an effective OD practitioner, internal and external change agents must have the knowledge, skills, and perhaps most importantly, the experiences to design and manage OD processes, implement action cycles, and evaluate outcomes. This requires education in the core knowledge and skill areas, intensive personal growth work in clinical and intrapersonal reflection, and enough practice to build a fund of tacit knowledge and skill to sense what to do and when to do it. This is a tall order, but if the field is to advance, setting high standards will help build a positive reputation and drive positive outcomes.

CONCLUSION

Over the past 50 years, OD has grown and evolved. The debates in the field have at times helped and at other times hindered that evolution, but they leave open the question, "Has OD matured?" To hasten its maturity, we believe the time is right to converge on some agreements.

We should not lose sight of the field's roots. The foundations are still important to the core of the practice. Choice, participation, human dignity, and learning values are powerful guides for design, interventions, and behavior. Action research and other data-driven methods are effective processes for engaging clients in purposeful change. Using the self as an instrument of change, keeping an eye on the client system's learning and capacity building, and working to transfer knowledge fulfills the development mission inherent in OD.

But the roots of the field should not act as blinders to its vision. The nature of today's strategic issues, including globalization and diversity, the proliferation of new technologies, the implementation of alliances and networks, and accelerated change, demand new solutions requiring much of what OD has to contribute (Greiner & Cummings, 2004). OD started where its founders perceived the need was the greatest at that time. They would certainly applaud the application of the essence of OD to today's most pressing organizational and human needs. Moreover, the questions about OD's effectiveness should not remain so ambiguous. The field needs better answers to the questions about how to improve organization performance and build change capabilities. They are part of the differentiators of OD and therefore warrant rigorous research attention.

Better practice and better-educated practitioners will also hasten the field's maturity. Our hope is that the theory proposed here will start a vigorous dialogue on what constitutes good OD practice. But good practice and better-educated practitioners are an integrated dilemma. Although most educational programs have adopted foundational skills and knowledge into their curricula, few go far enough in building the experience base. Given our proposal to use education as a proxy for credentialing, the best educational programs will require significant organization experience as an admission requirement and will find ways to increase the amount of supervised practice.

In other fields, such supervised practice is a required part of their credentialing process and entry requirements. OD does not have such a formal, structured entry process, but it does share some commonality with these fields in that each requires the practitioner to work with people in conducting their practice. It is where theory becomes action, circumstances must be factored in to action choices, and client feedback differs across situations and changes the diagnosis. In fields where self as instrument is a central concept, learning in real contexts is the only way to see what different situations look like and understand the intended and unintended results of interventions. When this can be done under the guidance of someone experienced, learning can be accelerated, and one situation can provide learning for numerous similar situations.

In OD education, this can be difficult and expensive to implement. It requires both experienced practitioners with enough time to supervise someone else and organization sites with real-time issues to work on. There are enough experienced people in the field now that there should be a way to use the universities, their alumni, and the professional associations to create a clearinghouse for connecting students and field mentors. Similarly, organization sites need to be identified through students, the professional association members, internal or external consultants, or OD program alumni.

Finding ways to add more experience-based learning will go a long way toward generating better-educated practitioners and enhancing the field's credibility. In addition to gaining experience under the watchful eye of experienced practitioners, we believe a few areas of learning need greater emphasis in developing competent practitioners because certain skills and knowledge seem to be less effectively used in practice.

- With or without T group–like experiences, practitioners need to work on the skills and attitudes associated with the self as instrument concept. In a field that involves working with change in people and human systems, this competence must rank high on the developmental list.

- Building effective client–consultant relationships, especially in contracting, boundaries, and power dynamics.
- In the area of consultation, more theory is needed to address what is consultation and what makes it effective. Specifically, there needs to be more work on the core, but less tangible, processes of diagnosis and intervention strategy and design.
- Finally, there is still much to learn about change in individuals, groups, and organization collectives. Both problem-based and appreciative changes have a variety of necessary conditions, motivations, phases, and needed interventions to be effective and sustaining.

Because the field has expanded in both the scope of targets and the substantive issues it addresses, today's practitioners cannot excel at all aspects of OD. There is room for some specialization by specific use of one's previous work life or other education degrees. This would be an additional sign of OD's maturity. In any case, what needs to be common among the diverse community of practitioners is their understanding of organizations, systems, change, consultation, and self and how to use the values of human dignity, learning, participation, and choice in the design of change processes, intervention cycles, and evaluation efforts. The theory of practice proposed here takes an important first step in integrating those issues into a single framework.

There is much to be done in improving both research and practice in OD. The field has grown and developed in many ways, and it must continue to evolve because organizations and their environments will keep changing. Despite recent criticisms, the current state of the field seems healthy in many ways. The number of OD program students and alumni is growing, the volume of OD-related jobs is up, membership in the professional associations is increasing, and many organizations consider OD interventions mainstream practice. We hope that our colleagues heed the recommendations and proposals outlined in this chapter.

NOTE

1. We use *human dignity* here to represent the value thread, derived from humanism, of the concern for the worth, respect, interests, needs, and welfare of humans and their capacities and potential.

REFERENCES

Anderson, M. (2003). *Bottom-line organization development*. Burlington, MA: Butterworth-Heinemann.

Argyris, C. (1965). Explorations in interpersonal competence. *Journal of Applied Behavioral Science, 1*(1), 58–83.

Axelrod, R. (2001). Why change management needs to change. *Reflections, the SOL Journal, 2*(3), 115–123.

Beckhard, R. (1969). *Organization development: Strategies and models*. Reading, MA: Addison-Wesley.

Beckhard, R. (1997). *Agent of change: My life, my practice*. San Francisco: Jossey-Bass.

Beer, M. (1980). *Organization change and development: A systems view*. Santa Monica, CA: Goodyear.

Bennis, W. (1969). *Organization development: Its nature, origins and prospects*. Reading, MA: Addison-Wesley.

Bennis, W., & Shepard, H. (1956). A theory of group development. *Human Relations, 9*, 415–457.

Block, P. (1999). *Flawless consulting* (2nd ed.). San Francisco: Pfeiffer.

Block, P. (2003). *The answer to how is yes: Acting on what matters*. San Francisco: Berrett-Koehler.

Bowers, D., & Franklin, J. (1972). Survey guided development: Using human resources measurement in organizational change. *Journal of Contemporary Business, 1*, 43–55.

Bradford, D., & Burke, W. (2004). Is OD in crisis? *Journal of Applied Behavioral Science, 40*(4), 369–373.

Bradford, D., & Burke, W. (Eds.). (2005). *Reinventing organization development*. San Francisco: Pfeiffer.

Bradford, L., Gibb, J., & Benne, K. (Eds.). (1964). *T-group theory and laboratory method: Innovation in re-education*. New York: John Wiley & Sons.

Brown, J., Isaacs, D., and the World Café Community. (2005). *The World Café: Shaping our futures through conversations that matter.* San Francisco: Berrett-Koehler.

Bullock, R., & Svyantek, D. (1987). The impossibility of using random strategies to study the organization development process. *Journal of Applied Behavioral Science, 23,* 255–262.

Bunker, B., & Alban, B. (1997). *Large group interventions: Engaging the whole system for rapid change.* San Francisco: Jossey-Bass.

Bunker, B., & Alban, B. (2005). Introduction to the special issue on large group interventions. *Journal of Applied Behavioral Science, 41*(1), 1–9.

Burke, W. (1982). *Organization development: Principles and practices.* Boston: Little, Brown.

Burns, T., & Stalker, G. (1961). *The management of innovation.* London: Tavistock.

Cameron, K., Dutton, J., & Quinn, R. (2003). *Positive organizational scholarship: Foundations of a new discipline.* San Francisco: Berrett-Koehler.

Cartwright, D., & Zander, A. (1954). *Group dynamics.* Evanston, IL: Row Peterson.

Church, A. (2001). The professionalization of organization development: The next step in an evolving field. In R. Woodman & W. Pasmore (Eds.), *Research in organizational change and development* (pp. 1–42). Greenwich, CT: JAI.

Cole, D. (2005). *Building the field of organization development into a profession.* Retrieved May 19, 2005, from http://www.odinstitute.org

Cooperrider, D., Sorenson, P., Yeager, T., & Whitney, D. (Eds.). *Appreciative inquiry: An emerging direction for organization development.* (2001). Champaign, IL: Stipes Publishers.

Cooperrider, D., & Srivastva, S. (1987). Appreciative inquiry in organizational life. In R. Woodman & W. Pasmore (Eds.), *Research in organization change and development* (*Appreciative inquiry: An emerging direction for organization development.* Champaign, IL: Vol. 1, pp. 1–57). Greenwich, CT: JAI.

Cummings, T., & Worley, C. (2005). *Organization development and change* (8th ed.). Mason, OH: Southwestern College Publishing.

Davis, M. (2001). *OD and change management consultants: An empirical examination and comparison of their values and interventions.* Working paper, Shenandoah University.

Dictionary.com (2006). Retrieved May 9, 2006, from http://dictionary.reference.com/search

Egan, T., & Gellermann, W. (2005). Values, ethics, and practice in the field of organization development. In W. Rothwell & R. Sullivan (Eds.), *Practicing organization development* (2nd ed.). San Francisco: John Wiley & Sons.

Eisen, S., Cherbeneau, J., & Worley, C. (2005). A future-responsive perspective for competent practice in OD. In W. Rothwell & R. Sullivan (Eds.), *Practicing organization development* (2nd ed.). San Francisco: John Wiley & Sons.

Ellinor, L., & Gerard, G. (1998). *Dialogue: Rediscover the transforming power of conversation.* New York: John Wiley & Sons.

Follett, M. (1941). In H. S. Metcalf & L. Urwick (Eds.), *Dynamic administration: The collected papers of Mary Parker Follett.* New York: Harper & Row.

French, W. (1969). Organization development: Objectives, assumptions, and strategies. *California Management Review, 12*(2), 23–34.

French, W., & Bell, C. (1999). *Organization development: Behavioral science interventions for organizational improvement* (6th ed.). Englewood Cliffs, NJ: Prentice Hall.

Galbraith, J. R. (2001). *Designing organizations: An executive guide to strategy, structure, and process.* San Francisco: Jossey-Bass.

Gladwell, M. (2001). *The tipping point.* New York: Little, Brown.

Golembiewski, R. (2002). *Ironies in organization development* (2nd ed.). New York: Marcel Dekker.

Golembiewski, R., & Munzenrider, R. (1976). Measuring change by OD designs. *Journal of Applied Behavioral Science, 12,* 133–157.

Greiner, L., & Cummings, T. (2004). OD more alive than dead! *Journal of Applied Behavioral Science, 40*(4), 374–391.

Holman, P., & Devane, T. (1999). *The change handbook: Group methods for shaping the future.* San Francisco: Berrett-Koehler.

Homans, G. (1950). *The human group.* New York: Harcourt Brace.

Jamieson, D. (2006). What makes OD different (and better) than other approaches to change? In N. Breuer (Ed.), *Wisdom of ASTD-LA 2006* (pp. 121–139). Los Angeles: ASTD-LA.

Jamieson, D., & Gellermann, W. (2006). Values, ethics and OD practice. In M. Brazzel &

B. Jones (Eds.), *The NTL handbook of organization development and change* (pp. 46–65). San Francisco: Jossey-Bass/Pfeiffer.

Katz, D., & Kahn, R. (1966). *The social psychology of organizing*. New York: John Wiley & Sons.

Kliener, A. (1996). *The age of heretics*. New York: Doubleday.

Lawler, E., & Worley, C. (2006). *Built to change*. San Francisco: Jossey-Bass.

Lawrence, P., & Lorsch, J. (1967). *Organization and environment*. Cambridge, MA: Harvard Business School Press.

Lewin, K. (1948). *Resolving social conflicts*. Washington, DC: American Psychological Association.

Lewin, K., & Lippitt, R. (1938). An experimental approach to the study of autocracy and democracy: A preliminary note. *Sociometry, 1,* 292–300.

Likert, R. (1961). *New patterns of management*. New York: McGraw-Hill.

Ludema, J., Whitney, D., Mohr, B., & Griffin, T. (2003). *The appreciative inquiry summit: A practitioner's guide for leading large group change*. San Francisco: Berrett-Koehler.

Macy, B., & Mirvis, P. (1982). Organizational change efforts: Methodologies for assessing organizational effectiveness and program costs versus benefits. *Evaluation Review, 6,* 301–372.

Magruder-Watkins, J., & Mohr, B. (2001). *Appreciative inquiry: Change at the speed of imagination*. San Francisco: Jossey-Bass.

Mann, F. (1957). Studying and creating change: A means to understanding social organization. In C. Arensberg (Ed.), *Research in industrial human relations*. Publication no. 17. New York: Industrial Relations Research Association.

Marshak, R. (1996). *Reclaiming the heart of OD: Putting people back into organizations*. Keynote address to the National OD Network Conference, Orlando, FL, October 6.

Maslow, A. (1954). *Motivation and personality*. New York: Harper.

Mayo, E. (1945). *The social problems of an industrial civilization*. Cambridge, MA: Harvard Business School Press.

McGregor, D. (1960). *The human side of enterprise*. New York: McGraw-Hill.

Miller, J. G. (1978). *Living systems*. New York: McGraw-Hill.

Mohrman, S. A. (2002). The organizational level of analysis: Consulting to the implementation of new organizational designs. In R. L. Lowman (Ed.), *Handbook of organizational consulting psychology* (pp. 54–75). San Francisco: Jossey-Bass.

Mohrman, S., & Cummings, T. (1989). *Self designing organizations: Learning how to create high performance*. Reading, MA: Addison-Wesley.

Nadler, D. (1977). *Feedback and organization development: Using data-based methods*. Reading, MA: Addison-Wesley.

Neilsen, E. (1984). *Becoming an OD practitioner*. Englewood Cliffs, NJ: Prentice Hall.

Old, D. (1995). Consulting for real transformation, sustainability, and organic form. *Journal of Organizational Change Management, 8*(3), 6–17.

Owen, H. (1992). *Open space technology: A user's guide*. Potomac, MD: Abbott.

Porras, J., & Robertson, P. (1992). Organization development: Theory, practice, and research. In M. Dunnette & M. Hough (Eds.), *Handbook of industrial and organizational psychology* (Vol. 3, 2nd ed.). Palo Alto, CA: Consulting Psychologists Press.

Reason, P., & Bradbury, H. (2001). *Handbook of action research: Participative inquiry and practice*. Newbury Park, CA: Sage.

Roethlisberger, F., & Dickson, W. (1939). *Management and the worker*. New York: John Wiley & Sons.

Rogers, C. (1961). *On becoming a person*. Boston: Houghton Mifflin.

Schein, E., & Bennis, W. (1965). *Personal and organizational change through group methods: The laboratory approach*. New York: John Wiley & Sons.

Seashore, S., Lawler, E. III, Mirvis, P., & Cammann, C. (Eds.). (1983). *Assessing organizational change: A guide to methods, measures, and practices*. New York: Wiley-Interscience.

Stacey, R. (2001). *Complex responsive processes in organizations*. New York: Routledge.

Tannenbaum, R., Margulies, N., Massarik, F., & Associates. (1985). *Human systems development: Perspectives on people and organizations*. San Francisco: Jossey-Bass.

Tannenbaum, R., & Schmidt, W. (1973, May–June). How to choose a leadership pattern. *Harvard Business Review, 51,* 162–180.

Tenkaski, R., Mohrman, S., & Mohrman, A. (1998). Accelerating organizational learning during transition. In S. Mohrman, J. Galbraith, & E. Lawler (Eds.), *Tomorrow's organizations* (pp. 330–361). San Francisco: Jossey-Bass.

Terborg, J., Howard, G., & Maxwell, S. (1982). Evaluating planned organizational change: A method for assessing alpha, beta, and gamma change. *Academy of Management Review, 7,* 292–295.

Thompson, R., & Hunt, J. (1996). Inside the black box of alpha, beta, and gamma change: Using a cognitive-processing model to assess attitude structure. *Academy of Management Review, 21,* 655–691.

Trist, E., & Bamforth, E. (1951, February). Social and psychological consequences of the long-wall method of coal getting. *Human Relations, 4,* 3–28.

Varney, G., & Darrow, A. (1997). Market position of master level graduate programs in organization development. *OD Practitioner, 27*(2), 39–43.

von Bertalanffy, L. (1969). *General systems theory* (rev. ed.). New York: G. Braziller.

Weidner, C., & Kulick, O. (1999). The professionalization of organization development: A status report and look to the future. In W. Pasmore & R. Woodman (Eds.), *Research in organizational change and development* (Vol. 12, pp. 319–371). Greenwich, CT: JAI Press.

Weisbord, M. (1987). *Productive workplaces.* San Francisco: Jossey-Bass.

Wheatley, M. (2001). *Leadership and the new science.* San Francisco: Berrett-Koehler.

Whyte, W., & Hamilton, E. (1964). *Action research for management.* Homewood, IL: Irwin-Dorsey.

Worley, C., & Feyerherm, A. (2003). Reflections on the future of organization development. *Journal of Applied Behavioral Sciences, 39*(1), 97–115.

Worley, C., Rothwell, W., & Sullivan, R. (2005). Competencies of OD practitioners. In W. Rothwell & R. Sullivan (Eds.), *Practicing organization development* (2nd ed.). San Francisco: John Wiley & Sons.

Worley, C., & Varney, G. (1998, Winter). A search for a common body of knowledge for master's level organization development and change programs: An invitation to join the discussion. *Academy of Management ODC Newsletter,* pp. 1–4.

Worren, N., Ruddle, K., & Moore, K. (1999). From organization development to change management: The emergence of a new profession. *Journal of Applied Behavioral Science, 35,* 273–286.

Yuchtman, E., & Seashore, S. (1967, December). A system resource approach to organizational effectiveness. *American Sociological Review, 32,* 891–903.

8

Action Research and Organization Development

K AT E   L O U I S E   M c A R D L E

P E T E R   R E A S O N

We approach this writing from opposite ends of our careers in action research and organization development (OD). Peter's first engagement with OD was in the late 1960s, when he moved into an internal consulting position to help implement a formal change management strategy in the UK-based multinational ICI, which at that time was a leader in the field. In contrast, Kate's early forays into organization change through action research have been explicitly formed by the literature and practice of a range of action research approaches during her doctoral studies with young women working as managers in a multinational company.

From these contrasting points in our careers we have two purposes in our writing. First, we want to contribute an action research perspective on OD, one that encourages continual inquiry, development, and curiosity in ourselves and in those we work with rather than seeing OD as a set of techniques. Second, we want to assert that at their best, by creating processes and structures for collaborative inquiry, action research and OD can be profoundly emancipatory.

We both bring to our work a strong bias that action research and OD are both pragmatic and rooted in democratic values: They aim to change things for the better through engagement of all those concerned (including, of course, deciding what needs to be changed and what *better* might mean). At their best, they are ways of reaching toward a world worthy of human aspiration, encouraging values of inquiry and learning, mutual respect for other people, and the wider ecology of which we are all a part (Reason & Bradbury, 2001). We start with a brief sketch of the history of OD and action research and of their relationship. We then move to some examples of action research practice and some suggestion of how we might frame these as OD interventions.

In some ways, early OD was quite sober and business oriented, as with the Blake and Mouton (1964) argument that organization success could be reached through "9.9 management," integrating a concern for people with a concern for production. But it also reflected some of the liberationist and utopian spirit of the 1960s, holding the possibility that individuals could flourish while contributing to organization purposes. Furthermore, it was often argued that organizations would be effective only if they fully engaged the skills and motivations of their members and that as people became better educated and expected more from employment, organizations would recruit and retain the people they needed only if they offered much more rewarding and challenging work experiences. OD practitioners of the day were strongly influenced by the motivation theories of McGregor, Maslow, and Hertzberg. OD therefore was often defined as the democratic mobilization of information, energy, and resources present in the organization—but currently diverted to nonconstructive channels—for organization improvement. Action research is similarly rooted in the view that we cannot generate valid understanding about people unless we engage with them as people in the fullest sense of the word.

A second significant influence shared by action research and OD in the early days was T group training. The apocryphal story is that a group of human relations trainers holding a staff meeting to discuss the progress of their group were asked by some of the trainees whether they could join in. The ensuing discussion revealed that people could learn much about their own behavior in learning to inquire together into the process of a group and their own contribution to this. T groups were not simply about training in human relations; they were about developing a capacity for self-reflective learning and the invitation to relate to others in more open, authentic, and equal relationships. However, there were significant difficulties in transferring the genuine learning from T grouping to a work situation, and OD specialists often struggled with the ideal of authentic relations in the face of unacknowledged power differentials, as action researchers sometimes do today. However, sensitivity training contained the seeds of an important idea: that people could learn to become researchers of their own life situations, an important parallel with action research.

Although one important origin of action research is the work of Lewin in the 1940s, modern action research has a long and diverse history, with origins in applications of social science to practical problems of wartime situations in Europe and America (Trist & Bamforth, 1951), in the social democracy of work research in Scandinavia (Toulmin & Gustavsen, 1996), in critical thinking (Kemmis, 2001), in liberationist thought and practice (Fals Borda & Rahman, 1991; Freire, 1970), in pragmatism (Greenwood & Levin, 1998; Reason, 2003b), in social construction (Gergen, 1999; Shotter, 1993), in systemic thinking (Flood, 2001; Pasmore, 2001), and in political activism of feminist (Maguire, 2001; Stanley & Wise, 1983), antiracist (Bell, 2001), and other liberationist movements. There are further links to psychotherapeutic thinking, group dynamics theory, and broadly to democratic traditions of social change going back to Tom Paine (1995). Action research is best understood not as a method or set of techniques but as an orientation to inquiry—a move to reexamine our understanding of the nature of human knowledge by reintegrating the dualisms that have haunted Western approaches to knowledge (Reason, 2003b; Rorty, 1999) splitting apart theory and practice, researcher and subject, everyday experience and academic knowledge.

Action research is a practice for the systematic development of knowing and knowledge but based in a rather different form from traditional academic research. It has different purposes, is based in different relationships, and has different ways of conceiving knowledge and its relationship to practice. We can define it broadly as

> a participatory, democratic process concerned with developing practical knowing in the pursuit of worthwhile human purposes, grounded in a participatory worldview. . . . It seeks to bring together action and reflection, theory and practice, in participation with others, in the pursuit of practical solutions to issues of pressing concern to people, and more generally the flourishing of individual persons and their communities. (Reason & Bradbury, 2001, p. 1)

This definition brings together five dimensions of action research: It is pragmatic, concerned with addressing practical issues and making links between theory and practice; it is democratic, both in the sense of involving people and in being liberationist, seeking to enable all people to create their own knowledge in learning organizations and communities of inquiry; it draws on an extended epistemology (Heron, 1996) of many ways of knowing, valuing the experiential, narrative, and aesthetic alongside the propositional and conceptual; it is value oriented, asking how we can contribute to the economic, political, psychological, and spiritual flourishing of people and communities and of the wider ecology of the planet; and it is developmental, evolving over time from tentative beginnings toward more significant influence (Reason & Bradbury, 2001).

VARIETIES OF ACTION RESEARCH

Action research typically involves creating spaces in which participants engage together in cycles of action and critical reflection. However, this basic process has been elaborated in different ways in different schools of practice. We outline some of the major ones in this section.

Organizational Change and Work Research. There is a longstanding tradition of action research in organization settings that aims to contribute to more effective work practices and better understanding of the processes of organization change. This approach draws on a variety of forms of information gathering and feedback to organization members, leading to problem-solving dialogue. This tradition is well represented in recent publications such as Toulmin and Gustavsen (1996), Greenwood and Levin (1998), and Coghlan and Brannick (2004).

Cooperative Inquiry. A cooperative inquiry group consists of people who share a common concern for developing understanding and practice in a specific personal, professional, or social arena. All are both co-researchers, whose thinking and decision making contribute to generating ideas, designing and managing the project, and drawing conclusions from the experience; and also co-subjects, participating in the activity being researched. Cooperative inquiry groups cycle between and integrate four forms of knowing: experiential, presentational, propositional, and practical (Heron, 1996; Heron & Reason, 2001).

Action Science and Action Inquiry. These related disciplines offer methods for inquiring into and developing congruence between our purposes, our theories and frames, our behavior, and our impact in the world; to put it colloquially, they ask us, "Do we walk the talk?" These practices can be applied at the individual, small group, and organizational level. Their overall aim is to bring inquiry and action together in more and more moments of everyday life, to see inquiry as a way of life (Argyris, Putnam, & Smith, 1985; Friedman, 2001; Marshall, 2001; Torbert, 2001).

Learning History. This is a process of recording the lived experience of those in an action research or learning situation. Researchers work collaboratively with those involved to agree on the scope and focus of the history, identify key questions, gather information through an iterative reflective interview process, distill this information into a form the organization or community can understand, and facilitate dialogue with organization members to explore the accuracy, implications, and practical outcomes that the work suggests (Roth & Kleiner, 1998).

Appreciative Inquiry. Practitioners of appreciative inquiry argue about the extent to which action research maintains a problem-oriented view of the world that diminishes people's capacity to produce innovative theory capable of inspiring the imagination, commitment, and passionate dialogue needed for the consensual reordering of social conduct. Devoting attention to what is positive about organizations and communities enables us to understand what gives them life and how we might sustain and enhance that life-giving potential. Appreciative inquiry begins with the unconditional positive question that guides inquiry agendas and focuses attention toward the most life-giving, life-sustaining aspects of the organization (Ludema, Cooperrider, & Barrett, 2001).

Whole System Inquiry. Large group interventions or processes are events designed to engage representatives of an entire system, whether it be an organization or a community, in thinking through and planning change (for descriptions see Bunker & Alban, 1997). What distinguishes them is that the process is managed to allow all participants an opportunity to engage actively in planning (Martin, 2001). Rather than aim at a single outcome, in dialogue conference design (Gustavsen, 2001) and whole system designs (Pratt, Gordon, & Plamping, 1999), the role of the researchers is to create the conditions for democratic dialogue among participants.

Participative Action Research. Usually used to refer to action research strategies emerging from the liberationist ideas of Paulo Freire (1970) and others in countries of the political South, participatory action research is explicitly political, aiming to restore to oppressed peoples the ability to create knowledge and practice in their own interests and therefore has a double objective. One aim is to produce knowledge and action directly useful to a group of people; another is to empower people at a deeper level through the process of constructing and using their own knowledge so they see through the ways in which the establishment monopolizes the production and use of knowledge for the benefit of its members. Participatory action research practitioners emphasize emergent processes of collaboration and dialogue that empower, motivate, increase self-esteem, and develop community solidarity (see Fals Borda & Rahman, 1991; Selener, 1997).

Art, Storytelling, and Theater as Action Research. Action research is increasingly linking with contemporary movements in a range of artistic practices in the community. Practices drawn from community art, theater, and storytelling offer starting places for inquiry based in presentational ways of knowing (Hawkins, 1988; Mienczakowski & Morgan, 2001).

Public Conversations. The aim of the public conversations movement is to foster a more inclusive, empathic, and collaborative society by promoting constructive conversations and relationships between those who have differing values, worldviews, and positions about divisive public issues. This might include activists in adversarial relationships who are interested in talking with each other directly, rather than through the media, in ways that reduce stereotyping and defensiveness; groups and networks who seek to more effectively collaborate despite differences of identity or perspective; and civic leaders, political officials, and educators who seek to build community and enhance democracy. (See http://www.publicconversations.org/pcp/index.asp?catid=54.)

STRATEGIES OF ACTION RESEARCH

Action research has encompassed the individual, the small group, and wider organization and social entities. At an individual level it has addressed issues of personal and professional change, of living life as inquiry (Marshall, 1999, 2001, 2004), and questions such as, "How can I improve my practice?" (Whitehead, 1989,

2000). In small groups, action research has allowed people to come together to address a common problem, to redesign work practices (Toulmin & Gustavsen, 1996), to explore issues of race and gender in organizations (Douglas, 2002), to pioneer professional change (Charles & Glennie, 2002; Reason, 1988), and so on. At the wider social and organizational levels, action researchers have explored a variety of large group processes as vehicles for action research (Martin, 2001), and there is lively debate among action research practitioners as to how action research can go beyond the singular and local to influence societal discourses and address issues of policy formation at the regional and national level (Gustavsen, 2001, 2003). Torbert refers to these three strategies when he asks,

> How may we intentionally enhance the effectiveness of our actions and the destructiveness of our inquiry (destroying illusory assumptions, dangerous strategies and self-defeating tactics)? How may we do so individually, in our face to face groups and in the larger organizations and collectivities to which we belong? How may we do so in the very midst of real-time actions of our every day lives—here and now? To what degree need such inquiry be explicit to ourselves and to others at each moment? (Torbert, 2001, p. 250)

We have found it helpful to refer to these three broad strategies as first-, second-, and third-person inquiry practices and to see them as mutually interpenetrating. Both action research and OD involve an interplay between "me" (my own experience and behavior), "us" (our immediate peers), and "them" (the wider organization) and encourage attention to be paid simultaneously to all three perspectives. We shall explore in some more detail what we mean by each of these strategies and then move on to illustrate them in practice.

First-Person Research Practice

First-person action research/practice skills and methods address the ability of the researcher

to foster an inquiring approach to his or her own life, to act awarely and choicefully, and to assess effects in the outside world while acting. (Reason & Bradbury, 2001, pp. xxv–xxvi)

Early work on first-person inquiry can be found in Argyris and Schön's now classic *Theory in Practice: Increasing Professional Effectiveness* (1974) and Schön's *The Reflective Practitioner* (1983). Much of this work centers around the distinction between espoused theories and theories in use—between what people say they do and what they actually do. Argyris called this work action science (Argyris et al., 1985).

> The goal of action science inquiry is to help practitioners discover the tacit choices they have made about their perceptions of reality, about their goals and about their strategies for achieving them. . . . By gaining access to these choices, people can achieve greater control over their own fate. . . . If people can find the sources of ineffectiveness in their own reasoning and behaviour, or their own causal responsibility, they then possess some leverage for producing change. Data are collected first and foremost for the purpose of helping people understand and solve practice problems of concern to them. (Friedman, 2001, p. 160)

Torbert distinguishes what he calls action inquiry from Argyris's action science by seeking congruence not just between espoused theories and behavior but between four territories of attention. He argues that any acting system, including an individual inquirer, needs valid knowledge of its purposes, thinking, behavior, and the outside world. Although this may seem obvious, in practice this takes a significant developmental effort. Our attention doesn't register a great deal of what occurs; we are rarely aware of our own behavior and others' reactions as we act, and what we know about the outside world is ordinarily about the past and is rarely tested in the present (Fisher, Rooke, & Torbert, 2000; Torbert, 2004). Essential to the notion of action inquiry is collaboration: In acting more awarely and inquiringly, we seek to increase mutuality between people, to develop communities of inquiry within communities of practice.

Torbert draws on developmental theory to articulate parallel stages of personal and organizational development. A person's frames of perception and action are narrow in early stages of development, focused on social membership and technical competence. Similarly, the early life of organizations often is focused on survival and efficiency, only later and rarely emphasizing processes of learning and development. However, in later stages both individual and organization become more concerned with the learning process itself: the way perceptions and practices are articulated and revised in interactions and how more people can be engaged in mutual learning and inquiry. These later stages can be called postconventional in that the intellectual and emotional processes they represent are infrequently found among those who have not undergone some form of intentional personal development, which might include spiritual practice, meditation, martial arts, and the process of action inquiry itself. Torbert argues that late-stage organizations are unlikely to arise without late-stage leadership.

Judi Marshall has contributed to inquiry as an everyday practice in a series of articles (Marshall, 1999, 2001, 2004) that have led her from articulating research as personal process through research as political process to inquiry as life process. The idea of living life as inquiry is that very little in life is fixed, finished, clear-cut, and the inquiring practitioner is living continually in process: adjusting, seeing what emerges, bringing things into question. This means attending to inner and outer arcs of attention, which on one hand seek "to notice myself perceiving, making meaning, framing issues, choosing how to speak out and so on" and on the other to one's own and others' behavior and the organizational context in which this takes place (Marshall, 2001, p. 431).

It is one thing to write about first-person inquiry and quite another to engage with it. It can be transformational to the point of being deeply disturbing. When Carlis Douglas explored how she, as a black woman, could not only survive but thrive in British organizations, she "uncovered ways in which my survival strategies colluded in maintaining my oppression rather than in negotiating my liberation" and as a consequence "experienced feelings of vulnerability and of being de-skilled" (Douglas, 2002, p. 252).

The practice of first-person inquiry is an ongoing life practice that can take place at the very moment of acting (online reflection) or at a later time (offline reflection). Reflecting online is very challenging for most people because it demands multilevel attention while acting: attending to what you are doing and how you are being, noticing what you believe is enabling or constraining in the situation, deliberately making changes in your behavior to change this, attending to how this change feels, and so on. Reflecting offline or after the event puts time and space between our action and our reflection on it. Tracking these reflections and the learning that comes from them in a journal is a popular method, as is arranging regular conversations with a trusted friend or colleague. This is distinct from engaging others in inquiry. Kate describes it thus: "Sometimes I need to hear my own voice articulate what I am thinking about—the act of speaking is one which helps me to do my figuring out. [With others I] talk myself through" (McArdle, 2004, p. 57). Some people use structured approaches such as the learning pathways grid (see Rudolph, Taylor, & Foldy, 2001) to encourage rigor and avoid the trap of "not noticing what I am not noticing," which we might easily fall into when inquiring alone. Others find less conventional methods more useful, seeing activities such as running as part of their reflective practice (McArdle, 2004; Roberts, 2003).

At the first-person level the sense that is made, both online and offline, is only "my" sense. This obviously shifts at the second-person level, where we make our sense evident to others and invite mutuality in deciding what is going on and how we might change it for the better. Whatever the approach, the point is that some kind of systematic process is adopted; it is this that makes the practice a discipline rather than just an anecdotal account of "what I remember." In addition, these practices are intended to be challenging, and their usefulness depends on our willingness to confront ourselves and to experiment, with changed behavior as a result. What might begin as some gentle observational notes should, over time, become an in-depth exploration of what is really going on?

So What Does This Look Like in Practice?

Marianne Kristiansen and Jørgen Bloch-Poulsen (2004) are Danish OD consultants who see their work as training members of organizations to enter into dialogue on topics in which they are deeply engaged so they can arrive at practical solutions that will receive general support. They describe how through reflective practice they saw that despite their espoused values of practicing democracy and dialogue with participants, their theories in use (Argyris & Schön, 1996) revealed how they behaved in such a way as to maintain unilateral power. They develop the concept of self-referentiality: interpreting others' behavior through one's own frames of reference:

> Self-referentiality means that you take your own actions and reactions for granted. You do not question your observations, bodily sensations, emotions, thoughts, intuition, and communication. They pass unattended and are not submitted to the scrutiny. (Kristiansen & Bloch-Poulsen, 2004, p. 372)

They arrived at these insights first by watching videotapes of conversations. They had already seen how rare dialogue was between managers, who regularly interpreted the perspective of their colleagues and employees from their own perspective without checking this. However, they also realized that this was often true of themselves:

> A closer look at video clips of our own inquiry practice in feedback conversations revealed that we, too, acted self-referentially in spite of our espoused value of practising dialogic research. (Kristiansen & Bloch-Poulsen, 2004, p. 377)

They saw in these videotapes how they interpreted nonverbal cues through their own framing rather than exploring with the managers how they themselves experienced them; they saw how their ostensibly open questions were actually biased, often in subtle ways, and how this established them in a superior position, as "uppers" devaluing others' experience as "lowers" (Chambers, 1997). They experienced this self-questioning as a vulnerable process.

Transcending self-referentiality is not only a question of changing one's own behavior; it is also about questioning a tendency to impose one's own regime of truth on others (Foucault, 2000) rather than treating others as co-participants in a learning process. As a result of these insights they continued to explore and challenge this tendency in themselves through continued offline review; collegial feedback and education in psychodynamic psychotherapy provide an understanding of transference and countertransference when working with participants.

Second-Person Research Practice

Second-person action research and practice addresses our ability to inquire face to face with others into issues of mutual concern—for example, in the service of improving our personal and professional practice both individually and separately. Second-person inquiry starts with interpersonal dialogue and includes the development of communities of inquiry and learning organizations (Reason & Bradbury, 2001, p. xxvi).

Second-person research and practice starts when we engage with others in a face-to-face group. One of the most clearly articulated approaches to second-person research and practice is cooperative inquiry (Heron, 1996; Reason,

2003a), which we outlined earlier; a typical inquiry group consists of between 6 to 15 people who work together as co-researchers and co-subjects.

Whereas cooperative inquiry is a clearly set out method, second-person research and practice is always present, albeit underdeveloped, in everyday life. In organizations, activities to develop effective teamwork, mentoring, and other forms of person-to-person and small group engagement are at their best forms of second-person inquiry, albeit tacitly. Indeed, most forms of professional practice are at their best forms of mutual inquiry. For example, the appraisal interview, which can be experienced as an exercise of power and defense, can be reframed as an inquiry to which both manager and managed bring their own different knowledge, skills, and perspective to the improvement of performance. Thus, a significant form of second-person research and practice may be to make explicit and systematic these everyday, tacit forms.

The shift from first- into second-person space involves a sense of going public with one's inquiry, of joining with others who have similar concerns or questions and engaging with them in exploring them. It is important to reiterate here that the shift into second-person inquiry is not a shift away from first-person inquiry. As discussed earlier, each generates and is sustained by the other, and working to figure out a balance of attention between the two is one of the many challenges for the action researcher. Indeed, as in Geoff Mead's (2002) example that we use here, the inquiry opens a second-person space that allows participants to attend to first-person practices.

At the time of his inquiry Geoff Mead was a senior police officer in Hertfordshire Constabulary in the United Kingdom. Among his concerns was leadership in the police force at a time when police services through the country were being accused of insensitivity, machismo, and institutional racism. He started from the premise that "improving the quality of leadership is a crucial issue for the police service.

Learning about theories of leadership is not enough. What really matters is for each of us to understand and improve our own unique practice as leaders" (Mead, 2002, p. 191). To explore this issue he initiated and ran an 18-month cooperative inquiry called "Developing Ourselves as Leaders," which was included in his doctoral research (Mead, 2001).

Initiating a cooperative inquiry is itself a delicate process (McArdle, 2002). After exploring the idea with senior colleagues and getting the formal endorsement of the chief constable, Geoff initiated a series of briefing meetings

> designed to help people make a positive decision to opt in to the action inquiry or to decide, without any stigma, that it was not for them. The underlying principle was that of voluntary, informed self-selection. . . . I talked about the possibility of transformative learning and asked people to decide if they wanted to take part using their head (Do you have enough information? Does it make *sense* for you to do it?), heart (Are you intrigued, curious, drawn? Does it *feel* right for you to do it?), and will (Are you able and willing to meet the commitment? Do you really *want* to do it?). (Mead, 2002, p. 196)

From these meetings an inquiry group was established that engaged in cycles of action and reflection over several months. Sometimes all members focus on the same issue, but often the inquiry is conducted as variations on a common theme:

> Each member of the [group] formulated his or her own individual inquiry question under the umbrella: "How can I improve the way I exercise leadership in the Hertfordshire Constabulary?" The focus on our own practice informed each subsequent cycle of action and reflection. . . .
>
> We found that the simple act of sharing our stories, telling each other how we had been getting on with our inquiries, was enormously powerful—both to deepen the relationships between us and as a way of holding ourselves and each other to account. . . . We

learned to trust the process of . . . inquiry and that, in an organisational setting at least, it needs to be sustained by careful cultivation and lots of energy. (Mead, 2002, p. 200)

The outcomes of the inquiry were varied. The following might be taken as typical: A colleague in the group was exploring his style as a leader and a manager, espousing a clear position of valuing other people and wanting to empower his staff. He was confronted suddenly one day by feedback from his boss: Rather than opening up and giving his staff space in which to work as he wished, they were concerned about the controlling influence he was retaining inappropriately.

When he talked about this in the group I could see that the work we had done together enabled him to hold the challenge and work with it. Instead of being either resistant to it or panicked by it, he took this as an opportunity to really reflect and with the group form an action plan as to how he would begin to try to change his behavior so that it was in accordance with his values. He began to learn how to let go of the reins and arranged to get systematic feedback from this person about how he was doing. Geoff also reflects on the difficulty of accounting for these kinds of changes:

Sometimes these stories which have such enormous import to us in our lives, as reported feel quite small. And I am also conscious that in the telling and the retelling of the story so much of the richness of that encounter, that learning, is inevitably dissipated. But part of the huge pleasure and privilege of working in an inquiry group in this way is that we do come together and share these problems and issues, these moments together. And then we move out again. We constantly converge and diverge, and at these points of convergence we can take sustenance and then take that energy out into the wider world. (transcribed and adapted from Mead, in Marshall & Reason, 2003)

The role of cooperative inquiry in OD has enormous potential, which has been applied

with medical practitioners (Reason, 1999), to explore ecologically sustainable practice in a construction company (Ballard, 2005), and interorganizational collaboration (Mullett, Jung, & Hills, 2004), organization culture (Marshall & McLean, 1988), gender and race in organizations (Aymer, 2005; Bryan, 2000; Douglas, 1999, 2002), and leadership in communities (Ospina et al., 2003).

Third-Person Research Practice

How can we move beyond the contained and small-scale practices of first- and second-person action research to stimulate inquiry in whole organizations and the wider society? The current debate in action research circles (Fricke, 2003; Greenwood, 2002; Gustavsen, 2003) suggests that although we have learned a lot about how to create inquiry at a personal, small group, and to some extent organizational level, we have been less successful in addressing large-scale issues of institutional change and scarcely touched the global issues of poverty, violence, and environmental degradation that are arguably the most pressing.

Some have suggested that there is an urgent need to develop strategies for developing larger scale in action research. To do this we may start from two perspectives: first considering ways to scale up small-scale inquiry at an organizational level and then asking whether action research can contribute at the level of social movement to address major issues of our time.

How might we scale up first- and second-person research practices? How can we build from the relative intensity of the cooperative inquiry group to engage large groups and whole systems in inquiry? Often, the move from an intimate inquiry group to larger participation is difficult. However, Kate McArdle's inquiry with young women was more successful in stimulating wider debate by inviting others into an inquiring space.

Kate initiated a cooperative inquiry within a multinational organization in the United Kingdom as part of her PhD research (McArdle,

2002, 2004) and as part of the OD move toward more effective management of diversity. The inquiry call invited young women from the organization to form a cooperative inquiry group through which they would deepen their understanding of their experience of the organization and enable themselves to act in more effective ways. The eventual inquiry group YoWiM (Young Women in Management) consisted of seven women who worked together in month-long cycles for 15 months. The group met together every 4 weeks on site at the host organization, sharing their stories and ideas from the action phase. In doing so, they opened space for new conversations about their experience, conversations that ranged from concerns about self-presentation, how they were addressed, the absence of female role models, and bullying—all underpinned with issues around voice and voicing.

From the very earliest days of the inquiry group, participants discussed their desire to include, in some way, a wider group of women in the process. There was a strong sense that this would validate their involvement in the inquiry group in the eyes of a larger membership of the organization rather than just key sponsors and that the involvement of a more diverse group of women (older, younger, more senior, more junior) would enable the inquiry group members to check out their own experiences in the light of new stories these women would bring. Furthermore, working the (by this stage, familiar) cooperative inquiry method with a new group of people who had not encountered it before offered the group the possibility of trying out new ways of being with others, a further validity check on their developing facilitative skills.

The YoWiM group conceived, designed, and conducted the half-day event with Kate, who had initiated and actively facilitated the YoWiM cooperative inquiry, almost entirely as an observer. The preceding 10 months of developing first- and second-person inquiry skills together in the intimate YoWiM inquiry group ultimately enabled the YoWiM women to facilitate and hold an inquiring space for more than 50 women from their organization with confidence. Translating their own processes of inquiry into the larger third-person space— a much bigger circle of chairs, structures to enable work in smaller, safer subgroups, setting expectations that participants would really listen to each other and would try to hear each other as equals, stating that experience is real and that stories told from it are therefore true, encouragement to offer opening comments and challenges, rather than judgmental closing ones—shifted the pattern of interactions and the types of stories that were possible to tell. The YoWiM women facilitated the deepening of engagement with the themes that emerged throughout the session, with Kate carefully intervening at times when they became drawn into noninquiring behaviors or hooked into other normative agendas.

The key point with this inquiry is how the development of first- and second-person inquiry skills over the preceding year enabled the YoWiM women to create and hold an inquiring space for others in which normative patterns of behavior can be named, inquired into, and resisted, alongside the emergence of behaviors that enable flourishing and an inquiring stance to become a reality.

An entirely different model of third-person inquiry comes from the Scandinavian experience under the leadership of Bjørn Gustavsen. Gustavsen suggests we need to extend beyond the small scale of individual action research cases so that "rather than being defined exclusively as 'scientific happenings' they (are) also defined as 'political events'" (Toulmin & Gustavsen, 1996, p. 11). More recently he has deepened this argument, stating that action research will be of limited influence if we think only in terms of single cases and that we need to think of creating social movements by adopting a distributive approach, generating efforts of some substantial size and focusing research on developing and sustaining the network rather than on individual interventions (Gustavsen, 2003).

If we use action research in a distributive way to create social movements it becomes more important to create many events of low intensity and diffuse boundaries than fewer events that correspond to the classical notion of a "case." Instead of using much resources in a single spot to pursue things into a continuously higher degree of detail in this spot, resources are spread over a much larger terrain to intervene in as many places in the overall movement as possible. (Gustavsen, 2003, pp. 96–97)

Gustavsen uses the dialogue conference (Gustavsen, 2001), which, like the range of large-scale and whole system conference designs—future search, the appreciative inquiry summit, open space, whole system events, and so on (Bunker & Alban, 1997; Pratt et al., 1999; Weisbord & Janoff, 1995)—broadens the "community of inquiry" definition, creating a forum for debate based on principles of participatory democracy, but without the intensity, intimacy, and duration of second-person inquiry designs.

Using the dialogue conference approach (Gustavsen, 2001), Marianne Ekman-Philips (2004) reports such a distributive intervention in the Swedish Health Service, focusing on dialogue generation between as many actors as possible. Participants represented the main professional groups, including nurses, doctors, assistant nurses, occupational therapists, and home service assistants. The main purpose was to expose the participants to each other, across professional as well as organizational boundaries, to explore the potential for learning from one another.

As an action research strategy, the health care programme can be seen as an effort to promote organisation development in as wide a range of workplaces as possible through the organisation of an external support structure. This support structure relied, furthermore, mainly on actors from the health services themselves and on activities unfolding between them. The main task of research was to help develop the support structure, not to intervene deeply in processes at the level of specific organisations. The main reason for this kind of strategy is the need to reach broadly out into working life to be able to give changes a critical mass and sustainability. (Ekman-Philips, 2004, p. 362)

CONCLUSION

After taking a look at some illustrated accounts of first-, second-, and third-person research practice, what are the themes that we can see, and how might they be useful for the OD practitioner?

The accounts offered in this chapter emphasize that action research is not a method but an approach that shapes methodological practices. As such it is full of choices, some of which are articulated in this chapter. Rather than thinking in terms of "getting it right or wrong," action researchers must try to make appropriate choices in different situations. A key dimension of quality is to be aware of the choices, consider them well, and make those choices clear, transparent, and articulate to yourselves, to your inquiry partners, and, when you start writing and presenting, to the wider world (Reason, 2006).

Action research and OD are close cousins. We argue that in remembering the way OD is in many ways born of action research, we can emphasize OD not only as a process of organization improvement but also as a process of mutual and liberating inquiry.

REFERENCES

Argyris, C., Putnam, R. W., & Smith, M. C. (1985). *Action science: Concepts, methods, and skills for research and intervention*. San Francisco: Jossey-Bass.

Argyris, C., & Schön, D. A. (1974). *Theory in practice: Increasing professional effectiveness*. San Francisco: Jossey-Bass.

Argyris, C., & Schön, D. A. (1996). *Organizational learning II*. Reading, MA: Addison-Wesley.

Aymer, C. (2005). *Black cultural renewal*. Unpublished PhD dissertation, University of Bath, Bath, UK.

Ballard, D. (2005). Using learning processes to promote change for sustainable development. *Action Research, 3*(2), 135–156.

Bell, E. E. (2001). Infusing race into the discourse of action research. In P. Reason & H. Bradbury (Eds.), *Handbook of action research: Participative inquiry and practice* (pp. 48–58). London: Sage.

Blake, R. R., & Mouton, J. S. (1964). *The managerial grid*. Houston, TX: Gulf Publishing.

Bryan, A. (2000). *Exploring the experiences of black professionals in welfare agencies and black students in social work education*. Unpublished PhD dissertation, University of Bath, UK.

Bunker, B., & Alban, B. (1997). *Large group interventions: Engaging the whole system for rapid change*. San Francisco: Jossey-Bass.

Chambers, R. (1997). *Whose reality counts? Putting the first last*. London: Intermediate Technology Publications.

Charles, M., & Glennie, S. (2002). Co-operative inquiry: Changing interprofessional practice. *Systemic Practice and Action Research, 15*(3), 207–221.

Coghlan, D., & Brannick, T. (2004). *Doing action research in your own organization* (2nd ed.). London: Sage.

Douglas, C. (1999). *From surviving to thriving: Black women managers in Britain*. Unpublished PhD dissertation, University of Bath, UK.

Douglas, C. (2002). Using co-operative inquiry with black women managers: Exploring possibilities for moving from surviving to thriving. *Systemic Practice and Action Research, 15*(3), 249–262.

Ekman-Philips, M. (2004). Action research and development coalitions in health care. *Action Research, 2*(4), 349–370.

Fals Borda, O., & Rahman, M. A. (Eds.). (1991). *Action and knowledge: Breaking the monopoly with participatory action research*. New York: Intermediate Technology Publications/Apex Press.

Fisher, D., Rooke, D., & Torbert, W. R. (2000). *Personal and organizational transformations through action inquiry*. Boston: Edge/Work Press.

Flood, R. L. (2001). The relationship of "systems thinking" to action research. In P. Reason & H. Bradbury (Eds.), *Handbook of action research: Participative inquiry and practice* (pp. 133–144). London: Sage.

Foucault, M. (2000). *Power. Essential works of Foucault 1954–1984* (Vol. 3). New York: The New Press.

Freire, P. (1970). *Pedagogy of the oppressed*. New York: Herder & Herder.

Fricke, W. (2003). Discussion forum. *Concepts and Transformation, 8*(3), 217–218, 255–302.

Friedman, V. J. (2001). Action science: Creating communities of inquiry in communities of practice. In P. Reason & H. Bradbury (Eds.), *Handbook of action research: Participative inquiry and practice* (pp. 159–170). London: Sage.

Gergen, K. J. (1999). *An invitation to social construction*. Thousand Oaks: Sage.

Greenwood, D. J. (2002). Action research: Unfulfilled promises and unmet challenges. *Concepts and Transformation, 7*(2), 117–139.

Greenwood, D. J., & Levin, M. (1998). *Introduction to action research: Social research for social change*. Thousand Oaks, CA: Sage.

Gustavsen, B. (2001). Theory and practice: The mediating discourse. In P. Reason & H. Bradbury (Eds.), *Handbook of action research: Participative inquiry and practice* (pp. 17–26). London: Sage.

Gustavsen, B. (2003). Action research and the problem of the single case. *Concepts and Transformation, 8*(1), 93–99.

Hawkins, P. (1988). A phenomenological psychodrama workshop. In P. Reason (Ed.), *Human inquiry in action*. London: Sage.

Heron, J. (1996). *Co-operative inquiry: Research into the human condition*. London: Sage.

Heron, J., & Reason, P. (2001). The practice of co-operative inquiry: Research with rather than on people. In P. Reason & H. Bradbury (Eds.), *Handbook of action research: Participative inquiry and practice* (pp. 179–188). London: Sage.

Kemmis, S. (2001). Exploring the relevance of critical theory for action research: Emancipatory action research in the footsteps of Jürgen Habermas. In P. Reason & H. Bradbury (Eds.), *Handbook of action research: Participative inquiry and practice* (pp. 91–102). London: Sage.

Kristiansen, M., & Bloch-Poulsen, J. (2004). Self-referentiality as a power mechanism: Towards dialogic action research. *Action Research, 2*(4), 371–388.

Ludema, J. D., Cooperrider, D. L., & Barrett, F. J. (2001). Appreciative inquiry: The power of the unconditional positive question. In P. Reason & H. Bradbury (Eds.), *Handbook of action research: Participative inquiry and practice* (pp. 189–199). London: Sage.

Maguire, P. (2001). Uneven ground: Feminisms and action research. In P. Reason & H. Bradbury (Eds.), *Handbook of action research: Participative inquiry and practice* (pp. 59–69). London: Sage.

Marshall, J. (1999). Living life as inquiry. *Systematic Practice and Action Research, 12*(2), 155–171.

Marshall, J. (2001). Self-reflective inquiry practices. In P. Reason & H. Bradbury (Eds.), *Handbook of action research: Participative inquiry and practice* (pp. 433–439). London: Sage.

Marshall, J. (2004). Living systemic thinking: Exploring quality in first person research. *Action Research, 2*(3), 309–329.

Marshall, J., & McLean, A. (1988). Reflection in action: Exploring organizational culture. In P. Reason (Ed.), *Human inquiry in action* (pp. 199–220). London: Sage.

Marshall, J., & Reason, P. (2003). *Introduction to action research* [CD]. Centre for Action Research in Professional Practice, School of Management, University of Bath, UK.

Martin, A. W. (2001). Large-group processes as action research. In P. Reason & H. Bradbury (Eds.), *Handbook of action research: Participative inquiry and practice.* London: Sage.

McArdle, K. L. (2002). Establishing a co-operative inquiry group: The perspective of a "first-time" inquirer. *Systemic Practice and Action Research, 15*(3), 177–189.

McArdle, K. L. (2004). *In-powering spaces: A co-operative inquiry with young women in management.* Unpublished PhD dissertation, University of Bath, UK.

Mead, G. (2001). *Unlatching the gate: Realising my scholarship of living inquiry.* Unpublished PhD dissertation, University of Bath, UK.

Mead, G. (2002). Developing ourselves as leaders: How can we inquiry collaboratively in a hierarchical organization? *Systemic Practice and Action Research, 15*(3), 191–206.

Mienczakowski, J., & Morgan, S. (2001). Ethnodrama: Constructing participatory, experiential and compelling action research through performance. In P. Reason & H. Bradbury (Eds.), *Handbook of action research: Participative inquiry and practice* (pp. 219–227). London: Sage.

Mullett, J., Jung, K., & Hills, M. (2004). Being, becoming and belonging: Getting to ambassadorship, a new metaphor for living and collaborating in the community. *Action Research, 2*(2), 145–165.

Ospina, S., Dodge, J., Godsoe, B., Minieri, J., Reza, S., & Schall, E. (2003). From consent to mutual inquiry: Balancing democracy and authority in action research. *Action Research, 2*(1), 45–66.

Paine, T. (1995). *Rights of Man, Common Sense, and other political writings.* Oxford, UK: Oxford University Press. Original work published 1791.

Pasmore, W. A. (2001). Action research in the workplace: The socio-technical perspective. In P. Reason & H. Bradbury (Eds.), *Handbook of action research: Participative inquiry and practice* (pp. 38–47). London: Sage.

Pratt, J., Gordon, P., & Plamping, D. (1999). *Working whole systems: Putting theory into practice in organizations.* London: King's Fund.

Reason, P. (1988). Whole person medical practice. In P. Reason (Ed.), *Human inquiry in action* (pp. 102–126). London: Sage.

Reason, P. (1999). General medical and complementary practitioners working together: The epistemological demands of collaboration. *Journal of Applied Behavioural Science, 35*(1), 71–86.

Reason, P. (2003a). Doing co-operative inquiry. In J. Smith (Ed.), *Qualitative psychology: A practical guide to methods.* London: Sage.

Reason, P. (2003b). Pragmatist philosophy and action research: Readings and conversation with Richard Rorty. *Action Research, 1*(1), 103–123.

Reason, P. (2006). Choice and quality in action research practice. *Journal of Management Inquiry, 15*(2), 187–203.

Reason, P., & Bradbury, H. (2001). Preface. In P. Reason & H. Bradbury (Eds.), *Handbook of action research: Participative inquiry and practice* (pp. xxiii–xxxi). London: Sage.

Roberts, P. (2003). *Emerging selves in practice: How do I and others create my practice and how does my practice shape me and influence others?* Unpublished PhD dissertation, University of Bath, UK.

Rorty, R. (1999). *Philosophy and social hope.* London: Penguin.

Roth, G. L., & Kleiner, A. (1998). Developing organizational memory through learning histories. *Organizational Dynamics, 27*(2), 43–61.

Rudolph, J. W., Taylor, S. S., & Foldy, E. G. (2001). Collaborative off-line reflection: A way to develop skill in action science and action inquiry. In P. Reason & H. Bradbury (Eds.), *Handbook of action research: Participative inquiry and practice* (pp. 405–412). London: Sage.

Schön, D. A. (1983). *The reflective practitioner.* New York: Basic Books.

Selener, D. (1997). *Participatory action research and social change.* Ithaca, NY: Cornell Participatory Action Research Network, Cornell University.

Shotter, J. (1993). *Cultural politics of everyday life: Social construction and knowing of the third kind.* Buckingham, UK: Open University Press.

Stanley, L., & Wise, S. (1983). *Breaking out: Feminist consciousness and feminist research.* London: Routledge and Kegan Paul.

Torbert, W. R. (2001). The practice of action inquiry. In P. Reason & H. Bradbury (Eds.), *Handbook of action research: Participative inquiry and practice* (pp. 250–260). London: Sage.

Torbert, W. R. (2004). *Action inquiry: The secret of timely and transforming leadership.* San Francisco: Berrett-Koehler.

Toulmin, S., & Gustavsen, B. (Eds.). (1996). *Beyond theory: Changing organizations through participation.* Amsterdam: John Benjamins.

Trist, E., & Bamforth, K. (1951). Some social and psychological consequences of the longwall method of coal-getting. *Human Relations, 4,* 3–38.

Weisbord, M. R., & Janoff, S. (1995). *Future search: An action guide to finding common ground in organizations and communities.* San Francisco: Berrett-Koehler.

Whitehead, J. (1989). Creating a living educational theory from questions of the kind: How can I improve my practice? *Cambridge Journal of Education, 19*(1), 41–52.

Whitehead, J. (2000). How do I improve my practice? Creating and legitimating an epistemology of practice. *Reflective Practice, 1*(1), 91–104.

9

Organization Development Diagnosis

CRAIG C. LUNDBERG

Ask members of the organization develop-ment (OD) community, especially expe-rienced OD practitioners and serious OD scholars, about the activities collectively called diagnostic and just about everyone will acknowledge that diagnosis is an essential stage of planned or managed change endeavors. The reasoning typically given for the importance of diagnosis is simple and straightforward: Without an appropriate diagnosis, how can managers and other change agents really know what is going on in the organization and what can or should be done to enhance current orga-nization functioning and effectiveness of future development? Ask further about what diag-nosis is and how it is accomplished and you are likely to hear a wide variety of responses, some simply general, some technique centered, some reflecting experiences with certain sizes and types of organizations or industries, some reflecting a personally preferred approach, and some suited to a certain type of change target or intervention.

Turning to the OD literature one quickly discovers that the diagnostic portion of it is surprisingly small, uneven, piecemeal, and scat-tered, that diagnosis usually is underempha-sized (given its acknowledged significance) and seemingly simplified. There are just a few books devoted exclusively to diagnosis, such as Levinson (1972), Mahler (1974), Weisbord (1978), Harrison (1987), and Howard and Associates (1994). OD textbooks and readers typically emphasize change management prac-tices and interventions and devote few chapters to diagnosis, mostly offering alternative diag-nostic models (e.g., Connor & Lake, 1988; Cummings & Worley, 2005). Academic OD books and articles almost invariably describe and example the author's inductively derived conceptual framework for understanding and assessing organizations, typically reflecting sys-tem theory (Cummings, 1980). These range in scope and complexity from the simple to mod-estly complex, for example, from Leavitt's (1965) four-component diamond (task, people, technology, and structure) through Weisbord's (1976) well-known six-box model (purposes, structure, rewards, helpful mechanisms, and relationships all around leadership and within an environment) to Burke-Litwin's (1992) well-known model with 12 major components and several feedback loops.

The very large OD practitioner's literature rarely discusses diagnosis per se—the exception being portions of case examples—emphasizing instead change management roles, relationships, and interventions (e.g., the well-known Addison-Wesley OD series). Perhaps most surprising of all is that the OD research literature neglects diagnosis (e.g., the annual volumes of *Research in Organizational Change and Development* from 1987 on).

If we agree about the importance of diagnosis in OD work and can acknowledge that the OD literature about diagnosis has neither coalesced conceptually nor standardized as to its practices, it may be time to pose and address the following three general questions. The first question asks for a review: What is our current understanding of what OD diagnosis is and how it is done? The second question inquires into meaning: How might we begin to conceptually understand diagnosis? The third question concerns the future: What appears to be the needed or predicted development of OD diagnostic conceptualization and practice? Our responses to these three questions will be elaborated in several sections. The first section discusses the metaphorical roots and the definitional variety of diagnosis. The next section argues for a sensemaking perspective of diagnosis, that is, diagnosis as sensemaking as well as a sequence of sensemaking frames with which to organize our diagnostic thinking and practices. In the third section we review and assess the diagnostic process in terms of its agents, its initiation, data acquisition, data sharing and meaning making, and its outcomes. In the fourth section we will suggest the challenges—technical, conceptual, and circumstantial—for enhancing OD diagnosis in the years ahead.

MANY MEANINGS OF DIAGNOSIS

In still developing fields of practice and knowledge, central ideas tend to be somewhat loosely and variously defined, with fragmented agreement on their definitional essence. In the field of OD, diagnosis is one such idea. Few OD scholars or practitioners share more than the most rudimentary meaning. Subsequently, diagnostic practices also vary greatly.

The major metaphorical image of the term *diagnosis* goes back to early medical practice. People feeling ill seek out a physician who listens, observes, takes a history, and does tests to clarify the patient's symptoms and current state. The physician then interprets the information gathered, comparing it to the current model of health, and names the illness to complete the diagnosis. The physician then prescribes some treatment that enables the patient to regain his or her health. OD diagnosis is generally understood to parallel medical diagnosis. We should take note of what is presumed in this metaphor. Ill health prompts the visit to the physician, who is an expert, who gathers information, and who uses a model of normal health on which to base his or her diagnosis—elements congruent with the early use of OD consultants by managers for reestablishing desired levels of internal efficiency and effectiveness and short-term development. As is well known, however, management, consultancy, and OD have all loosened their adherence to even general one-best-practice ideals.

Another, albeit very minor metaphorical image for the OD diagnostician is as a detective. As Steele (1975) reminds us, detectives search extensively for cues and evidence, are only temporarily involved with a set of people, sometimes actively intervene to create relevant information, often collaborate with one or more others in the investigation, and are quite expert and experienced in seeking and sifting through information even though it appears intuitive to observers. OD diagnosis is presumed to parallel detective investigations; passive and active fact finding and careful comparisons to a standard of normal behavior by skilled experts will reveal the motive, means, and opportunity behind organization problems. Like the physician image, the detective image of OD diagnosis probably reflects an older, conventional command-and-control management style and a content-focused, planned change consultancy.

If diagnosis is central to OD work, one might reasonably expect to find a clear definition of it. This is not the case. Much of the OD literature simply sidesteps defining diagnosis or defines it in idiosyncratic ways.

Examination of a variety of definitions suggests one major commonality and many, many differences (Alderfer, 1977; Burke, 1982; Connor & Lake, 1988; Cummings & Worley, 2005; French & Bell, 1999; Harrison, 1987; Rothwell, Sullivan, & McLean, 1995; Weisbord, 1978). They all seem to agree that diagnosis involves one or more processes (e.g., gathering, collecting, identifying, assessing, analyzing). However, they differ in many ways:

- Although many include the word *problem,* some say diagnosis begins with a problem, others say diagnosis sharpens or defines a change problem, and others say diagnosis identifies a problem area.
- Many definitions state that diagnosis involves data gathering or information gathering (and it is not clear whether *data* and *information* are meant to be synonymous). This data or information is about the current situation of an organization, opportunities for change, or problems previously identified.
- Diagnosis is also sometimes defined as assessing, understanding, or analyzing one or more of the following:
  - Causes of problems, gaps between actual and desired performances, or the situation in which change is anticipated
  - The clarification of change objectives
  - The parts or components of the change target system
  - The system's readiness and capacity for change
  - The system's resources available for pursuing change

- Definitions may or may not indicate that diagnosis is guided by a model of organizations.
- Similarly, definitions do or do not state whether diagnosis is done just once or may be repeated.
- Most definitions do not state who does a diagnosis or whether it is or can be done collaboratively.
- Diagnosis sometimes is defined as preceding action planning or as pointing to or suggesting some interventions.

Although perhaps we shouldn't expect too much from definitions of OD diagnosis, available definitions do leave much unclear, such as whether diagnosis is a descriptive or prescriptive activity, what is a problem, what might be the time frame of diagnosis, what methods are involved in diagnosis, what constitutes valid information or what amount or scope of information or data is appropriate, how conceptual models are to be used, and, significantly, who does a diagnosis.

For all of the definitional variety, however, there seem to be two themal meanings of OD diagnosis, seen separately or in combination in all definitions. One meaning of diagnosis can be called "analytic understanding": the more or less explicit, more or less systematic, use of ideas, models, and theories to describe the parts of organizations, their relationship to one another, the whole organization, and the organization's environments historically, or at present, or in a desired future. The other meaning of diagnosis can be called "issue identification and clarification" and refers to either the selection of some focal symptom or, more commonly, to the underlying dysfunctions of an organization, the basic problems behind observed symptoms, perceived gaps between current reality and goals, or unclear, inconsistent, or missing goals. Not contained in available definitions of diagnosis but implied in discussions of diagnostic activities is a third, albeit very minor set of meanings, namely "self-diagnosis" (Bartee & Cheyunsky, 1977), diagnosis as a process that sets expectations for organization members, sometimes energizes them, and occasionally prompts members to correct their own behavior.

As discussed earlier, there is probably one major metaphor for diagnosis (i.e., what physicians do) and one other, much more minor one (i.e., what detectives do). Both of these images are longstanding ones, more appropriate to OD as simple planned change, and thus restrictive for the contemporary array of organization change thinking and practice. Both definitional avoidance and variety in OD diagnosis and the definitions people tend to use leave organization diagnosis more of an art than systematic practice.

MAKING SENSE WITH AND ABOUT DIAGNOSIS

The two themal process meanings in OD diagnosis definitions, analytic understanding and issue identification and clarification, share a common fundamental process: making sense. In a very fundamental way, diagnosis is about making sense of change situations and making sense of the focus of change.

How to make sense of the world we inhabit and our experience of it has fascinated and puzzled scholars (James, 1890; Strauss, 1956) and managers (McCaskey, 1982) for a very long time. However, only in recent decades has sensemaking begun to be deemed important for organization studies (Louis, 1980; Starbuck & Milliken, 1988; Weick, 1995; Westley, 1990).

The main features of sensemaking are as follows: Sensemaking is grounded in identity (i.e., who the sensemaker is and is becoming appears to be highly determinant); sensemaking is a process of human construction that begins when a person notices something (a cue) in the ongoing flow of his or her experience, and the sensemaker uses his or her learned sociocultural experience as a conceptual frame to retrospectively create a plausible, coherent interpretation or explanation of noticed cues. Thus sensemaking has just three elements: a frame, a cue, and the relationship between frame and cue. Frames are past moments of socialization, of learned precedent and tradition. Cues are present moments of perceived experience; they exist within and are noticeable in terms of a frame learned from first- and second-hand experiences in sociocultural systems (e.g., family, schools, projects, organizations, occupations, and communities, all such systems at least partially the creation of the sensemaker). Sensemaking thus is more about sociocultural plausibility than factual reality; that is, the sensemaking process generates meaning by relating a cue to a frame.

Frames are configurations of beliefs, assumptions, values, and factual knowledge. Frames can and do vary greatly in their phenomenological scope (e.g., from a very small event to a whole era) and in their fidelity to reality. Cue noticeability within a frame is a function either of learned symbolic importance or cue interruption (i.e., when something expected to happen didn't or when something not expected to happen did). Cues are more or less emotionally arousing and energizing depending on the operative frame.

We can now understand OD diagnosis as a process whereby a diagnostician uses a frame about organizations, their purpose, external relations, structure, functioning, and member behavior to notice cues relevant to appropriate or desirable performance and then understand them. In addition, a sensemaking perspective enables us to further see that one's choice of a diagnostic model (a frame) is likely to be selected largely in terms of a salient organization change strategy (an encompassing frame), which in turn is selected in accordance with some ongoing OD practitioner mindset (an even wider sociocultural frame). OD diagnosis thus is a process composed of several activities that uses an organization model (a diagnostic frame) in accordance with an OD strategy (a frame about organization change), which in turn reflects the mindset of an OD practitioner (a subcultural frame). Figure 9.1 graphically shows this set of OD's nested sensemaking frames.

Figure 9.1   The Nested Frames of Organization Development

A diagnostic frame is a set of related ideas or categories of ideas that guide data acquisition and meaning making. There are many available, typically called an organization model. They vary from simple to complex in terms of the number of their ideas and focus on one or more levels of analysis (i.e., individual, group, and, most commonly, a whole organization) and usually include the focal phenomena's context. Most such models today reflect a general system perspective (Burke & Litwin, 1992; Nadler & Tushman, 1977; Tichy, 1983). They ostensibly promote systematic data attention, categorization, and interpretation, although in practice only parts of the model may actually be used. Such models guide diagnostic work in that they specify what information is considered data, leaving the amount of data and the people and methods for gathering it unspecified.

The choice of a diagnostic organization model and its use will almost always reflect the agent of change's preferred frame about how to accomplish organization change. The major known change strategies—planned change (Burke, 2002), action research (Elden & Chisholm, 1993), process consultation (Schein, 1987), and guided change (Kerber, 2001)—represent the major frame archetypes. Change strategies differ in several basic, consequential ways, such as whether organization change is considered to be naturally episodic or continuous; the ratio of attention to content or process data; whether the stimulus for organization change resides in external changes or internal change opportunities; whether internal organizational difficulties are assumed to be mostly about the distribution of power, the mobilization of energy, or communication patterns

(Lippit, Watson, & Westley, 1958); whether their focus is on observable reality or on socially constructed meanings; the preferred model of the change agent–client relationship (e.g., doctor–patient, supplier–purchaser, or facilitator–peer) (Lundberg & Finney, 1987; Schein, 1999); and the strategy's focus on one or some combination of the organization's fundamental tasks: internal readjustment, external realignment, or anticipation of the future (Lundberg, 1989).

Preferences among change strategy frames reflect the subcultural frame we call OD practitioner mindset. The organization's dominant coalition, those who make the major decisions about organization affairs and resource allocations, typically but not always top management, and the relevant OD professionals, almost always share a set of beliefs, values, assumptions, and ways of thinking, derived from industry and occupational experience, that prompt them to embrace one or another organization change strategy. Mindsets are above all ideologies. They bundle preferred organization metaphors (Bolman & Deal, 1997; Morgan, 1986), preferred strategic beliefs about how to govern, compete, satisfy stakeholders, and conduct change (Lorsch, 1985), assumptions about the nature and interests of organization members (McGregor, 1960; Miles & Creed, 1995), and the degree to which consequentially oriented, rational, analytical thinking is valued and practiced (Ingersol & Adam, 1992; March, 1994). Although no classification of mindsets yet exists, some sense of their variety is revealed by contrasting characterizations of managerial style, from command and control to facilitator, from administrator to liberator, from authoritarian to steward.

We emphasize that diagnosis in its essence is sensemaking, both the sensemaking that produces analytical understanding and the sensemaking that is issue identification and clarification. Because sense is always made by means of a socioculturally learned cognitive–emotional frame, diagnostic sensemaking relies on frames that say what data are and imply how, when, and where they may be gathered. For sensemaking, frames matter.

DIAGNOSTIC PROCESS

At base, OD is concerned with perceived current or anticipated uncertainty and its associated emotional arousal (Lundberg, 2002). Generally, organization change therefore is either reactive to current uncertainty or proactive to thwart anticipated uncertainty. Organization change intentionally attempts to reduce or preclude the distress associated with felt anxiety. Uncertainty-fueled distress occurs when organization members do not understand what is or is not going on or why things are happening or not happening as expected or desired. Organization change ideally makes internal or external circumstances less ambiguous and less distressing.

Uncertainty and distress are in the eye of the beholder, however, seen through the lens of one's sensemaking frames. Organization members, especially central, influential ones and their internal and external agents, hold and share ideas of what constitutes acceptable ranges of personal and organizational action and inertia. Although it is a truism to state that organizations and their environments are always in flux through evolutionary and intended changes, it is the deviations from the expected that bring the uncertainty that initiates OD. Deviations from expected and hoped-for performance and outcome levels thus cue the threshold need for possible organization changes. The cues triggering diagnosis are of several kinds: frame-defined discrepancies, such as goal overachievement or underachievement

(problems) and goal conflicts or inconsistencies (predicaments); frame-defined symbols of what is organizationally valued and hence to be sought or avoided, such as retrenchment; and frame-defined tipping points (Gladwell, 2000), where a critical mass is suddenly and unexpectedly jolted out of its quasiequilibrium into a new state (e.g., morale plummets, a new market takes off). Triggering cues often are emotionally arousing. Although they usually mobilize concern and energy in support of change endeavors, when they are extreme they may paralyze both thought and action.

Cues of deviations, when recognized, may or may not prompt enough concern or felt distress to do something about the situation. If so, initial decisions are whether to do something sooner or later, whether to seek assistance, and whether the present understandings of the cues and situation are sufficient. The prevailing mindset thus will lead either to taking some action or to initiating planned change. If the latter, diagnostic planning is the first step. Diagnostic planning—explicit or not, detailed or not—specifies the who, how, where, and when, and what information will be acquired and used. The alternatives about who, how, when, and where are many; the choices between them largely reflect the preferred planned change strategy.

The goals of diagnosis have been variously described. They range from simply providing specific information, to solving a specific problem (Block, 1981, p. 141, goes so far as to assert that "the purpose of a diagnosis is to mobilize action on a problem"), to assessing organization effectiveness, to recommending ways to improve effectiveness, to contributing to organization learning (Harrison, 1987). Such goals probably reflect the perceived validity and importance of triggering cues. If the presenting problem is presumed to be clear, then diagnosis focuses on analytic understanding as a basis for intervention planning. If the triggering cues are unclear concerns, then diagnosis can initially focus either on immediate issue clarification followed by intervention planning or on first acquiring via analysis a better understanding of the situation as a basis for issue clarification.

However, it should be noted that today much OD is conducted in the midst of change efforts already under way, such as reengineering, mergers and acquisitions, strategic alliances, diversity programs, new leadership, and internationalizing markets. Surprisingly often, these sorts of changes run into trouble, and OD is initiated to help. In these situations, the luxury of doing a diagnosis before intervention planning isn't feasible; it's really diagnosis on the run to swiftly fix management-identified problems (Burke, Javitch, Waclawski, & Church, 1997). Judicious sampling and increased member involvement in data gathering and analysis often can overcome the time constraints and data paucity of midstream diagnosis.

Diagnostic agents, the "who" of a diagnosis, may play several roles. Some are organizational support roles (e.g., OD champion, resource provider, nonclient monitor) performed by one or more managers or staff personnel. There are also usually several roles associated with the unit of diagnostic focus (e.g., clients, informants, and representatives of those affected). And there are the several diagnostic roles (e.g., for diagnosis planning, data collection, data analysis, data feedback, and dissemination of the diagnosis). Because diagnosis always involves more than one person, the quality of their relationships is important. Whether or not there are third parties (e.g., external consultants, internal staff), helping and trust are key considerations, not always easy to establish and maintain given the inevitable differences in power and status between diagnostic players.

As for other phases of OD, we can ask of diagnosis, "Which activities may be usefully shared?" There are obviously many alternative patterns of involvement depending on the diagnostic project's size and scope, available diagnostic competencies, time availability and project commitment, and so on. These involvement alternatives can range a great deal, from one extreme of a dedicated team with joint collaborative responsibility for all diagnostic activities, to a designated set of people who may individually take part in one or some aspects of diagnosis, to a solo diagnostician who relates to others just to gather data and feed it back. Involvement in diagnosis, especially real collaboration, is widely believed to accomplish much: to reduce resistance to change, to overcome pluralistic ignorance (Margulies & Wallace, 1973), to overcome the semisecretive manner of most top managements, to mobilize energy for interventions, to improve the quality of a diagnosis, to provide opportunities for diagnostic skill building among organization members, and to increase ownership of the diagnosis.

These agent considerations apply to diagnoses that range from a superficial scan to a detailed, in-depth assessment. Sampling here is determinate: from a small convenience sample of member opinions on what is going well and what is not to larger, representative samples of people, places, activities, and events. Diagnoses may be episodic or continuous; for example, French and Bell (1999, p. 50) define diagnosis as the "continuous collection of system data." Today, more organizations regularly survey members about their attitudes, the organization's climate, group work and interunit relationships, and the like (Mahler, 1974). Data acquired in this way are almost always viewed as benefiting management even if they are not shared widely or used for change diagnosis. Regular survey data may point to possible issues and to benchmarking some types of change but are suspect if solely relied on for a deeper diagnostic understanding.

Data collection in service of diagnosis has the generic objective of providing valid and useful information (Argyris, 1970). Valid information has credibility because it is descriptive and verifiable by others and by multiple methods. Useful information is that which is relevant to the user, that which refers to things that are acceptable and manipulatable (Newstrom & Lillyquist, 1979). Data is information specified by the ideas and categories of an organization model. But how much data? Data collection is subject to sampling decisions and to methodological, resource, and relationship constraints. The four basic methods (interview, questionnaire, observation, and secondary data, all of which can be more or less structured) all have different advantages and problems. These are nicely compared in Table 9.1, borrowed from Nadler (1977, p. 119). In addition, there are some seldom used methods (e.g., unobtrusive measures) and several invented for OD-using groups to gather and order data of varying degrees of specificity (e.g., force-field analysis technique, organization mirror, focus groups).

Data gathering methods can be compared along several dimensions (Margulies & Wallace, 1973), from direct to indirect, from structured to unstructured, from time-consuming to less

so, from easy to administer to difficult, from gathering data useful mostly for analysis to mostly useful for problem solving. Data collection methods can be evaluated in terms of many criteria: whether they provide respondent confidentially, whether they are flexible and efficient (in terms of time and money), whether they convey the concern and interest of the diagnostician, whether they elicit rich data, whether they guard against bias by either the informant or collection agent, and whether their data are easy to categorize, summarize, and represent (cf. Beer, 1980). However, the choice of methods will be made primarily because they provide the kind of data needed by the organization model in use given time and resource constraints. Because model categories tend to be somewhat general, mixing methods is common diagnostic practice.

With data collected, diagnosis moves to sensemaking and meaning sharing. The generic objective of this phase of diagnosis is for the

Table 9.1   Comparison of Data Collection Methods

Method	Major Advantages	Major Potential Problems
Interviews	Adaptive; allow data collection on a range of possible subjects.	Can be expensive.
	Sources of rich data.	Interviewer can bias responses.
	Empathic.	Coding and interpretation problems.
	Process of interviewing can build rapport.	Self-report bias.
Questionnaires	Responses can be quantified and easily summarized.	Nonempathic.
	Easy to use with large samples.	Predetermined questions may miss issues.
	Inexpensive.	Data may be overinterpreted.
	Can obtain large volume of data.	Response bias.
Observations	Collect data on behavior rather than reports of behavior.	Interpretation and coding problems.
	Real time, not retrospective.	Sampling is a problem.
	Adaptive.	Observer bias and reliability.
		Costly.
Secondary data and unobtrusive measures	Nonreactive; no-response bias.	Access and retrieval possibly a problem.
	High face validity.	Potential validity problems.
	Easily quantified.	Coding and interpretation.

data and its meanings to be owned by all stakeholders (i.e., personally accepted as a basis for thought and action). This usually initially requires that the data be ordered and synthesized (i.e., put into the categories and relationships of the organization model, sometimes statistically manipulated, then summarized or subjected to theme extraction). The reconstituted data are then fed back to organization participants in oral or written form, with timing and confidentiality crucial concerns. This feedback may go to just the diagnostic sponsors or may cascade downward and outward to everyone potentially touched by the data, depending on the OD mindset frame and time availability.

Data feedback forms the basis for issue identification and clarification and the basis for situational understanding. The meaning of the data, raw or synthesized, becomes interpreted as a function of the operative organization model in combination with perceptions of issue urgency, system inertia or receptivity, and readiness for change of the dominant coalition and members. Diagnostic sensemaking is about situational understanding in light of identified issues. Diagnostic data, analysis, and clarified issues may or may not be disseminated within or outside the focal analytic unit at this point, typically depending on the mindset of the managers and OD professionals involved. If dissemination is viewed as desirable, the design questions of when, how, to whom, and what become pertinent. Dissemination of synthesized data is believed to serve several purposes, such as creating a sense of urgency for action, co-opting key people, justifying the OD work begun, and giving attention to matters little thought about.

The outcomes of a diagnosis as implied earlier are several. The manifest outcomes reflect the twin sensemaking themes of diagnosis: a better, perhaps deeper, understanding of how things work and how they got that way (usually including change resource availability, change champions, and system readiness) and issue clarification and ownership. Most reasonable

diagnoses also hold some leads for intervention planning. Commonly there are latent outcomes from a diagnosis, too. Data collection and analysis skills and issue identification and clarification skills are likely to be enhanced by diagnostic involvement. Management or member motivation for change undoubtedly will be affected—up or down. If the data suggest that little change is needed or that the change probably won't threaten individuals or units with job, status, or power losses, then resistances tend to fade, and the motivation that comes from feasible challenges will rise. In general, expectations for the initiation of change, small or large, specific or general, are likely to increase with knowledge that a diagnosis has occurred.

As described earlier, the OD diagnosis process is not conceptually very well specified or rationalized. Nothing appears to have become standardized—from diagnostic purpose to who is involved, from how data are collected to how they are made sense of, and so on. Diagnostic practice is still an art; alternatives of practice and organization models have not yet been assessed comparatively. However, the guidance in the literature for bundling and sequencing the variety of diagnostic activities often seems plausible when prescribed by experienced OD contributors. However, the centrality of diagnosis for OD suggests that we soon have to move beyond the rules that constitute contemporary diagnostic practice.

DIAGNOSTIC CHALLENGES

As the practice of OD goes forward, what sorts of challenges are likely to be in store for diagnosis? To respond to this question we will widen our lens beyond diagnosis per se. We begin by briefly reviewing the emerging trends in organization environments and how they are reflected in new and emerging organization forms and the changing nature of managerial work. Next we speculate on what these sorts of changes imply for the three nested types of frames that influence diagnosis (i.e., shifts in OD practitioner mindsets, organization strategies, and the organization models that guide diagnostic practices). Finally, we begin to speculate on the technical challenges to diagnosis frame modifications imply.

The business environment of organizations has recently been characterized as dynamic and hypercompetitive (D'Aveni, 1994) or hyperturbulent (Mohrman, 2001). These dramatic labels refer to the globalization of markets and industries; shortening planning and product life cycles; the sophistication of technologies, especially in communication and logistics; rapidly changing talent pools in terms of demographics and diversity; fluctuations in the cost of capital; changes in employee attitudes about such things as their psychological contract, career trajectories, and work–life balance; the greatly increased proliferation of information and access to it; political uncertainties; and much more.

The impact of environmental changes on organization structures and practices has also been widely reported. Whereas traditional organization forms emphasized the advantages associated with greater size, role clarity, formalization, and specialization, new environmental conditions promote the emergence of new forms that supposedly encourage speed, flexibility, innovation, and boundaryless integration (Clarke & Clegg, 1998; Volberda, 1996). There has been an outpouring of new organization form labels from *postbureaucratic* to *self-managing*, from *cellular* to *boundaryless*, from *virtual* to *holonomic*, from *horizontal* to *centerless*. Recently, Palmer and Dunford (1997) identified eight recurring aspects of these new organization forms: collaborative networks or alliances, outsourcing of noncore activities, disaggregation of business units, delayering, reduced internal and external organization boundaries, flexible work groups, empowerment, and short-term staffing. These features constitute many of the goals of contemporary OD and the contexts of diagnostic work.

The sweeping and dramatic transformations of the workplace as just indicated have also ushered in changes in the nature of managerial work itself. Recent views see managerial work as becoming more intensive in response to changes in the business environment and organization structures. Managers say that their work and the demands placed on them have changed greatly, and they have had little training to help them cope with the changes (Cooper, 1998). For example, delayering takes out some managers but rarely takes out the work they did. Most managers today report that their units have fewer, less secure people doing more with more task fragmentation. Most managers also report having to deal with much more information, spending more time dealing with organization politics, having to rely less and less on positional authority, and dealing with more work-related change even as their own jobs become more fragmented. Longer hours, role overload, and reduced role clarity lead more to manager stress.

The changing circumstances sketched here constitute many of the opportunities for and the contexts of contemporary OD. Managers have to make sense of what their organization's environments require organizationally and to make sense of what new organization forms and practices mean for work, employees, and their own roles. Traditional mindsets are unlikely to suffice. Preferences for rational, analytic, command-and-control managerial practices and episodic, lightly disguised imposed change no longer seem very appropriate. Moving toward a managerial mindset that is somehow more positive, experimental, and organizationally liberating (Cameron, Dutton, & Quinn, 2003), more existential, and more transformational now seems more essential, perhaps mandatory. At minimum, the beliefs, values, and assumptions of emerging mindsets probably will have to embrace ongoing multilevel change; pursue complexity rather than simplicity, recursiveness rather than linearity, shaping rather than managing; and rely on adaptation rather than design. Indicators of the contemporary mindset movement include the attention being given to such things as continuous quality improvement, organization learning, customer-focused service, and employee empowerment.

Moving away from overformalized, overfunctionalized, over–output determined organization forms and practices—and their associated managerial mindsets—probably will also mean a shift in preferred organization change strategies. Until quite recently, OD has been dominated by a strategy of planned change. As suggested earlier, however, emerging external and internal organization circumstances probably are altering the managerial mindsets that dominant coalition members use to choose between change strategies. It seems easy to predict less planned change and more short-cycle, more process-oriented, more collaborative strategies (e.g., the several varieties of action research and process consultation). These types of change strategies are also becoming more embedded in normal managerial practice. Perhaps soon we will be able to explicate and codify the change strategies that directly affect efficacies and uncertainties.

If environmental changes result in new organization forms and practices and changes in mindsets, then we can anticipate the creation of a new generation of diagnostic organization models also. To enhance the analytic understanding and issue clarification of diagnosis, we will probably need organization models that are more complex, more explicitly environmentally contingent, and more attuned to nuances of mindset and emotion and permit the identification of syndromes instead of just the causes associated with particular symptoms, change targets, or interventions. Diagnostic models of the future will more often be dynamic process models than static variance ones (Mohr, 1982) and probably reflect complexity (Svyantek & Brown, 2000), chaos (Prigogine & Stengers, 1984), and self-synchronizing system theories (Strogatz, 2003) and their kin. The presumption prevalent today that any organization model is appropriate for most or all situations seems increasingly specious. Perhaps the time

has come for more multilevel frame variety about organization models.

The sorts of challenges noted earlier in external and internal organization circumstances, the predicted shifts in organization forms and practices, and the probable frame changes in managerial mindsets, change strategies, and organization models in turn will prompt many changes in diagnostic practices. Although some of these practices can be reasonably anticipated, such as assumption surfacing techniques (Mitroff & Linstone, 1993), the creation of system benchmarking metrics (Mackenzie, 2003), and the standardization of cause-maps, most cannot. Computer-assisted data display and analysis techniques are appearing frequently. How to systematically acquire and analyze important new sorts of data (e.g., network, cultural, and emotional) are technical challenges just now being seriously attempted (cf. Davey & Symon, 2001). Similarly, techniques for explicating syndromes, self-correcting issues, transorganization phenomena, and the like, though desirable, remain beyond reach at present. However, it does seem safe to predict that a variety of new diagnostic data gathering and analysis practices will soon appear.

CONCLUSION

This chapter has reminded us that organization diagnosis is both central to and crucial for OD. Regardless of the importance of diagnosis, however, we have noted that at present it consists of a potpourri of loosely rationalized practices and that diagnosis remains conceptually glossed. To provide a common understanding of what diagnosis is and does, we have begun to reconceptualize it through the lens of sensemaking.

The twin meanings of organization diagnosis, that is, coming to an analytic understanding of the situation and identifying and clarifying any issues in the situation, are both, in essence, sensemaking activities. Diagnosis thus depends on the sensemaking derived from an organization model, which in turn reflects both a change strategy frame and the shared mindset frame of the organization's OD practitioners. This nested sequence of sensemaking frames—mindset, organization change strategy, and organization models—begins to bring some order to the diagnostic process and alert us about how to move toward a more conceptually anchored diagnosis.

The ongoing, perhaps accelerating changes in organization environments present many challenges to OD diagnosis. As new organization forms and practices continue to evolve, the frames that guide OD will also require deliberate development. We can anticipate more diagnostic frame variety and more kinds of diagnostic practice. Perhaps we stand at the threshold of a real diagnostic systemization.

REFERENCES

Alderfer, C. P. (1977). Organization development. *Annual Review of Psychology, 28*, 197–223.

Argyris, C. (1970). *Intervention theory and method: A behavioral science view.* Reading, MA: Addison-Wesley.

Bartee, E. M., & Cheyunski, F. (1977). A method for process-oriented organizational diagnosis. *Journal of Applied Behavioral Science, 13*, 53–68.

Beer, M. (1980). *Organization change and development.* Santa Monica, CA: Goodyear.

Block, P. (1981). *Flawless consulting: A guide to getting your expertise used.* San Diego, CA: Pfeiffer.

Bolman, L., & Deal, T. E. (1997). *Reframing organizations: Artistry, choice and leadership* (2nd ed.). San Francisco: Jossey-Bass.

Burke, W. W. (1982). *Organization development: Principles and practices.* Boston: Little, Brown.

Burke, W. W. (2002). *Organization change.* Thousand Oaks, CA: Sage.

Burke, W. W., Javitch, M., Waclawski, J., & Church, A. H. (1997). The dynamics of midstream consulting. *Consulting Psychology Journal: Practice and Research, 49*(2), 83–95.

Burke, W. W., & Litwin, G. H. (1992). A causal model of organizational performance and change. *Journal of Management, 18*(3), 532–545.

Cameron, K. S., Dutton, J. E., & Quinn, R. E. (2003). *Positive organizational scholarship: Foundations of a new discipline.* San Francisco: Berrett-Koehler.

Clarke, T., & Clegg, S. (1998). *Changing paradigms: The transformation of management knowledge for the 21st century.* London: HarperCollins.

Connor, P. E., & Lake, L. K. (1988). *Managing organizational change.* New York: Praeger.

Cooper, C. L. (1998). The changing psychological contract at work. *Work & Stress, 12*, 97–100.

Cummings, T. G. (1980). *Systems theory for organization development.* New York: John Wiley & Sons.

Cummings, T. G., & Worley, C. G. (2005). *Organization development and change* (8th ed.). Cincinnati, OH: Southwestern College Publishing.

D'Aveni, R. A. (1994). *Hypercompetition: Managing the dynamics of strategic maneuvering.* New York: Free Press.

Davey, K. M., & Symon, G. (2001). Recent approaches to the qualitative analyses of organizational culture. In C. Cooper, S. Cartwright, & R. C. Early (Eds.), *The international handbook of organizational culture and climate* (pp. 123–142). New York: John Wiley & Sons.

Elden, M., & Chisholm, R. (1993). Emerging varieties of action research: Introduction to the special issue. *Human Relations, 46*, 121–142.

French, W. L., & Bell, C. H. (1999). *Organization development: Behavioral science interventions for organization improvement* (6th ed.). Englewood Cliffs, NJ: Prentice Hall.

Gladwell, M. (2000). *The tipping point: How little things can make a big difference.* Boston: Little, Brown.

Harrison, M. I. (1987). *Diagnosing organizations: Methods, models, and processes.* Beverly Hills, CA: Sage.

Howard, A., and Associates. (1994). *Diagnosis for organizational change.* New York: Guilford Press.

Ingersoll, V. H., & Adam, G. B. (1992). *The tacit organization.* Greenwich, CT: JAI.

James, W. (1890). *The principles of psychology* (Vols. 1 & 2). New York: Dover.

Kerber, K. W. (2001). Change in human systems: From planned change to guided change. In A. F. Buono (Ed.), *Current trends in management consulting* (pp. 145–170). Greenwich, CT: Information Age Publishing.

Leavitt, H. J. (1965). Applied organizational change in industry. In J. G. March (Ed.), *Handbook of organizations* (pp. 1144–1170). New York: Rand McNally.

Levinson, H. (1972). *Organizational diagnosis.* Cambridge, MA: Harvard University Press.

Lippit, R., Watson, J., & Westley, B. (1958). *The dynamics of planned change.* New York: Harcourt, Brace.

Lorsch, J. W. (1985). Strategic myopia: Culture as an invisible barrier to change. In R. H. Kilman, M. J. Saxton, & R. Serpa (Eds.), *Gaining control of the corporate culture* (pp. 84–102). San Francisco: Jossey-Bass.

Louis, M. R. (1980). Surprise and sensemaking: What newcomers experience in entering unfamiliar organizational settings. *Administrative Science Quarterly, 25,* 226–251.

Lundberg, C. C. (1989). On organizational learning: Implications and opportunities for expanding organizational development. In R. W. Woodman & W. A. Passmore (Eds.), *Research in organizational change and development* (Vol. 3, pp. 61–82). Greenwich, CT: JAI.

Lundberg, C. C. (2002). Consultancy foundations: Toward a general theory. In A. F. Buono (Ed.), *Developing knowledge and value in management consulting* (pp. 153–168). Greenwich, CT: Information Age Publishing.

Lundberg, C. C., & Finney, M. (1987). Emerging models of consultancy. *Consultation, 6*(1), 32–42.

Mackenzie, K. D. (2003). Dynamic congruency. In M. A. Rahim, R. Golembiewski, & K. D. Mackenzie (Eds.), *Current topics in management* (Vol. 8, pp. 19–42). New Brunswick, NJ: Transaction.

Mahler, W. R. (1974). *Diagnostic studies.* Reading, MA: Addison-Wesley.

March, J. G. (1994). *A primer on decision making.* New York: Free Press.

Margulies, N., & Wallace, J. (1973). *Organizational change: Techniques and applications.* Glenview, IL: Scott Foresman.

McCaskey, M. B. (1982). *The executive challenge.* Marshfield, MA: Pitman.

McGregor, D. (1960). *The human side of enterprise.* New York: McGraw-Hill.

Miles, R. E., & Creed, W. E. D. (1995). Organizational forms and managerial philosophies: A descriptive and analytic review. In L. L. Cummings & B. M. Staw (Eds.), *Research in organizational behavior* (Vol. 17, pp. 333–372). Greenwich, CT: JAI.

Mitroff, I. I., & Linstone, H. (1993). *The unbounded mind.* New York: Oxford University Press.

Mohr, L. B. (1982). *Explaining organizational behavior.* San Francisco: Jossey-Bass.

Mohrman, S. A. (2001). Seize the day: Organizational studies can and should make a difference. *Human Relations, 54,* 57–65.

Morgan, G. (1986). *Images of organization.* Newbury Park, CA: Sage.

Nadler, D. A. (1977). *Feedback and organization development: Using data-based methods.* Reading, MA: Addison-Wesley.

Nadler, D. A., & Tushman, M. L. (1977). A diagnostic model for organization behavior. In J. R. Hackman, E. E. Lawler, & L. W. Porter (Eds.), *Perspectives on behavior in organizations* (pp. 85–100). New York: McGraw-Hill.

Newstrom, J. W., & Lillyquist, J. M. (1979). Selecting needs analysis methods. *Training Development Journal, 33,* 52–56.

Palmer, I., & Dunford, R. (1997). Organizing for hyper-competition. *New Zealand Strategic Management, 2*(4), 38–45.

Prigogine, I., & Stengers, I. (1984). *Order out of chaos: Man's new dialogue with nature.* New York: Bantam.

Rothwell, W., Sullivan, R., & McLean, G. (1995). *Practicing organizational development.* San Diego, CA: Pfeiffer.

Schein, E. H. (1987). *Process consultation.* Reading, MA: Addison-Wesley.

Schein, E. H. (1999). *Process consultation revisited.* Reading, MA: Addison-Wesley.

Starbuck, W. H., & Milliken, F. J. (1988). Executive perceptual filters: What they notice and how they make sense. In D. C. Hambrick (Ed.), *The executive effect: Concepts and methods for studying top managers* (pp. 33–65). Greenwich, CT: JAI.

Steele, F. (1975). *Consulting for organizational change.* Amherst: University of Massachusetts Press.

Strauss, A. M. (Ed.). (1956). *The social psychology of George Herbert Mead.* Chicago: University of Chicago Press.

Strogatz, S. (2003). *Sync: The emerging science of spontaneous order.* New York: Hyperion.

Svyantek, D. J., & Brown, L. L. (2000). A complex-systems approach to organizations. *Current Directions in Psychological Science, 9,* 69–74.

Tichy, N. M. (1983). *Managing strategic change: Technical, political, and cultural dynamics.* New York: John Wiley & Sons.

Volberda, H. W. (1996). *Towards the flexible firm: How to remain competitive.* Oxford, UK: Oxford University Press.

Weick, K. E. (1995). *Sensemaking in organizations.* Thousand Oaks, CA: Sage.

Weisbord, M. R. (1976). Organizational diagnosis: Six places to look for trouble with or without a theory. *Group and Organization Studies, 1,* 430–447.

Weisbord, M. R. (1978). *Organizational diagnosis: A workbook of theory and practice.* Reading, MA: Addison-Wesley.

Westley, F. R. (1990). Middle managers and strategy: Micro dynamics of inclusion. *Strategic Management Journal, 11,* 337–351.

10

Conceptual Underpinnings of Intervening in Organizations

JEAN M. BARTUNEK

JOHN R. AUSTIN

MYEONG-GU SEO

A major contribution of organization development (OD) for the past several decades has been the creation and implementation of novel ways of intervening in organizations using means designed to foster their effective behavior. The interventions OD practitioners develop represent a primary way in which OD portrays itself.

Particular humanistic principles are clearly core to OD and have been since its beginnings (Church, Burke, & Van Eynde, 1994; Fagenson & Burke, 1990; French & Bell, 1995; Worley & Feyerherm, 2003). Nevertheless, when practitioners and clients talk about OD they often identify it with interventions that are current in practice. For example, Burke (1976) suggested that perhaps the name *organization development* should change to *quality of working life*.

Porras and Silvers (1991) suggested that second-generation OD should be identified with organization transformation. Worren, Ruddle, and Moore (1999) suggested that change management had superseded OD. Moreover, OD units in organizations have sometimes taken other names (e.g., *organization effectiveness* or *quality*) that are consistent with current popular interventions. The importance of interventions to OD's identity can even be seen in the table of contents of this book: A whole section is devoted to particular types of OD interventions. Understanding OD interventions is crucial for understanding OD.

In this chapter we summarize some ways interventions have been defined and discussed in the past 40 years. We will indicate in the summary some material that is often discussed in conjunction with interventions, such as effectiveness criteria and contingencies affecting their success, although these will not be our major emphasis.

Some discussions of interventions (especially in materials training practitioners to implement them) treat interventions as formalized, discrete, perhaps off-the-shelf recipes for sequences of events (Weick, 2000). An intervention can be described, materials (often including precise logistical information) can be written about how to carry it out in articles, chapters, and books, and the intervention is expected to unfold as described. However, there is much more to the design and underlying processes associated with interventions than is often portrayed. In particular, throughout OD's history its interventions have been based on underlying concepts about how best to accomplish particular types of change in organizations. These concepts have evolved in a time-based way; interventions designed at about the same time often are based on some common principles. Therefore, the primary focus in this chapter is on the conceptualization underlying intervention processes.

INTERVENING AND INTERVENTIONS

There are at least two kinds of approaches to intervention in OD literature. One focuses primarily on the intervening process and the other focuses more on the content of particular interventions. Although this chapter focuses more on interventions than intervening, it is important to have a basic understanding of intervening.

Intervening

Argyris (1970, p. 15) formulated a definition of intervening that is still cited frequently several decades later (Burke, 1987; Harvey & Brown, 2001). He said, "To intervene is to enter into an ongoing system of relationships, to come between or among persons, groups, or objects for the purpose of helping them." This definition was similar to one by Beckhard (1969, p. 13): "moving into an existing organization and helping it, in effect, 'stop the music'; examine its present ways of work, norms and values, and look at alternative ways of working, or relating, or rewarding." Thus, the general expectation is that the OD intervention process is an interruption in some way; it lets the client system know that the current situation is not business as usual and is aimed at helping the system function more successfully (Cummings & Worley, 2005). Almost all intervention methods are designed in ways that pull organization members out of their present work to reflect on and consider differing approaches. This definition situates OD within larger categories of events aimed at interrupting organization functioning in some manner (Okhuysen, 2001).

Furthermore, Argyris (1970; also see Cummings & Worley, 2005) describes three processes that must be present regardless of the substantive issues with which the intervention deals if it is to be helpful (effective) with clients. These processes are consistent with OD's humanistic ideals.

The first is that the intervener and client system have and generate valid information about the factors, including their interrelationships, that create problems for the client system. This depends in part on adequate diagnosis. Second, the client must have a clear map of what it wants to accomplish and must choose freely to try to accomplish this aim. That is, members of the client system are involved in making decisions about changes that affect them, and may choose or not to participate in them. Third, the client must be internally committed to the choices made and their implications.

These processes describe some of the implicit contractual issues involved in the client–intervener interaction. The client expects some change in the system, has a say over the aims of the change effort, and is committed to this effort. Others (e.g., Burke, 1987) describe similar criteria for assessing the effectiveness of intervening.

Interventions

Focusing on their content, French and Bell (1995, p. 156) define interventions as "the planned activities clients and consultants participate in during the course of an OD program. These activities are designed to improve the organization's functioning by helping organization members better manage their team and organization cultures and processes." Similarly but more generally, Cummings and Worley (2005, p. 143) describe an intervention as "a sequence of activities, actions, and events intended to help an organization improve its performance and effectiveness." These activities may last over a long or short time; they may be multiple years in length (Bartunek, 2003; Grubb, Silvestro, & Ward, 1994a, 1994b) or a few minutes. They may involve complex sequences of events or simple individual activities. They may be oriented toward one or multiple levels of organizational or interorganizational functioning. They may involve a small group of people or many thousands. Their major characteristic is that they are planned and aimed at improving the organization's functioning in a way that is generally consistent with OD's principles and the criteria developed by Argyris (1970).

Contingencies Affecting the Success of Interventions. Large numbers of interventions have been designed in the past several decades, and multiple contingencies affecting their success have been discussed. Cummings and Worley (2005) include individual differences between organization members and organization factors such as management style. Other factors that make a difference are organization members' readiness for change and capacity for change, the cultural context, and the capabilities of the change agent. If clients are not ready for change (Armenakis, Harris, & Mossholder,

1993), and if they do not have the capacity to change in a certain way, if a particular kind of intervention planned is not suitable for a particular cultural context, including national culture (Lau & Ngo, 2001), if change agents are trying to do something beyond their levels of competence, an intervention will not succeed. French and Bell (1995) add additional features of intervention activities that lead to effective interventions, such as the right people participating, a clear goal, and an initially high probability of successful goal attainment. Beer, Eisenstat, and Spector (2000) suggest that an intervention must be closely linked with the actual work of the organization in order to succeed. Weick (2000) suggests that planned change will be more effective if it acknowledges and links with already ongoing and emergent organization change processes rather than separating itself from them.

Almost all of these contingencies could be the focus of study themselves, and the references given indicate that some of them have received scholarly attention. They begin to indicate some of the myriad ways in which the course of an intervention may be affected by factors that have little to do with its design. It is likely that these factors apply to a range of change processes well beyond those associated with OD.

Categories of Interventions. In the past 30 years or so there have been a number of category schemes for OD interventions. The schemes in use have evolved, as a brief glance makes evident.

Roger Harrison (1970) developed an early, influential category scheme that focused on the depth of interventions. Harrison defined depth in terms of how private, individual, and hidden were the issues and processes about which a consultant would attempt to obtain information and would seek to influence. If the focus is only on public and observable aspects of behavior, the intervention strategy would be classified as closer to the surface.

If the focus is on very deep and private perceptions, attitudes, or feelings, the intervention strategy would be classified as one of great depth. Harrison differentiated interventions according to five levels of depth. His category scheme was cited regularly in OD literature in the 1970s.

This classification scheme tended to treat structural interventions in organizations as superficial; the most important interventions, such as sensitivity training, focused on the interpersonal and intrapersonal. Such an approach was consistent with many OD classifications that, despite the fact that they defined OD as system-wide, saw the primary work of OD as very focused on the individual and the group. For example, Burke and Hornstein (1972, p. xii) classified the types of OD interventions then in wide use as team building, managing conflict, technostructural, data feedback, training, and other potential interventions.

Over time, the category schemes for OD interventions have expanded. There has been much more recognition that interventions aimed at publicly observable structures, roles, functions, and goals may have profound depth and impact on organization members (Galbraith, 2000). The interventions originally rated as the most in depth are still seen as important but have become much less prevalent and less likely to be more valued than other types of interventions.

Thus, in a recent study of OD interventions used in multinational corporations, for example, Lau and Ngo (2001) distinguished four types of interventions: individual development (which was least frequently used), human resource system planning, individual and group work, and system redesign. In their recent book, Cummings and Worley (2005) also include four types of interventions: strategic change interventions (including competitive and collaborative strategies and organization transformation), human resource interventions (interventions addressing performance management and developing and assisting others), human process interventions (which deal with

interpersonal, group, and organization processes), and technostructural interventions (those that deal with restructuring organizations, employee involvement, and work redesign). The contemporary expectation is that all these kinds of interventions are important. In fact, the chapters of this handbook that deal with individual interventions are organized generally around this classification scheme. Because many of the individual chapters describe the intervention types in detail, we focus more on conceptualizing that is pertinent to many types of interventions.

Another way of classifying interventions is to suggest that they fall into multiple generations of planned change (French & Bell, 1995; Porras & Silvers, 1991; Seo, Putnam, & Bartunek, 2004). These generations are based primarily on when particular planned change approaches began to be implemented widely and on the assumptions that underlie approaches developed at similar times. Seo et al. (2004) conducted an in-depth exploration of multiple OD interventions developed in the past several decades and concluded that there have been three generations of OD approaches.

The differences between the generations are based in large part on their differing conceptual bases. This chapter now turns to the conceptual foundations of various interventions. We address this topic in two ways. First, we describe the kinds of conceptualizing that underlie OD interventions. Then we suggest ways this conceptualizing has evolved through multiple generations.

CONCEPTUALIZING INTERVENTIONS

Most OD interventions are based on a theory of behavior and behavioral change. That is, they are based on an expectation that a given intervention accomplishes change in the intended direction by means of certain processes or structures that are built into the intervention or evoked by it.

Sometimes these expectations are well described by and explicitly linked with academic theories that focus on variables that play causal roles in change. For example, Porras and Hoffer (1986) developed a complex model of the types of individual changes in behavior that occur in successful OD interventions and through which the expected outcomes of the interventions are accomplished. However, conceptual models underlying many OD interventions are based on somewhat different causal mechanisms and sequences than standard academic theories.

In 1966 Bennis distinguished between theories of change and theories of changing. He suggested that theories of change attempt to answer the question of how and why change occurs; they are primarily academic. Theories of changing attempt to answer the question of how to generate change and guide it to a successful conclusion; they are primarily concerns of practitioners. Porras and Robertson (1987) relabeled the two different approaches change process theory and implementation theory, terms that are easier to distinguish.

Porras and Robertson (1987, 1992) described change process theory as explaining the dynamics of the change process; it focuses on the multiple types of variables involved in the accomplishment of planned change, however they are generated. With regard to the Porras and Hoffer (1986) article, for example, successful change from OD efforts is considered to occur through the mediation of individual behavior change. In contrast, implementation theory focuses on activities change agents take in accomplishing organization change. It is this kind of theorizing that most characterizes the work of OD practitioners.

In 1995, Van de Ven and Poole significantly advanced change process theory by describing four different motors of change, four "fundamentally different event sequences and generative mechanisms" (p. 511) to explain how and why changes unfold. They proposed that most theories of change are based on one or more of these motors.

The motors Van de Ven and Poole uncovered as applicable to a very wide variety of change processes were teleological (development of an organization entity involves movement toward a purposefully chosen goal or an end state), dialectic (stability and change are explained by reference to balances of power between opposing entities), evolutionary (cumulative changes in structural forms of populations of organization entities across communities, industries, or society at large), and life cycle (a developing entity has within it an underlying form, logic, program, or code that regulates the process of change and moves the entity from a given point of departure toward a subsequent end that is prefigured in the present state). OD is generally characterized as reflecting teleological processes of change; it is explicitly aimed at helping organizations reach a chosen end state.

The Van de Ven and Poole (1995) article was a very important contribution that enables theorists to understand much more fully why change occurs. However, change process motors as they are described in academic literature are not easily manipulable by change agents; there often is not much one can directly do with them. With regard to the Porras and Hoffer (1986) article, for example, knowing that individual behavior change mediates the impact of an OD intervention does not give specific direction regarding what the intervener should do to affect individual behavior. Thus, inspiration for OD interventions rarely comes directly from change process theories.

Austin and Bartunek (2003) propose as analogous to the Van de Ven and Poole (1995) model four implementation theory motors of change. These are four underlying intervention approaches that are prevalent in multiple categories of OD interventions, whether designers are fully cognizant of them or not. On the whole, these motors are more explicit in literature written for practitioners than in literature written primarily for academics. These are participation, self-reflection, action research, and narrative or rhetorical intervention. As is the case with the conceptual motors that Van de Ven and Poole (1985) describe,

OD interventions typically make use of multiple motors of change. A summary of these implementation motors, adapted in part from Austin and Bartunek (2003), is presented here.

Participation

Participation in organization change efforts and, in particular, participation in decision making formed some of the earliest emphases of OD (French & Bell, 1995) and remains its most enduring characteristic, one of the necessary features Argyris (1970) describes. However, over time there has been expansion in ways such participation is understood and takes place. Earlier rationales for participation often centered around the expectation that employees were more likely to accept decisions in which they had participated. Currently, however, there is much more explicit emphasis on employees participating in inquiry about their organizations and contributing necessary knowledge that will foster the organization's planning and problem solving (Seo et al., 2004). This is illustrated in the roles of employees in the various large-scale interventions such as future search, open space, and real-time strategic change (Bunker & Alban, 1997). It is also illustrated in the expectation that employees contribute to learning in their organizations, such as through the various exercises designed to foster organization capacity (Senge, Kleiner, Roberts, Ross, & Smith, 1994) and in their contribution to learning histories (Roth & Kleiner, 2000). Creative new means of participation such as General Electric's workout sessions (Bunker & Alban, 1997) acknowledge and are based much more on employee knowledge than was typically the case in the past.

Self-Reflection

The growing interest in large-scale transformation in organizations has been accompanied by a similar interest in the leadership of organization transformation and thus in the development of leaders who can blend experience and reflection in order to create lasting organization change. Senge (1990) emphasized the importance of personal mastery for creating learning organizations and collaborated with others to develop several means (Senge et al., 1994) by which leaders might reflect on and learn from experience. Egri and Frost (1991), Torbert (1999; Torbert & Associates, 2004), and Quinn, Spreitzer, and Brown (2000) suggest the importance of leaders' developing self-reflection and self-inquiry.

For example, advanced change theory (Quinn et al., 2000) proposes that by modeling a process of personal transformation, leaders and change agents enable deeper organization change. This process demands that change agents be empowered to take responsibility for their own understanding (Spreitzer & Quinn, 1996) and develop a high level of cognitive complexity (Denison, Hooijberg, & Quinn, 1995). Leaders who model this process are constantly shifting perspectives and opening up values and assumptions for questioning. The more skilled organization leaders are at generating deep personal cognitive change, the more likely it is that they will be able to support or create deep organization change.

Action Research

Action research, developed in the 1940s (Collier, 1945), has been one of the core components of OD since its beginnings (Burke, 1992; French & Bell, 1995; Pasmore & Friedlander, 1982). It is an intervention in itself, and its stages make up an underlying process for multiple types of interventions.

The typical stages of action research interventions include systematically collecting research data about an ongoing system relative to some problem, objective, need, or goal of the system, followed by feeding the data back to the system (sometimes by means of formal survey feedback processes), performing collaborative diagnosis based on these data, taking action based on the diagnosis, and evaluating the results of the action (French & Bell, 1995;

Frohman, Sashkin, & Kavanagh, 1976) in a manner that may lead to a reiteration of the process. All of these must be present in some collaborative way for action research truly to be present.

Original models of action research tended to focus on organization or group problems as the starting point for change. Over the past two decades, however, descendants of action research such as participatory action research, action inquiry, and action science have expanded its emphasis. For example, the emphasis has moved toward future vision and aspirations and toward triggering change through comparison of action and theory. In addition, in original models of action research, diagnosis and survey feedback often used quantitative measures (Bowers, 1973; Seashore, Mirvis, Lawler, & Cammann, 1983). However, the ways data are gathered have also expanded. Regardless of the starting point or the type of diagnostic data collected, for an action research implementation motor of change to be present, the four stages of action research—starting with some purpose (be it a problem, vision, or comparison of action and theory), data collection, diagnosis based on the data, and action—must all be carried out, and all of this done collaboratively.

Narrative and Rhetorical Intervention

Narrative interventions emphasize the roles of rhetoric and writing in generating organization change. This approach finds its roots in sensemaking (Weick, 1995) and interpretive perspectives on organizations (Boje, 1991). Organization actors partially create their reality through the retrospective stories that they tell about their experience and through future-oriented stories that they create as a pathway for action. Convergence of narratives by organization members drives collective sensemaking (Boyce, 1995). The stories thus offer a goal toward which organization actors can work, and the role of the change agent is to help organization members reconceive their understandings (Frost & Egri, 1994) by creating new stories.

Several current OD practices rely on a narrative approach to changing. For example, appreciative inquiry draws on narrative OD theories by challenging organization members to generate local theories of action (O'Connor, 2000). Future search (Weisbord & Janoff, 1995) and search conferences (Emery & Purser, 1996), two prominent large group interventions, engage participants in telling stories of their organization's past and future.

Almost all OD interventions use one or more of these underlying motors of change, individually and in combination. As hinted at earlier, the ways in which these motors are used have evolved over time, typically in ways that are informed by the various implementation motors rather than the change process motors. We will now turn to a discussion of generations of OD interventions.

GENERATIONS OF OD INTERVENTIONS

We noted earlier that authors have identified multiple generations of OD efforts. As surrounding environmental circumstances have evolved and as academic and practitioner knowledge about change have expanded, OD practitioners have developed new interventions and modified to some extent the ways more established interventions are used.

We will summarize very briefly multiple types of intervention approaches that have been developed in each generation. We will also discuss their underlying conceptual bases, the implementation motors they tend to use (Table 10.1).

As noted earlier, Seo et al. (2004) suggest that to this point in the early 21st century there have been three generations of OD interventions: first-generation planned change, including sensitivity training, team building, sociotechnical systems, and quality of work life; second-generation planned change, including organization transformation and large group interventions; and third-generation planned change, including learning organizations and appreciative inquiry.

Table 10.1 Implementation Motors Associated With Generations of Interventions

Generations of Interventions	Participation	Self-Reflection	Action Research Stages	Narrative
First-generation approaches				
Sensitivity training	X	X		
Team building	X	X	X	
Sociotechnical systems	X		X	
Quality of work life	X		X	
Second-generation approaches				
Organization transformation	X	X		
Large group interventions	X		X	X
Third-generation approaches				
Learning organizations	X	X	X	X
Appreciative inquiry	X	X	X	X

SOURCE: Parts of this table are adapted from Austin & Bartunek (2003).

According to Seo et al. (2004) the generations are distinguished in part by their primary targets of and impetuses for change, such as whether they are more internally or externally oriented or focus more on the individual or small group or the organization. They are also distinguished by the change processes they use, such as whether these processes focus more on reacting to problems or proactively addressing the future.[1] Interventions developed in earlier generations continue to be implemented later, sometimes in ways that differ from their original designs. However, there has been evolution in types of change interventions over time.

First-Generation Approaches and Their Conceptual Bases

First-generation OD emerged from and incorporated advances in behavioral science knowledge that appeared in the 1940s and 1950s, including sensitivity training, team building, sociotechnical systems, and survey feedback. As noted earlier, action research began in the 1940s, sensitivity training was an outgrowth of Lewin's work with the Connecticut interracial commission in the 1940s (Marrow, 1967), and team building was a more organization-oriented adaptation of sensitivity groups. Sociotechnical system approaches derived from Trist's work with coal mines in the late 1940s (Trist & Bamforth, 1951), and survey feedback arose in part from Mann's work with Detroit Edison in the 1940s and 1950s (French & Bell, 1995). Although quality of work life interventions were not implemented until the 1970s in the United Sates, they were based in part on the sociotechnical system approach and evolved from work done in Scandinavia in the early 1960s.

Despite their labeling as organization development, the primary focus of many of the first-generation activities was the small group or individual. This focus is reflected in Harrison's (1970) classification of the depths of intervention.

As Table 10.1 shows, three of the implementation motors were present in one or more of the prominent intervention approaches of this generation. Participation of some kind was present in all of the interventions, as it has been throughout the generations of planned change.

For most of the first-generation change efforts participation was based on the expectation that people should have say in the events that affected them under the assumption that they will be more likely to accept decisions if they have participated in the decisions (Lewin, 1951; Vroom & Yetton, 1974). In contrast, participation in the T group sessions in first-generation OD focused more on the open-ended exploration of participants' potential.

Most of the first-generation interventions also made use of action research. Team building, sociotechnical system approaches, quality of work life interventions, and similar efforts were based on models that included the various steps of action research, including collaborative diagnosis, often through survey feedback, along with problem solving and action. Only sensitivity groups did not necessarily include all these components.

Finally, sensitivity training made extensive use of self-reflection, and this continued when sensitivity training was adapted for team-building efforts. Sensitivity training and team building were both aimed at helping individuals, aided by group members, to reflect on and learn about their behavior in their group context.

Second-Generation Approaches and Their Conceptual Bases

At least since the 1980s, organizations have faced particularly intense and ongoing environmental change. Business environments have been increasingly global, competitive, and turbulent, forcing many companies to rethink their purposes and directions (Fagenson & Burke, 1990; Kilmann & Colvin, 1988). As a result, the scale and occurrence of organization change have increased (Nadler, Shaw, & Walton, 1995), and there have been fundamental shifts in how organization change is understood, approached, and handled. New approaches designed to respond to these changes include organization transformation (Kilmann & Colvin, 1988) and large-scale

interventions (Bunker & Alban, 1997; Weber & Manning, 1998).

A primary distinguishing characteristic of second-generation OD approaches is their explicit attention to the organization environment and the organization's alignment with it (Bunker & Alban, 1997; Mirvis, 1988, 1990; Woodman, 1989). Frameworks that emphasized the organization's environment as a vital factor for organization development and change were developed earlier (Beckhard, 1969). However, it was in the 1980s that these ideas and prescriptions became widely adopted among OD researchers and practitioners. Since then, OD practitioners have increasingly reframed their work within a strategic framework and adopted relevant techniques, such as environmental scanning, competitive analysis, stakeholder analysis, and business planning (Mirvis, 1988; Tichy, 1983; Woodman, 1989). This emphasis has led to change initiatives focused broadly on transformation of the whole system (Kilmann & Colvin, 1988) as a way of responding to the external environment more than internal needs.

There are multiple approaches to transformation but substantial agreement that it depends on the leadership of the CEO and a new vision of the future to which the CEO subscribes. Thus, the capacity for CEO reflection is crucial, and some of the transformation approaches include explicit emphasis on developing the capacity of the CEO.

Large-scale interventions are also playing an important role in accomplishing transformational change (Bunker & Alban, 1997). A large number of system-wide, large group intervention approaches have been developed and adopted by OD researchers and practitioners (Bunker & Alban, 1997; Weber & Manning, 1998) such as future search, the search conference, the Institute of Cultural Affairs strategic planning process, fast cycle full participation work design, simu-real, and workout. These are based on a somewhat different premise than the original problem-focused orientation of action research. They typically begin by asking people to reflect on what future state they would like for their organization (Lippitt, 1980). Moreover, as noted earlier, some of these large-scale interventions have incorporated narrative methods in which organization members tell the story of the organization from the past and into the future.

As Table 10.1 indicates, participation remains a central feature in this generation of interventions. However, participation in second-generation OD is not like the participation in first-generation OD efforts, in which it refers to open-ended exploration or is oriented toward greater acceptance of decisions made, regardless of their content. Instead, second-generation OD approaches focus more on participation relating to strategic goals of an organization. Moreover, especially in large group interventions, second-generation OD begins to emphasize the importance of incorporating multiple organization members' and stakeholders' knowledge.

The kinds of interventions associated with second-generation OD emphasize a central role for leaders, especially in terms of developing their capacity. Authors such as Torbert (1999; Torbert & Associates, 2004) and Quinn et al. (2000) argue that, for leaders, developing their capacity necessarily involves enabling them to reflect on themselves and their actions. These authors have developed multiple means of fostering such self-reflection. Large group interventions do not incorporate individual self-reflection, although reflection on the organization is certainly a component.

Transformation approaches, though varied, do not necessarily incorporate action research. Many of them are top down, without a strongly collaborative component. However, large group interventions generally include action research steps. Some type of collaborative component that involves formulation of a goal, data gathering, joint action planning, and then action is a part of most of the large group interventions.

Finally, it was during this generation that narrative approaches to change began to develop. Narrative approaches are especially evident in the storytelling associated with some of the large group interventions.

Third-Generation Approaches and Their Conceptual Frameworks

To state the case simplistically, first-generation approaches to OD aimed to help organizational groups do better, typically (implicitly) within an already-accepted framework for action and responding to employee needs without attention to an organization's past. Second-generation approaches focused more on transformational change, movement away from a particular framework or set of behaviors and toward a very different framework or set of behaviors in response to environmental shifts. This approach has been based on the implicit and sometimes explicit expectation that the past has to be discarded for future success. Third-generation OD approaches also focus on major change and transformation. In contrast to transformational change approaches, however, these types of changes are based on the assumption that the past can play an important role in the organization's ongoing life and change effort; it should not be discarded. Two important illustrations of third-generation interventions are learning organizations and appreciative inquiry. Although they have some aspects in common, they also differ in many aspects. Thus, their conceptual bases are summarized individually.

Learning Organizations. Peter Senge's (1990) best-selling book, *The Fifth Discipline,* has been most responsible for bringing the learning organization into the mainstream of business thinking. For Senge, a learning organization is "an organization that is continually expanding its capacity to create its future" and for which "adaptive learning must be joined by generative learning, learning that enhances our capacity to create" (p. 14). Senge describes five different disciplines as the cornerstone of learning organization: system thinking, personal mastery, mental models, building shared vision, and team learning. Several means have been identified that help accomplish this vision. These include use of the "ladder of inference" and the "left hand column" to help develop understanding of mental models. They also include learning histories (Roth & Kleiner, 2000), book-length descriptions of major organization changes that are written in a way designed to help organization members reflect on and learn from their experiences. These book-length histories reflect both a narrative approach and a means of self-reflection.

Learning organizations create a significant extension of action research by their commitment to continuous, collective learning. In addition, the fundamental approach of learning organizations involves participation, based on the assumption that capacity must be increased throughout the organization.

Learning organizations share several components with second-generation OD approaches. For example, adaptation to or alignment with the organization's environment is a core impetus for building learning organizations. In addition, despite its emphasis on developing individual and group learning capacity, the ultimate focus of the learning organization approach is at the system level, making the entire organization capable of continuous learning. In contrast to second-generation approaches, however, as the use of learning histories makes clear, past experiences are regarded as valuable resources in learning organizations.

Appreciative Inquiry. Appreciative inquiry is the newest of the approaches considered here. It is based on several important assumptions: that social systems are socially constructed, that every social system has multiple positive elements, that members of a system draw energy for change much more by focusing on positive aspects of the system than by focusing on its negative, problematic aspects, and that it is quite possible for organizations to build consensus around positive elements (Cooperrider, 1990; Watkins & Mohr, 2001). Based on this philosophy, appreciative inquiry includes five generic processes: Choose the positive as the focus for inquiry, inquire into stories of life-giving forces, locate themes that appear in stories and select topics for further inquiry, create shared images for a preferred future, and find innovative ways to create that future (Watkins & Mohr, 2001). Appreciative inquiry illustrates the use of narrative and self-reflection. It does so by asking participants to talk about their stories and, on the basis of the material gathered, to reflect on their organization.

The strong belief in social construction that characterizes appreciative inquiry explicitly rejects the problem orientations of many other approaches to organization change. Rather, this approach makes use of narrative methods, depending to a large extent on stories, narratives, dreams, and visions that stimulate human imagination and meaning systems and thus expand the possibilities for new social constructions. The four stages of appreciative inquiry include an adaptation of action research that focuses on a positive goal, data gathering related to it, planning based on the data gathering, and action. As with learning organizations, appreciative inquiry is participative throughout. In fact, means have recently been developed to conduct appreciative inquiry as a large group intervention method (Ludema, Whitney, Mohr, & Griffin, 2003). Finally, both learning organizations and appreciative inquiry extend self-reflection in ways that incorporate the organization and the individual.

DISCUSSION

When people talk about the values of OD and their concerns that the values remain the same (Worley & Feyerherm, 2003), they often do not talk about what it means to express the values in action. However, it is in action—in interventions—that these values are expressed. More precisely, as we have demonstrated, it is in the underlying implementation motors of interventions that the values of OD are expressed. Therefore, understanding its interventions is crucial for understanding what OD means in practice.

The material we have presented suggests that OD interventions over the past 30 or 40 years have evolved in ways that appear to represent three overlapping generations. As they have evolved, they have used somewhat different combinations of participation, self-reflection, action research, and narratives, the implementation motors we have described here.

Understanding the evolution of interventions sometimes has been addressed solely by focusing on specific interventions, how popular they are at any given time, how they change over time, and how new interventions might be developed to enable adaptation to changing circumstances (French & Bell, 1995). As this chapter has made evident, however, evolution in interventions can also be explored by addressing each of the motors, how they have been implemented, and how they have evolved in conjunction with different generations of interventions.

First, as we have made evident, the rationale for and expectation of participation in OD interventions in the early 21st century is quite different from the rationale for and expectation of participation in the late 1960s and early 1970s. Participation has been present in almost all the interventions. Initially the rationale for participation was greater acceptance of decisions; more recently, however, the rationale has been more on the necessity of incorporating a wider range of knowledge in order to determine best approaches.

Second, self-reflection has been present in one way or another throughout most of the interventions. However, it too has taken on different meanings, from an open-ended focus on human potential, to developing leadership capacity in order to be able to lead transformation efforts, to shared reflection on significant organization events and their meanings.

Third, action research, also present throughout the generations, has also taken on different meanings. In particular, action research has shifted from being primarily problem driven to being more positive oriented; in learning organizations, it has also shifted from taking place episodically to being considered a continuous process.

Finally, narrative, which was not present in early intervention initiatives, is currently salient in a manner similar to ways in which quantitative survey research methods were salient in the first-generation approaches. Rather than distributing and scoring questionnaires, planned change interveners have developed ways of coding narratives to find common themes. This is particularly evident in large-scale interventions and in appreciative inquiry.

This description suggests that exploring how implementation motors are associated with interventions, which motors are used at particular times, what they mean in practice, how their meanings evolve, which motors become more prominent and which become less salient, and how they are combined is a valuable way to study interventions. Such exploration enables classification of multiple types of interventions that appear on the surface to be somewhat different but that actually have some underlying mechanisms in common. Outward appearances of change may differ over time, but the change efforts may still be using similar motors to those developed before. An approach such as action research that has existed for decades may take on new life through adaptations and development in other implementation motors. Understanding OD and its development requires appreciation of these processes.

OD interventions continue to evolve. At the time of this writing, design approaches to change are being developed (Boland & Collopy, 2004; Romme, 2003; van Aken, 2004). Among other things, these approaches address the action dimensions of action research more than many of other interventions do (Bartunek, 2004). At the same time, some questions have been raised about how participative they are (Pasmore, 2004). It will be interesting to observe how the various implementation motors are expressed as design approaches become more fully developed as interventions.

CONCLUSION

In this chapter we have looked to past generations of OD interventions to make sense of present and, perhaps, future interventions. Combining the implementation motor framework (Austin & Bartunek, 2003) with the temporal sorting of interventions into generations (Seo et al., 2004) reveals the common mechanisms that drive many interventions while also highlighting how interventions evolve over time. Third-generation approaches draw from multiple motors and build on many aspects of successful interventions from earlier generations.

Recognizing and making intelligent use of common implementation motors can enable OD practitioners to combine OD approaches appropriately to match the contexts of their implementation. In this fashion, the practitioner can skillfully call on first-generation techniques in the midst of a second- or third-generation implementation process.

The framework that we use in this chapter also begs the question, "What of the future? What will the next generation look like?" As we noted earlier, design approaches are starting to be discussed, and undoubtedly other types of interventions are also being developed. There are many possible directions for future OD interventions that build from past successes.

First, it is reasonable to believe that contemporary and prior approaches will continue to be widely adopted and adapted by OD practitioners. Academic researchers, especially those whose emphases are on change process theories, probably will be slower to attend to these interventions.

Although learning organizations and appreciative inquiry are enjoying widespread popularity, for example, they have yet to be fully explored in the academic literature on organization change (Austin & Bartunek, 2003). Previous generations of OD implementation approaches (team building, quality of work life, large group interventions) likewise experienced delayed attention by organization researchers; academic attention to these earlier approaches often appeared in tandem with the emergence of the next-generation implementation approaches. If present trends continue, change process–oriented research will continue to trail the development of OD intervention strategies.

Second, much as the past decade has offered the emergence of the narrative implementation motor, we can anticipate new implementation motors emerging from research or, more likely, practice. In light of how second- and third-generation approaches built on earlier implementation approaches, we would expect new implementation motors to find their way into OD practice in the form of an incremental improvement on previous approaches (e.g., the use of qualitative data in addition to quantitative data in survey feedback) and gradually grow in significance over time (e.g., to a full-blown appreciation of narrative approaches).

Third, as newer implementation approaches grow in complexity, practitioners and clients may begin to seek less holistic approaches to OD and refocus activity on first-generation, single- or dual-motor approaches to OD. Such a recursive cycling through generations could strengthen the field by refining motors and solidifying connections between disparate OD methods.

The past several decades have seen the introduction of a dizzying array of organization implementation techniques that are linked by a small number of common implementation motors whose use has evolved over time and whose evolution is reflected in multiple generations of interventions. It is these implementation motors and others that may evolve from them that will build the practice foundation for OD.

NOTE

1. Seo et al. (2004) note that the types of change processes used all reflect some way of handling dualities and tensions, polar opposites or oppositional pulls that vary in degree in any planned change initiative. How the interventions deal with dualities suggests characteristic features of the different generations of change.

REFERENCES

Argyris, C. (1970). *Intervention theory and method.* Reading, MA: Addison-Wesley.

Armenakis, A. A., Harris, S. G., & Mossholder, K. W. (1993). Creating readiness for organizational change. *Human Relations, 46,* 681–703.

Austin, J., & Bartunek, J. (2003). Theories and practices of organization development. In W. Borman, D. Ilgen, & R. Klimoski (Eds.), *Handbook of psychology: Industrial and organizational psychology* (Vol. 12, pp. 309–332). New York: John Wiley & Sons.

Bartunek, J. M. (2003). *Organizational and educational change: The life and role of a change agent group.* Mahwah, NJ: Lawrence Erlbaum.

Bartunek, J. M. (2004). *Is design science better at creating actionable research and knowledge than action research is?* Symposium presented at the Academy of Management meeting, New Orleans.

Beckhard, R. (1969). *Organization development: Strategies and models.* Reading, MA: Addison-Wesley.

Beer, M., Eisenstat, R. A., & Spector, B. (1990). Why change programs don't produce change. *Harvard Business Review, 68*(6), 158–166.

Bennis, W. G. (1966). *Changing organizations.* New York: McGraw-Hill.

Boje, D. (1991). The storytelling organization: A study of story performance in an office-supply firm. *Administrative Science Quarterly, 36*(1), 106–126.

Boland, R., & Collopy, F. (2004). *Managing as designing.* Stanford, CA: Stanford University Press.

Bowers, D. (1973). OD techniques and their results in 23 organizations: The Michigan ICL study. *Journal of Applied Behavioral Science, 9,* 21–43.

Boyce, M. E. (1995). Collective centering and collective sensemaking in the stories of one organization. *Organization Studies, 16*(1), 107–137.

Bunker, B. B., & Alban, B. T. (1997). *Large group interventions.* San Francisco: Jossey-Bass.

Burke, W. W. (1976). Organization development in transition. *Journal of Applied Behavioral Science, 12,* 22–43.

Burke, W. W. (1987). *Organization development: A normative view.* Reading, MA: Addison-Wesley.

Burke, W. W. (1992). *Organization development: A process of learning and changing.* Reading, MA: Addison-Wesley.

Burke, W. W., & Hornstein, H. A. (1972). *The social technology of organization development.* Fairfax, VA: NTL Learning Resources.

Church, A. H., Burke, W. W., & Van Eynde, D. F. (1994). Values, motives, and interventions of organization development practitioners. *Group and Organization Management, 19,* 5–50.

Collier, J. (1945). United States Indian Administration as a laboratory of ethnic relations. *Social Research, 12,* 275–276.

Cooperrider, D. L. (1990). Positive image, positive action: The affirmative basis of organizing. In S. Srivastva & D. L. Cooperrider (Eds.), *Appreciative management and leadership: The power of positive thought and action in organizations* (pp. 91–125). San Francisco: Jossey-Bass.

Cummings, T. G., & Worley, C. (2005). *Organization development and change* (8th ed.). Cincinnati, OH: Southwestern.

Denison, D. R., Hooijberg, R., & Quinn, R. E. (1995). Paradox and performance: Toward a theory of behavioral complexity in managerial leadership. *Organization Science, 6*(5), 524–540.

Egri, C. P., & Frost, P. J. (1991). Shamanism and change: Bringing back the magic in organizational transformation. In R. W. Woodman & W. A. Pasmore (Eds.), *Research in organizational change and development* (Vol. 5, pp. 175–221). Greenwich, CT: JAI.

Emery, M., & Purser, R. E. (1996). *The search conference: A powerful method for planning organizational change and community action.* San Francisco: Jossey-Bass.

Fagenson, E. A., & Burke, W. W. (1990). Organization development practitioners' activities and interventions in organizations during the 1980s. *Journal of Applied Behavioral Science, 26,* 285–297.

French, W. L., & Bell, C. H. (1995). *Organization development* (5th ed.). Englewood Cliffs, NJ: Prentice Hall.

Frohman, M. A., Sashkin, M., & Kavanagh, M. J. (1976). Action research as applied to organization development. *Organization and Administrative Science, 7,* 129–142.

Frost, P., & Egri, C. (1994). The shamanic perspective on organizational change and development. *Journal of Organizational Change Management, 7,* 7–23.

Galbraith, J. R. (2000). The role of formal structures and processes. In M. Beer & N. Nohria (Eds.), *Breaking the code of change* (pp. 139–159). Boston: Harvard Business School Press.

Grubb, I. M., Silvestro, N. W., & Ward, D. F. (1994a). Stop the organization—I want to change it! Part 1. *Industrial and Commercial Training, 26*(1), 23–27.

Grubb, I. M., Silvestro, N. W., & Ward, D. F. (1994b). Stop the organization—I want to change it! Part 2. *Industrial and Commercial Training, 26*(4), 15–21.

Harrison, R. (1970). Choosing the depth of organizational intervention. *Journal of Applied Behavioral Science, 6,* 181–202.

Harvey, D., & Brown, D. R. (2001). An experiential approach to organization development (6th ed.). Upper Saddle River, NJ: Prentice Hall.

Kilmann, R. H., & Colvin, T. J. (1988). *Corporate transformation: Revitalizing organizations for a competitive world.* San Francisco: Jossey-Bass.

Lau, C., & Ngo, H. (2001). Organization development and firm performance: A comparison of multinational and local firms. *Journal of International Business Studies, 32,* 95–114.

Lewin, K. (1951). *Field theory in social science.* New York: Harper & Row.

Lippitt, R. (1980). *Choosing the future you prefer.* Washington, DC: Development Publishers.

Ludema, J. D., Whitney, D., Mohr, B. J., & Griffin, T. J. (2003). *The appreciative inquiry summit: A practitioner's guide for leading large-group change.* San Francisco: Berrett-Koehler.

Marrow, A. J. (1967). Events leading to the establishment of the National Training Laboratories. *Journal of Applied Behavioral Science, 3,* 145–150.

Mirvis, P. H. (1988). Organizational development: Part I—An evolutionary perspective. In W. A. Pasmore & R. W. Woodman (Eds.), *Research in organizational change and development* (Vol. 2, pp. 1–57). Greenwich, CT: JAI.

Mirvis, P. H. (1990). Organizational development: Part II—A revolutionary perspective. In W. A. Pasmore & R. W. Woodman (Eds.), *Research in organizational change and development* (Vol. 4, pp. 1–66). Greenwich, CT: JAI.

Nadler, D. A., Shaw, R. B., & Walton, A. E. (1995). *Discontinuous change: Leading organizational transformation.* San Francisco: Jossey-Bass.

O'Connor, E. S. (2000). Plotting the organization: The embedded narrative as a construct for studying change. *Journal of Applied Behavioral Science, 36,* 174–192.

Okhuysen, G. A. (2001). Structuring change: Familiarity and formal interventions in problem-solving groups. *Academy of Management Journal, 44,* 794–808.

Pasmore, W. A. (2004). Action research: More necessary than ever? In J. M. Bartunek, *Is design science better at creating actionable research and knowledge than action research is?* Symposium presented at the Academy of Management meeting, New Orleans.

Pasmore, W. A., & Friedlander, F. (1982). An action-research program for increasing employee involvement in problem solving. *Administrative Science Quarterly, 27,* 343–362.

Porras, J. I., & Hoffer, S. J. (1986). Common behavior changes in successful organizational efforts. *Journal of Applied Behavioral Science, 22,* 477–494.

Porras, J. I., & Robertson, P. J. (1987). Organization development theory: A typology and evaluation. In R. W. Woodman & W. A. Pasmore (Eds.), *Research in organizational change and development* (Vol. 1, pp. 1–57). Greenwich, CT: JAI.

Porras, J. I., & Robertson, P. J. (1992). Organizational development: Theory, practice, research. In M. D. Dunnette & L. M. Hough (Eds.), *Handbook of organizational psychology* (Vol. 3, pp. 719–822). Palo Alto, CA: Psychology Press.

Porras, J. I., & Silvers, R. C. (1991). Organization development and transformation. *Annual Review of Psychology, 42*, 51–78.

Quinn, R. E., Spreitzer, G. M., & Brown, M. V. (2000). Changing others through changing ourselves: The transformation of human systems. *Journal of Management Inquiry, 9*, 147–164.

Romme, A. G. L. (2003). Making a difference: Organization as design. *Organization Science, 14*, 559–573.

Roth, G., & Kleiner, A. (2000). *Car launch: The human side of managing change*. New York: Oxford University Press.

Seashore, S. C., Mirvis, P., Lawler, E., & Cammann, C. (1983). *Assessing organizational change: A guide to methods, measures, and practices*. New York: John Wiley & Sons.

Senge, P. (1990). *The fifth discipline: The art and practice of the learning organization*. New York: Doubleday Currency.

Senge, P., Kleiner, A., Roberts, C., Ross, R., & Smith, B. (1994). *The fifth discipline fieldbook: Strategies for building a learning organization*. New York: Currency Publishers.

Seo, M., Putnam, L., & Bartunek, J. (2004). Dualities and tensions of planned organizational change. In M. S. Poole & A. H. Van de Ven (Eds.), *Handbook of organizational change and innovation* (pp. 73–107). New York: Oxford University Press.

Spreitzer, G. M., & Quinn, R. E. (1996). Empowering middle managers to be transformational leaders. *Journal of Applied Behavioral Science, 32*, 237–261.

Tichy, N. M. (1983). *Managing strategic change*. New York: Wiley-Interscience.

Torbert, W. R. (1999). The distinctive questions developmental action inquiry asks. *Management Learning, 30*, 189–206.

Torbert, W. R., & Associates. (2004). *Action inquiry: The secret of timely and transforming leadership*. San Francisco: Berrett-Koehler.

Trist, E., & Bamforth, K. (1951). Some social and psychological consequences of the long wall methods of goal-getting. *Human Relations, 4*(1), 1–8.

Van Aken, J. E. (2004). Management research based on the paradigm of the design sciences: The quest for field-tested and grounded technological rules. *Journal of Management Studies, 41*, 219–246.

Van de Ven, A. H., & Poole, M. S. (1995). Explaining development and change in organizations. *Academy of Management Review, 20*, 510–540.

Vroom, V. H., & Yetton, P. W. (1974). *Leadership and decision-making*. Pittsburgh, University of Pittsburgh Press.

Watkins, J. M., & Mohr, B. J. (2001). *Appreciative inquiry: Change at the speed of imagination*. San Francisco: Jossey-Bass.

Weber, P. S., & Manning, M. R. (1998). A comparative framework for large group organizational change interventions. In R. W. Woodman & W. A. Pasmore (Eds.), *Research in organizational change and development* (Vol. 11, pp. 225–252). Greenwich, CT: JAI.

Weick, K. E. (1995). *Sensemaking in organizations*. Thousand Oaks, CA: Sage.

Weick, K. E. (2000). Emergent change as a universal in organizations. In M. Beer & N. Nohria (Eds.), *Breaking the code of change* (pp. 223–241). Boston: Harvard Business School Press.

Weisbord, M. R., & Janoff, S. (1995). *Future search*. San Francisco: Berrett-Koehler.

Woodman, R. W. (1989). Organizational change and development: New arenas for inquiry and action. *Journal of Management, 15*(2), 205–228.

Worley, C. G., & Feyerherm, A. E. (2003). Reflections on the future of organization development. *Journal of Applied Behavioral Science, 39*, 97–115.

Worren, N. A. M., Ruddle, K., & Moore, K. (1999). From organizational development to change management: The emergence of a new profession. *Journal of Applied Behavioral Science, 35*, 273–286.

11

Groups as Agents of Change

J. RICHARD HACKMAN

AMY C. EDMONDSON

Groups are prominent in the field of organization development. Classic studies in organizational behavior document that it is awkward, at the very least, to try to accomplish meaningful organization change without addressing group dynamics (Coch & French, 1948; Roethlisberger & Dixon, 1939). At the same time, the use of groups in organization development sometimes dissipates change efforts. For example, senior managers often form a project management group and charge it with responsibility for disseminating throughout the organization some innovation in how work is designed, managed, or supported. Even when that innovation has proven effective in initial trials, it may not survive the group-managed dissemination process. We explore in this chapter the various uses of groups as tools for organization change, with special attention to what can be done to increase their chances of success.

Although organization development traditionally has been defined as the use of behavioral science methods to achieve system-wide

change (Beckhard, 1969; Beer, 1980), in practice, groups are among the most common targets of intervention. Two kinds of group-focused interventions are especially common. First are those that seek to improve the functioning of existing teams. Examples include the use of coaching and other process-focused techniques to improve teamwork (Hackman & Wageman, 2005; Schein, 1988; Schwarz, 1994; Schweiger, Sandberg, & Ragan, 1986), in-depth consultations intended to help senior executive teams perform better (Argyris, 1993), and diagnosis-based assessments of work team functioning (Wageman, Hackman, & Lehman, 2005). Beyond their direct effects on the focal teams, interventions of this type potentially can generate broader organization change indirectly by strengthening the culture of the social systems within which the teams operate.

A second common type of group-focused intervention involves creating teams to deal with organization problems that have defied resolution using existing structures and processes.

Examples include sociotechnical interventions with front-line teams (e.g., Cummings, 1978; Trist, 1981), creating cross-disciplinary groups to develop new products or processes (Wheelwright & Clark, 1992), forming "inflexibly diverse" groups to ensure that all relevant perspectives are brought to bear on a particular change problem (Tucker, Nembhard, & Edmondson, 2007), creating of top management teams to foster coordination between units (Wageman, Nunes, Burruss, & Hackman, in press), and spawning grassroots teams to provide the social foundation for broad programs of political, labor, or religious organizing (Ganz, 2004; Gladwell, 2005; Staggenborg, 1998). Such teams are intended to be solutions to organizational problems, rather than tools for generating solutions.

Although organization development practice appropriately includes interventions of both types just described—consulting to groups to help members work together more productively and creating groups to solve particular problems—these kinds of interventions are not addressed in this chapter. Nor do we address large group methods, in which members of an entire system are brought together to assess and take action to improve that system (Bunker & Alban, 2006; Gilmore & Barnett, 1992). Instead, we focus here on the two primary ways in which groups are used as tools in organization development: as diagnostic tools for assessing the state of a social system and as intervention tools for facilitating change processes.

GROUPS AS DIAGNOSTIC TOOLS

When one encounters the word *diagnosis,* one of the first images to come to mind is that of an individual clinician—a physician, a psychotherapist, or an organization consultant—who gathers, integrates, and interprets data that then are used to guide treatment. Groups also can conduct diagnoses and, in organization development practice, often are the diagnostic tools of choice.

There are some significant potential benefits of using teams rather than individuals to conduct diagnoses of social systems. For one thing, groups always consist of multiple individuals who have different knowledge, skills, and experience, which means not only that they have *more* resources but, when properly composed, that they have *more diverse* resources to apply to the diagnostic task than would be the case for any single person. Moreover, because diagnostic teams have flexibility in how they deploy their resources, the diagnostic process can proceed even when individual team members become unavailable or preoccupied with other matters.

When a diagnostic team includes people who are members of different identity groups or organization units, as is the case for what Alderfer and Smith (1982) call microcosm groups, relationships between team members often mirror the dynamics of relationships that exist in the client system. That is, processes that are characteristic of the larger social system also unfold and are available for inspection within the diagnostic team itself, in part because of its representative composition (Alderfer & Smith, 1982). Attentiveness to the internal dynamics of that team therefore can provide insights about the client system that would be unavailable to individual diagnosticians or to compositionally homogeneous teams.

An additional advantage of team-managed organizational diagnosis is the learning that can occur for members of the team. Groups of various kinds are among the most significant sources of personal learning, starting with family relations for children and extending throughout adulthood. Working with others to develop understanding of a social system can be a rich source of learning about relationships, groups, and organizations for participating individuals and can result in a level of peer coaching among members that can significantly enhance diagnostic team performance (Hackman & O'Connor, 2005). And, finally, there is the possibility that the team will generate a truly synergistic insight, a way of understanding the client system that both orders what had seemed chaotic and points the way to the design of constructive social interventions.

Types of Diagnostic Teams

Positive examples of team-driven diagnostic work abound in organization development practice and in the research literature. Consider the work by Alderfer and his associates on the diagnosis of race relations in the managerial ranks of a large corporation (Alderfer, Alderfer, Tucker, & Tucker, 1980). The four researchers served as the core diagnostic team (a white man, white woman, black woman, and black man), assisted by a 12-person advisory committee of managers with the same mix of gender and race. As part of its diagnosis, the team developed an empathic questionnaire (Alderfer & Brown, 1972) about race relations in the firm. The survey addressed the issues that had emerged in preliminary diagnostic work as especially salient, using items that were specifically constructed to include phrases and linguistic conventions that were in common use by organization members. Diagnostic findings were provided to the senior managers who had commissioned the study, who then initiated an action program to address the issues that the diagnosis had shown to be most problematic.

Alderfer's work both draws on and advances behavioral science research and theory about organization dynamics, with special emphasis on the role of intergroup dynamics (for a comprehensive discussion of this perspective and its implications for organizational diagnosis and change, see Alderfer, forthcoming). Other team-driven organizational diagnoses may appear at first reading to be quite distinct from what is commonly meant by the phrase *organizational diagnosis*. The structure and operation of National Transportation Safety Board (NTSB) accident investigation teams illustrates this.

The NTSB is legally mandated to collect data about major accidents, to thoroughly analyze those data, and to suggest probable causes of each accident. For aviation accidents, an NTSB "Go Team," is always on call and ready to travel immediately (National Transportation Safety Board, 2002). A fully staffed Go Team consists of 13 members, with specialties including air traffic control, human performance, aircraft maintenance, and meteorology. The team is clearly bounded, with each NTSB specialist on the team also serving as chair of a separate investigating group in his or her area of expertise. Go Teams have clear and strong norms (from which members almost never deviate) that guide and constrain key aspects of the investigative processes, including confidentiality, relations with others who have a stake in the investigation, and standard procedures to be followed in assessing and integrating diagnostic data. Although far more structured than those that diagnose group and organization dynamics, NTSB investigation teams are widely recognized as a model of effective diagnostic work.

Yet another example of team-based diagnosis, one that appears to have little in common with analyses of intergroup relationships or aircraft accidents, is seen in total quality management (TQM) programs. As set forth by TQM founders W. Edwards Deming, Joseph Juran, and Kaoru Ishikawa, TQM focuses heavily on the use of data about work processes to reduce variability in work systems, improve quality, and ultimately serve customers well (for an overview of TQM, see Crosby, 1989; for an evaluative assessment, see Hackman & Wageman, 1995). In the early stages of TQM programs, cross-functional teams are formed to gather and analyze data about quality problems in existing work processes, focusing especially on the vital few issues that the team finds to be most consequential for quality. These diagnostic teams are trained in the use of a variety of scientific tools and rely heavily on them in analyzing the work system. After diagnostic work is completed, the team works with senior management to fashion changes in how the work is designed and managed to reduce variability and improve quality.

Although the rhetoric of TQM emphasizes learning and continuous improvement, in practice most of the learning is done by the cross-functional teams that conduct the diagnosis. Rank-and-file workers are expected to adhere closely to the new work procedures once they have been implemented, and have little opportunity to exercise initiative or judgment in generating additional changes in how the work is structured or performed (Hackman & Wageman, 1995). The main leverage of teams in TQM programs, then, has mostly to do with their contribution to the diagnostic assessment of the work system, and the outcomes of such programs depend heavily on how well these teams carry out their diagnostic work.

Types of Diagnostic Tasks

As these examples illustrate, diagnostic teams are instances of a broader class of team tasks that involve collaborative analysis. Woolley and Hackman (2006) define collaborative analytic work as that which requires team members to use data that may be incomplete or of uncertain reliability to generate collective conclusions about something that has happened, is happening, or may happen. On the basis of interviews with members of analytic teams in the intelligence, medical, and financial communities, Woolley and Hackman identified three dimensions on which analytic tasks vary: the scope of the problem or issue being investigated, the temporal urgency of the work, and the degree to which the analysis requires team members to work together interdependently. These three task attributes cluster into separate zones of collaborative analysis, and the dynamics of analytic work in each of those three zones are remarkably similar across the intelligence, medical, and financial domains.

Analytic tasks in the first or inner zone are narrow in scope, have temporal urgency, and

necessitate highly interdependent work among team members (e.g., intelligence analysis to make sense of a specific crisis, emergency room diagnostic work, and back-room financial analyses in preparation for an impending merger or acquisition). Because the structural conditions needed for effective work generally are naturally present for inner-zone teams (see Hackman, 2002, for an exposition and discussion of these conditions), the main challenges faced by inner-zone analytic teams is management of their own group processes.

Analytic tasks in the second or outer zone are the opposite of those in the first zone: wide scope, little time pressure, and little need for members to work interdependently. Examples include tracking data on a particular topic or issue to document trends that could signal an impending change from the status quo in the financial or intelligence communities or continuing monitoring of patients' health by primary medical care physicians. The main challenges faced in the outer zone involve obtaining, weighting, and integrating data provided by a broad range of experts who are not directly involved in the analytic work. Dealing with these challenges often can be facilitated by contextual supports, such as the formation of social networks, that help analysts locate relevant experts and incorporate their inputs into the analysts' own assessments. Real teamwork is rare for outer-zone tasks.

Middle-zone tasks are moderate in scope, with low to moderate temporal urgency and moderate interdependence. Examples include generating overview intelligence estimates, collecting and assessing financial data for use in making recommendations to clients, and dealing with patients who have chronic illnesses. Sometimes middle-zone teams follow up on issues surfaced by outer-zone analysts; other times they take over the monitoring of a crisis that has become less urgent and broader in scope. Although teams in this zone are less vulnerable to the special challenges experienced by inner- and outer-zone analytic teams, they encounter problems of their own. They do not enjoy the inherently well-designed tasks of inner-zone teams, nor are they as free from the need to work closely together as are outer-zone teams. Therefore, Woolley and Hackman argue, how the analytic work is structured and supported is especially critical to the success of middle-zone teams.

In sum, as one moves from the inner zone to the middle and outer zones, the main points of leverage for improving collaborative analytic work also change, from interventions into team processes, to improving the team's structure, to providing contextual resources. If supported by further empirical research, these conclusions appear to be as germane for diagnostic teams in organization development activities as they are for teams that are assessing and making sense of intelligence, medical, or financial data.

For example, the NTSB investigative teams discussed earlier clearly fall into the inner zone and therefore could benefit from team process interventions intended to help members take full advantage of their favorable structure and context. By contrast, the race relations and TQM teams appear to fall into the middle zone, with moderate scope, time pressure, and interdependence. The success of these teams should depend heavily on how well they are designed as performing units. And, finally, a diagnostic team that is given a highly general charge, such as "identify and explore some of the main issues that this organization needs to deal with," clearly would fall into the outer zone: broad scope, little time pressure, and little necessary interdependence of members. For these teams, helping individual members become aware of, value, and have ready access to others who are working largely independently on their own aspects of the task could increase the chances that the final product is more than the mere splicing together of members' separate analyses and conclusions.

Diagnostic Team Effectiveness

For all the potential advantages of team-driven diagnoses, it is far from certain that a diagnostic team will generate a valid and useful assessment of a client system. For one thing, a diagnostic team can fall victim to the particular challenges that confront teams in each of the three zones discussed earlier. And even the special advantages enjoyed by diagnostic teams, described at the beginning of this section, can become obstacles to their effectiveness. Within-team mirroring of the processes that characterize the client system can indeed prompt valuable diagnostic insights. But mirroring also brings the risk that the diagnostic team will fall victim to the organization and intergroup dysfunctions it is supposed to be assessing. The fact that multiple people are involved in the conduct of team diagnoses can indeed provide both extra resources and flexibility in deploying them. But team tasks bring at least some risk of free-riding and slippage in coordination between members. And it is true that diagnostic teams sometimes generate synergistic insights unlikely to be stumbled on by any individual working alone. But such teams also run the risk of smoothing over member disagreements by generating lofty, abstract conclusions that are indeed acceptable to everyone but are far from the best that the team's most competent member could produce on his or her own.

Therefore, the design and leadership of diagnostic teams deserve as much management care and competence as are given to front-line teams that perform mission-critical work. The work of a diagnostic team, like that of any other task-performing team, is facilitated when those who create the team make sure that it is well designed and supported— matters that we discuss in some detail at the end of this chapter. But diagnostic teams also can be significantly helped by straightforward and easy-to-implement process guidelines. Examples include having one member serve as devil's advocate as the group nears an analytic conclusion (Priem, Harrison, & Muir, 1995; Priem & Price, 1991), using the dialectical inquiry method in which subgroups develop their own assessments before the team as a whole meets to discuss its overall analysis (Schweiger et al., 1986) or drawing on any of a number of other procedures that help structure group discussions and increase the chances that members will be able to express their views free from pressures to conform to a dominant position (Delbecq, Van de Ven, & Gustafson, 1975; Janis, 1982). It takes both a proper team design and good team processes to generate an organizational diagnosis that can point the way to constructive, high-leverage interventions.

GROUPS AS INTERVENTION TOOLS

Some group-managed interventions seek mainly to change individual organization members in hopes that these changes gradually will spawn organization-wide improvements. Other group-managed interventions focus directly on improving work and organization processes. We discuss these two types of interventions separately in this section.

Changing Individuals

Traditionally, interventions that aspire to develop individuals in organizations have used methods that directly address the target people without explicit reference to their group memberships. Individuals' personal capabilities are assessed relative to their task or role requirements, gaps are identified, and those for whom developmental work is indicated are dispatched to training courses to obtain it. Both the characterization of the problem and the remedy are at the level of the individual.

As noted earlier, however, what one needs to know to function well in social systems is obtained more often by interacting with others than by reading books, attending lectures, or engaging in other solo training activities. Group methods therefore have special advantages for developmental work that seeks to enhance individuals' capabilities to operate skillfully in groups and organizations. Indeed, such learning is almost impossible to obtain

without the active involvement of other people (Hackman, 1992; Kemper, 1968). The methods and targets of change are congruent in this approach also, because both the focus (social behavior) and the change strategy (interventions that centrally involve interaction with other trainees) are at the level of the group.

Group-based training is especially valuable for learning *how* (acquiring skills) as opposed to learning *that* (acquiring content knowledge). As Ryle (1949) pointed out long ago, learning *that* can be accomplished through direct instruction, whereas learning *how* is obtained only gradually, through ongoing coaching, practice, and example. In his book *The Making of a Surgeon,* William Nolen (1970) describes the many ways in which fledgling surgeons are dependent on their medical teammates as they develop the capability to execute surgical procedures with even minimum adequacy.

Skill training for surgeons occurs naturally as part of training activities that, by their nature, require group interaction. Using groups for developing individuals also can be a planned and deliberate development strategy, as was the case at the startup of a new engine manufacturing facility. Managers took very seriously the need for new employees to learn how to work in teams using sophisticated metalworking equipment. Before employees were assigned to production units, they spent time offline in core skill groups that used metalworking equipment to construct various objects. The tasks the groups performed merely provided a vehicle for members to gain experience with the equipment they later would use on the production floor, and to develop their skills at working in teams (Eisenstat, 1984).

Group methods also are commonly used in developmental work with experienced senior managers. Among the historically most popular group-mediated training programs is the class of programs variously known as laboratory training, sensitivity training, or, most commonly, T-group training (Argyris, 1964;

Bradford, Benne, & Gibb, 1964; Schein & Bennis, 1965). T-group training, which typically involves a dozen or so trainees, has three phases: unfreezing, change, and refreezing. During the unfreezing phase, the trainer maintains a very low profile, thereby providing a wide-open opportunity for members to generate behaviors that are not attributable to his or her requests or expectations. Rather than provide direct instruction about desired behaviors, the trainer helps members obtain data from their fellow students about the impact of their behavior. Members typically are surprised and dismayed as they discover that the impact of what they said or did is widely discrepant from what they meant or intended. Once they are unfrozen from their existing, well-learned behavioral repertoires, trainees begin to explore behavioral alternatives that might yield fewer unexpected and unwanted responses. Initially, they are likely to mimic the style or phraseology of the trainer, but with the encouragement of both the trainer and other group members, they gradually develop new ways of speaking and behaving that are more authentic and empathic than the behaviors they exhibited in the early stages of the group experience. Finally comes the refreezing phase, in which members elaborate their new behaviors, incorporate them into their personal behavioral repertoires, and rehearse how they will behave once they return to a workplace where the new behaviors may be both unfamiliar and unwelcome.

Members typically report that their T-group experience has helped them develop useful new skills, fresh perspectives on themselves, and a strong commitment to apply what they have learned in their back-home organization settings. Empirical research affirms that well-led T-group training has a positive effect on participants' beliefs, attitudes, and behavioral intentions (Campbell & Dunnette, 1968).

The problem is with the transfer and persistence of what members have learned. The new skills and good intentions of the returning executive are no match for the situational pressures, role demands, and interpersonal expectations that pervade the back-home work context. That context did not change while the executive was away, and it does not take long before things are back to normal. Moreover, the executive is least likely to exhibit the newly learned behaviors at precisely the times when they are most needed, namely for highly consequential matters in stressful situations. Dealing with such matters invariably puts the executive under stress and therefore increases the likelihood that his or her historically dominant response, rather than the newly learned and potentially more constructive behaviors, will be exhibited (Hackman, 1992; Zajonc, 1965). The problems of transfer and persistence may be among the most important reasons why T-group training is no longer nearly as popular and pervasive as it once was.

Research and organization development practice in the decades since the heyday of T-groups suggest four different strategies for dealing with the transfer and persistence of group-mediated training of individuals.

Adjust Expectations. It is widely recognized that there are significant differences between individuals in the degree to which they are helped by training interventions. Group-mediated development activities take hold more rapidly and have more profound effects for some people than for others. Less widely recognized is the fact that differences in back-home environments also significantly shape the degree to which the lessons learned transfer and persist. Edmondson and Woolley (2003) point out that organization interventions tend to be globally assessed as either successes or failures when, in fact, they may be differentially successful in different parts of an organization. Organization learning interventions, in particular, are more likely to succeed in units that have a climate of psychological safety (Edmondson & Woolley, 2003). The degree to which the effects of group-mediated training are seen in back-home environment therefore depends not only on how competently the training was designed and executed or on how much individual participants learned from the training but also on the level of psychological safety in the setting where the lessons are to be applied. In some organization units, application of the learning occurs without difficulty; in others, it may be impossible for participants to use what they have learned because the behavior changes required of them seem too risky.

Make the Group a Continuous Presence for Participants. Alcoholics Anonymous (AA) is widely recognized as quite powerful in maintaining the sobriety of participants who commit themselves to the program. This occurs even for participants whose home environments are either unsupportive or rich with cues that historically have been associated with alcohol consumption. Committed AA members attend meetings many times a week—often every day or, during especially risky periods, even more than once a day. Regular attendance keeps the group extremely salient for members and thereby significantly lessens the likelihood that the norms and values of the program will give way to those associated with daily life in one's home or work environment. In effect, the AA group is a continuous presence in the life of its members, and the same is true for many of the more successful weight loss programs. By contrast, most off-site training and development programs for organization members are not. Although training group members often vow to have reunions and to check in with one another regularly, these commitments tend to dissipate in response to the pace and pressures of the back-home work setting. To counter this tendency, some group-mediated training programs take explicit steps to keep the training group alive for alumni. For example, change expert Larry Wilson and his associates have designed programs in which 2- or 3-day

training sessions are followed by monthly modules that bring groups back together to discuss new and old content in a structured team meeting format, facilitated by workbooks and other media. Recent advances in information technology offer additional possibilities for this kind of continued group engagement in learning.

Train Intact Teams. One popular alternative to group-mediated individual training is for training to be provided, either in the home organization or off site, to intact organization teams. The idea is that team members will provide a supportive context for one another as they all seek to use in their regular work what they have learned. Moreover, precisely because the training teams also are a part of participants' usual work environments, they should provide an even more continuous presence for members than do programs such as AA. The evidence on the efficacy of team-based learning programs is mixed, but overall it suggests that training intact teams is much more likely to persist than is off-site, group-mediated training of individuals. One change program used company-specific sessions to trigger a process of personal growth and reflection for individuals, followed by the creation of small learning teams that then met monthly both to make the group a continuous presence and to work on improvement tasks such as reducing costs, increasing revenue, or reducing material waste in production (Casciaro, Edmondson, & McManus, 2006).

High-fidelity simulations are a special type of intact team training that appears to have great promise for ameliorating the transfer and persistence problems that can compromise participants' use of lessons learned in off-site training. Such simulations have been used with success both in aviation and in medicine (Gaba, Howard, Fish, Smith, & Sowb, 2001; Hackman, 1993). Simulations provide a hybrid of online and offline learning; they eliminate the risk (e.g., to patients or passengers) of learning new skills on the job while mitigating the problem of transfer from the classroom to the real organizational task—although effective debriefing appears to be essential to the transfer of insights and skills from the simulation to the real job (Rudolph, Simon, Dufresne, & Raemer, 2006).

Although participants in high-fidelity simulations are not working with the specific people with whom they will be interacting in the operational environment, the *roles* of group members are exactly the same. A captain in a line-oriented flight simulation, for example, might never be rostered with the particular individuals who are serving as his or her first officer and flight engineer in the simulation, but every actual flight will involve working with people who occupy those same two roles. Although additional research is needed on the transfer and persistence of this type of group-mediated training, it appears to have great potential for obtaining the benefits of intact team training in settings where team composition changes frequently.

Alter Individuals' Personal Theories of Action. Although Chris Argyris was deeply involved in the theory and practice of T-group training, he gradually came to understand that this type of training was not having the enduring effects in participants' back-home organizations that training practitioners had hoped for. In exploring the reasons for this outcome, he concluded that achieving personal change that would transfer and persist would require more fundamental change than typically occurs in group-mediated training. Specifically, he articulated two different models of personal intervention: Model 1, which involves unilateral actions to achieve one's objectives (and is characteristic of almost all people he assesses), and Model 2, which is predicated on the values of valid information, free and informed choice, and internal commitment to choice (Argyris, 1976, 1982). His recent research has shown that it is indeed possible to use group methods to achieve fundamental changes in individuals' theories of action but also that achieving this high developmental aspiration takes extraordinary investment

and commitment, sometimes taking years to accomplish (Argyris, 1993).

Recent research has built on Argyris's theory of action to examine the use of groups to change entrenched beliefs and thought patterns through practicing reflection offline, which can gradually increase the chances of reflective practice online (Rudolph, Taylor, & Foldy, 2001). Drawing on a case study of their own "reflection group," the authors present transcript data showing how they worked together to examine unintended consequences of their implicit theories of action for influencing others' behavior. This offline reflection, removed from the stresses of real work, promoted new habits of attention and analysis that improved participants' online effectiveness.

What remains to be explored in research and practice is the possibility of combining group-mediated individual development with simultaneous alteration of organization structures and systems to create contexts in which newly learned behavioral strategies are welcomed rather than viewed as aberrations and discouraged. We turn next to a discussion of what is involved when groups are used as a tool for organizational rather than individual change.

Improving Work and Organization Processes

Groups often are asked to implement substantive organization change, such as improving work processes through which products or services are produced for customers, implementing new technologies, or changing the organization's culture. The desire to improve an organization's culture—that is, to alter fundamental assumptions, norms, and attitudes that shape the way people work (Schein, 2004)—may be the most frequently espoused organization change goal. Initiatives to substantially alter work processes—that is, procedures and communication patterns that transform work inputs into outputs—may be less popular but, we suggest, are no less important to understand. In both cases, the change is organizational because it affects multiple people, relationships, or processes.

Organization change is notoriously difficult to accomplish, however, especially in large or well-established organizations (Beer, Eisenstat, & Spector, 1990). A range of psychological, interpersonal, and structural factors present obstacles to change (Argyris, 1993; Goodman, Bazerman, & Conlon, 1980; Walton, 1975). In general, individuals are reluctant to alter well-practiced, skilled, or routine behaviors (Argyris, 1982), and changing group or organization routines can be even more challenging (Edmondson, Bohmer, & Pisano, 2001; Gersick & Hackman, 1990). First, given a general preference for the status quo, people are unlikely to change without strong motivation to do so. This might come in the form of a compelling rationale for the new way of doing things or evidence that a respected leader or role model is doing things a new way. Second, an intended change might not appear to be an improvement right away. Many times, organization changes produce performance decrements before members gain enough experience to improve them (Edmondson, 2004; Senge, 1990). Moreover, transferring an innovative technology or work practice to a different setting almost always entails adjustments or adaptations (Tucker et al., 2007), which may put the change in a bad light and reduce engagement by those targeted for the change. Third, the people acting as change agents or change leaders may lose interest, become distracted by other responsibilities, or prematurely assume a change has taken hold.

These barriers to organization change can be lowered by the use of groups, rather than individuals, as change agents. We illustrate this claim with case studies that document instances of groups attempting to design and implement organization change efforts. These studies range from efforts to change corporate cultures to projects targeting work process improvements, and they include both successful and unsuccessful initiatives.

Using Teams to Lead Organization Change. Compared with individuals, teams assigned the task of leading organization change have several advantages. First, the change effort's momentum is less vulnerable to turnover; a single individual leading change might be out sick, lose interest, or leave for a new job, unlike a team of people, who can cover for each other and help each other sustain momentum and commitment to the change. More generally, a team has greater flexibility for deploying its attention, assistance, skill, or effort at varied times and in varied locations than does any single change agent.

Second, if team members are deliberately selected to represent key constituents targeted for change, the initiative is likely to have greater credibility in the organization than it would if it were led by even a very persuasive individual. Thus, rather than relying on a single senior executive with expertise in a single function such as marketing or finance, change teams can include people from multiple functions and levels. This can foster legitimacy and fairness by engaging people throughout the organization and provides additional resources for working through the details of implementation (Beer, 1980; Kotter, 1996).

Third, the task of successfully producing organization change almost certainly requires a diverse set of skills. Leading change involves design, planning, analysis, communication, and interpersonal skill. These capabilities are more likely to be distributed across individuals than found in any one person.

Finally, members of a group working together to produce organization change can use other members as sounding boards to check their ideas, plans, or reactions to field experiences. Similarly, after they encounter a challenging or puzzling experience while working to implement a change, team members can report back to their colleagues and get help in deciphering what happened. As is seen in the three case studies of group-led organization change described next, these shared sensemaking experiences can significantly improve the quality and effectiveness of the change initiatives.

Promoting Patient Safety. In a case study of an organization-wide patient safety initiative, Edmondson, Roberto, and Tucker (2002) documented the activities of a change team created by a new chief operating officer, Julie Morath, at Children's Hospital and Clinics in Minnesota in the late 1990s. Morath communicated a vision of achieving 100% patient safety in an era in which medical errors were just beginning to attract policy and managerial attention in the U.S. health care community.

To realize her vision, Morath created a change leadership team, called the Patient Safety Steering Committee (PSSC). The PSSC was a diagonal slice of the organization. The team included members from key functions such as medicine, administration, and nursing, spanning all levels from the executive ranks to the front lines and including important constituents such as union representatives. This team, not Morath, was designed to be the driver of change. Three change goals were identified: to transform the culture to create an environment conducive to discussing medical accidents in a constructive manner, to develop the infrastructure needed to implement safety improvements, and to overhaul the hospital's medication administration system.

To change the culture from one characterized by blame and silence about errors to one in which people could more easily learn from them, the PSSC instituted a new policy of blame-free reporting and taught people to replace threatening terms such as *errors* and *investigations* with less emotionally laden terms such as *accidents* and *analyses*. Very gradually, the culture of the organization was altered by these efforts. More concretely, the change team generated a number of task-focused projects aimed at improving patient safety in various clinical areas throughout the hospital. These smaller change projects, tailored to the particular needs of specific areas, embedded the culture change in the context of task-focused work.

Creating a Climate for Speaking Up. Arthur Ryan, CEO of Prudential in the late 1990s, wanted to change the culture of the 100-year-old insurance company after taking the firm public (Edmondson & Hajim, 2003b). Believing that successfully operating as a public company would require a culture that supported direct, honest, and consistent communication between employees, Ryan asked his human resource group to create a program geared toward making the working environment one in which it was safe to speak one's mind. A small group of consultants from Prudential's Learning Center (one of eight groups in human resources) led the charge. Through a series of integrated training programs, meetings, and other communication initiatives, the learning center team worked vigorously to make the work culture safe for speaking up. Although many employees spoke positively of the learning center's efforts, few signs of substantial change in the culture could be found. An internal culture survey revealed remarkably stable scores on items pertaining to the ability to speak up, although response rates did steadily increase, possibly indicating that greater numbers of people felt safe enough to complete the survey. It was not clear whether employees understood in a tangible way the value of openness to excellence in financial services. The learning center team's enthusiasm waned over time, and some consultants eventually left the company.

Comparing the Cases. One obvious difference between the two cases just described is the composition of the change team: At Children's the team was designed to be representative of the population of the hospital, thereby obtaining multiple views and ensuring a broad network of contacts, whereas at Prudential the change team came exclusively from human resources. Moreover, the change effort at Children's was explicitly task focused in that members of the organization were encouraged to examine the work processes in their own areas to identify hazards that might pose harm to patients. At Prudential, by contrast, change group members were less able to make crucial connections between safety for speaking up and specific organization tasks because their shared human resource backgrounds limited their expertise in other aspects of the work of a diverse financial service organization. People throughout the organization who were the targets of the "safe to say" program never came to view the change as either relevant to or integrated into their day-to-day tasks.

Creating a Lean, Efficient Organization. The value of having both a representative change team and an explicit task focus is seen in a third case, this one involving an organization-wide change effort in a public utility. The Washington Suburban Sanitation Commission (WSSC), founded in 1918, operated water and sewer services for households and businesses in Maryland. John Griffin, general manager, was recruited in 1999 at a time of crisis: The WSSC, an organization that had previously relied on both a growing population and an ability to raise rates in lieu of running a leaner organization, had been under review for privatization by local government, which was concerned about the organization's high-cost operations after a period of population stability.

Soon after Griffin joined the WSSC, he began to communicate a vision of the utility as a lean, efficient, competitive organization. Two years later, the organization had changed as follows: headcount reductions of 30%, cross-trained employees who were rewarded for learning new skills, self-managed teams throughout operations, and restructuring that transformed functional silos into cross-functional units. As a result, a 21% gap in operating efficiency between the WSSC and best of private industry was reduced to 3.5%, and customer confidence in the organization increased substantially.

To lead his change initiative, Griffin had put together a steering committee consisting of about 12 members representing a cross-section of work functions and hierarchical levels. The new change team started by reviewing best-in-class practices in the industry and creating a Competitive Action Program (CAP), designed to "reduce costs and staff without sacrificing quality or impacting employee safety" (WSSC Annual Report, 2000, quoted in Edmondson & Hajim, 2003a, p. 4). Although outside consultants were engaged to provide training to help the organization's cultural shift gain traction, the consultants were not members of the steering team. With the consultants' help, the WSSC sent several groups of managers to a local training facility for a 3-day program to build commitment, teamwork skills, and personal awareness of the change process. Immediately after this program, organization members were quickly marshaled to implement aspects of the CAP, including concrete changes in how they executed their tasks and cross-training to learn new tasks in newly formed teams.

Taken together, these three cases suggest that change teams are more effective when they are roughly representative of the constituents whose behaviors, interactions, or work processes they seek to change and when they help these constituents make essential connections between the aims of the change efforts and their day-to-day work activities. Although these cases do not allow comparison of the relative efficacy of change teams and individual change agents, it does appear that the diverse composition of both Children Hospital's PSSC and the WSSC's steering committee helped change team members figure out, and then communicate, how the intended organization changes would play out in their organizations' different work areas. The diverse positions and roles of change team members gave them legitimacy in the eyes of those targeted for change, and their diverse skills and expertise gave them actual knowledge of the organizations' varied tasks.

WHAT IT TAKES TO USE GROUPS AS AGENTS OF CHANGE

Our discussion thus far has identified a number of significant benefits that can be obtained when groups are used as tools for change in both the diagnostic and the action phases of organization development activities. Group-driven change is not without risks, however. Unless the groups that manage change processes are themselves well designed and competently led, an organization development initiative may devolve into an uncoordinated or misdirected set of activities that are, at best, ineffectual.

A central challenge in designing and leading change teams is that they must be able to do two things at once: get specific change tasks accomplished and continuously learn and adapt in a context that is inherently fluid and unpredictable. If a change team cannot get specific pieces of work accomplished well and on time, then the change program is almost certain to become entropic; the energy present when the program began diminishes, and eventually the initiative fades away without having made a discernible difference. And without continuous learning, the team's efforts are likely to be undermined by unanticipated developments, resulting in changes that are misdirected or that spawn unintended consequences. Both learning and performance are essential for teams that manage change.

Our own previous work has focused on one or the other of these two imperatives: Hackman (2002) on the conditions that foster excellent task performance by teams and Edmondson (1999, 2003) on what is needed for teams to learn from, rather than be subverted by, novelty, failure, or unexpected outcomes. Specifically, Hackman has identified five conditions that, when present, increase the chances (but do not guarantee) that task-performing teams will perform well: The team is a *real* team rather than a team in name only; the team has a clear and compelling direction that engages and orients members; the team is properly structured, especially regarding its composition, the design of its task, and basic norms of member conduct; the organization context supports rather than impedes the team's work; and the team has competent coaching available to facilitate members' collective work.

Edmondson's research suggests that a team climate of psychological safety enables learning

behaviors such as discussing mistakes, asking questions, and sharing ideas. Through team learning behaviors, teams master new tasks and improve work processes and performance in a changing context. By contrast, when team members operate in a climate of fear, when all are worried about the consequences of mistakes or of promoting ideas that others view as wrong or inappropriate, then the natural response is to duck down, pull back, and protect oneself. Such a climate significantly compromises learning and thereby lessens the likelihood that the team will generate truly innovative avenues for change.

In the paragraphs that follow, we integrate findings from our separate research programs to identify the main conditions that, as a set, should foster both learning and performance specifically for teams that manage organization change and development. In establishing these conditions, those responsible for change programs must navigate between two opposing poles, each of which invites group processes that can subvert the achievement of change objectives. Between the opposing poles lies a preferred, balanced state, which we also describe.

Bounded Change Team

A change team is likely to encounter difficulties when its boundaries are so diffuse or fluid that it is not clear who actually is on the team or when it is so tightly bounded that members focus far more on their own interactions than on exchanges with others in the surrounding organization. As Alderfer (1980) documents, these two difficulties are characteristic of underbounded and overbounded systems, respectively.

Underbounded. The membership of underbounded change teams may change frequently, or even if it does not, there might be great variance over time in who is present and actively involved in the group's work. For example, it is not uncommon for different subsets of change team members to come to different meetings, and to do so unpredictably, which can make it nearly impossible for the team to generate a coherent diagnosis or to achieve continuity in executing change activities. Although a change team's boundaries must be permeable enough to receive the ideas and concerns of different members of the organization, they should not be so fluid that the team's continuity and structure are too weak to support task accomplishment.

Overbounded. The boundaries of the group are sufficiently impermeable—or are seen by others as such—that the group becomes something of an island unto itself, out of touch with other groups that also are important to the change effort. In an organization one of us has studied, for example, a heavyweight product development team was created in hopes that its intense and singular project focus would lead to a breakthrough product and, moreover, would help forge a new approach to product development. But the team came to be viewed as elitist and overly exclusive, which, perversely, resulted in it having *less* influence than expected. The team did generate an innovative outcome, but the rest of the organization reacted negatively to its exclusivity and standoffishness and rejected it as a model for broader process changes. Overbounded teams also run the risk of insisting on homogeneity of views within the group, which can stifle learning and dissent and invite dysfunctional conflict with other groups that also are involved in planning and executing change activities.

Ideal. A group that has distinct but permeable boundaries, which allow both continuity in pursuing change objectives and cross-boundary transactions that can help the group develop valid diagnoses of the focal social system, generates appropriate change strategies and tactics and self-corrects when plans go awry. The PSSC at Children's Hospital and Clinics, discussed earlier, illustrates this kind of balanced permeability, recognizing the need for new members (e.g., parents) and for imperfect attendance

(because of clinical schedules and responsibilities) while maintaining a committed core membership that drove the change process.

Clear and Challenging Vision for Change

Groups that manage change need a clear and compelling vision of the end states that are sought. Aspirations that are either too modest or excessively challenging can compromise a change team's work.

Too Modest. Members of groups whose vision for change is diffuse or excessively modest are likely to find it difficult to generate the motivation to do much of anything. It always will feel as if there are more important or urgent matters to attend to, which can result in change activities not getting done or, in some cases, not even being initiated. In one organization with which we are familiar, for example, a change team was formed to gather members' views about the logo on certain official documents and possibly to recommend a change in font. That matter was of symbolic importance for the organization, but it might more appropriately have been handled by a professional designer. It was not something that challenged, excited, or engaged change team members.

Too Challenging. Perversely, aspirations that members experience as being beyond the group's reach also may result in the group never actually getting started on a program of organizational diagnosis and change. When a task is viewed as likely to become all-consuming or as impossible to accomplish, anxieties escalate and actual work often is deferred until "never." Statements of change vision such as "go global," "double our size," or "create new markets using new technologies" are at once too diffuse and too challenging to meaningfully engage team members. And when a change team does take on an overly challenging change task, there is a real risk of frustration, disillusionment, and disengagement as members gradually come to realize that the project is unlikely to be brought to a successful conclusion.

Ideal. A vision for change that is clear, challenging, and within the realm of plausible is ideal. As is the case of individual task motivation, a group task for which members feel that they have about a 50–50 chance of success may be optimal. The objectives to be pursued by change management groups should be as clear and meaningful as possible but also require significant effort and the deployment of the full complement of members' knowledge, skill, and experience.

Adequate Autonomy

Groups in organizations vary in how much autonomy they have to control the behavior of their own members and to get things done in the broader organization. Change teams need sufficient autonomy to manage both their own processes and their relationships with external individuals and groups—but not so much that members feel authorized to deviate substantially from agreed-upon change objectives or from organization norms and values.

Too Constrained. Members of groups that are excessively constrained by prespecified procedures, activities, or rules may have many discussions about what they would like to do, but when the time comes to actually do it they find they cannot. Such groups may be unable even to develop and enforce norms about the behavior of their own members, let alone to get other individuals and groups to make decisions or take actions at the group's request. Although low-autonomy groups may persist indefinitely, the degree to which they are taken seriously by external entities or by their own members is likely to diminish over time. The change team at Prudential, discussed earlier, can be described as overly constrained by the CEO's

focus on creating safety for speaking up. This mandate may have prevented the group from diagnosing and intervening in critical aspects of the organization's work processes and norms in a way that might have altered employees' beliefs about speaking up in the context of doing work rather than as an end in itself.

Too Few Constraints. By contrast, some change management groups are told that they can do whatever is needed to get change accomplished, with essentially no constraints on what they ask of their own members or of others in the organization. Members of such groups have a lot of muscle, and they are likely to use it—to keep members in line, to be a significant force in the larger system, or both. Such groups are so effective at enforcing behavioral norms that they risk falling into a pattern of what Barker (1993) calls "concertive control." Because deviance is rare in groups that exert concertive control, member-generated innovations are infrequent, and such groups are likely to be far more orderly than they are interesting. The external relationships of unconstrained groups are another story. Such groups risk spinning out of control, pursuing objectives that may not be aligned with the purposes of the overall system, and exhibiting a level of deviance in the larger system that would never be allowed within the group itself.

Ideal. A group that is able to develop and execute a coherent strategy for deploying member resources to achieve its purposes but whose focus and scope are limited and explicitly directed toward the change objectives of the larger social system is ideal.

An Organization Culture That Supports Real Change

Organizational diagnosis and change activities, by their nature, require both exchanges with and support from the broader system where the changes will occur. Yet a change management team should not be so tightly linked to its context that members have difficulty envisioning distinctive alternatives to the status quo.

Unsupportive Cultural Context. The unavailability of organizationally provided information, access, and resources can compromise the work even of well-designed teams that have a clear and compelling vision for change. It is as common as it is perverse that the very organization culture that senior leaders hope to alter itself undermines the work of the team that was created to promote change. Change activities cannot be successfully executed by free-standing groups that are neither linked to nor supported by their organization contexts, as was illustrated in the case of the homogeneous human resource change team at Prudential. Nor can such groups learn what is needed to manage the change process if the broader organization culture gives higher priority to covering over problems than to learning from them. One of us studied a hospital team that emphasized the appearance of excellent performance at the expense of opportunities to catch, correct, and learn from errors. As a result, team members got the message that mistakes were to be quickly corrected but not shared or used as a point of departure for improving existing systems. Thus, the faulty systems that gave rise to errors remained intact.

Too Embedded in Existing Culture. A group that is too deeply embedded in its surrounding system is unlikely to be able to initiate and carry out substantial change of that system. Because change management activities are subject to the very systems, policies, and practices for which change is sought, the sharp edges of proposals for change generated by highly embedded change teams risk being gradually sanded down in discussions with colleagues in the broader organization. Simmons Mattress CEO Charlie Eitel recognized the importance of change teams having some level

of independence from the existing culture. Therefore, he created a leadership team to turn company performance around that included both long-time Simmons managers and new executives with experience in other turn-around companies and other industries. The presence on the team of the new executives decreased the chances that the team would unthinkingly perpetuate existing ways of operating (Casciaro et al., 2006).

Ideal. A group that is a clearly independent entity but whose membership roughly mirrors the makeup of the larger organization is ideal. When the composition of a group responsible for change is a diagonal slice of the organization, for example, the group will have within its boundaries a broad spectrum of change-relevant perspectives. Moreover, membership will include people who are positioned to help the group obtain the resources and support it needs in its work and to assist in developing change strategies that can challenge but not be rejected by their home units.

Leadership That Fosters Both Performance and Learning

The hands-on coaching of change team leaders is a major determinant of whether the team focuses mainly on getting its change tasks accomplished well and on time, on harvesting as much learning as possible from the work, or, ideally, on both.

Performance Only. Some change management groups become so intently focused on accomplishing the tasks they have set for themselves that they do not notice the emergence of unanticipated problems and opportunities—or, in some cases, that they suppress or explain away developments from which they should be learning. The traction that emerges when a group is proceeding vigorously down some path that members have committed themselves to can, if uncorrected by learning, result in the work getting completed as planned but with consequences that are unfortunate and unanticipated. Change team leaders who focus their behavior exclusively on task performance run a significant risk that their team's work will generate unintended dysfunctional consequences for the broader social system. The leaders of U.S. government teams who attempted to bring democracy and a market economy to Iraq may have fallen victim to precisely this problem. Some of these teams were so intently focused on accomplishing their change tasks that they overlooked or dismissed data about unanticipated outcomes that could have helped members generate more efficacious change strategies or tactics.

Learning Only. As Edmondson (1999) has shown, learning requires that the climate of a group be sufficiently safe that members can raise and explore issues that are risky, worrisome, or anxiety arousing. However, some change management groups develop a climate that is so focused on learning that the team's actual change tasks get overlooked. Even member contributions that are outrageous or irrelevant may elicit a response along the lines of "Thank you for sharing that," followed by discussions in which members explore what can be learned from the member's comments. In such circumstances, the likelihood that a group will generate and implement a provocative and interesting avenue for organization change is essentially nil. Leaders who focus their behavior and their groups' attention exclusively on learning run a real risk that the group's change objectives will never be achieved.

Ideal. Leadership that simultaneously creates a safe climate within which learning can occur and promotes competent collective work on the group's actual tasks is ideal. The kinds of leadership behaviors that promote continuous learning within teams have been explicated by Edmondson (2003). Coaching behaviors that promote task performance effectiveness, as well

as the times in a team's life cycle when such coaching behaviors are most efficacious, have been identified by Hackman and Wageman (2005). Leaders of change teams need to do both simultaneously: develop and sustain an internal climate that supports an intent focus on task requirements and performance and a shared commitment to explore and learn from new ideas, dissenting views, and unanticipated problems and opportunities.

LEADING GROUPS THAT LEAD CHANGE

The implications of these prescriptions for those who create groups to lead change activities are clear. The first order of business is to establish the purpose, structure, and links to the broader organization and then to create and sustain an internal culture that both fosters task performance effectiveness and provides the safety that is needed for appropriate risk taking and learning.

The order is important: Vision and design come before hands-on coaching. As Wageman (2001) and others have shown, the quality of a team's design is a significantly stronger determinant of team performance than is a leader's hands-on coaching behavior. Members of teams that are set up right experience fewer problems in working together than do members of poorly designed teams. And the problems that do develop are more amenable to correction. By contrast, even highly competent coaching makes little constructive difference for teams that have been poorly designed. Indeed, attempting to coach a structurally flawed change team to greatness can do more harm than good because it can divert members' attention from fundamental flaws in the team's purpose, design, or context.

Those who lead groups that are responsible for organization change must recognize and manage the ongoing tension between reflective learning and task execution in such teams. Managing this tension may involve frequent shifts between learning and execution modes. For example, some turnaround situations require teams to invent new approaches (thus innovating and learning) and implement a change (with demonstrable progress) simultaneously or in rapid sequence. Shifting modes in this way is challenging, both intellectually and emotionally. Whereas learning is a reflective state (preferably an unhurried one) that requires consideration of alternative possibilities, execution involves focused action to achieve specific objectives. A key leadership task is to help change teams navigate between these modes and appreciate their different but equally critical contributions to the overall change program.

Even well-designed and well-led change teams occasionally stumble and make mistakes. Because such teams are forging new directions, it is unrealistic to expect that they will get everything right on the first try. Another key leadership task, therefore, is to help change teams embrace mistakes and small failures for their learning value. Although it is human nature to distance oneself from failure, it is failure rather than success that offers the greatest opportunity for learning. Therefore, effective leaders of change teams do not stop with getting in place the structural and contextual conditions that foster the effectiveness of such teams. They also help their teams learn how to operate in ways that take full advantage of those favorable conditions— and, perhaps most importantly of all, they help their teams approach, explore, and learn from things that go wrong as the change process unfolds.

REFERENCES

Alderfer, C. P. (1980). Consulting to underbounded systems. In C. P. Alderfer & C. L. Cooper (Eds.), *Advances in experimental social processes* (Vol. 2, pp. 267–295). New York: John Wiley & Sons.

Alderfer, C. P. (forthcoming). *Intergroup relations and organizational diagnosis*. Manuscript submitted for publication.

Alderfer, C. P., Alderfer, C. J., Tucker, L., & Tucker, R. (1980). Diagnosing race relations in management. *Journal of Applied Behavioral Science, 16,* 135–166.

Alderfer, C. P., & Brown, L. D. (1972). Designing an "empathic questionnaire" for organizational research. *Journal of Applied Psychology, 56,* 456–460.

Alderfer, C. P., & Smith, K. K. (1982). Studying intergroup relations embedded in organizations. *Administrative Science Quarterly, 27,* 35–65.

Argyris, C. (1964). T-groups for organizational effectiveness. *Harvard Business Review, 42*(2), 60–74.

Argyris, C. (1976, Winter). Leadership, learning, and changing the status quo. *Organizational Dynamics,* 29–43.

Argyris, C. (1982). *Reasoning, learning, and action.* San Francisco: Jossey-Bass.

Argyris, C. (1993). *Knowledge for action.* San Francisco: Jossey-Bass.

Barker, J. R. (1993). Tightening the iron cage: Concertive control in self-managing teams. *Administrative Science Quarterly, 38,* 408–437.

Beckhard, R. (1969). *Organization development: Strategies and models.* Reading, MA: Addison-Wesley.

Beer, M. (1980). *Organization change and development: A systems view.* Glenview, IL: Scott, Foresman.

Beer, M., Eisenstat, R. A., & Spector, B. (1990). Why change programs don't produce change. *Harvard Business Review, 68*(6), 158–166.

Bradford, L., Benne, K., & Gibb, J. (1964). *T-group theory and laboratory method.* New York: John Wiley & Sons.

Bunker, B. B., & Alban, B. T. (2006). *The handbook of large group methods.* San Francisco: Jossey-Bass.

Campbell, J. P., & Dunnette, M. D. (1968). Effectiveness of T-group experiences in managerial training and development. *Psychological Bulletin, 70,* 73–104.

Casciaro, T., Edmondson, A. C., & McManus, S. (2006). *Leading change at Simmons (A).* Boston: Harvard Business School Case No. 406-046.

Coch, L., & French, J. R. P., Jr. (1948). Overcoming resistance to change. *Human Relations, 1,* 512–532.

Crosby, P. B. (1989). *Let's talk quality.* New York: McGraw-Hill.

Cummings, T. G. (1978). Self-regulating work groups: A socio-technical synthesis. *Academy of Management Review, 3,* 625–634.

Delbecq, A. L., Van de Ven, A. H., & Gustafson, D. H. (1975). *Group techniques for program planning.* Glenview, IL: Scott, Foresman.

Edmondson, A. (1999). Psychological safety and learning behavior in work teams. *Administrative Science Quarterly, 44,* 350–383.

Edmondson, A. C. (2003). Framing for learning: Lessons in successful technology implementation. *California Management Review, 45*(2), 34–54.

Edmondson, A. C. (2004). Learning from failure in health care: Frequent opportunities, pervasive barriers. *Quality and Safety in Health Care, 13,* 3–9.

Edmondson, A. C., Bohmer, R. M., & Pisano, G. P. (2001). Disrupted routines: Team learning and new technology implementation in hospitals. *Administrative Science Quarterly, 46,* 685–716.

Edmondson, A. C., & Hajim, C. (2003a). *Large scale change at the WSSC.* Boston: Harvard Business School Case No. 9-603-056.

Edmondson, A. C., & Hajim, C. (2003b). *"Safe to say" at Prudential Financial.* Boston: Harvard Business School Case No. 9-603-093.

Edmondson, A. C., Roberto, M .R., & Tucker, A. L. (2002). *Children's Hospital and Clinics.* Boston: Harvard Business School Case No. 9-302-050.

Edmondson, A. C., & Woolley, A. W. (2003). Understanding outcomes of organizational learning interventions. In M. Easterby-Smith & M. Lyles (Eds.), *The Blackwell handbook of organizational learning and knowledge management* (pp. 185–211). London: Blackwell.

Eisenstat, R. A. (1984). *Organizational learning in the creation of an industrial setting.* Unpublished doctoral dissertation, Yale University, New Haven, CT.

Gaba, D. M., Howard, S. K., Fish, K. J., Smith, B. E., & Sowb, Y. A. (2001). Simulation-based training in anesthesia crisis resource management (ACRM): A decade of experience. *Simulation and Gaming, 32,* 175–193.

Ganz, M. (2004). Why David sometimes wins: Strategic capacity in social movements. In D. Messick & R. Kramer (Eds.), *The psychology of leadership: New perspectives and research* (pp. 209–238). Mahwah, NJ: Lawrence Erlbaum.

Gersick, C. J. G., & Hackman, J. R. (1990). Habitual routines in task-performing teams. *Organizational Behavior and Human Decision Processes, 47,* 65–97.

Gilmore, T. N., & Barnett, C. (1992). Designing the social architecture of participation in large groups to effect organizational change. *Journal of Applied Behavioral Science, 28,* 534–548.

Gladwell, M. (2005, September 12). The cellular church. *New Yorker.*

Goodman, P. S., Bazerman, M., & Conlon, E. (1980). Institutionalization of planned organizational change. *Research in Organizational Behavior, 2,* 215–246.

Hackman, J. R. (1992). Group influences on individuals in organizations. In M. D. Dunnette & L. M. Hough (Eds.), *Handbook of industrial and organizational psychology* (Vol. 3, pp. 199–267). Palo Alto, CA: Consulting Psychologists Press.

Hackman, J. R. (1993). Teams, leaders, and organizations: New directions for crew-oriented flight training. In E. L. Wiener, B. G. Kanki, & R. L. Helmreich (Eds.), *Cockpit resource management* (pp. 47–69). Orlando, FL: Academic Press.

Hackman, J. R. (2002). *Leading teams: Setting the stage for great performances.* Boston: Harvard Business School Press.

Hackman, J. R., & O'Connor, M. (2004). *What makes for a great analytic team? Individual vs. team approaches to intelligence analysis.* Washington, DC: Intelligence Science Board, Office of the Director of Central Intelligence.

Hackman, J. R., & Wageman, R. (1995). Total quality management: Empirical, conceptual, and practical issues. *Administrative Science Quarterly, 40,* 309–342.

Hackman, J. R., & Wageman, R. (2005). A theory of team coaching. *Academy of Management Review, 30,* 269–287.

Janis, I. L. (1982). *Groupthink: Psychological studies of policy decisions and fiascoes* (2nd ed.). Boston: Houghton Mifflin.

Kemper, T. D. (1968). Reference groups, socialization, and achievement. *American Sociological Review, 33,* 31–45.

Kotter, J. P. (1996). *Leading change.* Boston: Harvard Business School Press.

National Transportation Safety Board. (2002). *Aviation investigation manual*. Washington, DC: NTSB.

Nolen, W. A. (1970). *The making of a surgeon*. New York: Random House.

Priem, R. L., Harrison, D. A., & Muir, N. K. (1995). Structured conflict and consensus outcomes in group decision making. *Journal of Management, 21*, 691–710.

Priem, R. L., & Price, K. H. (1991). Process and outcome expectations for the dialectical inquiry, devil's advocacy, and consensus techniques of strategic decision making. *Group and Organization Studies, 16*, 206–225.

Roethlisberger, F. J., & Dickson, W. J. (1939). *Management and the worker*. Cambridge, MA: Harvard University Press.

Rudolph, J. W., Simon, R., Dufresne, R. L., & Raemer, D. B. (2006). There's no such thing as "nonjudgemental" debriefing: A theory and method for debriefing with good judgment. *Simulation in Healthcare, 1*, 49–55.

Rudolph, J. W., Taylor, S. T., & Foldy, E. G. (2001). Collaborative off-line reflection: A way to develop skill in action science and action inquiry. In P. Reason & H. Bradbury (Eds.), *Handbook of action research* (pp. 405–412). Newbury Park, CA: Sage.

Ryle, G. (1949). *The concept of mind*. London: Hutchinson.

Schein, E. H. (1988). *Process consultation: Its role in organization development* (2nd ed.). Upper Saddle River, NJ: Prentice Hall.

Schein, E. H. (2004). *Organizational culture and leadership* (3rd ed.). San Francisco: Jossey-Bass.

Schein, E. H., & Bennis, W. (1965). *Personal and organizational change through group methods*. New York: John Wiley & Sons.

Schwarz, R. (1994). *Team facilitation*. Englewood Cliffs, NJ: Prentice Hall.

Schweiger, D. M., Sandberg, W. R., & Ragan, J. W. (1986). Group approaches for improving strategic decision making. *Academy of Management Journal, 29*, 51–71.

Senge, P. (1990). *The fifth discipline: The art and practice of the learning organization*. New York: Doubleday.

Staggenborg, S. (1998). Social movement communities and cycles of protest: The emergence and maintenance of a local women's movement. *Social Problems, 45*, 180–204.

Trist, E. L. (1981). The evolution of sociotechnical systems as a conceptual framework and as an action research program. In A. H. Van de Ven & W. F. Joyce (Eds.), *Perspectives on organization design and behavior*. New York: John Wiley & Sons.

Tucker, A. L., Nembhard, I. M., & Edmondson, A. C. (2007). Implementing new practices: An empirical study of organizational learning in hospital intensive care units. *Management Science, 53*(6), 894–907.

Wageman, R. (2001). How leaders foster self-managing team effectiveness: Design choices versus hands-on coaching. *Organization Science, 12*, 559–577.

Wageman, R., Hackman, J. R., & Lehman, E. V. (2005). The team diagnostic survey: Development of an instrument. *Journal of Applied Behavioral Science, 41*, 373–398.

Wageman, R., Nunes, D. A., Burruss, J. A., & Hackman, J. R. (forthcoming). *Senior leadership teams: What it takes to make them great*. Boston: Harvard Business School Press.

Walton, R. E. (1975, Winter). The diffusion of new work structures: Explaining why success didn't take. *Organizational Dynamics*, 3–21.

Wheelwright, S. C., & Clark, K. B. (1992). *Revolutionary product development*. New York: Free Press.

Woolley, A. W., & Hackman, J. R. (2006, July 29). *Defining analytic zones in organizations*. Paper presented at the Interdisciplinary Network for Group Research Conference, Pittsburgh.

Zajonc, R. B. (1965). Social facilitation. *Science, 149*, 269–274.

12

Assessing Organization Development and Change Interventions

RICHARD W. WOODMAN

JOHN B. BINGHAM

FEIRONG YUAN

"There was no 'one, two, three, and away,' but they began running when they liked, and left off when they liked, so that it was not easy to know when the race was over. However, when they had been running half an hour or so, and were quite dry again, the Dodo suddenly called out, 'The race is over!' and they all crowded round it, panting and asking, 'But who has won?'"

—Lewis Carroll, *Alice's Adventures in Wonderland*

Evaluation of organization development (OD) interventions and other planned change initiatives in complex social systems is a tricky business. Because organizational change is a continuous process, assessing OD may sometimes take on an Alice in Wonderland quality. In a manner similar to Alice's experiences, we may find it challenging to identify when the change actually begins and when it ends. In addition, it is seldom easy to measure the outcomes of interventions. Furthermore, it may be difficult to convince the major players that rigorous evaluation is necessary. Even with appropriate support and reliable and valid measures, it is typically quite challenging to design and carry out a scientifically sound assessment strategy such that we might have reasonable confidence in the results. Assessing OD is not for the faint of heart.

The reasons for these difficulties are many and complex. For starters, there are at least two basic, sometimes conflicting goals for evaluation of change programs (Woodman, 1989a, 2005). In a practical vein, OD seeks to develop evaluation methods that allow valid inferences about effective and ineffective organizational change efforts. At the same time, the field needs to understand change processes, dynamics, and phenomena in complex organizations in order to contribute to theory development in the organizational sciences. Approaches that are effective in program evaluation may or may not contribute as much to theory development as we would like, and vice versa.

Closely related to this dilemma, a variety of actors are involved in the change drama: top executives, other managers, human resource professionals, internal change agents, OD consultants, academic researchers, and employees (on whom the success of improvement efforts ultimately depends). Not surprisingly, values, perspectives, and insights vary a great deal between these people both in terms of practical concerns and in terms of philosophical and scientific concerns. Everyone involved in change programs and change evaluation does not necessarily have the same agenda. There is hope, of course, for bridging these differing values and perspectives (cf. Rynes, Bartunek, & Daft, 2001).

Our intention in this chapter is to explore the constraints and challenges facing organizational change evaluation and to provide a number of examples as to how such evaluation efforts might proceed. In addition, we make suggestions for conducting valid evaluation research on OD and similar change programs.

ARGUMENTS FOR THE IMPORTANCE OF EVALUATION

At some level of abstraction, organizational effectiveness is the goal of all OD interventions (Woodman, 1989b). Similarly, understanding and explaining the antecedents of organizational effectiveness is the goal of much applied research on organizational change. Thus, to be concerned about both implementing and evaluating OD programs is to be concerned about fundamental issues of organizational effectiveness (Carnall, 1986).

Certainly for many in the field the desirability of validly assessing the usefulness and outcomes of an OD effort seems obvious. Nevertheless, it makes sense for both change agents and change scientists to be able to articulate the need for rigorous evaluation of organizational change. First, one might argue that effective organizational change begins with a valid diagnosis (Woodman, 1990). It is difficult, if not impossible, to change what you do not understand. This diagnosis leads quite naturally into creating the assessment strategies, identifying change levers and variables of interest, developing measurement tools, and planning the research design that, in turn, should be part of the action planning process that is a precursor to the actual implementation of the change program. Furthermore, in practical managerial language, it should be logically possible to sell the notion that every significant change effort, using and absorbing some portion of the organization's resources, should be accompanied by an assessment of whether the flame is worth the candle. Also, if the field is to contribute appropriately to theory development in the organizational sciences, then scientifically rigorous assessment of the antecedents, context, and consequences of change processes and phenomena must be done (Woodman, 2005). We mention these straightforward notions here because, as we closely examine the parameters of the many constraints on and problems with evaluation in OD, it is good to remember why we are engaged in this exercise. Perhaps this will keep us from getting discouraged.

DYNAMICS REDUCING THE PROBABILITY OF VALID OD ASSESSMENT

A variety of dynamics within the organization mitigate against the valid evaluation of change programs. We group these into two broad categories: technical constraints and sociopolitical constraints.

Technical Constraints on Evaluation

Rigorous research (including evaluation research) is not easy to do. A plethora of technical issues limit both the ability and the enthusiasm of organization members for rigorous evaluation of their change programs. A large percentage of the constraints and limitations on effective evaluation can be summarized in two words: *resources* and *difficulty*. More specifically, constraints in this category can be grouped into resource limitations, measurement difficulties, consistency in treatment across organizations (and across time), and evaluation biases.

Resources. Evaluating change has costs. In addition to monetary resources, evaluating change costs time, talent, and energy. When the organization judges that talent employed in the firm is insufficient for diagnosing and implementing change, outside talent typically is employed (McMahan & Woodman, 1992; Toegel, 2005). Under such circumstances, an organization may resist undertaking a rigorous evaluation because of a perception that outside consultants are attempting to extend their contract, pad their fees, or some such. Internally, there are always opportunity costs for everyone involved with the change program because, obviously, people

are investing their time in this manner rather than doing something else. Pressures to get closure on the change effort may limit the enthusiasm of management for follow-up assessments, particularly when such assessments are sophisticated and, perhaps, costly in time and money. In sum, organizations may sometimes make decisions with regard to implementing an assessment strategy that are driven by false notions of cost reduction or invalid notions about the ability of experienced managers to know when something has been improved (which is not to deny, of course, that experienced managers or other change agents are capable of valid judgments in this regard). Although it may seem illogical to expend significant resources on a change effort and then seek to compensate for this expense by stinting on evaluation, such a scenario is too common.

Measurement Issues. It is difficult to know what to measure and to understand how to go about it. One of the most basic measurement problems in organizational change occurs when employee perceptions are used to assess organizational change. The well-known typology of alpha, beta, and gamma changes was developed as a way of understanding problems that accompany perceptual judgments about change (Golembiewski, Billingsley, & Yeager, 1976). In this typology, alpha change represents an actual change in behavior or some other variable perceptually assessed. Beta change represents a scale recalibration in the sense that the employee (e.g., responding to a survey questionnaire) has recalibrated some scale in her mind such that what is objectively identical behavior before and after the OD intervention is nevertheless judged to be different. The behavior has not changed; what has changed is the observer's perception of the behavior. (Alternatively, behavior that is actually different might be perceived as unchanged.) Gamma change, representing the most severe threat to the validity of a perceptual measure, is defined as a situation in which the OD intervention has caused concepts to be redefined in the respondent's mind in such a way that the variable being measured after an intervention is no longer the same construct as the variable measured before the intervention. For example, a team member has redefined the meaning of group effectiveness after being exposed to team building in such a dramatic fashion that a perceptual measure of effectiveness taken before the team building cannot be meaningfully compared with a perceptual measure after the team building. Team effectiveness has now come to mean something dramatically different to the respondent. We are not totally at sea with regard to these issues. Using measures that have been carefully pilot tested to improve their psychometric properties will go a long way toward protecting against beta and gamma changes being mistaken for alpha change (the goal of the intervention). Furthermore, a number of sophisticated statistical and procedural approaches can reduce the probability of the occurrence of beta and gamma change or, at a minimum, measure such changes when they occur (Armenakis, 1988).

It seems that the possible existence of these problems with perceptual measures argues strongly for the use of more objective indicators of change. Although that is typically an excellent idea, it is unfortunately no panacea. Objective criteria may be difficult to measure. For example, willful absenteeism is notoriously difficult to measure accurately because it is often problematic to disentangle willful absences from illness absences (Martocchio & Harrison, 1993). At the risk of stating the obvious, there is no reason why an intervention designed to reduce willful absenteeism would reduce legitimate illness. Thus, unless we can partial one from the other, it becomes impossible to validly assess the effects of the change program.

Also, seemingly objective criteria may change in subtle ways across time, unbeknownst to the researchers. One of the authors of this chapter was once involved in a longitudinal

OD evaluation using productivity data that appeared to be an excellent measure of the effects of the change program. Sadly, these data were found to be seriously flawed because the organization had changed its productivity index three times over several years, rendering comparisons across time periods nearly worthless. As a rule, we should certainly seek to develop objective measures of changes in variables of interest, but it is important to avoid blind confidence in such indicators. Change agents and change scientists should avoid being lulled into a false sense of security with regard to statistical conclusion validity simply because measures are "objective."

Yet another measurement issue stems from the quite straightforward question of when to measure. Pettigrew, Woodman, and Cameron (2001) argue that time has played an insufficient role in attempts to understand and measure organizational change. Recognizing that organizational changes represent processes that unfold across time suggests both that longitudinal research designs, as opposed to cross-sectional ones, are often most effective and that timing of assessment may be crucial. For example, measurement times may be too widely or too narrowly spaced to adequately sample the process of change. A classic problem in OD interventions has been the distressingly common phenomenon of some change target variable returning to its original state after assessment occurs but having this fact unknown to the evaluators, who have already drawn their conclusions about the efficacy of some change effort based on a measurement made in the warm afterglow of the intervention.

Inconsistent Treatment Across Interventions. In addition, the OD field has its own version of validity problems stemming from the inconsistent application of OD technologies across interventions. That is, the field has long been plagued by change agents—who often come from quite different paradigms—describing what is essentially the same intervention using different names and using the same label to identify interventions that, on close examination, turn out to be markedly different (Woodman, 1980). This can create serious problems when one is attempting a meta-analysis or even a narrative review designed to accumulate findings across studies. A corollary problem exists when multiple change agents or consultants are involved in a large-scale change effort or the intervention unfolds across time. Some interventions are particularly susceptible to the skill with which the OD intervention is led. These types of interventions may be more likely to be susceptible to erroneous evaluation; that is, evaluators may conclude that a change technology was ineffective when, in fact, the intervention is potentially capable of causing desired change but has been implemented poorly (Woodman, 1989a).

Evaluation Biases. All research, including evaluation research, is subject to a variety of potential biases stemming from sampling, measurement, design and procedures, and even interpretation of findings. The *Devil's Dictionary of Behavioral Science Research Terms* defines *bias* as the sugar in the gas tank of measurement (Woodman, 1979). But the issue here is much broader than just measurement error, although that is problem enough. A paradox that exists throughout the social sciences is that there can be (in the eyes of some critics) an inverse relationship between methodological rigor and the importance of research findings. That is, research questions that seem to be rich and important in content seem particularly difficult to investigate in a rigorous fashion; more trivial research questions often appear to lend themselves more readily to rigorous research designs and strategies. The cynic thus argues that the field often seems to be choosing between answering trivial questions with confidence or providing invalid answers to important questions.

In the change and development arena, a related problem emerged and was addressed some time ago, although not to everyone's satisfaction. For example, Terpstra (1981) posits

the existence of a positive findings bias in OD research: The less rigorously an intervention was evaluated, the more likely it was to report positive outcomes. An evaluation of 52 published OD studies appeared to support the positive findings bias hypothesis. Bullock and Svyantek (1985) analyzed 90 OD studies in an attempt to replicate Terpstra's research but reached the opposite conclusion; they reported no evidence of a positive findings bias. Building on Terpstra's and Bullock and Svyantek's work, Woodman and Wayne (1985) analyzed 50 evaluations of OD interventions using a larger number of judges and an improved scale to assess methodological rigor. In general, their work supported the Bullock and Svyantek findings. There was no support, overall, for the existence of a positive findings bias in published work. Unfortunately, when process interventions (e.g., survey feedback, team building, process consultation, laboratory training) were analyzed separately from technostructural interventions (see Friedlander & Brown, 1974), there was some marginal evidence for the positive findings bias. There is reason for concern here. Process interventions often rely somewhat more on perceptual assessments and less on objective indicators of change than do technostructural interventions. In general, evaluation biases are also very much related to the sociopolitical constraints to be discussed next.

Sociopolitical Constraints

In addition to the numerous limitations discussed earlier, a variety of constraints and limitations arise from the nature of human beings and the patterns of social interaction typical of organizations and other complex social settings. We categorize these constraints into individual differences, political behavior, and the phenomenon of evaluation apprehension.

Individual Differences. As mentioned previously, there are many players in the organizational change arena. All decision makers, including those who must make decisions about implementing and evaluating OD, are influenced by their past experiences, their educational backgrounds, their current situations, and by a host of individual differences (e.g., personality, attitudes, values) that influence their judgments (Woodman & Dewett, 2004). For example, it is simply not realistic to expect a line manager faced with rigid deadlines and scarce resources to come to the same decisions about the value of rigorous assessment that a student pursuing her PhD might make. A crucial issue in evaluating OD and other change interventions is the management of the differences between the various interests, perspectives, agendas, and so on of the people involved. This management begins with an understanding of and appreciation for these individual differences.

Political Behavior. Organizations are political systems. We must expect that people in organization settings will attempt to meet their own needs, to advance their own agendas, to accomplish their own goals, and to behave in a political fashion particularly when there are finite resources (as there always are), when situations, decision rules, and policies are ambiguous, and when there are differences in power between the participants. After a somewhat slow start as the field developed, these dynamics are now fairly well understood (cf. Cummings & Worley, 2005, pp. 163–168). A host of issues of a political nature can threaten the effective design and implementation of an assessment strategy. Some people may judge (perhaps even correctly) that rigorous evaluation of change programs is not in their best interests.

Evaluation Apprehension. Somewhat related to political behavior, it is very understandable that people may be threatened by an evaluation of their decisions, actions, degree of effort, and so on, in OD as in any other work endeavor. Whereas the organizational scientist may think of the research design solely in terms of scientific findings, organization participants may

look at the same assessment strategy and see something quite different. A lack of progress, significant improvement, or change when resources have been expended may threaten those responsible for design and implementation. One should anticipate some concerns about and resistance to rigorous evaluation stemming from the phenomenon of evaluation apprehension. This resistance may even be somewhat unconscious and unrecognized by organization participants. The normal fear of evaluation must be understood and managed if effective assessment is to take place.

APPROACHES TO EVALUATION AND ASSESSMENT STRATEGIES

There are multiple ways to categorize evaluation research in OD. In Table 12.1 we suggest a straightforward typology of research types, settings, and approaches that will help to make sense of the possibilities. In each category, studies are shown that provide examples of approaches using this setting or method. The categories shown here are not mutually exclusive; that is, a given study could appear in more than one category. For example, a study could be longitudinal and explore cross-cultural comparisons; a study could use a quasiexperimental design with data collected at multiple times (longitudinal).

Our intention is not to comprehensively review the change and development literature but rather to identify and describe studies that can serve as exemplars of each assessment approach or research design. These exemplars are drawn from the planned change literature and from published evaluations of specific OD techniques.

True Experimental Designs

True experimental designs are a particularly powerful class of research design in terms of establishing causality (Campbell & Stanley, 1966). In general, experimental designs represent an

Table 12.1   Research Exemplars

True Experimental Designs

    Cooke & Coughlan, 1979

    Orpen, 1979

    Woodman & Sherwood, 1980

Quasiexperimental Designs

    Schuster et al., 1997

    Sommer, 1987

    Wanous & Reichers, 2001

Nonexperimental Survey Research and Field Studies

    Bernstein & Burke, 1989

    Daly, 1995

    Waclawski, 2002

Longitudinal Field Research

    Arthur & Aiman-Smith, 2001

    Beard, Woodman, & Moesel, 1998

    Coyle-Shapiro, 1999

Cross-Cultural Comparative Research

    Fagenson-Eland, Ensher, & Burke, 2004

    Lillrank et al., 1998

Meta-Analyses

    Bullock & Tubbs, 1990

    Macy & Izumi, 1993

    Robertson, Roberts, & Porras, 1993

Qualitative Research

    Denis, Lamothe, & Langley, 2001

    Falkenberg, Stensaker, Meyer, & Haueng, 2005

    Ferdig & Ludema, 2005

Combined Paradigm Research

    Manning & DelaCerda, 2003

    Whelan-Berry, Gordon, & Hinings, 2003

ideal assessment form for evaluation research that has the objective of determining the effects of some programmatic effort. The internal validity of the research is paramount ("What are the effects of X?"), and true experimental designs have the highest internal validity of any form or category of research commonly used in the organizational sciences. Several criteria must be met for a design to qualify as a true experimental design (Kerlinger & Lee, 2000). Specifically, the researcher must have the ability to directly control at least one independent variable,[1] the ability to form control groups or conditions, and the ability to randomly assign individuals, groups, or organizations to either the treatment or control condition. In addition, we might note that the study must have a sufficient number of subjects for the randomization process to distribute error variance equally across the experimental design.

It has been argued that true experimental designs are impossible in OD (Bullock & Svyantek, 1987) because of the impossibility of randomly assigning individuals or work groups within existing organizations. However, this position is not supported by all researchers (see Seashore, 1984). Indeed, examples of true experimental designs, though rare, can be found in the change literature.

Cooke and Coughlan (1979). Cooke and Coughlan (1979) described and assessed an organization development program for educational systems. Specifically, they measured the impact of a "survey feedback–problem solving–collective decision" intervention on 24 elementary schools and their teaching staffs. The OD program was designed to establish collective decision-making structures in schools and to initiate survey feedback and group problem-solving processes at the faculty level.

Researchers used 24 elementary schools: three survey feedback controls, seven pretest–posttest controls, and seven posttest-only control schools. Seven randomly selected schools received the full intervention and were evaluated within the framework of the four-group

experimental design. A survey was administered as a pretest to all teachers in three of the four groups of schools. Shortly after, profiled results were provided to schools in the two experimental groups. Leaders in each of these groups were trained in data feedback techniques, problem-solving processes, effective communication, and group leadership. About 6 months later, interviews were conducted with the experimental schools to evaluate program effectiveness. One year after the pretest administration, the survey was again administered as a posttest to all teachers in all four groups of schools.

Results suggest that the intervention affected the full-treatment schools and their staffs in the ways expected. More specifically, the program was generally successful in establishing collective structures and increasing the perceived adequacy of collective decision processes in the schools and faculty members in the full-treatment group. The program effectively established complementary collective structures in the majority of schools, which were associated with organizational health improvements and improved teachers' attitudes toward important aspects of the work environment. Favorable outcomes also resulted from a variety of faculty-initiated changes.

Orpen (1979). Orpen (1979) examined the effect of a job enrichment intervention on employee satisfaction and improved performance among clerical employees in a federal agency. Participants were randomly assigned to either an enriched or unenriched condition, with measures taken both before and after the systematic program of job enrichment. In the enriched condition, a systematic attempt was made to increase the extent to which the employees' jobs possessed each of the dimensions of skill variety, task identity, task significance, autonomy, and feedback. In the unenriched condition, the employees performed their original duties and tasks. The study was conducted in four phases: initial data collection, random assignment, a 6-month period during which subjects in both conditions performed their jobs, and a final data collection period by which the effect of enrichment was examined.

Using analysis of covariance, Orpen showed that employees in the enriched condition perceived their jobs as more enriched than before, and enrichment caused significant favorable increases in employee job satisfaction, job involvement, and intrinsic motivation. Enrichment also led to significant decreases in absenteeism and turnover. However, results did not show effects for enrichment on the work outcomes of performance and productivity, whether assessed by superiors' ratings or by actual output. These findings present evidence that enrichment may cause substantial improvements in employee attitudes, but these benefits may not necessarily lead to greater productivity.

Woodman and Sherwood (1980). Woodman and Sherwood (1980) undertook a rigorous experimental study of a team development intervention with 67 work groups in an engineering survey course. Groups were randomly assigned to one of three experimental conditions: team development, a placebo treatment (designed to control for possible Hawthorne effects), or control. The intervention was designed to improve the effectiveness of the work group by diagnosing problems facing the work group, providing feedback for those diagnoses, identifying key problems and setting priorities, and designing action planning strategies to address them. Researchers randomly assigned subjects to work groups, which were then, in turn, randomly assigned to treatment, placebo, or control conditions. Over a 6-week period, people in the work groups were assigned one surveying project per week. Two team development interventions were conducted during the fourth and fifth weeks, followed by a posttest measurement during the week after completion of the final group project.

Multivariate analysis of variance suggested that although there were positive effects on some perceptual measures of group functioning and dynamics, team development had no

significant impact on work group performance. Follow-up qualitative analysis revealed that approximately one-third of the surveying parties chose to not try to increase their performance effectiveness because information gathering and sharing revealed no issues or problems of any significance or because the cost of solving a problem appeared greater than the perceived benefits from the solution. However, results from this study also showed that people in the experimental group perceived their group as more effective and reported greater participation than members of control groups. The placebo condition revealed that a Hawthorne effect was not a rival explanation for the findings.

Quasiexperimental Designs

Whereas true experimental designs are somewhat rare, a larger number of evaluation studies of organizational change fall into the category of quasiexperimental designs (Cook, Campbell, & Peracchio, 1990). This research design is called quasiexperimental because researchers typically lack the ability to randomly assign individuals, groups, organizations, or parts of organizations to treatment or control conditions, although they still have the ability to control at least one independent variable (such as the change intervention). Quasiexperimental designs typically take one of two major forms: the use of nonequivalent control groups or the use of time series analysis. In the first of these, even though random assignment is impossible, the research is designed such that individuals, groups, or settings (e.g., offices, facilities) are withheld from the treatment to serve the function of a nonequivalent or comparison condition. Sometimes, even creating a reasonably valid comparison group is impossible, and researchers must rely on multiple measures made across time in order to develop inferences about the effects of an intervention. A valid time series design certainly entails more than a single pretest and posttest, however. Ideally, several measures of variables of interest must be made over time, both before and after the intervention.

Schuster et al. (1997). Schuster et al. (1997) examined a largely anecdotal proposition in OD: that conscious interventions to move an organization toward high levels of employee involvement and enhanced emphasis on meeting employee needs can produce higher motivation, commitment, and organization performance. Their study reports a single time series quasiexperiment in a Canadian firm and evaluates the effect of implementing a structured, seven-step strategy to obtain improved organization performance through employee-centered management. An intervention strategy to produce increased employee involvement and attention to the needs of employees, they suggest, may produce significant improvement in hard financial measures.

Using a subject pool from a diversified dairy product processing and marketing firm of about 3,000 employees in Canada, researchers used the Human Resources Index to implement and assess employee-centered management. A participative management intervention was introduced into the system to complement corporate strategy restructuring focused on developing and maintaining competitive advantage in the global marketplace. A significant change in the condition of the human organization resulting from the intervention was measured over a 5-year period and was shown to be correlated with a 66% increase in profitability. That is, improvement in the motivation, morale, and commitment of employees in the firm led to significantly improved organization performance, rather than vice versa. Results further indicated that in the Canadian and U.S. context, employee-centered management is compatible with high performance and competitive advantage. Additional evidence also suggested that in some instances, organization performance can be significantly enhanced through the participation and contribution of employees in problem-solving and decision-making processes.

Sommer (1987). Sommer (1987) also studied an intervention's effect on outcomes, but this study used an action research model. Four memorial and funeral cooperative societies were studied to evaluate their dissemination and use of membership survey results under conditions of high and low client involvement and technical assistance. Sommer suggested that a survey undertaken with client involvement and followed by technical assistance from professional researchers will be more likely to result in the dissemination (discussion or publication of the survey findings initiated by the client organization's leadership, either within or outside the organization) and use (tangible changes in the organization's policy or practice that could be attributed to the survey findings) of the findings than will a survey conducted without client involvement or outside technical assistance. Two of the societies were assigned to the experimental condition, in which the client was significantly involved, and the remaining two groups were assigned to a control condition of low client involvement. Consistent with Lewin's conceptualization of action research, the experimental societies had greater involvement in the survey process followed by technical assistance. The control societies, on the other hand, had an outside group conduct the survey for them, received results through the mail without prescriptions for action, and received no technical assistance.

A multimethod approach for evaluating the surveys was used, which included available quantitative indices supplemented by historical analysis of events occurring before and after the surveys were administered. Followup interviews with management suggested that societies highly involved in survey planning and those that received technical assistance disseminated and used the results most often and had more favorable attitudes toward the researchers than did the societies characterized by low involvement or no assistance. Sommer suggested that the dissemination and use of survey results could be improved if members of the organization are closely involved in developing and executing the project and the researcher provides technical assistance to the organization during and after the survey.

Wanous and Reichers (2001). Wanous and Reichers (2001) conducted a 3-year action research OD project in an automotive part manufacturing plant. They designed the project to increase employee participation and solve certain organization problems. More specifically, management sought to increase employee participation while increasing the visibility of the OD effort. Four issue-specific task forces were formed as a result of an action planning meeting. Each task force was assessed in terms of its visibility to employees, given that it was assumed project visibility would be directly related to its success. Wanous and Reichers suggested that the greater the number of employees affected and the more the project could be directly observed by employees, the greater the OD project's visibility.

This quasiexperimental field study involved a large organization with more than 1,000 employees. The OD effort was directed at the largest of four internal business units in the experimental group, called the Plant. The other three business units formed the comparison group. The study was also longitudinal, conducted over a 3-year period, with two survey data collection points. Employees of the Plant were highly involved in the action research OD process to varying degrees throughout the project's 3 years. Employees had the opportunity to provide initial input during open-ended interviews. Data collected from the interviews aided in the development of survey items that reflected local issues and concerns. Employees were then asked to complete two separate surveys before and after the intervention. Small groups of employees then examined and discussed the survey results during feedback sessions that were directed at addressing plantwide problems that were believed to be highest priority. The experimental group was involved in additional meetings, and group members who attended town hall meetings were asked to nominate members for the task force groups. Together with the research team, task force members met to plan specific actions and determine how to meet specific goals.

Two way analyses of variance were used to assess possible differences in attitudes and behavior between the experimental and comparison groups. Measures of participation, decision making, and management effectiveness significantly increased in both the experimental and comparison groups over the 21 months that elapsed between the two surveys. Furthermore, the results of the second survey suggested the overall OD effort was viewed as significantly positive on two of the three indicators (i.e., being aware of the effort and believing that it was beneficial). This latter finding supported the author's arguments with regard to the importance of visibility of the OD effort.

Nonexperimental Survey Research and Field Studies

A great deal of field research in the organizational change arena, and research in the organizational sciences in general, takes the form of survey research. Another term for what we are calling nonexperimental survey research is simply *field studies*. This research is nonexperimental because researchers lack control of independent variation or lack the ability to create comparison or control groups (Kerlinger & Lee, 2000). Some authors restrict use of the terminology of survey research to research that is limited to description only; that is, samples of a population are surveyed and inferences made about population values from the values of some variable of interest discovered in the sample. However, in the organizational sciences in general, it seems that nonexperimental field research—research conducted in real organizations—is most frequently referred to as survey research when, as is typically the case, survey questionnaires are used to collect data from organization participants. Organizations survey their employees all the time, of course, to determine levels of job satisfaction, organizational commitment, intentions to turnover, attitudes toward specific firm policies, and the like. What distinguishes this pervasive activity from the research category being discussed here is the pursuit of scientific hypotheses. Lacking the ability of experimental design to deal directly with causality, researchers rely on sophisticated statistical approaches, such as structural equation modeling, to address causal research questions in these field studies.

Bernstein and Burke (1989). Bernstein and Burke (1989) examined the way beliefs regulate behavior. In this extensive three-part study, the authors discussed the theoretical and methodological assumptions underlying a new strategy for discerning organization members' performance-relevant beliefs.

Using three case interventions, Bernstein and Burke suggested that researchers can uncover a standard set of beliefs used by most people to understand organization events and the relationships between the beliefs of various subgroups, including managers and subordinates. The first intervention examined executives' beliefs about themselves and how those beliefs relate to their own beliefs about corporate strategy; it involved 68 managers of a top management group of a large financial institution that was considering strategic options. The second study, involving an agency of the U.S. government interested in management development, concerned managers' perceptions of themselves and how their self-perceptions related to subordinates' and superiors' perceptions of them. The third case intervention was a Fortune 500 manufacturing company attempting to radically transform itself in response to drastic internal and external change. This particular intervention involved managers' and subordinates' perceptions of management behavior, group climate, and organization culture. In all three cases, data were collected on employees' beliefs about specific content areas, and then attempts were made to find systematic relationships between the beliefs.

The study examined different uses of multivariate statistics including regression and path analysis to better discern the idiographic belief systems of individual employees in work systems. The authors noted that most OD specialists tend to use qualitative data and depend essentially on clinical intuition. However, by creating diagnostic models using quantitative multivariate methods, Bernstein and Burke suggested that when people associate one belief with another, they begin thinking in a systematic fashion. When OD consultants and practitioners can gain appreciable knowledge about belief systems, a new stage of development is attained, one that helps organization development change from a passive to an active process.

Daly (1995). Daly (1995) examined Kotter and Schlesinger's (1979) "education" as a method for adapting to change. The intervention, which involves explaining why the change is occurring and how it affects employees, is purported to increase commitment to a change initiative. One hundred eighty-three employees from seven relocated organizations were surveyed and asked about their judgments of a relocation decision. Analyses of variance assessed the degree to which there were organization-level differences on the three major variables in the study (justification, outcome fairness, and procedural fairness). Moderated hierarchical regression was then used to test the hypotheses, and results indicated that when employees are evaluating the fairness of change outcomes, they expect explanations only when the outcomes are negative. The relationship between justification and outcome fairness was moderated by outcome favorability, suggesting that Kotter and Schlesinger's (1979) "education" intervention does not always have the intended effect. Daly also found that employees expect explanations as a means of evaluating decision procedures, even when outcomes are favorable. That is, employees are likely to expect an explanation for a change decision regardless of whether the outcomes are positive or negative.

Waclawski (2002). Waclawski (2002) used a unique approach to evaluate large-scale organizational change interventions and to determine the effects of such change on organization performance. Waclawski explored the idea that organizational change occurs through modifications in the behavior of organization members. This framework was tested using survey data, financial measures, and customer service ratings collected in 26 different business units in the same organization. Using the Burke and Litwin (1992) model of performance, Waclawski tapped large-scale organizational change using 18 items evaluating mission and strategy, leadership, culture, and structure. Large-scale organizational change was measured as a significant change in scores over a 1-year period in each of these four domains.

Results showed that organizations experiencing large-scale change performed better financially than organizations that experienced incremental change, no change, or negative change. Results also demonstrated significantly greater improvement in managerial competence. Thus, in order to implement change that positively affects performance, organizations must consider each of the domains of mission and strategy, culture, leadership, and structure (as large-scale organizational change is defined in this study). Focusing on one or a subset of these elements, as many executives and consultants have been known to do, may not produce significant performance increments over time. The importance of changing managers' behaviors as a primary means of driving performance is clearly supported; the identification and modification of desired management practices are critical for organizations planning fundamental organizational change.

Longitudinal Field Research

As previously mentioned, Pettigrew et al. (2001) argued for a greater emphasis on assessing organizational change as a process that occurs over time. To adequately examine change across time requires the use of longitudinal research. Such research can be quite costly because it entails the involvement of researchers and organizations for months, if not years. Significant longitudinal designs can be a difficult sell to organizations anxious to get quick closure on the results of evaluation research.

Arthur and Aiman-Smith (2001). Arthur and Aiman-Smith (2001) answered a call by researchers to develop a better understanding of how gainsharing programs work and showed that it is possible to distinguish between two types of employee suggestions resulting from a gainsharing program that represent two different types of learning in organizations. Arthur and Aiman-Smith lamented the absence of a strong theory-based understanding of gainsharing programs given that such programs represent a complex intervention that requires firms to make a large number of choices about their implementation and measurement.

Using data from a large manufacturing plant, they chose a 48-month period to analyze the impact of the gainsharing plan. Union and management parties were extensively involved in the development and implementation of a gainsharing plan that would prevent the plant from being shut down or sold. Consistent with a Scanlon plan format, the plant introduced a formal procedure for soliciting and processing employee suggestions as part of the plan. Employees would submit a suggestion on a standard form to a joint union–management review team. The review team could accept, decline, or ask to investigate the suggestion further. Of the 495 suggestions made, 436 were coded and content analyzed. First-order learning suggestions were categorized as those that did not challenge the status quo thinking in the plant or change the basic way in which work was performed. Second-order suggestions were categorized as those containing ideas for increasing productivity by changing the way employees performed their tasks or by redesigning a product or manufacturing process. To test the hypotheses about the changes in volume and proportion of gainsharing suggestions, the authors summed the total number of suggestions and the number of first- and second-order suggestions for each month. Data were initially analyzed using time series procedures to ensure a stationary noise structure and then tested using ordinary least squares regression.

Results suggested that the plan was successful when the average level of performance was compared for the 2 years before gainsharing with the average for the first 4 years of the plan. However, the majority of the gains from gainsharing occurred in the first 2 years of the plan. From a learning perspective, the declining gainsharing payouts and suggestions were not evidence of a failed short-term program but the foundation for the generation of second-order learning and change in the organization. By disaggregating the pattern of overall suggestion making into first- and second-order learning suggestions, the authors found that the type of suggestions shifted over time, from being predominantly first-order material savings and new work suggestions in the earlier period to predominantly second-order learning production process changes by the end of 4 years. Consequently, from an organizational learning perspective, the program could be judged a success.

Beard, Woodman, and Moesel (1998). Beard et al. (1998) explored a behavioral modification intervention at an electronics manufacturing facility where absenteeism had been interfering with productivity and cost goal achievement. Addressing the problem in ways congruent with the facility's prevailing work culture philosophy, a task force established a baseline for attendance and then conducted a major survey of employee attitudes and opinions to identify salient work and nonwork factors in employee attendance patterns. Based on survey data gathered within the organization, the task force designated an organizational behavior management (OBM) intervention to modify and reinforce workforce attendance patterns.

The OBM intervention relied on a combination of positive reinforcers, negative reinforcers, and punishers to improve overall employee attendance. Positive reinforcement was used with those who fell into the top two attendance categories: perfect (100% attendance) or good to excellent (97–100% attendance). In the third and fourth categories (needing improvement, 95–96.9% attendance and unacceptable, below 95% attendance) employees began to experience negative reinforcement, including counseling sessions with supervisory personnel and actions plans to improve performance followed by progressive discipline if attendance did not improve.

Preintervention and postintervention data were collected from a 2-year period to evaluate the effects of the intervention. The organization summarized attendance data by week, and nonmissing data were aggregated for a total of 104 consecutive weeks. The primary measure used to assess attendance was the percentage of hours actually worked out of the 40-hour workweek. Attendance was expected to increase as a direct result of the intervention.

The researchers used a Box–Jenkins time series to address possible autocorrelation in the data and to account for seasonal, holiday, weather-related, and widespread illness effects. Furthermore, a time series intervention model was estimated to capture the change in the nature of the series with the formal interpretation of the intervention and the duration of program effects in the series. The percentage of overall attendance was estimated to have increased permanently by approximately 0.4%, a level that was marginally significant. Using the formula proposed by the firm of $80,000 in gross program savings from each percentage point increase in attendance, the firm gained a total of $43,627 in gross savings from the first five quarters of data after the intervention. In the final analysis, the intervention at the organization was hailed as a modest success based on this strict economic accounting.

Based on the aggregated efforts of individual teams, firm managers observed healthy increases in team attendance averages. Furthermore, the models developed to represent absenteeism behavior of this population of employees showed that external factors, many of which are beyond the control of employees, may contribute more to changes in absenteeism after an intervention than a person's discretionary behavior. Some of the implications of this study are that withdrawal behaviors are symptomatic of potentially deeper underlying organization problems. Creating a complex array of reinforcers and punishers, the researchers suggest, is unlikely to fundamentally alter employee behavior in the absence of strategies that deal with the underlying problems that may be driving the behavior.

Coyle-Shapiro (1999). Coyle-Shapiro (1999) used a three-part longitudinal design to examine total quality management (TQM) and its effect on commitment. The research design included the survey of employees from a U.K.-based multinational supplier of engineering and electrical components. The site launched development groups in the 1990s as a way for employees to contribute to continuous improvement on a voluntary basis. Yet given the sporadic participation in these groups, the site embarked on a TQM initiative. Previous changes had focused on the visible reorganization of work methods, systems, and structure. The objective of the current change initiative was to change the culture of the site toward continuous improvement through the participative involvement of all employees.

The change intervention, focusing on education and training, was designed with the assistance of a TQM proponent from within the organization and a group of outside consultants. It was assumed that as a consequence of the training and education program, which included Theory X and Y leadership styles, empowerment, leading and managing groups, and tools and techniques of TQM, a series of changes would occur throughout the site. The initiating point for the training and education programs was to facilitate the cascade of the training throughout the managerial hierarchy

and support the subsequent cascade from managers to employees.

The intervention was met with some supervisory reluctance, resulting in the integration of the intervention into the annual performance objectives and performance appraisals. Consequently, all new employees were required to participate in the intervention. The method for evaluating employees included a before-and-after study of TQM interventions with three measurement occasions: 6 months before the commencement of the intervention and 9 months and 32 months after the initiation of the intervention. A random sample of 40% of employees stratified by work area was asked to participate in the research. A total of 118 employees completed questionnaires from all three time periods. To assess employee participation in the intervention, employees were asked to indicate the extent to which they participated in the intervention activities along a five-point scale, which permitted a more accurate representation of the degree of employee participation in the intervention. Qualitative data were also collected during the intervening period to record reactions to the introduction of the TQM intervention and monitor the progress of implementation. Perceived benefit, organizational commitment, supervisory participative style, perceived management commitment, and improved support for TQM were other measures used in addition to demographic indicators.

Hypotheses for the study were measured using hierarchical regression. Results suggested that supervisors have an important role to play in getting employees involved in TQM. The extent of employee involvement was positively related to the assessment of benefits of TQM. Furthermore, how employees assess the beneficial impact of TQM was more important in predicting subsequent participation in TQM than was their initial participation. That is, employees who did not see a change intervention as beneficial in the early stages of implementation were unlikely to participate subsequently. Contrary to the proposed relationships, enhancement of organizational commitment did not occur as a consequence of employee participation in TQM. In sum, this study suggests that TQM involves different interest groups relinquishing some authority, suggesting that strategies for dealing with potential resisting forces must be integrated as part of the change process. Given that people resist change for a number of reasons, a multi-faceted change intervention, which may involve a reconceptualization of TQM, may increase the likelihood of achieving the desired change.

Cross-Cultural Comparative Research

In their introduction to the *Academy of Management Journal* special issue on organizational change, Pettigrew et al. (2001) identified cross-cultural comparative research as one of the six major areas of challenge for the organizational change and development field. They decried the paucity of international comparative work on organizational change and urged scholars to do more work of this type. Only by comparison of research results across cultures can the field ensure that its research-generated knowledge base and its change management practice are not culture bound.

Fagenson-Eland, Ensher, and Burke (2004). This study used Hofstede's (1980) four dimensions of culture as a framework to compare the use of different OD interventions in seven different countries: Finland, Ireland, the Netherlands, New Zealand, South Africa, the United Kingdom, and the United States. The authors predicted and tested different levels of usage of different types of OD in these seven countries based on their differences in national cultures.

Data about the use of interventions were collected via surveys of internal OD practitioners (OD practitioners providing consultation to their respective organizations) in these countries. Following the criteria and definitions provided by the researchers, a local investigator in each country identified OD practitioners in his or her country, distributed the surveys to them, and returned the surveys to the researchers. OD practitioners were recruited from different industries and companies to complete the survey through different methods (e.g., at OD conferences and workshops, through mailings to members of OD organizations and associations, and through selected newsletters and colleague referrals). Five hundred forty-seven surveys were completed. Sample sizes varied from country to country (22 from Ireland, 75 from Finland, 42 from the Netherlands, 79 from New Zealand, 51 from South Africa, 35 from the United Kingdom, and 243 from the United States).

In the survey, OD practitioners reported information about themselves, their organizations, and the interventions they engaged in. For each of the 55 OD interventions listed in the questionnaire, they indicated the degree to which they were currently using, have used, or have been involved in these interventions and activities in the past 3 years. The majority of the authors' hypotheses were at least partially supported. For instance, as predicted, OD practitioners in high-masculine countries such as the United States, the United Kingdom, New Zealand, and South Africa were more likely to use training and development and career development initiatives than practitioners in low-masculine countries such as Finland and the Netherlands. The overall results suggested that Hofstede's theoretical approach is a useful framework for comparing OD practices across cultures.

Lillrank et al. (1998). Lillrank et al. (1998) compared the design of successful continuous improvement (CI) programs at eight companies in eight different countries: Canada, France, Italy, Japan, Spain, Sweden, the United Kingdom, and the United States. This research project was conducted over a period of 3 years. The research team arrived at a list of seven design requirements for achieving CI based on a synthesis of the literature and comparative analysis of the companies studied. They then developed seven corresponding design dimensions, representing different possible ways to respond to these design requirements. The seven design dimensions for CI programs are as follows: Is CI part of ordinary work (integrated) or not (parallel)? Is CI work performed at a permanent group or a task group? Are the group members from one or several functions? Are the group members from the same or different levels? Is goal setting made centrally or in groups, and is it process guided or free? Are decisions about implementation made by the management hierarchy or the group? Are incentive system compensations for effort or rewards for results?

The eight cases of CI implementation were compared along these seven design dimensions. The comparative analyses revealed that at least two different ways to design CI programs emerged for each design dimension. For example, it was found that two of the eight companies had chosen to integrate CI activities in ordinary work, whereas the other companies had developed special forums for CI activities that are distinct from and parallel to ordinary work. The authors provided potential explanations for these different design choices by analyzing the impact of contextual factors such as history, economy, labor market institutions, and cultural norms in these different cases. This cross-cultural comparative study suggests that no one correct or best design for CI exists. The authors called for careful contextual analysis before transferring CI programs across national or cultural borders.

Meta-Analyses

For some time, many areas of the organizational sciences have benefited from the development and application of meta-analysis as a way of accumulating research findings across studies. Replication is essential for the "truth value" testing that advances science, although social science in general and the organizational sciences in particular have sometimes suffered from the difficulty scholars have of getting the pure replication into print. Meta-analysis has offered us a way out of this conundrum, allowing researchers to find studies that have investigated the same relationship in differing contexts and to combine these studies into a "meta" study that, theoretically, allows a good approximation of the "true score" value of the relationship. The literature contains excellent work that informs researchers about effective, statistically valid ways to conduct such analyses (e.g., Hunter & Schmidt, 1990; Hunter, Schmidt, & Jackson, 1982; Rosenthal, 1991).

Bullock and Tubbs (1990). This case meta-analysis study tested the effects of structural, implementation, and situational factors on the success of gainsharing plans as OD interventions. Structural features of gainsharing refer to the specific components of the involvement system (e.g., formal or informal) or the financial formula (e.g., productivity-oriented or profit-oriented, the employees' share of the gains). *Implementation* refers to how gainsharing plans are developed and installed (e.g., the use of outside practitioners, employee involvement in plan design, favorable employee votes). Situational factors include organization size, union status, organization technology, favorability of external environment, and management style. The success of gainsharing plans was measured by program retention, organization effectiveness, employee attitudes, labor–management cooperation, and pay and rewards increases.

Data were derived from 33 case studies of gainsharing plans implemented over 50 years. Five structure variables, three implementation variables, five situational variables, and six outcome variables were coded. In most cases, the authors tested for the presence or absence of a factor (e.g., whether the case study reported employee involvement in design and implementation) using a 0–1 coding scheme, but for two variables (organization size and payout percentage) continuous measures were used. All the available published literature was acquired for each of the 33 case studies. Three raters independently coded this published literature.

Different relational statistics were calculated to assess the effects of the structure, implementation, and situational variables on gainsharing success. Phi was used when both variables were dichotomous, and point-biserial correlations were used to assess relationships between dichotomous and continuous variables. When both measures were continuous, zero-order correlations were used. All these relation statistics reduce to a product–moment coefficient, which allows a direct comparison of the effects of individual factors on gainsharing success.

Results indicated that several structural features and implementation practices significantly predicted gainsharing success: employee involvement in plan design, use of outside practitioners, formal involvement structures, and employee favorability toward the plan. With the exception of participative management style, situational conditions did not correlate with gainsharing's success. Success was robust across organization size, union status, technology, and environment.

Macy and Izumi (1993). Macy and Izumi (1993) used meta-analytic procedures to evaluate organizational change, design, and development efforts based on 131 North American field studies from 1961 to 1991. A four-member research panel consensually identified the most commonly implemented action levers (i.e., specific change efforts) and outcomes found in the organizational change and work innovation literatures based on a collection of approximately 1,800 field studies. Three broad categories of action levers were examined in the study: structural, human resource, and technological. The structural category includes 17 action levers that change an organization's power and control (i.e., organization hierarchy) systems (e.g., the implementation of self-directed semiautonomous or autonomous work teams, goal setting). The human resources category includes 14 change efforts that are carried out within the existing organization's hierarchical structure but ultimately change the

way people are viewed, the way people view their job, or the way people do their job (e.g., job enrichment or enlargement, team building). The technological category includes 14 change efforts that occur in the mechanical or electronic, information, and process technologies of an organization (e.g., management information systems, just-in-time manufacturing). Outcomes or results from organizational change efforts were classified into three categories: financial (quantity, quality, and cost), behavioral (counterproductive behaviors), and attitudinal (employee attitudes and perceptions toward the work environment, group characteristics, and individual characteristics).

Empirical North American field studies were included in this meta-analysis if they met the following six criteria:

1. The studies are longitudinal field studies or change efforts across time, attempting to transform or change the work system, subsystem, or individuals.

2. The field study site is a naturalistic field setting functioning as a work organization.

3. The number of people in the organization affected by the change effort is at least 15 employees.

4. Sample sizes (Ns), t values or F values, means, and standard deviations are reported or were available from the original authors in order to calculate the individual d-effect scores.

5. Data are provided for either a postintervention–preintervention contrast or a postintervention contrast between an experimental and an equivalent comparison group.

6. The field study is published and is generally available to other researchers. One hundred thirty-one studies out of the approximately 1,800 field studies in the sample population were included in this meta-analysis based on these selection criteria.

Field study findings were calculated as standardized d-effects. The effect of the change effort was standardized before any *d*-effect aggregation. This prior standardization of mean scores followed by the calculation of the *d*-effect score made it possible to compare financial, behavioral, and attitudinal outcomes across the 131 field studies on the same metric. Meta-analysis was conducted to assess the overall impact of change efforts on each type of organization outcome, how change efforts in different categories relate to organization outcomes, how the number of action levers and their respective design categories are related to organization outcomes, whether or not there were clusters of action levers that were commonly implemented together in field research, the relationship between specific action levers and specific organization outcomes, and the impact of change efforts across three types of organizations (manufacturing, nonmanufacturing profit, and nonmanufacturing nonprofit).

Results of the meta-analysis indicated an overall positive effect of change efforts on outcomes (mean effect size = .77), which remained highly positive across different types of organizations. This overall positive impact was extremely large for financial performance outcomes (mean effect size = 1.27), moderately so for behavioral outcomes (mean effect size = .89), and small for attitudinal outcomes (mean effect size = .42). The extremely large improvement in financial performance outcomes came from a combination of structural, human resource, and technological change efforts. This finding suggested that the real impact of OD is through organization-level system-wide transformation efforts, not individual- or group-level change efforts.

Robertson, Roberts, and Porras (1993). Robertson et al. (1993) meta-analyzed 52 evaluation field studies to test a set of hypotheses derived from a theoretical model of the dynamics of planned organizational change (Porras, 1987; Porras & Robertson, 1992). Based on this theoretical model, an organization work setting comprises four major interrelated subsystems: organizing arrangement

(i.e., formal elements of organizations developed to provide the coordination and control necessary for organized activity, such as formal structures and reward systems), social factors (i.e., individual and group characteristics of the people in an organization, their patterns and processes of interaction, and the organization's culture), technology (i.e., everything associated with the transformation of organization inputs into outputs, such as work flow design and job design), and physical setting (i.e., the characteristics of the physical space in which organization activity occurs). Change interventions are viewed as the activity that changes elements of the work setting. Characteristics of the work setting then influence individual behavior, which in turn determines outcomes (organization performance and individual development).

Three hypotheses derived from this theoretical model were tested in this study: Planned organizational change interventions will generate positive change in work setting variables (Hypothesis 1), the relationship between the amount of positive change in work setting variables and the amount of positive change in individual behavior will be positive (Hypothesis 2), and the relationship between the amount of positive change in individual behavior and the amount of positive change in organization outcomes will be positive (Hypothesis 3).

Fifty-two evaluation studies from 1967 to mindset 1988 were included based on the following selection criteria: Only published studies were included, only evaluations of interventions occurring in ongoing organization settings were included, and studies were included only if they reported quantitative data on measures of dependent variables that were statistically analyzed and tested.

Change efforts were classified as intervening primarily in any of four subsystems: organizing arrangements, social factors, technology, and physical setting. In five cases, the interventions consisted of a dual thrust and were coded as multifaceted interventions. Each dependent variable in the 52 studies was coded as belonging to one of the following three classes: variables assessing work setting, individual behavior, or organization outcomes. This analysis didn't present results separately for the four categories of work setting dependent variables or for different categories of organization outcomes.

An effect size (r) was calculated for each dependent variable. The 52 studies yielded a total of 555 effect sizes. The effect sizes, weighted by sample size, were then cumulated across studies. Consistent with Hypothesis 1, the results supported an overall positive impact of change interventions (all combined) on work setting variables (effect size = .10). The effects on work setting variables were also positive for all intervention categories except for physical setting. The correlation between positive change in work setting variables and the amount of positive change in individual behavior was positive but not significant (r = .15). Social factors and organizing arrangement interventions had significant, positive effects on both work setting and individual behavior. Technology interventions had a significant positive impact on work setting variables and a significant, negative impact on individual behavior variables. Thus the overall pattern of findings provided mixed support for Hypothesis 2. There was a significant, positive correlation between the amount of positive change in individual behavior and the amount of positive change in organization outcomes (r = .53), thus supporting Hypothesis 3. Social factors and organizing arrangement interventions both yielded significant, positive change in individual behavior and organization outcomes. However, technology interventions had a significant, negative impact on individual behavior and a nonsignificant impact on organization outcomes. Overall, except for technology interventions, the pattern of findings was consistent with the theoretical model of planned organizational change. The results supported the basic viability of this model and suggested that future evaluation analysis be performed to assess causality in the relationships between interventions, work setting, individual behavior, and organization outcomes.

Qualitative Research

Qualitative studies are increasingly appearing in leading journals in the organizational sciences. For example, the special issue on organizational change and development published in the *Academy of Management Journal* in 2001 contained 10 articles focused on various aspects of organizational change (Woodman, Cameron, Ibarra, & Pettigrew, 2001). Of these 10, 5 were wholly, or in part, qualitative analyses. The field has become much more sophisticated in recent years with regard to conducting qualitative research in a systematic, replicable manner (cf. Denzin & Lincoln, 2005; Lincoln & Guba, 1985).

Denis, Lamothe, and Langley (2001). Denis et al. (2001) used a replicated case study method to assess the dynamics between collective leadership and strategic change processes in pluralistic organizations where leadership roles are shared, objectives are divergent, and power is diffuse. The first set of three cases studied involved first-order strategic changes (altering internal practices and redefining missions without threatening the integrity and existence of the hospitals) in three Canadian hospitals from the late 1980s to the early 1990s. A second set of cases included two hospital mergers (i.e., second-order changes) that took place in the late 1990s. For the five cases, the authors conducted 100 interviews, observed 54 meetings, and collected information from documents.

The cases were analyzed using a temporal bracketing strategy. The authors decomposed chronological data for each case into successive discrete time periods, or phases, which became comparative units of analysis. The boundaries of the chosen periods were defined either by changes in the key people involved (the leadership constellation) or by a major change in the environment. For each period, each case was analyzed based on three categories: the characteristics of the leadership during that period (who the important members were, what roles they played), the actions of the leadership group (what was done, what kinds of tactics were used), and the effects of these actions and tactics (symbolic, substantive, and political consequences of leaders' actions). As the first step, a comparative analysis was conducted for the first set of three cases based on these periods and categories. The analysis led to several theories about the dynamics of collective leadership and strategic change. As the second step, the authors analyzed the two merger cases using the same comparative approach and examined the extent to which theoretical understanding emerging from the first set of cases is useful in the context of second-order change.

The analysis of the five cases suggested that major substantive change in pluralistic organizations is more likely to be established under unified collective leadership in which each member of a "leadership constellation" plays a distinct role and all members work together harmoniously. However, unified collective leadership is fragile in a context of diffuse power and multiple objectives. In particular, a constellation may be shattered by internal rivalry (strategic uncoupling), by dislocation from its base (organizational uncoupling), or by poor adaptation to the needs of the environment (environmental uncoupling). Because it is difficult to maintain coupling at all levels simultaneously, change tends to occur in a cyclical manner, driven by the effects of leaders' actions on their political positions.

Falkenberg, Stensaker, Meyer, & Haueng (2005). Drawing on three cases of strategic change in one telecommunication company and two major divisions of an oil company, Falkenberg et al. (2005) developed the phenomenon of excessive change and assessed its individual and organizational consequences. The authors discovered consistent perceptions of excessive

change in three cases, which were originally studied to investigate implementation issues of information technology–related strategic change. Inspired by this finding, the authors undertook a systematic approach to deliberately explore the concept of excessive change and its consequences.

Data on the three cases were collected through interviews (with informants from multiple organization levels and subgroups), documents (e.g., project reports for the change program, internal newsletters), and observations of organization meetings. Using a grounded theory approach, open coding was used to form initial categories of information about excessive change. Three members of the research team coded empirical data into two broad categories: descriptions of too much change and statements revealing consequences of too much change. All four authors then worked together in further categorizations of the definition and consequences of excessive change. After the open coding, axial coding was used to explore the links between the phenomenon of excessive change and its consequences. Finally, selective coding was used to write a story that integrated the categories in the axial coding model.

Excessive change was defined as occurring when organizations pursue several seemingly unrelated and perhaps conflicting changes simultaneously or when organizations introduce new changes before previous changes have been completed. This phenomenon was defined as the subjective perceptions of individuals. The analyses discovered different perceptions of excessive change in organizations, where the perceptions of excessive change existed among low-level organization members and middle managers but not among top-level managers. Different employee reactions to excessive change found were classified and analyzed based on two categories: passive (paralysis, passive coping, cynicism, loyalty) or active responses (sabotage, exit, self-control) and whether the responses make the change attempt likely or unlikely. Bend Over, Here It Comes Again (BOHICA), or passive coping by waiting it out, was found to be the most popular individual response to excessive change in these three cases. The findings indicated three structural consequences of excessive change for organizations: rotating responsibility (managers being moved around or eliminated), nonfunctioning middle management, and structural instability of the organization. Excessive change was also found to result in organization performance outcomes of implementation failure (failure of actually changing the organization) and loss of organization effectiveness (because the organization's attention focused on the change rather than on their customers, markets, and operational tasks). These findings suggested the need to conduct a careful diagnosis of organization needs before initiating change and the importance of planning in implementing change.

Ferdig and Ludema (2005). Based on complexity and social constructionist theories, this study illustrated how the U.S. Nuclear Regulatory Commission (NRC) engaged a wide range of stakeholders in a successful dialogue process to recreate a new system for monitoring nuclear reactors: a revised reactor oversight process (ROP). The purpose of the study was to examine how participants made sense of their reality and chose to interact with one another in the process of designing the industry-wide ROP change. Using narrative analysis, Ferdig and Ludema (2005) focused on what participants paid attention to, how they interpreted what was going on around them, and how they chose to interact with others in their present moment interactions, thus influencing the direction and quality of emerging outcomes.

Data were collected during the period from December 1999 to April 2001 through open-ended interviews with 61 participants representing three constituency groups (the NRC, the nuclear industry, and public activists);

observations of 18 meetings; informal conversations with people in the NRC, the industry, and public; documents such as meeting transcripts, reports, and letters; and journal notes recorded during this period. Data were analyzed based on the convention of grounded theory and generative theory, including narrative development and analysis. Thematic patterns of interaction were identified, categorized, and further studied for interpretive content and meaning through iterative communication encounters with informants.

Findings of this study illustrated how five qualities of conversation—a spirit of freedom, inclusion, inquiry, spontaneity, and possibility—shifted the way people involved in the ROP communicated with each other and thereby freed up energy for transformative, self-organizing change. Having freedom of choice—to engage or not to engage—gave participants the power to speak their minds about the issues that mattered to them; commitment to inclusion resulted in diverse perspectives that contributed to a more comprehensive picture of reality. A spirit of inquiry led to ongoing exploration of the purpose, principles, and deep structures that governed the oversight process, past, present, and future. Maintaining spontaneity allowed participants to remain flexible and experimental in the face of the uncertainties associated with emergent cocreation; and a persistent belief in the possibility of finding novel solutions through cooperation and dialogue sustained the momentum and energy needed to arrive at mutually satisfactory outcomes. This analysis shows how the five conversation qualities produced transformative change by increasing levels of interconnectivity, shared identity, and collective capacity among participants. Follow-up interviews with selected participants involved in the change process indicated that the shift in the relationship developed among the NRC, nuclear industry, and public activist groups during the 3-year ROP process has been sustained.

Combined Paradigm Research

OD is both a field of social action and a field of scientific inquiry (Woodman, 1989a). Therefore, a number of dualities, paradoxes, and tensions influence the nature of research done in the field. For example, the tension between action and research in the action research model that underlies many organizational change efforts is well known. Additionally, organizational change is a complex process, not easily measured under the best circumstances, as discussed at some length previously. A solution to the complexity and duality of organizational change, proposed some time ago (with only minimal or no impact), is to use both quantitative and qualitative evaluation methods when assessing OD interventions.[2] Sometimes people do this, as we can see in the following studies.

Manning and DelaCerda (2003). Manning and DelaCerda (2003) assessed the applicability of whole systems change (WSC) using large group interventions in an emerging economy. From 1999 to 2002, the authors participated in 20 large group interventions in Mexico as facilitators. The results of two applications of WSC were examined in detail based on both quantitative and qualitative data. One application was a large group conference in a small, privately held software development company in Guadalajara (the Parnet Case). The other was a large change intervention process to enhance the national forest product industry held in various locations throughout Mexico (the Conafor Case).

The Parnet Case involved a large-scale participative design conference conducted to redesign the company's work processes and to improve service quality, cost-efficiency, and delivery effectiveness. The change method applied is known as WSC, which means that a company's entire internal and external system meets in one place, with no other agenda, with no departmental interfaces or job hierarchies, to work together full-time as long as necessary on designing the change that the company needs in order to be competitive in its market. The 2-day participative work design conference ended with a new work design for Parnet. This design involved the creation of multidisciplinary teams formed around clients and product lines, and a new organization structure for performing core work processes. One main outcome resulting from this intervention was that the company found ways to cut costs by eliminating unnecessary processes and getting consulting, engineering, training, and installation jobs done faster. Throughput process time for client projects was cut from an average of 8 months to at most 3 or 4 months. Estimates by managers of these achieved efficiencies go as high as 50% of former process costs. Aside from these quantitative indicators of intervention results, individual interviews with Parnet owners, managers, chief software engineers, and other stakeholders were also conducted 2 years after the design conference to gather subjective evaluations. Parnet managers considered the conference a turning point for the company that awoke the potential for change and improvement. Everyone interviewed agreed that clients are clearly better off with the company's improvement: Services are done faster and more efficiently, client satisfaction indexes went up, and complaints went down.

Conafor is the National Forest Commission in Mexico. One of Conafor's main projects is the development of production supply chains in an attempt to enhance the competitive stance of the Mexican forest industry. As part of Conafor's supply chain project, future search and participative design conferences were carried out as pilot interventions in five different regions in Mexico. Both survey and in-depth interviews were conducted to evaluate the results of these large group interventions. In the survey, participants evaluated these large group conferences on the following four questions: Were the conference goals achieved?

Were the supply chain shareholders represented in the conference? How do you evaluate facilitation and methods applied in the conference? and What is your overall evaluation of the large-scale conference? The survey data gathered indicated that more than 80% of the participants gave very positive answers to these four questions. For example, overall evaluation of conferences averaged 31% as excellent, 53% as high, and 16% medium. No one rated any of the conferences as low or very low on the overall evaluation. In-depth follow-up interviews were conducted with prominent conference participants (i.e., those who stood out during the conference to motivate or support other participants or who were critical about the process at times) about their perceptions of the conferences. Interviewees agreed that large-scale conferences generated great expectations among the participants about what they could achieve by working together and that increased trust resulted from this collective action. On the limitation side, one general perception shared by most interviewees was the lack of attendance of critical business participants. The authors concluded that large-scale and highly participative change interventions are appropriate to facilitate change in Mexican society.

Whelan-Berry, Gordon, and Hinings (2003). Using both quantitative and qualitative data collection and analysis methods, Whelan-Berry et al. (2003) examined the relative effect of leadership, participation, training, and communication as change drivers and their relationship to individuals' adoption of the change initiatives. This study was part of a large research project that examined four separate but intertwined change initiatives in the corporate audit department of FBC, one of the 20 largest banks in the United States. These four initiatives were adopting a national line-of-business–based approach to work, organizing into a team-based work environment, reengineering the audit process, and implementing a new performance development system.

Three sources of data were used: The FBC case tracked the change initiatives over 2 years, survey data were gathered from all FBC corporate audit employees at four times during those 2 years; and qualitative interviews were conducted with a sample of corporate audit employees at the time of the first three surveys. The FBC case was developed based on data from interviews, surveys, observations, and information from written documents following standard case method. Corporate audit employees completed questionnaires approximately every 4 months. The authors analyzed data from three of the four surveys administered (the first survey that focused on prechange data was not used). For each of the four initiatives, corporate audit employees reported in the surveys their perceptions of the degree to which they had personally adopted the initiative and their perception of the significance of each change driver to this adoption. Structured interviews 30 to 90 minutes long were conducted with a smaller sample of employees a few weeks after each of the first three surveys, at approximately 4-month intervals from spring 1996 through early 1997. Interviewees described each initiative's progress and its impact and their perceptions of planned events related to specific change initiatives. The study focused its analyses on answers to the following three interview questions: "What events and experiences have contributed to your understanding and adopting the change initiative?" "How do you believe organizational change occurs and what are the major steps or events in the process?" and "What two or three events and experiences have been most significant to your adoption of the change initiatives?"

The authors first used the FBC case to provide a general understanding of the FBC corporate audit initiatives and change drivers. Then, they analyzed survey data using Wilcoxon two-related-samples statistical analysis to test for differences in the perceived significance of various change drivers to individual adoption and used Kendall's Tau-*b* to test the relationship between the change drivers and individual adoption of the initiative. Finally, they used the interview data (number of employees who named each change driver and details of their responses) to understand employees' perception of the change drivers in more detail and to complement and explain the quantitative data.

The results suggested participation as the most highly rated change driver that had the strongest overall impact across change initiatives. In addition, participation as a change driver also had the most consistent relationship with individual adoption of change initiatives during the FBC corporate audit change effort. Contrary to expectations, neither department nor initiative-specific leadership was the most highly rated change driver on the surveys, although leadership was the most frequently mentioned change driver in the interviews.

SUGGESTIONS FOR EVALUATION RESEARCH ON OD

Fully mindful of the constraints on and challenges to valid assessment of the effects of OD interventions, we nevertheless propose that this endeavor is worth doing and can be improved. Specifically, we think that progress with regard to both the development of change theory and the application of actionable change knowledge would be enhanced by greater attention to the following ideas.

More Use of True Experimental and Quasiexperimental Designs in Evaluation Research on OD

Often, in the field we are too quick to assume that experimental research designs cannot be used. This judgment is largely based, we think, on the extremely problematic nature of random assignment of either individuals or groups in organization settings. Without a doubt, there are few opportunities to use randomization in the context of a change program. At the same time, more extensive experience with quasiexperimental designs (with a good

literature available to educate ourselves about their use and to support their efficacy) suggests that there are many reasonable ways to use either nonequivalent comparison groups or some form of time series analysis. For example, it is not necessary that individuals or parts of the organization be withheld from the treatment forever—only that the intervention be delayed for some groups or units while they serve this important control function. And, as can be seen from the exemplars reviewed (see Table 12.1), there *are* possibilities to use true experimental design in field research as well. This design is not limited to laboratory investigations, although it is admittedly much easier to use in that setting. The tremendous strengths in internal validity—what are the true effects of the intervention, and can we have high confidence in these results?—that stem from experimental research suggest that this should be the first thing we try to do when evaluating intervention effects in OD. When this simply can't be done, we move on to other options.

Explore the Possibilities for Combined Paradigm Research

Although this seems to be somewhat more popular than a few decades ago, few studies have been done that successfully combine normal paradigm (quantitative) research with qualitative assessment approaches. A big part of the problem here probably stems from the reality that researchers tend to be skilled in either one domain or the other but not often in both. An obvious solution to this dilemma is to form teams of researchers where both skill sets can be represented. As we stated previously, "Managing organizational change effectively is both an art and a science, so perhaps our evaluation paradigms need to better reflect this reality. Similarly, there is art even in the most rigorous, systematic research act as reflected in the imagination and skill needed to design and successfully carry out such research. Further, the fundamental dualities that appear in the change and development area, as well as the nature of change itself as a second-order abstraction, would seem to require research paradigms that, at least, attempt to match the complexity that is being investigated" (Woodman, 1989a, p. 177).

Use Longitudinal Research Designs Whenever Possible

The ability of cross-sectional (single-time) measures to validly assess the complex processes of organizational change is limited. In the early stages of any research discipline, one is more likely to see cross-sectional work (even in the best journals) as scholars are just beginning to develop their understanding about some phenomenon of interest. And, depending on the research question, cross-sectional analyses may be all that is needed to investigate some hypotheses. However, in evaluation research, we are examining the effects of an intervention that takes time to unfold and time to assess. We certainly recognize the (sometimes enormous) costs associated with research that is seriously longitudinal. Still, the field has advanced to the point where much more longitudinal work is needed in order to advance our theory and practice.

Invest Considerable Time and Energy in Developing Reliable and Valid Measures for Explanatory Variables and Change Outcomes

Drawing valid inferences about the effects of some change program requires construct validity in our measures. Absent this validity, the most rigorous experimental design and procedure are rendered valueless. There is also a wealth of new information about the approaches and techniques that can be used to draw statistical inferences about the fundamental judgment of when things have changed and when they have not (e.g., Collins & Sayer, 2001). Evaluation researchers in OD need expertise in measurement theory, the development of measurement instruments, the use of

sophisticated statistical inference techniques, and the knowledge to engage in qualitative research in a sound, scientific manner. Equally needed is valid organization knowledge so that the field knows which questions are worth asking and which change outcomes matter.

Develop Research Partnership Opportunities Between the Academic and Practitioner Groups Operating in the Change and Development Arena

The idea of improving knowledge transfers between practitioners and academics is a common call to make yet one that the organizational sciences continue to struggle with (cf. Rynes et al., 2001). Nowhere in the organizational sciences is the potential greater for developing a deeper sense of collaboration on solving problems and generating knowledge of mutual interest than in the change and development arena. Pettigrew et al. (2001) identified the need for greater engagement between scholars and practitioners as one of the six major challenges facing the field. The potential payoffs are enormous: A lot more change occurs in organizations than gets examined, written about, shared, used to develop and improve theory, and so on. Tell your change management practitioner friends that you will work for free if they will allow you to develop and carry out their assessment strategy.

NOTES

1. Typically in evaluation research on OD this independent variable is the intervention itself.

2. The statistics used in a combined paradigm study may be descriptive (as in Manning and DelaCerda, 2003) or inferential (as in Whelan-Berry, Gordon, & Hinings, 2003). As another option, Bullock and Tubbs (1987) propose a case meta-analysis method for OD that combines the qualitative case study with the quantitative analysis strategy of meta-analysis. See our review of Bullock and Tubbs (1990) presented earlier for an example of this application. If more widely used, case meta-analysis could inform the field because

there is an extensive published case study literature in OD.

REFERENCES

Armenakis, A. A. (1988). A review of research on
the change typology. In W. A. Pasmore &
R. W. Woodman (Eds.), *Research in organizational change and development* (Vol. 2,
pp. 163–194). Greenwich, CT: JAI.

Arthur, J. B., & Aiman-Smith, L. (2001). Gainsharing
and organizational learning: An analysis of
employee suggestions over time. *Academy of
Management Journal, 44,* 737–754.

Beard, J. W., Woodman, R. W., & Moesel, D.
(1998). Using behavioral modification to change
attendance patterns in the high-performance,
high-commitment environment. In R. W.
Woodman & W. A. Pasmore (Eds.), *Research
in organizational change and development*
(Vol. 11, pp. 183–224). Stamford, CT: JAI.

Bernstein, W. M., & Burke, W. W. (1989).
Modeling organizational meaning systems. In
R. W. Woodman & W. A. Pasmore (Eds.),
*Research in organizational change and devel-
opment* (Vol. 3, pp. 117–159). Greenwich, CT:
JAI.

Bullock, R. J., & Svyantek, D. J. (1985). Analyzing
meta-analysis: Potential problems, an unsuccessful replication, and evaluation criteria.
Journal of Applied Psychology, 70, 108–115.

Bullock, R. J., & Svyantek, D. J. (1987). The
impossibility of using random strategies to
study the organization development process.
Journal of Applied Behavioral Science, 23,
255–262.

Bullock, R. J., & Tubbs, M. E. (1987). The case
meta-analysis method for OD. In R. W.
Woodman & W. A. Pasmore (Eds.), *Research
in organizational change and development*
(Vol. 1, pp. 171–228). Greenwich, CT: JAI.

Bullock, R. J., & Tubbs, M. E. (1990). A case meta-
analysis of gainsharing plans as organization
development interventions. *Journal of Applied
Behavioral Science, 26,* 383–404.

Burke, W. W., & Litwin, G. H. (1992). A causal
model for organizational performance and
change. *Journal of Management, 18,* 532–545.

Campbell, D. T., & Stanley, J. C. (1966).
*Experimental and quasi-experimental designs
for research.* Chicago: Rand McNally.

Carnall, C. A. (1986). Toward a theory for the
evaluation of organizational change. *Human
Relations, 39,* 745–766.

Collins, L. M., & Sayer, A. G. (Eds.). (2001). *New
methods for the analysis of change.* Washington,
DC: American Psychological Association.

Cook, T. D., Campbell, D. T., & Peracchio, L.
(1990). Quasi experimentation. In M. D.
Dunnette & L. M. Hough (Eds.), *Handbook of
industrial & organizational psychology* (2nd ed.,
Vol. 1, pp. 491–576). Palo Alto, CA: Consulting
Psychologists Press.

Cooke, R. A., & Coughlan, R. J. (1979).
Developing collective decision making and
problem-solving structures in schools. *Group
& Organization Studies, 4,* 71–92.

Coyle-Shapiro, J. A.-M. (1999). Employee participation and assessment of an organizational
change intervention: A three-wave study of
total quality management. *Journal of Applied
Behavioral Science, 35,* 439–456.

Cummings, T. G., & Worley, C. G. (2005).
Organization development and change (8th
ed.). Mason, OH: South-Western.

Daly, J. P. (1995). Explaining changes to employees: The influence of justifications and change
outcomes on employees' fairness judgments.
Journal of Applied Behavioral Science, 31,
415–428.

Denis, J.-L., Lamothe, L., & Langley, A. (2001). The
dynamics of collective leadership and strategic
change in pluralistic organizations. *Academy of
Management Journal, 44,* 809–837.

Denzin, N. K., & Lincoln, Y. S. (Eds.). (2005). *The
Sage handbook of qualitative research* (3rd
ed.). Thousand Oaks, CA: Sage.

Fagenson-Eland, E., Ensher, E. A., & Burke, W. W.
(2004). Organization development and change
interventions: A seven-nation comparison.
Journal of Applied Behavioral Science, 40,
432–464.

Falkenberg, J., Stensaker, I., Meyer, C. B., &
Haueng, A. C. (2005). When change becomes
excessive. In R. W. Woodman & W. A.
Pasmore (Eds.), *Research in organizational
change and development* (Vol. 15, pp. 31–62).
Oxford, UK: Elsevier.

Ferdig, M. A., & Ludema, J. D. (2005).
Transformative interactions: Qualities of conversation that heighten the vitality of self-organizing
change. In R. W. Woodman & W. A. Pasmore

(Eds.), *Research in organizational change and development* (Vol. 15, pp. 169–205). Oxford, UK: Elsevier.

Friedlander, F., & Brown, L. D. (1974). Organization development. *Annual Review of Psychology, 25,* 313–341.

Golembiewski, R., Billingsley, K., & Yeager, S. (1976). Measuring change and persistence in human affairs: Types of change generated by OD designs. *Journal of Applied Behavioral Science, 12,* 133–157.

Hofstede, G. (1980). Motivation leadership and organization: Do American theories apply abroad? *Organizational Dynamics, 9*(1), 42–63.

Hunter, J. E., & Schmidt, F. L. (1990). *Methods of meta-analysis: Correcting error and bias in research findings.* Newbury Park, CA: Sage.

Hunter, J. E., Schmidt, F. L., & Jackson, G. B. (1982). *Meta-analysis: Cumulating research findings across studies.* Beverly Hills, CA: Sage.

Kerlinger, F. N., & Lee, H. B. (2000). *Foundations of behavioral research* (4th ed.). Fort Worth, TX: Holt, Rinehart and Winston.

Kotter, J., & Schlesinger, L. (1979, March–April). Choosing strategies for change. *Harvard Business Review,* pp. 106–114.

Lillrank, P., Shani, A. B., Kolodny, H., Stymne, B., Figuera, J. R., & Liu, M. (1998). Learning from the success of continuous improvement programs: An international comparative study. In R. W. Woodman & W. A. Pasmore (Eds.), *Research in organizational change and development* (Vol. 11, pp. 47–71). Stamford, CT: JAI.

Lincoln, Y. S., & Guba, E. G. (1985). *Naturalistic inquiry.* Beverly Hills, CA: Sage.

Macy, B. A., & Izumi, H. (1993). Organizational change, design, and work innovation: A meta-analysis of 131 North American field studies—1961–1991. In R. W. Woodman & W. A. Pasmore (Eds.), *Research in organizational change and development* (Vol. 7, pp. 235–313). Greenwich, CT: JAI.

Manning, M. R., & DelaCerda, J. (2003). Building organizational change in an emerging economy: Whole systems change using large group interventions in Mexico. In W. A. Pasmore & R. W. Woodman (Eds.), *Research in organizational change and development* (Vol. 14, pp. 51–97). Oxford, UK: Elsevier Science.

Martocchio, J. J., & Harrison, D. A. (1993). To be there or not to be there? Questions, theories, and methods in absenteeism research. In G. R. Ferris & K. M. Rowland (Eds.), *Research in personnel and human resources management* (Vol. 11, pp. 259–328). Greenwich, CT: JAI.

McMahan, G. C., & Woodman, R. W. (1992). The current practice of organization development within the firm: A survey of large industrial corporations. *Group & Organization Management, 17,* 117–134.

Orpen, C. (1979). The effects of job enrichment on employee satisfaction, motivation, involvement, and performance: A field experiment. *Human Relations, 32,* 189–217.

Pettigrew, A. M., Woodman, R. W., & Cameron, K. S. (2001). Studying organizational change and development: Challenges for future research. *Academy of Management Journal, 44,* 697–713.

Porras, J. I. (1987). *Stream analysis: A powerful way to diagnose and manage organizational change.* Reading, MA: Addison-Wesley.

Porras, J. I., & Robertson, P. J. (1992). Organization development: Theory, practice, and research. In M. D. Dunnette & L. M. Hough (Eds.), *Handbook of industrial and organizational psychology* (2nd ed., Vol. 3, pp. 719–822). Palo Alto, CA: Consulting Psychologists Press.

Robertson, P. J., Roberts, D. R., & Porras, J. I. (1993). Dynamics of planned organizational change: Assessing empirical support for a theoretical model. *Academy of Management Journal, 36,* 619–634.

Rosenthal, R. (1991). *Meta-analytic procedures for social research.* Newbury Park, CA: Sage.

Rynes, S. L., Bartunek, J. M., & Daft, R. L. (2001). Across the great divide: Knowledge creation and transfer between practitioners and academics. *Academy of Management Journal, 44,* 340–355.

Schuster, F. E., Morden, D. L., Baker, T. E., McKay, I. S., Dunning, K. E., & Hagen, C. M. (1997). Management practice, organization climate, and performance. *Journal of Applied Behavioral Science, 33,* 209–226.

Seashore, S. E. (1984). Field experiments with formal organizations. In T. S. Bateman & G. R. Ferris (Eds.), *Method and analysis in organizational research* (pp. 222–231). Reston, VA: Reston Publishing.

Sommer, R. (1987). An experimental investigation of the action research approach. *Journal of Applied Behavioral Science, 23,* 185–199.

Terpstra, D. E. (1981). Relationships between methodological rigor and reported outcomes in organization development evaluation research. *Journal of Applied Psychology, 66,* 541–543.

Toegel, G. (2005). Consultancy. In N. Nicholson, P. G. Audia, & M. M. Pillutla (Eds.), *The Blackwell encyclopedia of management: Organizational behavior* (2nd ed., Vol. 11, pp. 64–67). Oxford, UK: Blackwell.

Waclawski, J. (2002). Large-scale organizational change and performance: An empirical examination. *Human Resource Development Quarterly, 13,* 289–305.

Wanous, J. P., & Reichers, A. E. (2001). A quasi-experimental study of an action-research project: The effect of project visibility. In R. W. Woodman & W. A. Pasmore (Eds.), *Research in organizational change and development* (Vol. 13, pp. 169–194). Oxford: Elsevier Science.

Whelan-Berry, K. S., Gordon, J. R., & Hinings, C. R. (2003). The relative effect of change drivers in large-scale organizational change: An empirical study. In W. A. Pasmore & R. W. Woodman (Eds.), *Research in organizational change and development* (Vol. 14, pp. 99–146). Oxford: Elsevier Science.

Woodman, R. W. (1979). A devil's dictionary of behavioral science research terms. *Academy of Management Review, 4,* 93–94.

Woodman, R. W. (1980). Team development versus T-group training. *Group & Organization Studies, 5,* 135–142.

Woodman, R. W. (1989a). Evaluation research on organizational change: Arguments for a "combined paradigm" approach. In R. W. Woodman & W. A. Pasmore (Eds.), *Research in organizational change and development* (Vol. 3, pp. 161–180). Greenwich, CT: JAI.

Woodman, R. W. (1989b). Organizational change and development: New arenas for inquiry and action. *Journal of Management, 15,* 205–228.

Woodman, R. W. (1990). Issues and concerns in organizational diagnosis. In C. N. Jackson & M. R. Manning (Eds.), *Organization development annual, volume 3: Diagnosing client organizations* (pp. 5–10). Alexandria, VA: American Society for Training and Development.

Woodman, R. W. (2005). Change, evaluation. In N. Nicholson, P. G. Audia, & M. M. Pillutla (Eds.), *The Blackwell encyclopedia of management: Organizational behavior* (2nd ed., Vol. 11, pp. 37–38). Oxford, UK: Blackwell.

Woodman, R. W., Cameron, K. S., Ibarra, H., & Pettigrew, A. M. (Eds.). (2001). Special research forum: Change and development journeys into a pluralistic world. *Academy of Management Journal, 44,* 697–925.

Woodman, R. W., & Dewett, T. (2004). Organizationally relevant journeys in individual change. In M.S. Poole & A. H. Van de Ven (Eds.), *Handbook of organizational change and innovation* (pp. 32–49). Oxford,UK: Oxford University Press.

Woodman, R. W., & Sherwood, J. (1980). Effects of team development intervention: A field experiment. *Journal of Applied Behavioral Science, 16,* 211–227.

Woodman, R. W., & Wayne, S. J. (1985). An investigation of positive-findings bias in evaluation of organization development interventions. *Academy of Management Journal, 28,* 889–913.

PART III

Organization Interventions

13

Process Wisdom
The Heart of Organization Development

PETER B. VAILL

The following striking remark is taken from Elton Mayo's *The Social Problems of an Industrial Civilization,* where the author draws broader conclusions from the famous Western Electric Hawthorne researches, which he had recently directed:

> The enthusiasm of the efficiency engineer for the organization of operations is excellent; his attempt to resume [*sic*] the problems of cooperation under this heading is not. At the moment, he attempts to solve the many human difficulties involved in wholehearted cooperation by *organizing the organization of organization* without any reference whatever to the workers themselves. This procedure inevitably blocks communication and defeats his own admirable purpose. (Mayo, 1945, p. 80; italics added)

The first time I read the highlighted phrase in this quotation, I thought it might be a misprint. But then I realized that this is Mayo's well-known darting, puckish intelligence, punning on the word *organization* to make his point.

In the context, Mayo is discussing the second of the two great findings of the Hawthorne researches of the late 1920s and early 1930s. The first great finding was that work motivation and productivity do not depend on the physical factors of the workplace, a discovery that Fredrick Herzberg later developed as the difference between "hygiene" factors and "motivators" (Herzberg, 1959). The second great finding is that there is something else, called social organization, which powerfully influences work attitudes and productivity, and that this social organization is not a matter of

AUTHOR'S NOTE: I am indebted to my colleague Bill Monson of the University of St. Thomas for insightful comments on earlier drafts of this chapter.

management fiat or, as Mayo says, of the organizing or front-end designs of efficiency experts.

It is hard to imagine what it was like not to have available the idea of social organization and thus not to be able to think systematically about social life and social processes. To be sure, many managers realized that there was more going on in the plant than met the eye, whether called an underground, or a grapevine, or just "the way things work around here." There is no telling how far back into history this awareness goes, for it is undoubtedly ancient. But what Mayo and his colleagues did was to make social organization a phenomenon for study and thus vastly expand the tools we had for understanding how and why human organizations operate as they do.

The other thing that the explication of social organization did was to forever render pointless and ineffective the attempts by management to control social organization by fiat from the top down, or to finesse it with rationalistic designs (as Mayo's efficiency expert is attempting). Unfortunately, this lesson of Hawthorne is one that has to be relearned over and over again. The temptation to "organize the organization" by fiat is too strong; more importantly, as Mayo and his descendants, including today's OD consultants, are repeatedly asked, what is the alternative? If you can't design cooperative work systems, what can you do?

For a decade or two after Hawthorne, research continued on the nature of social organization in industry and other formal work settings. Survey data and case studies accumulated. The original findings were broadly supported over and over again: Human beings in continual proximity to each other tend to form social systems that have identifiable and stable patterns of interaction and, within members of these systems, identifiable sentiments (or feelings). The "wholehearted cooperation" mentioned by Mayo, though not always evident in these systems, appears frequently, as is amply documented in modern studies of high-performing systems (Collins & Porras, 1994; Peters & Waterman, 1982; Vaill, 1978). "Wholehearted

cooperation" clearly is not some rare piece of exotica but rather something that human beings are quite capable of under the right conditions. Leadership emerges from these systems that is not necessarily designated by any outside authority. The productivity of these social systems is one manifestation of their existence and operation but not the only one. Numerous other kinds of informal social behavior signal the existence of the underlying social system. By the late 1940s it was possible to create general theories of the operation of social systems that were not merely speculative but instead were grounded in extensive empirical data (Homans, 1950; Radcliffe-Brown, 1948).

But let us return to "wholehearted cooperation" for a moment. What is it? How does it arise? How much and what kind of external influence does it need? Is there anything special in the education or natural abilities of system members needed for it to arise? Can "leadership" make it happen? Why can't it be engineered, as Mayo's remark says it cannot be? These are just a few of the questions a curious managerial leader might ask as he or she thinks about the needs in his or her own organization for "wholehearted cooperation." For make no mistake, any practicing manager in any kind of organization can point to innumerable places in the work flow where better human cooperation is needed. Such a manager will also be conscious of how much the lack of cooperation is costing in wasted capital, lost time, low product quality, workplace injuries, and stress for everyone involved. And these would be just the visible manifestations. Today we know that there are as many invisible points where the degree of cooperation makes a difference. Moreover, we know now that cooperative relations can extend across the boundaries of an organization into its environment. It is not just a matter of the workers at the bottom of the hierarchy; social organization is something everyone is involved in, and the need for more cooperation extends throughout the organization, including at the very top.[1]

By the 1950s the question of how to shape and influence social organization had become increasingly pressing. Postwar organizations were pursuing new missions, and they were doing it with increasingly new and untried technologies. New methods of manufacturing appeared continually. New quasiprofessions were arising in all of an organization's functions, putting organization members into new kinds of relations to each other. Women were entering the workforce as professionals, and members of diverse ethnic and cultural backgrounds were arriving in what had been previously all–white male environments. People were doing new kinds of work with new kinds of work associates, and they were doing it under increasingly competitive conditions against increasingly ambitious objectives. Social organization was becoming more and more problematic everywhere, a perception that Mayo elaborated quite vividly in *The Social Problems of an Industrial Civilization.*

It was against this background of changes that OD arose. Practitioners of the early OD were educated in what had become known about social organizations, particularly small groups and two-person relationships. Much of the need for better cooperation was apparent in various work groups in organizations. Groups composed of highly trained technical professionals[2] seemed particularly in need of help in managing their internal relationships. Management would get an order from a customer to build a complex new technical system. The company would create a project team to do the work and appoint a project manager to lead the effort. Then the group would set about its task and too often fall into chronic conflict and recrimination, turf battles, and professional jealousies. Resistance to the project manager's leadership attempts was common. Budgets would be overrun, timelines would slip, and the customer's specifications often would get lost in the shuffle.

This sort of scenario occurred often enough that senior managers knew they had to do something to create professional work teams that could do the work the company was contracting for. Enter OD, although of course not as the full-blown body of theory and practice that we now call the profession.

THE IDEA OF SOCIAL PROCESS

"When Douglas McGregor came to Antioch [in 1948], all he could talk about was 'process,' 'process,' 'process.' We all said, 'What is this "process'?" (Weisbord, 1987, p. 126; see also Seashore, 2004). It was social organization and social structure that actually had flowered as concepts in the 1920s and 1930s, fueled by the data of the Hawthorne researches and many other sociological and anthropological studies (Parsons, 1951; Roethlisberger & Dickson, 1939, Chapter 24). The ongoing, concrete social relationships and processes that underlay the concepts of social organization and social structure were much more difficult to talk about, even though these social relationships are much more observable in everyday life. The idea of social process was and is an elusive idea. Social organization and social structure are much easier to visualize. They can even be pictured and diagrammed. It is much easier to specify a status hierarchy, for example, than it is to describe and make vivid the innumerable ongoing social processes by which this hierarchy is created and maintained. It is much easier to describe a role abstractly than to catch the flavor of the way it is being played (its process) in the concrete behavior of a specific person.

One of the most important early contributors to our gradual understanding of the reality of social process was Kurt Lewin. In a landmark essay in 1947, he said the following:

> It is important that a social standard to be changed does not have the nature of a "thing" but of a "process." A certain standard of consumption, for instance, means that a certain action—such as making certain decisions, buying, preparing, and canning food in a certain family—occurs with a certain

frequency within a given period. Similarly, a certain type of group relations means that within a given period certain friendly and hostile actions and reactions of a certain degree of severity occur between the members of two groups. Changing group relations or changing consumption means changing the level at which these multitude of events proceed. In other words, the "level" of consumption, of friendliness, or of productivity is to be characterized as the aspect of an ongoing social process. (Lewin, in Bennis, Benne, & Chin, 1961, p. 235)

It is an "ongoing social process" one is trying to change in some human organization, not a fixed thing. Moreover, as is easily deducible from Lewin's comment, this ongoing social process is the live operations of conscious human beings. A wolf pack is also an ongoing social process, no doubt, but it is a very different matter when we are dealing with human beings who can make their own evaluations of what is being done and aid and abet or vigorously oppose the proposed change.

It is not the purpose of this chapter to write a history of OD and social process. That can better be achieved by consulting such histories as Weisbord (1987) and Kleiner (1996). Rather, the point here is to suggest that the idea of social process and its static counterparts, social organization and social structure, are fundamental notions in the understanding of organization change processes. Moreover, it is not an exaggeration to suggest that process awareness, process consciousness, or, as Weisbord calls it, process thinking *is the distinctive contribution of the OD field to our understanding of organization change*. Of course there is much more to OD than simply "process." But without this idea, the danger is that those initiating change will revert to the method of Elton Mayo's benighted efficiency engineer, trying to "organize the organization of the organization." The "organization of the organization" is not a matter of issuing fiats from on high, nor is it the province of lengthy reports

issued by outside consultants, popular as the two methods have been and continue to be. No, *the* achievement of the wholehearted cooperation Mayo speaks about is a social process, a multitude of social processes in fact. You don't organize it; you don't design it in anything like the ways the efficiency engineer is used to. OD has brought to organization leaders and managers this understanding. It is no exaggeration to say that without understanding social process, without process consciousness and process wisdom, there is no OD. Moreover, and far more importantly, OD brings ideas and methods for how one can work with social process, for this is the real question: If you can't organize it and design it and mandate it, what can you do? Are you simply condemned to letting social process be what it is: a natural phenomenon of extraordinary complexity and subtlety?

This question in various forms will occupy us for the rest of this chapter, for note that "working with social process" is itself a social process—a collaborative enterprise between various organization members and internal or external consultants and observers.[3]

SOCIAL PROCESS: A WORKING DEFINITION

When we say we are "working with process," what do we mean? I have said this ability is OD's distinctive contribution to organizations. The idea is a difficult one for several reasons. For one thing, it presumably can include everything that is going on among human beings in some organization context. But to say it includes everything that is going on is to say it includes everything that one might be able to say about an organization either from an inside point of view or from that of an external observer. Another thing that makes process difficult is that it is a mixture of things that are supposed to be happening—management's directions, for example, or the requirements of job descriptions—but it also includes things that are not mandated by official directives. Roethlisberger and Dickson (1939) famously gave these nonmandated patterns the name *informal organization*. Some of these patterns are actually prohibited; they break the rules of the system and may warrant punishment. But a much larger set of informal patterns aren't illegal or improper; they have just naturally emerged from people's proximity and the feelings that exist between them: the noon card game, for example, or the way people decorate their cubicles, the kinds of informal helping relationships that grow up between people, or the tensions that arise between people and the ways they are expressed in behavior. The discovery and clarification of informal patterns was one of the Hawthorne researches' greatest contributions to management thought, although at first many managers probably were not happy to hear about how little control they actually had.

In addition to being all-inclusive and a mixture of formal and informal patterns, social process is dynamic through time. This means that it can be difficult to detect the central tendency of a social process, as opposed to random variations that don't represent the main process. It is often tempting to equate some particular event with the overall process, when in fact that particular event may not be very representative at all. This also means that when trying to understand a social process, it is necessary to select from everything that is going on the particular events and happenings that best express the overall process.

Because it involves everybody, social process is through and through a matter of perception, not just the perceptions of one person but the perceptions of everyone. Each person is viewing the organization through their own glasses and acting on what they see, acting on the meanings that they perceive people, things, and events to have. *An organization is a place where everybody's right and everybody's wrong.* Each person understands some of the truth of the social process. No one understands all the truth of it. It is yet another instance of the famous story of the blind man and the elephant.

In this chapter I mean by social process the meanings people attach to themselves, to other people, things, and events, and the actions they take on those meanings. The totality of such actions by the members of some portion of the organization, or all of it, is the social process. Social process consists of myriad interactions. Thus, "working with process" is paying attention to all this meaning making, bearing in mind that it is both visible behavior and also inner thoughts and feelings of organization members and, in the first instance, accepting the reality of all of it rather than getting caught up in who is right and who is wrong, as regular organization members are prone to do. The OD person does have to make some choices, but at the outset all the meaning making that is occurring is valid, not just that of some chosen few.

THE VALUE OF PROCESS CONSCIOUSNESS AND PROCESS WISDOM

Process consciousness has many values. Because social process is what it is, process consciousness looks in many directions, concerns itself with many different kinds of phenomena, and operates continually. As suggested earlier, the principal thing that OD brings to the organization is its process consciousness. An OD professional is paying attention to process full time—not just when advising on the implementation of change but full time from the moment one walks through the door.

High-quality process consciousness I call *process wisdom* (Vaill, 1998b). It truly is wisdom we are talking about, and not just technical knowledge, because so much creativity, imagination, and interpersonal skill are involved. To some extent these qualities can be formally trained. To some extent they can be called competencies. But when one stops to think what truly is involved in being able to envision myriad human relationships evolving through time, imagine their reactions under various conditions, and communicate these insights in terms that nontechnical people can understand and act on, we clearly are talking more about what has been called wisdom than anything else.

There are at least eight values that process wisdom brings to the organization in the process of change. First, and most importantly, process wisdom is the handmaiden of whatever the organization is trying to do. The essence of a formal organization is its goal directedness. It is set up to do something. Its major parts and its formal structure are presumably in service of its goal directedness. But as discussed earlier, the sheer establishment of a formal structure is only half the battle. The other half is to operate these structures in such a way that the goals are achieved. This is the "wholehearted cooperation" Mayo speaks of. Moreover, the establishment of goals in the first place is itself a social process, a very important one. Often no one can quite explain how the goals came to be what they are, or indeed whether there are any goals at all. Process wisdom can bring such a situation into view if need be.

Second, if process wisdom is being used by an OD person in some context of change, it can call attention to the changes in social relationships that are directly needed or indirectly implied by the intended change. Usually it is some aspect of the social process itself that the OD person has been called in to help with. Examples might be to strengthen leadership, improve communication, restore trust, help manage conflict between two or more groups, or help discover more positive sources of motivation. Mayo's efficiency engineer can't rationally design any of these things, much as he might like to. Moreover, because social process occurs as a system of relationships, more things will be affected by changes than just the target behaviors that the leadership would like to change. Process wisdom understands that systemic change is involved and that what people

end up working on may be much deeper and more pervasive than the original statement of the problem.

Third, process wisdom identifies unanticipated consequences of initiatives by an organization's leadership. There probably are few ways in which an OD person is more helpful than in helping organization leaders think through the likely effects on social process of actions they are considering.

Identifying key kinds of events that need to happen if some overall change process is going to succeed is a fourth kind of benefit that process wisdom brings an organization. Process wisdom is able to anticipate what some action is likely to mean to those affected. Maybe there are meetings that need to occur, key people who need to be briefed, guarantees that need to be made to one group or another, or forecasts of further downstream effects of some change. The OD process mentality is continually anticipating how people are going to react to something management is considering and what further things need to be done in taking account of these reactions. Process wisdom is distinctly imaginative even as it is rooted in concrete events.

Fifth, process wisdom does not stop at the boundaries of some action management is taking or has taken. It reaches out to the broader context. It asks what other things might be on people's minds beside the immediate particular action. Often management would like people to stay focused narrowly on a particular action, but process wisdom knows that people's meanings don't stay neatly within management's boundaries.

Combining this contextual awareness with the ability to anticipate downstream consequences yields a sixth kind of value: the ability to identify or imagine disruptions to the social process—what I have called "permanent white water" events (Vaill, 1996). There is never the kind of tranquility and predictability management might like to have surrounding its initiatives. Its control is never that good, and surrounding events are never that docile. Process wisdom can take note of the turbulence people are experiencing, the confusion, the wondering what is going to happen next. Turbulence hits people especially at the level of their need for meaning. Things can become so turbulent that no one knows exactly what is going to happen next. All of this is still a social process of intense interaction and mutual questioning. None of it is invisible to a well-developed process consciousness. In fact, it is not an exaggeration to say that in times of extreme turbulence, process wisdom is one of the most important defenses any person has and thus it is a time when an OD person can be most helpful. It is process wisdom that sees what people are doing for and with each other, recognizes the need for leadership and identifies it when it arises, and sees how important the daily rituals and conventions can be in maintaining people's sense of order and coherence.

Seventh, process wisdom recruits colleagues, so to speak. It teaches process wisdom to others. It provides a vocabulary with which organization members can discuss what their problems are and what would be more desirable states of affairs. Process wisdom gives organization members something to reflect on together and helps them see that everyday slang and jargon often are insufficient for capturing the subtleties of what they are involved in and what they would like to see change. Indirectly, process wisdom helps organization members to value each other more highly, which is one of OD's most cherished values: to help people get beyond the superficialities of everyday life and encounter each other more deeply as people.

Finally, process wisdom knows what it doesn't know, that is, when for whatever reason the organization has moved into a social space that no one understands very well, where many of the former norms and values of the previous social process have been superseded. I call this state a process frontier (Vaill, 1996, pp. 135–136; 1998a, Chapter 8). On a process frontier, no one is exactly sure how to act. Everyone is experimenting, whether they

are quite able to admit it to themselves and each other or not. When the organization is on a process frontier, it is especially important that the experimental frame of mind be maintained and that things not be nailed down too quickly. The process frontier can be many different kinds of things, but three that are especially important are where the organization is entering new markets with new customers and competitors, where the organization is operating a new technology it has no experience with, and where the organization is encountering an entirely new culture, either by taking in new members who carry the new culture or by engaging another organization whose social process is that of a very different culture. Many organizations in the modern world, both business and nonbusiness, are on process frontiers where all three of these factors are operating simultaneously. The key qualities on process frontiers are experimentation, mindfulness, and learning together in community. It is an OD frame of mind that can bring this awareness to an organization.

Because process wisdom extends throughout an organization's operations and over the entire span of its life, there are other values of process wisdom than these eight. But these can be expected to arise continually.

Obviously, all eight of these values are matters of growth and development both for an OD professional and for other organization members. This is why it is appropriate to speak of the process wisdom, rather than just the process consciousness of someone who has been working with process for some time.

And to repeat once more, process consciousness—process wisdom—is the principal frame of mind OD brings to an organization's affairs. It is the OD person who is thinking about these things all the time and the OD person who defines his or her own development in terms of increasing process wisdom as the way to increase his or her value to the organization. There is a lot of talk among OD people about increasing their "tool kits" and doing things that "add value" for the client.

Sometimes process wisdom is a difficult thing to put a price tag on, and an OD person may be tempted to market something more tangible, such as a particular workshop design, a set of computerized slides about motivation, or a complex simulation for organization members to go through. But these kinds of services risk being irrelevant, or worse, if they are not rooted in some wisdom about the organization's social process and what this process needs for the organization to get where it is trying to go.

WORKING WITH PROCESS: THE ROLE OF THEORY

Given that understanding and working with social process is the principal skill of the OD professional, the problem is how to understand such a complex phenomenon as social process. As a result of the research of the past century, we have a great deal of theory, research findings, and miscellaneous concepts available to understand process. OD brings this knowledge to bear on particular organization conditions for the purpose of understanding both why the social process is as it is and how it might be changed in some way—some way that is still consistent with what we know about the ways people form and act on meanings in social contexts. For OD is not just management's tool to get the social process to "behave itself" and do what management wants it to do.

One might think that after its near half century of existence OD would have evolved a unified theory of social process that would handle most situations an OD consultant might face. But this has not occurred.[4] If anything, more theories and concepts are available now than there ever were, and there does not seem to be any let-up in the proliferation. Unfortunately, the plethora of concepts and diagnostic techniques tend not to distinguish between a snapshot of how things are and a more dynamic view of how things are evolving

over time. The latter kinds of concepts are much more useful for understanding process than the former.

It is probably desirable that we continue to seek simplicity and comprehensiveness of theory as much as possible, but there seems to be a characteristic of organizations, not often commented on, that works against this goal: Organizations are recalcitrant. Sociologist Robert Merton calls them intractable. Organizations elude control. They keep behaving in unexpected ways. An intervention at one point of an organization may generate effects that appear somewhere else and that do not exist in the same conceptual terms as the intervention that generated them. For example, an intervention at the level of trying to strengthen the vision that inspires organization members may lead organization members to enumerate all the particular problems an organization has. Their concerns are at a lower level of abstraction than the effort to stimulate vision, and they are coming out of personal meanings and feelings rather than sweeping vision of the organization. A different kind of theory is needed to understand these concerns; otherwise, the danger is that they will seem to be merely whining and carping. It is as if the one intervention generates the need for the other, for indeed the effect can work the other way, also: Preoccupation with particular problems is just as likely to stimulate someone to suggest that the real problem is lack of an overarching vision. In other words, a theory about the importance of vision and an attendant intervention designed to generate more vision can also generate more consciousness of particular problems, for which a different body of theory is needed. Similarly, a theory based on strong support from the top of the organization may generate a concern for more bottom-up participation. An intervention based on the formal, structural aspects of the system may generate concern for the informal, sociocultural aspects—again, two different bodies of theory and again, cause and effect can work either way. Theories of leadership often generate a need to know more about followership, which takes us into issues of group membership and group dynamics. Changes in technology and job design affect social process, and vice versa.

What we are suggesting is a kind of polarization process: Use of one kind of theory may tend to create a need for another kind of theory that deals with polar opposite phenomena. The pieces of theory that are needed for one pole have not been integrated with the pieces of theory needed for the other pole. So, the OD practitioner uses both fragments without worrying too much that they are not formally integrated. This is at least one reason why OD has found it so difficult to create one unified theory of social process that will undergird efforts to initiate change: Any actual change process generates a need for a huge variety of pieces of theory at a variety of points in the system and at a variety of times.

Nonetheless, social process cannot be addressed at all without some kinds of theory. Because social process as defined earlier involves all the human relationships of the organization and entails the behaviorally expressed meanings that people are continually ascribing to themselves, to others, and to things and events, this is too complex a phenomenon to embrace without some theory as a way of managing all the data that would be showering a consultant as he or she entered the organization. What we need, though, is theory that preserves the process quality, so to speak, of the data. We do not want theory that freezes the data into fixed categories. We need a movie, not a snapshot.

Moreover, an OD person needs an approach that will help him or her understand a change process, for that of course is what OD is really interested in. However, this chapter takes the position that the social process as we have been discussing it and the change process that OD fosters are not two different phenomena. They are forms of the same thing; put another way, the change process OD seeks is a particular kind of social process, but it does not escape being itself a social process. This is a very important point. This is the mistake Mayo's efficiency engineer who would "organize the organization of the organization" makes: He tries to escape social process. OD knows, or should know, that it can't be done. This mistake is made over and over again. It is made when it is believed that sufficiently strong leadership will be able to overcome any resistance in the ranks. It is made when it is assumed that a work group will be able to change its norms and rituals overnight and start working in some new way. It is made when it is believed that members can be added or subtracted from the organization without any effects on the other members. It is made when it is believed that an external consultant will have instant understanding of the system and credibility in it and can just begin immediately suggesting changes.

In this chapter neither one grand theory nor even a particular set of theoretical fragments is going to be offered. For one thing, there are many other chapters in this book that contain useful theories and research findings. But we refrain from suggesting a set of theories for a more important reason: When working with social process, most OD people seem to have evolved their own working theories, which I have elsewhere called "practice theories," following Kurt Lewin (Vaill, 1975). It doesn't mean they don't use the ideas of others. What it means is that they evolve a personal way of interpreting and using theories and concepts that helps them to work with social process. Notice that the aim is not the prediction and control that is the essence of truly scientific theories. The aim is for the OD practitioner to be able to synchronize with process, get a feel for how it is operating, understand intuitively what various process events mean, and sense where process is going. The OD practitioner is not unlike the anthropologist entering and learning to live in an entirely new society or the clinician who does not know what new syndromes are going to appear in the examining room. What is seen and heard is new and different enough to make any systematic theorizing and hypothesizing quite risky. The aim is to understand the dynamic whole, to come as close as possible to experiencing it the way members are experiencing it, so that when various changes are being considered, the OD person will have a good feel for what will be received positively and what will not. Furthermore, he or she will have a good feel for the way in which new concepts can be introduced to the organization in the interest of increasing the process wisdom of other organization members.[5]

From time to time over the years, various practicing OD people have written down their practice theories. One of the most famous and influential has been Edgar Schein's (1988) work on what he calls process consultation. Process consultation is working with the social processes of the organization of which Schein names nine, centered heavily around small group processes. Another major contribution was Weisbord's Six Box Model (Weisbord, 1978). Yet another well-known model was created by Nadler et al. (1994). Though not OD consultants per se, Peters and Waterman (1982) published what became a very influential seven-element framework, the "Seven S's" model. While working with what I called high-performing systems in the 1970s and 1980s, I developed an eight-element model for helping me understand groups and organizations that were performing at a very high level of excellence (Vaill, 1998a). Maslow, whose hierarchy of needs is a wonderful example of a practice theory, never drew a diagram to express it, but many other people have drawn ladders and step diagrams and truncated pyramids to show Maslow's five levels of needs. Kouzes and Posner (2002) have synthesized an impressive set of five principal things leaders do. Deming's (1982) famous 14 points are another example, an unusually good one because they were offered as working guidelines rather than as a grand theory of the change process.[6]

There are many such frameworks. Some may be found in this book. Some are admittedly fragmentary, but some purport to be comprehensive.[7] But none of these models were or are formal theories from which hypotheses can be deduced. Generating hypotheses for rigorous testing is not their purpose. Rather, their function is to help a practitioner understand some social process so that he or she can advise on the kinds of changes that might make sense in that system.

These models for helping an OD practitioner understand and work with process often exist as boxes connected by lines. Usually the lines go in all directions so that every box is connected to every other box. Or maybe they are set up in a rough flow, but then feedback arrows are drawn in such a way that all of the boxes or most of them are influenced by the output end of the flow process. Another common form of expressing practice theories is in a simple list of factors. The great value of a list is its flexibility. The user can mix and match in any way that seems appropriate for the situation. Either way, whether a diagram or a list, what the model reflects is the modeler's sense of the complexity and interdependence in the system. The boxes and the lists name the phenomena the modeler has learned are important. The lines depict relationships the modeler has learned need to be paid attention to. The diagrams and lists themselves do not depict social process. Social process is the combination of the visual names and connections and the modeler's intuitive grasp of their dynamics. Thus, it is the OD practitioner's values and behavior that make the movie; the diagrams and lists of key factors are the snapshots that name what we are talking about. This feel for the dynamics is another way of describing what we have been calling process wisdom.

THREATS TO PROCESS WISDOM

It was noted earlier that the OD professional is continually paying attention to process. This is a somewhat idealistic statement, for undoubtedly there are plenty of occasions when the OD person is not particularly conscious of process but is rather simply participating in it pretty much like everyone else. But beyond such natural immersion, there are genuine threats to process wisdom, threats that may impair it even when the OD professional is trying hard to stay in touch with process and work with it to the organization's benefit. The list that follows is somewhat speculative, although it is based on experience and the comments of other OD professionals. If working with process is as important as this chapter has made it out to be, though, this clearly is an area we need to know more about.

In the history of OD one kind of problem that has arisen repeatedly is that the client organization doesn't know that it is hiring process wisdom when it first retains an OD consultant. It has tended to think it is hiring an expert in some kind of content or technique, although this is often left somewhat vague. As performance pressure has increased on organizations, so has this tendency to think there must be some substantive expertise somewhere that will solve their problems. However, as detailed in this chapter, working with process is not a matter of deductive theory or the technical application of some treatment. Helping the client organization to come to see that there is a social process that needs to be understood, and that is the key to successful change, is itself a social process. The experienced OD consultant understands this and evolves various methods for conveying the importance of process. Sometimes it is playing back information about the organization that the client is unaware of. Sometimes it is helping various voices in the organization to be heard. Sometimes through a game or simulation the client can come to see how important process is. There are many different methods. Sometimes the consultant never does publicly surface the importance of process but instead works with it in the context of doing something more publicly

valuable, such as conducting an offsite retreat or giving a talk to a management group. Process wisdom can be used with amazing effects while one is ostensibly giving a speech to some large assemblage. Indeed, large group process work has become one of the fastest-growing areas of OD practice. (See Bunker & Alban, 1996; Owen, 1997; Weisbord, 1992.)

Related to this first problem is the danger that process wisdom will be seen as some kind of "touchy-feely" focus that the client does not want to get involved in. This issue was not so much of a concern for OD in its first couple of decades of existence. But gradually through the 1970s and into the 1980s, there evolved a kind of cultural contempt, at least among some would-be "hard chargers," for anything that has to do with looking closely at how people are acting and how they are feeling. OD's reliance on sensitivity training groups in its early years did not help the situation. OD had to detach itself from the stereotype that all it was interested in was probing into psyches. The temptation then became one of going too far in the other direction and abandoning concern for process entirely in favor of some presumed commitment to the bottom line.

A third kind of problem is the consultant's tendency to get too involved in content issues and forget the role of process. This may result from the consultant's desire to be seen as tough and no-nonsense, it may derive from client expectations, it may result from the consultant's lack of understanding of the importance of process. In any event, if the consultant abandons a concern for process, the changes he or she recommends and takes part in implementing will encounter the organization's social process, and at that point someone will have to address it. A variation on this problem, hinted at in the Mayo quotation with which we began, is the idea that if the change program is sufficiently rational, if it takes into account enough of the key variables and is sufficiently well thought-through, then somehow process will be finessed, and it will not need to be worked with along the way, or at least working with it will be merely tactics, a bit of tweaking here and there, managing a few over-sized egos, not really having to rethink and reshape the program as it proceeds because of process issues.

Perhaps that really is the nub of it: the rethinking and reshaping as a change process proceeds as a result of the way various parts of the organization are reacting. Those who would "organize the organization of the orga-nization" don't think such rethinking and reshaping should be necessary if we are suffi-ciently rational at the outset. But the whole history of the OD profession runs counter to this idea. The OD point of view, from the days of Kurt Lewin forward, is that if we really want to seat new ideas and new procedures deeply in the fabric of the organization, we have to involve organization members as we go along. Involving organization members means work-ing with the social processes that exist among them and being willing to rethink and reshape a change project as various aspects of social process manifest themselves.

In an article that was quite prophetic in its day, Beer et al. (1993) explained why change programs don't produce change. They showed that it all has to do with mistaken assumptions about what the social process of the organiza-tion can be made to do by top management. These authors' answer is that the social process can't be made to do anything. What you can do is work with it. The authors offer six prin-ciples for managing change, every one of which entails working with the social process of the organization:

1. "Mobilize commitment to change through joint diagnosis of business problems."

2. "Develop a shared vision of how to organize and manage for competitiveness."

3. "Foster consensus for the new vision, com-petence to enact it, and cohesion to move it along."

4. "Spread revitalization to all departments without pushing it from the top."

5. "Institutionalize revitalization through for-mal policies, systems, and structures."

6. "Monitor and adjust strategies in response to problems in the revitalization process" (Beer et al., 1993, pp. 269–273).

This list is an example of what was earlier called a practice theory. Notice that each of the verbs involves interaction with other members of the organization rather than doing things to them, or for them for that matter. The list of principles powerfully communicates that a change project, no matter how rationally and comprehensively conceived, depends on the skill with which it can be integrated with the ongo-ing social process of the organization. Each verb names a kind of skill that an OD professional needs to be able to practice.

At the other extreme from being unmindful of process might be the problem of being too mindful, with too many competing views of what to pay attention to in an organization's social process. One way this problem manifests itself is when the organization's culture is being taken into account. Culture is very much in the eye of the beholder: Depending on one's expe-rience in an organization, cultural norms can have different forms, meanings, significance, and strength. Various artifacts of culture can have different degrees of importance. Because cultures often contain status rankings of vari-ous groups, which group one is a member of can powerfully affect what one thinks of the culture and what one thinks ought to be changed (or not). In short, social process can itself become a matter of contention. Another mani-festation of this phenomenon is competition between various theories for influence on a change process. If one is a "group dynamics" disciple (Cartwright & Zander, 1960), one is not likely to be sympathetic to a change strat-egy grounded in the psychodynamic theories of Wilfrid Bion (1961), and vice versa. Elliott

Jaques's (1998) theories about executive development lead in one direction, Warren Bennis's (Bennis & Nanus, 1985) in another.[8] Again, if a change process is to have coherence, the theoretical grounds must have coherence, understanding, and commitment from organization members. As management groups have themselves become more sophisticated about social process, the variety of available concepts has become more and more of a problem for OD. For some years it has not had a monopoly on how to think about change.

The first step in dealing with the problem of plethora of available change concepts is to recognize that the problem exists. Members of the organization need to understand that this is an area of choice, that there is not just one best theory to fit their situation. This is mainly a matter of education of organization members in which an OD consultant can play a very important role. It then follows as a second step that organization members together with their consultants need either to choose a particular conceptual scheme or, better yet, fashion their own working theory.

It is important to remember a principle that Harvey articulated early in the life of the OD profession: "Theory dictates the process of change and the value system underlying that process" (Adams, 1975, p. 188). The change we are talking about is largely a matter of helping people learn to think differently as a basis for acting differently. Therefore, the process of developing a new way of thinking about the organization and its change processes should be a matter of careful development. This new way of thinking should not just be chosen quickly because it is available, popular, or verbally impressive. If organization members understand that the theory is the intervention, then those involved in leading the change can trust that the process of choosing a conceptual basis is time well spent. Theories and concepts need not be set in win–lose competition; synthesis, integration, tailoring to local culture, and their appeal to organization members can

be the criteria by which the conceptual basis is developed.

Turbulence and chaos in organizations—what I call "permanent white water" (Vaill, 1989, 1996)—is a final kind of threat to process consciousness and process wisdom. The idea of social process evolved out of studies of the social structure of organizations and societies, as sketched at the beginning of this chapter. These social structures had evolved in some cases over millennia, but at least over many decades in the case of American companies and other organizations. It was possible to identify stable lines of communication between stable roles that people were playing in stable status hierarchies. It had become possible to write down some very predictable characteristics of bureaucratic structures (see Bennis, 1966, pp. 5–6; Bolman & Deal, 2003, pp. 45–46). But what happens when formal structures are continually changing through reorganizations, mergers and acquisitions, outsourcing, and proliferation of staff functions? What happens when there is a high degree of turnover in organization leadership, leading to articulations of new visions and mission and a continuing stream of structural initiatives? What happens both structurally and in terms of morale and cohesion in the midst of continual downsizing (see Noer, 1993)? What about extreme degrees of turbulence in the environment, first noticed by Emery and Trist (1965), necessitating non-stop "adaptive change," as Heifetz (1994) has called it, that is, continual reinvention of what the organization is trying to be and do?

With the advent of chaos theory a number of books have applied these ideas to organizations. For the most part, however, these books do not delve deeply into existing social processes or the question of what social processes under conditions of chaotic change looks like. However, in a well-received book, Stacey (1992) devoted a chapter to how to structure an organization that is undergoing chaotic change. His ideas about structure try to take account of the impact of chaotic change on social process, but he does not address social process directly. Similarly, in a book about how to stimulate creativity and innovation in organizations in the midst of turbulence, Gryskiewicz (1999) devotes a chapter to "strategies for managing positive turbulence," but he too takes social process for granted and speaks only about managing in relation to it.

In what may turn out to be one of the most prophetic OD books of the decade, Olson and Eoyang (2001) have undertaken to apply chaos theory and what they call complex adaptive systems theory to the social process of organizations and to the way in which change agents can work with these processes. Given turbulence, chaos, and continual disruptive change, say these authors, let us fashion a conceptual scheme that makes these events their central focus. Most other theories of social process treat continual change as an aberration or exception to the primary nature of the system. Not so, say Olson and Eoyang. If the primary nature of the system is continual change, then we need theories and concepts that focus on that. This is what complex adaptive systems theory does.

As the pace of change continues and stresses on organizations and the people in them increase, we can expect to see more studies of how social process operates in the midst of chaos. We know from natural disasters and from the consequences of wars and other human-made disasters that social process does survive; it does not evaporate. OD consultants can be the sources of new knowledge about social process in organizations undergoing chaotic change.

These are a few of the major threats to social process and OD's ways of working with it. Undoubtedly other threats are occurring now or will occur in the future. It is paradoxical that so pervasive a phenomenon should also be so fragile in terms of managers' ability to address it directly and OD's ability to keep the skill of working with process alive. If working with process does pass into eclipse for a time, it seems safe to say that the theory and practice of working with process will just have to be reinvented. It is the key to intentional leadership and management of organizations.

LEARNING MORE ABOUT WORKING WITH PROCESS

We close this chapter with a few thoughts about the how working with process can be strengthened as a way of doing OD. Certainly working with process in chaotic conditions is a topic that warrants a great deal of further research and concept development. Beyond this point, I discuss a few ideas for how the OD profession and its clients can learn more about working with process.

There aren't nearly as many first-person accounts of doing OD work as there need to be. I have said several times that working with process is both central to OD practice and difficult to define and describe. The best source of knowledge about working with process is the practitioner himself or herself. Weisbord has been one who has contributed in major ways to our understanding of OD practice (Van Eynde, Hoy, & Van Eynde, 1997, pp. 107–118). *The O.D. Practitioner,* the journal from which the Van Eynde et al. book is compiled, has recently been publishing more first-person accounts of OD practice (as opposed to objective case studies of OD projects). Bellman (2002) is another practicing professional who has contributed important information about OD practice. Indeed, he comes very close to fulfilling the vision of this entire present chapter in three chapters about working with organizations. These accounts by Weisbord and Bellman are consistent with what has been said here about working with process.

Beyond first-person narratives, we need more interviews with OD consultants about how they work, even though interviews are once removed from the point of action. Though not focusing on working with process, Kaplan (1994) did show that a variety of rich insights into OD practice can be generated through interviewing methods that are open ended and phenomenological in approach. Interviewing practicing consultants is an excellent method of teaching students of OD what the work is all about.

It is difficult to systematically observe an OD consultant working with process. However, there are occasions when it can be done. In meetings where the consultant is present as a facilitator, it is sometimes possible for another person to observe the facilitation. These opportunities are especially present where the meeting is itself a key part of the change process, as is the case in Weisbord's (1992) "Future Search" conferences and in the "Open Space" conference design invented by Harrison Owen in the 1980s. "Open Space" is now widely used by OD consultants as a method of involving large numbers of organization members in various stages of the change process (Owen, 1997). Somebody manages the "Open Space" concept, and that person is working with process in just the sense that this chapter has meant it.

CONCLUSION

As was suggested earlier, "working with process," "being aware of process," and "paying attention to process," are phrases that OD consultants use all the time. Ironically, however, the profession has not spent nearly as much time discussing what these phrases mean as one might think, given the centrality of these attitudes and actions. This chapter has taken up the challenge to try to say what we mean and to locate the notion of working with process in the broader practice of OD and of organization change in general. The idea of process wisdom has been a key notion—the ability to work with process effectively—despite the fact that it is not a technical skill that can be defined and efficiently transmitted in education and training. Process wisdom is something every effective OD consultant possesses. Describing what it is, how it operates, and why it is important has been this chapter's objective.

NOTES

1. Ideally, the practicing manager in the trenches should be the one who works effectively with all the social processes that are going on in the course of performing the work. For a variety of reasons, many of which are mentioned in this chapter, the strength, complexity, and dynamism of today's social processes continually threaten to outrun a manager's ability to comprehend and influence them. This is why the professional perspective and help of an OD consultant often are needed. The ideal of a practicing manager who does possess process wisdom, as discussed in this chapter, remains a worthy vision, however.

2. This is not to say that there weren't many other places in the organization where help was needed. For example, Walker and Guest (1952) clearly demonstrated how many problems there were at the blue-collar level where OD values and skills could be helpful.

3. It is worth noting here that "Trust the process!" is one of the most fundamental values of OD work. The phrase usually is uttered when the OD consultant perceives that there is movement, however subtle, in the direction of the "whole-hearted cooperation" Elton Mayo speaks of. It is a statement of hope grounded in data, says my colleague Bill Monson.

4. Blake and Mouton (1976) made a heroic effort to encompass OD in relation to the entire social process of an organization in something they called the Consulcube. The Consulcube was a 100-cell framework generated by five different consultant styles times five different kinds of organization settings times four different issues to focus on. The authors sought to show what working with process looked like in each cell, drawing from published research. However, the Consulcube did not become the standard framework that the authors intended it to become.

5. This is why doing OD is not really applied behavioral science, despite the popularity of this phrase in the history of OD. With a true applied science, as in engineering, for example, different practitioners can use the same theory or model. With OD, however, the practitioner's values and personality are part of the change process, and this is why a personal practice theory is necessary.

6. Interestingly, most of Deming's famous 14 points were about the organization's social process, not its business factors or technology. Process wisdom was needed in order for Deming's total quality management to work.

7. In fact, there are probably thousands of such models, for they are what professors create to communicate their own ideas about some organization situation. Most go unpublished, but undoubtedly they are regularly fed back to their creators on final exams and term papers.

8. In a quite remarkable piece of scholarship, Segal (1997), himself a respected OD scholar-practitioner, assesses the relevance of nine major schools of personality theory to the kinds of organization change problems a consultant and client might be facing.

REFERENCES

Adams, J. D. (Ed.). (1975). *New technologies in organization development 2*. La Jolla, CA: University Associates.

Beer, M., Eisenstat, R. A., & Spector, B. (1993). Why change programs don't produce change. In T. D. Jick (Ed.), *Managing change: Cases and concepts* (pp. 264–276). Chicago: Irwin.

Bellman, G. M. (2002). *The consultant's calling* (rev. ed.). San Francisco: Jossey-Bass.

Bennis, W. G. (1966). *Changing organizations*. New York: McGraw-Hill.

Bennis, W. G., Benne, K., & Chin, R. (Eds.). (1961). *The planning of change*. New York: Holt, Rinehart, and Winston.

Bennis, W. G., & Nanus, B. (1985). *Leaders: Strategies for taking charge*. New York: Harper & Row.

Bion, W. R. (1961). *Experiences in groups*. New York: Basic Books.

Blake, R. R., & Mouton, J. S. (1976). *Consultation*. Reading, MA: Addison-Wesley.

Bolman, L. G., & Deal, T. E. (2003). *Reframing organizations* (3rd ed.). San Francisco: Jossey-Bass.

Bunker, B. B., & Alban, B. T. (1996). *Large group interventions: Engaging the whole system for rapid change*. San Francisco: Jossey-Bass.

Cartwright, D., & Zander, A. (1960). *Group dynamics: Research and theory* (2nd ed.). Evanston, IL: Row, Peterson & Co.

Collins, J. C., & Porras, J. I. (1994). *Built to last*. New York: HarperBusiness.

Deming, W. E. (1982). *Out of the crisis*. Cambridge: MIT Press.

Emery, F. E., & Trist, E. L. (1965). The causal texture of organizational environments. *Human Relations, 8*, 21–32.

Gryskiewicz, S. S. (1999). *Positive turbulence*. Greensboro, NC: Center for Creative Leadership.

Heifetz, R. A. (1994). *Leadership without easy answers*. Cambridge, MA: Belknap.

Herzberg, F. (1959). *The motivation to work*. New York: John Wiley & Sons.

Homans, G. C. (1950). *The human group*. New York: Harcourt, Brace.

Jaques, E. (1998). *Requisite organization*. Gloucester, MA: Cason Hall Publishers.

Kaplan, K. L. (1994). *An exploration of the experiences and perceptions of women organization development consultants*. George Washington University PhD dissertation. Ann Arbor: UMI Dissertation Services.

Kleiner, A. (1996). *The age of heretics: Heroes, outlaws, and the forerunners of corporate change*. New York: Doubleday.

Kouzes, J. M., & Posner, B. Z. (2002). *The leadership challenge* (3rd ed.). San Francisco: Jossey-Bass.

Mayo, E. (1945). *The social problems of an industrial civilization*. Boston: Harvard Business School Division of Research.

Nadler, D. A., Shaw, R. B., & Walton, A. E. (1994). *Discontinuous change: Leading organizational transformation*. San Francisco: Jossey-Bass.

Noer, D. M. (1993). *Healing the wounds*. San Francisco: Jossey-Bass.

Olson, E. E., & Eoyang, G. H. (2001). *Facilitating organization change: Lessons from complexity science*. San Francisco: Jossey-Bass.

Owen, H. H. (1997). *Open space technology: A user's guide*. San Francisco: Berrett-Koehler.

Parsons, T. (1951). *The social system*. Glencoe, IL: The Free Press.

Peters, T. J., & Waterman, R. W. (1982). *In search of excellence*. New York: Harper & Row.

Radcliffe-Brown, A. R. (1948). *A natural science of society*. Glencoe, IL: The Free Press.

Roethlisberger, F. J., & Dickson, W. J. (1939). *Management and the worker*. Boston: Harvard University Press.

Schein, E. H. (1988). *Process consultation: Its role in organization development* (Vol. 1). Reading, MA: Addison-Wesley.

Seashore, E. W. (2004, August 10). Remarks to a seminar of the Antioch University PhD program in Leadership and Change, Yellow Springs, OH.

Segal, M. (1997). *Points of influence: A guide to using personality theory at work*. San Francisco: Jossey-Bass.

Stacey, R. D. (1992). *Managing the unknowable*. San Francisco: Jossey-Bass.

Vaill, P. B. (1975). Practice theories in organization development. In J. D. Adams (Ed.), *New technologies in organization development 2* (pp. 71–84). La Jolla, CA: University Associates.

Vaill, P. B. (1978). Toward a behavioral description of high-performing systems. In M. W. McCall Jr. & M. M. Lombardo (Eds.), *Leadership: Where else can we go?* (pp. 103–125). Durham, NC: Duke University Press.

Vaill, P. B. (1989). *Managing as performing art*. San Francisco: Jossey-Bass.

Vaill, P. B. (1996). *Learning as a way of being*. San Francisco: Jossey-Bass.

Vaill, P. B. (1998a). *Spirited leading and learning*. San Francisco: Jossey-Bass.

Vaill, P. B. (1998b). The unspeakable texture of process wisdom. In S. Srivastva & D. L. Cooperrider (Eds.), *Organizational wisdom and executive courage* (pp. 25–39). San Francisco: Jossey-Bass.

Van Eynde, D. F., Hoy, J. C., & Van Eynde, D. C. (1997). *Organization development classics*. San Francisco: Jossey-Bass.

Walker, C. R., & Guest, R. H. (1952). *The man on the assembly line*. Cambridge, MA: Harvard University Press.

Weisbord, M. R. (1978). *Organizational diagnosis: A workbook of theory and practice*. Reading, MA: Addison-Wesley.

Weisbord, M. R. (1987). *Productive workplaces*. San Francisco: Jossey-Bass.

Weisbord, M. R. (1992). *Discovering common ground*. San Francisco: Berrett-Koehler.

14

Team Building

R. WAYNE BOSS

MARK L. McCONKIE

Because organizations are composed of individuals working together as teams, team effectiveness is central to both organization change and organization effectiveness. One chief means of increasing team effectiveness is the process known as team building, wherein members of teams, or natural work groups, work together to strengthen their interaction patterns and processes in ways that enhance overall organization productivity. Given the dramatic increase in the use of teams in organization life (Gordon, 1992; Lawler, Morhman, & Ledford, 1995), coupled with the fact that teams seem pivotal to organization success (Katzenbach & Smith, 1993; Peters, 1988; Reich, 1987), it is clear that one of the skills most needed to increase organization effectiveness is the ability to work with others (Capelli & Rogovsky, 1994).

THE BEGINNINGS OF TEAM BUILDING

Modern team building as a systematic set of human interaction processes aimed at shaping the behaviors of individual team members has multiple roots. The first was the emergence of the National Training Laboratories, with its focus on small groups as laboratories in which group behaviors and emotions could be identified, understood, and altered in order to improve interactions within the group and the organization. These training groups came to be called T groups. Group members learned such skills as behavior diagnosis, giving and receiving feedback, self-awareness, self-disclosure, communicating at substantive and emotional levels, goal setting, action planning, and problem solving (Blake, 1995, pp. 24–25). This "laboratory learning" legitimated small groups, and eventually teams, as forums for behavioral exploration, correction, and improvement (Golembiewski & Blumberg, 1967). With the passage of time, the use of T groups as organization development (OD) interventions has declined, but the movement's lessons on group behavior and using groups to elicit change have become important foundation stones in team-building processes.

A second root of the team-building movement reached into the practical experience of men and women working to solve organization problems, such as the early work of Alfred J. Marrow (1974) on Project Accord at the U.S. Department of State. The State Department had received five decades of criticism for its failure to function properly and was so slow in decision making that President John F. Kennedy called it a bowl of Jello (Marrow, 1974). In 1963 Kennedy appointed William J. Crockett as deputy undersecretary of state for administration, and Crockett hired a team of behavioral scientists to conduct T group training and other group-related interventions. Though only infrequently called team building, the design used very closely resembled that described by Beckhard (1967) in what has become a classic model for team building. Soon thereafter Crockett was replaced, and his replacement deliberately sought to undo the effects of Crockett's work by returning to an authoritarian, control-centered management style. Nevertheless, empirical results of these early interventions showed small improvements in performance and attitudes and generated enthusiasm for team building as a mechanism for resolving organization problems (Argyris, 1967; Marrow, 1974).

In work similar to what Marrow reported at the State Department, Douglas McGregor, working as a consultant to one of the management groups at Union Carbide, set out to build an effective management team. McGregor collected data from team members and used a crude scale of his own making to monitor attitudes and progress, focusing on such matters as the degree of trust, the quality of communication, the degree of mutual support for group member activity, means of controlling conflict, clarity of team objectives, means for using resources, and the degree of freedom felt within the work group. The feedback that the scale provided became the basis for group discussion and action planning. McGregor (1967, pp. 106–111) published his results, and they became one of the early demonstrations of effective team building (Bennis, 1969, pp. 2–6).

A third important factor contributing to the acceptance of team building was a growing body of research and practical literature studying groups and analyzing group processes. The research literature began in social psychology, where studies of group dynamics suggested insights into group behaviors that researchers and practitioners could integrate into work with groups and teams (see Cartwright & Zander, 1953). Argyris (1957, 1965, 1967), for one, insisted on scientific rigor as the basis for the study of groups and organizations in order to ensure that the theory thus generated was reliable. Rensis Likert (1961) concurred and described organizations as systems of interlocking groups connected by "linking pins," or people who are simultaneously members of two groups, being subordinates in the one and supervisors or superiors in the other. It was through these interlocking groups that the organization's work was accomplished, because, Likert reasoned, people functioned not less as individuals than as members of teams or groups. He developed a scale for measuring human behavior, which he argued was the central variable in all organization behavior. The scale measured interaction style along a continuum from "exploitative authoritarian" through "benevolent authoritarian" to "consultative" and finally to "participative, group-based" behavior (Likert, 1967). This scale meant not only that group or team behavior could be measured but that it could be tracked, and changes in behavior therefore could be verified. Ultimately, this meant that team-building effectiveness could be measured.

DIFFERENT APPROACHES TO TEAM BUILDING

The principal purpose of team building is to improve team effectiveness (Woodman & Sherwood, 1980), and most team-building designs are based on Kurt Lewin's (1946) action research model, which envisions a cycle of data collection, data analysis, data feedback, and action planning (Beckhard, 1969a; Beer, 1976). Team building is based on the assumption that a team's participation in its own problem diagnosis, planning, and goal setting will increase team members' commitment to those processes (Coch & French, 1948; Lewin, 1965) and that those closest to the problem are best suited to resolve it (Beckhard, 1969a, p. 14). As a general rule, the values and assumptions underlying team building are those of humanistic management philosophies (for an expanded discussion, see Liebowitz & DeMeuse, 1982).

One of the central purposes of team building is trust building because many, if not most, of the variables responsible for team and organization effectiveness grow out of high-trust relationships (see Golembiewski & McConkie, 1975; Spreitzer, Shapiro, & Von Glinow, 2002). Giffin (1967) found, and Mishra (1996) later confirmed, that trusting relationships are those in which competence is exhibited, openness exists, concern for the well-being of others is manifest, and the parties to the relationship are consistent or reliable. Because team building is designed to build skill levels and increase competence, create greater openness in problem solving and interpersonal relationships, hold people accountable for commitments made, and increase people's concern one for another, it is not surprising that team building is an effective means of building trust (Boss & McConkie, 2004).

In a more general sense team-building activities are intended to strengthen organization health and effectiveness by building trust and creating more open climates where problems are confronted and resolved. By increasing participants' sense of ownership of organization goals and objectives, they simultaneously increase commitment to those purposes. Team building is also designed to increase collaboration between interdependent people and interdependent groups. Where competitive relationships exist, for example, they can be managed to the benefit rather than to the detriment of the organization, as is often the case when limited resources are involved. Team building typically seeks to increase participants' awareness of group processes and their implications for group performance. An underlying theme is empowerment: helping people understand what power they possess and how they can maximize their control over their environment, expand their choices, and gain skills that facilitate cooperation with others (Boss, 1991).

Because different teams have different needs and goals, different team-building designs have different foci. Thus Beer (1976) considers four basic approaches to team building, each based on the primary focus of the team building design. These include goal-setting designs, designs to improve interpersonal relations, designs to reshape group members' roles, and problem-solving designs. Variations and combinations of these four basic designs also exist (see Buller, 1986; Dyer, 1995), but Beer's classification grasps the major differences in approach. Goal-setting approaches to team building assume that if individual or group goals are redefined, team culture will inevitably shift and team effectiveness will improve. Interpersonal approaches assume that greater interpersonal effectiveness will lead to greater team effectiveness (Argyris, 1962). A primary interest in these approaches is building trust and creating mutual support. Role approaches focus on role negotiation and role definition, assuming that role clarity intensifies work focus and therefore team effectiveness. Role approaches further assume that teams involve interlocking and overlapping roles, which can be clarified and coordinated for optimum performance, and that team behavior often is best understood in terms of how people perceive their assigned roles (Homans, 1950). Problem-solving approaches assume that teams become more effective as they solve problems together (Buller & Bell, 1986) by generating and analyzing data, planning, and conducting action steps. Interpersonal problems, role conflicts, goal differences, or other problems may be resolved en route to task accomplishment, but the principal focus is the task. Early on, McGregor (1960) listed some of the characteristics of effective groups:

- The atmosphere tends to be relaxed, comfortable, and informal.
- The group's task is well understood and accepted by group members.
- Group members listen to one another; a great deal of task-relevant discussion occurs, and most group members participate in it.
- Group members express feelings and ideas.
- Conflict and disagreement exist, but they center on task-related issues rather than on personal differences and personalities.
- The group has a high degree of self-awareness about its own functioning.
- Decisions usually occur by consensus rather than majority vote.
- When action items are generated, clear assignments are made and accepted by group members.

Defining the characteristics of an effective group, as McGregor did, was an important step in setting the standards against which team effectiveness could be measured. It also meant that team-building efforts in different kinds of teams could be conducted differently and would logically have different foci. For example, French and Bell (1984, p. 140) argue that the team-building needs of family groups—that is, "intact, permanent work teams composed of a boss and subordinates"—are more likely to focus on task accomplishment, including problem

solving, decision making, role clarification, and goal setting, or perhaps on relationship building, understanding and managing group culture and processes, role clarification, and role negotiation techniques.

On the other hand, special groups such as startup teams are more likely to need attention to task accomplishment, especially for special problems, such as role and goal clarification; resource use; relationship issues, such as interpersonal and interunit conflicts and the underuse of each other as resources; or processes such as communication, decision making, and task allocation. Golembiewski (1972, pp. 169–170) provided an early, typical typology of team building designs:

- *Team diagnostic meeting:* The learning group is an organizational family, a manager and his or her immediate work group. The diagnosis may center on specific tasks or problems, or it may have a summary quality, as in asking, "What do we do best? What do we do worst?"
- *Goal-setting and planning groups:* These may be either individual pairs of superiors and subordinates or individual family teams throughout the organization. The focus is on systematic review of performance that leads to mutual setting of targets or goals, with mutual review of progress.
- *Interface groups:* The learning groups may combine different functional specialties, such as sales and engineering, labor and management, the managements of two organizations working through a merger, or organization insiders and an outside group such as customers and clients. A hundred or more people may participate, usually meeting for a day or less, and the emphasis is on groups rather than individuals. These three factors limit the intensity of the design. As Sherwood (1972, p. 156) explains, such groups are "a problem-solving mechanism when problems are known to exist. An action-research format is used. The entire management group of an organization is brought together, problems and attitudes are collected and shared, priorities are established, and commitments to

action are made through setting targets and assigning task forces." Three subtypes of interface groups are common:

o *Mirror groups:* This design allows some inside group to get feedback from one or more key clientele groups to which it relates (e.g., customers, suppliers, or inside users of the target group's services). This is a one-way confrontation. The target group sees itself mirrored by the clientele group. The target group does not mirror back. Proposals to improve conditions usually are generated by mixed teams, each with members from both target and clientele groups. The mixed teams report their suggestions to the whole group.

o *Goal-setting interface groups:* Representatives from several related groups of organization units meet to set goals for action or change, usually on quite specific issues. The basic work typically is done in mixed subgroups of five or six members representing each group of units. The subgroups report back to the total population of participants, and some known procedure is used to integrate the results. For example, a manager might take the results as inputs to guide his or her decision making. Or a steering committee composed of one representative from each subgroup might prepare a composite report for all participants or for some manager or group of managers.

o *Confrontation groups:* Here two or more groups, such as black employees and white employees, are brought together to begin building a relationship or to repair a defective one. The groups share how they see themselves and others, with the intent of exposing issues, letting the groups know how they are perceived, and permitting groups to compare their own group concepts with perceptions of others. The intent of such a design is to clear the air, to provide a realistic and open base on which to build relationships. Such a meeting typically concludes with an action phase: What can be done to do what needs to be done?

• *Internal team building:* The learning group consists typically of a manager and one or more levels of his or her immediate subordinates, up to a limit of 15 or so participants. The focus is on identifying and solving work problems. The broad emphasis is on interpersonal, procedural, and organizational blockages to effective functioning. The design is distinguished by depth of analysis, scrutiny of interpersonal relations, and focus on individuals. Interpersonal relations aims include increasing openness and owning of ideas and feelings; heightening mutual trust, acceptance, and understanding of team members; and changing patterns of communication. Procedural and organizational improvements might include adapting different procedures for different tasks or analyzing patterns of delegation to isolate and possibly eliminate their awkward consequences.

• *Interface team building:* Two or more separate organization units simultaneously deal with the same kinds of issues that are encountered in internal team building. This design is extremely complex and demanding because it deals with complex intergroup phenomena such as intergroup competition or the presence of two or more coequal authority figures. (For additional information on various team-building designs, see Agnew & Boutwell, 1995; Eggleton & Rice, 1996; Elledge & Phillips, 1994; Fordyce & Weil, 1971; Pfeiffer, 1991; Phillips & Elledge, 1989; and Weiss, 1991.)

What the Research Says

The literature reviews examining team building generally note its popularity but emphasize that measurements of its productivity vary, with some reviews pointing to its strengths and some to its weaknesses. Team building typically receives a mixed review: Sometimes it works, and sometimes it does not (Bettenhausen, 1991, pp. 366–370; Buller, 1986; Rushmer, 1997b; Salas, Rozell, Mullen, & Driskell, 1999; Tannenbaum, Beard, & Salas, 1992). Early reviews, which were largely anecdotal testimonials or subjective evaluations often made by participants in team-building sessions immediately after the session itself (Davis, 1967; Kuriloff & Atkins, 1966), evoked calls for more empirical rigor in evaluating team-building effects (Buller, 1986; DeMeuse & Liebowitz, 1981; Terpstra, 1982). Some scholars also complained that it would be difficult to accurately measure team-building effects until OD and team building were better defined (Buller, 1986; DeMeuse & Liebowitz, 1981).

Through the 1970s and 1980s team building widened its reach in the corporate, government, and not-for-profit worlds. It was described as useful in wilderness settings (Long, 1987; Neeley & Kling, 1987), in an airline cockpit (Margerison, Davis, & McCann, 1987), in religious settings (Athey & Hautaluoma, 1988), in medical settings (Bair & Greenspan, 1986; Boss, 1989), and in a multiculturally staffed headquarters (Ratiu, 1986). In another instance, the effects of team building were tracked in seven Israeli command teams (Eden, 1986). One study even described five people working together without a leader or advisor to solve work-related problems (Segal-Horn, McGill, Bourner, Bourner, & Frost, 1987). Books appeared that outlined strategies and various team-building designs, assuming that team building was an applicable intervention in organizations of all kinds, although its application would have to be tailored to organization needs (see Dyer, 1987).

Meanwhile, scholars paid increasing attention to methodological and other details. Masterson and Murphy (1986) outlined steps for improving self-awareness and skills working with employees from diverse cultures, and Boss and Mariono (1987) noted that many successful American team-building designs and conflict management constructs failed in Italy because of cultural differences. Rideout and Richardson (1989) proposed a model for team building that was sensitive to gender differences and personality types, building on the fact that differences in group composition tend to influence differences in group interaction abilities and strategies.

In reviewing the empirical studies on team building, Tannenbaum et al. (1992) found a total of 67 studies: 14 conducted in the 1960s,

36 in the 1970s, and 17 in the 1980s. They found that most of the work on team building had been conducted with white-collar teams, with the fascinating exception of Buller and Bell (1986), who reported on a team-building experience within a blue-collar community. Tannenbaum et al. also reported a consistent pattern of low empirical rigor in the measurement of team-building effectiveness, specifically noting that more than half the studies mentioned in an earlier review used pre-experimental designs that made it difficult to attribute causality, and no pre-1980 study used a true experimental design (DeMeuse & Liebowitz, 1981; Woodman & Sherwood, 1980). They also found that most of the pre-1980 research had small sample sizes, and they voiced concerns about the types of outcome measures used. By the 1980s, there was some improvement in research methods; 11 of the 17 studies conducted in that decade used quasiexperimental designs, and 2 used true experimental designs.

Although the 1980s brought increased attention to the measurement of team-building outcomes, most of the focus was on team or individual process changes. This reliance on process measures as indicators of team-building effectiveness is perhaps troubling, if only because it diverts attention from the need for other measures of effectiveness. A team may improve its processes without improving its performance. Still, most of the studies in the 1980s yielded positive results, and they even began to pay attention to variables that extended beyond the team building itself, recognizing that team performance is related to the larger organization context. It became apparent that team building was but one of multiple interventions affecting team performance and that successful OD involved multiple interventions. Thus we have instances of team building joining with a goal-setting program (Buller & Bell, 1986) and of team building as part of larger OD interventions (Paul & Gross, 1981; Porras & Wilkins, 1980) that reported improvements in morale and productivity.

At the same time, even when coupled with other interventions, team building does not always yield positive results.

The question, of course, is why? Or, what combination of OD interventions should be coupled with team building to ensure that results endure? The initial answer to that question has been provided by Boss (1983, 1985), who found that when team building is coupled with follow-up sessions in which team-building commitments are reinforced and renewed, the positive effects of the team building are prolonged. Indeed, it appears that the effects can be retained as long as the post–team building meetings are conducted. This suggests that team building should not be considered as a one-shot deal but rather as part of a larger process wherein participants meet regularly for follow-up discussions.

Thus, although the 1980s saw less research on team building, they also saw more rigorous research. The focus of the research remained on intact, white-collar teams, but more studies were multidimensional. A review of the studies suggests that the assumed connection between process and productivity is not always warranted, but team-building interventions, in general, were deemed fairly effective. Team building seemed to change perceptions and attitudes more than behavior, although later intervention could reinforce the effects of the team building.

Tannenbaum et al.'s (1992, p. 118) summary review of the existing research described an "input, throughput, output" model. In a disciplined definition of teams, they noted that "while all teams are groups, not all groups can be considered teams" and that for a group to qualify as a team "its members must rely on each other and share a common goal." They defined a team "as a distinguishable set of two or more people who interact dynamically, interdependently, and adaptively toward a common and valued goal/objective/mission, and who each have some specific roles or functions to perform." This meant that groups of people could attend a common meeting and not constitute a team.

Also, teams evolved over time, and as they did, their shape and purpose would change, as would team interaction patterns.

Differences in team composition, goals, purpose, and structure influence how well teams function and how well team building works. In reviewing the major work on teams (see Hackman, 1983; Nieva, Fleishman, & Rieck, 1978; Steiner, 1972), several researchers concluded that team building can influence every level of team functioning. Team building thus affects and is affected by input variables such as team task, work structure, the individual characteristics of team members (attitudes, motivation, personality, and mental models), and team characteristics such as member homogeneity or cohesiveness. Team building can also shape throughput variables such as communication, coordination, conflict resolution processes, and training. Output variables such as team changes (including things such as new team norms, new team member roles, new processes) and team performance variables, as well as individual behavior changes, make team building one of the more potent change strategies in the OD panoply. Changes in team behavior, including those impelled by team building, always occur in a context, so team building is also affected by reward systems, management control systems, levels of stress, the quality of intergroup relations, and environmental uncertainties.

The literature of the 1990s continued the themes developed in the 1980s, suggesting the maturation of OD as a field and the depth to which team-building interventions had penetrated the mindset of OD practitioners. One review of the OD work conducted in the 1990s, which included some 414 references, found "a continuing emphasis and interest in team building and outcomes in team-related performance" (Piotrowski & Armstrong, 2004, pp. 52–53). Other reviews contained similar results, and Golembiewski (2003) thought it one of the ironies of OD that OD success rates, which often included team-building interventions, were so high and yet so underreported.

The things we have learned about team effectiveness—for instance, that the type of team matters in determining the criteria for team effectiveness, that self-directed work teams generally are more effective than teams pulled together from different units of an organization, that group cohesiveness is positively related to performance—relate to the kinds of variables team building is designed to strengthen (Cohen & Bailey, 1997, 2000) and thus further suggest the value of team building.

Rather than simply reiterating the need for team building or producing much in the way of new designs, team building was expanding its reach, and the literature reported applications in international settings, including such places as South Africa (Preston & Armstrong, 1991), Ireland (Kakabadse, Alderson, & Gorman, 1992), Canada (Bourgault, Dion, & LeMay, 1993; Gilbert et al., 2000), Czechoslovakia (Cakrt, 1993), England (Currie, 1994), France and Morocco (Hatch, 1995), Scotland (Rushmer, 1997a), Nigeria (Samawicz, 1998), and Korea (Yoon, 2001). At the same time, the 1990s produced an occasional study that focused on cultural differences in a given country, such as Hispanic and non-Hispanic comparisons in the United States (Boss & McConkie, 1995).

All in all, team building has become an accepted part of the OD arsenal, both in the United States and abroad. Furthermore, the reported use of such designs far transcends those published in our literature. For example, McLean (2005) found team-building interventions to be widely used in Australia, Canada, France, Hong Kong, Israel, Jamaica, Japan, Jordan, Kenya, Korea, Kyrgyzstan, Malaysia, Mexico, New Zealand, Pakistan, People's Republic of China, Russia, Saudi Arabia, Singapore, South Africa, Sri Lanka, Taiwan, Thailand, the Netherlands, the United Kingdom, and the United Arab Emirates. Given what we know about its use in Europe, Scandinavia, Central and South America, and the Pacific Rim countries, the application of team building appears to be worldwide.

Confrontation Designs

Unfortunately, there is a dearth in the literature of multiple reports that validate the effectiveness of specific designs, particularly in different contexts. The exception to this is the use of the confrontation design (Golembiewski & Blumberg, 2000), which focuses on both behavior and attitudes of team members. This approach has produced positive results in a variety of settings (see Beckhard, 1967; Blake, Mouton, & Sloma, 1965; Boss, 1979a; Boss, McConkie, & Boss, 2004; Golembiewski & Kiepper, 1988; Greiner, 1967; Marrow, 1974). Although confrontation designs vary in format, a number of core features typically characterize their implementation (Golembiewski & Blumberg, 2000, pp. 579–580):

• "Confrontation designs involve as participants individuals who are hierarchically and/or functionally involved in some common flow of work. . . .

• Confrontations involve two or more organizational entities, whose members have real and unresolved issues with one another. . . .

• Confrontation designs involve the mutual development of 'images' as a basis for attempting to work through unresolved issues . . . with relevant others, i.e., any position or unit with whom more effective relations are necessary to do a more effective job. For each of these relevant others, participants [are asked] to develop '3-dimensional images' based on these questions: (a) How do we see ourselves in relation to the relevant other? (b) How does the relevant other see us? (c) How do we see the relevant other?

• Relevant designs involve sharing such images. This confronting via images is the first step toward mutually working through any relational problems. . . .

• Confrontation designs assume that significant organizational problems often rest on blockages in communication. Confrontations 'free up' people 'to level' in communicating, and thus set the stage for authentic interaction and problem solving.

- Confrontations are short-cycle affairs. . . .

- Confrontation designs typically are seen as springboards for organizational action."

This confrontation design, or variations thereof, has been applied in a variety of settings, industries, and cultures and has proven to be highly successful intervention, particularly when combined with such activities as contracting, problem solving, training, and skill development. For example, Boss and McConkie (2004) report the results of a 3-day confrontation-team-building design with 3,679 participants in 369 teams, representing 72 different organizations. The before–after measures produced statistically significant improvement in organization climate, group effectiveness, burnout rates, interpersonal trust, job involvement, role ambiguity, self-esteem at work, job satisfaction, empowerment, and employee engagement.

Making Team Building Work

Successful team building is not accidental. It happens because a number of essential elements are present before the meeting is ever held. First, it depends on the commitment and participation of the team leader. Consider, for instance, a study (Boss, 1978a) that reports the impact of leader absence on a confrontation team-building design. Six natural teams (or family groups) and one cousin group participated in a 6-day confrontation team-building design. However, five of the six natural teams met without the CEOs of their respective organizations. Although each team experienced design and environmental constraints, only the team with the leader present evidenced growth during the 6-day session. Similar results were obtained in a cross-cultural application of a team-building design in the United States, South Africa, and Japan, where only the team lacking leader participation (the Japanese) experienced failure, and the others

experienced productivity increases (Boss, Gouws, & Nagai, 1978).

Boss and McConkie (2004) reinforced the important role of the leader in their study of 3,679 participants in team-building meetings. When asked which single person played the most important role in their team-building sessions, 3,384 (92%) identified the team leader. Furthermore, team members consistently reported greater concern about their relationships with their immediate supervisors than about those with their colleagues.

The importance of the leader centers on issues of power; leaders have access to multiple sources of power and thus to multiple mechanisms for reinforcing action steps and commitments made during team building. Therefore, the commitment and participation of the team leader are the single most important factor in successful team-building designs. Without the leader's support, by both precept and example, the intervention is doomed to failure (Boss & Golembiewski, 1995).

Second, the team must be culturally prepared. That is, psychologically the team must be predisposed to achieving rather than derailing organization goals and purposes. This is an issue of commitment, and sufficient levels of cultural preparedness assume some measure of interpersonal trust between employees, a willingness to confront and resolve problems, and a willingness to be held accountable.

Third, expectations must be realistic. Behavior change requires significant effort and emotion, and where participants do not have realistic expectations, the likelihood of success is dramatically reduced.

Fourth, group members must experience internal tension and pain, or what might be called a felt need. Change grows out of discomfort, and unless group members are uncomfortable with where they are, they will not have the psychological energy to move to where they could or should be. Organization change efforts have a high probability of success only when those involved have been experiencing internal stress (Dalton, 1980).

Fifth, successful team building has a dual focus: first on problem resolution and second on building the skills necessary to solve other problems later on. Building skills in communication, decision making, motivation, and leadership frees participants from an otherwise dangerous dependence on consultants or whoever is conducting the team-building sessions.

Sixth, there must be some means of holding people accountable for commitments and goals. Personal management interviews, or what are sometimes called "win–win agreements" (Covey, 1990), and leader follow-up are important mechanisms for maintaining accountability.

Seventh, the team building must be tied to organization goals and purposes to increase accountability and reinforce both organization and team-building commitments. Integrating the individual and the organization increases productivity and reduces the propensity for unethical behavior (Argyris, 1964).

Eighth, successful team building occurs where it is seen as being part of a larger change effort. Few team-building changes remain in force unless they are tied to purposes larger than the team building itself.

Ninth, successful team building depends on the cooperation of the team's most powerful members. They play a central role in setting expectations and in following up and holding others accountable to commitments (Boss, 1991, pp. 41–42).

Finally, effective team building almost always requires the help of an objective third party. This person should have, at a minimum, the credentials, training, and professional skills to build effective teams and the interpersonal skills necessary to build a trusting, open relationship with team members.

The absence of any one of these essential variables can seriously undermine the effectiveness of a team-building design. The omission of a number of them, particularly the commitment of the team leader, can prove disastrous to the intervention. Additional contributors to team-building failures include short-sighted or incomplete designs, culture shock over letting go of preferred ways of doing things, and misguided design of an organization's evaluation and reward system, to which action planning items are tied (Roth, 2002).

The Problem of Regression

Even the presence of these essential elements does not guarantee successful team-building meetings. Team-building activities are, by nature, brief. At their conclusion the team returns to the workplace to fulfill its normal function, that is, to solve the organization's ongoing problems. And because those problems usually are serious (or the organization would not have resorted to team building in the first place), the process of addressing them normally entails negotiation and rarely produces solutions that are equally satisfactory to all parties. Thus, over the long haul the problem-solving process itself tends to generate further interpersonal problems within the team. In short, its members accumulate emotional debts and grudges. This happens even if the offsite team-building session has fully worked through all of the previously existing interpersonal problems.

The result is that teams often experience marked regression after an offsite team-building session (Boss, 2003; Burke, 1995; Cummings & Worley, 2005; Dyer, 1995; Golembiewski, 2000; Katzenbach & Smith, 1993; Marx, 1982). High levels of cooperation may last for several weeks but then begin to decrease as team members encounter problems, and if steps are not taken to address these problems, group effectiveness can deteriorate to pre–team building levels. A number of interrelated variables contribute to this tendency toward regression (Boss, 1983, pp. 68–70):

• *Unfulfilled expectations:* Participants often return home with high expectations about changes that are scheduled for implementation. When these expectations go unrealized, communication begins to break down, interpersonal trust decreases, and the progress achieved during the offsite session is neutralized because of the incongruity between people's expectations and what they see happening back home.

- *Low tolerance for error:* Participants often have unrealistic expectations about both the extent to which fellow team members are able to change their undesirable behavior and the speed with which positive changes will take place. Mistakes inevitably are made, and when those errors occur and people exhibit former undesirable behavior patterns—though with less frequency and intensity than before—participants often become discouraged, resolve that nothing really has changed, and therefore stop trying to improve their own behavior.

- *Lack of process skills among team members:* Essential elements of effective teams include the ability to manage the leadership, motivation, decision-making, goal-setting, and control processes of the group (Likert, 1967) and competence in fulfilling the necessary task and maintenance functions (Schein, 1969). A short-team-building session usually is inadequate to equip personnel with the skills necessary to implement the changes they would like to make. Therefore, without effective follow-up and additional skill building, the pressures toward regression are substantial.

- *Lack of accountability:* An implicit part of effective management is the ability to hold subordinates accountable. This skill is particularly relevant after team-building sessions. In the absence of effective methods for supervisors to hold personnel accountable, the tendency to continue the old and often less productive behavior patterns undermines any success that may have been achieved during the team-building session.

- *Team building as a one-shot activity:* To prevent regression, a team-building session must be seen as part of a larger and ongoing change effort. Research shows that one-shot team-building efforts do not produce the desired long-range results and that few, if any, changes take place without effective follow-up (Beer, 1980; Dyer, 1977).

- *Consultant dependency:* Hiring a consultant automatically creates dependency. In situations where the consultant, rather than the team, becomes the focus of the change effort, an unhealthy dependency occurs in the sense that the client becomes overly dependent on the consultant and cannot function effectively in his or her absence. This is particularly true when skill building is not a goal of the team-building session. Under such circumstances, when the consultant leaves, team effectiveness naturally deteriorates.

- *Turnover among key staff members:* Changes in team membership, whether caused by employee turnover or by modification in the organization's structure, usually cause off-site agreements to become invalid for the new members and therefore require that the team-building process begin again. Furthermore, when key staff members are replaced by those who have no idea of the history of the change effort or the theory underlying those changes, the potential for regression is substantial. This is particularly true if the team gets a new leader because research shows that the leader is the single most important person responsible for successful team-building sessions.

- *Changes in policies and procedures:* Common byproducts of team-building sessions are resolutions to improve the way team members work together by implementing new policies and procedures. If such changes are inconsistent with current policies and practices, the potential for successful implementation of these new ideas is minimal.

- *Lack of cultural preparedness back home:* Often cultural forces in the organization as a whole oppose the change effort, particularly as they relate to the unwillingness of key personnel to resolve problems and deal with issues of accountability, their lack of trust for one another, and their poor psychological health. In such situations, the transfer of learning is difficult because the organization is not culturally prepared to support a healthy, productive team (Boss, 1979b).

• *Lack of political support:* The change effort must be supported by the key people in the organization in general, and the CEO in particular. Without that support, any long-range change effort is doomed to failure.

• *Lack of a clear reward system:* For desirable behavior to continue, that behavior must be rewarded (e.g., though promotion, formal recognitions, or pay). Such a clear reward system validates the importance of the change effort. On the other hand, if participants perceive that new behaviors will not be accepted and rewarded by others, particularly their superiors, they will not use those behaviors. Furthermore, if they perceive their careers to be in jeopardy for engaging in such behavior (something that may be implied by the lack of rewards for new behaviors), the regression process is accelerated (Beer, 1980).

• *Lack of consultant availability:* Situations often arise in which team members need help in resolving problems and overcoming obstacles to effectiveness. If the consultant is not available when needed to reinforce learning and facilitate additional skill development, group members may be left to fend for themselves in a trial-and-error manner, often producing feelings of frustration and creating problems that must be resolved in subsequent team-building sessions (Boss & McConkie, 1979).

The Personal Management Interview

Collectively, these problems constitute a strong push toward regression. Therefore, it is not surprising that so few data substantiate the long-term impact of team building or the connection between team building and performance. In most cases, the results don't last long enough to be meaningful. Without a counterforce against regression, the team members will lose most of what they learned at the offsite session. One such counterforce is a simple intervention called a personal management interview (PMI) (Boss, 1983). When implemented after team-building meetings, it can prevent regression for as much as 29 years with no additional interventions (Boss, 2003).

The PMI is a regular, private meeting between the leader and each of his or her direct reports, and its implementation involves two phases. First, the leader and each subordinate participate in an initial, 1-hour, private, role-negotiation meeting wherein they articulate their expectations of one another and define how they will work together. Although they will have addressed some of these expectations in the team-building session, the role-negotiation meeting gives the participants the opportunity to explore the full range of these expectations. It also ensures a clear understanding of and agreement on exactly what each expects of the other and what each party is willing to deliver. In most cases the consultant (who participates in the team-building session) both facilitates the role negotiation session and keeps a detailed account of all decisions reached during it, and both the leader and the subordinate receive a copy of that material at the conclusion of the meeting (Boss, 1983, p. 70).

However, successful implementation of PMIs does not always require separate role-negotiation meetings. Further research (Boss, 2003) has shown that when the team-building design includes the clarification of expectations, a separate role-negotiation meeting can be skipped, and a clarification of remaining expectations can take place during the first PMI.

Once the roles have been clarified, regular PMIs are implemented. These meetings, held weekly, biweekly, or monthly, depending on the need, normally last from 30 minutes to 1 hour. The major objectives of the PMI are to increase communication between the superior and the subordinate, resolve problems, give each party feedback from the other, build trust, and increase employee accountability.

A number of agenda items make up the central part of the PMI. The first few minutes of each meeting are spent in following up on action items generated during the previous session. When assignments have not been completed, detailed plans are made to ensure their completion before the next meeting. Although the format for the remainder of the PMI varies, depending on the need, each interview consistently includes the following:

- Discussion and, where possible, resolution of administrative and organizational problems currently faced by the subordinate.
- Training the subordinate in administrative and management skills. (The CEO takes an active role in helping subordinates resolve technical, administrative, and personnel problems.)
- Resolution of interpersonal problems between the CEO and the subordinate. Implicit in each PMI is the expectation that such problems will be dealt with and resolved when they are small rather than being allowed to fester and create additional difficulties and misunderstandings.
- Information sharing in order to bring both parties up to date on what is happening in the organization.
- Identification of individual and organizational needs.
- Discussion of personal problems faced by the subordinates, as appropriate.

The last item on the agenda of each PMI is a review of the action items generated during that meeting. This summary ensures that all parties clearly understand their assignments and guarantees the accuracy of the documentation (which is performed by one of the two parties attending the PMI or by a trusted third party whose only responsibility is to document the proceedings of the meeting) before its distribution at the end of the meeting (Boss, 1983, pp. 71–72).

Boss (2003) reports the results of using PMIs in 200 natural teams over a period ranging from 3 months to 29 years. The data represent the responses of 2,281 participants (1,326 experimental and 955 comparison group members) to Friedlander's (1966, 1968) Group Behavior Inventory (GBI) and the Likert Profile of Organizational and Performance Characteristics (Likert, 1967). The results indicate that regular PMIs can prevent regression for as long as 29 years with no additional interventions after off-site team-building meetings.

LINKING TEAM BUILDING AND PERFORMANCE

Several factors make it difficult to link team building and performance. For example, most OD projects include a number of interventions, making it impossible to isolate the impact of team-building sessions. As Cummings and Worley explain,

> Team building rarely occurs in isolation. Usually it is carried out in conjunction with other interventions leading to or resulting from team building itself. For this reason it is difficult to separate the effects of team building from those of the other interventions. (2005, p. 239)

In addition, many teams, such as management teams, do not have objective outcomes by which their individual performance can be measured. Even where team production can be measured, the outputs often exist too far in the future for clear performance data to be captured (Sundstrom, McIntyre, Halfhill, & Richards, 1990).

Nevertheless, an emerging body of evidence links team building with increased productivity. For example, Trufant, Boss, and McConkie (2005) report the results of team building with staff members in the operating rooms of two major hospitals. Results include decreased turnaround time of rooms between cases, increased use of rooms, increased monthly case volume, increased average number of minutes in surgery per month, decreased overtime costs, and decreased turnover.

Boss, McConkie, and Trufant (2005) describe a 2-year change project in the perioperative services division of a medical center. Results included the implementation of a surgery scheduling protocol, the development of a block schedule, the establishment of data audit method, the implementation of a surgery information system, the training of physician office staffs, the development of a performance process for new products, the establishment of an effective loan–borrow policy, the improved management of surgical supplies, the implementation of an electronic tracking instrumentation system, a significant reduction in instrument repair and replacement costs, the consolidation and standardization of instrument sets, the development of protocols for the postanesthesia and ambulatory care departments, the standardization of an admission history database, the formulation of setup and teardown protocol, the standardization of anesthesia orders and consent, the development of postanesthesia nursing protocols, and outstanding physician satisfaction ratings in the areas of preadmission screening, anesthesiology, operating room nursing care, medical administration, instrumentation and equipment, and nursing.

Trufant and Lawrence (2004) describe the impact of team building on a 2-year transformation of a sterile processing department in a major medical center. Subjective results included significant improvements in organization climate and group effectiveness, interpersonal trust and job satisfaction, and reductions in burnout, intent to turnover, and powerlessness. Objective results included an annual reduction of $456,000 in duplicate and wasted supplies, a savings of $80,000 a year in case cart replenishment, a 45% increase in the availability of surgical products, a 48% increase in customer service approval rating, a $50 per case reduction of instrument expenses, and a decrease in annual turnover from 40% to 5%. The department also received the "National Department of the Year Award" from *Healthcare Purchasing News*.

Hutton, Angus, Angermeier, and Boss (2004) report the results of a 2-year change effort in a major medical center employing 5,000 people, where the major interventions were survey research and team building. Results included significant improvements in a number of attitudinal measures; a movement from the 46th to the 96th percentile in overall patient satisfaction scores and the 99th percentile in patient satisfaction with oncology, restorative

care, and hospice care; a 98% increase in the number of nurses recruited; a 60% decrease in turnover among nurses; a 30% decrease in the registered nurse vacancy rate; and a $5.3 million decrease in spending on agency nurses. Additional improvements included significant increases in total and operating margins, higher net revenue per adjusted discharge and net revenue per full-time employee, and a decrease in net days in accounts receivable. There were also decreases in postoperative infections (infections caused by medical care), cardiac arrests, uterine ruptures, stroke average length of stay, ischemic stroke mortality rates, adult pneumonia mortality rates, and acute myocardial infarction mortality rates. In addition, the hospital constructed two ambulatory surgery centers and became one of the 100 Top Hospitals in Cardiovascular Benchmarks for Success. During the same 2-year period, it gave $7 million each year in revenue sharing to its employees.

In each of these projects, three interventions took place: a thorough and accurate diagnosis of the problems facing the unit or organization, participation in team-building meetings by work teams, and PMIs between leaders and their direct reports. In follow-up interviews, team-building participants almost unanimously stated that when properly held, PMIs prevented regression and contributed significantly to improved individual and organizational performance.

Virtual Team Building

With the advent of the electronic age, managers and workers interact in ways previously unimagined. E-mail, desktop video conferencing, collaboration software, and Internet or intranet systems, for example, have created non–face-to-face teams that are nonetheless interdependent. Such organizationally and often geographically dispersed teams, using an assemblage of telecommunication technologies to accomplish a common task, are called virtual teams. Virtual teams face the same pressures to increase productivity that confront other teams but are burdened with the added weight of diverse cultural backgrounds, distance between team members, differing time zones and schedules, and communication technology, all of which affect productivity, culture, satisfaction, interpersonal dynamics, and trust (Connell, 2002; Hart & McLeod, 2003; Hart & Saunders, 1997).

Virtual teams are unique in that they lack the interpersonal contact on which face-to-face teams are so dependent (Kiesler & Sproull, 1992; Siegel, Dubrovsky, Kiesler, & McGuire, 1986). Although they are often separated geographically, they are nonetheless bound by a common mission, vision, values, and goals. This implies that in their contact, team members build relationships and communicate with different emphases. The absence of interpersonal contact is important, for we perceive different data points interpersonally than we do virtually: Interpersonal contacts provide much with body language, eye contact, voice tone, and speech pauses, all of which clarify intent and meaning. Still, virtual teams can achieve shared communication, mutual goals, a performance orientation, close personal relationships, high levels of trust, and respect of and appreciation for co-workers. They simply use a different medium.

Team building among virtual teams becomes a necessity because trust between virtual team members is far more volatile and people are less forgiving when communicating virtually (Jarvenpaa, Knoll, & Leidner, 1998). Therefore, leaders must understand the need to build virtual teams right in the first place and then put mechanisms in place to maintain trust and resolve problems as they arise. This can best be accomplished in a face-to-face meeting. As Freedman and Leonard explain,

> Virtual teams require significant face-to-face time to get beyond basic information sharing to develop into highly performing teams. Teams will receive the greatest payoff from investment in time and money if team members

are brought together for a significant period of time (two or three days) during the [early phases] . . . of the team's life. By meeting together for several days when the team is initially launched, the team can get the interaction time [necessary to] . . . achieve the cohesiveness, focus, and collaboration required for the high creativity and productivity expected during the mature performing phase of the team's life cycle. Meeting again for several days just prior to delivery of the team's work products will allow team members to reengage with each other, realign themselves regarding mission and deliverables, and celebrate their accomplishments in preparation for adjournment or renewal/redirection. (2002, p. 41)

During the initial face-to-face meeting, team members can profit by openly discussing cultural differences and similarities, becoming familiar with each other's competence and unique personal attributes, carefully planning advanced technology use, developing communication norms that facilitate technology use and bridge differences, and building trust (Gibson & Cohen, 2003, pp. 418–419).

SOME CLARIFICATIONS

Using the phrase "team building" with multiple meanings often creates confusion (Tannenbaum et al., 1992). First, team building is sometimes confused with team development. Historically, team-building interventions have been conducted almost exclusively by an outsider who is a professional consultant in the field of human resource development or OD. This outsider may be someone from outside the organization or someone who is inside the organization but outside the work group participating in team building. A team development facilitator usually is the team's formal leader or a designated team member. As Pfeiffer explains,

> The activities that can be conducted by a team leader or member, who is generally not . . . [a] professional, are, of necessity, different from

those designed to be facilitated by a professional: they are less intense, produce less affect, and demand less of the person who is facilitating and the team members as participants. After a team's members have been introduced to team building by [an outside consultant], that professional can suggest that they follow up with team-development activities to enhance their ability to resolve their own issues. (1991, pp. 4–5)

Dyer (1987, p. 52) suggests, "The use of a consultant is generally advisable if a manager is aware of problems, feels he or she may be one of the problems facing the work unit, and is not sure exactly what to do or how to do it, but feels strongly that some positive action is necessary to pull the work group together for more effective operation."

Second, team building and team training are not the same thing. Team building deals with making stronger teams, enabling people to work more effectively as a unit; team training has to do with some systematic effort to develop job-related knowledge, skills, and attitudes. The skills thus acquired may help people perform in ways that strengthen teams, but unless the team has been strengthened, no team building has occurred (Tannenbaum et al., 1992, p. 126).

Third, team building also differs from process consultation (Cummings & Worley, 2005, p. 222). (See Schein's [1969] definition of process consultation as both a set of skills and an approach to organization change.) Process interventions aim at helping individuals and groups work on their own behavior and relationships. Again, such improvements in individual behaviors may give people skills that make them more effective in group interactions, but they are not team building.

Fourth, in training circles many group activities have been labeled "team building" that are not. Trust walks, rope exercises, T groups, decision-making games and simulations, to name a few, may be useful in their place, but they do not in themselves constitute team building.

CONCERNS ABOUT TEAM BUILDING

A number of problems continue to plague practitioners. First is quality control of practitioners. In medicine, one can assume that when physicians pass their state boards, they have the minimum qualifications to practice medicine. Unfortunately, no similar governing body exists that requires team-building consultants to meet minimum standards of knowledge, skills, and abilities. As a result, those who choose to label themselves as team-building consultants can sell themselves as professionals and, in the short term, get away with it if clients are willing to hire them. Predictably, unqualified practitioners often do much damage. For example, Boss (1990) reports a case in which a client exploded and threatened to beat the consultant to a pulp because of a poorly timed process intervention during a team-building meeting. Indeed, the field is filled with anecdotal accounts of problems caused by the unqualified. Team-building activities can generate intense feelings, depending on the degree to which participants confront problems, particularly those that are interpersonal. These interventions require an extensive knowledge of group dynamics and a high level of skill in facilitating group processes and managing conflict. Unfortunately, the burden of finding high-quality team-building professionals falls on the consumers, and "most individuals are more astute in selecting a new refrigerator or a car than they are in retaining a [very expensive] consultant" (Dyer, 1977, p. 3).

Second, practitioners and leaders often underestimate the power of an effective, collaborative team, and this newfound power can unbalance an organization. As Cummings and Worley explain,

As a team becomes more cohesive, it usually exerts a stronger influence on other groups within the organization. This can lead to intergroup conflict. Because that is one in which team building can have negative effects, the process consultant must help the group understand its role within the larger organization, develop it own diagnostic skills, and examine alternative action plans so that intergroup tensions and conflicts do not expand. (Cummings & Worley, 2005, p. 237)

Indeed, a markedly successful offsite session, precisely because it was so successful, can exacerbate ongoing difficulties in the home organization. For example, Boss and McConkie (1981) examined a confrontation team-building intervention that successfully built the supervisors of a public agency into a cohesive, trusting, and unified group. However, the team became the most important variable, with little consideration given to the rest of the organization. As a result, the whole organization was crippled and had to be completely rebuilt—something that could have been avoided had the consultant understood the need to make certain that the team-building intervention strengthened both the team and the organization.

Third, consultants must avoid obeying "The Law of the Hammer," which states, "If you give a child a hammer, everything he sees will need to be pounded." Team building should never take place without a diagnosis that substantiates the need for it. As Cummings and Worley explain, "If the problem is a structural or technical one, an intergroup issue, an administrative mistake, or a conflict between only two people, team building would not be an appropriate change strategy" (2005, p. 232). The diagnosis produces data that warrant the use of a specific design. Without an accurate diagnosis, continuous evaluation, and follow-up, the chances of an effective outcome are slim.

IMPLICATIONS FOR FUTURE RESEARCH

Although we have learned a great deal about how to make effective teams, the fields of future research are ripe for the harvest. Earlier reviews of the research on team-building effectiveness

were cautious at best, suggesting the need for more research to confirm the power of team building as an OD intervention (Salas et al., 1999, pp. 322–325). As of 2005, we have already amassed ample research to conclude that when conducted with appropriate reinforcement mechanisms, such as PMIs, team building can change both individual and group behavior, facilitate group growth and development, and increase group productivity over extended periods of time.

Still, additional research would teach us just how to conduct effective team building in different settings. In their review of the empirical work on work groups, for example, Sundstrom et al. (2000) ask what happens when team boundaries are fluid or when there are varied degrees of external support for team accomplishments. What are the effects of team building on different kinds of teams, such as production teams, service teams, or support teams? What is the role of organization support systems in reinforcing team-building commitments (e.g., by making resources available)?

In addition, some of the concerns of Tannenbaum et al. (1992, pp. 146–147) are still valid:

- More non–self-report measures would increase our confidence in the ability of team building to change behavior in positive directions.
- The nature of the relationship between process and performance still needs clarification, and perhaps the scrutiny of longitudinal, time series analysis.
- "Two variables that could moderate the effectiveness of team building interventions are task type and stage of team development." Little or no research has examined the effects of these variables.
- Because accurate diagnosis is so central to team development, more research is needed on validly diagnosing team inputs, processes, and products.
- Because it seems unlikely that one intervention alone will have the power to change behavior that multiple interventions do,

research on the relationship of team building to other interventions seems highly valuable.

- Negative findings are also important, to enable researchers and practitioners to learn from team-building failures.

Moreover, in our increasingly globalized information age, characterized by interdependent markets, economic transfers, and government ties, the importance of studying virtual teams and team building cannot be overstated. Some initial results suggest the viability of team building via satellite (Cornish et al., 2003). But most team-building designs deal with issues of disclosure, trust building, response to individual feedback, and other interpersonal variables and assume eye-to-eye contact. How does a virtual setting affect such interaction variables? People tend to pick up on different pieces of information when they interact interpersonally than when they interact electronically. What does that imply for team building?

Virtual team building may also involve cross-cultural interplay (Hurn & Jenkins, 2000). Culture has a strong impact on group behaviors. For example, Asians appear to be less able than Westerners to develop relationships via long-distance learning (Tuan & Napier, 2000). What are the implications of such cultural differences for team building?

CONCLUSION

Team building is here to stay; it has become an accepted and vibrant part of many, if not most, organization change intervention strategies. It is popular as a means of bringing people together, creating stronger relationships, breaking down interpersonal barriers, solving team and organization problems, and setting goals. Every year an estimated $51 billion is spent on corporate training, and a conservative estimate suggests that at least 20% of that amount, or roughly $10 billion, is spent on team-building activities. These numbers will change over time, but the need to develop stronger teams will not. Indeed, we anticipate that with increasing pressures to perform, the need for effective team building will increase. In an age of globalization and increasingly technical problems, work teams of highly trained and specialized workers will be needed to respond to market pressures and government strictures, many of which cross national boundaries. Technology has made organization life more complex. In many ways it has also complicated team member relationships, which in turn increases the need for effective team building.

Empirical studies also show the effects of team building as mixed, including both failures and successes. The critical issue, therefore, is to distinguish effective from ineffective team building. Successful team-building interventions appear to be those with strong leader commitment and involvement, in teams that are culturally prepared and recognize a felt need to change. Such projects set realistic expectations, focus on both problem solving and skill building, include mechanisms for reinforcing commitments, tie action steps to the reward structure and to a larger change effort, engage the commitment of the team's most powerful members, and involve a third-party facilitator who has the necessary skills to develop a group of people into a collaborative, trusting unit. It falls to the team leader to manage these variables advantageously.

REFERENCES

Agnew, P. G., & Boutwell, S. P. (1995). *How to make teams work*. Watertown, MA: American Management Association.

Argyris, C. (1957). *Personality and organization: The conflict between system and the individual*. New York: Harper & Row.

Argyris, C. (1962). *Interpersonal competence and organizational effectiveness*. Homewood, IL: Dorsey.

Argyris, C. (1964). *Integrating the individual and the organization*. New York: John Wiley & Sons.

Argyris, C. (1965). *Organization and innovation.* Homewood, IL: Dorsey.

Argyris, C. (1967). *Some causes of organizational ineffectiveness within the Department of State.* Washington, DC: Department of State, Center for International Systems Research, Occasional Paper No. 2.

Athey, T. R., & Hautaluoma, J. E. (1988). Team building in religious organizations. *Organization Development Journal, 6,* 62–65.

Bair, J. P., & Greenspan, B. K. (1986). Teamwork training for interns, residents, and nurses. *Hospital and Community Psychiatry, 37,* 633–635.

Beckhard, R. (1967). The confrontation meeting. *Harvard Business Review, 45,* 25–27.

Beckhard, R. (1969a). *Organization development: Strategies and models.* Reading, MA: Addison Wesley.

Beckhard, R. (1969b). An organization improvement program in a decentralized organization. *Journal of Applied Behavioral Science, 2,* 3–25.

Beer, M. (1976). The technology of organization development. In M. D. Dunnette (Ed.), *Handbook of industrial and organizational psychology* (pp. 937–994). Chicago: Rand-McNally.

Beer, M. (1980). *Organization change and development: A systems view.* Glenview, IL: Scott Foresman.

Bennis, W. G. (1969). *Organization development: Its nature, origins and prospects.* Reading, MA: Addison-Wesley.

Bettenhausen, K. L. (1991). Five years of group research: What we have learned and what needs to be addressed. *Journal of Management, 17*(2), 345–381.

Blake, R. R. (1995). Memories of HRD. *Training and Development, 49*(3), 22–28.

Blake, R. R., Mouton, J. S., & Sloma, R. L. (1965). The union–management intergroup laboratory. *Journal of Applied Behavioral Science, 1,* 25–27.

Boss, R. W. (1978a). The effects of leader absence on a confrontation-team building design. *The Journal of Applied Behavioral Science, 14*(4), 469–478.

Boss, R. W. (1978b). Trust and managerial problem solving revisited. *Group and Organization Studies, 3*(3), 331–342.

Boss, R. W. (1979a). Essentials for successful organization development efforts. *Group and Organization Studies, 4*(4), 496–504.

Boss, R. W. (1979b). It doesn't matter if you win or lose, unless you are losing: Organizational change in a law enforcement agency. *The Journal of Applied Behavioral Science, 15*(2), 198–220.

Boss, R. W. (1983). Team building and the problem of regression: The personal management interview as an intervention. *Journal of Applied Behavioral Science, 19,* 67–83.

Boss, R. W. (1985). Just between you and your boss. *Training and Development Journal, 39*(11), 68–71.

Boss, R. W. (1989). *Organization development in health care.* Reading, MA: Addison-Wesley.

Boss, R. W. (1990). Addressing the obvious: Its role in effective consultation. *Consultation: An International Journal, 9*(4), 329–331.

Boss, R. W. (1991). Team building in health care. *Journal of Management Development, 10*(4), 38–44.

Boss, R. W. (2003). *Team building and the problem of regression: The 29-year-impact of personal management interviews.* Paper presented at the annual meeting of the Academy of Management, Seattle, WA.

Boss, R. W., & Golembiewski, R. T. (1995). Do you have to start at the top? The chief executive officer's role in successful organization development efforts. *The Journal of Applied Behavioral Science, 31*(3), 259–277.

Boss, R. W., Gouws, D. J., & Nagai, T. (1978). The cross-cultural effects of an OD intervention: A conflict-confrontation design. *The Southern Review of Public Administration, 1,* 486–505.

Boss, R. W., & Mariono, M. V. (1987). Organization development in Italy. *Group and Organization Studies, 12,* 245–256.

Boss, R. W., & McConkie, M. L. (1979). An autopsy of an intended OD project. *Group and Organization Studies, 4*(2), 187–200.

Boss, R. W., & McConkie, M. L. (1981). The destructive impact of a positive team building meeting. *Group and Organization Studies, 6*(1), 45–56.

Boss, R. W., & McConkie, M. L. (1995). Building productive teams in cross-cultural settings: An intervention with Hispanic and non-Hispanic managers. *Organization Development Journal, 13*(2), 59–69.

Boss, R. W., & McConkie, M. L. (2004, March). *Creating high performance work teams: Team building results from 3,679 participants.* Paper presented at the Eleventh International Conference on Advances in Management, Orlando, FL.

Boss, R. W., McConkie, M. L., & Boss, A. D. (2004, August). *Sustainable change in the public sector: Three decades of success in a law enforcement agency.* Paper presented at the Academy of Management Annual Meeting, New Orleans, LA.

Boss, R. W., McConkie, M. L., & Trufant, J. E. (2005, July). *Revolutionizing a perioperative services department.* Paper presented at the Twelfth International Conference on Advances in Management, Washington, DC.

Bourgault, J., Dion, S., & LeMay, M. (1993). Creating a corporate culture: Lessons from the Canadian federal government. *Public Administration Review, 53*(1), 73–80.

Buller, P. F. (1986). The team building–task performance relation: Some conceptual and methodological refinements. *Group & Organization Studies, 11*(3), 147–168.

Buller, P. F., & Bell, C. H. (1986). Effects of team building and goal-setting on productivity: A field experiment. *Academy of Management Journal, 29,* 305–328.

Burke, W. W. (1995, Winter). Organization change: What we know, what we need to know. *Organization Development and Change Newsletter,* pp. 1, 3–5.

Cakrt, M. (1993). Team development programmes for top management groups in Czechoslovakia. *Journal of Organizational Change Management, 6*(2), 11–25.

Capelli, P., & Rogovsky, N. (1994). New work systems and skill requirements. *International Labour Review, 133*(2), 205–220.

Cartwright, D., & Zander, A. (1953). *Group dynamics: Research and theory.* New York: Harper & Row.

Coch, L., & French, J. R. P., Jr. (1948). Overcoming resistance to change. *Human Relations, 11,* 512–533.

Cohen, S. G., & Bailey, D. E. (1997). What makes teams work: Group effectiveness research from the shop floor to the executive suite. *Journal of Management, 23*(3), 239–290.

Cohen, S. G., & Bailey, D. E. (2000). Making teams work. In R. T. Golembiewski (Ed.), *Handbook of organizational consultation* (2nd ed., pp. 219–233). New York: Marcel Dekker.

Connell, J. B. (2002). Organizational consulting to virtual teams. In R. L. Lowman (Ed.), *The*

California School of Organizational Studies handbook of organizational consulting psychology (pp. 285–311). San Francisco: Jossey-Bass.

Cornish, P. A., Church, E., Callanan, T., Bethune, C., Robbins, C., & Miller, R. (2003). Rural interdisciplinary mental health team building via satellite: A demonstration project. *Telemedicine Journal and e-Health, 9*(1), 63–71.

Covey, S. R. (1990). *Principle-centered leadership.* New York: Simon & Schuster.

Cummings, T. G., & Worley, C. G. (2005). *Organization development and change* (8th ed.). Mason, OH: Thompson/Southwestern.

Currie, G. (1994). Evaluation of management development: A case study. *Journal of Management Development, 13*(3), 22–33.

Dalton, G. W. (1980). Influence and organizational change. In A. R. Negandhi (Ed.), *Modern organizational theory* (pp. 343–372). Kent, OH: Kent State University and the Comparative Administration Research Institute.

Davis, S. A. (1967). An organic problem-solving method of organization change. *Journal of Applied Behavioral Science, 3,* 3–21.

DeMeuse, K. P., & Liebowitz, S. J. (1981). An empirical analysis of team-building research. *Group & Organizational Studies, 6*(3), 357–378.

Dyer, W. G. (1977). So you want to hire a consultant. *Exchange, 1*(2), 2–5.

Dyer, W. G. (1987). *Team building: Issues and alternatives* (2nd ed.). Reading, MA: Addison-Wesley.

Dyer, W. G. (1995). *Team building: Current issues and new alternatives* (3rd ed.). Reading, MA: Addison-Wesley.

Eden, D. (1986). Team development: Quasi-experimental confirmation among combat companies. *Group and Organization Studies, 11,* 133–146.

Eggleton, C. H., & Rice, J. C. (1996). *The fieldbook of team interventions.* Amherst, MA: HDR Press.

Elledge, R. L., & Phillips, S. L. (1994). *Team building for the future.* San Diego, CA: Pfeiffer.

Fordyce, J. K., & Weil, R. (1971). *Managing with people: A manager's handbook of organization development methods.* Reading, MA: Addison-Wesley.

Freedman, A. M., & Leonard, E. S. (2002). Organizational consulting to groups and teams. In R. L. Lowman (Ed.), *The California School of Organizational Studies handbook of organizational consulting psychology* (pp. 27–53). San Francisco: Jossey-Bass.

French, W., & Bell, C. H. (1984). *Organization development: Behavioral science interventions for organization development*. Englewood Cliffs, NJ: Prentice Hall.

Friedlander, F. (1966). Performance and interactional dimensions of organizational work groups. *Journal of Applied Psychology, 50*(3), 257–265.

Friedlander, F. (1968). A comparative study of consulting processes and group development. *Journal of Applied Behavioral Science, 44,* 377–399.

Gibson, C. B., & Cohen, S. G. (2003). The last word. In C. B. Gibson & S. G. Cohen (Eds.), *Virtual teams that work* (pp. 403–421). San Francisco: Jossey-Bass.

Giffin, K. (1967). The contribution of studies of source credibility to a theory of interpersonal trust in the communication process. *Psychological Bulletin, 68,* 104–120.

Gilbert, J. H. V., Camp, R. D., Cole, C. D., Bruce, C., Fielding, D. W., & Stanton, S. J. (2000). Preparing students for interprofessional teamwork in health care. *Journal of Interprofessional Care, 14*(3) 223–235.

Golembiewski, R. T. (1972). *Renewing organizations: The laboratory approach to planned change*. Itasca, IL: F. E. Peacock Publishers.

Golembiewski, R. T. (2000). *Handbook of organizational consultation* (2nd ed.). New York: Marcel Dekker.

Golembiewski, R. T. (2003). *Ironies in organization development* (2nd ed.). New York: Marcel Dekker.

Golembiewski, R. T., & Blumberg, A. (1967). Confrontation as a training design in complex organizations: Attitudinal changes in a diversified population of managers. *Journal of Applied Behavioral Sciences, 3,* 525–547.

Golembiewski, R. T., & Blumberg, A. (2000). Confrontation design: Training and relational learning. In R. T. Golembiewski (Ed.), *Handbook of organizational consultation* (2nd ed., pp. 579–583). New York: Marcel Dekker.

Golembiewski, R. T., & Kiepper, A. (1988). *High performance and human costs*. New York: Praeger.

Golembiewski, R. T., & McConkie, M. L. (1975). The centrality of interpersonal trust in group processes. In C. L. Cooper (Ed.), *Theories of group processes* (pp. 131–185). New York: John Wiley & Sons.

Gordon, J. (1992, October). Work teams: How far have they come? *Training*, pp. 59–65.

Greiner, L. E. (1967). Antecedents of planned organization change. *Journal of Applied Behavioral Science, 3,* 51–85.

Hackman, J. R. (1983). *A normative model of work team effectiveness* (Technical Report No. 2). New Haven, CT: Yale University Press.

Hart, P., & Saunders, C. (1997). Power and trust: Critical factors in the adoption and use of electronic data interchange. *Organizational Science, 8*(1), 23–42.

Hart, R. K., & McLeod, P. L. (2003). Rethinking team building in geographically dispersed teams: One message at a time. *Organizational Dynamics, 31*(4), 352–361.

Hatch, E. K. (1995). Cross cultural team building and training. *Journal for Quality & Participation, 18*(2), 46–51.

Homans, G. (1950). *The human group*. New York: Harcourt-Brace.

Hurn, B. J., & Jenkins, M. (2000). International peer group development. *Industrial and Commercial Training, 32*(4), 128.

Hutton, D., Angus, L., Angermeier, I., & Boss, R. W. (2004, March). *Achieving strategic objectives using real-time data*. Paper presented at the American College of Healthcare Executives 2004 Congress on Healthcare Management, Chicago.

Jarvenpaa, S. L., Knoll, K., & Leidner, D. E. (1998). Is anybody out there? Antecedents of trust in global virtual teams. *Journal of Management Information Systems, 14*(4), 29–64.

Kakabadse, A., Alderson, S., & Gorman, L. (1992). Cream of Irish management. *Journal of Managerial Psychology, 7*(2), 18–47.

Katzenbach, J., & Smith, D. (1993). *The wisdom of teams*. Cambridge, MA: Harvard Business School.

Kiesler, S., & Sproull, L. (1992). Group decision making and communication technology. *Organization Behavior and Human Decision Processes, 52*(1), 96–123.

Kuriloff, A. H., & Atkins, S. T. (1966). T-group for a work team. *Journal of Applied Behavioral Science, 2,* 63–93.

Lawler, E. E., III, Morhman, S. A., & Ledford, G. E., Jr. (1995). *Creating high performance organizations: Practices and results of employee involvement and total quality in Fortune 100 companies.* San Francisco: Jossey-Bass.

Lewin, K. (1946). Action research and minority problems. *Journal of Social Issues, 2*(4), 34–46.

Lewin, K. (1965). Group decision and social change. In H. Proshansky & B. Seidenberg (Eds.), *Basic studies in social psychology* (pp. 423–437). New York: Holt, Rinehart & Winston.

Liebowitz, S. J., & DeMeuse, K. P. (1982). The application of team building. *Human Relations, 35,* 1–18.

Likert, R. (1961). *New patterns of management.* New York: McGraw-Hill.

Likert, R. (1967). *The human organization.* New York: McGraw-Hill.

Long, J. W. (1987). The wilderness lab comes of age. *Training and Development Journal, 41,* 30–39.

Margerison, C. J., Davis, R., & McCann, D. (1987). High-flying management development. *Training and Development Journal, 41,* 38–41.

Marrow, A. J. (1974). *Making waves in Foggy Bottom.* Washington, DC: NTL Institute.

Marx, R. D. (1982). Relapse prevention for managerial training: A model for maintenance of behavior change. *Academy of Management Review, 7,* 433–441.

Masterson, B., & Murphy, B. (1986). Internal cross-cultural management. *Training and Development Journal, 40*(4), 56–60.

McGregor, D. (1960). *The human side of enterprise.* New York: McGraw-Hill.

McGregor, D. (1967). *The professional manager.* New York: McGraw-Hill.

McLean, G. N. (2005, Summer). Expansion of organization development principles in international settings. *ODC Newsletter,* pp. 12–14.

Mishra, A. K. (1996). Organizational responses to crisis: The centrality of trust. In R. M. Kramer & T. R. Tyler (Eds.), *Trust in organizations: Frontiers of theory and research* (pp. 261–287). Thousand Oaks, CA: Sage.

Neeley, M. A., & Kling, E. B. (1987). Effect of leadership training during wilderness camping. *Small Group Behavior, 18,* 280–286.

Nieva, V. F., Fleishman, E. A., & Rieck, A. (1978). *Team dimensions: Their identity, their measurement and their relationships* (Contract No. DAHC 19-78-C-0001). Washington, DC: Advanced Research Resources Organization.

Paul, C. F., & Gross, A. C. (1981). Increasing productivity and morale in a municipality: Effects

of organization development. *Journal of Applied Behavioral Science, 17,* 59–78.

Peters, T. (1988). *Thriving on chaos.* New York: Harper & Row.

Pfeiffer, J. W. (Ed.). (1991). *The encyclopedia of team-building activities.* San Francisco: Jossey-Bass.

Phillips, S. L., & Elledge, R. L. (1989). *The team-building source book.* San Francisco: Jossey-Bass.

Piotrowski, C., & Armstrong, T. R. (2004). The research literature in organization development: Recent trends and current directions. *Organization Development Journal, 22*(2), 48–54.

Porras, J. I., & Wilkins, A. L. (1980). Organization development in a large system: An empirical assessment. *Journal of Applied Behavioral Science, 16,* 506–534.

Preston, J. C., & Armstrong, T. R. (1991). Team building in South Africa: Cross cultural synergy in action. *Public Administration Quarterly, 15*(1), 65–82.

Ratiu, I. S. (1986). A workshop on managing in a multicultural environment. *Management Education and Development, 17,* 252–256.

Reich, R. B. (1987). Entrepreneurship reconsidered: The team as a hero. *Harvard Business Review, 65*(3), 77–83.

Rideout, C. L., & Richardson, S. A. (1989). A team building model: Appreciating differences using the Myers–Briggs Type Indicator with development theory. *Journal of Counseling and Development, 67,* 529–533.

Roth, W. (2002). Three reasons why your team building efforts aren't producing. *Journal for Quality and Production, 25*(1), 36–41.

Rushmer, R. K. (1997a). How do we measure the effectiveness of team building? Is it good enough? Team management systems: A case study. *Journal of Management Development, 16*(2–3), 93–110.

Rushmer, R. (1997b). What happens to the team during teambuilding? Examining the change process that helps to build a team. *Journal of Management Development, 16*(5), 316–327.

Salas, E., Rozell, D., Mullen, B., & Driskell, J. E. (1999). The effect of team building on performance: An integration. *Small Group Research, 30*(3), 309–329.

Samawicz, P. S. (1998). Cross-cultural team building: The impact of leadership and technology on an industrial project in West Africa. *Dissertation*

Abstracts International, Section A: Humanities and Social Sciences, 59(5), 1666.

Schein, E. (1969). *Process consultation: Its role in organization development.* Reading, MA: Addison-Wesley.

Segal-Horn, S., McGill, I., Bourner, T., Bourner, T., & Frost, P. (1987). Non-facilitated action learning. *Management Education and Development, 18,* 277–286.

Sherwood, J. J. (1972). An introduction to organization development. In J. W. Pfeiffer & J. E. Jones (Eds.), *The annual handbook for group facilitators* (pp. 153–156). Iowa City, IA: University Associates.

Siegel, J., Dubrovsky, V., Kiesler, S., & McGuire, T. (1986). Group processes in computer mediated communication. *Organization Behavior and Human Decision-Making Processes, 37*(1), 157–187.

Spreitzer, G. M., Shapiro, D. L., & Von Glinow, M. A. (2002). Helping transitional team member to sense trust: A counterintuitive approach to leadership. In H. Sondak (Ed.), *Toward phenomenology of groups and group membership* (pp. 203–233). New York: JAI.

Steiner, I. D. (1972). *Group process and productivity.* Orlando, FL: Academic Press.

Sundstrom, E., McIntyre, M., Halfhill, T., & Richards, H. (2000). Work groups: From Hawthorne studies to work teams of the 1990s and beyond. *Group Dynamics: Theory, Research and Practice, 4*(1), 44–67.

Tannenbaum, S. I., Beard, R., & Salas, E. (1992). Team building and its influence on team effectiveness: An examination of conceptual and empirical developments. In K. Kelley (Ed.), *Issues, theory, and research in industrial/ organizational psychology.* Warsaw, Poland: Elsevier Science Publishers B. V.

Terpstra, D. E. (1982). Evaluating selected OD interventions: The state of the art. *Group and Organization Studies, 7*(4), 402–417.

Trufant, J. E., Boss, R. W., & McConkie, M. L. (2005, July). *Quality improvement in two operating rooms: The impact of team building on performance.* Paper presented at the Twelfth International Conference on Advances in Management, Washington, DC.

Trufant, J. E., & Lawrence, J. (2004, March). *Redesign of sterile processing: A collaborative approach for success.* Paper presented at the 2004 Annual Meeting of the Association of Operating Room Nurses, San Diego, CA.

Tuan, V. V., & Napier, N. K. (2000). Paradoxes in Vietnam and America: Lessons-learned, Part II. *Human Resource Planning, 2*(2), 9.

Weiss, D. H. (1991). *How to build high-performance work teams.* Watertown, MA: American Management Association.

Woodman, R., & Sherwood, J. (1980). The role of team development in organizational effectiveness: A critical review. *Psychological Bulletin, 88,* 166–186.

Yoon, J. I. (2001). OD applications in Korea. *Public Administration Quarterly, 25*(2), 154–167.

15

Large Group Interventions

Whole System Approaches to Organization Change

RONALD E. PURSER

THOMAS J. GRIFFIN

In the last decade, large group interventions (LGIs) have gained prominence and legitimacy in the field of organization development (OD) (Bunker & Alban, 1997). LGIs involve anywhere from 40 to 300 people at a time, usually for several consecutive days, as a means of creating a collaborative process for creating alignment around future strategic directions and mobilizing large system change. Although there are many differences and varieties of LGI methods, they all share in common the values that have informed OD theory and practice, particularly the imperative for inclusiveness and widespread participation in the change process. LGIs have been used as an integral component in numerous organization change efforts across a variety of applications, such as organization development, organization redesign,

restructuring, strategic planning, visioning, value and principle clarification, process improvement, customer–supplier relations, global learning and development, and formation of collaborative alliances.

Many case studies describe how these organization change methods have been used in diverse industries, such as transportation (Ford, Amtrak, United Airlines, Boeing, Northwest Airlines), hospitality (Marriott), financial services (World Bank, Bank of Montreal, Richmond Savings, Amalgamated Bank of South Africa), health care (Inova Health Systems, Columbus Regional Hospital), telecommunication (GTE, Lucent, AT&T, U.S. West, Motorola, SBC/Ameritech, and U.S. Cellular), retail (Levi Strauss, Liz Claiborne, General Electric, Donnelly, Xerox, Whole Foods), energy

(Mobile, Detroit Edison, Pacific Power), government (U.S. Department of Agriculture), nongovernment organizations (Save the Children, World Vision), education (George Washington University, University of Minnesota, Keene State University), computers and electronics (Microsoft, Hewlett-Packard), chemicals (Dupont), and many local, regional, and state government organizations (Bunker & Alban, 1997; Chase, 1995, 1996, 1997, 1998; Holman & Devane, 1999; Sullivan, 1997). Unfortunately, empirical research, such as longitudinal studies, quasiexperimental field studies, and studies of large sample sizes across a wide variety of LGIs, are severely lacking. Data that are available tend to be anecdotal or single case studies from practitioners and consultants who have a commercial stake in promoting their own methods.

BASIC THEORETICAL ASSUMPTIONS INFORMING LGIS

LGIs, also known as critical mass events, large group interactive events, whole system change, and large-scale organization change, grew out of the field of OD, evolving from OD practices that emerged in the 1950s. OD is a set of concepts and techniques for improving organization effectiveness and individual well-being that had its genesis in the behavioral sciences and was tested in real-world organizations (French, Bell, & Zawacki, 1995). The theoretical influences that have informed LGIs can be traced to open system theory and system thinking (Bertalanffy, 1998; Emery & Trist, 1965; Katz & Kahn, 1978; Senge, 1990), social constructionism (Berger & Luckmann, 1994; Gergen, 1994), value theory (Maslow, 1943; McGregor, 1960), futuring (Lippitt, 1983; Schindler-Rainman & Lippitt, 1980), group dynamics (Bennis & Shepard, 1956; Bion, 1961; Lewin, 1951; Smith & Berg, 1987), and large group dynamics (Alford & Klein, 1989; Gilmore & Barnett 1992; Pasmore & Fagans, 1992; Turquet, 1975).

System Thinking

System thinking and open system theory have played a central role in the theoretical basis of LGIs. A system thinking perspective considers processes, relationships, and interactions across the system as a whole. The essence of system thinking according to Senge (1994) is that an organization is a whole system that cannot be reduced into independent parts. System thinking is based on the following assumptions:

- An organization is a complex puzzle.
- No single person or group understands the entire puzzle, but everyone holds a piece of the puzzle that is important to the overall picture.
- When viewed collectively, the pieces provide a more holistic understanding of the system and its potential for change.
- To understand the entire puzzle, all piece holders (larger groups) must meet and work together.
- If everyone works on the system together to implement the change, it will happen more quickly and effectively.

A system cannot be understood by looking at its isolated parts because this leads to an incomplete and fragmented picture of the system's operation. To understand the system, one must understand how the parts of the system interact and what they make up collectively. System insights emerge when the whole is studied in relation to its parts and its parts in relation to the whole (Wheatley, 1999).

LGIs represent an integrated and comprehensive approach to organization change that uses system thinking to develop awareness of the whole. Going beyond isolated, linear, cause-and-effect thinking, LGIs strive to involve all components of the system simultaneously. To evoke system-wide change, the parts of the system have to understand the behavior and operation of the whole, and to understand the whole, the system must understand the behavior and operation of the individual parts. As described by physicist David Bohm (1980), everything is enfolded into everything else, each part contains information about the whole, and each part is a subtotal of the entire whole and participates in its dynamic and interactive processes.

Senge further states that a system thinking perspective is integral to the development of a learning culture and that first-hand experience of undivided wholeness is important to the development of a system thinking perspective. LGIs give organizations a means to put system thinking into practice and to be part of a larger, more holistic strategy for change. This is also consistent with the findings of Miller and Friesen (1984), who assert that a holistic perspective for changing organization structures and management systems entails an analysis of overall patterns rather than a narrow focus on isolated organization properties. By intervening at the whole system level we understand more than just the individual dynamics and ripple effects (Manning & Binzagar, 1996). LGIs get the whole system or a significant part of it in the room at the same time and design changes in shorter periods of time compared with traditional methods (Weisbord & Janoff, 1995).

Group Size and Participation Effects

The use of these methods required a paradigm shift on the part of the traditional change management practitioners about large group dynamics. A body of critical work related to large group dynamics has been emerging over the last 25–30 years. Groups are defined as large groups when it becomes impossible for each group member to maintain eye-to-eye contact with the others (Alford & Klein, 1989; Turquet, 1975). Gilmore and Barnett (1992) state that large group dynamics begin once a group exceeds 15 participants.

System change using large groups of people held a contrary view to what was normally accepted: that group size and participation were inversely related (Gilmore & Barnett,

1992; Pasmore & Fagans, 1992). According to these theories, large groups induce stereotyping, decrease ownership of ideas, increase abstraction, and generate hesitation to express unique thoughts (Weick & Quinn, 1999).

The conventional justification for using these processes is that people tend to support what they help create (Weisbord & Janoff, 1995) and that the diversity of knowledge generated through these high-involvement practices leads to greater creativity and innovation in both the technical and social system arena (Bunker & Alban, 1997). The use of LGIs may also ensure that the necessary changes in attitudes, skills, beliefs, and behaviors happen simultaneously (Levine & Mohr, 1998). Inherent in the design of large group methods are the underlying assumptions that people want and will accept responsibility, have the creative ability and organization knowledge to help solve problems and devise new ways of doing things, and will take action toward the achievement of goals that they feel committed to.

Large group methods extend high-involvement management practices (Lawler, 1986) to their maximum in regard to decision making, sharing of information, sharing of power, and employee participation. These beliefs are also consistent with Lewin's (1951) notion that the validity of research improves when people in the setting become active participants in the meaning-making process.

The participatory assumptions cited here reflect many of the principles that have been the cornerstone of OD theory and practice. However, such values of inclusiveness, participation, egalitarianism, and power sharing are not universally shared across national cultures. As Hofstede's (2004) research shows, national cultures that are high on power distance probably would not be receptive or supportive of LGIs designed to equalize power sharing, minimize status differences, and promote high degrees of participation.

Generative Dialogue

Dialogue in LGIs involves sharing experiences, telling stories, and making private assumptions public. According to Hatch (1997, p. 368), dialogue involves collective thinking: interactions that result in a transcendence of individual points of view. Senge (1994) asserts that in dialogue, groups are able to explore difficult and complex issues because they learn to suspend their own assumptions.

Through generative dialogue, people are capable of experiencing change that becomes the source of collective action and collaboration. In the context of LGIs, interorganizational dialogue goes beyond provincial boundaries and helps to construct shared meaning, promote learning, foster greater understanding, and strengthen cooperative spirit. Dialogue moves beyond traditional forms of communication that favor debate, argumentation, competition, and single-minded avocations. These forms of communication produce fragmented and incoherent interchanges (Bohm, 1996) that reinforce cultures (shared values, attitudes, and practices) of individuality, oversimplification, and either–or thinking. Bohm's thinking about dialogue was based on the experience that as people became more aware of their collective thinking and the meaning it produced, it coherently moved them toward a sense of the whole (Ellinor & Gerard, 1998).

Hazen (1993) suggests that organizations can be understood as socially constructed verbal systems composed of stories, discourses, narratives, and texts. In these verbal systems, each person has a different voice and ability to contribute to the organization narrative. Through dialogic resources and techniques used in LGIs, viewpoints are expounded, recounted, interpreted, and even questioned. In a similar sense Barrett, Thomas, and Hocevar (1995) posit that discourse is the core of any organization change process. It is through patterns of discourse (dialogue) that relational bonds are formed and viewpoints are shaped. They further state that communication is much more than just a way of transmitting information between people. Instead, they believe that communication forms the basis by which organizing produces co-constructed meaning. In this sense, communication helps to establish organizing processes. This means, then, that words themselves do not necessarily create meaning, but rather meaning is created through dialogic processes in relational practice.

According to Schein (1993), organization effectiveness is progressively dependent on effective communication across subcultures and boundaries. Because LGIs create opportunities for effective conversations across subcultures and boundaries, organizations can maximize their potential for innovation and creative change. Coordination and integration then become a function of the ability to develop a common lexicon and a sense of shared meaning. Schein states that the practice of dialogue brings about new possibilities for effective communication. In summary, LGIs' use of dialogue as a practice across subcultures and boundaries helps organization members think more generatively, creatively, and with a greater sense of the whole in mind.

Real-Time Diagnosis for Unfreezing

Another common feature of LGIs is that they all involve participants directly in conducting a diagnosis of their system in real time. One LGI method, called real-time strategic change (RTSC), is a type of LGI developed by Dannemiller, James, and Tolchinsky (1999) in work done at Ford Motor Company. This approach is highly structured and organized, with events grounded in giving participants a common database of information from which to work. Designing an RTSC intervention, though customized around a specific issue, is based on Beckhard and Harris's change formula (revised by Dannemiller, 2000):

$$Change = (Dissatisfaction)(Vision)(First\ steps) > Resistance$$

Change is given the opportunity to occur when three elements are in place simultaneously, including

- Dissatisfaction with the present situation
- A compelling vision of how the change will create a better future
- First steps for reaching the vision

If any of these elements is missing, or collectively they are less powerful than the resistance to the change, then change will not take place. Thus, LGIs focus a portion of the time on creating a common database and the foundation for the dissatisfaction. After that, LGIs typically shift focus to dialogue on creating a future that is far more desirable than that which caused the dissatisfaction. LGI sessions usually conclude with participants discovering the steps that are necessary for moving the organization and themselves forward.

Alignment and Common Ground

Jacobs (1994) further elaborates that the significance of the common database is that as diverse perspectives are shared, creative insights and new possibilities for strategic action emerge. This is often called *alignment*, the point at which people begin to understand how the whole organization fits together as a total system.

Weisbord and Janoff (1995) call the sense of alignment participants of a future search conference experience "common ground." They say these events are designed to help organizations to collectively discover their ideal future and then design that future. In the future search conference, they claim that groups acknowledge their differences, work despite them, and move forward in areas where they find alignment and common ground.

Using different language, Dannemiller (2000; Dannemiller & Jacobs, 1992; Dannemiller et al., 1999) calls this sense of alignment and common ground the "one brain, one heart" effect. She describes this as a very complex association of brain and heart that brings

together a diverse group of people for a common purpose. Whitney and Cooperrider (2000) assert that in these events the search is not for common ground but for a higher sense of possibility that excites, inspires, and drives action. They call this sense of higher possibility "higher ground." In the appreciative inquiry method (or appreciative inquiry summits), people are asked to identify the most moving, innovative, and meaningful ideas and possibilities, not the most common. Doing so evokes excitement, hope, and inspiration to envision such higher possibilities about the future and the energy and momentum to follow through with actions, decisions, and planned changes.

Shared Values and Organization Identity

In LGIs, participants experience the highs of joy, hope, inspiration, connectedness, affiliation, and empathy and the lows of confusion, discomfort, and conflict. This rise and fall of emotion combined with creative thinking and the launching of action initiatives produces what has been previously described as alignment, common ground, creating community, the one brain, one heart effect, and higher ground. When these effects are produced, people have a better understanding of how the whole system fits together and in turn can affect it in more profound and effective ways. The modes of organizing what LGIs represent also facilitate the alignment of both individual and organization core values and beliefs. Mohrman and Lawler (1985) suggest that a set of shared values and beliefs is critical to fostering cooperation, collaboration, and learning during change processes. When individual and organizational values and beliefs are closely aligned and integrated into organization change efforts, ownership, commitment, and support for the change are intensified and resistance is minimized.

The alignment of values and beliefs between individuals and organizations is consistent with the concept of perceived organization identity (Dutton, Dukerich, & Harquail, 1994).

Perceived organization identity is what the organization member perceives to be distinctive, central, and enduring about the organization. It is an identification process that is socially constructed and represents the extent to which organization members define themselves by the same attributes they believe define the organization. Dutton et al. (1994) further argue that organization members identify with an organization when their identity as an organization member is more important than alternative identities and their self-concept contains many of the same attributes they believe define the organization as an entity or social group. This identification leads organization members to participate in and support activities that are congruent with that identity (Ashforth & Mael, 1989), resulting in favorable outcomes (Cialdini et al., 1976).

Social Constructionism

Social constructionism maintains that our knowledge of the world is derived from the conversations and relational practices we engage in (Burr, 1995; Cooperrider & Srivastva, 1987; Gergen, 1982, 1990, 1994, 1998). Our words (language) create our worlds and govern our external actions and behaviors. In other words, meaning making occurs in our relatedness with one another (Gergen, 1991). Our conversations serve as linguistic instruments that promote interpersonal connection, sense of purpose, and greater understanding.

LGIs use relational and participative methods to involve stakeholders, explore and test assumptions, generate feedback, and drive action. At the heart of LGI practices is the assumption that the knowledge needed for successful organization change resides within its stakeholders. Inherent in this knowledge creation process is the notion that people produce through discourse (dialogue, conversation, or language processes) the conditions by which their thoughts and actions are determined and how their reality is constructed. In LGIs, dialogue and conversation are the primary medium

through which collective wisdom and coordinated action are produced. LGIs, then, focus on active interaction and social processes as ways of helping organization members see and think differently. LGIs create the conversational space where people can change the way in which they talk to one another, constructing new images of the organization in their collective minds. Language thus is a powerful way of shaping organization reality; social knowledge and organization destiny are interwoven (Cooperrider & Srivastva, 1987).

Viewing LGIs through the social constructionist lens helps to promote inclusiveness and innovation into the design of the change process. The social constructionist viewpoint with its emphasis on dialogue and relationship is essential in helping organization members understand that meaning is created through social context rather than being a given. Because knowledge creation is at the heart of most organization development and change activities, organization scholars and practitioners must be skilled in creating new and more effective ways of using language as a form of social action. In the realm of politics, Lakoff (2002) recently criticized the Democratic party in the United States for not understanding the power of language through the use of metaphors to shape political agendas and the public consciousness. In contrasts, Lakoff credits the Republican party's ability to control the political agenda of the United States to their skillful and strategic use of metaphors to rename issues. For example, the bill to clear-cut old-growth forests was renamed "The Healthy Forests Act." A political phrase such as "compassionate conservatism" reframes the issue to suit the proponent's advantage. The power of language to shape social reality can be used to create Orwellian doublespeak or to honestly evoke the passion, energy, and commitment of people.

Self-Management

LGIs create the right type of conditions for people to take ownership and responsibility for the success of the change effort. They become part of the change they want to see. An important aspect of adult learning theory popularized by Marv Weisbord (1995) is that people tend to support what they help create. When people are given opportunities to take greater levels of responsibility for task and process outcomes, their personal learning is deepened and contributions are maximized. LGIs provide participants with many applied learning opportunities to self-manage small group tasks, dialogues, presentations, and action planning. The more participants are involved in capturing, organizing, managing, and taking action on system data, the more inspired and committed they are to follow through and implement.

Use of self-managing methods has the added benefit of building system capability once the event is over. Allowing small groups to choose process roles and functions such as leader, facilitator, timekeeper, recorder, and presenter fosters a sense of shared leadership and promotes the learning of new behaviors and skills. The more people are given the opportunity to manage themselves in these events, the more they will rise to the occasion and produce results beyond what is expected. The use of self-managing methods also provides organization members with a greater understanding of the organization's conditions, environmental forces, and internal system issues.

Self-management flourishes in a psychologically safe environment. A safe environment exists when people feel free to speak openly without fear that their viewpoints will be marginalized, judged, or arbitrarily rebuked. This means inviting disagreement and encouraging dissenting opinions (Axelrod, 2000). For a safe environment to exist people must be willing to suspend their own assumptions, listen for deeper levels of understanding, and allow room for new ideas to rise up and be heard. A safe environment creates a holding space where individual and organizational learning blossoms, collaboration grows, and system appreciation thrives in spirit of the whole. Openness, teamwork, caring, commitment, respect, mutual trust, connection,

understanding, creativity, imagination, creative breakthrough, and coordinated action are the primary fruits of a safe environment.

VARIETIES OF LGI METHODS

Bunker and Alban (1997) identified 12 LGI methods for whole system change (Search Conference, Future Search, Real Time Strategic Change, Institute of Cultural Affairs Strategic Planning Process, the Conference Model, Fast Cycle Full Participation, Real Time Work Design, Participative Design, Simu-Real, Work-Out, Open Space Technology, and Large Scale Interactive Events). They divided these LGIs into three categories:

- Large-scale system methods for creating the future
- Large-scale system methods for work redesign
- Large-scale system methods for discussion and decision making

Similarly, Holman and Devane (1999) outlined 18 large-group, high-leverage (their term) methods for navigating through change (Search Conference, Future Search, ICA, Strategic Forum, Participative Design Workshop, Gemba Kaizen, Fast Cycle Full Participation, Whole Systems Approach, Preferred Futuring, SimuReal, Organization Workshop, Whole-Scale Change, Dialogue, Open Space, Appreciative Inquiry, Conference Model, Think Like a Genius, and Real Time Strategic Change). They also divided these large-scale system models into three categories:

- Planning methods to help set a direction for an organization or a community
- Structuring methods to redefine working relationships between organization members and create new structures for doing work
- Adaptable methods that vary, including planning, structuring, and other complex, important purposes

Both sources describe each method in detail, their distinguishing features and theoretical roots, potential use applications, and suggested resources for further study. There is much commonality across these methods: They all use a system approach to tap into organization members' creative intelligence for shaping the future in meaningful and empowering ways through high levels of participation and information sharing; purposeful dialogue to create shared meaning, understanding, and context; shared decision making to build commitment; and focused action planning for timely implementation.

Bunker and Alban (1997) discuss four dynamics of large groups that practitioners need to pay special attention to:

• The dilemma of voice (amount of individual airtime and the feeling of being heard) occurs primarily because in large groups people may feel as if they have not had a real opportunity to speak or be heard. Therefore, people may feel marginalized and further withdraw from the group; even when they do have the opportunity to speak, they don't take advantage of it. Bunker and Alban also note that the dilemma of voice possibly results in what has been described as diffusion of responsibility. Diffusion of responsibility is a phenomenon that asserts that, as the number of people in a group increases, their sense of individual responsibility for the success of the group decreases, and this affects their behavior.

• The dilemma of structure (amount needed to manage anxiety in the room and active individual participation) can occur when there is either too much or not enough structure. Paradoxically, they state that if not enough structure is present in a situation that needs more structure, anxiety will increase and people may act out. Alternately, if too much structure is present in situations that don't need it, anxiety will increase and people may act out. The dilemma is not knowing how much anxiety is present in a group and how much structure is needed to manage it.

• The egocentric dilemma (each person acting as though his or her reality is the only true reality) occurs because people often view their worlds through their own limited experiences and filters. When people experience this dilemma they fail to view differences as potentially productive ones that could lead to more healthy and vital outcomes.

• Affect contagion (experiencing and expressing feelings because one feels them vicariously in others) can occur in a large group setting. Contagion occurs when people who had differing experiences are fused with the same emotions. Turquet (1975, p. 375) describes the contagion effect as a condition of oneness in which "members seek to join in a powerful union with an omnipotent force, unobtainably high, to surrender self for passive participation, and thereby feel existence, well-being, and wholeness."

LGIs manage these considerations by using many small group processes to stimulate and encourage involvement and participation, using principles of self-management and democratic methods to take responsibility for task outcomes, maximizing opportunities for individual choice making through voting and other individual selection methods, use of large group report-out to create shared understanding and group learning, considering the right amount of structure to contain anxiety and maximize productiveness, and encouraging diversity, holistic thinking, and collaboration through group member selection.

Rather than attempting to offer an exhaustive comparative review of LGIs, we focus on two methods: the search conference and the appreciative inquiry summit. The search conference could be considered the first LGI in the field of OD, pioneered more than 45 years ago by Fred Emery and Eric Trist at the Tavistock Institute (Trist & Emery, 1960). The appreciative inquiry summit (Whitney & Cooperrider, 2000) is perhaps the most recent of the LGIs.

SEARCH CONFERENCE

Trist and Emery (1960) discovered how a system approach to planning, coupled with democratic, task-oriented work groups, created a motivating force for strategic change. In the Barford Conference, Emery and Trist created the first search conference to assist managers with the merger of two British aircraft engine makers in 1960. Rather than limiting participation to select experts or a handful of senior executives, Emery and Trist structured the event to create an even playing field so that managers from both organizations could speak freely about common strategic issues. Based on their action research orientation and experimentation with search conferences over the next decade, Emery and Trist developed a deeper theoretical understanding of the design of effective search conferences.

The search conference can be viewed as a temporary organization that locates responsibility for the coordination, control, and implementation of planning tasks in self-managing work groups. Unlike in traditional strategic planning retreats, there is no hand-off or division of labor between thinkers and doers. The search conference is based on a fundamental assumption that organizations are purposeful and need to be organized so as to maximize the probability that the people in them can make the best choices about the means and ends that are critical to the survival of the enterprise. The search conference is designed to elicit full participation, actively engaging the people who attend to take responsibility for making choices and decisions that are in the best interests of the whole. But in order to maximize the probability that this occurs, people in LGIs must become ideal seeking. Ideals represent shared aspirations people have toward mutually acceptable ends and goals that constitute the common ground for cooperation and coordinated action. The democratic design philosophy, future focus, and open conditions for communication are

deliberate attempts to create a social atmosphere conducive to the creative expression of human ideals. In short, the search conference is an example of an LGI that enables people to fully participate in shaping the destiny of their organization and to make decisions for the common good.

Search conferences have been used in a wide variety of organizations as an alternative approach to traditional corporate strategic planning meetings. Other uses of the method include kicking off organization renewal or transformation initiatives; mergers of companies and hospitals; planning the future of cities, regions, industries, and professional associations; managing conflict between contentious parties and diverse interest groups; forging long-term partnerships with customers, suppliers, or government regulators; and developing system-wide plans for school reform and reinventing government (Emery & Purser, 1996).

The search conference normally is a two-and-a-half-day event, usually held offsite in a retreat setting. Twenty to 60 people are selected to participate in a search conference based on such criteria as their knowledge of the organization, whether they offer a diverse perspective on the strategic issue under consideration, and their potential for taking responsibility for implementation. In many cases, participants are selected from multiple levels of the organization and span membership across widely dispersed departments and functions. Furthermore, defining the purpose of the conference is crucial because such definition will inform the criteria for participant selection. Participants in a search conference work on planning tasks in a mixture of large group plenary sessions and small groups. The search conference proceeds in three phases: scanning the external environment, focusing on the present system, and developing strategic goals and action plans (Figure 15.1).

As a whole community, participants scan their external environment, review their history, and analyze the strengths and weaknesses of

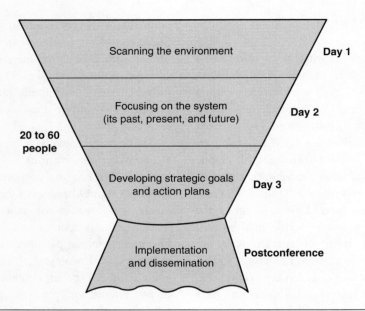

Figure 15.1   Search Conference Overview

SOURCE: Emery, M., & Purser, R. E. (1996). *The search conference: A powerful method for planning organizational change and community action.* San Francisco: Jossey-Bass. Used with permission of John Wiley & Sons, Inc.

their current system, which provides a shared context for their most important tasks: the development of strategic goals and action plans. Strategic issues relevant to the organization are debated and discussed by the entire conference community, and areas of agreement and common ground are mapped out through a process of generating, analyzing, and synthesizing data into an integrated community product.

The overall goal of the search conference is to develop a committed group of knowledgeable people who have a deep understanding of the challenges confronting their organization, a set of solid agreements about the ideals that the change and strategy are supposed to serve and action plans that are in alignment with these ideals, and a social mechanism for a participation and dissemination process to engage the target system in the implementation of planned change.

APPRECIATIVE INQUIRY SUMMIT

The appreciative inquiry (AI) summit method is an LGI method for accelerating organization change by involving a diverse group of

stakeholders (internal and external) in the change process. It is a collaborative inquiry and action research process designed to get the "whole system" in the room to discover its positive core (life-giving forces) and then build on these forces to create a new, more exciting, and more fulfilling future. In an AI summit, people with common interests come together in robust dialogue to discover an organization's positive core, that is, its most cherished values, beliefs, competencies, strengths, successes, and best practices; envision and a dream more desirable and fulfilling future; design a new organization form (systems, structures, approaches, and practices) to bring about the new vision; and create the infrastructure to manage and sustain the change. The AI summit approach suggests that human organizing and change, at its best, is a relational process of inquiry, grounded in affirmation and true appreciation. By tapping into accounts of organizations when they are functioning at their best, AI unleashes information and commitment that together create the energy for positive and widespread sustainable change.

AI summits typically range from 2 to 4 days and flow through the 4-D cycle: Discovery,

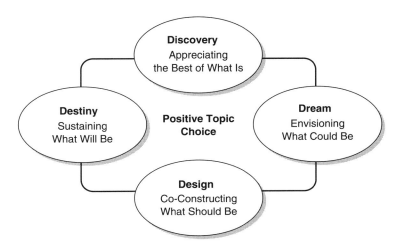

Figure 15.2   Appreciative Inquiry Cycle

Dream, Design, and Destiny (Figure 15.2). A summit can involve as few as 30 or as many as 2,500 or more. Each AI summit takes on a life of its own because of its distinctive topic focus and unique design considerations. Because the AI summit approach focuses on individuals' personal experience and the organization's history, members learn how to repeat their successes. Therefore, the AI summit approach is a generative learning process, always evolving, always growing, and always future focused.

Table 15.1 describes the key activities that occur in a typical AI summit as groups move through the 4-D model.

Among the most important concepts underlying the AI summit model approach are the basic AI principles (Cooperrider & Srivastva, 1987). These principles are fundamental to the success of any AI summit, and any practitioner who designs an AI summit should understand the nature of these principles and how they affect its success.

Constructionist Principle

The constructionist principle indicates that reality is socially constructed through conversation and relational interaction: Our language and cultural practices give rise to our interpretations and ultimately determine our actions. At the heart of the constructionist viewpoint is the belief that the knowledge needed for change resides in the people and systems that make up that system. As we are talking to one another in a positive and inspiring way, we are simultaneously constructing a more positive and inspiring view of the world around us. If words are the basic building blocks of social reality, why not use words that inspire, motivate, illuminate, and highlight the best of things instead of remaining gripped in the deficit-based language that permeates organizations and society at large?

Principle of Simultaneity

The principle of simultaneity says that inquiry and change happen at the same time—that the minute we begin to ask questions, we begin to bring about change. The kind of questions you ask determine what you find and set the stage for future discovery. This has enormous implications for OD practitioners: If inquiry is a form of intervention, then what type of questions should be asked to bring about successful change? Should we look for what is wrong or what is right? AI practitioners frame questions as a means for generating hope and inspiration.

Table 15.1   Key Activities in an AI Summit

Phase	Key Activities
Discovery	• The primary task of discovery is to identify and highlight an organization's life-giving factors—its positive core.
	• Through appreciative interviews and storytelling, participants illuminate the best of what is by focusing on peak times or organization excellence from their own experience.
	• By reflecting on the success factors gleaned from the interviews (e.g., leadership, relationships, technologies, core processes, structures, values, learning processes, partnerships, planning methods) that made the high points possible, people discuss the aspects of their organization's history that they most value and want to bring to the future.
Dream	• The primary task of dream is to envision a more desired and fulfilling future.
	• Compelling images of the future emerge out of positive examples from an organization's past; they are vibrant, new possibilities based on extraordinary moments of excellence in previous times.
	• Through appreciative and future-focused dialogue, evocative dreams are shared and acted out.
	• In a very practical sense, the dream phase can galvanize an organization and expand its most positive potential.
Design	• The primary task of design is to create the structural design (organizational architecture or arrangement) for the change.
	• Organization members identify the design features (strategies, systems, structures, relationships, leadership styles, policies, and procedures) that will facilitate the change and position the organization for implementation success.
	• By crafting provocative propositions or design possibility statements, the organization links the vision of a more desired future (dream) with its positive core (discovery).
Destiny	• The primary task of destiny is to create the specific action plans to carry forward the new vision crafted through discovery, dream, and design.
	• Innovation (action) teams are formed to identify resource needs and plan the next steps.
	• Energy usually is incredibly high by this point in the process. Because positive images of the future have been co-created, everyone is ready to be aligned, committed, and motivated to work in support of the whole.

Poetic Principle

The poetic principle says that organizations are like open books, open to multiple interpretations and understanding. It indicates that organizations are not fixed systems that are unable to change. People in organizations create the systems, processes, and practices that produce their results and successes, and therefore they have the potential to change. The organization stories that are produced are constantly being rewritten in the moment by those who are interacting with them.

Anticipatory Principle

The anticipatory principle says that what we look for or anticipate is what we find (good or bad), so why not anticipate, look for, or imagine the times in which we felt most alive, most effective, and most positively affected? By engaging in positive and productive dialogue, we can produce more positive images of the future we want to create and in turn generate more positive and meaningful actions toward the fulfillment of that future.

Positive Principle

The positive principle says that organizations move in the direction of their most hopeful and satisfying images. The more affirmative the topic of inquiry, the more positive the guiding images of the future that are produced and the more powerful the commitment and action that follow. This principle has enormous implications for the OD practitioner; it points out that framing the topic of inquiry is an important task that takes forethought and careful handling. To maximize success, an AI summit must have an unconditional focus on the positive during inquiry, analysis, and action.

FUTURE DIRECTIONS OF LGIS IN OD

Gergen (1982, 1999) believes that if patterns of action are to be changed, one significant means of doing so is by altering forms of discourse and social interaction. The implications for the future direction of LGIs are very clear: If wholeness (individual or organizational) is inseparable from social engagements and relationships, if meaning making occurs through relational (social constructionist) practices, then OD scholars–practitioners must continually strive to transform and improve the process by which people become aware of how they co-construct their collective identity as an organization in a dynamic environment. Social constructionist practices have already made inroads in the field of OD, as noted in the AI summit. However, the field has much more work to do in this area. The emerging field of positive organization psychology undoubtedly will inform innovations and spur new types of LGIs in the next few years.

The opportunities for future research on wholeness in the context of organizations are many. Varying theoretical, academic, and practical perspectives suggest that the "organization wholeness" or "organization health" is a phenomenon that is not fully understood and

perhaps never will be through detached forms of second- and third-person inquiry (Torbert, 2002). Questions such as, "What does it take to become whole again?" "How do organizations become whole?" or "How can organizations continuously promote a sense of wholeness?" provoke multifaceted, complex responses. Indeed, organization wholeness cannot be conceptualized in the abstract because it also requires understanding what constitutes wholeness at the individual level in organizations. In some respects, this appears to be "going back to the future," revisiting such classic OD theories as Chris Argyris's (1964) notion of organization–individual fit.

Another fruitful area of exploration that could reinvigorate the theory and practice of LGIs (and the process of organization change) is developing more powerful approaches to connecting to the dynamic of time and the future (Purser & Petranker, 2005). OD, and theories of change in general, are based on a number of unexamined assumptions about the temporality of change, particularly our embodied and socially conditioned view of the future. Based on our review, all current LGIs in some way or another attempt to create desirable images of the future, whether by creating a shared vision, an image of the best of what could be, and so on. The future state LGIs aim to bring into being through visioning turns out to be a hypothetical version of the past. Ironically, attempts to know or envision the future (as conventionally understood) actually depend on "analogous actions in the past" (Weick, 1979, p. 102). This point was clearly worked out by sociologist and phenomenologist Alfred Schutz (1932/1972), who claimed the future is available to us only when we imagine it to have been already completed, only in the "future perfect."

The stark and perhaps unpopular reality is that the actual future is unknown, and when it emerges into the present, it rarely conforms perfectly to the images or visions conceived in

LGI events. The future perfect is a past-centered version of the future and is entirely subjective. Even as Das (1986) makes clear in his analysis of the subjective side of strategic decision making, the future perfect has everything to do with the way we think about or project the future and nothing to do with the actuality of the future as such. It is often said that the present is real in a way that the past and the future are not, but in this context it makes more sense to say that the past and present are real in a way that the future is not. For the past is what really happened, but the future is simply what we expect, imagine, or project will happen. We have to honestly ask whether such attempts at visioning—which is usually the focus of LGIs—is at some level merely a collective ritual to reduce anxiety rather than to actually develop the human capacities for engaging the dynamic of changing in time.

We propose that LGIs need to focus on the future as a unique temporal dynamic that does not involve projecting a vision forward based on our thoughts, hopes, desires, or imagined expectations. Rather, we contend that participants need to learn first-person forms of inquiry that help them appreciate and embody time and the future on its own terms as a creative dynamic that they can master as a force for individual and organizational change. The proposition being made here is that it is possible to know the real future not simply in terms of projections of the future based on past constructs (the future perfect)—the stuff visions, predictions, scenarios, or desirable images are made of—but the actual dynamic of the future in unfolding flow of time. Tulku (1994, p. 93) distinguishes the "future infinitive" from our conventional conceptualization of the future:

> But this constructed future has little to do with the future as time's transitional indeterminacy: the future infinitive of time. The future located "up ahead," projected forward along linear lines of force, is not the same as the future that will never arrive and thus never restrict. It is in this "never arriving" of

the future that the dynamic and power of time makes themselves available.

The future must be viewed and approached as a temporal dimension that is unconditioned, unknown, and indeterminate. Such an unconditioned future is not arrived at by projecting forward a "future perfect" by creating a shared vision but by tapping into the "never-arriving" dynamic and indeterminacy. Rather than continuing to project forward from the past and into the future, LGIs in the future can focus on heightening participants' awareness of time as the indeterminate, "nonarriving" dynamic of the future to inform collective thinking and action. Purser and Petranker (2005) call this capacity a form of "deep improvisation." Exploring first-person methods that allow participants to engage in deep improvisation through the "future infinitive" provides a theoretical framework for understanding how LGIs can develop more appropriate and effective methods for dealing with emergent and continuous change.

REFERENCES

Alford, C., & Klein, M. (1989). *Social theory*. New Haven, CT: Yale University Press.

Argyris, C. (1964). *Integrating the individual and the organization*. New York: John Wiley & Sons.

Ashforth, B. E., & Mael, F. (1989). Social identity theory and the organization. *Academy of Management Review, 14*, 20–39.

Axelrod, R. (2000). *Terms of engagement: Changing the way we change organizations*. San Francisco: Berrett-Koehler.

Barrett, F. J., Thomas, G. F., & Hocevar, S. P. (1995). The central role of discourse in large-scale change: A social construction perspective. *Journal of Applied Behavioral Science, 31*(3), 352–372.

Bennis, W. G., & Shepard, H. A. (1956). A theory of group development. *Human Relations, 9*, 415–437.

Berger, P., & Luckmann, T. (1994). *The social construction of reality*. New York: Doubleday.

Bertalanaffy, L. (1998). *General systems theory*. New York: George Braziller.

Bion, W. R. (1961). *Experiences in groups.* New York: Basic Books.

Bohm, D. (1980). *Wholeness and the implicate order.* London: Ark.

Bohm, D. (1996). *On dialogue.* New York: Routledge.

Bunker, B., & Alban, B. (1997). *Large group interventions: Engaging the whole system for rapid change.* San Francisco: Jossey-Bass.

Burr, V. (1995). *An introduction to social constructionism.* London: Routledge.

Chase, T. (Ed.). (1995). *Large group interventions for organizational change: Concepts, methods, and cases.* Unpublished readings from the 1995 OD Network Conference.

Chase, T. (Ed.). (1996). *Large group interventions for organizational change: Concepts, methods, and cases.* Unpublished readings from the 1995 OD Network Conference.

Chase, T. (Ed.). (1997). *Large group interventions for organizational change: Concepts, methods, and cases.* Unpublished readings from the 1995 OD Network Conference.

Chase, T. (Ed.). (1998). *Large group interventions for organizational change: Concepts, methods, and cases.* Unpublished readings from the 1995 OD Network Conference.

Cialdini, R. B., Borden, R. J., Thorne, A., Walker, M. R., Freeman, S., & Sloan, L. R. (1976). Basking in the glory: Three field studies. *Journal of Personality and Social Psychology, 34,* 366–375.

Cooperrider, D. L., & Srivastva, S. (1987). Appreciative inquiry in organizational life. In W. A. Pasmore & R. W. Woodman (Eds.), *Research in organizational change and development* (Vol. 1). Greenwich, CT: JAI.

Dannemiller, K. (2000). *Whole-scale change toolkit: Tools for unleashing the magic in organizations.* San Francisco: Berrett-Koehler.

Dannemiller, K., & Jacobs, R. (1992). Changing the way organizations change: A revolution of common sense. *The Journal of Applied Behavioral Science, 28,* 480–498.

Dannemiller, K., James, S., & Tolchinsky, P. (1999). *Whole-scale change.* San Francisco: Berrett-Koehler.

Das, T. K. (1986). *The subjective side of strategy making: Future orientations and perceptions of executives.* New York: Praeger.

Dutton, J. E., Dukerich, J. M., & Harquail, C. V. (1994). Organizational images and member identification. *Administrative Science Quarterly, 39,* 239–263.

Ellinor, L., & Gerard, G. (1998). *Dialogue: Rediscover the transforming power of conversation.* New York: John Wiley & Sons.

Emery, F., & Trist, E. L. (1965). The causal texture of organizational environments. *Human Relations, 18,* 21–32.

Emery, M., & Purser, R. E. (1996). *The search conference: A powerful method for planning organizational change and community action.* San Francisco: Jossey-Bass.

French, W. L., Bell, C., & Zawacki, R. A. (1995). *Organization development and transformation: Managing effective change.* New York: Irwin/McGraw-Hill.

Gergen, K. (1982). *Toward transformation in social knowledge.* New York: Springer-Verlag.

Gergen, K. (1990). Toward a postmodern psychology. *The Humanistic Psychologist, 18,* 23–34.

Gergen, K. (1991). Toward reflexive methodologies. In F. Steier (Ed.), *Research and reflexivity* (pp. 76–95). London: Sage.

Gergen, K. (1994). *Realities and relationships: Soundings in social construction.* Cambridge, MA: Harvard University Press.

Gergen, K. (1998). Constructionism and realism: How are we to go on? In I. Parker (Ed.), *Social constructionism, discourse and realism.* Thousand Oaks, CA: Sage.

Gergen, K. (1999). *An invitation to social construction.* Thousand Oaks, CA: Sage.

Gilmore, T., & Barnett, C. (1992). Designing the social architecture of participation in large groups to effect organizational change. *The Journal of Applied Behavioral Science, 28,* 534–548.

Hatch, M. J. (1997). *Organization theory: Modern symbolic and postmodern perspectives.* New York: Oxford University Press.

Hazen, M. A. (1993). Towards polyphonic organization. *Journal of Organizational Change Management, 6*(5), 15–26.

Hofstede, G. (2004). *Culture and organizations: Software of the mind.* New York: McGraw-Hill.

Holman, P., & Devane, T. (1999). *The change handbook: Group methods for shaping the future.* San Francisco: Berrett-Koehler.

Jacobs, R. (1994). *Real time strategic change.* San Francisco: Berrett-Koehler.

Katz, D., & Kahn, R. (1978). *The social psychology of organizations*. New York: John Wiley & Sons.

Lakoff, G. (2002). *Moral politics: How liberals and conservatives think*. Chicago: University of Chicago Press.

Lawler, E. E. (1986). *High involvement management*. San Francisco: Jossey-Bass.

Levine, L., & Mohr, B. J. (1998). Whole system design (WSD): The shifting focus of attention and the threshold challenge. *Journal of Applied Behavioral Science, 34*(3), 305–326.

Lewin, K. (1951). *Field theory in social science*. New York: HarperCollins.

Lippitt, R. (1983). Future before you plan. In *NTL Manager's Handbook* (pp. 36–45). Arlington, VA: NTL Institute.

Manning, M., & Binzagar, G. F. (1996). Methods, values, and assumptions underlying large group interventions intended to change whole systems. *International Journal of Organizational Analysis, 4*(3), 268–284.

Maslow, A. H. (1943, July). A theory of human motivation. *Psychological Review*, 370–396.

McGregor, D. (1960). *The human side of enterprise*. New York: McGraw-Hill.

Miller, D., & Friesen, P. (1984). *Organizations: A quantum view*. Englewood Cliffs, NJ: Prentice Hall.

Mohrman, A. M., & Lawler, E. E. (1985). The diffusion of QWL as a paradigm shift. In W. G. Bennis, K. D. Benne, & R. Chin (Eds.), *The planning of change*. New York: Holt, Rinehart, & Winston.

Pasmore, W. A., & Fagans, M. R. (1992). Participation, individual development, and organizational change: A preview and synthesis. *Journal of Management, 18*, 375–397.

Purser, R., & Petranker, J. (2005). Unfreezing the future: Exploring the dynamic of time in organizational change. *Journal of Applied Behavioral Science, 41*(2), 183–203.

Schein, E. H. (1993). On dialogue, culture, and organizational learning. *Organizational Dynamics, 22*(2), 40–51.

Schindler-Rainman, E., & Lippitt, R. (1980). *Building the collaborative community: Mobilizing citizens for action*. Riverside: University of California, Extension.

Schutz, A. (1972). *The phenomenology of the social world* (trans. G. Walsh & F. Lehnert). London: Heinemann. (Original work published 1932)

Senge, P. (1990). *The fifth discipline: The art and practice of the learning organization*. New York: Doubleday.

Senge, P. M. (1994). Personal transformation. *Executive Excellence, 11*(1), 17–18.

Smith, K., & Berg, D. N. (1987). *Paradoxes of group life*. San Francisco: Jossey-Bass.

Sullivan, R. (1997). *The facilitation of large group interactive events: The most impactful change management intervention since the inception of teambuilding*. Unpublished paper.

Torbert, W. (2002). *Learning to exercise timely action now*. E-publication, available from torbert@bc.edu.

Trist, E., & Emery, F. (1960). *Report on the Barford course for Bristol/Siddeley*, July 10–16, 1960 (Tavistock Document 598). London: Tavistock Institute.

Tulku, T. (1994). *Dynamics of time and space: Transcending limits on knowledge*. Berkeley, CA: Dharma.

Turquet, P. (1975). Threats to identity in the large group. In L. Kreeger (Ed.), *The large group: Dynamics and therapy*. London: Constable.

Weick, K. E. (1979). *The social psychology of organizing*. Reading, MA: Addison-Wesley.

Weick, K. E., & Quinn, R. (1999). Organizational development and change. *Annual Review of Psychology, 50*, 361–386.

Weisbord, M. (1995). *Discovering common ground*. San Francisco: Berrett-Koehler.

Weisbord, M. R., & Janoff, S. (1995). *Future search: An action guide to finding common ground in organizations and communities*. San Francisco: Berrett-Koehler.

Wheatley, M. (1999). *Leadership and the new science: Learning about organizations from an orderly universe*. San Francisco: Berrett-Koehler.

Whitney, D., & Cooperrider, D. (2000). The appreciative inquiry summit: An emerging methodology for whole system positive change. *Journal of the Organization Practitioner: OD Network, 32*(1), 13–26.

16

Sociotechnical Systems

Designing and Managing Sustainable Organizations

FRANS M. VAN EIJNATTEN

A. B. (RAMI) SHANI

MYLEEN M. LEARY

Like everything in today's business world, organizations are changing more than ever before. The potential of profound and continuous renewal of the organization and management provides a unique competitive advantage. Because the world has become a global marketplace and technology is continuing to advance rapidly, organization change is the rule rather than the exception. A multitude of models were developed in the 20th century, but whether they are real innovations or just management fads often has been difficult to assess. At the same time, the literature on organization strategy, design, development, and change shows some theoretical crystallization points. Taylorism certainly was the first grand theory in the field of organization renewal (Daft, 2005). This approach has been applied to many organizations over the course of nearly a century, and it is still present in a significant number of firms in the new millennium. Sociotechnical system theory provides an alternative paradigm.

SOCIOTECHNICAL SYSTEMS

Since its inception in the 1950s, three major sociotechnical system (STS) subfields emerged: STS theory, STS design, and STS change and development process (Pasmore, 1988). STS theory is a developed and still developing body of academic literature (Adler & Docherty, 1998). Its main activity is advancing research in the field of management, organization, change, and development. STS design is the pragmatic and applied cousin of STS theory. Specific sets of design principles have been advanced over the years that guide the design or redesign of an existing organization or the design of a new organization—the actual architecture of the firm (Cherns, 1976, 1987; Davis & Cherns, 1975; Hanna, 1988; Pasmore 1988; Taylor & Felten, 1993). The relationship between STS design and STS theory is both implicit and explicit. Although it is not design, STS theory informs STS design. On occasion, STS theory and STS design are tightly coupled. At other times the relationship is tenuous (Kolodny & Shani, 2004).

The third subfield is STS change and development process. This subfield is devoted to processes of creating or transforming an organization. Specific sets of phases and steps have been advanced over the years that guide the redesign process of an existing organization or the design process of a new organization. STS provides a comprehensive planned change process with analytical tools and methods that were developed to facilitate the transformation of an organization toward a more STS-based design entity. The design processes, methods, and tools are elaborate and multilevel in nature. They use an action research orientation and provide links between business environment analysis, vision and strategy statements, system analysis and diagnosis, exploration of new alternatives for joint optimization, experimental implementation, and system-wide dissemination. Parallel learning structures, composed of steering, study, and action groups, plan and carry out the learning and redesign process (Bushe & Shani, 1991; Kolodny & Stjernberg, 1986; Pasmore, 1994). The relationship between STS change, STS design, and STS theory also is both implicit and explicit. In most cases STS design and theory serve as the conceptual guide for the design or change process (Stebbins, 2003; Susman & Chase, 1986).

At the core of the STS field one can find two key concepts: semiautonomous work groups

and joint optimization. The semiautonomous work group concept was developed into a basic prototype for the design of team-based organizations (Cummings & Srivastva, 1977; Mohrman & Cummings, 1989; Pasmore, Francis, Haldeman, & Shani, 1982; Pasmore & Sherwood, 1978; Trist & Murray, 1990; Trist, Murray, & Emery, 1997; Trist, Murray, & Trist, 1993). The concept of joint optimization is the backbone of the paradigm: An organization will function best if the social and technological systems are designed to fit the demands of each other and of the environment (Adler & Docherty, 1998; van Eijnatten, 1993; Taylor & Felten, 1993).

Firms around the globe are increasing their engagements in a large variety of continuous improvement programs and system-wide change efforts. At the most basic level, continuous improvement is a purposeful and explicit set of principles, mechanisms, and activities within an organization, designed to achieve positive and continuous change in deliverables, operating procedures, and systems by the people who actually perform these procedures and work under these systems (Lillrank et al., 1998). A careful review of the many reported continuous improvement and system-wide change efforts reveals that many of the STS theoretical concepts, design, and planned change processes are integrated into these efforts. This signifies for us that STS may have moved through the stages of introduction, experimentation, and evaluation into the stage of general acceptance, implementations, and dissemination.

Over the last 50 years, STS applications have spread over most continents of the globe. Today STS comes in many different forms for all kinds of conceptual thinking and applications, from industrial to knowledge work (van Eijnatten, 1993, 1998, 1999; Pasmore 1988; Pava, 1983a, 1983b; Taylor & Felten, 1993; Trist, 1981). Principally, STS is about kinds of division of work that explicitly respect human values. Some commentators suggest that STS probably is the other candidate for the nomination of grand theory in the field of organization and management science (van Eijnatten & van der Zwaan, 1998; Munkvold, 2000). On the basis of analysis of a comprehensive bibliography of English-language STS literature references (van Eijnatten, Eggermont, Goffau, & Mankoe, 1994; Pasmore et al., 1982), Emery (1995) refutes Scarbrough's (1995) grave–tomb thesis, which states that STS is dead. Furthermore, Emery concludes that the STS paradigm is very much alive, considering the observed explosion of publications in the late 1980s and early 1990s and the dissemination of many STS concepts into a variety of hybrid models and theories.

ACTION RESEARCH CONTEXT

STS came into existence in the 1950s, as semi-autonomous work groups accidentally were rediscovered in a British coal mine (Trist & Bamforth, 1951; Trist, Higgin, Murray, & Pollock, 1963). The classic STS theory was first articulated at the Tavistock Institute of Human Relations in London (Emery, 1959; Herbst, 1959; Miller, 1959; Trist et al., 1993), and the first real experiments with industrial democracy took place in Norway in the 1960s (Emery & Thorsrud, 1964, 1976). Figure 16.1 introduces the primary theoretical developers and depicts the spread of STS to the different continents.

Region-specific variants were developed in the 1970s to accommodate different work contexts in Europe (Scandinavian STS or "Democratic Dialogue," Dutch STS or "Integral Organizational Renewal"), Australia (Australian STS or "Participative Design"), and the United States ("North American STS"). Although there were exceptions, these local varieties developed mainly in isolation, propagated by distinct groups of authors, as can be seen in Figure 16.1. Later on, more frequent professional contacts resulted in cross-fertilization of these different STS streams of thought.

STS evolved primarily in conjuncture with and based on action research orientation (Elden & Chisholm, 1993). Changing behavior and learning were some of the concerns that led Kurt Lewin in the development of action research (Lewin, 1951; Pasmore, 2001). Lewin's attempt to solve social problems using systematic data collection, feedback, reflection, and action was pioneering and is at the foundation of learning by design (Mohrman & Cummings, 1989; Shani & Docherty, 2003). In the last 50 years, action research—just like STS—has developed as a major field of research composed of a variety of activities and streams that integrates research and action in living systems (Adler, Shani, & Styhre, 2004; Reason & Bradbury, 2001). Action research is viewed as an emergent inquiry process, embedded in partnership between researchers and organization members, for the purpose of addressing a problem and simultaneously generating scientific knowledge (Susman & Evered, 1978). Moreover, action research seeks to improve the organization's ability to understand itself and develop self-help competencies, or learning by design (Coghlan & Brannick, 2005; Elden & Chisholm, 1993; Friedlander & Brown, 1974; Shani & Pasmore, 1985).

WORLDVIEW OF PARTICIPATIVE DEMOCRACY

Changing the division of labor within firms to achieve a participative democracy is a focus of all STS varieties, (van Eijnatten, 1993). The notions of participation and democracy are embedded in most of the STS literature. The assumption is that democratization of work will elicit commitment, which subsequently will lead to multiskilling and will result in better productivity and quality (Emery, 1989). At the most basic level, participative democracy is a vision that the responsibility for coordination should be put with those whose efforts need coordination (Abrahamsson, 1977).

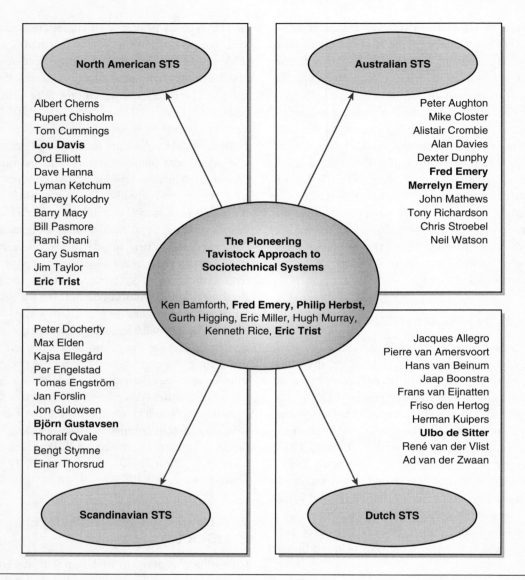

Figure 16.1   Some Contributors to Classic Sociotechnical Systems and Its Local Varieties (authors listed in boldface are the prime theoretical developers)

The following STS pioneers echo the basic social and technical inspirations: social scientists Eric Trist, Fred Emery, Björn Gustavsen, Tom Cummings, and Jim Taylor and technical engineers Lou Davis, Ulbo de Sitter, Bill Pasmore, and Harvey Kolodny. They all share the STS ideal of designing sociotechnical organizations in which people can continuously learn, improve, and develop. These authors initiated the development of distinct STS

schools of thought, each with many followers. The USA-based STS Roundtable played a central role in fostering the STS research and consultancy community in the 1980s and 1990s (Savage, 2004). Its yearly conferences triggered a number of new initiatives and a series of proceedings volumes compiled by Tom Chase (1991–2000). This series of readings documents the development of the STS paradigm in North America.

SOCIOTECHNICAL SYSTEMS: A SYNOPSIS OF BASIC KNOWLEDGE AND CURRENT STATE OF THE FIELD

Building on the work of van Eijnatten (1993), we distinguish between four distinct conceptual developments or regional variants of modern STS around the globe: North American STS, Australian STS or "Participative Design," Scandinavian STS or "Democratic Dialogue," and Dutch STS or "Integral Organizational Renewal." Although they all share the basic themes discussed earlier—semiautonomous work groups, joint optimization, action research, and participative democracy—the particular STS concepts that emerged on each continent seem to differ and tend to be based on a distinct emphasis, culture, and business contexts. Of course, there also is much multiformity and internal variety, so any attempt to generalize at a metalevel (continent level) runs the risk of being perceived as oversimplified. The effort put forth in this section is to use, to the extent possible, the language advanced by the original contributors.

Undertaking this review, we recognize that STS has become eclectic, drawing on a large array of cultural orientations and behavioral, organizational, and management science concepts, theories, and techniques. Thus, for the purpose of presenting an overview of the field, we made hard choices about what should and should not be included and where to include what. In this section we focus on what we view as direct and distinct contributions to the field in the different world regions.

The basic assumptions, specific guiding principles, basic assumptions about change, and phases of the change process for each of the four variants of STS examined in this chapter are summarized in this section. Each perspective of STS is discussed in turn to identify commonalities and differences.

North American STS[1]

Three comprehensive studies have focused on the major evolution of STS in the North American context: Pasmore et al. (1982) provide a review of 132 STS experiments, Macy and Izumi (1993) provide a comprehensive meta-analysis of 131 field studies covering 30 years of evaluation research, and Taylor and Felten (1993) provide a historical account of the STS field that focuses on the evolution of STS through the examination of the roles of industrial practice, government and private foundations, academic centers, and private practice. The early STS development in the North American context is based on the early work of Eric Trist and Lou Davis (see Cummings & Srivastva, 1977; Pasmore & Sherwood, 1978). Intellectual origins of this STS variant are open-system thinking (OST), classic STS theory, and the theory of organization; national origins are Great Britain and North America. The essence of North American STS interventions is summarized as a thorough and equal consideration of both social and technical subsystems in order to creatively meet the needs of the external environment through the use of a variety of mechanisms (e.g., self-managed teams) that enhance worker performance, commitment, and satisfaction.

The North American variant of STS views new plants as a particularly fertile ground for experimentation with STS design principles. The intended outcomes of the North American design school of thought seem to focus on joint optimization of the social and technical subsystems, empowerment of employees, improvement of the quality of work, development of worker's understanding of the industry in which the organization is involved, enhancing the workers' competence in controlling key variances and product development and delivery, and addressing significant change opportunities and threats.

The North American variant of STS views study groups and line management teams as the key actors of change. The researcher's role is as a design and change expert who guides the redesign process and helps apply changes. The major change mechanism is the steering group and study and design teams. North American STS knowledge and competence acquisition are accomplished by developing employee capacity for understanding the business environment, developing employee competencies for controlling key variances, and increasing work group control of product and production process (variance control).

BOX 16.1   Summary of North American STS

Assumptions

- There is not one best way to design an organization.
- Designs should be aimed at joint optimization of social and technical subsystems.
- Organization constituencies should be included in the design process.
- Decisions on work flow and structure are made by managers and employees.

Guiding Principles

- Compatibility
- Minimum critical specification
- Variance control
- Multifunctionalism and multiskilling
- Boundary location
- Information flow
- Power and authority
- Support congruence
- Design and human values
- Bridging and transition
- Implementation

Assumptions About Change

- The process is led by a design team.
- Incompletion: The need for change and redesign is ongoing.
- Change is necessary for growth and renewal.
- Continual adaptation is an essential competency for renewal.
- Continuous feedback is the heart of holistic renewal.

Phases in the Change Process

- Discovery of existing paradigm, system model, and method and structure
- Open-system scan to specify the boundary and the environmental demands and define the purpose
- Technical analysis through variance matrix or a variance control table
- Social analysis of the network's role, the social system grid, and quality of work life criteria
- Joint optimization design to identify design principles, feedback, problems, and constraints
- Provisional design
- Implementation of the subsystem design along with evaluation of the plan and redesign

Australian STS[2]

A second dominant STS stream centers on the notions of "Participative Design" that emerged in the Australian context, based on the early work of Fred and Merrelyn Emery (see F. Emery, 1959, 1979; Emery & Emery, 1974; M. Emery, 1994). Intellectual origins of this STS variant are OST, classic STS theory, and redundancy of skills; national origins are Great Britain and Australia. The essence of the Australian STS approach can be summarized as follows: Participative Design rests on a pure democratic model that seeks to overcome resisters to change in an organization by developing a group design (that leads the entire process to its completion) for the organization without the help of an outside expert. A significant portion of the Australian variant of STS occurs in public sector projects.

The intended outcomes of this design school of thought are a high level of trust between employers and employees, learning-to-learn and learning-to-participate skills, and a future for the organization's place within the environment.

In this stream of STS, the key actors in a change process are representatives from a cross-section of the firm (a vertical deep slice). The researcher's role is as process facilitator and co-learner (Emery & Purser, 1996; Griffiths, 1995). The major change mechanisms are the participative design workshop, the search conference, and the elected design team. Knowledge and competence acquisition is accomplished by developing the learning-to-learn competences of the employees and strengthening employees' learning-to-participate skills.

BOX 16.2   Summary of Australian STS

Assumptions

- Participants are equipped and given ownership and responsibility for the entire design process.
- The value of workers centers around their need to cope with increasing environmental complexity.

Guiding Principles

- Representatives are drawn from a vertical slice of the organization.
- Dissemination of the new principles must start within the existing structure and flow from one level of leaders to the next.
- The influence of external scientific advisors on the dissemination process is filtered through organization leaders.
- Oral and written communication is not sufficient to lead change beyond the leadership level.
- Dissemination depends on the impact of the leadership example; a well-respected person or group must be behind the example.

(Continued)

(Continued)

Assumptions About Change

- Failed attempts at change often result from insufficient support from within.
- Dissemination of change requires a deep slice of the organization (e.g., workers, manager, and union representatives).

Phases in the Change Process

- Election of design team members
- Redesign training
- Begin search process
- Establish design criteria and alternatives
- Evaluate alternatives
- Manage the redesign process
- Use interorganizational learning

Scandinavian STS[3]

The Scandinavian stream is the third STS emerging body of knowledge and practice. Two parallel lines of development can be seen in this context: the substream that focused on developmental processes and the substream that focused on design and design criteria. Although both are embedded in the "Democratic Dialogue" orientation, the evolution of the design school was more influenced by the dynamics with union organizations around the development of union policies as a result of labor displacement and employability issues (Adler & Docherty, 1998). The development school focused on developmental processes that are embedded in dialogue and communicative practices (Elden, 1986; Gustavsen, 1985; Thorsrud, 1970). Intellectual origins of this STS variant are participative democracy theory and linguistic and pragmatic discourse; national origins are Sweden and Norway. The essence of Scandinavian STS interventions is summarized as a broadened STS scope to include other relevant businesses in the wider environment, local knowledge through dialogue between partners (companies and academia) for the purpose of learning and knowledge generation, and emphasis on primary work group control, development of business control, employability for security, and increase in customer contact with work groups.

The intended outcomes of this stream are institutional commitment on the part of labor and management, establishment of knowledge-sharing partnerships between companies, increased primary work group control of business, increased interaction between customers and workers, increased employability of labor, health, wellness, and sustainability.

Key actors in the change process from the Scandinavian perspective of STS are multiple employees and managers. The researcher's role is as communication enabler. Knowledge and competence acquisition is established by developing work group capacity for increased business control and by increasing the employee–customer contact.

Box 16.3   Summary of Scandinavian STS

Assumptions

- The proper foundation for organization development is a theory of communication and a theory of design.
- Epistemologically, language and practice are linked by vocabulary, not by field experiment.
- As language is restructured, practice is reconfigured.
- Maintaining scope in the development process is accomplished through broad involvement and participation.
- Employability and sustainability are crucial.

Guiding Principles

- Meaningful exchange of ideas
- Organization mapping
- Local theories
- Design for employability and sustainability
- Equality of participants and ideas
- Experience as valid knowledge
- Shared understanding of key issues
- Legitimacy of arguments
- Vocal arguments
- Intellectual humility
- Work role assignment
- Tolerance for ambiguity
- Practical action as key output

Assumptions About Change

- All participants are equal regardless of their role or position in the organization.
- Key actors in the change process are multiple employees and managers.
- Continuous system and human development are critical to the development of sustainable work systems.

Phases in the Change Process

- Adoption in the branch network through project group establishment, demonstration conference, strategy forum, and regional promotion conferences
- Business development process through whole-company conference and the inclusion of a scholarship holder
- Expansion of supporting network through a network development conference to expand the number of participating and supporting institutions and the development of a project or action-learning process in each unit

Dutch STS[4]

The fourth dominant STS stream is the "Integral Organizational Renewal" design school of thought, initially developed by Ulbo de Sitter (1994). Intellectual origins of this STS variant are OST, modern sociotechnical theory, and the balance model; national origins are Sweden and the Netherlands. The essence of Dutch STS interventions is summarized as integral design of the organization's systems in order to enhance the quality of work, organization, and labor relations; shaping of the organization's structural context that is capable of acting on emerging business opportunities; and reduction of interference between multiple interaction cycles in order to enhance process control at every level such that the work group controls the entire product flow.

The intended outcomes of this design school of thought are improvement of the organization's control of key processes, mobilization of human resources, a reduction of organization complexity (enhanced flexibility), promotion of work group control of the entire product flow, and development of a holistic system architecture that optimizes the quality of work life (personnel), the quality of the organization (engineering), and the quality of labor relations (union management).

In the Dutch stream of STS, the researcher's role is to provide expert consulting and training. The major change mechanism is self-design by knowledge transfer. Knowledge and competence acquisition is established by developing work group capacity for increased control over purpose, context, and system dynamics, on-the-job training through teamwork and experiential learning, and employee self-design competencies.

BOX 16.4   Summary of Dutch STS

Assumptions

- The organization is modeled as a network of interaction cycles in which multiple functions are produced.
- The STS is composed of production-aspect, control-aspect, and information-aspect systems.
- An organization's viabilities for control should equal the environmental demands for control.

Guiding Principles

- Functional deconcentration
- Performance integration and performance generalization
- Integration of performance and control functions
- Integration and generalization of control
- Integration of all functions in a control cycle
- Simplification of the production structure of parallelization of process flows
- Quantitatively fitting the production structure for team work by segmentation of each process flow
- Building operational flexibility in every individual task
- Building feedback loops in each task and uncoupling feedback loops wherever possible

Assumptions About Change

- It is by logical necessity impossible to transform an undemocratic structure in a democratic manner.
- The sociotechnical problem refers to the question of whether structure conditions constitute the generic capacity for balanced (i.e., multifunctional) control.

Phases in the Change Process

- Identification of core problems through a global strategic analysis, global system analysis, and identification of bottlenecks
- Diagnosis of the problems by narrowing the system's boundaries, detailed strategic analysis, detailed system analysis, and diagnosis and specification of redesign objectives
- Action planning by reconsidering the product design and planning redesign of the production structure, the decision and control structure, and the information structure
- Intervention through implementation of the plan
- Joint optimization design to identify design principles, feedback, problems, and constraints

Partial Comparison, Practical Relevance, and Evaluation

From the previous paragraphs it is not difficult to see the compatibility and a few of the distinct features that emerged over time on the different continents. Table 16.1 attempts to capture, through a comparative lens, the development of STS theories (identified earlier as the first subfield), STS designs (second subfield), and STS change and development processes (third subfield).

Common to all the STS theories are general system theory and the view of organizations as open systems. The basic premise building on general system theory and open system theory is that organizations have common characteristics with all other living systems. Therefore, a basic set of fundamental concepts can be applied to our understanding of an organization. Some of the concepts include purpose or goal, boundary, input, transformation or throughput, outputs, feedback, environment, hierarchy, equifinality, and entropy (see Table 16.1.)

A careful review of the comparative table reveals that some other common concepts

center around self-regulation, democracy, and participation. For the rest, there is much multiformity. North American STS theory is closest to classic STS; Scandinavian STS is most distant. The potential scope of North American, Australian, and Scandinavian STS is the local and regional community; the scope of Dutch STS seems to be restricted to the organization or enterprise and its direct environment (customers and suppliers).

The STS design theories are viewed as comprehensive. That is, they provide a guiding macro framework, they articulate a set of design principles with which to evaluate a design or redesign of an organization or an organization unit, and they have an established track record (Stebbins & Shani, 1989). The STS design orientations and principles seem to vary along the area of emphasis: social, technical, task, and structural design dimensions. All four orientations seem to include all the areas, yet a careful review of the key concepts and theories used seem to indicate that they stress one over the others.

Although all varieties successfully combine social and technical dimensions, North American

Table 16.1   Comparisons of the Key Concepts, Design Principles, and Change Processes Across the Four Streams of STS

North American STS		
Key Concepts	*Design Principles*	*Planned Change and Development Processes*
Open system thinking	Compatible with STS goals and values	Expert and consultant approach
Organization choice		Open systems scan and environmental analysis
Joint optimization	Specification of what, not how	
Minimum critical specification	Local control of key variances	Establishment of design team (mechanism)
Quality of working life	Boundary set–support congruence	Technical analysis variance control matrix
Variance control	Information to point of action	
Self-managed teams	Employees' power and authority	Social system, role network analysis
Democratic decision making		Joint optimization design
	Multifunctional, multiskilled personnel	Provisional design
	Incompletion–bridging transition	Implementation of the design along with evaluation of the plan and redesign

Australian STS		
Key Concepts	*Design Principles*	*Planned Change and Development Processes*
Open system thinking	Establish design ownership	Antiexpert, do-it-yourself method
Redundancy of functions and skills	Rationalization of conflict	
Long-term directive correlations	Representative total design team	Class of job or skill grouping
Six psychological requirements		Multiskilling table
Participative democratic planning	Overcome resisters of change	Organizational deep slice
	Development of desirable futures	Desirable future scenarios
Self-generative puzzle learning		Participative design workshop
Semiautonomous groups	Learning to learn and participate	Search conference or multisearch
Dissemination through leaders	Cope with complex environment	Elected design team
	Impact of leadership example	

Scandinavian STS		
Key Concepts	*Design Principles*	*Planned Change and Development Processes*
Open system thinking	Design for employability and sustainability	Communication-enabling process
Meaningful exchange of ideas		Organization mapping
Linguistic and pragmatic discourse	Equality of participants and ideas	Dialogue conference method
Institutional commitment	Interactive, deep slice project	Network-development conference
Interorganizational learning	Experience as valid knowledge	Regional promotion conference

Key Concepts	Design Principles	Planned Change and Development Processes
Organization as local process Intellectual humility Connecting work and society	Inclusive and active participation Shared understanding and learning Tolerance for ambiguity Broad-based democratic dialogue	Strategy forum and demo conference Large-scale societal change Many leading actors

Dutch STS

Key Concepts	Design Principles	Planned Change and Development Processes
Open system thinking Balance model (Ashby's law) Concept of aspect systems Functional deconcentration Human resource mobilization Integration performance and control Whole-task groups Controllability and control capacity	Design for controllability Parallelization of order flows Segmentation of order flows Building control capacity in jobs Self-design by knowledge transfer Top-down allocation of P-tasks Bottom-up allocation of C-tasks Reduction of process interferences	Expert and participative approach Rough strategic and system analysis Demarcation of system boundaries Detailed strategic and system analysis Reconsideration of product design Top-down P-structure redesign Bottom-up C-structure redesign Implementation and evaluation

and Dutch STS have more explicit engineering design orientations and feature new plants as a particular ground for experimentation with STS design principles, whereas Australian and Scandinavian STS emphasize the social development dimension to a greater extent. Similarly, the task and structural design dimensions seem to be an area of emphasis in the North American and Dutch orientations and a little less of an emphasis for the Australian and Scandinavian orientations. The Australian and North American approaches seem to highlight the design principles for the creation of learning mechanisms, whereas the Dutch orientation seems to emphasize design principles that integrate intelligent expert systems.

The third subfield of STS is the planned change orientation. All four varieties stress a comprehensive orientation that takes into account the business environment, the industrial context, and the regional or national context. The respective STS change and development processes seem to differ mostly in line with the regional and national cultures.

North American STS shows the most explicit expert approach, led and executed by qualified consultants. Australian STS demonstrates a do-it-yourself, antiexpert approach to change. In Scandinavian STS, change is only facilitated by a researcher, whereas in Dutch STS a combination of expert knowledge and participative processes is being used and put into practice by process consultants and trainers. North American and Dutch STS share normative, highly structured, stepwise methods, whereas Australian and Scandinavian STS join more free-floating methods, which are open to the parties' discretion.

The four STS streams dominated the STS literature in the last three decades of the 20th century. An important characteristic of the period of modern STS is the relative isolation in which those varieties could develop. Initially, there were several contacts between the founders, but gradually the four varieties embarked on their own journeys, reinforced by their own regional and national cultures (European, American, and Australian). In the 1990s STS streams started to merge and became more eclectic, predominantly as a consequence of the introduction of new technologies, the Internet, and increasing pressures for the development of alternative managerial and theoretical paradigms (Figure 16.2).

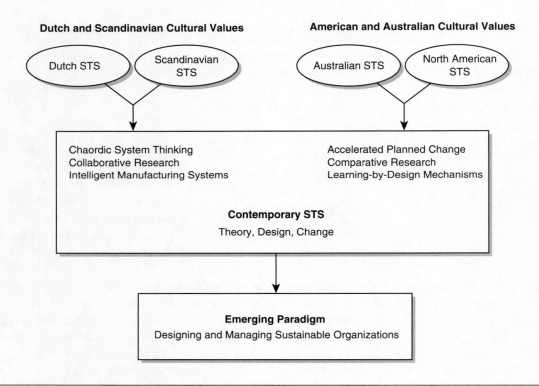

Figure 16.2   The Potential Merging of Regional STS Varieties Into a New Global Paradigm

A careful review of the literature suggests that in the past decade we witnessed the emergence of a new STS paradigm. The eclectic nature of what continues to emerge is worth pursuing as it sets the stage for the future creation of actionable knowledge and more sustainable work systems. As we have argued, the STS paradigm is well documented in the literature. This is true for its theories, its designs and change and development processes, and its practical applications and case studies (Table 16.2). This body of knowledge may serve as a future reference for human-centered organization renewal in industrial and office work.

Table 16.2 Partial Selection of Sociotechnical Applications Reported in the Literature, 1949–2004

Year	Details of Sociotechnical Application Literature	Reference
1949	Elsecar Mine, Haighmoor Seam, South Yorkshire, United Kingdom	Trist & Bamforth (1951)
1950	Bolsover Mines, East Midlands coalfield, United Kingdom	Shepherd (1951)
1952	Jubilee and Calico weaving mills, Ahmedabad, India	Rice (1953)
1959	Dutch Giro Service, The Hague, The Netherlands	Van Beinum (1959)
1962	Philips Audio/Video, assembly, Eindhoven, The Netherlands	Van Beek (1964)
1964	Christiania Spigerverk Wire Draw Plant, Oslo, Norway	Marek et al. (1964)
1965	Hunsfos Paper Mill, Vennesla, Kristiansand, Norway	Engelstad et al. (1969)
1965	NOBØ Household Appliances, Hommelvik, Norway	Thorsrud (1970)
1965	Alcan Aluminium Factory, Arvida, Kingston, Quebec, Canada	Gagnon & Blutot (1969)
1966	Coras Iompair Eireann, bus service, Dublin, Ireland	Van Beinum (1966)
1967	Norsk Hydro Fertilizer Plant, Heröya, Porsgrun, Norway	Gulowsen (1972)
1967	Shell Microwax Plant, Stanlow, Cheshire, United Kingdom	Burden & Derek (1975)
1968	Luv Pet Foods Plant, Sydney, Australia	Clark & Emery (unpublished)
1969	KNTU Textile Spinning Mill, Bamshoeve, Twente, The Netherlands	Allegro (1971)
1969	Philips Television Assembly Plant, Eindhoven, The Netherlands	Hertog & Kerkhof (1973)
1971	Gaines General Foods, pet food factory, Topeka, Kansas, United States	Ketchum (1975)
1972	Olivetti Components Factory, Ivrea, Italy	Butera (1975)
1972	Bang and Olufsen pick-up assembly, Stuer, Denmark	Larsen (1979)
1972	Saab-Scania engine factory, final assembly, Södertälje, Sweden	Norstedt & Agurén (1973)
1973	Community development project, Jamestown, New York, United States	Trist et al. (1978)
1973	General Motors Fisher body plant, Grand Rapids, Michigan, United States	Robison (1977)
1974	Volvo dock car assembly, Kalmar, Sweden	Agurén et al. (1976, 1984)
1974	South Australian Meat Corporation, Australia	Emery & Emery (1974)
1974	Community Planning Gungahlin, Canberra, NSW, Australia	M. Emery (1974)
1975	SEMA Pension Fund, executive services, Paris, France	Lefebvre & Rolloy (1976)
1975	Philips Machine Factory, Eindhoven, The Netherlands	Den Hertog & Wester (1979)
1975	Shell Polypropylene Plant, Sarnia, Ontario, Canada	Davis & Sullivan (1980)

(Continued)

Table 16.2   (Continued)

Year	Details of Sociotechnical Application Literature	Reference
1976	Rolls Royce automotive engineering works, Derby, United Kingdom	Mumford & Henshall (1979)
1977	Coal mine, Rushton, Pennsylvania, United States	Trist et al. (1977)
1978	Siemens Pneumatic Control Equipment, Karlsruhe, Germany	Schlitzberger (1978)
1978	Community development project, Sudbury, Ontario, Canada	Trist & Clarke (1981)
1979	Centraal Beheer Life Insurance, Apeldoorn, The Netherlands	Allegro & De Vries (1979)
1980	IHC Smit Shipyard, Kinderdijk, The Netherlands	Van Amersvoort (1982)
1980	Zilog (Exxon) microchip plant, Nampa, Idaho, United States	Taylor & Asadorian (1985)
1981	Railway Locomotives Maintenance Depot, Sennar, Sudan	Ketchum (1984)
1984	Signetics semiconductor plant, Sunnyvale, California, United States	Shani & Elliot (1988)
1985	Pratt & Whitney aircraft engines, Halifax, Nova Scotia, Canada	Betcherman et al. (1990)
1985	LOM Programme (80 enterprises), Work Environment Fund, Sweden	Gustavsen (1993)
1986	DAF Trucks final assembly, Eindhoven, The Netherlands	Van Eijnatten et al. (1986)
1988	HABUT Programme, Work Life Centre, Oslo, Norway	Qvale (1991)
1988	McNeil Consumer Products Factory CPC, Fort Washington, Pennsylvania, United States	Weisbord (1990)
1989	Volvo car assembly, Uddevalla, Sweden	Ellegård et al. (1991)
1989	Eagon Life Insurances, The Hague, The Netherlands	Boonstra (1992)
1992	Bendix Mintex pad moulding plant, Ballarat, VIC, Australia	Mathews et al. (1993)
1992	Swedish Railway repair shop, Hagalund, Sweden	Ehn (1995)
1992	Alcan Sheet Division, Granville, Australia	Dunphy & Berggren (1992)
1992	Philips Ceramic Multilayer Actuator Factory, Roermond, The Netherlands	Verkerk (2004)
1993	Xtree, software development firm, California, United States	Shani & Sena (1994)
1994	Telecom, California, United States	Terlaga (1994)
1995	Organon Pharmaceutics Industry, Oss, The Netherlands	Kollenburg (2003)
1996	Hope Project (SME's), European Commission, Brussels	Verweij (1997)
1997	Philips Glass Factory, Aachen, Germany	Verkerk (2004)
1997	Blue Shield of California, health care insurance company, United States	Stebbins & Shani (1998)

Year	Details of Sociotechnical Application Literature	Reference
1997	Multinational service corporation, United States	Taylor (1998)
1998	Celestica, international service company, Toronto, Canada	Halpern & Dyck (1999)
1998	Amberley Airforce Base, Queensland, Australia	Warne (2000)
1999	WCB Public Insurance Company, British Columbia, Canada	Painter (2004)
2000	Cases in Computer Supported Cooperative Work	Coakes et al. (2000)
2000	Global distance group work, Ann Arbor, Michigan, United States	Olsen & Olsen (2000)
2000	Machine industry, Switzerland	Grote et al. (2000)
2000	Superconducting electron accelerator lab, United States	Keating et al. (2001)
2001	PSIM project, European Commission, Brussels:	Van Eijnatten (2002)
	Volvo, Torslanda, Göteborg, Sweden	Davidsson et al. (2002)
	Finland Post, Helsinki, Finland	Little et al. (2002)
2002	Cases in Computer Supported Cooperative Work	Coakes et al. (2002)
2002	Seagate, California, United States	Sena & Shani (2002)
2003	Dutch Army, Breda, The Netherlands	Kramer (2004)
2003	Socio-Technical Interaction Networks, Bloomington, Indiana, United States	Kling et al. (2003)
2003	Integrated STS in complex systems, Sheffield, United Kingdom, and Germany	Waterson (2003)

CRITICAL REFLECTIONS

The STS paradigm originated in the post–World War II period and acted as a breakthrough of extreme Taylorist fractionation of work. Originally, production manufacturing was its main focus, and it offered solutions for mechanized processes in discrete manufacturing and process industries. As factory automation started in the 1970s, it was expected that STS solutions would expand and adapt. However, up until now—perhaps with the exception of some Dutch STS and North American STS (cf. van der Aalst et al., 2002; van Eijnatten, 2002; van Eijnatten, Berg, & Goossenaerts, 2000; van Eijnatten & Goossenaerts, 2004; Kolodny & Stjernberg, 1986; Loeffen & Wortmann, 1998; Pasmore et al., 1982; Pava, 1983a, 1983b; Shani & Elliott, 1988; Susman & Chase, 1986; Taylor & Felten, 1993) and some individual authors such as Mumford and Weir (1979) and Ehn (1988, 1989, 1992, 1995)—most STS variants stayed predominantly with the social psychological and sociological approaches to the design of work systems. STS increasingly lagged behind the dominant role information and communication technology (ICT) began to play in organizations. For instance, in the 1990s software tools such as work flow management systems began to take over the work allocation and control of office work by "secretly reinstalling" the Tayloristic fractionation and control of human work.

Increasing sophistication and complexity of technology, coupled with the increased emphasis on knowledge work, triggered the need to focus on nonlinear technical processes and R&D work. To date, we know remarkably little about STSs and professional and office work, despite the pioneering efforts of the late Cal Pava (1983a, 1983b) in North American STS and Lianne Simonse (1998) in Dutch STS. Knowledge-intensive firms are characterized by their emphasis on knowledge creation and use. Therefore, they have standard, routine, and nonroutine elements (Pasmore & Purser, 1993). At the most basic level, standards are applied to activities that are repetitive in an identical fashion. Therefore, a demonstrated best practice can be established by trial and error, tinkering the knowledge of underlying mechanisms and theories. Best practices can then be codified into manuals and verified through comparison of targets and actual outcomes. *Routine systems* are characterized as systems that address familiar but slightly dissimilar events through repetitive planning systems, decision rules, and algorithms that lead to routinized behavior. Measures of their success are efficiency criteria (i.e., cost, time) and customer satisfaction in variable situations that are expected to lead to market share and competitive strengths.

A *nonroutine system* is a system designed to address nonpredictable, surprising, and unfamiliar events through inquiry and learning systems with a capacity for problem solving. Success is evaluated by tracking resource mobilization, patience, innovation, and creation of new markets. Nonroutine systems are found in contexts that are continuously shifting, and the organization must deal with a high number of exceptions, high task variety, issues, and problems not addressed before. They have complex and difficult conversion processes. They need access to a variety of knowledge bases, need to mobilize networks both inside and outside the organization, and need to build mechanisms for integration of different specialties and are of an emergent character (Stebbins & Shani, 1995). Their conversion process cannot be described beforehand

but develops as the system encounters emergent challenges. Success can be determined only afterwards. Therefore, the STS body of knowledge is missing deeper insights into our understanding of nonroutine situations and the possible dynamic interplay between routine and nonroutine elements.

Recent literature seems to focus more on the integration of STSs and computer-supported cooperative work (Coakes, Willis, & Lloyd-Jones, 2000). Yet a careful review of the emerging body of knowledge reveals that most of the time the traditional, classic sociotechnical approach is embraced and applied without serious attempts to significantly modify the STS approach to the fundamentally changed work contexts.

The evolution of virtual work and contemporary work systems presents a new set of challenges. We do not know much about contemporary work systems or work systems that integrate permanent and temporary workers, in which the unity of time, place, and action is no longer present. This is the case in all virtual work systems. The new questions become "How do complex technical systems influence the work of people?" and "How can complex technical systems be influenced in order to create meaningful work?"

Currently, work–life challenges are significant. On one level, because of automation, personal autonomy has increased to more than optimal levels. Similarly, because modern ICT technology fundamentally broke the unity of place, time, and action, work and private life have blurred. As a consequence, work intensity has increased dramatically and has become the primary work–life problem in Europe at the beginning of the 21st century (Docherty, Forslin, & Shani, 2002; van Eijnatten, 2000). People feel overwhelmed by excessive, often self-induced mental workloads (Kira, 2003). Burnout is common among young professionals. STS simply does not specify what healthy work means under these new conditions.

In a reflective manuscript, Pasmore (1994) examines the necessary shifts from the STS paradigm in the 1950s to the application of STS today. He identifies eight significant shifts that have occurred:

1. From the primary concern being on the dominance of science and technology over human needs and contributions to the instability of organization arrangements and employment security

2. From technology being dominated by assembly lines, process technology, and large batch production to technology being dominated by computers

3. From employees' understanding of the technology and the need to develop empowerment to skills that lag behind technical and business developments where education is needed

4. From efficiency as the primary concern of intelligent managers to learning as the primary concern of intelligent managers

5. From the notions that ecological environments should be exploited to ecological environments that are to be protected

6. From organizations being viewed as independent actors in competition for survival to organizations being viewed as increasingly interlinked through alliances and networks, where collaboration for survival is the underlying truth

7. From culture as viewed primarily as male and national or continent-centric to culture that is diverse

8. From less-developed countries as sources of cheap labor and raw materials to less-developed countries as potential markets

The 55 years of STS theoretical development that have addressed design challenges and worked through complex planned change processes has advanced our understanding of the design and management of workplace complexity. Yet five areas merit further investigation for the creation of actionable knowledge: creating actionable knowledge that focuses on the integration of advanced information and communication technology; deeper theoretical development and understanding of knowledge-intensive firms' design (the nature of non-routine designs and the possible dynamic interplay between routine and nonroutine elements); the nature of contemporary work systems and work systems that integrate permanent and temporary workers in which the unity of time, place, and action is no longer present; creating actionable knowledge that focuses on the issues of sustainable systems as a countermeasure to work intensity that has increased dramatically and has become a major work–life problem; and deeper theoretical understanding of the transformation process, learning mechanisms, and time horizon.

EMERGING STS TRENDS AND FUTURE RESEARCH

The current business context, the changes in technological and social systems, and the emerging trends of the past 55 years necessitate the development of a new paradigm and the creation of new actionable knowledge about STS. In this section we identify and explore areas that emerge from this review as a possible starting point for future actionable knowledge creation and dialogue. This platform focuses on the integration of chaordic system thinking, the role of intelligent manufacturing, the challenge of designing and managing sustainable work systems, the challenges of collaborative and comparative research, accelerated planned change, and the integration of learning-by-design mechanisms.

Integrating Chaordic System Thinking Into STS

Historically, STS was based on OST, in which system change is seen primarily as the exception rather than the rule, a temporary unfreezing in a short journey from the old into a new steady state. OST's emphasis on stability increasingly became a dilemma in today's turbulent business contexts. A recent development is called chaordic system thinking (CST) (see van Eijnatten, 2001; van Eijnatten & Putnik, 2004a; Fitzgerald & van Eijnatten, 2002). Through this lens, change is viewed as the rule rather than an exception.

Organizations travel during their life cycles between multiple attractor states, ranging from order to chaos, and in order to prevent decay they may jump to higher levels of complexity in a constantly changing fitness landscape. This view is consistent with the way human beings learn through qualitative leaps in their thinking (van Eijnatten, 2004).

Although STS's terminology has changed dramatically in order to enable a dynamic, nonlinear approach, the basic STS purpose remains the same: to enable better use of people and technology and nurture participative democracy. The intent is to create organizations that are capable of enabling human development and growth and giving the human being, instead of the technology, discretion over the work. Integrating CST with STS thinking might provide a theoretical platform from which to launch a new research agenda that addresses the emerging challenges of today's work life.

Role of Intelligent Manufacturing

Intelligent manufacturing is slowly but steadily becoming a reality in contemporary production environments (van Eijnatten et al., 2000; Vink & van Eijnatten, 2002). In the highly competitive global marketplace, manufacturing companies are forced to optimize their production processes at an ever-increasing rate. However, specialized technical staff groups tend to improve only one single aspect, mostly technological, with suboptimal results. Therefore, a participatory and more integral approach must be developed to help companies improve their work organizations. But more importantly, contemporary sociotechnical prototypes should be embedded in state-of-the-art software. This ambition was realized in a recent project (van Eijnatten, 2002). The project, Participative Simulation Environment for Integral Manufacturing Enterprise Renewal (PSIM), was sponsored by the EU 5th Framework IST (information systems and technology) project and is a part of the global Intelligent Manufacturing Systems program.

The PSIM project resulted in a digital language to enable better communication between several software packages, and a navigator was built to make the PSIM system usable for different participants. Also, additional software was developed to enable the subtraction of data from the enterprise resource planning system (integrator). In this project, participative simulation was used in which workers exert direct influence over the product and process designs by bringing in their tacit knowledge to combine it with expert knowledge and to put the blend of both insights to the test. The moment these experimenting and problem-solving activities are supported by an attractive ICT interface, the resulting continuous improvement process may become even more intrinsically motivating for the workforce and will contribute to the competitive advantage of the enterprise (van Eijnatten & Goossenaerts, 2004).

The goal of participative simulation in general and of the respective simulation tools in particular is not to deliver factual solutions to users but to support them in reflecting on their own work situations and elaborating on their own tailor-made solutions. Those kinds of solutions are also highly desirable in knowledge work. Finally, a new generation of work flow–management systems is being developed, using Dutch STS principles in order to give the self-managed team some discretion over their work (van der Aalst, Rutte, & van Eijnatten, 2002). The integration of intelligent manufacturing and new software systems provides a unique opportunity for advancing the design and theoretical understanding of the new work environment.

Challenge of Designing and Managing Sustainable Work Systems

Promoting sustainable and competitive growth is today a key issue in many industrialized countries. At the core of sustainability is the notion that due weight is given to the legitimate needs and ambitions of all stakeholders. In business and working life, the stakeholders are employees, owners, customers, and society. The balancing of these interests is a main task for management. Failure to achieve balance can have negative effects for one or more stakeholders. At the individual level, it may result in increased intensity of work, limited creativity, stress, and ill health. At the organizational level, it may lead to decreased innovative capacity, market share, and profitability (van Eijnatten & Shani, 2000).

Managers at different levels, from the shop floor manager to the CEO, make judgments and decisions that affect the health of employees and the competitiveness of the organization. High and continuous levels of stress cause inferior decisions that result in bad working conditions. It has been shown that managers with a high level of stress exercise leadership that in itself creates bad health as they become unclear or authoritarian in their leadership and thus create insecurity and fear among their employees.

We use the term *sustainability* to describe the ability to maintain and develop an organization and its employees over a long period of time. In this context it refers to the purposeful design of processes and activities that give due weight to the legitimate needs and ambitions of the different stakeholders in a work context. In business and working life, the principal stakeholders are employees, owners, customers, and society. The needs and ambitions of the stakeholders may refer to ongoing activities in present conditions and planned changes and developments in activities to meet expected future conditions. The core concept of sustainable work systems is that the resources deployed are regenerated by the system. Human resources to be fostered include skills, knowledge, cooperation and trust, employability, constructive industrial relations, and broader institutional or societal prerequisites (Docherty et al., 2002). From an organization perspective the sustainability goals refer to competitiveness, innovativeness, productivity, value creation, and organization learning.

Organizations that act in competition are seldom sustainable over a long period of time. For example, very few organizations reach the age of 50. Industries are characterized by strong consolidation to a few dominating actors competing through cost and process efficiency (Utterback, 1994). The few successful and surviving organizations then get captured by their former success and develop strategies, structures, incentives, and capabilities that act primarily to protect the historical success. The organizations become less responsive to signals of upcoming changes in core technologies or market dynamics (Leonard-Barton, 1992), systematically underestimate the value of new opportunities (Christensen, 1997), and avoid opportunities that are perceived by the decision makers and opinion leaders to challenge the present technological skills and market relations. As some of the literature suggests, STS provides the framework, design principles, learning mechanisms, and change processes that can provide the foundation for facilitating sustainability. A research focus on the interplay between key features of STS and sustainability is likely to generate new insights and more sustainable work systems.

Challenge of Collaborative Research

Review of the current body of knowledge reveals that although action research stimulated the development of STS, most research on STS attempted to use traditional research approaches and methods. This orientation seems to have generated a static body of knowledge that is not always relevant (Stebbins & Shani, 2002). Parallel to the development of the traditional research approaches, we have witnessed the development of more participative research approaches that attempt to generate knowledge that satisfies both the scientific community and organization members. The growing body of knowledge about collaborative research suggests a variety of alternatives to create actionable knowledge about STS in which action research is only one stream. The origin of the collaborative research approaches can be traced to the work of John Collier and Kurt Lewin in the late 1940s and early 1950s, who, independently of each other, coined the term *action research* (Pasmore, 2001).

Collaborative research is defined as an emergent and systematic inquiry process, embedded in a true partnership between researchers and members of a living system, in which behavioral, social, organizational, and management scientific knowledge is integrated with existing organization knowledge for the purpose of generating actionable knowledge (Adler et al., 2004; Shani, Mohrman, Pasmore, Stymne, & Adler, 2008). At the most basic level, collaborative research brings about the challenge of balance and interdependence between actors, between academic research and actual applications, between knowledge creation and problem solving, and between inquiry from the inside and inquiry from the outside. It is a partnership between a variety of individuals forming a community of inquiry and is viewed as an emergent inquiry process that differs from the notion of scientific research as a closed, linear, and planned activity.

The ultimate success of knowledge creation about STS depends on how the different knowledge actor groups or microcommunities relate through the knowledge creation process. Collaborative research is viewed as an enabler for the understanding of STS because it provides the methods, mechanisms, and processes for interactions between the microcommunities of knowledge and other relevant individuals inside and outside the organization for the purpose of creating new knowledge.

Challenge of Comparative Research

Developing a deeper level understanding of STS can benefit from comparative-based research. Yet a review of the literature reveals very few comparative-based empirical studies that focused on STS. The multiple levels of complexity that surround the conduct of such research seem to be a major impediment to such initiatives. The complexity of the research process, although different in nature, seems to be part of both the traditional research and comparative research paths.

In a comparative study (Lillrank et al., 1998) that followed the more traditional research path, the authors examined the design of eight different organizations in a variety of locations on three continents. The team of six researchers developed a theoretical model and a comparative conceptual-based framework, had a set of hypotheses to be tested, collected the data, developed comprehensive cases that captured each organization, worked through the data as a team in order to develop shared meaning, and attempted to draw scientific conclusions. Although the researchers managed to develop a good picture of each organization, the complexity of the context in which an organization functioned limited the ability to draw clear and valid scientific generalizations about organization design.

The potential of coupling comparative-based and collaborative-based research orientations is intriguing. Yet the dynamic and emergent nature of collaborative research adds another layer of complexity to any attempt to conduct comparative-based research about STS. Our view is that developing the mechanisms and methods that will allow such research to take place will provide new insights and a deeper-level of understanding STS theory and design.

Accelerated Planned Change

A review of the planned change orientations that emerged on the different continents reveals that all have advocated a slow planned change process that can last anywhere from 6 to 24 months, based on the firm's size, culture, and business context. The reality of the changing global business context and increased global competition indicates that such a length of time for organization transformation is problematic. The challenge faced by planned change experts, designers, and researchers is to find new ways that can accelerate the process.

As was discussed earlier, the integration of software technology and search conference methods into the data collection and analysis phases seems to accelerate the process. In addition, a few accelerated STS-based approaches are being developed. For example, organization fitness profiling is an accelerated strategic organization learning process recently developed that enables senior management to assess the fit between the business environment and the organization's capabilities and realign the organization design toward a desired state (Beer, 2001; Beer & Eisenstat, 2004). Although the development of communities of inquiry and communities of action seems to take time and demonstrate multilevel benefits, a reexamination of the degree and practice of democratic dialogue and participation during the redesign process can add new insights and organization redesign alternatives.

Integrating Learning-by-Design Mechanisms Into STS

Almost at the opposite side of the continuum from accelerated planned change, one can find literature that advocates the development of organization learning mechanisms as a way to facilitate continuous design and redesign of the firm. Learning mechanisms are viewed as the formal and informal configuration—structures, processes, procedures, rules, tools, methods, and physical configurations—created within the firm for the purpose of developing, enhancing, and sustaining performance and learning. Just as there are many types of organization designs, there are also various ways to design and manage organization learning mechanisms. The design of a specific configuration is viewed as a rational choice between alternatives based on learning design needs and learning design dimensions. Recent research suggests that, in practice, organization learning mechanisms could be designed and managed in various ways. These ways have been described as a set of learning design dimensions, each of which fulfills a necessary learning requirement for achieving learning and performance. Thus, the learning design dimensions are a basic set of alternative solutions managers can choose from in order to meet the learning design requirements. The range of alternatives must be investigated by every organization and could integrate some alternative solutions from the literature and benchmark-existing solutions (Shani & Docherty, 2003).

The set of necessary but not sufficient learning requirements for achieving learning is called learning design requirements. Some examples of learning design requirements might include the following: A legitimate forum for exchange of ideas must be created; a specific set of processes that facilitate ongoing participation, dialogue, and conversations must be developed; a specific set of tools need to be developed or adopted that facilitate learning; the design forum and processes must reflect and incorporate the totality of the organization and not just parts; and goals and objectives that define the direction of the learning efforts must be formulated. Some examples of learning design dimensions might include the following: Is learning an integral part of ordinary work? Is learning work performed in a permanent working group or a specially formed task force? Are group members from one or several functions? Are the group members from the same or different levels? Is goal setting made centrally or in the groups? Is it process guided or free?

The learning design dimensions represent different possible ways to respond to the learning design requirements. Along each learning design dimension is a range of choices an organization designer can make. The conscious choices could be functionally equivalent ways to achieve the same objectives in a different context. An integral part of the rational decision-making process is to identify the external and internal conditions necessitating improvements in the existing learning mechanisms or the decision to create a new one, identify the specific learning design requirements that fit the business situation and business dynamics and investigate and explore the alternative most appropriate learning design dimensions for the firm. Learning mechanisms provide a platform for ongoing organization learning, reflection, and action and a way to advance the theoretical understanding of work and organization design and organization redesign process.

CONCLUSION

In the 55 years of its existence, the STS field evolved from the accidental discovery of a self-managed work team in a British coal mine, via an approach to industrial democracy in Scandinavia, into a modern system paradigm with multiple regional variants. We have clustered the distinct developments into regional areas: North American STS, Australian STS, or "Participative Design," Scandinavian STS or "Democratic Dialogue," and Dutch STS or "Integral Organizational Renewal." Within each, we have identified the people who have contributed to the development of the field, the key concepts and theories, the design principles that were advanced, and the planned change and development processes. A partial comparative discussion led to the identification and initial discussion of the emerging eclectic and more global STS framework. Some of the gaps that were identified include the need to create actionable knowledge that focuses on the integration of advanced information and communication technology; deeper theoretical development and understanding of knowledge-intensive firms' design (the nature of non-routine designs and the possible dynamic interplay between routine and nonroutine elements); the nature of contemporary work systems and work systems that integrate permanent and temporary workers in which the unity of time, place, and action is no longer present; creating actionable knowledge that focuses on the issues of sustainable systems as a countermeasure to work intensity that has increased dramatically and has become a major work–life problem; and deeper theoretical understanding of the transformation process, learning mechanisms, and time horizon. Next, areas for future research were identified and discussed, namely the integration of chaordic system thinking, the role of intelligent manufacturing, the challenge of designing and managing sustainable work systems, the challenge of collaborative research, the challenge of comparative research, accelerated planned change, and the integration of learning-by-design mechanisms.

In 2004 the North American STS Roundtable started a deliberation in order to develop a new sociotechnical approach (STS Roundtable, 2004). This network took a pivotal position and the responsibility to start renewal activities in the United States. STS continues to evolve as a dynamic paradigm that incorporates the changing business environment while building on the foundations and contributions that were generated in the past five decades. The path toward a future workplace that is more responsive to changing business needs, more informed about the unique characteristics of the business context, technology, and ICT, and characterized by optimal use and development of business, human potential, and creativity is challenging. The cumulative experience and knowledge created in the past 50 years provides the foundation as we embark on the challenges of designing and managing sustainable organizations in the new millennium.

NOTES

Note: The authors appreciate the input and suggestions from Niclas Adler, Tom Cummings, Peter Docherty, Jan Forslyn, Harvey Kolodny, Yoram Mitki, Bill Pasmore, Jim Sena, Mike Stebbins, and Bengt Stymne on an earlier version of this manuscript.

1. We used the following literature sources in preparing this section: Cherns (1976, 1987), Susman (1976), Cummings, (1978), Cummings and Srivastva (1977), Pasmore et al. (1982), Davis (1983), Pasmore (1988, 2001), Shani and Elliott (1989), Stebbins and Shani (1989), Kolodny (1990), Macy and Izumi, (1993), van Eijnatten (1993), Taylor and Felten (1993), Stebbins, Sena, and Shani (1995), Berniker (1996), Mitki, Shani, and Stjernberg (2000), and de Leede, Looise, and Verkerk (2002).

2. We used the following literature sources in preparing this section: F. Emery (1959, 1969, 1989), Emery and Emery (1974), M. Emery (1982, 1989), Stebbins and Shani (1989), Taylor and Felten (1993), van Eijnatten (1993), Dunphy and Griffiths (1998), and de Leede et al. (2002).

3. We used the following literature sources in preparing this section: Adler and Docherty (1998), Emery and Thorsrud (1964, 1976), Gustavsen (1991, 1992, 1993), Kolodny and Stjernberg (1986), van Eijnatten (1993), and de Leede et al. (2002).

4. We used the following literature sources in preparing this section: de Sitter, den Hertog, and van Eijnatten (1990), de Sitter, den Hertog, and Dankbaar (1997), van Eijnatten (1993), de Sitter (1994), van Eijnatten and van der Zwaan (1998), van Amersvoort (2000), and de Leede et al. (2002).

REFERENCES

Aalst, W. van der, Rutte, C. G., & Eijnatten, F. M. van. (2002, April). *Workflow management systems: Moving from process-centric to user-centric*. Research Proposal Institute for Business Engineering and Technology Application (BETA), Eindhoven University of Technology, The Netherlands.

Abrahamsson, B. (1977). *Bureaucracy or participation: The logic of organization*. Beverly Hills, CA: Sage.

Adler, N., & Docherty, P. (1998). Bringing business into socio-technical theory and practice. *Human Relations, 51*(3), 319–345.

Adler, N., Shani, A. B., & Styhre, A. (Eds.). (2004). *Collaborative research in organizations: Foundations for learning, change, and theoretical development*. Thousand Oaks, CA: Sage.

Agurén, S., Bredbacka, C., Hansson, R., Ihregren, K., & Karlsson, K. G. (1984). *Volvo Kalmar revisited: Ten years of experience*. Stockholm: Trykert Balder.

Agurén, S., Hansson, R., & Karlsson, K. G. (1976). *The Volvo Kalmar plant: The impact of new design on work organization*. Stockholm: The Rationalization Council SAF-LO.

Allegro, J. T. (1971). Socio-technische organisatieontwikkeling en veranderend leiderschap [Socio-technical organization development and changing leadership]. *M&O: Tijdschrift voor Organisatiekunde en Social Beleid, 47*(1), 39–54.

Allegro, J. T., & Vries, E. de. (1979). Project: Humanization and participation in Centraal Beheer. In A. Alioth, J. Blake, M. Butteriss, E. Elden, O. Ortsman, & R. van der Vlist (Eds.), *Working on the quality of working life: Developments in Europe* (pp. 223–237). Boston: Martinus Nijhoff/International Council for the Quality of Working Life.

Amersvoort, P. J. L. M. van. (1982). *Samen werken aan samenwerking: Een socio-technische procesanalyse van de sector werf van IHC-Smit b.v. te Kinderdijk* [Working together to accomplish cooperation: A socio-technical process analysis of the shipyard of IHC-Smit in Kinderdijk]. Eindhoven, The Netherlands: Eindhoven University of Technology.

Amersvoort, P. J. L. M. van. (2000). *The design of work and organization: The modern socio-technical systems approach*. Vlijmen, The Netherlands: ST-Groep.

Beek, H. G. van. (1964). The influence of the assembly line organization on output, quality and morale. *Occupational Psychology, 38*(3/4), 161–172.

Beer, M. (2001). Embrace the drive for results–capability development paradox. *Organizational Dynamics, 29*(4), 233–247.

Beer, M., & Eisenstat, R. (2004, February). How to have an honest conversation. *Harvard Business Review, 82*, 82–89.

Beinum, H. J. J. van. (1959). *Interim-rapport over de proefafdeling Zaanstraat* [Interim report on the test department Zaanstraat]. The Hague,

The Netherlands: Post-Cheque-en Girodienst (PCGD), Afdeling Sociaal Wetenschappelijk Onderzoek.

Beinum, H. J. J. van. (1966). *The morale of the Dublin busmen*. London: Tavistock.

Berniker, E. (1996). *Some principles of socio-technical systems: Analysis and design*. Tacoma, WA: Pacific Lutheran University, School of Business Administration.

Betcherman, G., Newton, K., & Godin, J. (1990). Systems and people: Managing socio-technical change at Pratt and Whitney Canada. In Canadian Publishing Centre (Ed.), *Two steps forward: Human resource management in a high-tech world*. Ottawa: Canadian Government Publishing Centre.

Boonstra, J. J. (1992). *Integrale organisatieontwikkeling: Vormgeven aan fundamentele veranderingsprocessen* [Integral organizational development: Shaping fundamental changes]. Utrecht, The Netherlands: Lemma.

Bregard, A., Gulowsen, J., Haug, O., Hangen, F., Solstad, E., Thorsrud, E., et al. (1968). *Norsk Hydro: Experiment in the fertilizer factories*. Oslo: Work Research Institute.

Burden, D. W. F., & Derek, W. E. (1975). Participative management as a basis for improved quality of jobs: The case of Microwax department. Shell U.K. Ltd. In L. E. Davis & A. B. Cherns (Eds.), *The quality of working life, vol. II: Cases and commentary* (pp. 166–200). New York: Free Press.

Bushe, G. R., & Shani, A. B. (1991). *Parallel learning structures: Increasing innovation in bureaucracies*. Reading, MA: Addison-Wesley.

Butera, F. (1975). Environmental factors in job and organization design: The case of Olivetti. In L. E. Davis & A. B. Cherns (Eds.), *The quality of working life* (Vol. 2., pp. 166–200). New York: Free Press.

Chase, T. (Ed.). (1991–2000). *The STS Roundtable readings*. Northwood, NH: STS Roundtable.

Cherns, A. B. (1976). The principles of socio-technical design. *Human Relations, 29*(8), 783–792.

Cherns, A. B. (1987). The principles of socio-technical design revisited. *Human Relations, 40*(3), 153–161.

Christensen, C. (1997). *The innovator's dilemma: When new technologies cause great firms to fail*. Cambridge, MA: Harvard Business School Press.

Coakes, E., Willis, D., & Clarke, S. (Eds.). (2002). *Knowledge management in the socio-technical world: The graffiti continues*. London: Springer Verlag.

Coakes, E., Willis, D., & Lloyd-Jones, R. (Eds.). (2000). *The new sociotech: Graphity on the long wall*. London: Springer Verlag.

Coghlan, D., & Brannick, T. (2005). *Doing action research in your own organization*. London: Sage.

Cummings, T. G. (1978). Self-regulating work groups: A socio-technical synthesis. *Academy of Management Review, 3*, 625–634.

Cummings, T. G., & Srivastva, S. (1977). *Management of work. A socio-technical systems approach*. San Diego, CA: University Associates.

Daft, R. L. (2005). *Organization theory and design* (7th ed.). Cincinnati, OH: Thompson/South-Western.

Davidsson, A., Little, S., Rhijn, G. van, & Rönnäng, M. (2002). Test at Volvo. In F. M. van Eijnatten (Ed.), *PSIM: Participative simulation environment for integral manufacturing enterprise renewal* (pp. 103–114). Hoofddorp, The Netherlands: TNO Arbeid/The PSIM Consortium.

Davis, L. E. (1983). Learning from the design of new organizations. In H. F. Kolodny & H. J. J. van Beinum (Eds.), *The quality of working life and the 1980s* (pp. 65–86). New York: Praeger.

Davis, L. E., & Cherns, A. B. (Eds.). (1975). *The quality of working life* (Vols. I and II). New York: Free Press.

Davis, L. E., & Sullivan, C. S. (1980). A labour–management contract and quality of working life. *Occupational Behaviour, 1*(1), 29–41.

Docherty, P., Forslin, J., & Shani, A. B. (Eds.). (2002). *Creating sustainable work systems: Emerging perspectives and practice*. London: Routledge.

Dunphy, D., & Berggren, C. (1992). *Industrial renewal at Alcan sheet division*. Unpublished manuscript. Sydney: University of New South Wales, Centre for Corporate Change, Australian Graduate School of Management.

Dunphy, D., & Griffiths, A. (1998). *The sustainable corporation: Organizational renewal in Australia*. Sydney: Allen & Unwin.

Ehn, P. (1988). *Work-oriented design of computer artifacts*. Stockholm: Arbetslivscentrum/Almqvist and Wiksell.

Ehn, P. (1989). *Work-oriented design of computer artifacts* (2nd ed.). Hillsdale, NJ: Lawrence Erlbaum.

Ehn, P. (1992). Setting the stage for design as action: Artifacts for participatory design in theory and practice. *Nordic Journal of Architectural Research (Nordisk Arkitekturforskning), 4*, 49–59.

Ehn, P. (1995). *On the right track: Report on the local planning system (LPS) project, 1992–1994* [Videotape]. Hagalund, Sweden: Railway Repair Workshop.

Eijnatten, F. M. van. (1993). *The paradigm that changed the work place*. Assen/Stockholm: Van Gorcum/Arbetslivscentrum.

Eijnatten, F. M. van. (1998). Developments in socio-technical systems design. In P. J. D. Drenth, H. Thierry, & C. J. de Wolff (Eds.), *Handbook of organizational psychology. Vol. 4: Organizational psychology* (pp. 61–88). Sussex, UK: Psychology Press.

Eijnatten, F. M. van. (1999). Design clássico de sistemas sociotécnicos: O paradigma organizacional do design sociotécnico [Classical sociotechnical systems design (STSD): The socio-technical design paradigm of organizations]. In M. P. Cunha (Ed.), *Teoria organizacional: Perspectivas e prospectivas* [Organization theory: Perspectives and prospects] (pp. 127–165). Lisbon: Publicações Dom Quixote, Biblioteca de Economia e Empresa.

Eijnatten, F. M. van. (2000). *From intensive to sustainable work systems: The quest for a new paradigm of work*. Keynote speech at the TUTB/SALTSA Conference "Working Without Limits: Re-Organizing Work and Reconsidering Workers' Health," Brussels, 25–27 September. In M. Sapir (Ed.), Conference proceedings: Plenary sessions (pp. 47–66). Brussels: TUTB.

Eijnatten, F. M. van. (2001). Chaordic systems for holonic organizational renewal. In W. A. Pasmore & R. W. Woodman (Eds.), *Research in organizational change and development* (Vol. 13, pp. 213–251). San Francisco: JAI/Elsevier.

Eijnatten, F. M. van (Ed.). (2002). *PSIM: Participative simulation environment for integral manufacturing enterprise renewal*. Hoofddorp, The Netherlands: TNO Arbeid/ The PSIM Consortium.

Eijnatten, F. M. van. (2004). Chaordic systems thinking: Some suggestions for a complexity framework to inform a learning organization. *The Learning Organization, 11*(6), 430–449.

Eijnatten, F. M. van, Berg, R. J. van den, & Goossenaerts, J. B. M. (2000). ICT-supported participative simulation to enable integrated intellectual capital management. In B. Stanford-Smith & P. T. Kidd (Eds.), *E-business: Key issues, applications and technologies* (pp. 659–665). Amsterdam: IOS Press.

Eijnatten, F. M. van, Buyse, J. J., Hendriks, H. J., & Desmares, J. G. W. (1986). *Grenzen voor productiecellen: Ervaringen met het formeren van pseudo-autonome groepen in een truck-eindassemblage-fabriek* [Boundaries for production cells: Experiences with designing pseudo-autonomous work groups in truck assembly]. Nijmegen, The Netherlands: Katholieke Universiteit, KWO-Research Groep.

Eijnatten, F. M. van, Eggermont, S. J. C., Goffau, G. T. A. de, & Mankoe, I. (1994). *The socio-technical systems design (STSD) paradigm: A full bibliography of 3082 English-language literature references (release FBEL 05T)*. Eindhoven, The Netherlands: University of Technology, Graduate School of Industrial Engineering and Management Science.

Eijnatten, F. M. van, & Goossenaerts, J. B. M. (2004). Towards human-profile based operations in advanced factory governance systems: Contemporary challenges for socio-technical systems design? In E. Aray & T. Arai (Eds.), *Proceedings of the 5th International Conference on Machine Automation, ICMA 2004, "Mechatronics for Safety, Security, and Dependability in New Era,"* Osaka University, Osaka, Japan, November 24–26, pp. 529–534.

Eijnatten, F. M. van, & Putnik, G. D. (Guest Eds.). (2004a). Chaordic systems thinking for learning organizations. *The Learning Organization, 11*(5, Special Issue).

Eijnatten, F. M. van, & Putnik, G. D. (2004b). Chaos, complexity, learning, and the learning organization: Towards a chaordic enterprise. *The Learning Organization, 11*(6), 418–429.

Eijnatten, F. M. van, & Shani, A. B. (Eds.). (2000). *From intensive to sustainable work systems: Beyond time limitations in the European context.* Symposium presented at the Academy of Management Annual Meeting, Toronto, August 4–9.

Eijnatten, F. M. van, & Zwaan, A. H. van der. (1998, March). The Dutch IOR approach to organizational design. An alternative to business process re-engineering? *Human Relations, 51*(3), 289–318.

Elden, M. (1986). Socio-technical systems ideas as public policy in Norway. Empowering participation through worker-managed change. *Journal of Applied Behavioral Sciences, 22,* 239–255.

Elden, M., & Chisholm R. F. (1993). Emerging varieties of action research, *Human Relations, 46*(2), 121–142.

Ellegård, K., Engström, T., & Nilsson, L. (1991). *Reforming industrial work: Principles and realities in the planning of Volvo's car assembly plant in Uddevalla.* Stockholm: Swedish Work Environment Fund.

Emery, F. E. (1959). *Characteristics of socio-technical systems.* London: Tavistock Institute.

Emery, F. E. (Ed.). (1969). *Systems thinking: Selected readings.* Harmondsworth, UK: Penguin.

Emery, F. E. (1974). *Participant design.* Canberra, NSW: Australian National University, Centre for Continuing Education.

Emery, F. E. (Ed.). (1979). *Systems thinking* (Vol. II). Harmondsworth, UK: Penguin.

Emery, F. E. (1989). The light on the hill: Skill formation or democratization of work. In M. Emery (Ed.), *Participative design for participative democracy* (pp. 89–89). Canberra, NSW: Australian National University, Centre for Continuing Education.

Emery, F. E. (1995, April). *Replies to reviews of volume two by Pasmore and Scarbrough (HR, 1995). Contrary perspectives to socio-technical theory.* Unpublished mimeo.

Emery, F. E., & Emery, M. (1974). *Participative design: Work and community life.* Canberra, NSW: Australian National University, Centre for Continuing Education.

Emery, F. E., & Thorsrud, E. (1964). *Form and content of industrial democracy. Some experiments from Norway and other European countries.* Oslo: Oslo University Press.

Emery, F. E., & Thorsrud, E. (1976). *Democracy at work. The report of the Norwegian industrial democracy program.* Leiden, The Netherlands: Martinus Nijhoff.

Emery, M. (Ed.). (1974). *Planning our town: Gungahlin.* Canberra, NSW: Australian National University, Centre for Continuing Education.

Emery, M. (1982). *Searching: For new directions, in new ways, for new times* (rev. ed.). Canberra, NSW: Australian National University, Centre for Continuing Education.

Emery, M. (Ed.). (1989). *Participative design for participative democracy.* Canberra, NSW: Australian National University, Centre for Continuing Education.

Emery, M. (1994). Workplace Australia: Lessons for the planning and design of multisearches. *Journal of Applied Behavioral Science, 28*(4), 520–533.

Emery, M. (1995). *Searching.* Amsterdam: John Benjamin.

Emery, M., & Purser, R. E. (1996). *Search conferences in action.* San Francisco: Jossey-Bass.

Engelstad, P. H., Emery, F. E., & Thorsrud, E. (1969). *The Hunsfos experiment.* Oslo: The Work Research Institute.

Fitzgerald, L. A., & Eijnatten, F. M. van (Guest Eds.). (2002, July). Chaos: Applications in organizational change. *Journal of Organizational Change Management, 15*(4).

Friedlander, F., & Brown, L. (1974). Organization development. *Annual Review of Psychology, 25,* 313–341.

Gagnon, J. J., & Blutot, E. (1969). *Autonomous groups in aluminium reduction.* Unpublished report.

Griffiths, A. (1995). Socio-technical interventions and teams in Australia: 1970s–1990s. *The Economic and Labour Relations Review, 6*(1), 73–93.

Grote, G., Ryser, C., Wäfler, T., Windischer, A., & Weik, S. (2000). KOMPASS: A method for complementary function allocation in automated work systems. *International Journal of Human–Computer Studies, 52*(2), 267–287.

Gulowsen, J. (1972). *Norsk Hydro.* Oslo: Work Research Institute.

Gustavsen, B. (1985). Workplace reform and democratic dialogue. *Economic and Industrial Democracy, 6*(4), 461–479.

Gustavsen, B. (1991). The LOM program: A network-based strategy for organization development in Sweden. In R. W. Woodman & W. A. Pasmore (Eds.), *Research in organizational change and development* (Vol. 5, 285–315). Greenwich, CT: JAI.

Gustavsen, B. (1992). *Dialogue and development: Theory of communication, action research and the restructuring of working life.* Stockholm/Assen: The Swedish Center for Working Life/Van Gorcum.

Gustavsen, B. (1993). Action research and the generation of knowledge. *Human Relations, 46*(11), 1361–1365.

Halpernn, N., & Dyck, R. (1999, September–October). Organization redesign at Celestica. *Journal for Quality and Participation,* 36–41.

Hanna, D. (1988). *Designing organizations for high performance.* Reading, MA: Addison-Wesley.

Herbst, P. G. (1959). *Task structure and work relations.* London: Tavistock.

Hertog, J. F. den, & Kerkhof, W. H. C. (1973). *Experiment work structuring television receiver factory, Eindhoven Part II: Evaluation of the social psychological effects of autonomous task-oriented production groups.* Eindhoven, The Netherlands: Philips Industrial Psychology Department.

Hertog, J. F. den, & Wester, P. (1979). Organizational renewal in engineering works: A comparative process analysis. In C. L. Cooper & E. Mumford (Eds.), *The quality of working life: The European experiment* (pp. 180–214). London: Associated Business Press.

Keating, C. B., Fernandez, A. A., Jacobs, D. A., & Kauffman, P. (2001). A methodology for analysis of complex socio-technical processes. *Business Process Management Journal, 7*(1), 33–49.

Ketchum, L. D. (1975). A case study of diffusion. In L. E. Davis & A. B. Cherns (Eds.), *The quality of working life* (Vol. 2). New York: Free Press.

Ketchum, L. D. (1984). Socio-technical design in a third world country: The railway maintenance depot at Sennar in the Sudan. *Human Relations, 37*(2), 135–154.

Kira, M. (2003). *From good work to sustainable development: Human resources consumption and regeneration in the post-bureaucratic working life.* Unpublished doctoral thesis, Royal Institute of Technology, Stockholm.

Kling, R., Kim, G., & King, A. (2003). A bit more IT: Scholarly communication forums as sociotechnical interaction networks. *Journal of the American Society for Information Science and Technology, 54*(1), 47–67.

Kollenburg, T. van. (2003). *Taakgroepen duurzaam verbeteren: Tien jaar praktijkervaring met socio-technisch organiseren* [Sustainable improvement of self-managed teams: Ten years of experience with socio-technical systems design]. Unpublished doctoral thesis, Eindhoven University of Technology, Eindhoven, The Netherlands.

Kolodny, H. F. (1990). Some characteristics of organizational designs in new/high tech technology firms. In L. R. Gomez-Meija & M. W. Lawless (Eds.), *Organizational issues in high technology management* (pp. 165–176). Greenwich, CT: JAI.

Kolodny, H. F., & Shani, A. B. (2004). *Organization design as a research topic.* Paper presented at Knowledge Production in Management Research Conference, April 26–27, Stockholm, Sweden.

Kolodny, H. F., & Stjernberg, T. (1986). The change process of innovative work designs: New design and redesign in Sweden, Canada and the US. *The Journal of Applied Behavioural Science, 22*(3), 287–301.

Kramer, F. J. (2004). *Self-organization and army units in crisis operations.* Unpublished doctoral thesis, Eindhoven University of Technology, Eindhoven, The Netherlands.

Larsen, H. H. (1979). Humanization of the work environment in Denmark. In C. L. Cooper & E. Mumford (Eds.), *The quality of working life in Western and Eastern Europe* (pp. 124–158). London: Associated Business Press.

Leede, J. de, Looise, J. K., & Verkerk, M. (2002). The mini-company: A specification of socio-technical business systems. *Personnel Review, 31*(3), 338–355.

Lefebvre, C., & Rolloy, G. (1976). *L'amélioration des conditions de travail dans les emplois administratifs* [Improving work in administrative organizations]. Paris: Chotard et Associés Editeurs.

Leonard-Barton, D. (1992). Core capabilities and core rigidities: A paradox in managing new product development. *Strategic Management Journal, 13*(5): 111–125.

Lewin, K. (1951). *Field theory in social science.* New York: Harper & Row.

Lillrank, P., Shani, A. B., Kolodny, H. F., Stymne, B. A., Figuera, J. R., & Liu, M. (1998). Learning from the success of continuous improvement change programs: An international comparative study. In R. W. Woodman & W. A. Pasmore (Eds.), *Research in organizational change and development* (Vol. 11, pp. 47–72). Greenwich, CT: JAI.

Little, S., Leskinen, T., Lehtelä, J., Kalamaa, P., & Tanninen, O. (2002). Test at Finland post. In F. M. van Eijnatten (Ed.), *PSIM: Participative simulation environment for integral manufacturing enterprise renewal* (pp. 115–124). Hoofddorp, The Netherlands: TNO Arbeid/The PSIM Consortium.

Loeffen, J. M. J., & Wortmann, J. C. (1998). IT challenges organizational design: How to connect manufacturing concepts to IT. *International Journal of Technology Management, 19*(6), 630–637.

Macy, B. A., & Izumi, H. (1993). Organizational change, design and work innovation: Meta-analysis of 131 North America field studies, 1961–1991. In R. W. Woodman & W. A. Pasmore (Eds.), *Research in organizational change and development* (Vol. 7, pp. 235–314). Greenwich, CT: JAI.

Marek, J., Lange, K., & Engelstad, P. H. (1964). *Report 1: Industrial democracy project. The wire drawing mill of Christiania Spigerverk.* Trondheim, Norway: IFIM, Institute for Industrial Social Research.

Mathews, J. A., Griffiths, A., & Watson, N. (1993). *Socio-technical redesign: The case of cellular manufacturing at Bendix Mintex.* Sydney: University of New South Wales.

Miller, E. J. (1959). *Technology, territory and time: The internal differentiation of complex production systems.* London: Tavistock.

Mitki, Y., Shani, A. B., & Stjernberg, T. (2000). A typology of change programs. In R. T. Golembiewski (Ed.), *Handbook of organizational consultation* (pp. 777–785). New York: Marcel Dekker.

Mohrman, S. A., & Cummings, T. G. (1989). *Self-designing organizations: Learning how to create high performance.* Reading, MA: Addison-Wesley.

Mumford, E., & Henshall, D. (1979). *A participative approach to computer systems design.* London: Associated Business Press.

Mumford, E., & Weir, M. (1979). *Computer systems in work design, the ETHICS method: Effective technical and human implementation of computer systems.* London: Associated Business Press.

Munkvold, B. E. (2000). Tracing the roots: The influence of socio-technical principles on modern organizational change practices. In E. Coakes, R. Lloyd-Jones, & D. Willis (Eds.), *The new sociotech: Graphity on the long wall* (pp. 13–29). London: Springer Verlag.

Norstedt, J. P., & Agurén, S. (1973). *The Saab–Scania report.* Stockholm: Swedish Employers' Confederation SAF, Technical Department.

Olsen, G. M., & Olsen, J. S. (2000). Distance matters. *Human–Computer Interaction 15*(2/3), 139–179. Reprinted in Carroll, J. M. (Ed.). (2002). *Human–computer interaction in the new millennium* (pp. 397–417). New York: ACM Press.

Painter, B. (2004). Socio-technical design of knowledge work: A case study. In W. S. Bainbridge (Ed.), *The encyclopedia of human–computer interaction.* Great Barrington, MA: Berkshire Publishing Group.

Pasmore, W. A. (1988). *Designing effective organizations: The socio-technical systems perspective.* New York: John Wiley & Sons.

Pasmore, W. A. (1994). Social science transformed: The socio-technical perspective. *Human Relations, 48*(1), 1–21.

Pasmore, W. A. (2001). Action research in the workplace: The socio-technical perspective. In P. Reason & H. Bradbury (Eds.), *Handbook of action research: Participative inquiry and practice* (pp. 38–48). London: Sage.

Pasmore, W. A., Francis, C., Haldeman, J., & Shani, A. B. (1982). Socio-technical systems: A North American reflection on empirical studies of the seventies. *Human Relations, 35*(12), 1179–1204.

Pasmore, W. A., & Purser, R. E. (1993, July–August). Designing knowledge work systems. *Journal of Quality and Participation,* 78–84.

Pasmore, W. A., & Sherwood, J. J. (1978). *Sociotechnical systems: A sourcebook*. La Jolla, CA: University Associates.

Pava, C. (1983a). Designing managerial and professional work for high performance: A socio-technical approach. *National Productivity Review, 2*, 126–135.

Pava, C. (1983b). *Managing new office technology: An organizational strategy*. New York: Free Press.

Qvale, T. U. (1991). *Participation for productivity and change: A multi-level, cooperative strategy for improving organizational performance*. Oslo: Norwegian Work Life Centre, SBA. Paper presented at the Workplace Australia Conference, Melbourne, February 24–28.

Reason, P., & Bradbury, H. (Eds.). (2001). *Handbook of action research: Participative inquiry and practice*. London: Sage.

Rice, A. K. (1953). Productivity and social organization in an Indian weaving shed: An examination of the socio-technical system of an experimental automatic loomshed. *Human Relations, 6*(4), 297–329.

Robison, D. (1977). General Motors business teams: Advance QWL at Fisher body plant. *World of Work Report, 2*(7).

Savage, J. (2004, May). *STS Roundtable history and heritage chart*. Available: https://www.sonoma.edu/phpbb/viewtopic.php?t=61

Scarbrough, H. (1995). Review article. *Human Relations, 48*(1), 23–33.

Schlitzberger, H. H. (1978). Plannung von Arbeitssysteme mit hilfe von Strukturierungsbausteine [Planning of labor systems with the help of structuring principles]. *Refa Nachrichten, 31*(3), 131–134.

Sena, J. A., & Shani, A. B. (2002). Integrating product and personal development: Sustainability at a software development firm. In P. Docherty, J. Forslin, & A. B. Shani (Eds.), *Creating sustainable work systems* (pp. 89–100). London: Routledge.

Shani, A. B., & Docherty, P. (2003). *Learning by design: Building sustainable organizations*. Bodmin, UK: MPG Books/Blackwell.

Shani, A. B., & Elliott, O. (1988). Applying sociotechnical system design at the strategic apex: An illustration. *Organizational Development Journal, 6*(2), 53–66.

Shani, A. B., & Elliott, O. (1989). Socio-technical system design in transition. In W. Sikes,

A. Drexler, & J. Grant (Eds.), *The emerging practice of organization development* (pp. 187–198). La Jolla, CA: University Associates/NTL Institute for Applied Behavioral Science.

Shani, A. B., Mohrman, S. A., Pasmore, W. A., Stymne, B., & Adler, N. (Eds.). (2008). *Handbook of collaborative management research*. Thousand Oaks, CA: Sage.

Shani, A. B., & Pasmore, W. A. (1985). Organization inquiry: Towards a new model of the action research process. In D. Warrick (Ed.), *Contemporary organization development* (pp. 438–448). Glenview, IL: Scott, Foresman.

Shani, A. B., & Sena, J. (1994). Information technology and the integration of change: Sociotechnical system approach, *Journal of Applied Behavioral Science, 30*(2), 247–270.

Shepherd, V. W. (1951, May). An experiment in continuous longwall mining at Bolsover colliery. *Transactions of the Institute of Mining Engineers, 8*.

Simonse, L. W. L. (1998). *Organisatie-ontwikkeling in productcreatie: Op weg naar een teamnetwerkorganisatie met parallel-ontwikkelteams* [Organization development in product creation processes: Towards a team-network organization]. Unpublished doctoral thesis, Eindhoven University of Technology, Eindhoven, The Netherlands.

Sitter, L. U. de. (1994). *Synergetisch produceren. Human resources mobilisation in de produktie: een inleiding in de structuurbouw* [Synergetic manufacturing. Human resources mobilization in production: An introduction in the sociotechnical design of structure]. Assen, The Netherlands: Van Gorcum.

Sitter, L. U. de, Hertog, J. F. den, & Dankbaar, B. (1997). From complex organizations with simple jobs to simple organizations with complex jobs. *Human Relations, 50*(5), 497–534.

Sitter, L. U. de, Hertog, J. F. den, & Eijnatten, F. M. van. (1990). *Simple organizations, complex jobs: The Dutch socio-technical approach*. Paper presented at the annual meeting of the American Academy of Management, San Francisco, August 12–15.

Stebbins, M. W. (2003). Learning in a networked organization. In A. B. Shani & P. Docherty (Eds.), *Learning by design: Building sustainable organizations* (pp. 145–162). Bodmin, UK: MPG Books/Blackwell.

Stebbins, M., Sena, J. A., & Shani, A. B. (1995). Information technology and organization design. *Journal of Information Technology, 10,* 101–113.

Stebbins, M. W., & Shani, A. B. (1989, Winter). Organization design: Beyond the "mafia" model. *Organizational Dynamics,* 18–30.

Stebbins, M. W., & Shani, A. B. (1995). Organization design and the knowledge worker. *Leadership and Organization Development Journal, 16*(1), 23–31.

Stebbins, M., & Shani, A. B. (1998). BPR at Blue Shield of California: The integration of multiple change initiatives. *Journal of Organizational Change Management, 11*(3), 216–232.

Stebbins, M. W., & Shani, A. B. (2002). Eclectic design for change. In P. Docherty, J. Forslin, & A. B. Shani (Eds.), *Creating sustainable work systems* (pp. 201–212). London: Routledge.

STS Roundtable. (2004). *Deliberation about the development of a new STS approach.* Sonoma State University Listserve, https://www.sonoma.edu/phpbb/viewforum.php?f=8&sid=8e53b64c229ccf135efe499226c7a76b

Susman, G. I. (1976). *Autonomy at work: A sociotechnical analysis of participative management.* New York: Praeger.

Susman, G. I., & Chase, R. B. (1986). A sociotechnical analysis of the integrated factory. *Journal of Applied Behavioral Science, 22*(3), 257–270.

Susman, G. I., & Evered, R. D. (1978). An assessment of the scientific merits of action research. *Administrative Science Quarterly, 23,* 582–603.

Taylor, J. C. (1998). Participative design: Linking BPR and SAP with an STS approach. *Journal of Organizational Change Management, 11*(3), 233–245.

Taylor, J. C., & Asadorian, R. A. (1985). The implementation of excellence: Socio-technical management. *Industrial Management, 27*(4), 5–15.

Taylor, J. C., & Felten, D. F. (1993). *Performance by design: Socio-technical systems in North America.* Englewood Cliffs, NJ: Prentice Hall.

Terlaga, R. (1994, Fall). Minimizing the risks in re-engineering: A socio-technical approach. *Information Strategy,* pp. 6–11.

Thorsrud, E. (1970). *Democratization of work organizations: Some concrete ways of restructuring the work place (at Nobø-Hommelvik).* Oslo: Work Research Institute.

Trist, E. L. (1981). *The evolution of socio-technical systems. A conceptual framework and an action research program.* Toronto: Ontario Quality of Working Life Centre.

Trist, E. L., & Bamforth, K. W. (1951). Some social and psychological consequences of the long-wall method of coal-getting. *Human Relations, 4*(1), 3–38.

Trist, E. L., & Clarke, L. (1981). *Sudbury 2001: An evolutionary analysis.* Toronto, ON: QWL Centre.

Trist, E. L., Eldred, J., & Keidel, R. W. (1978). A new approach to economic development. *Human Futures, 1*(1), 1–12.

Trist, E. L., Higgin, G. W., Murray, H., & Pollock, A. B. (1963). *Organizational choice: Capabilities of groups at the coal face under changing technologies; the loss, re-discovery and transformation of a work tradition.* London: Tavistock, reissued 1987, New York: Garland Press.

Trist, E. L., & Murray, H. (Eds.). (1990). *The social engagement of social science: A Tavistock anthology. Volume I: The socio-psychological perspective.* Philadelphia: University of Pennsylvania Press.

Trist, E. L., Murray, H., & Emery, F. E. (Eds.). (1997). *The social engagement of social science: A Tavistock anthology. Volume III: The socio-ecological perspective.* Philadelphia: University of Pennsylvania Press.

Trist, E. L., Murray, H., & Trist, B. (Eds.). (1993). *The social engagement of social science: A Tavistock anthology. Volume II: The socio-technical perspective.* Philadelphia: University of Pennsylvania Press.

Trist, E. L., Susman, G. I., & Brown, G. W. (1977). An experiment in autonomous groups working in an American underground coal mine. *Human Relations, 30*(3), 201–236.

Utterback, J. M. (1994). *Mastering the dynamics of innovation.* Cambridge, MA: Harvard Business School Press.

Verkerk, M. J. (2004). *Trust and power on the shop floor: An ethnographical, ethical, and philosophical study on responsible behavior in industrial organizations.* Delft, The Netherlands: Eburon.

Verweij, M. J. (1997). *Redesigning the production organization of SMEs: Development and test of a participative method.* PhD thesis, Eindhoven University of Technology, Delft, The Netherlands.

Vink, P., & Eijnatten, F. M. van. (2002). Participation: The key to intelligent manufacturing improvement. *Lecture Notes in Computer Science, 2465,* 1–9.

Warne, L. (2000). Understanding organisational learning in military headquarters: Findings from a pilot study. *Australian Journal of Information Systems, 7*(2), 127–142.

Waterson, P. E. (2003). *Socio-technical design of work systems.* Kaiserslautern, Germany: Fraunhofer.

Weisbord, M. R. (1990). McNeil consumer Fort Washington manufacturing: Work redesign case study, January 1988–June 1990. Ardmore, PA: Block/Petrella/Weisbord.

17

Musings on the Past and Future of Employee Empowerment

GRETCHEN M. SPREITZER

DAVID DONESON

In the most comprehensive, long-term study of empowerment-oriented practices, Lawler, Mohrman, and Benson (2001) empirically demonstrated the positive growth of empowerment practices in the last 15 years. Today, more than 70% of organizations surveyed have adopted some kind of empowerment initiative for some portion of their workforce.

Why the tremendous growth in employee empowerment? Faced with competitive demands for lower costs, higher performance, and more flexibility, organizations have increasingly turned to employee empowerment to enhance their performance. Empowerment practices often are implemented with the hopes of overcoming worker dissatisfaction and reducing the costs of absenteeism, turnover, poor-quality work, and sabotage (Klein, Ralls, Smith-Major, & Douglas, 1998). Their focus is aimed at overcoming the debilitating psychological effects of traditional bureaucracies through the creation of high-involvement organizations. Empowerment enables employees to participate in decision making, helping them to break out of stagnant mindsets to take a risk and try something new. Empowering practices allow employees to decide on their own how they will recover from a service problem and surprise and delight customers by exceeding their expectations rather than waiting for approval from a supervisor (Bowen & Lawler, 1995). And perhaps most importantly, empowerment is viewed as critical in the process of organization change. Rather than forcing or pushing people to change, empowerment provides a way of attracting them to want to change because they have ownership in the change process.

Yet despite this positive growth, more than 25% of the surveyed companies in Lawler et al.'s (2001) study still report no significant empowerment-oriented practices anywhere in their organizations. And even those that do introduce empowerment practices often find it difficult to build genuine employee empowerment (Spreitzer & Quinn, 2001). Some don't have the courage to begin. Some get lost along the way. Others stumble and decide to turn around when they are only part of the way there. Many confuse empowerment with a quick fix and give up before it has been successfully implemented. Clearly, there is a great deal more to be learned about how to empower employees.

We begin this chapter by reviewing and synthesizing what we know about empowerment in the workplace. We look across several related perspectives on empowerment in the literature. We then integrate key learnings on empowerment with a special focus on implications for organization change and development. Finally, we offer an agenda for future work on empowerment. As part of this agenda, we highlight some critical new directions in organization studies that have implications for empowerment theory.

WHAT WE KNOW: SYNTHESIZING THE LITERATURE ON EMPOWERMENT

In order to understand the aims and implications of empowerment, it is necessary to understand the origins of the concept in the intellectual and political history of the West. Although its modern form was derived principally from the civil and women's rights social movements of the 1960s, its philosophical lineage can be traced to the beginnings of modern political philosophy. Although it is often regarded as a revolutionary development in thinking even in contemporary times, empowerment's theoretical roots point to a longer progression than is commonly assumed. In myriad ways, empowerment theory is concerned principally with elucidating and applying the answers to the timeless questions of political philosophy itself—namely the nature of power, the role of the citizen in the polis, and the achievement of justice in civic life. From this vantage point, empowerment is a continuation of this theoretical search for elusive but critical answers to timeless human questions.

Sir Francis Bacon, best known for his work *New Atlantis,* is intrinsically bound to the study of empowerment because of his crucial contribution to the development of the Western democratic system (White, 1987). According to Bacon, humanity's existence in a world of scarcity will continually result in human deprivation and hostility without the conquest of nature. He argued that only by the "release of man's estate," namely the rational and scientific generation of greater goods from nature, could this cycle of constant political animosity and privation be ended. Freedom, enfranchisement, and harmony among citizens cannot be achieved without overcoming the aggression that is inherent in scarcity and issues of survival. By uniting people behind the common goal of creating better lives via reason and human invention, the common good is finally able to triumph over sectarian divisions. At the most fundamental level, liberal democracy and the concept of constant progress require the emancipation of workers and their empowerment. Without empowerment, the manual laborer (or serf or slave) is used to provide the inputs that political life necessitates, and the stratification of power is perpetuated.

Although Bacon helped to form the foundations of the modern commercial republic, he could not have foreseen many of the developments that this polity engendered. One has only to peruse the works of Dickens, Marx, or Sinclair to be made aware of some of the obstacles of this political order. The sublimation of economic efficiency and science may liberate humankind from the bounds of scarcity, but it also can transform people into servants of power. Moreover, it often leads to a form of consumerism that seems ill suited for providing citizens with meaning outside the bounds of the acquisition of material possessions and elevates labor itself into the focal point for personal significance. From this perspective, our economic and political order may be required to bear more weight and significance than it can bear. Modern empowerment literature, with its emphases on theory, results, and meaning, is focused on improving this state of affairs through a variety of different approaches and applications. As a discipline, it embraces modern methods in order to answer ancient and familiar questions with the intention of elevating both the individual and the organization (political or otherwise) simultaneously.

In recent years, workplace empowerment has increasingly become part and parcel of the lexicon of organization research and practice. The meaning of the term *empowerment* has evolved over the years from its more radical beginnings in the civil and women's rights movements to its current manifestations focused on organization performance (Bartunek & Spreitzer, 1999). In the next section of the chapter, we look across the most recent decades of writing on empowerment and highlight three contemporary theoretical perspectives.

THREE PERSPECTIVES ON EMPOWERMENT IN THE WORKPLACE

In broad terms, contemporary management scholars and practitioners have used three different lenses to study and understand empowerment: the social–structural perspective, the psychological perspective, and the critical perspective. We briefly review each in this section.

Social–Structural Perspective

The social–structural perspective has its roots in the values and ideals of democracy, broadly stated. In this perspective, empowerment is linked to a belief in a democratic polity where power resides in individuals at all levels of a system (Prasad, 2001). The success and legitimacy of empowerment as democracy rest

on a system that facilitates and promotes the participation of most, if not all, employees (Prasad & Eylon, 2001). Of course, in contrast to a formal democracy, where each person has an equal vote and majority rules, most organizations stop far short of following the principle of voting equality and majority rule of employees (Eylon, 1998).

Nevertheless, the focus of this social–structural perspective is on sharing power throughout a system, where power is conceptualized as having formal authority or control over organization resources (Conger & Kanungo, 1988). The emphasis is on employee participation through increased delegation of responsibility down through the organization's chain of command. In this perspective, employees aren't empowered because managers tell them they are or because companies issue statements saying that employees are empowered. Instead, the social–structural perspective emphasizes the importance of changing organization policies, practices, and structures away from top-down control systems toward high-involvement practices (Bowen & Lawler, 1995). The focus tends to be on how organizational, institutional, social, economic, political, and cultural forces can root out conditions that foster powerlessness. For example, Walsh et al. (1998) found that the nature of relationships in organization life creates meaningful connections, energizes people, and helps to remove barriers to empowerment. In addition, in a study of a teacher-led empowerment initiative in a federation of independent schools, Bartunek and Spreitzer (1999) found that participation in change interventions was critical for the empowerment intervention to work because participation facilitated the individual behavior change that was necessary for empowerment to take hold.

One well-known social–structural model of empowerment is by Bowen and Lawler (1995). They found that employee empowerment is a function of organization practices that distribute power, information, knowledge, and rewards down throughout the organization. The more power, information, knowledge, and rewards given to employees, the more empowered they are. Of course, because the four elements are interdependent, they must be changed together to achieve positive results. In other words, if an organization shares important information with employees but fails to share power, training, or rewards, empowerment will fail to take root.

Yet from a structural perspective, empowerment also represents a moral hazard for managers (Pfeffer, Cialdini, Hanna, & Knopoff, 1997). The success or failure of employee empowerment depends on the ability of managers to reconcile the potential loss of control inherent in empowerment practices with the need for goal congruence (Mills & Ungson, 2003). Setting clear limits for empowerment and building trusting relationships have been found to be effective mechanisms for reducing the risk of this kind of moral hazard (Blanchard, Carlos, & Randolph, 2001; Spreitzer & Quinn, 2001).

In summary, then, the social–structural perspective on empowerment is embedded in theories of social exchange and social power, with the emphasis on sharing authority between superior and subordinate. However, empowerment theorists have found this perspective to be limiting because it does not address the nature of empowerment as experienced by employees. In some situations, power, knowledge, information, and rewards were shared with employees, yet they still felt disempowered. And in other situations, people lacked all the objective features of an empowering work environment yet still felt and acted in empowered ways. These issues spurred the emergence of the psychological perspective on empowerment, which we describe next.

Psychological Perspective

Psychological empowerment is a set of psychological conditions necessary for people to feel in control of their own destiny. Conger and Kanungo (1988) were among the first to define empowerment from a psychological perspective. In contrast to the social–structural perspective, which equated empowerment with the delegation of authority and resource sharing, Conger and Kanungo (1988) viewed empowerment as enabling or enhancing personal efficacy. Thomas and Velthouse (1990) built on this initial psychological conceptualization by defining empowerment as intrinsic task motivation consisting of four dimensions: meaning, competence, self-determination, and choice.

Meaning involves a fit between the needs of one's work role and one's beliefs, values, and behaviors (Hackman & Oldham, 1980). Competence is self-efficacy specific to one's work, a belief in one's capability to perform work activities with skill (Bandura, 1989; Gist, 1987). Self-determination is a sense of choice in initiating and regulating one's actions (Deci, Connell, & Ryan, 1989). Self-determination reflects autonomy over the initiation and continuation of work behavior and processes (e.g., making decisions about work methods, pace, and effort) (Bell & Staw, 1989). Finally, impact is the degree to which one can influence strategic, administrative, or operating outcomes at work (Ashforth, 1989). Together, these four cognitions reflect an active, rather than passive, orientation to one's work role.

Independently, Spreitzer (1997) conducted an intensive review of the literature on empowerment across a variety of disciplines, including psychology, sociology, social work, and education. Her synthesis of these disparate literatures found support for the same four-dimensional conceptualization of psychological empowerment. Using the Thomas and Velthouse (1990) model as a theoretical foundation, Spreitzer (1995) developed a four-dimensional scale in an attempt to measure these four dimensions. This measure was further validated by Kraimer, Seibert, and Liden (1997). Unlike in the social–structural perspective, where there are multiple ways of measuring empowerment (including measures of delegation, participation, and decentralization), in the psychological perspective this single measure has dominated empirical research. As a result, empirical research has flourished on the psychological perspective on empowerment as research studies have clearly built on one another in the development of a nomological network of empowerment in the workplace.

Empirical research on the psychological perspective on empowerment has been conducted in a variety of different contexts: a large service organization (Liden, Wayne, & Sparrowe, 2000), a Fortune 500 manufacturing company (Spreitzer, 1995, 1996), lower-level employees in the insurance industry (Spreitzer, 1995), diverse employees in the hospitality industry (Corsun & Enz, 1999; Sparrowe, 1994), hospital employees (Koberg, Boss, Senjem, & Goodman, 1999; Kraimer et al., 1997), nurses (Brancato, 2000), employees of an Israeli bank (Kark, Shamir, & Chen, 2003), rehabilitation employees (Miranda, 1999), employees and managers in an aerospace corporation (Mishra, Mishra, & Spreitzer, 1998), and public employees in a state agency (Feldman & Khademian, 2003). Because the empirical evidence is from such a broad swath of contexts, we can conclude that the generalizability of the psychological perspective on empowerment has been clearly established. And recent work has also developed the notion of empowerment at a team level of analysis (Kirkman & Rosen, 1999).

Research on Antecedents of Psychological Empowerment

A variety of antecedents have been examined in relation to empowerment. Several features of organization design, including a wide span of control (Spreitzer, 1996), enriching job characteristics (Liden et al., 2000), and a supportive and affiliative unit climate or culture (Sparrowe, 1994; Spreitzer, 1996), have been found to be related to high levels of employee empowerment. Other research has shown that high-quality relationships, including leader–member exchange (Liden et al., 2000; Sparrowe, 1994), supportive peer and customer relationships (Corsun & Enz, 1999),

sociopolitical support from one's boss, peers, and subordinates (Spreitzer, 1996), and leader approachability (Koberg et al., 1999), are also important in facilitating empowerment. Still other research has examined the specific role of the employee as an enabler of empowerment: access to information about the mission and performance of the organization (Spreitzer, 1995), rewards based on individual performance (Spreitzer, 1996), and role clarity (Spreitzer, 1996). In addition, other research has found employee characteristics such as rank and tenure (Koberg et al., 1999) to be associated with higher levels of empowerment. Finally, Kark et al. (2003) found that transformational leadership by way of social identification enhanced employee empowerment.

This growing body of research suggests that leaders have a wide variety of levers for enabling psychological empowerment in their employees. Interestingly, many of these antecedents could be enveloped in the social–structural perspective on empowerment above. Yet what is different in the psychological perspective is that rather than being seen as an indication of empowerment themselves, the social–structural antecedents are viewed as enabling mechanisms that can facilitate the individual experience of empowerment. For example, a system may provide employees with access to important information—one of Bowen et al.'s (1995) four elements—but unless they realize they have value, having this information and knowing how to use it will not help them experience empowerment. So the two perspectives on empowerment are linked but have different viewpoints on what empowerment means.

Research on Consequences of Psychological Empowerment

The empirical literature on empowerment suggests that empowerment matters for both employees and their organizations. When employees feel empowered, they have more positive attitudes in terms of job satisfaction

(Spreitzer, Kizilos, & Nason, 1997) and organization commitment (Liden et al., 2000). In addition, Sparrowe (1994) found that when lower-level hospitality employees felt empowered, they had more pay satisfaction, more promotion satisfaction, and less propensity for turnover. Similarly, Koberg et al. (1999) found that empowerment perceptions were associated with increased work satisfaction and reduced propensity to leave the organization. Empowered employees also reported less job strain (Spreitzer et al., 1997). But empowerment does not only affect attitudes; it also affects performance, specifically, managerial effectiveness and innovative behavior (Spreitzer, 1995), employee effectiveness (Spreitzer et al., 1997), employee productivity (Koberg et al., 1999), and work unit performance (Seibert, Silver, & Randolph, 2004). Spreitzer, Noble, Mishra, and Cooke (1999) found that supervisors who reported higher levels of empowerment were seen by their subordinates as more innovative, upward influencing, and inspirational. And Kirkman, Rosen, Tesluk, & Gibson (2004) found that virtual teams perform better when empowered. All in all, the findings suggest a great deal of positive potential for psychological empowerment in a work context.

Yet in the literature on psychological empowerment there remains the issue of where the power is in empowerment. This is where the critical perspective comes in.

Critical Perspective

Critical and postmodern empowerment theorists contend that without the formal power structures of direct worker ownership and representation, typical empowerment interventions are disempowering (Wendt, 2001) because real power still resides at the top of the organization (Boje & Rosalie, 2001). These theorists argue that feeling empowered is not the same as being empowered (Jacques, 1996). They note that discussions of power are conspicuously absent in the literature on empowerment (Hardy & Leiba-O'Sullivan, 1998). Moreover, these theorists recognize that empowerment interventions sometimes create more controls over employees through less obvious means. For example, Barker (1993) found that an intervention focused on empowering employees by putting them into work teams resulted in extensive peer pressure that left employees feeling ever more controlled and disempowered. So unless power is granted to employees through real ownership and control in the firm (through industrial democracy interventions such as worker councils and cooperatives), critical theorists question the extent to which empowerment interventions ever can be truly empowering (O'Connor, 2001). In an effort to reconcile the debate between mainstream empowerment theorists and critical theorists, Boje and Rosalie (2001) draw on Mary Parker Follett's theory of co-power and Clegg's circuits of power theory to bridge the gap between these disparate perspectives in the empowerment literature. They describe how thinking about power as "power to" rather than "power over" reconciles the notion of where power is in empowerment theory. So although the critical perspective helps bring the notion power back to the dialogue on empowerment, it is still at an early stage of development and needs further attention.

Looking across these three perspectives, we see that although each one views empowerment a bit differently, they complement one another. Each provides a different lens for understanding empowerment in the workplace (see Table 17.1 for a summary). The social–structural perspective focuses on the organization. The psychological perspective drills down to the individual and his or her experience. And the critical perspective focuses on the political nature of empowerment and the potential for domination. The challenge is to provide a more integrative perspective on empowerment that blends the three perspectives and links empowerment theory more

Table 17.1   Three Perspectives on Empowerment

	Roots	*Essence*	*Level of Development*
Social–structural	Democratic principles and sociology	Sharing power and decision making	Extensive theoretical development and practitioner writing; some empirical research
Psychological	Social psychology and intrinsic motivation	Experiencing meaning, efficacy, self-determination, and impact	Extensive theoretical development and empirical research; rigorous measurement
Critical	Postmodern theory and deconstructionism	Understanding who controls formal power structures	Initial conceptual ideas

explicitly to organization change and development. In this vein, we now turn toward future directions for empowerment work that might cut across these different perspectives, particularly in the context of organization change.

AN AGENDA FOR THE FUTURE: NEW DIRECTIONS FOR EMPOWERMENT THEORY AND RESEARCH

Although research on empowerment has gained increasing momentum in the last decade, the links to organization change and development have been implicit at best. Yet empowerment has several important implications for understanding change processes. Rather than forcing or pushing people to change, empowerment provides a mechanism for attracting people to want to change because they have ownership of the change process. This logic of attracting people to change through empowerment is thus an important direction for future research (Weick & Quinn, 1999). In this section of the chapter we elaborate on two particular streams of research that seem particularly ripe for future theoretical and empirical work on empowerment as an attractor for personal and organization change.

Positive Organizational Scholarship (POS)

POS is a new movement in organization studies that focuses on the dynamics in organizations that lead to developing human strength, producing resilience and restoration, fostering vitality, and cultivating extraordinary people (Cameron, 2003). POS is based on the premise that understanding how to enable human excellence in organizations will unlock potential, reveal possibilities, and facilitate a more positive course of human and organization welfare. POS does not adopt one particular theory or framework but draws from the full spectrum of organization theories to understand, explain, and predict the occurrence, causes, and consequences of positivism. Research findings to date indicate that enabling positive qualities in individuals leads to exceptional organization performance. This positive approach does not ignore, deny, or denigrate the negative phenomena and problems found in organizations. Instead, it seeks to study organizations and organization contexts typified by appreciation, collaboration, vitality, and fulfillment, where abundance and human well-being are key indicators of success. It seeks to understand what represents the best of the human condition.

At its core, POS is about "positive deviance," or the ways in which organizations and their members flourish and prosper in extraordinary ways. Positive deviance is behavior at the right end of the normal curve (Cameron, 2003). What does it take for people to be positively deviant? Spreitzer and Sonnenshein (2003) argue that an empowered mindset is critical. We know that social systems are designed to preserve the status quo. The pervasive influence of norms provides a means of control over what people say and do. Positive deviance entails real risk. It entails departing from norms in a positive way, often making others uncomfortable. For example, when employees perform in ways that are truly great, co-workers often express jealousy and try to recalibrate the greatness so that it seems less impressive (Quinn & Quinn, 2002). Sometimes they even denigrate the exemplar. Given that exceeding norms is difficult and entails risk-taking behavior, it is important to understand the conditions that enable people to be positively deviant. In this way, it is clear that psychological empowerment is likely to be a key enabler of positive deviance.

Consider the case of Merck Pharmaceuticals as retold by Spreitzer and Sonenshein (2003). In 1978, Merck & Co., one of the world's largest pharmaceutical companies, inadvertently discovered a potential cure for river blindness, a disease that inflicts tremendous pain, disfigurement, and blindness on the 85 million people who are at risk. The medication was first discovered as an animal antibiotic, but it quickly created a major dilemma when Merck scientists realized it could be adapted to become a cure for river blindness. Because river blindness was indigenous to the developing world, Merck would never recover the millions of dollars it would have to invest to develop the right formulation for humans and conduct field trials in the most remote parts of the world. Additionally, the company risked bad publicity for any unexpected side effects of the drug, which in turn could damage the drug's lucrative reputation as an animal antibiotic (Business Enterprise Trust, 1991).

Empowerment was a key enabler for Dr. Roy Vagelos and his team of scientists to take on the risk of developing this new drug. Creating a cure for river blindness would provide deep meaning to the scientists. Drawing on their expertise, they were confident that a reformulation would be an effective treatment for river blindness and that they would encounter few serious side effects. They were confident their actions would have an extraordinarily positive impact on the developing world. And they were hungry for new knowledge as well; they wanted to learn as much as possible about a fledging class of compounds, avermectins. Departing from norms in the pharmaceutical industry, Merck decided to manufacture and distribute the drug for free in the developing world, costing the company millions of dollars. Consequently, Merck helped eradicate river blindness at its own expense.

The empowerment of employees is believed to be a key enabler for the kind of positive deviance we see at Merck (Spreitzer & Sonenshein, 2004). Empowerment infuses people with the deep sense of meaning or purpose necessary to risk greatness. The feelings of competence that empowerment affords give people the confidence to take on difficult tasks. The self-determination helps people feel in control of their own destiny, facilitating the potential for risk taking. And the potential to have real impact gives people a reason to take the risk in the first place.

In addition to the influence of empowerment on positive deviance, there are several other potential links for empowerment in the growing POS movement. First, the POS movement emphasizes holistic excellence—psychological, physiological, societal, and spiritual as well as instrumental. From our literature review of empowerment, we know that empowerment is related to traditional outcomes such as commitment and effectiveness in the workplace, but we know little about other relevant outcomes such as individual health (Heaphy & Dutton, in press) and virtuousness (Cameron, 2003). Prior research looked at stress as an outcome of empowerment, but future research should examine other critical health indicators that capture notions of positive health, such as flourishing and thriving (Spreitzer, Sutcliffe, Dutton, Sonenshein, & Grant, 2004).

Second, POS has focused on how to enable people to be resilient in the face of difficulty or threat (Fredrickson, Tugade, Waugh, & Larkin, 2003). There is a broad interest in how to help people bounce back from extraordinary physical and financial devastation and loss of human life (Sutcliffe & Vogus, 2003). We believe that empowerment may provide the resources of capability and psychological strength to help people to get through difficult times. Feelings of empowerment may moderate the threat and stress inherent in difficult times. Through empowerment, people experience the purpose and efficacy to allow them to persevere. Empowerment can facilitate a sense of real hope that things will get better (Spreitzer & Mishra, 2000) and buffer survivors from the debilitating effects of downsizing (Brockner et al., 2004). For these reasons we believe that the links between empowerment and resilience may also provide fertile ground for future research.

Third, one element of POS particularly relevant to issues of organization change is called appreciative inquiry (AI). AI is a composite of change practices that are based on the assumption that organizations have a positive core that, if revealed and tapped, unleashes positive energy and improvement (Cooperrider & Whitney, 2000). The change process proceeds by identifying past examples of peak performance, spectacular successes, or positive aspirations for the future. Key explanatory elements are identified that account for these past successes, and a vision of the future is crafted based on what was extraordinarily successful and what can be perpetuated in the future. We suspect that empowerment is a key part of

successful AI interventions. When people feel empowered, they are more likely to break out of their normal mindset to think in new ways about possibilities for the future because they have a deep sense of meaning and purpose. Moreover, because of their strong sense of efficacy or competence, empowered people are more likely to have a clear idea of their special strengths that can release positive energy for change. Again, for these reasons we believe that a productive area for future research will be on the links between empowerment and AI.

Of course, these are only some initial forays into how empowerment may play a role in the POS movement. Our hunch is that empowerment may be a foundational theoretical mechanism for explaining other POS-relevant outcomes; examples might include courage (Worline & Quinn, 2003), forgiveness (Cameron, 2003), and compassion (Frost et al., 2004). By focusing future empowerment research on POS, we can learn more about how to attract people to positive deviance. We can learn about the systems, structures, and processes that attract people to be empowered for greatness. In this way, we can begin to build a stronger bridge between the social–structural and psychological perspectives on empowerment.

Advanced Change Theory

Several years ago, Quinn, Spreitzer, and Brown (2000) introduced the notion of advanced change theory (ACT). The focus of ACT is on adaptive change where leaders must bring change that is personally painful and transformative. The authors derive their theory from a synthesis of how exemplary leaders in history (Jesus, Gandhi, and Martin Luther King, Jr.) led adaptive change. The theory challenges conventional wisdom on how leaders can change others. Traditional approaches to change include the empirical–rational approach (making logical arguments for change), the power–coercive approach (using forms of leverage such as incentives to force change), and the normative–reeducative approach (using participation and pursuing win–win strategies). In contrast, the ACT approach focuses on the need for the leader to fundamentally change himself or herself in order to attract others to change. The foundation of ACT is that leaders must look inside first and make painful adjustments in their own behavior to overcome hypocrisy between what they say and what they do (Quinn, 2004). ACT involves attracting others to change rather than coercing or forcing them to change.

To help to bring ACT alive to the reader, consider this short story offered in Quinn, 1996, p. 157; see also Quinn et al., 2000).

> A large corporation engaged in three downsizings over a short period. One senior executive (we'll call Paul) graphically described his fears of losing his job and not being able to maintain his standard of living, send his children to college, or keep his home. After months of agony, Paul began to confront his fears and clarify his values. In doing so, he concluded that he had an identity separate from the organization and that he could survive on a much smaller salary if necessary. This change in perspective had an empowering effect. Paul stopped worrying about the dangers of change and how he was seen by the organization. He began to ask himself what was needed in the present. Paul saw his immobilized colleagues and realized he needed to do something to empower them. He designed a new role for himself. Paul carefully selected people and invited them into meetings and asked them what they wanted the division to look like in 10 years. Initially, they were startled by his question, but gradually, they joined the process of designing the company's future. Paul's empowerment began to spread to others. Gradually, things began to change.

In many ways, ACT leaders are a type of positive deviants. They engage risk and "build the bridge as they walk on it" (Quinn, 2004, p. 9). But rather than forcing or coercing others to change, they ask nothing more of others than they ask of themselves. Leaders who practice ACT are empowering themselves to take responsibility, risk new behaviors, and evolve meaning (Spreitzer & Quinn, 1996). Organizations cannot empower people. People empower themselves. However, systems can be created that enable empowerment (Spreitzer, 1996).

In this way, we can understand more clearly how empowerment can facilitate change by attracting others to empower themselves to change. By bringing empowerment research together with ACT theory, we can interpenetrate the psychological perspective with the critical perspective. The foundational ideas of ACT are consistent with recent work in the critical perspective on empowerment (Boje & Rosalie, 2001), more specifically, Mary Parker Follett's theory of co-power and Clegg's circuits of power theory.

CONCLUSION

We believe that the three perspectives on empowerment have important things to contribute to the growing POS movement and to contemporary change theory. The variety of theoretical approaches taken in empowerment literature also point to a number of additional issues for consideration. Because of the close relationship and tension between technology, consumerism, and personal significance in modern life, empowerment theorists can also concentrate on understanding the mechanisms of their interaction in formulating the theoretical foundations of empowerment initiatives. Through emphasis on these central conceptual issues, empowerment theory can demarcate the limits and unintended consequences that recur during implementation of the theoretical models. By synthesizing practice and theory, with greater insight into the individual and organizational factors that influence empowerment realization, the discipline can increase efficacy in practice and broaden empowerment's relevance in emergent social and political arenas. Because of the insistent pressures faced by modern organizations, and consequently on workers, the cultivation of empowerment theory is poised to have a lasting effect on the evolution of organizations and the role of the individual in the workplace.

We close this chapter with some practical advice to organization development practitioners considering empowerment interventions. Many organizations have a fundamental misunderstanding of how people can be empowered. There is an implicit assumption in many empowerment interventions that managers or organizations can empower employees. In reality, it is clear from the growing research on empowerment that no one can truly empower anyone else. Telling people they are empowered or forcing empowerment on people only demonstrates that they don't have any power—that the authority figure is still in control (Spreitzer & Quinn, 2001). In short, most empowerment programs have been implemented in a way that is likely to disempower employees.

Instead, what managers and organizations can do is create environments where people are more likely to empower themselves. It's not so much about empowering the workforce as about releasing the power in the workers so they can take initiative, feel trusted, be flexible, and do the right thing. Linking to the POS approach, organizations and managers want to attract people to notions of empowerment by creating conditions that unleash, rather than squelch, the power, ideas, and creativity that are embedded in every person. Clearly empowerment is neither easy nor quick. Sustained, genuine empowerment involves practices that cut across all three empowerment perspectives.

REFERENCES

Ashforth, B. E. (1989). The experience of powerlessness in organizations. *Organizational Behavior and Human Decision Processes, 43,* 207–242.

Bandura, A. (1989, September). Human agency in social cognitive theory. *American Psychologist,* 1175–1184.

Barker, J. A. (1993). Tightening the iron cage: Concertive control in self-managing teams. *Administrative Science Quarterly, 38.*

Bartunek, J. M., & Spreitzer, G. (1999). *The career of a popular construct: A pluralistic journey of understandings of empowerment.* Paper presented at the National Academy of Management, Chicago, IL.

Bell, N. E., & Staw, B. M. (1989). People as sculptors versus sculpture. In M. B. Arthur, D. T. Hall, & B. S. Lawrence (Eds.), *Handbook of career theory.* New York: Cambridge University Press.

Blanchard, K., Carlos, J., & Randolph, A. (2001). *Three keys to empowerment.* San Francisco: Berrett-Koehler.

Boje, D. M., & Rosalie, G. A. (2001). Where's the power in empowerment? Answers from Follett and Clegg. *Journal of Applied Behavioral Science, 37*(1), 90–117.

Bowen, D. E., & Lawler, E. E. (1995). Empowering service employees. *Sloan Management Review, 36*(4), 73–85.

Brancato, V. (2000). *The relationship of nursing faculties' psychological empowerment and their use of empowering teaching behaviors.* Wilmington, DE: Widener University.

Brockner, J., Spreitzer, G., Mishra, A., Pepper, L., & Hochwarter, W. (2004). Perceived control as an antidote to the negative effects of layoffs on survivors' organizational commitment and job performance. *Administrative Science Quarterly, 49,* 76–100.

Business Enterprise Trust. (1991). Merck & Co., Inc. In T. Donaldson & P. Werhane (Eds.), *Ethical issues in business: A philosophical approach* (pp. 215–220). Upper Saddle River, NJ: Prentice Hall.

Cameron, K. (2003). Organizational virtuousness and performance. In K. Cameron, J. Dutton, & R. E. Quinn (Eds.), *Positive organizational scholarship* (pp. 48–65). San Francisco: Jossey-Bass.

Conger, J. A., & Kanungo, R. N. (1988). The empowerment process: Integrating theory and practice. *Academy of Management Review, 12,* 471–482.

Cooperrider, D. L., & Whitney, D. (2000). A positive revolution in change: Appreciative inquiry. In D. L. Cooperrider, P. F. Sorenson, D. Whitney,

& T. F. Yeager (Eds.), *Appreciative inquiry* (pp. 3–28). Champaign, IL: Stipes.

Corsun, D. L., & Enz, C. A. (1999). Predicting psychological empowerment among service workers: The effect of support-based relationships. *Human Relations, 52*(2), 205–224.

Deci, E. L., Connell, J. P., & Ryan, R. M. (1989). Self-determination in a work organization. *Journal of Applied Psychology, 74,* 580–590.

Eylon, D. (1998). Understanding empowerment and resolving its paradox: Lessons from Mary Parker Follett. *Journal of Management History, 4*(1), 16–28.

Feldman, M., & Khademian, A. (2003). Empowerment and cascading vitality. In K. Cameron, J. Dutton, & R. E. Quinn (Eds.), *Positive organizational scholarship* (pp. 343–358). San Francisco: Jossey-Bass.

Fredrickson, B. L., Tugade, M. M., Waugh, C. E., & Larkin, G. R. (2003). What good are positive emotions in crises? A prospective study of resilience and emotions following the terrorist attacks on the U.S. on September 11, 2001. *Journal of Personality and Social Psychology, 84*(2), 365–376.

Frost, P., Dutton, J., Maitlis, S., Lilius, J., Kanov, J., & Worline, M. (2004). The theory and practice of compassion in work organizations. In *Handbook of organizational studies* (pp. 843–866). Thousand Oaks, CA: Sage.

Gist, M. (1987). Self-efficacy: Implications for organizational behavior and human resource management. *Academy of Management Review, 12*(3), 472–485.

Hackman, J. R., & Oldham, G. R. (1980). *Work redesign.* Reading, MA: Addison-Wesley.

Hardy, C., & Leiba-O'Sullivan, S. (1998). The power behind empowerment: Implications for research and practice. *Human Relations, 51*(4), 451–483.

Heaphy, E., & Dutton, J. (in press). Social interactions and the human body at work. *Academy of Management Review.*

Jacques, R. (1996). *Manufacturing the employee: Management knowledge from the 9th to the 21st centuries.* London: Sage.

Kark, R., Shamir, B., & Chen, G. (2003). The two faces of transformational leadership: Empowerment and dependency. *Journal of Applied Psychology, 88*(2), 246–255.

Kirkman, B. L., & Rosen, B. (1999). Beyond self-management: The antecedents and consequences of team empowerment. *Academy of Management Journal, 42*(1), 58–74.

Kirkman, B. L., Rosen, B., Tesluk, P. E., & Gibson, C. B. (2004). The impact of team empowerment on virtual team performance: The moderating role of face-to-face interaction. *Academy of Management Journal, 47*(2), 175–192.

Klein, K. J., Ralls, R. S., Smith-Major, V., & Douglas, C. (1998). *Power and participation in the workplace: Implications for empowerment theory, research, and practice.* University of Maryland at College Park Working Paper, College Park, MD.

Koberg, C. S., Boss, W., Senjem, J. C., & Goodman, E. A. (1999). Antecedents and outcomes of empowerment: Empirical evidence from the health care industry. *Group and Organization Management, 34*(1), 71–91.

Kraimer, M. L., Seibert, S. E., & Liden, R. C. (1997). Psychological empowerment as a multidimensional construct: A test of construct validity. *Educational and Psychological Measurement, 59,* 127–142.

Lawler, E. E., Mohrman, S. A., & Benson, G. (2001). *Organizing for high performance: Employee involvement, TQM, reengineering, and knowledge management in the Fortune 1000.* San Francisco: Jossey-Bass.

Liden, R. C., Wayne, S. J., & Sparrowe, R. T. (2000). An examination of the mediating role of psychological empowerment on the relations between the job, interpersonal relationships, and work outcomes. *Journal of Applied Psychology, 85*(5), 407–416.

Mills, P. K., & Ungson, G. R. (2003). Reassessing the limits of structural empowerment: Organizational constitution and trust as controls. *Academy of Management Review, 28*(1), 143–153.

Miranda, M. F. (1999). *Relationship of organizational culture, organization climate, and burnout to perceived empowerment among workers in a human service organization.* Hempstead, NY: Hofstra University.

Mishra, K., Mishra, A., & Spreitzer, G. (1998). Preserving employee morale during downsizing. *Sloan Management Review, 39*(2), 83–95.

O'Connor, E. S. (2001). Back on the way to empowerment: The example of Ordway Tread and industrial democracy. *Journal of Applied Behavioral Science, 37*(1), 14–32.

Pfeffer, J., Cialdini, R. B., Hanna, B., & Knopoff, K. (1997). *Faith in supervision and the self-enhancement bias: Two psychological reasons why managers don't empower workers.* Palo Alto, CA: Stanford University Graduate School of Business.

Prasad, A. (2001). Understanding workplace empowerment as inclusion: A historical investigation of the discourse of difference in the United States. *Journal of Applied Behavioral Science, 37*(1), 51–59.

Prasad, A., & Eylon, D. (2001). Narrative past traditions of participation and inclusion: Historic perspectives on workplace empowerment. *Journal of Applied Behavioral Science, 37*(1), 5–14.

Quinn, R. E. (1996). *Deep change: Discovering the leader within.* San Francisco: Jossey-Bass.

Quinn, R. E. (2004). *Building the bridge as you walk on it: A guide for leading change.* San Francisco: Jossey-Bass.

Quinn, R. E., & Quinn, G. (2002). *Letters to Garrett: Stories of change, power, and possibility.* San Francisco: Jossey-Bass.

Quinn, R. E., Spreitzer, G., & Brown, M. V. (2000). Changing others through changing ourselves: The transformation of human systems. *Journal of Managerial Inquiry, 9*(2), 147–164.

Seibert, S. E., Silver, S. R., & Randolph, W. A. (2004). Taking empowerment to the next level: A multiple-level model of empowerment, performance and satisfaction. *Academy of Management Journal, 47*(3), 332–349.

Sparrowe, R. T. (1994). Empowerment in the hospitality industry: An exploration of antecedents and outcomes. *The Council on Hotel, Restaurant, and Institutional Education, 17*(3), 51–73.

Spreitzer, G. (1995). Psychological empowerment in the workplace: Dimensions, measurement, and validation. *Academy of Management Journal, 38*(5), 1442–1465.

Spreitzer, G. (1996). Social structural characteristics of psychological empowerment. *Academy of Management Journal, 39*(2), 483–504.

Spreitzer, G. M. (1997). Toward common ground in defining empowerment. In R. W. Woodman & W. A. Pasmore (Eds.), *Research in organizational change and development.* Greenwich, CT: JAI.

Spreitzer, G., Kizilos, M. A., & Nason, S. W. (1997). A dimensional analysis of the relationship between psychological empowerment and effectiveness, satisfaction, and strain. *Journal of Management, 23*(5), 679–704.

Spreitzer, G. M., & Mishra, A. (2000). An empirical examination of a stress-based framework of survivor responses to downsizing. In R. J. Burke & C. Cooper (Eds.), *The organization in crisis: Downsizing, restructuring, and privatization* (pp. 97–118). Oxford, UK: Blackwell.

Spreitzer, G. M., Noble, D. S., Mishra, A. K., & Cooke, W. N. (1999). Predicting process improvement team performance in an automotive firm: Explicating the roles of trust and empowerment. In E. Mannix & M. Neale (Eds.), *Research on managing groups and teams* (Vol. 2, pp. 71–92). Greenwich, CT: JAI.

Spreitzer, G., & Quinn, R. E. (1996). Empowering middle managers to be transformational leaders. *Journal of Applied Behavioral Science, 32*(3), 237–261.

Spreitzer, G., & Quinn, R. E. (2001). *A company of leaders: Five disciplines for unleashing the power in your workforce.* San Francisco: Jossey-Bass.

Spreitzer, G. M., & Sonenshein, S. (2003). Becoming extraordinary: Empowering people for positive deviance. In K. Cameron, J. Dutton, & R. E. Quinn (Eds.), *Positive organizational scholarship* (pp. 207–224). San Francisco: Berrett-Koehler.

Spreitzer, G., & Sonenshein, S. (2004). Toward the construct definition of positive deviance. *Applied Behavioral Scientist, 77*(6), 838–847.

Spreitzer, G., Sutcliffe, K., Dutton, J., Sonenshein, S., & Grant, A. (2004). *Enabling human thriving at work.* Ann Arbor: Michigan Business School.

Sutcliffe, K., & Vogus, T. (2003). Organization resilience. In K. Cameron, J. Dutton, & R. E. Quinn (Eds.), *Positive organizational scholarship* (pp. 94–110). San Francisco: Berrett-Koehler, p. 94-110.

Thomas, K. W., & Velthouse, B. A. (1990). Cognitive elements of empowerment. *Academy of Management Review, 15*, 666–681.

Walsh, K., Bartunek, J. M., & Lacey, C. A. (1998). A relational approach to empowerment.

In C. Cooper & D. Rousseau (Eds.), *Trends in organizational behavior*. New York: John Wiley & sons.

Weick, K. E., & Quinn, R. E. (1999). Organizational change and development. *Annual Review of Psychology, 50,* 361–386.

Wendt, R. F. (2001). *The paradox of empowerment: Suspended power and the possibility of resistance*. Westport, CT: Praeger.

White, H. B. (1987). Francis Bacon. In L. Strauss & J. Cropsey (Eds.), *History of political philosophy* (3rd ed., pp. 366–386). Chicago: University of Chicago Press.

Worline, M., & Quinn, R. (2003). Courageous principled action. In K. Cameron, J. Dutton, & R. E. Quinn (Eds.), *Positive organizational scholarship* (pp. 138–158). San Francisco: Berrett-Koehler.

18

Organization Design

JAY R. GALBRAITH

Organization design has been a complementary field to organization development. They both are prescriptive. They both
attempt to deliver usable knowledge to leaders
who are responsible for the stewardship of
society's institutions. Organization design gathers this useful knowledge from sociology, organization theory, applied psychology, consulting
practice, or anywhere else there is useful information. It is a very eclectic field. It then focuses
this knowledge on the design of organization
structures and processes. Initially the pairing
of organization design and organization development was one of destination and journey.
Organization design determined the end state
and organization development determined the
change process to get to it. But today with constant change and reconfigurable organizations
there is much more overlap. Leaders must engage
simultaneously in design and development.

In this chapter I show how this merging
occurred. Starting with some brief history, I trace
the development of organization design to its
position today. The field has gone through
cycles from being practitioner led, to being academic led, to today, when we are once again
practitioner led. The chapter ends with some
speculation about what might be the next cycle.

ORIGINS OF ORGANIZATION DESIGN

Origins of any specialty are always debatable.
But I believe the origins of organization design
were in the scientific management school, starting about 100 years ago. This school was led
by the leading practitioners of the day, one of
whom was Frederick Taylor. Many of Frederick
Taylor's ideas were about the design of work.
But one of his concepts was functional fore-
manship. He believed that the leadership of
the workforce should be broken up into specialties. Each worker should have a method
boss, a schedule boss, an administrative boss,
and so on. There were eight specialties of fore-
man in all. He believed that this specialization
would maximize the level of expertise and

scientific management that could be made available to the workforce.

Others, led by Henri Fayol, acknowledged the need for expertise but thought that multiple bosses would be too confusing. Their work led to two important developments: unity of command and line and staff roles. The principle of unity of command stated that all employees in an organization should have one and only one boss and that authority should pass in an unbroken chain of command from the top management to the worker. The acceptance of the unity of command principle established the basic structure of an organization to be a social hierarchy, a hierarchy of authority. Yet there continued to be a need for expertise. The need for expertise led to the creation of two roles in the structure: line roles with authority and staff roles with no formal authority. These new staff roles would be occupied by experts who would advise the line managers, but only line managers would decide to use this expertise and issue policies and directives. Today there is less discussion of line and staff roles and more debate about matrix relations. The issues are the same, and they started a long time ago.

Almost all organizations were small by today's standards and used functional structures. Most of the businesses were vertically integrated single businesses such as railroads, telephone companies, steel mills, and electrical equipment manufacturers. The functional structures were the appropriate form of organization for companies executing a single business strategy. The main organization design issue was one of centralization or decentralization. Do you locate decisions at headquarters, where most of the staff is located, and get a single consistent expert decision based on the company's best practices? Or do you locate decisions in the field and close to the action? The knowledge about centralization was accumulated from the experience of practitioners and consisted of a long list of advantages and disadvantages. Lists such as Table 18.1 are still used today in deciding whether to place decisions in the field or at headquarters. Today, however, there is

Table 18.1   Advantages of Centralized and Decentralized Decisions

Centralized	Decentralized
Based on company best practice and knowledge	Based on local differences or facts
Consistent across field units	Fast and immediate
Eliminates duplication	Attracts local talent
Coordinates interdependence	Allows independence and autonomy
Made by the most competent, experienced people	Made quickly on the spot

the added complication of the headquarters being located in another country.

After hundreds of empirical studies on centralization (Jennergren, 1981), the results are contradictory, and organization designers still rely on balancing the pros and cons as listed in Table 18.1.

The organization books of this first phase were written by thoughtful executives such as Henri Fayol (1916/1949) and Chester Barnard (1938). Consultants such as McKinsey hired experienced practitioners. This experience-led phase continued until the end of World War II.

RESEARCH ON ORGANIZATION DESIGN

A number of changes occurred during and after the war. First there was an appreciation for the application of abstract knowledge and technology. Mathematical models were used to design naval convoys and bomber squadron attack structures. As leaders transitioned from the military back to business, they brought this appreciation with them. Second, the business firms entered a period of growth and development and needed new organizations for these new strategies. Firms pursued diversification strategies that led to new forms of organization. In 1950, about 85% of the Fortune 500 companies were functional organizations (Rumelt, 1973). By 1970, 90% of the Fortune 500 companies had transitioned to the multidivision, multi–profit center structure. In 1954 the Treaty of Rome was signed, creating the European Common Market, which would reduce cross-border tariffs to zero by 1968. So in the late 1960s and 1970s the multidivisionals transitioned into multinationals. Under these conditions past experience in domestic functional organizations was of little help in designing new organizations for new strategies. The books, such as Peter Drucker's *Concept of the Corporation* (1946), Chandler's *Strategy and Structure* (1962), and Burns and Stalker's *The Management of Innovation* (1961), were written by academics. In 1953, McKinsey stopped hiring practitioners and began hiring MBAs.

The need for knowledge about and understanding of the new organizations was not lost on the people who fund research. The Ford Foundation, the Office of Naval Research, and the newly formed National Science Foundation all began to support research on organizations. As always happens in academia, various schools of thought develop, compete, and do not talk to each other. So, very quickly, knowledge about organizations increased yet became fragmented into a classic management group still debating unity of command and centralization; a mathematics, accounting, and computers group that coalesced around central planning and mathematical models; and a behavioral science group that focused on participative management and employee satisfaction.

Then James March tried to pull these fragmented schools together in his *Handbook of Organizations* (1965). One of the best chapters in that handbook was one by Harold Leavitt. He created a fictitious manager with a problem who called in a consultant for a recommendation. The initial consultant was portrayed as a classic strategy and organization consultant. The advice that the manager received was to divisionalize to profit centers and decentralize decision making. Leavitt's manager was conservative, so he called in another consultant for a second opinion before acting. The second consultant came from a consulting firm following the operation research and quantitative school of thought. Staffed with PhDs, this firm recommended the implementation of a long-range planning system, a computer-based information system, and several mathematical models to guide decision making. The confused manager called in a third consultant. The third consultant came from a firm staffed with PhDs in behavioral science. After looking at the situation, these consultants recommended the improvement of interpersonal relations to be implemented through a series of offsite meetings and feedback sessions.

Leavitt used a diagram like the one shown in Figure 18.1 to portray the manager's dilemma. That is, for the same problem, it was possible to receive different prescriptions from different consultants based on their consulting specialties. Leavitt's point was that these prescriptions were not wrong but that they were all only partially correct. That is, in order to make a successful change and solve the manager's problem, structures, planning processes, information systems, and interpersonal relations all had to be changed. Real managerial problems and tasks required a blending of all the specialists' areas. Real tasks and situations were not just structural issues or just interpersonal relationships.

Figure 18.2 shows schematically the point Leavitt was making. In order to solve a manager's

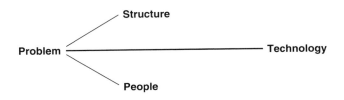

Figure 18.1   Leavitt's Manager

problem, consultants must deal with all the specialties simultaneously. This integration is one of the defining characteristics of organization design. It is integrative. That is, in order to be useful to leaders, organization design must integrate knowledge around the leaders' problems, not some academic school of thought.

Numerous models began to appear after Leavitt's initial works. Usually strategy was substituted for the problem box. Lawrence and Lorsch's (1967) work began to use a triangle of strategy, organization, and people. Lawrence and Lorsch and others who joined this effort added the idea that strategy, organization,

and people needed to fit together for high performance to occur. That is, the choice of organization and selection of types of people was contingent on the type of strategy that the firm chose to follow. Initially these ideas were called contingency theory. But eventually the school of thought came to be known as organization design. The star model, the author's version of the Leavitt model, is shown in Figure 18.3 (Galbraith, 2002). It states three of the ideas that provide the foundation for organization design.

First, different strategies require different organizations. Second, organization consists of

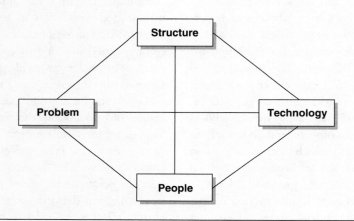

Figure 18.2   Leavitt Model

Figure 18.3   The Star Model
SOURCE: Copyright Jay R. Galbraith.

business and management processes, reward systems, and people practices in addition to structure. And the third idea is that the effective company is one that has aligned all of the elements of the star model. The various organization design frameworks then spelled out how to achieve alignment.

Consulting firms began to develop their own versions of these models. The most popular of these was the McKinsey "Seven S" model that achieved notoriety in Peters and Waterman's *In Search of Excellence* (1982). By 2000, almost every consulting firm was using its own version of the star model. The terminology and the graphics were all different but the models still were based on the three organization design ideas.

Contingency Theory

One of the characteristics of the academic-led phase two was the collection of empirical data on which to build the knowledge base. The researchers used comparative case studies, longitudinal case studies, and qualitative and quantitative data collected from real organizations. Then rather than debate on the basis of different experiences, the researchers used the logic of comparative analysis to see when one organization type worked better than another.

The study that has had the strongest impact is the one by Burns and Stalker (1961). These two British sociologists studied UK firms as they transitioned to peacetime commerce after the war. They found that the firms fall into two archetypes of structures. One was called mechanistic. This type was like the one articulated by the classic management school. It adhered to the unity of command principle, was very hierarchical, and used clearly defined roles and responsibilities. The other was the organic type. It was very flexible, used cross-departmental contacts and communication, and had few levels of structure. It was close to the type that behavioral scientists liked best. But rather than favoring one or the other, Burns and Stalker said each was appropriate

for different kinds of tasks. For work that was not well understood, that was constantly changing, and whose outcomes were uncertain, the organic type was superior. For work that was well understood, predictable, and repetitive, the mechanistic type was superior. Thus, the preferred type of organization was contingent on the nature of the task.

Another landmark study was the one by Lawrence and Lorsch (1967). Their work supported the Burns and Stalker findings about the nature of the work and the type of organization. But they also articulated the various coordination mechanisms that make up the organic type of structure. Their study looked at high- and low-performing companies in three different industries. The three industries varied in the amount of new product development work each conducted. The plastics industry had 35% of its revenues coming from new products. In contrast, the food industry had 15% and the container industry 0%. The percentage of new product sales was their indicator of how much change and uncertainty characterized the work in each industry. Therefore, the plastics companies would use organic structures and the container companies mechanistic structures, with the food companies somewhere between the extremes.

Table 18.2 displays the various coordination mechanisms used by the top performers in each industry. The container organization is the simplest structure, where all activities are coordinated through hierarchy and by voluntary and informal contacts between people in different departments. The food industry top performer also used the hierarchy and voluntary coordination, but it was not enough. The additional new product activity also required more coordination. This cross-departmental coordination took the form of cross-functional product teams (formal groups) and product managers (integrators). Lawrence and Lorsch articulated the features of the integrator role, which was very similar to the staff role. But the integrators were more than staff experts. They coordinated work in different departments. They

Table 18.2   Matching Strategy and Organization

	Plastics	Food	Container
Percentage of revenue from new products	35%	15%	0%
Coordination mechanisms used	Hierarchy	Hierarchy	Hierarchy
	Voluntary	Voluntary	Voluntary
	Formal groups at 3 levels	Formal groups	
	Integrating departments	Integrating roles	
Percentage integrators/managers	22%	17%	0%

were product managers, project managers, or brand managers. But like the staff role, they had no formal authority. The plastics industry high performer devoted even more resources to cross-departmental coordination because of the much higher level of new product activity. They used more cross-functional teams and had larger integrating departments. So Lawrence and Lorsch identified the voluntary communication, formal groups, and integrators as the flexible devices that supplement the hierarchy in organic organization forms. They also showed that the more variable the task, the more organic was the organization.

The author found similar mechanisms at Boeing's Commercial Airplane Division (Galbraith, 1973). Using a longitudinal case study to observe changes, the author found that the use of informal organization, liaison roles, teams, and integrators increased over time. The causes of the changes were the increase in the number of new aircraft programs and the large reductions in time to market. These studies set the stage for the articulation of the various types of lateral integrating mechanisms that make up the organic structures.

Lateral Coordination Networks

Lateral coordination mechanisms, now called networks, have become a key design tool for organization designers. Originally organic structures were thought to be informal and not controllable by designers. But as Lawrence and Lorsch showed, there are various types of lateral, cross-hierarchy coordination and communication practices. These practices can be arrayed as a continuum, as shown in Figure 18.4.

Originally the basic structure was a functional hierarchy. The lateral coordination was needed to coordinate the flow of products, particularly new products, across the functions.

The figure implies that these lateral forms are ordered along a continuum running from low (lower left) to high (upper right). The low end means that the informal networks have the lowest power and authority to get things done. But they are also the least expensive, most natural, and easiest to use. In contrast, the upper right end of the continuum has the most power and authority vested in the product champion. It is most likely to produce rapid time to market. But matrix forms and separate structures are the most costly and the most likely to generate conflicts. What drives organizations to move up the spectrum is the strategic priority they assign to the product development activity and the difficulty in achieving it.

The continuum begins with the informal networks that form voluntarily to coordinate the products. These networks are also called emergent networks, self-organizing networks, and communities of practice or interest. They are great at sharing information and ideas. However, the decision making still rests with the line structure. E-coordination simply

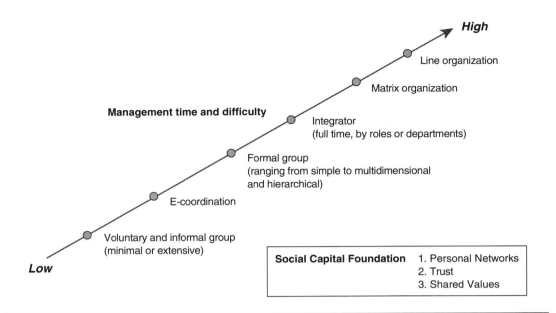

Figure 18.4   Lateral Coordination Networks

extends the networks and uses modern tele-conferencing, e-mail, and other technologies to support the informal organization.

Formal groups are just that. They are groups created by management rather than emerging from the working level. People are assigned to these teams. The teams create plans for their process or customer segment. The plan results in goals against which the team and team members are measured and rewarded. The cross-structural teams are thereby formalized. The teams are designed with certain principles, such as that team members should have the time to participate, and they must have the information and authority to represent the units from which they come. Formal groups are more expensive and more difficult to implement. They are more expensive because the organization is using informal networks and formal groups. The lateral networks shown in Figure 18.4 are cumulative. The organization adds more complex forms because the simple forms do not achieve the level of coordination that is desired to coordinate across functions and deliver new products on time. And when they add more complex lateral forms, organizations

do not eliminate the simpler forms. They use all the lateral forms that they deem necessary. And finally, formal groups require time and effort from talented people, and this time and effort are in addition to what these people invest in their full-time jobs. The formal groups are also likely to generate conflicts as they represent the product viewpoint in a functional structure.

The formal groups can be temporary, such as a project team, or permanent, such as a process team. The teams may be simple, such as an account team of all salespeople, or complex, such as the cross-function, cross-country product teams in the auto industry.

When organizations create many teams, an integrator or coordinator is appointed to represent the teams at the leadership level. For example, the food and plastics firms created integrator roles when they created 5 or more customer teams. The plastics industry used about 50 teams and grew an integrating department of 25 people. This integrating group creates common planning formats and accounting systems for tracking product revenues, costs, and project milestones. These units have no formal authority. They can be quite influential informally and participate on the management team. They can be quite active during the planning and goal-setting process. Often they get a budget to fund various activities.

The addition of the integrator role and the department increases the time, effort, power, and authority that are all focused on products. The organization still uses informal communication across units and product teams as well as the integrator role. This additional effort results in better coordination, more focus on individual products, and shorter time to market. The negatives are the increasing costs (25 people) and the increase in conflict with other units of the organization. There are opportunities for role conflicts if roles and responsibilities are not defined. The conflicts are a challenge for the leaders. The conflicts that are resolved can result in better decisions. But weak leadership and unresolved conflicts can degrade performance and focus the organization on itself rather than on the product. The strength of the leadership is more important as the organization uses lateral networks on the high end of the continuum.

The matrix organization is the next higher step along the spectrum. The move to a matrix is intended to put still more power and authority into the product dimension. The thinking is that better products result from a stronger product unit. The matrix is achieved when people on product teams report to the product department and to their functions. This dual authority is the defining characteristic of the matrix. Like the integrator role, the matrix is likely to cause confusion and conflict. These issues are the same ones we have dealt with under line and staff models. Definitions of roles and responsibilities and leadership processes to manage the conflicts are needed. Management processes for planning and goal setting are the forums in which this conflict is managed.

The last step along the spectrum is the creation of a separate product organization. The people on the product teams work for the product organization. The product unit often becomes a profit center. This step is taken when the company chooses a strategy in which developing a diverse line of products is the highest priority.

The pros and cons of the lateral forms are similar for each step on the continuum. The positives and negatives vary only in magnitude. That is, each product lateral network increases the quality of products and speed to market. Integrators provide more coordination than formal groups and e-coordination. But each lateral network on the spectrum increases in cost as one moves up to the higher end. Each high-end network adds a new voice to the decision process. The disagreements and debates increase. There is always the opportunity for confusion and conflict among the leaders. So the choice of which of the lateral networks to implement is a balancing of the time to market and the costs of coordination to achieve on-time performance.

The discussion in this section was centered on coordinating new products across functions. But the design of lateral networks is applied to many different situations in which cross-unit coordination is needed, such as coordinating processes across functions, products across countries, or customers across business units. It is the design of networks that drives the merging of organization design and organization development.

Merging Design and Development

The merging of the fields of design and development occurs when we design organic, flexible organizations using lateral coordination mechanisms. Organization development is needed for the skills that underlie lateral forms and for the constant change associated with these flexible forms.

First, in order to effectively use lateral networks, managers need a lot of the skills and tools of OD. Effective interpersonal skills and relationships with other departments are basic to lateral coordination. There is a need for team building and team working. There is a need for skills in group problem solving and conflict management. There is a constant need to define roles and responsibilities. In my experience the OD group at the client is my best friend.

The other connection is that companies can evolve new structures by moving up the continuum. Earlier I mentioned that companies start with single business strategies and functional organizations. When growth in their core business slows, they diversify. Then they reorganize into the multi–profit center divisionalized form. It is possible and probably preferable to evolve from a functional organization by creating product teams, product integrators, and then product profit centers in a multistep process. This slow stagewise process is certainly less disruptive than a big-bang change. It also allows the company to refine its strategy, develop management to think in portfolio terms, build product accounting systems, develop general managers, and create planning processes. This developmental sequence combines organization change and organization design. This use of lateral forms recognizes that change is constant and builds capability with each change in structure.

TOWARD MULTIDIMENSIONAL STRUCTURES

Historian Alfred Chandler (1962) initiated a line of research. He developed the thesis that structure follows strategy. We have already used some of his results. When he examined the histories of companies he found that those that remained vertically integrated single businesses organized themselves as single–profit center functional organizations. When they diversified into new businesses, they reorganized into multi–profit center divisions. Each division was itself a single-business functional organization. So Burns and Stalker (1961) discovered that the hierarchical functional organization became more organic when faced with changing and unpredictable tasks. Chandler discovered that the functional organization

was divided into multiple functional organizations when faced with diverse tasks. The diversity variable has been well researched. The rest of this section traces the design knowledge that has accumulated for designing corporate structures when companies execute strategies for diverse businesses, countries, and customers.

Multi–Profit Center Structures

A key study that extended Chandler's work was that of Richard Rumelt (1973). Using the list of Fortune 500 companies, he categorized each company's strategy according to the degree of diversity and the company's structure as being functional or multidivisional. In so doing, he replicated Chandler's historic findings.

Rumelt also distinguished between different kinds of diversification strategy. On one extreme were companies such as Procter & Gamble, which diversified into businesses that were all related to their core business. Procter & Gamble diversified from soap into paper, food, health care, and beauty care. But all products were consumer packaged goods, sold through the mass merchant channel and managed through a system of brand management. On the other extreme were the conglomerates that grew by acquisition and entered into very diverse businesses. The best example was ITT, which, from its base of monopoly telephone companies in Europe and South America, acquired Hartford Insurance, Continental Baking, Avis Rent-a-Car, Canadian paper companies, and so on. The significant point is that these different strategies lead to different organizations.

The different elements of organization, from the star model, are shown in Table 18.3 for the pure types of strategy (Galbraith, 1993). The single business strategy is implemented through the centralized functional structure. The related diversification strategy is implemented through the divisionalized structure. The unrelated, conglomerate strategy is implemented through the decentralized holding company structure. These structures are

Table 18.3 Matching Organization Attributes with Governance Models

Strategy	Structure	Centralization	Corporate Staff	Control Type	Business Processes	Compensation System	Bonuses	Careers	Subsidiary Culture	Division Name or Brand
Single business	Functional	High	Small	Operational	Common	Company	Company	Company	Company-wide	Company name
Related diversification	Divisional	Moderate	Large	Strategic Financial	Common	Company	Company	Company	Company-wide	Company name
Unrelated diversification	Holding company	Low	Small	Strategic Financial	Different	Subsidiary	Subsidiary	Subsidiary	Unique to subsidiary	Subsidiary

shown and contrasted in Figure 18.5. From Table 18.3 and Figure 18.5, it is clear that the large, corporate staff of the multidivision structure is the primary difference between the three models. Because the businesses are related, the multidivision form centralizes some activities and performs them for all divisions. There are common processes, a common brand, and common information technology systems. These common practices are needed because managers move from one business to another. Their bonuses are based on company results. In this way all organization policies are aligned with each other and with the strategy. For the holding company, there is a small corporate staff, which is primarily financial. Because the businesses are unrelated, most activities are decentralized to the business level. The processes are business specific. Managers do not move across the businesses. The cultures of the businesses are different, and so are the brands. Each business is an independent unit except for finance. This independence facilitates the buying and selling of these self-contained businesses. These policies too are aligned with each other.

The work of Chandler and Rumelt showed that different strategies led to different organizations. Specifically, they showed the difficulties of managing diversity in a single structure. They showed that the greater the diversity of business, the greater the decentralization of power. Much of the other work on the multi–profit center forms is summarized in Galbraith and Kazanjian (1986).

International Organizations

In the 1960s and 1970s, American multinationals expanded internationally. This international strategy added another dimension, a geographic dimension, to the organization. The stagewise development of these multinationals was traced by Stopford and Wells (1968). The European multinationals, which expanded internationally much earlier, were similarly traced by Franko (1976).

The two studies first confirmed the results of Chandler and Rumelt. They found that single business strategies are coupled with functional structures that are converted to multidivisional structures when companies diversify into new businesses. Then a new structure emerged as they expanded internationally. The American companies, as well as companies from home countries with large domestic markets, first formed an international division and added it to their divisional structures. They kept the international division until international sales and assets reached about 20% of the total (Egelhoff, 1988). At this time the international division was disbanded, and one of two structures emerged. If the company expanded internationally with only a single business, as automotive companies did, they adopted a regional structure. For example, Ford North America, Ford Europe, and Ford Rest of World was an early structure. If the company took its diversified product line into new geography, as General Electric did, they broke up the international division and gave the pieces to worldwide product divisions. So again portfolio diversification appears to be a determining factor.

Companies from countries with small home markets tended to reverse the growth process. That is, they expanded internally first, then diversified second. In the end they all evolved to a three-dimensional structure consisting of product lines, geographies, and functions. This three-dimensional matrix structure is shown in Figure 18.6.

The research of Prahalad and Doz (1987) and Bartlett and Ghoshal (1989) showed how power was best distributed across the geographic and product division dimensions. When the industry and strategic forces favored global integration, the power was best placed in the roles of those with cross-border responsibility. These roles are the business unit division heads and functional heads. The forces that favor global integration are high fixed costs,

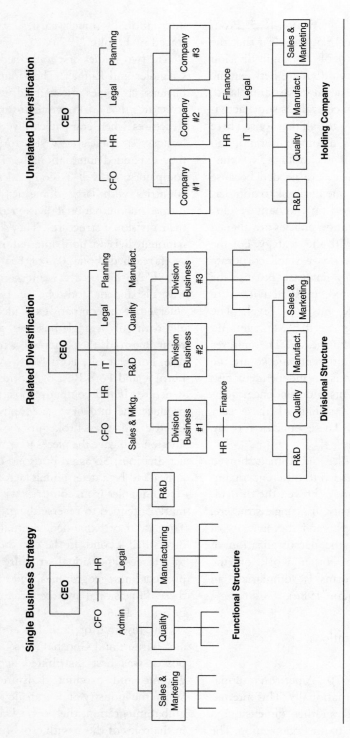

Figure 18.5   Alignment of Portfolio Strategy With Corporate Structure

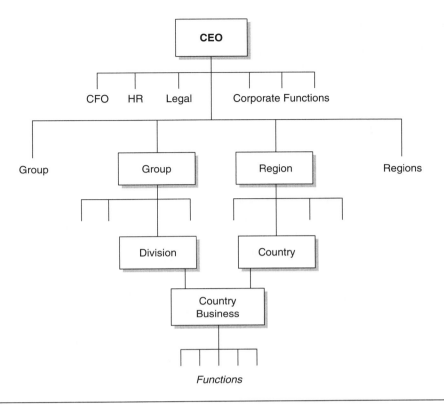

Figure 18.6   Country–Business Matrix Structure

homogeneous country markets, standard global products, and global customers. When these forces are the opposite, that is, low fixed costs, heterogeneous markets, varied national products, and local customers, they favor local responsiveness. Local responsiveness shifts power to the country managers. Another factor shifting power to country managers is the activity of host governments in the economic process. The matrix structure is appropriate when both global integration and local responsiveness are needed.

The 1980s and 1990s were a period of global integration, privatization, and deregulation. This was a time of shifting power from country managers to global business unit managers. In the new millennium the shift has stopped. It is a time of war, state-owned companies, and some reregulation. Countries have become more important. There is also the rise of the Brazil, Russia, India, and China (BRIC) bloc. In these countries we are seeing much stronger country managers and active host governments. The national oil companies in each of these countries are active on the global stage.

The strong country managers in the BRIC bloc illustrates another design principle, that of differentiation. That is, we do not have to organize the same way in every country and for every business. Very often business units are integrated across North America and Europe but use countries as profit centers in Latin America and Asia. Now it appears that some companies have global business units, country or regional coordinators in Europe and North America, and strong country managers in the BRIC bloc and other large developing countries.

The Rise of the Customer Dimension

Most multinational companies were operating with the differentiated three-dimensional structure shown in Figure 18.6 by the 1990s. But in the 1990s most of these companies experienced the rise in strategic importance of the customer. Customers were present in many countries and wanted the same level of service in each of them. Many customers preferred fewer, closer, longer-term relationships on a global basis. An increasing number of customers wanted to buy solutions rather than standalone products. With the rise in the power of the customer, most companies felt the need to organize around the customer in addition to business divisions, geographies, and functions.

The customer organization chosen varied with the strategic importance of the customer dimension. The various responses can be arrayed along the lateral network continuum shown in Figure 18.4.

1. Nestlé has chosen not to focus on global retailers. However, the account managers in various countries for Wal-Mart, Tesco, and Carrefour have chosen to create informal networks. They hold an annual meeting to exchange information about dealing with these global retailers. The account managers have also created Web sites and Internet discussion groups and use e-mail and other forms of electronic coordination. Each country still decides how to deal with these retailers.

2. ABB formed global accounts teams to coordinate the salespeople around the world who called on Shell, Daimler-Chrysler, and other companies. Procter & Gamble chose to focus on the global retailers and use a complex team structure. They have a multifunctional, multiproduct team of 200 people or so in Arkansas for Wal-Mart. There are subteams of 10 or 12 in Mexico, the United Kingdom, Germany, and other countries where Wal-Mart is present.

3. Citibank introduced global customer teams for customers who wanted them in the 1980s. They created an integrating department to coordinate roughly 400 teams in 1995.

4. Then in 1995 Citibank made the industry groups, which managed customer teams, the basic profit centers of the bank. However, they had significant business in many developing countries. Citibank used a matrix structure of customer segments and countries in the developing world.

5. Citibank took the profit-and-loss responsibility away from the countries in the developed world and made the industry groups the profit centers. They created a separate line customer structure. So as the strategic priority of the customer increases, firms move up the continuum and put more power and authority in the customer-facing unit. The customer dimension gives us another good example of how to deploy lateral networks.

When separate customer segment structures were created at Citibank, IBM, and eventually Procter & Gamble, a new structure emerged. These new structures are being adopted at other companies as well. This new structure was a four-dimensional structure, which we called the front–back model.

THE FRONT–BACK STRUCTURE

The front–back model is a type of dual structure in which both halves are multifunctional units. The structure for a manufacturer of diesel engines for ships is shown in Figure 18.7. The front half, which is organized around the customer, can be a geographic or country structure, or it can be focused on some market-segmentation scheme such as industries. The back half, which is usually organized around products or product lines, supplies all the customer units and achieves global scale.

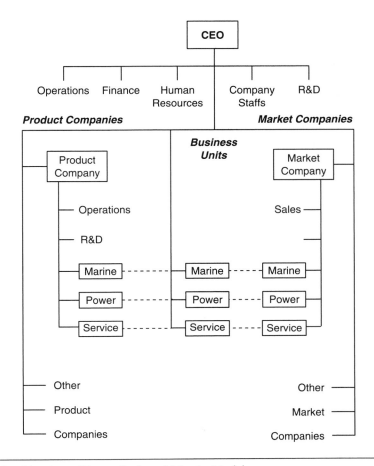

Figure 18.7   Combination of Front–Back and Matrix Models

Both the product and the market companies shown in Figure 18.7 are multifunctional profit centers, although each type of company has different functions. The front–back model separates the value chain for the business. The functions closest to the customer—the front-end functions such as sales, local marketing, customer service, and technical support—are focused and organized around the customer's needs. The functions upstream from the customer, such as R&D, operations, and product marketing, are organized to achieve product excellence and scale. In the example, none of these business functions are shared or have two bosses, so it is not a matrix organization like the one shown in Figure 18.6. Nor is it a country organization; the large engine product company, although located in the United Kingdom, is a separate profit center from the UK market company. Product companies are structured to serve all market companies equally; serving all market companies distinguishes the front–back from the worldwide business unit structure. Figure 18.8 contrasts the product flow of the front–back model with that of the business units of General Electric. General Electric's profit centers have dedicated sales and service functions for each business

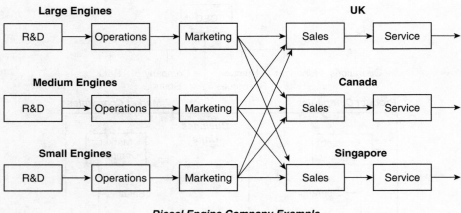

Diesel Engine Company Example

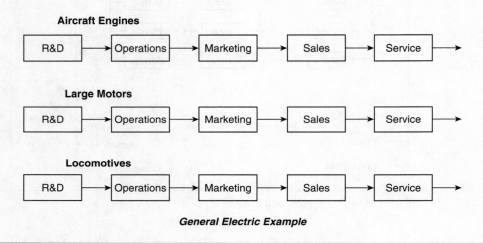

General Electric Example

Figure 18.8   Front–Back Model Compared With Business Units

unit; the diesel engine supplier uses its sales and service functions to sell and service all its products. The front–back model requires a much more complicated product flow than the business unit model does; managing this product flow is addressed in the last section of this chapter. The front–back therefore is a hybrid; it is not a country-based structure, nor is it a worldwide business structure but rather a combination of the two.

The corporate functions form a matrix across the product company and the market company profit centers. The operations and

R&D functions form a matrix across the product companies. The human resource and finance functions form a matrix across both product and market companies. So the diesel engine company has a three-dimensional structure: product, geographies, and functions. But only the functions form a matrix across both product and market companies.

Some form of matrix usually is used to tie the front and the back together; the diesel engine supplier illustrates the concept. The corporate function–profit center matrix just described is one form. In the 1980s, diesel engines began to be used to supply electric power, and some towns and factories found that they could use a smaller power plant than those supplied by power generation companies such as ABB (the diesel engine company whose organization is shown in Figure 18.8 focused on this power market). A diesel engine supplier could get an engine running and delivering power more quickly than a power generation company could by making product modifications so that its engines could more efficiently generate electricity; fully half the current diesel engine sales are to the power market (the remainder are for ship propulsion). Because the purchasers of power engines want only an electrical source, not all the headaches of running a power plant, the engine supplier started a service business to operate power plants for cities and factories and to provide engine maintenance. The resulting organization is shown in Figure 18.9.

The diesel engine supplier has added two new businesses—power and service—to what was the lone marine engine business. These global businesses link the product companies and the market companies through shared activities that form a matrix organization. For example, sales in the market companies are now specialized and divided into the marine market, the power market, and the service market. The marine sales unit in a country is shared and reports to the marine business manager and the country manager. In the product companies, product development, some manufacturing, and product marketing are now organized by power, service, and marine; in the product companies, there is sufficient volume to allow a business specialization. Purchasing and some component manufacturing remain separate and serve all businesses; the R&D and manufacturing resources are shared resources, collected into the businesses. The business manager in the product company reports to the global business manager and to the head of the product company. The businesses form a matrix structure across the product and market companies, with the business resources shared. The addition of the business matrix makes the diesel engine company a four-dimensional structure.

In some industries the front–back hybrid form has been around for some time, although it was not called front–back. The investment banking business has always had relationship management and product management components, but the front–back model now occurs in all types of businesses. What is causing this organization form to be the structure of choice?

A number of forces are pushing companies into the front–back structure, but the dominant one is the customer. A major effect of global competition has been a shift in the buyer–seller relationship to the buyer, who has learned how to use this power and now demands more value and more attentive service than previously. Sellers are responding to these demands by organizing their activities around customers and customer segments, although in many industries it is impossible to align and dedicate all functional activities to a customer segment and form a self-contained business unit; the semiconductor industry is an example.

Semiconductor manufacturers must now customize their products for buyers in the telecommunication, defense, computer, and automotive industries; these manufacturers have created sales, service, application engineering, and product design units dedicated to customers in these industries. However, a semiconductor factory costs $1 billion or more, and it is impossible to build a factory for each customer segment. Therefore, product units, which supply all customer segments, are created for the factories, as are product engineering and supporting activities. These achieve focus and responsiveness. This is the primary objective of the structure: to achieve customer focus and responsiveness along with product excellence and scale. The local customer, with uniquely local needs, can be supplied by global scale; this structure permits the supplier to be simultaneously global and local.

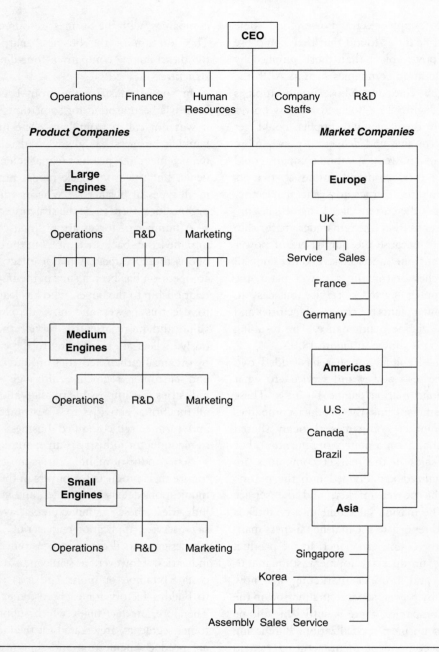

Figure 18.9   Front–Back Hybrid Structure

The factors that cause a multiproduct company to choose the front–back structure are as follows:

- Customers can buy all products.
- Customers want a single point of contact.
- Customers want a sourcing partnership.

- Customers want solutions and systems, not components and products.
- Opportunities exist for cross-selling and bundling.
- Value-added business is becoming increasingly customer specific.

- Advantage can be gained through superior knowledge about customers and customer segments.

The pressure for a market focus (and a separate structure) starts when customers buy—or can buy—all products. (If products are all purchased by different customers in different countries, there is no pressure for separate customer structures.) When customers can buy all products, the question arises whether each product group needs its own sales force, all of whom call on the same customer. Would it not be more economical to have one sales force sell all products to the customer? The answer depends, in part, on how the customer wants to do business. Some customers have different buyers purchasing different products from the same vendor; these companies may prefer to have separate, product knowledgeable salespeople calling on separate, product knowledgeable buyers. Some products may be sold to the customer end user, not to buyers from purchasing at all. Increasingly, however, customers are pooling their purchases and negotiating a total, single contract with multiproduct vendors. These customers want a single point of contact in the vendor organization for communication, negotiation, and coordination to lower their joint costs; these single interfaces are the beginning of the front-end customer structure.

An increasing number of customers are adopting sourcing policies like those of the auto industry; that is, they prefer to have fewer, closer, and longer-term vendor relationships. They choose one or two vendors for a product and dedicate their entire volume to those vendors, who become their partners. In return, the customer may prefer—and some will insist—that the vendor create a strong local manager or a dedicated organization unit with whom it can conduct its business (Lewis, 1995); this unit becomes a front-end customer unit.

Some customers want to buy systems rather than products. Wells Fargo Bank is buying products when it orders 250 personal computers from IBM, but Wells Fargo may actually want to buy a consumer banking system. A system consists of many products—desktop computers, teller terminals, automatic teller machines, high-volume transaction processors, disk drive storage—that are all manufactured by different units at IBM. When buying a system, Wells Fargo does not want a collection of products but a banking system that works. As a result, IBM will do the system integration for customers such as Wells Fargo who do not want to do it themselves. Therefore, vendors such as IBM need a system integration capability, which also becomes a front-end customer function.

Customers who do not currently buy all of a vendor's products may provide cross-selling opportunities for the vendor. By bundling products together for a single price, the vendor may win a greater share of the customer's business. Software companies create suites of programs in this way for selected segments. Citibank relationship managers package foreign exchange and cash management for global customers. Cross-selling and bundling usually require a single customer-focused unit in the front end to create and price the package for the customer.

These examples illustrate that more value-adding activities are being created that are best located in the front-end structure and focused on the local customer or global customer segment. In the past, sales was the one activity organized around the customer, but more customer-specific services and software are now being added. PPG used to sell paint to automobile manufacturers; today, it sells paint, provides application software for choosing paints, and runs the entire painting operation for General Motors. As the economies of developed countries become service and information oriented, companies will continue to add service and software as a source of growth. These services, which typically require customization for market segments and customers, are being located in the front-end local, or customer, structure.

Many companies are recognizing that a local customer or customer segment structure allows them to create superior information and knowledge about customers and to form close relationships with them. If the knowledge and relationships can be converted to superior products and services, the segment focus will become a competitive advantage.

IBM'S STRUCTURE

The most complex organization I have encountered is IBM. The structure I will describe has six dimensions to it. As shown in Figure 18.10, IBM is organized around functions, products, solutions, customers, geographies, and channels. It also is organized around a customer-facing front end and a product-and-solution back end. The front end of the structure consists of regions, customer segments based on industries, and channel partners through which IBM sells to its customers. The back end consists of the product lines, which are classified as hardware, software, and services. Also, generic or cross-industry solutions are organized as part of global services. For example a customer relationship management system is a type of solution consisting of a combination of hardware, software, and services and is sold to customers in all industries. Solutions that are industry specific are organized as part of the industry groups. This structure allows IBM to achieve global scale and leverage in the back end and local adaptation and customization in the front end. Indeed, the front–back structure is a means for implementing mass customization strategies.

MANAGEMENT PROCESSES

The front–back organization is a process-intensive organization. Success seems to require a strong customer-facing front end, a strong global back end, and an equally strong corporate management to integrate them into one company. The strong central leadership is enacted through five management processes discussed in this section. A standalone product company will have a business unit planning and budgeting process, a new product development process, and an order fulfillment process. A solution provider that adopts a front–back structure, such as IBM, needs to have those same processes with five modifications. These processes build on the lateral networks of the industry groups. In Figure 18.10, the consulting, software, and outsourcing units all show industry groupings as part of their structures. These units provide staffs that participate in the processes described below.

Strategy and Reconciliation

In addition to product strategies, the solution company must generate customer and solution strategies. At IBM the plans and strategies are created for servers, desktops, storage units, database software, Lotus software, and other products. There are also strategies for 1,000 global customers, which are aggregated into industry groups. In each industry the customers are prioritized according to profitability. Then the customer and solution strategies must be reconciled with the product strategies. A product general manager may feel that a customer unit is not featuring the manager's product line as it should. Usually the top management performs the reconciliation using a spreadsheet like the one shown in Figure 18.11.

The reconciliation requires a strong and active top management. In a business unit structure, the leader can interact with business units one at a time. In a front–back structure, the leader needs to get everyone around a table and manage the natural conflict. The result of the reconciliation is an aligned set of goals. The front and the back have the same goals to attain.

Product Portfolio

Each product unit develops its own products, but each unit's products must work together with the product of other units to provide a solution. For example, if Nokia is going to offer third-generation equipment,[1] it

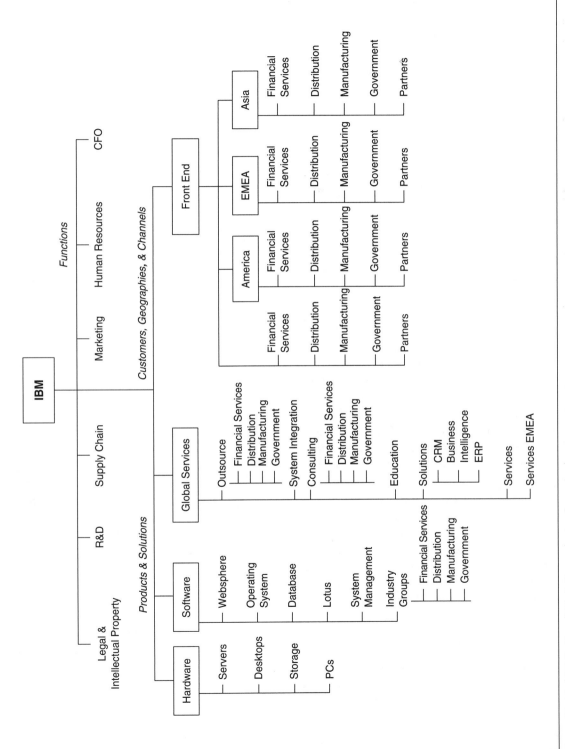

Figure 18.10 IBM's Front–Back Structure

Customer–Solution Units

	A	B	C	D
1	Revenues, Profits, Growth, etc.			
2			Revenues, Profits, Growth, etc.	
3		Revenues, Profits, Growth, etc.		
4				

Product Units (vertical axis label)

Figure 18.11   Spreadsheet to Reconcile Solution and Product Plans

must have switches and transmission products, software, consulting practices, customer service contracts, and handsets that all work together using 3G technology. The product units cannot independently develop their own product lines without a dialogue. Again, a strong top-management team is needed to guide the portfolio planning process. The Nokia software product business may want to challenge Microsoft. However, Nokia will also need a totally integrated product line in order to provide customer solutions. Through the portfolio planning process, the software and other product groups have to develop a strategy that advances their product line and integrates the products into solution offerings.

Solution Development

In addition to developing products, a solution strategy requires a solution development process. There are two aspects to this development process. The first is the choice of what solutions to offer. Usually the solution providers, such as IBM and Nokia, choose solutions that can be replicated. Replication then requires a process to create a solution that can be sold to other customers. If every solution is unique, the company cannot make much money on them. It needs to invest up front and then replicate the solution to get a return on its fixed investment.

The second aspect is an explicit process, like the new product development process, to develop a replicable solution. Usually a solution provider works with a lead customer and invests in the solution so that it can be sold to similar customers. For example, IBM tries to start with Swedish banks for its financial service solutions in Europe. They believe that innovation starts in the north of Europe and moves south. Often there are centers such as the Insurance Solutions Development Center, where IBM and the customers coinvest to create solutions.

Solution Fulfillment

The company usually has an order fulfillment or supply chain management process.

Solutions require an addition to the front end of this process. When a customer orders a solution, the solution must be broken into its product components, and each is assigned and scheduled for a product division. But the assignment of revenue to the product units usually becomes an issue. When a solution is created, it usually contains an estimated price and prices for all of the components. But when an actual order is won, the solution price may be different than planned in order to win the order. Then the allocation of revenue and pricing of components becomes an issue again. The issue arises on every sale that has a solution price change.

Pricing therefore is a major policy issue for solution providers. They usually have pricing committees or pricing centers. For example, at IBM the finance department is active in pricing and has models based on its experience for a pricing decision and allocation of revenue. To make the decision in a timely manner and resolve disputes, the finance people make the final decision at IBM. So the fulfillment process entails a computational change, which breaks orders for solutions into orders for products and a pricing decision process for determining revenue for solutions and products.

Assembly–Disassembly of Teams

A major addition to all solution companies' processes is one for mobilizing teams to capture opportunities for solution sales and their implementation when capture is successful. The size of the task of assembling teams of talent is directly related to the scale and scope of the solution. The larger the solution, the larger the capture team that must be marshaled. However, large solutions usually can be anticipated and planning begun before the actual request appears. The IBM account manager for Volkswagen should know that a new American assembly plant is in the works. The account team usually can talk to the CIO and predict what equipment and software will be

needed. So a lot of work for gathering a team and preparing a bid can be done in advance.

Timing sometimes can be predicted also. But when the request to bid is made, time is critical. The account team of salespeople needs to swing into action. But it also needs to be supplemented with people from the services, the partners, and the product lines. Often the services units are organized like a consulting firm where people routinely move from project to project. The product lines often have business development departments with people who are tasked with winning new business. These people join the capture team and work with the salespeople to win the opportunity. IBM forms quick response groups of technical people trained in solutions such as wireless field applications that can form and reform into capture teams. The important point is to have flexible resource units that can contribute to the constantly forming teams. The amount of revenue that comes from solutions is an important determining factor in the design of flexible resource units. The larger the revenue, the easier it is to get product and service units to create quick response teams. If the product and service units have growth goals, they are interested in providing talent for winning new business.

Another key feature of assembling teams is a short-run decision process to match resources with opportunities. Companies with a wide scope of solutions will engage many specialists. Invariably some of these specialists are in short supply and limit the number of opportunities a solution provider can address. A company needs to decide which opportunities will be pursued. The priority of the customer created in the customer strategy will be used in the decision process. Some companies assign a priority number from one to five to customers in the strategy process. Usually the priority is based on customer profitability. IBM uses its regional organization to allocate the limited talent to opportunities. All talent resources are organized regionally rather than by country. The European leadership team meets once or twice per week to match its limited resources to opportunities. Consulting firms have similar regional decision processes. These firms usually have a scheduling or staffing department that supports these decision processes.

Thus it is through management processes and lateral networks that the front–back units are integrated. These processes are the vehicles through which strong leadership is exercised. When this leadership and the requisite processes are missing, the company fails at solutions and the front–back model. Hewlett-Packard tried on five different occasions to implement the front–back model. Primarily because of the lack of top-down leadership and strategy, these five attempts were abandoned. HP was and is an effective product provider but is trying once again to become a solution provider.

So starting with Chandler, organization design research has generated a body of knowledge to match the increasingly complex strategies that companies are following. The complex organizations consist of multidimensional structures, extensive lateral networks, and many management process through which the leaders resolve the conflicting priorities.

THE NEXT ORGANIZATIONS

The field of organization design has developed along with the complexity of organizations. As long as managers need help with design, organization design will continue to develop. Some recent research and ideas give us some ideas about the future. One that we can see already is unbundling of the organization. Following the ideas of Treacy and Wiersema (1995), Hagel and Singer (1999) suggest that organizations will be unbundled into cost-centric, product-centric, and customer-centric portions. The reason is that each type is a different business model and requires a different form of organization. We have already seen the different structures for the front–back model. This structure consists of a customer-centric front end and a product-centric back end. But it is not just the structures that are different but the

entire star model. The contrasting organizations for the product- and customer-centric types are shown in Table 18.4.

By reading down the list of organization characteristics, one can see that they form an aligned star model. The product-centric company has product profit centers, a well-tuned product development process, product measures, and a product excellence culture.

The customer-centric company tries to find as many products and services as it can for its customer. It is organized around customer profit centers, customer relationship processes, customer retention measures, and a customer-friendly culture. It too is a completely aligned star model. The two types must be separated; otherwise, products would be compromised in one and customers compromised in the other. Companies can choose to be one or the other of these types. Or they can try to be both, but they must separate the two units into a front–back model.

Today companies are going a step further and separating out the cost-centric activities. The structure is shown in Figure 18.12. The pressures to be cost competitive are leading to the design of a complete star model for a cost-centric organization. The most repetitive and transactional activities are placed in this organization. These activities typically are those that are candidates for outsourcing. They are not sources of competitive advantage. They simply need to be performed reliably and at minimum cost. Initially these were shared services activities, but now more activities such as procurement, operations, and manufacturing are going into an infrastructure unit. Some or all of these activities may be outsourced. However, the management of the activities still remains in the cost-centric unit. Cisco is a company that is organized like the one shown in Figure 18.12. They outsource almost all of their manufacturing. However, they still have around 400 people in their manufacturing function to manage the vendors and the supply chain.

Table 18.4   Product-Centric Versus Customer-Centric

		Product-Centric Company	*Customer-Centric Company*
STRATEGY	Goal	Best product for customer	Best solution for customer
	Main offering	New products	Personalized packages of products, service, support, education, consulting
	Value creation route	Cutting-edge products, useful new applications	Customizing for best total solution
	Most important customer	Most advanced customer	Most profitable, loyal customer
	Priority setting basis	Portfolio of products	Portfolio of customers, customer profitability
	Pricing	Price to market	Price for value, risk
STRUCTURE	Organizational concept	Product profit centers, product reviews, product teams	Customer segments, customer teams, customer P&Ls
PROCESSES	Most important process	New product development	Customer relationship management and solution development
REWARDS	Measures	• Number of new products • Percentage of revenue from products less than two years old • Market share	• Customers share of most valuable customers • Customer satisfaction • Lifetime value of a customer • Customer retention
PEOPLE	Approach to personnel	Power to people who develop products • Highest reward is working on most challenging product • Manage creative people through challenges with a deadline	Power to people with in-depth knowledge of customer's business • Highest rewards to relationship managers who save the customer's business
	Mental process	Divergent thinking: *How many possible uses of this product?*	Convergent thinking: *What combination of products is best for this customer?*
	Sales bias	On the side of the seller in a transaction	On the side of the buyer in a transaction
	Culture	New product culture: open to new ideas, experimentation	Relationship management culture: searching for more customer needs to satisfy

A cost-centric organization is shown in Table 18.5. Like the product- and customer-centric models, the cost-centric model is an aligned Star Model. Starting with a strategy for achieving the lowest total cost, the structure is built around centralized functions, which manage the processes, especially the order-to-cash and other transaction processes. The people, rewards, and culture are all oriented toward continual cost reduction and minimization of total costs.

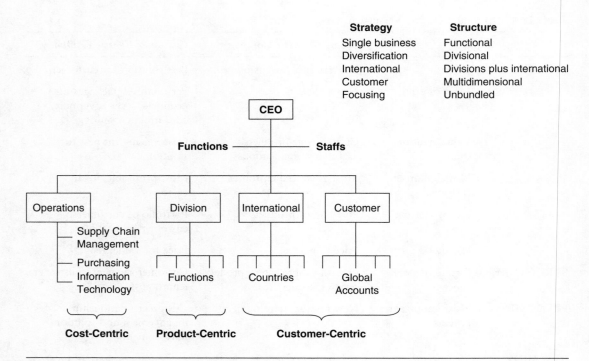

Figure 18.12   The Unbundled Model

Table 18.5   The Cost-Centric Organization

		Cost-Centric Company
STRATEGY	Goal	Lowest total cost
	Main offering	An acceptable product at the lowest price
	Value creation route	No frills offering for the middle of the market
	Most important customer	The value shopper
	Priority setting basis	Find the most efficient way to do everything
	Pricing	Guaranteed lowest price or everyday low price
STRUCTURE	Organizational concept	Strong centralized functions to standardize, economize, and achieve scale
PROCESSES	Most important process	Order-to-cash
		All transaction processes are efficiently reengineered
REWARDS	Measures	• Detailed measures of all costs • Total delivered cost • Constant improvement and cost reduction
PEOPLE	Approach to personnel	Power to discoverers of how to use scale and leverage • Highest rewards to the discoverers of cost-reduction ideas • Best if it is the frugal person who prefers Motel 6
	Mental process	Lean thinking: *How to eliminate time, waste, cost?*
	Sales bias	Anything that increases constant, level volume
	Culture	Constant search for improvement of costs through eliminating waste and variety and implementing repeatable processes.

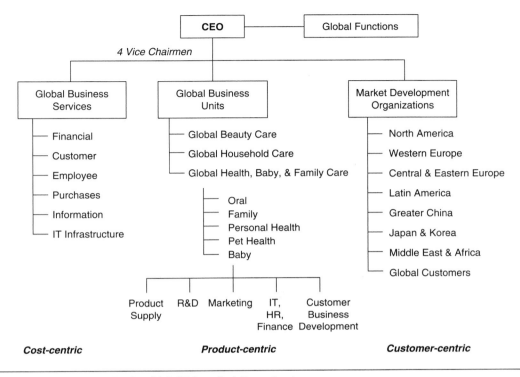

Figure 18.13   Procter & Gamble's Unbundled Organization

Another organization pursuing this unbundled model is Procter & Gamble. Their structure is shown in Figure 18.13. It consists of a customer-centric front end or market development organizations, which focus on products and brands. The cost-centric portion of the structure is global business services. These services are located in cost-effective places such as Costa Rica for the Americas. The corporate center and global functions round out the complete structure.

When asked how Procter & Gamble has achieved its superior performance in recent years, the CEO A. G. Lafley said that one of the reasons was their unique organization structure that creates an advantage. It currently creates an advantage because no other competitors are organized in this manner.

CONCLUSION

The field of organization design has developed from the principles of scientific management. It was the research in the 1960s, 1970s, and 1980s that laid the foundation for design. This period was led by academics researching the new forms of organization. Today firms are organizing around functions, products, countries, customers, and channels. They organize differently in each country and each business. The leading edge of design today is with companies such as IBM that are implementing these multidimensional, front–back designs and companies such as Procter & Gamble with its unbundled model. The rise of social networks and their design may be an opening for the academic research to move to the forefront again.

NOTE

1. Third generation (3G) is a wireless technology that will permit handsets to connect to the Internet and to various company databases.

REFERENCES

Barnard, C. I. (1938). *The functions of the executive.* Cambridge, MA: Harvard University Press.

Bartlett, C., & Ghoshal, S. (1989). *Managing across borders*. Boston: Harvard Business School Press.

Burns, T., & Stalker, G. M. (1961). *The management of innovation*. London: Tavistock.

Chandler, A. (1962). *Strategy and structure*. Cambridge: MIT Press.

Drucker, P. (1946). *Concept of the corporation*. New York: John Day.

Egelhoff, W. (1988). *Organizing the multinational enterprise*. Cambridge, MA: Ballinger.

Fayol, H. (1949). *General and industrial management*. London: Pitman. (Original French version published 1916)

Franko, L. (1976). *The European multinationals*. Greenwich, CT: Greylock.

Galbraith, J. R. (1973). *Designing complex organizations*. Reading, MA: Addison-Wesley.

Galbraith, J. (1993). The value-adding corporation. In J. Galbraith, E. E. Lawler, & Associates (Eds.), *Organizing for the future*. San Francisco: Jossey-Bass.

Galbraith, J. (2002). *Designing organizations: An executive guide to strategy, structure and process*. San Francisco: Jossey-Bass.

Galbraith, J., & Kazanjian, R. (1986). *Strategy implementation: The role of structure and process* (2nd ed.). St. Paul, MN: West.

Hagel, J., & Singer, M. (1999, March–April). Unbundling the corporation. *Harvard Business Review*, 133–141.

Jennergren, L. (1981). Decentralization in organizations. In W. Starbuck & P. Nystrom (Eds.), *Handbook of organization design*. Oxford, UK: Oxford University Press.

Lawrence, P. R., & J. W. Lorsch (1967). *Organization and environment*. Boston: Harvard Business School Press.

Leavitt, H. (1965). Applied organization change in industry. In J. March (Ed.), *Handbook of organizations*. New York: Rand McNally.

Lewis, J. D. (1995). *The connected corporation: How leading companies win through customer–supplier alliances*. New York: Free Press.

March, J. (1965). *Handbook of organizations*. New York: Rand McNally.

Peters, T. J., & Waterman, R. H. Jr. (1982). *In search of excellence: Lessons from America's best-run companies*. New York: Harper & Row.

Prahalad, C. K., & Doz, Y. (1987). *The multinational mission*. New York: Pergamon.

Rumelt, R. (1973). *Strategy, structure and economic performance*. Boston: Harvard Business School Press.

Stopford, J., & Wells, L. (1968). *Managing the multinational enterprise*. London: Longmans.

Treacy, M., & Wiersema, F. (1995). *The discipline of market leaders*. Reading, MA: Addison-Wesley.

19

Strategic Human Resource Management

EDWARD E. LAWLER III

A number of forces have converged to support the idea that human resource (HR) management should be a major strategic focus in most organizations. Many recent articles, books, and studies have argued that HR management can be an important source of competitive advantage if it becomes more strategic (Boudreau & Ramstad, 2007; Brockbank, 1999; Lawler, 1995; Lawler & Mohrman, 2003b; Ulrich, 1997). The reason for this is clear: Corporations are undergoing dramatic changes that have significant implications for how critical human resources are to their performance. Perhaps the most important of these changes is the rapid deployment of information technology (IT) and the increasing amount of knowledge work that organizations do. Also important are the rapidly changing business environment and the increasing complexity of modern organizations (Lawler & Worley, 2006). These and other changes have created a growing consensus that effective human capital management is critical to an organization's success (Jackson, Hitt, & DeNisi, 2003).

HR FUNCTION IN ORGANIZATIONS

The future of HR management is inseparable from the future of the HR function in organizations. It is the developer and deliverer of the HR practices and programs in most large organizations. There is little doubt that the ways in which the HR function is organized, managed, and positioned and operates in corporations today will change dramatically over the next decade. Significant changes are already occurring because of the willingness of companies to outsource staff functions that are not viewed as core to their missions, the increasing prevalence of electronic self-service Web tools, the complexity and variety of new organization forms, and the criticality of human capital for competing in the knowledge economy (Lawler, Boudreau, & Mohrman, 2006; Lawler, Ulrich, Fitz-enz, & Madden, 2004). These changes raise important questions about how human capital should be managed: What kind of functions should the HR staff perform? What should be done by non-HR managers? How should the HR function be organized in order to add the most value? How can and should HR influence business strategy?

We are entering or are already in a time of significant upheaval in the work and responsibilities of internal HR functions and in services and value that HR consulting firms can and do provide to companies. Although it is not clear how these changes will ultimately play out, what is clear is that there will be more and more strategic HR work to be performed and that there will be a significant difference between the work being done by HR functions in companies today and that which will be performed by them in the future (Lawler et al., 2006; Lawler & Mohrman, 2003a).

Staff functions in general are under fire in organizations because they are often perceived as controlling rather than adding strategic value and as not responding to operating units' demands for change. They are being asked to change to provide expert support to the strategic initiatives of the company and to take advantage of technology and other approaches to deliver more efficient and responsive services.

Despite compelling arguments supporting the view that HR management is the key strategic issue in most organizations, HR executives historically have not been strategic partners (Brockbank, 1999; Lawler, 1995; Lawler et al., 2006). The HR function has been an administrative function headed by people who focus largely on cost control and administrative activities (Ulrich, 1997).

A number of studies have investigated the potential for the HR function to be a strategic partner and found that it can be an important value-adding function. For example, work by Becker and Huselid (1998) found that there is a relationship between HR practices and firm performance. They found that firms with the greatest intensity of HR practices that reinforce performance had the highest market value per employee. They argue that HR practices are critical in determining the market value of corporations and that improvement in HR practices can lead to significant increases in market value. They conclude that the best firms are able to achieve both operational and strategic excellence in their HR systems and functions.

STRATEGIC AND BUSINESS PARTNERING

Perhaps the major champion of HR as a business partner is Dave Ulrich (1997). He has argued that the HR function must become strategically proactive and go beyond administrative expertise (Ulrich & Brockbank, 2005). It must be an expert in strategic business partnering, change management, and employee advocacy. Wright, Dyer, and Takla (1999) found that there is a growing consensus in support of Ulrich's model but that HR is not seen as able to execute on this model.

Given the changes that are occurring in the competitive environment of organizations, many significant opportunities exist for HR management to become more strategic. The creation and implementation of most business strategies depend on the quality of human input, usually from many parties possessing diverse knowledge and information about a complex and uncertain world. The effective execution of strategies depends on the quality of organization leadership and on widespread commitment in the workforce. Finally, even when a firm develops a viable and promising strategy that is well executed, its organization design and employees must be able to withstand and adapt to rapid and unanticipated changes in the marketplace (Lawler & Worley, 2006).

Exhibit 19.1 characterizes the three areas of HR management (see Lawler & Mohrman, 2003a). The first is the administrative one. It is the bread and butter of the HR function; it is the reason the function was created in the first place. The HR function in major corporations has a long history of offering administrative services while delivering little of value with respect to furthering their strategies. HR typically is positioned as a cost center with a ratio of one HR employee to about every 100 employees. The cost of HR administration is estimated to range from $900 to as much as

HR Roles

I. **Basic Administrative Services and Transactions involved with compensating, hiring, training and staffing**

   — *Emphasis on resource efficiency and service quality*

II. **Business Partner Services involved with developing effective HR systems and helping implement business plans, talent management**

   — *Emphasis on knowing the business and exercising influence--solving problems, designing effective HR systems to ensure needed competencies and talent.*

III. **Strategic Partner Role contributing to business strategy development and implementation based on considerations of human capital, organizational capabilities, and readiness. Developing HR practices as strategic differentiators**

   — *Emphasis on deep and broad knowledge of HR and of the business, competition, and market of business strategies*

Exhibit 19.1 HR Roles

$2,000 per employee in most large corporations. What do organizations get for this cost?

The evidence suggests that in many cases organizations do not get particularly good or cost-effective administrative services (Lawler & Mohrman, 2003a; Lawler, Ulrich, et al., 2004). It is not a core competency of corporations, and as a result the HR function does not possess the expertise and power needed to provide world-class service. In addition, the function is not large enough to achieve significant economies of scale in order to lower the cost of its services. It also doesn't have the expertise or capital to make significant investments in technology and system development. As a result, all too often HR ends up as a high-cost, low-quality bureaucratic provider of administrative services.

There is no question that HR administration needs to be done, but there is also no question that how well it is done is not likely to provide a competitive advantage. Because more and more firms are recognizing the nonstrategic nature of HR administrative services, outsourcing in transactional areas such as benefit administration is growing rapidly. This trend mirrors changes that are also occurring in other corporate staff areas, including accounting and information services. As companies realize that they cannot build world-class capabilities in all areas, they are turning to outsourcing in hopes of receiving higher-quality, less expensive services in the areas where they cannot be world class or decide not to make the investment needed to become world class.

The business partner and strategic partner roles shown in Exhibit 19.1 are newer and are the ones that HR functions seem to have the most trouble delivering (Brockbank, 1999). In some corporations it clearly does deliver on the business partner role, but rarely does it deliver on the strategic partner role. One of the reasons for this is that it often has to spend much of its time dealing with administrative issues (Lawler et al., 2006).

Figures 19.1 and 19.2 amplify the distinction between the business and strategic partner roles. They show that both have some of the same deliverables. The business partner role helps translate strategies into practices and helps with change management and implementation. Many organization development groups in organizations are already active in just this kind of work. Support for it can be found in a growing body of research that establishes links between organizational performance measures and the use of a wide range of HR management practices (Becker & Huselid, 1998).

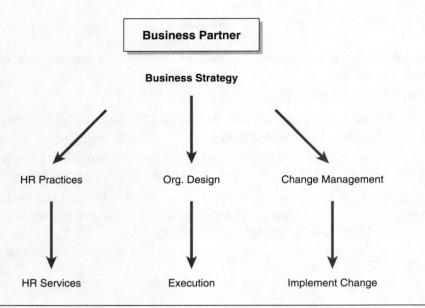

Figure 19.1   Business Partner

SOURCE: Copyright © 2005. Center for Effective Organizations, University of Southern California, EL67M.

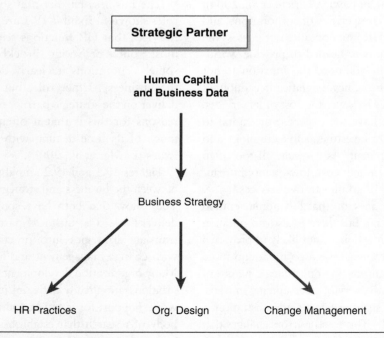

Figure 19.2   Strategic Partner

SOURCE: Copyright © 2005. Center for Effective Organizations, University of Southern California, EL68M.

The strategic partner role provides strong input and direction to the formation of business strategy and to the implementation of the business strategy. In order to have HR issues influence the strategy of organizations, an organization needs to have good metrics and analytic data about human capital, human capital management practices, organization capabilities, and core competencies (Boudreau & Ramstad, 2003; Lawler, Levenson, & Boudreau, 2004). It is a role that isn't well developed in many organizations and admittedly doesn't have as large a research base to draw on as does the business partner role. However, it has the ability to be a major value-adding activity if it improves the strategy development process.

IT AND HR MANAGEMENT

HR functions need to reinvent themselves if they are to deliver high-quality, low-cost administrative services and offer valuable strategic advice and services. They need to reinvent themselves in a world of increasingly rapid change and the movement of most company activities onto the Web. HR management needs to become part of the movement of business onto the Web. In addition to moving HR administrative functions onto the Web, organizations need to create Web-based metric and analytic models that provide the kind of human capital information that improves strategy formulation and implementation.

Figure 19.3 illustrates the relationship between IT and the three major roles that HR management can play in the modern corporation. These three roles range along a continuum from contributing to the company's strategy—highly uncertain, experience-based knowledge work that entails expert judgment—to transactional service work emphasizing production efficiency and service standards reflecting ease of use, responsiveness, and accuracy. The three HR roles entail different expertise, different mixes

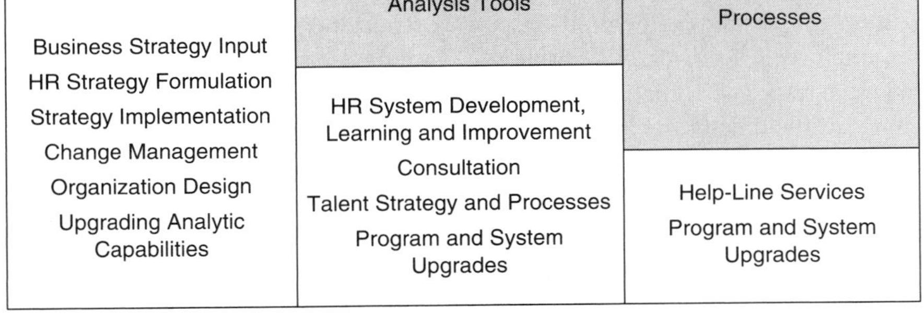

Strategic Partner Role	Business Support and Execution Role	Personnel Service Role
Data Analysis, Modeling, and Simulation Capabilities	HR System Administration Employee and Manager Tool, Information and Advice Data and Analysis Tools	Transactional Self-Service Processes
Business Strategy Input HR Strategy Formulation Strategy Implementation Change Management Organization Design Upgrading Analytic Capabilities	HR System Development, Learning and Improvement Consultation Talent Strategy and Processes Program and System Upgrades	Help-Line Services Program and System Upgrades

Figure 19.3   IT and HR Management

SOURCE: From *Handbook of management consulting, the contemporary consultant, insights from world experts,* by Greiner. 2005. Reprinted with permission of South-Western, a division of Thomson Learning: www.thomsonrights.com. Fax 800-730-2215.

Shaded = IT and HR enabled

of routine or nonroutine knowledge work, and different IT tools.

Transactional Personnel Services

For decades, the transactional work performed by HR has been largely paper based and labor intensive. It includes activities involved in advertising and filling a job, administering compensation and benefits, preparing personnel policies and distributing them, changing company records to keep up with employee changes, ensuring adequate records of performance appraisals, and even purchasing products from vendors. In addition, many kinds of training have been done in essentially a labor-intensive mode even when this learning is of a rote nature.

Today, almost all the transactional work of HR can be done in a self-service mode on computer-based intranet systems. The movement of these transactions to self-service on the Web is inevitable for several reasons. First and foremost, the traditional way this work has been done is costly and, in many instances, slow. It is often justified by emphasizing the importance of personal contact with employees, but it is not clear that this kind of personal contact is even desired by employees, much less worth the costs involved in delivering it.

As shown in Figure 19.3, the greatest overlap between IT and HR management occurs in the routine personnel administrative services role. By automating these simple transactional processes and fostering employee self-service, HR can eliminate multiple-step paperwork that consumes a large percentage of the time of the HR staff and reduce the costs of HR administration. However, even with the most advanced IT systems there is a need for some personally delivered knowledge-based services, often in the form of call centers or help lines, to deal with complex cases, answer questions, and to teach employees how to use the self-service systems.

To date it is the routine transactional area where IT and outsourcing firms have been active in the design, software development, implementation, and ongoing operations of HR systems.

There also is a large business in maintaining these systems, reprogramming them for changes in the parameters of the system, and upgrading their capabilities. Relevant knowledge and skill for performing these activities are not typically found in traditional HR departments, and therefore much of this work is outsourced. With outsourcing comes the need to establish contracts and to monitor contract performance. The skills and knowledge to do this often are not present in the HR organization but must be developed.

Some HR administrative functions have already been outsourced to vendors by many organizations. This is particularly true of benefit administration, around which Hewitt, Fidelity, and other firms have built large outsourcing businesses. They offer substantive knowledge about how to create a cost-effective system, and they deliver the administrative services. Outsourcers in this area typically operate their own call centers to answer employees' questions and try to migrate the employees they serve to Web-based interfaces. This is often done by putting kiosks at company locations or linking companies' networks into the outsourcer's computer systems.

There is every reason to believe that almost all HR transactional work will go on the Web and in most cases be outsourced (Lawler, Ulrich, et al., 2004). The reason is simple: HR administration is not a core competency of most organizations. Outsourcers and consulting firms now exist that either have or are developing this core competency. Outsourcers are also able to operate on a scale that no firm can, and in HR administration, there are significant economies of scale.

Of course, organizations can choose not to outsource any or all of their HR transactional work but still actively pursue the Web enabling them. There are four basic self-service solutions from which organizations can choose when it comes to using IT to handle HR administrative tasks. The four Web-enabled choices are home gown (companies develop their own software), best-in-breed (companies buy standalone applications from multiple vendors), integrated HR systems that are provided by enterprise resource planning companies (e.g., Oracle, SAP), and outsourcing. They all promise to deliver better HR services at lower costs by using Web-based systems, but they go about it in very different ways. It is likely that the last two will end up as the most popular approaches because they are best positioned to have low costs and well-developed systems.

Business Support

In the middle column of Figure 19.3 is the HR work involved in the development of HR systems and services that support the execution of the company's business strategy and, more generally, its business operations. These activities include the design and management of systems to secure needed talent, compensate and motivate people, train and develop them, and place them in the right jobs. It also includes internal consultation to line managers about their HR needs, questions, and issues. These are key HR knowledge areas and are the ones in which HR departments have a significant opportunity to add value. In order to operate effectively in this area, capabilities in HR system design and organization development are needed.

Some aspects of HR management systems can be codified and automated. For example, computer modeling tools that are based on the objectives of the compensation system can be provided to managers so that they can do their own compensation planning. Much of the work that HR has traditionally done in consulting to managers about HR staffing, training, development, and performance management issues can also be handled by putting information and tools on the Web while encouraging self-service. For example, a manager dealing with the potential transfer of an employee can be provided with procedures, criteria, and a diagnostic set of questions to help determine exactly what needs to be done to carry out the transfer.

Web-enabling HR systems and transactions make possible the systematic tracking and evaluation of HR systems. For example, they can help determine the relationship between compensation awards and performance evaluation results. They can help track the effectiveness of an organization management development program. Data-based analyses, tracking, and modeling capabilities also can provide a basis for improving HR systems. Having data-based capabilities that involve knowledge-orientated tools is critical to HR's ability to contribute to organization effectiveness.

The development and management of HR systems, whether they are Web based or not, entails a deep understanding of the principles, regulatory issues, and dynamics of HR systems and the strategy and the business model of the organization. There must be a close relationship between the way the work of employees is designed and HR systems such as job grades, career tracks, and incentive methods. Therefore, the crafting of effective HR systems cannot be accomplished without expert knowledge of HR and business strategy.

Strategic Partner

The strategic partner role is the one that is least well developed in most corporations and the newest. It also is the one that has the potential to add the most value. It is rapidly increasing in importance because of the growing importance of intangibles and human capital (Lev, 2001). It entails providing strategic advice and expertise. It includes providing input to the organization's business strategy and playing a key leadership role in developing the organization capabilities and core competencies that are needed in order to execute the strategy. Organization design, HR systems, and change management are all key to successful strategy execution.

HR can make a logical case for being an important part of strategy development because of the importance of human capital in the ability of the firm to carry out its strategy. Increasingly, talent limitations and limited organization flexibility in the application of scarce talent constrain the strategic options of the firm

(Mohrman, Galbraith, Lawler, & Associates, 1998). At least in theory, this should mean that HR can play an important role in formulating strategy by making explicit the human capital resources that are needed to support various strategies and strategic initiatives. It also can play a leadership role in helping the organization develop the necessary capabilities to enact the strategy and in implementation and change management.

Most strategies, like most mergers, fail not because of poor thinking but because of poor implementation. Implementation failures usually involve the failure to acknowledge and build the needed skills and organization capabilities, to gain support of the workforce, and to support the organization changes and learning needed to behave in new ways. In short, execution failures often are the result of poor human capital management. This opens the door for HR to add important value if it can deliver effective change strategies, plans, and thinking that aid in the development and execution of business strategy.

The HR function within companies potentially can play a key role by working closely with top management and consultants on strategy issues. There is much research to suggest that strategic planning and complex change efforts that do not consider and involve the human element are doomed to failure. HR can assist senior management in seeking out consultants who are especially skillful at including and involving people in strategic planning, organization design, and change management. And HR can work closely with consultants to provide internal knowledge.

HR can play a vital partner role in the use of IT for strategic planning development purposes. The ability to track and model the company's talent pool provides HR with compelling data about whether the human capital of the firm is adequate to enact a strategy, where talent is, and how it might be redeployed in order to carry out a changing strategy.

IT tools also can be useful for ongoing sensing of employee reactions to changes that are being implemented and for communication and solicitation of input to changes. Electronic HR systems can enable two-way communication with employees to help accelerate learning in the organization and consequently the implementation of fundamental changes. Again, however, the ability to use IT for these purposes depends on access to IT expertise in the HR domain.

Finally, HR scorecards can be developed that report on the overall condition of the workforce and the work systems of an organization (Huselid, Becker, & Beatty, 2005). Scorecards can be helpful in strategy development (they can indicate what is possible) and in the monitoring of strategy implementation.

STRUCTURING HR

Most HR organizations have struggled with the issue of how to organize in order to deliver their services. Indeed, it is quite likely that their failure to organize properly is one of the reasons why they have had trouble developing a high value-added strategic role. The skills that are needed to provide services concerning business strategy development, implementation support, and execution are significantly different from those needed for personnel services and HR administration. For this reason and a number of others, different people need to be involved, and the structure of the HR organization must be designed to provide these very different services. The best structure to do this is a version of the front–back design (Galbraith, 2005).

In the typical HR front–back structure, the administrative services are delivered by centralized shared services (or outsourced) processing units. The business partner and some strategic services are provided by senior HR managers, often called generalists, who are located in the key business units of the organization. The HR generalist is the major interface between the HR organization and the business unit. The generalists are available to help with picking the right HR practices, developing change management strategies, advising on talent development and deployment, and the other HR issues and organization effectiveness issues that come up as line managers try to implement and effectively manage their business units. They also have the responsibility for overseeing the delivery of administrative services to the business unit. Typically, the generalists who are in this role report jointly to the business unit manager, as well as to the HR vice president.

In order to execute the HR generalist's role effectively, HR managers need support. First and foremost, they need to be able to draw on expertise in the issues that they confront in their business support activities. This expertise can come from corporate centers of expertise in areas such as change management, organization development, leadership development, staffing, and metrics and analytics, or it can come from external consultants. Regardless of where the help comes from, it must be available, and the organization must be structured and resourced so that the HR generalists in the business units have the resources that they need to deliver their product line.

In many organizations where the generalist role has been established, the generalists have not been able to deliver the business partner and strategic services the organization needs. Often it is because they lack a depth of knowledge of the business. In some cases, it has to do with the resources that are available to them. They simply do not have the ability to access either the internal resources or the external resources to deliver on some of the complex issues that they face. They also often find it difficult to report to both the HR vice president and a business unit head.

Business strategy typically is developed at the corporate level in most organizations. Thus, the strategy implementation process begins there, and strategic input must be delivered to the senior executives of the corporation. HR input must include an analysis of the organization's strategic readiness and its ability to implement different strategies. In order to deliver these inputs, HR needs people at the corporate, senior executive level who can interact as peers with other senior executives and HR generalists and who can help with strategy development and implementation. This suggests that there must be staff at the corporate level that is focused on strategy analysis, development, and implementation—in effect, an organization effectiveness unit that has a small, full-time staff. This unit also must be chartered to draw on HR executives (e.g., generalists) from elsewhere in the organization and consultants to help with strategy development and implementation.

What should an organization effectiveness unit look like? It must be a multidiscipline center of excellence that focuses on business strategy, organization design, and human capital management. It should be staffed by people who have expertise in business strategy, organization design, organization capability development, knowledge management, HR analytics and metrics, financial modeling, and utility analysis. In short, it should have a broad range of analytic skills so that it can evaluate different strategic options and alternatives for the business, assess how effectively the current strategy is being implemented, and develop recommendations about how to improve the strategic position of the organization and the implementation of its current strategy.

FUTURE OF HR

For the last decade, the Holy Grail for HR functions in large corporations has been to become a business partner. Much of the writing on how HR can become a partner argues that the best way is for HR to focus on aligning the human capital management of an organization with its business strategy. This usually means being sure that there is an appropriate reservoir of leadership talent and technical talent to support the direction in which the business is heading. The associated HR activities include the development of a talent strategy and the design and ongoing operation of HR systems that contribute to business performance.

There clearly is a demand for business partner help from the HR function, as senior executives often report that they would like HR to be a partner with them in managing the talent strategy and the HR development agenda of the organization (Lawler et al., 2006). However, being a strategy implementation partner requires a broadening of the focus and expertise of HR beyond its traditional systems that are associated with human capital development.

Strategy implementation often entails the development of new organization capabilities and consequently entails organization design, development, and change management activities. Rather than focusing primarily on the individual employee's capabilities and motivation and the job as the unit of analysis, strategic HR must address system-wide requirements. It must focus on how a company can organize in a manner that optimally configures activities and uses talent to achieve business strategies and on enabling the organization to make changes in the way it functions.

Some HR functions have had organization development groups that profess to have expertise in organization design and development. However, most of them have been focused more on training and development than on change management and organization design.

Finally, there is the least developed area of HR, acting as a strategic partner that helps develop business strategy. Many of the writings on HR being a business partner fail to even mention the potentially important role HR expertise can play and should play in shaping the business agenda of corporations, particularly when human capital is the critical strategic resource in the firm. Research points out that execution often is the key problem when an organization tries to implement a business strategy. Sometimes, execution does fail because of the type of talent in the organization, but it fails more often because of the inability of the organization to change its systems to support the business strategy or because key design features of the organization are barriers to the development of the capabilities needed to implement the new strategy (Lawler & Worley, 2006).

Many of the implementation problems with the strategy can be avoided if a realistic assessment is made of the organization's ability to implement the strategy before it is adopted. HR potentially can play a key strategic role by identifying the existing performance capabilities of the employees and the organization and using this information in the strategy process. It also can contribute to the development of new strategic directions for the business by identifying the capabilities and competencies that the organization has that are not broadly recognized or currently used. If people from the HR function understand the business and the capabilities of the organization and have expertise in organization design and change, they may be in an unusually good position to recognize and develop promising new strategic directions.

There is a potentially close interplay between the expertise needed to be a strategic partner and IT tools. With the growth of Web-based HR systems, there is an increasing potential for the analysis of HR data to play a powerful role in the development and implementation of business strategies. Well-developed HR IT systems make possible employee and workforce analyses that are quite helpful in identifying the feasibility of entering new areas of business and developing key organization capabilities.

HR functions increasingly have metrics about how well the HR function is operating (Lawler, Levenson, et al., 2004). However, organizations need to go beyond simply having metrics that show how well HR administration is going. They need to have metrics that allow them to more effectively analyze and allocate their human capital (Boudreau & Ramstad, 2003, 2007). They need to include such things as competency models that identify personnel skills and help the organization move into new business areas.

HR measurement systems need to be used that provide complete data on the condition of the human capital. Measures are needed of how satisfied it is, how committed it is to the organization, the rate at which it turns over, and a host of other issues that assess the readiness and the ability of the organization to perform. These data, which are already collected by the HR organization in many companies, must become part of an integrated Web-based system and related to organization outcomes. This is how HR analytics can help an organization determine what is and what is not working and make improvements in its practices and programs and its strategy. It is a critical deliverable that HR must have in order to be a strategic partner (Lawler, Levenson, et al., 2004).

HR information systems should be particularly useful in helping strategy-driven change management efforts. They can provide powerful data on employee reactions to specific change initiatives and provide mechanisms for two-way communication about the business logic underpinning changes and their implications for employee career paths, rewards, and development. If they include training features, Web-based HR systems can also enable rapid implementation of training and development to support change. Because of the analytic power they can provide with respect to assessing HR programs, HR IT systems can be tools during times of change for accelerated learning and improvement of new HR programs that are put in place to support the strategy.

Despite the potential contributions HR can make to business strategy, there is very little evidence that the internal HR function in many companies is becoming more of a strategic partner (Lawler et al., 2006). This raises the key question of why it isn't changing. There are a number of possible answers to this, many of which have to do with the HR functions, strengths, and weaknesses.

On the strength side, HR managers almost always have a fine-grain knowledge of the organization's HR systems and may have an understanding of the work of the organization, its culture, and its capabilities, information that could make a significant contribution to the business strategy. On the weakness side, the HR function often has a poor reputation for its ability to deliver on business-related issues. This poor reputation often is well deserved, because people in the HR function do not have the business skills or business experiences that are necessary to link HR programs and processes to the business strategy. For most HR functions, business strategy, organization design, and change management are not core competencies.

BECOMING A STRATEGIC PARTNER

It is time for HR to become a strategic partner. For the last decade the focus has been on becoming a business partner; it is time to seek a new Holy Grail, being a strategic partner. Figure 19.4 depicts the constellation of factors that can help HR play a strategic partner role. These factors suggest the following very specific steps organizations can take to increase the degree to which HR issues are part of the strategy process (based on Lawler & Mohrman, 2003a, 2005).

Highlight the knowledge and competency aspects of the business strategy. Many companies in the knowledge economy rely on the processing of knowledge by skilled knowledge workers—on the development and use of human capital. On the other hand, many do not explicitly identify their competitive reliance on these resources or think of their strategy as maximizing the value they can derive from knowledge. The HR function can help make this reliance and this perspective obvious to line managers. Doing this will enhance the value it contributes and help it gain a partnership seat at the strategy table.

Increase HR's focus on planning, organization development, and organization design. The HR function is well situated to see the organization as a complex system in which the development and management of human capital is intricately intertwined with strategy and

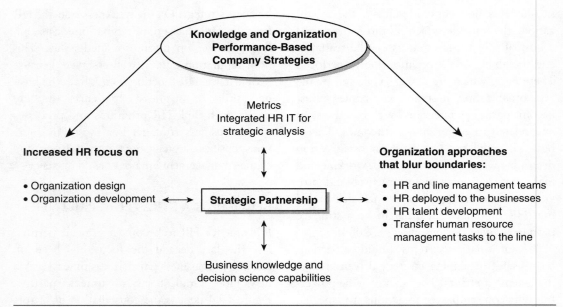

Figure 19.4   Factors Associated With HR as a Strategic Partner

SOURCE: From Edward E. Lawler III, John W. Boudreau, & Susan Albers Mohrman, *Achieving strategic excellence*. Copyright © 2006, by the Board of Trustees of the Leland Stanford Jr. University. All rights reserved. Used with permission of Stanford University Press, www.sup.org.

design. By overlaying a strategic perspective on the development of HR systems and by increasing the focus on developing organization competencies and capabilities, HR can play a unique role in the development of strategy and strategic capabilities.

Expand the vision and application of electronic HR capabilities beyond process improvement and efficiency to include a focus on analyses that can turn data into strategically valuable information. The development of electronic HR systems offers an unprecedented opportunity to examine what HR approaches and factors make a difference in business performance. Metrics must be developed that go beyond simply assessing the effectiveness of the organization's HR services and practices. They must involve the measurement of an organization's performance capabilities and competencies and how HR metrics relate to performance.

Increase the business knowledge of HR professionals and their link to the business. In today's world, addressing critical competitive issues requires the combination of specialized areas of knowledge and deep expertise. Rotation of HR professionals within HR ensures a broad understanding of HR, and placement of professionals close to the business and deploying them to joint line and HR task teams allows them to develop greater understanding of the business and to combine their expertise with the expertise of the line. HR functions should also focus on providing their HR professionals with development opportunities, including job rotations outside the HR function, special assignments, and formal educational experiences that broaden and deepen their knowledge and experience bases.

Ensure that the head of HR has the deep HR experience needed to be a strategic business partner. The head of HR must fully understand the complexity of the various aspects of human capital management in order to bring HR to the strategic planning table and to integrate HR activities with the business-oriented perspectives. Whereas there are other people at the table well versed in the business perspective, the HR vice president is likely to be the only person who is a deep expert in HR.

Don't forget the administrative and business partner product lines. Failure to deliver on the other two product lines can prevent HR from being a strategic partner in two ways. First, it can undermine the credibility of the function. Second, it can take time and attention away from strategic issues. Delivering these two product lines effectively can also provide data that are needed in order to execute the strategic role.

CONCLUSION

The knowledge economy, with the proliferation of companies that rely on knowledge-based competitive strategies, offers a special opportunity for strategic HR thinking and actions to move front and center in organizations. Advanced IT-based systems can offload transactional tasks, freeing HR professionals for larger value-adding roles. More importantly, they offer the potential for HR to collect and analyze data in ways that yield knowledge about the effectiveness of various HR approaches and about the feasibility of various strategic paths. The function must place a greater focus on planning, organization design, and development. It also must make greater use of approaches whereby HR professionals operate in proximity and partnership with the line and develop a broad and deep understanding of HR and business issues.

REFERENCES

Becker, B. E., & Huselid, M. A. (1998). High performance work systems and firm performance: A synthesis of research and managerial implications. *Research in Personnel and Human Resources Management, 16,* 53–101.

Boudreau, J. W., & Ramstad, P. M. (2003). Strategic HRM measurement in the 21st century: From justifying HR to strategic talent leadership. In M. Goldsmith, R. P. Gandossy,

& M. S. Efron (Eds.), *HRM in the 21st century* (pp. 79–90). New York: John Wiley & Sons.

Boudreau, J. W., & Ramstad, P. M. (2007). *Beyond HR: The new science of human capital.* Boston: Harvard Business School Press.

Brockbank, W. (1999). If HR were really strategically proactive: Present and future directions in HR's contribution to competitive advantage. *Human Resource Management, 38,* 337–352.

Galbraith, J. R. (2005). *Designing the customer-centric organization: A guide to strategy, structure, and process.* San Francisco: Jossey-Bass.

Huselid, M. A., Becker, B. E., & Beatty, R. W. (2005). *The workforce scorecard.* Boston: Harvard Business School.

Jackson, S. E., Hitt, M. A., & DeNisi, A. S. (Eds.). (2003). *Managing knowledge for sustained competitive advantage: Designing strategies for effective human resource management.* San Francisco: Jossey-Bass.

Lawler, E. E. (1995). Strategic human resources management: An idea whose time has come. In B. Downie & M. L. Coates (Eds.), *Managing human resources in the 1990s and beyond: Is the workplace being transformed?* (pp. 46–70). Kingston, Canada: IRC Press.

Lawler, E. E., Boudreau, J., & Mohrman, S. A. (2006). *Achieving strategic excellence.* Palo Alto, CA: Stanford University Press.

Lawler, E. E., Levenson, A., & Boudreau, J. W. (2004). HR metrics and analytics: Use and impact. *Human Resource Planning, 24*(4), 27–35.

Lawler, E. E., & Mohrman, S. A. (2003a). *Creating a strategic human resources organization: An assessment of trends and new directions.* Palo Alto, CA: Stanford University Press.

Lawler, E. E., & Mohrman, S. A. (2003b). HR as a strategic partner: What does it take to make it happen? *Human Resource Planning, 26*(5), 15.

Lawler, E. E., & Mohrman, S. A. (2005). Human resources consulting. In L. Greiner & E. Poulfelt (Eds.), *The contemporary consultant* (pp. 133–148). Mason, OH: Thomson.

Lawler, E. E., Ulrich, D., Fitz-enz, J., & Madden, J. (2004). *Human resources business process outsourcing.* San Francisco: Jossey Bass.

Lawler, E. E., & Worley, C. (2006). *Built to change.* San Francisco: Jossey-Bass.

Lev, B. (2001). *Intangibles: Management, measurement, and reporting.* Washington, DC: Brookings.

Mohrman, A. M., Galbraith, J. R., Lawler, E. E., & Associates. (1998). *Tomorrow's organization: Crafting winning capabilities in a dynamic world.* San Francisco: Jossey-Bass.

Ulrich, D. (1997). *Human resources champions.* Boston: Harvard Business School Press.

Ulrich, D., & Brockbank, W. (2005). *HR value proposition.* Boston: Harvard Business School Press.

Wright, P., Dyer, L., & Takla, M. (1999). *State-of-the-Art and Practice Council report.* New York: Human Resource Planning Society.

20

The Use of Strategic Career Development in Promoting Organization Effectiveness
A Multilevel Model

AYSE KARAEVLI

DOUGLAS T. HALL

Drastic changes in the social, economic, and technical environments, with the corresponding changes in customer preferences and demands, necessitate a high degree of adaptive capacity in organizations. Human resources have been identified as critical for achieving the capability to adapt to changing environmental contingencies (Wright & Snell, 1998). Although an organization development intervention might result in significant changes in basic systems or processes, unless the people whose work is part of those systems or processes are affected and experience some level of personal or behavioral change, those changes will not be sustainable.

Despite the strategic importance of career development in an organization's overall effectiveness,

however, human development is an untapped resource in contemporary organizations. This may be one of the reasons why established firms often have difficulty adapting to swift environmental changes. In the 1980s, at the beginning of the era of corporate restructuring, there was strong interest in finding ways to help employees find ways of adapting to smaller, flatter organizations, with fewer advancement opportunities. As a result, there were widespread initiatives to develop corporate career development programs and processes. Usually housed in the human resource organization, there were groups of career practitioners with titles such as "career development manager" and "career resource director." Sometimes career development was

AUTHOR'S NOTE: Work on this chapter was supported in part by the Executive Development Roundtable.

seen as an extension of organization development, and in other cases it was considered part of employee development and training. Examples of these initiatives can be found in Hall (1986b), Leibowitz, Farren, and Kaye (1986), and Gutteridge, Leibowitz, and Shore (1993). Figure 20.1 presents the spectrum of career development activities that were typically performed. Activities on the right-hand side of the continuum, at the organization level, are typically called career management, and those toward the left, done by individual employees, are called career planning.

We argue that this full spectrum of career activities must be performed in some way if the organization is to have an integrated career development system. In its simplest form, there

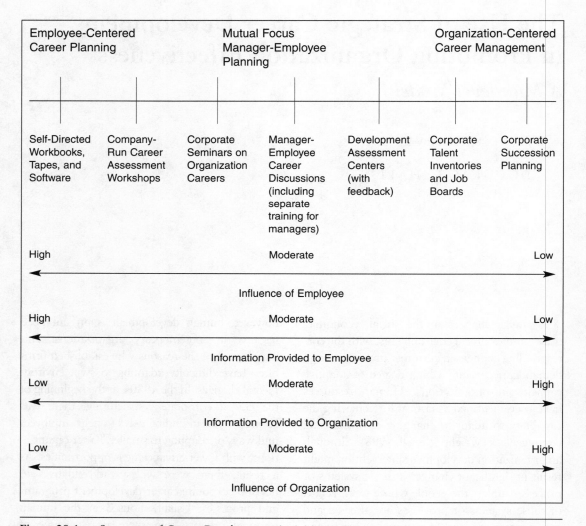

Figure 20.1   Spectrum of Career Development Activities

SOURCE: From D. T. Hall (1986). An overview of current career development theory, research, and practice. In D. T. Hall & Associates, *Career development in organizations* (pp. 1–20). San Francisco: Jossey-Bass. Used with permission of John Wiley & Sons, Inc.

NOTE: This is a sample of program activities to illustrate different points of the continuum between career planning and career management. This is not a complete list of possible career development activities.

must be a process whereby the organization plans the development and deployment of human talent to implement the business strategy, and this process must be informed by the desires, goals, constraints, and talents of its employees. This organization-level strategy implementation process is achieved through career management, and the employee linkage with career management is enabled through career planning.

It is our observation that most traces of career development are gone in contemporary organizations as formal activities. The function has been largely outsourced and is now being provided by professional firms that specialize in outplacement and career consulting. Another professional group that also performs the career development functions are executive and professional recruiters. Although recruiters technically are the agents of the employing organization, they often have their own stable of talent whom they follow—and indeed, often help move—from employer to employer.

Where we do currently see corporate career activities done in an explicit, formal way is in the more macro activities represented by human resource planning systems. At the managerial and executive levels, an example would be the succession planning process, which is definitely alive and well today (Karaevli & Hall, 2003). We also see career information systems, such as job boards and electronic résumé systems, which use information technology (Cappelli, 2002). And for career search and corporate staffing there is widespread use of information systems such as Monster.com.

Overall, however, we argue that as we move toward a recovery from an economic downturn, there would be a competitive advantage for the firm that actively promotes the career growth of its employees. Despite its strategic importance, though, theoretical and empirical inquiry into how career development affects organization outcomes has been very rare. In this chapter, therefore, we present a blueprint for an integrated approach to career and organization development. Our framework attempts

to delineate how combining two major elements of career development, career planning at the individual level and career management at the organization level, together can facilitate an organization's adaptive capacity. Because organizations have an impact on a person's career whether they consciously intend to or not, we argue for the wisdom of proactively including considerations of career development in a program of system-wide organization development. Thus, in our opinion, career development can be a key element of an organization development strategy. The next section attempts to explain the rationale behind the necessity of an integrated approach in more detail by focusing on the related goals of career and organization development.

TOWARD AN INTEGRATED MODEL: THE RELATED OBJECTIVES OF CAREER DEVELOPMENT AND ORGANIZATION DEVELOPMENT

Hall (1976) describes the remarkable similarity between the dimensions for evaluating career effectiveness and those for measuring organization effectiveness. However, when one considers the fact that the organization represents the sum of the people who make it up, perhaps this similarity is not so surprising.

According to social system theory, any human system has four functions that it must perform in order to survive. It has to attain its goals (perform effectively), it has to adapt (that is, to perform well over time), it has to integrate individuals into work roles, and it has to maintain its cultural patterns. Each of these system functions has an analog at the individual level. Goal attainment for the organization requires performance by the people in the organization. (To cite a specific case, Dell Computer has a goal of growing to a revenue of $62 billion by fiscal year 2007, and according to Peter Leddy [2003], head of leadership development, the critical factor in attaining this goal will be attracting and developing key talent.) Integration requires the attraction, retention, and development of the right employees for the right jobs, which requires the development of positive career attitudes, such as commitment and involvement. Maintenance of the organization's cultural patterns is analogous to the development

of the individual's identity over the years. And adaptation of the organization is clearly related to the adaptability of its employees. Both indicate an ability to respond quickly and appropriately to changes in the demands and opportunities presented by the business environment. These relationships between

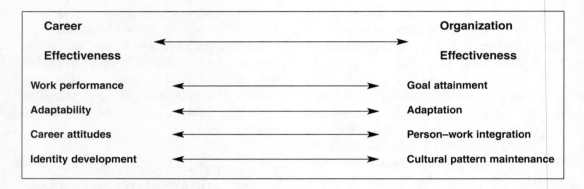

Figure 20.2   Relationship Between Career Effectiveness and Organization Effectiveness
SOURCE: From Hall (1976, p. 76). Reprinted by permission of the author.

career and organization effectiveness are shown in Figure 20.2.

As the reverse arrows indicate in Figure 20.2, these qualities of career and organization effectiveness are mutually enhancing. For example, the overall goal attainment of an organization depends on good work performance by its employees. At the same time, being a member of a high-performing system influences a person to perform at a high level. Similarly, being in an organization with a strong culture helps a person develop a strong sense of identity as a member of that organization. On the other hand, when the members of an organization, as a collective, are clear on their sense of identity as members, that helps them maintain the patterns and traditions of that organization's culture. Similar arguments can be made for adaptability and integration.

Thus, we are led to the following equation:

Organization effectiveness = f(Collective career effectiveness)

The question, then, is how the two facets of career development, organizational career management and individual career planning, contribute to achieve collective career and organization effectiveness. Figure 20.3 presents the relationships we feature here on the relationship between career development and organization effectiveness. First we will look at the individual end of the career development spectrum in Figure 20.1 by turning to contemporary approaches to the process of career planning and efforts focused on the individual employee. Then, we will shift gears and examine a range of issues and strategic options for

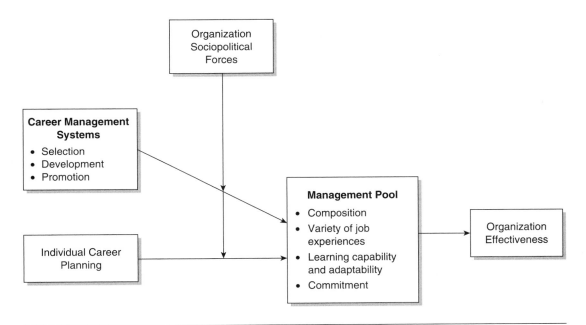

Figure 20.3   Integrated Model of Career Development and Organization Effectiveness

how the organizationally-centered career management process works. In the final two sections, we will present our assessment on the strategic role of career development in achieving organizational effectiveness.

CAREER PLANNING

Career planning is defined as

> A deliberate process for (1) becoming aware of self, opportunities, constraints, choices, and consequences, (2) identifying career-related goals, and (3) programming of work, education, and related developmental experiences to provide the direction, timing, and sequence of steps to attain a specific career goal. (Gutteridge, 1986, p. 54)

Traditionally, career planning includes activities such as self-assessment, career testing, and career counseling. These activities might be provided through mechanisms such as

self-directed workbooks, career resource centers, videotaped and audiotaped instruction, career planning workshops and seminars (either in the employing organization or external), mentors, career networks, and manager–employee discussions (Hall, 1986b). In a 1993 publication sponsored by the American Society for Training & Development (ASTD), Gutteridge and his colleagues reported that some of the more common career planning activities among American employers (of whom 47% had some type of career development program) were career counseling by human resource staff or supervisors, employee communications on career-related topics (educational assistance, company conditions and economic information, career paths and ladders, training and development options, and job vacancy information), job postings, training for supervisors on career counseling, career planning workshops, and computer software (Gutteridge et al., 1993). Most of these activities represented increases from the previous ASTD survey, which was conducted in 1978. However, only half of the respondents rated the overall effectiveness of their company's career development system as "somewhat effective" or "very effective."

What has been the more recent experience with career planning in industry? We are frankly in a bind in answering that question. Why? The reason is that if the new or current career deal is one in which the employee is self-directed, managing his or her own career, the notion of organization career planning is an oxymoron. If careers are protean and bound-aryless, what is the relevance of focusing on what happens to a person's career while he or she is in a particular organization? And, if the employee is acting like a free agent, free to move to the highest bidder and the best opportunity, why should any employer be motivated to provide resources to aid an employee's career planning? After all, if *We Are All Self-Employed,* as Cliff Hakim (1994) informs us, and if *The New Rules,* according to John Kotter (1995), include being entrepreneurial and keeping away from big bureaucratic organizations, or if, even more drastically, *The Career Is Dead* (Hall et al., 1996), what could a company do about career planning, even if it wanted to?

More recent research shows that the career contract has changed from an organization-based model to a more employee-based model (Arthur, Inkson, & Pringle, 1999; Arthur & Rousseau, 1996; Hall, 2002; Hall et al., 1996). One result is that employers are providing less career planning assistance to employees. A survey of 25 best-practice American employers found that nearly all (84%) believe that the employee has primary responsibility for his or her career (O'Connell, 1997). In interviews with employees of 17 major U.S. employers, Hall and Moss (1998) found agreement that the person, not the organization, now manages the career. They also found that the definition of *development* had changed. It is no longer upward mobility or formal training or retraining but rather continuous learning, self-directed and relational. Thus, the critical targets for development efforts have become the person's ability to learn and his or her employability. And organizations are using three primary methods to promote career development: challenging assignments, developmental relationships, and information resources.

It appears that the formal career planning activities found in the 1993 Gutteridge and associates survey have waned with the arrival of the "new deal." O'Connell (1997) reports that in his sample about half of the firms provide career information and support (48%), only 28% provide career coaching, 36% provide career self-assessment tools, and only 28% communicate about options within their organizations. Furthermore, only 24% of the firms reported that they have a clearly communicated philosophy of career development for their firms.

Similar trends were observed in a survey of 17 best-practice companies by Prior (1998). She found that few employers had mastered an integrated career development strategy (i.e., one that linked career planning and career management). One intriguing finding was that some of the more successful, less formal career practices were in entrepreneurial businesses. (By "formal" she meant systems that had a written, company-specific definition of career development, a written description of the roles and responsibilities of the employee, manager, and corporation, and evidence that the career development strategy is based on business need.) In companies where the culture was entrepreneurial, across industries their product cycle was short and their business was highly competitive. Their managers, focusing on whatever it took to get the job done, would coach their employees on career development. They would provide feedback on resumes and tip off employees to opportunities in other departments. Because business growth and the resulting need for people was so intense, Prior reports that these managers provided more career support than managers in nonentrepreneurial companies.

Prior also found that all companies responding agreed that employees are responsible for their own career development. However, all 17 companies reported that the organization is responsible for providing tools and resources to help employees understand business needs, along with programs to support employees' self-directed continuous learning.

Related to this self-directed learning, in a survey of companies that use competency models for development, Briscoe and Hall (1999) found evidence of this growing interest in fostering independent employee learning. They discuss two learning metacompetencies, which are competencies that enable people to develop competencies on their own. These learning metacompetencies are adaptability and identity development. If the person is capable of gathering and using feedback on his or her skills and other personal qualities in relation to what is required at work (i.e., feedback about himself or herself, for greater self-awareness and identity development), and if the person is capable of acting on this personal learning (i.e., adaptable), he or she will always be capable of learning what new qualities he or she needs to develop and of developing those qualities. (More detail on these career metacompetencies can be found in Hall, 2002.)

A major resource for helping employees learn about themselves and about career opportunities in their organization is information technology. Career information systems are now widely available to people at all levels of organizations. They can be either external, public sources, such as Monster.com or Hotjobs.com, or they can be internal to a company, in the form of job boards. Cappelli (2002, p. 1) describes these job boards (electronic systems for matching employees with job openings) as "arguably the most important new mechanism shaping careers inside organizations." He describes some specific corporate innovations in the use of these job boards as follows:

- JP MorganChase reports that all vacancies below the top 200 executive positions in the company are now posted on its "Job Connect" internal job board. Internal applicants apply online, and the application process includes many screening questions about applicant skills and experience. One-third of the vacancies in the company are filled through this system.
- Fidelity Investments has used the software associated with its internal job board system to produce a career planning tool for employees called "My Job Connection" that allows applicants to see the career paths that previous incumbents have taken to get to more senior positions in the organization.

Cappelli concludes that the easy availability of information through job boards has markedly raised the employee's autonomy and control over his or her career. They move the locus of control over information about positions from the organization to the employee, and they replace the control of the bureaucracy with internal labor markets as a guiding mechanism for career advancement:

> The implications are very important. Rather than a set of administrative rules determining how and when employees move through the organization and a human resources office deciding which individual moves where, the rules and the old paths are gone, and the interaction of applicant preferences and hiring manager options determines which individual go where. (Cappelli, 2002, p. 15)

Thus, one conclusion we would draw about the state of career planning in contemporary organizations is that there is less career activity now than there was 10 or 15 years ago. However, the good news is that what is there gives the employee greater self-control than he or she had in the past. To be more specific, the resources companies now are likely to provide to assist the employee with career planning are

- Self-assessment tools
- Challenging job assignments
- Relational support from managers, mentors, and career networks
- Technology-supported job opportunity information

CAREER MANAGEMENT

Career management can be defined as an ongoing process of preparing, implementing, and monitoring career plans undertaken in concert with the organization's career system (Gutteridge, 1986). The subprocesses of career management include recruitment and selection, development, and appraisal and promotion. At the extreme right side of the career management spectrum presented in Figure 20.1 is formal succession planning, which can be defined as "the systematic management of mobility patterns in an organization" (Kerr & Jackofsky, 1989, p. 158). Although the short-term purpose of succession planning is to fill the planned or unplanned vacancies in managerial jobs with people who possess the necessary skills and experiences, in the long-term, talented employees, usually called "high potentials," are provided with sequences of job experiences in order to prepare them for future upper-echelon roles in the organization (Hall, 1986a; Kerr & Jackofsky, 1989). Here the organization has high levels of information and control, and the employee has correspondingly little of both.

Moving a bit to the individual career planning end, we can find corporate talent inventories, which are formal human resource information systems covering employee skills, experiences, and interests and using some information provided by the employee (Hall, 1986a). Because much of the literature on careers has focused on the individual view, theoretical models on organizational career management practices are rare with the following exceptions.

Sonnenfeld and Peiperl (1988, p. 589) propose a four-cell typology of career systems,

reflecting the firm's supply flow (the movement into and out of the firm) and assignment flow (the movement across job assignments). They characterize the supply flow dimension as the openness of the career system to the external labor market at other than entry levels. The assignment flow dimension indicates which assignment and promotion decisions are made based on criteria such as individual performance or contribution to the general group (Sonnenfeld & Peiperl, 1988, p. 590).

As Sonnenfeld and Peiperl (1988) argue, it is very hard to have a uniform model of organization career systems because there are significant variations in career management activities responsive to the characteristics of different firms. However, their typology categorizes organizations based on the characteristics of their industry membership along the dimensions of supply flow and assignment flow. For example, organizations that they call the "Fortress" type, operating in industries such as hotels, retail, textiles, publishing, and natural resources, are at the higher end of the dimension of openness to hire employees from outside and assign and promote employees based mostly on their group contribution. On the opposite side, organizations grouped under "Academy," operating in industries such as consumer products, automobiles, electronics, pharmaceuticals, and office products, prefer to staff from within the organization and base their assignment and promotion decisions more on individual contribution.

Another career management model has been proposed by Baruch and Peiperl (2000), based on their empirical study of 194 companies in the United Kingdom. Their model comprises two dimensions: the level of sophistication of organization career management practices and the level of the involvement on the part of the organization necessary to put those practices into use (p. 358). In terms of the level of sophistication, organization career management practices range from what they call basic practices (e.g., job postings, formal education, lateral moves) to multidirectional practices (e.g., peer appraisal and upward appraisal). The elements of basic practices were most frequently reported by their survey participants and require a low level of sophistication, whereas those of multidimensional practices were reported least frequently by the survey participants and, in the authors' opinions, are the most sophisticated ones.

In terms of the level of involvement, according to the same study, organization career practices can be grouped into three categories. The elements of what they call formal practices (e.g., written personal career planning, dual career ladder, career books and pamphlets, common career paths) receive the least amount of involvement by the organizations, whereas the elements of what they call active planning (e.g., performance appraisal as a basis for career planning, career counseling, and succession planning) receive the highest level of involvement. The third group of career management practices, what they call active management (e.g., assessment centers, formal mentoring, and career workshops) receive a medium level of involvement by organizations (Baruch & Peiperl, 2000, p. 359).

Having covered the previous literature and the current state of the practice of individual career planning and organizational career management, now we turn our attention to the critical question of the extent to which career development practices are linked to achievement of the organization's strategic objectives.

ASSESSING THE ROLE OF CAREER DEVELOPMENT IN ACHIEVING ORGANIZATION EFFECTIVENESS

The most effective organizations are those that have capacity to adapt to changes in the environment (Pasmore, 1988). Therefore, our discussion here focuses on the effects of collective career development practices on an organization's adaptive capacity. Pfeffer (1997) also argues for the importance of studying career processes as sources of change in organizations. Based on Reed's (1978) and Stewman's (1988) arguments, Pfeffer contends,

Organizations' inability to adapt to changing circumstances are [*sic*] somewhat caused by opportunity structures (i.e., recruitment and promotion policies), which result in significant time delay when young managers move into higher levels where they can have expanded responsibilities and can bring new perspectives into the strategic decision making process. (1997, p. 86)

One of the most important differences between firms that are adaptive and those that fail in the face of environmental shifts is the ability to engage in exploration while maintaining some continuity with existing routines (Levinthal & March, 1993; March, 1991). We argue here that career development plays an important role in building an organization's capacity to explore while keeping its sense of identity.

How does this process unfold? We believe that organizations with diverse talent pools whose members have been groomed with highly varied career experiences are likely to achieve high exploration capability while maintaining some sense of identity, both of which are needed for successful adaptation to turbulent environments. On the other hand, because any reductions in variance-increasing activities prevents organizations from responding to environmental uncertainty effectively (Burgelman, 1994), we predict that organizations with career development processes that constrict the diversity of people for managerial and upper-echelon leadership roles and the variety in their experiences will have difficulty making successful adaptations in highly dynamic environments.

Furthermore, a major outcome of the lack of a strategic approach to career development in organizations is employee turnover (Hall, 1986a). Particularly with the changing psychological contract, security concerns are replaced by employability (Nicholson, 1996). Therefore, when companies take the responsibility to help employees acquire portable and marketable skills, employees feel more committed to the organization (Galunic & Anderson, 2000; Hall, Zhu, & Yan, 2001; Nicholson,

1996). As a result, the retention of valuable employees will help firms to maintain some behavioral routines and a sense of organization identity needed for successful adaptation. We will next attempt to explain how career development processes affect the characteristics of the management pool.

This is one reason why the integration of career management and career planning is so critical. The organization's career development system must contain a process that includes employee self-assessment and career conversations with higher management so that the employee will be informed of and have an opportunity to influence the organization's future plans for him or her, and the organization will be informed of the employee's future career goals and constraints as a reality check for the company's human resource plan.

Based on our discussions in the previous sections, our recent study (Karaevli & Hall, 2003), and the literature on strategic human resource management, strategic leadership, and careers, we argue that the career management practices of firms fall into a continuum ranging along the following dimensions:

Selection:	Fit-based	Potential-based
Development:	Business needs	Individual needs
Promotion:	Vertical	Lateral

We further argue that as the firm's selection, development, and promotion practices move from the left side of the continuum (fit-based selection, development focused on business needs, and vertical movement through the hierarchy) to the right (potential-based selection, development focused on individual needs, and lateral mobility as promotion), the organization's adaptive capacity will increase as well. However, these three processes of career management are not mutually exclusive; selection process has direct implications for development and promotion (i.e., organizations that

use fit-based selection are likely to develop people based primarily on business needs and link promotion primarily to vertical mobility). Therefore, our discussion here is centered on selection and its implications for development and promotion.

Selection Method: Fit Based Versus Potential Based

Most organizations select people on the basis of current competency models—basically, individual knowledge, skills, and abilities determined by current organizational needs and individual past performance (Briscoe & Hall, 1999). By "past performance" we mean a selection that favors candidates who have performed well on jobs very similar to the one currently being filled. This is in contrast to selection based on potential, in which the nod is given to candidates with the qualities and competencies that make them likely to perform well in future roles that may be quite different from any job they have performed in the past.

The importance of matching managers to the environmental context and to firm strategies is broadly acknowledged in the strategic management and organization theory literatures (e.g., Pfeffer & Salancik, 1978; Thompson, 1967). Selection and identification processes attempt to find people who fit with the current organization environment and strategies (Cascio, 1987) and particular requirements of a given job (Dunnette, 1966). The underlying assumption is that the variables related to people and jobs will stay stable for some time because it is hard to incorporate expectations of change on both sides with the current assessment of current abilities and job requirements (Kerr & Jakofsky, 1989). Because there are such good techniques for talent identification and selection, such as past and current performance appraisal results, 360-degree feedback, and competency assessments, it seems that selection as a matching technique can be used to bring the most appropriate managerial abilities and traits to the problem at hand.

In addition to the well-recognized advantages of fit-based selection, however, there are several disadvantages. For example, with a constantly changing environment, a person who is the best fit today may very well be a poor fit tomorrow. Therefore, an excessive focus on fit-based identification and selection might cause organizations to reduce their flexibility. Lengnick-Hall and Lengnick-Hall (1988, p. 457) also argue that the fit approach to managerial selection can be counterproductive from a competitive perspective because it may constrain the firm's repertoire of skills and thereby inhibit innovation.

There has been limited support for the normative view that firms that match top management characteristics to environmental contingencies (i.e., industry structure), for example, will realize better postsuccession performance than those with lower levels of fit (Datta & Rajagopalan, 1998, p. 848). Matching managerial characteristics with the general characteristics of the product and market or institutional environment is based on the premise that the environment will stay stable or change very slowly because managerial characteristics will not vary as much as environmental conditions (Lengnick-Hall & Lengnick-Hall, 1988). Therefore, it is not surprising to find that an improved fit between a particular environmental contingency and executive characteristics does not always yield better economic performance or competitive position of the firm (Datta & Rajagopalan, 1998). Based on their investigation of superintendents, March and March (1977) also argue that the matching approach has limited validity because of the commonality of certain general characteristics needed for successful top managers.

Management selection practices affect not only the knowledge, skills, and abilities of the management pool but also its modal personality profile. There has been empirical evidence on how excessive similarity on managerial personalities within a firm may have negative consequences. Argyris (1954, 1957) was the first scholar to argue that too much focus on "the right type" is dangerous for organizations. Schneider (1983, 1987) has also proposed a framework for understanding the negative consequences of a good fit. The logic of his attraction–selection–attrition framework is that, over time, organizations naturally attract, select, and keep people who are homogenous with respect to personality type. He argues that when selective attraction to organizations is followed by formal and informal selection based on fit and then finalized by attrition of those who do not fit, there will be a conformity in the outlook of organization members that yields organizations incapable of adapting to environmental changes. Thus, Schneider (1987) proposes that homogeneity narrows the perspectives from which the larger environment can be viewed. This, in turn, yields incomplete information about the changes the organization must make to adapt to the environment (Schneider, Goldstein, & Smith, 1995; Schneider, Smith, Taylor, & Fleenor, 1998).

Thus, when the emphasis is more on past performance and current organization strategies and environmental contingencies than on potential for development in the future, the organization is opting for risk reduction, and there is therefore less opportunity for surprise and creativity. Therefore, we believe that fit-based managerial selection processes tend to operate similarly to Denrell and March's (2001) explanation of how the restriction of information in a system may lead to adaptation failures in the long run:

> The basic adaptive mechanism that produces biases in favor of reliable alternatives and the status quo is the differential reproduction of actions that have led to success. Because alternatives with a record of good performance are reproduced, alternatives with high potential that initially do poorly are likely to be avoided in the future. . . . Because they are likely to require practice to realize their full potential, new alternatives are likely to be underestimated on the basis of a small sample of experience. Thus an adaptive system will

exhibit behavior that looks like risk aversion and resistance to change even in situations in which the long-run expected returns from new alternatives and risky alternatives are notably higher than those from existing alternatives and reliable alternatives. (p. 535)

This is also in line with the threat–rigidity hypothesis, which suggests that in the face of a threat, organizations often fail to consider alternative responses that are not well understood and whose outcomes are ambiguous (Ocasio, 1995; Staw, Sandelands, & Dutton, 1981). Based on all these discussions, we argue that excessive focus on fit in the managerial selection process reduces the diversity of the managerial pool and the variety in its career experiences.

Development Approaches: Business Focus Versus Individual Focus

The developmental activities of organizations include training and education, mentoring and coaching, and sequence of job experiences. As other studies that we will discuss later have found, a very clear trend from our research in best practice companies is that organizations believe that development is the employee's responsibility, and therefore the development process is increasingly becoming more individualistic (Karaevli & Hall, 2003). This is not surprising in this era of the "protean" (Hall & Associates, 1996) or "boundaryless" (Arthur & Rousseau, 1996) career.

However, we also found that there are still significant differences in the development strategies firms use. Firms in our sample differed mainly in whether their development activities are business focused or personal development focused. For example, at Dell Computer, regular structured discussions aim to facilitate the necessary movement around different business segments that people need in order to further their development. Motorola has a similar approach. By identifying common needs of business and employees and rotating

people to different business segments by providing them with specific training, the company is trying to balance business goals and individual needs. At Eli Lilly and Company, on the other hand, the development is targeted to individual needs.

What might be the implications of these two different approaches to development for organization adaptability? Aside from some obvious advantages, such as finding the right person for the immediate business problems, if it is done extensively for career development, development strategy focused on business needs may reduce an organization's adaptive capacity. Gabarro (1988) states that if an organization's goal is to develop a well-trained pool of leadership talent, then it must put managers in assignments that stretch them and broaden their experience base. However, this may mean putting the managers in charge of jobs in which they are expected to have less than optimal performance. Gupta (1986) also suggests that *mis*matching managers at various career stages may actually enhance organization performance in the long run.

We also believe that when organizations focus almost exclusively on finding the person whose past experience is seen as a perfect fit for the current job, their incentive to provide their managers with a variety of experiences for further development is reduced. Furthermore, when development is tied to fit-based selection, the diversity of people who have access to those assignments typically decreases. Both of these processes constrain the knowledge, skills, and behavioral repertoire of the talent pool and thereby decrease organization flexibility.

Promotion: Vertical Versus Lateral

Despite the new paradigm of the organization as a network rather than a bureaucracy, many organizations still value one kind of mobility: vertical movement through the hierarchy (Nicholson, 1996, p. 41). It is clear that the new forms of organizations, which are flattened and decentralized, require developmental mobility to be lateral rather than solely vertical. However, many organizations do not even link performance in the developmental activities to pay and promotion (Karaevli & Hall, 2003).

Because of bureaucratic promotion policies that recognize only vertical mobility, as people rise, they get more narrow in experience but more irreplaceable in their function or business unit as the expertise deepens (Lombardo & Eichinger, 2001). This results in a human capital pool with a narrow range of skills and behavioral repertoire, which decreases organization flexibility (Wright & Snell, 1998).

MODERATING INFLUENCES OF SOCIOPOLITICAL FORCES

Organization politics and institutionalized power have long been recognized as playing important roles in executive succession decisions (Ocasio, 1999; Pfeffer & Salancik, 1978). Similar processes play an important role in career development and succession planning as well. For example, it has been found that being in the high-potential pool depends partly on the power of business units and social networks to which an employee belongs, because more powerful business units have the ability to push their own people for inclusion in the high-potential pool (Karaevli & Hall, 2003). Empirical evidence has also shown that there is a tendency in many corporations for insider CEOs to be similar to their predecessors in important ways (Smith & White, 1987; Vancil, 1987), such as in their primary functional area (Ocasio, 1999; Ocasio & Kim, 1999; Smith & White, 1987). In a longitudinal study at large manufacturing firms in the United States (1981–1992), Ocasio and Kim (1999) found that in 100 out of 275 succession events, there was stability in the functional backgrounds of CEOs. Based on the theory of circulation of corporate control, Ocasio (1994, 1999) argues that the similar CEO functional backgrounds imply "institutionalization" within the organization.

Kanter (1977) warned three decades ago about homosocial reproduction. Hall describes this as an executive cloning process: "the tendency of a group of senior executives to try (often unconsciously) to perpetuate the organization's future leadership in their own images; to choose successors who are very much like themselves" (Hall, 1986a, p. 242). The rationale underlying this cloning process is to maintain not only consistency in strategic direction but also harmony within the organization (Vancil, 1987). However, the price for this harmony could be fewer sources of information variety within the firm.

For example, one reason why so few women are promoted to senior management positions in many firms may be that during their careers they experience fewer developmental job opportunities than men do (Ohlott, Ruderman, & McCauley, 1994). Accordingly, although men and women may have had similar career paths and held jobs at similar levels in an organization, women have not had the same responsibilities as men in similar jobs. Because being able to handle more task-related challenges becomes more important at higher levels, Ohlott et al. (1994) conclude that women might be eliminated from the candidate pool because they have not had the opportunity to show what they can do when faced with these types of challenges. Ruderman, Ohlott, and Kram's (1995) empirical study also indicates that decision makers choose candidates who are like them because of the comfort they feel, and this leads them to use different criteria in promoting men and women, which undermines women's career advancement.

In terms of minority groups, Thomas (2001, p. 99) found that "whites and minorities follow distinct patterns of advancement. Specifically, promising white professionals tend to enter a fast-track early in their careers, whereas high potential minorities take off much later, typically when they have reached middle management." The implication of this is that many high-potential minorities became discouraged when they were not selected into the high-potential pool early in their careers. They became "demotivated—especially when they saw their white colleagues receive plum assignments and promotions—and de-skilled" (Thomas, 2001, p. 101).

Therefore, when an organization's selection, development, and promotion practices fall toward fit-based selection, business-focused development, and exclusively upward mobility, because of the various conscious or unconscious sociopolitical forces in play, the diversity of people who are prepared for the managerial and leadership roles of the organizations and the variety of their experiences are likely to decrease further. Less diversity of people and less variety in the experiences of the managerial pool mean a lack of variety in perspectives, knowledge, and skills, which limits firms' ability to foresee and respond to sudden crises and changes effectively (Karaevli & Hall, 2003; Wright & Snell, 1998).

CONCLUSION

It appears that career development activities are not as much in evidence now as they were in the early 1990s. This seems to be in part because the new protean career contract puts more control in the hands of the employee and makes the guiding role of the employing organization less clear. Another factor is the economic recession, which has resulted in cuts in human resource development budgets and activities.

At the same time, however, companies still need to engage in the career management activities of making job assignments, doing succession planning and human resource planning, and assessing and engaging human talent. But if these activities are performed without being integrated with the career planning of individual employees, there is a great risk that these plans and systems will be merely paper tigers. Because career planning deals with the processes by which employees get in touch with

the passions that drive them in their work and with the directions and paths they want to follow, this activity has great potential to strengthen the integrative function of the system. Therefore, we argue that for a career development system to be integrated, it must contain elements that cover the full career development continuum shown in Figure 20.1.

As Gutteridge (1986, p. 55) points out, "career development is designed to be a joint process." It does no good for an employee to develop and become committed to detailed career plans if there is no career management process in the organization to help him or her implement those plans. And it is equally pointless for the organization to create detailed human resource planning and succession plans without knowing whether the key people in those plans are willing to accept the future job moves that are part of these plans. Thus, in theory and practice, career planning and career management should be integrated and comparable in their detail.

Furthermore, when the organization uses a strategy of career variety (Karaevli & Hall, 2006)—that is, human resource planning and selection systems that stretch people to perform in roles that would develop them (as opposed to roles very similar to those in which they have already had experience)—it is using career development for another critical system function: adaptation. Companies must put in place career development processes that will help them grow a large pool of well-trained and adaptable managers who see learning, mobility, and change as part of their identities and jobs. Bringing high-potential people with diverse backgrounds, different ways of thinking, and new competencies into key positions will introduce fresh, adaptive approaches to solving today's novel business problems. In this way organizations can use career development in a strategic and creative manner, and career development strategies will be more closely linked to corporate and business strategies.

REFERENCES

Argyris, C. (1954). Human relations in a bank. *Harvard Business Review, 32,* 63–72.

Argyris, C. (1957). *Personality and organization.* New York: Harper.

Arthur, M. B., Inkson, K., & Pringle, J. K. (1999). *The new careers: Individual action and economic change.* London: Sage.

Arthur, M. B., & Rousseau, D. M. (1996). Introduction: The boundaryless career as a new employment principle. In M. B. Arthur & D. M. Rousseau (Eds.), *The boundaryless career: A new employment principle for a new organizational era.* New York: Oxford University Press.

Baruch, Y., & Peiperl, M. (2000). Career management practices: An empirical survey and implications. *Human Resource Management, 39,* 347–366.

Briscoe, J. P., & Hall, D. T. (1999, Autumn). Grooming and picking leaders using competency frameworks: Do they work? An alternative approach and new guidelines for practice. *Organizational Dynamics,* pp. 37–52.

Burgelman, R. (1994). Fading memories: A process theory of strategic business exit. *Administrative Science Quarterly, 39,* 24–56.

Cappelli, P. (2002). *The path to the top: The changing model of career advancement.* Paper presented at the Harvard Business School Conference on Career Evolution, London, June 13–15.

Cascio, W. (1987). *Applied psychology in personnel management* (3rd ed.). Englewood Cliffs, NJ: Prentice Hall.

Datta, D. K., & Rajagopalan, N. (1998). Industry structure and CEO characteristics: An empirical study of succession events. *Strategic Management Journal, 19,* 833–852.

Denrell, J., & March, J. G. (2001). Adaptation as information restriction: The hot stove effect. *Organization Science, 12,* 523–538.

Dunnette, M. D. (1966). *Personnel selection and placement.* Belmont, CA: Wadsworth.

Gabarro, J. J. (1988). Executive leadership and succession: The process of taking charge. In D. C. Hambrick (Ed.), *The executive effect: Concepts and methods for studying top managers* (pp. 237–268). Greenwich, CT: JAI.

Galunic, C. D., & Anderson, E. (2000) From security to mobility: Generalized investments in human capital and agent commitment. *Organization Science, 11*(1), 1–20.

Gupta, A. (1986). Matching managers to strategies: Point and counterpoint. *Human Resource Management, 25,* 214–239.

Gutteridge, T. G. (1986). Organizational career development systems: The state of the practice. In D. T. Hall & Associates (Eds.), *Career development in organizations* (pp. 50–94). San Francisco: Jossey-Bass.

Gutteridge, T. G., Leibowitz, Z. B., & Shore, J. E. (1993). *Organizational career development: Benchmarks for building a world-class workforce.* San Francisco: Jossey-Bass.

Hakim, C. (1994). *We are all self-employed: The new social contract for working in a changed world.* San Francisco: Berrett-Koehler.

Hall, D. T. (1976). *Careers in organizations.* Glenview, IL: Scott, Foresman.

Hall, D. T. (1986a). Dilemmas in linking succession planning to individual executive learning. *Human Resource Management, 25,* 235–265.

Hall, D. T. (1986b). An overview of current career development theory, research, and practice. In D. T. Hall & Associates (Eds.), *Career development in organizations* (pp. 1–20). San Francisco: Jossey-Bass.

Hall, D. T. (2002). *Careers in and out of organizations.* Thousand Oaks, CA: Sage.

Hall, D. T., & Associates. (1996). *The career is dead—Long live the career: A relational approach to careers.* San Francisco: Jossey-Bass.

Hall, D. T., & Moss, J. E. (1998, Winter). The new protean career contract: Helping organizations and employees adapt. *Organizational Dynamics,* pp. 22–37.

Hall, D. T., Zhu, G., & Yan, A. (2001). Developing global leaders: To hold on to them, let them go! In W. H. Mobley & M. W. McCall Jr. (Eds.), *Advances in global leadership* (2nd ed., pp. 327–349). Oxford, UK: Elsevier.

Kanter, R. M. (1977). *Men and women of the corporation.* New York: Basic Books.

Karaevli, A., & Hall, D. T. (2003, Winter). Growing leaders for turbulent times: Is succession planning up to the challenge? *Organizational Dynamics, 32,* 62–79.

Karaevli, A., & Hall, D. T. (2006). How career variety promotes the adaptability of managers:

A theoretical model. *Journal of Vocational Behavior, 69,* 359–373.

Kerr, J. L., & Jackofsky, E. F. (1989). Aligning managers with strategies: Managerial development versus selection. *Strategic Management Journal, 10*(special issue), 157–171.

Kotter, J. P. (1995). *The new rules: How to succeed in today's post-corporate world.* New York: Free Press.

Leddy, P. (2003). *Succession planning at Dell.* Presented as a part of the Symposium on Innovations in Succession Planning: Theory and Practice. Industrial and Organizational Psychology Conference, April 10–13, Orlando, FL.

Leibowitz, Z. B., Farren, D., & Kaye, B. L. (1986, October). Overcoming management resistance to career development programs. *Training and Development Journal,* 77–81.

Lengnick-Hall, C. A., & Lengnick-Hall, M. L. (1988). Strategic human resource management: A review of the literature and a proposed typology. *Academy of Management Review, 13,* 454–470.

Levinthal, A. A., & March, J. G. (1993). The myopia of learning. *Strategic Management Journal, 14,* 95–112.

Lombardo, M. M., & Eichinger, R. W. (2001). *The leadership machine.* Minneapolis: Lominger.

March, J. C., & March, J. G. (1977). Almost random careers: The Wisconsin school superintendency, 1940–1972. *Administrative Science Quarterly, 22,* 377–409.

March, J. G. (1991). Exploration and exploitation in organizational learning. *Organization Science, 2,* 71–87.

Nicholson, N. (1996). Career systems in crisis: Change and opportunity in the information age. *Academy of Management Executive, 10*(4), 40–51.

Ocasio, W. (1994). Political dynamics and the circulation of power: CEO succession in U.S. industrial corporations, 1960–1990. *Administrative Science Quarterly, 39,* 285–312.

Ocasio, W. (1995). The enactment of economic diversity: A reconciliation of theories of failure-induced change and threat-rigidity. In L. L. Cummings & B. M. Staw (Eds.), *Research in organizational behavior* (Vol. 17, pp. 287–331). Greenwich, CT: JAI.

Ocasio, W. (1999). Institutionalized action and corporate governance: The reliance on rules of CEO succession. *Administrative Science Quarterly, 44,* 384–416.

Ocasio, W., & Kim, H. (1999). The circulation of corporate control: Selection of functional backgrounds of new CEOs in large U.S. manufacturing firms, 1981–1992. *Administrative Science Quarterly, 44,* 532–562.

O'Connell, D. (1997, May). *Career development in the age of the "new deal" for work.* Boston: Human Resources Policy Institute Technical Report.

Ohlott, P. J., Ruderman, M. N., & McCauley, C. D. (1994). Gender differences in managers' developmental job experiences. *Academy of Management Journal, 37,* 46–67.

Pasmore, W. A. (1988). *Designing effective organizations: The sociotechnical systems perspective.* New York: John Wiley & Sons.

Pfeffer, J. (1997). *New directions for organization theory.* New York: Oxford University Press.

Pfeffer, J., & Salancik, G. R. (1978). *The external control of organizations.* New York: Harper & Row.

Prior, L. A. (1998). *Evaluating organizational career development savvy.* Boston: Executive Development Roundtable Technical Report.

Reed, T. L. (1978). Organizational change in the American Foreign Service, 1925–1965: The utility of cohort analysis. *American Sociological Review, 43,* 404–421.

Ruderman, M. N., Ohlott, P. J., & Kram, K. E. (1995). Promotion decisions as a diversity practice. *Journal of Management Development, 14,* 6–23.

Schneider, B. (1983). Interactional psychology and organizational behavior. In B. M. Staw & L. L. Cummings (Eds.), *Research in organizational behavior* (Vol. 5, pp. 1–31). Greenwich, CT: JAI.

Schneider, B. (1987). The people make the place. *Personnel Psychology, 40,* 437–454.

Schneider, B., Goldstein, H. W., & Smith, D. B. (1995). The ASA framework: An update. *Personnel Psychology, 48,* 747–774.

Schneider, B., Smith, D. B., Taylor, S., & Fleenor, C. (1998). Personality and organizations: A test of the homogeneity of personality hypothesis. *Journal of Applied Psychology, 83,* 462–470.

Smith, M., & White, M. C. (1987). Strategy, CEO specialization, and succession. *Administrative Science Quarterly, 32,* 263–280.

Sonnenfeld, J. A., & Peiperl, M. A. (1988). Staffing policy as a strategic response: A typology of career systems. *Academy of Management Review, 13*(4), 588–600.

Staw, B., Sandelands, L., & Dutton, J. (1981). Threat rigidity effects in organizational behavior: A multilevel analysis. *Administrative Science Quarterly, 26,* 501–524.

Stewman, S. (1988). Organizational demography. *Annual Review of Sociology, 14,* 173–202.

Thomas, D. A. (2001). The truth about mentoring minorities: Race matters. *Harvard Business Review, 79*(4), 98–107.

Thompson, J. A. (1967). *Organizations in action.* New York: McGraw-Hill.

Vancil, R. F. (1987). *Passing the baton: Managing the process of CEO succession.* Boston: Harvard Business School Press.

Wright, P. M., & Snell, S. A. (1998). Toward a unifying framework for exploring fit and flexibility in strategic human resource management. *Academy of Management Review, 23*(4), 756–772.

21

Integrating Organization Development With Strategic Planning

Closing the Approach–Method Gap

L A R R Y   G R E I N E R

A troubling but promising oxymoron is reflected in the title of this chapter, where organization development (OD) is coupled with strategic planning. OD is about collaboration within the firm, whereas strategy is about competition outside the firm. The connection between these two important management activities has rarely existed in practice and seldom in the OD or strategy literature. Historically, they are odd bedfellows in both a practical and scholarly sense, yet I argue that they must be joined if organizations are to formulate and implement more effective strategies in the future.

Over time the OD field has been seen by managers as irrelevant to strategic planning because of its narrow and exclusive attention to behavioral topics confined to lower levels in organizations, reflecting OD's inability to address the substance of business planning.

At the same time, strategy scholars have not attempted to make links with OD, focusing more on the substance of strategy, emphasizing abstract macroeconomic and organization theories derived from research data collected in ways remote to contact with firms. Strategy consultants from consulting firms have also been isolated from OD, where they too have given priority to substance over process while engaged in lengthy data-gathering studies designed to yield analytical insights for clients.

If OD is to play a more vital role in the future of organizations it must become involved in strategic planning, which affects not only the direction of organizations but also the lives and careers of many employees (Buller, 1988; Worley, Hitchin, & Ross, 1996). Throughout its history, OD's raison d'être has been to develop human capital and improve organization effectiveness, which are clearly key leverage points for any strategic effort in today's competitive environment (Pfeffer, 1998).

Strategic planning is undergoing change in its approaches and methods to keep up with a fast-moving marketplace; detailed and lengthy plans prepared by specialists are being replaced by flexible guidelines developed by managers (Mintzberg, Ahlstrand, & Lampel, 2005). Critics of traditional planning approaches are advocating more real-time plans that have wider commitment from employees at all levels (Eisenhardt & Sull, 2001). This new environment provides an opening for OD to make a valuable contribution if it can first get its own house in order.

In this chapter I ask, "Why has OD in the past ignored or been excluded from strategic planning?" "What are the historical antecedents and current state of scholarly thinking about the substance and content of strategic planning?" "What are some recent steps taken by OD to address strategic planning?" and "How can OD connect better with strategic planning in the future?" When addressing the "how" question, I will describe one new OD approach to strategic planning, including a set of methods we have developed to engage substantive strategy content and close the gap. I also provide examples of our approach to strategic planning and other methods like it that show promise for improving the quality and implementation of strategic planning. As I see it, the answer lies in the details of the approaches and methods used in planning.

My contention is that the gap exists not because of a lack of theory or sound research or a lack of focus on execution (Hrebiniak, 2005); rather, it is the absence of concrete and useful methods to integrate process with content. *Methods* refers to two key features: a clear format for recording relevant strategic content for a firm and a designed process for key managers to input their content to the format. I address both in this chapter.

The search for greater concreteness in methods may seem to some like a mundane and overly practical task when compared with developing breakthrough theory, but I believe it may answer why so many firms fail to implement their strategies effectively.

SOURCES OF GAP

OD's Self-Destructive Tendencies

The inability of OD to engage the realism of strategic planning has been cited and widely criticized by others (Weidner & Kulick, 1999). Unfortunately, little has happened to bridge this gap, except for a few recent theories with OD origins (organization learning and appreciative inquiry), which will be discussed later. Throughout this chapter OD is discussed as if it were one thing, although there clearly remains variety around the OD core.

Much of OD's problem with strategic planning is of its own making for a variety of historical reasons. OD had its birth and ascendancy (French & Bell, 1972) in the 1950s and 1960s, and from its inception, OD focused largely on behavioral and organizational change issues, not on strategic content issues. Its emphasis has been on teamwork, intergroup relationships, and leadership styles (Argyris, 1964). The change methods used by OD have relied primarily on team building and interpersonal feedback (Blake & Mouton, 1964). Participative methods and group decision making were used by OD consultants in attempts to change organizations toward more humanistic practices, which were assumed to lead to higher performance (Likert, 1961).

Most OD consultants have not been trained in strategic content issues, so understandably they have not been able to make substantive contributions. A longstanding assumption of OD has been that business content issues will be solved if OD focuses on providing an open and trusting climate to facilitate decision making by others. The OD literature gives little attention to the issues of marketing, finance, and operations.

Perhaps the most damaging block to progress occurred in the mid-1970s when a backlash of critics depicted OD as soft, naive, and invasive of individual privacy. Many psychologists criticized OD for idealistically assuming that people could easily change their behavior after receiving interpersonal feedback (Armenakis & Field, 1975). Still others wondered whether more harm was done by pointing out a person's interpersonal flaws in public (Boris, 1978). This damaged reputation for OD greatly slowed its momentum and popularity.

In addition, OD developed an early reputation for focusing its work at the middle and lower levels of organizations, not at the top, where strategic planning occurs. The values espoused by OD were rarely those of senior management, advocating instead ways to redistribute power to lower levels through a greater use of participation, bottom-up management, and consensus decision making (Beckhard, 1969; Bennis, 1969). OD was often seen as championing the underdog and the less powerful and even being anticorporate (Argyris, 1957). Its advocacy of democratic values and methods proved threatening to many senior executives.

In response to its critics, OD began in the 1980s to move away from its emphasis on interpersonal relations to focus on self-managed work groups, career development, and cultural change in organizations. There was also a growing interest in structural design (Alpanger, 1995; Pasmore, 1994), and sociotechnical systems (Cohen & Ledford, 1994). However, OD was rarely involved in the formulation and analytical phase of strategic planning. During this time, OD's traditional methods of using T groups and interpersonal feedback to promote change lost their relevance for solving the macro issues of organization design and strategic change.

Management Blinders

Not all the causes of OD's lack of involvement in strategic planning are its own shortcomings. Senior managers typically have displayed more interest in the content and analytical side of strategic planning than in its process and implementation issues. In addition, consultants and academics have long relied on and proposed complex analytic models for new insights. The 1960s and 1970s saw the rise of large planning departments in organizations devoted exclusively to the content of strategic planning. At General Electric, just before Jack Welch became CEO, working in the corporate strategic planning department were about 300 people (Aguilar, Hamermesh, & Brainard, 1985), most of whom were removed by Welch.

Another hurdle for OD was erected by well-known management consulting firms; some firms devoted themselves primarily to strategic planning (e.g., Bain, BCG, Monitor), and others (the consulting divisions of accounting firms) offered it as a service. The consultants from these firms sold large projects, spent long hours with clients gathering data, applied their analytical models, and made substantive recommendations. Their billing practices typically relied on hours spent on a project, an economic formula that correlated time consumed with revenue growth.

Interestingly, many clients have been willing to spend large sums on strategy consulting in return for not only the content received but also the value of the consulting firm's reputation. Clients of strategy consulting firms often mistakenly assume that a consulting firm's brand name and the size of their expenditure will be matched by the quality of strategic content provided. This assumption by clients operates unfavorably for OD, where fees and revenues are not based on time; rather, OD tends to rely on "do-it-yourself" methods that use employees of the client firms to perform much of the work, such as through the use of retreats. Internal OD consultants suffer even more because they typically charge little or nothing for their services.

Another block to OD has come from the way strategic planning has traditionally been separated and sequenced by scholars and managers into two independent and sequential activities: a formulation stage and an implementation phase (Ansoff, 1965). The formulation stage has been reserved largely for top management to focus on content and analysis, and subsequent implementation and change phases typically have been delegated to middle and lower management. OD has occasionally contributed to the implementation stage when organization change is involved (Tichy, 1983), but rarely has OD been involved in the formulation stage.

BRIEF HISTORY OF STRATEGIC PLANNING

If OD is to make headway on strategic planning, it needs to better prepare itself by understanding the intellectual context of strategic theory and knowledge. Historically, three somewhat simplified phases tend to characterize the evolution of strategic thought and practice: the business policy phase, before 1970; the market and resources competitive advantage phase, 1970–2000; and the dynamic total systems phase, after 2000. Definitions of *strategy* have clearly evolved and been advanced with each era, although all are useful for our thinking.

Business Policy Phase, Before 1970

The origins of strategic planning are traceable to the first business policy course at the Harvard Business School after World War II (Cruikshank, 1987). Its focus was on the management problems facing a firm as it attempts to grow. The objective was to train future managers in the necessary diagnostic and judgmental skills to evaluate firms and their opportunities. The policy course was viewed as the capstone for the Harvard MBA program, drawing from all its business disciplines.

The policy course continued at Harvard into the early 1970s, having served as a model for launching similar courses at other business schools. Policy cases were developed for class discussion. The case teaching manuals and course syllabi gave little priority to the use of

formal theories to explain what was happening in a case. Instead, students were engaged in a Socratic and intuitive case discussion about the problems and solutions for the firm under study.

In essence, this phase might be characterized as a managerial problem-solving approach to setting the direction of the firm. In the Harvard cases, each company's strategic problems were considered to be unique, necessitating custom solutions. Class discussion centered more on internal issues of senior managers who set the direction and policies for moving forward (Andrews, 1971). The belief was that senior managers had the responsibility, knowledge, and skill to set future strategy. Theories and models for analyzing the market and competition were just being developed.

The Market and Resources Competitive Advantage Phase, 1970–2000

Michael Porter's books on achieving competitive advantage by analyzing market forces became the intellectual cornerstone of this phase (Porter, 1985). The major consulting firms—especially BCG, led by Bruce Henderson, with its models "growth share matrix" and "experience curve" (Stern & Deimler, 2006)—fueled an explosion of economic and marketing concepts for analyzing the competitive situation of firms. The focus of these models was largely external to the firm, helping clients to plan for their markets by locating a profitable niche relative to competitors (Slywotzky, 1996). Many of these planning models were complex and formalized (Ansoff, 1984). In addition, numerous organizations created large planning departments at the corporate level for the purpose of developing detailed planning books containing analysis and instructions to managers on actions they should take.

A critical backlash developed later in this phase, directed at the overemphasis on formal planning, especially at the detailed plans that were never implemented (Pettigrew,

Mintzberg, & Lorange, 1987). The term *analysis paralysis* was commonly used to criticize bureaucratic planning. As a result, attention shifted to implementation and using capabilities of the firm to achieve competitive advantage (Wernerfelt, 1984). Here the organization and its resources came more into the forefront as the target of change. Strategy was also increasingly viewed as a pattern of key political decisions that emerged over time (Pettigrew et al., 1987).

The Dynamic Total Systems Phase, After 2000

The new millennium ironically brings us partly back to the early business policy phase, where the focus was on leadership decisions; however, this new era learned from the prior era about the importance of recognizing and including the marketplace in any strategy. Thus, today's version of strategy has become more comprehensive, dynamic, and integrated to include the organization, the global marketplace, hypercompetition, and the fast pace of decisions (Eisenhardt & Sull, 2001).

We call this phase dynamic total systems, which suggests that strategy formulation is not separate from implementation; rather, the two activities occur simultaneously (Nadler & Slywotzky, 2005). For example, the content of the planning process can be influenced by a variety of implementation factors, such as the CEO's leadership style, the particular managers selected to participate in planning, a reliance on outside consultants, and the methods used to gather data (e.g., meetings, surveys, interviews)—all affect not only future commitment but also the quality of substance used in the formulation analysis (Greiner & Bhambri, 1989).

Dynamics are also accelerated by fast-moving events in today's global world. Rapid decisions often must be made to improve the link between strategy, organization, operations,

and systems. Interestingly, strategic planning efforts for time periods longer than 3 years have proven difficult to realize. Therefore, organizations faced with limited time horizons must become stronger and more flexible in their readiness to change rapidly, even learning to invent new strategies on the spot. An innovative and dynamic organization is likely to provide higher-quality and more real-time input to the content of planning than is a bureaucratic and slow-moving one (Brown & Eisenhardt, 1998).

At the same time, organizations cannot become chameleons. They need direction and coherence of effort; otherwise, they become reactive and disjointed. So strategic planning is still alive but in a different form that provides guidelines and goals for the firm and all its employees. Gone are the days of highly detailed strategies with long time frames. Explicit plans must be formulated for today's boards of directors who, because of their responsibility and liability, are expecting CEOs to develop strategic plans with accountability attached. Financial analysts and investors are also asking companies to explain where they are going in the short term. Finally, because of the frequency of CEO turnover, many new CEOs often begin their tenure with a strategic planning exercise.

OD, with its emphasis on process, organizations, and behavior, has a new opportunity to play a more valuable role in this new kind of strategic planning (Lawler & Mohrman, 2003). Will it respond effectively? That is the challenge.

HOW PREPARED IS OD TO CONTRIBUTE?

OD proponents and organization theorists have made recent forays into strategic thinking and practice (Hamel & Prahalad, 1989). Most of these efforts have been directed at using the underlying capabilities of organizations to implement new strategies. A comprehensive textbook on OD covers many of these efforts to strengthen organizations' receptivity to change (Cummings & Worley, 2005).

Many of these attempts have been made to facilitate strategic planning through team building at senior management levels by helping top teams become more ready to plan and engage in change activities. As before, the content side of planning in these efforts is left mostly to the managers involved. One recent OD foray into content has been to perform group "vision-setting" and "open space" exercises in which the participants discuss and offer perceptions and projections for what they want the company to become and look like in the future (Lipton, 1996). In my opinion, these exercises often lack substance by avoiding a realistic analysis of opportunities and threats based on economics, competitors, products, and financial and human resources.

Some OD progress has also been made recently on the theoretical and research levels. Several macro theories of strategic change have been advanced from research to describe what happens when organizations attempt to change their strategies (Greenwood & Hinings, 1993). All of these theories make clear that strategic planning is a top-down yet collaborative process, reaching out eventually to involve the entire organization with implementation. They also emphasize the importance of including substantive content in strategy making; Chapter 22 by Michael Beer in this book proposes a model that integrates Theory E (economics) with Theory O (organization). Beer also offers suggestions for holding a thoughtful planning discussion and advocating a number of general behavioral principles to follow in furthering E and O integration.

Other recently developed strategic change models involve stage theory with a sequence of interdependent phases as the top management plans and acts its way toward more complete strategic change. These models depend for their outcomes on the interaction between the situation and a series of interventions taking place.

One such model is called integrated strategic change, which is based on four phases (analysis, strategic choice, action plan, and implementation) that address both content and behavior involved in strategic planning (Worley et al., 1996). These same phases are commonly used in many normative strategic planning models; in addition, the authors advocate a traditional OD value of using extensive participation throughout the planning process.

A different change model, based on research, suggests seven descriptive phases of successful strategic change, beginning with the CEO "negotiating a mandate with the Board for strategic change" (Greiner, Cummings, & Bhambri, 2003). The seven phases represent one of the few change models, like Beer's and Worley's, that directly address and include the substantive content of formulation in strategic planning. The authors also identify certain contextual conditions that are likely to block or enhance strategic change efforts, such as external environments with more or less slack (e.g., high regulation equals low slack, meaning less space and support for change). Also, internal organization conditions affect progress, such as the degree of receptivity toward change based on whether the organization has had a successful experience with change in the past.

Unfortunately, these macro models are so broad and all encompassing without giving sufficient consideration to the micro concrete methods used to implement strategic change. Little is said about how the plan itself is created and defined through interactions in the top management group. The Greiner et al. (2003) model includes a phase in which the top management group collaborates to develop a new strategy that later provides the basis for defining action steps. However, the specific real-time behavioral dynamics of how management interaction addresses and resolves certain substantive issues during the strategy formulation phase is not clearly described or explained.

One recent and helpful theoretical contribution with OD implications is the literature on appreciative inquiry (AI) (Cooperrider, Sorenson, Yaeger, & Whitney, 2001). AI's basic premise is that organizations will change toward the direction in which they inquire. The connection between AI and strategic planning runs something like this: If members of an organization search for what they have done best in the past, that insight can be built on through visioning of a future centered on the organization's best practices from the past. AI is basically a worthy philosophy, a good building block for our approach that searches for the positive in people and strengths in the organization, assuming that the resulting insights will unblock people from negative thoughts and stimulate positive action (Cameron, Dutton, & Quinn, 2003). Some consultants have directly applied AI to the process of developing a vision for organizations (Lipton, 1996). Lipton proposes a sequential process to develop a positive vision before determining a mission and strategy; that is, if members of an organization can gain a better sense of purpose for the organization, this will energize them later when they are developing a specific strategy.

Closely related to AI is the concept of organization learning (OL), which is another building block for our real-time approach, relying on continuous experimentation and innovation to cause employees to increase their capability to learn and create solutions for changing conditions (Senge, 1990). OL seeks to harness the collective intelligence and experience of employees as they innovate, experiment, and reflect on their actions. When this creative behavior becomes widespread and continuously applied throughout an organization, the term *learning organization* is used to describe the functioning of the firm.

Both AI and OL theories have a behavioral and organizational focus for providing strategic insights. They tend to represent the Theory O side of Beer's model while neglecting the Theory E side. Underlying AI and OL thinking is OD's traditional but questionable assumption that if behavioral processes are working well, management will automatically make good strategic content decisions and perform effectively. Interestingly, academic scholars who study business strategy have not been of much help in integrating the E with the O side of planning, preferring to perform research that is quite technical, abstract, and remote from practice and managerial behavior.

Another theory related to AI and OL but incorporating more of the E side is the concept of strategic intent (Hamel & Prahalad, 1989). Basically, these authors see strategy as leveraging creatively a firm's internal resources while considering the realities of the marketplace. Like AI and OL, strategic intent exists in the heads and behavior of the firm's leaders, but these managers go further to assess realistically the competition and then use their own strengths to position, invest, and outcompete other firms. Strategic intent becomes a general long-term direction—a vision of what the firm should become—that guides the firm as employees invent new means to reach it. This strategy moves ahead by solving different challenges that emerge in succeeding eras over time. Emphasis is placed on winning against competition, including targets to gauge progress.

The downside of strategic intent, as it is described by its originators, is the lack of specificity in how intent is created in practice. In fact, the authors are critical of formal planning methods, believing that much of strategic intent occurs outside the planning process, depending more on the skills, minds, and hopes of leaders in the firm. The theory proposes general principles to follow instead of detailed plans. It leaves up in the air questions about how to get there.

CONTENT: FORMAT FOR A WRITTEN STRATEGY STATEMENT

We have served as strategy consultants to more than 12 organizations in the past 15 years, including a large academic association, a hotel chain, a major construction firm, a software company, a college of arts and sciences, an energy firm, a childcare company, a propane company, and an aircraft engine manufacturer. This consulting experience has been directed at fine tuning our strategic planning approach and methods, including a new format for a written strategy statement and an improved design of retreats where the statement is created. The format represents the content side of strategic planning, and the retreat design reflects the process side. The challenge for any consultant, and that of strategic planning in general, is to help the two sides interact and integrate effectively.

Strategy is a complex and abstract subject, which makes it very easy for managers, consultants, and academics to engage in an intellectual exercise without producing much in the way of concrete meaning and results. For this reason, we do not start our consulting by asking a client to develop a vague statement of "mission," which we regard as too passive and overly general (e.g., "We are in the propane distribution business throughout the United States"). Nor do we begin with a statement of "vision" built on the idealistic hopes of the participants (e.g., "We will become the dominant propane provider in our industry"). The difficult planning task for any management group is to avoid retreating into generalities or vague hopes and instead confront realistically their competitive situation and to search for a way to succeed in it. They must identify a profitable niche in the marketplace, especially where their firm can obtain a competitive advantage, and align the organization in ways that cause the strategy to be implemented.

This challenge brings us to our current format for developing a written strategy statement. Our consulting engagements have sought to find ways to simplify (but not oversimplify) the elusive subject of strategy into a coherent statement of strategic direction, which we currently divide into four key action elements. Without these four elements, any strategy statement is likely to remain vague and lacking in implementation. It must be comprehensive, recognizing and incorporating the

many factors that will ensure success for the outcomes (Mintzberg et al., 1998). Our experience suggests that the impact of strategy is maximized through internal consistency across the following four elements as they build on each other and are implemented as a whole.

1. Determine competitive logic:
   • Determine market position.
   • Determine customer tiebreakers.

2. Set key goals:
   • Set overall financial goal.
   • Create rallying goal.

3. Align organization and people:
   • Design organization structure.
   • Create shared values.

4. Launch action plan:
   • Determine key initiatives.
   • Specify action steps.

We arrived at these four elements based not only on our experience but after surveying the strategy formulation and implementation literature, examining the work of strategy consultants, and including interviews with senior executives for what they thought to be important and helpful. Although each element is not new by itself, the four here are rarely combined in a single comprehensive format.

Each element represents an important concept and leverage point in a viable strategic plan; for example, the concept of competitive logic and its subelements of market position and customer tiebreakers focuses the firm's strengths and resources on a niche where it can attract customers and win against competitors. The key goals concept points to the need to unify the organization in pursuing common metrics of accomplishment that are consistent with the competitive logic. Aligning the organization and people is necessary because it helps to structure the firm's human resources in ways to carry out and reinforce the logic and goals. The action plan begins to set everything in motion. Without it the strategic statement remains just that: a piece of paper without life. The preceding three elements establish a focus for the action plan. (See Appendix A for a completed statement for an energy firm.)

We establish several guidelines for the participants to follow in completing the four elements on a strategic statement. First, it must be in writing so as to solidify agreements reached in the management group. Simply asking managers to discuss it and adjourn without producing a written agreement allows for too much subjectivity and room for slippage that makes consensus illusory. We also ask that the statement be written in brief and clear terms, usually stated in bullet points on one page; otherwise, it can be obfuscated by too much verbiage with excessive room for compromises. Finally, it must also be worded in ways that managers and employees will understand and act on.

Each of the four elements is illustrated here with a hotel chain client. For its competitive logic, the chain's new management decided to limit growth to the western United States, where they saw openings to manage more hotels and focus on conferences and repeat customers from business organizations. This logic took the place of national or international expansion where an acquisition and capital were available for doing so. They also decided to price rooms just under those of competing five-star hotels. The chain's tiebreakers then became a new practice of "drop everything for the customer," "Western friendliness," and "comp their room if they are unhappy," along with pursuing highly profitable conference groups by offering exceptional service and favorable pricing. The prior management of the chain had sought to expand nationally, competing directly against five-star chains, and was centralizing its decisions at headquarters.

The new management team set a financial goal for each hotel to achieve 30% annual operating profit within 2 years. This goal was consistent with the competitive logic to grow and supported by a new organization that decentralized each hotel into a separate profit center. The former CEO had set a plethora of financial goals for the chain as a whole without making each hotel responsible for its local decisions and outcomes. The rallying goal became "Best Service in the West," which was consistent with the chain's competitive logic to focus solely on the western market, supported by conference business and repeat customers traveling up and down the West Coast.

Each hotel was led by a general manager whose compensation was closely tied to the chain's new financial goal of achieving 30% operating profit. Previously, the general managers in charge of each hotel were treated more as public relations people who implemented decisions made at headquarters. These managers lacked autonomy and responsibility for decisions affecting their bottom lines. In the new organization, the general manager's initiatives included service training of all employees and pursuit of conference business by hiring a conference marketing manager at each hotel location.

All these elements were created in two workshops and written as bullet points on one page of paper. By the end of 2 years, the chain had expanded by six new hotels, and all hotels had exceeded 30% operating profit.

PROCESS: RETREAT DESIGN AND CONDUCT

In addition to the format for developing strategic content, there are processes through which people contribute their knowledge to the strategy statement. Over the years, various approaches to planning have been tried in companies to develop strategic content, including relying on staff planning groups, turning to outside consulting firms, to holding meetings of the senior executive group. Common to many of these approaches is an intensive period of data gathering, then several meetings to analyze the data, followed by report writing and presentations. Too often CEOs set the format in their language and preferences with a preordained decision in mind. In addition, there are CEOs who believe the annual budget serves as a surrogate for a strategic plan, those who believe that corporate strategy is the sum of strategies from each business unit, and those who engage in political bargaining with key subordinates over whose vision will prevail (Pettigrew et al., 1987).

These different approaches often fail because of process breakdowns and conflicts between staff and line groups, between consultants and senior management, or between key managers, resulting in watered-down compromises. Many organizations simply give up trying because of an accumulation of bad experiences with plans that never got implemented. Some even engage in strategic planning as a meaningless exercise intended only to satisfy requirements of the board.

Retreats traditionally have been used by OD to facilitate effective discussion, and we use them for the same purpose. Retreats remove people from the distractions of the office so they can reflect and focus; they also help increase participation and commitment to decisions.

We design strategic planning retreats to produce different content from what is typically revealed in OD retreats; traditional OD topics such as team building and interpersonal relationships are replaced by strategic content about markets, competitors, products and services, and economics. To be sure, team building occurs as people interact, express their opinions, and then together create a strategic plan that they will own and implement as a team.

A poorly designed retreat can easily dissolve into disagreements with little progress. Five major considerations go into the actual design and conduct of our strategic retreats: goals of the retreat, preparation for the retreat, structure of the retreat, conduct of the retreat, and follow-up steps.

Retreat Goals

Our overriding objective for strategy retreats is to develop a written strategic plan that will

be implemented with successful results. We produce written products of key conclusions at the end of each day and distribute copies to all the members the next morning. We usually produce a final-draft strategic statement (without action plan) after no more than three retreats over 8–12 weeks. This statement is then used to guide creation of an action plan, including who does what and when, at a follow-up retreat.

Preparation for Retreats

Several preparation steps, ranging from pre-retreat interviews to simple logistics, are essential. Most important is for the consultants to perform a preliminary analysis of the company situation facing the participants. We hold interviews via the Internet with each attendee beforehand; the Web and e-mail permit a faster and less expensive way to interview each person. We send an e-mail message in advance to participants asking each to report his or her opinions about the firm's strengths, weaknesses, opportunities, and threats (SWOT) on one page, placing three to five bullet points under each category. We assure complete anonymity and receive responses directly by e-mail. Next, we identify the patterns running across all the SWOT responses, which typically indicate a lot of agreement (the Web-based results seem just as valid as those obtained from personal interviews). Then we use our SWOT summary to kick off the first retreat, where we ask the group whether our analysis of their responses represents an accurate picture of the company's current situation. This step facilitates a fast starting foundation to build on and reduces the probability of later disagreements about the state of the company.

Planning for the logistics should make sure that the right people attend and that the surroundings are conducive to discussion without outside disturbance. Who should attend? Our experience is that it should at least be the top team reporting to and including the CEO or head of the unit in question. Without the

CEO's involvement, the planning exercise becomes an empty one because of uncertainty about the CEO's opinions on strategy. We often add a few influential members from the next level of management below the top so as to correct for senior management bias. The total number of participants should be somewhere between 8 and 12 because a larger group is difficult to manage. Next, there is a choice of appropriate facilities. We prefer quiet locations not too far from headquarters yet far enough away so people don't run back and forth at night or during the day. There should be enough breakout rooms for subgroup meetings with sufficient media equipment to record comments and make presentations.

Structure of Retreats

The agenda for our retreats is organized entirely around the four elements that go into a written statement of strategic direction, beginning with the competitive logic. Sometimes we can accomplish a final draft in two retreats, and other times it may take up to four retreats, all depending on the length of each retreat and how fast the group comes to new insights and reaches consensus conclusions. The agenda for a retreat must be carefully planned. Appendix B gives a sample schedule for how we currently organize an opening retreat, which includes the following key points:

- We begin with an introduction by the CEO, who should express his or her seriousness about developing a new strategic plan. We then give a summary of the patterns in the SWOT analysis and ask for further discussion to test for agreement on the findings. Next we introduce the need to write a strategic statement as the main product of work. We explain the statement and its elements with a short lecture on the current state of knowledge about strategic planning so that everyone understands how and why we will approach each task as we do.
- We suggest that the statement should be worded more as a set of concrete guidelines in bullet points, instead of a highly detailed planning document. The environment surrounding most organizations is moving too quickly and in surprising ways to rule out needed flexibility. Strategy statements must be reviewed and revised frequently.
- We find that the quality of content is advanced and reinforced when two or three subgroups meet separately and report back to the total group. Our experience is that the subgroups usually agree in their overall conclusions, which adds credibility and validity to the points being made. Also, the feedback tends to be more honest and objective when we ask subgroups to meet in separate rooms instead of with the CEO. We usually ask the CEO to move around, observe the conversation, participate, but not dominate, and avoid staying in any subgroup for long.
- On the first evening, we often draft a statement of conclusions reached to that point about the elements covered. This draft is provided to the participants for review at the start of the second day. The group indicates areas of consensus and suggests revisions. They continue to work on the remainder of the five elements. If the group bogs down on one element, we often move on to the next one and recycle back later.

The first retreat ends with a volunteer first reading a rough draft statement prepared by a volunteer from the group. It is reviewed carefully and discussed by the group before they depart (if they have not completed work on a draft at the first retreat, we discuss what must be considered before the next retreat). Usually, we hope to complete work on a draft in two retreats.

In the final part of the retreat, we discuss the next steps. If there is a completed draft, we suggest reviewing it next with groups of middle managers for discussion and feedback, which is accomplished through a series of meetings run by pairs of senior managers who attend the first retreat. This begins the process of extending the change process to the larger workforce. These middle manager meetings ask whether the draft statement is sufficiently realistic and inspirational; will it work, and can they get behind it? And what suggestions would they make to improve it? Their reactions are fed back to a designated manager for preparation of a redraft to be presented at the second retreat.

- The second retreat (and a third or fourth if necessary) focuses on finalizing the draft strategy statement, beginning discussion of needed changes in organization structure, specifying key values, and outlining initiatives and action steps. The discussion of values usually is not difficult because they are closely related to the tiebreakers set earlier. However, the issue of organization structure is a sensitive topic for the participants because it may threaten people's power positions. We avoid talking about specific people for positions; rather, we ask the subgroups to identify alternative structures with pros and cons, including their preference. We remind the group that any chosen structure must be consistent with the competitive logic and goals. If there is wide disagreement on a proposed structure, the CEO can take the alternatives under advisement and make a decision later after the retreat ends. Personnel changes usually are decided by the CEO talking one-on-one with candidates outside the retreat structure.
- The last retreat normally is used to fine tune initiatives and action steps. All people in the group are asked beforehand to come prepared with proposals for initiatives and action steps. New subgroups are asked to meet, combine their individual ideas into one consensus report, making sure their recommendations are consistent with the other elements, and expand the change process to include lower levels in the organization.
- Once there is consensus across the group, we move on to issues of follow-up. Who will do what, when, and where? We also discuss how to communicate the statement widely to the employees and involve them in moving ahead. It is likely that two to four retreats over 2–3 months will be needed to complete the planning process, including the initiation of action steps.

Conduct of Retreats

Consultants and CEOs provide two key but differing roles in moving a retreat forward. The consultant provides expertise in retreat design, and the CEO intervenes only when his or her words can make a difference to the group. We prefer two consultants to complement each other's expertise, and they are responsible for consulting with the CEO on retreat design, conducting the Internet interviews, giving minilectures on strategy concepts to the group, introducing and summarizing each part on the agenda, writing drafts of the statement of strategic direction, intervening when the process is not going smoothly, and bringing the retreat to a close with planning for the next steps.

The consultants must be expert at both strategic content and OD process. As we indicated earlier, they cannot focus solely on process because the clients often are biased by past experience in thinking about the content of strategy. The client's knowledge on how to perform strategic planning often is parochial and confined to the firm's practices. An OD facilitator without strategic knowledge should team up with another consultant who is expert in strategic planning.

It is essential to have a supportive CEO present; a defensive or overcontrolling CEO is likely to inhibit participants, making them hesitant to speak up or likely to mimic whatever the CEO wants to hear. At the same time, an effective CEO will know when to step in to decide issues that cannot be decided by the group.

Follow-Up Steps

The real effects of a new strategy come to light only when the wider workforce embraces the strategy and acts consistently with it. In the hotel example described previously, we conducted large, follow-up, all-day meetings attended by as many as 100 front-line employees to hear the CEO and other managers discuss the strategy statement and its implications for the workforce. These large groups were then divided into subgroups to identify gaps between current practice and standards set in the strategy statement and determine what actions should be taken to close the gaps. Excerpts from the statement can also be used for public relations purposes, for presentations to analysts, for the annual report, and for advertising to the public.

It is important to appoint a small task force composed of managers from different levels to oversee follow-up and report directly to the CEO. Senior management must maintain a continuing focus on accomplishing major initiatives and goals articulated in the strategy statement. If they turn away, the rest of the organization will lose confidence and commitment. The CEO must behave as an enthusiastic supporter of the plan and make decisions consistent with it.

REMEMBER THE CONTEXT

We continually remind our clients and ourselves that any approach to strategic planning must match the situation in which it is applied. There are organizations that are more ready for planning and change than others. There are also organizations where strategic planning may be fruitless when the firm faces external barriers to growth outside its control, as may occur in highly regulated industries (Greiner et al., 2003). There are also autocratic CEOs who do not want to involve their senior managements, and there are senior managers who do not respect their CEOs and are unwilling to take direction from them (Greiner & Schein, 1989). There are small entrepreneurial organizations with dominant founders who haven't the patience to sit still and reflect, so they dictate strategy. Even the best OD approaches are not likely to overcome these difficult hurdles. As a result, good consultants must be skilled diagnosticians who first understand the client's situation before proposing OD methods to conduct strategic planning.

Another situational reminder is that strategic planning usually occurs within an overall change process. As mentioned previously from past research, successful strategic change tends to evolve in overlapping phases in which one phase supports the next (Greiner & Bhambri, 1989). For example, astute CEOs solidify their support with their boards before embarking on strategic change. In addition, sequential steps are necessary to ensure logical alignment of the key elements; the competitive logic must be set before changes in organization structure, and a revised organization is necessary before people move to new positions. Without subsequent positive results, people are likely to fall back to their old ways.

Not-for-profit organizations provide an interesting challenge for strategic planning. Nonprofit participants often look perplexed when asked to develop a competitive logic; however, this becomes clearer when they are asked who their customers (e.g., research funds, students) are and who else competes for their attention and money. All public organizations have competitors, although they are often unrecognized by their managers. Although profit is not in their charter, financial goals can still be stated in terms of operating costs or revenues from sources such as foundation grants, government subsidies, student tuition, and donations. There does not seem to be any difficulty for nonprofits in addressing the remaining key elements in the written statement.

Finally, any model for designing a strategy statement, including ours, should not be applied rigidly like a cookie cutter. We believe the four elements in our format reflect key issues that must be considered in any strategy exercise, whatever the format or retreat design. Some clients may already have a good understanding of their competitive logic and therefore need to begin work on goals, organization, and initiatives. A pre-engagement SWOT analysis will reveal a lot about the client situation and where to begin the strategic planning effort.

FUTURE CHALLENGES FOR OD AND STRATEGIC PLANNING

We have described only one approach to using our version of OD to close the gap with strategic planning. If any kind of OD is to make this integrative link in the future, it will need to move ahead on several fronts:

- OD must inform itself better about the content of strategic thinking (i.e., economics, marketing, finance, and operations) so as to become more competent and comfortable in dealing with strategic issues. It is these topics that OD needs to understand better so as to design formats to address them. For too long OD has focused on organizational and behavioral issues, but limiting itself to these issues is not enough.
- OD facilitators must gain greater access to the halls of senior management where strategic planning takes place. They can begin by acquiring the content expertise and reputation for being helpful with strategic planning at lower levels in organizations. Many large firms have divisions and profit centers that need strategies; these smaller subunits are good places to build credibility. Acquiring comfort in working with people in positions of power is important, especially for OD professionals who have worked for years at lower levels while championing the underpowered.
- OD must invent new methods beyond its traditional repertoire of team building, feedback, and participative decision making. These newer methods, similar to ones described here for the workshops, can facilitate a constructive discussion of strategic content. Retreats are a useful forum for a team to reflect and focus on the substance of planning, yet we need to know more about how to organize them to facilitate movement through the various phases of strategic change.
- With this preparation, OD advocates must convince senior management that the necessary knowledge to create a successful strategy resides more in the heads of their managers than the brainpower applied to an outside study. Much of this managerial knowledge

remains dormant and hidden, serving diverse personal agendas. An effective OD process can help to surface this knowledge in constructive ways and incorporate it into a consensus plan. By creating and owning a new strategic plan, even if imperfect, senior management is more likely to implement it. There are additional behavioral questions, such as who should participate in the planning process, how the process is to be organized, how commitment to implementation will be secured, and how the wider workforce can be motivated and encouraged to adopt new behaviors consistent with the espoused strategy.

- All of these questions suggest the need for more research on innovative approaches to strategic planning. We have presented here only one approach. Unfortunately, much academic research has ignored the application of strategic planning in organizations. Scholars who want to study the actual conduct of planning may have difficulty gaining access because of client sensitivity to being studied. So they may have to enter as consultants, as we did, with a research attitude (Schein, 2005).

OD CAN CLOSE THE GAP

The coming years will present a rich opportunity for OD to contribute to strategic planning; markets are changing daily because of global competition and technological advances. Senior managers cannot wait for consulting firms to perform lengthy studies to tell them what to do under short time frames. CEOs won't sit still for outside analysts engaged in weeks of data gathering and a search for analytic perfection. Managers want to become involved in charting their future. The key planning question facing these managers is, "How quickly can we work together as a team to share our knowledge openly, plan our strategy, and reach agreement on action steps?"

OD can provide an answer to this challenge. Tomorrow's high-performing organizations must create real-time strategies that are more focused, clear, flexible, dynamic, and widely adopted throughout the firm. There will undoubtedly be a tighter link needed between strategy, leadership, and organization, and this integrated link must be reviewed and revised frequently. These are characteristics that OD understands well, yet to contribute it must gain a seat at the table by embracing strategic planning and its content. If it does, traditional strategy consultants and their consulting firms will have a lot to learn from OD.

REFERENCES

Aguilar, F., Hamermesh, G., & Brainard, C. (1985). *General Electric.* HBS Case No. 385-315. Boston: Harvard Business School Press.

Alpanger, G. (1995). Culture, strategy and teamwork: The keys to organizational change. *Journal of Management Development, 14*(8), 4–18.

Andrews, K. (1971). *The concept of corporate strategy.* New York: Dow Jones-Irwin.

Ansoff, H. I. (1965). *Corporate strategy.* New York: McGraw-Hill.

Ansoff, H. I. (1984). *Implanting strategic management.* New York: Prentice Hall.

Argyris, C. (1957). *Personality and organization: The conflict between system and the individual.* New York: Harper & Row.

Argyris, C. (1964). T-groups for organizational effectiveness. *Harvard Business Review, 43*(2), 60–74.

Armenakis, A., & Field, H. S. (1975). Evaluation of organizational change using nonindependent criterion measures. *Personnel Psychology, 28*(1), 39–44.

Beckhard, R. (1969). *Organization development: Strategies and models.* Reading, MA: Addison-Wesley.

Bennis, W. (1969). *Organization development: Its nature, origins, and prospects.* Reading, MA: Addison-Wesley.

Blake, R. R., & Mouton, J. (1964). *The managerial grid.* Houston, TX: Gulf Publishing.

Boris, S (1978). OD evaluation: A different view. *G&OS, 4,* 396–398.

Brown, S. L., & Eisenhardt, K. (1998). *Competing on the edge.* Boston: Harvard Business School Press.

Buller, P. F. (1988). For successful change: Blend OD practices with strategic management. *Organizational Dynamics, 16*(3), 42–55.

Cameron, K., Dutton, J., & Quinn, R. (Eds.). (2003). *Positive organizational scholarship: Foundations of a new discipline.* San Francisco: Berrett-Koehler.

Cohen, S., & Ledford, G. (1994). The effectiveness of self-managing teams: A quasi-experiment. *Human Relations, 47,* 13–43.

Cooperrider, D., Sorenson, P., Yaeger, T., & Whitney, D. (Eds.). (2001). *Appreciative inquiry: An emerging direction for organization development.* Champaign, IL: Stipes.

Cruikshank, J. (1987). *A delicate experiment: The Harvard Business School, 1908–1945.* Boston: Harvard Business School Press.

Cummings, T., & Worley, C. (2005). *Organization development and change.* Mason, OH: Thomson/South-Western.

Eisenhardt, K., & Sull, D. (2001, January). Strategy as simple rules. *Harvard Business Review,* 107–116.

French, W., & Bell, C. (1972). A brief history of organization development. *Journal of Contemporary Business, 1*(3), 1–8.

Greenwood, R., & Hinings, C. (1993). Understanding strategic change: The contribution of archetypes. *Academy of Management Journal, 36*(5), 1052–1081.

Greiner, L., & Bhambri, A. (1989). New CEO intervention and dynamics of deliberate strategic change. *Strategic Management Journal, 10*(Special Issue), 67–86.

Greiner, L., Cummings, T., & Bhambri, A. (2003). When new CEOs succeed and fail: 4-D theory of strategic transformation. *Organizational Dynamics, 32*(1), 1–16.

Greiner, L., Olson, T., & Poulfelt, F. (Eds.). (2005). *The contemporary consultant casebook.* Mason, OH: Thomson/South-Western.

Greiner, L., & Schein, V. (1989). *Power and organization development.* Reading, MA: Addison-Wesley.

Hamel, G., & Prahalad, C. K. (1989, May–June). Strategic intent. *Harvard Business Review.*

Hrebiniak, L. (2005). *Making strategy work: Leading effective execution and change.* Upper Saddle River, NJ: Pearson.

Lawler, E., & Mohrman, S. (2003). *Creating a strategic human resources organization: An assessment of trends and new directions.* Palo Alto, CA: Stanford University Press.

Likert, R. (1961). *New patterns of management.* New York: McGraw-Hill.

Lipton, M. (1996). Demystifying the development of an organizational vision. *Sloan Management Review, 37*(4), 83–92.

Mintzberg, H., Ahlstrand, B., & Lampel, J. (1998). *Strategy safari: A guide through the wilds of strategic management.* New York: Free Press.

Mintzberg, H., Ahlstrand, B., & Lampel, J. (2005). *Strategy bites back.* Upper Saddle River, NJ: Pearson Prentice Hall.

Nadler, D., & Slywotzky, A. (2005). Strategy and organization consulting. In L. Greiner, T. Olson, & F. Poulfelt (Eds.), *The contemporary consultant casebook.* Mason, OH: Thomson South-Western.

Pasmore, W. (1994, July–August). An approach to successful integration. *Self-Managing Work Teams,* 15–23.

Pettigrew, A., Mintzberg, H., & Lorange, P. (1987). *Basil Blackwell series on corporate strategy, organization & change.* New York: Basil Blackwell.

Pfeffer, J. (1998). *Putting people first.* Boston: Harvard Business School Press.

Porter, M. (1985). *Competitive advantage: Techniques for analyzing industries and competitors.* New York: Free Press.

Schein, E., (2005). Clinical inquiry/research. In P. Reason & H. Bradbury (Eds.), *Handbook of action research* (pp. 228–237). Thousand Oaks, CA: Sage.

Senge, P. (1990). *The fifth discipline: The art and practice of the learning organization.* New York: Doubleday.

Slywotzky, A., (1996). *Value migration.* Boston: Harvard Business School Press.

Stern, C., & Deimler, M. (2006). *The Boston Consulting Group on Strategy: Classic concepts and new perspectives.* Hoboken, NJ: John Wiley & Sons.

Tichy, N. M. (1983). *Managing strategic change: Technical, political, and cultural dynamics.* New York: John Wiley & Sons.

Weidner, C., & Kulick, G. (1999). The professionalization of organization development: A status report and look to the future. In W. Pasmore & R. Woodman (Eds.), *Organization change and development* (Vol. 12, pp. 319–371). Oxford, UK: JAI.

Wernerfelt, B. (1984). A resource-based view of the firm. *Strategic Management Journal, 5,* 171–180.

Worley, C. G., Hitchin, D. E., & Ross, W. L. (1996). *Integrated strategic change: How OD builds competitive advantage.* Reading, MA: Addison-Wesley.

Appendix A

STATEMENT OF STRATEGIC DIRECTION: XYZ PETROLEUM COMPANY

I. Determine Competitive Logic

IA. *Market Position:*

- Self-service stations located in South (five southeastern states).
- Price gas at 5 cents below major competitors.
- Seek high volume and revenues.
- Focus on large cities and suburban high-traffic areas.
- Cash or ATM purchases only.
- All crude provided by Indonesian reserves.
- Highly efficient refinery in Louisiana.

IB. *Customer Tiebreakers:*

- No-hassle purchase: clean, efficient, safe service stations.
- Located within easy driving from home and on way to work.
- Strong customer orientation; act friendly and courteous at all times.
- Provide high-margin impulse soft drink and snack foods.

II. Set Goals

IIA. *Set Key Financial Goal:*

- Increase urban market share from 20% to 24% within 3 years.
- Reduce refinery operating cost by $50 million over 3 years.

IIB. *Create Rallying Goal for Employees:*

- #1 in South
- 100 new stations in 2 years

III. Align Organization, Values, and People

IIIA. *Design Structure:*

- Decentralize to cities as revenue centers.
- Lean corporate staff focused on serving operations.
- Incentives for achievement of financial goals.

IIIB. *Values and People:*

- Be environmentally conscious in all operations.
- Do not sacrifice quality or safety for earnings.
- Be good corporate citizen; support communities where we live.

IV. Lay Out Action Plan (Initiatives and Action Steps)

- Initiative #1: Replace all single-product pumps with high-speed multiple-product pumps by end of year.
- Action Steps:

  1. Set up task force to move project forward—complete in 6 months.
  2. Allocate $2 million to project.

- Initiative 2: Hire new advertising firm to enhance quality and price image.
- Action Steps:

  1. Select firm in 6 weeks, launch in 3 months.
  2. Appoint director to manage the project.

- Initiative 3: Institute new incentive pay plan for revenue increases and cost reductions.
- Action Steps:

  1. Human resources draw up plan.
  2. Complete for approval and implementation in 3 months.

Appendix B

CURRENT DESIGN OF STRATEGIC RETREAT

Day One

8:00   **Introduction to Retreat:** CEO
- Purpose of retreat
- Schedule of retreat
- Climate for discussion
- My role here
- Roles of Larry G. and Tom C.

8:15   **Presentation and Discussion of SWOT Analysis:** Tom C.
- SWOT as foundation for strategic statement
- Based on executive interviews
- Discussion of SWOT conclusions

9:15   **Break**

9:30   **Presentation on Elements to Prepare for Statement of Strategic Direction:** Larry G.
- Current state of knowledge on strategic planning
- Key elements in drafting a strategic statement
- Examples from other companies
- Small group assignment for developing *competitive logic*

10:15 **Small Groups Meet to Prepare *Competitive Logic***
- Select speaker and prepare feedback to total group.

12:00 **Lunch**

1:00   **Small Groups Present *Competitive Logic* to Total Group**
- Hear presentations.
- Discuss similarities and differences.
- Identify preferred elements.

2:15   **Break**

2:30   **Presentation on How to Develop Financial and Rallying Goals:** Tom C.
- Why specify goals?
- Difference between financial and rallying goals.
- Examples from other companies.
- Small group assignment.

3:00   **Small Groups Meet to Develop Financial and Rallying Goals**
- Meet in assigned rooms.
- Select speaker and prepare feedback for total group.

4:00   **Break**

4:15   **Small Groups Present Financial and Rallying Goals to Total Group**
- Hear presentations.
- Discuss similarities and differences.
- Identify preferred elements.

5:00   **Summary and Assessment of Day One**

5:30   **Adjourn**

6:30   **Drinks and Dinner**

Day Two

8:00   **Presentation by Consultants of Written Draft from First Day (Competitive Logic and Goals)**
- Total group reviews draft.
- Group makes suggested revisions.

9:00   **Presentation on How to Align *Organization and People:*** Larry G.
- Examples of management values
- Examples of organization structure alternatives
- Small group assignment

9:45 **Break**

10:00 **Small Groups Meet to Develop** *Organization Structure and Values*
- Meet in assigned rooms.
- Select speaker and prepare for total group.

11:30 **Small Groups Present Organization Structure and Values to Total Group**
- Hear presentations.
- Discuss similarities and differences.
- Identify preferred elements.

12:30 **Lunch**

1:30 **Presentation on How to Develop** *Action Plan:* Tom C.
- Guidelines for developing initiatives
- Examples from companies
- Small group assignment

2:00 **Small Groups Meet to Develop** *Strategic Initiatives*
- Meet in assigned rooms.
- Select speaker and prepare feedback for total group.

3:30 **Break**

3:45 **Small Groups Present** *Strategic* **Initiatives to Total Group**
- Hear presentations.
- Discuss similarities and differences.
- Identify preferred elements.

5:00 **Summary and Assessment of Day Two**

5:30 **Adjourn**

6:30 **Drinks and Dinner**
- Consultants prepare final written draft in evening.

Day Three

7:30 **Presentation by Consultants of Written Draft From First and Second Days (competitive logic, tiebreakers, goals, organization, values and initiatives)**
- Total group reviews draft.
- Group makes suggested revisions.

8:30 **Break**

8:45 **Instructions on How to Prepare** *Action Steps* **for Initiatives:** Larry G.

9:00 **Small Groups Meet to Prepare Tentative Action Steps (meet in assigned rooms)**
- Select speaker and prepare feedback for total group.

10:00 **Small Groups Present Action Steps for Each Initiative**
- Hear presentations.
- Discuss implications.

11:00 **Break**

11:15 **Final Review of Draft of** *Statement of Strategic Direction*
- Total group reviews draft.
- Group makes suggested revisions.

12:00 **Discussion of** *Next Steps:* CEO, Larry G., Tom C.
- Hold meetings to review statement with middle management.
- Final retreat date and plan to make modifications and plan action steps.

12:45 **Closing Comments:** CEO

1:00 **Adjourn and Lunch**

22

Transforming Organizations

Embracing the Paradox of E and O

MICHAEL BEER

W e live in a time of unprecedented change. Global competition and rapid changes in technology and markets force organizations to be adaptive, and capable of transformation. Of the original Forbes 100 in 1917, 61 had ceased to exist by 1987. Of the remaining 39, only 18 stayed in the top 100, and their return was 20% less than the overall market. Of the companies in the original Standard & Poor's (S&P) 500 in 1957, only 74 remained in 1997, and of these only 12 outperformed the S&P 500 between 1957 and 1998 (Foster & Kaplan, 2001). This astounding record of corporate destruction suggests that organizations generally are not adaptive. They are unable to transform their capabilities and behavior to fit a changing business environment.

The inability of corporations to produce sustained performance reflects top management's inability to transform their organization into high commitment *and* performance

systems: organizations that achieve sustained high economic performance and develop high commitment in their employees. A study of 1,435 companies in the Fortune 500 list between 1965 and 1995 showed only 11 companies that were able to attain and sustain high performance (cumulative stock returns 6.9 times the general market) for a 15-year period after the beginning of a corporate transformation (Collins, 2001). Failure to transform corporate performance is also reflected in the declining tenure of CEOs from 10.5 years in 1990 to 4.2 years in 2000—an indication that boards of directors, under pressure from capital markets, are increasingly impatient with their ability to lead change.

In this chapter I discuss two opposing theories of organization transformation, the failure of corporate leaders to integrate them, and an emerging theory and method of organization development (OD) for integrating these opposing perspectives (Beer & Nohria, 2000a). Theory E has as its goals economic value creation and focuses on the hard facets of organizations, financial performance, strategy, structure, and systems. Theory O has as its goal enhancing organization effectiveness and focuses on the organization's culture and its people. I call them theories because the purpose and means for change embedded in the two theories have very different underlying assumptions. I argue that a successful corporate transformation must embrace the paradox represented by these two theories of change. I also argue that the difficulty of enacting one theory *and also* the other necessitates a disciplined strategic change process led by an effective team with diverse perspectives. Without discipline the transformational process tends to favor the leader's dominant theory. Hierarchy, which creates distance between leaders and organization members and makes open dialogue across organization levels so difficult, prevents top management from testing their theory of transformation and revising it to incorporate the "and also." I offer a set of principles to guide such a disciplined process and evidence about their efficacy in helping organizations and their leaders embrace the paradox.

TWO THEORIES OF CHANGE

As the aforementioned data suggest, few senior executives seem to be able to lead a sustained transformation when a changing environment calls for dramatic change. The reason is that there is substantial lack of agreement, indeed confusion, about the purpose of and means for corporate transformations.

Theory E has as its advocates economists, investment bankers, and venture capitalists. The only way to transform an underperforming organization, according to this school of thought, is through a dose of tough, result-oriented, top-down initiatives: reengineering, restructuring, and layoffs driven by managers motivated by financial incentives that align their interest with those of the shareholders

(Jensen, 2000). Consider the following example (adapted from Gilson & Cott, 1996):

Scott Paper embarked on a journey of theory E change in 1994 when Al Dunlap took over as CEO. Scott had participated profitably in the forest product and paper industry since 1879 but ran into profitability problems in the early 1990s. International expansion had stretched resources at a time when the industry was again entering a period of overcapacity, a pattern that had repeated itself many times in this industry. Performance and shareholder returns dropped at an alarming rate. Bowing to pressure from capital markets, the board of directors recruited Dunlap, a turnaround manager with a record of success in restructuring companies. Dunlap immediately ordered a layoff of 11,000 employees, about 42% of Scott Paper's workforce. He sold a number of businesses and closed down a number of its less profitable plants. In the remainder he imposed a strict regime of efficiency measures with the help of external consultants. And within months he fired most of Scott's top management, often after chastising them in public.

At the end of two and a half years Dunlap sold Scott's remaining core business, the consumer packaging business, to competitor Kimberly Clark at three times Scott's market capitalization at the time he took charge ($9 billion compared with $3 billion). The financial community applauded Dunlap's efforts and pointed to Scott Paper's approach to change as a model to be emulated by others. Dunlap total compensation was more than $100 million, and many of the company's shareholders, including the senior executives he had fired, became much wealthier. However, a proud company ceased to exist. According to informal reports, Kimberly Clark's management was surprised by the condition of the company it had acquired. Scott Paper's many tangible assets were there, but its organizational capability and human assets had been depleted.

Theory O historically has been represented by academics and professional consultants in the field of OD (Beckhard, 1969; Beer, 1980;

Bennis, 1969; Burke, 1982; French & Bell, 1978). Commitment, coordination (teamwork), competence (particularly leadership skills), communication, creativity, and the capacity of employees to engage in constructive conflict must be developed if an organization is to achieve sustained high performance. The way to do this is through high involvement in the change process itself. Theory E change strategies are thought by O advocates to be inadequate if not destructive: They increase self-interest and thereby reduce trust, employee commitment, teamwork, and the capacity to learn (Senge, 2000). Consider the following example (adapted from Ault, Walton, & Childers, 1998; Beer & Weber, 2000):

> Champion International, a company also operating since 1893 in the forest product and paper industry, embarked on a journey of organization change in the early 1980s. Like Scott Paper, it found competing in an industry with frequent cycles of undercapacity and overcapacity extremely challenging. The company had operated for many years as a functional and hierarchical organization and had poor relations with its unions. Its shareholder returns lagged the average for companies in the Fortune 500 and its peers in the industry. CEO Andrew Sigler had resisted the revolution in capital markets that demanded that underperforming companies improve shareholder returns by restructuring.
>
> The transformation journey began with the articulation of a new set of values by Sigler, but he did not drive organization change from the top, despite the autocratic management style he had exhibited over the years. Instead, organization change began with low-profile changes at the periphery of the company. A new manufacturing plant was designed around principles of cross-functional self-managed teams organized along horizontal processes. With the help of a few sociotechnical consultants, managers and employees were involved in the design of the plant. This experiment led to similar change efforts in an ever-larger circles of new and old manufacturing facilities. Over more than a decade, change that started at the periphery spread to the corporate center. What had been at one time a deeply functional corporation

evolved into a matrix structure organized around product groups. All corporate functional activities were oriented through the matrix toward product and market businesses and customers. Few financial incentives were used to move change, and no reengineering efforts or layoffs were implemented, although key plant and functional managers who did not adhere to the new philosophy of management were asked to leave.

> The transformation was remarkable. Productivity, union–management relationships, and customer and employee satisfaction all improved. A long march, facilitated by a small number of OD consultants in cooperation with the human resource function, had succeeded in managing a change in culture and operating performance, particularly productivity and customer satisfaction. But these changes did not improve Champion's return to shareholders. In 1997 Sigler's successor stated that shareholder returns had to be the objective going forward. Two years later the company was sold at only one and a half times its market capitalization in 1981, when the long journey of change began.

Although most corporate transformations are not pure types, a close examination of these cases and others like them reveals important differences in assumptions about the purpose of business organizations, the motivation of people, and the best means for creating change in bureaucratic, underperforming organizations. These differences are summarized in Table 22.1 (Beer & Nohria, 2000a, 2000b).

Purpose

The purpose of Theory E transformations is to produce economic value, what is commonly called shareholder value.[1] Advocates of this theory believe companies fail because top management has not been an agent of the shareholder. What are needed are monetary incentives tied to shareholder return objectives that will motivate tough decisions about employees and businesses with whom managers have had a long-term relationship. A single-minded focus

Table 22.1   Theories E and O of Change

Purpose and Means	Theory E	Theory O
Purpose	Maximize economic value.	Develop organization capabilities.
Leadership	Top down.	Participative.
Focus	Strategy, structure, and systems.	Culture.
Process	Plan and establish programs.	Experiment and evolve.
Motivation	Motivate through financial incentives.	Motivate through commitment. Use pay as fair exchange.
Consultants	Large, knowledge driven.	Small, process driven.

on economic value is preferable to a multiple-stakeholder perspective because managers are unable to make quantifiable tradeoff decisions (Jensen, 2000). According to this theory, the marketplace ultimately will help managers attend to the development of the organization's capabilities if this is needed to enhance economic value. For example, if firm performance is hurt by low employee commitment and high turnover, managers will correct their change strategy to incorporate Theory O considerations (Jensen, 2000).

The effort of Al "Chainsaw" Dunlap to transform Scott Paper, described earlier, is arguably the best example of a pure Theory E corporate change effort. Dunlap was single minded in his objective of improving shareholder value, as exemplified by a speech in which he said, "Shareholders are the number one constituency. Show me an annual report that lists six or seven constituencies, and I'll show you a mismanaged company" (Beer & Nohria, 2000b, p. 135).

Theory E is the dominant approach to corporate transformations in the United States. For example, General Dynamics in the 1980s followed this model, as did General Electric in CEO Welch's first 6 years (Heskett, 1999; Murphy & Dial, 1993). Indeed, it is almost standard procedure for new CEOs to launch their change effort with restructuring: the sale of unrelated businesses, closure of underused facilities, and often huge layoffs. E strategies are now making their way to other countries, notably Japan and Europe, where societal values and practices have resisted them until now.

The argument for E strategies is that managers in many organizations, perhaps most, seek to enhance their power base, careers, rewards, and comfort at the expense of shareholders (Jensen, 2000). Recent revelations about how senior executives at Tyco accumulated money and privilege illustrate this. Interestingly, Theory O advocates largely agree with this perspective, although they typically point to the effect on employee commitment and organization learning, not shareholder value (Argyris & Schön, 1993; Deming, 1986; Senge, 2000). There is also evidence that managers, like all human beings, are defensive and therefore discourage open feedback about their own behavior (Argyris, 1990; Beer & Eisenstat, 2000b; Morrison & Milliken, 2000). This causes them to resist reform even when financial returns decline. It is this phenomenon, according to E theorists, that makes a strong market for corporate control essential. And it is the increasing power of this market that has led to E leadership and change approaches such as those exhibited by CEO Dunlap in the Scott Paper case. The results at Scott Paper and many other companies suggest that a single-minded focus on economic value creation quickly corrects excesses created by mismanagement and leads to lower cost, improved cash flows, and, at least in the short run, higher stock prices (Wruck, 2000). However, there is little evidence that downsizing and restructuring create long-term economic value (Cascio, 1993).

Theory O transformations are based on the assumption that the purpose of a corporation is to serve multiple stakeholders: shareholders, employees, customers, and community. By developing commitment of all stakeholders, particularly employees, the organization, it is thought, will achieve sustained performance. High commitment will cause everyone to work together collaboratively for the survival of the institution (Beer, Spector, Lawrence, Mills, & Walton, 1985; O'Reilly & Pfeffer, 2000; Pfeffer, 1998).

The change effort at Champion International is a nearly pure example of a Theory O transformation and could not be more different from the change strategy at Scott Paper. Although he acknowledged the importance of shareholder value, CEO Andrew Sigler thought that it could be achieved best by focusing on the transformation of organization behavior. In 1981 these goals were articulated clearly in a statement of values. These served as a broad vision and provided a roadmap for a diverse set of change initiatives over a 15-year period. Sigler believed that if the company focused on improving communication, coordination, conflict management, and a culture that encouraged creativity, learning, productivity, and performance would follow. Indeed, the bottom line did improve, but share price in relation to Champion's peers in the industry did not. The improvements were hampered by Sigler's reluctance to sell a number of businesses that did not fit the strategy, an example of how commitment to businesses, people, and communities can blind managers to necessary business decisions. Because of pressures from powerful capital markets, pure Theory O transformations are rare.

Theory O proponents argue persuasively that the human side of enterprise is essential to sustained high performance. Numerous studies do indeed illustrate that participative

and high-involvement work systems and cultures lead to extraordinary employee commitment, financial performance, and shareholder returns (Becker & Huslid, 1998; Denison, 1990; Gittel, 2003; Heskett, Sasser, & Schlesinger, 2003; Huslid, 1995; O'Reilly & Pfeffer, 2000; Pfeffer, 1998). Moreover, O theorists argue that because business and organization problems are nonlinear, circular, and recursive, learning should be the single-minded focus of transformation leaders (Argyris & Schön, 1993; Senge, 2000). In this way managers can overcome their inability to predict the future and the unintended consequences of their actions. And there is substantial evidence that to foster such a learning and decision-making process, organizations need to develop commitment and collaboration, characteristics that can easily be destroyed by E strategies (Miller & Lee, 2001).

Leadershsip

Al Dunlap's leadership at Scott Paper exemplifies how most outsiders typically go about implementing an E transformation. Dunlap set financial objective at the top. He ordered restructuring initiatives without involvement of Scott's key executives. Theory E leaders favor top-down change because of their need to show results quickly. "I have a [profit] goal of $176 million this year, and there is no time to involve others or develop organizational capability," explained one Theory E CEO (Beer & Nohria, 2000b. p. 136). Khurana (2002b) has shown that boards of directors bring in outsiders to manage top-down change because they believe that internal candidates are too close to past decisions and to executives they may need to replace. The reason for bringing in a new CEO, a director observed, was his "brilliance and that he would not waste time getting consensus" (Khurana, 2002a, p. 174). The prevailing theory appears to be that charismatic leaders who advocate a new direction and the solutions needed to move there are essential for a corporate transformation (Khurana, 2002a).

The sharp reduction in the length of CEO tenure mentioned earlier suggests that insiders do have difficulty making tough decisions. New CEOs brought in from the outside do not need to defend the past and are motivated to put a new stamp on the organization. Fundamental strategic change is indeed carried out by new managers, research suggests (Grinyer, Mayes, & McKiernan, 1990; Virany, Tushman, & Romanelli, 1992). They are able to maintain the psychological distance needed to make hard people decisions.[2] Theory E leaders may also prefer top-down change out of fear that if they engaged their employees, they would be talked out of needed changes. Indeed, Vroom, Jago, and Arthur (1988) have shown that for participation to be the right choice, employee support for the goals of the enterprise is essential. Support for painful restructuring is not common in failing companies. Conger (2000) argues for top-down change based on the unique perspective that a position at the top offers leaders. He also argues that the "romance of leadership"—the willingness and perhaps need of employees to attribute change to visible and heroic leaders—gives top-down leadership a unique advantage in managing change. Perhaps the most persuasive argument for top-down leadership is that there are almost no examples of slow and participative change efforts that lead to rapid organization transformations.

As the Champion case illustrates, Theory O transformational leaders have distinctly different assumptions. They assume that there is valuable knowledge in the organization about the problems that have blocked performance. Therefore, the best way to solve these problems is to engage key people in an open dialogue about problems and potential solutions. This approach is based on optimistic assumptions about human nature. People want to do a good job, know what blocks needed transformation, and are motivated to improve things as long as they are properly engaged. The central assumption of OD practitioners is that if the difficulty in getting people to speak

up honestly can be overcome, barriers to change can be identified and overcome (Argyris & Schön, 1993; Beer & Eisenstat, 2000b). Low performance is a function mostly of the system in which people are embedded, not of incompetence or lack of individual motivation (Deming, 1986).

Just as there is evidence that top-down leadership is needed to overcome resistance and achieve speed, many studies of organization change have illustrated the power of participation in work and change, although this approach works only when there is some level of trust and support for organization goals (Bennis, 2000; Coch & French, 1948; Miner, 2002). Without involvement, Theory O advocates argue, there can be no emotional commitment and true learning. Top-down changes result in compliance, not internalization of new attitudes and skills. Collins (2001) found that successful transformational leaders were humble about their role in the transformation, involved their people in the transformation, and gave them credit for it. Vroom et al. (1988) have shown that participative management is the right choice when developing commitment and competence is the goal. The result of such involvement is partnership and commitment. That is what happened at Champion International. Union leaders and members became partners in the change process, and this enabled the development of competence and commitment.

Focus

E transformations begin with changes in strategy (including changes in the portfolio of businesses), structure, processes, and systems—the "hardware" of the organization. At the core of corporate failures is a strategy that is not working or a bureaucratic organization that is unresponsive, E advocates argue. Dunlap sold some businesses and decided to eliminate a costly and unresponsive bureaucracy by outsourcing many of Scott Paper's services: benefits and payroll, information systems, medical services, and even some of its product research. Aside from the inherent validity of this argument, top management's focus on the harder as opposed to the softer aspects of organizations can be attributed to their personality. Most top executives are "Ts," for "thinking," on the Myers–Briggs Type Indicator. That style favors decisions based on critical analysis of objective facts as opposed to emotions with regard to community, relationships, and fairness, except for relationships that promise personal benefits (Hirsh & Kummerow, 1988).[3] Pressure from capital markets only exacerbates this tendency.

A focus on strategy, structure, and systems is supported by decades of organization research. These studies show that corporate performance is contingent on fit or alignment between a firm's business environment and its strategy and structure (Burns & Stalker, 1961; Chandler, 1962; Collins, 2001; Galbraith, 1978, 2000; Lawrence & Lorsch, 1967). Consider the transformation of IBM under Louis Gerstner. To move the company from a product orientation to a solution orientation, he had to create a matrix structure and supporting systems. These shifted accountability for profit and decision rights from product division and country heads to worldwide customer segment heads (Gerstner, 2003).

Theory O transformations focus on developing a culture that will foster commitment. Its supporters argue that such a culture is a source of sustained competitive advantage because culture, painstakingly developed over many years, is very hard for competitors to imitate (Barney, 1986). The assumption is that poor performance is attributable to alienation and low commitment brought about by top-down control (Pfeffer, 1998; Walton, 1985).

Although successful O transformations incorporate changes in strategy, structure, and systems, these changes occur late in the transformation process and with participation of employees (Beer, Eisenstat, & Spector, 1990a).

Champion International changed the nature of jobs and redesigned its manufacturing plant and corporate organizations, but it did so only after a high-involvement process fashioned after the sociotechnical theories and methods of Eric Trist (1969). By starting with shared values and high involvement, Champion International's management was able to reorient attitudes and behavior toward collaboration and teamwork. By involving people in an honest reexamination of business and management practices, the company's leaders were able to reduce skepticism and build trust. Because management encouraged truth to speak to power and responded accordingly, employees became convinced that management meant what they said.

A substantial body of knowledge supports Theory O's focus on culture. Numerous studies have shown that cultures, particularly high-commitment cultures, are associated with high performance (Collins & Porras, 1992; Denison, 1990; Kotter & Heskett, 1992). Hewlett-Packard (until 1999), SAS Institute, Southwest Airlines, and New United Manufacturing, a joint venture of General Motors and Toyota, are frequently cited examples (O'Reilly & Pfeffer, 2000). There is also substantial evidence that companies' fortunes decline if corporate culture and leadership are not transformed as the corporation grows or confronts new business realities (Miller, 1990; Schein 2003). Although it is difficult, there is evidence that corporate culture can be changed and that these changes lead to performance improvements (Beer et al., 1990a; Collins, 2001; Denison, 1990).

Process

Theory E executives launch top-down initiatives with the help of corporate staff groups and consultants to change the corporation. These programs are part of a "battle plan" by the CEO to force rapid change in the organization. This is typically done through standardized education and internal champions or external consultants who guide local leaders through the changes. If local leaders do not conform, they are moved out. At Scott Paper goals were set at the top, and managers were asked to achieve them by a given target date. Reengineering was mandated and systematically applied in every part of the company.

In following this programmatic approach, Theory E leaders assume that they cannot rely on subunit leaders to implement radical change. Programs are intended to change people's minds about the right way to work and manage. It is hoped that if they change minds, hearts will follow. Given the need for speed, this approach makes sense. It is unlikely that managers below the top who have been embedded in one set of practices will have the attitudes and skills needed to create and adopt a wholly different set of practices in their subunits. And Adler (1993) has shown that centrally established practices introduced through training can improve performance as long as it is done with concern for employees and they are involved in applying the new practices to their own situation. There is also evidence that centrally planned programs can create sustained change in subunits of the larger corporation when the unit's leadership team sees the program as instrumental to their objectives and the local culture is aligned with the program's purpose and substance (Beer et al., 1990a; Edmondson & Woolley, 2003).

Compared with E transformations, O transformations are more evolutionary and emergent. They start with the premise that large corporations cannot be changed at once or with the same top-down prescriptions; one size does not fit all. Organization change is treated as a process of experimentation beginning with a small number of units followed by adoption in many other units (Beer et al., 1990a). Innovation in one part of the organization can lead to learning in other parts if properly encouraged by top management (Walton, 1977). There was no master plan at

Champion when the transformation started in 1981. Innovations in work systems, union–management collaboration, and worker involvement began in a new "green field" manufacturing plant and spread from there, first to other new startups and later to older plants with more entrenched cultures. No single manager or function was seen as the central driver of change, not even CEO Sigler. Local unit managers and their people took responsibility for change, supported by a small cadre of internal and external consultants. Consistent with research on corporate renewal, innovations in organizing and managing at Champion spread from early adopters to other units (Beer et al., 1990a; Walton, 1987). Top management's role is to encourage the dissemination of innovation. They do it by supporting leading unit managers politically, orchestrating conferences where managers are exposed to the innovations, arranging for visits to innovative units, and promoting managers in leading units to run lagging units. This process is much slower. Champion's transformation took 15 years, compared to 2½ in the case of Scott Paper's E strategy.

The wisdom of slower and emergent corporate transformations is supported by evidence that top-down programs do not fundamentally transform large corporations (Beer, Eisenstat, & Spector, 1990b; Miller, Hartwick, & LeBreton-Miller, 2004; Shaffer, 1988). There are several reasons for this. In diversified multibusiness organizations the same management practice may not apply to all businesses. Even when the task across all subunits is the same (e.g., retail stores, manufacturing plants) and the content of the program is relevant, leaders of subunits comply but are not committed. This means that they will not engage their organization in an active learning process that adapts the programmatic solution to their particular circumstances (Beer, 2003; Beer et al., 1990b; Edmondson & Woolley, 2003).

There is also a developmental cost to top-down programs. Because centrally driven programs put subunit leaders in compliance mode, they do not learn how to lead change—mobilizing people in a common effort to identify, diagnose, and solve problems—a capability essential for long-term corporate success. At the same time, research shows that when managed effectively, transformations that follow the slower and emergent unit-by-unit strategy produce dramatic change in corporate culture, effectiveness, and performance (Beer et al., 1990a; Beer & Weber, 1997). Procter and Gamble used a slower unit-by-unit transformation strategy to gain a 40% cost advantage over its competitors in the 1970s, one that its competitors did not quickly replicate. Although they take longer, unit-by-unit strategies change minds *and* hearts and promise to lead to a high-commitment organization capable of sustained high performance (Beer, 2001).

Motivation

E transformations use monetary incentives such as bonuses and stock option plans as a prominent lead intervention. The first thing Dunlap did at Scott Paper was to introduce such incentives. Ultimately these incentives paid out large sums of money to many executives. Dunlap's compensation ultimately rewarded him with $100 million as a result of the increase in the price of Scott Paper stock. The assumption underlying the heavy early use of incentives linked to shareholder interests is that money will motivate managers to make quick, tough decisions. Pay-for-performance incentive systems, their proponents believe, will unfreeze and refocus existing behavior quickly because they are highly visible, tied to relevant performance outcomes, and substantial (Lawler, 2000). A second purpose for these pay system changes is to create larger differences in compensation between better and poorer performers and thereby to undermine the entitlement cultures that often reside in underperforming companies (Baker, 1993).

Much evidence supports the claims that financial incentives are desired by employees and lead to changes in behavior and performance. Employees believe that pay-for-performance systems are fair because they promise to differentiate between better and poorer performers (Beer & Gery, 1972). A meta-analysis of pay-for-performance studies found that performance improved in approximately two out of three pay-for-performance program introductions (Heneman, Gresham, & Ledford, 2000). Gibson (1995) reports on a study by Carla O'Dell and Jerry McAdams (sponsored by World at Work and conducted by the Consortium for Alternative Reward Strategies) that suggested that the average net return on money invested in pay-for-performance programs was an impressive 134%. Surveys of 500 companies reported in *The Economist* ("Business: Pay Purview," 1998) indicated that those actively using pay-for-performance programs showed twice the shareholder returns as those who were not actively using these programs. Lincoln Electric, for many years a high-performing Midwest manufacturing firm, demonstrated that variable pay, linked to measurable individual performance outcomes, improves quality and productivity, although an important aspect of their success, not always well understood, was the culture of cooperation in which the incentive system was embedded. Incentive payouts were contingent on an evaluation of the employee's cooperativeness.

However, the case for incentives is undermined by findings that monetary incentive systems have a positive effect initially but may ultimately be undermined by contextual factors beyond the control of the individual or group. These weaken the link between effort and the performance and make it hard to justify incentive payouts (Beer & Cannon, 2004; Lawler, 1971, 1981). When employees lose control of the factors affecting their performance, the perception that the compensation system is fair and that management can be trusted is undermined. To satisfy the requirements for fairness, incentive systems typically are redesigned frequently, raising their costs in time, money, and loss of trust and commitment, leading Theory O proponents to argue that the costs of these systems outweigh their benefits (Beer & Cannon, 2004; Beer & Katz, 2003; Lawler, 2000). In one high-commitment organization employees gave management a party when they discontinued a team-based incentive system (Beer & Cannon, 2004). Moreover, there is evidence that incentives can undermine teamwork and cause managers to manipulate goals, particularly when the incentives are focused on individual or individual unit performance (Beer & Katz, 2003; Hambrick & Siegel, 1997). They can also cause managers to focus narrowly on the goals to which the incentives are tied.

O transformations motivate primarily through the creation of meaning, involvement in the task, and participation in decisions. Pay is used to recognize effective behavior and performance and is far less central to motivation. Differences between top management and lower levels with respect to rewards such as offices, status symbols, and total compensation are minimized. At Champion International a skill-based reward system was used to encourage and reinforce the acquisition of new skills. A corporate profit-sharing plan applied equally at all levels was used to reinforce teamwork across the company and between management and production workers. Although executives at Champion received stock options and bonuses, they represented a smaller percentage of total compensation than a similar compensation system at Scott Paper.

Theory O assumptions about motivation are supported by evidence that financial rewards typically are ranked well below needs for meaningful work and good supervision (Beer et al., 1985). Evidence also shows that the nature of work itself motivates (Hackman & Oldham, 1980). Jobs that are perceived as significant and provide autonomy and feedback will involve and motivate people who value autonomy, achievement, and growth. Such a work setting may also develop these needs,

thereby developing a more motivation-ready workforce. An extensive review of the literature on high-involvement and high-performance work practices by Pfeffer (1998) shows that when people are given the freedom to make a difference in the context of extensive training, employment security, and comparatively high compensation contingent on organizational, not individual, performance, then productivity, quality, service, and organization performance improve.

Consultants

Theory E change strategies often rely heavily on external consultants. Large consulting firms with armies of experts are brought in to analyze the market and the company and suggest changes in strategy and organization. Most of these firms also offer help in implementing change. Consultants lead employee project teams in solving problems and formulating recommendations. In 1997 AT&T was reported to have spent $200 million on such expert services. Consultants were used by Dunlap to identify and manage cost-saving initiatives.

Large-scale consulting engagements make sense in a crisis (Miles, 2000). Capital markets demand rapid change. An infusion of experts will move change along rapidly. CEOs may not always be able to reframe strategic and organizational problems without the help of outsiders. Consultants also offer specialized talent that may not be available in the company, and they may offer psychological and political support to turnaround CEOs who do not trust their own managers to be objective. Finally, consultants may enable CEOs to legitimize their turnaround strategy with the board of directors.

Theory O transformations rely on a far smaller set of external process consultants to help managers identify, analyze, and solve problems themselves. At Champion, a very small number of these consultants were introduced early in the transformation and continued to be involved throughout the 15-year period. They came with Theory O tools and frameworks to facilitate the process of change.

Two arguments can be made for the process consulting approach (Schaffer, 2000). The first has to do with the problems created when outside experts enter a firm to offer advice, and the second has to do with the benefits of process consultation. The infusion of an army of experts may result in precise and well-crafted solutions but takes away ownership and learning opportunities for managers. Managers may comply for political reasons but avoid confronting deep organization and leadership problems that block implementation of recommended solutions (Beer & Eisenstat, 2000b; Schaffer, 2002).

Even if immediate implementation were not a problem, managers may grow dependent on consultants, particularly if they stay involved over a long time. One of the main problems with large-scale consultant interventions is that the firm and its managers may be prevented from developing the most critical capability they need: the capacity to lead a learning and change process (Miles, 2000). Solutions offered by consultants may also make it easier for managers to avoid confronting deeply rooted organization and leadership problems. Process consultation, on the other hand, enables such learning (Schein, 1969). The approach is very effective in creating cultural change but is slower, as the Champion case illustrates. It also may not challenge management sufficiently to reconsider hard economic and strategic realities. In the case of Champion senior management was not challenged by the Theory O process consultants to restructure the portfolio of businesses.

EMBRACING THE PARADOX OF E AND O

This discussion suggests that E and O strategies each have great strengths and equally great limitations. Therefore, the paradox of E and O must be embraced to obtain the benefits of both theories. But unless this is done carefully, integrating these theories is likely to yield the worst of both worlds. A typical failed approach to embracing the paradox is to compensate for E strategies that reduce commitment, trust, and teamwork by introducing top-down human resource management programs. As suggested earlier, these programs foster cynicism when no real change occurs, and they fail to engage unit managers at every level in leading a genuine transformation in their subunit (Beer et al., 1990a, 1990b).

The easiest way to combine these strategies effectively is to begin with Theory E and follow with O. At General Electric Jack Welch began the transformation by restructuring the company between 1981 and 1985. Businesses were told they had to be number one or two in their markets or they would be sold or closed. He also downsized the organization radically, reducing employment from 412,000 to 299,000. Sixty percent of staff groups were laid off. In this phase Welch became known as "Neutron Jack." However, he followed with Theory O strategies. With the help of OD consultants he began to launch a series of OD initiatives in 1986 to change the culture. Criteria for promotion were changed, and Welch introduced and institutionalized a rigorous review of key people known as "section C reviews." To be promoted managers had to produce financial results and also demonstrate that their managerial behavior was consistent with GE's Theory O values. Managers at all levels also had to go through a rigorous process called "Workout," which required them to be confronted by their own employees with feedback about barriers to their organization's effectiveness (Tichy & Sherman, 1993). In the last decade of his tenure, Welch spent 50% of his time on people and their development. However, sequencing works only when O strategies follow E strategies, not the other way around. If E follows O, it is highly likely that employees will feel betrayed. Draconian E initiatives would shatter the psychological contract built over many years by a participative O strategy.

The sequencing approach takes too long, however. Welch was fortunate to have 20 years at the helm of GE. Because most CEOs' tenure is far shorter, they must implement E and O strategies simultaneously and in an integrated manner. This will prove difficult for many turnaround managers. Temperamentally they find it difficult to embrace theory O, and their E strategies earn them distrust not easily overcome. Welch was an exception.

The solution is a diverse yet effective senior management team with a range of E and O perspectives. Consider the highly successful transformation of Asda, a UK grocery chain, led by a pair of managers, one with an E orientation and skills and the other with an O orientation and skills (adapted from Beer & Weber, 1997).

When Archie Norman took charge of British grocery chain Asda in December 1991, the company was 1.5 billion pounds in debt and near bankruptcy. Asda, like Scott Paper and Champion International, had a long and venerable past. It had sprung from a dairy farmers' association into one of Britain's leading grocery chains. It was the first to build superstores and one of the most successful in broadening its offerings to include clothing and other nonfood items. Although Asda offered value and therefore had lower profit margins than its high-end competitors, it had been consistently profitable. However, because of overcapacity in the industry, Asda experienced intense pressures on margins, and it experienced the slow growth characteristic of the industry, although it continued to be the grocer of choice for working-class shoppers looking for value. In the 1980s, in an effort to improve margins and grow the business more rapidly, management began to raise prices and acquire a number of nongrocery retail businesses. By borrowing money to purchase 60 stores instead of capitalizing the purchase, management caused the company to incur an unsustainable debt burden

when interest rates increased in the inflationary environment of the late 1980s. Top management's autocratic management style prevented store managers from confronting management with their views that these policies were potentially disastrous. When Norman arrived, he found a hierarchical and bureaucratic organization running out of cash. Store managers felt they had no influence on a trading (purchasing) group at headquarters that was buying high-end products Asda's working-class customers did not want to buy. Morale was extremely low, and the company was running out of cash.

Norman quickly moved to stem off bankruptcy. He fired the chief financial officer within hours of his arrival, stopped all capital expenditures, sold unrelated businesses and unprofitable stores, imposed a wage freeze, and laid off 10% of the workforce. Declaring to the financial community that it would take 3 years to see results, Norman visited stores in the first 2 weeks to talk with and listen to employees and store managers. He immediately reconfigured his top team by removing a layer of management and recruited two new senior executives. One of them, Allen Leighton, soon to become an equal partner in leading change, complemented Norman's strategic and intellectual capabilities with his down-to-earth style and personal leadership skills.

During the restructuring initiatives, Norman articulated a back-to-roots strategy and Theory O values that would govern the business in the years ahead. He authorized radical experimentation in one and then two other "renewal" stores and declared them "risk-free zones." These store managers would not be held accountable for short-term financial results, as other store managers were. A cross-functional task force was commissioned to work with store management reinventing the concept of an Asda store—its design, retail proposition, and approach to organizing and managing people. This began a renewal strategy that ultimately transformed most of Asda's 200 stores over 8 years. During this period a variety of improvement teams and task forces were institutionalized.

Throughout, Norman and Leighton spent enormous amounts of time in conversations with various groups of employees in the company, articulating their strategic goals and values, surfacing barriers to progress, and engaging people in developing solutions. During 8 years of change more than 50% of managers who were unable to adopt the Asda way of managing were replaced. According to Norman, 75% of his time in the first 3 years was spent on human resource and organization development issues.

Asda's financial performance turned around by 1994 and was followed by a long string of quarters in which it outperformed the industry in like-for-like sales improvement. The company soon began to be regarded as a leader in the retail industry, with profits and share price improving steadily. The culture was transformed from a hierarchical, bureaucratic organization with low morale to one in which employees and customers were being heard through a variety of institutionalized mechanisms for two-way dialogue. Asda developed the organization capabilities of coordination, commitment, competence, creativity, communication, and the ability to manage conflict in a productive way typically found in companies with sustainable competitive advantage.

In 1999 Asda was sold to Wal-Mart, a high-performing company with many of these capabilities, at eight times its market capitalization at the time Norman took charge. Wal-Mart managers were quoted as saying, "Asda is more like Wal-Mart than Wal-Mart is like Wal-Mart." Norman had successfully led a financial *and* cultural transformation that Wal-Mart executives recognized as the source of sustained performance.

Asda's successful transformation illustrates the means by which a leadership team with both Theory E and O perspectives can create an integrated strategy for change. Table 22.2 articulates the paradoxical combination in Asda's transformation. Change was led from the top through advocacy of a new business direction and also a new organization direction. Like

Scott Paper, Asda was restructured (though with a very different style), but as at Champion, a hierarchical culture was transformed to an open, egalitarian, and participative one. Top management created a broad plan for change at the top, but it enabled spontaneous innovation at the store level through radical store-level experimentation from which a new retail and cultural model emerged, one that Norman had not fully envisioned or planned at the beginning. This store-level innovation is very similar to Champion's experimentation in its manufacturing plants. Although managers received bonuses and stock options based on unit and company performance, Norman insisted that the vision of building a better Asda and high involvement at all levels was the key motivator. Finally, several large consulting firms were brought in for expert analysis and advice early in the transformation journey, but so were process consultants to help managers reinvent stores and managerial practices. In the third year of change Norman and Leighton began to cut back consultant involvement to prevent managers from becoming dependent on them.

The fact that Wal-Mart bought Asda at eight times the market capitalization of the company when the transformation began 8 years earlier (much more than the three-to-one paid for Scott Paper's E transformation and the one-to-one and a half paid for Champion International's O transformation) suggests that embracing the paradox of E and O yields superior economic returns. All stakeholders in the company benefited from this approach.

What enabled this rare outcome? It was an all too rare partnership between two leaders with different strengths, skills, and perspectives. Norman and Leighton learned from each other, and this enabled them to avoid the law of unintended consequences. All too often one leader and one theory dominate. This prevents the leader from learning about the unintended consequences of his or her dominant theory of change. Because E strategies are top down, they

Table 22.2   Integrating Theories E and O

Dimensions of Change	Theories E and O Combined
Purpose	Explicitly embrace the paradox between economic value and organization capability driven change.
Leadership	Set direction from the top and engage the people below.
Focus	Focus simultaneously on the hard (structures and systems) and the soft (corporate culture).
Planning	Plan for spontaneity.
Motivation	Involvement is used to motivate; compensation is used to recognize, not motivate.
Consultants	Consultants are expert resources who empower employees.

create a climate of silence that prevents lower levels from confronting top management with organizational and managerial barriers, particularly top management's own leadership behavior and policies (Beer & Eisenstat, 2000b; Morrison & Milliken, 2000). The unintended consequences of an O strategy, failures to confront hard strategic and business realities, are equally difficult to confront, short of pressure from capital markets that remove the O leader. Values that hold dear people, process, participation, and purpose are defended without regard to economic reality.

PRINCIPLES FOR EMBRACING THE CONTRADICTION OF THEORIES E AND O

Simply describing and urging the integration of E and O will not cause leaders to embrace the paradox of E and O. Leaders' past experience, values, and skills and their business and social context predispose them to lead with their dominant E or O assumptions. Managers in Japan, until very recently at least, have eschewed theory E because of strong societal values and traditions that favor the community over immediate economic outcomes. The results have been a disastrous 13 years of recession and underperformance. In the United States, and to a somewhat lesser extent in the United Kingdom, CEOs

lean strongly toward Theory E. However, an integrated E and O transformation is possible if leaders motivated to embrace the paradox can learn about the unintended consequences of their E or O assumptions and decisions. GE's Jack Welch did. He began to embrace Theory O after the limitations of his sole focus on an E strategy began to be apparent. Unfortunately, most organizations are programmed to prevent truthful discussions about the unintended consequences of their leader's change strategy (Argyris & Schön, 1993; Beer & Eisenstat, 2000b).

What is needed is a socially engineered leadership platform—a guided process for strategic leadership and change—that embraces and integrates the tensions between E and O. For leadership teams who do not have the perspectives or capacity to embrace a paradoxical strategic leadership stance (most, in our experience) such a leadership platform would specify the paradoxical change process leaders must follow if they are to achieve both strategic business and OD objectives. For the past 15 years Russell Eisenstat and I have worked to develop such a paradoxical leadership process. It enables a senior team to engage organization (O) issues in the context of strategic business (E) issues (Beer & Eisenstat, 2000b, 2004; Eisenstat & Beer, 1997). The Strategic Fitness Process (SFP) orchestrates a multilevel organization-wide public conversation (see Figure 22.1 for the key steps). The process falls into the genre of OD interventions, called large group or system-level interventions, that enable leaders to engage their organizations in honest conversations about potentially sensitive strategic, organizational, and management issues (Beckhard, 1967; Bunker & Alban, 1997; Ulrich, Kerr, & Ashkenas, 2002; Weisbord, 1991). Unlike these OD interventions, however, SFP is explicitly designed to create an integrated E and O transformation agenda. It departs from other organization-wide interventions by putting business strategy and gaps in business performance at the center of the change process.

The process begins with the top team (corporate or business unit) advocating E and O objectives and articulating these in a two- to three-page statement of business and organization direction. It then guides the senior team to inquire into organization realities that potentially block their E and O objectives through an inquiry carried out by a task force of eight of their best and highest potential managers, managers they will believe when they present their findings. This is done through interviews with 100 key people in the organization by the task force. Interviewees are asked to describe the organization's strengths and barriers to achieving top management's business and organization direction. A structured feedback process that has emerged from years of experimentation enables the senior team to learn the unvarnished truth about E and O issues. A central premise of this feedback process is that the only way truth can speak to power is if the task force can speak as a group and can validly claim to be speaking as reporters rather than as themselves. This is accomplished by asking the task force to discuss key themes in a "fishbowl," with the

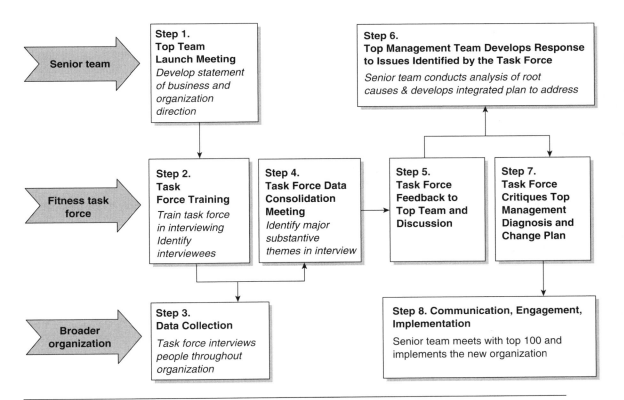

Figure 22.1 The Strategic Fitness Process: A Way to Have an Honest Conversation That Integrates Theories E and O

senior team seated around them, listening and taking notes, all in the context of explicit ground rules for dialogue (Beer & Eisenstat, 2000a; Eisenstat & Beer, 2002).

Feedback is followed by a systemic E and O diagnosis and an integrated action plan that addresses root causes. A number of analytic frameworks aid analysis of the fit between business strategy and the organization and present the senior team with the design and policy choices they face. In this way the hard substantive issues are integrated into the equally important soft cultural and commitment issues inherent in organization transformations. The learning loop continues when the senior team presents its change plan to the task force and receives a critique to which they must respond. Organization change is launched at a meeting at which the senior team and the task force communicate to the 100 key people interviewed—the dominant coalition—the outcomes of the process and how implementation will be carried forward and with whose involvement. Top teams meet with the task force once a quarter to review progress in change, and the full process is recycled once a year as part of the business planning process.

A decade of implementing and researching SFP has led us to extract a set of operating principles for implementing an integrated E and O transformation (Beer & Eisenstat, 2004). In this section I describe these principles briefly and explain what we have learned from implementing SFP in more than 200 organizations in 35 companies at the corporate and business unit level in the United States, Asia, Latin America, and Europe.

Demand a Lot and Give a Lot.[4] To change the behavior and performance of ineffective organizations, leaders must set new standards and demand that managers and workers live up to these new standards. Welch at GE articulated new performance standards ("Your business must be one or two or we will sell or close it"). But for new demands to stir commitment, senior management must also be willing to give

away more than economic rewards. It must send clear signals that it is willing to share power and control in the pursuit of excellence. This means giving employees a voice in the transformation and owning up to their own errors. Dunlap at Scott undermined the legitimate economic objectives of his transformation by paying himself $100 million while reducing the workforce by thousands, moving headquarters to his hometown for convenience, wielding absolute power, and verbally abusing employees.

An honest collective and public conversation about barriers to change prompted by SFP and the principles below produced the exact opposite result. An analysis of a dozen SFP applications shows that senior teams gain legitimacy by exposing their E and O objectives to inquiry, accepting honest feedback and responding with a plan for transformation, itself subject to critique. This occurs for three reasons. First the focus on business goals and strategies energizes employees to participate in what they know to be the keys to success and failure of the enterprise. Second, because the senior executives and their team make themselves vulnerable and show a willingness to change their policies and behavior for the good of the organization, hope is raised that change will be more than superficial. Third, engaging in a public inquiry process signals lower levels that the senior team is ready to sacrifice power based on position for power based on knowledge and centrality to successful implementation. Consider what Lynn Camp, vice president and general manager of Agilent Technology's Signal Source Delivery Unit (SGDU) told a "Fitness Task Force" that delivered the unvarnished truth about the state of the organization and consider the impact on commitment to the organization and its objectives:

> You lit a fire under us. Thank you for the unvarnished truth. . . . I take your feedback very seriously; it is my personal appraisal. . . . If the organization is going to change, I must change. The leader at the top casts a shadow. (Beer & Eisenstat, 2004, p. 7)

Embrace the Paradox With a Compelling Articulation of Business and Organization Direction. A failing business needs restructuring and a new business model with tough financial goals if it is to become economically viable (Collins, 2001). It also needs a new organization model and values to transform behavior. Without a redesigned organization, the new business model cannot be implemented. Without values, meaning, and commitment, sustained economic performance cannot be developed (O'Reilly & Pfeffer, 2000). Asda's long-term success can be traced to Norman's balanced E and O direction, articulated to his senior team on his first day. He made "securing value for the shareholder" and the revitalization of values and culture equal priorities. He launched a "renewal program" aimed at completely redefining how a store would be organized and managed on his first day as CEO, when he also announced sweeping restructuring goals and measures.

In almost all the organizations we studied, top teams had not developed an integrated E and O direction. New strategies were not accompanied by a clear idea of how the organization and leadership team had to change to enable implementation of the business strategy. Nor were organization changes solidly tied to economic goals and business strategy. With the help of six core questions, which focused on both E and O, top teams were able to create an integrated E and O direction that could then be challenged by inquiry into organization barriers. In many cases this was the first time the senior team had tried to create an integrated agenda. In all cases they discovered that they as a team did not fully understand the connection between E and O issues. In all cases senior teams and organization members acknowledged that the process of creating the integrated direction had clarified what needed to happen to create a successful transformation.

Underlying this principle and the SFP process is the belief, supported by research, that successful O transformations in culture and behavior must start with a focus on business goals and tasks. Transformations must be equally concerned with "hard" organization design issues and "soft" behavioral issues (Beer et al., 1990a; Collins, 2001). Disconnected from E objectives, O strategies are seen as idealistic and impractical. They lose credibility quickly. The failure of OD as a field to gain traction with senior executives may be traced in part to the fact that its theory and practice have not embraced the paradox of E and O.

Ownership and Active Leadership by a Diverse and Aligned Senior Management Team Are Essential. Transformations succeed only when the senior team embraces the E and O paradox as a team and leads the change in a unified manner (Tushman & O'Reilly, 1997). In too many E transformations leadership of change is delegated to consultants, staff groups, and task forces while senior management's priorities and behavior remain unchanged. To embrace the E and O paradox, top team members must have diverse perspectives: shareholder and employees, finance and human resources, and strategy and culture. Norman's success in embracing E and O at Asda was a function of his ability to build an effective team with diverse views that was deeply involved in leading the transformation as a team. When senior teams are effective in resolving their different perspectives through a fact-based dialogue, they can manage the "and also" so essential for a successful transformation (Beer & Eisenstat, 2000b; Eisenhardt, Kahwajy, & Bourgeois, 1977). All the senior teams that implemented these principles through SFP learned from their task forces that their business goals could not be implemented because they were not functioning as an effective team. Senior teams were perceived as unaligned with regard to strategic direction, priorities, and values. Too much of their time together was being spent on administrative matters and not enough time was being allocated to confronting difficult strategic and organizational issues that threatened the status quo and then leading change in them. Teams that changed the amount of time and energy they spent in resolving strategic business issues and at the same time the organizational and behavioral issues that prevented alignment were more successful in transforming their organization than those who did not. Consider the following quote from one of the most successful applications of these principles:

> Our top team has taken some big strides in becoming more effective. Scott [the general manager] looks to be taking more control of the reins and becoming the kind of leader the division needs. He and his staff will sit down as a group now and talk strategy where before they would have only talked about administrative detail. (Beer & Rogers, 1999, p. 4)

Enable Truth to Speak to Power. Without enabling lower levels to speak truthfully, leaders insulate themselves from the realities of their organization. They are unable to learn about the unintended consequences of their E or O theories of change. Leaders therefore should structure conversations that provide honest feedback. Welch held frequent no-holds-barred conversations with lower-level managers at GE's corporate education center. This is how he learned that his E strategy— "you have to be number one or two in your market or you will be sold or shut down"— was being undermined. General managers were simply redefining their markets narrowly to avoid being sold or shut down.

In all the organizations where SFP was applied, the inquiry surfaced the unvarnished truth about barriers to E and O goals that had not been in the open before. Confronting the truth energized senior teams to make changes in strategy and organization that promised to align the culture with the business's strategy. The truth about E and O quite often caused top management teams to make changes that were painful: selling a business, prioritizing projects, removing managers who did not conform to the new values, and redesigning the organization to enable teamwork even when it was politically difficult. The truth made managers more

accountable to shareholders, customers, and employees than they had been before. Consider the following top team member's view of how truth changed her organization:

> For instance we're now reviewing all the projects and making investment decisions, where before that would happen with one or two people in a side conversation. Those [had bad] ramifications all through our organization. (M. Beer, unpublished source)

Address Business, Organizational, Cultural, and Leadership Issues Holistically and Systemically. E and O theories of change address different but deeply connected sides of the enterprise. That is why a systemic approach to organization transformation is essential if the paradox of E and O is to be embraced (Cummings, 1980). The truth about the organization's capacity to achieve E and O goals, together with a systemic framework to analyze the gap, made it possible for managers who applied SFP to develop and implement an integrated agenda for change. Organization design and culture were transformed to enact strategy, and strategy was modified based on data about the organization's capabilities. New structures, particularly ones that necessitated cross-departmental or business teamwork, were accompanied by changes in the leadership team's role and behavior. And people were replaced or volunteered to leave when their motivation and skills did not match the transformational objectives.

At the Hewlett-Packard Santa Rosa Systems Division a root cause diagnosis, prompted by honest feedback, led to changes in multiple aspects of the system—the strategy, the leader's behavior, the senior team, the organization's structure, the resource allocation process and ultimately the culture (Beer & Rogers, 1999).

Sustain the Transformation Through Disciplined Cycles of Action, Learning, and Reflection. Transformational E and O goals espoused at the top often are not translated into reality at lower levels (Mallinger, 1993; Zbaracki,

1998). The only way to ensure that such a gap does not develop is to view corporate transformations as a continuous learning process. Managers can learn about unintended O consequences of E strategies and unintended E consequences of O strategies. Indeed, it is this principle that enables the organization to reinvent itself—the ultimate source of sustained competitive advantage. Of course, that is why the earlier principle of enabling truth to speak to power is so important. The Hewlett-Packard Santa Rosa Systems Division mentioned earlier used SFP to implement these principles every year for 5 years. Each year they discovered another deeper layer of E and O issues and how they interacted. And this is what enabled them to make an integrated E and O transformation over a 6-year period. Like others who followed these principles, they achieved dramatic changes in their financial performance and organization capabilities. Top management reported that they had risen from the worst division to among the best in the company (Beer & Rogers, 1999).

Apply These Principles in Every Unit of the Corporation From Top to Bottom. If corporate transformations are to incorporate both E and O strategies, top management must encourage, even demand, that unit leaders use the aforementioned principles to engage their organizations in a learning process from which they also learn. Faced with significant business challenges in Latin America, Grey Warner, Merck's senior vice president for Latin America, used the principles outlined earlier to lead successful E and O transformations in each of 10 Latin America country organizations. He did not launch a "one size fits all" solution for all countries in Latin America. Instead he asked each country manager and their top team to use SFP to define their business (E) and organization (O) direction and then use the aforementioned principles to learn about barriers and lead change. He held country managers accountable by meeting with them to review what they had learned about their organizations and their

leadership. To help them develop their organization, he supplied corporate resources when needed. Four years later the hierarchical cultures in all 10 organizations had moved significantly toward greater openness and participation, with substantial improvements in financial performance (Beer & Weber, 2001). A decade later a corporate-wide employee survey indicated that the Latin American region was higher than most other Merck organization units on a number of important human and business outcomes.

An analysis of a dozen organizations that used these principles showed that they were successful in surfacing and motivating E and O changes. O transformations occurred in coordination between functions or geographic regions, commitment to the organization, leadership effectiveness, openness of communication, and the capacity to manage conflict constructively. Improvements in financial performance could also be tied to organization changes in a number of cases, although without a control group one can never attribute causality. In one company, following SFP principles led the CEO and his team to spin off a business unit that constituted approximately 40% of the corporation's total revenue after they heard from the fitness task force that there were no synergies, something they suspected but had not acted on. This resulted in a rise in share price, demonstrating that these principles can have an immediate and direct effect on economic value, not just organization development. Fearing the difficulties of breaking up a company with a long history and tradition, the CEO had been putting off making this difficult decision, even in the face of a depressed share price and unenthusiastic stock analyst reports. The SFP principles changed economic value in a way that capital markets did not.

The principles outlined here were not equally successful in all organizations. The CEO or general manager had to be open to learning about his or her theory of transformation. Those who followed the operating principles for change discussed in this chapter were able to craft a transformation that embraced the E and O paradox. Not surprisingly, leaders in companies that historically had been exclusively E oriented and hierarchical did not embrace the principles as eagerly or easily. However, many that stuck with the principles learned from their experience about the side of the paradox that they were least committed to or skilled in implementing, were most often on the O side.

CONCLUSION

I have argued that only managers who embrace the paradox of Theories E and O can achieve a sustained transformation in economic performance and organization capability. I used three cases to illustrate this thesis. An E transformation at Scott Paper resulted in some significant immediate gains for shareholders but undermined the organization's capabilities. An O transformation at Champion International resulted in a remarkable change of the culture and improvements in a number of operating measures of performance but resulted in negligible changes in shareholder value. Finally, an integrated E and O transformation at Asda led to a fundamental transformation in organization capabilities and economic value. The study by Collins (2001) cited at the beginning of this chapter confirms these conclusions. Eleven companies (out of a possible 1,435) that achieved a sustained transformation did so through an integrated E and O transformation enabled by CEOs willing to confront the brutal facts about business and managerial issues. That only a small set of companies managed to achieve this result suggests that leaders clearly need help in integrating E and O change strategies. This chapter offered seven principles that leaders interested in learning how to integrate E and O might follow. By using these principles to engage their organizations in a strategic learning process, leaders were able to learn from lower levels about their theory of transformation and modify it to embrace the paradox of E and O.

Learning about one's own theory of change and moving to embrace the opposite theory proved difficult and painful for most of the managers in the companies we studied. A structured and carefully designed collective and public learning process (in this case SFP) that embraced the principles provided the essential discipline managers needed to embrace the paradox and learn. It provided guidance where leadership skills or knowledge about strategy and organizations were lacking. It created a mandate for change to which most leaders, who otherwise would avoid painful decisions, had to respond. Not doing so, they immediately recognized, threatened their credibility and legitimacy as leaders, something they instinctively knew they could not afford to do.

NOTES

1. An increase in the value of a company's stock price is not necessarily an indicator of increasing economic value. A stock price rise can be a function of the general movement of the stock market. Economic value is created by growth in profits net of the cost of capital.

2. There is some evidence that unlike most Theory E CEOs, Al Dunlap went beyond creating distance. He seems to have taken some pleasure in treating his key managers badly (Gilson & Cott, 1996).

3. Data from tens of thousands of executives who have taken the Myers–Briggs Type Indicator show that top managers are "thinking" types, who prefer to approach problems through analysis, as opposed to "feeling" types, who make decisions based on concerns about fairness and relationships. They also prefer control over spontaneous behavior (M. Beer, unpublished Myers–Briggs Type Indicator data from some 500 senior executives in Harvard Business School's Advanced Management Program).

4. I am indebted to my colleague Russell Eisenstat for this insight.

REFERENCES

Adler, P. A. (1993, January–February). Time and motion regained. *Harvard Business Review, 71*(1), 97–108.

Argyris, C. (1990). *Overcoming organizational defenses*, Needham Heights, MA: Allyn & Bacon.

Argyris, C., & Schön, D. (1993). *Organizational learning II*. Reading, MA: Addison-Wesley.

Ault, R., Walton, R., & Childers, M. (1998). *What works: A decade of change in Champion International*. San Francisco: Jossey-Bass.

Baker, G., III. (1993, November–December). Perspective: Rethinking rewards. *Harvard Business Review, 71*(6), 37–44.

Barney, J. B. (1986). Organizational culture: Can it be a source of sustained competitive advantage? *Academy of Management Review, 11*, 656–665.

Becker, B. E., & Huslid, M. (1998). High performance work systems and firm performance: A synthesis of research and managerial implications. In R. Ferris (Ed.), *Research in personnel and human resource management* (Vol. 16, pp. 53–101). Greenwich, CT: JAI.

Beckhard, R. (1967, March–April). The confrontation meeting. *Harvard Business Review, 45*, 149–156.

Beckhard, R. (1969). *Organization development: Strategies and models*. Reading, MA: Addison-Wesley.

Beer, M. (1980). *Organization change and development: A systems view*. Santa Monica, CA: Goodyear.

Beer, M. (2001). How to develop an organization capable of sustained high performance: Embrace the drive for results–capability development paradox. *Organizational Dynamics, 29*(4), 233–247.

Beer, M. (2003, Fall). Why total quality management programs do not persist: The role of management quality and implications for leading a TQM transformation. *Decision Sciences, 34*(4), 623–642.

Beer, M., & Cannon, M. D. (2004, Spring). Promise and peril in implementing pay for performance. *Human Resource Management Journal, 43*(1), 3–48.

Beer, M., & Eisenstat, R. A. (2000a). The organizational fitness profiling process. *Comportamentao Organizacional e Gestao, 6*, 1.

Beer, M., & Eisenstat, R. A. (2000b). The silent killers of strategy implementation and learning. *Sloan Management Review, 41*(4), 29–40.

Beer, M., & Eisenstat, R. A. (2004, February). How to hold an honest conversation about your strategy. *Harvard Business Review, 82*(2), 82–89.

Beer, M., Eisenstat, R. A., & Spector, B. (1990a). *The critical path to corporate renewal*. Boston: Harvard Business School Press.

Beer, M., Eisenstat, R. A., & Spector, B. (1990b, November–December). Why change programs do not work. *Harvard Business Review, 68*(6), 158–166.

Beer, M., & Gery, G. J. (1972). Individual and organizational correlates of pay system preferences. In H. L. Tosi, R. J. House, & M. Dunnette (Eds.), *Managerial motivation and compensation* (pp. 325–349). East Lansing: MSU Business Studies, Graduate School of Business Administration, Michigan State University.

Beer, M., & Katz, N. (2003). Do incentives work? The perceptions of a worldwide sample of senior executives. *Human Resource Planning Journal, 26*, 30–40.

Beer, M., & Nohria, N. (2000a). *Breaking the code of change*. Boston: Harvard Business School Press.

Beer, M., & Nohria, N. (2000b, May–June). Cracking the code of change. *Harvard Business Review, 78*(3), 133–141.

Beer, M., & Rogers, G. (1999). *Hewlett-Packard's Santa Rosa Systems Division, (A) (A1) (A2) (A3) (A4) (B3), case studies*. Boston: Harvard Business School.

Beer, M., Spector, B., Lawrence, P. A., Mills, D. Q., & Walton, R. (1985). *Managing human assets*. New York: Free Press.

Beer, M., & Weber, J. (1997). *Asda (A) (A1) (B) (C), case studies*. Boston: Harvard Business School.

Beer, M., & Weber, J. (2000). *Champion International, case study*. Boston: Harvard Business School Press.

Beer, M., & Weber, J. (2001). *Merck Latin America (A) (B) (C) (D), case studies*. Boston: Harvard Business School.

Bennis, W. (2000). Leadership of change. In M. Beer & N. Nohria (Eds.), *Breaking the code of change* (pp. 113–122). Boston: Harvard Business School Press.

Bennis, W. G. (1969). *Organization development: Its nature, origins, and prospects*. Reading, MA: Addison-Wesley.

Bunker, B., & Alban, B. T. (1997). *Large group interventions: Engaging the whole system in rapid change*. San Francisco: Jossey-Bass.

Burke, W. W. (1982). *Organization development: Principles and practices.* Boston: Little, Brown.

Burns, T., & Stalker, G. M. (1961). *The management of innovation.* London: Tavistock.

Business: Pay purview. (1998). *The Economist, 348*(8083), 59–60.

Cascio, W. F. (1993). Downsizing: What do we know? What have we learned? *Academy of Management Executive, 7*(1), 95–104.

Chandler, A. D. (1962). *Strategy and structure: Chapters in the history of the American industrial enterprise.* Cambridge: MIT Press.

Coch, L., & French, J. R. P. (1948). Overcoming resistance to change. *Human Relations, 1,* 512–533.

Collins, J. (2001). *Good to great: Why some companies make a leap and others don't.* New York: HarperBusiness.

Collins, J. C., & Porras, J. I. (1992). *Built to last.* New York: HarperCollins.

Conger, J. A. (2000). Effective change starts at the top. In M. Beer & N. Nohria (Eds.), *Breaking the code of change* (pp. 99–112). Boston: Harvard Business School Press.

Cummings, T. G. (1980). *Systems theory for organization development.* New York: John Wiley & Sons.

Deming, E. W. (1986). *Out of the crisis.* Cambridge: Massachusetts Institute of Technology, Center for Advanced Engineering Study.

Denison, D. R. (1990). *Corporate culture and organizational effectiveness.* New York: John Wiley & Sons.

Edmondson, A., & Woolley, A. (2003). Understanding outcomes of organizational learning interventions. In M. Easterby-Smith & M. Lyles (Eds.), *International handbook of organizational learning and knowledge management* (pp. 195–211). London: Blackwell.

Eisenhardt, K. M., Kahwajy, J. L., & Bourgeois, L. J., III. (1977, July–August). How management teams can have a good fight. *Harvard Business Review, 75*(4), 77–85.

Eisenstat, R. A., & Beer, M. (1997). *Organizational fitness profiling manual.* Waltham, MA: Center for Organizational Fitness.

Eisenstat, R. A., & Beer, M. (2002). *The strategic organizational fitness process handbook.* Waltham, MA: Center for Organizational Fitness.

Foster, R., & Kaplan, S. (2001). *Creative destruction: How companies that are built to last underperform the market—and how to successfully transform them.* New York: Currency.

French, W. L., & Bell, C. H., Jr. (1978). *Organization development: Behavioral science interventions for organizational improvements.* Englewood Cliffs, NJ: Prentice Hall.

Galbraith, J. (1978). *Organization design.* Reading, MA: Addison-Wesley.

Galbraith, J. (2000). The role of formal structure and process. In M. Beer & N. Nohria (Eds.), *Breaking the code of change* (pp. 139–158). Boston: Harvard Business School Press.

Gerstner, L. V. (2003). *Who says elephants can't dance: Inside IBM's turnaround.* New York: HarperBusiness.

Gibson, V. M. (1995). The new employee reward system. *Management Review, 84*(2), 13–18.

Gilson, S. C., & Cott, J. (1996). *Scott Paper, case study 9-296-048.* Boston: Harvard Business School.

Gittel, J. H. (2003). *The Southwest way: Using the power of relationships to achieve high performance.* New York: McGraw-Hill.

Grinyer, P. H., Mayes, D., & McKiernan, P. (1990). The sharpbenders: Achieving a sustained improvement in performance. *Long Range Planning, 23,* 116–125.

Hackman, J. R., & Oldham, G. R. (1980). *Work redesign.* Reading, MA: Addison Wesley.

Hambrick, D., & Siegel, P. (1997). *Compensation patterns within top management groups: On the harmful effects of executive pay disparities in high-technology firms.* Paper presented at the Academy of Management Meetings, Boston.

Heneman, R. L., Gresham, M. T., & Ledford, G. E., Jr. (2000). The changing nature of work and its effect on compensation design and delivery. In *Compensations in organizations* (Chapter 6). San Francisco: Jossey-Bass.

Heskett, J. L. (1999). *GE: We bring good things to life (A) (B), case studies.* Boston: Harvard Business School.

Heskett, J. L., Sasser, E. W., & Schlesinger, L. A. (2003). *The value profit chain: Treat employees like customers and customers like employees.* New York: Free Press.

Hirsh, S., & Kummerow, J. (1988). *Introduction to type in organizations*. Palo Alto, CA: Consulting Psychologists.

Huslid, M. (1995). The impact of human resource management practices on turnover, productivity and corporate financial performance. *Academy of Management Journal, 38,* 645.

Jensen, M. (2000). Value maximization and the corporate objective function. In M. Beer & N. Nohria (Eds.), *Breaking the code of change* (pp. 37–58). Boston: Harvard Business School Press.

Khurana, R. (2002a, September). The curse of the superstar CEO. *Harvard Business Review,* 3–8.

Khurana, R. (2002b). *In search of a savior.* Princeton, NJ: Princeton University Press.

Kotter, J. P., & Heskett, J. L. (1992). *Corporate culture and performance.* New York: Free Press.

Lawler, E. E. (1971). *Pay and organizational effectiveness: A psychological view.* New York: McGraw-Hill.

Lawler, E. E. (1981). *Pay and organization development.* Reading, MA: Addison Wesley.

Lawler, E. E. (2000). Pay system change: Lag, lead or both? In M. Beer & N. Nohria (Eds.), *Breaking the code of change* (pp. 323–336). Boston: Harvard Business School Press.

Lawrence, P. R., & Lorsch, J. W. (1967). *Organization and environment: Managing differentiation and integration.* Boston: Graduate School of Business Administration, Harvard University Press.

Mallinger, M., as reported in Argyris, C., & Schon, D. A. (1993). *Organizational learning II: Theory, method and practice* (pp. 234–236). Reading, MA: Addison Wesley.

Miles, R. H. (2000). Accelerated organizational transformation: Balancing scope and involvement. In M. Beer & N. Nohria (Eds.), *Breaking the code of change* (pp. 381–389). Boston: Harvard Business School Press.

Miller, D. (1990). *The Icarus paradox: How exceptional companies bring about their own downfall.* New York: HarperBusiness.

Miller, D., Hartwick, J., & LeBreton-Miller, I. (2004). How to spot a management fad. *Business Horizons, 47*(3), 7–16.

Miller, D., & Lee, J. (2001). The people make the process: Commitment to employees, decision-making, and performance. *Journal of Management, 27,* 163–189.

Miner, J. B. (2002). Participative decision making. In J. B. Miner (Ed.), *Organizational behavior: Foundations, theories and analysis* (pp. 291–319). New York: Oxford University Press.

Morrison, E. W., & Milliken, F. J. (2000). Organizational silence: A barrier to change and development in a pluralistic world. *Academy of Management Review, 25*(4), 706–725.

Murphy, K., & Dial, J. (1993). *General Dynamics: Compensation and strategy (A) (B) case studies.* Boston: Harvard Business School Press.

O'Reilly, C. A., & Pfeffer, J. (2000). *Hidden value: How great companies achieve extraordinary results with ordinary people.* Boston: Harvard Business School Press.

Pfeffer, J. (1998). *The human equation: Building profits by putting people first.* Boston: Harvard Business School Press.

Schaffer, R. H. (1988). *The breakthrough strategy: Using short-term success to build the high performance organization.* Cambridge, MA: Ballinger.

Schaffer, R. H. (2000). Rapid-cycle success versus the Titanics: Ensuring that consulting produces benefits. In M. Beer & N. Nohria (Eds.), *Breaking the code of change* (pp. 361–380). Boston: Harvard Business School Press.

Schaffer, R. H. (2002). *High impact consulting: How clients and consultants can work together to achieve extraordinary results.* San Francisco: Jossey-Bass.

Schein, E. H. (1969). *Process consultation: Its role in organization development.* Reading, MA: Addison-Wesley.

Schein, E. H. (2003). *DEC is dead, long live DEC: The lasting legacy of Digital Equipment Corporation.* San Francisco: Berrett-Koehler.

Senge, P. (2000). *The puzzle of paradoxes and how living companies create wealth: Why single value objective functions are not quite enough.* In M. Beer & N. Nohria (Eds.), *Breaking the code of change* (pp. 59–82). Boston: Harvard Business School Press.

Tichy, N. M., & Sherman, S. (1993). *Control your destiny or someone else will.* New York: Harper Business.

Trist, E. (1969). On socio-technical systems. In W. Bennis, K. D. Benne, & R. Chin (Eds.), *The planning of change* (pp. 269–282). New York: Holt, Reinhart & Winston.

Tushman, M. L., & O'Reilly, C. A. (1997). *Winning through innovation: A practical guide to leading organizational change and renewal.* Boston: Harvard Business School Press.

Ulrich, D., Kerr, S., & Ashkenas, R. (2002). *The GE work-out: How to implement GE's revolutionary method for busting bureaucracy and attacking organizational problems—fast!* New York: McGraw-Hill.

Virany, B., Tushman, M. L., & Romanelli, E. (1992). Executive succession and organizational outcomes in turbulent environments. *Organizational Science, 3,* 72–91.

Vroom, V., Jago, A. J., & Arthur, J. (1988). *The new leadership: Managing participation in organizations.* Englewood Cliffs, NJ: Prentice Hall.

Walton, R. E. (1977, Spring). Successful strategies for diffusing work innovations. *Journal of Contemporary Business,* 1–22.

Walton, R. E. (1985). From control to commitment in the workplace. *Harvard Business Review, 64*(2), 76–84.

Walton, R. E. (1987). *Innovating to compete: Lessons for diffusing and managing change in the workplace.* San Francisco: Jossey-Bass.

Weisbord, M. R. (1991). *Productive workplaces: Organizing and managing for dignity, meaning and community.* San Francisco: Jossey-Bass.

Wruck, K. H. (2000). Compensation incentives and organizational change. In M. Beer & N. Nohria (Eds.), *Breaking the code of change* (pp. 269–305). Boston: Harvard Business School Press.

Zbaracki, M. J. (1998). The rhetoric and reality of total quality management. *Administrative Science Quarterly, 43,* 602–638.

23

A Process for Changing Organization Culture

KIM CAMERON

Much of the current scholarly literature argues that successful companies—those with sustained profitability and above-average financial returns—are characterized by certain well-defined external conditions. These conditions include having high barriers to entry (e.g., the difficulty of other firms entering the market, so few competitors exist), nonsubstitutable products (e.g., others cannot duplicate the firm's product, and few alternatives exist), a large market share (e.g., the firm can capitalize of economies of scale and efficiencies by dominating the market), buyers with low bargaining power (e.g., purchasers of the firm's products become dependent on the firm because they have no other sources), suppliers with low bargaining power (e.g., suppliers to the firms become dependent because they have no other customers), rivalry between competitors (e.g., incentives to improve are a product of rigorous competition), and rare products or services (e.g., offering something that no other company provides) (Barney, 1991; Porter, 1980).

Unquestionably, these are desirable features that clearly should enhance financial success. A substantial amount of research supports the importance of these factors. However, what is remarkable is that several of the most successful U.S. firms in the last 20 years have had none of these competitive advantages. The top five performers in the last two decades of the 20th century—before the dot.com bubble, which blew away the competition in financial returns—were not the recipients of any of the so-called prerequisites for success. These highly successful firms included Southwest Airlines (21,775% return), Wal-Mart (19,807% return), Tyson Foods (18,118% return), Circuit City (16,410% return), and Plenum Publishing (15,689% return).

Think of it. If you were going to start a business and wanted to make a lot of money, what markets would you be most likely to avoid: airlines, discount retailing, consumer electronics, publishing, and food distribution. The list of industries represented by these five companies looks like an impending disaster for new entrants: many competitors, horrendous losses in the industry, widespread bankruptcy, almost no barriers to entry, little unique technology, many substitute products and services, and a nonleadership position in market share. Yet these five firms outperformed everyone, even with none of the special competitive advantages.

What differentiates these extraordinarily successful firms from others? How have they been able to succeed when others failed? How did Wal-Mart take on Sears and K-Mart, the two largest retailers in the world at the time, and almost drive them out of business? While Wal-Mart prospered, its largest rivals were forced to sell off divisions, replace CEOs (more than once), downsize dramatically, close stores wholesale, and even file Chapter 11 bankruptcy. How did Southwest thrive while several of its strongest competitors went belly-up (e.g., Eastern, Pan-Am, TWA, Texas Air, and People's Express)? How did Circuit City, Tyson Foods, and Plenum Publishing succeed when their competitors went out of business so rapidly that it's hard to keep up?

The key ingredient in every case is something less tangible, less blatant, but more powerful than the market factors listed earlier. The major distinguishing feature in these companies, their most important competitive advantage, the factor that they all highlight as a key ingredient in their success, is their organization culture. The sustained success of these firms has had less to do with market forces than company values; less to do with competitive positioning than personal beliefs; less to do with resource advantages than vision. In fact, it is difficult to name a single highly successful company, one that is a recognized leader in its industry, that does not have a distinctive, readily identifiable culture.

With very few exceptions, almost every leading firm has developed a distinctive culture that is clearly identifiable by its key stakeholders. This culture is sometimes created by the initial founder of the firm (e.g., Disney or Microsoft). Sometimes it is developed consciously by management teams who decide to improve their company's performance in systematic ways (e.g., G.E. or McDonald's). But almost all successful companies have developed something special that supersedes corporate strategy, market presence, or technological advantages. They have found the power that resides in developing and managing a unique corporate culture.

Not all organizations automatically possess a strong and highly effective culture, of course, so this chapter discusses a method for leading a culture change effort in an organization. A definition of organization culture is first provided, followed by the explanation of a framework for understanding culture in the context of organizations. Finally, a process for initiating culture change is described that can be used in organization development interventions.

DEFINITION OF ORGANIZATION CULTURE

Although more than 150 definitions of culture have been identified (Kroeber & Kluckhohn, 1952), the two main disciplinary foundations of organization culture are sociological (e.g., organizations *have* cultures) and anthropological (e.g., organizations *are* cultures). In each of these disciplines, two different approaches to culture were developed: a functional approach (e.g., culture emerges from collective behavior) and a semiotic approach (e.g., culture resides in individual interpretations and cognitions). The primary distinctions are differences between culture as an attribute possessed by organizations and culture as a metaphor for describing what organizations are. The former approach assumes that researchers and managers can identify differences between organization cultures, can change cultures, and can empirically measure cultures. The latter perspective assumes that nothing exists in organizations except culture, and one encounters culture any time one rubs up against any organization phenomenon. Culture is a potential predictor of other outcomes (e.g., effectiveness) in the former perspective, whereas in the latter perspective it is a concept to be explained independent of any other phenomenon.

A review of the literature on culture in organization studies reveals that a majority of writers agree that *culture* refers to the taken-for-granted values, underlying assumptions, expectations, and definitions that characterize organizations and their members (i.e., they have adopted the functional, sociological perspective). Most discussions of organization culture (Cameron & Ettington, 1988; O'Reilly & Chatman, 1996; Schein, 1996) agree that culture is a socially constructed attribute of organizations that serves as the social glue binding an organization together. Culture represents "how things are around here," or the prevailing ideology that people carry inside their heads; thus, culture affects the way organization members think, feel, and behave.

Importantly, the concept of organization *culture* is distinct from the concept of organization *climate*. Climate consists of temporary attitudes, feelings, and perceptions of individuals (Schneider, 1990). Culture is an enduring, slow-to-change, core characteristic of organizations; because it is based on attitudes, climate can change quickly and dramatically. *Culture* refers to implicit, often indiscernible aspects of organizations; *climate* refers to more overt, observable attributes of organizations. Culture includes core values and consensual interpretations about how things are; climate includes individualistic perspectives that are modified frequently as situations change and new information is encountered. The approach to change in this chapter focuses on culture attributes rather than climate attributes. It considers the "links among cognitions, human interactions, and tangible symbols or artifacts typifying an organization" (Detert, Schroeder, & Mauriel, 2000, p. 853), or, in other words, "the way things are" in the organization rather than people's transitory attitudes about them.

Unfortunately, most people are unaware of their culture until it is challenged, until they experience a new culture, or until culture is made overt and explicit through, for example, a framework or model. For example, most people did not wake up this morning making a conscious decision about which language to speak. Only when confronted with a different language or asked specific questions about language do people become aware that language is one of their defining attributes. Similarly, culture is undetectable most of the time because it is not challenged or consciously articulated. Measuring culture therefore has presented a challenge to organization scholars and change agents.

MEASURING ORGANIZATION CULTURE THROUGH COMPETING VALUES

The competing values framework has proven to be helpful for assessing and profiling the dominant cultures of organizations because it helps people identify the underlying cultural dynamics that exist in their organizations. It helps to raise consciousness of cultural attributes. This framework was developed in the early 1980s as a result of studies of organization effectiveness (Quinn & Rohrbaugh, 1981), followed by studies of culture, leadership, structure, and information processing (Cameron, 1986; Cameron & Quinn, 2006). The framework consists of two dimensions. The first differentiates a focus on flexibility, discretion, and dynamism from a focus on stability, order, and control. For example, some organizations are effective because they are changing, adaptable, and organic, whereas other organizations are effective because they are stable, predictable, and mechanistic. This dimension ranges from versatility and pliability on one end to steadiness and durability on the other end.

The second dimension differentiates a focus on an internal orientation, integration, and unity from a focus on an external orientation, differentiation, and rivalry. That is, some organizations are effective because they have harmonious internal characteristics, whereas others are effective because they focus on interacting or competing with others outside their boundaries. This dimension ranges from cohesion and consonance on one end to separation and independence on the other.

Together these two dimensions form four quadrants, each representing a distinct set of effectiveness indicators. Figure 23.1 illustrates the relationships of these two dimensions to one another along with the resulting four quadrants. These dimensions have been found to represent what people value about an organization's performance and what they define as good, right, and appropriate. However, these dimensions have also been found to accurately describe how people process information, what fundamental human needs exist, and which core values are used for forming judgments and taking action (Beyer & Cameron, 1997; Cameron & Ettington, 1988; Lawrence & Nohria, 2002; Mitroff, 1983; Wilber, 2000). Hence, they describe some of the fundamental underlying dimensions that make up organization culture (Cameron & Quinn, 2006).

What is notable about these dimensions is that they represent opposite or competing assumptions. Each continuum highlights a core value that is opposite from the value on the other end of the continuum (e.g., flexibility versus stability, internal versus external). Therefore,

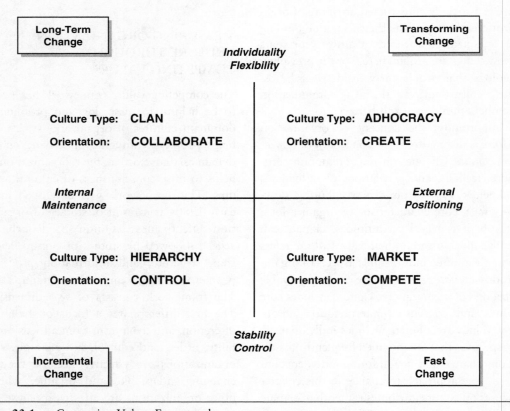

Figure 23.1   Competing Values Framework

the dimensions produce quadrants that are also contradictory or competing on the diagonal. The upper left quadrant identifies values that emphasize an internal, organic focus, whereas the lower right quadrant identifies values that emphasize external, control focus. Similarly, the upper right quadrant identifies values that emphasize external, organic focus whereas the lower left quadrant emphasizes internal, control values. These competing or opposite values in each quadrant give rise to the model's name.

Each of the four quadrants has a label that characterizes its most notable characteristics: *clan, adhocracy, market,* and *hierarchy*. These quadrant names were derived from the scholarly literature and identify how, over time, different values have become associated with different forms of organizations, such as Weber's (1947) hierarchy, Williamson's (1975) market, Ouchi's (1981) clan, and Mintzberg's (1979) adhocracy. (Similar dimensions have emerged in other scholarly domains—such as organization quality, child development, leadership roles, information processing, management skills, organic brain functioning, and philosophy—suggesting that the dimensions and the quadrants are very robust in explaining core values and human orientations [Hampton-Turner, 1981; Lawrence & Nohria, 2002; Mitroff, 1983; Piaget, 1932; Wilber, 2000].)

Organizations tend to develop a dominant orientation and value set—or culture—over time as they adapt and respond to challenges and changes in the environment (Sathe, 1983; Schein, 1996). Just as people who face threat, uncertainty, and ambiguity reassert their own habituated behavior with redoubled force (Staw, Sandelands, & Dutton, 1981; Weick, 1993), institutions tend to respond to challenges by amplifying their core cultural values. As competition, change, and pressure intensify, organization culture becomes more solidified and is given more prominence and emphasis (Cameron, 2003).

Culture Types

As noted in Figure 23.1, the competing values framework identifies four distinct types of cultures in organizations. The clan culture, in the upper left quadrant of Figure 23.1, is typified as a friendly place to work where people share a lot of themselves. It is like an extended family with best friends at work. Leaders are thought of as mentors, coaches, and perhaps even parent figures. The organization is held together by loyalty, tradition, and collaboration. Commitment is high. The organization emphasizes the long-term benefits of individual development, with high cohesion and morale being important. Success is defined in terms of internal climate and concern for people. The organization places a premium on teamwork, participation, and consensus.

In the upper right quadrant of the competing values framework is the adhocracy culture. It is characterized as a dynamic, entrepreneurial, and creative workplace. People stick their necks out and take risks. Effective leadership is visionary, innovative, and risk oriented. The glue that holds the organization together is commitment to experimentation and innovation. The emphasis is on being at the leading edge of new knowledge, products, or services. Readiness for change and meeting new challenges are important. The organization's long-term emphasis is on rapid growth and acquiring new resources. Success means producing unique and original products and services.

A market culture in the lower right quadrant is a result-oriented workplace. Leaders are hard-driving producers, directors, and competitors. They are aggressive and demanding. The glue that holds the organization together is an emphasis on winning. The long-term concern is on competitive actions and achieving stretch goals and targets. Success is defined in terms of market share and penetration. Outpacing the competition, escalating share price, and market leadership dominate the success criteria.

The organization culture in the lower left quadrant, the hierarchy culture, is characterized as a formalized and structured place to work. Procedures and well-defined processes govern what people do. Effective leaders are good coordinators, organizers, and efficiency experts. Maintaining a smooth-running organization is important. The long-term concerns of the organization are stability, predictability, and efficiency. Formal rules and policies hold the organization together.

Cameron and Ettington's (1988) review of the literature found more than 20 dimensions of organization culture, including dimensions such as internal–external focus, speed, riskiness, participativeness, clarity, power distance, masculinity, and individualism. Each of these dimensions helps establish a profile or pattern for an organization's culture. By far the three most dominant and common pattern dimensions in the literature are cultural strength (the power or preeminence of the culture), cultural congruence (the extent to which the culture in one part of the organization is congruent with the culture in another part of the organization), and cultural type (the specific kind of culture that is reflected in the organization). Cameron and Ettington (1988, p. 385) found that "the effectiveness of organizations is more closely associated with the *type* of culture present than with the congruence or the strength of that culture."

Profiling Organization Culture

Cameron and Quinn (2006) report a great deal of evidence that people can accurately describe the cultures of their organizations according to the competing values framework and that the resulting culture profiles predict multiple performance factors such as effectiveness (Cameron & Freeman, 1991), the success of mergers and acquisitions (Cameron & Mora, 2003), and quality of life in organizations (Quinn & Spreitzer, 1991). In other words, the manner in which organization culture is described and

experienced by individuals is congruent with the dimensions of the competing values framework (Mason & Mitroff, 1973; Mitroff & Kilmann, 1975). Therefore, the key to assessing organization culture is to identify aspects of the organization that reflect its key values and assumptions and then give people an opportunity to respond to these cues. The Organizational Culture Assessment Instrument (OCAI) was developed to identify an organization's culture profile. It has now been used in almost 10,000 organizations worldwide in most sectors (e.g., private sector, public sector, education, health care, new startups, nongovernment organizations). Examples of the kinds of profiles that result from this instrument are shown in Figure 23.2.

In the OCAI, organization members are provided with a set of scenarios that describe certain fundamental cultural indicators in organizations. People rate their own organization's similarity to these scenarios by dividing 100 points between four different scenarios, each descriptive of a quadrant in the competing values framework. Six dimensions are rated: the dominant characteristics of the organization, the leadership style that permeates the organization, the glue or bonding mechanisms that hold the organization together, the strategic emphases that define what areas drive the organization's strategy, the criteria of success that determine how victory is defined and what gets rewarded and celebrated, and the management of employees or the style that characterizes how employees are treated and what the working environment is like. In combination, these content dimensions reflect fundamental cultural values and implicit assumptions about the way the organization functions. They reflect how things are in the organization. This list of six content dimensions is not comprehensive, of course, but it has proven in past research to provide an adequate picture of the type of culture that exists in an organization. For example, these 6 dimensions have been found to be as predictive as 8, 12, or 16

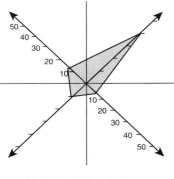

High-Tech Manufacturer

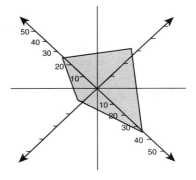

Fast-Growing Bancorp

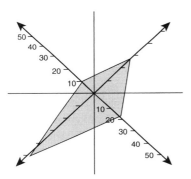

Standardized Part Producer

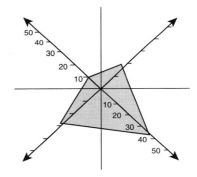

Multinational Manufacturer

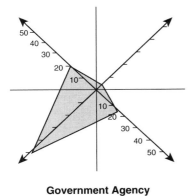

Government Agency

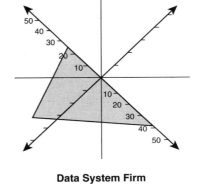

Data System Firm

Figure 23.2   Examples of Culture Profiles for Six Organizations

dimensions (Cameron & Quinn, 2006). When organization members respond to questions about these dimensions, the underlying organization culture can be uncovered. The items in the OCAI are reproduced in the Appendix.

An important caveat in culture assessment is that it may make little sense to assess the culture of the overall Ford Motor Company, for example, inasmuch as it is too large, heterogeneous, and complex an organization. Consequently, people are directed to target a specific organization unit as they respond to the questions on the OCAI. This organization unit is one in which unit performance is a relevant factor—not wholly dependent on a larger unit—and one that possesses its own identity. Evaluations should be done by people in the organization who have a perspective of the relevant organization's overall culture, who will be engaged in implementing change initiatives, and whose acceptance is necessary for ensuring a successful culture change effort. These people assess the current culture of their organization.

Using individual scores on the instrument, respondents participate in a discussion to generate a consensus view of the current organization culture (not an *average* view), with everyone having input into the profiling process. Discussing and highlighting the potentially disparate perspectives of individual raters is a rich and enlightening part of culture assessment because it uncovers multiple perspectives and a variety of aspects of the organization that may go unnoticed otherwise. This discussion builds understanding, opens lines of communication, and reveals elements of the organization's culture that a single individual or task force may miss.

After this consensus-building discussion focused on the current culture, this same group of evaluators completes the OCAI a second time. This time they rate the OCAI items in response to this question: "If your organization is to flourish, to achieve dramatic success, and to accomplish its highest aspirations in, say, 5 years, what kind of culture will be

needed?" After individual culture scores are produced a second time, a consensus-building process occurs again in which a preferred future culture profile is developed by the respondent group by using the same discussion process. The current and the preferred future culture profiles can then be compared to determine the extent to which a culture change process is needed. In most organizations, some culture change is desired, as indicated by a difference in the culture profiles produced by the two consensus-building discussions.

A Process for Changing Organization Culture

Changing organization culture is very difficult, not only because culture is largely unrecognized but because once set, commonly shared interpretations, values, and patterns are difficult to modify. However, once it has been determined that culture change is a desired objective, members of an organization can engage in a set of steps that will put a culture change process in motion. The outcome of these steps is a process for moving an organization's culture from the current state to the preferred future state. These steps are based on the work of several authors who have described successful change interventions aimed at organization culture change (e.g., Cameron & Quinn, 2006; Denison, 1989; Hooijberg & Petrock, 1993; Kotter, 1995; Trice & Beyer, 1993). These steps initiate change in individual and organizational processes, conversations, language, symbols, and values, none of which by itself ensures that culture change will occur, but in combination they create a great deal of momentum toward fundamental culture change in organizations.

To explain these seven steps, an (anonymous) example is provided, with its current and preferred future cultures illustrated in Figure 23.3. The solid line represents the organization's current culture, and the dotted line represents the preferred culture. The results of the culture assessment process indicated that

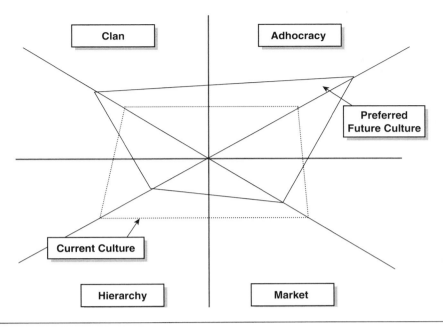

Figure 23.3   Comparing an Organization's Current and Preferred Future Culture Profiles

this organization desired to change its culture toward the clan and adhocracy cultures and away from the hierarchy and market cultures. Examples of how this organization engaged in a seven-step culture change process follow.

1. Clarifying Meaning. The first step in culture change is to clarify what it does and doesn't mean for the organization's culture to change. This is an interpretation and meaning-making step. Moving toward one particular type of culture does not mean that other culture types should be abandoned or ignored. It means only that special emphasis must be placed on certain factors if the culture change is going to be successful. Questions that may be addressed when determining what culture change means and doesn't mean include the following: "What attributes should be emphasized if the culture is to move toward the preferred quadrant?" "What characteristics should dominate the new culture?" "What attributes should be reduced or abandoned in the move away from a particular quadrant?" "What characteristics will be

preserved?" "What continues to be important about this culture type even though there will be an emphasis on another culture type?" "What are the most important tradeoffs?"

The purpose of this step is to clarify for the organization the things that won't change and the things that will. Wilkins (1989) identifies the importance of building on corporate character in any change effort, that is, on the core competencies, the unique mission, and the special identity that has been created over time. An organization should not abandon core aspects of what makes it unique, whereas some other aspects of the organization must be transformed. Identifying what culture change means and doesn't mean helps remind the organization about what will be preserved and what will be changed. It attaches specific meaning to the idea that culture change will occur.

By way of illustration, the organization profiled in Figure 23.3 interpreted a culture change toward the clan quadrant to mean more employee empowerment, more participation and involvement in decision making, and more cross-functional teamwork. More clan emphasis did not mean lack of standards and rigor, an absence of tough decisions, or a tolerance for mediocrity. In addition, moving away from the hierarchy quadrant was interpreted to mean fewer sign-offs on decisions, less micromanagement, and less paperwork. It did not mean lack of measurement, accountability, or performance monitoring.

2. *Identifying Stories.* Because organization culture is best communicated through stories (Martin, 1992; Martin, Feldman, Hatch, & Sitkin, 1983), a second step in the culture change process is to identify one or two positive incidents or events that illustrate the key values that will characterize the organization's future culture. That is, real incidents, events, or stories are recounted publicly in order help people capture a sense of what the new culture will be like. What will the new culture feel like? How will people behave? What events consistent with the preferred future culture occurred in the past? The key values, desired orientations, and behavioral principles that are to characterize the new culture are more clearly communicated through stories than in any other way. Not only do these stories help clarify the culture change, but people are less anxious about moving into an unknown future when they can carry parts of the past with them. When the parts of the past being carried forward are examples of best practices, peak performance, and aspirational levels of achievement, organization members are motivated to pursue them, they are clear about what is to be accomplished by the change, and they can identify with the core values being illustrated.

In the organization illustrated in Figure 23.3, the most common and motivational story associated with the preferred future culture was of a special project that had recently been accomplished approximately 75% ahead of schedule and 80% under budget, with extremely high morale and identification among employees.

Numerous examples of innovation and entrepreneurship made that achievement possible. In fact, the project team's watch cry was, "Make the impossible possible." Elements of that story were used to illustrate what the organization as a whole was shooting for as being indicative of their future culture.

3. *Determining Strategic Initiatives.* Strategic initiatives involve the activities that will be started, stopped, and enhanced. They are actions designed to make major changes that will produce culture change. What new things must be begun? What activities will be stopped, or what would have been done that will now not be done as a result of the culture change initiative? Most organizations have much more difficulty stopping something than starting it, so identifying what won't be pursued is a difficult but critical step. What resource allocation changes does this imply? What new resources will be needed? What processes and systems must be designed or redesigned to support the change initiatives? In what ways can the organization's core competencies be leveraged and magnified so that the culture change produces a sustained competitive advantage?

Identifying what is to be started is a way to help the organization think of strategic initiatives that have not been previously pursued. Identifying what is to be stopped helps focus resources and energy so that non–value-added activities—usually characteristic of the previous culture—will not inhibit the change process. Identifying what is to be enhanced implies that some current activities can engender change if they are enhanced with more resources, more attention, or more leadership.

Examples of strategic initiatives in the case illustrated in Figure 23.3 include the development of a leadership development program, a unique employee ownership program, and a budgeting process that set aside funds for entrepreneurial ventures and experimentation in the company.

4. Identifying Small Wins. The rule regarding small wins is to find something easy to change, change it, and publicize it. Then, find a second thing easy to change, change it, and publicize it. Small wins are immediate actions that represent baby steps in the direction of culture change. They can be implemented immediately, but none of them by itself represents substantial change. Small successes create momentum in the desired direction, limit resistance (because seldom do people resist small, incremental changes), and create a bandwagon effect so that additional supporters get on board. When people see that something is changing, even if it is small in scope, a sense of progress and advancement is created, and that sense helps build support for the larger and more fundamental changes. The biggest mistake made by organizations instituting a small wins strategy is that the first two steps are achieved but not the third. That is, small changes are initiated, but they are not publicly acknowledged and celebrated. The publicity accompanying the small wins is the chief momentum creator.

In the illustrative case (Figure 23.3), part of the culture change effort involved the dismantling of an old program, including some physical structures. Certain of these visible physical structures were dismantled even though doing so was not a necessary part of the new strategy, nor did their demolition create any particular advantage. The removal of the structures was simply part of a small wins strategy to show progress, create a sense of momentum, and build support for the larger initiatives. Other small wins included things as simple as changing a color scheme in buildings, painting offices, decorating work spaces, and eliminating (or creating) special parking spaces.

5. Crafting Metrics, Measures, and Milestones. Determining the key indicators of success, what to measure, how to measure it, and when certain levels of progress will be noted is a crucial part of the change process. An important shortcoming in most change processes, especially when the target of change is as soft and amorphous as organization culture, is the neglect of hard measures of achievement and progress. Change requires the identification of indicators of success in culture change and interim progress indicators. A data-gathering system and a time frame for assessing the results are needed. What gets measured gets attention, so the key initiatives and outcomes must have metrics and measuring processes associated with them. Of course, overloading systems with multiple measures is a sure way to kill change initiatives, so the key to good metrics, measures, and milestones is to identify enough to be helpful, attach them to decisions and resource allocations, attach them to the key levers and indicators of change, and ensure that they are understood by those involved in the culture change process.

For example, the organization in the case illustration specified times for specific changes to be completed, designed follow-up and reporting events, and developed mechanisms such as a monthly interview program in order to ensure that individuals and organization units followed through on personal commitments and assignments.

6. Communicating and Creating Symbols. It is certain that resistance to culture change will occur in organizations. Employees' basic ways of life will be challenged and changed, and familiar territory will be altered. Fundamental aspects of the organization will be changed, so culture change is sure to generate stiff resistance. Therefore, communicating the culture change process is a critical step in overcoming resistance and generating commitment. Explaining why the culture change is necessary and beneficial probably is the most vital step in generating commitment. Research suggests that people tend to explain "why" to people they care about and hold in high esteem. They tend to tell "what" to those they care less about or hold in low esteem. Explaining "why" communicates both caring and esteem to those involved in the culture change process.

Sometimes, in order to make a case for change, the current or past state is criticized or denigrated. The problem is, most organization members were a part of the previous condition. Criticism of the past diminishes commitment because it is interpreted as a criticism of organization members' previous best efforts. Instead of criticism, holding a funeral—celebrating the best of the past but outlining a future in which certain parts of the past will not be carried forward—is a more effective way to move beyond aspects of the old culture that will be left behind.

Building coalitions of supporters among key opinion leaders, involving the people most affected by the changes, and empowering people to implement aspects of the change process are also ways to help reduce resistance. Sharing as much information as possible on a regular basis, and as broadly as possible, limits the tendency to make up information in the presence of ambiguity or uncertainty. Reducing rumors by providing factual information, providing feedback on initiatives, and holding public events to share updates are all ways to engender support.

Finally, among the most important initiatives that accompany culture change is a change in symbols. Symbols are visual representations of the new state, so identifying symbols that signify a new future is an important part of culture change. Symbols help organization members visualize something different, provide a new interpretation of the organization, and provide a rallying point for people supportive of the change. New logos, new structures, new events, new charters, and other symbolic rallying points can be used.

The organization in Figure 23.3 produced videotapes featuring people working on the culture change to highlight progress in the change efforts, held regular town meetings to share updated information, sent teams of representatives to various parts of the organizations to address

questions and hold focus groups, and created numerous symbols—including specific company songs—signaling the successful culture change initiative.

7. Developing Leadership. All organization change requires leadership, champions, and owners. Culture change seldom occurs randomly or inadvertently in organizations, and it requires leaders who are consciously and consistently directing the process. A great deal has been written on the role of leaders in change processes, of course, and it will not be reviewed here. However, two key points should be made. One is that each aspect of the culture change process (e.g., each strategic initiative, each communication process) needs a champion or someone who accepts ownership for its successful implementation. Accountability is maintained best when specific people are designated as owners of the initiative, and an array of owners helps ensure broad participation and commitment. Second, not only must current leaders champion the culture change, but a cohort of future leaders must be prepared to lead the organization when the culture change has been put in place. The new leadership competencies that will be needed in the preferred future culture must be specified. Differences between current leadership and future leadership requirements should be articulated. Then, learning activities, developmental experiences, and training opportunities must be put in place to develop the needed leadership competencies. Selection processes must be aligned with the strengths needed in the future culture, not just the way things are at the present time.

The organization illustrated in Figure 23.3 implemented activities such as the following to help ensure that sufficient bench strength existed in their leadership ranks to lead the transformed organization culture: ongoing 360-degree feedback processes with sponsorship and coaching, formal mentoring by (mainly) senior executives, management development and training programs, assigned reading material outside the normal work-related material, attendance at professional conferences each year, a formalized support group for high-potential leaders, developmental and stretch assignments at work, and nonwork service opportunities aimed at giving back to the community.

SUMMARY

Almost all organizations develop a dominant type of organization culture over time, and these culture types can be reliably and validly assessed using an instrument based on the competing values framework (see Cameron & Quinn, 2006). Particular types of cultures form as certain values, assumptions, and priorities become dominant when organizations address challenges and adjust to changes. These dominant cultures help the organization remain consistent and stable as well as adaptable and flexible in dealing with a rapidly changing environment. Although organization cultures often evolve in predictable ways over time (Cameron & Whetten, 1981; Quinn & Cameron, 1983), organizations face the need to change cultures as a result of environmental jolts, mergers and acquisitions, new marketplace opportunities, or the need to implement certain kinds of strategic or structural changes. Without a change in culture, for example, most change initiatives such as total quality management, downsizing, mergers and acquisitions, and teamwork often fall short of expectations (Cameron, 1997). The problem with trying to change organization culture is that it is so amorphous and vague. It is hard to know what to target and where to begin. Culture often is the catch-all concept for almost anything in organizations that is difficult to specify or assess. This chapter has explained one well-accepted process for effectively leading organization culture change. An instrument has been discussed that helps assess the organization's current culture, its preferred future culture, and the strategic leadership activities that are needed to help culture change occur.

The main objective in outlining this assessment process, including the seven steps for implementing culture change, is to help ensure that the organization is clear from the outset about what its current culture is and why it needs to change. A common mistake in organizations desiring to improve is that they do not create a common viewpoint of where the organization is starting and how that differs from an ideal future state. Unsuccessful organizations often launch a change initiative without considering the need to develop a consensual view of the current culture; the need to reach consensus on what change means and doesn't mean; the specific changes that will be started, stopped, and enhanced; the small wins and celebrations that are needed; the measures, metrics, and milestones needed for accountability; the communication system needed; and the ongoing leadership demands faced by organizations in the midst of culture change (Cameron, 1997). This explanation provides a short but well-tested formula for overcoming the common obstacles to culture change and helping to make the process of culture change more systematic.

RESEARCH DIRECTIONS

This culture change process, though used widely in hundreds of organizations, also gives rise to a variety of research questions that necessitate systematic investigation. A comparison of the OCAI and other culture assessment instruments has never been undertaken, for example, so the relationships between various dimensions of organization culture have not been clarified. Comparing the validity and reliability of a variety of culture assessment instruments has never been undertaken. Moreover, identifying the effects of various dimensions of culture on organization performance warrants more systematic investigation. Although some research has been conducted on these relationships (e.g., Cameron & Freeman, 1991), too little is known about the relationships between various dimensions of culture, their impact on performance, and the effects of changes in cultural dimensions. In-depth case studies of successful culture change initiatives are rare in the literature, as are other forms of systematic measurements of cultural dimensions. More qualitative and quantitative measures of organization culture will certainly lead to a richer understanding of culture and its key dimensions.

The culture change process itself also begs for systematic assessment. Which of the steps is most crucial, which has the most impact on performance, which must be achieved in collaboration with other steps as opposed to being independent in its effect, and which sequence the change process must follow to be most effective all are areas in which systematic investigation can produce additional insight. The sources of data—top managers opposed to a diagonal slice of employees, for example— may affect culture profiles, but various samples of evaluators have not been compared systematically. The extent to which evaluators must also be implementers of culture change initiatives is also an area of controversy and needed investigation.

As in any endeavor in which complex and ambiguous concepts are being studied along with their complex and ambiguous relationships to performance, research on organization culture and the change process is neither simple nor necessarily straightforward. It requires careful definitions, measurements, and theoretical frameworks. The competing values framework discussed here is one such useful framework. Empirical evidence highlights the importance and effectiveness of culture change efforts, and the crucial role culture plays in accounting for the success of other kinds of organization change initiatives is unequivocal. Consequently, continuing research on the measurement and process of changing organization culture is an important and worthwhile endeavor.

Appendix

ORGANIZATIONAL CULTURE ASSESSMENT INSTRUMENT

SOURCE: From Cameron, K. S. "Ethics, virtuousness, and constant change." In Tichy, N., & McGill, M. (Eds.) *The ethical challenge* (pp. 85–94). Copyright © 2003, San Francisco: Jossey-Bass. Reprinted with permission of John Wiley & Sons, Inc.

1. Dominant Characteristics
    A. The organization is a very special place. It is like an extended family. People seem to share a lot of themselves.
    B. The organization is a very dynamic and entrepreneurial place. People are willing to stick their necks out and take risks.
    C. The organization is very production oriented. A major concern is with getting the job done. People are

very competitive and achievement oriented.
    D. The organization is a very formalized and structured place. Bureaucratic procedures generally govern what people do.

2. Organizational Leaders
    A. The leaders of the organization are generally considered to be mentors, facilitators, or parent figures.
    B. The leaders of the organization are generally considered to be entrepreneurs, innovators, or risk takers.
    C. The leaders of the organization are generally considered to be hard-drivers, producers, or competitors.
    D. The leaders of the organization are generally considered to be coordinators, organizers, or efficiency experts.

3. Management of Employees
   A. The management style in the organization is characterized by teamwork, consensus, and participation.
   B. The management style in the organization is characterized by individual risk taking, innovation, flexibility, and uniqueness.
   C. The management style in the organization is characterized by hard-driving competitiveness, goal directedness, and achievement.
   D. The management style in the organization is characterized by careful monitoring of performance, longevity in position, and predictability.

4. Organization Glue
   A. The glue that holds the organization together is loyalty and mutual trust. Commitment to this organization runs high.
   B. The glue that holds the organization together is orientation toward innovation and development. There is an emphasis on being on the cutting edge.
   C. The glue that holds the organization together is the emphasis on production and goal accomplishment. Marketplace aggressiveness is a common theme.
   D. The glue that holds the organization together is formal rules and policies. Maintaining a smooth-running organization is important.

5. Strategic Emphases
   A. The organization emphasizes human development. High trust, openness, and participation persist.
   B. The organization emphasizes acquiring new resources and meeting new challenges. Trying new things and prospecting for new opportunities are valued.
   C. The organization emphasizes competitive actions and achievement. Measurement targets and objectives are dominant.
   D. The organization emphasizes permanence and stability. Efficient, smooth operations are important.

6. Criteria of Success
   A. The organization defines success on the basis of development of human resources, teamwork, and concern for people.
   B. The organization defines success on the basis of having the most unique or the newest products. It is a product leader and innovator.
   C. The organization defines success on the basis of market penetration and market share. Competitive market leadership is key.
   D. The organization defines success on the basis of efficiency. Dependable delivery, smooth scheduling, and low cost production are critical.

REFERENCES

Barney, J. B. (1991). Firm resources and sustained competitive advantage. *Journal of Management, 17,* 99–120.

Beyer, J., & Cameron, K. S. (1997). Organizational culture. In D. Druckman, J. Singer, & H. Van Cott (Eds.), *Enhancing organizational performance* (pp. 65–96). Washington, DC: National Academy Press.

Cameron, K. S. (1986). Effectiveness as paradox: Conflict and consensus in conceptions of organizational effectiveness. *Management Science, 32,* 539–553.

Cameron, K. S. (1997). Techniques for making organizations effective. In D. Druckman, J. Singer, & H. Van Cott (Eds.), *Enhancing organizational performance* (pp. 39–64). Washington, DC: National Academy Press.

Cameron, K. S. (2003). Ethics, virtuousness, and constant change. In N. Tichy & M. McGill

(Eds.), *The ethical challenge* (pp. 85–94). San Francisco: Jossey-Bass.

Cameron, K. S., & Ettington, D. R. (1988). The conceptual foundations of organizational culture. In *Higher education: Handbook of theory and research* (pp. 356–396). New York: Agathon.

Cameron, K. S., & Freeman, S. J. (1991). Cultural congruence, strength, and type: Relationships to effectiveness. In *Research in organizational change and development* (Vol. 5, pp. 23–58). Greenwich, CT: JAI.

Cameron, K. S., & Mora, C. M. (2003). *Corporate culture and financial success of mergers and acquisitions.* Working paper, University of Michigan Business School.

Cameron, K. S., & Quinn, R. E. (2006). *Diagnosing and changing organizational culture.* San Francisco: Jossey-Bass.

Cameron, K. S., & Whetten, D. A. (1981). Perceptions of organizational effectiveness across organizational life cycles. *Administrative Science Quarterly, 27,* 524–544.

Denison, D. (1989). *Corporate culture and organizational effectiveness.* New York: John Wiley & Sons.

Detert, J. R., Schroeder, R. G., & Mauriel, J. J. (2000). A framework for linking culture and involvement initiatives in organizations. *Academy of Management Review, 25,* 850–863.

Hampton-Turner, C. (1981). *Maps of the mind.* New York: Macmillan.

Hooijberg, R., & Petrock, F. (1993). On cultural change: Using the competing values framework to help leaders to a transformational strategy. *Human Resource Management, 32,* 29–51.

Kotter, J. P. (1995, March–April). Leading change: Why transformation efforts fail. *Harvard Business Review,* 59–67.

Kroeber, A. L., & Kluckhohn, C. (1952). *Culture: A critical review of concepts and definitions.* New York: Vintage.

Lawrence, P. R., & Nohria, N. (2002). *Driven: How human nature shapes our choices.* San Francisco: Jossey-Bass.

Martin, J. (1992). *Cultures in organizations.* New York: Oxford University Press.

Martin, J., Feldman, M., Hatch, M. J., & Sitkin, S. (1983). The uniqueness paradox in organizational stories. *Administrative Science Quarterly, 28,* 438–452.

Mason, R. O., & Mitroff, I. I. (1973). A program of research in management. *Management Science, 19,* 475–487.

Mintzberg, H. (1979). *The structuring of organizations.* Englewood Cliffs, NJ: Prentice Hall.

Mitroff, I. I. (1983). *Stakeholders of the organizational mind.* San Francisco: Jossey-Bass.

Mitroff, I. I., & Kilmann, R. H. (1975). Stories managers tell: A new tool for organizational problem solving. *Management Review, 64,* 18–28.

O'Reilly, C. A., & Chatman, J. A. (1996). Culture as social control: Corporations, cults, and commitment. In B. M. Staw & L. L. Cummings (Eds.), *Research in organizational behavior* (Vol. 18, pp. 157–200). Greenwich, CT: JAI.

Ouchi, W. G. (1981). *Theory Z: How American business can meet the Japanese challenge.* Reading, MA: Addison-Wesley.

Piaget, J. (1932). *The moral development of a child.* New York: Harcourt Brace.

Porter, M. E. (1980). *Competitive strategy: Techniques for analyzing industries and competitors.* New York: Free Press.

Quinn, R. E., & Cameron, K. S. (1983). Organizational life cycles and shifting criteria of effectiveness. *Management Science, 29,* 33–51.

Quinn, R. E., & Rohrbaugh, J. (1981). A special model of effectiveness criteria: Towards a competing values approach to organizational analysis. *Management Science, 29,* 363–377.

Quinn, R. E., & Spreitzer, G. M. (1991). The psychometrics of the competing values culture instrument and an analysis of the impact of organizational culture on quality of life. In *Research in organizational change and development* (Vol. 5, pp. 115–142). Greenwich, CT: JAI.

Sathe, V. (1983). Implications of corporate culture: A manager's guide to action. *Organizational Dynamics, 12,* 4–23.

Schein, E. (1996). Culture: The missing concept in organizational studies. *Administrative Science Quarterly, 41,* 229–240.

Schneider, B. (1990). *Organizational climate and culture.* San Francisco: Jossey-Bass.

Staw, B. M., Sandelands, L., & Dutton, J. E. (1981). Threat-rigidity effects in organizational behavior:

A multilevel analysis. *Administrative Science Quarterly, 26,* 501–524.

Trice, H., & Beyer, J. (1993). *The cultures of work organizations.* Englewood Cliffs, NJ: Prentice Hall.

Weber, M. (1947). *The theory of social and economic organization* (Trans. K. Henderson & T. Parsons). New York: Free Press.

Weick, K. E. (1993). The collapse of sensemaking in organizations: The Mann Gulch disaster. *Administrative Science Quarterly, 38,* 628–652.

Wilber, K. (2000). *A theory of everything: An integral vision for business, politics, science, and spirituality.* Boston: Shambhala.

Wilkins, A. (1989). *Developing corporate character.* San Francisco: Jossey-Bass.

Williamson, O. (1975). *Markets and hierarchies: Analysis and antitrust implications.* New York: Free Press.

24

Organization Development at the Top of the Enterprise

DAVID A. NADLER

The ideas presented in this chapter trace back to a set of experiences that are almost 30 years old. In the mid-1970s I was the project manager on a research effort at the University of Michigan related to organization change. The project I happened to be leading concerned organization change in health care delivery. My research team watched as a separate team of consultants worked to improve the quality of health care and the quality of working life for health care workers through planned changed focused on a surgical unit of a major metropolitan medical center. For 4 years we observed the diagnosis, the involvement of labor and management, the use of different interventions, and the engagement of different individuals and groups in the hospital. At the end of this time, we came to the conclusion that the effort was a failure (Hanlon, Nadler, & Gladstein, 1985).

The insight that we drew from this was that it was difficult, if not impossible, to make profound and lasting change occur in a unit that was embedded in a larger organization. No matter how good the consultants were, too many of the variables that affected behavior on the unit were constrained by the larger system.

Several years later, we received a call from the president of this same hospital. Having observed the work that was done, he said he was interested in it and now wanted to retain me in a consulting role to address the issues for the whole hospital. We undertook a major diagnosis and developed an approach that would address the structural, process, and behavioral issues related to change of health care delivery in the hospital. However, within a few months, the initiative was stalled because of resistance by the management of the medical center that was the parent organization of the hospital itself. The faculty and disciplinary departments were threatened by the new cross-disciplinary and team-based approach to delivering care. Once again, the larger system had been a constraining factor on the implementation of organization change.

In contrast to this case of the hospital, along with my partners at Delta Consulting (later Mercer Delta), I became engaged with David Kearns, the CEO of Xerox, on a major organization change related to quality improvement. Beginning work in 1982, we were able to contribute to significantly changing the organization in relation to quality, culminating in Xerox winning a Baldrige National Quality Award in 1989. In the case of Xerox, change was driven from the highest levels of the organization. This work is described in detail elsewhere (Kearns & Nadler, 1992).

From these experiences and others over the subsequent years, we arrived at certain conclusions about organization change:

- Organizations are complex and interdependent systems (Katz & Kahn, 1978), and therefore change must be addressed at the system level.
- Addressing change at the system level means engaging "the top"—the leadership of the institution.
- Therefore, working with "the top" (institutional leadership) is a means to an end, not an end in itself. The ultimate objective is significant transformation of the whole organization, or enterprise change.
- Enterprise change involves a whole range of different elements and interventions, not just working at the top. Working with the top is necessary but not sufficient.

With that perspective, this chapter addresses the issue of how organization development (OD) applies at the top of the organization, with institutional leadership. I begin by talking about the concept of enterprise change and how the OD practitioner comes to engage with the client around enterprise change. I identify what I see as the key critical components of enterprise change. I then focus on three specific elements of enterprise change that are particularly relevant to the top. I discuss a way of thinking about consulting to the CEO. I outline some of the unique issues of working with the executive team, the highest-level management team of the organization. Finally, I address the emerging area of applying OD to the board of directors.

CONCEPT OF ENTERPRISE CHANGE

The ultimate objective of the OD practitioner working at the top is to be able to assist in bringing about change that ultimately affects the entire enterprise. In this section, I describe my way of thinking about this concept of enterprise change, starting with a focus on who are the clients for this work and ending up with a description of the role of the OD consultant. This point of view reflects my experiences and what I think is an effective way for the OD consultant to think about the challenge of having an impact on the whole organization.

My starting point is a way of thinking about organizations and change. I have written about this topic elsewhere (Nadler, 1998), but it is important to note three important assumptions. The first is that I think about the organization as an open system with interdependent elements that include work, people, formal organization arrangements, and the informal organization. This approach to organization and change is called the congruence model of organizations (Katz & Kahn, 1978). Efforts to bring about organization change must take account of those systemic properties (as noted in the opening vignette about the medical center). The second assumption is that as open systems, organizations basically change in response to (or anticipation of) changes in the environment. Ultimately, organizations face a change imperative that causes them to change or die (Nadler, Shaw, & Walton, 1994). The third assumption is that leaders of the enterprise are critical players in bringing about change (Nadler, 1998) and that our role as OD consultants is to help those leaders engage the whole organization in the process of change. Changing the organization is the role of the leader, not the consultant, who at best can be of assistance to the leader and others in bringing about change in response to the demands of the environment.

In this context, we have developed a way of thinking about enterprise change and what it involves. Of necessity, the clients for enterprise change are CEOs and leaders of organizations, both private and public. The focus is on CEOs because of their unique ability to create real change and to have a profound impact at the enterprise level; consequently, the OD work is most successful, and the client relationships most impactful, when the CEO is the client.

More broadly, the clients constitute the executive leadership at the public company or public enterprise level—the CEO, COO, executive team, and board—but the relationships extend beyond that level and out into the organization. The OD practitioner may work with different functions, different specialties, and different operating units as part of the broader change effort.

What makes a client? The potential for true clientship occurs when certain conditions exist:

- The potential client (I'll use the CEO as proxy for this role) recognizes the need for change.
- The need for change has created enough pain or frustration that the CEO feels the need to do something about it.
- The CEO is aware of his or her own limitations, or the limitations of his or her team or leadership group, and realizes that he or she cannot do it alone.
- The CEO has crossed the bridge to realize that he or she needs some outside assistance and has begun to search for help.

When these conditions exist, there is the potential for a relationship with a client around the challenge of enterprise change. What exactly is enterprise change? It is organization change that focuses on the system as a whole and that will create value rather than destroy it. This change is profound and pervasive; it touches on a number of ways in which the organization functions. It is understood and owned by the enterprise leadership, but it cannot be imposed by a single person or even by a small group. It is addressed to the organization as a total system and includes elements of both the organization's "hardware" (the technical systems such as structure and strategy) and the "software" (the social system). It is high-impact, lasting change that increases the organization's effectiveness.

CHANGE STRATEGY

As the executive leaders begin to see the need for enterprise change, they also begin to appreciate that this comes about ultimately through the development of a change strategy. Successful change depends on a strategy that is data based and diagnostic. It depends on leaders who, through their ownership and participation, become the instruments of change. It is both top down and bottom up. It is evolutionary, both planned and opportunistic; you can't sit and build a 3- or 4-year change plan down to every level because the world is also changing and you are always aiming at a set of moving targets.

ENTERPRISE CHANGE ELEMENTS

Enterprise change is a term that covers a multitude of activities. In actuality, successful organization change must touch on all the elements of the congruence model. However, a selected set of points of intervention constitute the vital few in bringing about enterprise change. Specifically, we have focused on 10 elements of enterprise change that we consider critical and where the bulk of our work occurs.

We have thought about this in terms of a sophisticated client who is thinking, "In order to effectively make this change, I will need to. . . ." Each of the possible answers describes the change elements. The elements, the core question (in client terms), and a description are presented in Table 24.1.

Table 24.1   Elements of Enterprise Change: The Vital Few

Element	In the Words of the CEO, "How Do I . . ."	Explanation
CEO effectiveness	. . . maximize my positive impact as a leader?	Working with CEOs to help them become more effective in their various roles
Executive team development	. . . get the right players around the table and working together?	Shaping the composition of the executive team
Corporate governance	. . . engage the board on the challenges we face and the change needed?	Building an effective and appropriate engaged board of directors and a collaborative CEO–board relationship
Strategy	. . . develop a compelling strategic direction the leadership owns?	Developing corporate strategy in a way that engages the leadership and creates a foundation for effective execution
Organization design	. . . design structures and processes capable of implementing the strategy?	Developing an organization architecture that fits and supports the strategic direction
Management process	. . . define roles and rules for critical decision making?	Designing the way the leadership will perform critical leadership tasks, including decision making and resource allocation
Organization culture	. . . create shared expectations about how people work together?	Creating an operating environment in the organization that reflects the espoused values and beliefs and supports the strategic vision
Leadership development	. . . ensure that we have leaders aligned with and capable of executing the strategy?	Assessing the leadership gap and developing approaches to ensure that the enterprise has the needed leadership and that the leadership is aligned with the strategic direction
Communication	. . . effectively communicate our intentions and actions, internally and externally?	Developing core messages to help constituencies understand change, getting information from constituencies, and broadly communicating strategies
Change metrics	. . . determine whether the actions we're taking are creating the necessary results?	Developing the metrics and data-gathering methods that help leaders monitor progress of the changes they are trying to implement

DUAL ROLES: CHANGE ARCHITECT AND TRUSTED ADVISOR

In this view of OD, the practitioner must successfully and simultaneously fill the roles of both change architect and trusted advisor. Playing both roles at once is the ultimate art of OD consulting. The change architect role entails the ability to both recognize and anticipate the client's needs and to design and develop interventions to help the client successfully address those needs. The change architect helps the client develop a deliberate, sequenced plan for addressing the various elements of enterprise change, and as the work proceeds, constantly lays the groundwork for subsequent streams of work that will help the client achieve its objectives. To be successful, the change architect must be adept at developing, scoping, deploying, and managing multiple and varied streams of work in new and existing client systems.

In successful engagements, another role emerges: The client grows to view the OD practitioner as a trusted advisor (Maister, Green, & Galford, 2000). That's not easy; few CEOs are actively or consciously looking for more people to add to their inner circle. This is a privileged status that must be earned during the course of doing real work; it is based on experience, maturity, candor, confidentiality, empathy, and the ability to put the client's best interests first while subsuming one's own ego and personal agendas.

Many OD consultants naturally gravitate toward one role or the other. Both are valuable, but it is the combination of the two that creates deep, long-lasting relationships that can weather the inevitable ups and downs of client relationships while leveraging the full range of the consultant's capabilities to help the client.

The dual role imposes tremendous responsibility on OD practitioners; they must constantly avoid abusing the client's trust by overcharging or underperforming. It becomes a delicate balancing act between seeking ways to deploy one's own resources while being mindful that the trusted relationship is not a license to sell work the client does not really need or to cut corners on delivering what has been promised. Ultimately, the truly successful OD consultants—the ones who maintain long-term, high-impact relationships—are those who consistently put the client's interests first.

Enterprise Change and Working With the Top

In the first section, I provided a brief overview of enterprise change as a context for working at the top. (See Figure 24.1 for a summary view of this concept.) OD work at the top is a critical, necessary, but not sufficient aspect of bringing about enterprise change. In some ways, all 10 elements need to be addressed by the top, but 3 of them in particular involve in-depth consultation with the top as the direct client of the work:

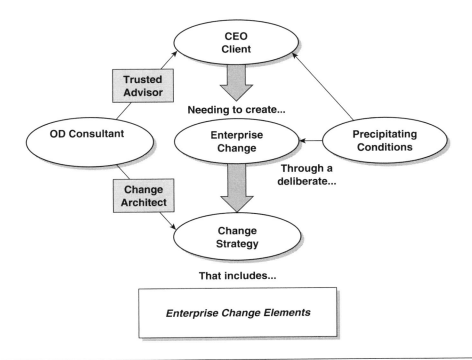

Figure 24.1   The Enterprise Change Concept

- CEO effectiveness: The OD consultant works with the CEO directly to help him or her become a more effective leader of the organization and leader of change.
- Executive team development: The practitioner engages with the most senior team of the organization to help it become more effective.
- Corporate governance: The consultant works with both the CEO and the board to help develop more effective processes of governance for the enterprise.

In the remainder of this chapter I provide perspectives, concepts, and a point of view of applying OD to each of these three elements.

Working With CEOs

The key to working with CEOs, particularly CEOs of large, complex public companies, is to understand the world in which they operate. It is a world like no other. The popular image of a CEO is that of an all-powerful figure—a ship's captain, for instance, setting a course and issuing orders to a crew that responds without question or pause. Nothing could be further from the truth.

In reality, the CEO sits at the center of a universe of stakeholders, both internal and external, who constantly attempt to impose difficult and often conflicting demands on the CEO and the organization (see Figure 24.2). Each set of stakeholders has its own expectations, its own interests, and its own standards for assessing the CEO's performance. The CEO's challenge is to constantly weigh the importance of those stakeholders and balance their demands against his or her own vision, strategy, and expectations.

The exact nature and relative importance of the stakeholder groups vary by organization, but some of these constituencies are always present. At the most basic level, they can be identified as either internal or external stakeholders. The external stakeholders include the "value chain constituencies": customers, suppliers, strategic partners, and the financial community. The external social constituencies, which very often exert demands that conflict with those of

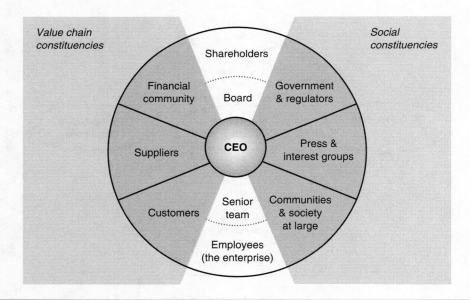

Figure 24.2   The World of the CEO

SOURCE: Nadler, D. A., Spencer, J. L., & Associates (Eds.). *Executive teams.* Copyright © 1998 San Francisco: Jossey-Bass, 1998. Reprinted with permission of John Wiley & Sons, Inc.

the value chain constituencies, include government agencies and regulators, the press, interest groups, local communities, and society at large. Internally, the CEO deals with several stakeholder groups that often impose conflicting demands: the board, senior management, and the general workforce. The final stakeholder group, which encompasses both internal and external constituencies, is the shareholders, ranging from huge institutional investors to day traders to employees and retirees.

So one aspect of the CEO's job that makes it unique is that he or she is the only person in the organization who is in direct contact with—and is directly held accountable by—the full universe of stakeholders. No one else in the organization has a job that comes close in terms of scope and complexity. On a daily basis, the CEO, more than anyone else, is dealing with the demands, concerns, and expectations of multiple constituencies. In every interaction of every day, CEOs are confronted with issues that represent either a personal or institutional agenda. They are surrounded by people seeking access, attention, and approval. And the job has become even more demanding. CEOs are now acutely aware that more than ever before, any misstep can dramatically increase the chances of failure.

There is one other factor that defines the world of the CEO: The notion that "it's lonely at the top" may be a cliché, but it's absolutely true. Anyone who has worked closely with CEOs can attest to the loneliness and isolation experienced by these powerful executives. They have no peers in their organization. There is rarely anyone in the company with whom they can temporarily step out from behind the desk and share their fears and concerns. Recently, a new CEO said, "The thing that was the greatest surprise to me in this job was the intense and profound loneliness." They are convinced—and rightly so—that every person who comes to see them is there for a reason and has a personal agenda that will color the tone and substance of their interactions. They can never allow themselves the luxury of accepting advice or suggestions at face value.

That is a very difficult way to live and work. Many CEOs harden themselves to that reality and conclude that the only way to do the job is to keep their own counsel and trust their own instincts. But a growing number of CEOs have come to realize that they need unbiased advice, feedback, coaching, new ideas, and fresh perspectives. So they look to professionals who can provide any or all of that. The most prominent among these advisors are lawyers, investment bankers and, of course, management consultants, including OD practitioners.

CEOs Are Attractive Clients

Many OD consultants seek CEO clients for the status this level of work confers. If you are working with the top of the organization, it must mean you are at the top of your own profession. The nature of the issues involved is challenging and intellectually stimulating. A vicarious thrill comes from being personally involved—even from the sidelines—in decisions that shape a company's future. And if we are frank with ourselves, we will admit the personal satisfaction that comes from having these important, powerful, and sometimes magnetic personalities turn to us for guidance and advice. It would be both silly and dishonest to discount the personal gratification that often comes with applying OD at this level.

But more importantly, working directly with CEOs offers the greatest opportunity for providing real value to organizations because the CEO is the real driver of organization change. Populist change theories notwithstanding, our experience clearly indicates that profound, sustainable, enterprise-wide change is led from the top. As frustrating as the CEO's job might be, only he or she has access to all the levers that drive change—the ability to shape the strategy, the structure, the culture, and the talent. The CEO enjoys more freedom of action than any other leader in the organization.

In most situations, he or she is the final decision maker and the ultimate arbiter of all appeals. Working directly with the CEO acknowledges that leaders lower down in the organization lack the leverage to sustain change and chart strategy for the organization.

By virtue of his or her unique position, the CEO is in greater need of outside advice. He or she has no peers to turn to in the organization, no internal aide whose advice is not colored by some agenda. The CEO needs the advice and counsel of an experienced OD professional whose only agenda is one of enhancing the CEO's effectiveness and likelihood of success.

Quite often, the nature of OD consulting that the CEO needs depends on certain stages that operate in parallel with the CEO's tenure in office. To be sure, these scenarios vary with changing business conditions, but in general there are four critical time periods in a CEO's tenure where the consulting needs are different:

1. *Perplexed New CEO.* Many CEOs spend much of their careers working and hoping to land the top job. But once they find out they are actually going to get it, their first reaction is often, "Now what do I do? How do I get started, and what should I do first?" Depending on the circumstances—whether they have been promoted from within or recruited from the outside, whether they are assuming control of a company that is doing well or one that is in deep trouble, whether they have landed the job through an orderly succession plan or been appointed to replace a predecessor who has been suddenly removed, whether they are an industry veteran or newcomer, whether they are inheriting an intact senior team or need to create one overnight—the new CEO may need OD help on any number of fronts, ranging from organization assessment to turnaround advice and strategic planning.

2. *Frustrated Sophomore CEO.* In many cases, a new CEO takes office with a clear strategy and plan of action, only to find after the first year in office that none of the projected changes is actually happening. A few years ago, the second-year CEO of a large pharmaceutical company came to visit us, complaining that he felt that he was on the bridge of a large ship, pulling at the controls and finding that they were not attached to anything. This man was confronted by a syndrome that frustrates many sophomore CEOs: They are doing all the things they thought were necessary to set a new course or change the culture or improve performance, but none of their tactics seem to have much impact. They turn to OD practitioners for help in identifying the barriers and using the real levers of organization change.

3. *Worried Midterm CEO.* Given the nature of today's business environment, it is inevitable that every CEO will experience at least one—and probably more than one—episode of significant crisis that necessitates radical, large-scale change in the organization. It might result from new forms of competition, disruptive technologies, or shifts in public policy, but whatever the cause, the organization has to find fundamentally new ways of doing business. Few organizations have the internal capacity to design, lead, manage, and sustain that kind of transformational change without outside professional help.

4. *Reflecting Late-Term CEO.* As they approach the natural end of their tenures, many CEOs become concerned with two issues: managing the selection and development of their successor and shaping their own legacy. On numerous occasions we have been approached by CEOs with very few years to go, realizing that they had significant succession problems yet no one to talk to about the candidates and criteria, except perhaps an uninformed and passive board. These CEOs need confidential advice and candid soul-searching that only outside OD experts can help with.

Understanding the Spectrum of Consulting Roles

The ability of OD practitioners to provide value beyond their particular areas of expertise underscores the paramount importance of the relationship between them and the client and highlights the critical relationship between the content of the consulting and the consultative approach that is used to engage the client with the content. In other words, every outside OD consultant interacts with the CEO on two dimensions:

Ideas versus actions: Does the OD practitioner bring fresh perspectives, information on best practices, or a new "Big Idea," or is she or he helping the CEO identify specific actions to take in order to address a specific issue?

Prescriptive versus facilitative: Does the consultant recommend a specific decision or course of action, or does she or he see the role as helping the client identify a range of alternatives and provide a process through which the client selects the most appropriate choice?

The work of every OD consultant, specialist, and advisor to CEOs combines some mix of these two dimensions (Figure 24.3). The interplay of the two dimensions suggests that most CEO-level OD work falls into six categories, which we define as follows:

Technician: Highly prescriptive about specific actions the CEO should take (e.g., crisis communications, legal strategies for handling specific litigation).

Guru: Also highly prescriptive but with regard to concepts or ideas at an abstract level rather than specific actions.

Content expert: Somewhat prescriptive, offering strategic advice on broad areas such as leadership or organization change.

Process facilitator: Brings skills and approach to help clients identify problems and develop solutions.

Coach: A pure facilitation role focusing on the client's personal development rather than on broader organization issues.

Sage: A rare and unique role in which the CEO has a relationship with an OD advisor who brings new ideas but interacts in a facilitative manner to help the CEO think through significant issues. This role usually is enacted in combination with one or more of the other roles.

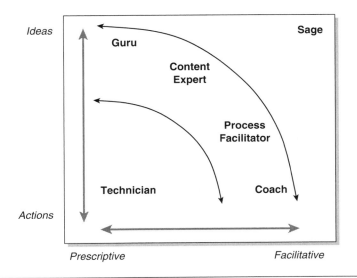

Figure 24.3   Consulting Roles With CEOs

Of course, these role designations are somewhat narrow and arbitrary; OD consulting relationships, particularly those that extend over a period of years, become quite complex, and the dividing lines between categories grow fuzzy. And that is our point: Consulting relationships, like any other relationships, are dynamic and evolving. If they are successful, they change, deepen, and grow with the passage of time.

Roles and Relationship Building

As we reflect on these different approaches and roles, we assume that the OD practitioner is ultimately interested in two objectives. First, she or he seeks to have impact. The real measure of professional and personal effectiveness is whether anything changes as a result of the engagement with the client. Second, at the CEO level, the complexity of the problems and context usually means that impact cannot occur without continuity of the relationship. Most of the critical problems that the CEO encounters are not amenable to one-shot, single interventions. Building on those assumptions and using this approach as a general depiction of the range of possible CEO consulting relationships, I offer three observations.

First, successful, long-term OD consultants can start in almost any of the roles but almost invariably end up combining two or more roles. Less effective ones tend to get stuck where they started, in terms of both their content domain and a single form of delivery.

Second, to apply OD successfully in some combination of these modes, the practitioner must fill the role of trusted advisor. In their insightful book *The Trusted Advisor,* Maister et al. (2000) suggest that trustworthiness results from the interplay of four components: credibility, reliability, intimacy, and the one to be wary of, self-orientation. It's an interesting way of defining a complex relationship; as the term "trusted advisor" continues to gain currency, there will undoubtedly be others. But the underlying idea is right: Technical expertise, in the absence of a trusting relationship, will result in a severely limited OD consulting role with seriously diminished opportunity for impact.

Finally, for OD practitioners who operate primarily in the process facilitator and coach roles, it is the relationship that actually becomes the content rather than a means to communicate the content. The skills and personal attributes needed to develop and sustain meaningful, long-term relationships become infinitely more important than any specific content knowledge or expertise.

Developing the CEO Relationship

The role of trusted advisor to a CEO is the goal, not the starting point, of an OD relationship. Almost always, the relationship starts with a specific assignment and a particular piece of work. If the relationship progresses well, the focus moves from narrow, segmented work to a much broader role that might involve helping the CEO develop and implement an agenda. The important point is that the relationship has to evolve naturally; OD practitioners who walk into the room for the first time and immediately attempt to create an artificial trusted advisor relationship are almost always doomed to failure.

Experience suggests that several elements are critical to building this relationship—a list not too different from that suggested in *The Trusted Advisor* (Maister et al., 2000). First and foremost, the relationship must be built on a foundation of substantive, high-quality work and beneficial advice. It doesn't matter how terrific the personal chemistry is between the OD consultant and the CEO; if the work does not add value and the advice does not make sense, the relationship is not going anywhere.

The second critical element is the tone of the engagement process: The OD consultant should be respectful of the client yet willing to confront him or her on critical issues. It is a delicate balance, to be sure, but early on the consultant is not just another member of the CEO's staff and must be prepared to push back—and push back aggressively—if the CEO seems to be avoiding an issue or discounting important data.

Trust is the third critical element. Over time, the OD practitioner must demonstrate a commitment to total confidentiality and the ability to consistently deliver information accurately, completely, and dispassionately, without distortion, exaggeration, or spin. The CEO must become completely confident that the consultant is not taking advantage of their special relationship to either send inappropriate messages to others in the organization or, conversely, to act as a conduit for underlings who want to pursue personal agendas by conveying information through the consultant.

The final element is positive personal engagement. In essence, this is the corollary of the first element. Without substantive, value-added work and advice, the relationship goes nowhere, yet as one of our clients once observed, "If I don't enjoy the personal relationship, it doesn't matter how smart you are, I won't keep working with you." Personal chemistry is critical to the trusted advisor relationship.

Process Determines Content

The process of working with CEOs has certain similarities to OD consultation with other clients, but there are also some important differences. For one thing, asking questions often can be far more effective than providing answers. By nature, most CEOs tend not to be highly introspective; they are oriented toward action. In their role, it is essential to be able to make decisions and then move on quickly, not spending much time on reflection or second-guessing. Given their range of responsibilities, CEOs have to be able to do that. The OD practitioner can play an important and unique role by providing the CEO with a safe space in which to step back and reflect privately and confidentially on concerns, doubts, and

sources of anxiety that may be crucial to impending business decisions. The simple question, "What's keeping you awake in the middle of the night?" may sound a bit trite, but it is amazing what responses it sometimes elicits.

A second key point is that the process of working with CEOs emphasizes discussion. The real value of this consultation comes from informal give and take, not formal presentations. Certainly, there are situations, generally in group settings, where the CEO will want to see data presented in a formal way. Nor does the idea of discussion diminish the importance of preparation for each private meeting with the CEO. But these meetings have to be tailored to the CEO's schedule, energy, and priorities, and the OD consultant must have the flexibility to use whatever time is available in the most beneficial way.

Third, a good deal of the value that the OD practitioner provides comes from structuring information so as to give a fresh viewpoint. It is not that she or he brings brand new information (although this may be the case) but that she or he provides a cognitive structure to make the information more meaningful. One can think of the consultant as not only gathering data but also transforming these data into information, information into knowledge, and ultimately knowledge into action. The value, therefore, comes from helping the client to look at an existing situation in a new way.

Finally, sometimes the most important service the OD consultant provides to the CEO is simply to listen. As mentioned previously, the CEO experiences a tremendous sense of loneliness and isolation; her or his day is filled with issues and problems that cannot be discussed candidly with anyone in the organization. Like any of us, the CEO sometimes needs an outlet to just vent anger, frustration, or anxiety. The practitioner should understand that there are times when the best way to help is just to listen, because the CEO is not really looking for advice—just a safe audience.

Dilemmas in Working With CEOs

Applying OD to CEOs not only entails some unique processes, it also presents the real possibility of handling difficult dilemmas that often arise in the relationship. These are among the most challenging:

Insulation: During their tenures, CEOs tend to become somewhat isolated. As time passes and they become more comfortable in their jobs, they tend to rely on a limited number of trusted subordinates for their information. OD practitioners must be wary of duplicating that same pattern. All too often, in the later stages of the relationship, consultants restrict their interactions to the CEO and perhaps one or two other senior executives, which severely limits the value they can bring to the CEO in terms of objective information and different perspective.

Clientship: Sooner or later when working with CEOs, many OD consultants face an incredibly difficult question: Who is the real client, the CEO or the organization? The simplistic answer is that there is no conflict; by helping the CEO perform effectively, the consultant is providing value to the entire enterprise. But in some situations, it becomes evident that the CEO is incapable of providing the kind of leadership the organization needs in order to address severe challenges, and no amount of coaching or advice will change that. Consequently, the consultant may conclude that the organization would be better off with a different CEO. There is no easy solution to this problem; it is just important to recognize that it is a perplexing dilemma that comes with the territory. One approach we have taken is to consciously and deliberately discuss with the CEO whether he or she is able and willing to undertake the actions that are necessary. If not, then we have, at times, terminated our relationship with the CEO and the organization rather than collude with the CEO to sustain the perception that issues are being worked constructively.

Influence balance: In working with CEOs, OD consultants run the constant risk of being perceived in the organization as having either too much or too little influence. The role entails an endless balancing act. If consultants are perceived as having insufficient influence, it becomes difficult to get on people's calendars, to get invited to the right meetings, to be privy to necessary information. On the other hand, OD practitioners can sometimes be perceived as a kind of Svengali, the mysterious figure behind the curtain who is really pulling all the strings—a role people come to resent and one that severely limits the consultant's effectiveness.

Backstairs channel: As mentioned previously, people who perceive a close relationship between the OD consultant and the CEO will seek ways to use her or him as a conduit to the executive office. The consultant must be careful to maintain relationships with others in the organization without being used as a tool for advancing other people's agendas.

Overidentification: It is inevitable, over time, that a close association with the CEO can color the OD practitioner's view of people and issues in the organization. That is a natural consequence of being privy to information that others do not have; you begin to tell yourself, "If they knew what the CEO knows (and what I know), they'd understand his decision." It is essential not to become so close to the CEO, or so reliant on the same sources of information as the CEO, that the OD consultant's perspective becomes indistinguishable.

Inflated ego: In working with CEOs, some OD practitioners tend to forget that they are consultants, not CEOs. They get carried away with their own sense of influence, power, and access. They become insufferably arrogant; they forget that they are in the room to give advice, not to make decisions. The consultant becomes intoxicated as a result of the closeness to the throne and the perception of influence that goes along with that proximity.

Assessing people: In the course of the OD relationship, as the CEO gains trust in the consultant's judgment, it's inevitable for the CEO to seek her or his assessment of people in the organization. The consultant's role needs to be clear, and if executives are to be assessed, it should be through an explicit and well-thought-out process, not through random interactions and narrow impressions. But the fact remains that the CEO will want to know what the OD practitioner thinks and will continue to ask.

Clearly, the relationship between the CEO and the trusted OD advisor is fraught with danger. To be successful, and to provide real value to the client, the practitioner must bring to the table a rare combination of content knowledge and process skills. He or she must understand that working with CEOs depends on all the abilities they needed to succeed with clients at lower levels, and then a whole set of unique capabilities beyond that. It is a professional OD role that demands maturity, confidence, keen intellect, and emotional insight. Few can play successfully at this level, but those who do earn the satisfaction of influencing the direction and performance of entire organizations.

WORKING WITH THE EXECUTIVE TEAM

As we think about the world of the CEO (Figure 24.3), the team of direct reports to the CEO, or the executive team, is a critical part of the CEO's world. In many ways, the executive team is the link between the CEO and the rest of the organization. Although the CEO has many direct interactions, much of the work of leadership happens through others, and for the CEO, those others constitute the executive team. Over the past decade the growing use of executive teams has underscored the unique problems involving this most senior team of all. This group of powerful men and women encounters the full range of problems and challenges that face every other team. Above and beyond those universal issues, however, this team's performance is complicated by the unique dynamics that exist only at the very top of the organization. Those dynamics, in turn, create a set of special demands on CEOs in the role of leader of the executive team and special challenges for the OD practitioner who seeks to provide assistance in this setting.

Much of what has been written about executive teams has focused primarily on their structure and function (Finkelstein & Hambrick, 1990; Hambrick, Cho, & Chen, 1996; Michel & Hambrick, 1992). Without question those are important issues. Yet they fail to come to grips with the reality of what goes on when these ambitious, powerful, and political people assemble behind closed doors. Indeed, both in the room and when they are apart, team members' behavior plays out a complex web of relationships—relationships between the members themselves, relationships between the CEO and individual members, and the relationship of the CEO to the group as a collective entity. The degree to which the CEO understands, shapes, and successfully manages the interpersonal dynamics of this pivotal group invariably has a major bearing on the ultimate success of the entire organization.

CEO as Team Leader

It is important to keep in mind that although CEOs are, by definition, the chief executives of the entire enterprise, they must also shoulder the responsibility of leading their own team. In general terms, the CEO plays this role in three basic venues: as the designer of the team, as the active leader in the room when the team is together, and as the leader, coordinator, and shaper of dynamics when the team is not in session.

First, the CEO is, again by definition, the designer of the team. The CEO makes the initial decision whether to have an executive team and then goes about creating it in whatever form she or he deems useful. It is the CEO who determines the composition of the team and its structure, who plays which roles, and the team's work processes, the specific ways in which the team members will work together.

Second, the CEO is the leader of the team when it meets in the room. She or he convenes the group, wields the gavel, and plays the primary role in shaping the team's dynamics.

The CEO serves as both participant and leader and makes the crucial decisions about both content and processes—what the team will work on and how it will go about its work.

Third, the CEO is also the leader of the team out of the room. For a host of reasons, the most powerful team in any organization is also the team that tends to spend the least time meeting face to face. Certainly, team members spend some time together, in both regularly scheduled and periodic offsite meetings. But they might get together only weekly or even monthly. In the physical sense, you will rarely find all members of the executive team working near each other; in fact, the more they operate as a cloistered team, the less effective they are likely to be in their roles as leaders of their respective operations. Often, they are separated by geography, in both micro and macro terms.

Consequently, the CEO's leadership of the team has to extend beyond the time members spend together in the room. She or he must also shape the team through individual interactions and by managing the team's structures and processes. So it is the responsibility of the CEO to do all the things necessary to oversee those team processes—including those that go on even when the team is not working face to face—that have tremendous implications for the rest of the organization.

Special Aspects of the Executive Team

As CEOs pursue these various functions as leaders of their executive teams, they have to keep in mind the factors that differentiate this team from all others to which they have been exposed over the course of their careers. To be sure, the executive team exhibits all the traits of any other team and has to be understood first and foremost as a team (Schein, 1969). As with any team, it operates at the levels of content (what it does), process (how it does it), and affect (the emotions that people bring to or develop in the team).

Obviously, all three—content, process, and affect—exert powerful influences on each other and on the effectiveness of any team. However, to differentiate the executive team from all other teams, our main interest is in the team's process and affect: what goes on and how it is dealt with. In that context there are three fundamental differences between the executive team and other senior-level teams.

The first difference has to do with power and more specifically the relative distribution of power between the team leader (the CEO) and the team members. There is always some imbalance of power between leaders and members, but in the case of the executive team the distribution of power is disproportionately tilted in favor of the leader. Unlike any other team leader, the CEO wields power that is nearly absolute. There are several reasons for this.

To begin with, almost all the CEO's decisions are final; there are no avenues of appeal. As the organization's ultimate administrator of sanctions and rewards, the CEO enjoys tremendous flexibility with fewer external controls than any other manager. What is important, however, is the general perception among team members that the CEO possesses unlimited power—and the perception of power is tantamount to reality.

The second factor that skews the distribution of power in executive teams involves the tenure of the CEO, which tends to be longer and more determinate than that of other team leaders. On most teams, senior or otherwise, the members really have no idea how long the leader is likely to be around. Leaders might be due for a promotion or transfer, they might be job hunting, or they might be on the way out—there is really no way of knowing. That is usually not the case with the CEO (with the exception of CEO removals in crises). Based on how long the CEO has already been in the job, her or his age, and the company's traditional tenure for CEOs, team members usually can make some fairly safe assumptions about how much longer the CEO is likely to remain on the scene. Moreover, CEOs tend to stay in the same job longer than most managers, who are still in the process of moving up, down, sideways, or out. So if the team is formed fairly early in a CEO's regime, the members probably can assume that the CEO is going to be around for years—perhaps a decade or more in some companies. Building a good relationship with the CEO becomes an absolute necessity because this powerful person is about to become a permanent fixture in your life—or as close to permanent as you are likely to get in the business world.

The third factor that gives the CEO disproportionate power is that executive team members have fewer low-cost outs. Typical managers who decide they do not like working for someone and want to make a move usually can figure out some lateral shift to another division or business unit. But for those reporting directly to the CEO, the alternatives are severely limited: They can move either down or out. For an executive who has reached the top ranks of an organization, the costs of leaving are enormous. On one hand, there is the loss of benefits: pension, restricted stock, and all the other "golden handcuffs" that go with membership in the exclusive senior club. On the other hand, starting over somewhere else presents huge risks involving a new job, new colleagues, a new culture, and possibly even a new industry. The upshot is that when the CEOs' direct reports become restive, they review their options, begin to feel trapped, and convince themselves that the only logical option is to continue to satisfy the boss.

The outcome of these three factors—the power implicit in the CEO's position, the CEO's unique tenure, and the limited exit options for team members—is that the CEO enjoys both real and perceived power in relation to the executive team far beyond anything experienced by other team leaders. Simply put, the CEO can do things no other leader can in terms of shaping the agenda, setting the rules, declaring issues off limits, and making decisions.

Along with this unusual distribution of power, the executive team is unique because of the psychological characteristics typically found in any group of people who have risen to the top ranks of a major institution. Not surprisingly, these people tend to have unusually high needs for power and achievement. Many are driven by ambition and the desire to succeed in a public arena. What is more, they tend to have well-honed interpersonal skills when it comes to "playing the game," maintaining public facades, and waging office politics. These are not rookies; on the whole, these are smart, ambitious veterans of the corporate wars, and they are immune to the typical team leader's normal bag of tricks.

In addition to the distribution of power and the makeup of the team, a third factor that sets the executive team apart from all other teams: succession. Within this team, those who are actively playing the game are all jockeying for the only prize that really counts: the CEO's job. All the team members are aware that they are engaged in a zero-sum game; there can be only one winner.

Issues and Implications

Take the unbalanced distribution of power between the executive team and the CEO and the psychological characteristics commonly found in team members, then superimpose the combustible ingredient of succession, and the result is a volatile set of dynamics that complicates the work of almost every executive team (Figure 24.4). On the basis of our experience and observation, we can predict that nearly every executive team will experience at least some, and possibly all six of the following problems. The good news is that there are effective ways to address each of them, and I present those solutions as well.

Problem 1: Bloated Membership. The cachet associated with the executive team inevitably leads top managers to imbue a seat at the big table with special importance and immense symbolic value. There is constant pressure from those clamoring for an invitation to join and also pressure from those already on the team who are lobbying for the inclusion of

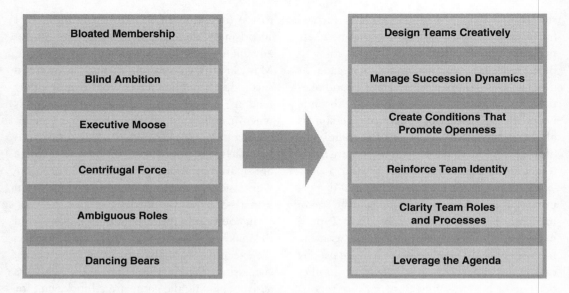

Figure 24.4   Problems and Solutions in Executive Teams

SOURCE: From Nadler, D. A., & Heilpern, J. D. (1998). The CEO and the executive team: Managing the unique dynamics and special demands. In D. A. Nadler, J. L. Spencer, & Associates, *Executive teams* (pp. 83–111). San Francisco: Jossey-Bass. Used with permission.

friends and supporters. That pressure for expanded membership is being exacerbated in many organizations by the move toward flatter hierarchies and broader spans of control. Instead of having 4 or 5 direct reports, as in the past, the CEO now might have 10 or 12. Along with the higher number of direct reports comes the assumption that anyone who is a hierarchical peer of a team member ought also to be a member. Too often membership on the executive team is extended in the interests of maintaining symmetry; that does not necessarily ensure that the right people are included and the extraneous ones are left out.

All too often, membership on the executive team becomes an end in itself rather than a means to an end. It is common to hear members complain loudly that the executive team eats up valuable time that they would rather be spending on their "real" work. Maybe so, but the fact is that the only thing they would consider worse than being on the executive team is not being on it. Ironically, once many of the people who lobby long and hard to be

named to the team are appointed, they go out of their way to find excuses not to attend meetings.

The result of expanded, diluted, and ritual membership is a team that is too big and largely dysfunctional. In my 25 years of experience working with CEOs and their senior teams, I have seen that the optimal group size for real problem solving and decision making ranges from 7 to 9, yet it is not uncommon to see executive teams with 15 or 20 members. Not only is the group too big to work efficiently, but with so many aggressive and ambitious people in the room, the competition for limited "airtime" can become fierce and counterproductive. There are just too many people jockeying for their moment in the limelight, resulting in a constant progression of performances rather than substantive give and take.

Solution 1: Design Executive Teams Creatively. One way to avoid bloated, unproductive executive teams is to think in terms of different teams for different tasks. There is nothing that says there can be only one executive team. Some CEOs design concentric rings of executive teams, such as a policy team involving the entire executive team and an operating team consisting of a small subset of the full team. The policy team would meet periodically and deal with matters suitable for large groups, such as communication, information sharing, gaining alignment around new policies, or building ownership of new strategies. The operating team would meet frequently and handle issues that call for problem solving or decision making.

The subsets of the executive team do not have to be permanent groups. Many CEOs often use ad hoc subgroups of the executive team to tackle specific issues and then disband these groups once the matter has been resolved. Another technique currently gaining the interest of CEOs concerned about their oversized executive committees is the appointment of a chief staff officer (CSO). The specific responsibilities vary from one organization, but in general the CSO is a senior executive whose direct reports include the managers responsible for critical staff functions, such as strategy, information technology, human resources, public affairs, communications, and legal affairs.

Problem 2: Blind Ambition. As noted earlier, executive teams typically include people who are unusually ambitious and achievement oriented. A few join the team in their 30s, but most come aboard in their early 40s to early 50s. These days they are extremely conscious of the probability that they have only a limited amount of time in which to realize their career objectives; it is not unusual to hear these people wonder, "How much runway do I have left?" Their career clocks are ticking, intensifying the competitive atmosphere in a naturally competitive group.

As the anticipated date of the succession decision draws near, this entire cast of characters can easily be swept up in a tidal wave of political behavior. The maneuvering, positioning, and competing intensify. Contenders often decide it

is not enough to present themselves in the best light; they feel compelled to go after their competitors, sometimes head on, other times through subtle feints and sneaky subterfuges. Depending on the intensity of the competition and the personalities involved, the behavior can easily become irrational and self-destructive.

The issue here is that the anticipation of a succession fight is a major spectator sport; onlookers love to watch what they perceive as competition, even when it is not there. When it really exists, particularly when it is positioned as an outright horse race, matters can get out of hand. The competition has a corrosive effect on relationships within the team, weakening and sometimes even demolishing the trust that is crucial to productivity.

Solution 2: Manage Succession Dynamics. To some degree, the succession dynamics we just described are unavoidable. They flow directly from powerful forces of human nature: power, control, competition, self-esteem, survival. What the CEO can do is, to the extent possible, manage the dynamics in ways that soften their impact on the team's effectiveness.

The primary challenge is to avoid the appearance of a public horse race. Time and time again we have seen CEOs create situations in which the leading contenders are pitted against each other with the clear expectation that it is up to each of them to demonstrate the desire, ambition, drive, and know-how to pull ahead of the pack. Perhaps that satisfies some internal notion of the dog-eat-dog nature of corporate natural selection. In reality, placing top executives in a position where they are actively and explicitly competing against one another is misguided, destructive, and detrimental to the organization's long-term interests.

Moreover, a succession horse race is inconsistent with the goal of an effective executive team. In any situation, the success of the executive team relies on each member's belief that the greater good is more important than immediate self-interest and the conviction that in the long run, individual success will be determined by collective triumph. In most situations that is absolutely true, but not when it comes to succession. Once a team member has been designated as an active contender and lined up in the starting gate, there is no way to make that person feel good about losing. So the challenge to the CEO is to keep as many options open for as long as possible and to actively discourage the perception of a head-to-head contest. CEOs attempting to manage succession dynamics must be as explicit as possible—as early as possible—about what kind of behavior is acceptable, both inside and outside the room.

Problem 3: Executive Moose. Almost every team, regardless of its position in the organization, faces the problem of "undiscussables" (Argyris, 1990). These are sensitive, volatile issues that are on everyone's mind and generally have a direct bearing on the team's work, and yet the group goes to incredible lengths to avoid discussing them or even mentioning them. My colleague Dennis Perkins (1988) developed the inspired metaphor of "the moose on the table" to describe this phenomenon. He likens these embarrassing, touchy, or unpleasant issues to a huge, hairy, smelly moose that is standing on the conference table, but not one member of the team will acknowledge its existence. The team goes about its business, people talk to each other between and around the moose's legs, but nobody makes any reference to the massive animal standing on the table. By unanimous but unspoken agreement, people decide to ignore the moose.

When the executive team gets together, there is likely to be a herd of moose crowded on top of the big table; some of them embodying the points of tension we have already discussed. In general, we can expect to see at least four of these shaggy beasts on the table.

The first is the distribution of power between the CEO and the team. Where are the boundaries, for both the CEO and the team? What kinds of issues are negotiable and which are off limits? How far can team members go in attempting to lead or influence the group without encroaching on the CEO's turf? How broad are the limits of dissent, and how deep is the need for consensus?

The second moose—and a huge one—is succession. In some situations, depending on the timing and circumstances, the succession issue may be uppermost in everyone's mind, coloring every statement, vote, presentation, and expression of support. Nevertheless, the executive team may go for months on end without acknowledging what is going on.

The third moose is the relationships between team members: their relative power, influence, competence, and performance. In most executive teams, there are certain unspoken taboos involving criticism of peers and open conflict between them. In most cases such criticism is simply off limits. Everyone around the table may be fully aware that a peer is running his operation into the ground or has been placed in a difficult situation and is clearly in over his head; even if other team members would like to raise the issue to see whether there is a way they can offer assistance, there is no acceptable method for bringing it up.

The fourth moose is failure—failure of individuals, strategies, projects, or initiatives. In too many executive teams, any open discussion of failure is simply off limits. Long-time members of the team can disappear like discredited Kremlin bosses, their departure marked solely by a note that the executive has decided to pursue other interests. Naturally, all the team members talk about the departed in private, but all too often there is no serious discussion of why the person was asked to leave or what lessons the others might learn from that experience.

Any or all of these moose can seriously hamper the executive team members' ability to work together effectively. Over time the failure to confront the moose creates an implicit conspiracy of silence. Important issues are sidestepped; vital concerns remain unsurfaced, unspoken, and unresolved. Dark emotions and destructive conflicts fester. Meanwhile, the team wastes extraordinary amounts of time and energy as people posture to talk around the issues sitting between them on the table.

Solution 3: Create Conditions That Promote Openness. The key to openness is trust, an often scarce commodity at the executive team level, where the stakes are so high and competition so intense. We are not advocating some New Age concept of warm and fuzzy acceptance based on spiritual affirmation of each member's intrinsic worth. The issue here is performance and competence; those who demonstrate their continuing value should be consistently validated and supported.

A sense of trust and openness is more essential at the executive team level than anywhere else in the organization. Day after day, these are the people who are asked to mount the high wire and perform death-defying acts for all to see. Consequently, it is up to the CEO to provide a safety net by building and sustaining supportive relationships with each person and with the team as a whole. It is up to the CEO to create a fundamental platform of assurance of team members' validity. Even more than the members of other teams, the executive team members have to feel they enjoy sufficient support to gamble on speaking out and being wrong or out of line.

It is not enough for team members to feel confident about the CEO's support. In order for the team to honestly tackle the most sensitive issues, there has to be a sense of trust and respect between the team members as well. Again, the CEO can play a crucial role, supporting people when they take risks, exercising sanctions when others try to undercut the risk takers through open attacks or peripheral potshots.

From a practical standpoint, CEOs can start to tackle the moose through the norms and rules of engagement that they lay out for the team. At the outset of each meeting, they can be explicit about what kind of meeting it

is—information sharing, problem solving, decision making, and so on—and what issues can and cannot be raised. The CEO needs to make that clarification a normal part of the team's work process, declaring at the outset what the ground rules will be.

Finally, the CEO can design specific ways to aggressively go after the moose, through moose hunts, roundups, or whatever name you want to attach to a variety of techniques for shattering the wall of silence.

Problem 4: Centrifugal Force. Complicating the work of any executive team is a set of factors that exert an inexorable pull on each team member, a centrifugal force drawing him or her farther from other team members and from the team's collective responsibilities. To begin with, each team member, by definition, is a leader in her or his own right, heading up an operating unit or major staff function. Each holds a job that imposes tremendous demands in terms of time, energy, and attention. Members' interests and areas of expertise differ widely. They feel subject to constant pressure, and time spent with the executive team working on other people's problems often is viewed as time that could be better spent on the job at hand.

Although job demands are the biggest forces pulling teams apart, there are others. Obviously, geography can present major obstacles to maintaining close contact. Another issue is the weak task interdependence that exists at the top of the corporation. In self-directed teams in the factory or office, each team member is directly and clearly dependent on the others for getting the job done. By the time you reach the team at the top, each team member is responsible for running his or her own operation. The situations in which team members are directly dependent on each other for getting their work done are minimal, particularly on the operational side. Finally, executive team members tend to be subject to huge external demands; they spend large amounts of time with customers, suppliers, and all the other outside constituencies that come into play in a major organization.

Taken collectively, then, the internal and external forces tearing at the fabric of the executive team can be enormous. They are constantly at work, eroding the time, energy, and commitment of each member.

Solution 4: Reinforce Team Identity. It is essential for the CEO to create conditions under which the team members are spending time together, doing the right work. This can be either formal time in conventional work settings or informal time at offsites or social events or when traveling together, for example. Along the same lines, teams benefit from the value of casual serendipitous encounters. The cohesiveness that results from these routine interactions ought to be a goal in decisions about the physical layout of executive offices so that the resulting design brings key people together.

Problem 5: Ambiguous Roles. Assuming the executive team members have been convinced to devote the necessary time and attention to their responsibilities as a team, there is still the problem of figuring out precisely what defines appropriate participation. We are referring here to participation beyond mere physical presence at the table. In one situation after another, we have witnessed confusion and frustration on the part of team members who are totally in the dark about the role they are expected to play once they are at the table.

On one level, team members are trying to discern their proper roles in the context of the politics, interpersonal dynamics, and power distribution we have described. They often feel they are in the dark about what kind of behavior the CEO and the other team members will consider acceptable. What are the real boundaries for argument, dissent, pointed questioning, and direct conflict? How will the CEO and team members react to any attempt to exert leadership or overt influence? How passive are team members expected to be? In the

absence of clear signals, team members tend to hang back and lie in the weeds because the potential cost of overstepping some unstated boundary is so incredibly high.

A second level of ambiguity concerns agenda items. One of the most serious problems that crops up time and time again on executive teams is a basic misunderstanding about the nature of the work on the table, resulting in ambiguous roles and inappropriate participation. This can and does happen in teams at every level, but again, the stakes are infinitely higher in the executive team.

At any point in the work of a team, different types of agenda items are on the table. The CEO may be asking for input or may be engaging the entire team in collaborative problem solving. In each of these situations team members are expected to play very different roles. Sometimes, they might be expected to simply listen and occasionally ask questions for purposes of clarification. At other times, they might be expected to articulate a strongly held point of view. What happens when people are confused about the nature of the work on the table? They may engage the CEO in debate or start offering divergent opinions when all the CEO wants is for them to sit and listen. Or they may hold back and seem stupefyingly passive at a time when the CEO is looking for ideas and alternative opinions.

Solution 5: Clarify Team Processes and Roles. The key to generating purposeful participation is for the CEO to make sure everyone is absolutely clear about how the team will operate, what kinds of decisions it will make, and what roles each member will be expected to play. This is not a new concept; it has been discussed for decades (Tannenbaum & Schmidt, 1958). Research and experience illustrate that within teams, not all decisions should be made the same way (Vroom & Yetton, 1973); consequently, we often counsel CEOs to be extremely careful about how they go about making decisions in the team setting because different kinds of decisions demand different decision-making processes.

In general, the CEO and the team encounter four different decision modes. Some decision making is *unilateral:* The CEO makes the decision on her or his own and then, in a timely manner, shares with the team the decision and the reasoning behind it. The second kind of decision making is *consultive:* The leader seeks input from the team but makes the final decision alone. The third form of decision making is *consensus:* The CEO participates as a team member rather than team leader, and the group works toward a collective decision. The final form of decision making is *delegation:* Others are empowered to make the decision as long as this process clearly falls within the CEO's comfort zone.

It is not enough for CEOs merely to recognize these different kinds of decisions; they need to be absolutely clear with their teams about what kind of decision is on the table and the ground rules for getting it resolved. One key to maintaining clarity in the process is to develop a common language system. It really does not matter what terms are used, as long as everyone in the room knows what the terms mean and is completely clear about what kind of work the team is about to do and what role it is expected to play.

Problem 6: Dancing Bears. It is inevitable that the executive team periodically becomes a stage for all kinds of performances. Invariably, one of its functions is to act as a review committee, the place where other managers and teams come to present their cases for new projects or expanded budgets or simply to share information and provide updates and status reports. Ideally, these ought to be working sessions in which the executive team extracts necessary information and acts accordingly. Unfortunately, the opportunity to perform in front of the organization's most influential audience is too much for many people to pass up. As a result, the executive team is treated to an endless spectacle of carefully staged presentations marked by posturing, positioning, and an obsession with scoring points rather than solving problems and making

decisions. And the consequence of all this misdirected activity is that gatherings of the organization's most valuable and highly paid executives, people whose time is an incredibly scarce resource, become wasteful exercises in self-aggrandizement, with precious little value created for the organization.

Solution 6: Leverage the Agenda. For executive teams caught in the grip of dancing bears, the answer is clear: The CEO has to manage the agenda process in ways that ensure the team is engaged in value-added work. The first step in this agenda management is understanding the balance of costs and benefits involved in the team's work. Assuming that each member of the executive team holds a responsible job that is critical to the organization's performance, a serious opportunity cost is associated with the time these executives spend with the team. Some of the things the team members do together as a group are of discernible value; in other cases the value is harder to determine.

The job of the CEO as team leader is to ensure that the marginal value of the team members working together is greater than the marginal cost of taking them away from their primary jobs. We constantly urge CEOs to weigh this equation and figure out other ways to accomplish the tasks that offer no added value. Typically, the value-added group tasks concern strategy decisions, major moves involving people, large resource allocation issues, portfolio moves, and issues involving the management of the organization's values and ethics. These are concerns that have to be handled in the executive team setting, with this group of people at the table, and cannot be done anywhere else. Issues that fall outside these concerns should be handled outside the group setting, leaving most of the team members to go back to their offices and do their jobs.

So the first issue involves the content of the agenda. The second issue deals with process: the kinds of work the team is being asked to do. To some extent process involves the proper balance of agenda items. If the majority of

items simply transmit information, you probably do not need to bring the team together; just
send them the information and eliminate most
opportunities for showboating and dancing
bears. If enough items do require the team to
meet, then it is important to set some strict
rules. For example,

- Limit presentations to no more than 20 minutes.
- Any time the team is being asked to make a
  decision, require the presenter to provide
  members with background material in
  advance of the meeting, to hold that material
  to a limited length, and not to repeat it during the live presentation.
- Make the first slide in the presentation the
  same as the last; in other words, the discussion is to begin by specifically identifying
  what form of action the team is being asked
  to provide.
- Carefully manage the presence of outsiders;
  hold them to strict time limits to avoid grand-
  standing and to allow serious deliberations
  without an audience.

Those are just a few examples of the kinds of
rules that can be used to manage the executive
team's agenda and process. The critical point is
that this group, more than any other, needs
absolute clarity about the kinds of items on its
agenda and how it is going to deal with them.
Just as CEOs should be explicit about the kinds
of decisions on the table, they need to set the
ground rules for each piece of business on the
agenda. That entails rigorous management of
the agenda, both before and during the meeting.

The OD Consultant
and the Executive Team

In the end it is the CEO who is critical to the
team's success. The CEO must seriously pursue
his role and responsibility as the designer of the
team, its leader in the room, and the shaper of
its dynamics outside the room. Beyond that,
the CEO must act as the quality assurance officer for the team. If left to their own devices,

these teams invariably will run out of gas: Their
processes will deteriorate, and their dynamics
will become dysfunctional. It is up to CEOs to
constantly assess what is working and what is
not, to bring in a fresh set of eyes when he or
she has gotten too close to an issue, and to
make the continuous improvements that are
vital to the team's continued success.

Having said that, it is difficult to be the
leader and also work on the process of the
team. Here is where the OD practitioner can
add tremendous value in several ways. She or
he can assist the CEO as

- Diagnostician: collecting data and assessing
  where the team is, what it does well and
  poorly, and where change is needed
- Designer of the team: helping with critical
  executive team design decisions
- Process consultant: helping the team, in the
  room, to develop new and more effective
  ways of working together
- Advisor or coach: helping the CEO understand and perform the role

However, the ultimate goal is to enable the
CEO to be a more effective designer, leader, and
facilitator of his or her own team.

WORKING WITH THE BOARD

Working with the CEO and the executive team
has been a significant part of OD at the top for
some time. Recently, however, a new aspect to
this work has come to the fore: working with
the board of directors. This has come about as
a direct consequence of the changes in U.S. corporate governance (also in Canada, the United
Kingdom, and to some extent in Western Europe)
in the past few years.

The pressure on boards to accept greater
accountability for their companies' performance has grown dramatically through the
1990s and into the new century. Spurred by
shareholder demands for consistently high
stock performance, by outside pressures from
"good governance" groups such as the CalPERS

pension fund, and by greatly intensified scrutiny by the business press, boards began paying closer attention to "scorecard" issues such as board composition, compensation, and meeting frequency. Then came the Enron collapse and renewed attention to board oversight issues (e.g., revised NYSE and NASDAQ corporate governance rules and the Sarbanes–Oxley Act), and directors quickly started paying closer attention to the legal exposure related to their handling of board oversight responsibilities.

As was already the case with CEOs, boards began looking to outsiders for guidance and expert help. But the content and process of OD consultation with boards offers some marked contrasts with the CEO applications I have been discussing up to this point.

Content of Board Work

To date the legal responsibilities of corporate boards in the United States have been minimal. According to the respected legal handbook *Liability of Corporate Officers and Directors* (Kepper & Bailey, 1998), the board's role generally encompasses six basic responsibilities:

- Approving major corporate actions (e.g., acquisitions, divestitures, stock splits)
- Providing counsel to senior management
- Overseeing management's performance, setting executive compensation, and hiring and dismissing the CEO
- Ensuring effective audit procedures
- Ensuring that nonmanagement perspectives are heard and considered when major decisions are made
- Regularly monitoring the company's investments for legal compliance

A board can limit its activities to those six areas and comply with its statutory obligations. However, growing public concerns for board performance suggest that this may not be enough. In *Corporate Boards: Strategies for*

Adding Value at the Top, Conger, Lawler, and Finegold (2001) argue that boards should go beyond their legal mandates to focus on additional areas that will ensure better governance:

- Strategic direction and advice: a largely advisory role to the CEO and executive team but one that can capitalize on the variety of business skills and backgrounds assembled around the board table
- Oversight of strategy implementation and performance: approving major financial and capital investments, setting benchmarks for organization performance, holding the CEO and executive team responsible for meeting strategic goals
- Developing human capital: overseeing succession planning and compensation strategies for senior management, evaluating CEO performance, exercising ultimate authority on hiring and dismissal of CEOs
- Crisis management and prevention: planning for the board's role in various crises, brainstorming crisis scenarios, instigating processes that will raise red flags that might signal potential crises
- Procuring resources: assisting management, particularly in smaller or newer companies, in obtaining the necessary financing, talent, technology, and strategic relationships

The Board's Unique Process Issues

Both of the frameworks just discussed—the chartered legal obligations and additional areas where, ideally, boards ought to be active—focus on the content of the board's work. But one of the most interesting developments in the evolution of corporate governance over the past decade has been the growing realization that the board's working processes—the ways in which its members engage each other and senior management—are a critical component of board performance and effectiveness. There are two reasons for this.

The first is that in legal proceedings—a cause of increasing concern to boards—the courts have established the so-called business judgment rule as a legal defense that can be invoked by directors in liability cases. Recognizing that judges and courts are not necessarily qualified to second-guess the correctness of complex business decisions, the courts have chosen instead to focus on a board's decision-making processes. In other words, rather than trying to evaluate the content of board decisions, the courts are weighing the processes and procedures used in reaching decisions. Special attention is being given to whether the board acted with the corporation's best interests in mind, was well informed, acted within the bounds of the law, and avoided conflicts of interest (Conger et al., 2001).

The second factor that has increased interest in board processes is the growing emphasis on the need for boards to do "real work" as opposed to performing purely ceremonial duties. When boards were merely disparate groups of people who gathered four times a year to rubber stamp management's recommendations and then adjourn for cocktails, it didn't really matter whether the board's work processes were designed to achieve high performance; it was simply irrelevant. Now, as boards feel growing pressure to demonstrate their active involvement and sharp oversight of major corporate issues, the board's ability to collectively perform substantive work, and to perform it well, has become a serious issue. In fact, new regulations and guidelines create clear responsibilities for the board, and specifically for certain committees, such as the audit committee and the nominating or corporate governance committee.

Implications for Working With Boards

Traditionally, boards have sought the assistance of outside specialists whose technical expertise was directly related to activities encompassed by the boards' legal obligations. These generally included lawyers, auditors, investment bankers, compensation experts, and executive recruiters. Over time, the "good

governance" groundswell led more boards to seek out a small group of consultants, primarily academics and single practitioners, to advise them on the issues that were of prime importance to the self-appointed watchdogs, such as board composition, committee roles and structures, meeting frequency, and agendas.

Today, the growing emphasis on board processes and the new corporate governance requirements are creating demand for a new form of consulting—new at least in the realm of corporate governance. In particular, some boards are beginning to ask for OD help with two sets of processes affecting governance and performance. The first involves the board's own internal processes: how the directors engage with each other to fulfill their legal obligations and pursue their other governance activities in ways that truly add value. The second area concerns the board's interactions with the CEO and the chair, who might or might not be the same person.

Taken together, these new developments have four major implications for OD practitioners working with boards.

Although boards will continue to need and to seek out technical expertise in a variety of legal and financial areas directly related to their statutory obligations, there will be a dramatic expansion of board interest in improving the process and dynamics of governance itself.

The key to process improvement involves dynamics rather than mechanics. If the board is willing, the mechanics of its work processes—composition, committee structures, meeting agendas—can be fixed fairly easily with help from management consultants operating in the content expert role. But the essence of board performance lies in the group's dynamics, not the mechanics. You can fix the mechanics but still fail to achieve high performance if the dynamics are wrong.

Consequently, the OD work with the biggest payoff to boards will take what we already know about high-performing executive teams and adapt the relevant concepts to the unique dynamics of the board. This approach implies a fundamentally new view that an effective board should operate as a real team: a group of people who work collectively to accomplish outcomes that they couldn't achieve individually. That view assumes that board members will interact and actively engage to perform real work, a marked difference from the traditional pattern of one or two board members acting in concert with senior management to lay the groundwork for periodic meetings that consisted of nothing more than perfunctory votes and well-rehearsed presentations.

Without question, boards differ in significant ways from other teams; the board's work tends to be episodic, takes place in a unique legal context, involves varying patterns of inclusion because of the committee structure, and generally takes place in the room when the team is together rather than in the periods between meetings. But there are also major similarities involving the dynamics of leadership, the importance of communication, and the diffuse distribution of power (Nadler et al., 1998). As stated earlier, the key for effective OD consultants will be to understand both the differences and similarities and to adapt what we already know from executive team building to the board's unique needs.

Corporate governance will be enhanced when the board functions as an effective team, with appropriate levels of engagement, and when there is a collaborative relationship between the board and the CEO. The idea of a collaborative relationship between CEOs and boards differs dramatically from what has been the norm in many companies. Some CEOs view their board as a necessary evil at best or as an interfering nuisance at worst. Others view their board as a valuable sounding board but little more. Conversely, for the many directors who believe they have been anointed with an honorary position that requires nothing more than filling a seat at occasional meetings, the idea of partnering

with other directors and the CEO to do real work will take a large attitudinal shift.

Board Building

One way of thinking about working with boards is to build on the existing knowledge, experience, and tools for consulting with teams in general and executive teams in particular. If we can think about working to improve the effectiveness of teams as a process of team building, then the parallel work with boards might be thought of as board building.

The approach we have used for board building is shown in Figure 24.5. It begins with taking stock of where the board is, through an in-depth diagnosis. That diagnosis may lead to many different directions, but typically the starting point is to clarify the work of the board as a team. Specifically, this involves work with the board and the CEO to determine where the board can add value through different levels of engagement. This involves an analysis of the different areas in which the board might become involved and a clarification of the roles of the board and corporate management in each of those areas.

Having clarified the work of the board, there are four key leverage points. First is the composition of the board. As in any team, having the appropriate skills, capabilities, and experience is critical for effectiveness. The second leverage point includes the various formal structures and processes of the board. This involves the design of the board's committees, agendas, and critical work processes related to potential core content areas, such as succession, executive compensation, and strategy. Third is information. Boards are in a unique situation in that outside directors are only partially included in the organization. They have episodic interaction with the company, yet to contribute they need the appropriate information and knowledge about the company. Fourth is board culture, the emergent or informal structures and processes that shape so much of the interaction in the board.

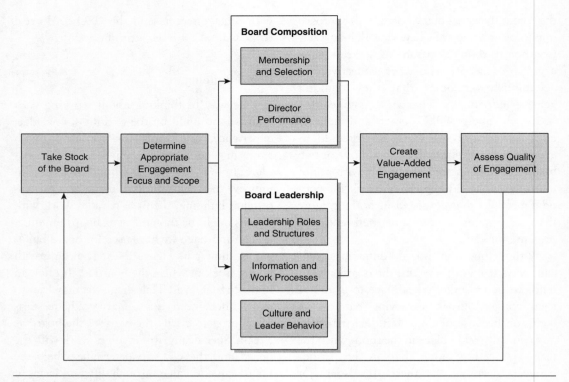

Figure 24.5   Board Building

SOURCE: From Nadler, D. A., Behan, B. A., & Nadler, M. B. (Eds.). (2006). *Building better boards: A blueprint for effective governance.* San Francisco: Jossey-Bass. Used with permission.

These four elements are dramatically shaped by board leadership—both leadership by the chair or CEO or leadership by other key people, including independent directors who have designated leadership roles.

Over time, working those leverage points, in the context of appropriate, clear, and agreed-upon areas for board involvement, will result in value-added engagement by the board. Of course, as in any team, it is critical to assess performance over time, both regularly and periodically in more depth, to keep the cycle of board building going.

CONCLUSION

Applying OD at the top of the enterprise is challenging yet potentially very impactful. As

we have discussed, it is important to think of the enterprise as a whole rather than myopically focusing on the top in a vacuum. Working with the top usually is a means to a larger end, that of enterprise change. Having said that, work with the CEO, the executive team, and the board presents unique issues and challenges and requires specific concepts, tools, skills, and experiences for successful OD practice.

REFERENCES

Argyris, C. (1990). *Overcoming organizational defenses: Facilitating organizational learning.* Boston: Allyn & Bacon.

Conger, J. A., Lawler, E. E., III, & Finegold, D. L. (2001). *Corporate boards: Strategies for adding value at the top.* San Francisco: Jossey-Bass.

Finkelstein, S., & Hambrick, D. C. (1990, September). Top management team tenure and organizational outcomes: The moderating role of managerial discretion. *Administrative Science Quarterly*, pp. 484–503.

Hambrick, D. C., Cho, T. S., & Chen, M.-J. (1996, December). The influence of top management team heterogeneity on firms' competitive moves. *Administrative Science Quarterly*, pp. 659–684.

Hanlon, M., Nadler, D. A., & Gladstein, D. (1985). *Attempting work reform: The case of "Parkside" hospital*. New York: John Wiley & Sons.

Katz, D., & Kahn, R. L. (1978). *The social psychology of organizations*. New York: John Wiley & Sons.

Kearns, D. T., & Nadler, D. A. (1992). *Prophets in the dark: How Xerox reinvented itself and beat back the Japanese*. New York: HarperCollins.

Kepper, W. E., & Bailey, D. A. (1998). *Liability of corporate officers and directors*. Charlottesville, VA: Michie.

Maister, D. H., Green, C. H., & Galford, R. M. (2000). *The trusted advisor*. New York: Free Press.

Michel, J., & Hambrick, D. C. (1992, March). Diversification posture and the characteristics of the top management team. *Academy of Management Journal*, 412–438.

Nadler, D. A. (1998). *Champions of change: How CEOs and their companies are mastering the skills of radical change*. San Francisco: Jossey-Bass.

Nadler, D. A., Behan, B. A., & Nadler, M. B. (Eds.). (2006). *Building better boards: A blueprint for effective governance*. San Francisco: Jossey-Bass.

Nadler, D. A., Shaw, R. B., & Walton, A. E. (1994). *Discontinuous change: Leading organizational transformation*. San Francisco: Jossey-Bass.

Nadler, D. A., Spencer, J. L., & Associates. (1998). *Executive teams*. San Francisco: Jossey-Bass.

Perkins, D. N. T. (1988). *Ghosts in the executive suite: Every business is a family business*. Branford, CT: Syncretics Group.

Schein, E. H. (1969). *Process consultation*. New York: Addison-Wesley.

Tannenbaum, R., & Schmidt, W. H. (1958). How to choose a leadership pattern. *Harvard Business Review*, 95–101.

Vroom, V. H., & Yetton, P. W. (1973). *Leadership and decision-making*. Pittsburgh, PA: University of Pittsburgh Press.

25

The Order and Chaos
of the Learning Organization

GEORGE ROTH

A quality unique to humanity is our ability to accumulate and use knowledge. Our societal progress depends on a developing knowledge base. We use, relearn, and add to knowledge by learning from our ongoing efforts and experiences. Business organizations are no exception. A competitive marketplace requires them to learn. Arie De Geus (1988, p. 74), head of planning for the Royal Dutch Shell Group, predicts, "The only competitive advantage the company of the future will have is its managers' abilities to learn faster than its competitors." Ray Stata (1989, p. 64), CEO of Analog Devices, emphasizes a similar point: "The rate at which individuals and organizations learn may be the only sustainable competitive advantage." Adler and Cole (1993, p. 85) found that "a consensus is emerging that the hallmark of tomorrow's most effective organizations will be their capacity to learn."

Looking historically, the average life of a Fortune 500 company is less than 50 years; what makes for long-lived companies involves organizing for learning (De Geus, 1997).

There is little doubt that learning is an important characteristic of successful firms. Management research and practice have long been interested in learning in organizations and more recently in the idea of a learning organization. Scholarship on organization learning first appeared in the 1960s (Cangelosi & Dill, 1965; Cyert & March 1963), and dramatic increases in this literature began in the late 1980s (Crossan & Guatto, 1996; Mirvis, 1996). Although more articles were published, there was little effort to accumulate or synthesize this research (Huber, 1991), and there is a lack of convergence on what organization learning means or how to do it (Crossan, Lane, & White, 1999; Kim, 1993). People reading these literatures are likely to find that it raises as many questions as it answers. Ulrich, von Glinow, and Jick (1993, p. 57) found what was written to be so broad that they conclude, "The concept of the learning organization has become a management Rorschach test. One sees whatever one wants to see." Leading scholars find "more reviews of organizational learning than there is substance to review" (Weick & Westley 1996, p. 440). If readers struggle with the organization learning literature, these comments should at least provide some consolation that their experience is not unique.

The purpose of this chapter is to draw insights and lessons for organization development from the writing on organization learning. To do so requires a review of the important contributions of what has become a large literature.

VARYING PERSPECTIVES ON ORGANIZATION LEARNING

Why should we care about the concept of the learning organization, and what does it add to our thinking, study, and practice of organization development? The concept has practical relevance, as the quotes by managers and academics attest, to the performance, competitiveness, and longevity of organizations. The title of this chapter takes the position that there is order and chaos in the concept and literature on learning organizations. Why reinforce order and chaos and the ambiguity that two opposed concepts imply? It is because the strength of the concept of a learning organization, for both practice and scholarship, might fundamentally be in embracing these opposites.

Weick and Westley (1996, p. 440) propose that *organization learning* is an oxymoron: "To learn is to disorganize and increase variety. To organize is to forget and reduce variety." Examination of this oxymoron entails holding the inherent tension between learning and organizing as a core concept that could be the basis for building more realistic and satisfying organization theories. Weick and Westley use the

word *affirming* in their article on organization learning to address noted failures in management literature. In the introduction to a special issue of *Organizational Science*, Allison argues that most rigorous management theories are built on rational choice assumptions, yet much of the empirical management research shows the faults of these assumptions (e.g., Allison, 1971, quoted in Cohen & Sproull, 1991, p. i; Kahneman, Slovic, & Tversky, 1982). However, this empirical work does not propose a basis for new theories, which leaves the management field stuck with many examples that illustrate the nonrational nature of organizations. Without careful attention, the same could happen to organization learning and leave researchers with not much more than examples of organizations as nonlearners. Better organization learning theories provide promise of a positive alternative theoretical approach. Those theories rest on confirming the oxymoron of organization learning and recognizing that we need to "keep organizing and learning connected despite the fact that they pull in opposite directions" (Weick & Westley, 1996, p. 456).

The challenge inherent in juxtaposing organizing with learning is accompanied by the need to make sense of an extensive and divergent literature. Why does nearly every author on the subject write another literature review? The reason is that literature is diffuse, and authors seeking to locate their position within one or across several of the many disciplinary perspectives need to describe and explain organization learning. Depending on their chosen perspective, they define the boundary between what they study and the organization learning outcomes and processes on which they concentrate. New researchers approach learning organizations from different perspectives and create more diversity. It is not surprising to find that there is no organization literature that has not received criticism or been noted as having problematic features.

We can reframe the challenges of these organization learning literatures by resetting our expectations. Why should we expect convergence on organization learning? What if instead of an integrated field with a convergent literature we expected a literature based on different disciplinary perspectives and applied interests? Most people write from a particular disciplinary base and find that others are writing on the topic from other disciplinary bases. Although this reframing does not make the literature less difficult, it does provide varied insights into organization learning processes. What we then see are parallel research efforts, based on research perspectives, disciplines, and methods, that could potentially provide complementary contributions. These different contributions can then become the basis for a rich set of intellectual resources for organization development scholars and practitioners to draw on in their efforts to study and develop people and organizations.

What can we learn from research on individual learning? More than a half century of research "has seen the emergence and demise of many theories" (Shrivastava, 1983, p. 8). Behaviorists promoted stimulus–response models, proposing learning as a change in the probabilities of responses. Neobehaviorists extended these ideas using stochastic models of learning processes, viewing learning as the acquisition of associations and stimulus–response bonds. Later research applied these ideas to verbal learning, memorizing, and concept identification. Cognitive psychology linked learning to problem solving and states of knowledge rather than probabilities of response. Individual learning research then shifted to memory, information processing, knowledge organizing, and information acquisition in problem solving. Methodological changes have become influential as the research has gone from theorizing, to laboratory experimentation, to computer simulation and modeling. More recent research, enabled by advances in medical diagnostic technology, examines responses in brain activities as part of learning.

The organization learning literature seems to have followed a similar trend over time: theorizing, experimentation, simulation, and empirical studies. Some authors have expressed concerns about the viability of individual learning as a basis for organization learning. "People in organizational theory began to talk about learning (Cangolesi & Dill 1965) just about the time psychologists began to desert the concept. I worry that scholars of organizations . . . [adopted] a concept that didn't work for others, and will not work for them" (Weick, 1991, p. 116). After considering this individual learning literature, Weick proposed two strategies for organization learning. One strategy is to retain traditional definitions of learning, conclude that organization learning is rare, and search for organizations and contexts where there is success in these traditional conditions. The other strategy is to develop a definition for learning more appropriately tied to organization properties and pursue studies of organization change involving learning.

A review of the literature provides a foundation of the various ideas that make up organization learning. Table 25.1 presents a grouping of this literature into four broad perspectives, showing the core ideas and, in keeping with our organization development orientation, factors for each perspective that enable or inhibit learning in organizations. The next four sections present each perspective based on key contributions, followed by a discussion distinguishing organization learning from the learning organization. This chapter concludes with directions for future organization learning research and practice and the implications for organization development.

Organization Learning as Accumulated Experience

Taylor's (1911) development of scientific management provided the basic principles and practices for measuring and improving organization work. Measurement allowed us to link

Table 25.1   Perspectives on Organization Learning

Organization Learning Perspective	Core Ideas	Enablers of Learning	Barriers to Learning
As accumulated experience	Learning curve extended to management decisions, efficiency, and productivity improvement.	Time and experience, better measurement and analysis, learning in sociotechnical systems	Linkage between measurement and behavior, limitations in applying physical world insights to social science
As adaptation to environmental changes	Organizations adapt to changes in the environment by readjusting goals, attention rules, and search algorithms.	Analysis of environment, planning, engaging more of the organization in planning, more and better experiments	Inappropriate understanding of environment, social and satisficing behaviors
As assumption sharing	Theories in use that result from shared assumptions, changing these assumptions and learning about learning.	Reflection and tools or techniques that make individual and collective thinking explicit	People's defensive routines, needs to unlearn worldviews, enactment
As a developing knowledge base	Knowledge about action–outcome relationships is developed and used in various settings.	More and better experiments, acquiring and processing information and knowledge	Incomplete learning cycles, superstition, not unlearning, holding onto past success

SOURCE: Adapted from Shrivastava (1983, p. 10).

learning with production and efficiency improvements. One of the first to write about the learning curve, Wright (1936) observed that as the units manufactured doubled, the number of direct labor hours to produce units decreased at a uniform rate. That uniform rate of decrease is what he called the learning curve. All manufacturing processes exhibit this kind of learning curve behavior— improvement in the resources needed to produce a unit declining with the log of cumulative volume produced—although the shapes of these curves might differ.

Factors influencing the shape of the learning included the "inherent susceptibility of the labor in an operation to improve and the degree to which this susceptibility is exploited by the organization" (from Yelle, 1979, p. 306, referencing Hirschmann, 1964). Early studies examined operations with high labor content being operator paced and found that they have steeper learning curves than machine-paced operations. Learning curves have been used predominantly to explain variation in learning rates within organizations, although they have been applied as evidence of organization learning through examination of the factors that influence their slope and curvature (Epple, Argote, & Devadas, 1990). Learning curves and production measures continue to be used extensively in industry. However, there is recognition that measures of output may overlook other important factors, such as the means by which improvements are made (Argote, Beckman, & Epple, 1990). There is also a challenge in that exogenous factors may be more important than endogenous ones in explaining performance improvements.

Measures can be used for systematic problem solving and ongoing experimentation. Without measures, learning efforts can be utopian (Garvin, 1993). Efforts such as total quality management rely on good measures of output and improvement over time. Any quantifiable approach has limitations if it is used in organizations to focus on what is measurable and emphasize outputs (ends) rather than contributing processes (means) (Johnson, 1993).

Productivity measures provide indications of results but not of the underlying process. Adler and Cole (1993) propose that greater specialization and shorter work cycles in the Toyota/GM New United Motors Manufacturing, Incorporated plant created greater learning opportunities than the less structured and longer work cycle found in the Volvo Uddevalla plant. The higher productivity of the NUMMI plant illustrated that it is better at learning than Uddevalla. NUMMI also had better documentation, which allowed workers to be more explicit about what they know and to reexamine and improve it. Berggren (1994) challenges these conclusions, arguing that the time frame of analysis was too short because Uddevalla later saw dramatic rates of productivity improvement and that productivity measures do not capture organization learning processes. Adler and Cole (1994, p. 46) agree in part and continue to argue that NUMMI's form of work organization (lean production, see Womack, Jones, & Roos, 1990) "better supports the kind of sustained rapid organizational learning necessary for world-class competitive performance."

Weick and Westley (1996, p. 450) comment on this analysis, proposing that Alder and Cole missed cultural factors in explaining learning. They propose two types of learning: explorative and exploitive. Explorative learning feeds on the unexpected events but atrophies in the face of tight, centralized control. This distinction, explorative learning as being in opposition to exploitive learning, refers to March's (1991) insights about organizations needing to make choices about the refinement of existing technologies and methods or creation of new ones. The exploration of new alternatives reduces the speed with which existing skills are improved, and improvements in competence of existing procedures make experimentation with alternatives less attractive (Levitt & March, 1988).

Organization development makes important contributions to views of organization learning as accumulated experience. Accumulating performance information, analyzing it, and creating feedback processes has been a vital part of organization development practices (Nadler, 1977). The research that contributes to the accumulated experience view of organization learning has been based largely on operational data. Organization development can expand these efforts to build on accumulated experience with its methods in workforce measures and feedback processes. A developmental approach to feedback, such as establishing trust between the people collecting data and the people to whom the data are provided, is a process that is explicit in organization development methods. Developing broader measures and creating more effective feedback processes can enhance the understanding and use of accumulated experience and thus organization learning.

Organization Learning as Adaptation to Environmental Changes

Cyert and March's (1963) behavioral theory of the firm proposed that an organization's changing behavior provides evidence of organization learning. Adaptation in the firm's behavior occurs over time in terms of changes in the firm's goals, in the attention given to different parts of the environment, and in the use of existing and development of new search procedures for solutions to problems. The firm develops a knowledge base from its experience that contains elements that it must learn, unlearn, and relearn. Effective organizations have members who have a capacity to predict environmental changes, search for suitable strategies to cope with these changes, and develop appropriate structures to implement these strategies (Shrivastava, 1983, p. 11). Organization learning is a process of successfully coping with environmental changes by linking them with organization contexts.

However, organizations do not face clear signals from their environments; ambiguities about what is going on in the environment arise because of people's cognitive and evaluative limits. March and Olsen (1975, 1976) examined organization conditions for learning, identifying many factors that affected outcomes of managerial choices and made learning difficult. They argued that "organizational intelligence," like individual intelligence, rests on two processes. One is rational calculation, involving activities such as planning, analysis, and forecasting. The second process is learning from experience, involving practices such as experimentation, assessment, and evaluation. Both of these processes suffer from the limitations on rationality, such as awareness of alternatives, precision of information, and clarity of goals; (Cyert & March, 1963; March & Simon, 1958; Simon, 1957). March and Olsen used rationality

limitations in developing and evaluating the implications for organization learning.

As is the case with individuals' limitations, people in organizations often act on incomplete or incorrect information, are not aware of all alternatives, and do not have well-defined preferences. Although people in organizations act based on what they have learned from experience, that process requires an interpretation of experience. A model that March and Olsen call the complete cycle of organization choice (Figure 25.1) posits four important relationships in an organization learning process. The cycle is a closed system involving how individuals' thinking and preferences affect their behavior, how individual behavior affects organization choices, how organization choices affect environmental acts, and how environmental acts affect individuals' thinking and preferences.

This cyclical model of learning is similar to most other individual and organizational learning models. It involves memory, perception (cognition), action, response, and feedback that affect future states of memory, perception, and action. Problems result when outside factors interrupt the learning cycle, the

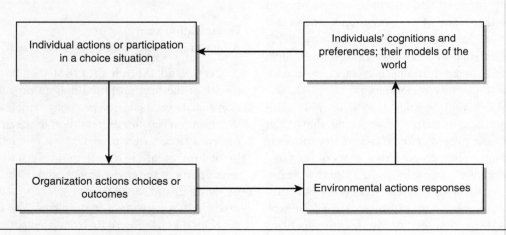

Figure 25.1   Complete Cycle of Choice

SOURCE: From March, J. G., & Olsen, J. H. (1975). The uncertainty of the past: Organizational learning under ambiguity, in *European Journal of Political Research* 3:150. Used with permission from Blackwell Publishing.

cycle is not accurate, or it is not complete. Role-constrained learning occurs when individual learning has little or no effect on individual behavior; superstitious learning occurs when the link between organizational action and environmental response does not function; audience learning occurs when individual actions do not influence organization action; and learning under ambiguity occurs when individuals do not understand environmental responses. When it is unclear what happened or why it happened, people have limited information from which to consider modifying their behavior. However, even if they have accurate information, people often believe what they want to believe and impose order and attribute a meaning that suits them.

Incomplete or wrong learning cycles explain why organizations seem to muddle through (Lindbloom, 1959). People make reasonable decisions that are satisfactory at some level, although criteria or consequences for effectiveness are not well known or enforced. The satisficing process is a limited view of learning, one that, although descriptively accurate, does not provide a systematic basis for organization learning. Individual learning within organizations is fraught with problems of incomplete and inaccurate information and multiple decision makers with different preferences and goals.

Various approaches have been developed to improve the learning cycle and the organization's abilities to perceive its environment and changes. Michael (1973) focuses on mismatches between long-range planning and short-run organization efforts. Short-run efforts for control and predictability are in direct conflict with long-run realities of ambiguity and uncertainty. Scenario planning efforts developed at Royal Dutch Shell sought to prepare managers to see possible futures and develop appropriate responses to possible futures (Schwartz, 1991). Future search conferences (Weisbord, 1993) bring whole systems together in a large group setting to examine, develop, and take action on their perspectives for possible futures. In addition to surfacing and developing perspectives on the future environment, these efforts also surface and question assumptions people hold for the current environment.

The view of organization learning as adapting to its environment has implications for the effectiveness of top teams and their abilities to perceive and gain information on their environment, create strategies, and implement changes through the organization's governance processes. Organization development work has created processes that engage a broader constituency beyond top managers and direct reporting relationships on issues of strategy and its fit to environmental conditions. The engagement of a broader constituency provides feedback on the effectiveness of strategies and environmental changes to top management. Greater involvement by people at multiple organization levels also creates better conditions for implementing change through the development of shared understanding.

Organization Learning as Assumption Sharing

Organizations are settings in which multiple levels of learning can take place. One level of learning is improvement within the existing structure: improving actions and behavior to attain better results more reliably. Another level of learning involves examining and changing the cognitive conditions or structure within which action and behavior take place. This change involves altering the thinking that produces action and behavior, or changing the beliefs, values, or worldviews that influence thinking. Argyris and Schön (1978) described the importance of these different levels—behaviors, thinking, and worldviews—of learning. They explained organization behavior as guided largely by the shared assumptions, most often implicit, that guided people's actions. They used the term "theories in use" to describe the "programs" or worldviews individuals and organizations have that produce their behavior.

Their research involved changes in these shared theories in use. First-order learning occurs when people and organizations learn within their theories in use, and second-order learning occurs when they learn about their theories in use. First-order learning might be a reaction to a problem and correction of an error. First-order learning is important because it is much of what people in organizations do. However, it is limited because the complexity of the situation may have changed (new theories may be needed) or because there are flaws in the existing theories in use. Second-order learning—changing theories in use—is more difficult. Argyris and Schön (1978) also describe learning about learning, or double-loop learning. The multiple levels and attention to shared assumptions is a different approach to organization learning from March and Olsen's (1975) adaptive learning. The differences are rooted in the same distinctions between behavioral and cognitive approaches found in individual learning.

Early research on individual learning came from the behaviorist tradition (Watson, 1914), whose focus was limited to what could be observed. These early studies developed theories based on animal experiments and extended them to human learning. Researchers thought that learning processes were universal, using experimental laboratory conditions to manipulate environmental factors and observing results. This approach obviated any reliance on introspective reports. Cognitive theories consider that stored environmental information directs action; they seek to explain behavior in terms of mental events such as purposes, beliefs, and decisions. Whereas behaviorists treat a person's mental state as irrelevant (because it cannot be observed), the cognitivist sees mental states as directly manipulating operant responses.

Studies on social cognition develop the concept of schemas as a general mental framework through which people impose structure and impart meaning to facilitate understanding (Gioia & Poole, 1984; Graesser, Woll, Kowalski, & Smith, 1980). Cognitive theories include goal-seeking or purposefully regulated behaviors that tend to be neglected in behavioral theories. Cognitive theories imply that people learn conceptual relationships and have mental maps that interpret and give meaning to environmental stimuli. Simon (1947) and his colleagues from Carnegie Mellon used schemas and cognitive maps concepts to examine decision making in organizations.

Cognitive theories of individuals do not directly translate to organizations. Concepts that are collective, such as paradigms (Kuhn, 1970), myths (Meyer & Rowan, 1977), metaphors (Smith & Simmons, 1983), schemata (Weick, 1979), ideologies (Starbuck, 1982), and culture (Cook & Yanow, 1993; Pettigrew, 1979; Schein, 1985) are all examples illustrating conceptual orientations to organizations. This cognitive orientation also plays strongly in applied work. Building on concepts of tacit knowledge ("we know more than we can tell," Polanyi, 1966, p. 4), Nonanka (1994) describes conversion of tacit to explicit knowledge as learning. Others have developed applied frameworks for using these concepts, such as Senge, Kleiner, Roberts, Ross, and Smith's (1995, p. 59) notions of "wheels of learning" and Dixon's (1999) cycles of organization learning. These applied perspectives all build on Argyris and Schön's (1978) theory of action, Kolb's (1984) experiential learning research, or Revans's (1980) action learning writings.

Argyris and Schön's organization learning theory (1978, 1996) is based on their discovery that there are widespread flaws produced by people's guiding values that inhibit individual and organizational learning. When confronted with difficult or embarrassing information, people react defensively. Defensive reactions include continuously protecting oneself from criticism, exposure of one's shortcomings, or other real or perceived threats to one's self image. Defensive behaviors limit what a person hears, keeping him or her ignorant of the consequences of his or her own behaviors. Defensive behaviors often are accompanied by aggressive counterbehaviors; they are antilearning, over-protective, and self-sealing. At an organization level, defensive routines are "actions or policies that prevent individuals or segments of the organization from experiencing embarrassment or threat. Simultaneously, they prevent people from identifying and getting rid of the causes of the potential embarrassment or threat" (Argyris, 1990, p. 25).

What guides these defensive routines is a set of values or governing variables that Argyris and Schön call Model I. In Model I, behaviors are governed by achieving the purpose as an individual has defined it, winning and not losing, suppressing negative feelings, and emphasizing rationality. These governing variables lead to actions that emphasize unilateral control of environment and tasks and unilateral protection of oneself and others. The consequence of Model I is escalating errors and decreased effectiveness in problem solving. There is low freedom of choice and difficulty in producing valid information, resulting in defensive interactions and relationships. Learning is inhibited because there is little public information and testing to determine whether strategies are achieving desired results. When managers make mistakes in organizations, the facts surrounding those mistakes are undiscussable. Not only are the mistakes undiscussable, but the undiscussability of mistakes is itself undiscussable. All three levels—mistakes, the fact that they are undiscussable, and the undiscussability of the undiscussable—contribute to a self-sealing system that cannot learn.

In developing a social system that produces conditions and behaviors consistent with learning, Argyris and Schön propose values based on what they call a Model II theory in use. The governing variables are valid information, free and informed choice, and internal commitment. Although these governing variables are often espoused, they are not often practiced. Model II behaviors involve sharing control with participants who are competent and have a role in designing and implementing their actions. Surfacing conflicting views is encouraged, and thoughtful consideration is given to creating conditions for public testing. As the proponents themselves recognize (Argyris, Putnam, & Smith, 1985, p. 102), "at an espoused level Model II [values] . . . sounds like mother-hood and apple pie . . . the trick is to produce them in the real world."

Argyris and Schön's development and testing of their theory have implications for their research methods. They developed a method they call action science. A conceptual understanding of this method is needed to initiate and sustain learning. These ideas are seemingly simple conceptually (easy at an espoused level) yet complex at an action level (difficult to consistently produce). Action science requires an interventionist to help an organization learn by creating conditions for a Model II theory in use. This principle extends back to the early research and writing by Argyris (1970) wherein he proposes that creating the conditions in which these appropriate values are realized in the organization is the primary work of the interventionist. The emphasis in action science is on producing actions consistent with these theories as part of studying organization learning.

One of the criticisms of a cognitive orientation is the question of how this concept moves from individual to collective or organizational levels. Kim (1993) proposes that this linkage can take place by having people share and make their private mental model explicit. Going from tacit to explicit requires tools that are shared by organization members. Argyris and Schön (1978, 1996; Argyris, 1993; Argyris et al., 1985) developed tools—such as an action map for organizations' defensive routines, the left-hand right-hand column case, and the ladder of inference—that are taught, shared, and used by teams and organizations to improve their collective learning. Many variations of these tools have been developed (see Senge et al., 1995).

In describing nearly three decades of their research, Argyris and Schön (1996) note their concern about the literature and lack of research progress. In two studies—research on naturally occurring innovations (medical field innovation and strategic decision making about dynamic random access memory markets) and intervention research (decentralization, activity-based costing, total quality management, reengineering, and strategic human resource management)—they found the consistent outcome to be limited learning (Argyris & Schön, 1996). These mixed results come from gaps of explanation (how organization kept undiscussable the issues raised by knowledge privately held by members) and gaps of implementation (interventions that provide only partial or temporary improvement). The basis for these problems is disconnections between organization learning theory and research methods, which were normal and not action science, used to study and improve learning in organizations.

Organization development shares a common intellectual foundation with these approaches to organization learning. The process of organization development—entering, contracting, diagnosing, analysis, feedback, designing interventions, leading change, and evaluating interventions—seeks to surface and test managers' and employees' assumptions. At its essence, an organization development effort is explicit about formalizing a process by which people go beyond what they are doing to discuss what they are thinking and feeling. Alternatively, the theory and methods to surface and test assumptions from this organization learning research can be part of and complement those OD efforts. People use many of the techniques for surfacing and testing assumptions in organization development efforts.

Organization Learning as a Developing Knowledge Base

Duncan and Weiss (1979) critique Argyris and Schön (1978) for focusing on the process of learning and not addressing how learning takes place, the outcomes of learning, and the fit between organization environment and structure. Organization learning, they propose, is the process by which the organization is designed to deal with its environment. Learning explains why organizations are differentially effective even though they "operate in environments which are relatively the same in terms of the components, demands on the organization, and other characteristics" (Duncan & Weiss, 1979, p. 76). There are three levels to examine effectiveness: organization success in attaining its goals (profit, growth, productivity, return on investment), adaptation to changes in the environment (organization activities change as a response to changes in the action–outcome relationships), and individual–organization interfaces (roles are defined to have low conflict and low ambiguity; otherwise people are overly stressed and do not perform well).

Duncan and Weiss developed what they call a middle range theory of organization learning by linking it to organization design processes. Studying learning processes requires an understanding of

- The efforts to predict changes in the organization's environment
- A search for alternatives such as raw materials or markets
- Maintaining memory about possible changes
- Discovering what changes are needed
- Undertaking changes that are expected to succeed

Organization learning is more than an aggregation of individual members; it includes articulation, communication, and acceptance of action–outcome relationships that becomes a form of organization knowledge. Managers act on that knowledge as the legitimate basis for action, and this knowledge forms the basis for control and coordination at many levels in the organization.

Hedberg (1981) makes the connection between individual and organizational levels by noting that organizations develop worldviews and ideologies through members. Although individual members and leaders come and go, organizations preserve certain behaviors, norms, and values. Hedberg describes the result of learning as being more effective in coping with problems, specifically in the environment of the organization. Learning occurs when organizations increase their understanding of their environment by observing the results of their actions or accepting others' experiences as relevant to them. Using March and Olsen's (1975; see Figure 25.1), he notes that it is individuals who act and learn, and organizations are stages where this acting takes place.

Organizations' environments change frequently. Understanding the environment involves learning new knowledge and discarding obsolete knowledge. Discarding old knowledge, or unlearning, is as important as gaining new knowledge. Slow unlearning is a crucial weakness in organizations (Hedberg, 1981, p. 3), especially in contexts where environments change quickly and existing knowledge becomes obsolete. Although they adjust to changes, organizations also create change in their environment through their actions. They may use their knowledge offensively to create changes in the environment that result in better fits with their own capabilities. Organization learning includes adaptation (the use of a firm's knowledge to adjust to the reality of the environment) and manipulation (the use of the firm's knowledge to change the environment to improve the organization's fit). In either of these situations, cognitive limitations of people in organizations distort their interpretations such that learning cycles are blocked and incomplete.

Building on the idea of a knowledge base, Hedberg (1981) draws many parallels from individual concepts and extends them to collective or organizational levels. For example, individual behaviors and habits link to organization operating procedures, traditions and norms link to customs and symbols, memories link to myths and sagas, and beliefs and values link to social systems and cultures. These phenomena influence individual learning within organizations and then transmit organization conditions to individuals. Based on the contingency that performance is linked to the fit of the organization to its environment, Hedberg proposes four design strategies to facilitate organization learning and unlearning. Organizations should seek to be more experimental, linking strategies and development to environmental conditions. They should seek to become more sensitive to change signals, removing perceptual filters and increasing communication channels. Little can be done to change the external environment, but organizations can internally encourage and reward risk taking to stimulate experiments. Efforts should be made to destabilize organizations, providing counterbalancing forces to consensus, contentment, affluence, faith, consistency, and rationality. All of these design strategies create movement from the organization's status quo. Experimentation provides variation and means to challenge accepted solutions and goals, regulating awareness reduces consensus, and redesigning environments reduces consistency and challenges worldviews. These are all efforts to explain how organizations learn, unlearn, and relearn; all three of these must be operating together if organizations are to develop.

In noting that the conception of organization learning may be too narrow, Huber (1991, p. 89) proposes a broader definition of learning: "An entity learns if, through its processing of information, the range of its potential behaviors is changed." This conception of learning entities applied to organizations becomes the following: "An organization learns if any of its units acquire knowledge that it recognizes as potentially useful to the organization" (Huber, 1991, p. 81). The key concern for organization learning is the gathering and processing of information. As information is distributed through the organization, people piece together patterns that may not have been evident.

Information becomes knowledge as it becomes part of the know-how of the organization. Nonaka (1994) builds on this concept to examine tacit and explicit knowledge. Explicit knowledge is captured and stored in information systems, but tacit knowledge resides with people; it is acquired through experience and can be communicated only through experience. Both explicit and tacit knowledge are important in organizations, and attention to the conversion of tacit to explicit knowledge is the basis for work on knowledge creation processes (Nonaka & Takeuchi, 1995). Nonaka and Takeuchi distinguish knowledge creation from organization learning largely because of their critical view of the organization learning literature and its roots in extending individual learning to organizations.

Knowledge management is proposed as a key to competitive advantage (Easterby-Smith, Crossan, & Nicolini, 2000). Nonaka and Takeuchi's work has led to a continuing stream of research and writing on knowledge management. Perhaps because of their critical views, knowledge management literature has remained distinct from organization learning. Yet "the key outcome of organizational learning processes is organization knowledge" (Cummings & Worley, 2005, p. 505). Information technology specialists or consultants focusing on technical aspects of system design or their services have written most of the knowledge management articles. Reviews of knowledge management projects (Davenport, De Long, & Beers, 1998) report that social factors—leadership and change management skills—were of critical importance to their success. However, the concepts underlying organization learning and knowledge management are largely similar.

Developing a knowledge base and knowledge management are new perspectives in organization development. As companies seek to improve their management of knowledge by implementing technical solutions, managers have recognized that their failures in achieving expected benefits relate to shortcomings in their associated social and behavioral efforts. Organization development provides a well-known framework and process to complement the implementation of capabilities in technical systems. An organization development framing of these issues is especially important when knowledge is at stake; to change and share their existing knowledge or adopt new knowledge, people need conditions of trust and safety. Organization development has developed processes for creating interventions and conditions that further trust and safety as a context for initiating and sustaining organization changes.

Organization Development Applied to Organization Learning Perspectives

Each of the four streams of literature reviewed illustrates a broad perspective on organization learning. Based on these perspectives' core ideas, there are specific factors that enable and inhibit learning (Table 25.1). Through an applied stance on what enables and inhibits learning, organization development practices can be used to improve organization learning processes. When viewed as accumulated experience, organization development can improve learning by revealing important historical conditions and by developing processes with metrics to capture performance and providing these data as feedback to current efforts. When viewed as adaptation to environmental changes, organization development can help, by linking internal processes with external conditions, to improve people's understanding of their organization's environment. When viewed as assumption sharing, organization development can help in the communication and processes that improve the abilities of people in the organization to surface and test their assumptions. Finally, when viewed as a developing knowledge base, organization development can help develop processes for valuing and retaining experience and for integrating newcomers' skills and capabilities into the organization. The application of organization development and an applied stance on organization learning are developed more broadly in the literature on the learning organization.

THE LEARNING ORGANIZATION

A way to understand the literature on the learning organization is to see it as a part of a longer history of management thought (Mirvis, 1996). Rather than being seen as a revolutionary concept distinct from other management research, Ulrich et al. (1993) propose that the learning organization be thought of as an evolutionary concept that integrates, builds on, and enhances decades of management thought (Figure 25.2). In building on historical management knowledge, the application of organization learning is part of "an evolutionary process whereby managers think and rework their organizations" (Ulrich et al., 1993, p. 59).

To this point, I have purposefully side-stepped the distinction between organization learning and the learning organization. The literature (Easterby-Smith et al., 2000; Easterby-Smith, Snell, & Gherardi, 1998; Sun & Scott, 2003; Tsang, 1997), though critical of these differences, has found that the differences have not amounted to much. These terms are two sides of the same coin. Organization learning is the study of learning processes in organizations, including individual, group, and organization-wide levels of analysis. This work, which is what has been reviewed, is largely descriptive and the domain of academics. It includes individuals learning in organizations and organization-level learning. No one has questioned that organization learning includes individual learning. The debate has been on the extent to which individual learning can be extended to organization learning and the extent to which organization learning should go beyond the learning of the people within organizations.

The writing on the learning organization focuses improving the learning of organizations,

1990s	Learning capability
	Learning organization
	Culture change
	Strategic unity
	Core competence
	Organizational capability
	Empowerment
1980s	Japanese management
	Quality circles
	Excellence
	Mission/vision/values
	Cycle time (competing through time)
	Customer service
	Intrapreneuring
1970s	Strategic planning
	Life cycles
	Value chain
	Zero-based budgeting
	Matrix management
	Participative management
1960s	Management by objectives
	Transaction analysis
	Team building
	Job enrichment
1950s	T groups
	Theory X and Theory Y
	Managerial grid
	Forecasting

Figure 25.2   Evolution of Management Thought

SOURCE: From Ulrich, D., von Glinow, M. A., & Jick, T. (1993), High-impact learning: Building and diffusing learning capability, in *Organizational Dynamics*, Autumn 93, Vol. 22 Issue 2, p. 58.
Copyright 1993, with permission from Elsevier.

including the individuals in the organization and the behavior, or learning, of the organization as a whole. According to Sun and Scott (2003, p. 203) there is some agreement on this definition in the work of Senge (1990), Pedler, Burgoyne, & Boydell, (1991), Garvin (1993), Stewart (1992) in Hill (1996), Tucker, Edmondson, & Spear, (2002), Agashae and Bratton (2001), and Overmeer (1997) in Stewart (2001). However, there is great diversity in the prescriptions for the learning organization. By describing processes through which managers enhance organization learning, this literature created the idea of the learning organization as an ideal type of organization. Most authors on the learning organization are practitioners, writing about the learning organization as a practical and applied concept, proposing what organizations should be like based on their experience. This work is naturally prescriptive because the inherent desire is to improve the transfer of knowledge from individuals to collectives to organizational to interorganizational levels. Unfortunately, the prescriptions in some of the writing lack an empirical basis.

The learning organization concept provides a framework consistent with basic goals of organization development: improving problem solving, responsiveness, quality of working life, and effectiveness (Cummings & Worley, 2005). It can be classified as a strategic intervention, involving individual, group, and organization-level interventions in enhancing capabilities to produce and use new knowledge. As an intervention, it aims to move organizations beyond just solving current problems to creating capabilities for continuous improvement and change. In their methods and approaches, learning organization prescriptions have many similarities to organization development. Much of the writing on the learning organization applies behavioral knowledge to help people and organizations build their capacities to change and become more effective through their learning.

What is notable in the history of this literature is the influence of the concept of the learning organization. "There is a new tradition of literature on *the learning organization* which is largely distinct from the literature on organizational learning" (Easterby-Smith, 1997, p. 1086). Corresponding to the 1990 time frame in which there has been a rapid increase in articles on organization learning (Crossan & Guatto, 1996) was writing that made the concept applied-and-action oriented. The literature on organization learning "boomed since publication of Senge's (1990) influential volume on the 'art and practice of the learning organization'" (Mirvis, 1996, p. 13). "Based

in part on the popularity of Senge's work and its impact on management, the study of learning organizations has received increasing attention" (Ulrich et al., 1993, p. 53).

It is likely that the popularity of the applied literature influenced the research literature, as was the case with organization culture (Barley, Meyer, & Gash, 1988). "Inspired by the success of Senge's *The Fifth Discipline* (1990), many management consultants and researchers have jumped on the bandwagon" (Tsang, 1997, p. 74). What made Senge's (1990) work different? Why is it connected to an increase in the popularity and impact on management? When *The Fifth Discipline* was published in 1990, academics were onto an important topic but very critical of their own literature. Cohen and Sproull wrote in their introduction to the *Organization Science* special issue on organization learning that there was "insufficient agreement among those working in the area on its key concepts and problems" (1991, p. i). These challenges were predominantly in describing learning in organizations and the various teleological, ontological, epistemological, and technological lenses used by researchers (Easterby-Smith et al., 1998).

Senge's (1990) book built indirectly on the literature, and it set a new course with a wider audience. In writing for a broad management audience, he popularized the idea of the learning organization as an ideal type, "an organization that is continually expanding its capacity to create its own future" (Senge, 1990, p. 14). Senge prescribed a set of principles, which he called disciplines, that would help people and organizations in their learning efforts. These ideas combine "the systems variant of the management science perspective with a strong reliance on OD" (Easterby-Smith, 1997, p. 1104).

As Easterby-Smith correctly identifies, OD practices are at the foundation of Senge's book and its influence on the popularity of the learning organization. Senge's writing integrates practices developed by organization development scholars and practitioners. The five disciplines are mental models (testing ingrained assumptions), shared vision (desirable future views developed and shared by key leaders), personal mastery (commitment to lifelong learning and innovation), team learning (group dynamics and collective behaviors), and system thinking (seeing integrated patterns in events and actions). In addition, the concept of improving the human interface to system dynamic models to create "microworlds" (Morecroft, 1987) for managers to learn from provided the basis for the managerial practice fields. The managerial practice field was an innovation in organization learning practices. These practice fields, although based on interactions with system dynamic computer simulations, conceptually built on the same notions behind organization development interventions using role-plays.

The basis for Senge's ideas came from his management science research on developing and applying system dynamic models (see Forrester, Graham, Senge, & Sterman, 1983). Senge's interest in addressing vexing societal problems led him to a complex system view and the study of system dynamics with Jay Forrester. Using computer models, Forrester showed that policymakers' efforts to solve problems by focusing on symptoms could cause worse long-term consequences. Work that was initially in the public sector shifted to business organizations as leaders of these organizations visited the Massachusetts Institute of Technology (MIT) research group to learn more about system thinking. "We all believed that the tools of systems thinking could make a difference in companies. As I worked with different companies, I came to see why systems thinking was not enough by itself" (Senge, 1990, p. 15).

A challenge for applying system dynamic models in organizations has been the complex system of feedback, misattribution, and judgment errors of managers and policymakers (Sterman, 1994). Senge worked with colleagues

in developing leadership programs along with system thinking teaching (Senge & Keifer, 1984). When *The Fifth Discipline: The Art and Practice of the Learning Organization* was published, he had 11 years of experience in developing and conducting workshops that have been attended by more than 4,000 managers, combining system thinking and building shared vision and personal mastery. "I take no credit for inventing the five major disciplines of this book. The five disciplines . . . represent the experimentation, research, writing, and invention of hundreds of people. But I have worked with all the disciplines for years, refining ideas about them, collaborating on research, and introducing them to organizations" (Senge, 1990, p. 14). Given that these disciplines were learned from colleagues in practice, written about with an emphasis on the fifth discipline, system thinking, and targeted for a general management audience, the organization development–based practices are recognizable but not identified as such.

Three factors contributed to making Senge's work a popular milestone. One factor was 30 years of literature and research work by academics on organization learning. As noted many times in this book, much of the behavioral science research has been developed, practiced, or applied as part of organization development. There was a solid interest and academic research in learning in organizations, diffuse and divergent as it is or may have been. Senge's writings draw on the interest and promise of this research. He was not writing about a new concept but taking an existing concept that had many adherents and providing clarity by writing about successful experiences in applying the ideas under the umbrella concept of the learning organization.

The second factor was his focus. His book and articles were for managerial audiences; he developed and tested these ideas with colleagues in teaching them to managers. Many of the concepts were linked to longstanding research streams, concepts that drew on organization development research and practices. The confidence about the ideas that comes through in the writing is based on an empirical grounding in practices that were proven with managers.

A third factor contributing to the popularity was the continuing efforts to broaden both research and practice. The popularity of *The Fifth Discipline* drew much interest from corporate executives, many of whom wanted to learn more and were willing to fund a research effort at the MIT Sloan School for Management. A center was established in 1991 to develop the learning organization concepts more fully with corporate sponsors through research projects (Roth & Senge, 1996). This center, the Center for Organizational Learning, had goals and processes in the tradition of what Lewin (1945) established more than 40 years earlier as the Research Center for Group Dynamics[1]:

- To integrate work across multiple research disciplines
- To address important societal problems
- To move beyond the level of description and into bringing about desired changes
- To cooperate with industry in field settings
- To be devoted to the development of scientific concepts, methods, and theories

Developing, testing, and studying the application of learning principles involved cooperative relationships between researchers, managers, and consultants. A framework was developed and tested to link learning to action, proposing that organizations develop infrastructure, guiding ideas, and methods (Senge et al., 1995). Values that broadly engaged people in organizations to enable learning (Kofman & Senge, 1993) were developed and described. A broad, strategic model of organization change based on learning capabilities emerged from company learning projects (Senge et al., 1999). Many of these publications were not traditional research articles but a "fieldbook" management genre that had hundreds of contributors detailing first-hand their practice and experience. The series of publications, based on combined work of academics,

managers, and consultants, reinforced and helped create the popularity of Senge's initial writing on the learning organization.[2]

A focus on applying prescriptions in organizations, popularity in the business press, working with consultants, attention of researchers at other universities, and long research cycle times created controversy about academic research standards. The center's administrative staff and sponsoring organizations started the nonprofit Society for Organizational Learning (SOL) in 1997. SOL was designed to integrate research, management, and consulting (capacity building) efforts in creating learning organizations. Since its founding, many chapters of SOL have been started in countries all over the world. Each of these chapters includes company members, academics from neighboring universities, and local consultants. The combination of a diverse group of professionals can be powerful in creating new insights and knowledge (Roth, 2005a). What makes for success in a project is different for academics than it is for consultants, and in order to work together, people must not only collaborate but also individually meet the criteria of their constituent disciplines.

FUTURE OF ORGANIZATION LEARNING

Organization learning has established itself as an area of study and practice. "Twenty-five years ago, organizational learning was a rare species among ideas . . . largely absent from the scholarly literature of organizational theory. . . . Well-respected scholars . . . found the idea confusing and, in some ways, repugnant. Now, in the mid 1990s, it is conventional wisdom that business firms, governments . . . are all subject to a 'learning imperative,' and in the academic as well as the practitioner world, organizational learning has become an idea in good currency" (Argyris & Schön, 1996, p. xvii). As I have repeatedly suggested in my review of the organization learning literature, the concepts and practices often go back to, or have similar roots to, organization development literature. Numerous authors took advantage of the interest in organization learning to develop a popularized literature for a general management audience. This literature extends, unfortunately often without reference, principles and processes from organization development. Given its common heritage, the directions, trends, and future of the organization learning literature have important implications for organization development.

As organization learning literature has grown, the nature of the debate on various topics has become well known, although not resolved. Easterby-Smith et al. (2000) recently reviewed more than 100 papers submitted for an organization learning conference. Notably absent were longstanding debates on levels of learning, cognitive versus behavioral change, the single- and double-loop learning relationship, learning and unlearning, and organization learning versus the learning organization. "These debates have not been abandoned, but become the taken-for-granted background . . . and now simply provide a point of departure for researchers to address their own assumptions about organizational learning" (Easterby-Smith et al., 2000, p. 784). This finding is an indication that we have not made much progress toward a more complete or integrative theory of organization learning. Writers continue to define specialized areas and address organization learning from their own perspectives. It is interesting to note that this inward-looking trend of the organization learning literature is similar to Varney's observation (Cummings & Worley, 2005, p. 611) that recent organization development writing focuses more on the status of the field than on evaluations of research or practice.

To deal productively with a lack of convergence, we could take a page from the book on the learning organization. Among others, Kofman and Senge (1993, p. 16) argue, "There is no such thing as a learning organization"; it is an ideal type and a linguistic creation and therefore not something that is or can ever be realized. In taking this view, organization learning researchers might come to realize that the phenomenon of organization learning is very broad and unlikely to rest with any conclusive findings given the various disciplinary lenses and different research methods used to investigate it. As in the study of organizations, there are so many variants and perspectives from which to see organizations (Morgan, 1986) that we become more interested in insights that the variants give us than in any conclusive, and what would be very narrow, definition.

In 1989, as I prepared my dissertation research proposal, Edgar Schein gave me advice that I did not like very much at the time but came to appreciate later. He suggested that I not even try to study organization learning. The basis for his advice was that developing an appropriate conception of organization learning would be too complex and would take too long. I should frame my fieldwork as a study of change, get my dissertation done, and then have a career in which to develop theories for organization learning. I did get my dissertation done, and I am still working on conceptions of organization learning. In his own analysis of organization learning research, Schein (1996, p. 1) maintains, "The literature is all over the map. . . . We have so many methodologies and paradigms for looking at these phenomena. . . . I have reached the conclusion over the last several decades that the only way out of this confusion is to go back to real data, based on intensive observation of real phenomena." He advocates a clinic approach: in-depth observations made during times of change with the observer collaborating with managers studying and understanding interventions, paying attention to process and structure, and assuming a system view over a linear, causal model.

Many scholars have made similar recommendations that apply equally to organization learning or organization development research. In their criticism of change research, Pettigrew, Woodman, & Cameron (2001) suggest that it needs to include multiple contexts and levels of analysis; focus on the role of time, history, and process; link processes to outcomes; provide international comparisons; pay attention to receptivity and pacing of change; and link scholarship and practice. These recommendations, if followed, would take us from the "how" that theoretical orientations develop and give us better accounts and data from which to better discern the "what" of organization learning. This change research recommendation is consistent with many requests others have made for more empirical, in-depth, longitudinal studies of organization learning (Dodgson, 1993; Fiol & Lyles, 1985; Levitt & March, 1988; Shrivastava, 1983; Sitkin, 1996; Tsang, 1997; Weick & Westley, 1996).

In looking for emerging directions in organization learning, Easterby-Smith et al. (2000) found three trends in the submissions: using practice as a unit of analysis, embracing issues of diversity, and including power and politics. Practice as a unit of analysis relates to the idea that knowledge is situated in practice, so that learning takes place in a workplace or performance settings (Brown & Duguid, 1991; Lave & Wenger, 1991). Related ideas have been proposed in the work on learning communities (Kofman & Senge, 1993), communities of practice (Wenger, 1998), and learning networks (Levin & Knutstad, 2003). The practice dimension connects people in their learning more strongly than in their affiliation, and these social networks develop learning that crosses organizations (Wenger, McDermott, & Synder, 2003).

Issues of diversity become prominent when it is recognized that organizations are entities with unstable boundaries rather than homogeneous and functional units. Challenges then become ones of coordination and learning in the presence of incoherent practices and cultures and the need to create alignment across organization boundaries. What influences which culture and which practice dominates in coordinating or learning across organization boundaries? Power and politics are well-known aspects of organization life (Zaleznik, 1989), but in the study of organization learning, power and politics have remained largely ignored (Lawrence, Mauws, Dyck, & Kleysen, 2005). Rarely is the question asked, "Whose purposes are being served?" (Easterby-Smith et al., 1998, p. 262). Are companies using the rhetoric of organization learning to obtain compliance and commitment from employees, as Neilsen (1996) suggests? Some critics suggest that the ideology implicit in a learning organization is one that lets managers build and safeguard their power (Coopey, 1995). A more explicit treatment of power and politics in organization learning research would improve our understanding of these issues.

These directions for organization learning research illustrate the lack of connection to efforts to define professional values and ethical guidelines. The many varied backgrounds and fields of people studying organization learning make any convergence difficult. Organization development has several organizations (such as the Organization Development Institute, Organization Development Network, American Society for Training and Development, and Academy of Management Organization Development and Change Division) that provide venues for the development of values and ethical standards to which their members subscribe. As a future direction, these organizations and their values and ethics could benefit organization learning researchers and practitioners.

Challenges for future research on learning organizations mirror broader challenges faced by most organizations. Technological capabilities and market shifts have created a networked, globalized economy that requires organizations to be interconnected and interdependent with one another. As the inner workings of organizations are more outwardly connected, companies conceptualize themselves and their conversion process as part of a value stream that connects raw materials to finished goods and services used by customers.

A value stream, like any chain, is only as strong as its weakest link. Organization learning and change to improve products and services have to take place across the interdependent set of organizations that make up an enterprise.

The assumptions on which much of our organization theories and change practices rest no longer hold when applied across sets of organizations (Roth, 2005b). Multiorganization enterprises need learning processes that cross organization boundaries to lead to needed sets of interdependent improvements. Making improvements across sets of organizations in a value stream or economic region is also a future direction for research and practice. Several scholars have written about these issues in organization development (Chisholm, 1998; Cummings, 1984), and these concepts could be helpful in extending their work to organization learning practices.

These concepts of levels of learning, learning about learning, and the context for learning are applicable to the challenges identified for improving complex engineered systems. Complex engineered systems are large-scale, technologically enabled, dynamic, and socially interactive systems such as the communication, energy, transportation, and financial systems of the U.S. government. These complex engineered systems are increasingly important to the quality of life in our highly industrialized societies. MIT President Charles Vest (2000, p. 1) wrote, "Humankind's advances will depend increasingly on new integrative approaches to complex systems, problems, and structures." One of the directions for the improvement of complex engineered systems comes from research in software development (Moses, 2003). Software engineers developed the term *ilities* (so named because many of the concepts end in -*ility*) to describe nonfunctional (i.e., going beyond function, cost, and performance) system requirements such as flexibility, reliability, affordability, usability, and maintainability. The application of ilities to organizations in general, and learning organizations

in particular, provides a conceptual direction for assessing progress. As organizations learn to embed the new capabilities in the ways in which they operate, they become adept at creating order through which to be more efficient and at creating chaos through which to become more effective. Ilities provide a concept through which to embrace order and chaos, to characterize progress, and to think about new frontiers for learning organizations and organization development.

To reflect on the future for organizations and learning, I return to the "organization learning" oxymoron: To organize is to forget and reduce variety, and to learn is to disorganize and increase variety (Weick & Westley, 1996). Organizing implies taking what is being done and improving by reducing variety; learning, on the other hand, implies a search for alternatives and being sure that you are doing the right things. These two concepts— doing the right things and doing things right— are what Drucker (1967, 1974) proposes as the management challenges of efficiency and effectiveness. Therefore, we might think about progress in organizations as improvements in the tradeoffs between efficiency and effectiveness or organizing and learning. Organization development research has been active in this domain—in countering too much management effort pushing toward efficiency with interventions to improve and sustain organization effectiveness. Many of the technical capabilities, focused on operational and financial results, have had dehumanizing effects on the workforce. Organization development, with its associated change practices, has sought to address these challenges through its attention to social responsibility and humanistic values.

NOTES

1. The Group Dynamics Research Center, which moved to form the Institute for Social Research at the University of Michigan, was a part of the lineage of people at MIT who influenced,

by their interaction, discussions, and presentation of research, Jay Forrester's development of system dynamics, and later organization learning. In addition to people associated with group dynamics research—Kurt Lewin, Dorwin Cartwright, Ron Lippitt, John French, and Leon Festinger—several other people influential to organization development worked at MIT. Among these people were Douglas McGregor, Dick Beckhard, Warren Bennis, and Edgar Schein.

2. These publications included a book on methods and tools for learning (Senge et al., 1995); the quarterly journal *Reflections*, edited by Ed Schein starting in 1998; a book on change through organization learning (Senge et al., 1999); a book on dialogue (Isaacs, 1999); in-depth case studies on corporate learning projects with commentaries (Kleiner & Roth, 2001; Roth & Kleiner, 2000); and a book on application of learning principles in schools (Senge et al., 2000).

REFERENCES

Adler, P. S., & Cole, R. (1993, Spring). Designed for learning: A tale of two auto plants. *Sloan Management Review,* 85–94.

Adler, P. S., & Cole, R. E. (1994). Rejoinder. *Sloan Management Review, 35*(2), 45–49.

Agashae, Z., & Bratton, J. (2001). Leader–follower dynamics: Developing a learning environment. *Journal of Workplace Learning, 13*(3), 89–103.

Allison, G. (1971). *Essence of decision.* Boston: Little, Brown.

Argote, L., Beckman, S., & Epple, D. (1990). The persistence and transfer of learning in industrial settings. *Management Science, 36*(2), 140–154.

Argyris, C. (1970). *Intervention theory and method.* Reading, MA: Addison-Wesley.

Argyris, C. (1990). *Overcoming organizational defenses, facilitating organizational learning.* Boston: Allyn & Bacon.

Argyris, C. (1993). *Knowledge for action: A guide to overcoming barriers to organizational change.* San Francisco: Jossey-Bass.

Argyris, C., Putnam, R., & Smith, D. (1985). *Action science: Concepts, methods, and skills for research and intervention.* San Francisco: Jossey-Bass.

Argyris, C., & Schön, D. (1978). *Organizational learning: A theory of action perspective.* Reading, MA: Addison-Wesley.

Argyris, C., & Schön, D. (1996). *Organizational learning II: Theory, method, and practice.* Reading, MA: Addison-Wesley.

Barley, S., Meyer, G., & Gash, D. (1988). Cultures of culture: Academics, practitioners and the pragmatics of normative control. *Administrative Science Quarterly, 33*(1), 24–60.

Berggren, C. (1994, Winter). NUMMI vs. Uddevalla. *Sloan Management Review,* 37–45.

Brown, J. S., & Duguid, P. (1991). Organizational learning and communities-of-practice: Toward a unified view of working, learning, and innovation. *Organization Science, 2,* 40–57.

Cangelosi, V. E., & Dill, W. R. (1965). Organizational learning: Observations toward a theory. *Administrative Science Quarterly, 10*(2), 175–203.

Chisholm, R. (1998). *Developing network organizations: Learning from practice and theory,* Reading, MA: Addison-Wesley.

Cohen, M., & Sproull, L. (1991). Editor's introduction. *Organization Science, 3*(1), i–iii.

Cook, S. D., & Yanow, D. (1993). Culture and organizational learning. *Journal of Management Inquiry, 2,* 373–390.

Coopey, J. (1995). The learning organization: Power, politics and ideology. *Management Learning, 26*(2), 193–213.

Crossan, M,. & Guatto, T. (1996). Organizational learning research profile. *Journal of Organizational Change Management, 9*(1), 107–115.

Crossan, M., Lane, H., & White, R. (1999). An organizational learning framework: From intuition to institution. *Academy of Management Review, 24*(3), 522–537.

Cummings, T. G. (1984). Transorganizational development. In B. M. Staw & L. L. Cummings (Eds.), *Research in organizational behavior* (Vol. 6, pp. 367–422). Greenwich, CT: JAI.

Cummings, T., & Worley, C. (2005). *Organization development and change* (8th ed.). Mason, OH: South-Western.

Cyert, R. M., & March, J. G. (1963). *A behavioral theory of the firm.* Englewood Cliffs, NJ: Prentice Hall.

Davenport, T., De Long, D., & Beers, M. (1998). Successful knowledge management projects. *Sloan Management Review, 39*(2), 43–57.

De Geus, A. P. (1988, March–April). Planning as learning. *Harvard Business Review, 66,* 70–74.

De Geus, A. P. (1997). The living company. *Harvard Business Review, 75*, 51–61.

Dixon, N. (1999). *The organizational learning cycle.* London: Gower.

Dodgson, M. (1993). Organization learning: A review of some literatures. *Organization Studies, 14*(3), 375–394.

Drucker, P. F. (1967). *The effective executive.* New York: Harper & Row.

Drucker, P. F. (1974). *Management tasks, responsibilities, practices.* New York: Harper & Row.

Duncan, R. B., & Weiss, A. (1979). Organizational learning: Implications for organizational design. In B. M. Staw (Ed.), *Research in organizational behavior* (pp. 75–123). Greenwich, CT: JAI.

Easterby-Smith, M. (1997). Disciples of organizational learning: Contributions and critiques. *Human Relations, 50*(9), 1085–1116.

Easterby-Smith, M., Crossan, M., & Nicolini, D. (2000). Organizational learning: Debates, past, present and future. *Journal of Management Studies, 37*, 783–796.

Easterby-Smith, M., Snell, R., & Gherardi, S. (1998). Organizational learning: Diverging communities of practice? *Management Learning, 29*(3), 259–272.

Epple, D., Argote, L., & Devadas, R. (1990). Organizational learning curves: A method for investigating intra-plant transfer or knowledge acquired through learning by doing. *Organization Science, 2*(1), 58–70.

Fiol, C., & Lyles, M. (1985). Organizational learning. *Academy of Management Review, 10*(4), 803–813.

Forrester, J., Graham, A., Senge, P., & Sterman, J. (1983, October). *An integrated approach to the economic long wave.* Position papers for Conference on Long Waves, Depression, and Innovation, Siena-Florence, Italy.

Garvin, D. (1993, July–August). Building a learning organization. *Harvard Business Review*, 78–91.

Gioia, D. A., & Poole, P. P. (1984). Scripts in organizational behavior. *Academy of Management Review, 9*, 449–459.

Graesser, A. C., Woll, S. B., Kowalski, D. J., & Smith, D. A. (1980). Memory for typical and atypical actions in scripted activities. *Journal of Experimental Psychology, 6*, 503–515.

Hedberg, B. (1981). How organizations learn and unlearn. In P. C. Nystrom & W. H. Starbuck (Eds.), *Handbook of organizational design* (Vol. 1, pp. 3–27). New York: Oxford University Press.

Hill, R. (1996). A measure of the learning organization. *Industrial and Commercial Training, 28*(1), 19–25.

Hirschmann, W. (1964). Learning curve. *Chemical Engineering, 71*(7), 95–100.

Huber, G. P. (1991). Organizational learning: The contributing processes and the literatures. *Organizational Science, 2*(1), 88–115.

Isaacs, W. (1999). *Dialogue and the art of thinking together: A pioneering approach to communicating in business and in life.* New York: Doubleday Currency.

Johnson, T. (1993). *Relevance regained: From top-down control to bottom-up empowerment.* New York: Free Press.

Kahneman, D., Slovic, P., & Tversky, A. (1982). *Judgment under uncertainty: Heuristics and biases.* Cambridge, UK: Cambridge University Press.

Kim, D. (1993). The link between individual and organizational learning. *Sloan Management Review, 34*, 37–50.

Kleiner, A., & Roth, G. (2001). *Oil change: Perspectives on corporate transformation.* New York: Oxford University Press.

Kofman, F., & Senge, P. (1993, Autumn). Communities of commitment: The heart of learning organizations. *Organizational Dynamics*, 5–23.

Kolb, D. (1984). *Experiential learning: Experience as the source of learning and development.* Englewood Cliffs, NJ: Prentice Hall.

Kuhn, T. (1970). *The structure of scientific revolutions.* Chicago: University of Chicago Press.

Lave, J., & Wenger, E. (1991). *Situated learning: Legitimated peripheral participation.* Cambridge, MA: Harvard University Press.

Lawrence, T., Mauws, M., Dyck, B., & Kleysen, R. (2005). The politics of organizational learning: Integrating power into the 4i framework. *Academy of Management Review, 30*(1), 180–191.

Levin, M., & Knutstad, G. (2003). Construction of learning networks: Vanity fair or realistic opportunities. *Systemic Practice and Action Research, 16*(1), 3–19.

Levitt, B., & March, J. (1988). Organizational learning. *Annual Review of Sociology, 14*, 319–340.

Lewin, K. (1945). The Research Center for Group Dynamics at the Massachusetts Institute of Technology. *Sociometry, 8,* 126–135.

Lindbloom, C. (1959). The science of muddling through. *Public Administration Review, 19,* 79–88.

March, J. G. (1991). Exploration and exploitation in organizational learning. *Organizational Science, 2,* 71–87.

March, J. G., & Olsen, J. P. (1975). The uncertainty of the past: Organizational learning under ambiguity. *European Journal of Political Research, 3,* 147–171.

March, J. G., & Olsen, J. P. (1976). *Ambiguity and choice in organizations.* Bergen, Norway: Universitetforlaget.

March, J. G., & Simon, H. (1958). *Organizations.* New York: John Wiley & Sons.

Meyer, J., & Rowan, B. (1977). Institutionalized organizations: Formal structure as myth and ceremony. *The American Journal of Sociology, 83*(2), 340–363.

Michael, D. (1973). *On learning to plan & planning to learn.* San Francisco: Jossey-Bass.

Mirvis, P. (1996). Historical foundations of organization learning. *Journal of Organizational Change Management, 9*(1), 13.

Morecroft, J. (1987, September). System dynamics and microworlds for policymakers. *European Journal of Operational Research,* 301–320.

Morgan, G. (1986). *Images of organization.* Beverly Hills, CA: Sage.

Moses, J. (2003). *The anatomy of large scale systems.* Unpublished working paper 2003-1.25. Cambridge, MA: MIT Engineering Systems Division.

Nadler, D. (1977). *Feedback and organization development: Using data-based methods.* Reading, MA: Addison-Wesley.

Neilsen, R. (1996). *The politics of ethics: Methods for acting, learning and sometimes fighting with others in addressing the problems of organizational life.* New York: Oxford University Press.

Nonaka, I. (1994). A dynamic theory of organizational knowledge creation. *Organization Science, 5*(1), 14–37.

Nonaka, I., & Takeuchi, H. (1995). *The knowledge-creating company: How Japanese companies create the dynamics of innovation.* New York: Oxford University Press.

Overmeer, W. (1997). Business integration in a learning organization: The role of management development. *Journal of Management Development, 16*(4), 245–261.

Pedler, M., Burgoyne, J., & Boydell, T. (1991). *The learning company.* London: McGraw-Hill.

Pettigrew, A. (1979). On studying organizational cultures. *Administrative Science Quarterly, 24*(4), 570–581.

Pettigrew, A., Woodman, R., & Cameron, K. (2001). Studying organizational change and development: Challenges for future research. *Academy of Management Journal, 44*(4), 697–713.

Polanyi, M. (1966). *The tacit dimension.* Garden City, NY: Doubleday.

Revans, R. (1980). *Action learning: New techniques for management.* London: Blond & Briggs.

Roth, G. (2005a). Creating new knowledge by crossing theory and practice boundaries. In W. Pasmore & R. Woodman (Eds.), *Research in organizational change and development* (Vol. 15, pp. 135–167). New York: Elsevier.

Roth, G. (2005b, Winter). Enterprise change and development. *Academy of Management ODC Newsletter,* 3–7.

Roth, G., & Kleiner, A. (2000). *Car launch: The human side of managing change.* New York: Oxford University Press.

Roth, G., & Senge, P. (1996). From theory to practice: Research territory, processes and structure at an organizational learning center. *Journal of Change Management, 9*(1), 92–106.

Schein, E. (1985). *Organizational culture and leadership.* San Francisco: Jossey-Bass.

Schein, E. (1996). *Organizational learning: What is new?* Unpublished working paper #3912. Cambridge, MA: MIT Sloan School of Management.

Schwartz, P. (1991). *The art of the long view.* New York: Doubleday.

Senge, P. (1990). *The fifth discipline: The art and practice of the learning organization.* New York: Doubleday.

Senge, P., Cambron-McCabe, N., Lucas, T., Smith, B., Dutton, J., & Kleiner, A. (2000). *Schools that learn.* New York: Doubleday Currency.

Senge, P., & Kiefer, C. (1984). Metanoic organizations. In J. Adams (Ed.), *Transforming work: A collection of organization transformation readings* (pp. 68–84). Alexandria, VA: Miles River.

Senge, P., Kleiner, A., Roberts, C., Ross, R., & Smith, B. (1995). *The fifth discipline fieldbook.* New York: Doubleday Currency.

Senge, P., Kleiner, A., Roberts, C., Roth, G., Ross, R., & Smith, B. (1999). *The dance of change: The challenges to sustaining momentum in learning organizations.* New York: Doubleday Currency.

Shrivastava, P. (1983). A typology of organizational learning systems. *Journal of Management Studies, 20,* 7–28.

Simon, H. (1947). *Administrative behavior: A study of decision-making processes in administrative organization.* New York: Macmillan.

Simon, H. A. (1957). *Models of man.* New York: John Wiley & Sons.

Sitkin, S. B. (1996). Learning through failure: The strategy of small losses. In M. D. Cohen & L. S. Sproull (Eds.), *Organizational learning.* London: Sage.

Smith, K., & Simmons, V. (1983). A Rumpelstiltskin organization: Metaphors on metaphors in field research. *Administrative Science Quarterly, 28*(3), 377–392.

Starbuck, W. (1982). Congealing oil: Inventing ideologies to justify acting ideologies out. *Journal of Management Studies, 19*(1), 3–27.

Stata, R. (1989). Organizational learning: The key to management innovation. *Sloan Management Review, 30,* 63–74.

Sterman, J. (1994). Learning in and about complex systems. *System Dynamics Review, 10*(2–3), 291–330.

Stewart, T. (1992). GE keeps those ideas coming. In R. Kanter, B. Stein, & T. Jick (Eds.), *The challenge of organizational change* (pp. 474–482). New York: Free Press.

Stewart, T. (2001). *The wealth of knowledge: Intellectual capital and the twenty-first century organization.* New York: Currency.

Sun, P., & Scott, J. (2003). Exploring the divide: Organizational learning and learning organization. *The Learning Organization, 10*(4), 202–215.

Taylor, F. (1911). *The principles of scientific management.* New York: Harper.

Tsang, E. (1997). Organizational learning and the learning organization: A dichotomy between descriptive and prescriptive research. *Human Relations, 50*(1), 73–89.

Tucker, A. L., Edmondson, A. C., & Spear, S. (2002). When problem solving prevents organizational learning. *Journal of Organizational Change Management, 15*(2), 122–137.

Ulrich, D., von Glinow, M. A., & Jick, T. (1993). High-impact learning: Building and diffusing learning capability. *Organizational Dynamics, 22*(2), 52.

Vest, C. M. (2000). *MIT President's report for AY 99/00.* Cambridge: MIT Press.

Watson, J. B. (1914). *Behavior: An introduction to comparative psychology.* New York: Holt, Rinehart & Winston.

Weick, K. E. (1979). *The social psychology of organizing* (2nd ed.). New York: McGraw-Hill.

Weick, K. (1991). The nontraditional quality of organizational learning. *Organization Science, 2*(1), 116–124.

Weick, K. E., & Westley, F. (1996). Organizational learning: Affirming an oxymoron. In S. R. Clegg, C. Hardy, & W. R. Nord (Eds.), *Handbook of organization studies* (pp. 440–458). Thousand Oaks, CA: Sage.

Weisbord. M. (1993). *Discovering common ground: How future search conferences bring people together to achieve breakthrough innovation, empowerment, shared vision and collaborative action.* San Francisco: Berrett-Koehler.

Wenger, E. (1998). *Communities of practice: Learning, meaning and identity.* Cambridge, UK: Cambridge University Press.

Wenger, E., McDermott, R., & Synder, B. (2003). *Cultivating communities of practice: A guide to managing knowledge,* Cambridge, MA: Harvard University Press.

Womack, J., Jones, D., & Roos, D. (1990). *The machine that changed the world.* New York: Macmillan.

Wright, T. (1936). Factors affecting the cost of airplanes. *Journal of Aeronautical Sciences, 3*(4), 122–128.

Yelle, L. E. (1979). The learning curve: Historical review and comprehensive survey. *Decision Sciences, 10*(2), 302–308.

Zaleznik, A. (1989). *The managerial mystique: Restoring leadership in business.* New York: Harper & Row.

26

Learning by Design

Key Mechanisms in Organization Development

A. B. (RAMI) SHANI

PETER DOCHERTY

The field of organization development (OD) continues to evolve as it is embedded in the firm and its context. The immense forces of technological, societal, and global changes have resulted in a variety of labels that attempt to capture the changing work life reality, such as *postindustrial society, the information revolution, the postcapital society,* and *the knowledge age.* Although we may not be able to fully comprehend the magnitude of these changes, organizations and managers around the world are struggling to find the balance between economic performance pressures and business and human sustainability while managing business transformations.

In the last decade thousands of companies have jumped on a variety of OD and management methods such as empowerment, business process reengineering, self-managed or self-directed teams, sociotechnical system redesign, and total quality management (TQM) as a means for improving business performance and competitiveness. In many cases their application probably reflects an interest in fashion, or what some call management fads or quick fixes (Abrahamson, 1996, 1999; Gibson & Tesone, 2001). Though immensely popular in the business press, there is a growing recognition that many OD approaches have failed to deliver on their promises (Beer & Eisenstat, 2000). Furthermore, business competitiveness has been sustained in only a few successful implementations (Stebbins & Shani, 2002). In many cases, the learning potential embedded in the change programs never materialized.

Some argue that the impacts of many OD intervention methods, tools, and processes that aim to help organizations enhance their productivity, quality, and workers' quality of life usually are very short lived (Lillrank, Shani, & Lindberg, 2001). At the heart of most of the failed OD and change interventions one can find the inability to create, develop, and sustain learning mechanisms (Shani & Docherty, 2003). Learning mechanisms are institutionalized cognitive, structural, and procedural arrangements that initiate, facilitate, and support learning of individuals, groups, and the organization as a whole.

This chapter attempts to bring to the forefront learning mechanisms that are at the core of OD interventions. Most OD interventions create learning mechanisms by design, yet our understanding of their creation, nature, development, and sustainability seems to receive limited attention. This chapter reviews the relevant literature and explores the nature of learning requirements, design dimensions, and learning mechanisms in OD interventions. We examine the learning mechanisms that were used in four specific OD initiatives, one from each intervention cluster. We conclude with a discussion of the implications for OD practice and the creation of actionable OD knowledge.

MANAGING OD:
THE PLACE OF DESIGN

The basic premise of this chapter is that OD efforts that prioritize the development and full use of personnel and simultaneously aim to achieve optimal and sustainable business performance (economic results) must explore alternative design configurations. Such organizations make purposeful choices about the design and implementation of specific learning mechanisms that fit their change efforts, goals, culture, and business context. The basic assumptions behind the organization learning mechanisms and methods are that the development and use of human capital entail exploring and thinking through specific organization design choices of structures and processes, the most effective business strategies and work

designs are developed and implemented when employees are involved directly in the redesign process, and achieving sustainability—of continuous competitive economic performance and continuous development of human potential—entails ongoing investment in the full use and regeneration of human resources.

From an OD perspective, the learning organization results in a flexible structural alternative to bureaucratic organization, and its power lies in the simplicity of the mechanisms that enable ordinary people to create systemic, fundamental, and sustainable learning processes and actions. The design process focus provides a vehicle for experiential and conceptual learning about the genotypical features of the learning organization alternatives. It is only from people pooling their knowledge that a learning organization can evolve. When the people involved work out their own designs, they are highly committed and motivated to sustainable, effective implementation.

How do we relate learning to learning mechanisms? Marsick and Watkins (1990) make the distinction between formal and informal learning. Formal learning typically is institutionally sponsored, classroom based, and highly structured. Informal learning is not usually classroom based or highly structured, and control of the learning rests primarily in the hands of the learner and usually is deliberately encouraged by an organization (the employer in a workplace context). Company strategies for promoting informal or experiential learning are planning for learning, creating mechanisms for learning, and, as mentioned earlier, developing an environment conducive to learning. Planning makes learning more conscious, focuses effort, and increases measures of accountability, as long as learning does not become an end in itself, with only a loose connection to the work processes. Planning allows people to nurture learning strategically and to take advantage of a wide range of learning strategies that might otherwise be overlooked.

Marsick and Watkins (1997) indicate several difficulties that may hinder informal learning:

Organizations do not always let people follow their natural inclinations to learn in different ways. People differ in their capacity to seek needed information and skills, and there is disagreement about what learning to learn means and therefore about how to help people learn how to learn. The topic of learning might require the assistance of outside experts. Organizations may not provide clear guidance about what people must know and how this will help them in their career paths.

Sustained competitiveness at the company level requires competence or capabilities on the cutting edge, which entails continuous learning. However, many workers do not see the opportunity to learn as a generous fringe benefit but rather as a threat, To make things worse, the demands for learning are increasing (e.g., manufacturing companies report that in 2001 they had 80% of the personnel they will have in the year 2010 and only 20% of the technology), and the conditions for learning are less favorable. In a study of about 60 companies, Lundgren (1999) found that the demands on the speed of learning had tripled (i.e., time to proficiency had been cut by two-thirds).

Yet despite all the energy, time, and money companies spend on attempts to transform organizations through a variety of OD and change programs, the reality is that few succeed in sustaining the reinventing process (Beer, 2001). Mastering the art of learning in such contexts is not a quick fix. We contend that one of the main reasons for the failure is that most change efforts and companies do not develop and nurture learning mechanisms that allow them to challenge the basic assumptions about the key or core business processes and thereby change their mental models and actions. Developing this kind of managerial and organizational capability takes time and strong conviction in order to overcome what Schein (2002) calls survival anxiety and learning anxiety.

The inherent challenge of OD and change fosters the need for managers and practitioners to have access to and develop a basic understanding of the ideas and theory behind the learning mechanisms, including an understanding of their origins and evolution. The realization that many choices must be studied and that many design alternatives can be created can help overcome some of the anxiety that seems to hinder successful implementation. This chapter provides a window into and a snapshot of the large variety of choices executives have made that resulted in many learning mechanisms in four different types of OD interventions.

LEARNING BY DESIGN: KEY FEATURES

In recent decades, the demands on companies for flexibility and responsiveness have increased at all levels and in both the short term and the long term. Managers constantly face the need for change and development, which constitute the core of dynamic effectiveness, a concept that has emerged from the debate on the rise of Japanese industry as a serious force among the OECD countries. This is further reflected in the inclusion of development, innovation, and learning as specific areas in many companies' management systems (e.g., balance scorecard [BSC] systems). Today the demands for sustainable competitiveness include the following learning requirements for the majority of personnel in change situations:

- The behaviors that define learning and the activities that define being productive are now identical. Learning is not something preserved for a managerial group. Personnel must have a broad spectrum of cognitive, technical, business, social, and learning skills.
- The work situation must promote workers' commitment to their work with a personal readiness to use their initiative, to take risks, to tolerate differences of opinion, to accept change, and to continually learn new things.
- They must focus on the integration of learning in their work.

Zuboff's excellent formulation of this point is even truer today than when she wrote it:

The (truly successful) organization is a learning institution, and one of its principal purposes is the expansion of knowledge that
comes to reside at the core of what it means
to be productive. Learning is no longer a separate activity that occurs either before one
enters the workplace or in remote classroom
settings. Nor is it an activity that requires
time out from productive activity. To put
it simply, learning is the new form of labor.
(Zuboff, 1988, p. 395)

Learning is a process that is embedded in all
change and development activities that concern people's attitudes, behavior, beliefs, competence, and knowledge, whether it be a radical
change such as an organization transformation or the incremental changes emerging from
continuous improvement groups in production. It is also present in change processes and
their outcomes. This is well illustrated in
all planned change models. For example, in
Kurt Lewin's phase model of change processes,
the first phase, unfreezing, indicates the
insights, attitude changes, and even new knowledge and skills that are prerequisites for the
coming change process. The refreezing phase
has similar implications, including the acquisition of the competences, norms, and values
necessary for the new system to function efficiently and effectively. The same reasoning
applies to incremental changes. In continuous
improvement, the suggested improvements are
the result of collective reflection in teams. The
implementation of the suggestions may involve
more or less learning on the part of the individuals and teams concerned. In many instances
an important object of change and development processes is to adapt the skills and knowledge of the organization to new demands
from the marketplace or to improve the learning ability of the organization through the
introduction or development of various learning mechanisms.

We maintain that learning is an essential
feature of OD and its outcomes. As such developments aim to realize sustainable improvements in organization performance, they

should lead to improved learning or at least
not endanger or impair learning. Such outcomes may be realized by actively planning for
learning, creating mechanisms for learning,
and, as mentioned previously, developing an
environment conducive to learning. Planning
makes learning more conscious, focuses effort,
and increases measures of accountability.
However, learning must not become an end in
itself, with only loose connection to the work
processes. Planning allows people to nurture
learning strategically and to take advantage of
a wide range of learning strategies that might
otherwise be overlooked. Therefore, it is advisable to make learning an explicit area for consideration and development in the directives
for OD projects. This should apply to all personnel categories affected by the changes.
Often learning is confined to management and
professional staff, through formal training or
feedback in the new organization. This should
apply to both change processes and their
outcomes. Often participation in development
projects is seriously undermined by insufficient
training, support, or time to allow workers to
acquire and use the skills they need to participate meaningfully in the development process.

Defining learning needs for the new organization requires careful consideration. New
technologies and new markets often clearly
indicate requirements of a professional and
technical character. However, important
development opportunities may be missed if
present assumptions and unrecognized behaviors are not uncovered. Marsick and Watkins
(1997) indicate several difficulties that may
hinder informal learning: organizations do not
always let people follow their natural inclinations to learn in different ways, people differ in
their capacity to seek needed information and
skills, and there is disagreement about what
learning to learn means and therefore about
how to help people learn how to learn.

At the most basic level, learning mechanisms are formalized strategies, policies, guidelines, management and reward systems, methods,
tools and routines, systems, allocations of

resources, and even the design of physical work space that have been designed, formulated, and ratified in order to promote and facilitate learning in the organization and its networks (Lipshitz, Popper, & Oz, 1996; Popper & Lipshitz, 1998). Learning mechanisms can be routinized only up to a point. Because learning demands ongoing inquiry into current and future practices, it can be viewed as a continuous disturbance of existing routines that were developed for the purpose of stability, predictability, and efficiency. Faced with the decision to focus on learning, managements range from having little or no interest in learning to regarding it as a principal means of competition (De Geus, 1997; Garvin, 2000; Schein, 2002).

Learning mechanisms are elements in the learning infrastructure or system that reflect management's intention to prioritize learning in the organization and its networks (Shani & Mitki, 2000). Therefore, management actions can be viewed on a continuum from facilitative to prescriptive. Facilitative aims indicate for individuals, groups, and the organization as a whole means and opportunities to support their learning. Prescriptive aims are achieved by formulating standard operating procedures, rules, and management systems that detail obligatory goals and methods for learning to be carried out by specific individuals and groups in the organization. Management emphasis on the need for and desire to use or engage in different learning activities is reflected in increasing numbers of and emphasis on learning mechanisms in the company.

Learning mechanisms can be regarded as being integrated or nonintegrated and designated or dual purpose. Integrated mechanisms allow organization members to analyze their own and others' experiences in order to improve their performance. Mechanisms that are used by personnel to collect, analyze, store, and disseminate information primarily for the benefit of others are called nonintegrated mechanisms. Mechanisms that operate separately from organization performance are regarded as designated or learning specific.

Those that act in conjunction with task performance are dual purpose. Thus local management planning systems in teams are the basis for the economic and operational activities in the teams and provide the essential feedback for reflection and learning for these activities (Friedman, Lipshitz, & Overmeer, 2001; Shani & Docherty, 2003). Dual-purpose, integrated learning mechanisms fuse learning and task structures, creating a community of reflective practitioners (Schön, 1983).

Learning mechanisms are the formalized, institutionalized results of active decisions by management based on the company's position regarding various aspects of learning. Three broad categories of learning mechanisms are cognitive, structural, and procedural (Table 26.1).

Cognitive mechanisms provide language, concepts, models, symbols, theories, and values for thinking, reasoning, and understanding learning issues. For example, the strategy discipline reasons about change and development in terms of dynamic capabilities and seldom uses the vocabulary of learning. The learning language is used mainly in the human resource field, where the term *learning capability* is also found (DiBella, 2001; Helfat, 2003). Examples of important concepts that have important bearing on learning strategies and plans are formal and informal learning, single- and double-loop learning, and tacit and explicit knowledge. These mechanisms may be manifested or formalized in organizations as company value statements, strategy documents, management–union agreements, intercompany contracts, and management and reward systems, such as BSC and human resource development (HRD) systems.

Structural mechanisms concern organizational, technical, and physical infrastructures. These include feedback channels; communication channels; databanks and databases; the work organization; formal (and even informal) forums, arenas, and networks; and learning-specific structures such as parallel learning structures, bench learning structures, continuous

Table 26. 1   Learning Mechanisms: Categories, Types, and Examples

Categories	Types	Examples
Cognitive mechanisms	Language, concepts, models, symbols, theories, and values	Cognitive, behavioral
		Single-loop, double-loop
		Tacit, explicit
		Company value statements
		Strategy documents
		Management–union agreements
		Intercompany contracts
		Human resource development system
Structural mechanisms	Feedback channels	Reward systems
	Communication channels	Spatial design
	Technical structure	Parallel learning structures
	Physical structure	Bench-learning structures
	Forums, arenas, networks	Continuous improvement
	Work organization	Teams
		Online learning applications
		Learning centers
		Data warehouses
Procedural mechanisms	Methods, models, procedures, rules, and tools	Tests, e.g., learning style
		Assessment methods
		Support infrastructure
		Standard operating procedures

improvement, and quality circles. Technology mechanisms may take the form of learning centers, e-learning programs, databases and data warehouses, and e-mail, document, and data-sharing systems. The physical structure may take the form of the layout of the work space to facilitate (spontaneous) contact between members of the organization (Bushe & Shani, 1991).

Procedural mechanisms concern the rules, routines, methods, and tools that have been institutionalized in the organization to promote and support learning (Pavlovsky, Forslin, & Rienhart, 2001). These may include tests and assessment tools and methods, standard operating procedures, methods for specific types of learning (e.g., action learning), and debriefing routines.

Learning mechanisms usually are designed to promote, facilitate, and support learning. Basically, people learn either individually or collectively. If they are not motivated or committed, then there is a strong probability that they will not learn. However, there are mechanisms that prescribe learning, such as BSC systems and certain compensation systems (Cressey & Docherty, 2002; Shani & Docherty, 2003).

Company strategies for promoting informal or experiential learning are planning for learning. Planning makes learning more conscious, focuses effort, and increases measures of accountability, as long as learning does not become an end in itself with only a loose connection to work processes. Planning allows people to nurture learning strategically and take advantage of a wider range of learning strategies that might otherwise be overlooked (Marsick & Watkins, 1997; Shani & Docherty, 2003).

OD INTERVENTIONS AND LEARNING MECHANISMS

The OD literature encompasses a large variety of well-documented and well-researched interventions. Attempts to cluster the OD interventions resulted in few maps or classifications. Some of the groupings include French and Bell's (1999) clustering by target group (individuals, dyads or triads, teams and groups, intergroup relations, total organization); Friedlander and Brown's (1974) clustering by technostructural and human processual; Mitki, Shani, and Stjernberg's (2000) clustering by level of impact (limited, focused, and system wide); and Cummings and Worley's (2005) clustering by the organization issues that the OD interventions address (human process interventions, human resource management interventions, technostructural interventions, and strategic interventions). For the purpose of this chapter we use the clustering proposed by Cummings and Worley (2005). For illustration purposes, in each cluster we focus on one specific intervention, as was implemented in an organization, provide a brief review of the context in which the intervention took place, briefly describe the change process and phases, identify and briefly discuss the learning mechanisms that were used or created by design, and capture the major outcomes of the initiative.

Technostructural Interventions: TQM Intervention at the Israeli-American Paper Mill Corporation

The technostructural intervention cluster includes interventions that focus on the technology and structure (design) of the organization. At the most basic level, interventions aimed at the structural design of the organization include helping the organization move from traditional ways of organizing work to more flexible and integrative forms such as process-based and network-based structures. Some of the OD interventions in this cluster include employee involvement interventions such as parallel structures and TQM, interventions aimed at restructuring organizations such as downsizing and business process reengineering, and work design and redesign interventions such as work design and sociotechnical systems.

For the purpose of this chapter we focus on the TQM effort at the Israeli-American Paper Mill Corporation. The Paper and Board Manufacturing Division includes three plants for manufacturing paper (white paper, brown paper, and household paper) and three support and service units (engineering, projects, and administrative). There are 800 employees in the division, making it the largest of the corporation's units. The Paper and Board Manufacturing Division's business strategy is derived from the targets set by the corporation's management and stresses several elements: the centrality of the customer in organization perception, which means viewing product quality as the highest value; introducing an approach and habits for continuous improvement; involving workers in developing advanced processes and innovative technologies; widespread implementation of teamwork; creating channels of communication at all levels and in all directions; and the management commitment to achieve these aims and to adopt and lead the necessary changes.

The initiative for this program was led by the divisional general manager. He chose to rely on an approach that would facilitate the development of quality improvement, achieve continuous improvement, and generate worker involvement as individuals and as teams. Starting with the development of a quality circle program was perceived as a safe first step that would be likely to yield the targets set by corporate management and set in motion a developmental orientation. In particular, changes could be brought about in organization culture, teamwork, and the provision of tools for managers and workers, with whose assistance the quality level of products would be improved. The risk of introducing quality circles is low, and the necessary investments for its implementation are also low. A quality circle structural configuration was established to house and guide the change effort. By the end of the first year, 9 quality circles operated in the Paper and Board Manufacturing Division, and by the end of seventh year the program encompassed 51 quality circles, involving 665 workers, or approximately 88% of all workers in the paper mills. The success of the quality circle program earned the division first prize as an organization excelling in the implementation of quality circles in Israel. The quality circles provided the infrastructure for TQM effort.

A system-wide TQM program was launched at the end of the seventh year. The program had the following objectives: The system will supply products and services that answer customer demands and expectations; every worker will accept and take full responsibility for his or her part in executing the work process; everyone is responsible for quality; the company will choose suppliers who meet and conform to the quality policy and requirements; the management and the workers, as one, lead the company to work quality improvement and to fulfilling the aims and targets set in its policy; and the quality assurance procedure will be prepared according to the ISO-9002 principles and the corporation's quality policy. A 12-year follow-up study at the company indicates impressive results in terms of performance measures, process development, and attitude-based measures. For example, the work time needed to produce a ton of paper was reduced from 16 to 8.2 work hours per ton, in a 10-year period. Furthermore, the average output of the four major paper production machines was raised during the same period by 14.9%. The water consumption for manufacturing a ton of paper decreased by 47.3% without damaging the production process or paper quality. Water conservation is a national goal in Israel.

The raw material for paper manufacturing comes from two sources: cellulose imported from overseas and waste fibers collected in Israel. The corporation's objective was to reduce the use of cellulose as much as possible and to increase the use of waste fibers. The improvements suggested by the process improvement teams resulted in a decrease of 9% in the same 10-year period in the percentage use of cellulose fibers for paper manufacture, and the percentage use of recycled fiber rose by almost 6%. Finally, in the paper production industry, quality of products is measured by defect ratio per 10,000 sheets of paper. The defect ratio was reduced from 6.2 to 2.2 in the same 10-year period. Customer satisfaction is measured in the industry by the number of complaints per month. In the same period, the average of complaints per month was reduced from 8.8 to 1.7.

A few learning mechanisms were created at the Israeli-American Paper Mill Corporation as a part of the TQM change program. Some of the cognitive learning mechanisms included a new value statement and a strategic business planning process. As part of the structural learning mechanisms, a parallel learning structure was created that included a steering committee and project study teams that focused on improvement, learning, and the establishment of quality circles and improvement teams. The formalization of goal-setting and progress review processes and the periodic review of progress and quality assurance procedures in the parallel learning structure and the formal organization top management are examples of procedural learning mechanisms.

Human Resource Management Interventions: Performance Management at Fossil Fuels Co. Ltd., United Kingdom

The human resource management intervention cluster includes interventions that focus on personnel practices used to integrate people into organizations and people development.

At the most basic level, these interventions include performance management systems, career planning and development, goal setting, reward systems, and employee wellness. For the purpose of this chapter we chose to focus on a performance management system intervention that was implemented at Fossil Fuels Co. Ltd., United Kingdom.

Fossil Fuels, a petroleum and chemical company, had started a shift in its corporate strategies to become more competitive in a fast-changing global environment. Its first steps were uncoordinated: Different parts of the company were working with different models and focusing on different issues. To rectify this, management drafted a new corporate mission and vision and also outlined a corporate change strategy. A key component in this was the transformation of the company's human resource management practices as a strategic business tool. The lead focus effort was the performance management (PM) system, which was viewed as a catalyst for change that could set the whole human resource context for the new company. Thus the main focus of the OD was a system that often is a key learning mechanism and certainly is in companies where learning is regarded as an important aspect of performance.

As partner in this development effort, management chose the Center for Effective Organizations, a California research center whose work was based on the ideas that organizations are best created by the self-designing activities of their members and that organizations are best understood by a dual focus on the structures and processes that make up the organization and on its members. The cooperation between the center's researchers and the company's personnel was seen as a joint learning process.

The development process in focus here was not an administratively driven human resource project. Top management appointed a nine-member task force consisting of the heads of seven of the corporation's companies and two heads of corporate functions, all members of the senior management team. They were selected to represent conservative, command-and-control industry traditionalists and more progressive, change-oriented, participative factions of top management. The task force was to recommend appropriate changes to the highest corporate management committee. It had a support team of three members of corporate human resources and two senior researchers. The company's aim was to design a new way in which to manage performance.

To lay a foundation for the strategy-driven redesign, the task force decided at the outset to establish a relevant company value base, a key cognitive learning mechanism. This would identify the values that would guide the design activities. Criteria for the design were also generated. The human resource values to support the new strategic direction were applicable to the PM system. They included respect for individuals, developing their potential, promoting understanding and contribution to the business, participation in decision making, fair rewards, risk taking, innovation, and ethical behavior.

The task force conducted extensive studies of PM systems in other companies. The PM system they designed was tested with respect to links between organization levels and the mutuality achieved between employees and their managers in the PM process in terms of shared perceptions and the development of shared understandings. Shortcomings in the existing system were explicitly addressed in the design of the new system. An extensive survey was carried out based on earlier research to assess strengths and weaknesses in the current practice. A top-down, bureaucratic process was to be replaced by meaningful interactions between managers and employees.

Criteria for the new system included such aims as to motivate, build trust and commitment, and be fair, credible, and flexible. The design of the PM system naturally covered the entire cycle: performance definition, development, and performance review. The importance of mutuality and participation entailed more equal two-way roles at all stages for the employee and manager. Individual and team goals and performance were explicitly linked to business plans and corporate goals. Groups were dealt with before individuals. Implementation entailed extensive materials and training efforts for all managers and all interested employees. The training included role playing. Ninety-seven percent of all employees received training at implementation. A systematic follow-up was carried out after 24 months. This showed that employee–management mutuality, employees' understanding of their situation, and their satisfaction with career opportunities had all increased significantly. Performance was also better.

Fossil Fuels used cognitive, structural, and procedural mechanisms to extend and reinforce learning at the individual and group levels in its organization. The foundation for its efforts was a new value statement from top management that spelled out management's perception of the position and value of personnel in the company and its development. This underlined respect for individuals, developing their potential, promoting understanding and contribution to the business, and increasing participation in decision making. New criteria for performance management also were formulated. The structural and procedural mechanisms took the form of a new performance management system. The structure included the formation of a human resource management and performance management task force. The procedures for a new performance management system were coordinated at the corporate level, and a broad training program for its introduction and a follow-up program were implemented to ensure its smooth running.

Human Process Interventions: Search Conference at Xerox

The human process intervention cluster includes interventions that focus on people within organizations and the processes through which they accomplish goals. Some of the OD interventions in this cluster include T groups,

process consultation, third-party intervention, team building, intergroup relations interventions, and large group interventions. Within the large group interventions one can find such interventions as search conferences, open space meetings, open system planning, and future search interventions.

For the purpose of this chapter we chose to focus on the search conference intervention implemented at Xerox (as reported by Emery & Purser, 1996). After the recent reorganization and downsizing at Xerox Customer Business Unit, management expressed a strong need to develop a strategic business plan from the bottom up. The search conference was considered to be a timely and appropriate method for organization renewal and for developing a clear vision for the newly formed business unit. Management established a planning team to design and facilitate the process. The planning team designed a two-and-a-half-day excursion to an off-site location. Employees from all functions and levels in the unit were asked to participate. The planning team selected 50 people as representatives of all the functions, areas, and levels.

The first day, which centered on the first phase, environmental appreciation, started in the afternoon and focused on environmental scanning, with Xerox members exploring the global environmental context. Participants were asked to identify the changes, trends, events, and forces that they perceived as being significant or novel in the last 3 to 5 years. Next, in small groups, participants were asked to formulate desirable and probable futures. Half of the groups were asked to focus on developing desirable future scenarios and the other half to focus on probable future scenarios for the world in 10 years. Each group presented its input in a plenary session. Next, the session focused on scanning the task (or business) environment for the unit. This was followed by a session that focused on identifying the most important trends in their task environment, the probable future of the unit, and possible strategic responses to these trends.

The second phase, system analysis, shifted the focus to the internal affairs of the unit, beginning with a look at the historical evolution that resulted in the creation of the unit. Toward the end of the historical exploration, people were asked to identify the best aspects of their history that they should continue as they planned their future. This shifted the discussion to aspects of the system that participants wanted to keep, drop, or create. The next task was to conduct a quick system analysis and identify a short list of quick fixes: items for quick improvements and changes that could be implemented immediately without a lot of time and resources. At that point the focus shifted to a small group focus on developing four or five strategic goals describing the most desirable future state for the unit 3 years out. After the reports from the small groups, the whole community was asked to develop the criteria for prioritizing the strategic goals. Intense work resulted in 10 different long-term strategic goals, and the top 5 were agreed upon.

The third phase, action planning, started with the participants creating small self-selecting groups around a strategic goal. In this phase, participants developed specific strategies and action plans for implementation; obstacles were identified and strategies on how to overcome them were explored and finalized. All action plans included specific mechanism and timelines for implementation. In the last part of the session, the participants agreed to reconvene in 45 days to conduct a progress review session.

Emery and Purser (1996, p. 206) report that 6 months after the search conference, the manager of the unit made the following assessment of the most significant results achieves thus far:

> We used the output from the Search Conference action planning teams in our annual planning process to develop the business strategy for the next three years. Our culture has engineered a big shift. We have moved from being highly dependent on top-down planning to acting like entrepreneurs. This is an incredible breakthrough for our front-line employees. Each action planning team and the associates they recruited devoted countless hours to integrate their output into the business plan. I put one of our top sales managers on special assignment to work full time to integrate the work of all the action teams into our business practices. From the best practices point of view, the Xerox World-Wide Service chose our unit as one of two sites as a pilot for future work to improve customer loyalty because of the results we achieved with the Search Conference. We are now implementing the cross-functional design strategies that came out of the Search Conference so Xerox can organize around tasks rather than functions. I am excited about the next year as people carry the plan forward.

As can be seen in the case, a few learning mechanisms were created at the Customer Business Unit at the Xerox search conference change program. Some of the cognitive learning mechanisms included the adoption of new concepts and symbols such as environmental appreciation, environmental scanning, system analysis, reflection, and action planning. As a part of the structural learning mechanisms, the design and planning team served as a steering committee, and many small functional and cross-functional task forces were created to focus on learning, the development of strategic goals, and action plans. The formalization of the development of strategic planning process and the establishment of a formalized progress review process represent examples of procedural learning mechanisms.

Strategic Interventions: Learning Organization at Telecom Services Co., Sweden

The strategic intervention cluster includes interventions that focus on improving the interface between the organization and its larger

environment such that the organization develops the capabilities to adapt better to its changing environmental context. At the most basic
level, these interventions include high-performance
systems, integrated strategic change, transorganization development, merger and acquisition integration, culture change, self-designing
organizations, and organization learning. For
the purpose of this chapter we chose to focus
on the organization learning intervention
implemented at Telecom Services Company
(TSC), Sweden.

Radical systemic changes often are called
transformations. Kochan and Useem (1992)
point out that such changes usually involve
four interdependent activities: strategic restructuring, using technology to strategic advantage,
redesigning structures and boundaries, and
using personnel as strategic resources. One path
that may be chosen for this organization transformation is to establish a learning organization to engage systemic change on a continuing
basis (Useem & Kochan, 1992). This approach
enables the engagement of many constituencies
or stakeholders.

The transformation case presented here is
that of a public utility struggling to establish
itself in a deregulated market economy as a
limited company while the basic technologies
in the sector are changing rapidly. This entailed
determined efforts to establish a learning organization while the company changed its business strategy, its organization, its technology,
and its relations with employees and their
unions. Action taken throughout the organization, from top management to the shop and
office floor, involved changes in all these areas
that acted to promote learning and the emergence of a learning organization.

Dismissals in 1990–1994 had resulted in
dramatic demographic consequences for the
company: The average employee was about
50 years old, with 20 years of service in the
company. A radical transformation necessitated a new strategy. The company's new CEO
appointed a new vice president for business

and competence development, responsible for
designing and implementing a new human
resource management strategy and policies.
A new Vision 2001 project was initiated in
1995. Line managers would have responsibility for all issues related to personnel, from
recruitment to competence switching, mobility, and possible outplacement. Human capital
is measured every year using an extensive
survey questionnaire sent to all employees,
covering such issues as values and culture,
competence, motivation, responsibility and
initiative, leadership, cooperation and process,
and organization effectiveness.

The second major change concerned new
conditions for the social dialogue: Cooperation,
commitment, and development were values
that would permeate the organization. In the
mid-1990s the social partners in TSC signed
two local joint agreements that manifested the
new direction in their joint efforts. The first
regulated the formal work practices for development processes, both business and competence development processes. The second was
a change and security agreement. During the
3-year period all personnel were guaranteed
employment security.

The agreements embraced all members currently in the organization, even those who were
at risk of redundancy. Competence development plans were to be made for all. General
policies, methods, and routines were to be
drawn up for the company as a whole, but
units were given freedom in the application of
these solutions to their particular contexts.

The company used a range of cognitive,
structural, and procedural learning mechanisms to steer the transformation process
toward a learning organization. A major cognitive mechanism was the reformulation of
management's clearly identifiable values, especially regarding personnel. Management made
it clear that it respected personnel's need for
security by ensuring security through employability (i.e., that personnel whose employment
was at risk would be given the opportunity for

retraining for a future position in TSC or, via outplacement, in another organization). This gave the company greater flexibility. This and a partnership with personnel were confirmed in two joint agreements. A second aspect of the learning organization as an ordinary feature of the company was its use of language regarding its new approach to learning in the company. It became a matter of "integrating learning in work" or "learning-where-you-are." Similarly, the adaptation of learning to personal learning styles was called "learning-as-you-are." This focused competence development as a strategic issue in the company.

The company also introduced several new structural mechanisms, which were complemented with procedural mechanisms in the form of new routines and management systems. All organization units participated in a corporate "competence network." This had a double function: to support management's formulation of policies and guidelines for competence development and to identify and disseminate best practice in the company. The network provided dialogue opportunities as a method for competence development. A standard frame of reference and basic routines for competence development were applied to the entire organization. These included a competence development process (HRD system), a common model for describing the competence profiles, and integration of competence and business development. The human resource management systems were not the only management systems to be altered. A new BSC system focused on human capital as one of its four principal areas. This addressed acquiring, developing, and removing competences in the company and the integration of competence and business development. Thirty to forty percent of managers' bonuses were coupled to human capital issues.

Some divisions prioritized the formation of an "interactive academy," an intranet offering online courses and providing information on experts who are prepared to answer questions and discuss problems. These experts may be more competent colleagues or people from TSC's partners or suppliers. The name *interactive academy* indicates the extent to which it has replaced traditional education. The range of courses covers practically every professional area from information and communication technologies to topics such as rhetoric and mental training.

TSC's requirements for the creation of the learning organization consist of the management philosophy and values around learning, its corporate strategy, management systems, and the total learning environment. The design dimensions concerned the social dialogue (between management and unions), work organization and roles, and various aspects of the planning, conduct, and follow-up for learning processes. These, in their turn, were supported by the specific mechanisms described earlier. The focus was on critical design specifications, that is, creating a structure that ensures understanding, acceptance, and enthusiasm while allowing discretion for adjustment to the specific conditions prevailing in different parts of the organization.

A Personnel Development Division was formed in 1996 with responsibility for the employability policy. In the 3-year period 1996–1998, 6,550 people passed through the division. An independent evaluation estimated a net profit for TSC of about $150 million through investing in retraining and outplacement instead of traditional downsizing (Hansson, 1999). This included the creation of goodwill both within and outside the company. The partnership between management and the unions had created a win–win situation. Both parties gained something from the competence strategy.

Personnel administration was changed to human resource management, and under the label *total leadership* line managers received responsibility for handling their staffs. TSC has a system approach to HRD. It has striven to create a total learning environment. Management's aim was to create a win–win–win situation for the individual, the investor, and society, generating goodwill externally and contributing to a positive company culture.

DISCUSSION

Learning mechanisms, in one variation or another, are an integral part of any OD program. The illustrations provided in the previous section attempted to highlight the learning mechanisms created in each of the four interventions, from each of the four intervention clusters proposed by Cummings and Worley (2005). Table 26.2 summarizes key features of the individual cases with respect to the organization context, the main focus chosen for development, key actions taken, and outcomes achieved. Table 26.3 presents the different

types of learning mechanisms—cognitive, structural, and procedural—used by each company in its development efforts. All companies used each of the three types of learning mechanisms. Regarding the cognitive mechanisms, all four companies made important changes in their value statements and introduced new management systems to steer, coordinate, and control the development of learning.

This section identifies and discusses three of the issues that need to be addressed by managers and scholars: the interplay between OD and change, learning by design, and learning mechanisms; the interplay between OD and change, collaborative research, and learning by design; and alternative learning mechanisms.

Table 26.2   OD Interventions: Summary of Case Illustrations

	Focus	Context	Key Intervention Features	Outcomes
Human process intervention: search conference at Xerox, USA	Developing a strategic plan for the organization from the bottom up	Increase competitive business environment Create a new business unit	Development of design and planning group High degree of involvement, by design Participants chosen based on representation of the whole unit Progress review mechanism and process Three major phases in the intervention process: environmental appreciation, system analysis, and action planning	Increase profit by 15% and revenue growth by 20% Bottom-line planning as a means of continuous learning and improvements Shift from top-down planning to acting like entrepreneurs Chosen as a pilot site (1 of 2) for the implementation of innovative solutions for the global organization
Technostructural intervention: TQM at Israeli-American Paper Mill Corporation, Israel	Translating strategic quality targets and continuous improvement practice to the overall	Dynamic business context More competitive business environment	Development of shared vision Implementation of a system-wide quality control structure Establishment of a parallel learning	Reduce time to produce paper from 16 to 8.2 hours/ton of paper in 10 years Reduce work-related accidents from 83 to 37 per year in 10 years

	Focus	Context	Key Intervention Features	Outcomes
	business operations	Changes in government policy around protection from imports	structure with steering committees and many study and project teams organized to focus on specific key business processes	Reduce absenteeism from 1,442 to 798 days/year in 10 years Reduce defect ratio from 6.2 to 2.2/10,000 sheets of paper in 10 years
Human resource intervention: performance management system at Fossil Fuels Co., Ltd., UK	Transforming human resource management practices to drive and coordinate business and organization strategy	Increasing competition in a fast-moving global environment Need for greater coordination of organization development efforts	Creation of top management task force with researcher support Focus on performance management Extensive internal survey and external review of performance management practice Design, test, and implement performance management system Follow-up	Information and training reached 97% of personnel Significant improvements in employee–management mutuality, employee understanding, employee satisfaction, and performance levels Performance management lead system for new human resource manager with better coordination
Strategic intervention: learning organization at Telecom Services Co., Sweden	Establishing a learning organization to engage systemic change on a continuing basis	Need for radical transformation because of deregulation and new technology Critical demographic problems	New CEO, new vision, and new joint agreements New learning mechanisms: values (employability), management systems, competence models, tools, networks	Successful employability program Competence issues better Strong cooperation between social partners Learning mechanisms functioning Local adaptation of central models and methods

OD, Learning by Design, and Learning Mechanisms

How are the different OD interventions related to learning by design and to the different use of learning mechanisms in the case illustrations presented here? Naturally these are positive, successful examples, so it is not surprising from an OD perspective that the CEO and top management were deeply involved in all the cases, all of which concerned clearly sanctioned, strategic leaps forward. In fact, at the outset all made clear couplings to important management values, which were explicitly referenced as cornerstones for the strategic effort at hand. In all cases the entire staff was concerned, and the OD activities included all personnel or representatives from all categories of personnel; participation was a key value. Other values cited in the different cases were respect for personnel's security, well-being, development, fair compensation, and influence. In one case this took the form of special joint agreements, and in others it took the form of new or revised vision statements (Table 26.3).

As noted earlier, OD processes entail learning, even if the learning processes per se are not formally acknowledged. The human process intervention example was of a search conference. Usually these develop into occasions for collective reflection on the perceptions and experiences of different parties about what has happened and may happen in the company and its environment. At best this is a very positive learning process that may continue after the conference. In this case the company reported that the conference had a beneficial impact on its learning climate, with improvements in people's willingness to participate, to experiment, and to change (Table 26.2).

Table 26.3   OD Interventions and Learning Mechanisms: Brief Summary

	Learning Mechanisms: Cognitive	Learning Mechanisms: Structural	Learning Mechanisms: Procedural
Human process intervention: search conference at Xerox, USA	Involve large number of employees in strategic business planning and implementation Shift from top-down planning to acting like entrepreneurs	Create the design and planning team as a steering committee and many small functional and cross-functional task forces to focus on the development of strategic goals, learning, and action plans	Formalized developmental strategic planning process Establishment of a formalized progress review processes
Technostructural intervention: TQM at Israeli-American Paper Mill Corporation, Israel	Involve large number of employees in business development activities (empowerment value)	Create parallel learning structure with steering committees and many study and project teams organized to focus on the key business processes	Formalized developmental goal-setting and progress review processes Periodic review of progress within the parallel learning structure
Human resource intervention: performance management system at Fossil Fuels Co., Ltd., UK	New learning-relevant value base New criteria for performance management	New human resource and performance management task force	New performance management system Broad training and follow-up program
Strategic intervention: learning organization at Telecom Services Co., Sweden	Value system (employability) New joint agreements New Vision 2001 New learning language	New management–union cooperation structure for retraining of "risk" personnel New competence network New intranet e-learning support system	New balance scorecard system New human resource development system New models, tools, and methods for learning

The examples of the other three types of interventions were of launching processes that were seen as important first steps in processes that were planned to be extended and disseminated through time. Such has happened in practice in all the cases, with TQM in the technostructure intervention and with learning mechanisms in the human resource and strategic interventions (Table 26.2). In all three cases the mechanisms were both contextual and operational. Among the changes implemented, all cases included new or revised management systems designed to initiate and support learning. These included performance, human resource development, and BSC management systems (Table 26.3). The cases resulted in better performance at individual, group, and business unit levels.

OD, Collaborative Research, and Learning by Design

The concept of learning mechanisms is embedded in most of the OD literature, without the actual use of the label. A careful examination of the OD literature reveals that the focus on learning can be traced to work in collaborative research efforts (Shani, David, & Willson, 2004). One of the many streams of collaborative research that can be found in most of the OD literature is action research (Lewin, 1946). For action research to hold true to its historical roots, it must be concerned with using knowledge derived from scientific inquiry (Coghlan & Brannick, 2001; Reason & Bradbury, 2001). The basic logic of action research is to give the learner access to a much deeper level of data about organization processes through the closeness to the process that comes from being an active participant and contributor. Action research is viewed as an inquiry process in which behavioral and organizational science knowledge is integrated with existing organization knowledge and applied to address real organization problems. It is simultaneously concerned with bringing about change in organizations, developing self-help competencies, and adding scientific knowledge (Susman & Evered, 1978).

Developing self-help competencies is viewed as the development of learning mechanisms that fit with the organization mission and culture that nurture continuous self-design, inquiry, renewal, and improvement. Thus, the learning mechanisms that are created as a part of the OD intervention have the potential to set in motion a continuous learning process. As we have seen in the illustrations in this chapter, the learning mechanisms implemented in the Israeli-American Paper Mill Corporation set in motion continuous learning, improvements, and scientific knowledge, whereas the learning mechanisms implemented at Fossil Fuels set in motion continuous improvements in both performance and employee satisfaction.

Collaborative research orientation that is embedded in an OD effort advocates clear focus on a specific organization issue, involves collaboration and inquiry, involves the learner in the process, involves mutual education, strives for continuous system development, generates valid knowledge, and lays the foundation for a learning organization. At its most basic level, collaborative research involves unlocking information or data trapped in the minds of people, generating shared understandings of the data, and applying the data effectively toward organization issues. Therefore, the learning mechanisms that are chosen are critical because all involved put themselves in a position of being accountable to both the future development of the system in which they work and to the wider community in which the knowledge is developed and transmitted.

Exploring Alternative Learning Mechanisms

As can be seen from the examples in this chapter, learning mechanisms are viewed as key organization capabilities. Capabilities are viewed as key elements of the firm's internal environment. At the business level, authors such as DiBella and Nevis (1998) and De Geus (1997) argue that development and organizing capabilities are the source of competitive advantage. Thus, the key emerging issue centers on matching the firm's capabilities with the opportunities that arise in the external environment. A company can look at an existing business context and examine the current strategy to determine what will make it more successful. Alternatively, the company can look at its existing way of using its capabilities and specify what might be a better way to take advantage of them or develop internal mechanisms to ensure successful.

Based on their assessments of their learning capabilities, organizations may choose to develop learning mechanisms to address the firm's strategic agenda (Adler, Shani, & Styhre, 2004). The designers of the OD effort are faced with few choices as they determine the direction, scope, and structural learning mechanisms to be developed. As the most basic level, they may choose to build on existing capabilities and build their own learning mechanisms, they may choose to build new mechanisms that seem to have worked elsewhere, or they might choose any combination thereof. The critical issue is not so much which choices are made but the learning process that is followed in making the choices.

What learning mechanisms are chosen when learning by design is considered in OD interventions? As our brief review of the four interventions illustrates, building on existing learning capabilities is critical. Careful examination of "what" and "how" the organization learns and an in-depth study of existing learning mechanisms that evolved within the firm over time seem critical. An assessment of the potential match and mismatch between the organization culture, the strategic agenda, and the different learning mechanisms can set the stage for exploration of alternative paths and mechanisms. As pointed out previously, cultural mechanisms, focusing key values for the stakeholders concerned, especially personnel, are of prime importance. They mobilize personnel's interest and commitment and set in motion system development and learning. Achieving the optimal fit between the organization's strategic agenda, culture, design, learning capability, and learning mechanisms for continuous system development is a complex process. As we can see from the four cases, each organization chose learning mechanisms as they saw fit. Yet, although the benefits of collaborative research orientation to guide the process are attractive, attaining them is not easy and certainly never guaranteed.

CONCLUSION

We maintain that learning must be embedded in development processes if they are to be viable and sustainable. The understanding of the importance of learning in a development context depends in turn on management's understanding of the concepts of complexity and sustainability. One important aspect of complexity is the need to pay attention to the needs and ambitions of the various stakeholders. The members of the organization—its employees—often draw the short straw in this context. Therefore it is important to note the role of explicit management values as cornerstones for the successful OD. Positive values express a respect for and appreciation of employees as key potential contributors to development and production in the organization.

Another feature of these cases is their relationship to time. Their view of development may well require direct and immediate actions, but they see development as an ongoing process and have to a great extent focused their attention on learning mechanisms to support such ongoing learning and development. The Japanese Productivity Institute states that in the development of TQM in an organization it is the first 20 years that are the most difficult. The Israeli-American Paper Mill Corporation case shows the benefits of learning mechanisms that were designed with a long-term perspective of ongoing development processes.

Learning by design is a crucial element of OD that warrants more scientific and practice attention. The cases illustrated four different interventions in different industries, geographic locations, and continents, within which a specific set of learning mechanisms was developed. Designers and OD practitioners made choices about the appropriate learning mechanisms to create, develop, and focus on. Coupling learning mechanisms with OD and collaborative research as a triangular area of emphasis sets in motion a sharper, more complex field of study and practice that is likely to generate new actionable knowledge.

REFERENCES

Abrahamson, E. (1996). Management fashion. *Academy of Management Review, 21*(1), 254–285.

Abrahamson, E. (1999). Lifecycles, triggers, and collective learning processes. *Administrative Science Quarterly, 44*(4), 708–740.

Adler, N., Shani, A. B., & Styhre, A. (2004). *Collaborative research in organizations: Foundations for learning, change, and theoretical development*. London: Sage.

Beer, M. (2001). How to develop an organization capable of sustained high performance. *Organizational Dynamics, 29*(4), 233–247.

Beer, M., & Eisenstat, R. (2000). The silent killers of strategy implementation and learning. *Sloan Management Review, 41*(4), 29–40.

Bushe, G. R., & Shani, A. B. (1991). *Parallel learning structures: Increasing innovations in bureaucracies*. Reading, MA: Addison-Wesley.

Coghlan, D., & Brannick, T. (2001). *Doing action research in your own organization*. London: Sage.

Cressey, P., & Docherty, P. (2002). Feedback, intangibles, and sustainable performance. In P. Docherty, J. Forslin, & A. B. Shani (Eds.), *Creating a sustainable work organization: Emerging perspectives and practices* (pp. 165–178). London: Routledge.

Cummings, T. G., & Worley, C. G. (2005). *Organization development and change* (8th ed.). Cincinnati, OH: Thompson/South-Western.

De Geus, A. (1997). *The living company: Habits for survival in a turbulent business environment*. Boston: Harvard Business School Press.

DiBella, A. J. (2001). *Learning practices: Assessment and action for organization improvement*. Upper Saddle River, NJ: Prentice Hall.

DiBella, A. J., & Nevis, E. C. (1998) *How organizations learn*. San Francisco: Jossey-Bass.

Emery, M., & Purser, R. (1996). *The search conference*. San Francisco: Jossey-Bass.

French, W. L., & Bell, C. H. (1999). *Organization development*. Upper Saddle River, NJ: Prentice Hall.

Friedlander, F., & Brown, L. D. (1974). Organization development. *Annual Review of Psychology, 25,* 313–341.

Friedman, V. J., Lipshitz, R., & Overmeer, W. (2001). Creating conditions for organizational learning. In A. B. Antal, M. Dierkes, J. Child, & I. Nonaka (Eds.), *Handbook of organizational learning and knowledge* (pp. 757–774). New York: Oxford University Press.

Garvin, D. A. (2000). *Learning in action*. Boston: Harvard Business School Press.

Gibson, J. W., & Tesone, D. V. (2001). Management fads: Emergence, evolution, and implications for managers. *Academy of Management Executive, 15*(4), 122–133.

Hansson, R. (1999). *Personalförsörjningsmodellen— Ett project I tiden: Övertalighetshantering* [Personnel flow model—A timely project: Redundancy management]. Stockholm: Svenska Strukturforskningsinstitutet HB.

Helfat, C. E. (Ed.). (2003). *The SMS Blackwell handbook of organizational capabilities: Emergence, development and change*. Oxford, UK: The Strategic Management Society and Blackwell.

Kochan, T., & Useem, M. (1992). Achieving systemic organizational change. In T. Kochan & M. Useem (Eds.), *Transforming organisations* (pp. 3–14). New York: Oxford University Press.

Lewin, K. (1946). Action research and minority problems. *Journal of Social Issues, 2,* 34–36.

Lillrank, P., Shani, A. B., & Lindberg, P. (2001). Continuous improvement: Exploring alternative organizational designs. *Total Quality Management, 12*(1), 41–55.

Lipshitz, R., Popper, M., & Oz, S. (1996). Building learning organizations. *Journal of Applied Behavioral Science, 32*(3), 292–305.

Lundgren, K. (1999). Kortare lärotider och ett nytt lärande system [Shorter learning times and a new learning system]. *Arbetsmarknad och Arbetsliv, 5*(4), 287–302.

Marsick, V., & Watkins, K. (1990). *Incidental and informal learning.* London: Routledge.

Marsick, V., & Watkins, K. (1997) Lessons from informal and incidental learning. In J. Burgoyne & M. Reynolds (Eds.), *Management learning: Integrating perspectives in theory and practice.* London: Sage.

Mitki, Y., Shani, A. B., & Stjernberg, T. (2000). A typology of change programs. In R. Golembiewski (Ed.), *Handbook of organizational consultation* (pp. 777–785). New York: Marcel Dekker.

Pavlovsky, P., Forslin, J., & Rienhart, R. (2001). Practices and tools of organizational learning. In M. Dirkes, A. B. Antal, J. Child, & I. Nonaka (Eds.), *Handbook of organizational learning and knowledge* (pp. 61–89). Oxford, UK: Oxford University Press.

Popper, M., & Lipshitz, R. (1998). Organizational learning: Mechanisms, culture and feasibility. *The Learning Organization, 7,* 235–248.

Reason, P., & Bradbury, H. (2001). *Handbook of action research.* London: Sage.

Schein, E. H. (2002). The anxiety of learning. *Harvard Business Review, 80*(3), 100–106.

Schön, D. A. (1983). *The reflective practitioner.* New York: Basic Books.

Shani, A. B., David, A., & Willson, C. (2004). Collaborative research: Alternative roadmaps. In N. Adler, A. B. Shani, & A. Styhre (Eds.), *Collaborative research in organizations: Foundations for learning, change, and theoretical development* (pp. 83–100). London: Sage.

Shani, A. B., & Docherty, P. (2003). *Learning by design: Building sustainable organizations.* London: Blackwell.

Shani, A. B., & Mitki, Y. (2000). Creating the learning organization: Beyond mechanisms. In R. Golembiewski (Ed.), *Handbook of organizational consultation* (pp. 911–919). New York: Marcel Dekker.

Stebbins, M., & Shani, A. B. (2002). Eclectic design for change. In P. Docherty, J. Forslin, & A. B. Shani (Eds.), *Creating sustainable work systems: Emerging perspectives and practice.* London: Routledge.

Susman, G. I., & Evered, R. (1978). An assessment of the scientific merit of action research. *Administrative Science Quarterly, 23,* 583–603.

Useem, M., & Kochan, T. (1992). Creating the learning organization. In T. Kochan & M. Useem (Eds.), *Transforming organizations* (pp. 391–406). New York: Oxford University Press.

Zuboff, S. (1988). *In the age of the smart machine: The future of work and power.* Oxford, UK: Heinemann.

27

Designing Organizations to Lead With Knowledge

SUSAN ALBERS MOHRMAN

Organization development practitioners in the knowledge economy must bring frameworks and development processes that help organizations build and sustain knowledge leadership. Today's sustainable competitive advantage is knowledge: creating it, importing it, and leveraging it to deliver higher value to the marketplace than one's competitors can provide. For example, financial service firms depend on broad and deep expertise in various kinds of financial instruments, models, and transactions, on growing that knowledge through data collection and analysis, on keeping current the understanding of laws and regulations in many countries, and on combining this technical knowledge with deep knowledge of customers' needs to guide the development of products and services that yield high value. Product, process, and service innovation in all industries is based on technical, organizational, and customer knowledge.

Knowledge defines and is embedded in the competencies of the corporation, yet sustaining knowledge leadership entails explicit focus and the intentional building of an organization's knowledge capabilities. Knowledge management—the building of a context that brings knowledge into the firm, uses it, grows and enhances it, and leverages it for competitive advantage—is a key strategic competence in today's organizations.

This chapter goes beyond the perspective that knowledge is a key resource and that the organization needs to take steps and develop programs to attain it and leverage it. It looks carefully at how knowledge translates into organization value, builds on the perspective that knowledge is practice based, and makes the case that the work structures and work processes should be designed with knowledge management in mind. It is argued that all elements of an organization should be designed

519

with an eye to how knowledge underpins the firm's capabilities and translates into organization value.

KNOWLEDGE AND CAPABILITIES

Almost any product or process can be copied or improved by competitors. Strategic leadership entails ongoing innovation, creativity, learning, and improvement that yield distinctive product, solution, and service offerings and effective and efficient technical and organization processes that leave competitors behind. The corporate world has been full of companies that have struggled on this dimension, some of which no longer exist. For example, Digital Equipment Corporation failed to detect the full significance of the trend toward small computers. Despite its wealth of technical talent, it did not develop knowledge and capabilities to respond to that trend. Bell Laboratories produced a great deal of ground-breaking scientific and engineering knowledge but failed to use much of that knowledge to develop services and products to deliver value to customers. These two companies no longer exist. Despite being the early developer of digital photography, Eastman Kodak failed to build the capability to turn this into a viable business until much later, after competitors had staked out the market. Despite having impressive advanced research laboratories, Hewlett-Packard has recently experienced problems with its innovation capabilities and its ability to deliver solutions that customers value. These examples illustrate the extreme consequences of not developing and leveraging knowledge effectively—of not building knowledge into new and enhanced capabilities.

The knowledge-based theory of competitive advantage focuses on the ability of firms to obtain sustainable advantages through the creation of knowledge-based resources and routines. These may include search routines, decision routines, and operating routines that are argued to constitute organization capability

(Nelson & Winter, 1982). Knowledge-based views of the firm also stress the importance of transforming old capabilities into new ones, both by sharing and recombining existing knowledge (Kogut & Zander, 1992) and by absorbing knowledge from outside the organization (Cohen & Levinthal, 1990).

Rather than being discrete skills, capabilities are composite bundles of competences, skills, and technologies and are coherent when various organized activities combine to enable particular salient performances (Hamel, 1994). For example, recent research in the pharmaceutical industry finds that a firm's success in introducing new drugs to the market depends not only on advancing particular specialized technical skills and knowledge but also on the firm's facility at combining capabilities such as research, clinical testing, and marketing (Henderson, 1994; Liyanage, Greenfield, & Don, 1999; Pavitt, 2003). Organization designs and work processes that enable the organization to grow, share, and combine knowledge from many disciplines and functions underpin new drug discovery, development, and commercialization.

Despite much corporate and academic attention to the topic of knowledge management, continually growing knowledge, leveraging it, and embedding it in the performance capabilities of the firm remain a challenge. In part this is because the management of knowledge has been treated as separate from the management of the organization; indeed, there are often special groups tasked with knowledge management. Much of the knowledge management literature has dealt with specific knowledge management programs and topics, such as organization memory (Cross & Baird, 2000), knowledge transfer (Dixon, 2000; Szulanski, 1996), the technology infrastructure for knowledge sharing (Davenport & Prusak, 1998), building the social networks that foster knowledge (Brown & Duguid, 1991; Wenger, 1998), developing the relational skills to collaborate effectively across boundaries (Liedtka, Haskins,

Rosenblum, & Weber, 1997), and developing a knowledge strategy (Zack, 1999). The success of these knowledge management approaches depends on a supportive context (Davenport, DeLong, & Beers, 1998). Such a context often is lacking because firms tend to focus on current performance requirements and are designed to support current capabilities, at the expense of focusing on the growth and leverage of their underlying knowledge-creating capabilities as a core competence. Knowledge management programs often are seen as add-ons to the processes that "get the work done."

Because capabilities are tightly embedded in the routines and design features of the organization, the task of increasing the organization's ability to compete on knowledge cannot be handled through add-on programs. One study of knowledge in new product development firms finds that the knowledge outcomes of the firm—innovative products and services and improved processes—are linked to four core knowledge processes that are tightly embedded in the way work is carried out in the firm (Mohrman, Finegold, & Mohrman, 2003): focusing members' attention on overall system performance; dynamic embedding of knowledge in standard processes, which then become the platform for improvement; sharing and combining knowledge across the organization; and experiential learning, or trying out new approaches and learning from them (innovating). Core organization and work design features, not special knowledge management programs, create the dynamics of knowledge sharing and knowledge combination that underpin these four core processes and lead to innovation and process improvement.

Human and social capital are key elements of the effective knowledge firm. The leaders of today's knowledge firms face a basic tension. While they depend on their knowledge workers to create value by applying and growing knowledge, these workers are more mobile than ever before, and they sense decreased loyalty from their firms. Unlike other corporate

investments, such as capital improvements, information technology (IT), or brand identity, knowledge workers can walk out the door at any time, taking their knowledge and their social network connections with them. Nonetheless, if companies do not invest in the development of human and social capital for fear of losing the investment, they run the risk of falling behind in their knowledge-based capabilities. This dilemma exists because the scarce resource in the knowledge economy is talent. In today's economy, knowledge workers are keenly aware that their knowledge and skills have value in the labor market, and they are focused on working in an environment where they can continue to develop marketable skills (Finegold, Mohrman, & Spreitzer, 2002). They actively work to build their professional networks, which provide valuable links for knowledge access but also for becoming aware of career opportunities and making job changes. While the firm is concerned with deploying and developing their competencies effectively to attain firm performance, the workers are striving to use their knowledge in a setting where they can best achieve their personal goals.

Given this tension, the effective organization and management of knowledge workers is central to the success of knowledge enterprises in general (Quinn, Anderson, & Finkelstein, 1996) and of the knowledge creating capabilities of an organization in particular (Dougherty, 2001; Leonard-Barton, 1995; Nonaka & Takeuchi, 1995). At any time a firm has access to a workforce with a particular array of knowledge and a limited number of knowledge hours. The firm faces several business challenges with respect to its human capital: to deploy knowledge workers and use their hours most effectively to accomplish its mission, to continue to build the human capital available to the firm by sourcing employees or partnering with other organizations that have new needed knowledge, to continually grow its human capital through the development experiences and enhanced tools and work processes that are provided to knowledge workers, and to retain the human capital it builds and needs by creating a fit between the personal goals of key knowledge talent and the needs of firm.

This depiction of the knowledge firm makes evident that organization development professionals must go well beyond the general interpersonal, teaming, task integration, and change capabilities of the organization. They must understand the business in terms of the key expertise and knowledge processes that underlie organization capabilities and their enhancement and develop interventions that optimize the value the organization derives from knowledge. The rest of this chapter describes the organization and work design issues of competing on knowledge. It takes the position that the management of knowledge is integral to the functioning of the knowledge firm and as such must be a major criterion in the design of all facets of the organization, not just of special programs. It first provides a perspective on knowledge and knowledge processes to frame the work and organization design approaches that constitute the main contribution of the chapter.

KNOWLEDGE IN PRACTICE

We start with the perspective that knowledge is contextual and relational: People construct knowledge as they interact in a social context, such as a work setting, and this knowledge in turn influences their behaviors, perceptions, and cognitions (Berger & Luckmann, 1966). Knowledge has been defined as "information combined with experience, context, interpretation, and reflection" (Davenport et al., 1998, p. 44). The knowledge that exists in a firm not only is rooted in the formal education and training of employees but also is grounded in and developed through practice and influenced by the context in which work is carried out. Knowledge grows as employees individually and collectively interpret their experiences and as they reflect on and derive meaning from those experiences. Sensemaking (Weick, 1995) is the process by which meaning is attached to a stream of experiences, data, information, insights, and ideas. Sensemaking underpins individual and collective learning and the creation of new knowledge.

Because of the active sensemaking role of employees in the apprehension, use, and creation of knowledge, the knowledge management approaches of the firm cannot be separated from its business management and operational processes. Comprehension of knowledge is both intellectual and practical. Although knowledge may be explicitly articulated in the form of methods, systematic processes, frameworks, and guidelines, in use the explicit always has an implicit, or tacit, dimension (Polanyi, 1966). Acquiring formal knowledge does not necessarily lead to being able to use it (Dixon, 2000). We learn how through practice. Practice-based learning theorists describe learning as situated and claim that learning and doing cannot be separated (Brown & Duguid, 2000; Polanyi, 1966; Schön, 1983). Information yields knowledge when it becomes "anchored in the beliefs and commitments of its holder" (Nonaka & Takeuchi, 1995, p. 58) through active involvement in its creation or through collective sensemaking and local learning as it is applied (Orlikowski & Robey, 1991).

Nonetheless, knowledge-based firms are particularly dependent on expert knowledge bases that come from formal education and training. For example, scientists, engineers, accountants, logistics and supply chain experts, physicians, and many others bring to their work formal and articulated discipline expertise: content and methods knowledge that have been socially constructed through time by a particular professional or academic community. This discipline-based knowledge frames what employees attend to when they approach a problem. But by making sense of particular problems and of the information they encounter in the particular context they are dealing with, and by taking action, seeing what is effective, and revising their interpretations and understandings, these knowledge workers develop tacit knowledge that greatly extends their formal discipline knowledge. This combination of discipline-based and experience- and firm-based knowledge underpins the capabilities of the firm and constitutes the knowledge base of the firm.

Although most firms are characterized by a "work breakdown" logic that aims to divide work processes into individual jobs and responsibilities, the effective knowledge-based organization is far more than a collection of knowledge workers with their individual stocks of knowledge, tools, and methods that they apply to individual tasks. The intersection of the knowledge of the individual practitioner and the knowledge of the firm through collective processes is paramount in deriving value from knowledge. Collaboration enables the sharing of the tacit and explicit aspects of knowledge and the development of new routines that become part of an organization's extended capability (Hamel, 1991; Ingram & Baum, 1997; Pavitt, 2003). By talking with other engineers, a person may become aware of warning patterns in test results that indicate a potential structural breakdown. An accountant well versed in the definitions and substance of fraud may learn from a colleague to pay attention to certain subtle (perhaps tacit) indicators in financial records that such fraud may exist. The knowledge-creating firm has been characterized as having a cycle of activity through which a person's often tacit knowledge becomes explicit and shared with others. The accrual of tacit knowledge and the process of sharing may occur as work is carried out. The individual's knowledge becomes the organization's knowledge as it becomes accessible to the larger team or unit going about solving its problems and is combined with the knowledge of others to yield new knowledge that can then be shared throughout the organization in the form of new methods and frameworks (Liedtka et al., 1997; Nonaka & Takeuchi, 1995).

In today's world, many of the most important problems and consequently much knowledge

creation and innovation occur at the intersection of multiple disciplines and functions and of deep discipline knowledge bases with the world of applications (Brown & Duguid, 2000; Iansiti, 1995). As a consequence, practice entails work processes that cut across disciplines and functions. For example, using modeling and simulation capability to greatly increase the speed of such diverse tasks as oil exploration and running a hedge fund requires deep substantive content knowledge about what is being modeled (e.g., about geology, petrochemistry, economics, and finance), mathematical knowledge to build algorithms to underpin models and analyses, and computer knowledge to build software architectures that can take advantage of large-scale computing capabilities. These knowledge bases must be combined in practice to generate an effective modeling approach. Collaboration across boundaries in shared problem solving and knowledge creation is core to creating value from knowledge (Boland & Tenkasi, 1995; Brown & Duguid, 1991; Kanter, 1988; Leonard-Barton, 1995). The importance of collaboration has grown as customers demand more integrated solutions (e.g., devices that can not only measure health indicators but can input data simultaneously to an electronic medical record and a population-level database). Integrated solutions increase the interdependencies in the knowledge system. Joint sensemaking and knowledge combination occur through sharing of knowledge within and across teams and through the "creative abrasion" (Leonard-Barton, 1995) and "mutual perspective taking" (Boland & Tenkasi, 1995) that occur when people with different knowledge successfully join forces to solve a problem or create an innovative approach. In today's world, where no one organization is likely to have cutting-edge knowledge in all necessary fields, practice-oriented communities and working relationships that extend across organization boundaries also create a vital link between the organization and changes emerging outside the organization.

Organizations are complex systems that have been hierarchically broken into subsystems, implying multiple traditions of practice, multiple forms of problem-solving behavior, and multiple communities of practice (Dougherty, 2001). The division of labor needed to create a complex technological system or deliver a complex service creates a system of interdependent communities. For example, Dougherty describes the new product development firm as an overall "practice" (2001, p. 624) in which practitioners with a variety of knowledge bases apply their knowledge to the solution of customer and market problems. She identifies four interrelated subpractices, which are defined by the set of problems they have to solve: the strategic practice that defines the overall value creation proposition of the firm and converts it into strategies, standards, and investment decisions to ensure long-term viability; the product and service development practice, which concerns itself with the matching of technology and customer needs in the creation and delivery of products and services; the business management practice, which worries about deploying resources, investing in projects, and creating a product portfolio to address market and competitive needs while making a profit; and the competency management practice, which ensures that the firm has the expertise and organization competencies needed to carry out the strategy. These four practices are highly related. They set the context for one another and interact in practice with one another, and a shared understanding and overlapping knowledge must be developed across them if the firm is to carry out its intended strategy and grow its intended competencies.

Shared understandings in the form of codified standards and organization-wide frameworks such as strategies, goals, and processes provide one way in which bridges are built between the different practices of the organization, attention is focused, and broader meaning is attached to the work that is done in each. These may be shared with employees through formal human resource processes such as training and development and formal management-driven processes such as strategic planning and goal setting. Yet work experiences and person-to-person collaboration continually enrich the knowledge of the participants and yield knowledge that can update and supplement the formal frameworks and shared understandings based on what is being learned through the organization. The knowledge organization must be designed to enable the generation and leveraging of knowledge from within the organization and from external connection—knowledge that becomes embodied in the shared frameworks and routines that guide collective action. Thus, it is not enough for knowledge workers simply to apply their formal knowledge and firm-specific processes. The organization depends on the collective and individual learning of its employees to generate knowledge to continually enrich and update its formal processes with new knowledge. Organizations must be developed to enable and accelerate this relentless cycle of advancement of organization knowledge.

DESIGNING FOR KNOWLEDGE LEADERSHIP

Given the centrality of knowledge in today's economy—its relationship to the capabilities and performance of the organization and the fact that it is developed in practice through social processes—clearly the capacity to advance knowledge should be a major criterion for both organization and work designs. Embodying knowledge-enhancing approaches in organization effectiveness interventions should be core to the practice of organization development. Organizing to compete on knowledge does not yield new forms of organization; rather, it means examining the organization through a knowledge lens and fine tuning the organization's design so that each feature supports the functioning of the organization as a knowledge-creating and knowledge-leveraging system.

Perhaps the largest change of mindset for designers and managers is to think of work not only as the application of knowledge to carry out particular tasks efficiently and effectively but perhaps more importantly as the venue in which knowledge is created and leveraged. Knowledge outcomes such as innovations and improved processes are closely related to firm performance and are attained by building knowledge processes into the fabric of the organization (Mohrman et al., 2003). The four knowledge processes mentioned earlier are particularly critical to performance and can be used as design criteria for the organization (see Criteria 1–4 in Box 27.1). Criteria 5 and 6 in Box 27.1 address the human and social capital imperatives that underpin and result from effective knowledge processes. They address the need for the organization to be designed in a way to attain, grow, develop, and retain needed human capital, to keep knowledge workers up-to-date in their professions, and to promote the building of social capital by enabling the internal and external networks that foster accelerated access to needed knowledge and collaborators. Design features can be assessed in terms of whether they foster these criteria.

Box 27.1 Design Criteria Related to the Knowledge Capabilities of the Firm

Does the design foster the following knowledge processes?

1. Attending to overall system performance so that each individual and unit is carrying out tasks with an eye to how they fit into the overall strategy and mission

2. Continually embedding new knowledge into updated processes and shared frameworks, turning individual knowledge into organizational knowledge

3. Sharing and combining knowledge with co-workers, both within and across boundaries

4. Experiential learning or trying out and learning from new approaches (innovating)

Does the design foster the stocks and flows of knowledge needed for competitive leadership in its chosen domains by

5. Building human capital?

6. Building social capital?

Figure 27.1 presents an adaptation of the classic star model of organization design developed by Jay Galbraith (1994b). The major premises of this design framework are that the organization is a complex system and that its design determines its capabilities to achieve desired outcomes. Organization strategy is the major input to design decisions around the star because strategy determines what competencies and capabilities are needed, how quickly they must be grown and evolved for market success, and thus how the organization is best configured for effective performance. In this figure, knowledge capacity is identified explicitly as an outcome of the design, consistent with the argument that the knowledge capacity of the firm is a critical competitive variable in today's economy. The design of each of the elements depicted on the star model affects knowledge capacity in some manner. Design features may result in connecting or disconnecting knowledge, focusing employees on narrow aspects of

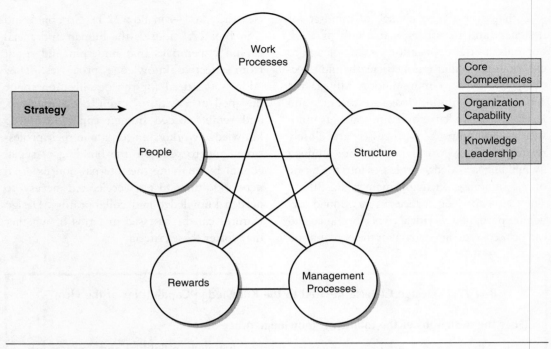

Figure 27.1   Strategy and Design

SOURCE: Adapted from Galbraith, J. R. (1994b). *Designing organizations: An executive briefing on strategy, structure, and process.* San Francisco: Jossey-Bass. Reprinted with permission of John Wiley & Sons, Inc.

the system or focusing them more broadly, building human and social capital or restricting them, and enabling knowledge processes or constraining them.

Each of the elements of the star model will be discussed from the perspective of how the design of that element contributes to knowledge leadership capabilities.

Strategy

The organization's strategy is potentially the most important of the frameworks that embody and create shared understandings in the organization. It focuses members' attention on what the organization is trying to accomplish in order to achieve competitive leadership, on the critical performances that are needed, and on the problems that must be solved in order to carry out that strategy. Like the other core frameworks guiding behavior in the organization,

the strategy must be continually infused with new knowledge. It must also identify new capabilities that are needed. It does not stop with the identification of the markets in which the company will compete, the kinds of new valued offerings that will be developed to surpass competitors' offerings and address customer needs, and the kinds of financial and market share targets that will be obtained. The strategy should identify strategically important knowledge, including knowledge in the areas where the firm needs to build and sustain industry-leading capability, and should serve as the basis for knowledge objectives in areas in which the organization intends to achieve knowledge leadership (Zack, 1999). For example, a hospital system may have a strategy of maintaining global leadership in three developing therapies through knowledge generation and innovation and of maintaining state-of-the-art capabilities in all related therapies by rapidly importing knowledge and building unparalleled experience-based expertise so that for the treatment of certain disease states the hospital system is second to none. Its strategy may also include maintaining sound, contemporary professional treatment competencies in other areas, although not investing to attain a leadership role in knowledge creation in these areas.

Knowledge strategies provide umbrella frameworks for decisions in each of the other star design features. The organization must facilitate the building of knowledge underpinning the ongoing development and delivery of valued products and services by enhancing and connecting the necessary knowledge bases in the context of the market problem. The next two elements of the star are particularly important in this regard.

Work Processes

The strategy of the organization determines which work processes are particularly important to the firm and what standards of performance are important for these processes. For example, a strategy that segments a financial service market into basic transactional consumers and larger institutional or high-wealth customers needs at least two different kinds of service delivery processes. One emphasizes low-cost, efficient self-service and the provision of clear information that enables customers to choose between standard products. The other emphasizes the provision of integrated systems of products and services that meet multiple and total portfolio needs of large customers and emphasizes customer relationships and understanding. The work processes to provide service to these two segments will be quite different from one another. As an organization moves from a strategy that emphasizes products or services to one that emphasizes solutions, integration processes become increasingly important.

Much organization knowledge is embedded in work processes (Leonard-Barton, 1995), and one of the important design elements to support

a knowledge strategy is the choice and use of systematic processes. These are the explicit and orderly approaches, often facilitated by IT, for carrying out operational processes, conducting projects, solving problems, making decisions and tradeoffs, and learning through practice. They are among the core frameworks of the organization that lead to shared understanding and guide integrated performance and shared sensemaking. Work processes should be designed explicitly to include the sharing of knowledge that is generated as work is done and as problems are encountered and solved, including documentation of anomalies, periodic work-group exchanges, and sharing of lessons learned, so that existing knowledge can be leveraged and tacit knowledge can become explicit and embedded in the shared knowledge of the system. These knowledge management approaches should be viewed as steps in the work processes rather than a separate set of activities—in essence meaning that the work processes are self-improving. Embedding knowledge in work processes and tools entails capturing learning from across the organization and creating and continually updating standard but appropriately flexible knowledge platforms to guide work. Flexibility in the processes stimulates the trying out of new approaches and the local adaptation and learning that are the source of new knowledge and of innovation. Systematic processes are not only a way to leverage process knowledge and to create organization memory but also the foundation for process innovation. They create ease of communication and coordination within and across boundaries, access to knowledge, and improvement (Cross & Baird, 2000; Leonard-Barton, 1995).

Knowledge work processes are also closely related to the tools knowledge workers use, especially to various kinds of IT enablers. Knowledge is built into these tools, which are task enablers and knowledge worker productivity enhancers. The extent to which various kinds of work processes will be enabled by IT tools is a key aspect of the design of knowledge work processes. These tools play an important role in the knowledge system by facilitating the key knowledge processes and providing information and knowledge that influence how people do work and what they focus on (Mohrman et al., 2003). They are also important to the development and support of human capital and therefore will be discussed further as part of the "people" star design point.

Structure

The structural challenge is that knowledge transfers more easily and work processes are more easily coordinated within boundaries than across boundaries. The most fundamental structural decision for an organization is what the core units of the organization should be in order to foster ease of performance of the most strategically critical processes and growth of the most strategically and operationally critical knowledge and capabilities. Technical organizations that depend first and foremost on continually advancing knowledge in technical disciplines may organize with technical disciplines as the core unit in order to facilitate ongoing advances of this critical knowledge and secondarily focus on the development of cross-discipline knowledge such as integration capabilities or innovation capabilities through the establishment of lateral linkages, networks, and teaming structures. Structuring to advance both kinds of knowledge and to ensure collaborative cross-unit problem solving requires that the organization structure simultaneously along multiple dimensions: discipline, customer, geography, product or service, and solutions (Galbraith, 1994a). This entails sophistication in designing formal lateral structures and processes and enabling informal ones to emerge.

Cross-boundary work is particularly important in light of the breadth of knowledge and amount of technical integration needed to solve many technical, market, and business problems in today's world (Iansiti, 1998). By implication many organizations have a critical need to grow complex, multidisciplinary knowledge such as that needed to develop new drugs and to run manufacturing facilities for biotech drugs. Various kinds of teams should be designed that house members with the requisite knowledge to carry out these complex integrated processes and solve problems with cross-functional elements. For some organizations this cross-functional and cross-discipline knowledge is the key strategic differentiator, and cross-functional units such as customer-, product-, or solution-focused units may be the core business units of the organization. Alternatively, these cross-functional tasks may be carried out in lateral structures that overlie the core functional and discipline units and include members with different "home bases" (Mohrman, Cohen, & Mohrman, 1995). The new product development literature in particular has stressed the importance of integrating the organization by using a dynamic series of lateral structures that includes heavyweight teams (Clark & Fujimoto, 1991), quasiformal structures (Jelinek & Schoonhoven, 1990), and semistructures (Brown & Eisenhardt, 1997). Research in the pharmaceutical industry has stressed the need for rapid capability development through multiple within-company and cross-organizational networks (Powell, 1998) and for the ability to move information rapidly across the boundaries of the firm and across the boundaries of scientific disciplines and therapeutic areas within the firm (Henderson & Cockburn, 1994).

In the global economy, structures are likely to be geographically dispersed, and work is increasingly virtual, with key work processes flowing across locations. Underpinning the ability to structure dynamically along multiple dimensions is another structural element that is especially salient in such dispersed work systems—the architecture of the IT systems that support task performance, integration, management, and knowledge exchange. Indeed, many knowledge management authors have stressed IT underpinnings and solutions to knowledge management challenges (e.g., Davenport, 1993; Davenport & Prusak, 1998)—and the simultaneous design of reengineered work processes and the supporting IT systems—in part to be able to take advantage of dispersed talent and capacity. Elements of the IT infrastructure—such as compatibility between subsystems and geographies, how open or closed it is, how user friendly the interface is that permits access to various knowledge repositories, how easy it is to update processes and knowledge, and how flexible and compatible the various modules are—will determine the extent to which it fosters or inhibits knowledge leverage and growth.

Lateral structure alone is insufficient to catalyze the knowledge system. Bringing people together in cross-boundary structures can only set the stage for knowledge-creating sensemaking by bringing together diverse experts to address common issues and solve common problems. In at least one study, participation in cross-boundary structures has only a weak direct relationship to knowledge processes and outcomes (Mohrman et al., 2003). Without well-defined work processes and managerial processes, people will have trouble making sense of the importance of lateral work in the organization and operating effectively within lateral structures (Mohrman et al., 1995). One can think of the structure as the skeleton of the organization that isn't able to operate without the messages sent by and systemic integration enabled by the other messages that employees receive from the processes of the organization, which might be thought of as the circulatory and neurological systems.

Management Processes

Under "Work Processes" we discussed one of the process elements of the organization: the processes by which the inputs of the organization are transformed into the products and services that are valued in the environment, or the operational system of the organization. The "management processes" star point deals with the regulation, governance, and integration of the activities of the system as a whole. Again, to effectively compete on knowledge, an organization must consider the management processes as regulating not only the operating characteristics of the system but also its knowledge-enhancing characteristics.

Direction-Setting Processes

The direction-setting processes of the organization (by which strategy is set and translated into goals and objectives, metrics and review processes) are the most critical determinants of where attention is focused and how information is interpreted. Because they provide standards of performance and define the problems that the organization must focus on, these direction-setting processes provide an important context for sensemaking. Through the objective-setting process a shared operating framework can be established that provides guidelines for the local interpretation and sensemaking that occur as a natural part of doing work. Aligning objectives throughout the organization facilitates knowledge sharing and collective problem solving, assuming that the objectives framework is openly shared and that collective objectives guide collective work.

Iansiti (1998) and others have found that defining goals and problems broadly contributes to breadth of input and efficiency of integration in technical work, in part by fostering knowledge sharing and combination. The breadth of focus and of the embedded knowledge that systematically guides how problems are approached are prime movers leading to absorptive capacity: the ability to absorb knowledge from other organizations and other organization units (Cohen & Levinthal, 1990; Szulanski, 1996). These features enable the sharing and the absorbing of knowledge from elsewhere and its application in new approaches. Sense is made of new knowledge in context of what is already known and in the process of systematically searching for new approaches that is driven by defining the problem in broad terms (Iansiti, 1998).

Communication

Communication is a key management process both for providing information that is needed for effective task performance and also for knowledge sharing and integration purposes. There is a voluminous literature on communication processes, communication networks, and various modalities of communication. For our purposes the critical issue is broad and open communication that provides insight into the bigger picture within which tasks are being performed and knowledge is being used and leveraged. Communication paints the picture of the context in which knowledge workers are using their skills and is a key focusing device, focusing not only on the operational activities but also on search and innovation processes.

Decision Making

The business decision-making processes that determine how the organization will go about being profitable and sustainable constitute another key management process. This process includes how scarce resources will be distributed among the various parts of the organization, how the organization will position itself among the various possible environmental and market opportunities, and the organization's architecture, or design. These decisions create the context for the knowledge work that is carried out in the firm and provide the resources for various tasks, including setting the stage for the extent to which knowledge creation, leverage, and leadership will be emphasized and supported. For example, investment decisions determine where there are slack (non–operationally constrained) funds and other resources available to build new capabilities.

The management processes in the knowledge firm reflect the complex and dynamic nature of the work and the changing environment in which the firm is competing. It has become impossible for the management of a firm to have access to all the knowledge needed to guide and glue together the activities of a complex firm. Individuals and teams are continually making sense of their situation and determining a course of action based on what they know of the context in which they are operating and the strategic intent of the firm. Management processes must define the context clearly enough to allow such self-regulation by providing and encouraging the sharing of information, broad direction, and standards and by providing the resources, competencies, and expectations to support and encourage ongoing local collective sense-making and knowledge creation. Motivational issues are closely related to self-regulation.

Rewards

Much knowledge management literature mentions the need to align motivational practices, and rewards in particular, with the knowledge management goals of the organization (e.g., Davenport et al., 1998; Quinn et al., 1996). This is another area where there is a voluminous literature. Here only the reward issues pertaining to competing on knowledge will be discussed.

Because of knowledge worker mobility and the strategic value of knowledge to the firm, it is essential in the knowledge economy that the company's reward system accurately acknowledges the value of its human and social capital. Failure to do so runs the risk of losing key employees who may feel they are more highly valued in the labor market. They will take with them not only the professional and discipline competences they brought to the job but also the networks and the experience- and firm-based skills they have developed (Finegold et al., 2002). The amount of human capital represented by knowledge workers holding similar positions can vary dramatically based on their depth and breadth of professional training, the professional networks they have maintained that enable the importing and sharing of knowledge, and the tacit and explicit knowledge they have picked up through various experiences. Thus, the firm must have new ways to describe valued knowledge and skills that are independent of level, position, and even of educational attainment—through what the person knows and is able to do what has value for the firm.

An important aspect of rewarding knowledge workers is valuing the way in which they contribute to the knowledge capabilities of the organization. It is critical for knowledge workers to be rewarded for the knowledge they have, for the generation of new knowledge, for the effective application of knowledge to achieve objectives, and for sharing and leveraging knowledge. As was discussed earlier in the chapter, deriving value from knowledge involves collective behaviors. The individual therefore must be assessed in the context of technical or business problems being solved by the team and the effectiveness of the product, service, or solution being produced—not simply for individual performance. Rewards for collective performance at the team, unit, or organization level are important not only to recognize valued contribution but also to focus individuals on the larger system and open them up to the processes of collective interpretation and sensemaking that are inherent in the generation, leverage, and value derived from knowledge.

Rewarding performance is both a core business process and a critical human resource process. Our studies of knowledge workers and countless others have found that employee retention and commitment are affected by perceptions that one's individual and collective contributions are being justly rewarded. Pay for organization performance is particularly linked to commitment, which may reflect a keen awareness of the dependence of the firm on the knowledge of its employees and a sense that one should therefore share in the firm's success (Finegold et al., 2002). Yet despite this clear relationship of rewards to the retention

and commitment of the firm's employees, other human resource factors are equally important in the knowledge-based firm, as discussed next.

People

The knowledge firm depends fundamentally on attracting, motivating, developing, and retaining employees who possess the knowledge and skills it needs to carry out its strategies and operate effectively as a knowledge system. One key people design element is the development of approaches to ensure that employees are kept up to date with the codified discipline and cross-discipline knowledge and skills that underpin the capabilities needed to deliver on the company's value proposition. The development and updating of deep technical skills and of breadth skills that allow effective managerial, cross-discipline, and cross-functional problem solving are critical to the effective functioning of the knowledge firm (Iansiti, 1995). A development-rich environment promotes employee retention and commitment (Finegold et al., 2002; Mohrman, Boudreau, Levenson, & Benson, 2004), although both of these cited studies also found that knowledge workers believed that informal, on-the-job experiences provided more valuable development than formal training and development. This is evidence of the amount of knowledge acquisition that occurs through the experiences and related sensemaking involved in carrying out work. It also argues that designers should think more centrally of job experiences and job progressions as knowledge development tools and be attuned to the different kinds of knowledge that are developed through different progressions.

Many knowledge workers are highly dependent on advanced analysis, modeling, and communication tools. Knowledge workers, tools, and tasks are linked together to deliver value (Argote & Ingram, 2000). Tools that embody knowledge have become extensions of the knowledge worker and the knowledge work team and may be significant productivity enhancers. For example, powerful tools have been created for actuaries to model risk and determine net present value, embodying sophisticated mathematical and statistical algorithms. Three-dimensional models and system simulation tools incorporate sophisticated engineering knowledge and serve as powerful productivity enhancers. Having the opportunity to master up-to-date tools is critical to the professional identity and employability of knowledge workers. Just as important is the relationship of such tools to the collective knowledge capabilities of the firm. Knowledge workers depend on their tools to be able to tap into knowledge communities, work teams, and projects from remote locations and with a shifting group of co-workers. These professional tools, combined with sophisticated groupware capabilities, have also made it possible for knowledge workers to physically locate anywhere in the world and still work interdependently with teammates in other locations, to have access to dispersed knowledge, and to participate in dispersed knowledge-generating interactions and experiences.

Career paths and career advancement opportunities are another key element of the human capital framework in the knowledge firm. Finding new ways to describe career advancement that acknowledge contribution to the knowledge system may be the most important human capital measure the firm can take. The opportunity for career advancement has been found to relate to retention and commitment for employees of all ages (Finegold et al., 2002). This poses tricky career path design challenges, however, because the employee's knowledge value and contribution can be unrelated to years of experience or hierarchical level in the firm or to managerial versus nonmanagerial contribution. Some kinds of knowledge are not enhanced by progression through managerial levels, and managers at various levels may find the need to develop knowledge that naturally is created at lower levels in the firm.

This is well illustrated in a research laboratory, where employees fresh from the university, with state-of-the-art knowledge and training, may bring new knowledge that, alone or combined with the existing expertise in the firm, is needed for the breakthroughs the labs seeks (Mohrman, Galbraith, & Monge, 2004). Such employees are not senior or managerial, and indeed they may not have the necessary interpersonal or managerial skills for rapid advancement, but they may have brought a contribution to a team that moved the work of the project forward immensely and as a result may have career expectations that cannot be met in a traditional hierarchical progression. Conversely, managers in the organization may need to develop an understanding and appreciation of the new approaches being brought by these younger knowledge workers and may find themselves gradually becoming obsolete if they are constrained to an environment in which they focus exclusively on the use and development of managerial knowledge. Dual ladders for progression—technical and managerial—are one way to provide a more varied concept of career pathing and valuing of employees than is possible with a uniform managerial hierarchy, but even dual ladders may not be adequately flexible to provide the human capital necessitated by dynamic waves of strategically important knowledge-based capabilities.

The proper valuing of rotational sequences, retraining, and other kinds of lateral movement and broad exposure are critical aspects of the people systems of knowledge firms. Lateral moves may bring far more value to a knowledge firm than our traditional human resource systems acknowledge, and hierarchical level may be much less closely associated with value than is traditionally assumed. The networks and multiple knowledge bases that come from rotational experience may be as critical or more so to the firm and its integration capabilities than managerial and leadership skills gained by hierarchical progression, in part because having broad knowledge and being able to draw on the knowledge of others in broad networks provides the knowledge foundation for self-regulation and knowledge combination.

Recent studies also point out the importance of work–life balance, especially for employees in their early career stages (Finegold et al., 2002; Mohrman, Boudreau, et al., 2004). This concern relates to the knowledge capabilities of the firm because it relates to the ways in which employees can and will contribute. In both the United States and in Europe, there are social forces—such as dual-career families and an affluence level and exposure to information that permit broader horizons and interests— that work against members of this generation of employees becoming totally committed company people. Furthermore, knowledge workers are hooked into broad social and professional networks, so they better understand the value of their knowledge hours, are aware of job alternatives, and see themselves as able to sell their skills in the labor market and perhaps to move into other kinds of job settings where they may be better able to achieve their career and personal interests. They may be decreasingly willing to stay with a job if it requires them to expand their time commitment to the organization at the expense of their other interests or to sacrifice their career values.

One approach a firm might take to deal with this problem is to adopt policies and programs that emphasize work–life balance, such as providing help to the employee in the form of child care and other services that help achieve such balance and providing guidelines so that managers are encouraged to respect employees' personal time. Another approach is to make better use of the scarce resource: the hours of the firm's knowledge workers. Using knowledge worker time more effectively through such means as improving work processes and tools, creating more effective shared understandings in the organization that

enable efficient coordinated action, and increasing self-governing capability is another approach to addressing the desire of employees to balance their work and personal life. These measures seek to enable balance by increasing productivity and decreasing the waste of time that is inevitable if the system is not well integrated and if accountabilities and responsibilities are not optimally designed to enable self-regulation.

Thus, we go full circle to work processes and then around the points of the design star, to make sure the organization is designed to use its human capital optimally. This underscores the need for a well-designed organization and well-designed work if the firm is to benefit optimally from the human capital it has helped develop, engage employees maximally in the knowledge processes of the firm, provide a careful use of knowledge worker hours, and retain talent. Figure 27.2 summarizes the major knowledge-related aspects of each of the star points discussed in this chapter.

CONCLUSION

This chapter has described the nature of the knowledge firm and of knowledge processes and has provided a framework for understanding how the design of the organization affects knowledge in practice. It has argued that competing on knowledge demands work processes and organization design that fit that strategy. Attracting and retaining critical talent is not sufficient because organizations can be significantly unequal in their ability to effectively use and enhance the knowledge of their talented workforce. These capabilities depend on how the workforce is deployed and whether the organization and the work are designed to effectively derive value from, share, and combine knowledge and to motivate employees to participate effectively in the knowledge system. Special knowledge management programs that are not related to the work processes of the organization will have

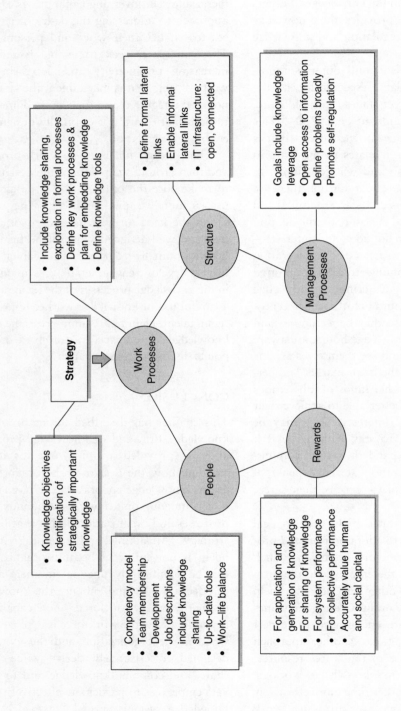

Figure 27.2   Design for Knowledge Enterprises

SOURCE: Adapted from Galbraith, J. R. (1994b). *Designing organizations: An executive briefing on strategy, structure and process.* San Francisco: Jossey-Bass. Reprinted with permission of John Wiley & Sons, Inc.

limited impact and limited longevity. The effectiveness of the knowledge system depends on the creation of an organization context that fosters the importing of knowledge, the generation of new knowledge, and the application and leveraging of knowledge to deliver value to the customers.

Organization development practitioners working with companies that compete based on knowledge leadership must be alert to opportunities to help design their work systems and the organization to foster knowledge processes and the ongoing engagement of human capital. The commitment of employees and the performance of the knowledge-based organization are closely linked to the effectiveness of the knowledge system, including employees' collective involvement in the sense-making processes that underlie the use and generation of knowledge. Through collaboration in the generation of knowledge, employees may create innovations that define the future of the organization. In a sense, they are re-creating or rejuvenating the organization, and in the process they are creating meaning. The knowledge that is created becomes embedded in their beliefs and actions, internalized in the organization's processes and routines, and available as a platform for further knowledge generation.

The business organization may be seen as a community guided by the shared meaning that is collectively created by employees in the process of doing work. The glue that holds the diverse activities of a firm together is the company's intent, as manifested in its strategy (Nonaka & Takeuchi, 1995), which shapes the shared meaning that develops as people work together toward desired outcomes for customers and for each other (Liedtka et al., 1997). Thus, the collective activities of knowledge workers both derive meaning from the purpose of the firm and create meaning. This underscores how important it is that knowledge management researchers and organization development practitioners focus on how

work is defined and carried out in the context of the business system and less on special programs. The design of work and of the organization are critical to the effectiveness of the knowledge-based firm.

Knowledge processes (sharing of knowledge, system perspectives, embedding knowledge in processes, and trying new approaches) are easy to describe and easy to discourage through the creation of work contexts that do not enable and encourage them. Fortunately, many of the design variables over which managers have the most direct control can have a large impact on the effectiveness of the knowledge system. For example, a clearly articulated strategy, well-designed work processes, providing clear direction and system performance information, and emphasizing employee and organization development have significant impacts on the effectiveness of the knowledge system (Mohrman et al., 2003). This chapter has described the criteria for the design of knowledge firms and relevant characteristics of various design features. In today's knowledge economy, it is imperative for organization development practitioners to incorporate these in organization diagnoses and interventions aimed at increasing effectiveness and to support transformations that entail the development of new and enhanced knowledge-based capabilities.

REFERENCES

Argote, L., & Ingram, P. (2000). Knowledge transfer: A basis for competitive advantage in firms. *Organizational Behavior and Human Decision Processes, 82*(1), 150–169.

Berger, P. L., & Luckmann, P. (1966). *The social construction of reality.* Garden City, NY: Doubleday.

Boland, R. J., & Tenkasi, R. V. (1995). Perspective making and perspective taking in communities of knowing. *Organization Science, 6*(4), 350–372.

Brown, J. S., & Duguid, P. (1991). Organizational learning and communities-of-practice: Toward a unified view of working, learning, and innovation. *Organization Science, 2*(1), 40–57.

Brown, J. S., & Duguid, P. (2000). *The social life of information*. Boston: Harvard Business School Press.

Brown, S., & Eisenhardt, K. (1997). The art of continuous change: Linking complexity theory and time paced evolution in relentless shifting organizations. *Administrative Science Quarterly, 42*(1), 1–35.

Clark, K., & Fujimoto, T. (1991). *Product development performance: Strategy, organization, and management in the world auto industry*. Boston: Harvard Business School Press.

Cohen, W. M., & Levinthal, D. A. (1990). Absorptive capacity: A new perspective on learning and innovation. *Administrative Science Quarterly, 35*(1), 128–152.

Cross, R., & Baird, L. (2000). Technology is not enough: Improving performance by building organizational memory. *Sloan Management Review, 41*(3), 69–78.

Davenport, T. H. (1993). *Process innovation: Re-engineering work through information technology*. Boston: Harvard Business School Press.

Davenport, T. H., De Long, D. W., & Beers, M. C. (1998). Successful knowledge management projects. *Sloan Management Review, 39*(2), 43–59.

Davenport, T. H., & Prusak, L. (1998). *Working knowledge: How organizations manage what they know*. Boston: Harvard Business School Press.

Dixon, N. (2000). *Common knowledge: How companies thrive by sharing what they know*. Boston: Harvard Business School Press.

Dougherty, D. (2001). Re-imagining the differentiation and integration of work for sustained product innovation. *Organization Science, 12*(5), 612–631.

Finegold, D., Mohrman, S. A., & Spreitzer, G. (2002). Age effects on the predictors of technical workers' commitment and willingness to turnover. *Journal of Occupational Behavior, 23*(1), 1–20.

Galbraith, J. R. (1994a). *Competing with the lateral, flexible, organization*. Reading, MA: Addison-Wesley.

Galbraith, J. R. (1994b). *Designing organizations: An executive briefing on strategy, structure and process*. San Francisco: Jossey-Bass.

Hamel, G. (1991). Competition for competence and interpartner learning within international strategic alliances. *Strategic Management Journal, 12*, 83–103.

Hamel, G. (1994). The concept of core competence. In G. Hamel & A. Heene (Eds.), *Competence-based competition* (pp. 11–33). Chichester, UK: John Wiley & Sons.

Henderson, R. (1994). The evolution of integrative capability: Innovation in cardiovascular drug discovery. *Industrial and Corporate Change, 3*(4), 607–630.

Henderson, R., & Cockburn, I. (1994, Winter). Measuring competence? Exploring firm effects in pharmaceutical research. *Strategic Management Journal, 15*, 63–84.

Iansiti, M. (1995, Fall). Shooting the rapids: Managing product development in turbulent environments. *California Management Review, 38*, 37–58.

Iansiti, M. (1998). *Technology integration: Making critical choices in a dynamic world*. Boston: Harvard Business School Press.

Ingram, P., & Baum, J. A. C. (1997). Chain affiliation and the failure of Manhattan hotels, 1898–1980. *Administrative Science Quarterly, 42*(1), 68–102.

Jelinek, M., & Schoonhoven, C. (1990). *The innovation marathon: Lessons from high technology firms*. Oxford, UK: Basil Blackwell.

Kanter, R. (1988). When a thousand flowers bloom: Structural, collective, and social conditions for innovation in organizations. *Research in Organizational Behavior, 10*, 169–211.

Kogut, B., & Zander, U. (1992). Knowledge of the firm, combinative capabilities and the replication of technology. *Organization Science, 3*, 383–397.

Leonard-Barton, D. (1995). *Wellsprings of knowledge: Building and sustaining the sources of innovation*. Boston: Harvard Business School Press.

Liedtka, J. M., Haskins, M. E., Rosenblum, J. W., & Weber, J. (1997). The generative cycle: Linking knowledge and relationships. *Sloan Management Review, 39*(1), 47–58.

Liyanage, S., Greenfield, P. F., & Don, R. (1999). Towards a fourth generation R&D management model: Research networks in knowledge management. *International Journal of Technology Management, 18*(3, 4), 372–393.

Mohrman, S. A., Boudreau, J., Levenson, A., & Benson, G. (2004). *The value of human capital in a professional services firm.* Los Angeles: University of Southern California, Marshall School of Business, Center for Effective Organizations.

Mohrman, S. A., Cohen, S. G., & Mohrman, A. M., Jr. (1995). *Designing team-based organizations: New forms for knowledge work.* San Francisco: Jossey-Bass.

Mohrman, S. A., Finegold, D., & Mohrman, A. M., Jr. (2003). An empirical model of the organization knowledge system in new product development firms. *Journal of Engineering and Technology Management, 20*(1–2), 7–38.

Mohrman, S. A., Galbraith, J. R., & Monge, P. (2004). *Network attributes impacting the generation and flow of knowledge within and from the basic science community.* (Final report to the U.S. Department of Energy, Office of Science, in fulfillment of Research Contract 84882.)

Nelson, R. R., & Winter, S. G. (1982). *An evolutionary theory of economic change.* Cambridge, MA: Harvard University Press.

Nonaka, I., & Takeuchi, H. (1995). *The knowledge-creating company.* New York: Oxford University Press.

Orlikowski, W. J., & Robey, D. (1991). Information technology and the structuring of organizations. *Information Systems Research, 2*(2), 143–169.

Pavitt, K. (2003). Innovative routines in large firms: What the evidence suggests. In C. Helfat (Ed.), *The SMS Blackwell handbook of organizational capabilities* (pp. 264–268). Malden, MA: Blackwell.

Polanyi, M. (1966). *The tacit dimension.* London: Routledge & Kegan Paul.

Powell, W. W. (1998). Learning from collaboration: Knowledge and networks in the biotechnology and pharmaceutical industries. *California Management Review, 40,* 228–241.

Quinn, J. B., Anderson, P., & Finkelstein, S. (1996). Leveraging intellect. *Academy of Management Executive, 10*(3), 7–27.

Schön, D. A. (1983). *The reflective practitioner.* New York: Basic Books.

Szulanski, G. (1996, Winter). Exploring internal stickiness: Impediments to the transfer of best practice within the firm. *Strategic Management Journal, 17,* 27–43.

Weick, K. (1995). *Sensemaking in organizations.* Thousand Oaks, CA: Sage.

Wenger, E. (1998). *Communities of practice: Learning, meaning, and identity.* New York: Cambridge University Press.

Zack, M. H. (1999, Spring). Developing a knowledge strategy. *California Management Review, 41*(3), 125–145.

PART IV

Special Applications of Organization Development

28

The Status of OD in Public Administration

Another Case of Practice Being Ahead of Theory

ROBERT T. GOLEMBIEWSKI

GENE A. BREWER

When it comes to planned change, most observers see public administration (PA) as determinedly stuck, and awkwardly so. This basic proposition here is evaluated via a basic orientation to planned change: organization development (OD), which some prefer to call organization development and change (ODC), to which much of the surrounding text gives robust illustration. This targeted family of theory, values, and experience relates to supervisory levels of organization and higher. Similar values-cum-theory focus on workday levels, along with unions and other associated institutions and dynamics, and such work often is classified as quality of working life (QWL).

Here, all of the intellectual traditions of PA follow relaxed rules for inclusion. Thus, these traditions include institutional and constitutional features; several clusters of ideation that have influenced PA practice and study over the years since Woodrow Wilson's (1887) seminal essay, often seen as PA's birth certificate; and even some of the shoptalk common among PA practitioners.

Overall, the present sampler of intellectual traditions in PA will be shown to serve planned change only in limp and limited ways, if at all. This overall assessment encompasses several intellectual traditions, more conveniently than exhaustively assembled. In all cases, much other literature could be fitted under each rubric, but the inclusions are broadly illustrative.

SEVERAL MAJOR PA INTELLECTUAL TRADITIONS

The poor fit of OD to PA's traditions may seem an awkward prelude to OD applications to planned change, especially given the optimistic orientation of this chapter. Nonetheless, one fact seems indisputable: OD got only a modicum of attention in yesterday's PA, and matters have improved recently, but progress remains limited. In one recent text meant for general readers (Tompkins, 2005), for example, OD gets very modest attention and is excluded from PA traditions.

Three major traditions get attention here. Thus, attention shifts from mainstream political science to neoclassical economics and concludes with contemporary thinking on PA and public policy. In this chapter we explore three literatures in brief and catalogue some of the reasons they usually imply feeble expectations about encompassing change.

Aspects of Mainstream Political Science

Many PA observers highlight numerous reasons to believe that ODC efforts will be more successful in business firms than in government agencies and nonprofit organizations. In fact, several well-developed literatures bearing on the topic suggest that government is one of the most inhospitable settings imaginable.

To illustrate, mainstream political science often advocates a "bureaucratic politics" perspective on public organizations, which portrays the government process as a combination of zero-sum games and as rationally technical. That is, politics provide the compass for administration, with the former "on top" and the latter "on tap." Much conflict comes from the very features of government that many attribute to making it democratic: federalism, the separation of powers, checks and balances, interest

group pluralism, political–bureaucratic tensions, and citizen participation in policymaking, among other sources. In its extreme form, the mainstream view maintains that there is no value in seeking more effective administration. In this view, inefficiencies make administration more susceptible to control by politics.

In sum, notes an influential elite, conflict may prevent the bureaucracy from functioning smoothly, and that is a good thing. Rather, conflict may be seen as the byproduct of a truly functioning democratic bureaucracy. Some proponents of democratic theory thus view OD as dangerous because it might reduce conflict in government, thus undermining the basic separation of powers. For a review of such treatments, see Golembiewski (1969, pp. 370–371). This neglects the possibility that effective planned change would facilitate the counterpart checks and balances, of course.

The bureaucratic politics perspective posits that public agencies are wedged in a dense constellation of powerful political actors and influences, and the more incautious versions suggest there never can be too much conflict. Without respite, then, public agencies must fight for their survival, purely and simply, so they are characterized as acting in their own self-interest and trying to advance an "agency view," which neglects the fact that in so doing administration might achieve a range of discretion that may be seriously inconsistent with the desires of elected officials and the public interest. But so much the worse for the mainstream theory.

Scholars of bureaucratic politics often use "neutral administration " or "principal agent" frameworks to study political–bureaucratic relations because these frameworks incorporate the top-down view of accountability that most political scientists seem to prefer. Elected officials often hold similar views and try to establish and maintain overhead political control of the bureaucracy by limiting bureaucratic discretion by risking micromanaging of agency operations (Bendor, 1990; Gruber, 1987; Lowi, 1969; Pratt

& Zeckhauser, 1985; Redford, 1969; Spence, 1997; West, 1995; Wood & Waterman, 1994). The resulting political–bureaucratic tensions are believed to lower agency performance and effectiveness and to lower expectations for humanistic reforms such as OD. But that is seen as merely tough for bureaucracies and an inevitable cost of representative systems. In other words, the tensions are nevertheless preserved because they are thought to be bellwethers of accountability.

One does not have to reach very far to discover that this first perspective presents a basic conceptual problem: The bureaucratic politics perspective rests on fundamental (but not necessarily accurate) assumptions about accountability in democratic government. In any case, this perspective does not offer a serviceable view of public agencies or employees. In some instances, agencies are portrayed as timid and ineffective bastions of inertia. In other cases, they are viewed as imperialistic and prone to overregulate society and even to trump the public. Relatedly, some observers describe public employees as lazy and incompetent, and others view them as reckless and aggressive in their actions.

Clearly, all of these stereotypes cannot be correct, and, far worse, mainstream views do not provide guidance for dealing with them. Public agencies cannot be both innocuous and intrusive, and employees cannot be both passive and active—at least not at the same time (Brehm & Gates, 1997; Brewer, 2001). Put another way, such variations suggest the common need for a theory of learning and change like that encompassed by OD or ODC, even as they undercut the major available approach to them.

Of primary importance here, the possibility of OD and planned change seems diminished in almost any bureaucratic politics scenario. This first perspective suggests that agencies are caught up in an out-of-control political system and have little reason to think about accountability to the public interest. Agency employees are believed to be fixated on self-interest, however defined, and thus they are portrayed

as instruments to be controlled, not as assets to be liberated and deployed strategically. Other observers may be content with the view of neutral and protected civil servants, but it implies both philosophical and empirical questions. In one popular view, autocratic bureaucracies at work are the price paid for democracy outside work hours. This seems a curious and even self-defeating combination.

How often does the prototype exist, and with what range of consequences for citizens in representative governments? Too often, and too fundamentally. Thus, the mainstream political science view of bureaucratic politics inclines toward a theoretical and practical straitjacket that can stifle the possibilities of successful change efforts in public agencies.

Neoclassical Economics

Neoclassical economics—both in its original form and as "public choice theory"—provides equally poor prospects for OD and change. From a macroeconomic perspective, business firms are seen as inherently dynamic: They must die if they do not respond to market incentives and develop ever more efficient and effective forms of organization. Businesses are thus more likely to adopt ODC-related strategies, some argue, particularly if these strategies promise to improve efficiency and productivity, which OD and ODC clearly do, as we will show later. In sharp contrast, government agencies are not subject to the rigors of market discipline. These organizations tend to be self-serving rather than approaching the self-correcting consequences of OD and ODC, and microeconomic theory helps to explain why.

According to microeconomic theory, bureaucrats favor expansion, and they are likely to maximize their budgets and to generate an oversupply of public goods and services to further their own self-interest (Buchanan & Tullock, 1962; Dahl & Lindblom, 1953; Downs, 1967; Dunleavy, 1991; Niskanen, 1971). This market disconnect undermines efforts to enliven the civic character of the public workplace or to empower public employees. This second perspective also triggers a vicious cycle: Perceptions of inefficiency lead to self-defeating reforms that emphasize cutback management and budget austerity, which tend to crowd out any possibility for OD and change. Indeed, even some supporters of OD view it as a luxury, perhaps affordable only (or mostly) in flush economic times when OD is less needed.

From a microeconomic perspective, consequently, public employees are likely to grow their bureaus, maximize their budgets, and act in self-interested and self-serving ways (Buchanan & Tullock, 1962). Anthony Downs (1967) was one of the first political economists to formulate a unified theory of public organizations. He described bureaucratic behavior as mostly self-interested, although bureaucrats might be climbers, conservers, advocates, zealots, or statesmen. Significantly, all of these bureaucratic archetypes are portrayed as externally driven. They are not sensitive people who care about human growth and self-actualization through their work.

In terms of OD, this second instrumentalist mindset is clearly misguided and perhaps even self-defeating. Indeed, OD's aspirations are seen as wasted to the degree that they are lofty and hence outside neoclassical economics. Conversely, one can easily urge that microeconomic views not only tend to profit from OD but may positively require them, to the degree that public personnel act as the second approach prescribes.

In sum, in this second tradition, the public sector cannot win for losing, which strains credulity. Different accounts of public choice theory portray government agencies and public employees in sometimes different but mostly negative ways. In some instances, agencies are portrayed as do-nothings. In other cases, they are viewed as predatory and likely to run amok or even to hijack the public interest. Similarly, different observers describe public employees as hapless laggards or as helmeted,

jackbooted oppressors of the citizenry, especially in some of the literature of supply-side economics or "individualist" variants. For a critique, see Golembiewski (1996), and Kettl (1990).

Clearly, all of these stereotypes cannot be correct even if one accepts them as describing an ideal condition. Agencies cannot be both underactive and hyperactive, at least not simultaneously. For additional details on these two sets of stereotypes, see Brehm and Gates (1997) and Brewer (2001).

Thus, the public sector organizations described in the second intellectual tradition are not ideal settings for planned OD and change, and government employees are not seen as either properly motivated or trustworthy enough. To a common point, almost any variation of these assumptions seems to work against the possibility of successful ODC. This may strike some as curious, because at least hypothetically one might propose that this second PA perspective defines exactly the set of conditions for which OD can credibly be seen as the antidote.

Variants of Traditional PA

Several variants of what we will call traditional PA provide no more comfortable home for OD. These newer incarnations of neologisms are related to formulation and implementation and here can be introduced in terms of only a few exemplars.

The core approach—traditional PA—builds on Max Weber's classic writings about the bureaucratic form of organization, whose rational and legal bases are combined with highly centralized and ultimately oppressive forms (Geerth & Mills, 1946; Whyte, 1956; also see Merton, 1957, pp. 195–206). In contrast to the private sector, OD interventions in the public are said to be especially burdened by archaic structures and behavioral patterns (Carnevale, 2002; Golembiewski, 1969, 2003).

Patently, this Weberian base promises no take-off point for a positive emphasis on OD, but Weberian bureaucracy is a useful point of departure for considering several successors of a similar spirit.

New Public Management

The new public management perspective builds on and enlarges this bleak view of bureaucracy (Hargrove & Glidewell, 1990; Rainey, 2003, chapter 6). Agencies are believed to be arthritic and low-energy collectivities resistant to change but, paradoxically, as lasting forever (Kaufman, 1991).

In recent years, the new public management perspective has emphasized—you guessed it—managerialism and its allegedly heroic role in transforming public organizations and improving their effectiveness. This movement often exhorts public managers to become risk-taking entrepreneurs who can slash red tape, implement best practices, and drive their organizations toward some mysterious bottom line that promises to improve performance while creating public value but whose scope and reach remain elusive and hard to define (Gore, 1993; Moore, 1995; Osborne & Gaebler, 1992). This single-minded emphasis on efficiency, economy, and effectiveness has overshadowed the importance of making public organizations more humanistic and accommodating for workers, and it has tended to overlook or at least underemphasize other important administrative values such as fairness, justice, and social equity, let alone a concern with the general will or civic virtues.

Policy and Its Implementation

The policy implementation perspective poses dismal probabilities for OD and change agents. From the outset, policy implementation scholars often see decision making as the primary unit of analysis in PA. Although it takes little creativity to conclude that OD should be central to the implementation literature, it can be fairly characterized—as Wildavsky urges (1979)—as neglecting organizations as well as people in its narrow view of policy and implementation. In contrast, OD directs forceful attention to networks and their components: chunks and clusters of government, nongovernment, and business organizations that must work in concert to implement policy effectively (Hjern & Porter, 1981). These networks usually are larger and more complex than single organizations, and they often violate several cardinal rules of Weberian bureaucracy: They challenge basic principles of hierarchy, centralized authority, and unity of command, among other features.

Even though intense debate over the top-down perspectives of policy implementation leaves little room for the possibility of planned OD and change, some OD practitioners have made notable progress, given the difficulties (Chisholm, 1998). Nonetheless, in the top-down view public agencies are depicted as subservient and responsive to overhead political forces, and they often get bogged down in politics and the policymaking process (Pressman & Wildavsky, 1984; Ripley & Franklin, 1986). In the bottom-up view, entrepreneurial public managers and street-level bureaucrats are among the central actors, and interorganizational networks are the primary units of analysis, as explained in many places (for details, see Hill & Hupe, 2002, chapter 3; Matland, 1995; Mazmanian & Sabatier, 1989, postscript).

Summary Considerations

Different theoretical accounts of PA and public policy portray government agencies and public employees in radically different ways. In some instances, agencies are viewed as ineffective or obstructionist. In other cases, they are viewed as narrowly instrumental, mere vehicles of elite or popular will. Other observers describe public employees as entrepreneurs, fixers, negotiators, bargainers, changers, or central nodes in complex interorganizational and intraorganizational networks.

A final emerging minority view deserves brief mention. Its proponents believe that public servants are actually public-spirited people who are motivated to serve society, protect the public interest, and increase the public weal (see Brewer, Selden, & Facer, 2000). This latter view suggests public employees are strongly motivated and therefore in modest need of OD practitioners, change agents, or anyone else.

Clearly, all of these stereotypes cannot be correct—at least not all at once. To note one contrast only, agencies cannot be both instrumental and purposive, and employees cannot be both risk averse and entrepreneurial, engaging in self-sacrifice and risk taking to advance the public interest. For additional details on these two broad sets of stereotypes, many sources are of service (Brehm & Gates, 1997; Brewer, 2001; Goodsell, 2003). For present purposes, however differentiated, all of these scenarios seem less than optimal for encouraging OD and change in public organizations. Notably, much contemporary thinking on PA and public policy may be the worst enemy of planned change, even where the need is presented as great. Of course, the selections in this chapter simplify as well as present an overview. Thus, Light (1999) contends that government agencies should rely on an increased number of private sector contractors and nonprofit organizations to perform the public work and to fulfill their missions. This type of third-party service delivery also can be used to finesse a concern for OD and change or at least direct attention away from such targets.

TESTING SOME OPINIONS ASSOCIATED WITH OD IN PA

This brief excursion through mainstream PA literatures strongly implies that the prospects for planned OD and change are pretty slim in the public sector, but this intellectual end has great practical costs. In sharp contrast to the selected views, increasingly widespread reports about OD success rates seem to tell a different story, or at least one that is much more nuanced. The focus in this section is on North American settings, but similar evidence is available for a range of cultures and work settings, such as the

Confucian work ethic and the contemporary Hindu work ethic (Golembiewski, n.d.).

In addition to the shortfalls in PA literatures providing a comfortable home for OD, more general shoptalk about OD in PA also helps discourage applications. Three are considered here:

- Opinion I: OD success rates are low in public sector applications in U.S. work settings.

- Opinion II: OD success rates may be somewhat higher in U.S. business, but not much so.

- Opinion III: OD applications are culturally bound; consequently, success rates are lowest in non-U.S. public settings, probably by large margins.

No single way of testing such opinions is fully satisfactory, but one approach can be useful here. For this purpose, a large panel of OD cases rates each application in one of four categories of success, as in Table 28.1:

- Category I generally means that almost all consequences of an application fall in the expected directions, and (where statistical tests are run) more than 50% of the cases achieve statistical significance.
- Category II falls short of I only in the sense that around a third or so of any statistical tests achieve significance, and few or none fall in a contrary direction.
- Category III is self-explanatory.
- Category IV includes cases in which a substantial proportion of effects falls in an opposite direction and all cases in which more than a few contrary measures achieve statistical significance.

No similarly large populations exist, and all panels with small numbers of cases reflect patterns like those in Table 28.1. In sum, patterns of effects of OD applications seem substantially positive. To be more specific, consider Table 28.1 in terms of the three opinions just

Table 28.1   Success Rates in Three Panels of OD Applications

Categories of Rated Success	A. Western Countries, Largely U.S. (N = 574)[a]		B. Developing Countries (N = 240)[b]		C. Korean Applications (N = 61)[c]
	Public Sector	*Business Sector*	*Public Sector*	*Business Sector*	
I. Highly positive and intended effects, with 2/3 being statistically significant when tests are available	41%	40%	26%	13.6%	28.2%
II. Definite balance of positive and intended effects	43%	49%	48%	63.6%	56.4%
III. No appreciable effects, or balance between intended and contrary effects	7%	5%	17%	9.1%	—
IV. Contrary effects, especially in applications with even a small proportion of estimates in a contrary direction that attain statistical significance	10%	6%	5%	4.5%	0%
Results not available	2.6%	0%	4%	9.1%	12.8%

SOURCES: [a]Golembiewski (1990, pp. 22–23).
[b]Golembiewski (2000).
[c]Yoon (1999); Yoon & Lee (2002).

described. Overall, the common opinion in PA stands at odds with the results of evaluative studies, which, as far as the present authors recognize, no one has refuted. Perhaps most tellingly, the cases of OD applications in subcategories B and C come from a total of 61 countries. Note also that public versus business sector estimates of success are quite similar, and both are substantial.

In sum, PA shoptalk in PA has little to recommend it when it comes to OD.

FACTORS BUOYING OD SUCCESS RATES IN PUBLIC SECTOR

What helps account for the sharp division between opinion about public OD applications and results such as those reflected in Table 28.1? No one can be absolutely sure at this stage of the game, for one thing. And we authors will let critics of OD in public sector applications make

their own case. Here we note only a few factors that may take some of the sting out of the surprise that some may see as appropriate for the substantial success rates in Table 28.1.

Four points only will illustrate the major factors that contribute to the buoyant trend obvious in Table 28.1. First, OD designs encompass a broad range, as Table 28.2 reflects. It describes five levels of democratic experience, and applicable OD designs are available at each of them. Discussions of such designs and more are available elsewhere (e.g., Golembiewski, 2003). And readers will find many of these designs referred to in this volume. Commonly, wherever the broad context of Table 28.2 is reflected, the result will be an enhanced fit of OD to specific situational features and hence a heightened success rate. One kind of design does not suit the diversity of situations to which OD can be applied any more than one size provides the close fit of socks to the diversity of human feet.

Table 28.2 Five Classes of Democratic Experiences and OD Designs Assignable to Them

Enhanced individual freedom and responsibility	Flexible work hour programs, which can increase control over work, commuting, and even family life
	Career planning, which can increase a sense of ownership and commitment to goals, permits response to changing stages of life, and so on
Committee democracy, in which all members have a roughly equal say while in face-to-face contact	Team-building or sensitivity training with intact work teams to surface and resolve both instrumental and process issues at work
	Group decision making to heighten involvement in and ownership of policies and goals, as in quality circles
	Autonomous teams, which organize around work flows so as to heighten self-discipline and self-control in many areas (e.g., recruitment, training, compensation)
Referendum democracy, in which all viewpoints are represented, although individuals do not necessarily speak out themselves	Various designs toward self-correcting cultures that seek to build norms and skills relevant to inducing valid and reliable data, such as self-enforcing large subsystems (e.g., plants or offices)
	Interview and feedback to a team or teams
	Survey and feedback, followed by a cascade of action planning
Representative democracy, in which a small, selected group speaks out for a larger collectivity	Group decision making by representatives in policymaking, or associated with latitude concerning ways of implementing policies, as in "Work Out"
	Joint labor–management committees (e.g., in an office) that seek to improve the quality of working life, as by planning changes in interpersonal and technostructural processes, often using survey methods to assess needs
	Some forms of collateral organizations that provide alternative vehicles for reinforcing opinions and exerting influence
Polyarchical democracy, which includes the aforementioned forms and also provides roles for diverse interest groups and complex delegations of authority	Large agenda- and norm-setting meetings with diverse participants from various levels of one or more organizations or nation-states, often using survey methods to assess needs
	Conflict resolution between representatives of nation-states (e.g., between officials of Israel and Egypt at Camp David)
	Enhancing complex forms of labor–management interaction at multiple levels, focusing on quality of working life and on pay and fringes
	Experiments with macro-problems (e.g., territorial disputes in Africa, conflict resolution between Jew and Arab in Israel or Catholic and Protestant in Ireland)

Second, Table 28.2 contains three classes of designs—interpersonal, structural, and policies and procedures—alone and in multiple combinations. Variants of these classes of designs will enhance the close fit of designs to settings. Therefore, success rates also may be expected to get an upward boost. To illustrate, interaction-centered designs are more appropriate for more permissive settings, or structural designs may be more suitable for traditional and autocratic settings, as De and other Indian natives have observed. Overall, this multiple situational flexibility of designs serving the same set of values is consistent with heightened success rates.

Third, some OD designs can be tailored to even very different cultures, again with positive impact on success rates. Thus, in most U.S. team-building designs, participants often give other members real-time and direct feedback. However, this may poorly serve the Confucian values of saving face and respect of elders. In Korea, then, objectives similar to U.S. variants can be met by participants drafting long letters to each other member for their review after the conclusion of a long training session (e.g., Ha, 1986). In Confucian cultures, then, OD applications may suffer in immediacy, but the evidence strongly suggests that the respect of common traditional culture emphases has counterbalancing effects. In Korea, the traditional cultural features include respect for authority and personal face saving.

Fourth, and finally only for the present purposes, there seem to be lesser differences between various work environments than is usually assumed. For example, substantial similarities exist between an OD work ethic in North America and several other broadly defined work contexts: Confucian settings associated with Korean and other Southeast Asian countries, a Hindu work context in Indian settings, and an Israeli work ethic (see Golembiewski, n.d.). The total effect is to make OD more applicable cross-culturally than is often acknowledged, with consequent increases in success rates resulting from essential similarities between many work situations to which OD can be applied. Suggestively, the evaluative studies summarized in Table 28.1 come from 61 different nation-states. Of course, this cross-cultural comparability suggests a more targeted OD and hence higher success rates.

In sharp contrast, much opinion among OD practitioners once ensured the narrow cultural relativity of applications, a position comfortable to expectations about low success rates. Indeed, substantial opinion often claimed that only a North American OD existed.

This is not the place to even attempt the necessary full treatment of the point that is under way in various other places (e.g., Golembiewski, n.d.). To illustrate, the basic theory of learning is essentially the same in several OD work settings. In the North American tradition, small learning collectivities often are central, and much the same is the case in Confucian variants, in which the family unit plays a prominent role and reflects a Southeast Asian form of the common theme of the small group in developing authentic and authoritative relationships in Southeast Asian settings. Nine other basic features also tend to reveal substantial similarities between cultural settings, (e.g., Golembiewski, n.d.), in sharp contrast to much opinion and consistent with the aggregate success rates in Table 28.1.

CONCLUSION

In sum, this approach to public sector OD applications builds on and around three propositions. First, major intellectual traditions in PA provide no firm roots for planned change, even as (in their own ways) they often imply the need for planned change. Second, ironically, much literature supports substantial success rates in public sector applications, broadly if certainly not worldwide or in all cultural and belief settings. Third, there seem to be credible reasons for such success rates, given the character of OD values, theory, and knowledge about applications.

REFERENCES

Bendor, J. (1990). Formal models of bureaucracy: A review. In N. B. Lynn & A. Wildavsky (Eds.), *Public administration: The state of the discipline* (pp. 373–417). Chatham, NJ: Chatham House.

Brehm, J., and Gates, S. (1997). *Working, shirking and sabotage: Bureaucratic response to a democratic public.* Ann Arbor: University of Michigan Press.

Brewer, G. A. (2001). *A portrait of public servants: Empirical evidence from comparisons with other citizens.* Unpublished doctoral dissertation, University of Georgia, Athens.

Brewer, G. A., Selden, S. C., & Facer, R. L., II. (2000). Individual conceptions of public service motivation. *Public Administration Review, 60*(3), 204–214.

Buchanan, J. M., & Tullock, G. (1962). *The calculus of consent: Logical foundations of a constitutional democracy.* Ann Arbor: University of Michigan Press.

Carnevale, D. G. (2002). *Organizational development in the public sector.* Boulder, CO: Westview.

Chisholm, R. T. (1998). *Developing network organizations.* Reading, MA: Addison-Wesley.

Dahl, R. A., & Lindblom, C. E. (1953). *Politics, economics, and welfare.* New York: Harper & Row.

Downs, A. (1967). *Inside bureaucracy.* Boston: Little, Brown.

Dunleavy, P. (1991). *Democracy, bureaucracy and public choice: Economic explanations in political science.* Hemel Hempstead, England: Harvester Wheatsheaf.

Geerth, H. H., & Mills, C. W. (Eds.). (1946). *From Max Weber: Essays in sociology.* New York: Oxford University Press.

Golembiewski, R. T. (1969). Organization development in public agencies: Perspectives on theory and practice. *Public Administration Review, 29*(4), 367–377.

Golembiewski, R. T. (1990). *Ironies in organizational development.* New Brunswick, NJ: Transaction.

Golembiewski, R. T. (1996). The future of public administration: End of a short stay in the sun? Or a new day a-dawning. *Public Administration Review, 56*(2), 139–148.

Golembiewski, R. T. (2000). *Handbook of organizational consultation.* New York: Marcel Dekker.

Golembiewski, R. T. (2003). *Ironies in organizational development* (2nd ed.). New York: Marcel Dekker.

Golembiewski, R. T. (n.d.). *Toward world-wide OD: Similar success rates and comparative work ethics.*

Goodsell, C. T. (2003). *The case for bureaucracy: A public administration polemic* (4th ed.). Chatham, NJ: Chatham House.

Gore, A. (1993). *Creating a government that works better and costs less: Report of the National Performance Review.* New York: Times Books, Random House.

Gruber, J. E. (1987). *Controlling bureaucracies: Dilemmas in democratic governance.* Berkeley: University of California Press.

Ha, M. (1986). *Self-overcoming training in Korean public administration.* Unpublished seminar paper, University of Georgia, Athens.

Hargrove, E. C., & Glidewell, J. C. (Eds.). (1990). *Impossible jobs in public management.* Lawrence: University Press of Kansas.

Hill, M., & Hupe, P. (2002). *Implementing public policy: Governance in theory and practice.* Thousand Oaks, CA: Sage.

Hjern, B., & Porter, D. O. (1981). Implementation structures: A new unit of administrative analysis. *Organization Studies, 2*(3), 211–227.

Kaufman, H. (1991). *Time, chance, and organizations: Natural selection in a perilous environment* (2nd ed.). Washington, DC: CQ Press.

Kettl, D. F. (1990). The perils—and prospects—of public administration. *Public Administration Review, 50*(4), 411–419.

Light, P. C. (1999). *The true size of government.* Washington, DC: The Brookings Institution.

Lowi, T. J. (1969). *The end of liberalism: Ideology, policy, and the crisis of public authority.* New York: Norton.

Matland, R. E. (1995). Synthesizing the implementation literature: The ambiguity-conflict model of policy implementation. *Journal of Public Administration Research and Theory, 5*(2), 145–174.

Mazmanian, D., & Sabatier, P. (1989). *Implementation and public policy: With a new postscript.* Lanham, MD: University Press of America.

Merton, R. K. (1957). *Social theory and social structure*. Glencoe, IL: Free Press.

Moore, M. H. (1995). *Creating public value: Strategic management in government*. Cambridge, MA: Harvard University Press.

Niskanen, W. A. Jr. (1971). *Bureaucracy and representative government*. Chicago: Aldine.

Osborne, D. E., & Gaebler, T. (1992). *Reinventing government: How the entrepreneurial spirit is transforming the public sector*. Reading, MA: Addison-Wesley.

Pratt, J. W., & Zeckhauser R. J. (Eds.). (1985). *Principals and agents: The structure of business*. Boston: Harvard Business School Press.

Pressman, J., & Wildavsky, A. (1984). *Implementation* (3rd ed.). San Francisco: Jossey-Bass.

Rainey, H. G. (2003). *Understanding and managing public organizations*. Somerset, NJ: John Wiley & Sons.

Redford, E. (1969). *Democracy in the administrative state*. Reading, MA: Addison-Wesley.

Ripley, R. B., & Franklin, G. A. (1986). *Policy implementation and bureaucracy* (2nd ed.). Chicago: Dorsey.

Spence, D. B. (1997). Agency policy making and political control: Modeling away the delegation problem. *Journal of Public Administration Research and Theory, 7*(2), 199–219.

Tompkins, J. (2005). *Organization theory and public management*. Belmont, CA: Wadsworth.

West, W. F. (1995). *Controlling the bureaucracy: Institutional constraints in theory and practice*. Armonk, NY: M.E. Sharpe.

Whyte, W. H. Jr. (1956). *The organization man*. New York: Simon & Schuster.

Wildavsky, A. (1979). *Speaking truth to power*. Boston: Little, Brown.

Wilson, W. (1887). The study of administration. *Political Science Quarterly, 2*, 197–222.

Wood, B. D., & Waterman, R. W. (1994). *Bureaucratic dynamics: The role of bureaucracy in a democracy*. Boulder, CO: Westview.

Yoon, J.-I. (1999). *OD applications in Korea*. Unpublished manuscript, University of Georgia, Athens.

Yoon, J.-I., & Lee, J.-W. (2002). *OD applications in Korea, II*. Unpublished manuscript, University of Georgia, Athens.

29

Organization Development in Family-Owned and Family-Controlled Companies

ERNESTO J. POZA

Family businesses are ubiquitous; they make up a significant part of the U.S. and global economy. Many family businesses are small; approximately 17 million[1] of them operate in the United States alone, and only 35,000 of them register annual revenues of $25 million or more (Poza, 2007). Family-owned firms may be privately held or publicly traded. Privately held businesses include such common brands as Mars, Inc., a $17-billion manufacturer of confectioneries, snacks, and pet foods; Cargill, the largest grain and agricultural commodity distributor in the world, with annual revenues of $50 billion; and S.C. Johnson, the $5-billion cleaning and consumer products company that brings us Pledge, Windex, Raid, and Off. Family-controlled publicly traded firms include Ford Motor, Wal-Mart, Marriott Corporation, The Washington Post Companies, and, until recently, Hewlett-Packard. In fact, 60% of all publicly traded companies and 34% of the S&P 500 are family controlled (Astrachan & Shanker, 2003). Family businesses are responsible for 54% of the gross domestic product of the United States and more than 75% of the gross domestic product of the economies in Europe, Asia, and Latin America.

Family businesses are essential to the livelihood of millions of entrepreneurs and enterprising families and, perhaps more significantly, to 85% of the world's private sector employees (Poza, 2007). Collectively, entrepreneurial and family businesses are the largest employers, the most significant creators of jobs, and the primary engines of economic activity throughout the world. Contrary to the widespread notion that family business is an oxymoron, family-controlled companies have been shown to be stellar performers. Family-controlled firms on the S&P 500[2] outperformed management-controlled companies on the list with a 6.65% higher return on assets and a 10% higher shareholder value created in the last decade (Anderson & Reeb, 2003).

Family firms are familiar to us; nationally, they create products whose brands are household names. Locally, family-owned enterprises often include the local car dealership, hardware store, and assorted retailers and merchants. This chapter introduces the unique characteristics of family firms and many of the challenges that accompany them. Two theoretical frameworks are introduced and are applied to interventions in family businesses.

THE NATURE OF FAMILY BUSINESS

Family firms may seem simple in comparison to other forms of enterprise (because of their often smaller size and the widespread stereotype that they are nothing more than mom and pop operations). In reality they are quite complex, especially because of the unique relationship between the owners and the business (see Box 29.1).

BOX 29.1   Characteristics of a Family Firm

- Ownership control (15% or higher) by two or more members of a family or a partnership of families
- Strategic influence by family members in the management of the firm, whether by being active in management, continuing to shape the culture, or serving as advisors or board members
- Concern for family relationships
- The vision of continuity across generations

Family ownership and control can influence how entrepreneurial and family firms are managed, even when they are publicly traded companies. Prominent examples of family leadership are evident in the Hewlett and the Packard families' open opposition to the merger between Hewlett-Packard and Compaq Computer and by the Ford family's role in appointing William Clay Ford, Jr. as CEO and then chair of the Ford Motor Company during a period of turmoil at the large auto producer. In the media industry, observers have witnessed strong commitment by families to great enterprises. Generational transitions and turmoil wrought by economic, natural, and technological forces have been no match for family ownership with a long-term perspective. Katharine and Don Graham, the mother-and-son team of the *Washington Post*, amply displayed this commitment during Watergate and the Pentagon Papers in the 1970s

and a generational transfer of power in the 1990s. The Blethens family of the *Seattle Times* exemplified stewardship responsibility when the fifth generation of the family recommitted itself to continuity in the face of a financially debilitating strike. The Ferré-Rangel family of *El Nuevo Día* in Puerto Rico, publisher of two leading newspapers and other media, created a model for succession in Latin America by transferring power and the entrepreneurial spirit to the next generation in 2006.

But achieving continuity across generations of family owners can be extremely difficult. Most family businesses (estimated at approximately 67%) do not survive beyond the founding generation under the ownership and control of the same family, and only about 12% survive to the third generation (Ward, 1987). Of course, companies in general do not enjoy long, successful lives. When Standard and Poor's Index of

90 major U.S. corporations was first created in the 1920s, the firms on the original list stayed there for an average of 65 years. By 1998, the expected tenure on the larger S&P 500 list was a mere 10 years (Foster & Kaplan, 2001). On the NASDAQ, 25% of the listed companies were delisted between 2001 and 2002 (Graham, 2000).

Despite these long odds, the fundamental intention of many family businesses is to continue family ownership across generations (see Box 29.2). This drive for continuity can result from personal and family legacy wishes, tax considerations, or the founder's dream of building an institution. Business continuity, and the transitions it entails, is the primary focus for much organization development (OD) practice in family businesses. OD practitioners can help family businesses deal effectively with succession and build an organization that will last across generations.

BOX 29.2   Essential Differences of Family Businesses

- The presence of the family
- The owner's dream to keep the business in the family; the objective of business continuity from generation to generation
- The overlap of family, ownership, and management, with its zero-sum (win–lose) propensities, which render family firms particularly vulnerable during management or ownership succession
- The unique sources of competitive advantage derived from the interaction of family, management, and ownership, especially when family unity is high

---

FRAMEWORKS FOR UNDERSTANDING FAMILY FIRMS

The primary objective of OD is to help an organization manage change and increase its effectiveness. OD relies on conceptual frameworks to diagnose organizations and help them improve. For family businesses, two perspectives are particularly helpful: system theory and resource-based theory. Both provide useful insights into the functioning and effectiveness of family firms.

System Theory

As shown in Figure 29.1, family businesses can be viewed as complex systems composed of three key subsystems that overlap and interact in unique ways: family (F), management (M), and owner (O) (Gersick, 1997). The primary mission of the family subsystem is to nurture individual members until differentiation, individuation, and interdependent adulthood are achieved. The core work of the management subsystem is to optimize profits, create shareholder value, and provide the infrastructure for continued competitiveness. The key objective of the owner subsystem is to maximize returns on invested capital and to provide oversight of management as the shareholders' agent. Each subsystem maintains boundaries that separate it from the other subsystems and the external environment within which the firm operates. In order for the organization as a whole to be effective, the subsystems must function together in a unified and coordinated manner (Alderfer, 1976). Integration is achieved through reciprocal adjustments of the subsystems. For example, the family subsystem can be expected to have a strong impact on the owner and management subsystems and vice versa. Because one subsystem cannot be fully understood apart from the others, OD practitioners focus on the interaction of the three subsystems and on the integration mechanisms used to coordinate them.

Depending on the position each member of the family and firm has in the system, his or her

**The Systems Theory Model
of Family Business**

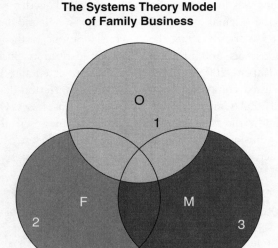

Figure 29.1   Systems Theory Model of Family Business

SOURCE: From *Family Business,* Second Edition by Poza, E. J., 2007. Reprinted with permission of South-Western, a division of Thomson Learning: www.thomsonrights.com. Fax 800-730-2215.

perspective understandably will be different. A family member who is a parent, CEO, and majority owner (position 1 in Figure 29.1) is likely to view things differently than a family member who is not active in management and does not own any shares in the business (position 2). Similarly, a nonfamily manager (position 3) is likely to have a different perspective on a situation the firm is facing as a result of her or his unique placement in the family business system. In its extreme form, these singular perspectives can lead to family businesses that have a family-, owner- or management-first perspective. This can result in significant suboptimization of the overall system and thus to poorer performance than the business and the family are capable of achieving.

Because of the complexity inherent in the interactions between the family, owner, and management subsystems, each with potentially different goals and operating principles, entrepreneurial and family businesses are vulnerable to the consequences of blurred boundaries between the subsystems. Research in psychology and economics has highlighted the power of emotion to lead to behaviors that rational thought would seldom support (Axelrod, 1980). As a result, family dynamics, which often have a large emotional content, can readily override the logic of business management or ownership. Similarly, lack of awareness of the different assumptions that go into decision making on the basis of whether an issue is considered a family, ownership, or management issue, can create incongruent policies and untenable decisions for family businesses.

A family business that exists primarily for the purpose of family benefit may offer extensive perks to family members. To support this situation, financial systems may intentionally obfuscate the firm's financial data, and secrecy may become paramount. The lack of financial transparency may enable practices that benefit family members beyond what standard compensation policies and Internal Revenue Service rules would deem reasonable. The business then becomes part of a lifestyle for the owning family. The Rigas family and Adelphia Cable were prosecuted by the Securities and Exchange Commission and other federal and state authorities for extensive self-dealing that illegally benefited the Rigas family. Of course, shareholder returns or managerial interests (e.g., for more rapid growth) could just as easily predominate and make the firm an owner-first or management-first system.

The absence of balance or clear boundaries between family, owners, and management can also lead to zero-sum dynamics or "me-ism" in family firms. This involves some stakeholders winning at the expense of others. In family firms, zero-sum mentality often is a precursor to business failure and broken families (Poza, Hanlon, & Kishida, 2004). It can be a corrosive influence that often overrides the goodwill and best intentions of even the healthiest families. There is evidence that such divisiveness and family conflict can set in easily in declining businesses (Cameron, Whetten, & Kim, 1987). Smaller family businesses, by virtue of their size, are much more susceptible to the effects of decline than are larger, publicly traded corporations (Cameron et al., 1987). When the pie is not growing, family shareholders often shift to fighting over the size of their slice. A regeneration that addresses the business's decline may involve renewed strategic planning activity and ownership and management structures that give greater control to some and change the nature of the participation of others. It is essential that overall responsibility for the firm and the authority to foster change be linked (regardless of family relationship and position in the family hierarchy) in any such reorganization.

After almost a hundred years of operation, the McIlhenny Company, makers of the peppery Tabasco Sauce, decided to execute strategies for the growth of the company. The decision to grow responded to the family's tradition of having good dividends from operations to distribute to shareholders. As the number of shareholders grew to more than 90, dilution of dividends loomed large among shareholders. Leaders of this family-owned company decided that the risk of unhealthy conflict between family members dictated that the company grow in order to avoid the zero-sum family dynamic. New products and product-line extensions were created, and the Tabasco label now graces not just the little bottle of red hot sauce but bottles of green sauce and ready-to-add spicy mixes for Cajun cooking at home.

Implicit in system theory is the capacity to jointly optimize interrelated subsystems in such a way that the larger system, in this case the family business, can be most effective. Putting strategic plans, sound business practices, and governance bodies (such as boards with independent[3] outsiders and family councils) in place, while promoting strong cultures and family unity, can inspire commitment to something greater than unbridled self-interest by individuals or groups in a family business.

For example, Edgepark Surgical, a leading family-owned medical device distribution company led by the Harrington Family and a team of very capable nonfamily managers, has developed the following statement of company values that displays a deep understanding of the powerful effects of jointly optimizing family, management, and ownership:

We are:

- Family-owned
- Professionally managed
- A family acting in the company's best interest

We believe in:

- Integrity: We do what we say we will do.
- No walls: We have no barriers to communication.
- Tenacity: We have an unrelenting determination to reach objectives.
- Profitability: We are committed to performance and results.
- Improvement: We are never satisfied.
- Service: We are loyal to our customers & respect them.

The mission statement acknowledges the three subsystems of family, management, and owner while reminding each of their shared goals and objectives.

Resource-Based Theory

From the resource-based perspective, family firms can gain competitive advantage by having valuable and nonsubstitutable resources that are unique to them and not easily imitated by other firms (Cabrera-Suarez, Saa-Perez, & Garcia-Almeida, 2001). These resources, often called organization competencies, are embedded in the firm's internal processes, human resources, or other intangible assets (Box 29.3.)

A unique source of competitive advantage in family-owned and family-controlled businesses is the interaction between the business and the

---

BOX 29.3   A Resource-Based View of Family Firms

- Owner–manager overlap and company size enable speed to market.
- Focus on market niches results in higher returns on investment.
- Concentrated ownership structure leads to higher overall corporate productivity.
- Desire to protect the founder's or family name and reputation often translates into high relative product or service quality and higher return on investment.
- The nature of the family–ownership–organization interaction and family unity supports longer time horizons in investor expectations, lower administrative costs, transfer of skill and knowledge across generations, and agility in rapidly changing markets.

---

family, which results from the relationships between members of these groups. When this interaction is characterized by a shared management, ownership, and family vision of business opportunity, companies are likely to engage in managerial and governance practices that control agency costs and take advantage of unique resources that produce idiosyncratic organization capabilities.

To better understand this unique aspect of family businesses, the Discovery Research for Family Business was initiated 14 years ago as part of a comprehensive learning partnership between family firms and the Weatherhead School of Management at Case Western Reserve University. Discovery Research is a multiyear action research process in which the actions taken by a firm in response to the often iterative feedback and action process are tracked and studied. Discovery Research uses a family firm questionnaire and a separate family questionnaire that together make up the Family Business Diagnostic Survey.[4]

The Discovery Research team studied the extent to which the unique interaction between the family and the business can be measured and the extent to which this interaction is associated with the behavior of the firm (Poza et al., 2004). We found that family unity and a positive family–business interaction were correlated with the implementation of effective management and governance practices, including planning activity, performance feedback, disclosure of succession plans, and the use of advisory boards and family meetings. (See Poza et al., 2004, for a more extensive discussion of the study, methods, and findings.) The findings seem to indicate that investing in the family's health and harmony by establishing guidelines for family participation in the business pays off for the firm. Issues considered in family guidelines include rules about the employment of family members and standards and processes for succession and ownership transfer. The Discovery Research findings further support research suggesting that family meetings, retreats, and family councils can play an important role in family-owned business effectiveness and continuity by creating a new reality for family members (Habbershon & Astrachan, 1997).

Other resources that tend to be unique to family businesses include the overlapping owner and management relationship, which can lead to advantages including powerful and efficient monitoring mechanisms, reduced administrative and financial control costs, speedy decision making, and longer time horizons for measuring firm performance. The transfers of industry, business, and product knowledge and skills from one generation to the next, along with ownership commitment over the long term, have also been recognized as idiosyncratic resources characteristic of family enterprises (Poza et al., 2004). These unique resources can be turned into competitive advantages that can enhance firm performance.

APPLYING OD TO FAMILY BUSINESSES

Family business members seldom examine or reflect on their organization practices, culture, or communication processes. They tend to be private, secretive, and conflict avoidant; consequently, there is little impetus for the kind of thorough diagnosis and open feedback common in OD practice. The action research process discussed earlier, the Discovery Research on Family Business, was created to address this problem.

The survey findings are shared in feedback sessions that are attended by owners, family, and key nonfamily managers. In these sessions, family members and participating nonfamily managers are provided with a profile of the firm's managerial practices and organization culture. The owners also receive a profile of the family culture, its communication practices, and CEO succession process. The survey results and discussion in the feedback session can influence which corrective actions a firm or owner takes. They can guide the creation of new practices, solutions, experiments, or

learning activities. Survey feedback has led to educational interventions, family meetings, business consultation, and changes in managerial practices and governance structures.

Action research in family businesses has helped break the hermetic seal that constrains so many of these firms. The process has added value to firm members by bringing an outsider's perspective to the analysis and discussion of how their company is operating. It has helped build bridges across generations of owner–managers and between family and nonfamily management. The process has promoted healthy dialogue and created new communication processes for both the shareholders and the organization. It has also promoted understanding of the different perspectives held by family members depending on whether they are family, management, or owners. Finally, it has provided a platform for planning actions that respond to the unique challenges and issues identified for each firm.

In the following pages, several OD concepts and processes applied to family business are discussed. Four key OD applications are presented: change management, leadership succession, strategic planning, and governance of the family–business relationship.

Change Management

A perspective on systemic change and the management of change that has proven very useful in family business settings is Richard Beckhard's three states of change: the present or current state, the transition state, and the desired or future state (Beckhard & Pritchard, 1992). Examples of this perspective in assisting family businesses with their change efforts follow the discussion of each of the three states.

The Present State

To drive the firm from its present to its future state, it is essential to identify the key subsystems or parts of the organization and family that will have a bearing on the change process or be affected by it. These key subsystems may be departments or divisions in the company, branches of the family, individual top managers, or shareholder family members. Two factors weigh heavily in the overall assessment of the subsystem's ability to change: its readiness, the level of support for the proposed change in that subsystem; and its power or capability, the human resources, funds, and family or organization influence it has available to either support or block the proposed change.

The utility of this assessment can be seen in the story of a recent corporate acquisition. Several years ago, a medium-sized material-handling family business acquired another privately held company. After performing a readiness assessment in preparation for the integration of the two companies, the acquiring company decided not to consolidate both companies in the same site (a move that would have entailed moving personnel across the country). Using information from the assessment, the acquiring company created a project management structure and gave leadership of the project to the president of the acquired company. The project structure allowed the gradual transfer and eventual consolidation of key technology. The readiness assessment had revealed both the tremendous value of the individual programmers at the acquired company and their low readiness for a coast-to-coast move. Upon successful completion of the change process, most of the programmers happily moved across the country to the headquarters facility.

The Transition State

The work to be done during the transition period in the evolution across generations within a family business is quite unique and different from the work the leader has to do in defining the desired future state and assessing the present. Once he or she has decided what must be changed as part of the assessment of the present, the leader's primary responsibility in the transition state is to decide where to begin the process:

Management. Should the change process begin with top management? Should the CEO begin by changing the makeup of the top team, the roles of the individual members, or the goals the top team pursues? Knowing who is "on the bus" in top management and what travel plans they make has a significant bearing on the ultimate destination of the family business.

Family. Should the change process begin with family? Should the leader begin by convening the family, making more information available, educating family members not active in the business about business matters, creating a family council, or developing policies guiding the family's participation in the business?

Ownership. Should the change process begin with ownership? Should the leader begin by restructuring ownership, changing who owns voting and nonvoting stock, educating heirs on the estate plan, developing or updating buy–sell agreements, or renegotiating existing dividend or distribution expectations? Because family members provide the enterprise with its growth capital, family unity and the nature of the family–business interaction have a huge bearing on the firm's ability to keep the long-term patient capital shareholder perspective.

Readiness. Should the change process begin with the most ready systems? Should the leader begin with the people, departments, or groups of people most ready for the change? Their readiness may be the result of alignment with the desired future or dissatisfaction with the status quo. Beginning with high-readiness parts of the system can create some early wins and develop momentum for the change process.

New Structures. Should the change process begin with new teams, units, or governance bodies? Should the leader leverage the initial phase of the change process by relying on new bodies that lack history and do not over-rely on past practices? A third-generation team, a strategic planning committee, a committee of the family council, or the newly formed advisory board can all be promising platforms for creating the desired future state.

The transition state entails developing and moving through a series of processes that support initiating the movement of stakeholders from the present state to the desired state. Significant changes may be part of the transition state. Near the end of the transition state, family, management, ownership, and the relationship between them must begin to look more like those envisioned in the desired future state. In order to get them there, each of the three subsystems must be assessed separately and in relation to the others (Figure 29.2). Following are examples of the kinds of changes that are often included in transition plans.

The family, through the policies it develops in its family council, for example, can renegotiate the criteria family members need to meet in order to be considered for management positions in the company. Similarly, a family considering a young heir as its next-generation CEO could support the development of that person by building some flexibility into the family structure, aware that the family's hierarchy traditionally has stood for primogeniture.

On the management front, the company could initiate a strategic thinking and planning process and "gun the engines" of growth. It could hire new nonfamily talent that better complements the skills the next-generation leader brings to the top team and further professionalizes management while giving the new leader his or her own hire. From an ownership perspective, a buy–sell agreement could be drafted and dividend policies could be changed to support reinvestment in growth. Alternatively, vehicles for financing the execution of an estate plan could be identified, insurance policies purchased, and buy–sell agreements drafted.

The Future State

The future state is a composite of the organization's and the family's plans, dreams, and hopes. Unlike a vision, which is usually somewhat abstract and longer range, the future state is equivalent to mapping out results or changes expected in a 1-, 2-, or 3-year period. A statement of the desired future state is equivalent to a midpoint scenario and should be developed bearing in mind both the vision and the core mission of the enterprise and the owning family.

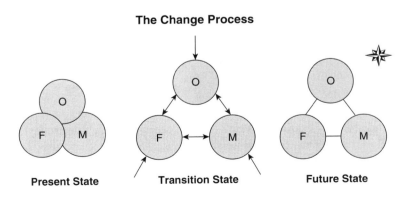

The Change Process

Present State — Transition State — Future State

Figure 29.2 Change Process

SOURCE: From *Family Business,* Second Edition by Poza, E. J., 2007. Reprinted with permission of South-Western, a division of Thomson Learning: www.thomsonrights.com. Fax 800-730-2215.

For example, a family business's statement of its desired future state begins this way:

> On November 1, 2010, Premier Corporation signed the papers acquiring a resort in Florida and announced third-quarter results showing a comparable property revenue increase of 15% and a profit increase of 18% over the same period last year.

The most helpful future state scenarios are quite concrete. They are also an honest reflection of what the leader wants for his or her future and the future of the family and business.

Excellent future state scenarios paint a detailed picture of the goal. The Premier Corporation, through its family owners, defined the extent to which it wanted to own and operate additional properties, manage real estate assets owned by others, and own and manage properties that were not in the resort and recreation sector, where it currently operated. The statement of the desired future state also defined the management structure and set standards for selecting a new CEO. The family coalesced on the principle that a family CEO would be preferable to a nonfamily CEO and agreed to a process for making the decision. The owning family also defined family participation on the corporate board. Two family members were to represent the interests of the family on the corporate board, and every other member was either in top management or an independent outsider. Shareholder expectations on returns were also discussed and established in the desired future state scenario. Family members then discussed and defined the nature of the desired relationships between them and between the extended family and the business. Finally, the family's commitment to business continuity across generations and to giving back to the community through family philanthropy was established.

Developing a shared definition of the desired future state is an ideal task for a family meeting or family retreat. At a later stage, key nonfamily managers can also be involved in the process,

particularly as it relates to strategic and managerial issues. Building bridges between groups with potentially different perspectives, such as family shareholders and nonfamily managers, is essential. If the company has a board with independent outsiders, providing board members with this direction from the shareholders, owner–managers, and key nonfamily managers means that the board will be better able to serve the company and its shareholders.

An advantage of defining the future state concretely in family business change efforts is that it provides directional information to those not involved in the drafting of the statement. It improves their ability to understand how they fit into that future. Uncertainty and misperception of the implications of change on a person's future role are a major source of resistance to change.

Another advantage to beginning with defining the future state is that people tend to be more optimistic about future opportunities than about fixing current problems. These positive prospects provide a positive tension. They pull the organization and the family toward something desirable that begins to provide the fuel for the engine of change, particularly if there is a sharp contrast between the desired future state and the present state.

For an OD practitioner working in a family business setting, leadership succession, strategic planning, and governance are all essential to understanding the present and creating the desired future.

Leadership Succession

Leadership succession is one of the leading concerns of family firms today. OD can provide a value-adding perspective on succession by emphasizing the benefits of conceiving of it and planning for it as a process, not an event. Unfortunately, for many understandable reasons, avoidance, delay, and denial are the order of the day when it comes to succession. This often makes succession an ill-timed event. Another important contribution relies on the systemic perspective OD can bring to the subject. When they are willing to confront the subject at all, family firms often define the need for an orderly succession as the need to find the right person, the successor. A much more realistic and useful framework is one that makes succession a whole system (ownership–management–family) challenge. This section begins with descriptions of a variety of systemic OD interventions in the leadership succession process in family-owned or family-controlled corporations. The section ends with an example from an individual family firm. OD interventions may include various types of consultation.

Individual Consultation With the CEO and the Successor Candidate or Candidates

The ability of next-generation members of family firms to lead the organization must be accompanied by an ability to lead family members in subordinate management positions and those who make up the shareholder group. Many heirs resist this as a prerequisite to success in their leadership role. They would rather just run the business and be judged by the financial outcomes. But there is ample evidence that active leadership of these additional stakeholders is essential for success (Poza, 2007). As a result, besides overcoming the natural resistance by successors to assume more and not less responsibility, individual consultation may be directed at their taking initiatives through the family council to promote the engagement of other family members in committees, community relations, family philanthropy, and board service.

Individual consultation with the CEO often is focused on helping the CEO let go of his or her leadership position and facilitating the transfer of power (embedded in longstanding customer, supplier, and employee relationships) and the creation of structures and processes to govern the relationship between the family and the business in the vacuum created by the incumbent leader's absence.

Dyadic Consultation With the CEO and Successor or Successors

The task here is often to help establish a timeline for the transfer of power while acknowledging that succession is best conceived of as a process rather than an event. OD consultation may facilitate a renegotiation of goals and roles as the succession process develops and the transfer of power becomes more imminent. OD consultation may also help develop creative approaches to the coaching and supervision of the successor-in-development while instilling accountability after the transfer of power to the new CEO.

Group Consultation With the Family or Owner Group

Interventions with the family or owner group often help them develop a family participation and employment policy in preparation for leadership succession. This policy guides the entry, development, compensation, and exit of owners from the management subsystem. After all, owners can be employees, suppliers, subcontractors, professional advisors, or board members of the corporation.

Shareholder loyalty and patient capital are very important to family businesses, and yet there is a natural tendency for suboptimal differentiation between owner and manager roles. The family participation policy may be part of a document, sometimes called the family charter or constitution, created by family firms primarily to regulate the relationship between the owner and management subsystems before a possible leadership vacuum engulfs the family business in the transition across generations.

Intergroup Consultation With the Family and Nonfamily Management

OD interventions here aim primarily to increase the stability of firm and family by having professional managers assume increased responsibility during leadership succession in the family firm. By raising awareness and promoting understanding of the critical role of non-family management in the growth and professionalization of the family firm, during a potentially turbulent period, such interventions increase stability. This intergroup work may also clarify the standards to which owner–managers are held and raise the standards for family members in the business. Recognition increases of the different but complementary contributions owners and managers make to the enterprise increases. Bridging interventions between owners and key managers can enhance ownership oversight of management so that managers are held accountable for corporate performance and the pursuit of shareholder interests (something that the Sarbanes–Oxley Act, developed in the wake of the Enron, WorldCom, and Tyco scandals, tries to legislate in management-controlled corporations). Intergroup interventions with owners and key managers can also symbolically support the transfer of power to the next generation and reassure investors (family members) that the enterprise is in good hands, even if the successor CEO is still in the process of acquiring the full authority to lead.

Development of Interpersonal Skills

The development of interpersonal skills in the next generation often is the subject of leadership succession consultation. After all, in order to succeed, successors need to earn the respect not just of employees and customers but of other family members, often shareholders, who may be older or for a variety of other reasons higher in the family hierarchy (Barnes, 1988). The incongruence between the family and organization hierarchy, the newness of the job, and the nature of the parent–child relationship all pose a unique set of challenges for effective leadership by successors.

Ultimately, there are two often very different generations of leaders in every family business. The critical leadership tasks for each generation involved in succession and continuity efforts are also very different. The CEO generation is responsible for building institutions of governance, promoting trust, family unity, and communication, promoting shareholder loyalty, and finally transferring power to the next generation. In contrast, next-generation leaders are called to perform the delicate task of respecting the past while advocating change and adaptation through a new strategic vision, a vision that will serve the company well in the ensuing generation.

Madco Industries, a fictitious name used to protect the privacy of this family company, found itself stuck in the middle of a strategic dilemma. The CEO's son, vice president of finance and third-generation member of the family, was convinced that their regional distributor of high-priced industrial equipment could grow and prosper if only it complemented its existing operations with the creation of a new channel of distribution via the Internet. His father, the CEO, was equally convinced that doing so would be a bad idea for two reasons: It would set up a competitive situation between the new company and the existing one and potentially between father and son, and it could damage relationships with other distributors in other parts of the country with whom, in the absence of competition, relationships and competitive dynamics were cordial.

The situation first came to the author's attention when the son and potential successor called with the news that he was leaving the firm. After obtaining his MBA and returning to the family firm, he had implemented a new financial information and control system. Because that assignment was finished, and he wanted to have a little entrepreneurship in his life, the idea of starting a Web-enabled company fit him fine. He described how he had suggested the new digital strategy to the CEO and how the latter had quickly dismissed it with the words "Over my dead body." The son could not refrain from responding to this ultimatum, so he said, "If we don't do it, somebody else will, and then somebody outside our family will be eating our lunch." So the author suggested a lunch meeting for the three of them.

The two generations could hardly speak to each other at the beginning of the luncheon meeting, even with the assistance of a third party. Emotions were running high. By the end of the afternoon, though, the CEO and his potential successor had crafted what seemed like a reasonable plan. The heir would write a business plan for his new venture idea, price shares in the new company on the basis of the seed capital needed, and get a 20-minute slot on the agenda of a meeting of the eight independent U.S. distributors. This meeting, held every year in one of the distributor's hometowns, was scheduled to take place 2 months later. This year it was Madco's turn to host the study group meeting. Because these eight distributors had assigned territories and did not compete with each other but rather with distributors for other manufacturers throughout the country, this forum had a proud tradition of member education and candid conversations. The potential successor would thus get his opportunity to present the business plan and see whether others in the industry considered it a viable idea, that is, to see whether they would buy shares in the new venture. The CEO closed the extended lunch meeting by telling his son, "If you manage to sell as little as one share in the project, I am in too."

Though quite a challenge to the young man, it seemed like a reasonable turn of events. The potential successor might get an opportunity to be an entrepreneur, and in the meantime, his decision to leave the family business was at least delayed. His father, the CEO, felt strongly that the only way he would be willing to change his mind was if the idea passed the marketplace test, especially among people he respected and whose relationships he wanted to protect.

During the industry study group meeting, the successor successfully sold three shares in the new business venture, his father/CEO then acquired one share, and the e-commerce company was launched as a collaborative venture between four of the distributors. The successor became the new venture's president. About a year after its successful launch, the publisher of a trade publication in their industry made an offer to acquire the new company. On the basis of that offer, it appeared that the successor had managed to create more shareholder value in about 18 months than the CEO had created in a whole generation. Very impressed with the offer and cognizant that it may take another lifetime to achieve such returns in the absence of the transaction, the successor and his partners, including his dad, decided to sell.

Although the new venture did not remain in the family company's fold for long, it represented a great growth and value-creation opportunity for the company's shareholders and a tremendous learning opportunity for the successor. Without a dyadic intervention that facilitated a very difficult conversation and the subsequent new strategic business plan, the son's idea probably would have died because he had called the author to announce his departure from the family firm.

In sharp contrast, conflict-averse families often include parents who attempt to squelch or resolve sibling rivalry or intergenerational conflict. They avoid the difficult conversations. They therefore avoid strategic planning activity. Strategic planning is inherently conflictual because of the very different time horizons of the two generations on board and their very different perspective on the implications of changes in the competitive environment. But if there is a conflict worth having in a family-controlled enterprise, it is a disagreement on strategy as the enterprise faces the next 10 or 20 years. Those difficult conversations free the next generation from feelings of dependency and powerlessness, the exact opposite of the entrepreneurial and enterprising behavior so often desired of next-generation business leaders.

Strategic Planning: A Parallel Process for Owners and Managers

> I don't think it's an accident that the newspapers best known for quality in this country . . . are, or were until recently, family controlled. It seems that certain attributes essential to quality are more easily provided by families than by public companies. These are the qualities that I think are most important: First deep roots. Families offer longevity and thus a knowledge of, and commitment to, the local community that's hard to get from professional managers who come and go. . . . Second, a perspective that extends beyond the next quarter's earnings per share. . . . Finally, family ownership provides the independence that is sometimes required to withstand governmental pressure and preserve freedom of the press.

SOURCE: *Katharine Graham*, late chairman, The Washington Post Company. (*The Wall Street Journal*, March 20, 2001, p. A34)

Strategic planning is executed differently in entrepreneurial and family-controlled corporations than in nonfamily firms. The uniqueness of the approach responds to the need to engage both the owners and management in thinking about the future. This engagement often entails a parallel planning process that involves the owning family group working alongside the more traditional management strategic planning process. In a family meeting or family council, for instance, the family may recommend the adoption of certain family-based company values, as in the case of Edgepark Surgical discussed earlier. Or it may establish return on equity, dividend distribution, or revenue and profit growth targets. The family may even advocate diversification of the business, given the highly undiversified position of most entrepreneurs' and private family business leaders' net worth. (Equity in privately held family firms is highly illiquid and unmarketable, and business continuity requires continued reinvestment in the firm, which keeps most of the owners' assets concentrated in just one company; this is precisely the position most financial advisors recommend that shareholders in publicly traded corporations avoid.)

Facilitation of these family–ownership planning meetings requires the OD practitioner to be skilled not only in group facilitation but also in the complex systemic interaction between owner, family, and management subsystems. Only then can the various stakeholders hope to achieve an optimal outcome from the parallel planning process that represents shareholder–family and management interests. Specific OD interventions may promote joint meetings between a family council and a board of directors to promote synthesis of the parallel planning process or may simply establish a linking function where at-large representatives of the family serve on the board and communicate the family's intentions to other board members.

In entrepreneurial companies when the owner is also the CEO, ownership is already well represented in any strategic planning done by the organization. In family-owned and family-controlled organizations, the family–shareholder group needs to establish its own goals and define the nature of the relationship between it and its enterprise going forward. For example, do family members intend to continue to own and manage the business in the next generation, or would they rather own and control the business but have professional nonfamily management run it for them (Figure 29.3)?

The uniqueness of the parallel strategic planning approach in family-controlled companies should never lead an ownership group to go astray in its strategic planning activity by becoming inward focused and losing sight of what is most valuable to do from the customer's perspective. The potential for developing this inward focus is perhaps the strongest rationale for engaging in strategic planning activity in a family-controlled company facing generational transition. Strategic thinking is the best antidote to inward thinking. It represents

Strategic Planning in the Family Business

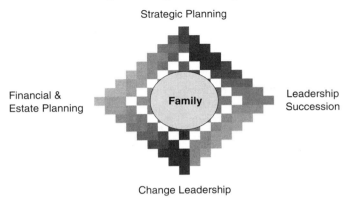

Figure 29.3   Strategic Planning in the Family Business

SOURCE: From *Family Business,* Second Edition by Poza, E. J., 2007. Reprinted with permission of South-Western, a division of Thomson Learning: www.thomsonrights.com. Fax 800-730-2215.

a breath of fresh air in what could otherwise be a vacuum-sealed system without a clue as to what is changing in its competitive environment.

From a strategic perspective, family-owned enterprises are most susceptible to accelerated decline and failure precisely because of their reliance on the individual entrepreneur or next-generation CEO. The entrepreneur is a hero who founded and led the young business to accelerated growth. He or she displays a natural disdain for organization architecture, systems, professional managerial practices, and governance mechanisms. Though not always the case, next-generation heroes often exhibit some of this same disdain for managerial discipline as they engage in the strategic regeneration and growth of the business. After all, professional managerial practices are considered the relatives of bureaucracy; bureaucracy is the dreaded disease that the privately held company CEO fled from in the world of management-controlled corporations.

When a family group is added to the equation, that is, when multiple members of a family become active in management or engaged as shareholders in thinking about the future of the enterprise, disagreement, conflict, and ultimately paralysis often occur. The different perspectives on the future result in conflict, and the different tolerances for differences held by active and inactive shareholders may lead to an impasse (Poza, 1989).

Speed is one of the family firm's strongest competitive advantages. More than in other forms of enterprise speed is the competitive advantage that is often sacrificed across generations of family-controlled companies. The author's experience as an educator, consultant, and family board member suggests that speed in decision making and execution suffers tremendously when ownership control is diluted as firms move from one generation to the next. To counteract this development in later generations, family councils and advisory boards may be launched. These forums often educate shareholders on business strategy, finance, estate planning, and the different roles of owners and managers. But these new forums should never lead shareholders to usurp top management's responsibility for thinking and acting strategically on behalf of the corporation and its shareholders. Because of this challenge, we now turn our attention to the role OD can play in creating appropriate governance of the family–owner–management relationship.

Governance of the Family Business

Governance is a complex subject when it comes to family business. Some forms of governance are provided for through the ownership structure and different classes of voting and nonvoting stock. The Washington Post, a family-controlled and publicly traded company, has both voting A shares and nonvoting B stock. Voting control rests in the A stock, owned by Don Graham and his three siblings. Other family members and other investors own the publicly traded B shares. In publicly traded family-controlled companies, many aspects of governance are legally prescribed, especially after passage of the Sarbanes–Oxley Act. In private family firms, there is greater latitude in the mechanisms of governance and a greater role for those deemed independent and neutral to help govern across system boundaries. OD practitioners often are in a unique position to add value in this way, given the marginality of their role and their sophistication with structural and systemic approaches.

Governance can be enhanced by creating institutions that can help govern the relationship between the family, the organization, and the company's shareholders. In the following section, the functions of governance are reviewed and OD interventions in the governance process are discussed. Given the family company's propensity for blurred boundaries between family and organization, it is difficult to imagine a finer legacy and contribution to family business continuity from its current CEO than the creation of appropriate governance bodies and processes.

Launching of a Board of Directors or Advisory Board With Independent Outsiders. The board of directors' primary functions are to review the financial status of the firm, review and deliberate on the strategy of the company, look out for the interests of shareholders, ensure the ethical management of the business, be a respectful critic of management, hold the CEO and top management accountable, provide advice to the CEO on a variety of subjects, bring in a fresh outsider perspective to issues, and, as the firm approaches succession, assist in the objective planning and managing of the multiyear succession and continuity process.

Boards of directors are legal entities, usually prescribed in the articles of incorporation. Although this unique status gives the board of directors unique rights and responsibilities, such as reviewing CEO performance and conceivably initiating termination of the CEO, these events are highly unusual in the world of entrepreneurial and family-owned companies. These same rights and responsibilities expose directors to a larger sphere of liability to litigation. For this and other reasons, many small and mid-sized family-owned companies launch advisory boards to serve alongside the statutory board of directors. Advisory boards often are implemented when family-owned businesses prefer to have membership on the board of directors remain exclusive to family members. Use of independent advisors, either through the statutory board or the board of advisors, is a very healthy development. The presence of independent advisors creates a change that positively influences managerial accountability and succession and continuity planning in the firm (Schwartz & Barnes, 1991).

OD interventions in this arena may include helping the next-generation CEO define the skills and capabilities desired on the board, assisting in the recruitment and selection of board members, helping the newly formed board develop a mission statement and ground rules or protocols for effective board meetings, formulating a process for the evaluation of board member performance, and facilitating board meetings and board retreats. OD practitioners with business acumen often serve on boards of family firms and provide ongoing support in deliberations about successor development, succession planning, and strategic planning.

Creating a Family Council and Promoting Frequent Meetings of the Owning Family. The family council is a governance body that focuses its activity on family matters. It is to the family what the board of directors is to the business. Family councils focus primarily on promoting communication, providing a safe harbor for the resolution of family conflicts, and supporting the education of the next-generation family members in family dynamics and ownership issues. OD interventions in this arena often are akin to team-building activities with a family group. But because families share a much greater sense of common history (for better and worse), OD practitioners need to be more alert to the limits of their skills and abilities in facilitating the family's work. Referrals to practitioners with a family therapy or social work background are not uncommon in this context. The organization work at the heart of the relationship between a family and its business can then proceed in parallel with any psychological or behavioral intervention deemed appropriate.

Family councils often concern themselves with family participation policies, the resolution of family disagreements, the promotion of family unity, issues of liquidity, diversification of the estate, and estate planning. The business ownership education of family members not active in the management of the business often is an important task for family councils. Again, OD practitioners with business acumen can play a key role in this developmental task of the ownership subsystem. The family council is responsible for ensuring that both the economic and the noneconomic goals of the family are articulated, sometimes via a family constitution or family charter, and given the importance they deserve vis-à-vis the family's ongoing relationship to the business. Family councils seldom vote on issues but rather deliberate and develop recommendations or policies to guide decisions to be made in other governance bodies such as the board and the shareholders' meeting.

Family councils often are a vehicle for the organization of family philanthropy and the creation of family offices to oversee trusts, next-generation scholarship funds, and other financial matters of the owning family. By providing a vehicle for family members to have a voice, family councils offer an alternative to the pressure for inclusion that leads other families to appoint family members to the board.

Designing and Facilitating Whole-Family Forums. Large multigenerational families sometimes use a family forum called a family assembly. Because of the size of the family, not all family members can be together in the policy and education committee format of a working family council. As a result, the family assembly is created to operate parallel to the family council. Family assemblies almost always include spouses and children. Family councils in large extended families, on the other hand, sometimes are limited to direct descendants and representatives of each branch of the extended family. Family assemblies are another vehicle for extended family education, communication, and the renewal of family bonds. The role of OD practitioners in this forum is similar to the developmental roles played in the family council: educator, facilitator, neutral third party, and shuttle diplomat when appropriate. Family assemblies create participation opportunities for all family members at least once a year, often scheduled to coincide with the annual shareholders' meeting. The smaller group of members that make up the family council can work on behalf of the assembly during its two or three meetings per year and then report on its progress during the annual family assembly.

Appreciative inquiry (Cooperrider & Whitney, 1999) also holds great potential as a method that enhances whole-family meeting deliberations and the healthy establishment of boundaries in the family–ownership–management system. In an environment where the quality of relationships in the family is more likely to be strained as the result of the complex set of demands imposed by multiple roles, its positive bias provides a sound alternative to the traditional deficit- or problem-focused models of change. The author has found appreciative inquiry processes particularly useful during precarious circumstances that put family business survival at risk and as part of a developmental process for family councils and family assemblies that had recently confronted significant conflict or significant loss in the family or the enterprise.

Examples of appreciative topics explored by several family council and family assembly retreats have included the following:

- "Family shareholders are operating with full information and enjoying full voice."

- "This is a trusting and loving family enjoying enlightened leadership and the gift of a wealth- and job-creating enterprise."

- "The sale of the business realizes shareholder value through liquidity and creates a positive-sum dynamic for the extended family."

The search for a brighter future among extended family members can create a foundation for significant improvement in a family business. In conjunction with a systemic review of leadership succession, competitive and strategic considerations, the management of change, and the governance of the family business

relationship, it constitutes a holistic and respectful approach to increasing the effectiveness of the complex system called a family business.

CONCLUSION

Family companies are complex and quite unique in their attributes. As a result, they embody unique assets and vulnerabilities. The boundaries between the family, ownership, and family subsystems present unique challenges; migration across the boundaries is seldom illegal but often highly problematic for long-term health, competitive fitness, and continuity of the business across generations of owners. The resources exclusively available to entrepreneurial and family businesses present the opportunity to achieve sustainable (or at least hard to replicate) competitive advantages.

An OD practitioner ideally works with a family firm in a variety of settings and subsystems (Figure 29.4). The work takes place with a variety of family and business leaders. In the OD practitioner role, through interventions and his or her very presence, the practitioner can play a significant role, reminding key decision

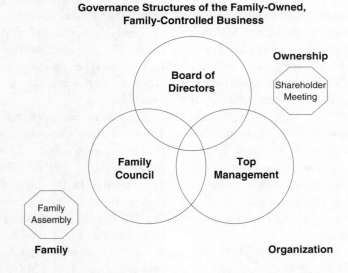

Figure 29.4   Governance Structures of the Family-Owned, Family-Controlled Business

SOURCE: From *Family Business*, Second Edition by Poza, E. J., 2007. Reprinted with permission of South-Western, a division of Thomson Learning: www.thomsonrights.com. Fax 800-730-2215.

makers of the appropriate boundaries between ownership, family, and management of the organization. OD practitioners can also assist in jointly optimizing the interaction between sub-systems in order to improve the performance of the family business.

The importance of jointly optimizing ownership, management, and family and of exploiting the unique resources available to family businesses in order to achieve competitive advantage and continuity across generations provides the theoretical framework for much education and consultation with family business leaders. It is all very much in the tradition of OD and its contributions to understanding complex systems and the management of change.

The study of family firms is a complex subject, but it would be a disservice to give up on the study of these organizations and instead dwell on the problems and stereotypes of family businesses. These are already quite prevalent in the business and family business literature. It is my hope that the reader can take away from this chapter a variety of sound organization, governance, and ownership practices that can increase the odds that entrepreneurial and family-controlled companies will reach sustainability and the desired level of continuity from generation to generation.

NOTES

1. Nine million of these firms are sole proprietorships.

2. Sixty-six percent of the companies on the S&P 500 are management controlled, and 34% are family controlled.

3. Independent directors receive no fees or compensation from the firm or family other than those associated with board service.

4. For additional information on Discovery Research and a preliminary report of its results, see Poza, Alfred, and Maheshwari (1997).

REFERENCES

Alderfer, C. (Ed.). (1976). *Change processes in organizations.* New York: Rand.

Anderson, R. C., & Reeb, D. M. (2003). Founding-family ownership and firm performance: Evidence from the S&P 500. *The Journal of Finance, 58*(3), 1301.

Astrachan, J. H., & Shanker, M. C. (2003). Family businesses' contribution to the U.S. economy: A closer look. *Family Business Review, 16*(3), 211.

Axelrod, R. (1980). Effective choice in the prisoner's dilemma. *Journal of Conflict Resolution, 24,* 3–25.

Barnes, L. B. (1988). Incongruent hierarchies: Daughters and younger sons as company CEOs. *Family Business Review, 1*(1), 9–21.

Beckhard, R., & Pritchard, W. (1992). *Changing the essence: The art of creating and leading fundamental change in organizations.* San Francisco: Jossey-Bass.

Cabrera-Suarez, K., Saa-Perez, P. D., & Garcia-Almeida, D. (2001). The succession process from a resource- and knowledge-based view of the family firm. *Family Business Review, 14*(1), 37–47.

Cameron, K. S., Whetten, D. A., & Kim, M. U. (1987). Organizational dysfunctions of decline. *Academy of Management Journal, 30*(1), 126–138.

Cooperrider, D. L., & Whitney, D. (1999). *Appreciative inquiry.* San Francisco: Berrett-Koehler.

Foster, R., & Kaplan, S. (2001). *Creative destruction.* New York: Currency/Doubleday.

Gersick, K. (1997). *Generation to generation.* Cambridge, MA: Harvard University Press.

Graham, K. (2000, March 20). Journalistic family values. *Wall Street Journal,* p. A19.

Habbershon, T. G., & Astrachan, J. H. (1997). Perceptions are reality: How family meetings lead to collective action. *Family Business Review, 10*(1), 37–52.

Poza, E. J. (1989). *Smart growth: Critical choices for business continuity and prosperity.* San Francisco: Jossey-Bass.

Poza, E. J. (2007). *Family business* (2nd ed.). Mason, OH: Thomson/South-Western.

Poza, E. J., Alfred, T., & Maheshwari, A. (1997). Stakeholder perceptions of culture and management. *Family Business Review, 10*(2), 135–155.

Poza, E. J., Hanlon, S., & Kishida, R. (2004). Does the family-business interaction factor represent a resource or a cost? *Family Business Review,* *17*(2), 99–118.

Schwartz, M. & Barnes, L. B. (1991). Outside boards and family firms: Another look. *Family Business Review, 4*(3), 269–275.

Ward, J. L. (1987). *Keeping the family business healthy: How to plan for continuing growth, profitability and family leadership.* San Francisco: John Wiley & Sons.

30

Sustainable Organizations

DEXTER DUNPHY

The 21st century brings challenges for the corporation as least as profound as those that reshaped corporate identity in the last century. The corporation is not a fixed entity but a social artifact that has evolved throughout its history to meet the changing demands of its environment. Corporations were originally formed primarily for foreign trade and licensed by kings and republican governments. However in the last century they faced the challenges of industrial mass production, globalization, cultural diversity, discontinuous change, and the move to knowledge-based service economies. These challenges reshaped the corporation. Organization development (OD) emerged in the first half of the 20th century and became a significant social movement in the second half. It was shaped by the evolving nature of the corporation and itself contributed to that evolution. Now there are new challenges, for the corporation and for OD, and their survival and growth depend on evolution and transformation.

Two challenges in particular are crucial. The first represents a natural evolution for the OD movement. As developed economies move steadily into the knowledge-based society, the traditional roles of capital, technology, and labor shift. Capital is less problematic because investment funds are seeking entrepreneurial opportunities. Buildings and technology are no longer the basis of wealth creation; owning major buildings is more likely to impede strategic repositioning than to facilitate it, and although advanced technology is critical to success, it can be readily bought or acquired. The critical success factor in the new economy is human capital and the development of strategically relevant human skills. OD has always emphasized the importance of people and developing human capability in the workplace. Associated with this internal emphasis on human capital creation is a broadening of the external role of the corporation beyond being responsible to shareholders alone to meeting the expectations of a wider group of stakeholders—the move to stakeholder capitalism. With the demise of firms such as Enron, WorldCom, and Andersen, issues of governance and social responsibility are now firmly on the agenda. There are new demands involved in responding to this challenge of creating human sustainability, but on the whole they are consistent with the values and professional skills of many OD practitioners.

The second challenge is to create corporations that nourish the biosphere rather than despoil it. Corporations bring major benefits, particularly to those in developed economies. But they are also the source of environmental degradation that threatens the viability of life on this planet. Corporations are part of the problem, and therefore they must also be part of the solution. Traditional ways of doing business are unsustainable, so we cannot continue to conduct business as usual. Most OD practitioners have shown little concern for environmental issues and, like the corporations they serve, have taken the planet's resources for granted. I argue here that there is a need to bring OD practitioners and environmentalists together to develop an integrated approach to human and ecological sustainability. This is the greatest challenge for the OD movement because it threatens the comfortable relationship that has developed between traditional managers and OD practitioners. It is nevertheless a challenge that must be met if humans and other species are to survive and thrive on this planet. Fortunately, this is already beginning to happen: In 2003 I gave the opening keynote address to the U.S. OD Network's annual conference in Portland, Oregon. The theme of the conference was sustainable organizations, and a variety of papers on that theme indicated that the OD movement was already opening up to this emerging need as it has responded to other needs in its 60-year history.

But first, I want to revisit the origins of the OD movement and trace how it has evolved. We need to understand the trajectory we are currently on and how to modify this so that the OD movement can play a vital role in shaping a sustainable future, a future in which every organization will be accountable for its social and environmental footprint.

EARLY ORIGINS AND FOCUS OF OD

The origins of OD lie in the development of the human relations approach to management at Harvard in the 1930s. Elton Mayo, Fritz Roethlisberger, George Homans, and others were early social scientists who sought to apply their theory and research about human behavior to the workplace, particularly to practical issues such as employee morale and work satisfaction, supervisory relationships, work group behavior, and worker productivity. Mayo in particular had the ongoing financial support of the Rockefeller Foundation throughout his long Harvard appointment. World War II intervened, and many social scientists found themselves involved in applying their knowledge to the war effort. On return to civilian life they sought active involvement in the process of rebuilding the economy by direct involvement in organization change or through consultancies.

If these social scientists provided much of the theoretical foundation for OD, Kurt Lewin (1951) provided what would become the core principle for OD intervention theory. Lewin is usually credited with starting OD proper through his development, with a number of colleagues, of laboratory training (Cummings, 2004). Its most distinctive feature was the involvement of both social scientists and participants in joint exploration of behavior in the participants' learning groups. This established the heady mix, so characteristic of the early OD movement, of participative action research and direct behavioral feedback as a stimulus for personal and collective change. In the 1950s sensitivity training, a development from Lewin's T groups, began to influence the practice of early OD consultants who were moving into organizations and designing and carrying out change programs (Warner Burke, 2002).

With most social scientists in business schools and early business consultancies being trained in clinical and social psychology, it was natural that their attention was directed primarily to individual, interpersonal, and small group behavior. After World War II there was an emphasis also on support for participative practices and opposition to authoritarianism. Many of those attracted to the early OD movement brought strong humanistic values and a commitment to social reform, often derived from upbringing in liberal Judeo-Christian families. Their interventions in organizations were at first simplistic: job rotation, job enrichment, group-based work, the provision of counseling and leadership training for frontline supervisors, team skills for work groups, and participation in decision making. Their work initially was mostly at the grassroots in organizations, and they favored incremental change because it gave time for workforce involvement and adjustment.

The expanding human relations tradition provided theorists who created the intellectual agenda and justification for these interventions. For example, Maslow (1954), Herzberg (1966), and MacGregor (1960) created new motivation theories that stimulated interventions around work design.

INTERNATIONALIZATION OF OD

The OD movement developed in the United States but spread rapidly to countries with other democratic traditions, in Europe and in the United Kingdom, Canada, and Australia. In these countries similar but independent movements emerged around the same time and eventually interchanged ideas with the OD tradition. In particular, in the United Kingdom, Scandinavia, and Australia there was active exchange between a number of social scientists around the development of what came to be known as sociotechnical systems (STS) theory and its associated ideology of industrial democracy. Key figures in the development of this approach were Fred Emery (an Australian, as was Mayo), Eric Trist, and several other British social scientists at the Tavistock Institute of Human Relations (established in London in 1940). Their applied research in mines and factories in the United Kingdom and Scandinavian countries had a profound effect on the development of work reform and industrial democracy practices in Europe, particularly in Sweden and the Netherlands. Subsequently there was active government-sponsored exchange of practitioners between Sweden and Australia. OD dominated the practice of organization change in the United States, whereas STS dominated practice in Europe. In the United Kingdom, Australia, and Canada there was fusion of ideas from both traditions.

Meanwhile, OD practitioners, particularly consultants, were following the expanding U.S.-based multinationals as they internationalized, crisscrossing the world on consulting assignments. Social and behavioral scientists were also becoming strongly established in schools of management around the world and developing a repertoire of more sophisticated applied research techniques and intervention strategies. Firms of consultants were also replacing or supplementing the traditional Taylorist time and motion study experts with the new OD professionals.

Gradually some leading OD practitioners began to operate at higher organization levels and increasingly to work with the organization as a whole rather than only with smaller subunits. By the late 1970s the movement was experiencing success, developing a sense of shared identity, and practitioner numbers were growing rapidly. Within organizations new human resource management functions were emerging to replace the old personnel departments, and these were more supportive of OD and often incorporated OD practitioners. Both OD and STS as practiced at this time might best be described as incremental humanist approaches to corporate change.

CHALLENGES TO TRADITIONAL OD

The world was changing, however. Major world recessions occurred in the 1970s and 1980s. Simultaneously, tariff barriers were coming down around the world, many companies were rapidly internationalizing, and global competition created new pressures for lower costs and more rapid innovation. Waves of new technologies were also arriving faster, eliminating whole industries and occupational categories; acquisitions and mergers became a veritable feeding frenzy among larger corporations. At this time the existing incremental, humanist approaches to change that had emerged around the world, in the forms of OD and STS, were challenged.

The Japanese, leading the first wave of Asian industrialization, developed very distinctive management strategies and techniques. One of the core features of their approach to organization change was continuous and incremental improvement using small, supervisor-centered problem-solving teams. These teams were not driven by a concern for worker satisfaction, as in the OD model, or by concerns for industrial democracy, as in the STS model. The Japanese approach was strongly driven by business concerns and focused on work process redesign and supply line reorganization. The approach was spectacularly successful in producing high-quality products for international markets. This sparked a debate in the West about whether more humanistic approaches could produce comparable results. In the United States, particularly in the tougher economic times, managers switched from improving work satisfaction to raising productivity in order to meet the Japanese challenge. It was a shock to American executives to face the fact that Japan, rather than the United States, was becoming number 1 (Vogel, 1975).

Another challenge to the OD approach (although less so for STS) came from the application of advanced technologies in the workplace. These technologies became powerful driving forces for change so that technical specialists, industrial engineers, information technology specialists, and others became rival change agents competing with OD practitioners. The dominance of OD by those trained in the social sciences meant that most OD practitioners did not have technological training and interests and therefore failed to seize the opportunities the new technologies provided for organization transformation. They were increasingly bypassed by technical change agents who were often unaware of and unconcerned about the impact of their new technologies on the social system of the corporation, particularly the resistance to change created in the workforce by their own interventions. As a result, many multi-million-dollar technological investments failed to produce the anticipated results.

A major example of what was initially a competing approach to OD is the total quality management (TQM) movement. This approach was developed initially by Edwards, Dodge, and Shewhart in the Bell Laboratories, was exported to Japan by Deming and Juran, but then returned to the United States and other countries and rapidly spread throughout industry. TQM had a whole cadre of change agents who were largely unaffected by OD concepts. Eventually many OD practitioners adopted some of the tools and techniques of TQM, enriching the range of intervention strategies and change tools available to OD practitioners. More recently, business process reengineering has been another change approach competing with OD. However, its directive, even coercive "crash through" approach was less compatible with the basic values of OD practitioners (Dawson, 2003; Dunphy & Griffiths, 1998).

A third challenge to OD arose as many executives faced the increasing torrent of change from volatile, unpredictable environments and realized that the kinds of incremental changes advocated by OD practitioners were the equivalent of rearranging the deck chairs on the *Titanic*. Incremental OD interventions often failed to realign organizations to the new and transformed economic conditions. In many cases external changes dictated transformational rather than incremental change for survival.

The rise of strategic management posed the problem very clearly. Corporate strategy emerged in the 1960s from the work of a number of U.S. managerial thinkers, particularly Selznick, Andrews, and Ansoff (Dunphy & Griffiths, 1998). It rose to prominence in the 1980s as the pace of change quickened dramatically and the direction of change became less predictable. Strategic change management challenged both the incrementalism of the OD approach and its ideological adherence to bottom-up change. Strategic management advocated fast and often revolutionary shifts, including divestment of whole divisions and acquisitions of new operations. It also advocated strong executive direction of this process. The term *strategy* derives from military usage, and the emphasis was on waging the competitive battle for market supremacy. This was a tough-minded approach that contrasted with the humanistic approach of OD, and it created a crisis of values in the profession. There is insufficient space here to discuss how this debate evolved and was resolved, but many leading practitioners seized the opportunity to modify the traditional values of OD to fit the demand for more executive control of change programs and to retool by introducing transformation strategies. Those who did so often found themselves in executive boardrooms.

The intellectual agenda was changing, and the OD movement was now being challenged from within its own ranks to transform itself to become OT (organization transformation) (Harrison, 1983; Porras & Robertson, 1987). The link made by an increasing number of OD practitioners to strategy helped OD play a more significant role in executive decision making and in the implementation of large-scale transformational change. This became the main game in town, as shown by Kanter's (1985) *The Change Masters* becoming a runaway best seller.

REDIRECTION: OD AS STRATEGIC PARTNER

From the late 1980s two issues dominated the debate about the future of OD. One was the issue of the scope and speed of change, that is, the dilemma of whether to change incrementally or transformationally. The other debate was around the style of change management—the issue of the use of power in organizations. This can be summed up as the dilemma about whether change should be top down or bottom up, directive or even coercive on one hand or consultative or collaborative on the other. These debates still take place, having become endemic in the OD movement (Beer & Nohria, 2000). Clearly thousands of OD practitioners around the world are still practicing OD much as it has always been done. Their work is still focused at the lower levels of organizations around traditional issues such as supervisory training, team building, and conflict negotiation and are mainly incremental. However, many of the best-known OD practitioners have developed a very different model that has them spending a good deal of time working with the CEO and top executive team, being directly involved in decisions about strategic repositioning, and designing and overseeing the implementation of top-down transformational change.

In the United States the intellectual agenda for change management has been strongly dominated by applied behavioral scientists based in management schools and by management consultants, including major firms such as Pricewaterhouse Coopers, McKinsey & Company, KPMG, and Deloitte and Touche. (Most of these organizations have been taken over or merged.) The predominant models have been simplistic *n*-step models of the one-size-fits-all type. Most are associated with the name of a change guru with at least one best-selling book. These include Kotter's (1995) *Leading Change,* Kanter's (1985) *The Change Masters,* and Peters and Waterman's (1997) *In Search of Excellence.* Few of these modern change gurus describe themselves as engaged in OD; rather, they see themselves as organization change practitioners. Their models often are based not on systematic research but on their own consulting practice. Where their work is based on research, the research approach usually is case analysis, and there is seldom a systematic basis for case selection. There has been no serious attempt to evaluate the validity or usefulness of the competing models; practitioners tend to choose a model on the basis of what they were taught, where they trained or studied, the model's appeal to their own value set, or their personal response to a particular guru.

Meanwhile, in the mainstream social sciences (as distinct from applied behavioral sciences in management schools) there has been a strong move to abandon such simple, linear models in favor of contingency or situational models (Dawson, 2003). One such model is that developed by Dunphy and Stace in Australia in the 1980s and 1990s. The central feature of this approach is a contingency matrix with scale of change on one dimension (from fine tuning to corporate transformation) and style of change management (from collaborative to coercive) on the other. Stace and Dunphy (2001) have used a systematic research design to select and research public sector organizations and private sector organizations across a variety of industries. These authors deal realistically with issues of power in organizations, in contrast to the work of many U.S. academics, particularly with OD backgrounds, who tend to gloss over power issues and see participative processes as inevitably bringing about win–win solutions.

An alternative approach to change that originated in the United Kingdom and now has a following in Europe, Australia, and more recently in North America is the processual approach to change. This is more a descriptive, analytical model than a prescriptive approach.

Its founder was Andrew Pettigrew (1985); other major contributors are Ropo, Eriksson, and Hunt (1997), Van de Ven and Huber (1990), and Dawson (2003). The processual theorists and researchers favor longitudinal case studies using qualitative analysis with a strong emphasis on contextual factors. Dawson's (2003) approach to the analysis of organization change in particular closely follows Lewin's change model of unfreezing, moving, and refreezing. The processual approach favors detailed historical analysis, but its exponents have developed no systematic link between their analysis and intervention strategies. The title of Dawson's book *Understanding Organizational Change* emphasizes that the aim of these researchers is primarily making sense of organization change rather than influencing its direction. As a result there has been little adoption of these ideas by change practitioners.

From the 1980s, change management, including OD, emerged as an important profession, a recognized field of study, and increasingly part of the prevailing managerial orthodoxy. OD professionals were no longer heretics outside the gates of the corporate world, struggling to gain recognition, desperate to be asked in, and, when they were, content to be given minor roles in the corporate change agenda. As they were increasingly accepted and involved, they added to their repertoire of incremental change interventions, contributing to the development of corporate strategy and to its expression in large-scale transformational change programs. By the end of the 20th century the OD movement had gained a glittering prize: a set of intellectual models of the organization change process and varied sets of intervention strategies and tools (Warner Burke, 2002). These theories and tools will be critical to managing the major changes faced by corporations in this century. But to what ends should they be applied?

Growing institutionalization brings with it increasing orthodoxy. Orthodoxy is current practice and implies comfort. Social movements come into being to challenge and are prickly by nature. As a movement's agenda is accepted in the mainstream, it is either absorbed into the status quo or reinvigorated by some new ideal. The strategic approach to change has been instrumental in legitimizing the OD movement and its practitioners. Is it time to declare that the goals of the movement have been accomplished and that the effort to establish change management as a profession has been successful? Indeed, the decreasing use of the OD label by many change practitioners supports the notion that this is already happening. The other alternative is to renew the movement itself, to find a new ideal, to establish a new direction. I now turn to this latter alternative.

SUSTAINABILITY: THE CHALLENGE OF THE 21ST CENTURY

Every century has its defining theme. The 20th century's defining theme was economic growth; all ideologies—capitalism, socialism, communism, fascism—agreed that the challenge for society was to continue the industrialization process in order to gain the productivity benefits made possible by the industrial revolution. The debates and the wars were attempts to resolve conflicting views about which sociopolitical system best supported this and how the gains were to be distributed.

The defining theme of this century will be sustainability, that is, how to limit or eliminate the negative impact of economic development on the biosphere and global society and to devise new production technologies and distribution systems that sustain the natural environment and develop human capabilities (Dunphy, 2002). One thing is certain: We cannot continue to conduct business as usual, for if we do we threaten the future of our own and other species and a decent way of life for the world's peoples (Beck, 2000; Diamond, 2005; Kennedy, 2000; Monbiot, 2000; Wright, 2004; Zuboff & Maxmin, 2002). At the point of the triumph of capitalism over alternative economic systems, we face the urgent need to remodel it substantially to ensure that its future

is sustainable. Economic growth has brought great benefits in the form of a higher standard of living and an improved quality of life— previously unsurpassed access to goods and services on a scale not envisaged by earlier generations. However, it has brought bad (e.g., pollution and weapons of mass destruction) as well as good, and disservices (e.g., widespread supply of addictive drugs and child prostitution) as well as services.

It is useful to distinguish two areas of sustainability mentioned at the beginning of this chapter. The first is human sustainability, that is, the development of human capability. In terms of creating sustainable corporations, this has an internal and an external agenda. The internal agenda often is called strategic human resource management or the building of human capital, that is, the development of strategically relevant human potential. The external agenda is called corporate citizenship or social responsibility and refers to the development of social policies that eliminate exploitive relationships and contribute to the well-being of society. The second area of sustainability is ecological sustainability. This involves constructing a corporate agenda that ensures that the organization uses the ecological resources of the biosphere that are inputs to the production process in such a way that waste is eliminated, there are no dangerous byproducts of the production process, and material goods are remanufactured or recycled. Another way of expressing this is that the organization reduces its footprint on the natural environment so that the impact of its activities and outputs is not destructive or, more positively, the organization constructs its business to support the regenerative processes of the biosphere.

ENRICHING THE CURRENT TRAJECTORY: BUILDING HUMAN CAPABILITIES WITHIN THE ORGANIZATION

Technologically advanced societies are moving rapidly into the postindustrial age. Their economies are increasingly dominated by the service sector, and the main sources of wealth are knowledge capital and social capital, that is, the knowledge and skills of the workforce and access to and influence over key relationships with stakeholders important for future success, respectively. What this means is that sustainable organizations must now focus on systematically enhancing the capabilities of organization members and accept responsibility for upgrading human knowledge and skill (Gratton, 2000). Increasingly, professionals in particular are realizing that future career success is built by seeking employment in or with companies that will enhance rather than reduce their portable knowledge and skills during the period of the employment relationship. For the organization, it is a great competitive advantage to be regarded as an employer of choice, for this enables the organization to assemble high-level capabilities needed for success in the knowledge-based economy.

As I noted earlier, developing strategies for building human capability is a natural extension of what OD practitioners have done in the past. People have always had a central place in OD change strategies; however, the new world of strategic human resource management demands a deep understanding of the repositioning strategies being pursued by the corporation, an ability to anticipate the profile of human capabilities that will be necessary to support those strategies, and a systematic set of customized interventions to transform the current capability mix toward future requirements on time. This kind of continuous upskilling contributes not only to the sustainability of the organization but also to building the pool of future relevant capabilities in society as a whole.

Capability enhancement includes developing the organization's capacity for reshaping and reinventing itself. The meta-capability needed by organizations of the future is the ability to anticipate and manage future change and demands the combination of incremental and transformational change strategies OD has developed. This innovative agility is fundamental to identifying future strategic opportunities,

redesigning and repositioning particular products and services, repositioning the organization as a whole or a particular division to take advantage of changing markets, or even proactively redesigning the industry as a whole or a significant part of it. But the skills involved in making changes of this sort go far beyond the traditional skills of, say, team building or conflict resolution. They need a profound understanding of the business imperatives faced by the organization and an ability to engage employees at all levels in developing the concrete change strategies needed to equip the organization for its emerging future.

Consistent with this emphasis on innovation is strong support for a policy of workplace diversity, participation in decision making, gender equity, and work–life balance. In addition, the organization architecture must reflect the emphasis on adaptability, flexibility, innovation, and speed of response. The success of companies such as Hewlett-Packard and Ericsson comes in part from their development of human resource policies of this kind.

EXTENDING THE CONSTITUENCY: CORPORATE CITIZENSHIP AND SOCIAL RESPONSIBILITY

The external focus of human sustainability involves adopting a strong and clearly defined ethical position based on multiple stakeholder perspectives. It identifies key stakeholders, builds positive relationships with them or their representatives, listens to their concerns, identifies their needs, and communicates the organization's mission and strategies to them. This ethical commitment makes good business sense as it provides, for example, an up-to-date customer knowledge base that signals emerging customer needs and interests; these represent future business opportunities. It also builds customer loyalty. Customers and other key stakeholders ask, "Why would we go elsewhere when our needs are being identified and met so effectively here?"

The sustainable organization seeks to exert influence on stakeholders, other industry participants, and society in general to pursue human welfare and equitable and just social practices and to create the social circumstances that contribute to the fulfillment of human potential in all citizens. The concern here is global and multigenerational: *Citizens* includes citizens of other countries as well as our own and future generations. Sustainable organizations are also sustaining organizations, that is, they use their influence to create a generative society. This is not considered an add-on to the organization's core activities, as a philanthropic or charitable exercise, but as a core business principle for any responsible corporate citizen. Patagonia is one well-known sports clothing and sports gear company that has consistently acted on this principle. The company's environmental commitment is evidenced, for example, by its decision to convert its entire sportswear line to organically grown fiber even though this incurs higher costs (Dunphy, Griffiths, & Benn, 2003, p. 72).

Traditionally OD practitioners largely confined their interventions to internal corporate change or, in some cases, engaged in community development. The modern organization has much more permeable boundaries than traditional 20th-century organizations. The core workforce may only be a fraction of those who carry out the work of the organization; there are often many subcontractors, consultants, alliance partners, and networked groups and individuals engaged in a kaleidoscopic array of interchanges. It no longer makes sense to limit human resource strategies to the core workforce. The modern organization is an open system, and human sustainability issues must be addressed in a coordinated way within the organization's full field of activity. This is an emerging challenge for the OD movement.

VENTURING INTO NEW TERRITORY: ECOLOGICAL SUSTAINABILITY

One fundamental reformulation of thinking is needed in the OD movement if it is to make its maximum contribution to solving the challenges of this century; this reformulation lies in the area of ecological sustainability. On the whole OD practice has reflected the training of most of its practitioners in the social sciences. I have already discussed how OD practitioners found themselves bypassed by change agents involved in the introduction of new technologies; without technical expertise, OD consultants tended to neglect the technical system of the corporation and concentrate their activities on modifying the social system. However, STS consultants emphasized the joint optimization of social and technical systems and, when trained as social scientists themselves, usually collaborated with technical experts in managing the introduction of changes in the technical systems in industrial plants and mines.

Today's organizations are increasingly exposed to pressures from governments and community activist organizations to modify supply chains and production and distribution processes to eliminate toxic emissions to the atmosphere, waste to landfills, and pollution to water (Dunphy et al., 2007). This requires attention to the design of products to reduce material intensity, eliminate waste and toxic elements, and make it possible to remanufacture or recycle products. Compliance with government health and safety regulations, energy guidelines, and so on is the minimum to earn a license to operate. But a sustainability focus has other major advantages that I outline in more detail later. It can identify unnoticed waste of resources in many organizations that regarded themselves as efficient and create new strategic business opportunities. But OD practitioners are likely to be bypassed once again because of their lack of awareness of the importance of these issues and their lack of scientific training. This time they need to engage with the environmentalists working in this area and develop collaborative projects. How easy it is to overlook the dependence of all organizations on the ecology is illustrated by the fact that Waddell, Cummings, and Worley (2000), in an otherwise excellent and comprehensive review of the OD field, omit any reference to the natural environment in a chapter titled "Organization and Environment Relationships."

When I have brought together OD practitioners with environmental activists and ecologists, I have been struck by how quickly the latter two groups recognize the potential contribution OD practitioners can make to the green agenda. Typically as views are exchanged, the environmentalists make statements such as, "We know the changes that need to be made, but we don't know how to bring these changes about" and "We have learned that it isn't enough to have the technical fix on environmental problems; the real challenge is to get people to recognize its value and adopt it." They are quick to perceive and acknowledge the expertise of experienced change agents, to seek their advice, and to involve them in the development of such projects as emission reduction, energy conservation, or redesign of factories around sustainability principles. This represents an enormous future opportunity for the OD movement. However, to take up this opportunity we need a model of change that maps the path to the sustainable organization. In the next section of this chapter I outline a model designed for this purpose. The model results from the collaboration of a number of social and natural scientists and has been developed over a period of about 7 years. It draws on the work of other theorists and researchers and on many research studies by practitioners from around the world. A fuller exposition of this model is given in Dunphy et al. (2007).

David Attenborough concluded a program on his life's work documenting the earth's ecology with these words: "Surely we have a responsibility to leave for future generations a planet that is habitable and hospitable to all species" (BBC TV, 2003). Boxes 30.1, 30.2, and 30.3 summarize the key agendas for human and ecological sustainability.

BOX 30.1   Human Sustainability: The Internal Agenda

- Adopt a strategic perspective to workplace development.
- Build the corporate knowledge and skill base (intellectual and social capital of employees—develop human potential).
- Foster productive diversity in the workplace (occupational health and safety, gender equity, participative decision making, work–life balance).
- Develop the capability for continuing corporate reshaping and renewal, including visionary change leadership.
- Create communities of practice to diffuse knowledge and skills.
- Provide relevant expertise in the best way to organize work for high performance and satisfaction.
- Represent employees' concerns to management while simultaneously giving employees an increased role in organizational decision making.

SOURCE: From Dunphy, D., Griffiths, A., & Benn, S., *Organizational change for corporate sustainability*. London, Routledge, pp. 291–92. Copyright © 2003, with permission of Thomson Publishing.

BOX 30.2   Human Sustainability: The External Agenda

- Reinterpret strategy around a wider range of stakeholders and develop co-operative strategies with them (responsiveness).
- Add rather than subtract value for all relevant stakeholders.

- Build a culture of workplace learning and commitment to a "generative society" through a declared and enacted value base.
- Initiate and sustain an ongoing dialogue with stakeholders to define key elements of social responsibility—set priorities (accountability).
- Define social goals, develop action plans to reach goals, monitor and disclose performance against key performance indicators (transparency).
- Seek genuine feedback on performance from stakeholders—welcome and learn from criticism.
- Win, by responsible informed action, the support of all stakeholders for the organization's continued existence and growth.

SOURCE: From Dunphy, D., Griffiths, A., & Benn, S., *Organizational change for corporate sustainability*. London, Routledge, pp. 291–92. Copyright © 2003, with permission of Thomson Publishing.

BOX 30.3   Achieving Ecological Sustainability

- Design a production system that is an integral part of the ecology (like an earthworm).
- Conduct life-cycle assessment and a policy of resource stewardship.
- Eliminate waste and pollution particularly by product redesign and developing an industrial ecology.
- Form active partnerships with "green," human rights and other community groups.
- Appoint independent experts to monitor the corporation's environmental "footprint" (environmental auditing).
- Link action on human sustainability with action on ecological sustainability to create an integrated, seamless approach to corporate sustainability.

SOURCE: From Dunphy, D., Griffiths, A., & Benn, S., *Organizational change for corporate sustainability*. London, Routledge, pp. 291–92. Copyright © 2003, with permission of Thomson Publishing.

PATHWAYS TO CORPORATE SUSTAINABILITY

One key contribution of OD theory has been the important role it assigned to the adaptiveness of organizations. Achieving fully sustainable corporations in this century will take even more adaptability and reshaping capability. However, the ultimate goal is clear: We must create organizations that are both sustainable and sustaining so that the corporation retains its proper place as an element in the economic system (as it is currently perceived to be) but becomes a constructive element in the social and ecological systems as well.

The phase model I outline here indicates how human and ecological sustainability are interrelated developments that jointly contribute to the well-being of the firm. (For a more detailed discussion of these phases, with case examples, see Dunphy et al., 2007.) The phases are ideal types that help organizations define where they are on the path and allow them to chart their way toward a more fully sustainable position. At each step of the way, there is a need to develop new human capabilities and organization characteristics, and these enable further progression toward ecological sustainability. We do not assume that a firm necessarily progresses through the phases step by step on an improving trajectory. Organizations can leapfrog phases or regress by abandoning previously established sustainability practices.

Changes such as the appointment of a new CEO, the loss of a key change champion, increased stakeholder pressure, or new legislation can trigger movement back and forth through the six phases.

The phases are as follows:

1. Rejection

2. Nonresponsiveness

3. Compliance

4. Efficiency

5. Strategic proactivity

6. The sustaining organization

I now discuss each of these in turn.

Rejection

In this phase the corporation's dominant elite regard all resources—employees, community infrastructure, and the ecological environment—as open to exploitation by the firm for immediate economic gain. On the human side, employees and subcontractors are exploited, and employees in particular are regarded as industrial cannon fodder. There is no commitment to knowledge and skill development, and health and safety measures are ignored or given lip service. Community concerns are rejected outright as irrelevant and illegitimate on the basis of a belief that the firm exists solely to maximize profit. The firm ignores any environmentally destructive aspects of its activities and resists any attempt by governments and green activists to place constraints on its activities. The environment is regarded as a free good to be exploited. Exxon and Mobil, for instance, are two of the companies that, with the National Association of Manufacturers, organized the Global Climate Coalition to rally opposition to the signing of the Kyoto Convention on Global Warming. Fortunately, most organizations do not begin at this phase of rejection and do not actively mobilize against sustainability initiatives.

Nonresponsiveness

Organizations in this phase regard sustainability as irrelevant to business activities, if they consider it at all, and concentrate on short-term profitability. However, this is changing as government regulations covering environmental and employee relations set increasingly high standards backed by heavy penalties for infringement. The corporate culture encourages the development of a passive and compliant workforce and defines human resource management narrowly as industrial relations. Wal-Mart, the U.S.-based chain store, has many of the characteristics, on the human sustainability side, of a nonresponsive organization. Nonresponsiveness usually results from lack of awareness or ignorance rather than from active opposition to a corporate ethic broader than financial gain. Many corporations in this category embody the culture of the past century, concentrating on business as usual. Community issues are ignored where possible, and negative environmental consequences of the firm's activities are taken for granted and disregarded.

Compliance

In this phase the corporation focuses on reducing the risk of sanctions for failing to meet minimum standards as an employer or producer. The organization's elite emphasizes being a "decent employer and corporate citizen" by ensuring a safe, healthy workplace and avoiding environmental abuses that could lead to litigation or strong community reaction directed toward the firm. The firm is primarily reactive to growing legal requirements and community expectations for more sustainable practices. Human resource functions such as industrial relations, training, and TQM are instituted but with little integration between them. Only ecological issues that are seen as likely to attract strong litigation or strong community action are addressed. Firms or industry associations in this phase often take a noncommittal position on politicized sustainability issues. For example, in Australia the Business Council of Australia, which represents the largest corporations, withdrew its support for the Australian federal government's persistence in refusing to sign the Kyoto protocol but did not adopt an alternative proposed by some members supporting signing. The council simply reported that its members could not agree, thus reflecting a move from rejection to nonresponsiveness. The organizations supporting a policy of signing are now attempting to move the council into the compliance phase.

Efficiency

This stage is the beginning of the process of incorporating sustainability as an integral part of the business. It reflects a growing awareness on the part of people at various organization levels that there are real advantages to be gained by proactively instituting sustainable practices. In particular, human resource and environmental policies and practices are used to reduce costs and increase efficiency. Investment in training may involve expense but result in compensating added value through increased quality of products and services. Technical and supervisory training is augmented with interpersonal skill training. Team building is encouraged for value-adding and cost-saving purposes, and external stakeholder relations are developed for business benefits. ISO 14000 systems are integrated with TQM and occupational health and safety systems with the aim of achieving eco-efficiencies.

Many managers argue that sustainability is a luxury they cannot afford. Their assumption is that they are currently operating efficiently and that implementing sustainability measures will only add significant costs. In fact, traditional "efficient" production operations often are extraordinarily wasteful when viewed through a sustainability lens (Dunphy et al., 2003). Many organizations are now discovering that there is a lot of low-hanging fruit to be picked when waste is analyzed. An example is Scandic Hotels, the dominant operator of, full-service, three- and four-star hotels in Scandinavia and one of Europe's leading hotel chains. The company adopted the Natural Step program to reduce the company's ecological footprint. Almost immediately employees identified major economies that could be achieved in the use soap and shampoo and through reduction in the use of energy and water. In addition, Scandic developed a 97% recyclable "eco-room" that has dramatically reduced the costs of refurbishing their hotels and eliminated the waste previously involved in this activity. With approximately 2,000 rooms refurbished every year, this made a major contribution to Scandic's bottom line (Dunphy et al., 2007).

Business controls the core technologies of production and the supply and distribution channels supporting production. Many traditional production processes, supply chains, and distribution channels have the unintended side effects of damaging the environment and reducing work satisfaction. What we need now are much more eco-efficient products and services, workplaces, and work processes designed to fulfill human needs rather than frustrating them. Newly developing production technologies can raise productivity, increase work satisfaction, and increase profitability, a win–win for all involved. New production systems are being forged that do not externalize costs to the community through waste and pollution, that dramatically reduce material throughput and energy use, and that replace physical products with services (Pears, 2000; Tibbs, 2000).

Strategic Proactivity

This phase moves the firm further along the path to corporate sustainability by making sustainability central to the firm's business strategy. Proactive environmental strategies are seen as a source of competitive advantage by firms in this stage, and the strategic elite views sustainability as providing competitive advantage. The commitment to sustainability is strongly embedded in the quest to maximize longer-term corporate profitability and is dictated by a broad view of corporate self-interest. In particular it is seen as moving beyond a single-minded focus on achieving efficiencies through cost reduction to value adding and innovation, including maximizing flexible responsiveness and speed of response to emerging market needs. Managers and change agents work to position the organization as a leader in sustainable business practices by instituting advanced human resource strategies that help make the organization an employer of choice, corporate citizenship initiatives that build stakeholder support, and innovative, high-quality products that are environmentally safe and healthy. Reflecting a growing awareness of the business possibilities associated with sustainable development, the environment industry now encompasses a wide range of products. In Europe alone, it is responsible for 3.5 million jobs.

In this phase, intellectual and social capital are used to develop strategic advantage through innovation in products and services. An innovation by an Australian company, for example, is the development of high value-added building material from waste tires. (Waste tires currently cost Australia Au$25 million per year in disposal costs.)

The Sustaining Corporation

In this final phase executives responsible for the strategic direction of the organization have strongly internalized the values of sustainability. They go beyond pursuing sustainability for its competitive advantage alone to making an ideological commitment to work more widely to create a sustainable world. If the organization is a for-profit company, it pursues the traditional business objective of providing an excellent return to investors but voluntarily goes beyond this to actively promote ecological values and practices in industry and society generally. The fundamental commitment is to facilitate the emergence of a society that supports the ecological viability of the planet and its species and contributes to just, equitable social practices and human fulfillment (Benn & Dunphy, 2007; Hart, 1997; Hawkins, Lovins, & Lovins, 1999; Kennedy, 2000).

The sustaining corporation works out a new deal that stands in marked contrast to the defining characteristics of most of today's corporations. Some important characteristics that define the conceptual shift are as follows:

An emphasis on meeting shareholder expectations alone is replaced by an emphasis on meeting stakeholder expectations (including, for public companies, shareholders).

A new social and ecological contract is developed that respects the rights of employees, the community, and the biosphere. This involves consulting stakeholders and securing their ongoing support for the organization's right to operate.

Corporate accountability to stakeholders, including future generations. This involves eliminating externalities such as waste and pollution.

A corporate culture of stewardship, involving the efficient and effective use of human and natural resources and contributing in a variety of ways to supporting a community that develops and enlarges human talent.

Abandoning the exploitation of people and the natural world for short-term gain and instead developing an active commitment to their health, renewal, and regeneration.

To many people this will seem like a dream. It is; the OD movement began with a dream of an organizational world that operated with more respect for people and provided them with greater opportunities for participation in decision making and the productive use of their capabilities. There are many organizations today in which that dream has become a reality. In our research we have identified a substantial number of organizations that have made progress toward the new ideal of being sustainable and sustaining organizations (Dunphy et al., 2007). If OD and other change practitioners are prepared to bring their substantial knowledge of change models and intervention strategies to this integration of the organization renewal movement with the movement for a more ecologically sustainable global economy, this dream too could become a reality. The challenge involved could also reinvigorate the movement so that it plays an even stronger role in reshaping the future of the corporation and capitalism.

BRINGING THE DREAM INTO REALITY

For many organizations the move to become sustainable and sustaining can take place through incremental change (Waddell et al., 2000). These organizations may be involved in industries that have limited impact on the natural environment, where the number of potentially mobile professionals has led to the development of leading-edge human resource strategies and where there is already active involvement with stakeholders. Alternatively, these may be organizations in industries where these issues are more problematic but where senior executives have seized industry leadership anyway. For example, a number of mining companies have moved strongly to establish forward-looking environmental and community relations policies. As the CEO of one large international mining company remarked to me, "If we don't establish a strong reputation for responsibility in these areas, we run the risk of never being able to open a mine again anywhere in the world." Other organizations, such as Nike, BP, and Shell, have experienced powerful international community criticism around specific controversial issues, have been through a resultant period of transformational change, and now are in a position to consolidate and progressively advance the gains made to date.

The OD movement has at least 50 years of experience in managing incremental change.

Incremental change strategies allow organizations to achieve what Weick describes as small wins:

> A small win is a concrete, complete, implemented outcome of moderate importance. By itself, one small win may seem unimportant. A series of wins at small but significant tasks, however, reveals a pattern that may attract allies, deter opponents and lower resistance to subsequent proposals. Small wins are controllable opportunities that produce visible results. (Weick quoted in Dunphy et al., 2007, p. 234)

Incremental change also has the advantage of providing opportunities for steady, systematic building of human capabilities (social and technological) in the organization through well-organized selection processes, training and development programs, career path planning, job placement, career planning, and ongoing appraisal systems linked to strategic goals. Incremental change allows steady improvement in efficiencies related to product and work design and process improvement and in the cumulative enhancement of team structures and intergroup relations. It also provides time for modifying corporate values and positive culture change through employee involvement and participation in decision making and innovative project work. This has been the bread and butter work of OD practitioners for decades.

Even the extension of OD work into the environmental area, a new venture for the OD movement, can be achieved naturally. As Orsatto points out,

> The majority of literature on corporate environmental management assumes reformism as the guiding principle for organizational change. Incrementalism is the basic principle of the standards of environmental management systems such as the ISO 14000 series. . . . These programs assume that through incremental improvements organizations would achieve eco-efficiency and, eventually, ecological sustainability. (in Dunphy et al., 2007, pp. 227–228)

Dunphy et al. (2007) outline the incremental strategies that are most useful to move organizations through the phase model outlined earlier in this chapter, applying these strategies to the development of both human and ecological sustainability.

Not all organizations will be able to become sustainable and sustaining through incremental steps. For example, this is true of organizations that are subjected to unanticipated and unprecedented public pressures to make radical change. Why? Because some of their current policies and practices are revealed as plundering and polluting the planet or destroying the human capital assets of the corporation or community or fracturing community relationships.

We are moving into a period of history when all organizations engaging in unsustainable operations will have their license to operate questioned by activist community groups or government watchdogs. If organizations persist in these behaviors, they will be forced into crisis mode to extricate themselves, to salvage their public image, and to retain market share. The community is increasingly suspicious of "greenwash" and manufactured public relations images; for example, before the exposure of unethical practices by its senior executives, Enron was widely publicized as a model in using triple-bottom-line accounting. In the modern world many employees may be more committed to sustainability principles than to their employer, and in the world of instant communication, organizations can neither run nor hide. In recent years we have learned that valuable corporate reputations built up over many years can crumble overnight.

There will be other organizations moving down the path to sustainability whose executives realize the benefits of reinventing the corporation and becoming industry leaders in sustainability. As a result, they will want to move rapidly to ensure that they secure these advantages. To do this they may have to reinvent the corporation or a significant part of it.

Dee Hock (1999) refers to modern organizations as chaordic, that is, as a mixture of chaos and order. Transformational change necessarily involves increasing the degree of chaos in order to redefine the business and reposition the company. For example, Interface, the international commercial carpet company, moved from manufacturing products based on petroleum products to manufacturing and recycling increasingly based on natural fibers. But it also built a new business based on leasing and servicing its carpets that eventually dwarfed its manufacturing business. BP relabeled itself as Beyond Petroleum rather than British Petroleum and moved heavily into alternative energy sources with the prospect of eventually phasing out oil altogether.

What we are addressing here is what Robert Quinn calls deep change:

> Deep change differs from incremental change in that it requires new ways of thinking and behaving. It is change that is major in scope, discontinuous with the past and generally irreversible. The deep change effort distorts existing patterns of action and involves taking risks. Deep change means surrendering control. (in Dunphy et al., 2007, p. 264)

Given the urgency and magnitude of many of the changes needed to move to a sustainable economy, many organizations will have to undergo corporate transformation. OD practitioners often have been ambivalent about transformational change because it raises serious questions about the possibility of widespread participation. Stace and Dunphy (2001) have shown that in most circumstances transformational change involves a shift of managerial style from participative and consultative to directive or even coercive, particularly with regard to the goals and major change strategies adopted throughout the organization as a whole. Most OD consultants are uncomfortable with this and often portray even coercive change as participative. For example, Jack Welch has been portrayed as a charismatic

CEO who used participative approaches to change G.E. However he became known as "Neutron Jack," "the human bomb that left the buildings intact while getting rid of people" (Ulrich, Kerr, & Ashkenas, 2002, p. 6).

The OD movement needs to face the controversial issues of power and conflict more directly than in the past if it is to play a significant role in the transformation of modern corporations toward being fully sustainable (Graetz, Rimmer, Lawrence, & Smith, 2002). There are two assumptions made by most OD consultants that need to be questioned. The first is that there can always be win–win strategies in organization change. Transformational change in particular often disadvantages some individuals and groups and advantages others. There are usually conflicts of interest that cannot be resolved by consensus. The second is that effective leadership is always participative and that everyone in the organization needs to be involved in significant decisions about the future of the organization. There can be insufficient time for widespread involvement. In addition, strategic reorientation of the enterprise is the responsibility of the board and senior executive team, not the general workforce. Of course, the strategic direction should be informed by others, particularly those at the interface with key stakeholders. It is also important that all members of the organization know and understand what the strategy is once it has been formulated and be given a part in its implementation when that depends on them. Stace and Dunphy (2001) provide guidelines for when participation and consultation are appropriate and when not. Jones, Dunphy, Fishman, Larne, and Canter (2007) provide a research-based model for achieving cultural transformation with widespread participation.

OD practitioners have come later to the world of transformational change than to incremental change, and their grasp of the strategies involved, such as mergers and acquisitions, changing the workforce capability mix, downsizing, and project management is less fully developed than in other areas, such as coaching, team building, and job redesign. There is scope here for collecting best practice and designing skill development processes for practitioners.

ROLE OF CHANGE AGENTS IN CREATING A MORE SUSTAINABLE CORPORATE WORLD

It is time for OD and other change practitioners to drop their professional boundaries and come together in a community of practice around a reenergized social movement. To recognize its more comprehensive membership, Andrew Griffiths and I have named this larger movement the organizational renewal movement (Dunphy & Griffiths, 1998). Who are the change agents who need to collaborate in this emerging attempt to create an integrated and comprehensive approach to corporate change? They include OD consultants, human resource managers, industrial engineers, information technology specialists, community activists, and environmental scientists who are applying their knowledge to creating more sustainable organizations. Only a movement that covers leading-edge knowledge of human, technological, and scientific change will be able to adequately meet the needs of the evolving corporation.

Other internal change agents who will be important in the evolution of sustainable corporations will be members of management boards, CEOs, senior executives, managers and supervisors, and general employees. Leadership at all levels will be vital. External change agent roles include politicians, bureaucrats and regulators, investors, and other stakeholders such as industry association leaders. There are increasing opportunities to lead through the formation of alliances between change agents working within an organization and outside it (Dunphy et al., 2007). Such alliances can create a pincer movement of pressure for change in the first three phases of change described earlier and so build momentum for compliance. In the latter three phases (efficiency, strategic proactivity, and the sustaining corporation) these alliances can create momentum by linking initiatives in different parts of the organization and in the community—initiatives that might otherwise be struggling for resources and support. It is vital to keep in mind that this is a social movement that extends beyond the corporation and, like all social movements, demands disciplined cooperation despite inevitable differences in values and skill bases.

As change agents and change leaders, we are only one source of influence in a complex changing reality. Nevertheless, let us not underestimate the potential transformative power we represent. As Korten states,

> The transformative power of the organism—both human and nonhuman—is the ultimate source of all that has value in the fulfillment of our own being. It includes not only the whole of the natural living capital, by which the planet's life support system is continuously regenerated, but also the human, social and institutional capital by which we utilize the wealth of the living planet to serve our needs and by which we may ideally come to lend our own distinctive capacities to further life's continuing journey. (Korten, 1999, p. 293)

The OD movement can try to continue to conduct business as usual, repeating the successes of the past, in which case it will simply fade away. The OD movement has always focused on change and has continued to change itself over time. It now faces not just incremental change but the need to transform and reposition itself in order to use its theoretical and practical heritage in meeting the emerging challenges of this century. Although this chapter has been assigned to the handbook section headed "Special Applications of OD," corporate sustainability is not, in my view, simply a special application of OD but the core business of OD in the future. OD practitioners and other change agents can lead in creating a new organization reality: the sustaining corporation that contributes to creating a more sustainable

world. Future generations deserve nothing less from us.

REFERENCES

BBC TV. (2003). Life on air—David Attenborough's 50 years on television [Television series episode]. In *The big picture*. London: BBC TV.

Beck, U. (2000). *The brave new world of work*. Cambridge, UK: Polity Press.

Benn, S., & Dunphy, D. (Eds.). (2007). *Corporate governance and sustainability: Challenges for theory and practice*. London: Routledge.

Beer, M., & Nohria, N. (2000). *Breaking the code of change*. Boston: Harvard Business School Press.

Cummings, T. G. (2004). Organization development and change: Foundations and applications. In J. J. Boonstra (Ed.), *Dynamics of organizational change and learning* (pp. 25–42). Chichester, UK: John Wiley & Sons.

Dawson, P. (2003). *Understanding organizational change: The contemporary experience of people at work*. London: Sage.

Diamond, J. (2005). *Collapse: How societies choose to fail or survive*. London: Allen Lane.

Dunphy, D. (2002). The sustainability of organizations. In S. Chowdry (Ed.), *Organization 21 C: Someday all organizations will lead like this* (pp. 259–271). New York: Pearson.

Dunphy, D., & Griffiths, A. (1998). *The sustainable corporation: Organizational renewal in Australia*. Sydney: Allen and Unwin.

Dunphy, D., Griffiths, A., & Benn, S. (Eds.). (2003). *Organizational change for corporate sustainability*. London: Routledge.

Dunphy, D., Griffiths, A., & Benn, S. (2007). *Organizational change for corporate sustainability*. London: Routledge.

Graetz, F., Rimmer, M., Lawrence, A., & Smith, A. (2002). *Managing organizational change*. Brisbane: John Wiley & Sons.

Gratton, L. (2000). *Living strategy: Putting people at the heart of corporate purpose*. London: Pearson.

Harrison, R. (1983). Strategies for a new age. *Human Resource Management, 22*, 209–335.

Hart, S. (1997, January–February). Beyond greening: Strategies for a sustainable world. *Harvard Business Review*, 67–76.

Hawkins, P., Lovins, A., & Lovins, H. (1999). *Natural capitalism: Creating the next industrial revolution.* London: Earthscan.

Herzberg, F. (1966). *Work and the nature of man.* Cleveland, OH: World Publishing.

Hock, D. (1999). *Birth of the chaordic age.* San Francisco: Berrett-Koehler.

Jones, Q., Dunphy, D., Fishman, R., Larne, M., & Canter, C. (2007). *In great company: Unlocking the secrets of cultural transformation.* Sydney: Human Synergistics.

Kanter, R. M. (1985). *The change masters: Corporate entrepreneurs at work.* London: Allen & Unwin.

Kennedy, A. (2000). *The end of shareholder value: Corporations at the crossroads.* London: Orion Business.

Korten, D. C. (1999). *The post-corporate world: Life after capitalism.* San Francisco: Kumarian Press and Berrett-Koehler.

Kotter, J. (1995). *Leading change.* Boston: Harvard Business School Press.

Lewin, K. (1951). *Field theory in social science.* New York: Harper & Row.

MacGregor, D. (1960). *The human side of enterprise.* New York: McGraw-Hill.

Maslow, A. H. (1954). *Motivation and personality.* New York: Harper.

Monbiot, G. (2000). *Captive state: The corporate takeover of Britain.* London: Pan MacMillan.

Pears, A. (2000). Technologies and processes for ecological sustainability. In D. Dunphy, J. Benveniste, A. Griffiths, & P. Sutton (Eds.), *Sustainability: The corporate challenge of the 21st century* (pp. 167–190). Sydney: Allen & Unwin.

Peters, T., & Waterman, R. (1997). *In search of excellence: Lessons from America's best run companies.* New York: Harper & Row.

Pettigrew, A. (1985). *Awakening giant: Continuity and change at ICI.* Oxford, UK: Blackwell.

Porras, J., & Robertson, P. (1987). Organization development theory: A typology and evaluation. In R. Woodman & W. Pasmore (Eds.), *Research in organization change and development* (Vol. 1, pp. 1–57). Greenwich, CT: JAI.

Ropo, A., Eriksson, P., & Hunt, J. (Eds.). (1997). Reflections on conducting processual research on management and organizations. *Scandinavian Journal of Management, 13*(4), 331–335.

Stace, D., & Dunphy, D. (2001). *Beyond the boundaries: Leading and re-creating the successful enterprise* (2nd ed.). Sydney: McGraw-Hill.

Tibbs, H. (2000). The technology strategy of the sustainable corporation. In D. Dunphy, J. Benveniste, A. Griffiths, & P. Sutton (Eds.), *Sustainability: The corporate challenge of the 21st century* (pp. 191–216). Sydney: Allen & Unwin.

Ulrich, D., Kerr, S., & Ashkenas, R. (2002). *GE workout.* New York: McGraw-Hill.

Van de Ven, A., & Huber, G. P. (1990). Longitudinal field research methods for studying processes of organizational change. *Organization Science, 1*(3), 213–219.

Vogel, E. F. (1975). *Japan as number 1: Lessons for America.* Boston: Harvard University Press.

Waddell, D. M., Cummings, T. G., & Worley, C. G. (2000). *Organization development and change.* Melbourne: Nelson Thompson.

Wright, R. (2004). *A short history of progress.* Melbourne: Text Publishing Company.

Warner Burke, W. (2002). *Organization change: Theory and practice.* Thousand Oaks, CA: Sage.

Zuboff, S., & Maxmin, J. (2002). *The support economy: Why corporations are failing individuals and the next decade of capitalism.* New York: Viking.

31

Organization Development for Social Change

L. DAVID BROWN

MARK LEACH

JANE G. COVEY

Organization development (OD) activity typically has focused on improving internal dynamics and their impacts on organization performance. For decades organization theorists have looked at how external contexts shape organization dynamics and performance and how organizations can deal effectively with those contextual forces (e.g., Lawrence & Lorsch, 1967; Nadler, Gerstein, Shaw, & Associates, 1992; Pfeffer & Salancik, 1978). But they have paid less attention to how external contexts (and, for our purposes here, social problems and issues) are themselves affected by organization activities.

This chapter focuses on how OD concepts and tools can be used for purposes of solving social problems and catalyzing constructive social changes. Twenty years ago two of us grappled with some of these issues as we worked with organizations that were committed to solving social, economic, and political development problems (Brown & Covey, 1987). We found that work with those agencies called for diagnosis and interventions that varied substantially from existing OD theory and practice. This chapter extends that analysis.

The external context for many organizations has shifted dramatically over the last 15 years. Politically the world has changed from the bipolar world of the Cold War to one now teetering between a U.S. hegemony and a more multipolar, pluralistic, regional international system (Nye & Donohue, 2000). The emergence of global markets has produced international competition, rapid growth in some countries, and mammoth increases in differences between the rich and the poor (Stiglitz, 2002; World Bank, 2000). The enormous expansion in communication and travel has encouraged both a shared global culture and increased concern with preserving local cultures (Steger, 2004). Ecological research has produced increasing recognition of the ecological limits to growth but not much political consensus on how to deal equitably with those limits (Goodland, Daly, & Serafy, 1992). The problems posed by technological change and expanding globalization have overwhelmed many of the organizational and institutional arrangements currently in place, creating intense demand for inventing and reinventing systems that are better equipped to cope with emerging complexities (Rischard, 2002; Social Learning Group, 2001). These events have created many opportunities to apply the insights of OD and other behavioral sciences to a variety of social and institutional change initiatives.

In the last two decades the authors have worked with dozens of agencies concerned with social problem solving and social transformation, including international development agencies (such as the World Bank and the U.S. Agency for International Development), nonprofit, nongovernment development agencies, environmental advocacy networks, transnational policy advocacy coalitions, and intersectoral partnerships concerned with intransigent social problems. Over that time we have been consistently engaged in work on large-scale, social problem solving and transformation, but our roles have varied from being external OD consultants, to third-party facilitators for interorganizational and intersectoral conflict management, to organizers of social learning networks, to activists in transnational advocacy coalitions. We worked together for more than a decade at the Institute for Development Research, a nonprofit, nongovernment think tank that provided organization research and consulting support to cause-oriented civil society organizations in North America, Asia, Africa,

and Latin America and in transnational contexts. We have continued those streams of work in our current organizations, and those activities have offered unique opportunities to explore the relevance of OD work to social change initiatives.

The next section briefly offers some conceptual background for OD in the service of social change, reviewing some of the elements of OD as it is currently understood. Then we turn to discussing and illustrating four leverage points at which OD may contribute to social change initiatives: strengthening organizations committed to social change, scaling up the impacts of successful social change organizations, creating new systems of organizations for societal purposes, and changing the contexts that influence strategic actors in social change processes. We illustrate these leverage points with cases from our experience and briefly discuss the kinds of interventions and change agent roles that emerge as critical. The final section articulates some emerging lessons about OD for social change.

OD AND SOCIAL CHANGE: CONCEPTS

What is social change? Obviously many kinds of change fall under the general term, including the rise of international terrorism, regime changes in Iraq, economic development in Thailand, democratization in South Africa, and women's liberation in the United States. At a minimum, social changes alter the structures, processes, and outcomes of domains larger than single organizations in ways that persist over time. Examples range from enhancing the capacities of a community to manage its resources, to altering national policies and practices to encourage more democratic participation in governance, to reshaping the institutions and assumptions of international trade to level the playing field for developing country producers.

Our work has focused on organizations concerned with poverty alleviation, human rights and democratization, and ecological sustainability, so *social change* in this chapter refers particularly to sustainable improvements in the lives and prospects of impoverished and marginalized groups. We have been particularly involved in efforts to enhance the opportunities and choices facing poor populations, increase the responsiveness of government, business, and civil society to citizens, and foster inclusive, sustainable, rights-based development.

Organizations are omnipresent actors in most societies today, critical to ongoing societal operations and pivotal actors in social problem solving and transformation. Some organizations, such as Amnesty International and Friends of the Earth, are organized around social change or problem-solving missions, and we will call them social change organizations. Other agencies are critical to various forms of social change, though not focused on change by their missions. The World Trade Organization and the U.S. Congress are strategic actors in the social changes under way in many developing countries, although those changes are peripheral concerns to those agencies. Still others have missions that position them to be either catalysts for change or bulwarks for stability: For example, the World Bank is seen as a force for alleviating poverty or a major contributor to immiserating the poor, depending on your perspective. So understanding organizations and intervening to change their behavior is potentially an important resource for social change initiatives.

How does OD become relevant to social change processes? We focus here on four leverage points at which OD has been useful in our experience. First, we look at OD to improve the functioning of social change organizations whose missions emphasize producing sustainable improvements for marginalized groups. OD work with such organizations resembles work with many organizations whose missions depend on accomplishment of complex tasks. Second, we discuss the use of OD in increasing or scaling up the impacts of social change organizations. Scaling up sometimes involves organization growth, an area to which OD may be

highly relevant. Scaling up may also involve more complex initiatives, which call for substantial extensions of OD theory and practice. Third, we consider the utility of OD for creating new systems that can solve problems or enable social changes beyond the capacities of existing organizational and institutional arrangements. Finally, we examine how OD can influence the contexts—and thereby the activities—of agencies that are critical to social changes. These different leverage points may pose different challenges to OD interventions and change agents.

There is much agreement on general families of interventions that OD practitioners use to help organizations (see Cummings & Worley, 2001; French & Bell, 1999). Those intervention families include the following:

- Work on human and organizational processes (e.g., process consultation, team building, and conflict management)
- Redesigning technical and structural arrangements (e.g., work design, business process redesign, or organization redesign)
- Developing human resources (e.g., training, building performance appraisal systems or reward systems, or coaching leaders)
- Organization-wide interventions (e.g., future search conferences, organization confrontation meetings, or large group strategic planning)

We examine examples in the next section of the kinds of interventions that appear to be critical to work with social change organizations, in part to see what families are particularly important and in part to identify interventions that are different from those common in present OD theory and practice.

There is also much agreement about the kinds of change agent skills needed for competence by current OD practitioners. Although early OD consultants tended to focus on being facilitators of OD processes rather than experts on the substance of organization change (French & Bell, 1999, pp. 257–259), over the last several decades OD roles have expanded from nondirective facilitators and process consultants to experts on designing and facilitating processes for team building or future search conferences or substantive resources on organization design, performance appraisal systems, or business process redesign. Distilling several analyses of core competencies and foundation competencies, Cummings and Worley (2001) concluded that OD change agents need four sets of skills:

- Intrapersonal skills that enable ongoing learning and effectiveness in ambiguous situations
- Interpersonal skills that allow effective relationships and trust development with individuals and groups in organizations
- General consultation skills that enable effective entry, diagnosis, intervention, and assessments of organizations
- OD theory that allows them to identify and use a range of OD tools and interventions (Cummings & Worley, 2001, pp. 46–50)

We will look at our examples to identify how this list may have to be amended for work with social change initiatives.

LEVERAGE POINTS FOR OD FOR SOCIAL CHANGE

This section offers brief descriptions of OD work with initiatives to catalyze social change. In each case we provide some background on the social change leverage points and briefly describe some illustrative cases. Then we explore the sorts of interventions and change agent skills that in our experience have been critical for that form of social change initiative. The leverage points, as presented here, move from focusing on internal organization dynamics, a perspective that is common to much of OD, to focusing on multiple organizations and on contextual forces that shape the actions of other agencies—perspectives much less common to existing OD.

Strengthening Social Change Organizations

Organizations that are focused on social change missions and strategies sometimes can

benefit from OD assistance, as do the businesses, government agencies, hospitals, and other agencies that use OD consultants. Our earlier work suggested that OD had much to offer social change and development organizations, even though some of their attributes might call for extensions of the existing OD paradigm. For example, we found that their organization around social visions and their responsiveness to diverse constituencies made social change organizations particularly vulnerable to ideological conflicts (Brown & Brown, 1983; Brown & Covey, 1987).

In the last decade there has been an explosion of work on the organization and management of social change organizations (Chadha, Jagadananda, & Lal, 2003; Ebrahim, 2003; Edwards & Fowler, 2002; Fowler, 1997; Human & Zaimann, 1995; James, 2001), much of it emphasizing the special challenges of strengthening social change actors for carrying out their work. We focus here on the challenges of everyday operation. Two examples illustrate some of the issues that arise for international organizations committed to fostering sustainable improvements in local choices and capacities in the developing world.

Authority and Conflict at the International Relief and Development Agency (IRDA). IRDA mobilizes resources in the United States to support grassroots development projects in the developing world, and it is widely recognized for innovative efforts to foster local self-reliance and democratic development. Its values and mission attract many young activists committed to ending poverty and oppression, but those staffs also resist deviations from participatory democracy in organizational decision making. In the late 1980s internal conflicts between IRDA departments and levels began to undermine its operational capacity, and the board asked an OD consulting team to help diagnose and manage tensions over racial and ideological differences and the use of authority. After a careful entry process with the board, management, and the staff, the consulting team developed a diagnostic report from interviews and questionnaires that linked conflicts to values and external relations and organized a series of feedback meetings. Stormy discussions of the report increased understanding of the perspectives of different parties and the impacts of conflict on mission attainment but produced few resolutions. In subsequent months, however, the intensity of conflicts declined. The agency continued to work with diverse constituents to support initiatives to enhance local self-reliance and collective action in the field.

Headquarters–Field Tensions at the International Child Sponsorship Agency (ICSA). ICSA delivers a variety of services to enhance the welfare of children in developing countries, with support from individual sponsors in industrialized countries. For many years it encouraged entrepreneurial leadership in field offices to develop local programs, but the proliferation of programs and activities became very difficult to control. A new CEO from the business sector was charged with improving headquarters' control over resources and programs, and he instituted new accounting and information systems. Although staff agreed that controls were important, they resisted what they saw as extreme and heavy-handed imposition of new roles. Increasing tensions between headquarters and the field and turnover of key staff led headquarters to commission a study of the situation. Organization diagnosis revealed differences between headquarters and field values that were exacerbated by the new "business-oriented" approach. Over the next several years the OD project enabled strategy formulation with significant field involvement, an organization design that devolved much decision making to regional and country offices, efforts to build a less "numbers-oriented" culture, and major shifts in leadership and leadership styles. Staff saw the changes as redressing an imbalance that favored fundraising over program development and so enabled more field influence over strategy and operations. ICSA continued to explore expanding its resources without compromising its programs for fostering local development.

These two cases describe organizations whose missions demand that they foster local capacities and programs for changing economic, social, and political contexts to benefit poor and marginalized communities. Four kinds of interventions have been helpful in working with these and other such organizations.

First, we have found that social change and development organizations often are clearer about their missions and their program activities than they are about the strategies that link them. External consultants or change agents can assist them in clarifying links between mission and activities so the relevance of immediate challenges can be understood in terms of larger organization values. It is easy in the press of carrying out high-stress, underresourced programs for staff to lose sight of how the work of different parts of the organization contributes to shared goals. At IRDA, for example, helping all the parties recognize how much their conflicts were counterproductive to the agency's mission, on which they largely agreed, was important to reducing tensions. Recognizing the importance of both developing programs and industrialized country fundraising and balancing local and central decision making were central to managing tensions between headquarters and field at ICSA. Providing strategic perspective can be a critical intervention in helping committed staff transcend the tensions of value-laden conflicts over organization changes.

In both cases, the consultants at the outset had to deal with intense internal conflicts, in which task differences were complicated by perceived differences in values and ideologies that encouraged "holy wars" between the parties. Managing conflict over fundamental power and value differences often is critical to work with social change organizations. What appear to be small differences to outsiders become crucial when they are infused with ideological meaning. At IRDA, for example, conflicts between board, management, and staff were complicated by perceptions of arbitrary and illegitimate use of power that catalyzed intense anger and mistrust. From the outset the credibility of the consultants was constantly tested by all the parties. Building links and understanding of common values across levels was a central concern. At ICSA a diagnostic survey demonstrated that field and headquarters staff shared similar values but perceived that headquarters policies favored accountability to donors over accountability to beneficiaries. The consultants focused particularly on creating conditions where previously unvoiced values and concerns could be heard, and the diagnostic process provided the bases for ongoing work to improve headquarters–field relations. Although conflict management is an important intervention in many organizations, it is particularly central to organizations that are mobilized around values and visions and that deal with constituencies whose interests often are in conflict with each other.

Few social change organizations place a high value on organization and management, at least until the need for better use of resources becomes overwhelmingly important. A third intervention that is often important to social change organizations is designing complex organization architectures. Once the agency is clear about its strategy, help in defining and fitting together needed tasks, formal structures and systems, informal arrangements, and human resources can be a major contribution. In IRDA, for example, management needed ideas for creating organization architecture that recognized board and management authority while preserving staff commitments to participation. Exploration of existing assumptions and alternatives consistent with the shared mission depended on external help. At ICSA efforts to impose more controls from headquarters had generated strong resistance from and turnover of key staff in the field. Neither the expertise nor the credibility was available inside the organization to define or implement needed design changes. So both the knowledge and the credibility to facilitate the development of new architectures may be central contributions of external OD resources.

Finally, in many social change organizations OD consultants may be asked to provide coaching to leaders who have little preparation for the challenges they face. Some leaders of social change organizations have little relevant management experience or training. For example, the chief executive of IRDA was a consultant to development projects and had little experience with managing a large dispersed organization with an activist board and a unionized staff. He used outside OD support to think about setting limits on both board and staff interference in management decisions. The chief executive of ICSA, on the other hand, had been a senior manager in large business organizations but was new to social change organizations with staffs accustomed to leadership based on values and collegial decision making. Consulting to ICSA involved helping the CEO understand the challenges of managing in value-based organizations.

The problems of social change organizations may demand change agent skills that are part of the normal OD repertoire of intrapersonal, interpersonal, organizational, and consulting skills—and others that are less common. For example, work with social change agencies often calls on change agents to have strategist skills for helping the organization understand the links between its mission and day-to-day activities. Although strategist skills may be included in the repertoires of many OD consultants, consultants with business or government experience may be less sophisticated about how organization activities can catalyze social change, and such links are central to managing the challenges facing social change organizations.

Although conflict management is important in many organizations, it is less common for OD consultants to participate (wittingly) in struggles over fundamental authority relations. In both the IRDA and ICSA cases, the change agents were hired to be third parties to escalated conflicts between management and staff. So skills as a mediator of organization authority relations can be critical to effective work in social change organizations. In this work, strategic perspective on the mission of the organization may be crucial as a basis from which to deal with the various parties.

The challenges of dealing with architectures for social change organizations may also expand the usual OD skills for structure and technical design. In addition to the usual challenges of organizing complex activities, social change organizations must coordinate across the demands of external constituencies whose diverse interests and expectations are reflected in internal subunits of the agency. So the role of OD in social change organizations may require that the consultant be an architect of external relations as well as authority relations. For example, improving headquarters–field relations at ICSA depended on an understanding of the interests of donors in industrialized countries, developing country communities, and civil society organizations. So the perspective needed of OD consultants can expand beyond the organization's boundaries to take in other actors in social change processes.

Despite these differences, many of the usual roles of OD consultants can be helpful in social change organizations. Indeed, counseling leaders in basic management approaches may draw heavily on ideas and tools developed in other kinds of organizations. So being a leadership consultant to social change organizations on issues that come up in the normal course of strategy implementation and program delivery is similar to OD in other settings. Of course, coaching leaders on the social change aspects of the organization's work may be a different story. In addition, when social change agencies seek to expand their social change impacts after initial successes, they may need different kinds of support, and the challenges to change agents may escalate.

Scaling Up Social Change Impacts

Social change organizations whose initiatives succeed as pilot programs often seek to scale up their impacts. Scaling up often is much more complex than it seems, and examinations of expanding impacts suggest that success relies on considerable sophistication (Rondinelli, 1983). Experience with scaling up development initiatives suggests several approaches: expanding coverage to affect more people, expanding functions to include more services or issues, packaging changes as easily disseminated and adopted approaches, training others to deliver similar services, spinning off new organizations, or building alliances to influence government agencies to expand program impacts (Edwards & Hulme, 1992; Uvin, 1995). Although the strategies involved are quite different, they all have implications for the agency involved and so might benefit from OD support.

Although expanding coverage and range of functions are common strategies for growth and impact in other sectors, often a more important strategy for social change initiatives is an indirect approach that influences other actors through alliances, training, or policy changes, without necessarily growing the original organization in size or resources (Uvin, Jain, & Brown, 2000). OD consultants could be assets in implementing such indirect strategies even when their long-term effect is to shrink the organization. Examples of OD initiatives to help social change organizations expand their impacts include the following:

Expanding a Support Organization Network in India. The Indian NGO Support Organization (INSO) began in the early 1980s to provide training, research, consulting, and other support to nongovernment organizations (NGOs) in many regions of India. INSO believed that such support was critical to strengthening grassroots and community-based organizations to carry out their own social change agendas. Although such services were an innovation with no obvious market appeal at the start, within 5 years demand exploded. INSO came under pressure to provide training and capacity-building programs in more languages and in more regions. After much discussion of the alternatives, INSO created a network of independent support organizations by spinning off new organizations, recruiting existing agencies with compatible philosophies and values, and acting as the center of a growing family of regional support organizations. INSO built network capacities by using support from international partners to provide advanced training in OD, strategic thinking, and action research to the network and strategic consultation to INSO itself. The resulting support organization network has been playing a catalytic role in decentralizing governance to local actors and in integrating women and marginalized groups into those governance processes. So the support organization network has become a national resource for enabling wider participation in local governance and development work.

Reorganizing IRDA for Transnational Policy Influence. IRDA recognized in the late 1990s that significant and sustainable poverty alleviation entailed more than success in the local self-reliance projects it had been funding for years. Many intransigent local poverty problems had deep roots, such as unfair terms of international trade, which could not be easily influenced at the local level. In cooperation with a family of like-minded organizations from other countries, IRDA launched international policy campaigns to change the terms of international trade, such as a multifaceted campaign to improve markets for small coffee producers. This shift of strategy entails a lot of organization change and capacity building: IRDA has used outside help to develop its new strategy, to build its capacity for policy campaigns, and to redesign and implement the architecture needed to mount campaigns in cooperation with international allies while continuing to support grassroots projects. IRDA is now implementing a plan developed with outside resources and is already demonstrating initial results from global campaigns. The changes in the agency position it to play a substantially enlarged role in shaping transnational policy and regulations for fairer trade.

Scaling up often involves fundamental changes in organization strategy and architecture. For example, scaling up involves clarifying social change theories that underlie organization strategies. Decisions to scale up by expanding coverage or functions may have largely organizational consequences, but scaling up by engaging other actors—such as training staff of other organizations, advocating for policy changes, or encouraging government agencies to adopt new programs—may depend on sophisticated knowledge about the other actors, their interests and incentives, and the forces that will resist or support expanding impacts. For example, INSO used consulting help to decide that a network of autonomous support organizations was more appropriate for responding to different regions than an expanded central organization. IRDA used consulting help to identify alternative approaches to expanding their impacts before opting to become a transnational campaign agency. Such consultations may provide critiques of existing theories of social change, alternatives to the currently dominant ideas, and suggestions about the implications of different choices.

Most strategies for scaling up impacts include designing architectures for expanding impact. Some scaling-up approaches involve organization growth to carry out larger and more complex operations—concerns for which OD theory and practice have a great deal to offer. Thus INSO's expansion entailed reorganizing the parent organization to provide resources and informational support to its emerging partners, advanced programs to enhance network capacities, and coordination of activities across the network. Other scaling-up strategies may involve expanding indirectly by disseminating innovations, affecting government policies, or training other agencies to undertake similar initiatives. Expanding impact by building policy advocacy coalitions at IRDA entailed reorganizing to coordinate new functions such as policy analysis and influence activities across regions and departments and learning to work within a multinational federation of allies. It also entailed building IRDA's capacity to participate in larger coalitions and to effectively engage policymakers. So internal changes to implement scaling-up strategies may include interventions to support organization growth or enable indirect impacts.

Finally, consultants involved in expanding social change initiatives by indirect means almost certainly will be called on to help with conceiving and building external relations. Expanding external relations may involve disseminating effective programs, spinning off new organizations, engaging with key actors in other sectors, or facilitating coalition building for collective action. INSO created a series of new organizations and built training programs to be used by many other agencies, and IRDA joined global coalitions to carry out transnational campaigns. Building external alliances is an area that can draw on interventions from the conflict management, intergroup relations, and team-building technologies of OD, but their use in the context of external alliances is much less common as an OD intervention in more traditional contexts.

These interventions in turn suggest change agent roles and skills that are not included in the personal, interpersonal, organizational, and consulting skills of traditional OD. When designing scaling-up strategies, consultants may be asked to take on the role of social change theorists who can help the agency conceptualize alternative ways to expand its social impacts. Familiarity with organization change theory is not the same as familiarity with social change theory. For example, social change theories involve understanding of large-scale political and social dynamics that are outside the training of many OD consultants. The social change theorist role calls on change agents to expand their horizons well beyond the viability of particular organizations.

Many OD consultants are quite familiar with the challenges of being an organization architect, and the challenge of changing organization systems in response to strategic shifts has drawn a good deal of attention. On the other hand, they are often less familiar with the strategic and organizational challenges associated with being a dissemination designer, particularly when those challenges may involve subordinating the organization to the larger change process and the concerns of many different stakeholders. INSO's creation of the support organization network in India involved sharing resources and building the capacities of autonomous organizations, which might take advantage of INSO's resources without returning much. The implementation of IRDA's commitment to transnational policy campaigns involved surrendering autonomy to transnational alliances and diverted resources from local initiatives to transnational campaigns whose value often was very controversial.

The role of facilitator of external relations can create significant tensions for consultants accustomed to serving a single client. Many approaches to scaling up social impacts involve relations with external actors, and that shift is particularly important for indirect scaling up. Being an external relations facilitator calls for the change agent to be aware of and effective in working with external actors who are relevant to the social change agenda—again necessitating a larger-system perspective on the organization and its work. Note that this role can dilute the change agent's relationship with the original client because facilitating external relations often calls for the facilitator to be neutral, particularly if the strategy involves creating multiorganization systems such as alliances or coalitions.

In short, scaling up impacts can call for change agent interventions and roles that are quite different from those demanded by "ordinary" OD with social change organizations. In such circumstances the focus of the work shifts in significant ways from dynamics and issues internal to the agency to issues encountered in interaction with key elements of the larger context that the organization seeks to transform.

Creating New Systems of Organizations

Some social change objectives necessitate the invention of new systems that organize a variety of actors who can together amass the necessary perspectives, resources, and capacities. OD perspectives, skills, and consultants can be very helpful in creating, leading, and maintaining multiactor systems for social change initiatives. Although there has been some attention to the possibilities of building interorganizational systems in the OD literature (e.g., Chisholm, 1998; Cummings, 1984; Trist, 1983), there has been more attention to these possibilities from students of negotiation and conflict management (e.g., Gray, 1989; Susskind & Cruikshank, 1987; Susskind, McKearnan & Thomas-Larmer, 1999) or social development (e.g., Brinkerhoff, 1999, 2002; Brown & Ashman, 1996; Leach, 1995). Such initiatives can construct multiorganization agencies with resources and capacities well beyond those of single agencies, but they may also suffer from problems that transcend those of single agencies as well.

Examples of multiorganization agencies constructed across diverse and autonomous organizations to work on complex problems include the following:

Creating the Urban River Collaboration (URC). This alliance between city agencies, community groups, and business associations was created to foster the development and maintenance of a riverside park in a midsized U.S. city. Despite strong support from the current city government, decades of distrust among key actors made action on the plan unlikely without a major effort to build cooperation across the sectors. An external consultant, recommended by a national conservation nonprofit that was providing technical expertise on the park, conducted interviews with representatives of all the parties and then convened meetings over several months to address underlying issues such as lack of understanding of the interests of

parties, concerns about hidden agendas, and unwillingness to entrust any party to take charge. Participants permitted the neutral consultant to facilitate a series of conversations and decisions, and that process built greater trust, a shared mission and work plan, and a joint fundraising plan. Despite these successes, the parties had difficulty creating an organization that could be efficient while balancing power among stakeholders. The consultant helped them generate shared criteria for a good structure, and they then interviewed representatives of similar collaborative ventures across the country for input on designing a well-understood and widely accepted structure. This process temporarily involved leadership from the consultant, and then shifted it back to group members when adequate trust developed. The intervention helped to reshape how member organizations enacted their roles in the city and broke down barriers to cooperation between political adversaries.

Convening the International Forum for Capacity-Building (IFCB) to Reshape Aid. This network of African, Asian, and Latin American development NGOs, international development NGOs, foundations, and bilateral and multilateral aid agencies was created to enable multiparty dialogues on building the capacities of civil society actors in the developing world. It was launched by a coalition of developing country NGO leaders, who perceived that the available capacity-building support was largely serving the needs of international actors rather than its local recipients. Over a 5-year period the IFCB created studies of capacity-building practice and needs perceived by NGOs in the three regions, international NGOs, and donor agencies; organized global, regional, and national conferences to discuss issues and negotiate improved approaches to capacity building; pioneered processes for constructive multiparty dialogue between key actors; and generated case studies of particularly successful examples.

The process reshaped conceptions of capacity building among the parties, fostered more active need assessment by recipients, and catalyzed new perspectives and policies among donor agencies and suppliers of capacity-building support, including an expanded commitment to civil society capacity building at the U.S. Agency for International Development and the World Bank.

Building new systems of organizations calls for interventions that bring and hold agencies together despite costs to their autonomy and resources. Whereas traditional OD starts from the assumption that there is an identifiable client—usually organization leaders—work with new systems at the outset may have to focus on a vision or problem because no client yet exists that can mobilize the right combination of resources to work on it. So a critical intervention may be convening a client system that has ownership and resources to achieve the vision or solve the problem. For example, the URC could not have come together without the intervention of a third-party consultant seen as credible and neutral with respect to the struggle that had blocked progress for years. Although many people were aware of the problems surrounding capacity building for Southern NGOs, the initiative by Southern NGO leaders with OD skills made action possible by a very diverse group of actors.

Convening key parties to consider social change initiatives is one thing; getting them to agree on problem definitions, let alone action strategies, can be another. Keeping the right parties engaged in a new system depends on building shared problem definitions and directions for action despite diversity in perspectives, power, and interests. Parties to the URC were willing to come together initially, and the consultant played a crucial role in facilitating agreement on mission, work plan, and fundraising activities across the chasms that initially separated the parties. The IFCB used the relationships between the conveners to bring many

actors together and encouraged key actors to organize studies of stakeholder views that could be synthesized into action plans at an initial international conference. In both cases a great deal of preparatory work went into setting the stage for constructive engagement by parties who might easily have destroyed opportunities for collective action at their initial meetings.

Once the parties can agree on basic definitions of objectives and strategies, change agents may play central roles in the construction of arrangements that will support further joint work. Change agents can play pivotal roles in creating formal and informal interface organizations to support multiorganization action. The consultant to the URC introduced the parties to previously unknown concepts of interorganizational collaboration, helped them generate criteria for assessing alternative structures, encouraged members to review alternatives used by other collaborations, and gradually shifted responsibility for leadership to collaboration members. The founders of the IFCB created an international steering committee and regional networks to carry out its activities and held a series of meetings at which the forum could be assessed. In the interim between international meetings members focused on regional and national activities designed to increase the relevance of capacity-building interventions to their Southern NGO clients.

For these new systems, the issue of creating new understanding and expanded alternatives for action was a central concern. Another key intervention by change agents was creating systems for network learning among people from diverse perspectives and experiences. The URC consultant played a central role in helping members invent and implement a learning process, increasing trust and expanding perspectives while relocating collaborative leadership within its members. The IFCB founders and resource consultants explicitly commissioned multiregional studies of key issues, such as the capacities needed to build civil society alliances, and they also commissioned consultants to develop approaches to multistakeholder dialogues on capacity-building issues. Results of these initiatives were disseminated through the IFCB Web site and conferences, enabling its far-flung membership and its steering committee to use them.

Creating new organizations calls for change agents to take on a number of roles beyond those envisioned by many OD practitioners. For example, the change agents in many of these initiatives acted as conveners and system entrepreneurs rather than external resources brought by already-organized clients. The founders of the IFCB brought the various parties together and created an unprecedented multiorganization initiative. The URC consultant created the conditions for a new system to be born out of the elements warring over the project. The roles of change agents in such circumstances are tricky in part because no widely acknowledged client exists, so creating a credible client is part of the work.

A major challenge for such change agents is to act as third-party mediators and system constructors. People in these roles bind conflict and hold together parties who threaten to explode rather than open up systems whose energies are blocked and suppressed. For such organizations, building trust and information sharing can be central. For the URC, for example, distrust was rampant, and the change agents had to build trust between change agent and members and between members. For the IFCB, the differences in perspectives and experiences that separated many forum stakeholders were huge. They met the challenge of spanning those differences by creating a steering committee that included different perspectives and that met often enough to develop mutual trust and shared norms to regulate potential tensions.

The importance of dealing with novel and evolving challenges calls on change agents' skills for acting as catalysts of network learning processes. That role demands both awareness of how to create the contexts for ongoing learning

and ability to keep learning oneself. It also entails the ability to synthesize shared understandings of competing views and mental models (Leach, 1995). The evolution of the URC presented continuing learning challenges, and the consultant provided much support in creating ways to gather and deal constructively with new information. In this process the participants developed substantive knowledge and at the same time built capacity and contacts to develop knowledge in the future, a capacity that would not have developed had the consultant acceded to their initial request to generate the information himself. The IFCB sought to catalyze learning among its stakeholders and across local, national, regional, and international levels by the network as a whole and by its members. It organized studies, commissioned conferences, fostered coalitions, and shared publications in this effort.

Creating new systems of organizations is particularly appropriate to emerging visions and new understandings of intransigent problems. In some circumstances, however, the relevant organizations already exist but do not see themselves as potential actors in social problem solving. In these circumstances, the resources of OD may be most useful in reshaping contexts that influence those actors.

Reshaping the Context of Strategic Agencies

We are interested here in OD work on contextual forces that influence strategic actors. In the previous three sections we focused on direct interventions with the strategic actors themselves. By contrast, here we focus on interventions with organizations that are part of the context of an agency that is strategic to social change. We have moved from a focus on the internal organizational dynamics common to much of OD to a focus on the external actors and forces that shape many of those internal dynamics.

So how can OD work with some organizations to influence others directly involved in a social change issue? One example is how the civil rights movement created the public opinion context that led the U.S. government to pass and enforce revolutionary civil rights legislation (Heifetz, 1994). Social movement theory has discussed in some detail the importance of organization building and resource management (e.g., Morris & Mueller, 1992; Tarrow, 1998), and organizations such as the Center for Community Change and the Industrial Areas Foundation have worked to strengthen grassroots agencies to exert pressure on government actors. When agencies have been identified as strategic actors in social change (Khandwalla, 1988), OD change agents may strengthen external actors to create contextual demand for social change.

Examples of initiatives that have used organization building to change external contexts of important social development actors include the following.

Promoting Participatory Development at the World Bank. The World Bank is widely recognized as a strategic actor in international development because of its financial resources and its credibility as a source of development theory and practice. It has sought to alleviate poverty through loans and technical assistance to governments, but the resulting projects have seldom mobilized the energies and resources of poor populations, and they often have little impact on long-term poverty. Within the World Bank reformers have argued for a more participatory approach to mobilize grassroots groups in defining and implementing projects intended to serve them. Those internal initiatives were stimulated and reinforced by external campaigns to promote more participatory approaches. The Participation Committee of the NGO Working Group on the World Bank, for example, organized transnational networks of NGOs to assess participation in existing participatory World Bank projects. The campaign assessed World Bank participatory experiments; monitored World Bank initiatives to implement pro-participation policies; recruited universities, NGOs, and other development agencies interested in participatory methods; and organized conferences with other international development agencies to share experiences and distill lessons for the future (Long, 2001). The campaign maintained ties with the internal reform groups to reinforce each other's efforts. Gradually World Bank policies and practices evolved, often against entrenched resistance, toward more participatory approaches and more responsive institutional arrangements. Because of the World Bank's prestige, its movement has also encouraged more participatory approaches in many other development agencies as well.

Fostering Responsive Education Systems in Mali. Decades of centralized one-party state control left the educational system in Mali plagued by lack of teachers, schools, books, and educational materials, especially in rural villages. Since the election of a reformist government in the early 1990s, international assistance from donor agencies and international NGOs has been directed toward organizing grassroots groups to improve their schools and secure policies responsive to rural needs. Supported by NGOs, local parent–teacher associations (PTAs) have been reorganized, members have been elected by the community and trained to manage their schools. The PTA assesses needs, sets priorities, and accesses resources needed to improve the accessibility and quality of education for their children. To support and extend the gains made at the community level, the NGO facilitators have organized conferences to bring together PTA representatives from different villages under ground rules that fostered democratic dialogue and decision making. As a result, newly unified regional federations of the PTAs can speak to government agencies with one voice. The NGOs have also provided basic training in policy analysis and advocacy to enable the federations to interact with the Ministry of Education in policy formulation. Contextual forces at the level of local schools have fostered increasingly effective local governance and management of schools and at the level of national Ministry of Education have increased attention on the concerns of rural village schools and increased local influence in curriculum and expenditure decisions.

Building contextual pressure for change in a strategic agency calls for interventions that may be quite different from work inside that agency. Whereas OD in organizations often is catalyzed by decisions and goals of top management, the choice to shape domain contexts grows out of articulating compelling visions for which it is possible to mobilize contextual resources and support. The NGO networks pressing the World Bank to become more participatory envisioned development initiatives characterized by local ownership and resources, sustainability based on local institutional commitment, and more attention to the concerns of grassroots populations. The Mali education initiative focused on a vision of an educational system responsive to the concerns of parents and students in the context of a more decentralized and democratic governance structure. These visions became the basis for defining desired changes in contextual forces that might achieve them.

A second set of interventions for shaping external contexts is identifying organizations strategic to change, recognizing contextual forces that influence those agencies, and building initiatives that mobilize those forces. OD experience can provide some (but not all) of the ingredients of building theories of contextual influence. In the campaign to influence the World Bank, for example, both insiders and outsiders recognized that the World Bank could be influenced by information and research. The civil society coalition developed a series of case studies of the World Bank's efforts to implement participatory development and organized workshops and conferences at which the lessons of those experiences could be discussed by representatives of the World Bank and other development agencies. This initiative built on the expectation that World Bank staff could be influenced by evidence about participatory approaches used by various agencies and by peer pressure from those agencies. In Mali the creation of effective and democratic PTAs and federations presented the Education Ministry at all levels with both carrots and sticks: The local associations could strengthen the positions of schools within communities and mobilize community support for their development, and they increasingly became an articulate and influential national lobbying force.

A critical activity for creating contexts that support change is mobilizing unorganized constituents for collective action. Often constituencies with large stakes in the behavior of strategic agencies have very little influence because they are not organized to speak cohesively or coherently on the issues. Interventions that help actors with shared interests build capacity for collective action can make a huge difference in the extent to which contextual voices are heard. The existence of NGO networks developing systematic data about World Bank projects and organizing highly visible events for sharing results created a setting for external voices being widely heard. Organizing regional federations and building capacities for policy analysis and advocacy in networks of PTAs created previously unavailable opportunities for voicing local perspectives to the Malian government. When key constituencies cannot make their voices heard, creating more voice can have a large impact on how issues are handled in the future.

A related intervention is creating alliances to support reform by target institutions. In part these alliances are reflected in the development of constituency organization, but they may also involve links across sectors (e.g., connecting with interested business leaders and government officials), across levels (e.g., local, regional, national, and international allies), or between outsiders and insiders in the target agencies. For example, alliances to influence

World Bank policies drew on links to many national governments and civil society actors from local, national, and international arenas. Reformers inside the World Bank made large contributions to assessing the shortcomings of existing models, articulating alternatives, demonstrating the potentials of participation, summarizing available research, and defining ways the World Bank might implement new priorities. The initiatives to strengthen parent and teacher roles in Malian education created alliances between national and international NGOs and between local and regional PTAs and sympathetic government officials. Influencing and reinforcing change at strategic agencies may involve alliances at many stages, from framing existing problems, to articulating alternatives, to testing options, to assessing impacts.

The nature of OD skills and roles also appears to shift across different leverage points for social change. For example, efforts to change contextual forces often are carried out by alliances of change agents with different sets of skills. Where much of OD responds to clients in organization leadership roles, social change initiatives may not have the resources to recruit consultants, and change agents may have to take more proactive roles in defining the issues and initial strategies. In crafting visions for alternative futures and mobilizing unorganized constituents, change agents may need activist visionary skills, grounded in their own values and commitments rather than in allegiance to existing organization or system interests. The creation of visions that challenge social problems may entail going beyond the perspectives built into existing social arrangements and resource allocations. Thus the NGO Working Group took the initiative to press the World Bank to live up to its own statements of participatory development. The democratic vision espoused by the new government of Mali was more rhetoric than reality before the NGOs initiatives to build local PTAs created pressures for better local schools and later policy campaigns

increased Ministry of Education responsiveness to rural concerns.

Social change theorist skills are also critical to efforts to create contexts that press strategic actors to act in new ways. External actors often do not understand how key agencies are influenced by their contexts. Assessing strategic organizations is a prelude to thinking about how contexts can be altered to foster desired change. Assessing the World Bank and the contextual factors that influence its choices for and against participatory development strategies calls for sophisticated understanding of international institutions and the politics that influence them. Similarly, understanding the Malian Ministry of Education and local schools calls for detailed knowledge about how contextual factors shape their activity. Extensive experience in OD may not prepare change agents for the conceptual or the situational analyses needed.

The mobilization of constituencies for collective action may call for organization-building skills that are common among OD consultants, but organizing contextual forces to affect strategic target organizations may call for movement-building leadership that is not so common to many OD activities. Reforming World Bank approaches to development involved creating new alliances to produce new information and discourses. Similarly, the resources to the PTAs and federations in Mali often took very active roles in assessing the capacities needed and how they might be developed. It is probably not an accident that both of these context-changing initiatives involved long-term alliances between actors with diverse resources and national backgrounds and so mobilized a great deal of information and resources relevant to their interventions.

A fourth set of important change agent resources in many of these initiatives is skills in bridge building for long-term change. The change agents in context-shaping initiatives may be pivotal to connecting alliances to supporters from other sectors, from other levels, or within the target institution. In the World

Bank case the NGO Working Group on the World Bank built bridges that linked outside challengers to other bilateral and multilateral development assistance agencies and to reformers within the World Bank. In the Mali initiative, change agents from national and international NGOs helped PTAs engage government actors in ways that supported the emerging democratic process. Creating bridges of understanding and support for change is central to the long-term sustainability of successful initiatives.

We have explored how OD interventions and roles may contribute to social change in four different ways. We turn now to implications for the field that emerge in looking across these different patterns.

EMERGING LESSONS: OD FOR SOCIAL CHANGE

We have argued that OD strategies and tools may be relevant to promoting social change at four leverage points: increasing the capacity of social change agencies to cope with organization problems, helping those agencies scale up their social change impacts, creating new systems of organizations to achieve social results, and changing the external contexts to influence agencies directly linked to such results. The first row of Table 31.1 summarizes the interventions and change agent skills described as central to existing practice by major texts in the field (Cummings & Worley, 2001; French & Bell, 1999). Subsequent rows summarize our discussion of the interventions and skills that appeared to be central to OD in social change initiatives at the different leverage points.

Some of the interventions and skills described in the first row appear in later rows as well, suggesting that much of OD theory and practice is relevant to organizations concerned with promoting social change. But there are also some important elements in lower rows (indicated with asterisks) that go beyond much of the existing theory and practice of OD. We focus briefly on some of the implications of this analysis for OD interventions, for OD skills, and for the field in general.

Implications for Intervention

The families of interventions that are staples of OD practice—improving processes, enhancing technical and structural systems, developing human resources, and fostering organization-wide diagnosis and change—appear in many of the rows of Table 31.1. Managing conflict is widely used as an intervention to improve organization processes, and redesigning organization architectures often involves tools from structural and system-wide OD interventions. Coaching leaders is widely used as a human resource development intervention in much OD. So many OD interventions are highly relevant to strengthening organizations that are involved in social change work.

On the other hand, some of the interventions listed in Table 31.1 suggest expansions of current OD theory and practice if it is to be effective in the social change arena. For example, many of the interventions described in Table 31.1 require that change agents ground their interventions in a theory of social change as well as a theory of organization change. Interventions that strengthen the organization without contributing to larger social results are not successful from a social change point of view. Social change theories explain the underlying causes of existing social and institutional arrangements and suggest how OD interventions applied in the right places can lead to desirable and sustainable change. Without such theories OD interventions may produce irrelevant or even harmful outcomes, such as strengthening organizations whose activities undermine desired social changes. Understanding and influencing social change processes and potentials is no small matter, and the topic is not treated by most OD training programs.

Although much OD assumes the existence of an organizational client, many of the

Table 31.1   OD Leverage Points, Interventions, and Skills for Social Change

Social Change Leverage Points	Common Interventions	Change Agent Skills
OD practice within organizations	Improving human and organization processes	Intrapersonal skills for working with ambiguity
	Improving technical and structural aspects of organization	Interpersonal skills for building relationships and trust
	Developing human resources	Consultation skills for entry, diagnosis, intervention, and assessment
	Intervening in the organization as a whole	OD theory for using tools and interventions
Enhance capacities of social change organizations	Clarifying links between mission and activities	Organization strategist skills
• Managing conflicts over authority at IRDA	*Managing conflict over fundamental power and value differences	*Mediating and synthesizing authority relations
• Improving headquarters–field relations at ICSA	Designing complex organization architectures	Designing and implementing changes in structure, roles, and culture
	Coaching leaders to deal with complexity and unfamiliar management challenges	Leadership consulting; skills in individual-level assessment and change
Scaling up impact of social change actors	*Clarifying social change theories	*Skills in analysis of power, policy, and social influence
• Expanding the reach of INSO and its network	Redesigning architectures for growth and external alliances	Design and implementation of intraorganizational and interorganizational structures and systems
• Organizing to influence transnational policy at IRDA	*Conceiving and building external relations	*Facilitator of external relationships
Creating new systems of organizations	*Convening and creating a new client system	*Temporary system leadership; system entrepreneurs
• Creating the URC to build support for an urban park	Building shared definitions and directions	*Mediating and synthesizing shared mental models and appreciations
• Convening the IFCB to catalyze learning for capacity building	*Creating interface organization	*Knowledge of collaborative and interorganizational design
	*Creating network learning systems	Catalyzing personal, organizational, and interorganizational learning and perspective sharing

(Continued)

Table 31.1   (Continued)

Social Change Leverage Points	Common Interventions	Change Agent Skills
Reshaping the context of strategic agencies • Promoting participation in World Bank projects • Promoting responsive education in Mali	Articulating visions of compelling future *Building theories of contextual influence *Mobilizing constituents for collective action *Creating alliances to support reform	*Activist visionary skills *Political and social analysis; advocacy and movement strategy *Organizing movement building *Building bridges for long-term change

*Indicates intervention or skill not called for in more traditions of OD practice.

interventions described in the lower rows of Table 31.1 are focused on influencing or even creating multiorganization systems rather than focusing on a single client. Much of the OD described here involves reorienting existing organizations to expand their impacts through alliances or creating multiorganization systems to deal with social challenges that will otherwise remain unmet. Building multiorganization systems and changing strategic contexts by definition involve more than one organization, and scaling up the impacts of social change organizations often involves expanding alliances and partnerships. We noted earlier that the internal dynamics of development organizations might be shaped by their external relations (Brown & Brown, 1983; Brown & Covey, 1987). It is increasingly apparent that external relations themselves may be shaped by the dynamics of multiorganization systems. Interorganizational relations, such as those in the URC, the IFCB, or the World Bank campaign, can alter institutional and social patterns of behavior. OD theory and practice derived from work with internal aspects of single organizations may need substantial elaboration or revision to deal with external contexts and multiorganization systems.

Most OD work at least implicitly assumes that the health and viability of the client organization are central to successful intervention, although change agents differ in how they define that health and viability. However, applying OD for social change can introduce different assumptions. For many actors in such initiatives, social change goals take precedence over organization interests, and change agents may find themselves pressed to support the larger initiative instead of a single organization. Change agents that begin working with single organizations and facilitate the creation of multiorganization initiatives often find themselves torn between their obligations to the initial client and their commitment to the success of the larger alliance. OD theory and practice do not yet offer much help for understanding or managing the dilemmas that can be posed by social change goals and multiorganization systems.

Implications for Change Agents

The descriptions of change agent interventions in Table 31.1 also suggest a need to expand or supplement past conceptions of OD skills if OD consultants are to be effective actors in social change settings. For example, the skills listed in Table 31.1 suggest that change agents in social change settings need skills for conceptualizing and framing organizational roles in larger social issues. Relevant capacities include conceptualizing social change initiatives, synthesizing values and articulating visions, understanding conflict over fundamental authority relations, and catalyzing ongoing learning. Conceptualizing social change problems and theories enables change agents to bring critical perspectives to key actors trapped in their own perspectives. Articulating visions that mobilize values across many constituents often is critical to sustainable change. Recognizing and mediating conflicts over power and authority can be critical to building relationships and trust in place of competition, distrust, and political exploitation. Creating and testing alternative frames to explain shifting patterns can help change agents and other stakeholders learn at both the organization and domain levels, without which sustainable changes become unlikely.

Change agents who practice OD in the service of social change often find that personal values and ideological commitments are critical to their credibility. In much OD work, negotiating entry with organization authorities establishes the legitimacy of change agents, particularly if conflict over authority is not a central issue. But in social change efforts it is often not clear who can confer legitimacy on change agents, and technical competence may be less important than skills for consensus building and working across boundaries. Concerns about values and ideologies can be particularly challenging when diverse constituencies regard quite different stances as credible. Histories of work with some parties may be grounds for dismissal by others. At a minimum, understanding of the political implications of past work and skills for building trust across diverse perspectives are important resources for change agents in conflicted social change arenas.

Much of OD work assumes that the change agent is a neutral and technical resource in building organization capacities. Although that description may be accurate for work with existing social change organizations, it is less accurate for creating new systems or

changing contexts of strategic agencies. In those settings change agents increasingly move from technical consultants for organizations to temporary leaders for underorganized systems or activists for social change, and from individual actors to members of teams or coalitions. Work with organizations such as IRDA and INSO may involve consulting to existing organization leaders, but convening new systems of organizations or mobilizing contextual forces to shape the behavior of strategic organizations involves more leadership or activist stances. As the demands increase for different kinds of expertise and work with wider networks, the importance of teams of actors may increase. The single-consultant model becomes less appropriate for describing the relevant actors as the work involves more multiorganization systems and more efforts to shape large-scale contextual forces. As creating organization systems and changing contexts become more common interventions, the skills of change agents may evolve away from familiar OD consulting approaches.

Implications for the Field of OD

The continuing market for OD texts, the growth and viability of professional networks such as the OD Network, the emergence of many educational programs to train OD consultants, and even this handbook are all evidence of a maturing professional field. It seems clear that there is continuing demand for OD resources to help organizations—particularly business organizations—continue to improve their capacities to deal with the challenges of global markets and international competition.

Should OD be concerned about applications to larger issues, such as problems of social problem solving and institutional transformation? It seems clear that such a path will entail significant investments in expanding and elaborating the range of OD interventions and skills. One plausible answer is that a better use of scarce resources is to focus on further professionalization of theory and practice for social actors who can afford to make good use of the field. This idea is implicit in a recent study that developed ideas about the future of the field from analysis of interviews with currently eminent practitioners (Worley & Feyerherm, 2003) in order to build better training for future practitioners. This initiative makes sense as an effort to build on best practices from the past to create standards and bodies of knowledge for the future.

An alternative, perhaps complementary approach, is to encourage OD theorists and practitioners to make forays into new domains where they will inevitably be operating at (and often over) the edge of their competence—but where new perspectives, alternatives, and possibilities may be revealed by their successes and failures. The field can grow from the experiences of mavericks and from the work of established practitioners; indeed, the OD field was founded largely by mavericks from better-established fields and professions who applied their insights to compelling social problems. So we argue for both processes: codifying and professionalizing on the basis of existing experience *and* exploring and inventing in the problem domains where OD might have value to add.

OD has been an important resource to organizations facing the increased demands for organization learning in an increasingly interdependent and competitive world. The ever-increasing gap between rich and poor, our difficulties in mobilizing action on global warming and HIV and AIDS, and the expanding concern with terrorism all reflect a growing need for innovations in social learning that can deal with problems beyond the grasp of individual organizations. We believe that OD for social change can play a central role in enabling more rapid and effective social learning. But developing that role will depend on the spirit of inquiry that motivated many of the field's pioneers and a tolerance for the ambiguities and risks of supporting a wide variety of innovative social change initiatives.

REFERENCES

Brinkerhoff, D. (1999). Exploring state–civil society cooperation. *Nonprofit and Voluntary Sector Quarterly, 28*(Suppl.), 59–86.

Brinkerhoff, J. M. (2002). *Partnership for international development: Rhetoric or results?* Boulder, CO: Lynne Rienner.

Brown, L. D., & Ashman, D. (1996). Participation, social capital and intersectoral problem-solving: African and Asian cases. *World Development, 24*(9), 1467–1479.

Brown, L. D., & Brown, J. C. (1983). Organizational microcosms and ideological negotiation. In M. H. Bazerman & R. J. Lewicki (Eds.), *Negotiating in organizations* (pp. 227–247). Newbury Park, CA: Sage.

Brown, L. D., & Covey, J. G. (1987). Development organizations and organization development: Toward an expanded paradigm for organization development. In R. W. Woodman & W. E. Pasmore (Eds.), *Research in organizational change and development* (Vol. 1, pp. 59–88). Greenwich, CT: JAI.

Chadha, P., Jagadananda, & Lal, G. (2003). *Organizational behaviour: A framework for nongovernmental organizations.* Bubaneshwar, India: Centre for Youth and Social Development.

Chisholm, R. (1998). *Developing network organizations: Learning from practice and theory.* Reading, MA: Addison-Wesley.

Cummings, T. G. (1984). Transorganizational development. In B. Staw & L. Cummings (Eds.), *Research in organizational behavior* (Vol. 6). Greenwich, CT: JAI.

Cummings, T., & Worley, C. (2001). *Organization development and change* (7th ed.). Cincinnati, OH: Southwestern College Publishing.

Ebrahim, A. (2003). *NGOs and organizational change.* Cambridge, UK: Cambridge University Press.

Edwards, M., & Fowler, A. (Eds.). (2002). *The Earthscan reader on NGO management.* London: Earthscan.

Edwards, M., & Hulme, D. (Eds.). (1992). *Making a difference.* London: Earthscan.

Fowler, A. (1997). *Striking a balance.* London: Earthscan.

French, W., & Bell, C. (1999). *Organization development* (6th ed.). Upper Saddle River, NJ: Prentice Hall.

Goodland, R., Daly, H. E., & Serafy, S. E. (1992). *Population, technology and lifestyle: The transition to sustainability.* Washington, DC: Island Press.

Gray, B. G. (1989). *Collaborating: Finding common ground for multiparty problems.* San Francisco: Jossey-Bass.

Heifetz, R. (1994). *Leadership without easy answers.* Cambridge, MA: Belknap.

Human, P., & Zaimann, A. (1995). *Managing towards self-reliance.* Dakar, Senegal: Phoenix.

James, R. (Ed.). (2001). *Power and partnership? Experiences of NGO capacity-building.* Oxford, UK: INTRAC.

Khandwalla, P. (1988). Strategic organizations in social development. In P. Khandwalla (Ed.), *Social development: A new role for the organizational sciences* (pp. 24–51). New Delhi: Sage.

Lawrence, P., & Lorsch, J. (1967). *Organization and environment.* Boston: Harvard Business School Press.

Leach, M. (1995). *Organizing images and the structuring of interorganizational relations.* Unpublished doctoral dissertation, Boston University.

Long, C. (2001). *Participation of the poor in development initiatives: Taking their rightful place.* London: Earthscan.

Morris, A. D., & Mueller, C. M. (Eds.). (1992). *Frontiers in social movement theory.* New Haven, CT: Yale University Press.

Nadler, D. A., Gerstein, M. S., Shaw, R. B., & Associates. (Eds.). (1992). *Organizational architecture: Designs for changing organizations.* San Francisco: Jossey-Bass.

Nye, J. S., & Donohue, J. D. (Eds.). (2000). *Governance in a globalizing world.* Washington, DC: Brookings Institution.

Pfeffer, J., & Salancik, G. (1978). *The external control of organizations.* New York: Harper & Row.

Rischard, J. R. (2002). *High noon: 20 global problems; 20 years to solve them.* London: Basic Books.

Rondinelli, D. (1983). *Development projects as policy experiments.* New York: Methuen.

Social Learning Group. (2001). *Learning to manage global environmental risks* (Vol. 2). Cambridge: MIT Press.

Steger, M. B. (Ed.). (2004). *Rethinking globalism.* Lanham, MD: Rowman & Littlefield.

Stiglitz, J. (2002). *Globalization and its discontents.* New York: Norton.

Susskind, L., & Cruikshank, J. (1987). *Breaking the impasse: Consensual approaches to resolving public disputes.* New York: Basic Books.

Susskind, L., McKearnan, S., & Thomas-Larmer, J. (Eds.). (1999). *The consensus building handbook.* Thousand Oaks, CA: Sage.

Tarrow, S. (1998). *Power in movement* (2nd ed.). New York: Cambridge University Press.

Trist, E. (1983). Referent organizations and the development of inter-organizational domains. *Human Relations, 36*(3), 269–284.

Uvin, P. (1995). Fighting hunger at the grassroots: Paths to scaling up. *World Development, 23*(6), 927–939.

Uvin, P., Jain, P., & Brown, L. D. (2000). Think large and act small: Toward a new paradigm for NGO scaling up. *World Development, 28*(8), 1409–1419.

World Bank. (2000). *World development report 2000/2001.* Washington, DC: Author.

Worley, C. G., & Feyerherm, A. E. (2003). Reflections on the future of organization development. *Journal of Applied Behavioral Science, 39*(1), 91–115.

32

Organization Development in Nongovernment Organizations

RAJESH TANDON

In the field of development, nonprofit non-government organizations (NGOs) have gained visibility in the past decades. When modern development enterprise began after World War II, the prime mover in each developing and developed country was the government. Problems of rural development, water, sanitation, education, health, environment, forests, agriculture, employment, tribal welfare, and women's rights were addressed predominantly by government ministries, departments, and agencies. Local voluntary agencies, community associations, and small indigenous development agencies existed at that time, too, but were largely invisible and marginal. With the rise of international aid for development in the South, Northern NGOs began to participate more actively in development programs in the South by the late 1960s. Voluntary development organizations or NGOs in countries of the South began to gain attention of international donor agencies and national governments in the mid-1970s. In comparison to large-scale, inefficient, top-down, at times corrupt government bureaucracies, NGOs were small and locally rooted, had rapport with local communities, were flexible and dynamic, and seemed to have greater impact in their development interventions.

This recognition slowly gained momentum, and NGOs (in both the North and the South) began to attract increasingly large amounts of bilateral and multilateral assistance, increased flow of private resources from Northern NGOs, and more programmatic provisions from national and provincial governments. At the same time, NGOs in the South began to develop a variety of roles and functions. Various typologies classify them differently. Many NGOs work at the grassroots level, others do research, training, networking, and advocacy. Some NGOs specialize (e.g., health, education, water, forestry, women's rights), others have integrated and multisectoral programs. Some NGOs provide relief and welfare services; others promote community organization and empowerment. Some are small, informal groups; others are large development agencies.

This phenomenon was further expanded to include a broader framework of civil society in the late 1980s. NGOs became a subset of civil society, which comprised of a variety of nonstate and nonmarket actors and associations (Clark, 1991; Tandon & Mohanty 2002).

In this context, the resources, outreach, visibility, impact, and presence of NGOs became a new social phenomenon throughout the world by the early 1990s. In the course of this development, strengthening capacities of NGOs to perform their tasks effectively began to gain certain significance in the mid-1980s. Concern with NGO capacity increased much more among donors in the early 1990s as increasingly greater resources and performance expectations were placed on NGOs. Training as an intervention to strengthen the capacity of NGOs staff received some attention in the mid-1980s but was largely limited to technical competencies.

Capacity-building of NGOs to manage their organizations more effectively gained attention only a decade ago (Community Development Resource Association, 1994–1995; IFCB, 1998; Tandon & Bandyopadhyay, 2003). Only in the last decade have institutional strengthening, institutional development, or organization development (OD) of NGOs begun to be discussed and practiced (Fowler, Campbell, & Pratt, 1992; MDF, 1994). As more and more NGOs learn about OD or undergo OD experiences, a larger body of knowledge will become available. However, in the current context of increasing demand for OD from NGOs and their donors, it is important to clarify the relevance and use of OD in NGOs and its implications.

MEANING AND DEFINITION OF OD

OD as a field of theory and practice in management science began nearly five decades ago with the practices of laboratory training methods (or T groups, as they became known later) in National Training Laboratories Institute for Applied Behavioral Science in the United States in the early 1950s. A more comprehensive organization focus (as opposed to mere individual focus of T groups) began to evolve in the actual practice of helping industrial organizations to improve their performance or solve human problems. A lot of initial practice in solving human problems of large-scale organizations occurred in military organizations (in particular coping with the post–World War II peacetime role of the military).

OD was defined and redefined with increasing practice in solving real-life organization problems in industry and government (Beckhard, 1969). As understanding about the nature and functioning of complex organizations grew, the scope and depth of OD and its interventions also expanded. Although many different definitions and frameworks have been adopted, certain key elements of OD have emerged.

Planned Change

Organizations change over time. Pressures for change generate from within and from outside the organization. OD implies proactive, anticipatory, planned change in some (or all) aspects of functioning of an organization, as opposed to ad hoc, haphazard, reactive change. In this sense, OD implies forward-looking and future-oriented planned change efforts.

Improved Effectiveness

The purpose of OD is to improve the long-term effectiveness of the organization. Short-term profit, efficiency in input and output, and growth are also part of the goals of OD. Improving the health of an organization and increasing its capacity to engage in planned change and ongoing self-renewal are part of this purpose of improving effectiveness. Gaining new technology, new products, new services, new markets, and new clients on one hand and improving employee morale and productivity, reducing costs, enhancing quality, and increasing competitiveness on the other hand have all been part of the framework of improving effectiveness of an organization.

Preferred Values

The practice of OD has emphasized certain preferred values about individuals, organizations, and society. Based on studies on motivation and human need, social relations, and group dynamics, OD professes the value of increasing individual autonomy, choice, creativity, and respect as necessary ingredients of improved organization effectiveness.

System-Wide Understanding

OD emphasizes the need for deeper understanding of underlying causes of visible problem symptoms faced by organizations. Therefore, OD starts with a diagnosis, which aims to improve a comprehensive, system-wide understanding of the organization. This process of diagnosis therefore makes OD a data-based change strategy that bases its interventions for organization improvements on the analysis generated from a systematic, system-wide diagnosis. In order for this diagnosis to be carried out, OD requires an explicit framework for understanding an organization. A variety of frameworks of organizations have been developed over the years in the now well-established management discipline of organization behavior. A clear and explicitly articulated framework describing what an organization is, how it functions, what outputs are caused by what inputs, and intervening variables therefore is necessary for OD.

Learning Process

Changes and improvements in organizations occur in a variety of ways. Large organizations typically use power and coercion, through executive orders and decrees, to effect desired changes. However, the process of changing an organization in OD follows an action research approach. Inquiry, learning, experimentation, education, and persuasion are preferred modes of bringing about change in OD. The processes of OD therefore are designed in such a way that the organization, its leaders, and its members actively participate in diagnosing, planning, and implementing changes and improvements needed on that basis (Grinnell, 1969). This ensures that change in organization is "owned" by it and has greater possibility of being sustainable. It also implies that organization's leaders and members undergo a learning and relearning process in order to appreciate the need for and directions of change needed to improve its effectiveness.

These key elements of OD are the foundation of any planned organization improvement effort. Thus, the practice and theory of OD emerged in a particular historical context from the experiences of certain types of organizations. Typically, these organizations were profit-making, large, commercial, industrial organizations (e.g., factories, mines, offices). Sometimes they included large government agencies, departments, or public corporations.

These organizations were large, complex bureaucracies with well-defined hierarchies, roles, rules, systems, and procedures. They operated in situations where the supply of raw materials, technology of production, and sale of outputs were reasonably stable and certain. Large government agencies or corporations operated in monopoly situations with unrestricted flow of resource inputs. Many of these organizations (for-profit corporations or government agencies) were designed and operated on the basis of the theory and principles developed in the 19th-century industrial revolution in Europe.

Principles of scientific management, efficiency through assembly lines, and bureaucracy as a nonfeudal form of organization evolved during the industrial revolution to create possibilities of managing efficiently and objectively these large production and service enterprises. The rise of organized labor and the increasing relevance of human motivation gave rise to theories and practices of human relations as an approach to effective management of an enterprise.

It is therefore significant that the practice of OD emphasized human values, organizational democracy, open and participative management, and learning orientation. The practice and theory of OD became concerned with practice and planned change as many industrial corporations grew volatile in changing, uncertain, and unpredictable social, political, economic, and technological environments. Because business as usual was no longer possible, OD interventions aimed to build the capacities of such organizations to proactively deal with anticipated future trends.

RELEVANCE OF OD IN NGOS

What is the relevance of OD in NGOs? As described earlier, NGOs are a diverse set of actors with varying functions, sizes, and approaches. Although no universal prescription is possible, certain typical pressures for change operate on many NGOs.

External Pressure

A number of external pressures for change affect NGOs today:

• NGOs are mission-oriented organizations. Typically, the mission of an NGO describes desirable social change in the community or society. Such a desirable change may imply changes in education, health, or employment. As social change organizations, NGOs intend to affect their external constituencies. As NGOs bring about that desirable change, they typically redefine their missions. Success in achieving an NGO mission results in social change, which in turn puts pressure on the NGO to change itself. Failure in achieving its mission also exerts pressure to redefine the NGO's strategy or mission. As social change-oriented organizations, NGOs live on and

promote change. Therefore, change is the very rationale of NGO existence and effectiveness. OD as a planned change intervention for NGO renewal and revitalization is necessary for its continued relevance.

• The core task of NGOs is to bring about some desirable change in an external constituency. By definition, that constituency is outside the jurisdiction and control of the NGO. Therefore, autonomous changes in that constituency generate renewed pressures for change in NGO (Uphoff, 1986). A local community may undergo social, economic, or political changes because of forces operating in the larger environment. Other actors in the community may change on their own. For example, economic liberalization may spur economic development of the community (or society), thereby bringing about significant changes in employment, income, poverty, migration, environmental degradation, and natural resource–use patterns. Government agencies operating in that community (or society) may change their policies, programs, laws, and strategies on their own, thereby increasing or reducing the space for NGO actions in that community (or society). In today's world of increasing globalization, changes in the community (or society) may emanate from multinational corporations or international bilateral and multilateral agencies, further augmenting the space for NGO actions in that community (or society). Thus, independent and autonomous forces create changes in these external constituencies where an NGO conducts its main business (or performs its core development functions). These changes generate significant pressures for change in NGOs, which could be helped through OD.

• Development, nonprofit NGOs often rely on external resources to conduct their business. These resources typically are mobilized from national and international donors, which are interested in bringing about certain desirable developmental impacts on the community (or society) with which an NGO does its main business. This constituency of resource-providers is different and distant from the local community constituency with which the NGO conducts its main business. Major changes and shifts in policies and programs of resource providers and donors have occurred over the past five decades as new lessons are derived from field experiences. As NGOs know well, donors emphasize different development problems at different points in time: Rural development, environment, women's status, microenterprise, and urban poverty are examples of some recent shifts in donor priorities. Priorities and the volume of resources available from international donors change in response to priorities, policies, public opinions, and macro trends in their host countries (Northern, industrialized, developed economies in most cases). Obviously, shifts in donor policies and priorities can significantly affect the functioning of an NGO, thereby necessitating organization change in NGOs. OD can make a contribution here.

• As NGOs gain visibility and prominence as development actors in a community or society, other relationships and expectations in society develop. NGO networks and associations evolve and generate expectations of mutual support and accountability. Media and the general public expect greater transparency and accountability of NGOs. Government agencies demand better data on NGO performance and impacts and make policy and legal regulations to govern NGO activities. Other actors in civil society (e.g., local associations, cooperatives, trade unions, professional associations, academia, and local governance institutions) also expect coordination and support from NGOs. Thus NGOs find themselves in a web of relationships with other autonomous actors and agencies, with conflicting expectations and demands placed on NGOs. These conflicting pressures from external constituencies generate pressures for change in NGOs. OD can help an NGO clarify these pressures (Brown & Covey, 1987b).

Internal Pressure

Likewise, NGOs experience a number of internal pressures for change:

• An NGO typically starts small in scope, coverage, and resources. As it succeeds in its mission, it grows. NGOs experience life cycles of birth, infancy, maturity, and possible decay. Growth in NGOs is generally associated with larger area of operation, a broader set of development interventions, and bigger staffs, budgets, and infrastructures. The methods of organization functioning appropriate for a small, informal group may not be appropriate for a large NGO. Pressures for change are inherent in growth, which itself is change. Typically, NGOs find themselves growing at a rapid pace, in unplanned ways. OD can be a relevant intervention in NGOs for both planning for growth and coping with growth.

• As social change-oriented organizations, NGOs are value driven. NGO staff often are attracted to the values of NGOs and the ideology of social change. The strong values and ideologies, the basis for NGO action, typically are surrounded by conflict and tension. NGOs relate to different constituencies and emphasize their different values accordingly. Enormous differences and conflicts arise in the debate over means and ends in NGOs. As an NGO gains experience, its staff review their theories and strategies of social change. For example, NGOs in South Asia in the late 1970s emphasized conscientization and organization of the poor and the marginalized. Over time, the need to bring community services, development inputs, and economic programs to the poor and marginalized became obvious. Previous staff committed to and experienced in conscientization and organization building came in conflict with newer staff skilled in health, education, and income generation. Differences in preferred ideologies are a typical ground for tensions, splits, and paralysis in NGOs. It is in this context that OD interventions can be helpful for planned change in NGOs.

• As NGOs gain experience and credibility over time, pressures for improved performance and demonstrable results are generated from within. Typically, there are major differences within an NGO about the meaning and indicators of performance results. Process-oriented development interventions, which are most often preferred by NGOs, are difficult to measure. Quantitative tangible targets are easier to measure but not necessarily an integral part of the NGO mission and plan. Pressure to demonstrate results and visible performance impacts generate pressures for change in NGOs (Fowler et al., 1992). OD intervention can be relevant at this juncture in an NGO.

• NGOs typically are set up by committed, idealistic, visionary people who want to make an impact on society. In important ways these people are social entrepreneurs as they take initiatives and risks to stake their values, capacities, reputations, and resources in setting up and nurturing NGOs. By investing their values, energies, and physical and emotional resources and by growing together with an NGO, the founders develop parallel life cycles with their organizations. A founder's association with an NGO reinforces the identity both internally and externally. In such situations, issues of transitions in leadership, building leadership at the level of NGO management, strengthening institutional mechanisms of NGO governance, and systematizing NGO functioning beyond the personal style and idiosyncrasies of the founder–leader gain significance. Therefore, many NGOs find themselves having difficulty with these issues, which generate enormous pressures for change. It is in this context that OD can make a contribution.

These external and internal pressures for change generate needs to restructure NGOs.

NGOs respond to these pressures for change in a variety of ways. Most tend to swim with the tide. They deal with these pressures as the waves come, allowing them to determine their direction or responding to such pressures for change by ignoring them and continuing with business as usual. The response, over time, ultimately results in the same tendency to respond to an outside pressure or an external agenda. Only in a few cases do NGOs recognize the need to change themselves. NGOs as social change organizations get so obsessed with changing others that they typically fail to take notice of the changes that have already occurred within them (e.g., growth) or to address the changes that they need to make in themselves (e.g., restructuring). Even in such situations, where the NGO responds to needed change in organization, it tends to looks for quick-fix partial and temporary solutions. This approach to organization change discourages systematic diagnosis and the development of a long-term perspective on organization renewal. Such a short-term focus was encouraged in the 1970s and 1980s by NGO thinkers, donors, and ideologues who typically viewed NGOs as temporary instruments to solve a limited problem. Such a misconception or narrow conception of NGO roles relegated them to "gap-filling" functions in response to failures of the government or market. It was generally assumed, and explicitly proclaimed, that NGOs should intervene in and withdraw from an area in a short-term, time-bound manner to play this gap-filling role. This conception assumed that NGOs had no role in the efficient functioning of government and market agencies. As a result, long-term organization capacity building, institutional strengthening, and organization development were never valued or supported by NGO leaders, their donors, and their evaluators. The instrument of NGO organization was seen as merely temporary, and therefore any investment in making this involvement valid, relevant, and functional over the long term was considered both unthinkable and undesirable. NGO leaders and their donors or patrons until very recently continued to support only the limited aspect of NGO capacity building that allowed effective execution of short (2- to 3-year) projects funded by a particular donor for a given point in time. This worldview significantly undermined NGO institutional capacity building and limited the possibility of OD interventions in NGOs.

However, beginning in the late 1980s with the advent of fresh thinking on the development trinity (state–market–civil society) and a new perspective of the role of NGOs in a perennially changing society, there is growing recognition of the significance and long-term role of civil society organization in ensuring democratic and equitable development (Brown & Tandon, 1994). This recognition has highlighted the existing reality of weak NGO institutional capacity. OD is being viewed as a possible intervention to build such capacity. Likewise, there is growing acceptance of the need for strong and effective local development institutions (outside the purview of the government) in order to ensure sustained benefits of any development project. This has further promoted the view of NGO institutional capacity building as an important requirement for bringing about desirable development. The analysis in this section helps put in perspective the rationale and timing of the growing interest in OD work with and in NGOs.

STEPS IN OD WITH NGOS

In a typical OD effort, three phases are distinct yet interrelated. What is the meaning of these three phases in OD with NGOs?

Recognizing the Need for Change

The first step in any OD effort is recognition of the need for change. Although pressures for change (both external and internal) operate in NGOs regularly, an NGO may or may not feel the need for change. Typically, the need for change in an NGO may be felt by field project staff, headquarters staff, leaders, or donors. Many times, a project evaluation triggers the need for change in an NGO. Sometimes, a long-term donor partner (which has worked with the NGO over a period of time) notices certain clear needs for change and may discuss them with NGO leadership and staff.

Recognizing the need for change is the first step in the OD process. The recognition of the need for change and commitment to planned change (a hallmark of OD) in an NGO ideally should be made throughout the NGO and its key external partners (such as donors). In reality, it is important to ensure that recognition of the need for and commitment to change are explicitly made by the top leaders of the NGO, preferably including its governing body.

It is also important that this decision to undertake OD as a systematic process of planned change be based on an informed choice of the possible long-term implications of OD on the NGO, its leaders, and future directions. If OD is initiated primarily because of donor pressures, without commensurate commitment from NGO leadership, it is likely to degenerate into a mere report that gathers dust on shelves of the NGO and its donors (as do most evaluation reports of NGO projects) (Agarwal & Tandon, 1996).

Any change from known, habitual ways of functioning to somewhat uncertain future ways generates resistance, anxiety, and apprehension among any set of individuals, groups, and organizations. Therefore, OD efforts to undertake planned change also provoke similar reactions. The nature and form of these reactions in NGOs vary, but it is important to recognize the reality of such reactions. To the extent that typical NGO leaders pay scant attention to the organization dynamics of their NGO, it is not uncommon to find NGO leaders somewhat insensitive to this universal phenomenon of initiating planned change.

Organization Diagnosis

Having articulated and established the need for change and commitment to OD as a vehicle for bringing about planned change, the next important (perhaps the most critical) step is diagnosis. Diagnosis is a systematic process of understanding the NGO, its problems, its future, and so on. Diagnosis typically starts with the aspect of an NGO that has prompted the need for OD. If a project evaluation report has pointed out the inadequate impact of NGO programs on the target group, project planning and implementation may become the starting point for diagnosis. If a donor has pointed out the imbalance in gender composition of senior staff, personnel policies and human resource development may be the starting focus of diagnosis. If a unit of field project focusing on income generation is unable to break even after 10 years of continuous investment, and the NGO chief functionary finds it impossible to raise more resources for that unit, this part of the NGO becomes the starting point of the diagnosis. If acrimonious conflicts between key staff members occur in all staff meetings, then interpersonal relations and team functioning become the starting point of the diagnosis.

Framework of the Diagnosis

Diagnosis implies systematic understanding of the underlying causes of visible problem symptoms. Therefore, whatever the starting point of diagnosis, it cannot be carried out without a clear, holistic, and systemic framework of the NGO as a whole. Understanding of part of an NGO can be enhanced if it is situated in an understanding of the NGO as a whole in its unique external environment. This is the most challenging requirement for an effective diagnosis. It therefore calls for developing and using a framework of understanding NGOs. The key issue here is not to blindly borrow the framework evolved from studies on private corporations or government agencies but to synthesize that theory of organization behavior with our own understanding of the unique features of NGOs. Such a synthesis alone will help in undertaking a diagnosis uniquely relevant to the NGOs (Brown & Covey, 1987a).

Although is not possible to espouse a complete theory of NGO organization here, it may be worthwhile to identify some unique features that must be incorporated in a framework of NGOs.

• As mission-oriented social change organizations, NGOs define desirable outputs in normative, qualitative, and processual terms. This entails establishing the relationship between the broadly defined desirable social changes an NGO stands for, its stated mission, and its program goals and operating strategies.

• As mission-oriented organizations, NGOs operate in a vaguely understood, complex social reality. Because its primary task or core business is conducted outside its boundaries, the organization's relationships with key constituencies in the external environment have a significant impact on its performance. This is further accentuated by the fact that an NGO may need operating and material resources from external donor constituencies, which are typically different and removed from the local community where the NGO intends to have an impact.

• As has been noted, an NGO attracts core staff on the basis of its values and ideology of social change. Such people have primarily a normative (as opposed to merely utilitarian) relationship with the organization. Certain functions, such as accounts and administration, may attract staff for more utilitarian reasons ("I am here for a job" vs. "I am here for a cause"). Among NGO staff, issues of morale, motivation, productivity, and organization culture are affected by this plurality.

- As mentioned earlier, an NGO's form and functioning in many cases reflect the personality of its founder. This makes the founder–leader a very powerful, perhaps central feature of an NGO. Decision making in an NGO therefore is much more personalized.

- Because leaders of most NGOs are committed to a vision, they have an inherent dislike and disregard for the secondary tasks of the NGO (e.g., financial management, office and infrastructure maintenance, personnel, and legal matters). These aspects, coupled with a quest for flexibility and responsiveness in relation to programs, makes NGOs rather unorganized systems (in contrast to an overorganized government bureaucracy or factory) (Brown, 1980). Many aspects of NGO functioning—its structure, rules, procedures, systems, role definitions, delegation, and accountability—remain fluid, ambiguous, and informal.

- Finally, as mentioned earlier, NGOs operate in a web of multiple stakeholders, many of whom are in conflict with each other. Besides its governing body, top leaders, core program staff, field workers, and other staff, local community groups, sociopolitical formations, donors and supporters, government development agencies and regulatory bodies, other NGOs, and the public at large all seem to have diverse and sometimes conflicting stakes in a given NGO (Gricar & Brown, 1981). Thus, effective NGO functioning sometimes implies a sensitive and delicate balancing of diverse stakeholders toward a well-activated and coherent mission.

Process of Diagnosis

A second set of issues in diagnosis relates to its processes. Diagnosis implies data collection and analysis. It is essentially a research exercise to deepen understanding of an NGO. By agreeing to initiate an OD process and by starting a diagnosis, an NGO initiates a certain type of intervention. So that the results of diagnosis can be used to improve NGO functioning, the process of conducting the diagnosis becomes crucial. Participation in diagnosis by key leaders and by the widespread membership of the organization helps to generate commitment to the findings and builds the basis for implementing organization change. It also ensures authentic data collection and analysis. This approach to diagnosis is distinctly different from the diagnosis of sickness by a medical doctor (in which the doctor as expert makes the diagnosis of a patient's condition and prescribes treatment) (Grinnell, 1969). The participatory process of diagnosis in OD therefore must be carefully planned and effectively facilitated.

Interventions

Based on the diagnosis, the analysis of the findings, and the decisions of the NGO members, concrete planning of interventions to improve the effectiveness and health of the NGO is undertaken (Friedlander & Brown, 1989). The nature, range, and depth of these interventions sometimes are linked to OD technologies and practices. However, the nature of the issues highlighted by the diagnosis determines the types of appropriate OD interventions. In a specific NGO context, OD interventions fall into four categories. Appropriate interventions in each category are briefly highlighted in this section.

Identity and Strategy

Common OD interventions to help clarify the identity and strategy of an NGO typically are included here. Given the nature of their changing external environment, NGOs find that they periodically need to rearticulate their vision, reformulate their mission, and redefine the broad components of their development strategy. This type of OD intervention is broadly called strategic planning. It entails a strength, weakness, opportunity, and threat analysis. It entails a systematic and comprehensive constituency mapping (identifying and elaborating the current and desired relationships with various key constituencies such as the local community, government agencies, donors, other NGOs, and other groups in civil society); it generates specific strategic options from which the NGO has to choose the one that will define its medium-term (3–5 years) posture, identity, and programs. The reformulated mission then becomes the basis for elaborating program objectives; the redefined strategy provides the basis of planning activities.

This type of OD intervention typically entails close involvement and decision making by NGO leaders, including the governing body. If an OD intervention starts with strategic planning, it creates a series of options and implications for rearranging the organization's planning, design and staff role allocations. This is a comprehensive organization-wide intervention that typically results in major renewal of the NGO as a whole.

OD interventions in this category sometimes involve search conferences. This method promotes a reformulation of external partnerships and relationships of an NGO with its external environment. This is an interorganizational intervention, typically bringing together diverse stakeholders to explore, analyze, and plan joint initiatives. Networking is another outcome of such an intervention. Typically, it helps build and strengthen an NGO's relationships with key segments of its external environment. This type of intervention is sometimes called institutional strengthening.

Human Processual

This category of OD interventions is the most popular and common feature of any OD exercise. These interventions focus on the human dimensions of an NGO. Such interventions help improve the processes of functioning of an NGO. These processes may be communication, participation, decision making, conflict resolution, individual motivation, commitment and morale, organization norms, values, culture, and leadership styles. Historically, OD interventions primarily addressed such human and process issues.

Human Resource Development. Human resource development (HRD), human resource management, human potential development, and training of individual staff is one subset of interventions in this category. It comprises of two aspects.

First, it entails establishing or strengthening HRD policies and systems in an NGO. Traditional personnel functions such as recruitment, induction, orientation, role allocation, service condition, compensation, individual career planning, and performance review are generally included here.

Despite their people-centered development philosophy, most NGOs have inadequate personnel policies and systems. The second category of interventions implies ongoing training and capacity building of staff. Specially designed training can reform attitudes, build awareness and knowledge, and develop professional, technical, and managerial skills. It may also include a focus on personal growth and development (Lynton & Pareek, 1990). Even when an NGO uses training as an OD intervention, it rarely looks at it as long-term human power planning and as HRD for people in the future. Hence, within the framework of OD and in response to organization diagnosis, this set of interventions is critical in many NGOs.

Process Consultation. The second subset of this category is interventions that help to improve processes in an organization (Schein, 1988). One common example is team building, which focuses on improving the functional processes of a team. Another example is role clarification and negotiation between supervisors and subordinates and between work team members.

Process consultation as a method facilitating understanding and improving the functioning of a manager, leader, work team, production unit, or NGO is a commonly practiced OD intervention of this type.

Third-party consultation or peacemaking and intergroup confrontation meeting or mirroring are other examples of OD interventions aimed at improving interdepartmental relations, collaboration, and processes. Such interventions are particularly suited to conditions in which interdepartmental conflict exists.

Certain OD interventions also aim at improving the informal culture of the organization to improve task performance and organization effectiveness. This entails changing and developing norms and values that are implicitly practiced in the NGO with a view to aligning them more closely with preferred norms and values and with requirements of organization effectiveness.

Technostructural

The third category of OD interventions focuses on technology and structure of an NGO. Technology means ways, techniques, and equipment needed for doing the core business or primary tasks of an NGO. For example, the technology of water harvesting is different from the technology of primary health care. This set of OD interventions attempts to build congruence between desired technology and organization structure. Structure means tasks (both primary and secondary), groupings of tasks into roles, role responsibility and accountability, reporting relationships, rules, procedures, and systems.

Typically, NGOs as underorganized systems need formalization of job and role descriptions, clarification and formalization of reporting relationships (e.g., the relationship of chairperson, treasurer, and chief functionary roles), formalization of certain routine decisions into component parts (e.g., hours of work, leave, approved expenditures), delegation procedures

(e.g., procedures for taking an advance from accounts), and systems (e.g., filing and record-keeping). Systems of program planning, monitoring, and evaluation, management information systems for decision making, and systems of financial management and reporting are other typical examples for NGOs. Instead of loosening existing rules, procedures, and systems, NGOs typically need interventions to formalize and systematize many of their ways of internal functioning.

Another set of OD interventions in this category focuses on improving staff creativity, responsibility, and morale through job design (for individuals) and work design (for work teams). Increasingly, some OD interventions in NGOs also address the introduction of new technology, particularly information technology; certain OD interventions aim at integrating that technology into the NGO. A common OD approach to this set of interventions is called the sociotechnical systems approach, in which the design of human, structural, and technical components of an organization is undertaken.

Overall, this set of OD interventions entails simultaneous attention to the technology and structure of an NGO.

External Relations

Development NGOs are facing a set of new pressures in relation to their external relationships. This fourth category of interventions focuses on strengthening this aspect of NGOs. The first type of interventions could be categorized under the broad theme of network building. In civil society as a whole, and among development NGOs more specifically, there is a growing need for networking. Building such relationships and types of mutual obligations through networking can be relevant at different levels, such as local, national, and global.

Another type of intervention focuses on building relations with other actors in civil society through coalitions, alliances, and partnerships. Interorganizational arrangements to pursue a common agenda in a time-, resource-, and activity-bound manner is a critical focus of such interventions.

Outside the development and civil society sector, NGO relations with government, media, academia, and private business have also acquired new priority. OD interventions aimed at helping build such relations and nurture them in pursuit of the NGO mission are becoming increasingly vertical. Interorganizational power and interinstitutional webs become key concepts to address in such OD interventions.

In sum, therefore, a wide range of OD intervention is available for use in NGOs in response to the diagnosis. Likewise, the planning for each of these OD interventions has to be undertaken in such a manner that those affected by it and the leaders of the NGO are fully involved and own the implementation of these interventions. Similarly, monitoring the implementation of OD interventions and evaluating the results must be planned in advance and undertaken in earnest in order to draw lessons for future improvements in the NGO.

PREREQUISITES FOR OD IN NGOS

There are several prerequisites for effective OD exercise in NGOs.

• A major issue in any OD exercise is the explicit commitment of the leaders to the challenges of revitalizing the organization. In the case of NGOs, this typically implies commitment of the founder–leader and the governing body of the NGO. Even when such a need is fulfilled, certain other needs must be addressed.

• One question invariably faced is the facilitation of OD. Who should do the diagnosis? Who has competence for OD interventions? The expertise and professional competence needed for OD diagnosis and intervention, and its acceptance as such, usually are not available in an NGO. Some large-scale private corporations and government agencies have in-house OD departments and competence. Even they periodically use external consultants for facilitation of some critical aspects of OD (such as top-management team-building exercises). NGOs may need to invite external facilitators for organization diagnosis and intervention if they opt for OD.

• Another prerequisite relates to time. When does an NGO do OD? How long does OD take? Clearly, OD is not a perpetual exercise. OD is undertaken periodically (every 3–5 years) in response to existing problems and anticipated internal and external pressures for change. The time taken by OD depends on its scope of coverage and depth of intervention. Typically, for a large NGO, a comprehensive OD exercise may take 12–24 months (if relying exclusively on external consultants).

• There is also the question of the resources needed for OD. Resources include the time of top leaders, other NGO staff who participate in diagnosis and interventions, resources for meetings, workshops, studies, and external consultants. Explicit and early commitment of resources for OD as an investment helps a great deal in undertaking such an exercise.

It is important for NGOs to pay attention to these prerequisites before committing themselves to an OD exercise.

FUTURE ISSUES FOR OD IN NGOS

As explained in the previous sections, OD with NGOs is a fairly new yet rapidly growing trend. In order for OD to be appropriate, relevant, and effective in strengthening and developing NGOs and their capacities, practitioners of OD and NGO leaders and their partners need to think carefully about some key issues.

• The first issue relates to the demand for OD with NGOs. Is this demand for OD with NGOs driven largely by donors? Are donors asking for OD for NGOs that they support in order to ensure optimum use of their funds for the partnered projects? Or is this demand also coming from the NGO's leaders? If it is merely the former (driven by donors' demand), then OD faces the risk of becoming short sighted (only for NGOs with funds to spend for a specific project) and short lived (only as long as major donors think OD is a panacea for the ills they face in working with NGOs). Sustained institutional development of the entire sector of NGOs and civil society should be promoted as the long-term goal of OD, not merely OD for a single NGO for short-term project implementation. Commitment to such an approach of OD requires both NGO leadership and donors.

• The available technology of OD is drawn largely from the practice and theory of large organizations of the market and the state. The frameworks for understanding the organization of civil society must be developed for more appropriate diagnosis of NGOs. Likewise, methods and techniques more appropriate to NGO size, culture, primary tasks, and leadership must be developed to use OD effectively in NGOs.

• This has also implications for the development of appropriate sets of ethics, values, and standards for OD with NGOs. The professionalization of OD and systematic standardization of the practice have occurred in mainstream OD work. More NGO-relevant values of OD must be articulated, and standards of professional conduct of OD with NGOs must be specified. Otherwise, unqualified people will be able to sell whatever they do to NGOs, calling all of it OD.

• Finally, there is a woeful shortage of trained and competent OD facilitators for NGOs. OD practitioners in private corporations and government bureaucracies are being drawn in as OD consultants and facilitators. Long-term capacity building of OD facilitators for NGOs must be undertaken to respond to the growing need for such professional competence. It also poses challenges for building in-house OD capacity in larger NGOs, their training units, and NGO support organizations. Long-term viability of civil society factors entails strengthening of their institutional base, and appropriate OD interventions can contribute to that process.

REFERENCES

Agarwal, S., & Tandon, R. (1996, May). CASA's experience from OD process: Challenges, advantages and constraints. *Journal of Institutional Development, 3*(1), 28–36.

Beckhard, R. (Ed.). (1969). *Organizational development.* Reading, MA: Addison-Wesley.

Brown, L. D. (1980). Planned change in underorganized systems. In T. G. Cummings (Ed.), *Systems theory for organization development* (pp. 181–203). New York: John Wiley & Sons.

Brown, L. D., & Covey, J. G. (1987a). Development organizations and organization development: Toward an expanded paradigm for organization development. In R. W. Woodman & W. E. Pasmore (Eds.), *Research in organizational change and development* (Vol. 1, pp. 59–88). Greenwich, CT: JAI.

Brown, L. D., & Covey, J. G. (1987b). Organization development in social change organizations: Some implications for practice. *IDR Reports, 4*(2), 1–12.

Brown, L. D., & Tandon, R. (1994, November). Institutional development for strengthening civil society. *Journal of Institutional Development, 1*(i), 3–17.

Clark, J. (1991). *Democratizing development.* London: Earthscan.

Community Development Resource Association. (1994–1995). Capacity building. In *Community development resource association annual report 1994/95* (pp. 2–21). Woodstock, South Africa: Author.

Fowler, A., Campbell, P., & Pratt, B. (1992). *Institutional development and NGOs in*

Africa: Policy perspectives for European development agencies. Oxford, UK: INTRAC.

Friedlander, F., & Brown, L. D. (1989). Organization development. In W. L. French, C. H. Bell, & R. A. Zawacki (Eds.), *Organization development: Theory, practice and research* (pp. 41–57). Homewood, IL: BPI/Irwin.

Gricar, B. F., & Brown, L. D. (1981). Conflict, power and organizations in a changing community. *Human Relations, 34*(10), 877–893.

Grinnell, S. (1969, Winter). Organizational development: An introductory overview. *The Business Quarterly,* 24–31.

IFCB. (1998). *Report of the first IFCB global conference, Brussels.* Washington, DC: Author.

Lynton, R. P., & Pareek, U. (1990). *Training for development.* Bloomfield, CT: Kumarian.

MDF. (1994, September 12–30). Institutional development & organizational strengthening. *MDF Conference Papers,* 128–142.

Schein, E. H. (1988). *Process consultation* (2nd ed.). Reading, MA: Addison-Wesley.

Tandon, R., & Bandyopadhyay, K. K. (2003). *Capacity building Southern NGOs: Lessons from the international forum on capacity building.* New Delhi: IFCB/PRIA.

Tandon, R., & Mohanty, R. (2002). *Civil society and governance.* New Delhi: PRIA/Samskriti.

Uphoff, N. (1986). *Local institutional development: An analytical source book with cases.* Bloomfield, CT: Kumarian.

33

Developing Interorganizational Networks

RUPERT F. CHISHOLM

Interorganizational networks assumed increasing importance in the 1990s, and the importance of them as a new form of organization will continue to grow well into the 21st century. Observers such as Alter and Hage (1993) predict that networks will become the key form of organizing over the next 25 years or so. And Castells (2000) indicates that networks are needed to provide disparate parties connectedness around shared, reconstructed identities. Many other writers (e.g., Aldrich, 1999; Clegg & Hardy, 1999) also note the growing relevance of networks for the foreseeable future. Given this heightened importance, it is crucial for organization development and change (ODC) scholars and practitioners to understand key features of these complex systems and ways of conceptualizing, planning, and conducting efforts to develop them.

This chapter gives an overview of the nature of networks, with special emphasis on features that distinguish the form of ODC needed to develop them from much past work in this field.

It also outlines a general process for approaching ODC in efforts to develop specific interorganizational networks. Although the specifics of each development process vary with context (e.g., surrounding environment, vision, stakeholder configuration, history of existing relationships), identifying phases and dynamics in a general development process should help inform future efforts. The chapter begins by describing the nature of networks and identifying key features of these systems that have important implications for ODC work. The final part of this section gives brief descriptions of three actual network organizations formed to meet the unique demands of situations in three different world locations. The next section provides the context for understanding the growing importance of networks by identifying several underlying forces operating in the general environment of organizations in the new century and the types of metaproblems that stem from these conditions. The next section presents a general process that has been used to develop several interorganizational networks in diverse settings. The next section covers the nature of action research needed to develop and maintain network systems. A concluding section summarizes the essential points from the chapter, captures learnings from earlier ODC efforts to develop interorganizational networks, and offers glimpses of the future.

NETWORK ORGANIZATIONS

The term *network* is commonly used in current writings on organizations and management. And common usage to refer to a variety of organization forms often leads to confusion about the identity and nature of network systems. Nohira and Eccles (1992) state that the network concept is used in so many different ways that it has lost much of its inherent meaning. These authors identify two different uses of the term *network*. The first use notes a new, highly organic form of organization that is coming into being to meet requirements of fast-paced, rapidly changing, information-rich environments that contain high levels of uncertainty. The second use involves electronic networks that rest on advanced forms of information processing and communication technologies (e.g., e-mail, computer databases, videoconferencing) (Nohira & Eccles, 1992). Other uses of *network* abound and include such terms as *strategic alliances, cluster organizations, networking, consortia,* and *virtual organizations*. Because of the wide variety of possible uses, it is necessary to clarify the meaning of network organization used in this chapter.

A network is all of the organizational or social units connected by a specific type of relationship (Jay, 1964). Conceptually, a network may develop at various levels. These levels include intergroup, interdepartmental, interorganizational, ecological, and international. In addition, a particular network may depend on one or more of the following types of relational content: communication content, the exchange of information between entities; exchange

content, the flow of goods or services between units; or normative content, shared expectations that network member units have of one another based on some social feature (Aldrich & Whetten, 1981). Networks also may develop to enable members to actuate increased political, social, or economic power and to legitimate new social structures (Gerlach & Palmer, 1981). Or networks may involve workflow, communication, or friendship links (Brass & Burkhardt, 1992). Following the concepts of Nonaka and Takeuchi (1995), experience suggests that networks also have the potential to create knowledge (i.e., developing a system that breaks with the past and discovers or creates new opportunities). Thus, networks may vary greatly by purpose or function as well as by level.

This chapter uses Eric Trist's socioecological perspective to conceptualize and discuss development of network organizations (Finsrud, 1995; Trist, 1983, 1985). Table 33.1 highlights key features of this view of interorganizational networks.

Several comments help explain key features identified in Table 33.1.

• A new frame: Interorganizational networks operate largely as abstract conceptual systems that enable members to perceive and understand large-scale problems in new ways. Developing deep, multifaceted shared appreciations (Vickers, 1965) makes it possible for members to create ways of organizing to deal with these complex large-scale problems. Networks enable members to engage in sensemaking (Weick, 1995) processes that lead to inventing ways of collaborating to deal with large-scale, complex problems or issues.

• Ecological level (beyond interorganizational relationships): Networks are different from mere interorganizational relationships. They operate at a higher level: the ecological level. Networks improve the ability of organizations to deal with ill-defined, complex problems or

Table 33.1 Key Features of Interorganizational Networks

Conceptual system	Member organizations consciously develop networks to help understand and deal with complex, ambiguous problems and issues ("messes").
	Primary work of networks involves devising ways for members to think about, create, plan, conduct, and evaluate collaborative activity.
System level	Networks exist at a level above interorganizational relationships.
	Member organizations come together to deal with complex metaproblems that necessitate collaborative work by many organizations.
	A shared vision and common purpose orient and guide a network and its work. These ground the network at the suprasystem level.
Loosely coupled	Member organizations belong to a network voluntarily and meet as needed to conduct work.
	A horizontal form of organization exists. Member organizations are equal, with no superior–subordinate relationships.
	Members control the network and its activities.
Self-regulating	Member organizations are responsible for developing a shared understanding of a problem or issue.
	Member organizations plan, initiate, and manage network activities.
Basic functions	Network organizations have three basic functions:
	Regulation: Maintaining orientation of the network to the shared vision and purpose; ensuring development and maintenance of network values and appropriate ways of organizing activities.
	Appreciation: Developing a shared understanding of changes to the network vision and purpose needed to incorporate issues and trends that emerge over time.
	Development support: Providing professional organization development resources needed to develop, maintain, and manage the network.

SOURCE: From Chisholm, R. F. *Developing network organizations: Learning from practice and theory,* © 1998, p. 7. Adapted by permission of Pearson Education, Inc., Upper Saddle River, New Jersey.

issues that individual members cannot handle alone. Network activity is grounded in the shared higher-level vision, purpose, and goals that bind member organizations together. These act as a superordinate goal (Sharif, 1962) that incorporates but transcends the interests of individual member organizations. Having a shared vision requires members to collaborate to bring about the vision that fosters positive intergroup relationships (Sharif, 1962). Forming and developing a system to achieve a shared larger purpose is the hallmark of network organizations from the socioecological perspective. This orientation affects the basic

worldview and all aspects of developing a network and conducting its activities.

• Loose coupling of member organizations: Members represent diverse organizations that are physically dispersed and meet from time to time to conduct activities needed to carry out the higher-level system purpose. Belonging to a network is voluntary, with few formal organization structures and processes that make involvement permanent. Networks also rest on a horizontal rather than a hierarchical organizing principle; one organization or member does not

have a superior–subordinate relationship
with another. In brief, these systems build on
Granovetter's (1973) concept of the strength
of weak ties.

• Self-regulation: Network organizations
are self-regulating. Members, not a centralized source of power, are responsible for
forming, developing, and maintaining the
system and for initiating and managing work
activities. Members direct and control activities, and the organization rests on a shared
understanding of issues. In short, the organization *is* the ways members devise to relate to
each other and the external environment in
carrying out work necessary to bring about a
shared vision of a desired future state. The
shared vision provides the context that orients
all network activity. Retaining this orientation through ongoing sensemaking (Weick,
1995) activities is critical to network survival
and development.

The following statements capture the essence
of network organizing principles:

• Participants are included because of
their interest in or ability to contribute to
constructive action.

• Network members are loosely coupled
and participate in system activities voluntarily.

• Activities and decisions revolve around a
broad vision or purpose and a set of general
goals that incorporate the interests of the
diverse organizations, groups, and individuals
involved in work of the system (Brown, 1987).

According to Trist (1983), interorganizational networks perform three basic functions.
The first function is regulating: ensuring
appropriate orientation, value maintenance,
and organization of the network. Regulating
involves maintaining the network as a unique
social system of stakeholders. Developing
a shared appreciation (Vickers, 1965) of a
desirable future and of trends and issues that

emerge over time is the second function. The
third function involves providing tangible
infrastructure support through expertise in
organizing, maintaining, and managing the
network. In one study (Chisholm, 1996), participants in a community economic and social
development coalition largely confirmed these
functions as appropriate for an interorganizational network.

EXAMPLES OF INTERORGANIZATIONAL NETWORKS

This section gives brief descriptions of three
interorganizational networks that were developed in three countries to deal with quite different situations. The Nordvest Forum has
functioned as a learning network of small and
medium organizations in the northwest coastal
region of Norway since 1989 (Hanssen-Bauer
& Snow, 1996). The second case, the Collaborative Alliance for Romanian Orphans,
emerged in 1990 to deal with a crisis following
collapse of the national government (Bilimoria,
Wilmot, & Cooperrider, 1996). The New
Baldwin Corridor Coalition has developed
over 12 years as a network of business, labor,
government, education, and community organizations and economic development agencies
that fosters broad economic and social development of the greater Harrisburg, Pennsylvania
area (Chisholm, 1998). Brief descriptions of
these networks are intended to communicate
the basic nature of real-life interorganizational
networks, how they operate, and the content
of their work.

Nordvest Forum (NVF)

NVF began as a collaborative effort of
employers in a remote region of Norway to
deal with a shortage of qualified managers.
Leading industries in the region include fish
processing, ship building, marine equipment,
and furniture manufacturing. Its coastal location and industrial mix make the region highly

dependent on international trade; consequently, the economy is especially sensitive to international competition.

The stated purpose of the NVF is "to improve regional competitiveness by upgrading the management capacity of (members) companies and other firms in the region" (Hanssen-Bauer & Snow, 1996, p. 417). Key features of the network include the following:

- Purpose: Increasing the competitiveness of the region as a whole (not just that of individual member companies).
- Membership: Open to all firms in the region. Organizations are loosely linked to the network and can join or leave it at will. Both members and nonmembers are included in the scope of NVF work.
- Strategy: Triggering and supporting learning to improve the professional capabilities of managers in the region.
- Resources: A full-time managing director and two part-time senior management training and development professionals have carried out much of the basic design, facilitation, and coordination work of the network. NVF relies heavily on professional resources of other organizations and institutions. This approach is consistent with the defined network role of identifying needed resources and providing strategic guidance rather than building up a large central staff of service providers.
- Programs: Two programs have been developed to stimulate and support management learning in the region. The Management of Change Program requires each manager to engage directly in an ODC project that increases some aspect of a company's capacity to compete internationally. An experienced manager serves as a mentor to each participant in the program. The Top Management Forum provides time, space, and designed activities that give senior executives opportunities to discuss regional issues, learn about international management topics, and develop personal and professional relationships. NVF also conducts work that builds the network and participating firms as learning organizations.

Action research shows that positive outcomes of network activities occurred at three levels: individual, helping managers form interpersonal relationships; organizational, fostering change through organization development; and regional, improving general perceptions of the region in the business press. Other positive outcomes include developing the capacity to influence key resource and policy institutions in the external environment and clusters of organizations spontaneously forming several mini-networks within NVF to foster information exchange, learning, and solutions to common problems. Based on these and other accomplishments, the Norwegian government chose several NVF projects as showcase examples of successful business development, and the National Research Council decided to fund action research to support, facilitate, and capture learnings from future NVF work.

Collaborative Alliance for Romanian Orphans

Network activity resulted from a crisis that surfaced in Romania in 1990 after the collapse of the national government and health care system. Part of the situation involved more than 140,000 infants and small children who were left to die in state-run institutions. After an edition of the ABC TV program *20/20* aired, large donations of money and goods (valued at more than $8 million) flooded World Vision, a private volunteer organization that had operated in Romania for many years. The size and complexity of the relief effort caused severe organization problems (e.g., overloading Romanian political, economic, and social agencies; intuitive "solutions," including orphan adoption, causing more problems than they solved; deteriorated health care system). Encountering these problems led to a change in strategy from providing direct assistance to developing Romanian capacity to conduct the necessary work.

Recognition of the need for strategic intervention through the health care system resulted in a knowledge alliance, Integrative Program Development (IDP). IDP developed a large network of formal and informal alliances of diverse organizations from various countries around the world. A shared vision of providing for the total developmental needs of Romanian children guided the network through four stages of development: emergency relief, rehabilitation, community empowerment, and knowledge alliance. Development stages demanded different primary concerns, time frames, actors, and organization roles. For example, the organization role changed from the doer role of relief work to the bridging role of the knowledge alliance (Bilimoria et al., 1996).

Developing IPD as a knowledge network involved creating vision and mission statements that fostered links between many organizations throughout the world. More than 125 diverse organizations joined the network with a three-organization consortium coordinating work. Two programs stemmed from this work:

- Romanian Orphans Social and Educational Redevelopment Project (ROSES) provided short-run assistance to children and training to service providers. Following IPD strategy, ROSES emphasized developing the capacity of Romanian agencies and institutions to provide necessary services.
- The Medical Education Redevelopment Project (MERP) replenished the Romanian medical information system, which government policy had isolated from other countries for more than 15 years. Advanced CD-ROM and video technologies enabled libraries of the eight medical schools to provide medical workers with the latest information in a short time period.

Several outcomes resulted from the work of the Collaborative Alliance for Romanian Orphans:

- Providing immediate emergency assistance: The estimated value of this immediate assistance exceeded $8 million.
- Developing the ROSES program: During the first year, this program trained 250 medical

students and academicians and 60 orphanage staff persons. This training improved the care of an estimated 40,000 children.
- Developing the MERP: In a short period, the libraries of the eight Romanian medical schools became current with the latest research and knowledge through advanced CD-ROM and video technologies.
- Building a global network: A network of more than 125 diverse organizations from many parts of the world was established, and a three-organization consortium to coordinate and manage the system was devised.
- Forming many mini-networks: Over time, many interorganizational networks began to emerge spontaneously to deal with the complexity inherent in coordinating and delivering services and to reflect particular stakeholders' strengths and values. Over time, these systems became increasingly self-managing.

New Baldwin Corridor Coalition (NBCC)

NBCC is a network of business, labor, government, education, and other key organizations and institutions that attempts to catalyze and support collaboration to develop a community for the 21st century. New Baldwin has evolved since 1992 from a series of open community meetings. The network vision emphasizes the need to involve all parts of the community in inventing new ways of thinking and taking action to bring about and sustain basic change in organizations and the total community. Initially, a steering committee of representatives of stakeholder organizations and a set of task forces carried out work. Over time, a board of directors, which meets monthly, has assumed the role of managing the network and relating activities to the larger community. Committees (e.g., education, community development, economic development, membership) are responsible for various key functions. A part-time coordinator at Penn State, Harrisburg, provides the only permanent staff. Member organizations give substantial in-kind support, and grants provide funds for projects and special activities.

Since its inception, NBCC has attempted to fill a unique role in the community. This role involves bringing representatives of key organizations, institutions, and groups together to identify essential development needs and help mobilize the resources needed to meet these basic needs. New Baldwin does not provide direct services (e.g., training) but identifies and helps identify or develop the types of services needed to advance basic organization and resource development. Specific activities that exemplify coalition work include convening several open community meetings to organize the network and gain community support through direct involvement and developing a mission statement adopted by representatives at an open community meeting.

The statement includes the following:

• Establish a coalition of government, labor, community, business, and education leaders.

• Involve every regional institution in the creation of a prototypical 21st-century community that can compete globally and provide an advanced standard of living.

• Acknowledge the need for major cultural change in our institutions and ourselves. Accept the need to think differently about how we deal with and solve problems.

• Prove that existing communities can convert to meet global realities.

• Focus on business revival, educational integration, human resource issues, governmental restructuring, housing and human services, and research and technology (Chisholm, 1998).

In essence, the statement defined a need for systemic change to occur through the involvement of all basic organizations and institutions in the community. It also indicated that a new form of organization (a network) and new ways of thinking and operating would be needed. Major coalition activities include the following:

• Sponsoring an interview survey of area business organizations to determine management perceptions of NBCC. Survey results were fed back to network members and the larger community to provide information for future work.

• Convening a search conference of 96 representatives of stakeholder organizations to identify factors needed for global competitiveness of the region, ways for network organizations to help each other, and ways for the coalition to help member organizations. The conference had a substantial impact on developing the network and its role and on establishing NBCC in the larger community.

• Forming an education committee with representatives from public education (seven school districts plus two vocational schools), Harrisburg Area Community College, and Penn State, Harrisburg. Committee work led to substantial collaboration in joint strategic planning, conducting a community education survey, and inventing ways of sharing resources and training between school districts.

• Forming a consortium of manufacturing organizations, unions, and education providers to identify common training needs and develop and offer training needed by area firms.

• Sponsoring a Family Sustaining Jobs Initiative to encourage local organizations to identify jobs, training, and potential employees who can benefit from focused skill development. The program emphasizes improving the area employee pool and helping people develop skills that enable them to hold jobs that provide sufficient income to support a family.

Important outcomes of coalition work include the following:

• Obtaining recognition in the community for identifying a crucial broad issue, focusing attention on it, and preparing and organizing a systemic approach to deal with it.

• Achieving a workable level of understanding among coalition members, its role compared with those of other organizations, and how it should be organized and managed.

• Demonstrating the ability to bring diverse groups of people together to begin building an industrial community for the 21st century in a conservative area.

- Developing the capacity to convene, design, and manage events that can have significant impacts on the community (e.g., development and planning conferences, meetings, surveys and feedback) using an action research approach.
- Demonstrating the capacity to carry out much work successfully with modest outside funding. This has been achieved through substantial contributions of in-kind services and pro bono work. These contributions, in turn, show a high level of commitment and motivation by many coalition members.

These brief descriptions of the three networks merely sketch some of the key features of these real-life organizations. These sketches provide real-life examples of interorganizational networks designed to carry out higher-level purposes and some aspects of how they function. Additional details appear in the references.

GROWING IMPORTANCE OF NETWORKS

Why are interorganizational networks becoming increasingly important in the 21st century? What forces are driving this phenomenon? This section attempts to answer this question.

Current environmental conditions place complex, often conflicting demands on organizations. Technological change, constantly expanding knowledge, globalization, and changing beliefs and values combine with other aspects of the environment to cause the turbulence many organizations face. System theory posits that a system or organization must have sufficient variety to match the variety present in its environment (Ashby, 1960). Similarly, organization theory (Lawrence & Lorsch, 1967) indicates that the design and structure of an organization must reflect the complexity of its operating environment. The network construct provides a basis for conceiving, designing, implementing, and managing development efforts in such highly complex situations.

Technology

Computers, microprocessors, and other rapid information-processing devices make up the lead technology of the postindustrial era (Emery, 1978). Increasingly, computers and rapid communication systems enable managers to link remote locations and integrate total work processes. Manufacturing organizations no longer have to hire large numbers of employees at one location to produce products. Insurance and financial service companies have data-processing units located in many other countries. Transportation technologies (e.g., ultrasonic aircraft, regional "supertrains," integrated multimodal transportation) also contribute to the diminishing importance of place (Knoke, 1996). In short, advanced technology is increasingly ushering in an era of placelessness. A placeless society has the capacity to make almost everything, including people, knowledge, and other resources, available anywhere in the world, often simultaneously (Knoke, 1996).

Castells (2000) asserts that advanced computer information technology is ushering in a new social paradigm. A key feature of this paradigm is the networking logic of any system that uses this technology. More important, he states that the "monopoly of the network seems to be well adapted to increasing complexity of interaction and to unpredictable patterns of development arising from the creative power of such interaction" (Castells, 2000, p. 70). Briefly stated, network structure and processes enable these systems to incorporate the differentiation, integration, and flexibility needed to use advanced computer information technologies effectively in complex, unpredictable environments.

Knowledge

More than a quarter century ago, Bell (1976) noted that advanced industrial societies around the world had entered a postindustrial era. Leading features of this transition include increased professionalism of the workplace, rising importance of theoretical knowledge, and a growing share of the economy providing services instead of goods. Knowledge creation and use, in turn, lead to more complex work roles that have several leading features:

- Customization: increased emphasis on quality and personalized service
- Information use: need for expanded search for information
- Skill levels: higher skill levels
- Discretion: increased employee discretion with fewer specific guidelines and rules (Hage & Powers, 1992, p. 51)

Although the growing importance of knowledge seems certain, emphasis to date has been on acquiring, accumulating, disseminating, and using existing knowledge. Creating new knowledge in organizations has been largely overlooked (Nonaka & Takeuchi, 1995). A properly designed network can help a set of organizations meet the need to generate new knowledge and use existing knowledge effectively (Powell, 1998). Potentially, this provides a network system and other entities affected by its activity with a competitive advantage in the global marketplace.

Globalization

Postindustrialism is generating changes in political and economic institutions. For example, as traditional nation-states decline in relative importance (Korten, 1995), transfers of responsibilities will occur, with some functions shifting to international organizations and others to subnational levels. Economic institutions also will change, showing a corresponding shift to multilevel arrangements. Many different arrangements will emerge.

American and European dominance of the world economy is rapidly passing, and in its place a global century has begun. Having world-class status to compete successfully in the new age entails several things:

- Concepts: the best and latest knowledge and ideas
- Competence: the ability to meet the highest operating standards that exist anywhere in the world
- Connections: effective links to other people, organizations, and institutions around the globe
- Cosmopolitanism: a comprehensive, complex view of the world (Kanter, 1995)

These changes in economic and political institutions cause many conflicting pressures on managers and political leaders in the new era. Private and public managers increasingly find it necessary to align activities with forces from various levels: local, regional, national, and international. Success under these circumstances entails collaboration, not singular activity. It also entails flexibility and the capacity to change organizations rapidly. Interorganizational networks have the potential of enabling managers to meet these complex, conflicting requirements of globalization.

Beliefs and Values

Several global trends are contributing to the need for a new set of beliefs (Laszlo, 1994). For example, rapid population growth poses a serious threat to the carrying capacity of the earth, and uneven population increases between industrialized and nonindustrialized countries make the problem worse. Deforestation, changing weather patterns, and energy production represent other basic threats to the planet. Faith in technological fixes and other industrial-era beliefs and values have led to the present situation; consequently, a new set of basic beliefs about how things work and how they should work is needed.

Laszlo (1994) identifies the following two key industrial-age beliefs and contrasts them with those needed in the postindustrial era:

- System orientation: Individuals, groups, organizations, and nations working together for the good of the whole (postindustrial) versus looking out only for self and belief in the "invisible hand."

- Type of system: Holistic view of organizations and social systems (postindustrial) versus machine model. The new view emphasizes total system design, contrasted with analysis and design of each component with little concern for its role in the system as a whole.

Although the industrial age is passing, its values and beliefs continue to guide most economic, social, and political organizations. New beliefs and values are needed to enable humankind to deal effectively with many large problems and to create a desirable future. Interorganizational networks provide a primary way of fostering new beliefs and values and inventing or discovering new ways of putting them into practice in specific situations.

CURRENT PROBLEMS

The changing environment leads to new types of problems. Many current socioeconomic problems are complex and share several important characteristics. National problems include sustainable community development, education reform, workforce development, an increasing gap between the very rich and very poor, and environmental quality. Global problems include environmental degradation, increasing numbers of marginalized people, and chronic hunger and poverty. Authors use various names for such recalcitrant problems. Trist (1983), for example, calls them problem domains, whereas Ackoff (1974) uses the term *messes,* and others call them wicked problems (Rittell & Webber, 1973). Despite different labels, these problems share several key features, including the following:

- Problems are "messes." Problems involve sets of problems that are interconnected.

Multiple links and the multifaceted nature of these problems make them impossible to solve with simple solutions; a solution to one aspect of the problem that fails to account for impacts on other interconnected organizations and groups usually fails. Complexity and interconnectedness also make them extremely difficult to conceptualize, analyze, and solve.

- Interorganization action is needed. Complexity and interdependence necessitate that many different organizations become involved in planning and implementing ways of improving the situation. Concrete, absolute solutions normally are impossible for such large-scale problems; only progress toward a more desirable future state is possible. Working toward a more desirable future requires the collaborative efforts of many organizations. In short, "social purposes in modern societies exceed the capacities of modern organizations and call instead for action by multiorganization complexes" (Thompson, 1967, p. 157).

- Problems are multisector and multilevel. Often the need to involve organizations from different sectors (e.g., public, private, labor, and higher education) and from different levels (e.g., federal, state, and local) adds to the complexity of dealing with large-scale socioeconomic problems. Work across regional and national boundaries encounters similar difficulties. Existing organization boundaries, budget and control systems, and preconceived views and feelings about other organizations typically make coordinated action difficult, and this difficulty grows when organizations from different sectors are involved. Adding requirements from the state and federal levels often compounds the difficulty.

- Multiple outcomes are possible. Actions to deal with complex problems often lead to a variety of outcomes over time, some positive, others negative. In addition, some outcomes can be predicted; others cannot. Often in complex, interactive systems, planned activities to reach desirable goals cause unintended, undesirable outcomes (Herbst, 1976). And seemingly logical solutions turn out to be wrong (Forrester, 1969). Consequently, attempts to deal with messes or problem domains must build in the capacity to monitor outcomes constantly. Online monitoring is needed to make rapid changes in the activities needed to continue to move the network in a positive direction.

The broad-scale, multifaceted nature of many key problems and the limitations of traditional attempts to deal with them indicate a need to develop and apply new approaches to these problem domains. As Aldrich (1999) indicates, in the emerging environment, single organizations are becoming increasingly isolated and supraorganizational entities are growing in importance. Interorganizational network development provides one approach to building necessary higher-level systems. Networks have the potential to create the knowledge and understanding needed to develop policies, programs, and actions that make progress in dealing with broad problem or issue domains. The network development approach rests on experience and research on developing networks as complex, ever-changing systems designed to help multiple parties deal with complex messes.

DEVELOPMENT PROCESS

Developing interorganizational networks involves developing appropriate links between groups and organizations that often have not worked together for a common purpose. That is, the starting condition of network development is an underbounded system, in contrast, to overbounded systems that exist for traditional organization development in traditional organizations (Brown, 1980). Consequently, the development process starts with a blank slate for conceptualizing, planning, and conducting system building. This condition leads to a high level of ambiguity regarding purpose, process, and outcomes. Almost every aspect of

the intended organization—such as vision, mission, goals, structures, processes, procedures—must be developed where none exists. And each aspect of development should meet the unique needs of the emerging system operating in its specific task environment (Thompson, 1967).

Phases in the general process of developing these complex, multiorganization systems include

- Recognizing the problem
- Holding informal discussions
- Planning network development
- Identifying stakeholders
- Forming a steering committee
- Visioning the future
- Convening system stakeholders (Chisholm, 1997)

The following sections discuss each of these phases. Recognizing that network building involves creating and maintaining an effective human organization that supports and meshes with allocating tangible resources (e.g., land, capital) is essential for understanding the development process. Developing a network organization involves building and enhancing the social capital (Burt, 2000) needed to address complex high-level problems or issues. "Social capital refers to connections among individuals—social networks and the norms of reciprocity and trustworthiness that arise from them" (Putnam, 2000, p. 19).

Recognizing the Problem

Often what appears to be the problem actually is a symptom of a more fundamental problem. Loss of jobs, for example, may result from a combination of factors that include lack of investment in new technologies, ineffective organization and management, lack of properly educated employees, or inappropriate ways of organizing overall community resources. Recognizing the problem thus entails tracing symptoms back to root causes to determine the broader and deeper factors that are operating. Recognition also entails including various perceptions of the problem from multiple perspectives to allow a deep, shared appreciation of the problem to emerge. Appreciation includes developing a thorough, deep understanding of the problem domain and placing high value on the understanding (Vickers, 1965). Maintaining openness to incorporating new views as the network develops also is crucial. Consequently, the shared appreciation tends to change over time. In brief, this phase involves making sufficient shared sense of the existing problem situation among a small group of people to enable basic development to begin.

Informal Discussions

Informal discussions play a critical role during early network development. Interest in starting a network development effort may come from a variety of sources. These include political leaders, labor union officials, executives and managers, educators, and citizens. The critical factor here is having at least one member of a community or system who spots the need for change and who can articulate and test support of a vision of the future. Ideally, this person will be an opinion leader in the system. Developing a shared sense of the need for change often occurs informally among a small group of people with existing relationships. For example, in the late 1960s, the mayor of Jamestown, New York, saw the need for action to reverse economic decline in the community and began talking with a few friends in local industrial organizations and labor unions. Informal discussions continued for several months and expanded to include several new members. Over time, these discussions led to the development of the Jamestown Area Labor Management Committee. Committee work developed a broad network of various organizations (e.g., business, public

education, health care, union) that collaborated to create conditions that stimulated economic development of the community (Trist, 1986).

Early meetings involve sharing views and feelings about the present situation and the need for change. Meetings also develop deep understanding of the problem domain and trust among participants. Meetings of this type may extend over 6 to 12 months or even longer. It is essential to support and facilitate these informal discussions and to allow them to percolate up from the bottom until those involved feel comfortable with each other, develop a sufficient level of trust and norms of collaboration, and are ready to begin reaching out to involve others. This helps ensure ownership of the problem and deep commitment to trying to bring about change. It also helps ensure and develop comprehensive, in-depth understanding of problems experienced, interests involved, motivation levels of various parties, and support for change.

Recognizing the problem and focusing community attention on it are essential during the early stages of developing a network. Defining the problem to capture interest that incorporates individual organization concerns and focuses on new network activities that can occur only through the joint work of many parties also is critical. Fostering informal discussions to develop a consensus on the need for collaborative action to deal with the problem situation is necessary during this phase.

Early Steps in the Development Process

Identifying stakeholders, forming a steering committee, and planning are critical steps early in the network development process. Ideally, informal discussions between leaders concerned about a problem create a preliminary shared definition of the problem and stimulate willingness of individuals or organizations to begin working on it. These discussions also should generate a tentative list of organizations, groups, and individuals that have a stake in the problem. Key questions for identifying stakeholders include the following:

- What organizations or individuals have critical involvement in the current problem domain?
- Whose support is absolutely essential to bring about change?
- What organizations and groups will be affected by outcomes?
- What organizations, groups, and individuals can block or retard progress?

Discussion and analysis of the first list of stakeholders usually lead to modification, and several rounds of identification, discussion, and change may be needed over time.

A steering committee includes representatives of stakeholder organizations and groups involved in a network. Individual steering committee members should have enough authority to speak for their organizations and commit them to network decisions. Committee functions include the following:

- Governing the network
- Guiding network activities and network development
- Linking the network continuously to the general outside environment and to member organizations

It is desirable to limit the size of the first steering committee to a maximum of 12 people. This enables small group dynamics to continue as the original group of involved people plans and expands network activity. Proceeding deliberately to identify formal and informal leaders who are motivated and can make a difference is in order.

Key issues and questions during this stage are as follows:

- What is the nature of the broad problem?
- What organizations and individuals should be involved to ensure that identified stakeholders

represent all critical aspects of the large-scale problem or issue?

- What knowledge, skills, and resources are needed to deal with the identified problem?
- What organizations or individuals can provide the needed skills, resources, and credibility or legitimacy?
- How should potential participants be invited to participate in the network development process? Who should invite them, and in what order, to develop a critical mass of mutually supportive individuals and organizations? What existing status and political sensitivities must be considered, and how will they be dealt with?
- What process will help members develop a broad and deep vision of a desirable future that will draw attention to improvement possibilities and help mobilize actions needed to bring about change?
- Who is the most appropriate person to voice the need for change and to communicate the tentative network vision?
- What strategy and action steps should be used to design, implement, and manage the change process to broaden and strengthen motivation of critical participants over time?

This short list of selected issues communicates the complexity involved in the early planning stage of developing a network. Careful attention to these issues is needed to increase the chances of success of the development effort. And commitment to revising existing thinking and planning based on experiences and learning is necessary.

Convening Network Members

The next stage in developing a network involves convening a meeting of the stakeholder representatives identified previously. The goals of this meeting include broadening involvement to additional stakeholder organizations, obtaining increased understanding of the existing situation and the external environment, developing a shared vision of a desirable future, testing and building increased motivation and commitment of participants to engage in a development process, and developing general change goals and several broad next steps for action.

"Searching," or holding a search conference (Emery, 1999; Emery & Purser, 1996; Weisbord, 1992), is one approach to meeting design and management that is highly consistent with the network development approach. A search conference rests on the assumption that the individuals, organizations, and groups that have a direct stake in a problem must provide the energy for change by becoming deeply involved in the development process. The process also assumes that they have the in-depth knowledge of the system needed for successful change. Although specialized expert knowledge may be needed at specific times during the change process, this expertise should respond to general guidance and requests from the stakeholders rather than drive the network development process. Stakeholders control the process during continuous cycles of designing, implementing, monitoring, and redesigning the effort. Search conference design aims to "help people restructure their views of reality to see beyond the superficial conditions and events into the underlying causes of problems—and therefore to see new possibilities for shaping the future" (Senge, 1990, p. 24).

Search conferences use the open system planning orientation of starting from the outside (the environment) and building inward. This approach helps to open participants' thinking, create an innovative learning environment, ensure that useful information about the environment is incorporated in network development, and maximize the likelihood that bridges across existing organization boundaries are identified. Such conferences are designed primarily to catalyze change by having stakeholders engage in an open process of exploring what the future might be and creating ways of bringing it into being. Properly designed and managed search conferences provide a new forum in which a different set of participants meet to deal with development in nontraditional ways.

A typical search conference involves six phases of activities that make up a holistic process. Table 33.2 shows the flow of work and purpose of the phases.

Table 33.2   Phases in the Search Conference Process

Phase 1	Preconference activities. Focal issue: design and planning search processes to develop networks.
Phase 2	Exploring the general environment. Focal issue: trends or forces that will affect the problem domain in the next 10 years.
Phase 3	Identifying current situation. Focal issue: key features—both positive and negative—of the existing system and its history.
Phase 4	Visioning a desirable future. Focal issues: creating a shared vision of an ideal system for the future.
Phase 5	Planning broad action steps. Focal issue: creating a strategy and defining goals and strategy to progress toward ideal future. Establish task forces on key issues identified.
Phase 6	Follow through: postconference work. Focal issues: conducting project work to implement plans and strategy. Maintaining the network organization as an effective system.

SOURCE: From Chisholm, R.F., Using large system designs and action research to develop interorganizational networks. In R. T. Golembiewski, *Handbook of organizational consultation*. New York, NY: Marcel Dekker. p. 204. Copyright © 2000. Reproduced by permission of Taylor & Francis, a division of Informa plc.

Phase 1 involves using a small team to design and plan the search process. Effective design work is critical to future development of the network and must be done with great care and skill. Key design issues include the following:

• What organizations should be included? What organizations must be involved to work on the problem successfully?

• Who should represent each invited organization? Who has the knowledge, interest, and capacity to speak for the organization?

• What organization or institution should convene the event, and which individuals should speak for it as a representative of the broad system?

• Content: What topics and issues to include?

• Process: How does conference design foster meaningful discussion, development of shared understanding, and motivation to collaborate for broad change?

• Resources: What financial, physical, and human resources and time are needed to design, plan, conduct, and follow up on the conference?

• Other: Location, timing (when), facilities, rooms, equipment, time of day.

Traditional search conferences take a substantial amount of time (e.g., 2–3 days). However, alternative designs are possible, and the exact amount of time needed depends on design decisions and how events unfold during the search process. One broad-based community economic and social development effort successfully used a 5-hour search process with 96 diverse participants (Chisholm, 1996, 1998). Another network effort that triggered change in a public school system used a 6-hour search process to convene stakeholders and start work by community groups (Chisholm, 2001b).

Phase 2 engages members of the total group in a broad exploration of the environment. Emphasis is placed on the future, and discussion of the past is excluded. A broad, open-ended question such as, "What trends will affect the U.S. economy or this community in the next 10 years?" elicits participants' perceptions of societal trends in technical areas, values, attitudes, and economic, demographic, and other critical areas. Following creative thinking guidelines for exploring issues, critical judgment is suspended, and all alternatives identified are simply listed without being evaluated. Using these guidelines is crucial to demonstrate the importance of everyone's inputs and to help ensure that all key environmental trends are included.

Phase 3 focuses attention on the present situation. For example, responding to a question such as "What are key features—both positive and negative—of this community, and what is its history?" helps build a shared picture of the system as it actually exists. Focusing discussion on positive and negative features of the system also helps root the search process in reality and ensure that valued unique features become incorporated in the emerging vision of a desirable future.

Phase 4 focuses on what could be in the community. This discussion builds on future trends identified during the exploration of the general environment (phase 1) and the reality testing of the existing system that occurred in phase 2. Developing several visions also elicits a set of values; these emerge as group members discuss possible alternative futures. Selection of general features of a shared vision of the future occurs in response to questions such as "What character do we want the community or region to have?" The shared vision serves as a superordinate purpose that elicits and supports collaboration between stakeholders.

Phase 5 identifies basic steps to take to bring about change with the desired characteristics. Discussion centers on future trends, constraints, and opportunities of the actual initiatives and the values expressed during earlier stages of the search process. It is crucial to discuss these areas adequately so that agreed-upon steps blend the desired balance of ideal, realistic, and value considerations.

Phase 6 represents an extension of the discussion process from the previous phase. Here, attention focuses on what action to take to implement the general vision agreed on in phase 5. Typically, task forces or project teams are formed to follow up on general action steps identified in the previous phase. Follow-up of activities generated here usually continues long after the search conference has ended.

Searching is only one way of designing and managing a general meeting of critical constituents. The search conference has been used in a variety of situations that involve bringing together organization representatives with diverse views from different types of organizations to create new approaches to broad social or economic problems. In addition, the search process is a way of directly involving stakeholders in taking responsibility for visioning, building, and managing the future of a new network. Other ways of involving stakeholders in developing interorganizational networks to address broad problems also exist (e.g., Bunker & Alban, 1997; Cooperrider & Whitney, 2000; March, Sproull, & Tamuz, 1991).

ORGANIZING FOR ACTION

Network development efforts include continuing careful attention to designing, organizing, and managing system activities. Although visioning the future and organizing for action represent the birth of a network system, the future existence and effectiveness of the new network are highly problematic. Each system also must devise ways of making progress on developing the network organization via creating and discovering effective ways of carrying out both task and maintenance activities. Visioning the future typically results in identifying several issues or topics that warrant more

detailed study. These in turn often lead to task forces formed to explore the areas and to develop information on alternatives. For example, one search conference created task forces on tourism, higher education, government relations, and long-term economic development. Task force work (e.g., discussion, collection, and analysis of data) is then brought back to the network through the steering committee or total group for discussion, development, and planning of the next steps.

Using task forces to report back to the steering committee is a natural way to bridge between the search conference and the next development stage, and, properly managed, this mode of organizing may continue to be an effective approach. It is critical that leaders recognize that a new phase of system development has been entered and that this new phase brings different needs. These include new ways of planning, coordinating, and managing task forces that are consistent with network principles and purpose. Paying attention to sustaining and developing the network over time also is essential.

The need for staff assistance generally increases substantially during this phase. Exploration of issues entails gathering, assembling, and distributing information and communication about meeting times and discussions. As the task forces develop projects and plans for specific sets of activities, the need to communicate and coordinate grows. In addition, demand for work on designing and facilitating meetings and workshops increases. This typically requires help from ODC professionals experienced in working with action research and large system development. Constant attention must be paid to working effectively on identified issues and problem areas and to developing the system. Ongoing attention to network development is essential to ensure support from the larger external environment and maintain the motivation of members to continue to participate. In short, carrying out project work assumes increased importance during this phase. At the same time, attention to maintaining and developing the network organization must continue. This organization maintenance work is essential to preserve the integrity of the network and maintain its viability and capacity to adjust to new external and internal demands. An action research (AR) approach is essential to developing and maintaining a network organization.

ACTION RESEARCH FOR NETWORK DEVELOPMENT

AR is an approach to system development, not a specific technique. Essentially, it attempts to generate knowledge about a network as an integral part of the development process. AR involves repeated cycles of diagnosis, planning, implementing, collecting and analyzing outcome data, reviewing and discussing data and reflections with network members, reaching conclusions, and defining new sets of action plans. Table 33.3 provides a starting point for discussing the nature of AR.

According to Table 33.3, AR involves an ongoing series of cycles that involve network members in determining the current state of the system, planning next steps to develop the network to a higher level of functioning, implementing action steps, collecting new data on outcomes, and analyzing and determining the meaning of the new data. Constructing the meaning of data serves as another diagnostic stage, which triggers another AR cycle.

Using an AR approach for network development extends well beyond using planned, clearly identifiable information feedback processes. Instead, AR includes almost every aspect of framing, exploring, designing, planning, implementing, collecting data, feedback, interpreting, reflecting on, learning, and modifying the organization processes needed to develop the network organization. In short, AR includes all the processes and activities that enable members to reach a shared appreciation (Vickers, 1965) of the large-scale problem and to conduct collaborative work on it. This means that sensemaking (Weick, 1995)

Table 33.3   Action Research Process

Diagnosing	*Planning*	*Implementation*	*Outcomes*	*Learnings*
Determining nature of current system	1. Action steps	1. Implement action steps	1. Collect additional data (qualitative and quantitative)	Use outcome information to determine changes to actions and organization
	2. Action research	2. Observe effects online	2. Organize information	
		Online reflections and learnings		

SOURCE: From James T. Ziegenfuss, Jr. & Joseph W. Sassani, *Portable health administration*, Academic Press. Copyright 2003, with permission from Elsevier.

is an essential part of using AR for network development. AR provides the primary process through which participants make sense of data and experiences and create the emerging network. In short, AR is the means for constructing a new shared social reality (Gergen, 2003), the network organization, and engaging the focal problem domain.

Network development requires an experimental frame of mind supported by an emerging network organization that is a learning system. Learning occurs when a system processes information that results in increasing its range of potential behaviors (Huber, 1991). This means that higher-level learning systems have a greater variety of responses to future events than lower-level ones. Fundamentally, they have a high capacity to learn from previous experiences and to perceive and adjust to new opportunities and pressures from the environment easily. Learning systems also are able to reach conclusions from the decision-making process itself, not only from observing the outcomes of earlier decisions (March, Sproull, & Tamuz, 1991). In effect, learning systems are able to distill deep, complex lessons from ongoing and previous work and to apply these lessons effectively to new circumstances. Such organizations build learning into all aspects of system functioning by focusing on "What can we learn from this?" rather than just "What have we accomplished?" This focus is essential to increase network capacity (and member capacity) to respond to future events and to develop useful knowledge in a turbulent world.

AR is needed to support development and maintenance of the network organization as a learning system. AR involves applying a dual focus on planning, taking action, and examining outcomes of these actions in every aspect of developing and managing the network. Using AR helps enable a developing network organization to be "less concerned with making 'correct' decisions than with making correctable ones; less obsessed with avoiding error than with detecting and correcting for error" (Reich, 1983, p. 107). Such a learning system orientation depends on a continuous flow of valid information about the basic outcomes of actions. It also entails reflecting on plans and actions to derive deep experience-based understandings of phenomena and have them assimilated into network thinking and future actions.

Obtaining a continuous flow of information about the effects of plans and actions does not occur automatically; rather, it entails legitimizing the need for AR, providing the necessary resources, and designing effective structures and processes for gathering the needed information and feeding it back to network members. In effective AR, examining the outcomes of plans and actions becomes an integral part of the planning and implementation process.

Over time, devising ways of determining the effects of plans and activities should become part of how the network organization functions (i.e., its culture); that is, network members should devise ways of determining outcomes automatically as a natural part of conducting work and managing the network development process. An AR perspective means that people are constantly asking the following:

- What needs to be done to create, maintain, and extend the shared vision and reach defined goals?
- How can we evaluate the total real effects of decisions and actions?
- What changes must be made based on feedback about actual outcomes?
- What have we learned from previous cycles of visioning, goal setting, planning, and implementation?
- How are learnings from earlier work incorporated into the developing network?

Establishing the value of AR is basic to developing a network organization. The AR process reinforces the concept of the organization as a learning system. AR also underlines the temporariness of specific goals, plans, activities, and arrangements and surfaces differences between espoused and actual values and guiding principles. And it highlights the ongoing need for system members to make sense of new conditions that arise over time and to construct shared meanings that enable the network to progress. Also, it provides the information about actual outcomes of earlier decisions that enable the system to learn for the future and make necessary adjustments. Stated differently, AR should become an integral part of the network development process. Chisholm (2001a) identifies several aspects of action research important for developing interorganizational networks.

In summary, rather than being a distinct activity, AR is a perspective or orientation for engaging in network development. Ideally, the approach pervades every network member, group, and activity. It also should become an integral part of the thinking and behavior of network members. Action research for network development is an ongoing process for planning, taking action, questioning, reflecting, searching, and creating and capturing learnings. Questioning, reflecting, and building learnings into the network can occur during any phase or part of the AR process. Using AR to create and maintain networks as learning systems emphasizes a process of proactive engagement, not simply reactive adjustment. The AR process is essential for developing, managing, and maintaining network organizations over time.

CONCLUSION

Interorganizational networks are an increasingly important type of organization in the early 21st century. This type of system is growing in importance to meet emerging conditions in the environments of organizations. General conditions that foster increased use of interorganizational networks include the complexity of issues and problems, increasing interdependence between organizations and institutions, and an accelerating pace of change. These conditions often create "messes" or problem domains: sets of interconnected problems that single organizations find impossible to deal with alone. The complexity of these problems typically defies simple solutions by individual organizations. Forming and developing interorganizational networks represents a way of dealing with these complex problems and issues that warrant collaborative work by various organizations.

Several factors apply pressures to create interorganizational networks, from technology, growth in knowledge, and globalization to changing beliefs and values. Existing and emerging information processing and communication technologies make possible the dispersal of organization units around the world. In addition, transportation and manufacturing technologies add further pressures toward placelessness—the capacity to make almost everything available anywhere in the world in very short time spans regardless of physical location. Growth in the importance of knowledge increases pressure to invent new work organizations that use and create knowledge, and joining other organizations to form networks can advance this quest. For example, the NVF in Norway illustrates an interorganizational network specifically developed as a learning system that increases knowledge in a large remote geographic region.

Realignment of economic institutions to international and subnational levels and the declining importance of nations per se also will encourage developing new organization forms. The interorganizational network is well suited to meet these new demands of globalization in many situations. Similarly, networks have the capacity to enable individuals, groups, and organizations to develop and put into practice a new set of postindustrial beliefs and values—beliefs that emphasize interconnection, holism, pluralism, and cooperation. These beliefs are highly congruent with the self-regulating, collaborative nature of interorganizational networks. Using AR to develop networks also enables members to create real meaning for these general values by creating ways of applying them in particular situations.

Although this chapter outlines a general process for developing a network organization, there are no prescriptions to follow. Steps in the process merely indicate stages of development that typically occur, not a neat step-by-step action manual. Similarly, insights from specific experiences merely provide general input for developing other networks in different settings.

Although the potential of interorganizational networks is great, they offer no magic solutions. But they do offer representatives of diverse stakeholders a way of organizing to make a difference in many key areas. In addition, the general approach to network development used in cases included in the book suggests ways for ODC practitioners to become involved in helping stakeholders create and develop these complex systems. Engaging in interorganizational network development will offer many of us serious challenges and much exciting work for years to come.

Laszlo briefly describes the future that lies ahead:

> We can now identify the post-modern age with a little more specificity. Ours will be a global society, integrated yet diversified, dynamic and complex, and organized on many levels, from the grass roots to the global. But, we must add, it may or may not come about in reality. (Laszlo, 1994, p. 52)

Our success depends largely on how we conceive of and develop organization forms that can be effective under the new conditions. Developing interorganizational networks via action research is one key to creating a desirable future.

REFERENCES

Ackoff, R. R. (1974). *Redesigning the future.* New York: Wiley Interscience.

Aldrich, H. (1999). *Organizations evolving.* Thousand Oaks, CA: Sage.

Aldrich, H., & Whetten, D. A. (1981). Organization sets, action sets, and networks: Making the most of simplicity. In P. C. Nystrom & W. H. Starbuck (Eds.), *Handbook of organization design* (pp. 385–408). New York: Oxford University Press.

Alter, C., & Hage, J. (1993). *Organizations working together.* Newbury Park, CA: Sage.

Ashby, W. R. (1960). *Design for a brain: The origin of adaptive behavior.* New York: John Wiley & Sons.

Bell, D. (1976). *The coming of post-industrial society: A venture in social forecasting.* New York: Basic Books.

Bilimoria, D., Wilmot, T. B., & Cooperrider, D. L. (1996). Multiorganizational and collaboration for global change: New opportunities for organizational change and development. In R. W. Woodman & W. A. Pasmore (Eds.), *Research in organizational change and development* (pp. 201–238). Greenwich, CT: JAI.

Brass, D. J., & Burkhardt, M. E. (1992). Centrality and power in organizations. In G. Moore & J. Whitt (Eds.), *Networks and organizations: Structure, form and action* (pp. 191–215). Cambridge, MA: Harvard Business School Press.

Brown, L. D. (1980). Planned change in underorganized systems. In T. G. Cummings (Ed.), *Systems theory for organization development* (pp. 181–203). Chichester, UK: Wiley.

Brown, L. D. (1987). *Development partnerships: Problem-solving at institutional interfaces.* Paper presented at the annual meeting of the American Society for Public Administration, Boston.

Bunker, B. B., & Alban, B. T. (1997). *Large scale interventions: Engaging the whole system for rapid change.* San Francisco: Jossey-Bass.

Burt, R. S. (2000). The network structure of social capital. In R. I. Sutton & B. Staw (Eds.), *Research in organizational behavior* (Vol. 22, pp. 345–423). Greenwich, CT: JAI.

Castells, M. (2000). *The information age: Economy, society and culture, Volume 1: The rise of the network society.* Oxford, UK: Blackwell.

Chisholm, R. F. (1996). On the meaning of networks. *Group and Organization Management, 21*(2), 216–235.

Chisholm, R. F. (1997). Building a network organization to foster economic development. *International Journal of Public Administration, 20*(2), 451–477.

Chisholm, R. F. (1998). *Developing network organizations: Learning from practice and theory.* Reading, MA: Addison-Wesley.

Chisholm, R. F. (2000). Using large system designs and action research to develop interorganizational networks. In R. T. Golembiewski (Ed.), *Handbook of organizational consultation* (pp. 197–211). New York: Marcel Dekker.

Chisholm, R. F. (2001a). Action research to develop an interorganizational network. In P. Reason & H. Bradbury (Eds.), *Handbook of action research* (pp. 324–332). Thousand Oaks, CA: Sage.

Chisholm, R. F. (2001b). Bringing about change in a public school system: An interorganizational network approach. In M. P. Mandell (Ed.), *Getting results through collaboration: Networks and network structures for public policy and management.* Westport, CT: Quorum.

Clegg, S. R., & Hardy, C. (1999). *Studying organization: Theory and method.* Thousand Oaks, CA: Sage.

Cooperrider, D., & Whitney, D. (2000). *Collaborating for change: Appreciative inquiry.* San Francisco: Berrett-Koehler.

Emery, F. E. (1978). *The fifth Kondradieff wave.* Canberra: Center for Continuing Education, Australian National University.

Emery, M. S. (1999). *The theory and practice of making cultural change.* Amsterdam: John Benjamins.

Emery, M., & Purser, R. E. (1996). *The search conference: A powerful way for planning organization change and community action.* San Francisco: Jossey-Bass.

Finsrud, H. (1995). How about a dialogue? Communication perspective meets socioecological perspective. In O. Eikeland & H. D. Finsrud (Eds.), *Research in action* (pp. 239–258). Oslo, Norway: Work Research Institute.

Forrester, J. W. (1969). *Principles of systems.* Cambridge, MA: Wright-Allen Press.

Gergen, K. (2003). Action research and orders of democracy. *Action Research, 1,* 39–56.

Gerlach, L. P., & Palmer, G. B. (1981). Adaptation through evolving interdependence. In P. D. Nystrom & W. H. Starbuck (Eds.), *Handbook of organization design* (Vol. 1, pp. 323–381). New York: Oxford University Press.

Granovetter, M. (1973). The strength of weak ties. *American Journal of Sociology, 78*(6), 1360–1380.

Hage, J., & Powers, C. H. (1992). *Post-industrial lives.* Newbury Park, CA: Sage.

Hanssen-Bauer, J., & Snow, C. C. (1996). Responding to hypercompetition: The structure and processes of a regional learning network organization. *Organization Science, 7*(4), 413–427.

Herbst, P. G. (1976). *Alternatives to hierarchies.* Leiden, the Netherlands: Nijoff.

Huber, G. P. (1991). Organizational learning: The contributing processes and the literatures. *Organization Science, 2,* 88–115.

Jay, E. J. (1964). The concept of "field" and "network" in anthropological research. *Man, 64,* 137–139.

Kanter, R. M. (1995). *World class.* New York: Simon & Schuster.

Knoke, W. (1996). *Bold new world.* New York: Kodansha International.

Korten, D. C. (1995). *When corporations rule the world.* West Hartford, CT: Kumarian.

Laszlo, E. (1994). *Vision 2020: Reordering chaos for global survival.* Langhorne, PA: Gordon and Breach.

Lawrence, P. R., & Lorsch, J. W. (1967). *Organization and environment.* Boston: Harvard Business School Press.

March, J. G., Sproull, L. S., & Tamuz, M. (1991). Learning from samples of one or fewer. *Organization Science, 2*(1), 1–13.

Nohira, N., & Eccles, R. G. (1992). Face to face: Making network organizational work. In N. Nohira & R. G. Eccles (Eds.), *Networks and organizations* (pp. 288–308). Boston: Harvard Business School Press.

Nonaka, I., & Takeuchi, H. (1995). *The knowledge creating company.* New York: Oxford University Press.

Powell, W. W. (1998). Learning from collaboration: Knowledge and networks in the biotechnology and pharmaceutical industries. *California Management Review, 40*(3), 228–241.

Putnam, R. D. (2000). *Bowling alone.* New York: Simon & Schuster.

Reich, R. R. (1983, April). The next American frontier. *Atlantic Monthly,* 97–108.

Rittell, H. W. J., & Webber, M. (1973). Dilemmas in a general theory of planning. *Policy Science, 4*(2), 155–169.

Senge, P. M. (1990). The leader's new work: Building learning organizations. *Sloan Management Review, 32*(1), 19–35.

Sharif, M. (Ed.). (1962). *Intergroup relations and leadership.* New York: John Wiley & Sons.

Thompson, J. D. (1967). *Organizations in action.* New York: McGraw-Hill.

Trist, E. L. (1983). Referent organizations and the development of interorganizational domains. *Human Relations, 36*(3), 269–284.

Trist, E. L. (1985). Intervention strategies for interorganizational domains. In R. Tannenbaum & F. Massarik (Eds.), *Human systems development: New perspectives on people and organizations* (pp. 167–197). San Francisco: Jossey-Bass.

Trist, E. L. (1986). Quality of working life and community development: Some reflections on the Jamestown experience. *Journal of Applied Behavioral Science, 22*(3), 223–238.

Vickers, G. (1965). *The art of judgment.* London: Routledge.

Weick, K. E. (1995). *Sensemaking in organizations.* Thousand Oaks, CA: Sage.

Weisbord, M. R. (1992). *Discovering common ground.* San Francisco: Berrett-Koehler.

34

Transorganizational Development

D A V I D   M .   B O J E

M A R K   E .   H I L L O N

Transorganizational networks emerge and transform through storytelling, yet until quite recently storytelling as an engine of transorganizational development (TD) has only seen limited attention by organization change consultants. The current consulting interest is in the use of storytelling for knowledge mining and management. As we shall demonstrate, transorganizational networks provide the virtual and face-to-face arenas in which storytelling transactions can take place. The transorganizational network is forever restorying, forgetting, and rehistoricizing to exploit its social and economic interfaces, and storytelling serves as the currency of exchange for collective memory. In essence, the fragmented bits of story are the narrative embodiment of organization.

This chapter is organized into three parts. The first reviews the origins and history of TD theory and practice from the early 1970s to today. The second explores storytelling organization theory

and presents two prevailing models of TD networks in order to connect antenarrative and narrative analysis to TD theory and practice. To conclude the chapter, we present an overview of current TD consulting methods and propose a new Story Space model of transorganizational networking as a tool to analyze a network of firms embedded in a community of storied action and development phases and cycles of network formation and metamorphosis.

HISTORY OF TD

Since its inception, TD as an academic field has been focused on how storytelling affects networking behavior and transformation in organizations. At the practical level, TD networking involves a very broad range of consulting strategies. Examples include information technology reengineering, knowledge management, learning organizations, appreciative inquiry, participative democracy, the socio-economic approach to management, sociotechnical systems, network organization design, supply and value chain management, military cyber–war game simulations, and various postmodern approaches such as restorying spectacles of mass production and consumption with more ecocentric and socially responsible ethics (Boje, 1999).

TD theory work began with the collaborative work of several University of California at Los Angeles (UCLA) faculty members. In 1972, UCLA's Samuel A. Culbert, J. Max Elden, Will McWhinney, Warren Schmidt, and Bob Tannenbaum called for transorganizational praxis as a means to go beyond traditional organization development.

> **Transorganizational networking** is defined as planned change in the collective relationships of a variety of stakeholders to accomplish something beyond the capability of any single organization or individual (Culbert, Elden, McWhinney, Schmidt, & Tannenbaum, 1972).

> **Transorganizational development** is defined as a collective story shaped and co-constructed by the network of participants. Each stakeholder organization negotiates the meaning of the collective story. Each story is a fragment, a perspective on the whole. Some are problem based, issue based, solution based, or just fantasy based. Each is a candidate to become the dominant collective story (Boje, 1979, 1981).

Thayer made a similar call for TD work in 1973. In 1978, Kurt Motamedi was visiting UCLA and joined in the wake-up call for the evolution from interorganizational design to TD (Motamedi, 1978). Boje joined UCLA in 1979 and began to work with TD, focusing on storytelling in grassroots TD interventions. Boje's (1979, 1981) story theory work with Michael Jones of the UCLA folklore and mythology department extended the storytelling aspects into the ICEND model of consultation to large interorganizational networks for long-term change:

I: Interactive, share stories around issues

C: Communicative, stories of the collective

E: Experiential, stories of joint actions

ND: Network development

The basis of the ICEND model is that when people convene to interact, communicate their stories, and form common experience, a network for action and change develops around their collective storytelling (Boje, 1982). Three subsystems are formed. In the first subsystem, an outside process consultant facilitates the formation of the second subsystem, an internal problem-solving networking cycle, so that people can crystallize issues, identify leaders, and form a temporary organization of organizations that will transform the current organizing patterns into the third subsystem, an extended network involvement cycle.

Cummings (1984) reconstructed Motomedi's and Boje's TD theory work into a sociotechnical system framework with a TD process model consisting of three stages: identification, convention, and organization. These three stages seem to have been adopted in some form or other by the majority of subsequent researchers (Sink, 1991). However, the initial thinking on TD assumed that the development of TD systems entailed a new approach in both theory and practice from OD in single organizations. Cobb (1991) and Sink (1991) showed through their work on organization coalition building that TD practice did not entail more than a broader perspective and a reassessment of some fundamental assumptions. Perhaps TD analytical research methods needed time to evolve, as Cobb's (1991) critique of organization coalition research characterized many studies as rigor without relevance because researchers tended to approach organization political processes from the rational utility-maximizing agent perspective.

The call for TD has been heard most recently by organizations awakening to the realities of global economic restructuring. Perlmutter (1991) speaks of the process of globalization as a growing system of networked interdependencies in every aspect of life. Likewise, Cooperrider and Pasmore (1991) argue that the rapid rate of global social change results in large part from thousands of non–bureaucratically organized groups seeking similar aims. They cite Perrow (1972) in their explanation that "bureaucracies are dedicated to eliminating all unwanted extra-organizational influences upon the behaviors of their members, are created to deal with stable, routine tasks in an efficient manner" (Cooperrider & Pasmore, 1991, p. 1044). Thus, assumptions of bureaucratic and hierarchical network organization may also have stymied past TD research efforts.

MONOLOGICAL AND DIALOGICAL MODELS OF STORY AND NARRATIVE METHODS FOR TD THEORY AND PRACTICE

Storytelling organization theory work had its beginning in 1991 with Boje's *Administrative Science Quarterly* study of storytelling in an office supply firm. The storytelling organization was defined as a "collective storytelling system in which the performance of stories is a key part of members' sense-making and a means to allow them to supplement individual memories with institutional memory" (Boje, 1991, p. 106; also see Boje, 1995). Storytelling organization writers come to the topic from a variety of philosophical positions. For example, Bob Gephart, Jr.'s (1991, p. 37) study of leader succession defines the storytelling organization as "constructed in the above succession stories as a tool or program for making sense of events." Mary Boyce's (1995) storytelling organization work is based in social construction philosophy. Michael Kaye (1996) worked with Boje's story writings to develop them into a successful consulting practice; Kaye says stories can shape the culture of organizations. For a review of the differences in these storytelling organization theories and studies, see Boje,

Alvarez, and Schooling (2001) and Boje (in press). Next, we will examine the two dominant storytelling organization models for TD theory and practice.

Model 1: Monological TD

The first model is called monological TD because it follows a control-based knowledge management approach to scan a network of multiple organizations through contracts and exchange relationships, retrieving tacit knowledge into a shared database. Attention to knowledge management and organization learning is not new, as the historical move toward globalization continually creates technological upheaval, resource discontinuities, and inefficiencies of crisis proportions for all forms of social and economic organization (Schein, 1996). Organization communication network analysts have long looked at individuals as nodes in day-to-day work processes. Transorganizational network analysis was a natural next step as nodes became whole organizations, even if represented by individuals. The governance of individuals in organizations also progressed to governance of organizations in transorganizational networks. A prominent example of this evolution is Porter's value chain or web, which is merely a transorganizational network governed by negotiated terms of exchange.

Storytelling is the currency or medium of exchange in both OD and TD relationships. Barry (1997) argues that storytelling and restorying past stories are major aspects of organization change, and TD consulting tends to focus on what Barry and Elmes (1997, p. 439) call the "technofuturist genre" of strategy as story. This genre is part of an epic narrative using quasiscience network mapping approaches such as temporal sequencing of who consults whom, who sends e-mail to whom, and who trades how much with whom. These are transactional data maps in which the domain of storytelling is at a very abstract and aggregate level. For example, Porter's "cost leaders" and "focusers" and Miles and Snow's "defenders" and "prospectors" are abstract characterizations of antagonists and protagonists that universalize and essentialize (Boje, 1995) system actor behavioral profiles into simple frameworks, typologies, and mappings.

This monological storytelling organization model is rooted in the knowledge management field rather than the narrative research just reviewed. There is a burgeoning field called knowledge engineering, a consulting practice that grows in the realization that knowledge is a tremendous business asset and that the way to get at this knowledge is through stories.

Nonaka and Takeuchi's (1995) four-part socialization, externalization, combination, and internalization (SECI) model was very influential in consulting circles in launching the knowledge engineering business. In knowledge (re)engineering, stories are increasingly thought of as a place to mine tacit knowledge assets. Knowledge engineers seek to develop data storage and retrieval systems to appropriate tacit knowledge from workers with specialized task knowledge, thereby making it redistributable instantaneously to whoever needs it at another time and place. The problem we observe is that stories are too elusive and contextualized to be captured like objects, and what ends up being storied often is not that useful.

One of the premier purveyors of storytelling knowledge management consulting is Dave Snowden, director of IBM's Cynefin Centre. He has discovered that narrative can be a pathway to tacit knowledge and "can also act as a source of understanding, disrupt entrained thinking, [and] provide a repository of learning" (Snowden, 2001, p. 4). He views this approach as an improvement over the failure of business process reengineering to deliver on its promised benefits for managerialist decision support (Snowden, 2002). The third generation (Snowden, 2002, p. 2) requires the clear separation of context, narrative, and content

management and challenges the orthodoxy of scientific management. Complex adaptive system theory is used to create a sensemaking model that uses the self-organizing capabilities of the informal communities and identifies a natural flow model of knowledge creation, disruption, and use.

Snowden (2002) became interested in storytelling in 1999 when he learned about the 3M work of Shaw, Brown, and Bromiley (1998), whose article made storytelling fashionable. Snowden sought to codify esoteric and tacit story knowledge using solicitation questions that could be analytically translated into levels of abstraction. Snowden adapted Polanyi's (1974) work on tacit knowledge to Nonaka and Takeuchi's (1995) four-part SECI model. The idea was to develop a technology to capture storied tacit knowledge. Snowden (2002, p. 12) summarizes,

> The ability to convey high levels of complexity through story lies in the highly abstract nature of the symbol associations in the observer's mind when she/he hears the story. It triggers ideas, concepts, values and beliefs at an emotional and intellectual level simultaneously. A critical mass of such anecdotal material from a cohesive community can be used to identify and codify simple rules and values that underlie the reality of that organization's culture.

Stories are collected in what Snowden calls story circles, a knowledge mapping exercise to gather the unofficial elements of knowledge in an organization. Snowden and Denning conduct an "Organizational Storytelling and Narrative Patterns" story elicitation and analysis master class for managers and executives. Participants learn how to assess tacit knowledge stories with archetypes and manage differences between official stated knowledge and the "shadow organization" of informal knowledge. Denning (2000) includes sessions on how to create and perform springboard stories. They end with how to create and exploit narrative databases.

In an Orwellian twist on the storytelling organization, concerns within the U.S. Homeland Security community for early detection of "strategic surprise" have fostered initiatives such as the Novel Intelligence From Massive Data program of the Advanced Research and Development Activity agency. According to project documents from the Information Awareness Office (2002, p. 21), data mining and the conversion of surveillance traces into story have advantages for analysts seeking to persuade policymakers:

> Conveying information in a story provides a rich context, remaining in the conscious memory longer and creating more memory traces than decontextualized information. Thus, a story is more likely to be acted upon than "normal" means of communication. Storytelling, whether in a personal or organizational setting, connects people, develops creativity, and increases confidence. The use of stories in organizations can build descriptive capabilities, increase organizational learning, convey complex meaning, and communicate common values and rule sets.

Thus, we see that whether for analytical or developmental objectives, the currency of influence and sensemaking in transorganizational networks is storytelling.

Model 2: Dialogical TD

The second approach built on storytelling organization theory is called dialogical TD because of its focus on developing a sense of multivoiced inclusion among multiple organizations. Instead of static networks, transorganizational relations are envisioned from Sloterdijk's (1993, 1998, 1999) new philosophical standpoint, looking at how organizations form spaces of togetherness and commonality called spheres. Our work here builds on Illich's (1993) research on oral society and its transition to image screens and Bakhtin's (1968, 1973, 1981) concepts of monophonic and polyphonic novels.

The second TD model includes the more polyphonic (multivoiced) strategy-as-story approaches, involving a dialogical and mutual authorship of strategic understanding of networking dynamics. This can mean "surfacing, legitimizing, and juxtaposing differing organizational stories" and differing stakeholder logics (Barry & Elmes, 1997, p. 444). Postmodernist and critical theory perspectives on collective narration and expert narration of strategy as story focus on how people are central to or marginal to the strategic discourse that dominates a given context. The dialogical approach is used to develop narrative spheres of common interest through such practices as search conferences and story networking. Storytelling is used to construct and restory network development and change rather than simply to extract tacit knowledge for unilateral competitive advantage. Thus, storytelling is essential to both consulting approaches, even though it is operationalized quite differently. However, the contribution we seek is an approach that looks at multiple storytellers in multiorganizational settings.

The dialogical approach develops the polyphonic (multivoice) and polylogical (multilogic) aspects of TD consulting to balance grassroots involvement with a rigorous appreciation of power dynamics. We see this balance as very much rooted in storytelling practices, for it is through story work that transorganizational participants develop their in and out groups and their potential willingness to engage in joint action.

Polyphony and carnivalization are two pivotal aspects of Bakhtin's (1981, p. 263) master trope, heteroglossia, the social diversity of speech types and multiple voices. Heteroglossia means that dialoging in and between storytelling organizations occurs in situ, in a matrix of a particular time and place, and in the nexus of contextual social, political, economic, and historical discourses that situate a given meaning then and there, versus any other meaning of the same word enacted under different circumstances. This is quite a contrast to the knowledge management model of storytelling organizations, where springboard stories are constructed and stories are mined and assembled into knowledge databanks, to be used to instruct and socialize employees.

The first aspect of heteroglossia, polyphony, refers not only to multiple voices but also to the presentation of multiple logics; the polyphonic and polylogic forces of dialogism are opposed by monological tendencies in social discourse. The consulting problem we see in transorganization work is how to bring organization participants with differing logics and perspectives together to fashion a shared collective story of themselves and their potential for action.

Dialogism (i.e., multiple logics) is the condition in which every word and gesture is understood as a part of the greater whole with a multiplicity of points of view. The consulting problem is how to create dialogue that results in collective storying and restorying. Dialogism is a force that is always naturally deconstructing social attempts to insulate participants into monological (i.e., one-logic) stories or entire monological storytelling organizations in which one story is the springboard enforced for all. In this way, the consulting process of TD becomes one of inviting more voices into the collective story construction, deconstruction, and reconstruction work of the network of players. At the same time that voices are invited into collective storying, the forces of monologism are attempting to cut off contact and marginalize voices of alternative logics to reduce all to the dominant story.

The second aspect of heteroglossia is carnival. Carnival has never been exploited as a theory of organization change and development, yet Bakhtin (1968, p. 11), points out that "all the symbols of the carnival idiom are filled with the pathos of change and renewal, with the sense of the gay relativity of prevailing truths and authorities." Carnival is not only the theatric and storied parody and mockery of spectacle power or the satire of the grotesque oppression of modernity; it is life itself finding a way to revive and renew the community. The TD consulting problem is how to approach a transorganizational community in ways that will unleash carnivalesque forces of transformation and renewal.

The application of stories to strategy is widely known; what is less apparent is how to move from monologic networking to more polyphonic storytelling organizing. Barry and Elmes (1997, p. 444) argue, "Above all, polyphonic texts arise from 'dialogical' rather than 'monological' authorship; in dialogical authorship, different logics not only coexist, but inform and shape one another." In the dialogical process of storytelling, the strategic narratives are read and written in ways that are participative and transparent for power moves. Barry and Elmes (1997, p. 447) observe that "a narrative view can also reveal how organizations become imprisoned by their strategic discourse—deconstructive analysis might be used to show how alternative meanings and constructions are silenced in favor of a dominant story, and suggest who benefits and who loses through such silencing."

The main differences between monological and polyphonic storytelling transorganizations are the lack of push by consultants for total consensus, opening up the process for more polylogical and inclusive dialogues with many points of view. The polyphonic storytelling organization is extraordinarily multivoiced and multilogical and encourages the intermingling of points of view without finalizing leaderly judgments that force monological consensus into some dominant story. As in *Tamara* (Boje, 1995), the dialogical storytelling activity occurs simultaneously in fragmented groupings in many rooms and buildings so that the essential activity of leadership (and consulting) is making sense of the unfolding separated dramas and the network of storylines.

The monological and dialogical storytelling TD approaches are ideal types and what consultants and narrative theorists contend with is the hybrid, the dialectic of the two. The consultant's role in the strategic process of a polyphonic transorganization is to transform monologic insulation into dialogic participation, which is an intervention into the political economy of storytelling. Sink (1991) boiled the TD practice down to two basic but critical areas: issues of power and issues of substance or meaning. For Foucault (1980), the two are more intertwined as power shapes what is socially and economically defined as knowledge; stories are normalizing truth fragments.

In sum, polyphonic transorganizational storytelling development is rich in prestory work, the formation of a story out of all the bits and fragments, called "antenarratives" (Barge, 2002; Boje, 2001; Vickers, 2002). Antenarratives are the bets storytellers make that an improperly fashioned prestory can change the world (Boje, 2001). This prestory work is rich in polylogical discourse and thus does not force monological narrative consensus. Antenarrative is what Bakhtin (1973, p. 27) might define as an uncompleted dialogue, not the "rounded-off and finalized monological whole" of the coherent and proper narrative. Narrative is the consensus that antenarrative emergence and exchange does not finalize. There is a highly practical side to antenarratives for consultants in that they reflect the cohesion and fault patterns in the collective stories of an emerging and transforming network.

STORYTELLING APPROACH TO TD CONSULTING

The first two sections of this chapter provided a general overview of the history and theoretical branching of transorganizational networks into two main storytelling models. This final section presents several alternative views on TD consulting practice.

The consulting side of storytelling has come a long way since the 1980s when Tom Peters recommended that CEOs learn 3-minute stump speeches to spur employees on to greater

acts of customer service and quality (Peters & Waterman, 1982). For example, David M. Armstrong (1992), president and CEO of a 100-year-old maker of steam, air, and water systems, systematically collected an arsenal of customer service stories that he used to train employees. Armstrong's (2002) latest book is titled *Chief Storytelling Officer: More Tales from America's Foremost Corporate Storyteller*. Peters wrote on the jacket of the book, "David Armstrong has elevated storytelling into a quasi-science."

Peters and Armstrong quickly emerged as proponents of the monological or managerialist approach to corporate storytelling. Storytelling consulting work has many other adherents. For example, Denning (2000) tells CEOs how to build, craft, and perform what he calls springboard stories. Springboard stories exploit tacit knowledge so that listeners will reinvent the knowledge in their own local contexts. Like the antenarrative described earlier, the springboard story can affect a change project, putting it back on track. The monological perspective is evident because the CEO is the principal or only storyteller of the organization. Gargiulo (2002) takes Denning's approach into a slightly more academic realm but follows the same managerialist thinking; stories are an object executives construct as a stump speech to influence social action but not something seen as part of the situated fabric of leading and organizing.

Boisot's (1998) information space (I-space) is a recent addition to the consulting arsenal. The three dimensions of Boisot's knowledge management I-space model attempt to describe the codification, abstraction, and dissemination of the tacit knowledge carried by organization stories. Codification of stories is a process of shedding excess data bits to the minimum necessary for categorization. Abstraction is a process of reducing a story to the minimum of categories necessary to capture its essence in a transferable array. Dissemination is a control process that depends not on the codified and abstracted story itself but on the number of agents or storytellers with access to the data. The control aspect is perhaps the most important feature of knowledge management, for without restrictions on dissemination, the carefully codified, abstracted, and destoried tacit knowledge ceases to be a firm-specific asset.

Transferring tacit knowledge is problematic in practice because, as Boisot (1998, p. 57) points out, once you abstract, reduce, and codify knowledge and shed its concrete context, the fragments that are communicated to another person no longer make sense to the end user. Only to the extent that stories can be standardized are they efficient for meaning transport, thereby resulting in economic utility in other contexts. Furthermore, a critical issue knowledge engineers ignore is that when creating transferable knowledge, you cannot just dispense with thorny legal issues of story ownership rights (i.e., stories are an intellectual property of the individual as well as of the enterprise). This is deskilling to extract surplus knowledge value. In this way, sharing story knowledge can make people victims of the global knowledge economy; people share the storyable asset that makes them most employable at living wages.

Case (2002, p. 93) argues that virtual organization consultants are promoting "the adoption of so called virtual organization, encouraging firms to enter into temporary 'networked' arrangements the better to create and exploit commercial opportunities." Case goes on to say, "From a dramatistic perspective the social fabric may be seen to be created, sustained, ruptured and transformed *by stories*" (Case, 2002, p. 96). Case is applying Burke's frames (or ideologies) and looking at how multiple frames evidenced in stories are able to dialogue into an emergent collective worldview. Case's work is rich in story texture as he details the virtual participants' efforts to story their context and manipulate their collective situation. Case reports that "the stories consultants

tell to illustrate the potential of [virtual] technology and virtual working are fantastical" (p. 109) and contends that participants are seduced into "telling virtual stories about virtual working and in so doing [deflect] attention away from alternative, and potentially more critical, accounts of the implications of 'virtual organization.'" Though virtual, such work environments still behave as storytelling organizations. More work is needed to study the practices by which consultants use and perhaps misuse story to facilitate new approaches to transorganizational development.

There is also confusion in I-space theory between the systemic knowledge, understanding, and democratic discourse that can result in collective wisdom. Knowledge is what people get from a book or lecture, and understanding comes only through the experience of using knowledge in one's life space, whereas wisdom is a rare insight that comes with time and ethos. We think stories can convey tacit knowledge but not understanding or wisdom, which require the experience of the story and its temporal in situ context and ethos to be interactively appreciated by the receiver of the story. This suggests that a more experiential and communicative approach to story, knowledge, understanding, and wisdom is needed. This is what we propose in the text that follows.

Story Space (S-Space) Model

Story Space (S-space) is defined as the collective experiential and communicative storytelling activity within and between organizations. Storytelling is a communicative currency that combines tacit knowledge with experiential understanding and the ethos that comes from time and interactive engagement. Narrative researchers and storytelling consultants can assess the S-space of storytelling organizations as knowledge, but attaining understanding and wisdom takes more development.

An important historical genealogy of knowledge must be explored before we can specify the S-space dimensions. There has been an almost unnoticed socioeconomic turn from knowledge that is oral to knowledge that is written and, more recently, to knowledge that is visual. The visual pattern analysis of storytelling and story networking is a new aesthetic allocation. This transition has followed a more spiral than linear succession as the visual theatrics of a story script and the oral aesthetic are quite different from those of the written story. To develop our concept of the transition from oral to visual storytelling and consulting will necessitate a slight detour into the history of storytelling.

The move from oral knowledge to written knowledge entailed a new collective understanding: We discovered the screen, the image of text that scrolls within our mind, something we in the age of TV and motion pictures take for granted. There is a point at which an oral story becomes a screen story, when story ceases to be oral and becomes a disembodied image scrolling on our mind screen.

Illich (1993, pp. 54–58) points out that until the late 12th century, the art of reading was an oral and body motion that did not involve mirroring the page of text onto the mind's screen; there was no such imagination. Reading in the 12th century was a highly physical activity in which people had to read out loud, in community, while mumbling and rocking their bodies. Knowledge from a written text became understanding in an oral community; reading alone and to oneself was unknown. Reading was done in the "communities of mumblers" (Illich, 1993, p. 54), and it had its analogy in bodily motor activity, "striding from line to line, or flapping one's wing's while surveying the already well-known page" (p. 54). "True, silent reading was occasionally practiced in antiquity, but it was considered a feat" (Illich, 1993, p. 87).

Reading for storying was also a task for the eyes: The eyes did the "picking," "bundling," "harvesting," and "collecting" of words (Illich, 1993, p. 58). People chewed words, making sounds as they turned words over in their mouths, tasting their sweetness, as they heard the sounds of their words mumbling and munching. This was oral storytelling culture, and only in the late Middle Ages did *sweetness* come to mean something to do with eating food; it was originally to do with the sweetness of chewing words (Illich, 1993, p. 56). In those early days, written textual knowledge was conveyed orally as a "vineyard and garden," and in the Middle Ages books often had gilded pages with organic images (Illich, 1993, p. 57). In short, knowledge transfer via stories (and reading) relied on community and the noise of people chewing their words and then swallowing knowledge to turn it into understanding. Wisdom was an act of tracing the word from text to oral and into the vineyard, into the space of understanding the world as a knowledge connection to letters on a page. The reader was helped to trace these connections by the ornamental drawings surrounding text. Thus, a network of relations from page to word to internalized knowledge was revealed through visual drawings to create an understanding of human relations. We have diverged briefly into history to offer the reader some idea of how different the ancient and the modern practices of storytelling and knowledge management have become. It is in this context that we would like to offer three dimensions of S-space that we think would constitute a return to the ancient collective storytelling process for sharing knowledge and gaining understanding.

Voices, Logics, and Meaning: S-Space Dimensions of Participation, Power, and Discursive Action

S-space is theorized to have three dimensions: logics of power, voices of participation, and discursive action or meaning. S-space can provide insufficient freedom of narration for one to perform anything but the dominant story; people's lives can be conscripted into a hegemonic S-space. As S-space expands from monophonic (one voice) to polyphonic (multiple voices) and from monologic (one logic) to polylogic (multiple logics), the discursive action of that space becomes richer in polysemy (multiple meanings).

Regarding voices of participation, elsewhere Boje has developed a four-voice model of leadership and storytelling. The four voices are the monological voice telling one story to all, the dialogic voice between self and other, the trio of voices that includes conscience, and the fourth voice, the "voice of the voiceless." To hear the voice of the voiceless requires us to hear what is not said, by people unable or unwilling to speak. The transorganization is a cacophony of these four voices, some from many spheres, some caught in spheres that dominate, others seeking to liberate.

To expand on discursive action and polysemy or multiple meanings, White and Epston (1990, p. 12) point out that "much of our stock of lived experience goes unstoried." That means that S-spaces have storied and unstoried regions. This can be because

- We do not yet understand experience until we can story it.
- No story conveys the full richness and depth of our lived experience (much remains unstoried).
- Much of the story is told and understood in its performance, not as abstractable, codifiable, reducible, or diffusible knowledge.

Power and control in knowledge management has more micro beginnings. Since Taylor's (1919) *Principles of Scientific Management,* we have known that a cadre of planners and engineers can be assembled to capture the knowledge of workers to increase centralized control of work planning. In Crozier's (1964) studies of tobacco factories in France, we have become aware that once the experiential knowledge of workers is captured in written manuals, workers have lower economic value. However, only recently have narrativists entered the debate. The codification and abstraction process is a narrative technology, an instrument of power to dehistoricize, decontextualize, and depersonify knowledge from encapsulated lived experience. However, the power of narrative and antenarrative technologies can also be used in a more humanistic manner to develop organizations and transorganizational networks.

Recent developments in qualitative data analysis technologies have facilitated research and consultant inquiry work with TD. Theodore Taptiklis is a former consultant at McKinsey, where Tom Peters got his start. In 2000 Taptiklis began work on an oral presentation software package called StoryMaker, a competitor to Groupware, N-Vivo, and Ethnograph. The competitive advantage is that StoryMaker is a mobile voice recording, retrieval, and presentation software platform. StoryMaker allows any conversation to be converted to a reusable knowledge resource, it supports detailed coding and analysis of recorded narratives, and it allows replay of story data in a variety of presentation formats. A network of computer users can upload recorded stories, analyze them, and share their notations on particular stories. Such developments are encouraging in that they may enable TD story consultants and researchers to venture further into the unstoried polysemic regions of S-space.

CONCLUSION

Storytelling is important to TD theory and practice in several ways. First, it is through story sharing that participants crystallize their experiences in the network under development. Visions of possible futures are formulated and alliances are contemplated in story. Second, the consultant can facilitate story sharing between the temporary organizations that undertake network change initiatives by disseminating stories throughout the extended network. As the extended network gets involved in the stories of the unfolding initiatives, the development of networking options continues. Storytelling therefore is the currency by which network development is achieved and large system change is realized. In the collective dynamics of TD, storytelling plays a critical role in facilitating change and in understanding the changes that are unfolding throughout complex networks.

In this chapter, we have traced the developments and transitions in narrative knowledge management from oral society to the global information economy. Before narrative technologization, stories resided in oral culture. Now stories are an exploitable written knowledge asset in an increasingly visual culture. Illich's (1993) work points out that the shifts from oral speech, to the record of written knowledge, and on to visual knowledge reflect dramatic changes in mentality and economy. The shift from oral to visual narration is part of the postmodern turn, and we have ways of glossing visually that are somehow different from those of oral and scribed glossing. Interstory glossing research is now possible in the computerized narrative software of N-Vivo, Ethnograph, and StoryMaker. However, how we use recording, storage, and retrieval technology has a tremendous impact on organization and human behavior. Narrative technologization is thus a new topic for theory and research in TD, and the use of narrative technologies to capture and transmit tacit knowledge has enormous consequences for the global economy.

To conclude, we have a self-critique. We are familiar enough with consulting methods to know what it will take for a dialogical approach to storytelling in TD to produce a marketable method. We recognize that mining tacit knowledge stories is an easier consulting road to follow. However, we also want to be part of the emerging field of critical management consulting that provides a more sociological understanding of the process of change and development. TD is about forming spaces in which organization actors can rediscover storytelling, it is a return to community and to interactivity, and it allows us to share the multiple voices and logics of collective memory.

We believe that this is an important contribution because the processes of global change involve a dialectic of transorganizational knowledge management and dialogical consulting practices.

REFERENCES

Armstrong, D. M. (1992). *Managing by storying around: A new method of leadership.* New York: Doubleday.

Armstrong, D. M. (2002). *Chief storytelling officer: More tales from America's foremost corporate storyteller.* New York: Doubleday.

Bakhtin, M. M. (1968). *Rabelais and his world* (H. Iswolsky, Trans.). Cambridge: MIT Press.

Bakhtin, M. M. (1973). *Problems of Dostoevsky's poetics* (R. W. Rotsel, Trans.). Ann Arbor, MI: Ardis.

Bakhtin, M. M. (1981). *The dialogic imagination: Four essays* (C. Emerson & M. Holquist, Trans.). Austin: University of Texas Press.

Barge, K. J. (2002). *Antenarrative and managerial practice.* Working paper, University of Georgia.

Barry, D. (1997). Telling changes: From narrative family therapy to organizational change and development. *Journal of Organizational Change Management, 10*(1), 30–46.

Barry, D., & Elmes, M. (1997). Strategy retold: Toward a narrative view of strategic discourse. *Academy of Management Review, 22*(2), 429–452.

Boisot, M. H. (1998). *Knowledge assets: Securing competitive advantage in the information economy.* Oxford, UK: Oxford University Press.

Boje, D. M. (1979, August). *The change agent as revolutionary: Activist interventions into inter organizational networks.* Transorganizational development session of the Academy of Management Meetings, Atlanta, GA.

Boje, D. M. (1981). *Organization lore in transorganizational praxis.* Invited paper for the Academy of Folklore Meetings, San Antonio, Texas, October 22–24.

Boje, D. M. (1982, December 31). *A networking approach to the problem of securing hi tech jobs for unemployed minority autoworkers.* Working paper, University of California at Los Angeles.

Boje, D. M. (1991). The storytelling organization: A study of storytelling performance in an office supply firm. *Administrative Science Quarterly, 36*, 106–126.

Boje, D. M. (1995). Stories of the storytelling organization: A postmodern analysis of Disney as "Tamara-land." *Academy of Management Journal, 38*(4), 997–1035.

Boje, D. M. (1999). *Who rules large system transorganizational development (TD) consulting?* Available at http://web.nmsu.edu/~dboje/TDforbes98.html

Boje, D. M. (2001). *Narrative methods for organizational and communication research.* London: Sage.

Boje, D. M. (in press). The antenarrative cultural turn in narrative studies. In M. Zachry & C. Thralls (Eds.), *The cultural turn: Communicative practices in workplaces and the professions.* Amityville, NY: Baywood.

Boje, D. M., Alvarez, R. C., & Schooling, B. (2001). Reclaiming story in organization: Narratologies and action sciences. In R. Westwood & S. Linstead (Eds.), *The language of organization* (pp. 132–175). London: Sage.

Boyce, M. (1995). Collective centering and collective sense-making in the stories and storytelling of one organization. *Organization Studies, 16*(1), 107–137.

Case, P. (2002). Virtual stories of virtual working: Critical reflection on CTI consultancy discourse. In T. Clark & R. Fincham (Eds.), *Critical consulting: New perspectives on the management advice industry* (pp. 93–114). London: Blackwell.

Cobb, A. T. (1991). Toward the study of organizational coalitions: Participant concerns and activities in a simulated organizational setting. *Human Relations, 44,* 1057–1079.

Cooperrider, D. L., & Pasmore, W. A. (1991). Global social change. *Human Relations, 44,* 1037–1055.

Crozier, M. (1964). *The bureaucratic phenomenon.* London: Tavistock.

Culbert, S. A., Elden, J. M., McWhinney, W., Schmidt, W., & Tannenbaum, B. (1972). Trans-organizational praxis: A search beyond organizational development. *International Associations, 24,* 470–473.

Cummings, T. G. (1984). Transorganizational development. In B. M. Staw & L. L. Cummings (Eds.), *Research in organizational behavior* (Vol. 6, pp. 367–422). Greenwich, CT: JAI.

Denning, S. (2000). *The springboard: How storytelling ignites action in knowledge-era organizations.* Woburn, MA: Butterworth-Heinemann.

Foucault, M. (1980). *Power/knowledge.* New York: Pantheon.

Gargiulo, T. L. (2000). *Making stories: A practical guide for organizational leaders and human resource specialists.* Westport, CT: Quorum.

Gephart, R. P., Jr. (1991). Succession, sensemaking, and organizational change: A story of a deviant college president. *Journal of Organizational Change Management, 4,* 35–44.

Illich, I. (1993). *In the vineyard of the text: A commentary to Hugh's* Didascalicon. Chicago: University of Chicago Press.

Information Awareness Office. (2002). *Total information awareness program (TIA) system description document (SDD).* Retrieved on June 18, 2005, from http://www.epic.org/privacy/profiling/tia/tiasystemdescription.pdf

Kaye, M. (1996). *Myth-makers and story-tellers.* Sydney: Business & Professional Publishing.

Motamedi, K. (1978). *The evolution from interorganizational design to transorganizational development.* Paper presented at the Academy of Management Meetings in San Francisco.

Nonaka, I., & Takeuchi, H. (1995). *The knowledge-creating company: How Japanese companies create the dynamics of innovation.* New York: Oxford University Press.

Perlmutter, H. V. (1991). On the rocky road to the first global civilization. *Human Relations, 44,* 897–920.

Perrow, C. (1972). *Complex organizations: A critical essay.* Glenview, IL: Scott Foresman.

Peters, T., & Waterman, R. (1982). *In search of excellence: Lessons from America's best-run companies.* New York: Harper & Row.

Polanyi, K. (1974). *Personal knowledge.* Chicago: University of Chicago Press.

Schein, H. (1996). Culture: The missing concept in organization studies. *Administrative Science Quarterly, 41,* 229–241.

Shaw, G., Brown, R., & Bromiley, P. (1998, May–June). Strategic stories: How 3M is rewriting business planning. *Harvard Business Review.*

Sink, D. W. (1991). Transorganizational development in urban policy coalitions. *Human Relations, 44,* 1179–1195.

Sloterdijk, P. (1993). *Weltfremdheit*. Frankfurt: Suhrkamp.

Sloterdijk, P. (1998). *Spharen I: Blasen*. Frankfurt: Suhrkamp.

Sloterdijk, P. (1999). *Spharen II: Globen*. Frankfurt: Suhrkamp.

Snowden, D. (2002, July). *Complex acts of knowing: Paradox and descriptive self-awareness*. IBM Global Services working paper.

Snowden, D. (2001). Narrative patterns: The perils and possibilities of using story in organizations.

Knowledge Management. Retrieved July 13, 2007, from http://www.kwork.org/Resources/narrative.pdf

Taylor, F. W. (1919). *Principles of scientific management*. New York: Harper.

Vickers, M. H. (2002). *Illness, work and organization: Postmodernism and antenarratives for the reinstatement of voice*. Working paper, University of Western Sydney.

White, M., & Epston, D. (1990). *Narrative means to therapeutic ends*. New York: W.W. Norton.

35

Reflections on the Field and Beyond

An Interview With Warren Bennis

THOMAS G. CUMMINGS

TC: Warren, you were there from the start of OD as an applied social science. What drew you to it? How did it pop into your life?

For my generation's cohort group, OD, group dynamics, and applied social science were sort of a loosely connected stew of ideas—intertwined, inseparable. I was drawn to it, as with so many other things in my life, through chance, best articulated by what Karl Weick has called in a marvelous phrase "eccentric precursors." For me, these precursors started at a small, very liberal college in the central Ohio town of Yellow Springs, Antioch College. I chose Antioch after returning from World War II, where I served in Germany as an infantry lieutenant. For an urban kid like me, Yellow Springs was not my vision of an ideal location. I like cities, and the closest big town I never heard of or could pronounce correctly was Xenia. Antioch College was always an adventurous, avant-garde place, founded in

1853 by Horace Mann, a close friend of Thomas Jefferson. It was the first "white" college to admit African Americans and, after Oberlin, the first to admit women.

I chose Antioch for two reasons: One of the men in my platoon, my runner, kept talking about this great college he had attended before the war. He never made it through, so I decided to visit his family, then living in Utica, New York. I learned from them that Antioch was a co-op college where you could work half the year and pay your way through college. I didn't know about the GI Bill, which would have paid my full tuition. In any case, that was the second reason I decided to go there.

During my sophomore year, a new president was appointed by the name of Douglas McGregor. He looked like a grad student, was 42 years old, from MIT's (pre–Sloan School days) Economics and Social Sciences Department. And with a Harvard PhD in social psychology. Seemed like an unusual choice: a burr of a reddish-brown hair, mustard-orangey mustache, tweedy, dashing, and unlike anybody's stereotype of what a college president should look like, certainly not mine. His first symbolic acts, as I now think about them, were either weirdly off-putting (to the faculty) or wondrously fascinating (to the students). At the second general assembly, held monthly for all 600 of us (the other 600 were out of town, on co-op jobs), he let us in on his strong feeling that his 4 years of psychoanalysis was a more powerful education than his 4 years of undergraduate study. At the second general assembly, he decreed that there would be no Friday classes for the remainder of the semester. All Fridays would be scheduled for Goals Discussions; that is, what should be the primary goals of our education for the next 4 years. These discussions plus the input from the returning co-op students would determine the destiny and future of Antioch College. After a while it became obvious that McGregor had been deeply influenced by the work of the German social psychologist Kurt Lewin, who he had recruited to MIT. In the late '40s, MIT established the first research center that focused on the social psychology of small groups. By the way, Doug is a very important part of this chronicle of OD because during his years at MIT, both pre- and after Antioch, he became, without knowing the term, what chaos theorists call a "strange attractor." He attracted some of the strangest and most creative types around, primarily a bunch of intellectual vagrants, soon to become a generation who shaped the intellectual contours of post–World War II social psychology.

Harvard, the story goes, passed on Kurt because he was too short, too Jewish, and too un-Cambridge. On top of that, his German accent was so thick that many thought it was his second language. One Harvard professor said he looked like an unmade bed. Definitely not a Harvard Man. He didn't much care for Harvard, either. So Doug lured him to MIT.

Then a number of Lewin's disciples followed him, Festinger, Schachter, Riecken, Back, Kelley, Lippitt, White, Leavitt, Bavelas, Shepard, Horwitz, and Cartwright among others.

After 6 years at Antioch, McGregor returned to MIT and helped establish the Sloan School of Management. Shortly after arriving he recruited Mason Haire from Berkeley, Bill Evan from Wharton, Don Marquis from Michigan, and president of the APA, Ed Schein from Harvard. Then for 1- or 2-year appointments he recruited Bob Greenleaf, who spent his time writing a book on "servant leadership"; Bob Kahn; and Harry Levinson. I forgot to mention one of his most unusual and important appointments, Joe Scanlon. Doug drafted him not from the Pittsburgh Steelers but from the U.S. Steelworkers of America, where Joe was head of research. He was a union guy through and through, without a college degree, and created the first postwar management–labor program for what was then referred to as (sounds rather quaint today) "participative management." Both Joe and Doug died young, in their late 50s, probably from a combination of smoking and the fatal habit of putting passion before health.

If Doug lived today, he would probably be called a "public intellectual" because he didn't do the usual—and today, the necessary—mainstream academic research after getting his PhD at Harvard under Gordon Allport. Harvard's social relations department was then loaded with prominent social scientists: Boring, Mundt, the Kluckhohns, Geertz, Parsons, Bales, Homans, Erikson, Mosteller, Bauer, Inkeles, and Murray were all there and many others I can't recall right now. Doug was part of that but then went to MIT and started writing a few essays, one of which led to his seminal book, *The Human Side of Enterprise* (1960).

It never crossed my mind that he would become my role model. I didn't think I had his passion to change the world or revivify human organizations. I was attracted to him and his brio but rather skeptical of all this new stuff.

What drew me to his work was his gift, both with students and faculty, to create what Jerry Bruner later called an "evocative community."

TC: So you didn't come out of the military, out of World War II, saying you want to be an academic?

Furthest from my mind. The only thing I was sure about was that I wanted to make something of myself. That plus, I suppose, a strong attraction to Doug McGregor's ideas, values, and cosmology. Basically "Theory X" and "Theory Y," for which he later became known, appealed to me: two views of humankind, virtually a black–white Manichaean view of what drives us. On the one hand, Theory Y reminds me of my favorite Emily Dickinson line, "I dwell in possibilities . . . a fairer house than prose." Theory Y views people as limitless reservoirs of strengths and capabilities waiting there, wanting to be pulled out of us or usefully deployed.

Theory X takes a Hobbesean, pessimistic view of human nature. People have to be coerced to work, are basically lazy and resistant to any purpose, noble or not, and based pretty much on coercive power. In a way, McGregor was Rousseauean, believing that if we could possibly create the right social system, the right conditions for growth, it would draw from our innate positive nature, our best selves.

Through the shining ether of time, we can observe that both worked under different conditions and that both are alive and well today. The difference is whether a social system or its leadership has a commitment toward creating "a culture of growth," which Doug likened to an "agricultural" model. Theory X, as Doug perceived it, favors a mechanical, bureaucratic, coercive view of motivation. Doug's genius was his ability to articulate that simple framework with clarity and empathy to a somewhat resistant cohort of 1950s and 1960s executives, most of whom thought he was either half crazy or half Bolshevik and probably both. I'm not exaggerating. As Abe Maslow later told me about Doug, "He shoved his ideas down the reluctant throats of thousands of American businessmen."

One brief and passing comment on where we are today: I wrote an article in 1959, for IBM's *Think* magazine, at a time when the company was considered to be the very model of the Weberian "ideal type" of bureaucracy. The article was titled "The Death of Bureaucracy," which forecast that in 50 years or so, it would be replaced by a more horizontal, collaborative model. (I figured that in 50 years or so, I would be proven right or dead.) Despite my noble aspirations, I recently was quoted in *The Economist*, "that the iron law of hierarchy remains in place as adamantine as a flawed diamond."

TC: What was it like at MIT during your doctoral studies and early years of your career?

It was an exuberant and nurturing environment for PhD candidates. I was able to combine my curriculum at MIT's strong economic and labor relations courses with Harvard's sociology and social psychology courses. I ended up with an MIT PhD in economics and social science. I was diligent at recruiting mentors and worked hard to become an unavoidable protégé. There were many older, supportive brothers, so to speak, like Doug and Alex Bavelas and economists like Samuelson, Modigliani, and Solow, who took the time to encourage and embolden me. So even when I was young and green, I was treated as if I might possibly become a contributor to our field. Certainly not in economic theory, as Samuelson regularly reminded me, but in the areas I eventually gravitated toward and thrived in: organizational change, group behavior, leadership with the romantic idea that through the behavioral sciences, we could influence the organizational terrain in positive directions. To a great extent the field of "positive psychology" and "positive organizational behavior" had its roots in the McGregorian chants.

I think I should say a little about the zeitgeist of OD and OB in the '40s through the

'60s. The title of the first book I co-authored and co-edited (1961) with Ken Benne and Bob Chin, *The Planning of Change,* signals what we were up to. The title itself seems ridiculously quixotic, at worst an episodic fit of adolescent hubris. The idea that significant change can be planned, with the right recipe or algorithm, is a charming aspiration but not exactly a revealed truth, then or now. That naïve hope, though, was energizing and in many ways fueled the social scientific world with the capacity to dream, we hoped, with our eyes wide open.

At that time those hopes were not totally unjustified. There were hundreds of extraordinarily bright and motivated academics who had served in various branches of the government during World War II. They served in research units such as the Office of Naval Research, the Office of Strategic Services (OSS), the Defense Advanced Research Projects Agency (DARPA), Office of War Information, and many others. Jim Miller, later president of the American Psychological Association, was a project leader at OSS, the predecessor of the CIA, developing ingenious personality test instruments for predicting intelligence agents' success. All the armed forces established research centers with enormously talented social scientists and statisticians working on social science and war-related problems, such as compatibility tests for personnel working in tight, isolated places like submarines; morale surveys, group cohesiveness, communication problems, persuasion techniques, etcetera. Mosteller, Stouffer, and Likert, with army support, produced the monumental, four-volume study *The American Soldier* (Stouffer, 1949); Paul Lazarsfeld, working with the Office of War Information, helped to develop the first political opinion surveys; other political scientists and social psychologists at Yale, Hovland, Janis, Lasswell, and others, were working on influence and persuasion issues. Anthropologists like Mead, Whorf, and Benedict studying the cultural attributes of the Germans and Japanese; linguists at MIT,

Columbia, Harvard, and other universities were working for our nascent intelligence agencies. Economists at Princeton, Chicago, MIT, and Berkeley were developing game theory and decision-making models and at places like Bell Labs, with DARPA money, coming up with some of the most advanced designs for computers and other technologies. And don't forget the work of the team of psychologists, philosophers, sociologists, and anthropologists (including Adorno, Frenkel-Brunswik, Levinson, and Sanford) that led to their seminal study, *The Authoritarian Personality* (Adorno et al., 1950).

Underlying all this urgent and energetic activity, to repeat myself, was the belief that with the new methods of statistics, especially nonparametric statistics, creative survey and experimental methods, the social science community could play a major role in bringing about a better world, a world that would make war obsolete, subdue prejudice, trump unbridled aggression through reason and reasonable interventions. Hopelessly, romantically naïve, probably, but we were all children of the Age of Enlightenment. We were, without knowing it, followers of a half-crazy monk, Pelagius (late 4th century), who felt that humans could draw resources from within, the core of natural purity that God had put there, and with that force, we could remake the world in our own lifetimes.

In the early '20s of the last century, the Johns Hopkins historian of ideas, Arthur Lovejoy, coined the term *metaphysical pathos* to describe the values, our underlying biases, which were embedded in and insinuated their way into our "value-free" research. Remember that all of the post–World War II researchers grew up under the shadow of Hitler. All of us were either running away from subhuman totalitarian states or frightened by their seductively toxic leadership, their power to control the masses, their fatal capacities to diminish human freedom and democratic values. Seared into the limbic zone of our brains were the eerily staticky sounds of the '40s, transmitted by short-wave radios; the scary Movietone News pictures of thousands of Germans goosestepping their way to the guttural pathologies of *der Führer*.

We also were able to understand our own vulnerabilities through what was occurring 3,000 or 7,000 miles away, across the Atlantic and then, later, the Pacific. Only by looking back can I understand the metaphysical pathos of those times and how that influenced and guided our research agendas. We focused on the positive and negative power of the human group; the necessity for democratic institutions; the power of collaboration and the small, primary group; the limits of and reverence for tolerance; the limits of and appeal of intervention; the passion for developing an applied behavioral science that could improve the human condition. That was the substrate that influenced almost all of our research efforts.

And it was that metaphysical pathos, as much as my attraction to McGregor, that led me to OB/OD, of that I'm pretty sure. It wasn't simply the conceptual excitement of OB/OD that drew me and others to it; it was the promise that if we didn't understand the phenomena sufficiently, the consequences would be fatal. We also felt that the human organization provided a laboratory, in situ, from which we could learn so much.

One other consideration to throw into the post–World War II mix: It was the era of the so-called Organization Man, millions of American men returning to jobs or taking jobs in factories for the first time in their young lives. And millions of women, raising children and buying kitchen appliances that the factories their husbands worked in were turning out by the millions. The movies and novels of the time are sadly telling: *Man in the Gray Flannel Suit, Executive Suite, Patterns,* and many sociological studies of the dreary flatness of the new suburban landscapes. Coincidentally, I'm writing this on March 8, 2007, International Women's Day, when I noticed in my neighborhood Costco more men than women buying those home appliances.

I still think we're a long way from developing a robust applied behavioral science. There was a time in the mid- to late '60s that I came close to rallying a small group of social scientists to build a University of Applied Behavioral Science, to bring together all relevant social sciences, which would illuminate the mysteries of change and leadership and the strategic leverage points of social system change. When you consider what's going on today in cognitive psychology, neurosciences, positive psychology, judgment and decision-making, negotiation and influence, computational biology and psychiatry, behavioral economics, brain mapping, and adaptive, complex systems, I think we're closer to a more scientific understanding of organizational behavior and leadership studies than ever. Am I once again being seduced by that Pelagian hubris to think that right now is the juiciest time ever for the possibility of an integrated, applied behavioral science? Do you see it that way, too?

TC: Absolutely, that research is very exciting. As you were talking, I was reflecting on what drew me into the OD field, and it is very parallel to your experience. Mine was around Vietnam, that was the zeitgeist in the 1960s. I happened to run into incredible people during my doctoral studies at UCLA, like Will McWhinney, Bob Tannenbaum, Eric Trist, Peter Vaill, and Jim Clark, who mentored me and kindled my interest in OD. Now, back to your early days in the field. What concepts drove your initial conceptions of OD?

First of all, because I was a returning vet, I started MIT 4 years later than most of my classmates. When I came to MIT, I don't think I had any fundamental concepts in mind at all. One aspect of growing up in the '50s was that I careened into psychoanalysis. I received foundation support for a "didactic analysis." And in those days, one didn't talk about that. And it wasn't just an intellectual pursuit. I was seriously anxious about a lot of things, most of all, whether I had the stuff to become an academic.

Like many of my doctoral student buddies, I thought I was a fraud. I should also admit, Tom, that a patient who was selected for a didactic analysis had to satisfy three criteria: 1, that he (no shes were eligible at that time) might possibly make a contribution to society; 2, that the applicant had to be neurotic enough to be interesting; and 3, not too neurotic to be helped. How that decision was made is still a mystery. All I can remember now—this was 1952—was that I was interviewed by three well-known analysts, each of whom were inscrutable, blew cigarette smoke in my face, and like many analysts of the time, coughed more than they talked. Additionally, I had to guarantee that I would not leave Boston for at least 3 years, would come daily and pay $5 for each session. That's cheap even figuring in inflation but ridiculously huge if your cash flow was a $1,300 fellowship.

I found some of the ideas of classical psychoanalysis marginally useful for understanding myself but far more helpful in my understanding of group behavior. I wasn't at all convinced, then or now, that it was a "cure." All the same, it was and is a fascinating, if reductive, way of looking at the world. I believe that even more today than I did a half-century ago. Freud himself said that, at best, psychoanalysis can strengthen your intellectual defenses.

At the same time, there really wasn't much theory in the applied social sciences. There was a lot of the work in survey research and group dynamics at the University of Michigan's Institute for Social Research with luminaries like Likert, Katz, Kahn, and Zajonc. There was a lot of solid research going on and theory building, what Merton would later call middle-range theory. There was also a ton of research going on in many research centers on group decision making, intergroup conflict, democratic versus autocratic leadership, and the beginning of cognitive social science by the likes of Festinger, Bruner, and Bavelas. Many of these experiments were ingenious, exemplified by the work of Asch, Sherif,

Carthwright, Newcomb, Hartley, Schein, and others.

There were also a lot of applied concepts that grew out of research on encounter and T groups. When researchers like R. R. Blake, H. A. Shepard, and others attempted to use T groups as an instrument to change large social systems, such as AT&T or Standard Oil, OD segued into the wider domain of complex, macrosystem dynamics.

TC: And the "causal texture of organizational environments," which led to interest in social ecology and transorganizational development.

So it is interesting to observe how we morphed from the individual to the organization qua system and to its relationship to the "causal texture" of the environment. I'm not as in touch with the younger people in our field as I'd like to be, so I don't know whether the same excitement that infused the field in the '50s and '60s is there today. I hope that's the case, and I'm encouraged by the work of our younger faculty and through interviewing recent candidates for our department. It seems to me right now we're at an axial point. I think the next phase is what we were talking about earlier, cognitive behavioral science and neuroscience. I think the future is going to be even more exciting, if more difficult.

In 1969, I wrote something about this being an age of change in managerial behavior requiring a new concept of man based on increased knowledge of her or his complex and shifting needs, which replaces an oversimplified, innocent, pushbutton idea of man; a new concept of power based on cooperation and reason, which replaces a model of power based on coerced and threatened behavior; and a new concept of organizational values based on democratic ideals, which replaces the depersonalized, mechanistic value system of bureaucracy. We're always in a struggle between bureaucratic solutions and new 21st-century conditions. Just take one example, social influence: distributing power and authority. The bureaucratic solution relies explicitly on legal, rational power with implied use of coercive power. In any case, it confused the often ambiguous and shifting sources of power: authority, coercion, and legal code. And Doug said it well: Power means that the leader controls the means of the subordinates' subjective well-being, such as pay, vacations, office space, and the like. But see how outdated that is with the changes taking place in the last third of the 20th century: the separation of management and ownership, the rise of trade unions, and the recognition of the negative and unintended effects of authoritarian rule. So when I think about the kind of changes going on, and have been going on for the last 50 years or so, it strikes me that it's going to take some time before we have anything like a grand theory. I think its going to take a while for us to say, "Here is *the* model of change."

TC: I just think there's a reason for the "D" in OD; to develop means that you have some idea of a more advanced state, meaning more open, more collegial; you name it. Change management just sits out there and uses whatever concepts and approaches are helpful to get things changed. It doesn't have a more developed state in mind.

That's true. I think the word *development* is the key. It's an important distinction you're making that I wasn't aware of when I coauthored *The Planning of Change* in 1961. When I read that question you proposed, I realized that in the late '50s and early '60s, that distinction was in full bloom but not fully recognized.

TC: So early on you're writing stuff on OD—very broad at that point. Then you start to zero down, what they call drill down, on leadership. Why? What led you to this topic?

Leadership has fascinated me since my childhood and was engraved in my thinking during and since my World War II experience as an infantry platoon leader in Germany. One of the most profound insights for me was the shift of the frame through which I began to understand the power of the group and of social norms. I began to realize that the morale of an individual, the courage of an individual, the cowardice of an individual are all influenced by the norms and expectations of the group and role expectations. Look up the word *courage* in your dictionary. I've tried just about every credible source, and all definitions exclusively endow the individual with bravery or courage. Now, there are some individuals who are courageous, and most of them I personally observed in combat were weirdly idiosyncratic, even borderline cases. What impressed me the most was that ordinary people can do extraordinary things due primarily to group bonding and role determinants. At that time, it was an amazing breakthrough in my thinking; nowadays, it's folk psychology. I was only mildly surprised in graduate school that a number of military sociologists were confirming my observations with their surveys of combat soldiers, some of which were reported in the earlier mentioned book, *The American Soldier*.

If you look at my work over the last half century or so, most frequently it addresses the *relationship* between the leader and the group, the leader in *relationship* to the organization, the leader in *relationship* to the self. I wrote an article recently, teasingly titled "The End of Leadership" (1999), where I go back and forth between the idea of leadership solely attributed to a person and leadership as a function of a relationship. Along with Geertz, I parted company with Weber on this. Charisma, as he wrote, was something endowed in an individual, a "gift of grace." I believe that charisma is a gift of a person capable of establishing a trusting relationship with willing followers.

Of course, that recognition I received for my writings on leadership, a "branding," if you will, encourages you to keep doing it, which is also a dangerous thing. Like a chef who does two or three really good dishes and then keeps doing those two or three dishes until they get stale. The truth is that I don't think you can fully get your conceptual arms around leadership without understanding the system. It's easy to be suckered into responding to the media and a vast lay audience by simply emphasizing *the* individual leader, *the* Carlylean "able man," as the sole agency for influence and power. Systems are just not sexy in a way that a person is. Honestly, Tom, I don't know of a single public intellectual who is known for insights about systems! Can you imagine a popular magazine, like *People,* called *Systems?* With the "peoplefication" of just about everything, we rarely, if ever, see articles about the system or group or ensemble in the media, including all business magazines. At the checkout counter of your supermarket, take a look— or better, don't—at the magazines on display. They all play into the celebrity, America's Top 40 Leaders, or the 30 Young Leaders, or the 50 Top Women Leaders, and so on and on, ad nauseam. I do not now, and never have believed, in the "great man theory," all this bullshit of one Rushmorean figure changing the world. There's probably at least a thousand definitions of leadership, but one I lean toward is that it is a process that motivates people to work collaboratively to accomplish great things. The key word is *collaboratively.*

One of the most interesting books I've read this past year is Don Tapscott's *Wikinomics* (Tapscott & Williams, 2006). It's about open source management, that is, working in collaboration with others outside the organization. It's interesting and controversial. Bill Gates and many others call it "collectivism" or "Bolshevik." That's rubbish. We had better understand and get ready for a different world than we OD types grew up in, know about, and have written about.

Let me give you one example taken from *Wikinomics.* It starts off with this anecdote: A newly appointed CEO of a failing gold mine company in northern Ontario, Canada, attends a weekend conference at MIT's Media Lab and hears a lecture by the founder of Linux on open source systems. He immediately gets excited about the possibilities for his firm. Shortly after his return, he tells his staff this is the strategy the company will take. He

persuades them that their only chance at resuscitating the company is through open source management, a new and inexpensive way of outsourcing. Which they promptly did. On the Internet, they invited one and all to help them find gold. They provided maps, access to the company lab, and worked out a formula of incentives based on what the new sources find. The formula was unclear and problematical, but outsiders found 75 tons of gold for the firm that existed on their property. The company reported huge profits for the first time in years.

For organizations, open source management is both a threat and a godsend. It threatens the hell out of in-house "experts" because now leaders have access to information not accessible to incumbents of the organization. I think this outsourcing of knowledge will increase exponentially in the coming years. Big time. Check it out on *Wikipedia.*

So when you read James Surowiecki's *The Wisdom of Crowds* (2004), it's hard to ignore how interconnected the world is and how we can mass collaborate to solve problems. I would love to teach a class using as texts *Wikinomics, The Wisdom of Crowds,* and Malcolm Gladwell's *The Tipping Point* (2002).

TC: *Freakonomics* (Leavitt & Dubner, 2006).

Yes, I should have mentioned that one, too. In a recent *New York Times,* a reporter covered the American Economics Association annual meeting. He talked to a young woman economist, only 26 years old, who was applying behavioral economic methods and findings to reduce the threat of AIDS in Africa. The reporter claimed that he's been going to these meetings for the last 6 years and found most of them dreary, boring, and esoteric. But now he's beginning to report things that can significantly impact some of the world's most serious problems. Can OD make the same kind of impact in organizations and public policy that are equivalent to the contributions of behavioral economics? Can the Academy of Management, for example, convene a

Manhattan-like task force to see how OD can be applied to our planet's problems and threats? Is this question just more hubris and grandiosity? Wouldn't it be helpful if we could work with a few less advanced and desperately poor countries where 90% of the population or more live on less than a dollar a day, with immunization and health organizations to make their efforts more effective and efficient? The Gates Foundation did support such a program for training immunization and health officers of six African countries and found a significant increase in the number of families and individuals who were inoculated. They all lived long enough to rise from that poverty level.

Tom, you said earlier that you thought that OD had lost much of its initial coherence in theory, value orientation, and practice. You asked what I make of all this. In a way, it has been a very prosperous age for OD. It's created lots of new roles and opportunities. Management consulting has grown and thrived. But I do think, as OD academics and practitioners, we do have common core values and principles. We do rely on ideas and evidence and a spirit of inquiry. We do work hard to develop more creative and productive organizations, with all of the gut-wrenching threats we are facing right now: terrorism and its partner, tribalism; global warming; the shrinking middle class; poverty; health care worldwide and in this country, with 45 million of our citizens without any health insurance; plus nuclear mayhem. Can we contribute actionable knowledge that could reduce the danger of these threats, even ameliorate them? Provide even some half-measure solutions? What's stopping us?

TC: Now you and Burt Nanus wrote the book *Leaders* (1984). What do you know today about leadership that you didn't know then? What have you discovered?

Based on extensive interviews with 90 leaders in the corporate, not-for-profit, and public sectors, we found four basic competencies of leaders: management of self, management of attention, management of trust, and management of communication. There are a couple of fundamental things that have changed in the meantime. One is implied. It refers to what I said earlier about open source management: the problem and the solution of mass collaboration. A lot of independent contractors or free agents are coming in to do things that both upset and benefit the organization. We didn't even think about this in the '80s when Burt and I started to discuss our book. I don't think we saw this coming until, maybe, the mid-'90s. We didn't take fully into account what is now taken for granted, the quotidian, everydayness of 24/7, adaptive complexity of social systems. Globalization, technological disruptive mischief, and a roiling world economy. Who knew? We didn't.

Let's take another example: Why do we have all these C-words today? When we wrote the book, Tom, Burt, and I wanted to call it *CEO*. The publisher said "No! in thunder. No," he repeated. "Who the hell knows what this acronym *CEO* means, for crissakes?" He was practically screaming at us. Twenty some years later, what sentient person doesn't know what *CEO* stands for? Nowadays we live with a dizzying proliferation of C-words, not just the common ones we're all familiar with by now, like *COO, CIO, CFO*. What about *CWO* (wisdom), *CSO* (security or spiritual), *CTO* (technology)? I'm not making these up. How come? Well, we all know the answer: because the tasks are more complicated, more far reaching and consequential these days. All of which make the top organization team more important than ever. Which is why the work of one of our colleagues, Nandini Rajagopalan, is so important. "No one is smarter than all of us" is an ancient Japanese adage. It is essential that leaders lead a team, that they must be interdependent and know that they can't succeed unless they can do this successfully. This isn't easy, never was easy, but made infinitely more difficult if one of the Cs is in Bangalore, another in Singapore, five other Cs in Europe, and three in Eastern Europe, and on and on and on.

So I don't think back in 1983, when we first started working on the book, that Burt and I had any idea of the magnitude and significance of all this, even though we were arguing against the intractable bureaucratic command-and-control machine systems which towered over the business landscape. Organizations today cannot be led the way they used to, not because it's, well, nice to be collaborative; not because it's wise or because it's humane, but because it's *necessary* to understand these interdependencies, those exogenous forces Eric Trist wrote about a half century ago. And if not understood, I just don't see how leaders will lead effectively. I remember asking Bob Galvin, before his son, Chris, succeeded him a few years ago, when Motorola was really "hot," how he thinks his bet on Iridium will do. He said, "Warren, until I figure out what's going on in South Korea, I'm not certain." Since when does a leader need to rely on Korea or China or Brazil to know if an innovation will succeed? Shakespeare, writing in the 16th century, talked about a "girdled globe." He had no idea.

Another thing: Because of the Internet and the mass of bloggers and other sources of information, transparency is inevitable. Secrecy just can't work any more; at least in the long run. What brought the CEO of Home Depot, Bob Nardelli, down? A smart *Wall Street Journal* writer and a perceptive blogger. I read in yesterday's *New York Times* that the add-on bonus for Goldman Saks and one other financial firm, which did $40 billion and $36 billion of business the last quarter, averaged about $300,000 per employee. How do you think that feels to someone who won't get close to that in a lifetime? More than 25% of CEOs of major companies were ousted involuntarily last year. This churning is due to a world I don't think any of us fully understand. Who knew about private equity firms a few years ago? It's not just disruptive technologies;

it's about lots of people all over the world getting an idea that could throw a monkey wrench into any business in the world and at any time. Who would have thought only 4 or 5 years ago that Ford would fall this drastically or that Toyota will be number 1, perhaps before this book's publication date?

Between the Internet and globalization, between the fight for talent and the complexity of organizations, what does this mean for leadership? It means that among other things, collaboration is a must because COP (control, order, and predict) organizations, no matter how audacious or smart, won't work. It means you have to get people to be open to the unbidden. It means that leaders have to create a culture of growth and candor. It means that leaders have to engender an adaptive capacity in themselves and their workforce.

We hinted at some of these things in our book, *Leaders,* and Phil Slater and I got closer to some of these changes in 1968 and wrote about some of these forces in *The Temporary Society.* But they weren't central.

TC: You are writing a book with Noel Tichy about judgment, which I think is the heart of leadership. I don't think we have a single course in the business school that has anything to do with judgment. What are you and Tichy trying to say?

We identified three domains where judgment is of utmost importance: people, strategy, and judgment calls during crisis. It's not that they are the only ones, but they are the most critical domains in making judgment calls. We're then refracting those three domains through the prisms of four types of knowledge. One is of self-knowledge: what the leader understands about herself, her needs, biases, abilities, aspirations, limitations, strengths, etcetera. Second is social network knowledge, meaning knowledge about his team, direct reports, his "curia," so to speak. Third is organization knowledge, and the fourth we're calling stakeholder knowledge, the understanding of the clogged cartography of stakeholders and the "causal texture of the environment," like Galvin's "South Korea" response. The third part of this three-by-four matrix is the judgment process through time: preparation, the call, and then evaluating and reflecting the decision. The book concludes with a template of factors to keep in mind when making critical decisions. We hope that our framework I've just outlined will increase the probability of leaders making good judgments. We're convinced that we barely touched the surface of this formidable topic. I feel now as if we are what the French call truffle dogs (actually, they're pigs) who scurry to find the ground where the truffles are. The farmer then has to do the grunt work, digging and digging to get the precious quarry.

TC: Judgment sounds like a skill that could be developed?

I think it's difficult but not impossible. I believe that the two hardest qualities to learn and use, maybe impossible to teach, are judgment and taste. I don't think you can learn either exclusively from readings or lectures. But we can use the written word and the classroom to help people use their experience to improve their capacity to make the right call.

TC: Just to wrap all this up, what do you want to be remembered for 20, 30, 40, 50 years from now?

I've been asked that question a number of times in the past, and my answer seems to change as I age. I'm editing this interview the day after my 82nd birthday, and I think I may be clearer now than ever before. I know that I am a master teacher and love doing that. I feel I can help engender, not always, but a lot of times, an evocative community. I want to be remembered as someone who touched people, students and colleagues. I want to be remembered as generous company. I want to be remembered as someone who is engaging and fun to be with. I want to be remembered as someone who never stopped questioning and

who was wandering through life in a state of wonder.

TC: I mean, how about traits? My recollection of you in the future will have nothing to do with your scholarly content.

What would you say about me?

TC: This guy was one of the hardest workers I've ever seen, pure hard work. Also, one of the best, keenest minds I ever met. And I liked him because he was open about his foibles and downsides, and not a vain human being. I never even hooked it to the content of your work.

Well, thank you. I would like to be remembered that way. I'm thinking of writing a short book called *Generous Company*. It's certainly a part of colleagueship and may even be an important, but an overlooked, facet of leadership. I'm so thankful that I've been encouraged to grow, never feeling pushed to do anything I wasn't keen on doing. In that respect, I feel that I've grown up and thrived here at USC. I came here when I was 55, and with the support of colleagues present when I got here in 1980, like O'Toole, Lawler, Nanus, Greiner, Mason, yourself, and others, USC has turned out to be the right place for me.

You're right. I honestly doubt—this is not false modesty—if I will be remembered for my scholarly contributions. When I read my students' yearly evaluations, year after year, only rarely does anyone mention my "good mind" or intellectual acuity. Most of the time, they write things like, "He's so attentive; sensitive; great listener"—nice, warm, fuzzy things like that. Another way of responding to your question is that I feel most alive when I teach. I also feel that way when I write something new, something freshly imagined, something I could find just the right words for that would make my thoughts sing. About a week before Abraham Maslow was stricken with a massive heart attack that took his young life, he told me why he left Brandeis and headed west to Palo Alto and Stanford. He said,

I think quoting Yeats, that he went west "to sing one last exultant song." I don't think I've sung mine yet.

REFERENCES

Adorno, T., Frenkel-Brunswik, E., Levinson, D., & Sanford, N. (1950). *The authoritarian personality*. New York: W.W. Norton.

Bennis, W. (1969). *Organizational development*. Reading, MA: Addison-Wesley.

Bennis, W. (1999). The end of leadership. *Organizational Dynamics, 28*(1), 71–80.

Bennis, W., Benne, K., & Chin, R. (Eds.). (1961). *The planning of change*. New York: Holt, Rinehart & Winston.

Bennis, W., & Nanus, B. (1984). *Leaders*. New York: Collins.

Bennis, W., & Slater, P. (1968). *The temporary society*. New York: Harper & Row.

Bennis, W., & Tichy, N. (2007). *Judgment: The essence of leader*. New York: Penguin Putnam.

Gladwell, M. (2002). *The tipping point*. Boston: Back Bay Books.

Leavitt, S., & Dubner, S. (2006). *Freakonomics*. New York: William Morrow.

McGregor, D. (1960). *The human side of enterprise*. New York: McGraw-Hill.

Stouffer, S. (1949). *The American soldier*. Princeton, NJ: Princeton University Press.

Surowiecki, J. (2004). *The wisdom of crowds*. New York: Random House.

Tapscott, D., & Williams, A. (2006). *Wikinomics*. New York: Portfolio Hardcover.

Name Index

Aalst, W. van der, 293, 296
Abrahamson, E., 499
Abrahamsson, B., 279
Abrams, L., 14
Ackoff, R. R., 638
Adam, G. B., 141
Adams, J. D., 231
Adler, N., 277, 278, 279, 284, 298, 301n3, 516
Adler, P. A., 412
Adler, P. S., 475, 479
Adorno, T., 668
Agarwal, S., 621
Agashae, Z., 487
Agnew, P. G., 241
Aguilar, F., 387
Agurén, S., 291 (tab)
Ahlstrand, B., 386, 392
Aiman-Smith, L., 193 (tab), 199–200
Alban, B., 101, 126, 133, 261, 262, 263, 267, 268
Alban, B. T., 28, 152, 156, 159, 168, 229, 419, 644
Alderfer, C. J., 169
Alderfer, C. P., 139, 168, 169, 179, 555
Alderson, S., 244
Aldrich, H., 629, 630, 639
Alford, C., 262, 263
Alfred, T., 571n4
Alinsky, S., 32
Allegro, J. T., 291 (tab), 292 (tab)
Allison, G., 476
Alpanger, G., 387
Alter, C., 629
Alvarez, R. C., 653
Amersvoort, P. J. L. M. van, 292 (tab), 301n4
Anderson, E., 375
Anderson, M., 107
Anderson, P., 521, 530
Anderson, R. C., 554
Andrews, K., 388
Angermeier, I., 250
Angus, L., 250
Ansoff, H. I., 387, 388

Argote, L., 478, 531
Argyris, C., 15, 17, 29, 30, 54, 56, 57, 58, 59, 60, 61, 63–64, 65, 71, 100, 125, 127, 129, 143, 152, 153, 156, 167, 172, 175, 176, 238, 239, 246, 273, 377, 386, 387, 408, 409, 410, 418, 464, 481–484, 490
Armenakis, A. A., 153, 190, 387
Armstrong, D. M., 657
Armstrong, T. R., 243, 244
Arthur, J., 410
Arthur, J. B., 193 (tab), 199–200
Arthur, M. B., 372, 378
Asadorian, R. A., 292 (tab)
Asch, S., 40
Ashby, W. R., 636
Ashforth, B. E., 266, 314
Ashkenas, R., 419, 589
Ashman, D., 602
Astrachan, J. H., 553, 559
Athey, T. R., 242
Atkins, S. T., 241
Ault, R., 407
Austin, J., 155, 156, 158(tab), 163
Axelrod, R., 110, 267, 556
Aymer, C., 131

Bailey, D. A., 469
Bailey, D. E., 244
Bair, J. P., 242
Baird, L., 520, 527
Baker, G. III., 413
Baker, T. E., 193 (tab), 196
Bakhtin, M. M., 655, 656, 657
Balazs, K., 86
Ballard, D., 131
Bamforth, E., 100
Bamforth, K. W., 124, 158, 279, 291 (tab)
Bandura, A., 314
Bandyopadhyay, K. K., 616
Barge, K. J., 657
Barker, J. A., 316

677

Subject Index

About the Editor

Thomas G. Cummings, professor, chair of the Department of Management and Organization, and director of the Leadership Institute, received his BS and MBA degrees from Cornell University and his PhD in business administration from the University of California at Los Angeles. He was previously on the faculty at Case Western Reserve University. He has authored 19 books, written more than 60 scholarly articles, and given numerous invited papers at national and international conferences. He was formerly editor-in-chief of the *Journal of Management Inquiry,* chair of the Organizational Development and Change Division of the Academy of Management, president of the Western Academy of Management, and member of the board of governors of the Academy of Management. He is past president of the Academy of Management.

About the Contributors

Chris Argyris, a director of the Monitor Group, is the James Bryant Conant Professor of Education and Organizational Behavior at Harvard Business School. He received his PhD in organizational behavior from Cornell University. His early research focused on the unintended consequences for individuals of formal organizational structures, executive leadership, control systems, and management information systems and on how people adapted to change in those consequences. He then turned his attention to ways of changing organizations, especially the behavior of executives at the upper levels of organizations. In the past decade, he has been developing a theory of individual and organizational learning in which human reasoning (not just behavior) becomes the basis for diagnosis and action.

John R. Austin earned his PhD in management from Boston College. For the past decade he has studied team and organization effectiveness. His work has examined the role of knowledge flows as a driver of team and organization performance. He has done work on understanding strategies for successful organization change. As an attempt to reconcile his management research and his finance interests, he developed the organizational indicators method for assessing financial performance. He is currently working to organize this research into a book that identifies publicly available red flags that may suggest hidden business risk within a company.

Katharina Balazs is an assistant professor in the Strategy and Organization Department at ESCP-EAP in Paris, France. She has a PhD degree from the Ecole des Hautes Etudes Commerciales in Jouy-en-Josas, France. She has worked as an organization consultant in Sweden, Denmark, France, Austria, Germany, and Hungary, where she has led strategic consulting assignments in companies in different business sectors. In her consulting work, she specializes in strategic and cross-cultural management issues in companies undergoing international mergers and acquisitions. She has also been active as a research associate in the Department of Leadership and Entrepreneurship at INSEAD.

Jean M. Bartunek is the Robert A. and Evelyn J. Ferris Chair and a professor of organization studies in the Carroll School of Management at Boston College. She received her PhD in theological ethics from the University of Chicago. She is also a member of the Religious of the Sacred Heart, an international women's Roman Catholic religious order. Her primary substantive research interests concern intersections of social cognition, conflict, and organization change and transformation. Her central methodological research interests concern insider–outsider research collaborations, with some representative publications that indicate her substantive and methodological interests.

Michael Beer is the Cahners–Rabb Professor of Business Administration Emeritus at the

Harvard Business School and chair of True-Point, a research-based consultancy he co-founded. The firm works with senior executives who aspire to transform their organizations into high-commitment, high-performance systems through honest conversations about their alignment with strategy and values. His teaching, research, and consulting activities are in the areas of organization effectiveness, change, and human resource management. Before joining the faculty of the Harvard Business School, he founded and served as director of the Organizational Research and Development Department at Corning Inc. He received his PhD at Princeton University.

Warren Bennis is a university professor and distinguished professor of business administration at the Marshall School of Business and founding chair of the Leadership Institute at the University of Southern California. He is a visiting professor of leadership at the University of Exeter and a fellow of the Royal Society of the Arts (UK). He earned his PhD in economics and social science at MIT. He has written 27 books, including the best-selling *Leaders* and *On Becoming a Leader*. In 1993 Addison-Wesley published a book of his essays, *An Invented Life: Reflections on Leadership and Change,* which was nominated for a Pulitzer Prize, and Jossey-Bass republished an updated version of his 1968 groundbreaking book, *The Temporary Society,* co-authored with Phil Slater.

John B. Bingham is an assistant professor of organization leadership and strategy at the Marriott School of Management at Brigham Young University. His research interests include organizational and individual ideology, contextual influences on employee behavior, employee–organization exchange, unethical behavior in organizations, and organizational justice. He is affiliated primarily with groups in organization behavior and human resources. He earned his PhD in management (organization behavior) from Texas A&M University.

David M. Boje holds the Bank of America Endowed Professorship of Management and is past Arthur Owens Professor in Business Administration in the Management Department at New Mexico State University. He received his PhD from the University of Illinois. He is described by his peers as an international scholar in the areas of narrative, storytelling, postmodern theory, and critical ethics of answerability. He has published nearly 100 articles in journals, including *Management Science, Administrative Science Quarterly, Academy of Management Journal, Academy of Management Review,* and the international *Journal of Organization Studies*.

R. Wayne Boss is a professor at the Leeds School of Business at the University of Colorado, Boulder. He received his DPA from the University of Georgia. His research interests include organization effectiveness, organization development, consultation skills, and organization behavior. His teaching interest areas include organization development, consultation skills, and organization behavior. His publications include "Antecedents and Outcomes of Empowerment: Empirical Evidence From the Healthcare Industry" in *Group and Organization Management* (in press), with Koberg, Senjem, and Goodman; and "Multiple Factors and Outcomes Associated With Mentoring Among Healthcare Professionals" in the *Journal of Vocational Behavior* (in press), with Koberg and Goodman.

Gene A. Brewer is a nationally recognized public management scholar who publishes in the top-ranked journals in the field. He earned his DPA from the University of Georgia. His current research interests include public sector reform, government performance, and bureaucratic accountability in democratic political systems. He is an editorial board member of the *Public Administration Review* and an overseas advisor for the UK's Advanced Institute for Management Research, Cardiff University, in Wales. He is an adjunct associate professor at the University of Georgia School of Public and International Affairs.

L. David Brown is a lecturer in public policy and director of international programs at the Hauser Center for Nonprofit Organizations at Harvard University. Before coming to Harvard, he was president of the Institute for Development Research, a nonprofit center for development research and consultation, and a professor of organization behavior at Boston University. His research and consulting have focused on institutional development, particularly involving civil society organizations, that fosters sustainable development and social transformation. He has written or edited *Transnational Civil Society: An Introduction* (with Srilatha Batliwala), *Practice–Research Engagement for Civil Society in a Globalizing World*, *The Struggle for Accountability: NGOs, Social Movements and the World Bank* (with Jonathan Fox), and *Managing Conflict at Organizational Interfaces*. He received his PhD in administrative sciences from Yale University.

W. Warner Burke is the Edward Lee Thorndike Professor of Psychology and Education and the education program coordinator of the graduate programs in social–organizational psychology at Columbia University. He earned his PhD at the University of Texas. His area of interest is behavioral practices associated with superior leaders and managers and their performance, which includes multirater feedback, organization culture, interorganizational relations, empowerment in the workplace, leading and managing organization change, and organization diagnosis and change.

Kim Cameron's past research on organization downsizing, organization effectiveness, corporate quality culture, and the development of leadership excellence has been published in more than 70 articles and 7 books. He earned his PhD at Yale University. His current research was funded by the Templeton Foundation and focuses on virtuousness in organizations, such as forgiveness, humility, and compassion, and its relationship to success. He is actively engaged in developing a new field in organization studies called positive organization scholarship, the examination of extraordinarily positive dynamics in organizations and the factors that unleash the highest human potential.

Rupert F. Chisholm (deceased) was a professor of management in the School of Public Affairs at Penn State, Harrisburg. He received his PhD in organization behavior from Case Western Reserve University. He wrote more than 40 scientific publications. His book *Developing Network Organizations: Learning From Practice and Theory* was published by Addison-Wesley in 1998. He was a frequent contributor to professional society meetings in the United States and Europe. At Penn State, Harrisburg, he was one of the founders of the doctoral program in public administration and served as its program coordinator since the mid-1990s.

Jane G. Covey is a nonprofit manager and consultant specializing in the strengthening of civil society organizations worldwide. Until 2002, she was executive director of the Institute for Development Research (IDR), an international civil society support organization. IDR undertook research and education to generate and disseminate civil society organizational theory in order to catalyze organization development and support leadership development in Asia, Africa, and, to a lesser extent, Latin America. Through partnerships with civil society support organizations, such as the Society for Participatory Research in Asia and MWENGO, IDR's work supports civil society capacity strengthening. Jane focuses on strategic planning, advocacy, non-government organization partnerships, and civil society–business engagement issues.

Peter Docherty holds a PhD in psychology from the University of London. He is a DSc (docent) in business administration at the Stockholm School of Economics and a senior researcher at the National Institute for Working Life, Stockholm, and the Fenix Programme at the Stockholm School of Economics. Recent developments in the economic contexts of many organizations, combined with popular management systems and practices, have resulted in a steady increase in the level of work intensity and an imbalance in the attention given the long-term development of organizations regarding learning, creativity, and innovation. A primary theme in his research is the development and management of sustainable work systems.

David Doneson is a graduate of Phillips Academy in Andover, Massachusetts. He received his BBA from the University of Michigan Business School with concentrations in organization behavior and corporate strategy. He currently works for Eli Lilly and Company's Diabetes Health Unit.

Dexter Dunphy is a distinguished professor at the University of Technology, Sydney. He earned his PhD in sociology from Harvard University, where he was an instructor in the Social Relations Department and the Graduate School of Business. He took a position as senior lecturer in sociology at the University of New South Wales. From there he chaired a small graduate department in the Faculty of Commerce and subsequently the Australian Graduate School of Management. These career moves represented his increasing interest in applying social theory to the practical issues of managing large, complex organizations.

Amy C. Edmondson is the Novartis Professor of Leadership and Management and chair of the doctoral programs at Harvard Business School. She is chair of the Committee of Higher Degrees in Business Studies at Harvard University. The Novartis Chair was established to enable the study of human interactions that lead to the creation of successful business enterprises for the betterment of society. Edmondson joined the Harvard

faculty as an assistant professor in 1996. Her research examines leadership influences on learning, collaboration, and innovation in teams and organizations. Her field-based approach includes research in contexts ranging from health care delivery and manufacturing to space exploration.

Frans M. van Eijnatten is associate professor of organization behavior at the Department of Technology Management, Eindhoven University of Technology, the Netherlands. He has a PhD from Radbout University Nijmegen, the Netherlands. He is a member of the Research School for Operations Management and Logistics and is engaged in research and development in human performance management, chaos and complexity in management, and organization development and change. His original research interest was in sociotechnical systems design, an ambition he pursued by initiating and coordinating design-oriented action research projects in R&D and information system design. Currently, he is exploring the implications of chaos and complexity theories for sociotechnical system design and organization renewal.

Jay R. Galbraith, PhD, is senior research scientist at the Center for Effective Organizations, Marshall School of Business, University of Southern California. He is internationally known as the primary expert on organization design. He is studying how companies redesign their organizations to deliver systems or solutions to customers who demand more than just individual products. He also focuses on rapidly reconfigurable organizations, front–back organizations, international organizations, joint ventures, and the role of the corporate center. He has partnered with several international universities and organizations, such as Institut Pendidikan dan Pembinaan Manajemen in Jakarta, Indonesia, and McKinsey & Company, on various research and consulting projects. He is professor emeritus at the International Institute for Management Development in Lausanne,

Thomas J. Griffin, Ph.D is vice president of organizational learning and chief teaching officer for U.S. Cellular, where he is responsible for the design and execution of the company-wide learning and organization development strategy. In this role, he ensures that associates and leaders at all levels are provided with the training, education and developmental experiences needed to deliver the ideal customer experience and build a culture of sustainable excellence.

Prior to being named vice president, he served as senior director of leadership and organization development, assuming responsibility for cultivating an effective leadership team, succession and performance management, and culture development. Before joining U.S. Cellular in 2000, he held a variety of positions focused on leadership & organizational development with SBC/Ameritech, Texas Instruments, and the U.S. Army. He has extensive experience in the leadership & organization development field, change management, and adult learning methodology.

He holds a bachelor of science degree in computer science from Fitchburg State College; master's degrees in general business and management of engineering technology from Amber University; a master's degree in organization development & change management from the University of Texas at Dallas; and a doctorate in organization development from Benedictine University. He is a published author, frequent conference speaker, and a U.S. Cellular President's Award winner. He and his wife reside in Algonquin, Ill.

Switzerland. He continues to consult for a diverse array of Fortune 500 companies worldwide.

Robert T. Golembiewski is a distinguished research professor at the University of Georgia. He received his PhD at Yale University. He is the author or editor of 77 books, with the latest being *Ironies in Organization Development* (2003), and he has published nearly 1,000 scholarly articles, case studies, and book reviews. His consulting work continues in business and government, with emphasis on a diversity and leadership project for the U.S. Centers for Disease Control and Prevention. Dr. Golembiewski's research interest is in behavior in large organizations. His teaching interests include organization development and change.

Larry Greiner is a professor of management and organization in the Marshall School of Business at the University of Southern California. He holds DBA and MBA degrees from the Harvard Business School. Professor Greiner served on the faculties at the Harvard Business School, Oxford University, University of Kansas, and INSEAD in Fontainebleau, France. He is a former chair of the Management Department at USC and chair of the Organization Development and Change Division and the Managerial Consultation Division of the Academy of Management. He is a fellow of the Managerial Consultation Division of the Academy of Management. He is the author of numerous publications on the subjects of organization growth and development, management consulting, and strategic change.

Thomas J. Griffin is a partner at the Goodwin Procter LLP firm. He has extensive experience in product liability and toxic tort litigation. Mr. Griffin is actively involved in continuing legal education programs outside the firm, both as a contributor to course materials and as a member of the teaching faculty. In 1987 he developed the curriculum and course materials and presented as faculty leader the inaugural

Deposition Skills Training Program for Massachusetts Continuing Legal Education. In 1988 he chaired the program, which is now an annual event. From 1987 to 1991, he directed the litigation department's training program for the firm's litigation associates.

J. Richard Hackman is the Edgar Pierce Professor of Social and Organizational Psychology at Harvard University. He received his doctorate in social psychology from the University of Illinois. He taught at Yale until 1986, when he moved to Harvard. He conducts research on a variety of topics in social and organizational psychology, including team dynamics and performance, social influences on individual behavior, and the design and leadership of self-managing groups and organizations. He is on the editorial board of several professional journals and has consulted to a variety of organizations on issues of work design, leadership, and team effectiveness.

Douglas T. Hall is the director of the Executive Development Roundtable and a professor of organization behavior in the Boston University School of Management. He is a core faculty member of the Human Resources Policy Institute. He has served as acting dean and associate dean of faculty development and faculty director for the master's programs at the School of Management. He received his graduate degrees from the Sloan School of Management at MIT. He has held faculty positions at Yale, York, Michigan State, and Northwestern universities. At Northwestern, he held the Earl Dean Howard Chair in Organizational Behavior and served as department chair.

Mark E. Hillon is an assistant professor of management at the University of Central Oklahoma, where he teaches graduate and undergraduate capstone strategy courses. He earned his PhD from New Mexico State University and from ISEOR/Université Jean Moulin (Lyon 3). His interests include socioeconomic management, socioecological strategic planning, small business development, emerging markets, and the improvement of critical and creative thinking in management education.

David W. Jamieson is president of the Jamieson Consulting Group and adjunct professor of management, Pepperdine University in their master of science in organization development program. He received his PhD from UCLA. He has more than 30 years of experience in consulting to organizations on change, strategy, design, and human resource issues. He is a past national president of the American Society for Training and Development, past chair of the Managerial Consultation Division of the Academy of Management, and former chair of the Practice Theme Committee of the Academy.

Ayse Karaevli is on the faculty at Sabanci University, Istanbul, Turkey. She received her DBA from Boston University and a postdoctorate from Northwestern University. Her areas of interest include corporate governance, industry evolution and strategic adaptation, organization design and change, executive succession, careers, and labor markets. Other interests include performance management system design, managerial and organizational cognitive functions, learning organizations, competitiveness analysis and strategy formulation, managerial epistemology, modeling and validation, and philosophy of operational research.

Manfred Kets de Vries is the Raoul de Vitry d'Avaucourt Professor in Human Resource Management at INSEAD. He received his DBA from Harvard University Graduate School of Business Administration. His research areas include the interface between psychoanalysis or dynamic psychiatry and management. Other specific areas of research include leadership, organization stress, career dynamics, entrepreneurship and family business, cross-cultural management, and the process of organization transformation and change. He teaches MBA and EDP leadership programs.

Edward E. Lawler III is a distinguished professor of business in the Management and Organization Department of the Marshall School of Business at the University of Southern California. He is director of the school's Center for Effective Organizations. After receiving his PhD from the University of California at Berkeley, he joined the faculty of Yale University and then the faculty at the University of Michigan. In 1978, he came to the University of Southern California and was subsequently named Distinguished Professor of Business. He has been honored as a major contributor to theory, research, and practice in the fields of human resource management, compensation, organization development, and organization effectiveness.

Mark Leach is Bro Professor of Regional Sustainable Development at Northland College. He earned his PhD from the University of Wisconsin at Madison. His approach to sustainable development emphasizes development not only of new buildings and roads but of the mature person as a moral and effective participant in society. His main research interest has been industrial plants and their conservation. Through his research, he has learned that scientific knowledge has never been sufficient; knowledge of how to be effective in organizations and agencies is also essential.

Myleen M. Leary is an assistant professor of management at California Polytechnic State University in San Luis Obispo. She earned her PhD in strategy and organization theory at the University of Wisconsin. Her research interests include boards of directors and strategic management, top management teams, strategic management of not-for-profit organizations, and new banks. She is also a member of the Academy of Management and the British Academy of Management. Some of her business experience includes an assistant position to the director of transportation planning at the Massachusetts Port Authority and assistant to the deputy secretary at the Massachusetts Office of Business Development.

Craig C. Lundberg recently retired from the School of Hotel Administration at Cornell University, where he was the Blanchard Professor of Human Resources Management. He earned his PhD from Cornell University. His distinguished academic career included faculty and administrative positions at Wharton, Southern Methodist University, Oregon State University, the University of Southern California, and SUNY Binghamton. He was president of the Western Academy of Management and chair of the Organization Development and Change Division of the Academy of Management. He has researched and published extensively about organization development and change, research methods, and human resource management. He is also a poet, cowboy, and mentor to many scholars in the field.

Kate Louise McArdle is a lecturer in organization behavior at the University of Bath, working on undergraduate management programs and the postgraduate program at the Centre for Action Research in Professional Practice (CARPP). Her PhD work at CARPP focused on second-person inquiry processes with young women managers in a multinational organization. She has explored her ensuing interests in the variety of issues involved in the development of inquiry practice (particularly around issues of quality, scale, facilitation practice, and skill building for change) through a broad spectrum of academic and consulting work.

Mark L. McConkie is a professor in the Graduate School of Public Affairs at the University of Colorado, Colorado Springs. He earned his DPA from the University of Georgia. Before joining the University of Colorado, he consulted with BankOne, NASA, the U.S. Navy, the U.S. Air Force (Special Forces), MCI Corp., Hewlett-Packard, and others. His teaching focuses on organization change and behavior, leadership, management development, and ethics; his research interests also include the myths and folklore of organization culture.

Susan Albers Mohrman is senior research scientist at the Center for Effective Organizations at the Marshall School of Business, University of Southern California. She received her PhD from Northwestern University. She is widely known for her research in organization design and effectiveness. Recently, she has focused on learning in organizations and design for knowledge management in the contexts of companies undergoing fundamental change and global technology firms. She examines the research process itself and how to create university–company partnerships to yield useful knowledge. She has been actively involved as a researcher or consultant to a wide variety of organizations implementing innovative management systems and organization designs. She has helped install innovative production and management systems in organizations.

David A. Nadler is vice chairman of Marsh & McLennan Companies, Inc. (MMC), a global professional service firm with annual revenues of approximately $12 billion. In addition, he serves as chair of Mercer Delta Consulting, LLC, a global consulting firm and an operating company of MMC that works with CEOs, boards of directors, and senior executives of major corporations on the design and leadership of large-scale organization change. He received his PhD from the University of Michigan. He is well known for his research and writing on organization change, corporate governance, organization design, and executive teams. He has written numerous articles and book chapters and has authored or edited 16 books.

Ernesto J. Poza is Thunderbird Professor of Family Business and faculty chair of the Global Family Enterprise Program at the Thunderbird Garvin School of International Management. His research and consulting challenges business owners to revitalize mature businesses through strategic thinking, succession planning, global entrepreneurship, and change. His areas of research interest include best practices in family business continuity, growing the family-led business, governance of the family business and entrepreneurship, family enterprise, and economic development. Other areas of interest include strategy in the privately held companies, managing change in the family-owned business, and next-generation leadership development.

Ronald E. Purser is a professor of management in the College of Business at San Francisco State University and an adjunct faculty member at Benedictine University, Fielding Institute, and Colorado Technical University. Before this, he was a tenured professor and graduate program director at the Center for Organization Development at Loyola University of Chicago. He earned his PhD in organization behavior from the Weatherhead School of Management at Case Western Reserve University. He is past division chair for the Organization Development and Change Division of the Academy of Management. He has published more than 60 refereed journal articles and book chapters on high-performance work systems, design of new product development organizations, environmental management, social creativity, and participative strategic planning.

Robert E. Quinn is Margaret Elliott Tracy Collegiate Professor in Business Administration and a professor of management and organizations at the Stephen M. Ross School of Business at the University of Michigan. He earned his PhD from the University of Cincinnati. He has published many papers and books on management and organization. He is particularly interested in issues of leadership, vision, and change. He has an applied orientation and has 25 years of experience in working with executives on issues of organization change. He has been involved in the design and execution of numerous large-scale change projects. He has worked with a large percentage of the Fortune 500 companies. He teaches in both the MBA and executive education programs at the University of Michigan and is known for

innovative instructional efforts. He is also a fellow of the World Business Academy.

Peter Reason is director of studies in the Postgraduate Programme in Action Research at the University of Bath, UK. He has been fascinated by the theory and practice of collaborative inquiry. The experience of conducting participatory research for his PhD at Case Western Reserve University led him to question the bases of Western epistemology: Research *with* people rather than *on* people means that the Cartesian separation of subject and object is no longer tenable. His current interests include the further development of this method and its application to personal and organizational learning, radical shifts in epistemology and consciousness, professional and managerial practice as inquiry, education as liberation, and high-quality postconventional personal behavior.

George Roth is a principal research associate at the MIT Sloan School of Management. He leads the Enterprise Change Research Program, a part of MIT's Lean Aerospace Initiative program, a joint MIT Management School and School of Engineering effort transforming aerospace companies and government. His research examines and develops initiatives that promote learning and improvement initiatives across multiple organizations. This current focus builds on his ongoing research in organization culture, leadership, learning, and change. He has a PhD in organizational studies from MIT.

Edgar H. Schein is a professor of management emeritus at MIT's Sloan School of Management, where he taught for nearly 40 years. He also consults on corporate culture, organization development, career and management development, team building, human resource planning, and related issues. Among other publications, Addison-Wesley has published two volumes of his book *Process Consultation* (1987 and 1988). He earned a PhD from the University of Chicago and a PhD in social psychology from Harvard University.

Myeong-Gu Seo is an assistant professor of management and organization at the University of Maryland's Robert H. Smith School of Business. He earned his PhD from Boston College. His primary areas of research include work-related emotions and organizational and institutional change. He received the 2001 Best Doctoral Student Paper award from the Academy of Management's Organizational Development and Change Division and was the 2002 second-place winner of the INFORMS Dissertation Proposal Competition. His work, which has received funding from the National Science Foundation, has been published in several journals, including *Academy of Management Journal, Academy of Management Review, Journal of Organizational Behavior, Journal of Applied Behavioral Science, Handbook of Organizational Change,* and *Academy of Management Learning and Education.*

A. B. (Rami) Shani is a professor of management at California Polytechnic State University. He received his PhD in organization behavior and theory from Case Western Reserve University. His teaching and research specializations include organization behavior, organization development and change, sociotechnical systems, organization design and theory, organization learning and knowledge management, design of nonroutine systems, research methods, and action research. He studies the management of change from a longitudinal perspective using collaborative research methods.

Scott Sonenshein is a PhD candidate in management and organizations at the Stephen M. Ross School of Business, University of Michigan. His research examines how interpretive processes contribute to understanding change. Scott's work on social change focuses on how sensemaking and sense-giving affect individuals' advocacy and responses to social and ethical issues. His work on strategic change draws from sensemaking and narrative perspectives to challenge existing models of change implementation predicated on a limited role of employees as information processors and resistors during change. His work on individual change investigates how employees narrate their growth at work as part of the self-adaptation process.

Gretchen M. Spreitzer is a professor of management and organizations at the Stephen M. Ross School of Business at the University of Michigan. She received her PhD from the University of Michigan. Dr. Spreitzer's research focuses on employee empowerment and leadership development, particularly in a context of organization change and decline. Her most recent work looks at positive deviance and how organizations enable employees to flourish. This work fits within a larger effort at Michigan's business school to develop a Scholarship of Positive Organizing that is dedicated to understanding how work organizations contribute to the development of human strengths and virtues.

Rajesh Tandon is an internationally acclaimed leader and practitioner of participatory research and development. He founded the Society for Participatory Research in Asia, a voluntary organization providing support to grassroots initiatives in South Asia, and continues to be its president. He received a PhD from Case Western Reserve University and an electronic engineer degree (IIT Kanpur) with a graduation in management (IIM Calcutta). He has specialized in social and organization change. His contributions to the enhancement of perspectives and capacities of many voluntary activists and organizations revolve around issues of participatory research, advocating for people-centered development, policy reform, and networking in India, South Asia, and beyond.

Peter B. Vaill, one of the nation's most influential organization change theorists, is a university professor of management at Antioch University. He received his DBA from the Harvard Business School. He is internationally known for his innovative approaches to organization behavior and has written extensively. He has consistently broken new ground in addressing issues of spirituality in the workplace and on the importance of lifelong learning. He has worked with many well-known corporations, most major agencies of the U.S. government, and many universities, health systems, and professional associations. He was formerly director of the PhD program at George Washington University's School of Business and Public Management. Most recently, he was distinguished chair in management education at the Graduate School of Business, University of St. Thomas, Minneapolis–St. Paul, Minnesota.

Richard W. Woodman is the Fouraker Professor of Business and a professor of management at Texas A&M University, where he teaches organization behavior, organization change, creativity and innovation, and research methods. He received his PhD from Purdue University. He is editor of the *Journal of Applied Behavioral Science* and co-editor of the annual series *Research in Organizational Change and Development,* published by Elsevier. He has been division chair and program chair of the Organization Development and Change Division of the Academy of Management and

is a former department head at Texas A&M. In a previous life, he was a military intelligence officer in the U.S. Army, worked in both the petroleum and banking industries, and served for several years as vice president of a financial institution.

Christopher G. Worley is a research scientist at the Center for Effective Organizations, Marshall School of Business, University of Southern California. He received his PhD from the University of Southern California and was on the faculty at the Graziadio School of Business and Management at Pepperdine University. He consults with organizations in the health care, high-technology, and natural resource industries on strategy and organization design. He is the co-author of *Organization Development and Change,* the best-selling textbook in the field. In addition, his book *Integrated Strategic Change* was co-authored with Dr. David Hitchin. He was chair of the Organization Development and Change Division of the Academy of Management. His presentations to the Academy of Management, the OD Network, and the Conference Board have focused on both scholarly topics and practical applications.

Feirong Yuan is an assistant professor of management at the University of Kansas School of Business. She earned a PhD at Texas A&M University. Her academic interests include human resource management, organization behavior, and organization development and change.